Introductory Course

HOLT
Literature
&Language
Arts

 Mastering the California Standards
Reading · Writing · Listening · Speaking

 HOLT, RINEHART AND WINSTON

A Harcourt Classroom Education Company

Austin · New York · Orlando · Atlanta · San Francisco · Boston · Dallas · Toronto · London

EDITORIAL
Project Directors: Kathleen Daniel, Mescal Evler
Project Editors: John Haffner Layden, Hester Weeden
Manager of Operations and Planning: Bill Wahlgren
Managing Editors: Marie Price, Mike Topp
Manager of Editorial Services: Abigail Winograd
Senior Product Manager: Don Wulbrecht
Executive Editors: Peter Letendre, Kristine E. Marshall
Senior Editor: Susan K. Lynch
Editorial Staff: Jane Archer Feinstein, Steven Fechter, Richard Kelso,
    Barbara Knaggs, Quraysh Ali Lansana, Rick Lucas, Sondra Maze,
    Jennifer Schwan, Michael Zakhar
Copyediting Manager: Michael Neibergall
Copyediting Supervisors: Mary Malone, Tamsin Nutter
Copyeditors: Christine Altgelt, Joel Bourgeois, Elizabeth Dickson, Emily Force, Julie A. Hill,
    Julia Thomas Hu, Jessica Keitlen, Jennifer Kirkland, Millicent Ondras, Evan Russell,
    Dennis Scharnberg, Kathleen Scheiner
Editorial Finance Managers: Lori De La Garza, Elizabeth LaManna
Editorial Support: Renée Benitez, Heather Cheyne, Louise Fernandez, Christine Han, Mark Holland,
    Bret Isaacs, Marcus Johnson, Ruth Hooker, Laurie Muir, Joie D. Pickett, Margaret Sanchez,
    Tom Ver Gow
Editorial Permissions: David Smith, Kimberly Feden

ART, DESIGN, AND PRODUCTION
Director: Athena Blackorby
Senior Design Director: Betty Mintz
Design and Electronic Files: Preface, Inc.; H&S Graphics, Inc.
Production Manager: Catherine Gessner
Production Assistant: Peter Sawchuk

For permission to reprint copyrighted material, grateful acknowledgment is made to the following sources:

Brandt & Hochman Literary Agents, Inc.: From "School Visits: The Author's Viewpoint" by Avi with Betty Miles from *School Library Journal,* January 1987. Copyright © 1987 by Avi.
Scholastic Inc.: From "Dr. Seuss" from *Meet the Authors and Illustrators,* edited by Deborah Kovacs and James Preller. Copyright © 1991 by Scholastic Inc.
Gary Soto: Autobiographical comment by Gary Soto. Copyright © 2000 by Gary Soto.

Sources Cited
From "Ghosts and Voices: Writing from Obsession" by Sandra Cisneros from *Americas Review* 15, Spring 1987 (Houston, TX).
From speech by Ann Petry from *Horn Book Magazine* (Boston, MA), April 1965, pp. 147–151.
Quote by Jacob Lawrence from "Simplicity Can Be Complicated: Jacob Lawrence Found Emotional Authority in Art and Life" by Michael Kimmelman from *The New York Times,* June 14, 2000.

ISBN 0-03-057363-7

2 3 4 5 6 048 05 04 03 02

Program Authors

Kylene Beers established the reading pedagogy for Part 1 of *Holt Literature and Language Arts* and wrote the lessons in the Reading Matters section of the book. A former middle-school teacher, Dr. Beers has turned her commitment to helping readers having difficulty into the major focus of her research, writing, speaking, and teaching. A clinical associate professor at the University of Houston, Dr. Beers is also currently the editor of the National Council of Teachers of English journal *Voices from the Middle*. She is the author of *When Kids Can't Read: The Reading Handbook for Teachers Grades 6–12* and co-editor of *Into Focus: Understanding and Creating Middle School Readers*. She has served on the review boards of the *English Journal* and *The Alan Review*. Dr. Beers currently serves on the board of directors of the International Reading Association's Special Interest Group on Adolescent Literature.

Lee Odell helped establish the pedagogical framework for Part 2 of *Holt Literature and Language Arts*. Dr. Odell is Professor of Composition Theory and Research and, since 1996, Director of the Writing Program at Rensselaer Polytechnic Institute. He began his career teaching English in middle and high schools. More recently he has worked with teachers in grades K–12 to establish a program that involves students from all disciplines in writing across the curriculum and for communities outside their classrooms. Dr. Odell's most recent book (with Charles R. Cooper) is *Evaluating Writing: The Role of Teacher's Knowledge About Text, Learning, and Culture*. He is Past Chair of the Conference on College Composition and Communication and of NCTE's Assembly for Research. Dr. Odell is currently working on a college-level writing textbook.

Special Contributors

Flo Ota De Lange and **Sheri Henderson** helped plan and organize the program and played key roles in developing and preparing the informational materials.

Flo Ota De Lange is a former teacher with a thirty-year second career in psychotherapy, during which she studied learning processes in children and adults. These careers have led to her third career, as a writer.

Sheri Henderson brings to the program twenty years of experience as a California middle-school research practitioner and full-time reading and language arts teacher at La Paz Intermediate School in Saddleback Valley Unified School District. She regularly speaks at statewide and national conferences.

Since 1991, DeLangeHenderson LLC has published forty-three titles designed to integrate the teaching of literature with standards requirements and state and national tests.

Writers

John Malcolm Brinnin, author of six volumes of poetry that have received many prizes and awards, was a member of the American Academy and Institute of Arts and Letters. He was a critic of poetry and a biographer of poets and was for a number of years Director of New York's famous Poetry Center. His teaching career, begun at Vassar College, included long terms at the University of Connecticut and Boston University, where he succeeded Robert Lowell as Professor of Creative Writing and Contemporary Letters. Mr. Brinnin wrote *Dylan Thomas in America: An Intimate Journal* and *Sextet: T. S. Eliot & Truman Capote & Others.*

John Leggett is a novelist, biographer, and teacher. He went to the Writer's Workshop at the University of Iowa in the spring of 1969, expecting to work there for a single semester. In 1970, he assumed temporary charge of the program, and for the next seventeen years he was its director. Mr. Leggett's novels include *Wilder Stone, The Gloucester Branch, Who Took the Gold Away?, Gulliver House,* and *Making Believe.* He is also the author of the highly acclaimed biography *Ross and Tom: Two American Tragedies* and of a biography of William Saroyan, *A Daring Young Man.* Mr. Leggett lives in California's Napa Valley.

Joan Burditt is a writer and editor who has a master's degree in education with a specialization in reading. She taught for several years in Texas, where her experience included work in programs for readers having difficulty. Since then she has developed and written instructional materials for middle-school language arts texts.

Madeline Travers Hovland, who taught middle school for several years, is a writer of educational materials. She studied English at Bates College and received a master's degree in education from Harvard University.

Richard Kelso is a writer and editor whose children's books include *Building a Dream: Mary Bethune's School; Walking for Freedom: The Montgomery Bus Boycott; Days of Courage: The Little Rock Story;* and *The Case of the Amistad Mutiny.*

Mara Rockliff is a writer and editor with a degree in American civilization from Brown University. She has written dramatizations of classic stories for middle-school students, collected in a book called *Stories for Performance*. She has also published feature stories in national newspapers and is currently writing a novel for young adults.

Program Consultants

SENIOR PROGRAM CONSULTANT
Carol Jago is the editor of CATE's quarterly journal, *California English*. She teaches English at Santa Monica High School, in Santa Monica, and directs the California Reading and Literature Project at UCLA. She also writes a weekly education column for the *Los Angeles Times*. She is the author of several books, including two in a series on contemporary writers in the classroom: *Alice Walker in the Classroom* and *Nikki Giovanni in the Classroom*. She is also the author of *With Rigor for All: Teaching the Classics to Contemporary Students* and *Beyond Standards: Excellence in the High School English Classroom*.

CONTENT-AREA READING CONSULTANT
Judith L. Irvin served as a reading consultant for the content-area readers for *Holt Literature and Language Arts: The Ancient World; A World in Transition;* and *The United States: Change and Challenge*. Dr. Irvin is a Professor of Education at Florida State University. She writes a column, "What Research Says to the Middle Level Practitioner," for the *Middle School Journal* and serves as the literacy expert for the *Middle Level News*, published by the California League of Middle Schools. Her several books include the companion volumes *Reading and the Middle School Student: Strategies to Enhance Literacy* and *Reading and the High School Student: Strategies to Enhance Literacy* (with Buehl and Klemp).

ADVISORS
Dr. Julie M. T. Chan
Director of Literacy
  Instruction
Newport-Mesa Unified
  School District
Costa Mesa, California

Cheri Howell
Reading Specialist
Covina-Valley Unified
  School District
Covina, California

José M. Ibarra-Tiznado
ELL Program Coordinator
Bassett Unified School
  District
La Puente, California

Dr. Ronald Klemp
Instructor
California State
  University, Northridge
Northridge, California

Fern M. Sheldon
K–12 Curriculum and
  Instruction Specialist
Rowland Unified School
  District
Rowland Heights,
  California

CRITICAL REVIEWERS
Diana Edie
Bret Harte Middle
  School
Hayward, California

Jennifer Oehrlein
Tewinkle Middle School
Costa Mesa, California

Judith Shane
Carr Intermediate
  School
Santa Ana, California

FIELD-TEST PARTICIPANTS
Kristina Chow
Martha Baldwin School
Alhambra, California

Katrina Hunt
Ida Price Middle School
San Jose, California

Candice Phillips
South Hills Middle
  School
Pittsburgh,
  Pennsylvania

iv

PART 1 **Mastering the California Standards in Reading**

Chapter

Structures:
Building Blocks of Meaning

Standards Focus

Vocabulary Development 1.4 Monitor expository text for unknown words or words with novel meanings by using word, sentence, and paragraph clues to determine meaning.

Reading Comprehension (Focus on Informational Materials) 2.1 Identify the structural features of popular media (for example, newspapers, magazines, online information), and use the features to obtain information.

Literary Response and Analysis 3.3 Analyze the influence of setting on the problem and its resolution.

Chapter 1
Mastering the California Standards:

Chapter

Characters: The People You'll Meet

Standards Focus

Vocabulary Development 1.3 Recognize the origins and meanings of frequently used foreign words in English, and use these words accurately in speaking and writing.

Reading Comprehension (Focus on Informational Materials) 2.4 Clarify an understanding of texts by creating outlines, logical notes, summaries, or reports.

Literary Response and Analysis 3.2 Analyze the effect of the qualities of the character (for example, courage or cowardice, ambition or laziness) on the plot and the resolution of the conflict.

Chapter 2
Mastering the California Standards:

A4 **Contents**

Contents   **A5**

Chapter

3

The Heart of the Matter:
Themes and Conclusions

 Standards Focus

Vocabulary Development 1.2 Identify and interpret figurative language.

Reading Comprehension (Focus on Informational Materials) 2.6 Determine the adequacy and appropriateness of the evidence for an author's conclusions.

Literary Response and Analysis 3.6 Identify and analyze features of themes conveyed through characters, actions, and images.

Chapter 3
Mastering the California Standards:

A6 Contents

Contents   A7

Forms and Patterns: Stories and Explanations

Standards Focus

Vocabulary Development 1.2 Identify and interpret words with multiple meanings.

Reading Comprehension (Focus on Informational Materials) 2.2 Analyze text that uses the compare-and-contrast organizational pattern.

Literary Response and Analysis 3.1 Identify the forms of fiction, and describe the major characteristics of each form.

A8 Contents

Chapter 4
Mastering the California Standards:

Contents **A9**

Biography and Autobiography: Looking at Lives

Chapter

Standards Focus

Vocabulary Development 1.4 Monitor expository text for unknown words by using word, sentence, and paragraph clues to determine meaning.

Reading Comprehension (Focus on Informational Materials) 2.3 Connect and clarify main ideas by identifying their relationships to other sources and related topics.

Literary Response and Analysis 3.5 Identify the speaker, and recognize the difference between first- and third-person narration (for example, autobiography compared with biography).

Contents   **A11**

Looking at Texts:
Uses of the Imagination

Chapter

 Standards Focus

Vocabulary Development 1.5 Understand and explain shades of meaning in related words (for example, *softly* and *quietly*).

Reading Comprehension (Focus on Informational Materials) 2.7 Make reasonable assertions about a text through accurate supporting citations.

Literary Response and Analysis 3.7 Explain the effects of common literary devices (for example, symbolism, imagery, metaphor) in a variety of fictional and nonfictional texts.

Chapter 6
Mastering the California Standards:

Contents A13

A14 Contents

Rhyme and Reason

 Standards Focus

Vocabulary Development 1.2 Identify and interpret figurative language.

Reading Comprehension (Focus on Informational Materials) 2.8 Note instances of unsupported inferences, fallacious reasoning, persuasion, and propaganda in text.

Literary Response and Analysis 3.4 Define how tone or meaning is conveyed in poetry through word choice, figurative language, sentence structure, line length, punctuation, rhythm, repetition, and rhyme.

Chapter 7
Mastering the California Standards:

Contents **A15**

Contents   **A17**

Chapter

8

You the Critic

Standards Focus

Reading Comprehension (Focus on Informational Materials) 2.5 Follow multiple-step instructions for preparing applications (for example, for a public library card, bank savings account, sports club, league membership).

Literary Response and Analysis 3.8 Critique the credibility of characterization and the degree to which a plot is contrived or realistic (for example, compare use of fact and fantasy in historical fiction).

Chapter 8
Mastering the California Standards:

Reteaching Lesson

PART 2   **Mastering the California Standards in Writing, Listening, and Speaking**

Introduction

 Standards Focus

Writing Strategies 1.0 Students progress through the stages of the writing process as needed.

Writing Strategies 1.1 Choose the form of writing (for example, personal letter, letter to the editor, review, poem, report, narrative) that best suits the intended purpose.

Peanuts reprinted by permission of United Feature Syndicate, Inc.

A20 Contents

Workshop

Narration

Standards Focus

Writing Applications 2.1 Write narratives.
Speaking Applications 2.1 Deliver narrative presentations.

**Mastering
the Standards**

Workshop

Exposition

Standards Focus

Writing Applications 2.2 Write expository compositions (for example, explanation).
Listening and Speaking Strategies 1.3 Restate and execute multiple-step oral instructions and directions.

Contents A21

Workshop 3

Response to Literature

Standards Focus

Writing Applications 2.2 Write expository compositions (for example, explanation).

Speaking Applications 2.3 Deliver oral responses to literature.

A22 Contents

Workshop

4

Research

Standards Focus

Writing Applications 2.3 Write research reports.
Speaking Applications 2.2 Deliver informative presentations.
Writing Strategies 1.4 Use organizational features of electronic text (for example, databases, keyword searches, e-mail addresses) to locate information.

Mastering the Standards

Workshop 4
Mastering the California Standards:

Workshop

Persuasion

Standards Focus

Writing Applications 2.5 Write persuasive compositions.
Speaking Applications 2.4 Deliver persuasive presentations.
Listening and Speaking Strategies 1.9 Identify persuasive and propaganda techniques used in television, and identify false and misleading information.

Mastering the Standards

Calvin & Hobbes © 1993 Watterson. Distributed by Universal Press Syndicate. Reprinted with permission. All rights reserved.

Workshop 5
Mastering the California Standards:

Workshop 6

Learning About Paragraphs

 Standards Focus

Writing Strategies 1.0 Students write clear, coherent, and focused essays. Essays contain formal introductions, supporting evidence, and conclusions.
Writing Strategies 1.2 Create multiple-paragraph expository compositions.
Writing Strategies 1.3 Use a variety of effective and coherent organizational patterns, including comparison and contrast; organization by categories; and arrangement by spatial order, order of importance, or climactic order.

Workshop 6
Mastering the California Standards:

Contents **A25**

Mini-Workshops

Standards Focus

Writing Strategies 1.2 Create multiple-paragraph expository compositions.

Writing Applications 2.0 Students write narrative, expository, persuasive, and descriptive texts.

Writing Applications 2.2 Write expository compositions (for example, comparison and contrast, description, problem and solution).

Writing Applications 2.2c Follow an organizational pattern appropriate to the type of composition.

Speaking Applications 2.5 Deliver presentations on problems and solutions.

Listening and Speaking Strategies 1.6 Support opinions with visual or media displays that use appropriate technology.

Mini-Workshops

Mastering the California Standards:

Writing

Listening and Speaking

Media

A26   Contents

Resource Center

Contents **A27**

SKILLS

Literary Response and Analysis Essays

Reading Matters: Strategy Lessons

Literary Skills

Reading Skills for Literary Texts

Reading Skills for Informational Texts

Vocabulary Skills

STANDARDS

 Review Standards from Earlier Grades

Vocabulary Development

SELECTIONS BY GENRE

A34 Selections by Genre

Your Road Map to Success:
Mastering the California Standards

Students today enter their middle school classrooms with a wide range of abilities and individual levels of preparation. Advanced learners, English-language learners, students with learning disabilities, and students who have reading difficulties all converge in the language arts classroom with a need to build solid reading, writing, listening and speaking, and grammar skills. Teaching this broad scope of skills while addressing students' individual needs can be a challenge.

Designed for California Teachers and Students

The *Holt Literature and Language Arts* program has been designed specifically to help you address these critical skills and to guide your students toward mastery of the California English–Language Arts Content Standards. This carefully researched, comprehensive language arts program covers all the standards without losing sight of the central focus of the language arts classroom: to help all students become good readers and writers, appreciate literature, and embrace the power of the English language in all its forms.

Comprehensive and Coherent Structure

Holt Literature and Language Arts is based on current and confirmed research that suggests that curriculum, assessment, instruction, and organization should be aligned and integrated in any language arts program. This approach ensures that all students are given opportunities to achieve the essential knowledge and skills required by the standards and that students are introduced to these skills in a way that fosters confidence and promotes success.

Giving All Students Access to Language Skills

So that every student has a supportive environment in which to build language arts skills, the *Holt Literature and Language Arts* program provides alternative methods of planning, instruction, and assessment to help you differentiate instruction for your classroom's specific needs. Suggestions for modifying instruction to address the particular needs of advanced learners, special education students, English-language learners, or those who need more help building reading skills are included throughout the program.

Second Course

HOLT
Handbook

Master... in Engl...

Second Course

HOLT
Literature & Language Arts

Mastering the
CALIFORNIA
STANDARDS

Introductory Course

HOLT
Handbook

First Course

HOLT
Handbook

Introductory Course

HOLT
Literature & Language Arts

Evaluation Materials Submitted is
Less Than
Final Format
Completed Materials
Available Soon!

Mastering the
CALIFORNIA
STANDARDS
• Reading
• Writing
• Listening
• Speaking

First Course

HOLT
Literature & Language Arts

Mastering the
CALIFORNIA
STANDARDS
• Reading
• Writing
• Listening
• Speaking

Evaluation Materials Submitted
Less Than
Final Format
Completed Materials Available Soon!

Program Organization

Covering All the
Standards in the
Language Arts

The *Holt Literature and Language Arts* program is logically organized and systematically sequenced so that students build the skills and master the content required by the California standards. The *Holt Literature and Language Arts Pupil's Edition* is the centerpiece for building the knowledge and skills required by the Reading, Writing, and Listening and Speaking standards. The *Holt Handbook Pupil's Edition* is the primary tool for building the knowledge and skills required by the Written and Oral English Language Conventions standards. Opportunities for practice and remediation and for reteaching, assessing, and connecting the standards are offered throughout the program.

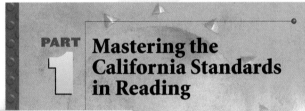

PART 1 Mastering the California Standards in Reading

HOLT LITERATURE AND LANGUAGE ARTS, PART 1

Part 1: Mastering California Standards in Reading is organized by chapters that cover standards instruction in vocabulary development, reading comprehension, and literary response and analysis. Each chapter uses a variety of related literary and informational texts to build students' understanding of grade-level standards. In addition, each chapter includes direct instruction of the standards, sustained practice and reinforcement of the standards, and assessment aligned with the standards.

 California Standards

Here are the Grade 7 standards you will study for mastery in Chapter 1. You will also review standards from earlier grades.

 Reading

Word Analysis, Fluency, and Systematic Vocabulary Development

1.3 Clarify word meanings through the use of definition, example, restatement, or contrast.

Reading Comprehension (Focus on Informational Materials)

2.1 Understand and analyze the differences in structure and purpose between various categories of informational materials (for example, textbooks, newspapers, instructional manuals, signs).

Grade 5 Review

2.2 Analyze text that is organized in sequential or chronological order.

2.3 Discern main ideas and concepts presented in texts.

Literary Response and Analysis

3.2 Identify events that advance the plot, and determine how each event explains past or present action(s) or foreshadows future action(s).

Grade 5 Review

3.2 Identify the main problem or conflict of the plot, and explain how it is resolved.

Grade 6 Review

3.7 Explain the effects of common literary devices (for example, symbolism) in fictional texts.

HOLT LITERATURE AND LANGUAGE ARTS, PART 2

Part 2: Mastering California Standards in Writing, Listening, and Speaking is organized by workshops that cover standards instruction in writing strategies, writing applications, listening and speaking strategies, and speaking applications. Each workshop covers a different genre of writing and directly correlates to a speaking and listening application standard. Each workshop includes direct instruction, sustained practice, and reinforcement of the standards. Assessment is aligned with the standards.

PART 2
Mastering the California Standards in Writing, Listening, and Speaking

WHAT'S AHEAD?

In this section you will learn how effective writers
- use the stages of the writing process
- read professional models
- create think sheets, outlines, and summaries
- create documents with correct manuscript style
- use editing symbols to edit and proofread manuscripts

Introduction

You use processes every day—when you play a game, follow a recipe, or make artwork. Writing, too, is a **process** that involves many steps to complete. This introduction to the writing process will prepare you for the workshops in this book. You will also learn about the following language arts standards.

California Standards

Writing

1.0 Students progress through the stages of the writing process as needed.

1.3 Use strategies of notetaking, outlining, and summarizing to impose structure on composition drafts.

1.6 Create documents by using word-processing skills and publishing programs.

1.7 Revise writing to improve organization and word choice after checking the logic of the ideas and the precision of the vocabulary.

2.0 Student writing demonstrates a command of standard American English.

2.5 Write summaries of reading material.

Writing as a Process

"Genius," wrote Thomas Edison, "is 1 percent inspiration and 99 percent perspiration." He was talking about inventing, but the same goes for writing. Writing is a process made up of many steps, and it takes effort. The chart on the next page summarizes the stages that usually take place during the writing process.

528 Introduction The Writing Process

HOLT HANDBOOK

The *Holt Handbook Pupil's Edition* focuses on the written and oral English-language conventions required by the standards. The grammar, usage, and mechanics chapters are based on John Warriner's time-tested system for instruction: Teach students the rule, show examples of the rule in action, and provide immediate practice.

The *Holt Handbook* is divided into three main parts:

- **Part 1: Grammar, Usage, and Mechanics**
- **Part 2: Sentences**
- **Part 3: Resources**

First Course

HOLT Handbook

Mastering the CALIFORNIA STANDARDS English Language Convention

HOLT
Literature
&Language
Arts

CONTENTS IN BRIEF

Contents in Brief **A1**

Take a Road Trip to
Literary and Real-World Fluency

Part 1 of **Holt Literature and Language Arts** prepares students to master the California reading standards by helping them build skills in reading comprehension, literary response and analysis, and vocabulary development. Each chapter offers culturally and historically significant literary works and a variety of high-interest informational pieces directly related to the literary selections—so that students understand how different structures are used to communicate meaning.

LITERARY RESPONSE AND ANALYSIS

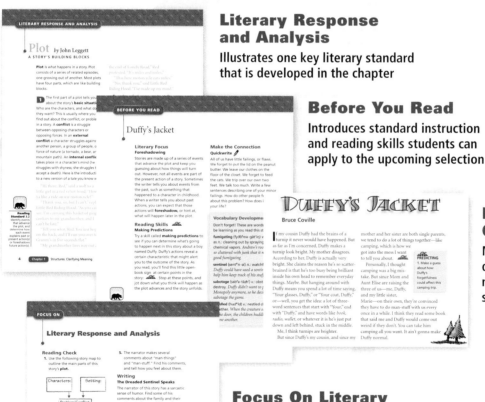

Literary Response and Analysis

Illustrates one key literary standard that is developed in the chapter

Before You Read

Introduces standard instruction and reading skills students can apply to the upcoming selection

Directed-Reading Questions

Models the thinking and questioning strategies students need to build strong reading skills

Focus On Literary Response and Analysis

Guides comprehension of the selection and key literary standard with **Reading Check, Interpretation,** and **Evaluation** questions, and a writing assignment

VOCABULARY DEVELOPMENT

Focus on Vocabulary Development

Focuses on the skills students need to build strong vocabularies with exposition and practice exercises

Test Practice

Tests mastery of multiple meanings, synonyms, or context clues using vocabulary learned from the chapter

READING COMPREHENSION

Reading Informational Materials

Teaches essential skills students need to analyze and evaluate information before each selection

Focus on Informational Materials

Tests students' mastery of the informational selection and standard with **Reading Check** and **Test Practice** questions

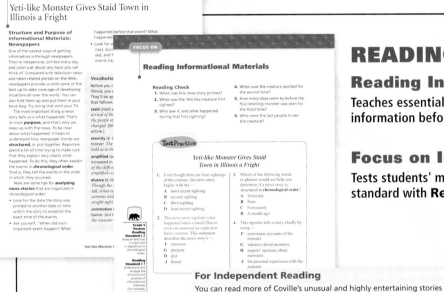

For Independent Reading

You can read more of Coville's unusual and highly entertaining stories in *Oddly Enough* and *Odder Than Ever*. You might also check out his wildly popular longer works: *My Teacher Is an Alien*, *Jennifer Murdley's Toad*, and *Jeremy Thatcher Dragon Hatcher*.

Read On:

Offers suggestions for independent reading of fiction and nonfiction

STANDARDS REVIEW

At the end of every chapter, reviews the literary and informational standards with new selections and questions in multiple-choice format

Explore Multiple Avenues to Reading Success

Universal Access: Interactive Reading offers alternative direct instruction in and practice of the grade-level standards taught in each chapter of *Holt Literature and Language Arts,* Part 1.

A BOOK FOR STUDENTS' THOUGHTS AND IDEAS

Universal Access: Interactive Reading, a consumable worktext, offers students a hands-on approach to reading. Additional readings related to core selections in the *Pupil's Edition* give students further reading practice. Graphic organizers for each reading selection in the *Pupil's Edition* strengthen comprehension and are ideal for additional instructional time, remediation, or review.

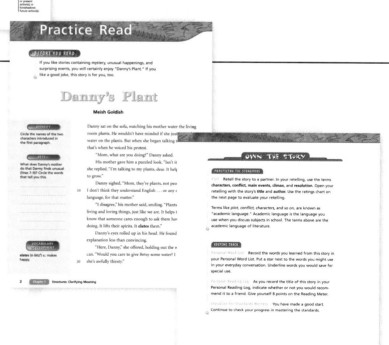

STEP 1: BEGIN WITH A PRACTICE READ

Practice Read

- Uses controlled vocabulary
- Formatted interactively
- Focuses on a reading strategy

Own the Story/ Text/ Poem/ Play

- Applies the reading strategy and literary focus
- Invites use of personal word list and reading log

STEP 2: TURN TO *HOLT LITERATURE AND LANGUAGE ARTS*

After students have completed the **Practice Read** and accompanying exercises, they will be prepared for the chapter selections in *Holt Literature and Language Arts.*

Interact with Informational and Literary Texts

- Includes graphic organizers for students to complete
- Offers reading strategies students can apply to the textbook selection

STEP 3: BUILD INDEPENDENCE WITH ADDITIONAL READING

New selections are presented in the same interactive format as the **Practice Read.**

Interact with New Selections

- Offers opportunities to apply strategies and reinforce skills
- Assigns projects to extend knowledge

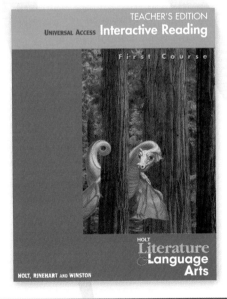

TEACHING SUPPORT FOR TAILORING INSTRUCTION

The *Universal Access: Interactive Reading Teacher's Edition* provides a variety of suggestions and plans to tailor instruction to suit your classroom's needs. This resource is divided into four parts:

- **Part 1: Guide to Teaching Interactive Reading**
- **Part 2: Annotated Edition**
- **Part 3: Graphic Organizers**
- **Part 4: Transparencies for Modeling**

Discover Miles and Miles of
Program Reading Support

CONTENT-AREA READERS

The Ancient World (Grade 6)
A World in Transition (Grade 7)
The United States: Change and Challenge (Grade 8)

Because the language arts can be—and should be—learned in all academic disciplines, the *Content-Area Readers* provide additional reading selections that help students build their reading skills within the context of the social sciences, science, and mathematics. Using interesting, grade-appropriate informational materials, such as newspaper and magazine articles, biographies and autobiographies, excerpts from nonfiction books, and even songs, the *Content-Area Readers* allow students to explore the wonders of history while building reading comprehension, analysis, and vocabulary skills.

Teacher's Guides

These guides include suggestions for differentiating instruction; ideas for building content-area vocabulary; tips for teaching reading strategies; before-, during-, and after-reading activities; and cross-curricular connections to the language arts, art, and social sciences. Also included for each selection are assessments that test for comprehension and vocabulary.

Audio CD Library

Dramatic readings by professional actors bring to life nearly every reading selection in *Holt Literature and Language Arts.*

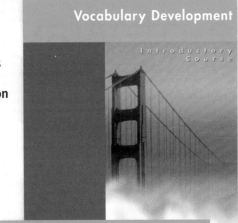

Vocabulary Development

- exercises
- worksheets
- decoding practice
- cumulative review

Visual Connections Videocassette Program

Author biographies, interviews, historical summaries, and cross-curricular connections enrich and extend learning.

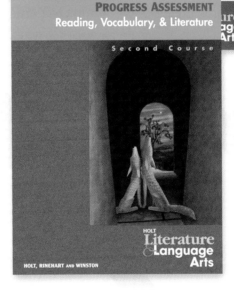

Progress Assessment of Reading, Vocabulary, & Literature

- tests for each *Pupil's Edition* reading selection
- cumulative chapter tests

California HRW Library Middle School Titles

- a collection of titles ideal for motivating readers and achieving the "million words" goal
- connections that extend themes of core literature
- connections drawn from essays, articles, interviews, and biographical sketches
- multicultural literature written for middle school students

Study Guides

- suggestions for differentiating instruction
- reproducible masters for reading, vocabulary, and literary response

Give Students the "Write-of-Way" to Standards Mastery

Part 2 of *Holt Literature and Language Arts* prepares your students to master the California writing standards by offering workshops that focus on different kinds of writing, such as narration, exposition, persuasion, research, and response to literature. Students choose the form of writing best suited to the purpose, develop strategies for organizing support for their main ideas or theses, and learn strategies for evaluating and revising and for using word-processing programs to refine and publish their work.

Professional Model

Introduces the genre of writing

Think About the Model

Working with a partner, discuss the following questions and write down your responses.

1. Do you think the character of Fausto is believable? Why or why not?

2. What details does the writer use to make the story seem true to life?

3. What is the main problem that Fausto faces in the story?

4. Organize the events of the story in a graphic organizer such as a diagram or time line. Below the graphic organizer, write down the theme, or main idea, of the story.

Think About the Model

Guides students to think about the craft of writing

Writer's Framework

Shows students how to structure their papers

Writer's Model

Models the workshop assignment

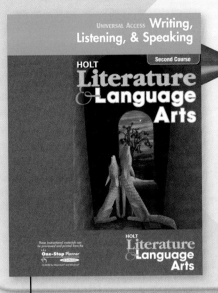

Universal Access: Writing, Listening, & Speaking

Designed to support instruction for students at various levels, this resource provides worksheets and transparencies for each **Writing Workshop.** Transparencies include Journal Warm-ups and motivating visual Writing Prompts.

Grammar Link

Punctuating Dialogue

In your story, you should include **dialogue,** the words that people speak. Punctuate dialogue correctly so your reader can tell the dialogue from the rest of the story.

- Use quotation marks to enclose a person's exact words.

Incorrect We'll hide in Danny's yard until he comes home he whispered.

Correct "We'll hide in Danny's yard until he comes home," he whispered.

- A direct quotation begins with a capital letter. Commas, a question mark, or an exclamation point can separate the dialogue from the rest of the sentence.

Example:

"I'm drenched!" she shouted.

- When the expression identifying the speaker interrupts a quotation, commas set off the expression. The quotation then continues with a small letter.

Example:

"Sonya," Rafael went on, "you hide by the controls for the sprinklers."

- A period or comma always goes inside the closing quotation marks.

Example:

"Here, puppy. Nice puppy," he called, trying not to laugh.

Mrs. Hernandez said, "Nice job watering the lawn."

PRACTICE

Punctuate the dialogue in each of [the fol]lowing sentences.

1. Where were you yesterday aske[...]
2. I'm sorry said Jack I had to stay h[...] school because I had a cold.
3. Too bad Melissa said because yo[...] the tryouts for the school play.
4. Jack sighed I know I guess I'll ha[...] until next year.
5. Why don't you go talk with Mr. [...] gested Melissa.

Reference Note

For more information and practice on [...] dialogue, see pages 322–327 in the Holt [...]

Grammar Link

Shows students how to identify and correct common grammatical errors

---

Short Story: Content and Organization Guidelines		
Evaluation Questions	▶ **Tips**	▶ **Revision Techniques**
❶ Does the story have an interesting plot, with an effective beginning, a conflict, rising action, a suspenseful climax, and a clear denouement?	▶ Place a **check mark** next to each of the following elements: beginning, conflict, rising action, climax, and denouement.	▶ **Add** or **elaborate** on elements of the plot as necessary. **Delete** any information that ruins the suspense.
❷ Is the point of view consistent throughout the story?	▶ **Identify** pronouns (*I, he,* or *she*) that show whether the point of view is first or third person. **Label** the story's point of view; then **circle** any information not given from that point of view.	▶ If any sentences are circled, **delete** them. If necessary, **add** the same information told from the narrator's point of view.
❸ Are the major and minor characters complex and realistic?	▶ **Underline** specific details about each of the characters.	▶ If necessary, **add** details about a character's appearance, personality, or background. **Add** dialogue and narrative actions that tell more about a character.
[...]a	▶ With a colored marker, **highlight** details about the setting.	▶ If there are few highlighted words, **elaborate** on the setting by adding descriptive details.
[...]anized [...] the [...]	▶ **Number** the major events in the story. Put a star next to transitional words and phrases such as *next* and *later that day.*	▶ **Rearrange** any events that are out of order. If there are few or no stars, **add** transitional words and phrases to show the order of events.

Editor in Charge

Poses questions that spark students to think about how to evaluate their papers, and offers tips and appropriate techniques for revising

---

Designing Your Writing

Using White Space Use **white space**—a couple of lines left blank—to show where one part of your story ends and another begins and to give readers' eyes a break. White spaces can show sudden changes in time or place and other shifts or breaks in the flow of a story. For example, a story might begin on Friday morning in a classroom and then move to Saturday evening at a school dance. To divide your story into chapters, start each chapter on a new page. On a computer, do this by inserting a page break.

Designing Your Writing

Teaches the most effective design and layout to convey a message

---

MINI-LESSON · WRITING

Using Narrative Strategies

All people have a complex way of communicating with others—not only with words but by their actions as well. The more you include details in your story about how your characters speak and move, the better your reader will be able to picture them. For example, here is one simple, short line of **dialogue:** *"I'm so glad to see you."* Look at how that simple line of dialogue changes when it is combined with different actions.

doing a cartwheel, running, or simply standing with crossed arms can reveal important information about a character's personality, mood, and intentions.

Gestures When Kara folds her arms, she is demonstrating that she is angry and does not want to be friendly. Like movements, gestures are a kind of body language, usually involving movements of the hands and arms, that can reveal much about your characters.

Writing Mini-Lesson

Offers students opportunities to practice the skills and strategies related to the writing assignment

Widen the Road to Excellent Oral Communication Skills

Part 2 of *Holt Literature and Language Arts* prepares your students to master the California listening and speaking standards with workshops that guide students in delivering focused, coherent presentations and in evaluating a variety of oral and media communications. Each workshop focuses on a different kind of presentation, such as narration, exposition, persuasion, research, and response to literature.

WHAT'S AHEAD?

In this workshop you will deliver an oral narrative. You will also learn how to

- **choose a story and plan how to tell it**
- **use a variety of speaking techniques**
- **listen to and give feedback on an oral narrative**

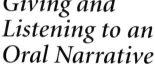
Listening and Speaking Workshop

Giving and Listening to an Oral Narrative

As his family celebrates his great-aunt's ninetieth birthday, Jeremy says, "Aunt Luba, tell us a story about when you were a kid." Aunt Luba smiles slyly and begins, "Well, when I was your age, we didn't have TV, and kids had to make their own fun. One day, my sister—your grandmother Marla—tried to play a trick on me, but I outsmarted her. . . ."

Aunt Luba is telling a story out loud, or sharing an **oral narrative**. In this workshop you will prepare and deliver an oral narrative. You will also evaluate a classmate's oral narrative.

Select a Story

Choose Wisely To plan your oral narrative, you must find the right story to tell. That story should have the following elements.
- **complex major and minor characters** that seem real
- **setting**, a definite time and place in which the story occurs
- **conflict**, a problem that the major character must solve
- **plot**, made up of a **beginning** that sets the scene, **rising action** that leads to the story's **climax**, and a **denouement** or outcome that shows how the conflict is resolved

Make sure the story also has **dialogue** that brings the characters to life, **suspense** that makes listeners wonder what will happen next, and **specific narrative action** that you can describe vividly or act out using movements, gestures, and facial expressions.

WHAT'S AHEAD?

In this workshop you will deliver an oral narrative. You will also learn how to
- choose a story and plan how to tell it
- use a variety of speaking techniques
- listen to and give feedback on an oral narrative

TIP Try to choose a story you know well—the story you wrote in the Writing Workshop or any story you have heard before.

Reference Note
For more on **elements of plot**, see pages 4–5.

Listening and Speaking 2.1a Establish a standard plot line (having a beginning, conflict, rising action, climax, and denouement). 2.1b Describe complex major and minor characters and a definite setting. 2.1c Use a range of appropriate strategies, including dialogue, suspense, and naming of specific narrative action (e.g., movement, gestures, expressions).

558 Workshop 1 **Narration:** Giving and Listening to an Oral Narrative

---

What's Ahead

Alerts students to the standards for each listening and speaking workshop and includes objectives for both strands in each workshop:

- Develop and deliver oral presentations

- Analyze and evaluate oral presentations

SPEAKING TECHNIQUES

Voice Modulation	Change the **tone** and **volume** of your voice to emphasize important moments, to build suspense, and to show emotion.
Inflection	Move the **pitch** of your voice up or down to express shades of meaning or to share your attitude about the subject of the story. For example, a rising inflection can show doubt, surprise, or curiosity. A falling inflection can express certainty.
Tempo	Change the **speed** at which you talk to communicate emotion. For example, you might increase your tempo when delivering a section of your story that involves a high-speed chase.
Enunciation	Say each word clearly and precisely. Be sure not to [___] For example, don't say "I'm gonna" when you mea[___] way a character speaks.
Eye Contact	Make eye contact with your audience members free[___] impression that you were speaking to each of them [___] contact for emphasis at important moments in you[___]

PRACTICE & APPLY 7 — Perform and Respond to an Oral Narrative

- Follow the instructions on pages 558–561 to plan and deliver an oral narrative.
- Pair up with a classmate to evaluate each other's oral narratives. As your partner delivers his or her presentation, make notes of your answers to the questions above. Use your notes to write a one-paragraph evaluation of the presentation. Trade evaluations with your partner and discuss each other's comments. Add notes from this discussion to your partner's evaluation of your presentation to help you improve future presentations.
- Reflect on your presentation. What would you do differently if you told the story again?

Quick Guides

Recap key listening and speaking skills that students will apply in their delivery or evaluation of oral presentations

Practice & Apply

Presents the workshop requirements at a glance and encourages constructive feedback and reflection on student performance

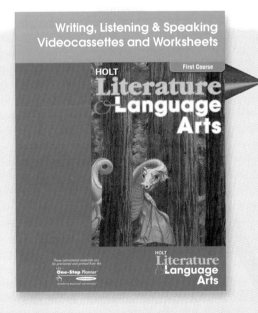

Writing, Listening & Speaking
Videocassettes and Worksheets

HOLT
Literature & Language Arts
First Course

Universal Access: Writing, Listening, & Speaking Videocassettes and Worksheets

- Designed to support instruction and assignments in Part 2 of the *Pupil's Edition*
- Provides support for each listening and speaking workshop
- Includes Think Sheets for the videos to help with previewing and analyzing each segment

Holt Handbook: Your Road Map to Success in Grammar, Usage, and Mechanics

An integral part of the *Holt Literature and Language Arts* program, the *Holt Handbook* answers the call for students to master language skills at levels demanded by the twenty-first century. This invaluable handbook offers teachers and students a method for focusing on the written and oral English-language conventions required by the standards.

Three Parts Cover the Basics

Part I: Grammar, Usage, and Mechanics helps students acquire the building blocks of language: words, phrases, clauses, capitalization, punctuation, and spelling.

Part II: Sentences is divided into two main areas of instruction: Writing Effective Sentences and Sentence Diagramming.

Part III: Resources includes History of English, Test Smarts, and Grammar at a Glance.

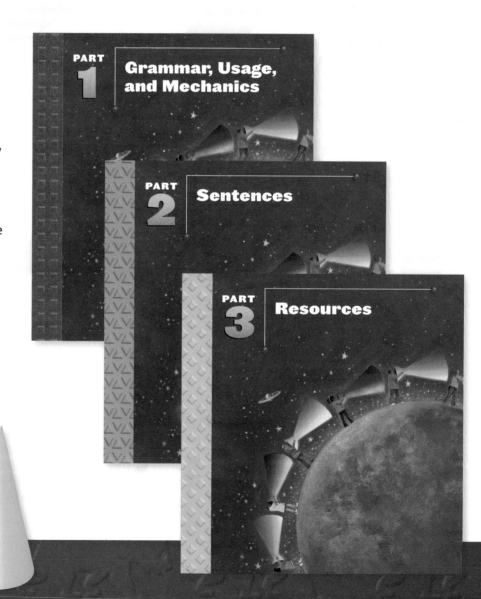

PART 1 Grammar, Usage, and Mechanics

PART 2 Sentences

PART 3 Resources

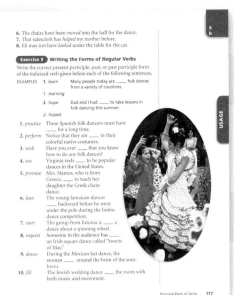

Warriner's Three-Step Approach

An English teacher for thirty years, John Warriner developed the original instructional approach used in the grammar, usage, and mechanics chapters. This logical approach is based on a three-step process:

- Teach students the rule.
- Show examples of the rule in action.
- Provide immediate practice and review to reinforce the skill.

Annotated Teacher's Edition: Suggestions That Keep All Students Involved

Suggestions for differentiating instruction are integrated with lessons to support all students.

Strategies are included to help students make connections between the grammar, usage, and mechanics skills you're teaching them and the writing, science, and social studies skills they need to succeed in other classes.

CONTENT-AREA CONNECTIONS

Social Studies
Places and Names. To give students practice in naming proper nouns, have students complete a team race on a social studies topic that they are studying. Divide the class into groups of four. Give each group a social studies category, and have the groups write ____ can in five ____ re responsible ____ le categories ls, continents, ____ ts, and

DIFFERENTIATING INSTRUCTION

Advanced Learners
Have students read and discuss John Gardner's "Dragon, Dragon" or another folk tale that uses common nouns rather than proper names for its characters. Ask students to consider why the author uses common nouns rather than proper ones for the characters in the story. [*Students may say that there are so many characters in the story that it is easier for the reader to remember them with descriptive common nouns than with proper ones. Common nouns may also make the characters seem more universal.*]

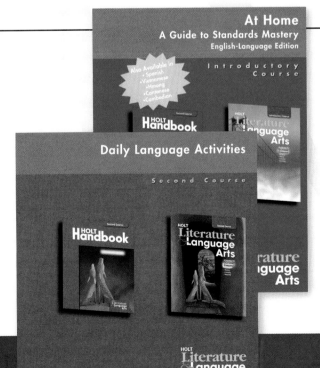

Additional Practice and Strategies to Help Students Succeed

Teaching resources for the program include

- *Universal Access: Developmental Language & Sentence Skills*
- *At Home: A Guide to Standards Mastery*
- *Daily Language Activities Transparencies*
- *Diagnostic and Summative Assessments, California Standards Mastery*
- *Language and Sentence Skills Practice*
- *Progress Assessment for the Holt Handbook*
- *Spelling Lessons and Activities*

Technology resources for the program include

- *One-Stop Planner® CD-ROM with Test Generator*
- **go.hrw.com** Web site

Universal Access

Pave the Way Toward
Each Student's Success

The *Holt Literature and Language Arts* program provides support to help you differentiate instruction for your classroom's specific needs so that every student has an equal opportunity to meet or exceed the California standards. This support is integrated throughout the program (in both the *Pupil's Edition* and the *Annotated Teacher's Edition,* and in the teaching resources), allowing you easy access to alternative methods of planning, instruction, and assessment.

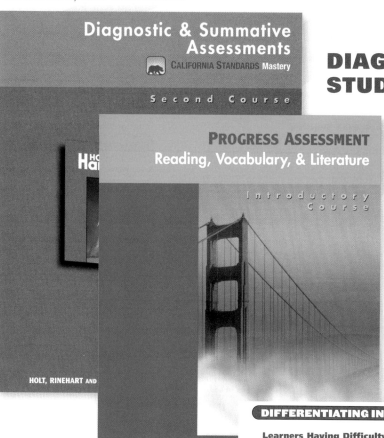

DIAGNOSE AND ASSESS STUDENTS' NEEDS

Diagnostic & Summative Assessments

Determines students' levels of preparation and standards mastery

Progress Assessment

Provides ongoing evaluations of students' skill development and understanding

---

DIFFERENTIATING INSTRUCTION

Learners Having Difficulty
Plot. To help students recognize and describe the plot of a story, suggest that they name a favorite fairy tale or folk tale and the main conflict or problem faced by the characters. As an alternative, provide students with a three- or four-frame cartoon strip, and have them describe the conflict or problem the characters face.

Advanced Learners
Acceleration. Help to move students toward the eighth-grade Standard 3.2, which requires that they determine the structural elements of plot. Ask students working in pairs to take a simple plot and brainstorm a subplot and its resolution to add to the story. Have students create a plot diagram that shows both the plot and the subplot.

Annotated Teacher's Edition

Offers strategies and techniques to tailor instruction for advanced learners, English-language learners, special education students, and learners having difficulty with content. Included are integrated assessments, guided practice, and links to alternative instruction.

OFFER SUPPORT FOR ALL STUDENTS

Universal Access: Interactive Reading

Offers students a consumable worktext to interact with reading selections

- **Reading Strategy** helps students meet a California standard
- **Practice Read** lets students apply the strategy
- **Graphic Organizer** facilitates directed reading

Universal Access: Writing, Listening, & Speaking Videocassettes and Worksheets

- Supports instruction and assignments in Part 2 of the *Pupil's Edition*
- Includes worksheets, transparencies, and video segments for each **Writing Workshop** and each **Listening and Speaking Workshop**

Universal Access: Developmental Language & Sentence Skills Support for the *Holt Handbook*

- Includes remedial worksheets for instruction, practice, and reinforcement of lessons in the *Holt Handbook*
- Targets those students who have not yet mastered specific grammar, usage, and mechanics concepts

Universal Access: Lesson Plans for Language Development

- Includes lesson plans with alternate teaching strategies
- Offers exercises for English-language learners and special education students

At Home: A Guide to Standards Mastery

- Offers letters to parents and guardians with activities related to the instruction in the reading chapters and writing workshops in *Holt Literature and Language Arts* and to lessons in the *Holt Handbook*

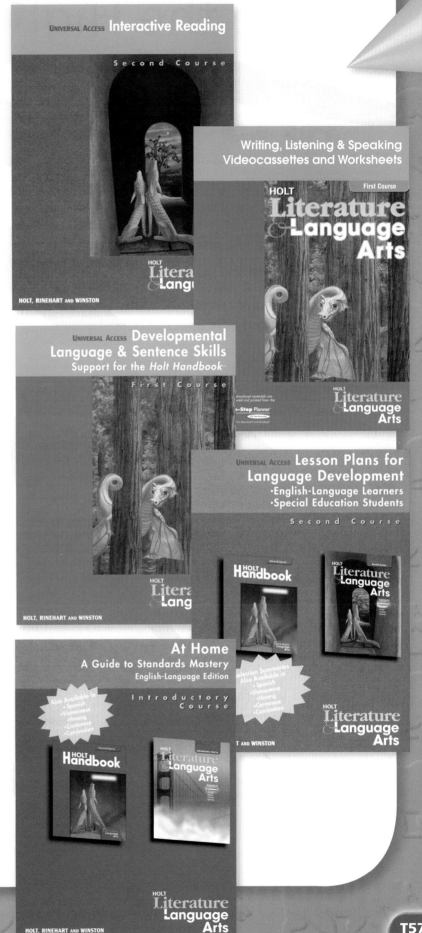

Take the High Road to Assessing Language Arts Proficiency

Because assessment is so important in determining what to teach, how much your students are learning, and whether your students have achieved mastery, *Holt Literature and Language Arts* provides a complete standards-based assessment package that is fully integrated into the program. Carefully planned and sequenced assessment options throughout the *Pupil's Edition, Annotated Teacher's Edition*, and assessment support materials provide the following:

- **entry-level assessments**
- **frequent ongoing assessments**
- **summative assessments**

STANDARDS REVIEW

Literary Response and Analysis

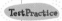 **TestPractice** DIRECTIONS: Read the following story. Then, read each question, and write the letter of the best response.

The Dinner Party
Mona Gardner

The country is India. A colonial official and his wife are giving a large dinner party. They are seated with their guests—army officers and government attachés[1] and their wives, and a visiting American naturalist[2]—in their spacious dining room, which has a bare marble floor, open rafters, and wide glass doors opening onto a veranda.

A spirited discussion springs up between a young girl who insists that women have outgrown the jumping-on-a-chair-at-the-sight-of-a-mouse era and a colonel who says that they haven't.

"A woman's unfailing reaction in any crisis," the colonel says, "is to scream. While a man may feel like it, he has that ounce more of nerve control than a woman has. That last ounce is what counts."

The American does not join in the argument but watches the other guests. As he looks, he sees a strange expression come over the face of the

hostess. She is staring straight ahead, her muscles contracting slightly. With a slight gesture she summons the Indian boy standing behind her chair and whispers to him. The boy's eyes widen; he quickly leaves the room.

Of the guests, none except the American notices this nor sees the boy place a bowl of milk on the veranda just outside the open doors.

The American comes to with a start. In India, milk in a bowl means only one thing—bait for a snake. He realizes there must be a cobra in the room. He looks up at the rafters—the likeliest place—but they are bare. Three corners of the room are empty, and in the fourth the se[...] waiting to serve the nex[...] is only one place left—

His first impulse is t[...] warn the others, but he [...] commotion would frigh[...] into striking. He speaks [...] tone of his voice so arr[...] sobers everyone.

"I want to know just [...] everyone at this table ha[...] to three hundred—that'[...] and not one of you is to [...]

 Reading Standard 3.2
Identify events that advance the plot, and determine how each event explains past or present action(s) or foreshadowing future action(s).

1. **attachés** (at'a-shāz') *n.:* diplomatic officials.
2. **naturalist** *n.:* person who studies nature by observing animals and plants.

96 | Chapter 1 | Structures: Clarifying Meaning

ASSESSMENT LINKED TO INSTRUCTION

The *Pupil's Edition* provides standards review tests at the end of each chapter and workshop for ongoing assessment of reading, writing, and listening and speaking standards.

The *Annotated Teacher's Edition* helps teachers make informed instructional decisions and provides additional opportunities to monitor students' progress.

GUIDED PRACTICE

Monitoring students' progress. Have each student create a sketch of what the story means to him or her. Emphasize that students should not draw a literal illustration of events of the story but rather should sketch symbols of what the story means. Have students share their drawings in small groups. Encourage group members to tell what they see in each drawing, and have each artist explain his or her intent to the group.

ENTRY-LEVEL, ONGOING, AND SUMMATIVE ASSESSMENTS TO TEST FOR PROFICIENCY

Diagnostic & Summative Assessments, California Standards Mastery

- Includes entry-level tests (pretests of essential prior knowledge and skills)
- Includes quarterly tests (summative assessments required by California)

Progress Assessment of Reading, Vocabulary & Literature

- Offers selection tests for reading comprehension, reading skills, literary elements, and vocabulary

Progress Assessment of Writing, Listening, & Speaking

- Includes assessment of writing, listening, and speaking standards in a variety of test formats, including standardized tests
- Provides scales and rubrics for each workshop assignment

Progress Assessment for the *Holt Handbook*, English-Language Conventions

- Contains chapter tests in standardized-test formats for the grammar, usage, and mechanics chapters in the *Holt Handbook*

One-Stop Planner®
with Test Generator
CD-ROM for Macintosh® and Windows®

- Provides a quick and useful way to find test items for each chapter and workshop in *Holt Literature and Language Arts* and for each chapter in the *Holt Handbook*
- Included as part of the *One-Stop Planner* **CD-ROM** program

Explore the World of Technology and the Information Highway

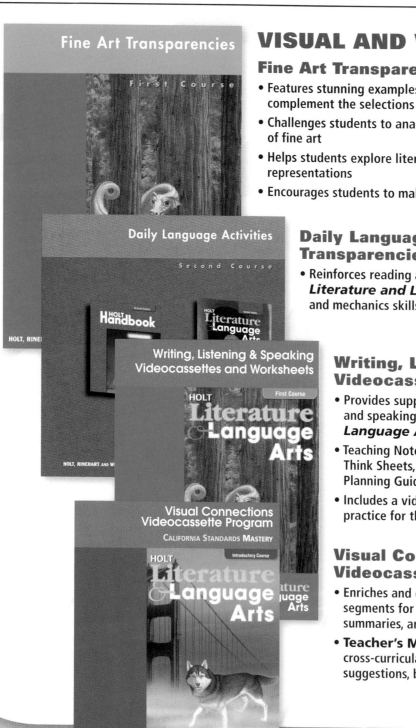

VISUAL AND VIDEO RESOURCES

Fine Art Transparencies

- Features stunning examples of classic and contemporary art that complement the selections in *Holt Literature and Language Arts*
- Challenges students to analyze ideas and culture using transparencies of fine art
- Helps students explore literary characters and ideas through visual representations
- Encourages students to make cross-curricular connections

Daily Language Activities Transparencies

- Reinforces reading and writing skills covered in *Holt Literature and Language Arts* and grammar, usage, and mechanics skills covered in the *Holt Handbook*

Writing, Listening, & Speaking Videocassettes and Worksheets

- Provides support and practice for the writing, listening, and speaking skills addressed in *Holt Literature and Language Arts*
- Teaching Notes pages include suggestions for using Think Sheets, Independent Practice worksheets, Project-Planning Guides, transparencies, and video segments
- Includes a videocassette that provides models and practice for the listening and speaking assignments

Visual Connections Videocassette Program

- Enriches and extends course content with video segments for biographies, interviews, historical summaries, and cross-curricular connections
- **Teacher's Manual** includes background information, cross-curricular connections, additional video suggestions, bibliographies, and worksheets

CD-ROM RESOURCES

Audio CD Library

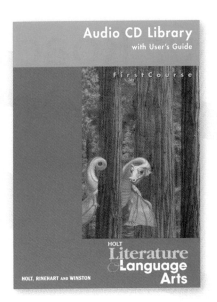

- Makes literature accessible with dramatic readings by professional actors of nearly every reading selection in *Holt Literature and Language Arts*

One-Stop Planner CD-ROM with Test Generator for Macintosh® and Windows®

- Simplifies lesson planning and management
- Includes all the teaching resources for *Holt Literature and Language Arts* and for the *Holt Handbook*
- Includes printable program resources and an easy-to-use test generator
- Offers previews of all teaching resources, including assessments and worksheets linked to the *Pupil's Edition*
- Launches directly to the **go.hrw.com** Web site

One-Stop Planner®

with Test Generator

CD-ROM for Macintosh® and Windows®

Keyword: HLLA

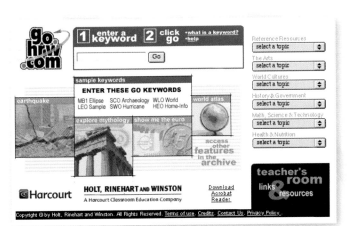

INTERNET RESOURCES

go.hrw.com

Internet references throughout the *Pupil's Edition* direct students to a new Web site for users of *Holt Literature and Language Arts.* This site provides activities and projects for each chapter and workshop and allows students to put their reading, writing, and speaking and listening skills into action in real-world situations.

When students see the **go.hrw.com** logo and a keyword in the textbook, they can go to the **go.hrw.com** site, enter the keyword, and connect instantly to activities and projects for the chapter or workshop they are studying. Additional references to the site appear in the *Annotated Teacher's Edition.*

Engaging interactive tutorials help students discover the elements of great literature, develop reading skills, and dissect the prose of professional writers. Students can also submit their work for publication in an online gallery.

Your Road Map to Teaching
the Literature You Love and the Standards Too

Helping your students learn to appreciate and participate actively in building reading, writing, and grammar skills while guiding them to meet and exceed the California standards may seem like a Herculean task. That's why the ***Holt Literature and Language Arts*** program is so carefully sequenced and why the ***Annotated Teacher's Edition*** provides such easy-to-use planning resources. Now you can teach the literature you love and rely on resources built into ***Holt Literature and Language Arts*** to make planning for, integration of, and preparation for standards mastery an easy, integral part of your time in the classroom.

Instructional Sequence That Helps You Cover It All

Holt Literature and Language Arts provides specific sequencing suggestions to ensure complete coverage of grade-level standards, prerequisite instruction, frequent and effective testing, and remediation and reteaching opportunities.

A variety of instructional options are carefully outlined in both the ***Annotated Teacher's Edition*** chapter interleaf pages and in the resource ***On Course: Mapping Instruction.***

Mastering the California Standards CHAPTER 1

Holt Literature and Language Arts: Mastering the California Standards

Chapter 1 Structures: Building Blocks of Meaning

Program Organization

Holt Literature and Language Arts provides a complete curriculum for standards-based instruction in vocabulary, reading, literature, writing, and speaking and listening. The instructional content of the program is divided into quarters to enable teachers to anticipate and administer the quarterly assessments required by California.

About Chapter 1

Standards-based lesson plans and suggestions for pacing the presentation of Chapter 1 and the related instructional material are provided in *On Course: Mapping Instruction*, Chapter 1.

- Before beginning Chapter 1, give the Entry-Level Diagnostic Test, *Diagnostic & Summative Assessments*. This test will help you determine whether or not your students will need additional instruction and intervention.
- Chapter 1 helps students analyze the influence of setting on plot, identify the structural features of popular media, monitor expository text for unknown words, and use context clues to determine their meaning.
- The related instructional material for Chapter 1 is shown on the chart. This related instructional material will also be covered in the first quarterly assessment.

Holt Literature and Language Arts

Pupil's Edition	Holt Handbook
Part 1, Chapter 1	**Chapter 1**
Structures: Building Blocks of Meaning, pp. 2–49	Parts of the Sentence
• Reading Standards 1.4, 2.1, 3.3	• Written and Oral Language Conventions Standard 1.1, pp. 4–16
• Writing Application Writing a Short Story	
Part 2, Workshop 1	**Chapter 2**
Narration Writing a Short Story, pp. 500–518	Parts of Speech Overview: Noun, Pronoun, Adjective
• Writing Standard 2.1	• Written and Oral Language Conventions Standard 1.2, pp. 30–35
Presenting and Listening to an Oral Narrative, pp. 519–524	• Looking Ahead, Gr. 7 Standard 1.3, pp. 25–41
• Listening and Speaking Standard 2.1	
Part 2, Mini-Workshop 5	
Writing a Personal Narrative, pp. 676–677	
• Writing Standard 2.1	

WORKSHOP RESOURCES

Writing Workshop

Planning
- *On Course: Mapping Instruction*
- *One-Stop Planner* CD-ROM
- *At Home: A Guide to Standards Mastery*, p. 17
- *At Home: In Five Languages*

- *Writing, Listening, & Speaking*, Teaching Notes, p. 1

Differentiating Instruction
- *Lesson Plans for Language Development*, pp. 251–252
- *Supporting Instruction in Five Languages*

Practice
- *Writing, Listening, & Speaking*, Wkshp. 1

Planning Made Easy

Point-of-use references to all chapter resources in the ***Holt Literature and Language Arts Annotated Teacher's Edition*** help you plan your lessons.

A Map to Chart Your Course

On-Course: Mapping Instruction, A Teacher's Guide for Planning charts the instructional path between ***Holt Literature and Language Arts*** and the ***Holt Handbook.***

- Includes planning charts that give overviews of the content covered for each quarter, chapter, and week

- Provides weekly lesson plans with annotated suggestions for the program features that address learners having difficulty, on-level learners, and advanced learners

Point and Click Your Way to Planning Lessons

The ***One-Stop Planner*** **CD-ROM with Test Generator** is an all-in-one planning CD-ROM and includes all the teaching resources for ***Holt Literature and Language Arts*** and for the ***Holt Handbook,*** as well as valuable planning and assessment tools.

Features of the ***One-Stop Planner*** include

- printable program resources

- easy-to-use test generator

- previews of all teaching resources, including assessments and worksheets linked to the ***Pupil's Edition***

- direct launch to the **go.hrw.com** Web site

Teaching resources are presented in point-and-click formats. To preview an assessment or to print out worksheets for your students, simply make your selection and click your mouse.

The road to success lies ahead.

You Can't Soar If You Can't Fly the Plane

by **Kylene Beers**

He was eighty-five years old when he stood in front of the younger man who was wearing a T-shirt that said "A-One Flyers." He told the flight instructor again, "I'm not leaving until you sign me up for flying lessons." The flight instructor said, "Sir, I just don't understand why, at eighty-five, you want to learn how to fly." The old man crossed his arms and said, "I'll never be able to soar if I can't fly the plane."

The man had a point, a good point: *Wanting* to soar wasn't enough to make the soaring happen. He had to know how to fly the plane if he really wanted to climb the clouds.

Think about the things you want to do—all the ways you want to soar. If you want to soar with your favorite computer games, you've got to know all the rules. If you want to soar with sports, you've got to practice. If you want to soar with your grades, you've got to study.

You Can't Soar If You Can't Read

Perhaps more than anything else in life, reading has the potential for letting you soar. With reading you can learn to do just about anything—from building an ark to repairing your zither (or even figuring out what a zither is). With reading you can step back in time, go forward in time, and travel to new lands. With reading you can meet characters who are just like you or as far removed from you as you can possibly imagine. Sometimes books act as mirrors, showing us characters who remind us of ourselves. At other times, books act as windows, showing us characters and situations that take us far beyond ourselves.

Sometimes we need lessons to help us accomplish all the things a skilled reader can do. This textbook is your manual for soaring—it's your pilot's lesson plan for helping you soar as high as you can.

Using the Standards to Set the Standard

This book is designed to help you master the skills you need to be a strong reader *and* writer. The California standards are your tour guide. They will lead you through this book, helping you learn the literacy skills you'll need for this year, for your remaining years in school, and for your life as a member of society.

Everyone who worked on this book—the people who chose the reading selections, the people who wrote the activities, the people who chose the artwork—continually asked themselves, "How do we create a book that not only meets the California standards but also *sets* the standard when it comes to helping students become readers and writers?" We think that as you read through this book, you'll find that we answered that question by providing you with

- interesting selections to read
- powerful models to help you learn to write
- lots of opportunities to practice new skills
- specific information about each

standard—so that you will always know what is expected of you
- the kinds of topics and art that middle-schoolers have told us interest them

In this book, then, you'll get practice in all kinds of language skills.

You will read all kinds of material, from ads to odes, from stories to Web pages.

You will learn better ways to talk, listen, and write.

You will understand more, sound better, and be more confident about what you know and understand.

What's in This Book?

Holt Literature and Language Arts has three parts:

- Part 1 covers reading of all types—literature and informational texts.
- Part 2 covers writing, speaking, and listening.
- The last part of the book is a reference section, full of special activities and information you might need as you work through Parts 1 and 2.

Part 1

The chapters in Part 1 begin with an essay that explains the key standards you'll be mastering in the chapter. After this introductory standards essay, you'll read several literary selections. Following almost every literary selection, you will find some readings, called informational texts. These might be newspaper or magazine articles, Web pages, maps, or other documents. All of these informational texts relate to the piece of literature. For example, in this book you'll read Ray Bradbury's fantasy story "All Summer in a Day," a story set on Venus. Along with this story, you'll find several informational texts, including a NASA Web page about the real-life Venus. Along the way you'll find help in acquiring new words.

Here is a diagram showing how a chapter in Part 1 might look:

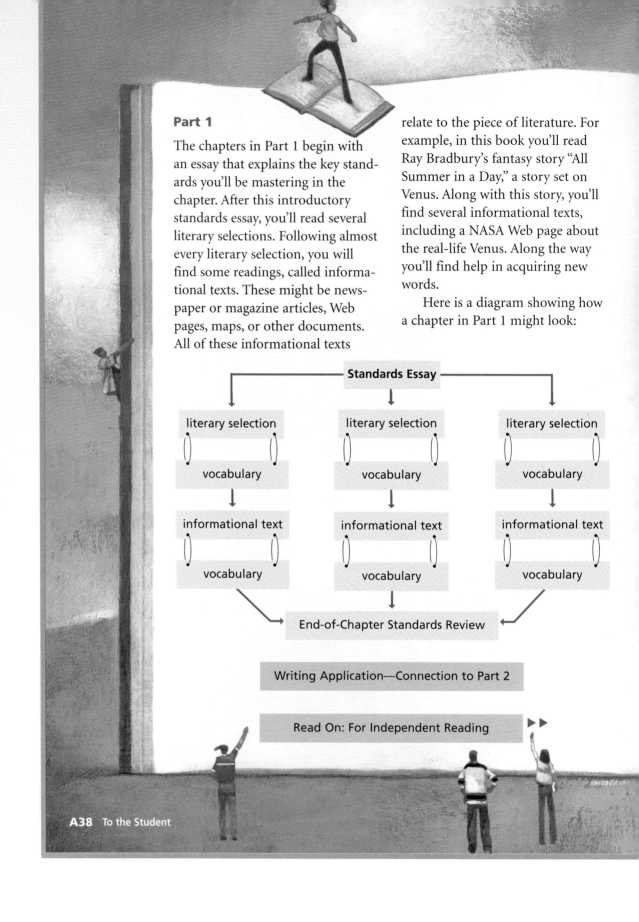

Part 2

Part 2 is a series of big and small workshops that will help you *write*. Here are workshops on writing narratives, essays, research reports, responses to literature—all the writing skills required by the California standards. Part 2 also includes workshops in listening and speaking. All of Part 2 will help you practice the writing, listening, and speaking skills that you are required to master by the end of this school year.

Part 3

Need help with a literary term? Could you use some tips for taking tests? Do you want to find out where to go for help in identifying the main idea of an informational text? Turn to Part 3. Part 3 includes a section called Test Smarts, with tips for test taking. Part 3 includes definitions of literary terms and of reading and informational terms. Part 3 includes a glossary and extensive indexes. Part 3 is your Resource Center.

A Book with a Big Idea

This is a book with a big idea—that you are going to learn a lot about your language.

This book came together because of the efforts of lots of people—writers, editors, artists, teachers, and even students like you.

Now it's time for us to hand the book to you, the reader. We hope you'll use it as a key to lifetime literacy and as a guide to lifetime reading. Enjoy!

 At our Internet site you can discover much more about the stories, poems, and informational materials in this book. You can look at how professional writers work. You can even submit your own writing for publication on an online gallery. As you use *Holt Literature and Language Arts* to master the standards, look for the very best online resources at **go.hrw.com.**

GO TO: go.hrw.com
KEYWORD: HLLA

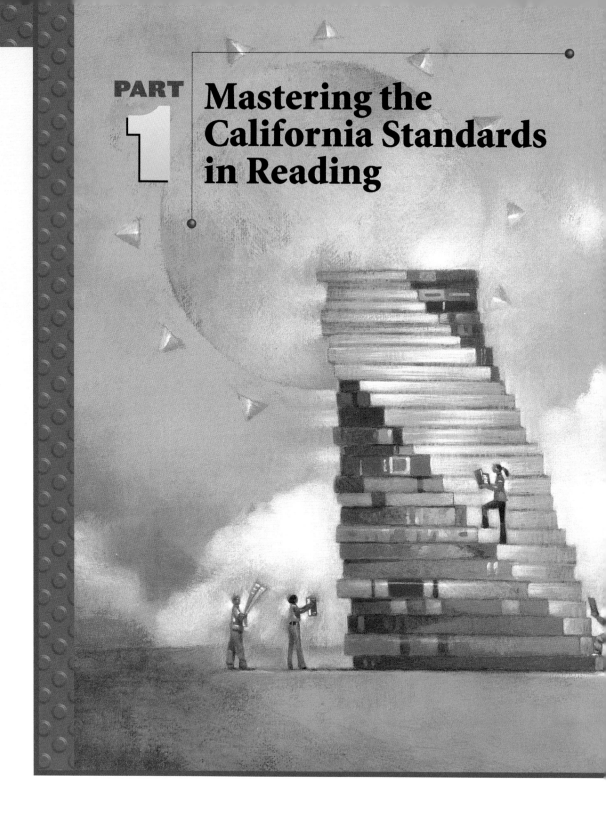

PART 1 Mastering the California Standards in Reading

vocabulary

informational
materials

literature

Chapters

1

Chapter 1 Structures: Building Blocks of Meaning

Program Organization

Holt Literature and Language Arts provides a complete curriculum for standards-based instruction in vocabulary, reading, literature, writing, and speaking and listening. The instructional content of the program is divided into quarters to enable teachers to anticipate and administer the quarterly assessments required by California.

About Chapter 1

Standards-based lesson plans and suggestions for pacing the presentation of Chapter 1 and the related instructional material are provided in *On Course: Mapping Instruction,* Chapter 1.

- Before beginning Chapter 1, give the Entry-Level Diagnostic Test, *Diagnostic and Summative Assessments.* This test will help you determine whether or not your students will need additional instruction and intervention.

- Chapter 1 helps students analyze the influence of setting on plot, identify the structural features of popular media, monitor expository text for unknown words, and use context clues to determine their meaning.

- The related instructional material for Chapter 1 is shown on the chart. This related instructional material will also be covered in the first quarterly assessment.

Holt Literature and Language Arts

Pupil's Edition

Part 1, Chapter 1

Structures:
Building Blocks of Meaning, pp. 2–49
- Reading Standards 1.4, 2.1, 3.3
- Writing Application **Writing a Short Story**

Part 2, Workshop 1

Narration
Writing a Short Story, pp. 500–518
- Writing Standard 2.1
  Presenting and Listening to
  an Oral Narrative, pp. 519–524
- Listening and Speaking Standard 2.1

Part 2, Mini-Workshop 5

Writing a Personal Narrative, pp. 676–677
- Writing Standard 2.1

Holt Handbook

Chapter 1

Parts of the Sentence
Written and Oral English-Language Conventions
- Grade-Level Standard 1.1, pp. 4–16

Chapter 2

Parts of Speech Overview:
Noun, Pronoun, Adjective
Written and Oral English-Language Conventions
- Grade-Level Standard 1.2, pp. 26–28; 34–35
- Looking Ahead, Gr. 7 Standard 1.3, pp. 25–42

Which vocabulary, informational reading, and literature standards are taught in Chapter 1?

In this chapter, students will master the following Grade 6 standards. They will also review a standard from Grade 5. Selections or features marked with a ✔ constitute the minimum course of study that provides coverage of all grade-level standards.

Grade 6 Standards

Word Analysis, Fluency, and Systematic Vocabulary Development

1.4 Monitor expository text for unknown words or words with novel meanings by using word, sentence, and paragraph clues to determine meaning.
✔ Using Context to Determine Meaning, p. 16
   Monitoring Comprehension, p. 27
   Using Glossaries and Dictionaries, p. 32
   Using Context Clues, p. 41

Reading Comprehension (Focus on Informational Materials)

2.1 Identify the structural features of popular media (e.g., newspapers, magazines, online information), and use the features to obtain information.
✔ "Suit Helps Girl Enjoy Daylight" (news article), pp. 28–31
✔ "What Will Our Towns Look Like?" (magazine article), pp. 33–36
✔ "Solar System Bodies: Venus" (Web page), pp. 37–40
✔ Standards Review: Reading Comprehension, pp. 44–45

Literary Response and Analysis

3.3 Analyze the influence of setting on the problem and its resolution.
✔ "Plot and Setting" (standards essay), pp. 4–5
✔ "All Summer in a Day" (short story), pp. 17–26
✔ Standards Review: Literary Response and Analysis, pp. 42–43

Review Standard Grade 5

Reading

3.2 Identify the main problem or conflict of the plot, and explain how it is resolved.
   "Just Once" (short story), pp. 6–15

Where do I locate lesson plans, additional resources, and other teaching aids?

- This Annotated Teacher's Edition and *On Course: Mapping Instruction* provide direction in planning and implementing a complete California standards–based curriculum. These components include instructions for administering diagnostic, progress, and summative tests; for presenting instruction of the standards; for differentiating instruction to provide universal access; and for locating and using the program's ancillaries.

- The program's resources are referenced at the beginning of each selection, in the bottom margin of this teacher's edition.

- Reminders for using additional resources appear in this teacher's edition at point of use.

- The *One-Stop Planner* CD-ROM with Test Generator contains editable lesson plans and all of the print ancillaries, available in PDF format.

What if I don't have time to teach all of Chapter 1?

- Most standards can be taught with a minimum number of selections and features. In the chart on p. 1B, the core lessons you need in order to provide complete coverage of the chapter standards are identified with a ✔.

- Use the Standards Review, pp. 42–45, for a quick review and informal assessment of the grade-level standards covered in Chapter 1.

What provisions have been made for students who have additional class time scheduled in language arts?

- *Interactive Reading* provides for additional direct instruction and practice of the grade-level standards taught in Chapter 1. It can be used as an introduction to instruction or as an opportunity for remediation.

- *Lesson Plans for Language Development*, Chapter 1, provides alternative teaching strategies and additional worksheets designed specifically for English-language learners and special education students. Many of the suggestions and activities in this ancillary will also be helpful to students in the regular classroom who are having difficulty with particular skills.

In addition to vocabulary, reading, and literature, what other language arts are covered in Chapter 1?

Writing Activities in Chapter 1
- The Way to the Prize: A Life Map (outline a life history), p. 15
- You Had to Be There (describe a bad-weather experience), p. 26

Writing Applications (p. 47)
- After They Let Margot Out . . . (short story)

- Another Choice: "A Dark and Stormy Night" (short story)

Grammar Links in Chapter 1
- Troublesome Verbs, p. 16
- Subject-Verb Agreement: Search for the Subject, p. 27

Universal Access

How do I differentiate instruction to ensure that all my students master the standards?

Holt Literature and Language Arts provides comprehensive, differentiated instruction for all types of students.

- Most of the general instruction and teaching strategies in the Annotated Teacher's Edition are at grade level. These instructions will work well with the majority of your students.

- In Chapter 1, suggestions for advanced learners are provided in the Annotated Teacher's Edition. Point-of-use suggestions for learners having difficulty, English-language learners, and special education students are also provided.

- *Interactive Reading* is designed to anticipate and/or remediate problems that students may experience in achieving mastery of the standards. *Interactive Reading* includes reading-strategy lessons, lower-level practice reads, and worksheets for every informational and literary text in *Holt Literature and Language Arts,* Pupil's Editions. *Interactive Reading* also contains three additional selections for each chapter and suggestions for extension projects, many of which are ideal for advanced learners working on their own. See *Interactive Reading,* Teacher's Edition, for specific information on using the reader to differentiate instruction in Chapter 1.

- *Lesson Plans for Language Development,* Chapter 1, offers teaching strategies and additional worksheets designed specifically for English-language learners and special education students.

Assessment

How do I determine whether or not my students are making progress in mastering the standards?

Progress Assessment

- Use the Standards Review at the end of Chapter 1, pp. 42–45, for an informal assessment of the informational reading and literature standards in Chapter 1.

- Use the Selection Tests for Chapter 1 in the *Progress Assessment of Reading* booklet to test comprehension and progress on mastering the standard(s) taught with a selection.

- Use Chapter Test 1 in the *Progress Assessment of Reading* booklet to test students' cumulative progress in mastering the standards taught in the chapter.

Summative Assessment

The content of *Holt Literature and Language Arts* has been divided into quarters to allow you to administer the four summative tests required by California. Chapters 1 and 2 and related instructional material constitute the quarter of instruction. At the end of Chapter 2, you may ask students to take the First-Quarter Test in the *Diagnostic and Summative Assessments* booklet.

Structures
Building Blocks of Meaning

STANDARDS FOCUS

(For grade-level and review standards taught in this chapter, see Pupil's Edition, p. 3)

Prerequisite Standards

- Grade 5, Vocabulary 1.2 **Use word origins to determine the meaning of unknown words.**

- Grade 5, Reading Comprehension 2.1 **Understand how text features (e.g., format, graphics, sequence, diagrams, illustrations, charts, maps) make information accessible and usable.**

Standards Coming Up in the Next Grade Level

- Grade 7, Vocabulary 1.3 **Clarify word meanings through the use of definition, example, restatement, or contrast.**

- Grade 7, Reading Comprehension 2.1 **Understand and analyze the differences in structure and purpose between various categories of informational materials (e.g., textbooks, newspapers, instructional manuals, signs).**

- Grade 7, Literary Response and Analysis 3.2 **Identify events that advance the plot, and determine how each event explains past or present action(s) or foreshadows future action(s).**

CHAPTER RESOURCES

Planning
- *One-Stop Planner* CD-ROM with Test Generator
- *On Course: Mapping Instruction*
  - Chapter 1
- *At Home: A Guide to Standards Mastery*
- *At Home: In Five Languages*
- *Supporting Instruction in Five Languages*

Reading
- *Interactive Reading*
  - Chapter 1

Differentiating Instruction
- *Lesson Plans for Language Development*
  - Chapter 1

Vocabulary and Spelling
- *Vocabulary Development*
  - Cumulative Vocabulary Review, p. 5

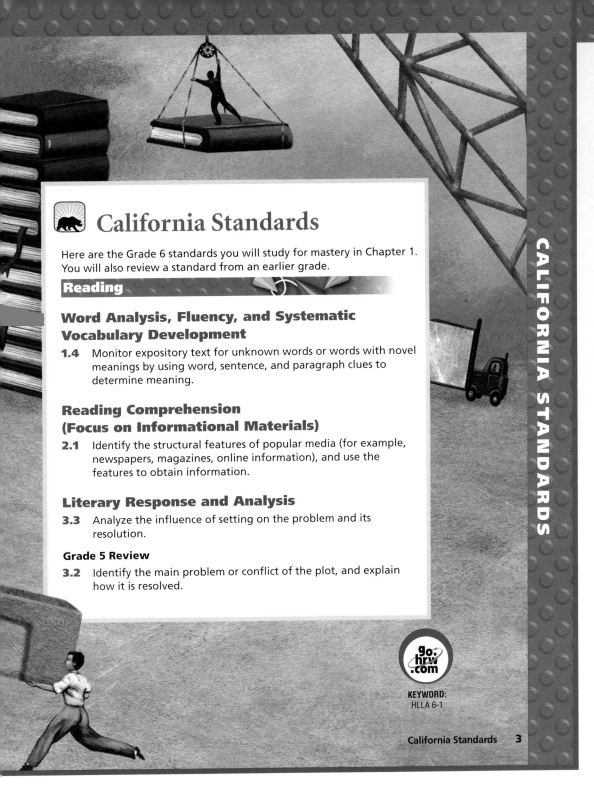

California Standards

Here are the Grade 6 standards you will study for mastery in Chapter 1. You will also review a standard from an earlier grade.

Reading

Word Analysis, Fluency, and Systematic Vocabulary Development

1.4 Monitor expository text for unknown words or words with novel meanings by using word, sentence, and paragraph clues to determine meaning.

Reading Comprehension (Focus on Informational Materials)

2.1 Identify the structural features of popular media (for example, newspapers, magazines, online information), and use the features to obtain information.

Literary Response and Analysis

3.3 Analyze the influence of setting on the problem and its resolution.

Grade 5 Review

3.2 Identify the main problem or conflict of the plot, and explain how it is resolved.

go.hrw.com

KEYWORD:
HLLA 6-1

California Standards   **3**

INTRODUCING THE CHAPTER

The stories in this chapter focus on things that happen just once—or at least very seldom. They invite readers to explore the implications of special or rare events and to appreciate the relationship between these events and the setting in which they occur. Three informational pieces follow the Ray Bradbury story "All Summer in a Day." As students read these informational pieces, they learn to identify and use structural features of newspapers, magazines, and online sources. The chapter ends with an opportunity for students to write their own short story, drawing inspiration from the thought-provoking plot and characters of "All Summer in a Day."

▶ Resources Reminder

Assessment

■ *Diagnostic and Summative Assessments*

  ■ Entry-Level Diagnostic Test, p. 6

This test will help you determine whether your students have mastered previous and grade-level standards.

Planning

■ *At Home: A Guide to Standards Mastery*

You may want to send home with students selected parent letters from this resource. Translations of these letters are available in *At Home: In Five Languages*. *Supporting Instruction in Five Languages* provides translations of the selection summaries.

Reading

■ *Interactive Reading*

  ■ Reading Log

The California framework requires students to read materials apart from in-class assignments. Additional reading suggestions are included on the Read On pages and on selected other pages in the Pupil's and Teacher's Editions. You may want to use the Reading Log to help students track their progress.

Grammar

■ *Holt Handbook*
  ■ Troublesome Verbs, pp. 150–159
  ■ Subject-Verb Agreement, pp. 124–137

Assessment

■ *Progress Assessment of Reading*
  ■ Chapter Test, p. 1
■ *Diagnostic and Summative Assessments*
  ■ Entry-Level Diagnostic Test, p. 6

■ *One-Stop Planner* CD-ROM with Test Generator

Internet

■ go.hrw.com
  Keyword: HLLA 6-1

STANDARDS FOCUS, pp. 4–5

(For the grade-level standard taught in this lesson, see Pupil's Edition, p. 4.)

Prerequisite Standard

■ Grade 5, Literary Response and Analysis 3.2 **Identify the main problem or conflict of the plot, and explain how it is resolved.**

Literary Focus: Plot and Setting

Review with the class the definitions of the terms *plot, conflict,* and *setting.* Invite students to imagine a familiar story in a new setting, such as *Robin Hood* set in Hawaii or *Star Wars* set during the Revolutionary War. Ask how the change in setting might change the conflicts and action. [Possible responses: Robin Hood fights polluters and surfs to the rescue. A bewigged Darth Vader masterminds redcoat schemes.]

▶ Resources Reminder

Reading

■ *Interactive Reading*

Before you teach Chapter 1 of *Holt Literature and Language Arts,* you may want to preteach the literary concept and a related reading strategy.

• To introduce students to the literary concept before they read this essay, assign p. 1 of *Interactive Reading.*

• To introduce students to a reading strategy that will help them grasp the literary concept, assign p. 1 of *Interactive Reading.*

• To give students practice applying the strategy to a short, vocabulary-controlled selection, assign the Practice Read on p. 2 of *Interactive Reading.*

Plot and Setting *by* Madeline Travers Hovland

Plot: The Story's Structure

Plot is the series of events in a story. Plot answers the question "What happened?"

1 The first part of the plot tells you about the story's basic situation. It often answers these questions:

• Who is the main **character**?

• What is the character's basic problem, or **conflict**?

A **conflict** is a struggle. One kind of conflict involves two characters opposing each other. Another kind of conflict involves a character struggling with a **setting**—a flood, a drought, a hurricane, a mountain, a dying space station. Conflict might also involve a character against a whole group of other people. Conflict can even result from a struggle inside a character—for confidence, for example, or for self-control.

Here's the beginning of a story in which the setting creates the problem:

As the hot July sun slipped below the horizon, a cooling darkness filled Central Valley. Lisa had just fallen asleep when the windows of the trailer rattled like a snake giving warning. The trailer swayed back and forth. Lisa could hear the baby screaming. Papa yelled, "Outside! Get out! Get out! It's an earthquake!"

Reading Standard 3.3 Analyze the influence of setting on the problem and its resolution.

2 As the story continues, the characters take action to solve their life-threatening problem. **Complications** arise, which means new problems come up. All of this creates suspense. We worry, "What will happen to the little family?"

The earth groaned, and a river of mud slid down the canyon. The family huddled together in the dark. Mama tore up a sheet to make a sling for Papa's broken arm. Papa shined his flashlight on the wreck that used to be the trailer. "It could explode," he warned. "Don't get any closer."

The baby kept screaming. Lisa's mother said, "I have nothing to feed him. What are we going to do?" Suddenly the earth rumbled again. Lisa looked back at the trailer and saw fallen electric wires dangling all around it.

3 When you read a good story, you become more and more involved with the plot as the characters try to solve their problems. You want to know what will happen next and how the conflict will turn out. At last you reach the **climax,** the most exciting moment of the story. This is the point where you find out how the conflict will be resolved.

Lisa stumbled down the side of the canyon. She could hear a siren coming

4

▶ DIFFERENTIATING INSTRUCTION

Learners Having Difficulty
Plot and setting. To help students understand how the setting of a story may create a conflict, suggest a couple of settings to them, such as an isolated farmhouse during a three-day blizzard or an abandoned, run-down mansion on a cold, wintry night. Invite students to brainstorm about a struggle that characters might face in that setting.

Advanced Learners
Acceleration. Help to move advanced learners toward the seventh-grade Standard 3.2, which requires that they explain how each event relates to past actions or foreshadows future actions. Have students look again at the plot diagram they have created. Have them consider how each event leads to the next event. Then, ask them to

closer. The lights of a helicopter shone on her like a spotlight. "Stop! Help us!" she cried, frantically waving her arms. The copter clattered to the ground.

4 In the **resolution,** the final part of the plot, the characters' problems are solved one way or another and the story ends. In this story we may find the family in their grandmother's home, a safe distance from the scene of the quake. We may see the family returning to their ruined home weeks after the earthquake and starting to rebuild their lives. What other resolutions can you think of?

Setting and Conflict

Setting is where and when the action of a story takes place. Some stories could take place almost anywhere, but in most stories, setting plays a more important role. Writers often use setting to create atmosphere: scary, peaceful, gloomy. In many stories, setting controls the action; it is so crucial to the plot that the story could not take place anywhere else.

In many stories the characters are in conflict with the setting. This is what happens in the little story you just read. In that story the family must struggle to survive an earthquake. Their very lives are threatened by their setting.

We see this kind of conflict a lot in the movies. You might have seen characters fight to survive on a cold mountain with no food. You might have seen a movie about people marooned in a rowboat in the middle of the Pacific

Ocean or trapped by a raging forest fire. All of these are conflicts with settings.

In these stories, if the characters can survive the threat posed by the setting, the story is resolved happily. If the setting is more powerful than the human characters, then the story's resolution is very sad indeed.

Practice

The main events of a **plot** can be charted in a diagram like this one:

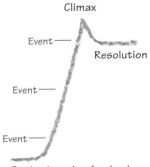

Fill out a diagram like this one, tracing the plot of a movie or book you know well. Try to find a story in which a character struggles with a setting that threatens his or her life.

explore what would happen if they changed one event near the middle of the story. How would this change lead to changes in future events? What changes in past actions are necessary to make the new event seem possible—or even inevitable? Ask students to create a plot diagram that outlines all of the revised events. Then, have students meet in a group to share and explain their revised diagrams.

Students might choose a story such as Scott O'Dell's *Island of the Blue Dolphins.* Possible diagram entries might include the following:

Basic situation—Twelve-year-old Karana's tribe abandons San Nicolas Island, and she must survive there alone.

First event—Karana sets sail from the island with her people, but her little brother Ramo is accidentally left behind, and she swims back to stay with him.

Second event—Wild dogs kill Ramo.

Third event—Karana finds a canoe and tries to reach the mainland but fails.

Fourth event—Karana tames a wild dog, who helps her hunt, fish, and gather survival materials.

Fifth event—When an enemy group lands on the island, Karana secretly befriends a girl, but the group leaves and does not return.

Climax—After several years, Spanish missionaries come to the island. Too lonely to hide, Karana agrees to sail with them to the mainland.

Resolution—Karana finds a new home at Mission Santa Barbara.

Apply

Encourage students to imagine new settings for the stories they have just diagrammed. Have students fill in new diagrams and speculate about how the change in setting might change the story's action and conflict.

▶ Resources Reminder

Differentiating Instruction

■ *Lesson Plans for Language Development*

For additional instruction on plot and setting for English-language learners and special education students, see *Lesson Plans for Language Development,* pp. 3–4.

STANDARDS FOCUS, pp. 6–16

(For grade-level and review standards taught in this selection, see citations on Pupil's Edition pages.)

Standard Coming Up in the Next Grade Level

■ Grade 7, Literary Response and Analysis 3.2 **Identify events that advance the plot, and determine how each event explains past or present action(s) or foreshadows future action(s).**

Reading Skills

■ Retell story events.

Summary ⬇ *below grade level*

Bryan Crawford, "the Moose," plays left tackle for the Bedford City Bears. His problem is that he wants to change his position and carry the ball. He longs to hear the fans cheer for him as they do for the fullback Jerry Dixon. Coach Williams good-naturedly denies the Moose's request, but the Moose launches a campaign to change the coach's mind. As a result, during a home game in which the Bears are leading 28–0 at halftime, the fans begin to yell, "Give the Moose the ball!" Hearing the crowd, the coach decides to give the Moose a chance. Although the lineman scores amid the cheers of the crowd, the Moose is surprised by the pummeling the opposing team's tacklers give him as he makes the touchdown. Once he experiences the painful reality of carrying the ball, the Moose decides "never again."

Just Once

Literary Focus
Plot and Conflict

In this story, Bryan "the Moose" Crawford, a high school football player, longs to hear the crowd roaring his name. His campaign to make this happen creates conflict. **Conflict** is the struggle that pulls us into a story and won't let us go until we find out who (or what) wins.

Reading Skills
Retelling

You can use a strategy called **retelling** to find the conflict and the important events in the plot. As you read this story, you'll see little open-book signs () alongside the text. At those points, stop and retell what has just happened. Focus on the major events that keep the plot moving. Jot down your retellings.

Make the Connection
Quickwrite ✏️

Have you ever dreamed of walking onstage to accept an Oscar? Do you long to be a basketball star? Would you give anything to be the best dancer at your school? We aim for many different goals in life. One dream that many of us share is to hear the crowd cheering, just once, just for us. You may have to fight your way to that moment of glory. Tell what you are willing to do—and not willing to do—to be a star.

Grade 5 Review Reading Standard 3.2 Identify the main problem or conflict of the plot.

Vocabulary Development

This story is easy to read, but it does contain a few words that might be new to you. See if you can make up a sentence of your own for each of the following words:

devastating (dev'ə·stāt'iŋ) *v.* used as *adj.:* causing great damage. *The Moose's devastating attack punched a hole through the opposing team's line.*

nurturing (nʉr'chər·iŋ) *v.:* promoting the growth of; nursing. *The Moose's teammates suspected that he had been nurturing his dream for a while.*

anonymous (ə·nän'ə·məs) *adj.:* unknown; unidentified. *The Moose was tired of being anonymous.*

tolerant (täl'ər·ənt) *adj.:* patient; accepting of others. *A less tolerant coach might have become angry.*

ponder (pän'dər) *v.:* think over carefully. *Coach Williams walked off to ponder the Moose's request.*

▶ Resources Reminder

Media
■ *Audio CD Library*
  ▪ disc 1

Reading
■ *Interactive Reading*
  ▪ Strategy Launch: Retelling, p. 1
  ▪ Practice Read: "Zoo," p. 2
  ▪ Graphic Organizer: Story Chart, p. 7

RESOURCES

Planning
■ *One-Stop Planner* CD-ROM with Test Generator
■ *On Course: Mapping Instruction*

Media
■ *Audio CD Library*
  ▪ disc 1

Reading
■ *Interactive Reading*
  ▪ Strategy Launch: Retelling, p. 1
  ▪ Practice Read: "Zoo," p. 2
  ▪ Graphic Organizer: Story Chart, p. 7
■ *Interactive Reading,* Teacher's Edition
  ▪ Transparency 1: Retelling

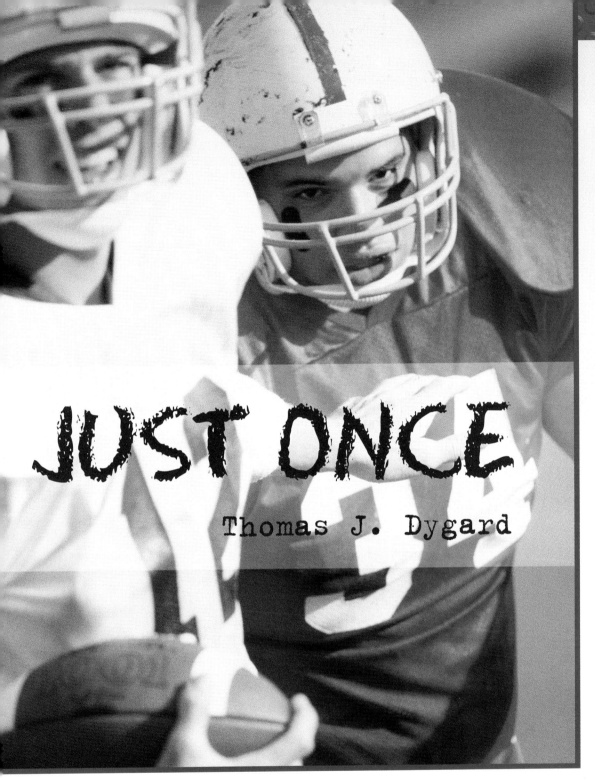

JUST ONCE

Thomas J. Dygard

Standards Starter

Motivate. Ask students if they have ever heard the expression "walk in another's shoes." Talk about what the saying means, and then ask, "Whose shoes would you like to walk in? Why? What would you expect this experience to be like?" Then, ask students to complete the Quickwrite activity.

Preview Vocabulary

Have students read the definitions of the Vocabulary words on p. 6. Then, have them explain their answers to the following questions.

1. Which would be a more important news story, a <u>devastating</u> earthquake or a mild earthquake?

2. Does <u>nurturing</u> a grudge seem like a good idea?

3. If you wrote a bestselling novel, would you want to be <u>anonymous</u>?

4. Do you like it when people are <u>tolerant</u> of your mistakes?

5. Would you make a serious decision quickly, or would you <u>ponder</u> it?

Assign the Reading

The syntax of this story is relatively simple, but the author uses colloquial language that may pose problems for English-language learners. Allow advanced learners and learners having difficulty to read the story independently while you work with students unfamiliar with colloquialisms such as *cinch,* meaning "a sure thing," and *hang-up,* meaning "problem."

Differentiating Instruction
■ *Lesson Plans for Language Development*
- English-Language Learners, pp. 5–7, 16, 21
- Special Education Students, pp. 8, 16, 21

Vocabulary and Spelling
■ *Vocabulary Development*
- Vocabulary Worksheet, p. 1

Assessment
■ *Progress Assessment of Reading*
- Selection Test, p. 1
■ *One-Stop Planner* CD-ROM with Test Generator

A English-Language Learners

Understanding football terminology. Ask one or more knowledgeable volunteers to explain the basics of football for any students who might not be familiar with the game. Make sure all students grasp the main point: that the linemen perform the job of blocking the opposing team, a task that enables the seemingly more glamorous runners to score touchdowns.

B Literary Focus
REVIEW STANDARD

❓ Conflict. What do you suppose the main struggle, or conflict, in the story is going to be about? [The Moose longs for the kind of recognition that goes with scoring a touchdown, yet doing that is not his job. He is a blocker.]

Everybody liked the Moose. To his father and mother he was Bryan—as in Bryan Jefferson Crawford—but to everyone at Bedford City High he was the Moose. He was large and strong, as you might imagine from his nickname, and he was pretty fast on his feet—sort of nimble, you might say—considering his size. He didn't have a pretty face but he had a quick and easy smile—"sweet," some of the teachers called it; "nice," others said.

But on the football field, the Moose was neither sweet nor nice. He was just strong and fast and a little bit devastating as the left tackle of the Bedford City Bears. When the Moose blocked somebody, he stayed blocked. When the Moose was called on to open a hole in the line for one of the Bears' runners, the hole more often than not resembled an open garage door.

Now in his senior season, the Moose had twice been named to the all-conference team and was considered a cinch for all-state. He spent a lot of his spare time, when he wasn't in a classroom or on the football field, reading letters from colleges eager to have the Moose pursue higher education—and football—at their institution.

But the Moose had a hang-up.

He didn't go public with his hang-up until the sixth game of the season. But, looking back, most of his teammates agreed that probably the Moose had been nurturing the hang-up secretly for two years or more.

The Moose wanted to carry the ball.

For sure, the Moose was not the first interior lineman in the history of football, or even the history of Bedford City High, who banged heads up front and wore bruises like badges of honor—and dreamed of racing down the field with the ball to the end zone[1] while everybody in the bleachers screamed his name.

But most linemen, it seems, are able to stifle the urge. The idea may pop into their minds from time to time, but in their hearts they know they can't run fast enough, they know they can't do that fancy dancing to elude tacklers, they know they aren't trained to read blocks. They know that their strengths and talents are best utilized in the line. Football is, after all, a team sport, and everyone plays the position where he most helps the team. And so these linemen, or most of them, go back to banging heads without saying the first word about the dream that flickered through their minds.

Not so with the Moose.

That sixth game, when the Moose's hang-up first came into public view, had ended with the Moose truly in all his glory as the Bears' left tackle. Yes, glory—but uncheered and sort of anonymous. The Bears were trailing 21–17 and had the ball on Mitchell High's five-yard line, fourth down,[2] with time running out. The rule in such a situation is simple—the best back carries the ball behind the best blocker—and it is a rule seldom violated by those in control of their faculties.[3] The Bears,

---

1. **end zone** *n.:* area between the goal line and the end line (the line marking the boundary of the playing area) at each end of a football field.
2. **fourth down:** In football the team holding the ball is allowed four downs, or attempts to carry the ball forward at least ten yards.
3. **faculties** *n.:* mental powers.

Vocabulary

devastating (dev′ə·stāt′iŋ) *v.* used as *adj.:* causing great damage.

nurturing (nur′chər·iŋ) *v.:* promoting the growth of; nursing.

anonymous (ə·nän′ə·məs) *adj.:* unknown; unidentified.

DIFFERENTIATING INSTRUCTION

Learners Having Difficulty
Modeling. Some students may need to read an easier selection before beginning "Just Once." Use the Practice Read in *Interactive Reading,* p. 2. You can use the transparency to model the reading skill of retelling. This skill can help students identify the events in the plot and the main conflict. Then, have students apply the skill to "Just Once." As they read, encourage

students to ask themselves, "What does the main character want, and what is stopping him or her from getting it?"

 Resources Reminder
Reading

■ *Interactive Reading,* Teacher's Edition
  ■ Transparency 1: Retelling

English-Language Learners
Enlist football fans in your class to explain terms such as *back* for the position of running back or fullback, *snap* for the play-opening pass of the ball from the center to the quarterback, and *huddle* for the team-strategy session before each play.

of course, followed the rule. That meant Jerry Dixon running behind the Moose's blocking. With the snap of the ball, the Moose knocked down one lineman, bumped another one aside, and charged forward to flatten an approaching linebacker. Jerry did a little jig behind the Moose and then ran into the end zone, virtually untouched, to win the game.

After circling in the end zone a moment while the cheers echoed through the night, Jerry did run across and hug the Moose, that's true. Jerry knew who had made the touchdown possible.

But it wasn't the Moose's name that everybody was shouting. The fans in the bleachers were cheering Jerry Dixon.

It was probably at that precise moment that the Moose decided to go public.

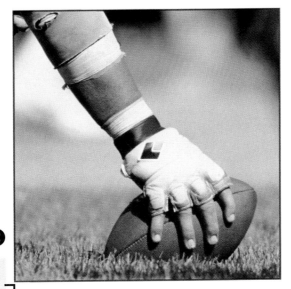

In the dressing room, Coach Buford Williams was making his rounds among the cheering players and came to a halt in front of the Moose. "It was your great blocking that did it," he said.

"I want to carry the ball," the Moose said.

Coach Williams was already turning away and taking a step toward the next player due an accolade[4] when his brain registered the fact that the Moose had said something strange. He was expecting the Moose to say, "Aw, gee, thanks, Coach." That was what the Moose always said when the coach issued a compliment. But the Moose had said something else. The coach turned back to the Moose, a look of disbelief on his face. "What did you say?"

"I want to carry the ball."

---

4. **accolade** (ak′ə·lād′) *n.*: something said or done to express praise.

RETELLING

1. What happens after Jerry scores a touchdown?

"I WANT TO CARRY THE BALL," THE MOOSE SAID.

Coach Williams was good at quick recoveries, as any high school football coach had better be. He gave a tolerant smile and a little nod and said, "You keep right on blocking, son."

This time Coach Williams made good on his turn and moved away from the Moose.

The following week's practice and the next Friday's game passed without further incident. After all, the game was a road game over at Cartwright High, thirty-five miles away. The Moose wanted to carry the ball in front of the Bedford City fans.

Vocabulary
tolerant (täl′ər·ənt) *adj.*: patient; accepting of others.

C Reading Skills

? Expressing an opinion. Is it true in real life that linemen go unnoticed? [Possible responses: Yes, they have always received less fame and money than quarterbacks, running backs, and receivers. No, informed fans are increasingly aware of their importance, and the best linemen are recognized and rewarded.]

D Reading Skills

Retelling. Stress that the skill of retelling can help students focus on the various conflicts in a story.

[Possible response to question 1: After Jerry scores a touchdown, he circles in the end zone for the cheering fans and then runs across and hugs the Moose.]

▶ Resources Reminder

For lessons designed for both intermediate and advanced English-language learners, see *Lesson Plans for Language Development,* pp. 5–7,16, 21.

Special Education Students

For lessons designed for special education students, see *Lesson Plans for Language Development,* pp. 8, 16, 21.

Advanced Learners

Acceleration. Use the following activity with advanced learners to move them toward the seventh-grade Standard 3.2, which requires that they identify events that advance the plot and determine how each event foreshadows future action.
Activity. Suggest that students note story events as they read—events that they think will affect the plot. Have students fill in a

two-column chart, recording the events in the first column and what they think might or should happen as a result in the second column. Ask students to look in the text for the phrase "just once," which is also the title. What do they predict this phrase will mean?

A Literary Focus
REVIEW STANDARD
? Conflict. How does the Moose make his wishes more apparent? [He repeats his demand to the coach.] What effect does this have on the conflict in the story? [It heightens the conflict by signaling that the Moose is not going to let the coach ignore his request.]

B Reading Skills
? Interpreting. What do you think the coach is really thinking at this moment? [Possible responses: He is thinking about how to answer the Moose; he is trying not to lose his temper.]

C Reading Skills
Retelling. [Possible response to question 2: The coach tells the Moose he is a "great left tackle, a great blocker" and to keep on blocking.] Because of this refusal, the conflict between the coach and the Moose continues.

D English-Language Learners
Building background knowledge. Ask a volunteer to explain the role of the quarterback in football. [The quarterback calls the signals for the plays that the team will execute and often passes the ball. This player is often a team leader.]

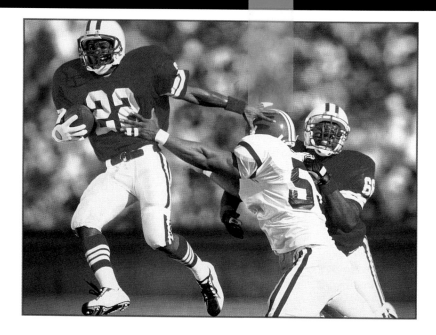

"SON, YOU'RE A GREAT LEFT TACKLE, A GREAT BLOCKER. LET'S LEAVE IT THAT WAY."

Then the Moose went to work.

He caught up with the coach on the way to the practice field on Wednesday. "Remember," he said, leaning forward and down a little to get his face in the coach's face, "I said I want to carry the ball."

Coach Williams must have been thinking about something else because it took him a minute to look up into the Moose's face, and even then he didn't say anything.

"I meant it," the Moose said.

"Meant what?"

"I want to run the ball."

"Oh," Coach Williams said. Yes, he remembered. "Son, you're a great left tackle, a great blocker. Let's leave it that way."

RETELLING
2. How does Coach Williams respond to the Moose's request?

The Moose let the remaining days of the practice week and then the game on Friday night against Edgewood High pass while he reviewed strategies. The review led him to Dan Blevins, the Bears' quarterback. If the signal caller would join in, maybe Coach Williams would listen.

"Yeah, I heard," Dan said. "But, look, what about Joe Wright at guard, Bill Slocum at right tackle, even Herbie Watson at center. They might all want to carry the ball. What are we going to do—take turns? It doesn't work that way."

So much for Dan Blevins.

The Moose found that most of the players in the backfield agreed with Dan. They couldn't

10 Chapter 1 Structures: Building Blocks of Meaning

"JUST ONCE," THE MOOSE PLEADED.

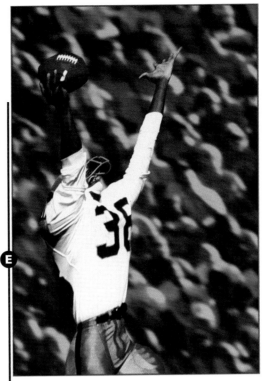

see any reason why the Moose should carry the ball, especially in place of themselves. Even Jerry Dixon, who owed a lot of his glory to the Moose's blocking, gaped in disbelief at the Moose's idea. The Moose, however, got some support from his fellow linemen. Maybe they had dreams of their own, and saw value in a precedent.[5]

As the days went by, the word spread— not just on the practice field and in the corridors of Bedford City High, but all around town. The players by now were openly taking sides. Some thought it a jolly good idea that the Moose carry the ball. Others, like Dan Blevins, held to the purist[6] line—a left tackle plays left tackle, a ball carrier carries the ball, and that's it.

Around town, the vote wasn't even close. Everyone wanted the Moose to carry the ball.

"Look, son," Coach Williams said to the Moose on the practice field the Thursday before the Benton Heights game, "this has gone far enough. Fun is fun. A joke is a joke. But let's drop it."

"Just once," the Moose pleaded.

Coach Williams looked at the Moose and didn't answer.

The Moose didn't know what that meant.

The Benton Heights Tigers were duck soup for the Bears, as everyone knew they would be. The Bears scored in their first three possessions and led 28–0 at the half.

___

5. **precedent** (pres′ə·dənt) *n.*: action or statement that can serve as an example.
6. **purist** (pyoor′ist) *n.*: someone who insists that rules be followed strictly.

The hapless[7] Tigers had yet to cross the fifty-yard line under their own steam.

All the Bears, of course, were enjoying the way the game was going, as were the Bedford City fans jamming the bleachers.

Coach Williams looked irritated when the crowd on a couple of occasions broke into a chant: "Give the Moose the ball! Give the Moose the ball!"

On the field, the Moose did not know whether to grin at hearing his name shouted by the crowd or to frown because the sound of his name was irritating the coach. Was the crowd going to talk Coach Williams into putting the

RETELLING

3. What's happening on the field and in the bleachers?

___

7. **hapless** *adj.*: unlucky.

DIRECT TEACHING

E **Literary Focus**
REVIEW STANDARD

❓ **Conflict.** How is the conflict in the story growing? [What began as the Moose's private struggle is now a topic of discussion for the football team, the school, and even the town. Everyone seems to have an opinion.]

F **Reading Skills**

❓ **Making inferences.** What do you think the coach's look means? [Possible responses: "Go away and stop asking"; "What am I going to do about this kid?"; "Well, we'll see."]

G **Vocabulary Development**
GRADE-LEVEL STANDARD

Using context clues. Encourage students to use the context—the Bears' wide lead—to guess the meaning of the expression "duck soup." [something that is handled easily, not a challenge]

H **Reading Skills**

Retelling. [Possible response to question 3: On the field, the Bears are easily winning the game—the Tigers are scoreless. In the bleachers the fans are beginning to chant, "Give the Moose the ball!"] This event increases the conflict between the coach and the Moose because the chanting irritates the coach.

MINI-LESSON Reading

Developing Word-Attack Skills
Remind students that the letter *e* at the end of a one-syllable word changes the vowel sound from short to long. Here are two examples:

mad   made
hop   hope

Review the spellings of *hop* and *hope* when *–ed* and *–ing* are added: *hop,*

hopped, hopping; hope, hoped, hoping.

Next, help students apply the following principles to the selection word *accolade.* The double consonant signals that the first *a* is short. The single consonant signals that the second *a* is long.

Then, compare *stifle* and *huddle.* Have students pronounce the words and explain

how the spellings told them if the first vowel in each word was long or short.
Activity. Have students decide whether the underlined vowels are long or short.

1. hyphen<u>a</u>te [long]
2. wh<u>i</u>ffle [short]
3. tr<u>i</u>fle [long]
4. scr<u>i</u>bble [short]
5. m<u>o</u>tto [short]
6. m<u>u</u>te [long]

A **Vocabulary Development**
GRADE-LEVEL STANDARD

Using context clues. To guess the meaning of the expression "runaway victory," have students use context clues in the next paragraph and in the phrase itself. [The word *runaway,* which suggests a big gap between contestants, and the score 42–0 imply that the winner's lead is very large—hence, an easy victory.]

B **Literary Focus**
REVIEW STANDARD

❓ Conflict. What part of the struggle has the Moose won? [He is being allowed to carry the ball.] What new conflict emerges now that the Moose has been given his chance? [The conflict is whether he will fail or succeed in his new position.]

C **Advanced Learners**

❓ Identifying cause and effect. How is the Moose himself the cause of five or six tacklers' being free? [If he were blocking, he would have stopped some of the tacklers. With the Moose running, the team's blocking isn't as good as it usually is.]

D **Reading Skills**

❓ Drawing conclusions. What has the Moose learned about football—and about life—that makes him want to thank the blocker? [Possible response: The Moose learned that in football blocking is important. He learned that in life everyone's role is important and that people need each other to succeed.]

Moose in the backfield? Probably not; Coach Williams didn't bow to that kind of pressure. Was the coach going to refuse to give the ball to the Moose just to show the crowd—and the Moose and the rest of the players—who was boss? The Moose feared so.

In his time on the sideline, when the defensive unit was on the field, the Moose, of course, said nothing to Coach Williams. He knew better than to break the coach's concentration during a game—even a runaway victory—with a comment on any subject at all, much less his desire to carry the ball. As a matter of fact, the Moose was careful to stay out of the coach's line of vision, especially when the crowd was chanting "Give the Moose the ball!"

By the end of the third quarter the Bears were leading 42–0.

Coach Williams had been feeding substitutes into the game since halftime, but the Bears kept marching on. And now, in the opening minutes of the fourth quarter, the Moose and his teammates were standing on the Tigers' five-yard line, about to pile on another touchdown.

The Moose saw his substitute, Larry Hinden, getting a slap on the behind and then running onto the field. The Moose turned to leave.

Then he heard Larry tell the referee, "Hinden for Holbrook."

Holbrook? Chad Holbrook, the fullback?

Chad gave the coach a funny look and jogged off the field.

Larry joined the huddle and said, "Coach says the Moose at fullback and give him the ball."

Dan Blevins said, "Really?"

"Really."

The Moose was giving his grin—"sweet," some of the teachers called it; "nice," others said.

"I want to do an end run," the Moose said.

Dan looked at the sky a moment, then said, "What does it matter?"

The quarterback took the snap from center, moved back and to his right while turning, and extended the ball to the Moose.

The Moose took the ball and cradled it in his right hand. So far, so good. He hadn't fumbled. Probably both Coach Williams and Dan were surprised.

He ran a couple of steps and looked out in front and said aloud, "Whoa!"

Where had all those tacklers come from?

The whole world seemed to be peopled with players in red jerseys—the red of the Benton Heights Tigers. They all were looking straight at the Moose and advancing toward him. They looked very determined, and not friendly at all. And there were so many of them. The Moose had faced tough guys in the line, but usually one at a time, or maybe two. But this—five or six. And all of them heading for him.

The Moose screeched to a halt, whirled, and ran the other way.

Dan Blevins blocked somebody in a red jersey breaking through the middle of the line, and the Moose wanted to stop running and thank him. But he kept going.

His reverse had caught the Tigers' defenders going the wrong way, and the field in front of the Moose looked open. But his blockers were going the wrong way, too. Maybe that was why the field looked so open. What did it matter, though, with the field clear in front of him? This was going to be a cakewalk;[8] the Moose was going to score a touchdown.

---

8. **cakewalk** *n.*: easy job.

CONTENT-AREA CONNECTIONS

Mathematics
Statistics. Students who like both football and mathematics might enjoy creating a presentation on football statistics. The presentation should include a brief explanation of the most important statistics and a discussion of why statistics are useful in sports.

Students may also discuss the effect of computers on sports statistics and how sports statisticians earn a living.

SMALL-GROUP

E Reading Skills

? **Making inferences.** Why does the Moose think of Jerry Dixon as he's running with the ball? [Possible responses: The Moose realizes that Jerry is good at what he does. Being smaller than the Moose, Jerry is able to elude tacklers; Jerry has more practice than the Moose at running with the ball.]

Then, again—"Whoa!"

Players with red jerseys were beginning to fill the empty space—a lot of them. And they were all running toward the Moose. They were kind of low, with their arms spread, as if they wanted to hit him hard and then grab him.

A picture of Jerry Dixon dancing his little jig and wriggling between tacklers flashed through the Moose's mind. How did Jerry do that? Well, no time to <u>ponder</u> that one right now.

The Moose lowered his shoulder and thundered ahead, into the cloud of red jerseys. Something hit his left thigh. It hurt. Then something pounded his hip, then his shoulder. They both hurt. Somebody was hanging on to him and was a terrible drag. How could he run with somebody hanging on to him? He knew he was going down, but

PLAYERS WITH RED JERSEYS WERE BEGINNING TO FILL THE EMPTY SPACE . . .

maybe he was across the goal. He hit the ground hard, with somebody coming down on top of him, right on the small of his back.

The Moose couldn't move. They had him pinned. Wasn't the referee supposed to get these guys off?

Vocabulary
ponder (pän′dər) *v.:* think over carefully.

Just Once **13**

DEVELOPING FLUENCY

Activity. Have students in small groups take turns reading the text aloud starting from the beginning of the game between the Benton Tigers and the Bears. While one student reads, the others can take notes on what happens in the game. Students can use these notes later to create their sports broadcast of the Bears-Tigers game. (See Writing/Oral Presentation on p. 15.)

SMALL-GROUP

A Reading Skills

Retelling. [Possible response to question 4: The Moose's conflict is resolved when he gets the opportunity to run with the ball and scores, but he decides to go back to being a blocker.]

GUIDED PRACTICE

Monitoring students' progress. To check students' comprehension of the story, guide the class in identifying these statements as true or false. Have students locate passages in the text that support their responses.

True-False

1. The Moose got his nickname because his real name is hard to pronounce. [F]

2. The Moose is an excellent line-man in football. [T]

3. The Moose wants to run with the ball. [T]

4. In the story the Moose doesn't get to run with the ball. [F]

5. The Moose decides he wants to be a lineman again. [T]

Meet the Writer

Background. A reporter and bureau chief for the Associated Press, Thomas Dygard published his first novel, *Running Scared,* in 1977. "I started writing young adult fiction for the fun and satisfaction of it, and it's still fun and satisfying, and I think it always will be."

For Independent Reading

If students liked the story of the Moose and his experiences as a football player, they might also enjoy *The Moves Make the Man* by Bruce Brooks, the story of a young African American man who plays basketball for his school.

Finally the load was gone and the Moose, still holding the ball, got to his knees and one hand, then stood.

He heard the screaming of the crowd, and he saw the scoreboard blinking.

He had scored.

His teammates were slapping him on the shoulder pads and laughing and shouting.

The Moose grinned, but he had a strange and distant look in his eyes.

He jogged to the sideline, the roars of the crowd still ringing in his ears.

"OK, son?" Coach Williams asked.

The Moose was puffing. He took a couple of deep breaths. He relived for a moment the first sight of a half dozen players in red jerseys, all with one target—him. He saw again the menacing horde of red jerseys that had risen up just when he'd thought he had clear sailing to the goal. They all zeroed in on him, the Moose, alone.

The Moose glanced at the coach, took another deep breath, and said, "Never again."

RETELLING

A 4. How is the Moose's conflict resolved?

MEET THE WRITER

Thomas J. Dygard

"I'm Not a Writer. I'm a Rewriter."

For **Thomas J. Dygard** (1931–1996), writing and editing newspaper articles was a full-time job; writing novels was the hobby he loved most. Dygard wrote seventeen novels, all sports related, for young people. In spite of his years of working with words, he said he always considered writing a challenge.

> My mistakes in my writing are so common that I'd bet I've thrown more pieces of paper in a wastebasket than any person alive. I'm not a writer. I'm a rewriter. As for having learned it all, I know that I haven't, and I also know that I never will.

For Independent Reading

Dygard wrote several novels about football. One, *Winning Kicker*, is about a girl who makes the team as a place kicker and the problems that arise. For more Dygard on football, try *Game Plan* and *Second Stringer*.

FAMILY/COMMUNITY ACTIVITY

Invite a coach from the community to visit the class and talk about his or her experiences trying to build team spirit. Has the coach ever encountered a situation like the one in "Just Once"? If so, how did he or she handle it? Also, discuss whether the coach ever orders players to change positions so they can appreciate the roles their teammates play.

Literary Response and Analysis

Reading Check

1. Use the following story map to outline the main parts of this story's **plot.**

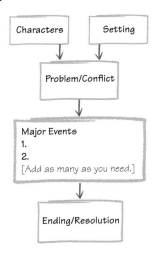

Interpretations

2. What is the **setting** of the story? Could a story like this take place in any other setting? Explain.

3. What does the Moose expect to happen when he carries the ball? How is his dream different from reality?

4. Describe the **conflict** the Moose faces when the crowd chants, "Give the Moose the ball!" (page 11). What does he want? What is keeping him from getting it?

5. **Theme** is what the story reveals to us about life. What would you say is this story's theme, or underlying message about life? Is it the same lesson that the Moose learns? Explain.

Evaluation

6. Is this a "boy's story," or does it appeal to both boys and girls? Conduct a survey of your classmates to find out what they think.

Writing/Oral Presentation
"And Carrying the Ball Is . . ."

Create a sportscast of the Bears-Tigers game. First, write a **summary** of what happened. Use details in the story to answer *who? what? when? where? why?* and *how?* questions. (You might want to use details from the story map you filled out for the Reading Check.) Give your report a snappy lead-in to capture your listeners' attention. Then, practice reading your report for a broadcast. Tape your sportscast, and play it for your classmates.

Writing
The Way to the Prize: A Life Map

As a high school senior, the Moose longs to hear the cheers of the crowd. People want different things at different times in their lives. Draw a life map as a kind of road or journey showing a person at one end and the prize or goal at the other end. Draw some of the forces that the person may have to overcome along the way. Then, write a paragraph explaining your map. (It does not have to be a map of the kind of life *you* want.) Look back at your Quickwrite notes for ideas for your map.

Grade 5 Review Reading Standard 3.2 Identify the main problem or conflict of the plot, and explain how it is resolved.

Reading Standard 3.3 Analyze the influence of setting.

Just Once **15**

INDEPENDENT PRACTICE

Literary Response and Analysis

Reading Check

1. *Characters*—the Moose, Jerry Dixon, Coach Williams. *Setting*—high school football. *Problem/Conflict*—The Moose wants to carry the ball; the coach won't let him. *Major Events*—Jerry's touchdown; the Moose asks the coach for ball and is turned down; the crowd chants for the Moose; the Moose gets the ball. *Ending/Resolution*—The Moose accepts his role as a lineman.

Interpretations

2. The story takes place during football games and in the locker room. Some students may think the story could involve any team sport. Others may feel another setting wouldn't have the drama of a football game.

3. The Moose expects to hear fans cheer him, but he experiences exhaustion, pain, and relief to be off the field.

4. The Moose is pleased by the crowd's support, but he is nervous because he knows the chants irritate the coach. He wants to carry the ball, but he thinks the coach won't let him to show who's boss.

5. Students might say the theme is that certain dreams are not always what they seem. The Moose realized his dream, but learned that it wasn't as wonderful as he thought.

Evaluation

6. Some students may feel that it is a boy's story because all of the characters are male. Others may feel that it appeals to both sexes because it involves a teenager who learns that his dream is not as wonderful as he thought it would be.

DIFFERENTIATING INSTRUCTION

Advanced Learners

Enrichment. Discuss the difference between appearance and reality when it comes to experiencing someone else's life. Have students think of a person whose identity they would like to take on for a week. Ask students to imagine living as their "assumed identity" and to record their thoughts on a pros and cons chart.

Activity. Have students create a diary entry for a day in the life of their imagined identity.

HOMEWORK

Vocabulary Development

Practice

- Clue for *anonymous* is "wondering who had written it."
- Clues for *ponder* are "time," "carefully," and "think."
- Clue for *devastating* is "ruin."
- Clue for *tolerant* is "fair."
- Clue for *nurturing* is "for months."

 Resources Reminder

Vocabulary and Spelling

- *Vocabulary Development*
  - Vocabulary Worksheet, p. 1
- *Lesson Plans for Language Development*
  - Vocabulary, p. 21

Grammar Link

Practice

1. *Incorrect verbs*—rised, seen. *Correct verbs*—rose, saw.
2. *Incorrect verb*—thinked. *Correct verb*—thought.
3. *Incorrect verb*—sayed. *Correct verb*—said.

Assessment

- *Progress Assessment of Reading*
  - Selection Test, p. 1

For a lesson reteaching plot, see **Reteaching,** p. 489B.

Vocabulary Development

Using Context to Determine Meaning

PRACTICE

Get into the habit of monitoring the text you are reading for unfamiliar words. If you find an unknown word, try to use the words and sentences around it—its **context**—to guess at the word's meaning. In the paragraph below, each underlined word has at least one **context clue.** Copy the paragraph, and circle the clues that would help a reader guess the words' meanings.

> The coach read aloud the <u>anonymous</u> note, wondering who had written it. "Please take some time to <u>ponder</u> our request carefully. You may think that it would have a <u>devastating</u> effect, but we're sure it won't ruin the sports program. It's time to be <u>tolerant</u> and fair. After all, we've been <u>nurturing</u> our dream for months. Please let girls try out for the team."

Reading Standard 1.4
Monitor text for unknown words by using word clues to determine meaning.

Word Bank

devastating
nurturing
anonymous
tolerant
ponder

Grammar Link MINI-LESSON

Troublesome Verbs

The **past tense** and **past participle** of most verbs are formed by adding *–d* or *–ed*, but **irregular verbs** change in sneaky ways. You just have to memorize them. (The past participle is the form you use with the helping verbs *has, have,* and *had.*)

Here are some irregular verbs from "Just Once":

Base Form	Past	Past Participle
rise	rose	(have) risen
say	said	(have) said
see	saw	(have) seen
think	thought	(have) thought

PRACTICE

In the following sentences, find the incorrect verb forms, and replace them with the correct forms.

1. The Moose rised from the field and seen a cloud of red jerseys.
2. The Moose thinked he wanted to hear the fans cheer for him.
3. Yesterday the Moose sayed to the coach, "I want to carry the ball."

For more help, see Irregular Verbs in the Holt Handbook, pages 150–159.

All Summer in a Day

Literary Focus
Setting

Setting is the time and place of a story. Setting can tell us about the weather, the time of day, and the historical period (past, present, or future). Setting can also tell us how people live, what they eat, how they dress, and where they work. In some stories, like this one, setting plays such an important part that it shapes the action from beginning to end.

Reading Skills
Making Inferences

An **inference** is a kind of guess. When you **make inferences** as you read, you look for clues in the story, and then you relate them to your own experience. You try to fill in the gaps by guessing about things the writer doesn't tell you directly. At certain points in this story, you'll see open-book signs alongside the text. When you see one, stop and make an inference about what you have just read.

You can make an inference about the **setting** of this story right now—just read the title. What do you think it means?

Make the Connection
Quickwrite 🖉

In this story the children of Venus (that is, Venus as Ray Bradbury imagines it) lead lives that are very different from the lives of kids on Earth. One thing is the same, though: Someone who differs from the rest of the crowd is treated like an outsider.

How does it feel to be an outsider? Why do people sometimes refuse to accept someone into their group? Jot down your thoughts on these questions.

Vocabulary Development

These are the words you'll be learning as you read this story. Are any other words in the story new to you?

slackening (slak'ən·iŋ) *v.* used as *adj.*: lessening; slowing down. *The rain fell in huge, heavy drops for hours without slackening.*

surged (sʉrjd) *v.*: moved in a wave. *The children surged toward Margot.*

resilient (ri·zil'yənt) *adj.*: springy; quick to recover. *The vegetation was resilient beneath their feet.*

savored (sā'vərd) *v.*: delighted in. *The pale children savored the warm sunshine.*

Reflex (detail) (1988) by William Baggett.

Reading Standard 3.3 Analyze the influence of setting on the problem and its resolution.

All Summer in a Day **17**

 STANDARDS FOCUS, pp. 17–27

(For grade-level and review standards taught in this selection, see citations on Pupil's Edition pages.)

Prerequisite Standard
■ Grade 5, Literary Response and Analysis 3.2 **Identify the main problem or conflict of the plot, and explain how it is resolved.**

Standard Coming Up in the Next Grade Level
■ Grade 7, Literary Response and Analysis 3.2 **Identify events that advance the plot, and determine how each event explains past or present action(s) or foreshadows future action(s).**

Reading Skills
■ Make inferences.

Summary ⟷ *at grade level*

On this imaginary version of Venus, the sun shines for two hours every seven years. Rain falls the rest of the time. Nine-year-old Margot anxiously waits with her class to witness the sun's brief appearance. She and her family moved from Earth five years earlier, so among her Venus-born classmates, only she remembers the sun. The children resent Margot for that, so they lock her in the closet when the teacher leaves the room. The sun appears, and the children spend two blissful hours playing in its warmth. Forced inside by the rain's return, the children release Margot, but it is too late—the sun will not return for another seven years.

RESOURCES

Planning
■ *One-Stop Planner* CD-ROM with Test Generator
■ *On Course: Mapping Instruction*

Media
■ *Audio CD Library*
  ■ disc 1
■ *Fine Art Transparencies*
  ■ Transparency 1

Reading
■ *Interactive Reading*
  ■ Graphic Organizer: Setting Circle, p. 8

Differentiating Instruction
■ *Lesson Plans for Language Development*
  ■ English-Language Learners, pp. 9–11, 17, 22
  ■ Special Education Students, pp. 12, 17, 22

▶ Resources Reminder

Media
■ *Audio CD Library*
  ■ disc 1
■ *Fine Art Transparencies*
  ■ Transparency 1

Reading
■ *Interactive Reading*
  ■ Graphic Organizer: Setting Circle, p. 8

Standards Starter

Motivate. Put students in small groups to fill out a diagram like the one below.

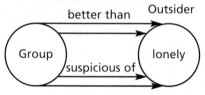

On the arrows leading from the Group circle, have students write words and phrases that describe how members of an in-group might feel toward an outsider. In the Outsider circle, have students write how the outsider might feel.

Preview Vocabulary

To reinforce students' understanding of the meanings of the Vocabulary words introduced on p. 17, have students use the words to complete the following analogies.

1. *increasing* is to *swelling* as *lessening* is to [slackening]

2. *river* is to *gushed* as *ocean* is to [surged]

3. *rigid* is to *flexible* as *unbending* is to [resilient]

4. *rejected* is to *accepted* as *disliked* is to [savored]

Assign the Reading

Because this is a powerful story, you might want to read it in class and discuss the ending.

VIEWING THE ART

John Marin (1870–1953) often painted New England landscapes and Manhattan skyscrapers. Casco Bay is in Maine.

Activity. Invite students to discuss how this painting of the sun makes them feel.

ALL SUMMER

Sunset, Casco Bay by John Marin.

The Roland P. Murdock Collection, Wichita Art Museum, Kansas.

IN A DAY

Ray Bradbury

RESOURCES

Vocabulary and Spelling
- *Vocabulary Development*
  - Vocabulary Worksheet, p. 2

Assessment
- *Progress Assessment of Reading*
  - Selection Test, p. 4
- *One-Stop Planner* CD-ROM with Test Generator

"Ready."

"Ready."

"Now?"

"Soon."

"Do the scientists really know? Will it happen today, will it?"

"Look, look; see for yourself!"

The children pressed to each other like so many roses, so many weeds, intermixed, peering out for a look at the hidden sun.

It rained.

It had been raining for seven years; thousands upon thousands of days compounded and filled from one end to the other with rain, with the drum and gush of water, with the sweet crystal fall of showers and the concussion[1] of storms so heavy they were tidal waves come over the islands. A thousand forests had been crushed under the rain and grown up a thousand times to be crushed again. And this was the way life was forever on the planet Venus, and this was the schoolroom of the children of the rocket men and women who had come to a raining world to set up civilization and live out their lives.

"It's stopping, it's stopping!"

"Yes, yes!"

Margot stood apart from them, from these children who could never remember a time when there wasn't rain and rain and rain. They were all nine years old, and if there had been a day, seven years ago, when the sun came out for an hour and showed its face to the stunned world, they could not recall. Sometimes, at night, she heard them stir, in remembrance, and she knew they were dreaming and remembering gold or a yellow crayon or a coin large enough to buy

the world with. She knew they thought they remembered a warmness, like a blushing in the face, in the body, in the arms and legs and trembling hands. But then they always awoke to the tatting drum, the endless shaking down of clear bead necklaces upon the roof, the walk, the gardens, the forests, and their dreams were gone.

All day yesterday they had read in class about the sun. About how like a lemon it was, and how hot. And they had written small stories or essays or poems about it.

I think the sun is a flower
That blooms for just one hour.

That was Margot's poem, read in a quiet voice in the still classroom while the rain was falling outside.

"Aw, you didn't write that!" protested one of the boys.

"I did," said Margot. "*I did.*"

"William!" said the teacher.

But that was yesterday. Now the rain was slackening, and the children were crushed in the great thick windows.

"Where's teacher?"

"She'll be back."

"She'd better hurry; we'll miss it!"

They turned on themselves like a feverish wheel, all tumbling spokes.

Margot stood alone. She was a very frail girl who looked as if she had been lost in the rain for years and the rain had washed out the blue from her eyes and the red from her mouth and the yellow from her hair. She was an old

---

MAKING INFERENCES

1. How do the children feel about the weather on Venus? Base your inference on their dreams.

Vocabulary

slackening (slak′ən·iŋ) *v.* used as *adj.*: lessening; slowing down.

---

1. **concussion** *n.*: violent shaking or shock.

All Summer in a Day **19**

Ⓐ Literary Focus
REVIEW STANDARD

❓ **Setting.** What do the descriptions here tell you about where the story is set? [Possible response: It is set on Venus. The planet's lush forests have been crushed, grown back, and been crushed again by seven years of incessant rain.]

Ⓑ Literary Focus
GRADE-LEVEL STANDARD

❓ **Influence of setting.** What effect does the setting seem to have on the children? [Possible response: The rain defines their lives. It is the single most important aspect of their environment.]

Ⓒ Reading Skills

Making inferences. Call attention to the words used to describe the sun: *gold, a yellow crayon, a coin large enough to buy the world with, a warmness.* Then, ask what these words suggest about how children feel about the sun. [They see it as wonderful and a source of wealth, warmth, and play.]

[Possible response to question 1: Since the children dream that the sun is wonderful, we can infer that they feel oppressed by the actual weather.]

Ⓓ Literary Focus
REVIEW STANDARD

❓ **Plot.** Why are the children clustered at the windows? [They want to see and feel the sun.]

Learners Having Difficulty
Modeling. To help students read "All Summer in a Day," model the reading skill of making inferences. Say: "Suppose you read that 'All Summer in a Day' is set in an imaginary place where the rain never stops. Knowing this, you can infer that the sky is always cloudy and the sun never shines." Encourage students as they read to ask

themselves: "How does the lack of sun affect the behavior of the characters?"

▶ **Resources Reminder**

Reading
■ *Interactive Reading*
  ■ Graphic Organizer: Setting Circles, p. 8

English-Language Learners
For lessons designed for intermediate and advanced English-language learners, see *Lesson Plans for Language Development*, pp. 9–11, 17, 22.

Special Education Students
For lessons designed for special education students, see *Lesson Plans for Language Development*, pp. 12, 17, 22.

A **Literary Focus**
GRADE-LEVEL STANDARD

❓ **Influence of setting.** How has the weather on Venus affected Margot? [Possible response: She has grown pale and frail and become unhappy and withdrawn.]

B **Literary Focus**
GRADE-LEVEL STANDARD

❓ **Influence of setting.** How is the weather on Venus contributing to a conflict between Margot and the other children? [Possible response: The fact that the sun is about to come out for the first time in seven years makes the other children "feverish"—sharper and more unruly than usual.]

C **Reading Skills**

❓ **Predicting.** What do you think might happen as a result of William's nastiness? [Possible responses: Nothing might happen; William might do something even more hurtful to Margot; the other children might join in and do hurtful things to her as well.]

D **Learners Having Difficulty**

❓ **Finding details.** Which details show how Margot is different from the other children? [Possible responses: She won't join their games; she won't sing with them, except about the sun and summer; she was born on Earth and remembers the sun.]

VIEWING THE ART

David Hockney (1937–   ) is a contemporary British painter. This work suggests the pebbles of a Japanese garden drenched in rain.

Activity. Ask students what they think the round objects are. [rocks, pebbles, slates] Where does the painter put the viewer? [right in the middle of the walkway or garden]

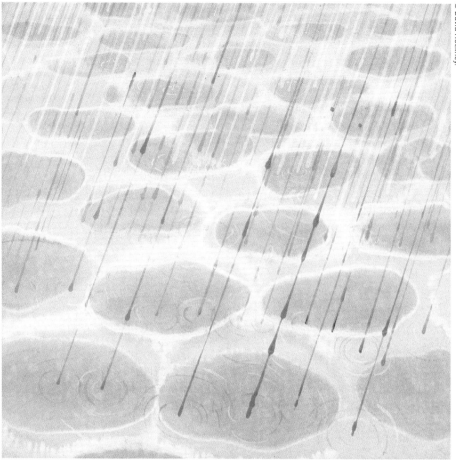

Japanese Rain on Canvas (1972) by David Hockney. Acrylic on canvas (48″ × 48″).

A photograph dusted from an album, whitened away, and if she spoke at all her voice would be a ghost. Now she stood, separate, staring at the rain and the loud wet world beyond the huge glass.

B "What're *you* looking at?" said William. Margot said nothing.

C "Speak when you're spoken to." He gave her a shove. But she did not move; rather she let herself be moved only by him and nothing else.

They edged away from her; they would not look at her. She felt them go away. And **D** this was because she would play no games with them in the echoing tunnels of the underground city. If they tagged her and ran, she stood blinking after them and did not follow. When the class sang songs about happiness and life and games, her lips barely moved. Only when they sang about the sun and the summer did her lips move as she watched the drenched windows.

And then, of course, the biggest crime of all was that she had come here only five years ago from Earth, and she remembered

DIFFERENTIATING INSTRUCTION

Advanced Learners
Acceleration. Use the following activity to move advanced learners toward the seventh-grade Literary Response and Analysis Standard 3.2, which requires that they identify events that advance the plot and determine how each event explains past or present action(s) and foreshadows future action(s).

Activity. As students read the story, direct them to sketch its main events in a storyboard format (a sheet of paper divided into four to six squares). After students finish, have them share their storyboards and discuss events that provide explanations for other events in the story.

© David Hockney.

the sun and the way the sun was and the sky was when she was four in Ohio. And they, they had been on Venus all their lives, and they had been only two years old when last the sun came out and had long since forgotten the color and heat of it and the way it really was. But Margot remembered.

"It's like a penny," she said once, eyes closed.

"No, it's not!" the children cried.

"It's like a fire," she said, "in the stove."

"You're lying; you don't remember!" cried the children.

But she remembered and stood quietly apart from all of them and watched the patterning windows. And once, a month ago, she had refused to shower in the school shower rooms, had clutched her hands to her ears and over her head, screaming the water mustn't touch her head. So after that, dimly, dimly, she sensed it, she was different, and they knew her difference and kept away.

There was talk that her father and mother were taking her back to Earth next year; it seemed vital to her that they do so, though it would mean the loss of thousands of dollars to her family. And so, the children hated her for all these reasons of big and little consequence.[2] They hated her pale snow face, her waiting silence, her thinness, and her possible future.

📖 **MAKING INFERENCES**

2. How is Margot different from the other children?

"Get away!" The boy gave her another push. "What're you waiting for?"

Then, for the first time, she turned and looked at him. And what she was waiting for was in her eyes.

"Well, don't wait around here!" cried the boy savagely. "You won't see nothing!"

Her lips moved.

"Nothing!" he cried. "It was all a joke, wasn't it?" He turned to the other children. "Nothing's happening today. Is it?"

They all blinked at him and then, understanding, laughed and shook their heads. "Nothing, nothing!"

"Oh, but," Margot whispered, her eyes helpless. "But this is the day, the scientists predict, they say, they know, the sun . . ."

"All a joke!" said the boy, and seized her roughly. "Hey everyone, let's put her in a closet before teacher comes!"

"No," said Margot, falling back.

They surged about her, caught her up and bore her, protesting, and then pleading, and then crying, back into a tunnel, a room, a closet, where they slammed and locked the door. They stood looking at the door and saw it tremble from her beating and throwing herself against it. They heard her muffled cries. Then, smiling, they turned and went out and back down the tunnel, just as the teacher arrived.

"Ready, children?" She glanced at her watch.

"Yes!" said everyone.

"Are we all here?"

"Yes!"

The rain slackened still more.

They crowded to the huge door.

The rain stopped.

It was as if, in the midst of a film concerning an avalanche, a tornado, a hurricane, a volcanic eruption, something had, first, gone wrong with the sound apparatus, thus muffling and finally

---

2. **consequence** *n.:* importance.

Vocabulary

surged (sʉrjd) *v.:* moved forward, as if in a wave.

All Summer in a Day   **21**

DIRECT TEACHING

E **Literary Focus**
GRADE-LEVEL STANDARD
❓ **Influence of setting.** What might Margot's reaction to the shower suggest about her struggle to cope with the weather on Venus? [Possible responses: She is losing the struggle; all the rain on Venus has caused her to fear and hate water; she is close to an emotional breaking point.]

F **Reading Skills**

Making inferences. Remind students to combine clues in the story (what it says) with their own knowledge (what they say) to figure out what's going on. [*The story says*—The children hate "her pale snow face, her waiting silence, her thinness, and her possible future." *Students may say*—People often resent others who have something they don't have.]
[Possible responses to question 2: Having lived on Earth and experienced the sun firsthand, Margot is more sensitive, gentle, and vulnerable than her classmates. She may be more hopeful too, because her family may return to Earth.]

G **Reading Skills**

❓ **Making inferences.** After locking Margot in the closet, the children turn away and smile as she beats on the door. From their actions, what do you infer about their feelings? [Possible responses: They hate her because she is special and different; they feel powerful.]

H **Vocabulary Development**
GRADE-LEVEL STANDARD
❓ **Using context clues.** Look at the word *muffling.* What words in the sentence can help you understand what *muffling* means? [Possible response: The phrases "something . . . wrong with the sound" and "finally cutting off all noise" suggest that *muffling* means "dulling or reducing the sound."]

All Summer in a Day   **21**

A Advanced Learners

? Identifying analogies. What analogy, or comparison, does Bradbury use to describe what it is like when the rain stops? [He compares it to a situation in which a film about an avalanche or other disaster suddenly has its sound cut off, and then the film is ripped from the reel and replaced with a slide of a peaceful tropical scene.]

VIEWING THE ART

David Finn is an artist, writer, and photographer. Some of his paintings have been inspired by works of literature, such as the poems of William Butler Yeats and T. S. Eliot.

Activity. Ask students to study the painting on this page and pretend to be Margot's classmates who have never seen the sun. Have them describe the painting from that point of view.

Large Sun by David Finn.

A cutting off all noise, all of the blasts and repercussions and thunders, and then, second, ripped the film from the projector and inserted in its place a peaceful tropical slide which did not move or tremor. The world ground to a standstill. The silence was so immense and unbelievable that you felt your ears had been stuffed or you had lost your hearing altogether. The children put their hands to their ears. They stood apart. The door slid back and the smell of the silent, waiting world came in to them.

The sun came out.

It was the color of flaming bronze and it was very large. And the sky around it was a blazing blue tile color. And the jungle burned with sunlight as the children, released from their spell, rushed out, yelling, into the springtime.

"Now, don't go too far," called the teacher after them. "You've only two hours, you know. You wouldn't want to get caught out!"

CONTENT-AREA CONNECTIONS

Science

Venus. Before the 1960s, our knowledge of Venus came from Earth-based telescopes. Since then, sophisticated space probes have provided new information. We've discovered, that Venus is the hottest planet in our solar system, about 860 degrees Fahrenheit. As a result of this heat, almost all the water on Venus has boiled away. Unlike Earth's atmosphere, which is mostly nitrogen and oxygen, the atmosphere of Venus is mostly carbon dioxide. It also contains sulfur dioxide, which combines with water vapor to produce poisonous sulfuric acid. There is no rain on Venus, yet the sun is always blocked by clouds. It does not shine even once every seven years.

Activity. Ask students to select another planet and find out more about its weather.

INDIVIDUAL

MINI-LESSON Reading

Developing Word-Attack Skills
Have students compare these two words from the selection: *concussion* (p. 19) and *repercussions* (p. 22). Point out that the tw words share the same root: *cussion*. Ask st dents to think of another familiar word w the word part *cussion*. [discussion]

Explain that *concussion, repercussion,* and *discussion* have Latin origins. Their root words mean literally "shake violently

But they were running and turning their faces up to the sky and feeling the sun on their cheeks like a warm iron; they were taking off their jackets and letting the sun burn their arms.

"Oh, it's better than the sun lamps, isn't it?"

"Much, much better!"

They stopped running and stood in the great jungle that covered Venus, that grew and never stopped growing, tumultuously,[3] even as you watched it. It was a nest of octopuses, clustering up great arms of fleshlike weed, wavering, flowering in this brief spring. It was the color of rubber and ash, this jungle, from the many years without sun. It was the color of stones and white cheeses and ink, and it was the color of the moon.

The children lay out, laughing, on the jungle mattress and heard it sigh and squeak under them, resilient and alive. They ran among the trees, they slipped and fell, they pushed each other, they played hide-and-seek and tag, but most of all they squinted at the sun until tears ran down their faces; they put their hands up to that yellowness and that amazing blueness and they breathed of the fresh, fresh air and listened and listened to the silence which suspended them in a blessed sea of no sound and no motion. They looked at everything and savored everything. Then, wildly, like animals escaped from their caves, they ran and ran in shouting circles. They ran for an hour and did not stop running.

MAKING INFERENCES

3. Why do you suppose Bradbury compares the children to animals?

And then—

In the midst of their running, one of the girls wailed.

Everyone stopped.

The girl, standing in the open, held out her hand.

"Oh, look, look," she said, trembling.

They came slowly to look at her opened palm.

In the center of it, cupped and huge, was a single raindrop.

She began to cry, looking at it.

They glanced quietly at the sky.

"Oh. Oh."

A few cold drops fell on their noses and their cheeks and their mouths. The sun faded behind a stir of mist. A wind blew cool around them. They turned and started to walk back toward the underground house, their hands at their sides, their smiles vanishing away.

A boom of thunder startled them, and like leaves before a new hurricane, they tumbled upon each other and ran. Lightning struck ten miles away, five miles away, a mile, a half-mile. The sky darkened into midnight in a flash.

They stood in the doorway of the underground for a moment until it was raining hard. Then they closed the door and heard the gigantic sound of the rain falling in tons and avalanches, everywhere and forever.

"Will it be seven more years?"

"Yes. Seven."

Then one of them gave a little cry.

"Margot!"

"What?"

Vocabulary

resilient (ri·zil′yənt) *adj.*: springy; quick to recover.

savored (sā′vərd) *v.*: delighted in.

---

3. **tumultuously** *adv.*: wildly; violently.

All Summer in a Day **23**

DIRECT TEACHING

B Literary Focus
REVIEW STANDARD

❓ **Setting.** What impressions do you get of the jungle? What words help create this impression of the setting? [Possible response: The jungle is loathsome. Note such phrases as "nest of octopuses," "arms of fleshlike weed," "color of rubber and ash," and "color of stones and white cheeses."]

C Reading Skills

Making inferences. [Possible response to question 3: The comparison catches the students' exuberance and feeling of freedom; it shows that they are unthinking, caught up in the joy of their sensory impressions; it might suggest that they have acted like animals by cruelly mistreating Margot.]

(concussio), "strike back" (repercussio), and "shake apart or scatter" (discussio). Then, discuss these three words: concourse, discourse, and recourse. With students, explore how the meaning of each prefix relates to the meaning of the word:

- con–, "together." A concourse is a flowing together of people or traffic.
- dis–, "apart." Discourse is presenting and taking apart ideas.

- re–, "back, again." Recourse is a means to get something back.

Activity. Write these items on the chalkboard. Have a volunteer select the word that fits each sentence and explain the choice.

1. dislocate   relocate
   Margot's family will _____ to Earth. [relocate]

2. compulsive   repulsive
   The constant rain was particularly _____ to Margot. [repulsive]

3. contribute   distribute
   The other children _____ to Margot's sadness. [contribute]

All Summer in a Day 23

A Reading Skills

? Making inferences. How do the children feel when they remember Margot? On which details in the story do you base your inferences? [Possible response: Their solemnity, downcast faces, and inability to meet each other's eyes might suggest that they feel shame and guilt.]

B Reading Skills

Predicting. [Possible responses to question 4: Margot will be emotionally broken; the teacher will scold the children; the children will apologize and say that they didn't mean to leave Margot in the closet; some of the children may become more compassionate as a result of this experience.]

GUIDED PRACTICE

Monitoring students' progress. Guide the class in answering these comprehension questions. Direct students to locate passages in the text that support their responses.

True-False

1. In this story, the sun shines on Venus once every seven years. [T]
2. Margot will not play with the other children. [T]
3. Margot was born on Venus. [F]
4. The other children are not interested in the sun. [F]
5. Margot is beating on the door when the children return. [F]

Reflex (1988) by William Baggett.

"She's still in the closet where we locked her."

"Margot."

A They stood as if someone had driven them, like so many stakes, into the floor. They looked at each other and then looked away. They glanced out at the world that was raining now and raining and raining steadily. They could not meet each other's glances. Their faces were solemn and pale. They looked at their hands and feet, their faces down.

"Margot."

One of the girls said, "Well . . . ?"

No one moved.

"Go on," whispered the girl.

They walked slowly down the hall in the sound of cold rain. They turned through the doorway to the room in the sound of the storm and thunder, lightning on their faces, blue and terrible. They walked over to the closet door slowly and stood by it.

B Behind the closet door was only silence. They unlocked the door, even more slowly, and let Margot out.

PREDICTING
4. What will happen now?

24   Chapter 1   Structures: Building Blocks of Meaning

FAMILY/COMMUNITY ACTIVITY

Ask groups of three students to form a "task force" to resolve the problem between Margot, the other children, and the teacher. As a group, students can brainstorm for ideas using a graphic organizer such as the one on the right. Then, invite a parent or community member trained in conflict resolution to talk to the class about their ideas.

Teacher	Children	Margot
have children apologize; take away their privileges	apologize; be nicer to Margot	try to make friends with the others and understand their problems

Ray Bradbury

Space-Age Storyteller

Ray Bradbury (1920–   ) has been called the world's greatest science fiction writer. It is not a label Bradbury agrees with. He describes himself more simply: "I am a storyteller. That's all I've ever tried to be."

Although Bradbury's stories are often set in outer space, his characters and their emotions are human and down-to-earth. For more than fifty years, Bradbury has produced fiction that reflects his deeply felt concern about the future of humanity.

Bradbury encourages young people to try to imagine the wonders the future will hold—just as he did when he was in school:

> Everything confronting us in the next thirty years will be science fictional, that is, impossible a few years ago. The things you are doing right now, if you had told anyone you'd be doing them when you were children, they would have laughed you out of school.... I was the only person at Los Angeles High School who knew the Space Age was coming. Totally alone among four thousand students, I insisted we were going to get the rocket off the ground, and that made me the class kook, of course. I said, 'Well, we're going to do it anyway.'

For Independent Reading

Bradbury's stories are collected in books such as *The Illustrated Man*, *R Is for Rocket*, *Twice Twenty-Two*, and *The Stories of Ray Bradbury*. Try starting with "Mars Is Heaven," "The Fog Horn," "The Sound of Summer Running," and "The Flying Machine." If you're interested in reading a Bradbury novel, try *Dandelion Wine*.

All Summer in a Day   **25**

Meet the Writer

Background. It's not surprising that Ray Bradbury has a shelf full of awards—including the O. Henry Memorial Award, the Benjamin Franklin Award, the World Fantasy Award, and an Emmy for his teleplay of *The Halloween Tree*. But he's also won a handful of surprising honors. The most astonishing? A moon crater has actually been named after his novel *Dandelion Wine*: Dandelion Crater. In addition, Bradbury's work helped inspire the creation of Spaceship Earth, EPCOT, and Disney World.

Bradbury advises young writers to write from their own experience: "Find out what excites and delights you, or what angers you most, then get it down on paper. After all, it is your individuality that you want to isolate. Work from the subconscious; store up images, impressions, data—then dip into this 'well of self' for your stories."

For Independent Reading

- Students interested in the theme of outsiders versus insiders might enjoy S. E. Hinton's *The Outsiders,* a story of teen conflicts written when the author was a teenager.
- For a contemporary story of two "new kids" ostracized by their classmates, students might read *Alan Mendelsohn, the Boy from Mars* by Daniel Pinkwater, whose quirky sense of humor and wild imagination are hard to resist.

▶ Resources Reminder

Reading

For another selection by Ray Bradbury, see "The Luggage Store" from *The Martian Chronicles* in *Interactive Reading*. You may want to assign this to advanced learners.

DIFFERENTIATING INSTRUCTION

Advanced Learners
Researching science fiction. Ray Bradbury believes "science fiction is the most important literature in the history of the world because it's the history of ideas, the history of our civilization birthing itself."
Activity. Encourage interested students to find out more about science fiction by researching the organization called the Science Fiction and Fantasy Writers of America. Every year this organization issues the Nebula Awards for the best scripts and fiction in the genre. Through this society, students can find out more about classic writers such as Ray Bradbury and up-and-coming authors just breaking onto the scene. If students are doing their research on the Web, have them input the keyword phrase *Science Fiction Writers of America* into a popular search engine.

INDEPENDENT PRACTICE

Literary Response and Analysis

Reading Check

1. The constant rain on Venus dominates the setting.
2. They expect the sun to come out for the first time in seven years.
3. Margot remembers the sun.
4. The sun comes out for two hours, and the children play outside.
5. The children let Margot out of the closet, aware that they have cheated her out of seeing the sun.

Interpretations

6. Students may infer that Margot, with her subdued nature, will be even more withdrawn, will refuse to come out, or will become hysterical (as she did in the shower). Some students may say that in her situation they would cry or lash out, but others may say that they would not express their pain verbally.
7. Possible answers: Margot's withdrawal and the children's lack of understanding or compassion combine to cause the conflict. She keeps to herself because she feels she does not fit in with her classmates.
8. The children may envy her memories of the sun, hate her for having the chance to return to Earth, or resent her for withdrawing from them.
9. The setting is crucial because the weather on Venus is the cause of Margot's depression; if the weather were fair, she would not be different and would not be targeted by the other children.
10. The title means that the sun comes out only once every seven years, so all of summer is compressed into one day. Students may like the title because it is unusual and catches their interest. Some

Literary Response and Analysis

Reading Check

1. The children in this story live on Venus. What is the outstanding feature of this **setting**?
2. Why are the children so excited at the beginning of the story?
3. What does Margot remember that the other children cannot remember?
4. What happens while Margot is in the closet?
5. What happens at the story's **resolution,** when the characters' problems are resolved in one way or another and the story ends?

Interpretations

6. From her behavior throughout the story, what do you **infer** Margot will say or do when she comes out of the closet? What would you do if you were in her situation?
7. Differences between people often cause **conflicts,** or clashes. What causes the conflict between Margot and the other children? Why does Margot keep to herself?
8. The **characters** in a story behave in certain ways for certain reasons. Why would the children lock Margot in the closet when they know how much the sun means to her? Think back to your Quickwrite notes as you answer this question.
9. Why is the **setting** of this story (including the weather) so important to the **plot**? Hint: Would there be a

Reading Standard 3.3
Analyze the influence of setting on the problem and its resolution.

story if the weather on Venus were like the weather in San Diego?
10. What do you think the **title** of Bradbury's story means? Do you think it's a good title? Why or why not?

Evaluation

11. Bradbury's ending leaves some questions unanswered. Do you think he should have shown what happened when Margot gets out of the closet, or do you like the story as it is? Explain.

Writing
You Had to Be There

What's the most extreme weather you've ever had to face? Tell about what happened to you that day or night. (If nothing much happened, use your imagination.) Describe what you saw, heard, tasted, felt, and smelled on your bad-weather day.

BONUS QUESTION

What is the weather like on the real Venus? Where would you find out?

may find it confusing. Encourage them to think of alternate titles, if they dislike this one.

Evaluation

11. Students might like the ending because it seems real and it invites them to imagine what happens next. Some may dislike it because it does not come to a conclusion and explain Margot's fate.

BONUS QUESTION

The weather on Venus is scorching, with little water vapor in the air. The atmosphere consists mostly of carbon dioxide, which traps heat. Students should visit the NASA Web site for more information.

Vocabulary Development

Monitoring Comprehension

A strategy called **semantic mapping** can help you learn new words you come across in your reading. (The word *semantic* means "having to do with the meaning of words.")

PRACTICE

Using the semantic map for *surged* below as a model, map the other words in the Word Bank. Before you begin, find each word in the story, and note how it's used. You can find related words for your maps in a **dictionary,** a **thesaurus,** or a **synonym finder,** another kind of reference book.

> **Word Bank**
> slackening
> surged
> resilient
> savored

surged — Definition: moved in a wave — Words with related meanings: flooded, rushed — Examples: Rivers surge. Energy surges.

Grammar Link MINI-LESSON

Subject-Verb Agreement: Search for the Subject

Once you find the subject of a sentence, you can decide whether you need a singular or a plural verb. Here are some tips for you:

- In a question the subject often comes *after* the verb. To find the subject, change the question to a statement.

  What was/were the children's deepest fear?

  The children's deepest fear was . . .

- The subject of a sentence is *rarely* part of a prepositional phrase. Cross out any prepositional phrases before looking for the subject.

  The sound of raindrops was upsetting to the children.

PRACTICE

Find the subject of each sentence, and then choose the correct verb.

1. The mood of the children match/matches the day.
2. What do/does Margot and the others think about the sun?
3. How friendly are/is Margot with the other children?
4. The dream of Margot and the others is/are to see the sun.

For more help, see **Agreement of Subject and Verb** in the *Holt Handbook,* pages 124–137.

All Summer in a Day **27**

DIFFERENTIATING INSTRUCTION

Advanced Learners

Enrichment. As students approach question 9, point out that Margot struggles with an internal conflict (her desperate need for sun) as well as an external conflict (the other children's dislike of her). Ask students to consider the roles of both conflicts in the story. [Margot's internal conflict leads her to alienate the other children. Their dislike of her drives the story's action; they ostracize her, pick on her, and finally lock her in the closet.]

Activity. Have students create symbolic drawings to express their understanding of the link between setting and conflict in "All Summer in a Day." A sun and a locked door might appear in these symbolic sketches.

HOMEWORK

Vocabulary Development

Practice

Possible Answers

- *slackening. Definition*—falling off. *Words with related meanings*—diminishing, lessening, slowing. *Examples*—Employment slackened. Ropes slacken.

- *resilient. Definition*—springy. *Words with related meanings*—elastic, buoyant, flexible. *Examples*—Resilient plastic. Willow is resilient.

- *savored. Definition*—delighted in, tasted, or smelled. *Words with related meanings*—enjoyed, relished. *Examples*—Savor youth! I savor chocolate.

► Resources Reminder

Vocabulary and Spelling

- *Vocabulary Development,* p. 2
- *Lesson Plans for Language Development*
  - Vocabulary, p. 22

Grammar Link

Practice

1. *Subject*—mood. *Correct verb*—matches.
2. *Subject*—Margot and the others. *Correct verb*—do.
3. *Subject*—Margot. *Correct verb*—is.
4. *Subject*—dream. *Correct verb*—is.

ASSESSING

Assessment

- *Progress Assessment of Reading*
  - Selection Test, p. 4

RETEACHING

For a lesson reteaching the influence of setting on plot, see **Reteaching,** p. 489B.

All Summer in a Day **27**

STANDARDS FOCUS, pp. 28–32

(For grade-level and review standards taught in this selection, see citations on Pupil's Edition pages.)

Prerequisite Standard

■ Grade 5, Reading Comprehension 2.1 **Understand how text features (e.g., format, graphics, sequence, diagrams, illustrations, charts, maps) make information accessible and usable.**

Summary *at grade level*

> Logan, a young girl, is forced to live her life indoors because she has a rare condition that makes her skin hypersensitive to ultraviolet light. Logan is excited about going outside for her first "play day" in the Florida sun in a specially made suit based on NASA technology.

PRETEACHING

Standards Starter

Build background. Hold up a page from a local newspaper, and ask students how they might find an article they want to read. Point out that the headlines grab the reader's attention and identify the subjects of articles. Read the beginning of one article, and explain that this is called the lead. You might also label headlines, bylines, datelines, and leads and circulate the paper.

 Resources Reminder

Media

■ *Audio CD Library*
  ■ disc 1

Reading

■ *Interactive Reading*
  ■ Graphic Organizer: Newspaper Features Chart, p. 9

Suit Helps Girl Enjoy Daylight

Structural Features of Popular Media: Newspapers

Fantasies like "All Summer in a Day" ask us to imagine "what if?" Informational materials—such as newspapers, magazines, and online information—help us think about "what is." They offer fact, not fiction.

Popular media are informational materials that share information with the general public. Newspapers are an example of popular media.

Features of a Newspaper

Follow these tips when you are looking for information in a newspaper.

- Learn about your newspaper's **sections.** A newspaper may be divided into sections for world and national news, local news, sports, entertainment, weather, and other subjects. Try to decide which section is most likely to have the information you want.

- Scan the **headlines.** Headlines of news stories are like titles of books. Newspaper headlines usually appear in large, heavy type and look like sentences with some words taken out. For example, a headline might read "TAXPAYERS DRAINED," instead of "AMERICANS ARE PAYING MORE IN TAXES." A good headline is attention-getting and clever.

Reading Standard 2.1 Identify the structural features of popular media (for example, newspapers, magazines, online information), and use the features to obtain information.

- Notice how the article begins. Beneath a headline you will sometimes find a **byline,** the name of the reporter who wrote the article. The article itself may begin with a **dateline,** the name of the place where the news event happened and often the date as well.

- For the most important information, check the **lead,** the beginning of the article. In most news articles, the farther you read, the less important the information becomes. That way, if the story has to be shortened to make room for late-breaking news, the editor can just cut from the bottom. News articles usually answer most or all of the *5W-How?* questions—*who? what? where? when? why?* and *how?*—and many of the answers can be found in the lead.

RESOURCES

Planning
■ *One-Stop Planner* CD-ROM with Test Generator
■ *On Course: Mapping Instruction*

Media
■ *Audio CD Library*
  ■ disc 1

Reading
■ *Interactive Reading*
  ■ Graphic Organizer: Newspaper Features Chart, p. 9

Differentiating Instruction
■ *Lesson Plans for Language Development*
  ■ English-Language Learners, pp. 13, 18, 22
  ■ Special Education Students, pp. 13, 18, 22

The **headline** tells you what the news story is about.

The **byline** tells you who wrote the article.

The **dateline** tells you where and (sometimes) when the news event happened.

The **lead** presents the most important information.

Suit Helps Girl Enjoy Daylight

by LISE FISHER

KEYSTONE HEIGHTS, Fla.—Tinted goggles and grayish green fabric covered the three-year-old's face while blocking sunlight from Saturday morning's hazy sky. The suit, however, couldn't hide her enthusiasm.

While other families record events like their children's first steps and words, Steve and Michele Williams will be marking down this day for their daughter, Logan. It was her first play day in the sunlight protected in a "Cool Suit" that blocks the sun's rays, and the event went better than the Williamses could have imagined.

"It just opens up a whole lot of doors," said Logan's father. "The burden is off," a tearful Michele Williams said.

Doctors determined Logan had a rare genetic[1] disease—xeroderma pigmentosum, or XP, as it is known—when she was eighteen months old. For the fewer than one thousand XP patients worldwide, exposure to ultraviolet radiation[2] can lead to deadly skin cancers. The disease has no known cure.

Since the diagnosis, Logan has lived in a world of tinted windows and terror caused by the "bad light."

Light streaming in from a front door and bouncing off their refrigerator frightens the family. Getting Logan to a doctor's appointment has involved padding Logan with a helmet and clothes and covering the car's windows with plastic bags and blankets. She hasn't seen stores, and she marvels that they stock more than one box of cereal and a few toys. Barbara Pellechio, a teacher at Keystone Heights's McRae Elementary School, visits the girl two to three times a week at night because that's when Logan is awake. Like any young child, Logan is afraid of the dark even though it has been the only time she can go outside and play.

The clothing is based on technology from NASA[3] and covers every inch of the little girl with tightly woven material to keep out the sun. Gloves outfitted with rough material for gripping hide her hands. An oversized shirt and pants that look and feel like a soft sweat suit cinch at her wrists and ankles. A hood

---

1. **genetic** (jə·net′ik) *adj.*: passed on as a characteristic by one's parents.
2. **ultraviolet radiation:** invisible energy waves that are present in sunlight.

3. **NASA:** National Aeronautics and Space Administration, the U.S. government agency that conducts research in space.

Suit Helps Girl Enjoy Daylight **29**

Vocabulary and Spelling
- *Vocabulary Development*
  - Vocabulary Worksheet, p. 3

Spelling Lessons and Activities
- *Vocabulary Development*
  - Using Dictionaries, p. 80

Assessment
- *Progress Assessment of Reading*
  - Selection Test, p. 7
- *One-Stop Planner* CD-ROM with Test Generator

A **Reading Informational Materials**
GRADE-LEVEL STANDARD
Structural features: Headlines, photographs, captions. Have students read the headline of the article and then look at the photograph and read the caption on p. 30. Ask what they think the article will be about based on what they read and observe. [Possible responses: It may be about a girl who enjoys the sun; it may be about a girl who wears an unusual-looking suit.]

B **Reading Informational Materials**
GRADE-LEVEL STANDARD
Structural features: Bylines, datelines. Ask students who wrote the article and where the events being reported happened. [Lise Fisher; Keystone Heights, Florida] Have them point to the byline and dateline that contain this information.

C **Reading Informational Materials**
GRADE-LEVEL STANDARD
Structural features: Leads. Have students read the lead—in this case, the first four paragraphs of the article. Ask how the lead answers the *5W-How?* questions. [*Who?*—Logan Williams; *Where?*—in Keystone Heights, Florida; *When?*—Saturday morning (no date); *What?*—played outdoors for the first time in daylight; *How?*—by wearing a "Cool Suit" that blocks the sun's rays; *Why?*—because she has a rare disease, XP, that can lead to death if the sunlight touches her.]

D **Reading Skills**
? Comparing and contrasting. How is Logan like Margot in Bradbury's "All Summer in a Day"? How is she different? [The sun plays a crucial role in both children's lives. Margot is prevented from seeing the sun by the cruelty of her peers; Logan is unable to go out in the sun because she suffers from a condition that makes the sun her enemy.]

Suit Helps Girl Enjoy Daylight **29**

A Advanced Learners

Acceleration. To move students toward the seventh-grade Standard 2.3, which requires that they recognize and analyze cause-and-effect patterns, ask what effects XP has had on Logan's life and how the suit will change her life. [XP has confined Logan indoors and limited her experience of the world. The suit will allow her to go out into the world, to play with groups of children, to experience nature, and possibly to attend regular school.]

B Reading Informational Materials
GRADE-LEVEL STANDARD
? Structural features: Credits and captions. Make sure students can distinguish a credit from a caption. Who took this photograph? [Jon Fletcher]

GUIDED PRACTICE

Monitoring students' progress. Invite students to create and explain similes showing the importance of the "Cool Suit" in Logan's life. Have students share their work in class. Help students who fail to create appropriate similes by re-reading key portions of the article. [Possible response: The "Cool Suit" is like a friend with superpowers. It goes everywhere with Logan and protects her from her enemy, the sun's ultraviolet light.]

secured with goggles conceals her freckled face.

Everything Logan did Saturday was a milestone for Logan's parents and for more than twenty of the family's friends and relatives. They kept pulling up in cars, in trucks, and even in the Keystone Heights fire engine.

Logan clutched purple and yellow flowers her parents bought and planted just for this day. She bounced on a trampoline with friends. Her hands found and clutched a lizard.

"This is probably the most special day of my life," said Alison Broadway, 33. The family friend was holding Logan when the girl spotted a butterfly. "I was holding her and she started squirming and screaming. . . . When they say miracles don't happen, they're wrong because one happened here today," said Broadway.

Logan Williams plays in her "Cool Suit."

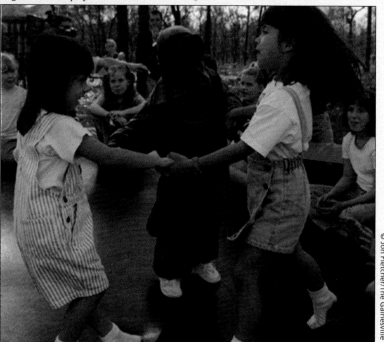

© Jon Fletcher/The Gainesville Sun.

> The **caption** explains what is shown in a picture.

> The photographer's **credit** is usually printed along the side of the photo.

CONTENT-AREA CONNECTIONS

Science
Point out that this article shows how innovations in materials designed for NASA benefited a sick little girl in an unexpected way. In science, research breakthroughs aimed at other purposes often have unexpected applications in health. For instance, Marie Curie's work with radioactivity at the beginning of the twentieth century led to unforeseen breakthroughs in the treatment of cancer.

Activity. Have groups of students of various ability levels research breakthroughs or inventions that unexpectedly have helped people struggling with diseases. Display the groups' findings in a bulletin-board collage.

MIXED-ABILITY

Reading Informational Materials

Reading Check

1. Why can't Logan go out in the sun?

2. When does Logan's teacher visit her? Why does she visit her at that time?

3. Describe Logan's "Cool Suit."

4. Name three things Logan did on her first play day in the sun.

Test Practice

Suit Helps Girl Enjoy Daylight

1. In which section of the newspaper would you be *most* likely to find this article?
   A   Health
   B   Sports
   C   Entertainment
   D   World news

2. The **byline** tells you —
   F   the most important information
   G   who wrote the article
   H   who made the "Cool Suit"
   J   what the story is about

3. You could say that the "Cool Suit" is like a space suit because —
   A   you can float when you wear it
   B   it protects the person wearing it from a deadly environment
   C   you need weeks of training before you can wear it
   D   you have to wear an air tank with it

4. Which of the following statements is *not* true of both "All Summer in a Day" and "Suit Helps Girl Enjoy Daylight"?
   F   The story is about a child who is different from other children.
   G   The story deals with a child who is treated cruelly by other children.
   H   The story has to do with the sun.
   J   The story is about a girl who yearns to play in the sun.

5. Which statement best sums up the point of the news story?
   A   Logan has lived in fear of the sun.
   B   Technology from NASA was used to make the "Cool Suit."
   C   The "Cool Suit" is a miracle for Logan.
   D   No cure has been found for XP.

Reading Standard 2.1 Identify the structural features of popular media (for example, newspapers), and use the features to obtain information.

Test-Taking Tips

For instruction on how to answer multiple-choice items, refer students to **Test Smarts,** p. 690.

INDEPENDENT PRACTICE

Reading Informational Materials

Reading Check

1. Logan has XP, a disease that makes sunlight deadly for her.

2. Her teacher visits her at night because Logan sleeps during the dangerous daylight hours.

3. Logan's grayish-green suit is made of light-blocking material developed by NASA. It is soft and baggy, and it includes goggles, a hood, and gloves.

4. Logan caught a lizard, saw a butterfly, held flowers, and bounced on a trampoline.

Test Practice

Answers and Model Rationales

1. **A**   Because this story is about a Florida girl with a rare disease, it would most likely appear in the health section.

2. **G**   Students have learned that a byline names the person who wrote the article. F and J describe a lead. H is too specific to the article to be correct.

3. **B**   Students must realize that a space suit is designed to protect astronauts from the cold vacuum of space, just as the "Cool Suit" is designed to protect people from the sun.

4. **G**   Students will recall that both Margot and Logan are different from other children and both yearn to play in the sun. Both stories depend on the sun. Thus, G must be correct.

5. **C**   The lead emphasizes that the "Cool Suit" changes Logan's life. Therefore, C is correct.

Vocabulary Development

Practice
Possible Answers

- *determined. Pronunciation—* di tʉr´mənd. *Glossary definition—* decided. *Additional dictionary definition—caused. Derivation—* Latin *de + terminare,* "to end."

- *exposure. Pronunciation—* ik spō´zhər. *Glossary definition—* the state of being unprotected. *Additional dictionary definition—a section of film for one photograph. Derivation—*Latin *exponere,* "to set forth."

- *marvels. Pronunciation—* mär´vəlz. *Glossary definition—* wonders. *Additional dictionary definition—wonderful things. Derivation—*Latin *mirabile,* "wonderful things."

- *milestone. Pronunciation—* mīl´stōn. *Glossary definition—* significant event. *Additional dictionary definition—stone set up on a highway to mark distance. Derivation—*Latin *milia,* "one thousand paces," + Old English *stan,* "rock."

 Resources Reminder

Vocabulary and Spelling
- *Vocabulary Development*
  - Vocabulary Worksheet, p. 3
- *Spelling Lessons and Activities,* p. 80
- *Lesson Plans for Language Development*
  - Vocabulary, p. 22

 ASSESSING

Assessment
- *Progress Assessment of Reading*
  - Selection Test, p. 7

Vocabulary Development

Using Glossaries and Dictionaries

A **glossary** is an alphabetical list of difficult words used in a book, along with their definitions. A glossary usually gives only meanings that apply to the way the words are used in the book. Look at the Glossary for this book (page 718). Besides the definition, what information about each word can you find?

For more information on the meaning of a word, look in a **dictionary.** Many dictionaries also give the **derivation** (der'ə·vā'shən), or origin, of a word. At the back or front of the dictionary, you'll find a list of definitions of symbols and abbreviations used in the derivations. One important symbol is <, which means "comes from." To show that the derivation of a word or word part is unknown, the symbols <? are used.

> **Word List**
> determined
> exposure
> diagnosis
> marvels
> milestone

PRACTICE

Here is a word map for the word *diagnosis.* Using the same labels, make word maps for three other words from the Word Bank.

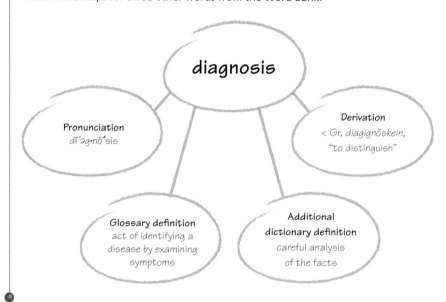

What Will Our Towns Look Like?

Structural Features of Popular Media: Magazines

You *can* judge a magazine by its cover. The next time you're in a library, take a look at the variety of magazines in the reference room. You can find magazines on news, sports, music, food, crafts, health, pets—there's one on just about any subject you can imagine.

Structural Features of Magazines

Magazines have special structural features that give you an overview of what's inside.

- **The cover.** The cover's art and main headline usually announce the lead article and other feature articles. The cover of *Archaeology's dig* magazine (see photo) tells you that the lead story is "Pyramid Power!" and that the issue includes articles on Hercules and King Arthur.

- **The contents page.** This page, at the front of the magazine, lists articles and tells you what pages they're on. The contents page is sometimes called simply "Inside This Issue." *Archaeology's dig* calls its contents page "dig into this!"

Before you read your next **magazine article,** take a minute to notice the way it's structured.

- **The title.** Most magazine articles have titles that are written to catch the reader's interest.

- **The subtitle.** An article may have a subtitle, a secondary title that tells you more about the article.

- **Headings.** Headings are words or phrases used to break up the text of an article into sections. They're often printed in a size or color intended to stand out. You can sometimes **outline** the main points of an article by listing the headings.

- **Illustrations.** Many articles are illustrated with drawings, photographs, maps, graphs, and tables. Illustrations are often used to help you picture something described in an article and to provide more information. They may be accompanied by brief printed explanations, called **captions.**

Reading Standard 2.1 Identify the structural features of popular media (for example, magazines), and use the features to obtain information.

STANDARDS FOCUS, pp. 33–36

(For grade-level and review standards taught in this selection, see citations on Pupil's Edition pages.)

Prerequisite Standard

- Grade 5, Reading Comprehension 2.1 **Understand how text features (e.g., format, graphics, sequence, diagrams, illustrations, charts, maps) make information accessible and usable.**

Summary ⟲ *at grade level*

This article reveals how changes in people's lifestyles in this century might make the environment cleaner and more healthful. Among the article's predictions: People will store energy drawn from the sun and the wind in clean fuel cells that produce hydrogen; food will be grown locally and organically, and wastewater will be recycled organically; town size and layout will favor walking and cycling, and many workers will telecommute. The article also points out that we already have the technology to make those changes happen: All we need to do is reorder our priorities.

PRETEACHING

Standards Starter

Motivate. Ask students to describe the ecological changes they would like to see in their communities over the next ten years. Have them speculate on how to bring those changes about.

RESOURCES

Planning
- *One-Stop Planner* CD-ROM with Test Generator
- *On Course: Mapping Instruction*

Media
- *Audio CD Library*
  - disc 1
- *Fine Art Transparencies*
  - Transparency 2

Reading
- *Interactive Reading*
  - Graphic Organizer: A Magazine Features Chart, p. 10

Differentiating Instruction
- *Lesson Plans for Language Development*
  - English-Language Learners, pp. 14, 19, 22
  - Special Education Students, pp. 14, 19, 22

Assessment
- *Progress Assessment of Reading*
  - Selection Test, p. 8
- *One-Stop Planner* CD-ROM with Test Generator

Resources Reminder

Media
- *Audio CD Library*
  - disc 1
- *Fine Art Transparencies*
  - Transparency 2

Reading
- *Interactive Reading*
  - Graphic Organizer: A Magazine Features Chart, p. 10

A Reading Informational Materials
GRADE-LEVEL STANDARD

❷ Structural features: Titles and captions. Point out that this article's title, "What Will Our Towns Look Like?" poses a question. Then, indicate the caption in large type below the illustration. What functions does this caption perform? [Possible response: It answers the question posed in the title, sums up the main idea of the article, and introduces the specific details in the numbered text below the illustration.]

B English-Language Learners

Interpreting idioms. Be sure students know that the *horizon* is the apparent line that separates earth and sky. Define the idiom *on the horizon* as "coming soon." To help students understand the expression, offer the image of an approaching ship that first appears on the horizon but then moves nearer and nearer.

C Reading Informational Materials
GRADE-LEVEL STANDARD

Structural features: Illustrations. Ask students how readers can quickly find out what the numbered parts of the illustration represent. [Possible response: Scan the columns of the text below the art for the corresponding numerals.]

What Will Our Towns Look Like? (If We Take Care of Our Planet)

The **title** is often a catchy phrase intended to grab your attention.

The **subtitle** tells you more about the article.

A **caption** explains what is shown in an illustration.

New inventions will help us build clean, green places to live.

Fantastic inventions made daily life easier in the past century but often at the expense of our natural resources. Gas-powered cars got us everywhere in a flash, but they polluted our air. Electric heat and light made our homes warm and welcoming but also burned up limited coal and oil. Factories revolutionized the way we worked, but industrial waste trashed rivers, streams, and oceans.

Lifestyle changes on the horizon for the next one hundred years may actually improve our planet's health. We can use cleaner energy and fewer chemicals while working, playing, and bringing up families in the towns of tomorrow. This is not an impossible dream. Most of the innovations shown here already exist or are being developed. If we put our minds to it, our towns can preserve Earth's natural riches and still be lovely places to call home. Here's how things might be—if we make the environment a top concern.

D Work/Transportation
More grownups will work in their homes ① and keep in touch with co-workers through computers. Others will make a short trip to a nearby office park ②. A few will ride swift electric trains ③ to the nearest city. Cars and trucks ④ will run on clean, hydrogen-powered fuel cells. Most entertainment and stores will be close by, so we'll often travel on old-fashioned, earth-friendly bicycles ⑤.

Food
We'll grow fruits, grains, and vegetables close to home, either in our gardens ⑥ or on nearby organic farms ⑦. Since the farms will use natural forms of pest control, such as predatory insects, there will be far fewer chemicals in the food supply.

34 Chapter 1 Structures: Building Blocks of Meaning

DIFFERENTIATING INSTRUCTION

English-Language Learners
Students who have come from farms and rural areas in less-developed nations may need help in understanding this article. You might explain some of the problems that industrialization has produced, including polluted air and water, the destruction of open green spaces, and long commutes. Then, encourage students to read the article, looking for solutions to those problems.

Advanced Learners
Enrichment. Invite students to create magazine advertisements "selling" a skeptical public on one of the changes mentioned in the article. Point out that, like magazine titles and headings, the copy for magazine advertisements must be both catchy and informative. Visual images, like the illustrations for magazine articles, need to grab readers and help them picture what is being discussed or described.

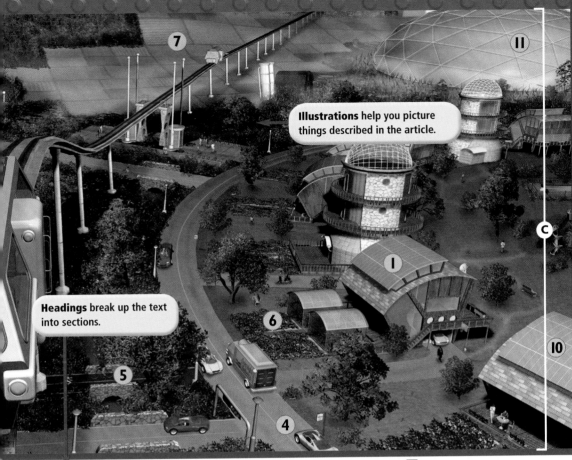

Illustrations help you picture things described in the article.

Headings break up the text into sections.

D Reading Informational Materials
GRADE-LEVEL STANDARD
Structural features: Headings. Ask students what information the five headings in the text give. [Possible response: They name the aspects or areas of life that will be greatly improved in the twenty-first century by new, earth-friendly inventions.]

E Reading Skills

? Speculating. Ask students which of the proposed changes they think will be least popular. For example, might people demand imported bottled water rather than recycled water for drinking? Might some people be unwilling to walk or cycle rather than ride in a car? Encourage students to provide reasons for their opinions.

GUIDED PRACTICE

Monitoring students' progress. Have students assume that "What Will Our Towns Look Like?" is the lead article in a special issue of a magazine that deals with life in the twenty-first century. Ask students to suggest other article topics and to create a cover and a brief table of contents for this issue.

Shopping

Even if online stores are here to stay, there will still be a mall ⑧. But it will be small, with sidewalks and bike racks instead of a giant parking lot. An airy place in which a flood of natural light will cut down on energy use, the mall will be one big recycling operation; when you're through using any product you buy there, the store will be required to take it back for recycling.

Energy

Our power will come from sources cleaner than coal, oil, and gas. Some energy will flow from windmills ⑨, but much of it will be generated in our own homes. Rooftop solar panels ⑩ will supply electricity to our appliances and to a basement fuel cell, which will produce hydrogen. When the sun is not shining, the cell will use the hydrogen to make electricity.

Waste **D**

Plumbing lines will empty into enclosed marshes ⑪, where special plants, fish, snails, and bacteria will naturally purify wastewater. Clean water will flow back into streams and reservoirs.

—from *Time for Kids*

E

What Will Our Towns Look Like? **35**

Encourage students to discuss this article with their families. What changes in the towns of the future do they anticipate most eagerly? Each student should return to class with one idea in mind.

INDEPENDENT PRACTICE

Reading Informational Materials

Reading Check

1. *Title*—"What Will Our Towns Look Like?" *Subtitle*—(If We Take Care of Our Planet). *Headings*—Work/Transportation, Food, Shopping, Energy, Waste.

2. *6*—a home garden; *7*—an organic farm. Look in the numbered text below the illustration.

3. They will make the planet healthier and cleaner.

Answers and Model Rationales

1. **B** Point out that A, C, and D all appear in the opening paragraphs. Thus, B is correct.

2. **G** The sentence is under the picture; students should conclude that it is a caption.

3. **C** "Egypt's Early Pyramids" is a topic from ancient times.

4. **J** Under "Shopping," it says "there will still be a mall." Therefore, J is correct.

5. **A** Explain that C and D are too specific; B is general but too negative. Therefore, A is correct.

Test-Taking Tips

Remind students that when *not* or *except* appears in an item, they should look for an answer that does not fit in with the others.

For more instruction, refer students to **Test Smarts,** p. 690.

ASSESSING

Assessment
- *Progress Assessment of Reading*
  - Selection Test, p. 8

Reading Informational Materials

Reading Check
1. Write down the **title, subtitle,** and **headings** of this article. (You should have seven in all.)

2. What are numbers 6 and 7 in the article's illustration? Where would you find out what the numbers mean?

3. How will lifestyle changes in the next hundred years affect the planet?

What Will Our Towns Look Like?

1. The article makes all of the following points *except* —
   A Lifestyle changes may help the environment.
   B Factories have made our daily lives harder.
   C Industrial wastes pollute streams, rivers, and oceans.
   D Coal and oil are burned to produce electric heat and light.

2. "New inventions will help us build clean, green places to live" is —
   F the magazine title
   G a caption
   H a heading
   J an illustration

3. In a special magazine issue on life in the twenty-first century, which article would you *not* expect to see?
   A "Next Stop: Mars"
   B "Staying Active After 150"
   C "Egypt's Early Pyramids"
   D "Robots Replace Teachers"

4. The article makes all of the following predictions *except* —
   F Malls will be smaller than they are today.
   G Malls will have bike racks instead of huge parking lots.
   H Malls will be lit by natural light.
   J There will be no malls in the future.

5. This article was written mainly to —
   A describe what life in the towns of the future will be like—if we take care of the environment
   B point out how desperate our environmental situation is
   C encourage people to grow their own food
   D suggest ways to clean up our water supply

Reading Standard 2.1 Identify the structural features of popular media (for example, magazines), and use the features to obtain information.

Solar System Bodies: Venus

Structural Features of Popular Media: The Internet

In the past, if you wanted to learn about the real Venus (not Bradbury's imaginary planet), you would probably look in a reference or science book. Today we have another important source of information literally at our fingertips—the Internet.

Using the Internet

There are several ways to find information on the Internet. You can go directly to a **Web site** if you know the URL (uniform resource locator), the address of the site. To find information about Venus, you might want to try the Web site of NASA (the National Aeronautics and Space Administration). NASA is the U.S. government agency that conducts space exploration. The information on Venus on pages 38 and 39 comes from NASA's Web site. There is an example of NASA's home page on page 44.

Sometimes you have to use a **search engine** when you do research. Using a search engine gives you access to a gigantic library of information. Because the computer can search very quickly, you get results faster than if you searched through books in a library.

A search will usually produce a list of **Web sites** relating to the topic of your search. Often you can just click on the site name and go directly to the site. If a search produces no useful results, you

may want to try another search engine. If a search produces too many results, you have to refine your search by choosing a more specific search term.

Online Skills: Getting Information

Most Web sites share some **basic structural features.** Knowing how to recognize these features can help you find information online. When you are at a Web site, keep these points in mind.

- Most of what a site offers is shown on the site's **home page.** Start out by finding and reading basic information about the site, usually at the top or center of the home page.

- Look for a **table of contents,** a list of the site's other pages. The table of contents often appears on the side of the home page. You can generally reach the other pages of a site by clicking on the items listed in the table of contents.

- Explore the other pages. You may find the information you're looking for presented in articles, charts, lists, and other formats.

- Look for **links,** Web sites related to the one you're exploring. You can often reach a link by clicking on its name. Not every Web site offers links, but you can usually find a "links" page in the table of contents.

Reading Standard 2.1 Identify the structural features of popular media (for example, online information), and use the features to obtain information.

Solar System Bodies: Venus **37**

STANDARDS FOCUS, pp. 37–41

(For grade-level and review standards taught in this selection, see citations on Pupil's Edition pages.)

Prerequisite Standards

- Grade 5, Vocabulary 1.2   **Use word origins to determine the meaning of unknown words.**

- Grade 5, Reading Comprehension 2.1   **Understand how text features (e.g., format, graphics, sequence, diagrams, illustrations, charts, maps) make information accessible and usable.**

Summary ⬆ *above grade level*

"Solar System Bodies: Venus" is a Web page full of facts and information about the planet Venus. The boxed labels explain how students can use the structural features of this Web page—a table of contents, a list of features, and a list of links to related Web sites—to locate online information about Venus. Those structural features are common to most Web pages. Once students can recognize and use them, they will be able to unlock online information from anywhere on the Internet.

PRETEACHING

Standards Starter

Motivate. Tell students that the Web page describes Venus as "a caldron of blistering heat." Encourage students to guess how hot they think Venus is and to write their guesses on slips of paper. After reading the Web page, students can compare their guesses to the actual temperature.

▶ **Resources Reminder**

Reading
- *Interactive Reading*
  - Graphic Organizer: Internet Search Chart, p. 11

RESOURCES

Planning
- *On Course: Mapping Instruction*

Reading
- *Interactive Reading*
  - Graphic Organizer: Internet Search Chart, p. 11

Differentiating Instruction
- *Lesson Plans for Language Development*
  - English-Language Learners, pp. 15, 20, 22

- Special Education Students, pp. 15, 20, 22

Vocabulary and Spelling
- *Vocabulary Development*, p. 4

Assessment
- *Progress Assessment of Reading*
  - Selection Test, p. 10
- *One-Stop Planner* CD-ROM with Test Generator

A **Reading Informational Materials**
GRADE-LEVEL STANDARD
Getting information from a Web page. Ask students how they can use the Web page to learn whether there have been any other recent discoveries about Venus. [by clicking on "News" in the table of contents]

B **Reading Informational Materials**
GRADE-LEVEL STANDARD
Getting information from a Web page. Ask students to read the "Profile" feature of the Web site and then identify the purpose of this section. [Possible response: to display useful or interesting facts about Venus that users can find quickly.]

Back Forward Reload Home Search

Location:

FEATURES HOME SEARCH FEEDBACK SITE MAP NASA

SOLAR SYSTEM EXPLORATION

Mercury • Venus • Earth • Mars • Jupiter • Saturn • Uranus • Neptune • Pluto • Asteroids • Comets

Romanticized as the morning and evening star, Venus is actually a caldron of blistering heat and noxious gases!

SOLAR SYSTEM BODIES: VENUS

SCIENCE GOALS –
NEWS –
MISSIONS –
TECHNOLOGY –
RESEARCH –
EDUCATION –

Venus, second planet from the sun, has sometimes been called Earth's sister planet because the two are so similar in size and mass. But there the similarities end. Venus is covered by thick, rapidly spinning clouds that trap surface heat, creating a scorched greenhouselike world with temperatures hot enough to melt lead, and pressure so intense that standing on Venus would feel like the pressure felt 900 m (3,000 ft.) deep in Earth's oceans.

These clouds reflect sunlight as well as trap in heat. Because Venus reflects so much sunlight, it is usually the brightest planet in the sky.

The atmosphere consists mainly of carbon dioxide (the same gas that produces fizzy sodas), virtually no water vapor, and droplets of sulfuric acid—not a great place for people or plants! In addition, the thick atmosphere allows the sun's heat in but does not allow it to escape, resulting in surface temperatures over 450°C (more than 800°F), hotter than the surface of the planet Mercury, which is closest to the sun. The high density of the atmosphere results in a surface pressure ninety times that of Earth, which is why probes that have landed on Venus have only survived several hours before being crushed ▶

PROFILE

Distance from the Sun (semimajor axis of orbit)
108,208,930 km
0.72333199 A.U.

Mean Equatorial Radius
6,051.8 km
(0.9488 of Earth's radius)

Mean Temperature at Solid Surface
730°K

Major Atmospheric Constituents
CO_2, N_2

Natural Satellites
None

Features: This band at the top of the page outlines the structure of the Web site.

Contents: This list tells you what other topics the site covers.

38 Chapter 1 Structures: Building Blocks of Meaning

Learners Having Difficulty
You may want to use the Internet Search Chart in *Interactive Reading*, p. 11, to help students work their way through the Web page. This graphic organizer calls out basic terms such as *URL* and *search engine*.

English-Language Learners
Make sure students understand the terms *planets* and *solar system* before beginning the selection.

Resources Reminder
For lessons designed for intermediate and advanced English-language learners, see *Lesson Plans for Language Development,* pp. 15, 20, 22.

Special Education Students
For lessons designed for special education students, see *Lesson Plans for Language Development,* pp. 15, 20, 22.

FEATURES

HOME | SEARCH | FEEDBACK | SITE MAP

NASA

SOLAR SYSTEM EXPLORATION

Mercury • Venus • Earth • Mars • Jupiter • Saturn • Uranus • Neptune • Pluto • Asteroids • Comets

Romanticized as the morning and evening star, Venus is actually a caldron of blistering heat and noxious gases!

SOLAR SYSTEM BODIES: VENUS

- SCIENCE GOALS –
- NEWS –
- MISSIONS –
- TECHNOLOGY –
- RESEARCH –
- EDUCATION –

by the incredible pressure. In the upper layers, the clouds move faster than hurricane-force winds on Earth.

Much of the surface is covered by vast lava flows. In the north, an elevated region named Ishtar Terra is a lava-filled basin larger than the continental United States. Near the equator, the Aphrodite Terra highlands, more than half the size of Africa, extend for almost 10,000 km (6,200 mi.). Volcanic flows have also produced long, sinuous channels extending for hundreds of miles.

Over 100,000 small shield volcanoes dot the surface, along with hundreds of larger volcanoes. Maxwell Montes, a mountain taller than Mount Everest, sits at one end of Ishtar Terra. Giant calderas over 100 km (62 mi.) in diameter are found on Venus. Calderas are basinlike depressions in the surface that occur after the collapse of the center of a volcano.

Venus's interior is probably very similar to that of Earth, holding an iron core about 3,000 km (1,900 mi.) in radius and a molten rocky mantle comprising the majority of the planet. Recent results from the Magellan spacecraft suggest that Venus's crust is stronger and thicker than had previously been thought.

RELATED LINKS

- *Exploring the Planets— Venus*
- *Missions to Venus*
- *NASA Planetary Photojournal: Venus*
- *National Space Science Data Center*
- *The Nine Planets*

Links: Clicking on an item in this list takes you to another Web site and more information.

Solar System Bodies: Venus **39**

Getting information from a Web page. After students have read the first three paragraphs, ask them which feature they would use if they wanted to compare the temperature of Venus with the temperatures of the other planets in our solar system. [They probably would use the related link "The Nine Planets."] Tell students to visualize the planet Venus as they read. Explain that it's possible for them to see what Venus actually looks like. Ask students how they might do this. [by going to the link "NASA Planetary Photojournal: Venus"]

GUIDED PRACTICE

Monitoring students' progress. Invite students to tell the most interesting thing they learned about Venus from the Web page. Then, ask students to write a feedback message to express their opinion of the page. Suggest they tell what features they like and why. Encourage students to include any suggestions they have for changes or additions.

Advanced Learners

Enrichment. Encourage students to create lists of questions on the topic of Venus that could be answered by features of this Web page. Have partners exchange lists and tell how they would use the Web page to find the answers.

Reading Informational Materials

Reading Check

1. In what ways is Venus like Earth?
2. Why have probes that have landed on Venus survived only a few hours?
3. What covers most of Venus's surface?
4. Find three places on the Web page where the writer describes a feature of Venus by **comparing** it to something we are familiar with on Earth.

INDEPENDENT PRACTICE

Reading Informational Materials

Reading Check

1. Venus is like Earth in size and mass, and it has a similar core.
2. Probes have survived only a few hours because Venus's surface pressure is ninety times that of Earth.
3. Lava flows cover most of Venus's surface.
4. The writer describes the size of Ishtar Terra as larger than the continental United States, the size of the Aphrodite Terra highlands as half the size of Africa, and Maxwell Montes as taller than Mount Everest.

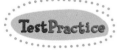

Answers and Model Rationales

1. **B** Students should realize that the main purpose of this Web site is to provide objective data. Therefore, they can eliminate A and D, which are basically persuasive. In choosing between B and C, students should select B because it sums up more of the information on the page.

2. **F** Explain to students that words such as *hideous* and *interesting,* which are subjective, cannot be factual. J contains the word *never,* and one can never say never about the future. Thus, F is correct.

3. **B** Students should find this piece of information at the end of the "Profile" feature.

4. **J** Students should find the word *missions* in the table of contents and in the "Related Links." Therefore, J is correct.

TestPractice

Solar System Bodies: Venus

1. The main **purpose** of this **Web page** is to —
   - **A** criticize scientific studies of Venus
   - **B** describe the characteristics of Venus
   - **C** explain how living things could survive on Venus
   - **D** encourage scientific probes of Venus

2. Which of the following is a **fact** about Venus—something that can be proved?
   - **F** Venus is the second planet from the sun.
   - **G** Venus is a hideous planet.
   - **H** Venus is more interesting than Earth.
   - **J** People will never colonize Venus.

3. What part of this **Web page** tells you that Venus has no natural satellites?
   - **A** The table of contents
   - **B** Profile
   - **C** Site Map
   - **D** News

4. In this **Web site,** where would you find information on missions to Venus?
   - **F** Features and the table of contents
   - **G** Feedback and Home
   - **H** Related Links and Profile
   - **J** The table of contents and Related Links

5. Which of the following statements best sums up the **main idea** of this **Web page**?
   - **A** Although Venus is similar to Earth in some ways, human beings could not survive the extreme conditions there.
   - **B** Venus should be romanticized as the evening star.
   - **C** Venus is Earth's sister planet.
   - **D** Venus's atmosphere consists mainly of carbon dioxide.

Reading Standard 2.1 Identify the structural features of popular media (for example, online information), and use the features to obtain information.

5. **A** Remind students that the main idea cannot be a detail. Since the Web page covers Venus's atmosphere, topography, and interior core, as well as information about missions, B and D cannot be correct. A and C resemble each other, but A covers more ideas in the article.

Test-Taking Tips

For instruction on how to answer multiple-choice items, refer students to **Test Smarts,** p. 690.

Vocabulary Development

Using Context Clues

When scientists write for the public, they often try to help readers understand specialized words. You can figure out the meanings of some of those words from clues in the text or in the word itself.

Look for definitions in the text.

"Giant calderas over 100 km (62 mi.) in diameter are found on Venus. Calderas are basinlike depressions in the surface that occur after the collapse of the center of a volcano."

Look for clues in the word itself.

"Venus is actually a caldron of blistering heat and noxious gases!"

> A definition is given in the second sentence.

> Noxious looks and sounds like obnoxious, which means "unpleasant or nasty."

PRACTICE

Study the context of the underlined word in each item below. Then, use **context clues** to select the best definition of the word. Do all the sentences contain context clues?

1. "Venus is covered by thick, rapidly spinning clouds that trap surface heat, creating a scorched greenhouselike world with temperatures hot enough to melt lead . . ."

   A damaged by intense heat

   B moist and warm

   C brightly lit

2. "The atmosphere consists mainly of carbon dioxide (the same gas that produces fizzy sodas) . . ."

   A a virus

   B a drink

   C a gas

3. "Volcanic flows have also produced long, sinuous channels extending for hundreds of miles."

   A winding

   B small

   C straight

Reading Standard 1.4
Monitor expository text for unknown words or words with novel meanings by using word and sentence clues to determine meaning.

Vocabulary Development

Practice

1. **A** "Heat" and "temperatures hot enough to melt lead" are clues to the meaning of *scorched.*

2. **C** The sentence explains in parentheses that carbon dioxide is a gas.

3. **A** When a liquid flows, it usually does not move in a straight line. When lava flows out of a volcano, "extending for hundreds of miles," one might assume that these flows are long and winding.

 Resources Reminder

Vocabulary and Spelling

- *Vocabulary Development*
  - Decoding Worksheet, p. 4
  - Cumulative Vocabulary Review, p. 5
- *Lesson Plans for Language Development*
  - Vocabulary, p. 22

ASSESSING

Assessment

- *Progress Assessment of Reading*
  - Selection Test, p. 10

Literary Response and Analysis

Literary Response and Analysis

STANDARDS FOCUS, pp. 42–43

(*For the grade-level standard reviewed in this lesson, see Pupil's Edition, p. 42.*)

INTRODUCING THE STANDARDS REVIEW

Use this review to assess students' grasp of the standards taught in this chapter. If necessary, you can use the annotations to guide students in their reading before they answer the questions.

DIRECT TEACHING

A Literary Focus
REVIEW STANDARD
❓ **Setting.** What impression do you get of the place where Ivan lived? What words help create this impression? [Possible response: The phrase "lonely shack" suggests a small, crudely built house where a poor person lives. The shack's location across from a cemetery evokes an uneasy feeling in the reader.]

B Literary Focus
GRADE-LEVEL STANDARD
❓ **Influence of setting.** When does the story take place, and how does this affect the mood of the tale? [The story takes place in the wintertime on a snowy, bitter cold, and windy night. This setting creates a somber mood.]

C Literary Focus
GRADE-LEVEL STANDARD
❓ **Influence of setting on conflict.** How does the setting influence Ivan's problem? [The cemetery has always frightened Ivan; the darkness and harsh weather make crossing it even more frightening, so Ivan shivers and starts to run. The setting seems to intensify his fear.]

 DIRECTIONS: Read the story. Then, read each question, and write the letter of the best response.

The Path Through the Cemetery
Leonard Q. Ross

Ivan was a timid little man—so timid that the villagers called him "Pigeon" or mocked him with the title "Ivan the Terrible." Every night Ivan stopped in at the saloon which was on the edge of the village cemetery. Ivan never crossed the cemetery to get to his lonely shack on the other side. That path would save many minutes, but he had never taken it—not even in the full light of noon.

Late one winter's night, when bitter wind and snow beat against the saloon, the customers took up the familiar mockery. "Ivan's mother was scared by a canary when she carried him." "Ivan the Terrible—Ivan the Terribly Timid One."

Ivan's sickly protest only fed their taunts, and they jeered cruelly when the young Cossack lieutenant flung his horrid challenge at their quarry.

"You are a pigeon, Ivan. You'll walk all around the cemetery in this cold—but you dare not cross it."

Ivan murmured, "The cemetery is nothing to cross, Lieutenant. It is nothing but earth, like all the other earth."

The lieutenant cried, "A challenge, then! Cross the cemetery tonight,

Ivan, and I'll give you five rubles—five gold rubles!"

Perhaps it was the vodka. Perhaps it was the temptation of the five gold rubles. No one ever knew why Ivan, moistening his lips, said suddenly: "Yes, Lieutenant, I'll cross the cemetery!"

The saloon echoed with their disbelief. The lieutenant winked to the men and unbuckled his saber. "Here, Ivan. When you get to the center of the cemetery, in front of the biggest tomb, stick the saber into the ground. In the morning we shall go there. And if the saber is in the ground—five gold rubles to you!"

Ivan took the saber. The men drank a toast: "To Ivan the Terrible!" They roared with laughter.

The wind howled around Ivan as he closed the door of the saloon behind him. The cold was knife-sharp. He buttoned his long coat and crossed the dirt road. He could hear the lieutenant's voice, louder than the rest, yelling after him, "Five rubles, pigeon! If you live!"

Ivan pushed the cemetery gate open. He walked fast. "Earth, just earth . . .

Reading Standard 3.3
Analyze the influence of setting on the problem and its resolution.

MINI-LESSON Reading

Reviewing Word-Attack Skills
Activity. Display these words and meanings. Have students use the prefixes to choose the correct meaning for each word.

1. disrupt [A]
   A "break apart or disturb the order"
   B "break in upon or hinder"

2. construct [B]
   A "build by putting parts back in place"
   B "build by putting parts together"

3. respond [A]
   A "answer back"
   B "answer quickly"

4. conspire [A]
   A "plan and work together"
   B "plan and work alone in secret"

5. dissipate [B]
   A "pay back or make amends"
   B "break apart and scatter"

like any other earth." But the darkness was a massive dread. "Five gold rubles . . ." The wind was cruel and the saber was like ice in his hands. Ivan shivered under the long, thick coat and broke into a limping run.

He recognized the large tomb. He must have sobbed—that was the sound that was drowned in the wind. And he knelt, cold and terrified, and drove the saber through the crust into the hard ground. With all his strength, he pushed it down to the hilt. It was done. The cemetery . . . the challenge . . . five gold rubles.

Ivan started to rise from his knees. But he could not move. Something

held him. Something gripped him in an unyielding and implacable hold. Ivan tugged and lurched and pulled— gasping in his panic, shaken by a monstrous fear. But something held Ivan. He cried out in terror, then made senseless gurgling noises.

They found Ivan, next morning, on the ground in front of the tomb that was in the center of the cemetery. He was frozen to death. The look on his face was not that of a frozen man, but of a man killed by some nameless horror. And the lieutenant's saber was in the ground where Ivan had pounded it—through the dragging folds of his long coat.

1. Ivan can best be described as —
    A brave
    B proud
    C fearful
    D sickly

2. Ivan's main **problem** is that he must —
    F carry the heavy saber
    G conquer his terror of the cemetery
    H fight the lieutenant
    J find the biggest tomb

3. When Ivan drives the saber into the frozen ground —
    A his heart gives out
    B he overcomes his fear
    C he sees a ghost
    D he pins his coat to the ground

4. By the **resolution** of the story, Ivan has —
    F claimed his five gold rubles
    G frozen to death
    H disappeared
    J been killed by the saber

5. The **setting** of this story creates an overall feeling of —
    A mockery
    B horror
    C peace
    D courage

6. Another good **title** for the story is —
    F "A Monstrous Fear"
    G "Ivan's Triumph"
    H "A Clever Soldier"
    J "The Lieutenant's Concern"

D Literary Focus
GRADE-LEVEL STANDARD
? Influence of setting on resolution. How does the setting affect the resolution of Ivan's problem? [Because the cemetery frightens Ivan, he is unable to tell that the saber is pinning his coat to the ground. The author suggests that Ivan is frightened to death by his own imagination.]

TestPractice

Answers and Model Rationales

1. **C** Students should eliminate A because Ivan is called timid. D is wrong because Ivan's protests are called sickly, not Ivan. C, *fearful*, is better than B, *foolish*, because the story suggests that panic causes Ivan's death.

2. **G** Students should realize that F, H, and J are irrelevant to the conflict. To win the rubles, Ivan must conquer his own fear.

3. **D** After re-reading the last paragraph, students should realize B and C do not happen. A does occur but *after* Ivan drives the saber tip into the ground. Therefore, D is correct.

4. **G** The last paragraph clearly states that Ivan was frozen.

5. **B** Students should be able to eliminate D and C immediately. B is a better answer than A because it is the overall feeling of dread and horror the setting creates.

6. **F** F is the best answer because it is Ivan's fear that kills him.

Test-Taking Tips

Remind students always to return to the passage when looking for an answer to a question about a specific detail in the text.

For more instruction on how to answer multiple-choice items, refer students to **Test Smarts,** p. 690.

Activity. Display each pair of words. Have students read them aloud. Then, have a volunteer circle the word that matches the definition.

1. fiber   fibber
    "one who lies about unimportant things" [fibber]

2. miller   miler
    "member of a track team" [miler]

3. follicle   foliage
    "leaves of a plant or tree" [foliage]

4. pillage   piles
    "plundering, looting" [pillage]

5. doggy   dogie
    "motherless calf" [dogie]

Standards Review

Reading Informational Materials

STANDARDS FOCUS, pp. 44–45

(For the grade-level standard reviewed in this lesson, see Pupil's Edition, p. 44.)

INTRODUCING THE STANDARDS REVIEW

Use this review to test students' grasp of the structural features of a Web page. Use these annotations only if you want to conduct this review orally.

DIRECT TEACHING

Ⓐ Reading Informational Materials
GRADE-LEVEL STANDARD
❓ **Getting information from a Web page.** Call students' attention to the "Features" section of the Web page. Which of these features would you click on to find out about missions to the moon? ["A History of Exploration"]

Ⓑ Reading Informational Materials
GRADE-LEVEL STANDARD
❓ **Getting information from a Web page.** What other way can you get information about missions to the moon? [Click on "Missions" in the table of contents.]

Ⓒ Reading Informational Materials
GRADE-LEVEL STANDARD
❓ **Getting information from a Web page.** Have students identify the part of the Web page where they could find reasons why space exploration is considered important. ["Science Goals" in the table of contents]

Reading Informational Materials

TestPractice DIRECTIONS: Read the Web page. Then, read each question, and write the letter of the best response.

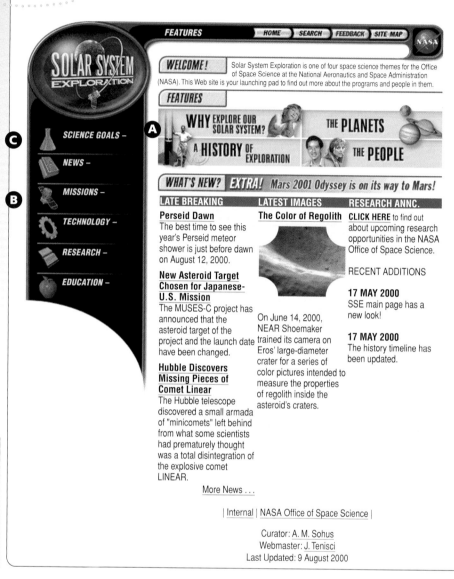

Reading Standard 2.1 Identify the structural features of popular media (for example, online information), and use the features to obtain information.

44 Chapter 1 Structures: Building Blocks of Meaning

1. The source of this home page is —
   A NASA (the National Aeronautics and Space Administration)
   B a group of amateur astronomers
   C the MUSES-C project
   D Solar System Exploration

2. This page was last updated on —
   F June 14, 2000
   G May 17, 2000
   H August 12, 2000
   J August 9, 2000

3. If you wanted to find out about the scientists who work at NASA, which feature would you go to?
   A A History of Exploration
   B The Planets
   C The People
   D Education

4. If you wanted to find out about research opportunities at NASA, what would you click on?
   F Recent Additions
   G Research Announcements
   H Latest Images
   J Late Breaking

5. If you wanted to find out about water on Mars, what would you click on?
   A The Planets
   B Latest Images
   C Recent Additions
   D A History of Exploration

6. Suppose you've read "Hubble Discovers Missing Pieces of Comet Linear." To read more about the Hubble telescope, you should click on —
   F "The Color of Regolith"
   G "The People"
   H "Recent Additions"
   J "More News"

7. Which of the following topics are listed in the contents of this Web page?
   A "Missions" and "Education"
   B "Feedback" and "Site Map"
   C "The Planets" and "The People"
   D "Welcome!" and "Features"

 TestPractice

Answers and Model Rationales

1. **A** The "Welcome" feature clearly cites NASA as the source of this page.

2. **J** The last item on the Web page is the "Last Updated" date.

3. **C** Since scientists are people, students should select C over A, B, and D.

4. **G** Through process of elimination, students should choose G because it is the only answer that mentions research.

5. **A** Since Mars is a planet, students should select A.

6. **J** Since the article on the Web page tells about the work of the Hubble telescope, the line "More News" is a link to additional information relating to the Hubble telescope. The other links provide connections to other kinds of information.

7. **A** The table of contents often appears on the side of the home page. In this example, "Missions" and "Education" are the two topics listed in the table of contents.

Test-Taking Tips

Point out that heads on Web pages usually signal links to a category of data or information. Encourage students to look carefully at the heads before answering the Test Practice items.

For more information on how to answer multiple-choice questions, refer students to **Test Smarts**, p. 690.

Test Practice

Vocabulary Development

Multiple-Meaning Words

Modeling. Model the thought process of a good reader getting the answer to item 1 by saying, "I know that a baby *shower* is a party for an expectant mother. I also know that 'to be caught in a shower' means 'to be exposed to rain.' In C, I think *shower* means 'an outpouring.' I also know that football players shower after practice. In that case, *shower* means 'to bathe in water from a shower nozzle,' which matches the sample sentence."

Answers and Model Rationales

1. **D** See rationale above.

2. **J** In F, *touch* means "affect." In G, it means "subtle effect or small detail." In H, it is part of the idiom "keep in touch." In J, *touch* means "make physical contact with." This is the same meaning *touch* has in the sample sentence.

3. **D** In A and C, *watch* means "look." In B, it is part of the idiom "keep watch," which means "to stand guard." In D, *watch* means "device worn on the wrist for telling time," as it does in the sample sentence.

4. **G** In F, *ground* means "earth." In H, it means "area of land." In J, it is part of the idiom "stand your ground," which means "do not back down." In G, "ground to a halt" means "gradually and noisily slowed to a stop," as it does in the sample sentence.

5. **C** In A, *flash* means "shine briefly." In B, it means "send rapidly." In D, it means "a streak." In C, it means "a moment in time," as it does in the sample.

Vocabulary Development

TestPractice

Multiple-Meaning Words

DIRECTIONS: Each of the sentences below is from "All Summer in a Day." Read the sentence. Then, choose the answer in which the underlined word is used in the same way.

1. "And once, a month ago, she had refused to shower in the school shower rooms. . . ."
   - **A** The baby shower is next Thursday.
   - **B** The children were caught in a shower and came home drenched.
   - **C** The singer smiled modestly as her admirers poured out a shower of praise.
   - **D** The players dashed off to shower after football practice.

2. "She . . . had clutched her hands to her ears and over her head, screaming the water mustn't touch her head."
   - **F** The movie didn't touch me at all.
   - **G** The bow tie added a jaunty touch to his outfit.
   - **H** We were glad to hear from you. Please keep in touch.
   - **J** Don't blame it on me. I didn't touch him.

3. "She glanced at her watch."
   - **A** Watch for Grandma; she should be here soon.
   - **B** As they worked, Jane kept watch over the door.
   - **C** Watch out! That foul ball almost hit you.
   - **D** What time is it by your watch?

4. "The world ground to a standstill."
   - **F** After the rain the ground was soaked.
   - **G** Slowly the train ground to a halt.
   - **H** The parade ground was deserted.
   - **J** Stand your ground or they will make you do it.

5. "The sky darkened into midnight in a flash."
   - **A** Flash your light over here.
   - **B** The boy saw his parents flash a glance at each other.
   - **C** He'll be with you in a flash.
   - **D** We saw a flash of purple light.

Vocabulary Review

Use this activity to assess whether students have retained the chapter Vocabulary. **Activity.** Have students select the correct word from the box to complete the following analogies.

nurturing	tolerant	slackening
anonymous	resilient	

1. *poor* is to *rich* as _____ is to *well-known* [anonymous]

2. *tentative* is to *aggressive* as *intolerant* is to _____ [tolerant]

3. *dull* is to *brilliant* as _____ is to *destructive* [nurturing]

4. *waxing* is to *waning* as *increasing* is to _____ [slackening]

5. *rigid* is to *flexible* as _____ is to *stiff* [resilient]

Mastering the
Standards

SHORT STORY

After They Let Margot Out . . .

Write a story about Margot and her classmates that starts when the children
let Margot out of the closet (page 24). Before beginning your story, think
about the elements of your **plot**: the **main character** and what he or she
wants, the **conflict** and **complications**, the **climax**, and the **resolution**.
You may want to choose someone other than Margot to be your main character—another child, the teacher, or even a new character. You may want to
keep track of the details of your story in a story map like the one below:

Story Map

Basic Situation	Setting	Main Character	Character's Want	Conflict and Complications	Climax	Resolution
Margot stands in doorway of closet facing the children.						

▷ Use "Writing a Short Story," pages 500–518, for help with this assignment.

Another Choice

SHORT STORY

"A Dark and Stormy Night"

On pages 34–35, you read about a town of the
future, and on pages 38–39 you read a Web
page describing conditions on Venus. Write a
story based on one of these informative texts.
The **setting** should play a major role in your
story: Your main character might be a sixth-
grader feeling trapped in the town of the
future or an alien creature living in a giant
caldera on Venus. Before you write, collect
details about your setting in a cluster diagram
like the one at the right. Use **sensory
language** to help your readers see, hear, smell,
feel, and even taste this strange setting.

▷ Use "Writing a Short Story," pages 500–518,
for help with this assignment.

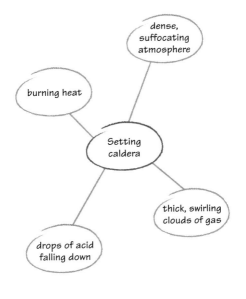

Evaluation Criteria

A good short story

1. centers on a major conflict that
   the characters must resolve
2. uses dialogue and actions to
   develop the characters
3. provides a description of the
   setting
4. ends with a resolution of the
   conflict
5. reveals a theme or makes a
   point

ASSESSING

Assessment

■ *Progress Assessment of Reading*
  ■ Chapter Test, p. 11

Writing Applications   47

Using Academic Language

Literary Terms
Ask students to look through the chapter to
find the meanings of the terms listed below.
Then, have students show their grasp of
Literary Response and Analysis Standard 3.3 by
citing passages from a story in the chapter that
illustrate the meanings of the following terms.
Plot (pp. 6, 15, 26, 47); **Conflict** (pp. 6, 15,
47); **Setting** (pp. 15, 17, 26); **Theme** (p. 15);
Resolution (pp. 26, 47); **Characters** (pp. 26–27);
Complications (p. 47); **Climax** (p. 47).

Informational Terms
As part of the review of Reading Comprehension Standard 2.1, ask students to look back
through the chapter to find the meanings of
the terms listed at right. Then, ask students
to use these terms to explain the structural
features of magazines, newspapers, and
online information. Ask students to point
out the features that are most useful for
obtaining information.

Popular Media (p. 28); **Newspaper** (p. 28);
Sections (p. 28); **Headlines** (p. 28); **Byline**
(p. 28); **Dateline** (p. 28); **Lead** (p. 28);
Magazine (p. 33); **Cover** (p. 33); **The
Contents Page** (p. 33); **Magazine Article**
(p. 33); **Title** (p. 33); **Subtitle** (p. 33);
Headings (p. 33); **Illustrations** (p. 33);
Captions (p. 33); **Internet** (p. 37); **Web Site**
(p. 37); **Home Page** (p. 37); **Table of
Contents** (p. 37); **Links** (p. 37).

Read On

For Independent Reading

If students enjoyed the themes and topics explored in this chapter, you might recommend these titles for independent reading.

Assessment Options

The following projects can help you evaluate and assess your students' outside reading. Videotapes or audiotapes of completed projects may be included in students' portfolios.

- **Make a conflict collage.** Point out that the conflict in each of these titles centers on a struggle with nature. Ask students who select different books to read to work together to create a collage illustrating the various threats that nature poses to the main characters. Encourage students to cut out illustrations from back issues of magazines to create their collages.

- **Write a letter.** Have students write a letter to Boy Regis, the main character in *Jungle Dogs*. Students should explain in their letter the approach they would have taken to resolve Boy's conflicts.

- **Create a Venn diagram.** *Survivor* was a reality-based TV show in which castaways competed to see who could survive on a deserted island. The show was wildly popular and spawned various copycat programs. Have students create a Venn diagram comparing and contrasting the character traits and survival skills that Phillip and Timothy display in *The Cay* with the traits and skills displayed by the castaways on *Survivor* or one of its imitators.

California Reading List Titles

Island of the Blue Dolphins
The Cay
Through My Eyes
How Would You Survive as an Ancient Greek?
Children of the Wild West

Fiction

Facing Your Fear

In *Jungle Dogs* by Graham Salisbury, Boy Regis, a sixth-grader, is scared of the wild dogs he sees in his Hawaiian village. Even worse, his older brother, Damon, always fights off the bullies who pick on him. As the confrontations become more violent, Boy needs to prove to Damon, and himself, that fighting is not the answer to his problems. Can he do it before somebody gets badly hurt?

Left Behind

What would you do if you were left totally on your own? In Scott O'Dell's *Island of the Blue Dolphins,* a twelve-year-old Native American girl named Karana is stranded on an island off the coast of California during the nineteenth century. She learns to build shelter and find food and wins an animal friend in this gripping tale of survival and self-discovery.

Shipwrecked

Phillip is traveling to Virginia when his ship is hit by a torpedo. Left blind in the middle of the ocean, he is rescued by Timothy, a West Indian man who leads Phillip onto a life raft. As they work together to survive on a deserted island, their friendship blossoms in *The Cay* by Theodore Taylor. If you like this story, you may also enjoy the prequel, *Timothy of the Cay.*

This title is available in the HRW Library.

The Shaking Earth

In *Earthquake at Dawn,* Kristiana Gregory looks back at the earthquake that devastated San Francisco in 1906. Fifteen-year-old Daisy and her friend Edith search for Daisy's father and try to help others amid the rubble and confusion. This historical novel is based on a letter written by a survivor of the earthquake and on photographs taken at the scene of the disaster.

48 Chapter 1 Structures: Building Blocks of Meaning

Toward Reading a Million Words Annually

Estimated Word Counts of Read On Books:

Fiction		Nonfiction	
Jungle Dogs	31,000	Through My Eyes	12,000
Island of the Blue Dolphins	38,000	Science in Ancient Egypt	18,000
The Cay	26,000	How Would You Survive	
Connections to The Cay	8,800	as an Ancient Greek?	20,000
Earthquake at Dawn	26,000	Children of the Wild West	17,000

Nonfiction

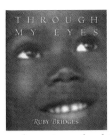

Battling Prejudice

In *Through My Eyes*, Ruby Bridges tells what it was like to be the first African American student in an all-white elementary school. In this moving memoir, we see her confronting abuse and isolation with remarkable courage. Newspaper articles, photographs, and quotations from the time provide a deeper understanding of her struggle.

Ancient Scientists

How did the ancient Egyptians build the pyramids? How did they mummify their dead? How did they use mathematics? Were there dentists? Find the answers to questions like these in *Science in Ancient Egypt* by Geraldine Woods. In this book you'll learn how the early Egyptians pioneered some of the key technologies of today.

Another Land, Another Time

Have you ever wondered what it would be like to live in the past? Fiona MacDonald shows you in *How Would You Survive as an Ancient Greek?* This interactive book, packed with useful information and colorful illustrations, tells you how you would eat, work, and travel in ancient Greece.

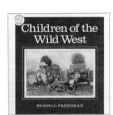

Children of Experience

In *Children of the Wild West*, Russell Freedman documents the lives of children in the American West during the nineteenth century. The book includes firsthand accounts by the sons and daughters of the pioneers. Unforgettable photographs present a moving portrait of family life and convey the special hardships faced by Native American and immigrant children.

Read On   **49**

- **Conduct a newspaper interview.** Have students pair off. One student will act as a newspaper reporter, and the other will be Ruby Bridges, the author of *Through My Eyes*. Ask the pairs to brainstorm for at least five questions the reporter can ask Ruby, such as "What was going through your mind when . . . ?" Videotape the pairs as they perform their interviews.
- **Create a storyboard for a documentary film.** Have groups who have read the same nonfiction book create a storyboard for a documentary film about the subject. Explain that their storyboard will be a series of pictures showing, in sequence, the scenes of the film. Tell students to include what they believe are the major points of interest about their subject.

 Resources Reminder

Reading

- *Interactive Reading* For additional readings that relate to the selections in this chapter, see *Interactive Reading*, Chapter 1.
- *The Ancient World:* A Content-Area Reader

DIFFERENTIATING INSTRUCTION

The Read On titles are categorized as shown below:

Below Grade Level ⬇
Jungle Dogs
How Would You Survive as an Ancient Greek?

At Grade Level ↔
The Cay
Earthquake at Dawn
Through My Eyes
Science in Ancient Egypt

Above Grade Level ⬆
Island of the Blue Dolphins
Children of the Wild West

Chapter 2 Characters: The People You'll Meet

Program Organization

Holt Literature and Language Arts provides a complete curriculum for standards-based instruction in vocabulary, reading, literature, writing, and speaking and listening. The instructional content of the program is divided into quarters to enable teachers to anticipate and administer the quarterly assessments required by California.

About Chapter 2

Standards-based lesson plans and suggestions for pacing the presentation of Chapter 2 and the related instructional material are provided in *On Course: Mapping Instruction,* Chapter 2.

- Chapter 2 helps students analyze the influence of characters on plot, clarify an understanding of informational texts by creating outlines, notes, summaries, or reports, and recognize and accurately use common foreign words in English.

- The related instructional material for Chapter 2 is shown on the chart. This related instructional material will also be covered in the first quarterly assessment.

Holt Literature and Language Arts

Pupil's Edition

Part 1, Chapter 2

Characters:
The People You'll Meet, pp. 50–113
- Reading Standards 1.3, 2.4, 3.2
- Writing Application **Writing an Explanation**

Part 2, Workshop 2

Exposition
Writing a "How-to" Explanation,
pp. 528–544
- Writing Standard 2.2

Following Oral Instructions and Directions, pp. 545–548
- Listening and Speaking Standard 2.2

Holt Handbook

Chapter 3

Parts of Speech Overview:
Verb, Adverb, Preposition,
Conjunction, Interjection
Written and Oral English-Language Conventions
- Grade-Level Standard 1.1, pp. 49–57
- Looking Ahead, Gr. 7 Standard 1.3, pp. 66–67

Chapter 4

The Phrase and the Clause
Written and Oral English-Language Conventions
- Grade-Level Standards 1.1, 1.3, pp. 89–100

Diagnostic and Summative Assessments: First-Quarter Test

Language Arts Content

In this chapter, students will master the following Grade 6 standards. Selections or features marked with a ✔ constitute the minimum course of study that provides coverage of all grade-level standards.

Grade 6 Standards
Word Analysis, Fluency, and Systematic Vocabulary Development

1.3 Recognize the origins and meanings of frequently used foreign words in English, and use these words accurately in speaking and writing.
   Developing Fluency in Word Usage, p. 63
✔ Words from Native American Languages, p. 68
   The Roots of English, p. 77
   Excluded People, Excluded Words, p. 85
✔ Foreign Words Frequently Used in English, p. 98
   Using Spanish Words in English, p. 107

Reading Comprehension (Focus on Informational Materials)

2.4 Clarify an understanding of texts by creating outlines, logical notes, summaries, or reports.
✔ "The Wind People" (history), pp. 64–67
✔ "Wartime Mistakes, Peacetime Apologies" (magazine article), pp. 78–84
✔ "Go for Broke: The Purple-Heart Team" (informational article), pp. 86–89
✔ Standards Review: Reading Informational Materials, pp. 108–109

Literary Response and Analysis

3.2 Analyze the effect of the qualities of the character (e.g., courage or cowardice, ambition or laziness) on the plot and the resolution of the conflict.
✔ "Characters: The Actors in a Story" (standards essay), pp. 52–53
   "Ta-Na-E-Ka" (short story), pp. 54–62
✔ "The Bracelet" (short story), pp. 69–76
   Blanca Flor (play), pp. 90–97, 99–106

Where do I locate lesson plans, additional resources, and other teaching aids?

- This Annotated Teacher's Edition and *On Course: Mapping Instruction* provide direction in planning and implementing a complete California standards–based curriculum. These components include instructions for administering diagnostic, progress, and summative tests; for presenting instruction of the standards; for differentiating instruction to provide universal access; and for locating and using the program's ancillaries.

- The program's resources are referenced at the beginning of each selection, in the bottom margin of this teacher's edition.
- Reminders for using additional resources appear in this teacher's edition at point of use.
- The *One-Stop Planner* CD-ROM with Test Generator contains editable lesson plans and all of the print ancillaries, available in PDF format.

What if I don't have time to teach all of Chapter 2?

- Most standards can be taught with a minimum number of selections and features. In the chart on p. 49B, the core lessons you need in order to provide complete coverage of the chapter standards are identified with a ✔.

- Use the Standards Review, pp. 108–109, for a quick review and informal assessment of the grade-level standards covered in Chapter 2.

What provisions have been made for students who have additional class time scheduled in language arts?

- *Interactive Reading* provides for additional direct instruction and practice of the grade-level standards taught in Chapter 2. It can be used as an introduction to instruction or as an opportunity for remediation.
- *Lesson Plans for Language Development*, Chapter 2, provides alternative teaching strategies and additional worksheets designed specifically for English-language learners and special education students. Many of the suggestions and activities in this ancillary will also be helpful to students in the regular classroom who are having difficulty with particular skills.

In addition to vocabulary, reading, and literature, what other language arts are covered in Chapter 2?

Writing Activities in Chapter 2
- Roger's Story (recount events in a letter), p. 62
- Another Point of View (retell events of a story using a different first-person narrator), p. 76
- A Change of Scenery (retell a story using a different setting), p. 106

Writing Applications (p. 111)
- The Human Seasons: Explaining a Ritual (an explanation)

- Another Choice: Onstage with Blanca Flor! (performance)

Grammar Links in Chapter 2
- Subjects and Verbs—in Perfect Agreement, p. 63
- Watch Your *Don'ts* and *Doesn'ts*, p. 89

Universal Access

How do I differentiate instruction to ensure that all my students master the standards?

Holt Literature and Language Arts provides comprehensive, differentiated instruction for all types of students.

- Most of the general instruction and teaching strategies in the Annotated Teacher's Edition are at grade level. These instructions will work well with the majority of your students.

- In Chapter 2, suggestions for advanced learners are provided in the Annotated Teacher's Edition. Point-of-use suggestions for learners having difficulty, English-language learners, and special education students are also provided.

- *Interactive Reading* is designed to anticipate and/or remediate problems that students may experience in achieving mastery of the standards. *Interactive Reading* includes reading-strategy lessons, lower-level practice reads, and worksheets for every informational and literary text in *Holt Literature and Language Arts,* Pupil's Editions. *Interactive Reading* also contains three additional selections for each chapter and suggestions for extension projects, many of which are ideal for advanced learners working on their own. See *Interactive Reading,* Teacher's Edition, for specific information on using the reader to differentiate instruction in Chapter 2.

- *Lesson Plans for Language Development,* Chapter 2, offers teaching strategies and additional worksheets designed specifically for English-language learners and special education students.

Assessment

How do I determine whether or not my students are making progress in mastering the standards?

Progress Assessment

- Use the Standards Review at the end of Chapter 2, pp. 108–109, for an informal assessment of the informational reading and literature standards in Chapter 2.

- Use the Selection Tests for Chapter 2 in the *Progress Assessment of Reading* booklet to test comprehension and progress on mastering the standard(s) taught with a selection.

- Use Chapter Test 2 in the *Progress Assessment of Reading* booklet to test students' cumulative progress in mastering the standards taught in the chapter.

Summative Assessment

At the end of this chapter, you may ask students to take the First-Quarter Test in the *Diagnostic and Summative Assessments* booklet. This test covers *Holt Literature and Language Arts,* Chapters 1 and 2, Workshops 1 and 2, and Mini-Workshop 5, "Writing a Personal Narrative," as well as the *Holt Handbook,* Chapters 1–4.

2 | Characters
The People You'll Meet

STANDARDS FOCUS

(For grade-level and review standards taught in this chapter, see Pupil's Edition, p. 51.)

Prerequisite Standards

■ Grade 5, Vocabulary 1.2 **Use word origins to determine the meaning of unknown words.**

■ Grade 5, Reading Comprehension 2.3 **Discern main ideas and concepts presented in texts, identifying and assessing evidence that supports those ideas.**

■ Grade 5, Literary Response and Analysis 3.3 **Contrast the actions, motives (e.g., loyalty, selfishness, conscientiousness), and appearances of characters in a work of fiction, and discuss the importance of the contrasts to the plot or theme.**

Standards Coming Up in the Next Grade Level

■ Grade 7, Vocabulary 1.2 **Use knowledge of Greek, Latin, and Anglo-Saxon roots and affixes to understand content-area vocabulary.**

■ Grade 7, Reading Comprehension 2.4 **Identify and trace the development of an author's argument, point of view, or perspective in text.**

■ Grade 7, Literary Response and Analysis 3.3 **Analyze characterization as delineated through a character's thoughts, words, speech patterns, and actions; the narrator's description; and the thoughts, words, and actions of other characters.**

CHAPTER RESOURCES

Planning

■ *One-Stop Planner* CD-ROM with Test Generator
■ *On Course: Mapping Instruction*
  ■ Chapter 2
■ *At Home: A Guide to Standards Mastery*
■ *At Home: In Five Languages*
■ *Supporting Instruction in Five Languages*

Reading

■ *Interactive Reading*
  ■ Chapter 2

Differentiating Instruction

■ *Lesson Plans for Language Development*
  ■ Chapter 2

Vocabulary and Spelling

■ *Vocabulary Development*
    ■ Cumulative Vocabulary Review, p. 9

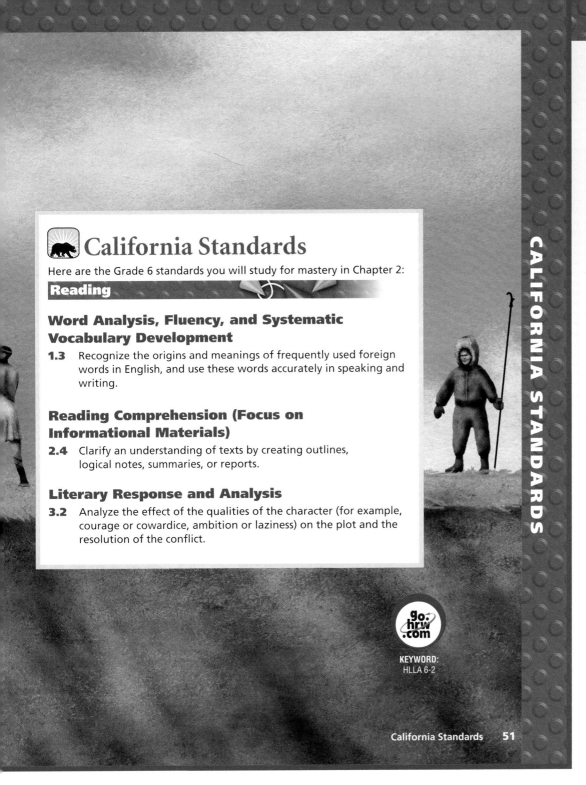

California Standards

Here are the Grade 6 standards you will study for mastery in Chapter 2:

Reading

Word Analysis, Fluency, and Systematic Vocabulary Development

1.3 Recognize the origins and meanings of frequently used foreign words in English, and use these words accurately in speaking and writing.

Reading Comprehension (Focus on Informational Materials)

2.4 Clarify an understanding of texts by creating outlines, logical notes, summaries, or reports.

Literary Response and Analysis

3.2 Analyze the effect of the qualities of the character (for example, courage or cowardice, ambition or laziness) on the plot and the resolution of the conflict.

go.
hrw
.com

KEYWORD:
HLLA 6-2

California Standards **51**

INTRODUCING THE CHAPTER

The selections in this chapter spotlight characters at major turning points in their lives. As students read, they are encouraged to connect the element of character to other elements of literature. This process gives students a sense of how characters come to life in a story and the roles they play in its conflict and plot. High-interest informational pieces enrich each story. These pieces are used to teach students to create outlines, notes, and summaries that further students' understanding of their reading. The chapter's culminating feature, Writing Applications, offers students the opportunity to write an explanation of a coming-of-age ritual or to perform scenes from *Blanca Flor*.

▶ Resources Reminder

Planning

■ *At Home: A Guide to Standards Mastery*

You may want to send home with students selected parent letters from this resource. Translations of these letters are available in *At Home: In Five Languages. Supporting Instruction in Five Languages* provides translations of the selection summaries.

Reading

■ *Interactive Reading*
  ▪ Reading Log

The California framework requires students to read materials apart from in-class assignments. Additional reading suggestions are included on the Read On pages and on selected pages in the Pupil's and Teacher's Editions. You may want to use the Reading Log to help students track their progress.

Grammar

■ *Holt Handbook*

Assessment

■ *Progress Assessment of Reading*
  ▪ Chapter Test, p. 34
■ *Diagnostic and Summative Assessments*
  ▪ First-Quarter Test, p. 41
■ *One-Stop Planner* CD-ROM with Test Generator

Internet

■ go.hrw.com
  Keyword: HLLA 6-2

(For the grade-level standard taught in this lesson, see Pupil's Edition, p. 52.)

Prerequisite Standard

■ Grade 5, Literary Response and Analysis 3.3 **Contrast the actions, motives (e.g., loyalty, selfishness, conscientiousness), and appearances of characters in a work of fiction, and discuss the importance of the contrasts to the plot or theme.**

Literary Focus: Character

Invite students to name their favorite movie characters. Ask them to identify the qualities, or traits, that make the characters memorable. How do these traits help or hinder the characters? Point out that films, like literature, feature characters in conflict. Many plots turn on the actions of clearly defined good guys and bad guys. In some plots, characters cannot be neatly classified as good or bad, but their personality traits lead them into conflict, and their conflicts drive the plot.

Resources Reminder

Reading

■ *Interactive Reading*

Before you teach Chapter 2 of *Holt Literature and Language Arts,* you may want to preteach the literary concept and a related reading strategy.

• To introduce students to the literary concept before they read this essay, assign p. 57 of *Interactive Reading.*

• To introduce students to a reading strategy that will help them grasp the literary concept, assign p. 57 of *Interactive Reading.*

• To give students practice applying the strategy to a short, vocabulary-controlled selection, assign the Practice Read on p. 58 of *Interactive Reading.*

Characters *by* Madeline Travers Hovland
THE ACTORS IN A STORY

Characters are the people or animals in a story. Characters are sometimes so lifelike that they seem to jump off the page at you. Like real people, characters in stories have qualities such as courage, laziness, or ambition. The character's qualities influence the events in a story—the way your qualities influence what happens to you in real life.

Who's Who?

Remember "The Three Little Pigs"? The characters in that story are three pigs, all members of the same family. Two of the pigs have similar qualities (sadly for them!). They're happy, good-natured fellows who mean well, but they're also timid, lazy, careless, and not very smart.

The third pig has more than his share of admirable qualities. He's hardworking, brave, intelligent, and determined to succeed.

The villain of the story, the wolf, has qualities that make him easy to dislike. He thinks he's a lot smarter than he is. He's mean and tricky, and he takes advantage of the weak and helpless (and the plump and delicious). He also likes to eat pigs for breakfast, lunch, and dinner.

Losers and Winners

The three pigs are the good guys. Even though two of them are losers, we feel sympathy for them—they're so foolish and scared. In fact, we might feel sympathy for these two pigs because they are a lot like us.

Even if you didn't know the **plot,** the series of related events that make up the story, you could probably predict what will happen. In this plot the characters' qualities set them on a collision course.

Characters in Conflict

The basic situation is set when the three pigs build their houses. The **conflict** starts when the wolf strolls by and decides to make the pigs his dinner. The character traits of the first two pigs create **complications** in the plot. The two happy-go-lucky pigs have thrown together houses of straw and sticks, which are not very sturdy. The third pig has taken the time and trouble to build a strong house of bricks.

The enemy easily blows down the houses of the two good-natured pigs. Whether he wolfs down those pigs or whether they get away to their brother's house depends on who is telling the story. But in every version of the tale, the wolf doesn't stop after he ruins the pigs' houses. His appetite for pork drives him on to the house of the third little pig.

This clever pig gets a pot of water boiling in the fireplace. At this point the wolf has given up trying to blow the brick house down and is squeezing himself

Reading Standard 3.2 Analyze the effect of the qualities of the character (for example, courage or cowardice, ambition or laziness) on the plot and the resolution of the conflict.

DIFFERENTIATING INSTRUCTION

Learners Having Difficulty

Character. To help students understand how character drives conflict, present a situation like the following: A mother has told her son to come directly home after school, but the boy is strongly tempted to join a game of softball. What will the boy do if he is responsible and honest? If he is conniving and deceitful? If he is rebellious? Have students discuss how different character traits can lead to problems and outcomes.

Advanced Learners

Characterization. To move students toward the seventh-grade Standard 3.3, discuss characterization. Point out that writers bring characters to life through the words, actions, and thoughts of the character portrayed; through description; and through the words, actions, and thoughts of other characters. **Activity.** Ask students to find examples in a story of each of the techniques of characterization that you have discussed.

© 1982 FarWorks, Inc. All Rights Reserved/Dist. by Creators Syndicate

"Listen out there! We're George and Harriet Miller! We just dropped in on the pigs for coffee! We're coming out! . . . We don't want trouble!"

down the chimney. The plot is now about to reach its **climax.** This is the moment when the tension in the story is greatest and when we learn how the conflict will be resolved. The wolf falls into the pot of boiling water, and the third little pig becomes the winner, not dinner.

Character Counts

A Greek philosopher, or thinker, named Heraclitus (her'ə·klīt'əs) once wrote, "Character is destiny." (Destiny is a person's fate or lot in life.) When Heraclitus wrote that 2,500 years ago, he was thinking about real people, not characters in a story. But you'll discover that what's true about life is often true about literature. Character *counts*. The qualities of characters in a story have a major influence on the plot.

Think about a story you've read in a book or seen on TV or at the movies. Try to pick a story that involves a **conflict** between two strong **characters** and that has a clear winner and loser (many stories don't). On a piece of paper, draw an outline of two heads like the ones below. These represent the two main characters in the story or movie. In each of the outlined heads, list three or four important traits of each character, just as in the model. Then, complete the sentence below the heads. Name the character who won the conflict, and explain how qualities of character affected the way the plot came out.

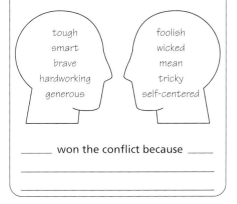

tough
smart
brave
hardworking
generous

foolish
wicked
mean
tricky
self-centered

_____ won the conflict because _____

_____

_____

Tell students to label each head with the name of the character it represents. Reassure students that rough drawings are fine. Note that students might reasonably list some of the same qualities for both characters since memorable conflicts can occur between characters who share certain traits. For students having trouble thinking of stories with clear winners and losers, you might suggest incidents from myths, legends, or folk tales (Athena versus Arachne, Japan's Momotaro versus the ogre king, the hare versus the tortoise).

Apply

Ask students how they would characterize George and Harriet Miller in the cartoon. [bland, cowardly, shallow, disloyal] Then, ask students, given what they know of the wolf, to predict how he might respond to the Millers and what might happen next. In other words, how might the inclusion of these two new characters change the plot and outcome of "The Three Little Pigs"? [Possible response: The wolf might offer the Millers safe passage but then eat them, get indigestion, and leave the pigs in peace.] Students should see that even minor characters can influence a story's plot.

► Resources Reminder

Differentiating Instruction

■ *Lesson Plans for Language Development*

For additional instruction on character for English-language learners and special education students, see *Lesson Plans for Language Development,* pp. 23–24.

STANDARDS FOCUS, pp. 54–63

(For grade-level and review standards taught in this selection, see citations on Pupil's Edition pages.)

Prerequisite Standard

- Grade 5, Literary Response and Analysis 3.3 Contrast the actions, motives (e.g., loyalty, selfishness, conscientiousness), and appearances of characters in a work of fiction, and discuss the importance of the contrasts to the plot or theme.

Standard Coming Up in the Next Grade Level

- Grade 7, Literary Response and Analysis 3.3 Analyze characterization as delineated through a character's thoughts, words, speech patterns, and actions; the narrator's description; and the thoughts, words, and actions of other characters.

Reading Skills

- Compare and contrast.

Summary *at grade level*

Grandfather is training eleven-year-old Mary and her cousin Roger for Ta-Na-E-Ka, an endurance test in which each must survive five days alone in the woods. The cousins think the test is outdated, but their elders insist on it. Roger follows tradition, but Mary secretly borrows money and spends all five days in a restaurant. After the ordeal, Mary alone is clean and well fed. She confesses what she did. In the end, Grandfather decides that Mary has passed the test in her own modern way.

▶ Resources Reminder

Media
- *Audio CD Library*
  - disc 2
- *Visual Connections*
  - Videocassette, Segment 1
- *Fine Art Transparencies*
  - Transparency 3

Ta-Na-E-Ka

Literary Focus
Character and Conflict

A **character** is a person or an animal in a story. Characters in stories have qualities—courage or cruelty, for instance—just as people do in real life. What happens in a story depends on the way the characters respond to a **conflict.** There are two basic kinds of conflict. **External conflict** is a struggle between a character and an outside force, such as a rival or an earthquake. **Internal conflict** is a struggle in a character's mind or heart. A character might struggle with shyness, for example, or fear or jealousy.

Reading Skills
Comparison and Contrast

As you read this story, you'll see little open-book signs and questions alongside the text. Some of these questions will help you **compare and contrast** the characters and the ways they deal with their conflicts. When you **compare,** you look for ways in which things are alike. When you **contrast,** you look for ways in which things are different.

Reading Standard 3.2 Analyze the effect of the qualities of the character (for example, courage or cowardice, ambition or laziness) on the plot and the resolution of the conflict.

Make the Connection
Quickwrite ✏️

Imagine that your family expects you to keep up a tradition they think is important but you're not sure you want to. Write a few sentences telling how you might deal with this conflict.

Background

This story has to do with the traditions of the Native Americans known as the Kaw or Kansa. Both names are forms of a word that means "People of the South Wind." The Kaw originally lived along the Kansas River.

Vocabulary Development

You'll be learning these words as you read "Ta-Na-E-Ka":

loftiest (lôf′tē·əst) *adj.:* noblest; highest. *Grandfather described endurance as the loftiest virtue.*

shrewdest (shrōōd′əst) *adj.* used as *n.:* sharpest; most clever. *Only the shrewdest could survive Ta-Na-E-Ka.*

grimaced (grim′ist) *v.:* twisted the face to express pain, anger, or disgust. *Roger grimaced at the thought of eating grasshoppers.*

gorging (gôrj′in) *v.:* filling up; stuffing. *During his Ta-Na-E-Ka the boy dreamed of gorging himself on hamburgers.*

audacity (ô·das′ə·tē) *n.:* boldness; daring. *Mary's parents were shocked at her audacity.*

RESOURCES

Planning
- *One-Stop Planner* CD-ROM with Test Generator
- *On Course: Mapping Instruction*

Media
- *Audio CD Library*
  - disc 2
- *Visual Connections*
  - Videocassette, Segment 1

- *Fine Art Transparencies*
  - Transparency 3

Reading
- *Interactive Reading*
  - Strategy Launch: Character Trace, p. 57
  - Practice Read: "Sparring," p. 58
  - Graphic Organizer: Character-and-Conflict Chart, p. 67

TA·NA·E·KA

MARY WHITEBIRD

As my birthday drew closer, I had awful nightmares about it. I was reaching the age at which all Kaw Indians had to participate in Ta-Na-E-Ka. Well, not all Kaws. Many of the younger families on the reservation were beginning to give up the old customs. But my grandfather, Amos Deer Leg, was devoted to tradition. He still wore handmade beaded moccasins instead of shoes and kept his iron-gray hair in tight braids. He could speak English, but he spoke it only with white men. With his family he used a Sioux dialect.[1]

Grandfather was one of the last living Indians (he died in 1953, when he was eighty-one) who actually fought against the U.S. Cavalry. Not only did he fight, he was wounded in a skirmish at Rose Creek—a famous encounter in which the celebrated Kaw chief Flat Nose lost his life. At the time, my grandfather was only eleven years old.

A

B

> **COMPARE/ CONTRAST**
>
> **1.** How is Mary's grandfather different from many younger Kaw Indians?

---

1. **Sioux** (so͞o) **dialect:** one of the languages spoken by the Plains Indians, including the Kaw.

■ *Interactive Reading,* Teacher's Edition
  ■ Transparency 2: Character Trace
Differentiating Instruction
■ *Lesson Plans for Language Development*
  ■ English-Language Learners, pp. 25–27, 40, 46
  ■ Special Education Students, pp. 28, 40, 46

Vocabulary and Spelling
■ *Vocabulary Development*
  ■ Vocabulary Worksheet, p. 6
Assessment
■ *Progress Assessment of Reading*
  ■ Selection Test, p. 19
■ *One-Stop Planner* CD-ROM with Test Generator

PRETEACHING

Standards Starter
Motivate. Invite students to describe family traditions that they find meaningful and those that they find meaningless. Point out that people's views of traditional activities sometimes change as they grow older. Then, ask students to complete the Quickwrite activity.

Preview Vocabulary
To help students master the Vocabulary words, assign the following exercise.
1. Discuss the character trait that you consider the <u>loftiest</u>.
2. Tell about the <u>shrewdest</u> action you have taken in the past year.
3. Describe a sight or sound at which you might have <u>grimaced</u>.
4. Draw a cartoon animal <u>gorging</u> on its favorite food.
5. Give an example of someone showing great <u>audacity</u>.

▶ Resources Reminder
Reading
■ *Interactive Reading*
  ■ Strategy Launch: Character Trace, p. 57
  ■ Graphic Organizer: Character-and-Conflict Chart, p. 67

DIRECT TEACHING

A Literary Focus
GRADE-LEVEL STANDARD
❓ Character and conflict. What internal conflict is giving Mary nightmares? [She is anxious about the upcoming Ta-Na-E-Ka ritual.]

B Reading Skills
Comparing and contrasting. Ask students to make a list of the ways the younger Kaw are the opposite of Grandfather. [Possible response to question 1: The younger Kaw are giving up the old customs, while Grandfather still honors Kaw traditions.]

DIRECT TEACHING

A Literary Focus
REVIEW STANDARD

? Theme. As an eleven-year-old, how was Grandfather different from Roger? [Grandfather was a warrior battling the U.S. Cavalry. Roger plans to become an accountant.] How do their differences reflect changing times, particularly in the challenges that face young people? [In the old days the challenge was to repel invaders, but today it is to succeed economically.]

B Literary Focus
GRADE-LEVEL STANDARD

? Character and conflict. What external conflict does Mary have with an adult? [Mary and her mother disagree about Mary's participation in Ta-Na-E-Ka.]

C Literary Focus
ADVANCED STANDARD

Characterization. Ask students what Mary's thoughts reveal about her character traits. [Possible responses: She is intelligent, independent, and ambitious; she enjoys escaping from reality through fantasy, and her fantasies draw upon European images of females being rescued rather than Native American images of women proving themselves.]

A *Eleven* was a magic word among the Kaws. It was the time of Ta-Na-E-Ka, the "flowering of adulthood." It was the age, my grandfather informed us hundreds of times, "when a boy could prove himself to be a warrior and a girl took the first steps to womanhood."

"I don't want to be a warrior," my cousin, Roger Deer Leg, confided to me. "I'm going to become an accountant."

B "None of the other tribes make girls go through the endurance ritual," I complained to my mother.

"It won't be as bad as you think, Mary," my mother said, ignoring my protests. "Once you've gone through it, you'll certainly never forget it. You'll be proud."

I even complained to my teacher, Mrs. Richardson, feeling that, as a white woman, she would side with me.

She didn't. "All of us have rituals of one kind or another," Mrs. Richardson said. "And look at it this way: How many girls have the opportunity to compete on equal terms with boys? Don't look down on your heritage."

C Heritage, indeed! I had no intention of living on a reservation for the rest of my life. I was a good student. I loved school. My fantasies were about knights in armor and fair ladies in flowing gowns being saved from dragons. It never once occurred to me that being an Indian was exciting.

But I've always thought that the Kaw were the originators of the women's liberation movement. No other Indian tribe—and I've spent half a lifetime researching the subject—treated women more "equally" than the Kaw. Unlike most of the subtribes of the Sioux Nation, the Kaw allowed men and

women to eat together. And hundreds of years before we were "acculturated,"[2] a Kaw woman had the right to refuse a prospective husband even if her father arranged the match.

The wisest women (generally wisdom was equated with age) often sat in tribal councils. Furthermore, most Kaw legends revolve around "Good Woman," a kind of supersquaw, a Joan of Arc[3] of the high plains. Good Woman led Kaw warriors into battle after battle, from which they always seemed to emerge victorious.

And girls as well as boys were required to undergo Ta-Na-E-Ka.

The actual ceremony varied from tribe to tribe, but since the Indians' life on the plains was dedicated to survival, Ta-Na-E-Ka was a test of survival.

"Endurance is the loftiest virtue of the Indian," my grandfather explained. "To survive, we must endure. When I was a boy, Ta-Na-E-Ka was more than the mere symbol it is now. We were painted white with the juice of a sacred herb and sent naked into the wilderness without so much as a knife. We couldn't return until the white had worn off. It wouldn't wash off. It took almost eighteen days, and during that time we had to stay alive, trapping food, eating insects and roots and berries, and watching out for ene-

---

2. **acculturated** (ə·kul′chər·āt′id) *v.* used as *adj.*: adapted to a new or different culture.
3. **Joan of Arc** (1412–1431): French heroine who led her country's army to victory over the English in 1429.

Vocabulary
loftiest (lôf′tē·əst) *adj.*: noblest; highest.

56 Chapter 2 Characters: The People You'll Meet

DIFFERENTIATING INSTRUCTION

Learners Having Difficulty
Modeling. Some students may need to read an easier selection before beginning "Ta-Na-E-Ka." Use the Practice Read in *Interactive Reading*, p. 58. You can then use the transparency to model the strategy of tracing character development. This strategy will help students see relationships between a main character and events.

Then, have students apply the strategy to help them read "Ta-Na-E-Ka."

 Resources Reminder

Reading
■ *Interactive Reading*, Teacher's Edition
  ■ Transparency 2: Character Trace

English-Language Learners
Point out that this story contains references to Native American culture (such as traditional dress and rituals) and history (such as battles with U.S. troops in the 1800s over land rights). Explain that the word *reservation* refers to a tract of land set aside by the U.S. government for Native Americans.

mies. And we did have enemies—both the white soldiers and the Omaha warriors, who were always trying to capture Kaw boys and girls undergoing their endurance test. It was an exciting time."

"What happened if you couldn't make it?" Roger asked. He was born only three days after I was, and we were being trained for Ta-Na-E-Ka together. I was happy to know he was frightened, too.

"Many didn't return," Grandfather said. "Only the strongest and shrewdest. Mothers were not allowed to weep over those who didn't return. If a Kaw couldn't survive, he or she wasn't worth weeping over. It was our way."

"What a lot of hooey," Roger whispered. "I'd give anything to get out of it."

"I don't see how we have any choice," I replied.

Roger gave my arm a little squeeze. "Well, it's only five days."

Five days! Maybe it was better than being painted white and sent out naked for eighteen days. But not much better.

We were to be sent, barefoot and in bathing suits, into the woods. Even our very traditional parents put their foot down when Grandfather suggested we go naked. For five days we'd have to live off the land, keeping warm as best we could, getting food where we could. It was May, but on the northernmost reaches of the Missouri River, the days were still chilly and the nights were fiercely cold.

Grandfather was in charge of the month's training for Ta-Na-E-Ka. One day he caught a grasshopper and demonstrated how to pull its legs and wings off in one flick of the fingers and how to swallow it.

I felt sick, and Roger turned green. "It's a darn good thing it's 1947," I told Roger teasingly. "You'd make a terrible warrior." Roger just grimaced.

I knew one thing. This particular Kaw Indian girl wasn't going to swallow a grasshopper no matter how hungry she got. And then I had an idea. Why hadn't I thought of it before? It would have saved nights of bad dreams about squooshy grasshoppers.

I headed straight for my teacher's house. "Mrs. Richardson," I said, "would you lend me five dollars?"

"Five dollars!" she exclaimed. "What for?"

> **COMPARE/ CONTRAST**
>
> **2.** What feelings do Roger and Mary share about Ta-Na-E-Ka?

Vocabulary

shrewdest (shrōōd′əst) *adj.* used as *n.:* sharpest; most clever.

grimaced (grim′ist) *v.:* twisted the face to express pain, anger, or disgust.

DIRECT TEACHING

D Reading Skills

? Expressing an opinion. Do you think the Kaw were too harsh toward the young people during Grandfather's youth? [Possible responses: Yes, it was cruel to send children out for so long with no assistance. No, the world that the Kaw lived in was harsh, and the endurance test was the best way of preparing the young for it.]

E Literary Focus
REVIEW STANDARD

? Theme. What does this passage suggest about how Kaw ways are changing? [Possible response: Change may be slow, but it is taking place. Ta-Na-E-Ka has been adapted from Grandfather's day to better suit the present-day world of the Kaw.]

F English-Language Learners

Interpreting idioms. The expression *to put one's foot down* means "to be firm or unyielding about something."

G Reading Skills

Comparing and contrasting. [Possible response to question 2: Both young people question the relevance of Ta-Na-E-Ka; both are frightened of the ordeal; both are sickened by the thought of eating grasshoppers.]

 Resources Reminder

For lessons designed for intermediate and advanced English-language learners, see *Lesson Plans for Language Development,* pp. 25–27, 40, 46.

Special Education Students
For lessons designed for special education students, see *Lesson Plans for Language Development,* pp. 28, 40, 46.

Advanced Learners
Acceleration. Use the following activity with advanced learners to move them toward the seventh-grade Standard 3.3, for which they analyze characterization.

Activity. Have students list two strong character traits that they see in Mary. For each trait, have students jot details from "Ta-Na-E-Ka" that show

- how Mary's words reveal the trait
- how Mary's actions reveal the trait
- how other people's responses to Mary indicate that she has the trait

A **Literary Focus**
GRADE-LEVEL STANDARD
❓ **Character and conflict.** How does Mary's independent nature add to the conflict in the story? [Possible response: Her decision to avoid eating grasshoppers and to borrow money to use for Ta-Na-E-Ka defy tradition.] **Would her grandfather approve of her ideas?** [Possible response: Grandfather, the traditionalist, would disapprove.]

B **Literary Focus**
REVIEW STANDARD
❓ **Theme.** How do Mary and Roger's attitudes at dinner differ from the adults'? [Possible response: Mary and Roger are subdued and anxious, the adults jovial and nostalgic.] **How do these differences suggest a clash between traditional and modern values?** [Possible response: The adults accept the value of Ta-Na-E-Ka unquestioningly, but the young people do not.]

C **Literary Focus**
GRADE-LEVEL STANDARD
❓ **Character and conflict.** How do Mary and Roger both show that they have courage? [Both are struggling with their fear of Ta-Na-E-Ka, but despite their fear, both are willing to go through with the test.]

A "You remember the ceremony I talked about?"

"Ta-Na-E-Ka. Of course. Your parents have written me and asked me to excuse you from school so you can participate in it."

"Well, I need some things for the ceremony," I replied, in a half-truth. "I don't want to ask my parents for the money."

"It's not a crime to borrow money, Mary. But how can you pay it back?"

"I'll baby-sit for you ten times."

"That's more than fair," she said, going to her purse and handing me a crisp, new five-dollar bill. I'd never had that much money at once.

"I'm happy to know the money's going to be put to a good use," Mrs. Richardson said.

A few days later the ritual began with a long speech from my grandfather about how we had reached the age of decision, how we now had to fend for ourselves and prove that we could survive the most **B** horrendous of ordeals. All the friends and relatives who had gathered at our house for dinner made jokes about their own Ta-Na-E-Ka experiences. They all advised us to fill up now, since for the next five days we'd be gorging ourselves on crickets. Neither Roger nor I was very hungry. "I'll probably laugh about this when I'm an accountant," Roger said, trembling.

"Are you trembling?" I asked.

"What do you think?"

"I'm happy to know boys tremble, too," I said.

At six the next morning, we kissed our parents and went off to the woods. "Which side do you want?" Roger asked. According to the rules, Roger and I would stake out "territories" in separate areas of the woods, and we weren't to communicate during the entire ordeal.

"I'll go toward the river, if it's OK with you," I said.

"Sure," Roger answered. "What difference does it make?"

To me, it made a lot of difference. There was a marina a few miles up the river, and there were boats moored there. At least, I hoped so. I figured that a boat was a better place to sleep than under a pile of leaves.

"Why do you keep holding your head?" Roger asked.

"Oh, nothing. Just nervous," I told him. Actually, I was afraid I'd lose the five-dollar bill, which I had tucked into my hair with a bobby pin. As we came to a fork in the trail, **C** Roger shook my hand. "Good luck, Mary."

"N'ko-n'ta," I said. It was the Kaw word for "courage."

The sun was shining and it was warm, but my bare feet began to hurt immediately. I

Vocabulary
gorging (gôrj′iŋ) *v.*: filling up; stuffing.

MINI-LESSON **Reading**

Developing Word-Attack Skills
On the chalkboard, write the selection words *reservation* and *liberation*. Point out that both words end with the letters *–ation*, pronounced ā′shən. Explain that both words are nouns formed by adding a suffix to a verb. Have students identify the base words and the letters that are added to form *reservation* and *liberation*. [reserve + –ation; liberate + –ion]

Compare the pronunciation of *reserve* and *reservation*. Discuss how the stress shifts from the second syllable in *reserve* to the third syllable in *reservation*. Similarly, compare the pronunciation of *liberate* and *liberation*. In *liberate*, the first syllable gets the greatest stress; in *liberation*, the third syllable gets the greatest stress.
Activity. Write these pairs of words on the chalkboard, without underlines. Have volunteers read the words and underline

the syllable in each word that is said with the greatest stress.

1. ad<u>mire</u>   admi<u>ra</u>tion
2. <u>in</u>novate   inno<u>va</u>tion
3. pre<u>pare</u>   prepa<u>ra</u>tion
4. <u>im</u>itate   imi<u>ta</u>tion
5. cre<u>ate</u>   cre<u>a</u>tion
6. ex<u>plore</u>   explo<u>ra</u>tion

spied one of the berry bushes Grandfather had told us about. "You're lucky," he had said. "The berries are ripe in the spring, and they are delicious and nourishing." They were orange and fat, and I popped one into my mouth.

Argh! I spat it out. It was awful and bitter, and even grasshoppers were probably better tasting, although I never intended to find out.

I sat down to rest my feet. A rabbit hopped out from under the berry bush. He nuzzled the berry I'd spat out and ate it. He picked another one and ate that, too. He liked them. He looked at me, twitching his nose. I watched a redheaded woodpecker bore into an elm tree, and I caught a glimpse of a civet cat[4] waddling through some twigs. All of a sudden I realized I was no longer frightened. Ta-Na-E-Ka might be more fun than I'd anticipated. I got up and headed toward the marina.

📖 PREDICTING

3. How do you predict Mary will handle her conflict with nature?

"Not one boat," I said to myself dejectedly. But the restaurant on the shore, Ernie's Riverside, was open. I walked in, feeling silly in my bathing suit. The man at the counter was big and tough-looking. He wore a sweat shirt with the words "Fort Sheridan, 1944," and he had only three fingers on one of his hands. He asked me what I wanted.

"A hamburger and a milkshake," I said, holding the five-dollar bill in my hand so he'd know I had money.

"That's a pretty heavy breakfast, honey," he murmured.

---
4. **civet** (siv'it) **cat** *n.*: furry spotted skunk.

"That's what I always have for breakfast," I lied.

"Forty-five cents," he said, bringing me the food. (Back in 1947, hamburgers were twenty-five cents and milkshakes were twenty cents.)

"Delicious," I thought. "Better 'n grasshoppers—and Grandfather never once mentioned that I couldn't eat hamburgers."

While I was eating, I had a grand idea. Why not sleep in the restaurant? I went to the ladies' room and made sure the window was unlocked. Then I went back outside and played along the riverbank, watching the water birds and trying to identify each one. I planned to look for a beaver dam the next day.

The restaurant closed at sunset, and I watched the three-fingered man drive away. Then I climbed in the unlocked window. There was a night light on, so I didn't turn on any lights. But there was a radio on the counter. I turned it on to a music program. It was warm in the restaurant, and I was hungry. I helped myself to a glass of milk and a piece of pie, intending to keep a list of what I'd eaten so I could leave money. I also planned to get up early, sneak out through the window, and head for the woods before the three-fingered man returned. I turned off the radio, wrapped myself in the man's apron, and in spite of the hardness of the floor, fell asleep.

"What the heck are you doing here, kid?" It was the man's voice.

It was morning. I'd overslept. I was scared.

"Hold it, kid. I just wanna know what you're doing here. You lost? You must be from the reservation. Your folks must be worried sick about you. Do they have a phone?"

Ta-Na-E-Ka   **59**

D **Reading Skills**

Predicting. [Possible responses to question 3: Mary will realize that she likes being in nature; she's not going to depend on nature to survive; she's going to have problems when she's really tested by nature.]

E **Vocabulary Development**
ADVANCED STANDARD

Latin roots and affixes. Tell students that *dejectedly* contains the Latin root *–ject–*, meaning "to throw or to cast"; the Latin prefix *de–*, meaning "down"; and the English suffix *–ly*, indicating an adverb. Ask students to formulate a definition for *dejectedly* that reflects the word's structure. [Possible responses: in a downcast way, sadly.]

F **Literary Focus**
ADVANCED STANDARD

? Characterization. In this passage, what character strengths do Mary's actions reveal? [Possible responses: She is clever, resourceful, and daring; in her own way, she is a survivor.]

Culture

Women's roles. Mary's wry description of the Kaw as "originators of the women's liberation movement" touches on the issue of gender equality. The Kaw were among several Native American groups in which women traditionally held positions of power. Among the Yurok, shamans were usually women. Among the Hopi and the Iroquois, women owned all the houses and land. Iroquois matriarchs also guided councils and chose the chiefs (and could remove them from office).

Activity. Encourage interested students to work together to research further the roles of women among the Yurok, Hopi, Kaw, Iroquois, or other Native American peoples.

SMALL-GROUP

History

The Sioux. The Kaw and their close relatives the Osage speak a Siouan language, but they are not among the tribes of the Sioux nation. The Sioux are a confederation of seven main tribal groups, each with many subgroups. Some migrated from the northeastern forests to Minnesota around the early 1600s. Gradually the Sioux spread through the upper Great Plains. In the 1860s and during the Black Hills gold rush of the 1870s, they fought the U.S. Cavalry under leaders including Sitting Bull, Red Cloud, and Crazy Horse.

Ta-Na-E-Ka   **59**

A **Reading Skills**

? Expressing an opinion. Do you agree with Ernie's view of Ta-Na-E-Ka or with Mary's? Why? [Possible responses: Ernie's, because the ritual ordeal is dangerous; Mary's, because the ritual ordeal is an important part of her heritage.]

B **Reading Skills**

Comparing and contrasting. [Possible response to question 4: Earlier, Mary would have been critical of Ta-Na-E-Ka, but now she understands the importance of this ceremony to Kaw tradition.]

C **Literary Focus**
REVIEW STANDARD

? Theme. What unexpected things does Mary gain from her "modernized" Ta-Na-E-Ka? [a new friend; cooking skills; the knowledge that she can take care of herself in today's world]

D **Literary Focus**
GRADE-LEVEL STANDARD

? Character and conflict. What worries Mary as she returns home? [She worries that Grandfather will discover that she didn't stay in the wilderness.] How is this both an internal and an external conflict? [The source of her anxiety is external because the conflict is between her and Grandfather and internal because she is struggling in her own mind to come to terms with how she should have handled her Ta-Na-E-Ka.]

E **Reading Skills**

? Interpreting. What was Roger's Ta-Na-E-Ka like? [He did what he was expected to do: He remained in the wilderness—cold, hungry, and frightened—for five days.]

"Yes, yes," I answered. "But don't call them." I was shivering. The man, who told me his name was Ernie, made me a cup of hot chocolate while I explained about Ta-Na-E-Ka.

"Darnedest thing I ever heard," he said, when I was through. "Lived next to the reservation all my life and this is the first I've heard of Ta-Na-whatever-you-call-it." He looked at me, all goose bumps in my bathing suit. "Pretty silly thing to do to a kid," he muttered.

That was just what I'd been thinking for months, but when Ernie said it, I became angry. "No, it isn't silly. It's a custom of the Kaw. We've been doing this for hundreds of years. My mother and my grandfather and everybody in my family went through this ceremony. It's why the Kaw are great warriors."

> 📖 **COMPARE/ CONTRAST**
> 4. How has Mary's attitude toward Ta-Na-E-Ka changed?

"OK, great warrior," Ernie chuckled, "suit yourself. And, if you want to stick around, it's OK with me." Ernie went to the broom closet and tossed me a bundle. "That's the lost-and-found closet," he said. "Stuff people left on boats. Maybe there's something to keep you warm."

The sweater fitted loosely, but it felt good. I felt good. And I'd found a new friend. Most important, I was surviving Ta-Na-E-Ka.

My grandfather had said the experience would be filled with adventure, and I was having my fill. And Grandfather had never said we couldn't accept hospitality.

I stayed at Ernie's Riverside for the entire period. In the mornings I went into the woods and watched the animals and

picked flowers for each of the tables in Ernie's. I had never felt better. I was up early enough to watch the sun rise on the Missouri, and I went to bed after it set. I ate everything I wanted—insisting that Ernie take all my money for the food. "I'll keep this in trust for you, Mary," Ernie promised, "in case you are ever desperate for five dollars." (He did, too, but that's another story.)

I was sorry when the five days were over. I'd enjoyed every minute with Ernie. He taught me how to make western omelets and to make Chili Ernie Style (still one of my favorite dishes). And I told Ernie all about the legends of the Kaw. I hadn't realized I knew so much about my people.

But Ta-Na-E-Ka was over, and as I approached my house at about nine-thirty in the evening, I became nervous all over again. What if Grandfather asked me about the berries and the grasshoppers? And my feet were hardly cut. I hadn't lost a pound and my hair was combed.

"They'll be so happy to see me," I told myself hopefully, "that they won't ask too many questions."

I opened the door. My grandfather was in the front room. He was wearing the ceremonial beaded deerskin shirt which had belonged to *his* grandfather. "N'g'da'ma," he said. "Welcome back."

I embraced my parents warmly, letting go only when I saw my cousin Roger sprawled on the couch. His eyes were red and swollen. He'd lost weight. His feet were an unsightly mass of blood and blisters, and he was moaning: "I made it, see. I made it. I'm a warrior. A warrior."

CONTENT-AREA CONNECTIONS

Science
Ecosystems. Point out that Mary's observations of plants and animals during Ta-Na-E-Ka provide clues about the local biome. Divide the class into small groups with students of mixed abilities. Challenge them to describe the ecosystem in which Ta-Na-E-Ka takes place based on Mary's observations. Good readers can identify descriptions of the ecosystem, and artists in the group can sketch. [Possible responses: The ecosystem includes a river and a forest; its plant life includes elm trees and berry bushes; its animal life includes rabbits, civet cats, redheaded woodpeckers, water birds, and grasshoppers. A food web might include elms and berry bushes as producers, with consumers such as grasshoppers and rabbits eating plants; woodpeckers eating grasshoppers and berries; and civet cats eating berries, grasshoppers, and rabbits.]

MIXED-ABILITY

My grandfather looked at me strangely. I was clean, obviously well fed, and radiantly healthy. My parents got the message. My uncle and aunt gazed at me with hostility.

MAKING INFERENCES
5. What "message" is Mary sending to her family?

Finally my grandfather asked, "What did you eat to keep you so well?"

I sucked in my breath and blurted out the truth: "Hamburgers and milkshakes."

"Hamburgers!" my grandfather growled.

"Milkshakes!" Roger moaned.

"You didn't say we had to eat grasshoppers," I said sheepishly.

"Tell us all about your Ta-Na-E-Ka," my grandfather commanded.

I told them everything, from borrowing the five dollars, to Ernie's kindness, to observing the beaver.

"That's not what I trained you for," my grandfather said sadly.

I stood up. "Grandfather, I learned that Ta-Na-E-Ka is important. I didn't think so during training. I was scared stiff of it. I handled it my way. And I learned I had nothing to be afraid of. There's no reason in 1947 to eat grasshoppers when you can eat a hamburger."

I was inwardly shocked at my own audacity. But I liked it. "Grandfather, I'll bet you never ate one of those rotten berries yourself."

Grandfather laughed! He laughed aloud! My mother and father and aunt and uncle were all dumbfounded. Grandfather never laughed. Never.

"Those berries—they are terrible," Grandfather admitted. "I could never swallow them. I found a dead deer on the

first day of my Ta-Na-E-Ka—shot by a soldier, probably—and he kept my belly full for the entire period of the test!"

Grandfather stopped laughing. "We should send you out again," he said.

I looked at Roger. "You're pretty smart, Mary," Roger groaned. "I'd never have thought of what you did."

"Accountants just have to be good at arithmetic," I said comfortingly. "I'm terrible at arithmetic."

Roger tried to smile but couldn't. My grandfather called me to him. "You should have done what your cousin did. But I think you are more alert to what is happening to our people today than we are. I think you would have passed the test under any circumstances, in any time. Somehow, you know how to exist in a world that wasn't made for Indians. I don't think you're going to have any trouble surviving."

Grandfather wasn't entirely right. But I'll tell about that another time.

RETELLING
6. How is Mary's conflict with the older generation resolved?

Vocabulary
audacity (ô·das′ə·tē) n.: boldness; daring.

Ta-Na-E-Ka   **61**

INDEPENDENT PRACTICE

Literary Response and Analysis

Reading Check

1. Its purpose is to test young people's endurance and worthiness.
2. She considers it uninteresting and irrelevant to her life.
3. It is shortened from eighteen days to five, and participants wear bathing suits instead of being sent out naked.
4. He is the restaurant owner; he feeds and shelters Mary for the five days of her Ta-Na-E-Ka.
5. He says that she should have done what Roger did, but she has strengths that will help her succeed "in a world that wasn't made for Indians."

Interpretations

6. Beforehand, Mary dreads the ritual. Afterward, she feels proud. She learns that she can survive and that she values her heritage.
7. *Arguments for*—Surviving will make you proud. It is an honored Kaw tradition. Girls compete on equal terms with boys. Endurance is a virtue. *Arguments against*—You don't need to be a warrior if you're going to work in an office. Wilderness survival is irrelevant in the modern world. The ordeal is too dangerous.
8. She feels the need to defend her people's tradition to Ernie, even though she really did not want to participate in Ta-Na-E-Ka.
9. Possible answer: Mary's independence and daring lead her to tell Grandfather the truth and to challenge him about the outdated aspects of the ritual, opening the door for his wise resolution of the conflict between traditional and modern values.
10. Possible answer: Traditions are worth keeping but may need to be altered to fit changing times.

Literary Response and Analysis

Reading Check

1. What is the purpose of Ta-Na-E-Ka?
2. At the beginning of the story, how does Mary feel about her Kaw heritage?
3. How has Ta-Na-E-Ka changed since Grandfather's day?
4. Who is Ernie? How does he help Mary?
5. What does Grandfather say to Mary after he learns how she survived her Ta-Na-E-Ka?

Interpretations

6. What is Mary's attitude toward Ta-Na-E-Ka before the ritual? after the ritual? What does Ta-Na-E-Ka teach her?
7. Mary and Roger face an **external conflict** with the older generation. What arguments do Mary's mother, grandfather, and teacher give in support of Ta-Na-E-Ka? What arguments do Mary and Roger give against it? **Compare and contrast** their arguments, using a chart like the one below. Whose side are *you* on? You might want to think about your Quickwrite response when you answer.

8. What **internal conflict** does Mary experience when Ernie says that Ta-Na-E-Ka is silly?
9. What qualities of Mary's **character** affect the **resolution** of the conflicts in the story?
10. The **theme** of a story is a truth about life or human behavior that is revealed through the action. What important truth about life does Mary discover from her Ta-Na-E-Ka?

Evaluation

11. What do you think of Mary? Does she seem like a real person? Does the story seem realistic? Explain your evaluation of the story.

Writing

Roger's Story

Roger suffers during his Ta-Na-E-Ka; Mary has a good time. How do you think Roger feels about that? Imagine that you're Roger. Write a letter to your best friend, telling about what happened to you and to Mary. Include a description of Mary's character, and tell what you think of her.

Reading Standard 3.2 Analyze the effect of the qualities of the character (for example, courage or cowardice, ambition or laziness) on the plot and the resolution of the conflict.

COMPARING ARGUMENTS	
For Ta-Na-E-Ka (Older Generation)	Against Ta-Na-E-Ka (Younger Generation)

Evaluation

11. Students' opinions of Mary will vary. Possible answers: She's realistic because she shows fear, cheats a little, scorns adult values, and ultimately grows and learns. The story seems unrealistic because everything works out too neatly: No harm comes to Mary, who never loses her perky attitude; Roger admires her instead of resents her; Mary wins Grandfather over instantly.

Literary Response and Analysis

Answer Column (Left)

Literary Response and Analysis

Reading Check

1. Its purpose is to test young people's endurance and worthiness.
2. She considers it uninteresting and irrelevant to her life.
3. It is shortened from eighteen days to five, and participants wear bathing suits instead of being sent out naked.
4. He is the restaurant owner; he feeds and shelters Mary for the five days of her Ta-Na-E-Ka.
5. He says that she should have done what Roger did, but she has strengths that will help her succeed "in a world that wasn't made for Indians."

Interpretations

6. Beforehand, Mary dreads the ritual. Afterward, she feels proud. She learns that she can survive and that she values her heritage.
7. *Arguments for*—Surviving will make you proud. It is an honored Kaw tradition. Girls compete on equal terms with boys. Endurance is a virtue. *Arguments against*—You don't need to be a warrior if you're going to work in an office. Wilderness survival is irrelevant in the modern world. The ordeal is too dangerous.
8. She feels the need to defend her people's tradition to Ernie, even though she really did not want to participate in Ta-Na-E-Ka.
9. Possible answer: Mary's independence and daring lead her to tell Grandfather the truth and to challenge him about the outdated aspects of the ritual, opening the door for his wise resolution of the conflict between traditional and modern values.
10. Possible answer: Traditions are worth keeping but may need to be altered to fit changing times.

Vocabulary Development

Developing Fluency in Word Usage

PRACTICE

We discover new words by reading; we develop **fluency,** or ease of use, by using those words as often as we can. How fluent are you with the Word Bank words? See if you can answer these questions.

1. In your opinion, what is the loftiest quality a person can have? What is the opposite of a lofty quality?
2. What is the shrewdest way to deal with a conflict? What adjective is the opposite of shrewd?
3. What would you do if someone grimaced at you? How is a grimace different from a smile?
4. Is gorging yourself acceptable or rude? Explain.
5. Name three deeds that require audacity to carry out.

Word Bank

loftiest
shrewdest
grimaced
gorging
audacity

Grammar Link MINI-LESSON

Subjects and Verbs—in Perfect Agreement

To find the right verb when a sentence has a **compound subject**—that is, two subjects joined by *and, or,* or *nor*—follow these rules:

- Subjects joined by the word *and* take a plural verb.

  Mary and Roger were afraid.

- Singular subjects joined by *or* or *nor* take a singular verb.

  Either Roger or Mary reaches the river.

- When a singular subject and a plural subject are joined by *or* or *nor*, the verb agrees with the subject nearer the verb.

  Neither Mary's parents nor her *grandfather* is able to predict how Mary will survive.

  Neither Mary's grandfather nor her *parents* are able to predict how Mary will survive.

PRACTICE

Choose the right verb for each sentence below.

1. Either Mary's teacher or her grandfather explains/explain that Kaw girls and boys compete on equal terms.
2. Both her mother and her teacher says/say that tradition is important.
3. Neither Mary's parents nor her grandfather knows/know that she has five dollars.

Ta-Na-E-Ka **63**

Practice
Possible Answers

1. Loftiest quality: honesty, love, compassion, mercy. Opposite quality: greed, intolerance, hatred.
2. Shrewdest way: to avoid it; to use reason. Opposite of shrewd: foolish, dull, senseless.
3. I would ask the person what's wrong; make a face back; walk away. Unlike a smile, which expresses pleasure, a grimace expresses pain or disgust.
4. In our culture, stuffing yourself is considered rude; in some other cultures, it is a compliment to the host.
5. Surviving in the woods alone; standing up to a bully; disagreeing on principle with a teacher.

▶ **Resources Reminder**

Vocabulary and Spelling
■ *Vocabulary Development*
  ■ Vocabulary Worksheet, p. 6

Grammar Link

Practice
1. explains
2. say
3. knows

ASSESSING

Assessment
■ *Progress Assessment of Reading*
  ■ Selection Test, p. 19

RETEACHING

For a lesson reteaching the influence of character on plot see **Reteaching,** p. 489B.

DIFFERENTIATING INSTRUCTION

Learners Having Difficulty
In class, have students write answers to the Reading Check questions. *Monitoring tip:* If students are unable to explain what Mary learns (question 6), have them re-read pp. 60–61, looking for the answers to these questions: What does Mary tell Ernie when he says Ta-Na-E-Ka is a "pretty silly thing to do to a kid"? What does Mary realize when the five days are over? Have student pairs collaborate on the remaining Interpretations questions. They can address the Evaluation question in a whole-class discussion.

Writing. For the Writing activity ("Roger's Story"), have the class brainstorm to make a list of Mary's character traits. Then, ask students to write their letters at home.

HOMEWORK

STANDARDS FOCUS, pp. 64–68

(For grade-level and review standards taught in this selection, see citations on Pupil's Edition pages.)

Summary *at grade level*

The Kaw, or Kansa, call themselves the People of the South Wind. In their creation story they lived on a cramped island until Kaw mothers asked the Great Spirit for more room. He ordered animals to enlarge the island, and it became the earth. When French explorers first encountered the Kaw in the early 1800s, Kaw territory spanned more than twenty million acres of the central Great Plains. The French recorded Kaw names for people and places, changing the spellings as they did so. European diseases and U.S. settlements soon ravaged the Kaw. In 1872, the United States forced most of the remaining Kaw from the Kansas River valley to an Oklahoma reservation. Leadership disputes further split the Kaw nation. In the year 2000, the last full-blooded Kaw died.

 Resources Reminder

Media
- *Audio CD Library*
  - disc 2

Reading
- *Interactive Reading*
  - Graphic Organizer: Outline Organizer, p. 68

The Wind People

Creating an Outline

Outlining is a good way to organize and record information in factual writing. **Outlining** usually involves three steps:

1. getting the main ideas
2. taking notes
3. putting the notes into outline form

Use the informational reading on the Kaw to practice taking notes and outlining. Before you start, get a stack of three-by-five-inch index cards.

1. **Getting the main ideas.** You'll probably have to read the article more than once to identify the main ideas. Note that the article has four **subheads.** You should look for a main idea and supporting details for each of these four sections of the article. As you read, ask **clarifying questions**—questions that clarify, or clear up, certain points for you. When you're finished, you should be able to answer questions like these: Who? What? When? Where? How? Why? What happened then? What caused this to happen? What were the effects of this event?

Now, read "The Wind People." Look for these four main ideas as you read the article:

- the Kaw creation story
- encounters with European explorers
- winds of change
- the end of the Kaw

Reading Standard 2.4
Clarify an understanding of texts by creating outlines and logical notes.

2. **Taking notes.** For a short article like this one, you can probably use one note card for each of the main ideas. Write down each idea at the top of a card; then, read the article again. When you find an important detail supporting one of the main ideas, stop and add it to the card for that idea. Try to write it in your own words. If you do use the author's exact words, put quotation marks around them.

3. **Putting the notes into outline form.** Now that you have four cards filled with notes, it is time to organize them in an outline. An outline is set up this way:

I. Main idea
  A. Detail supporting point I
    1. Detail supporting point A
      a. Detail supporting point 1

Make sure that there are at least two headings at each level.

You have four main ideas from the Kaw article. Now, finish outlining the content of the article by filling in supporting details. The first main idea has been outlined for you:

I. The Kaw creation story
  A. The Kaw nation lived on an island that was too small for them.
  B. Because of this, Kaw mothers prayed to the Great Spirit.
  C. As a result, beavers, muskrats, turtles were sent to make the island bigger.
  D. In time the earth became large, and plants and animals thrived.

Planning
- *One-Stop Planner* CD-ROM with Test Generator
- *On Course: Mapping Instruction*

Media
- *Audio CD Library*
  - disc 2

Reading
- *Interactive Reading*
  - Graphic Organizer: Outline Organizer, p. 68

Differentiating Instruction
- *Lesson Plans for Language Development*
  - English-Language Learners, pp. 29, 41, 46

- Special Education Students, pp. 29, 41, 46

Assessment
- *Progress Assessment of Reading*
  - Selection Test, p. 22
- *One-Stop Planner* CD-ROM with Test Generator

The Wind People

FACTS ABOUT THE KAW

by Flo Ota De Lange

William Mehojah.

On April 23, 2000, a sad story appeared in many American newspapers. William Mehojah, eighty-two years old, had died. Mr. Mehojah was the last member of the Sovereign Nation° of the Kaw. With his death, the Kaw people were gone forever.

The Kaw Creation Myth

According to a Kaw creation story, the Kaw originally lived on an island that was too small for their numbers. Because there were so many Kaw people in those days, the Kaw mothers offered prayers to the Great Spirit begging for more living space. The Great Spirit responded to their pleas. He sent beavers, muskrats, and turtles to enlarge the Kaw's island, using materials from the bottom of the great waters. In time the earth took shape. Plants and animals thrived. The world became spacious and vibrant. The Kaw population problem was resolved.

Encounters with European Explorers

By the early 1800s, the Kaw nation was prospering. Their land stretched over twenty million acres, from what is now Kansas east into Missouri and Iowa and north into Nebraska. The first Europeans who came in contact with the Kaw were French explorers. The French were interested in commerce, and that required a working knowledge of the geography of the Great Southern Plains and Mississippi Valley, as well as knowledge of the people who lived there and of the languages they spoke. To obtain this knowledge, the French (just like the English and Spanish explorers in other parts of the country) would ask for the names of the new animals, trees, rivers, and mountains they saw and of the new people they met. "What do you call this?" the French would ask. "And this? And this?" Then the French would eagerly record the answers in their ledgers and on their maps. But though the names they wrote down might have sounded roughly like the original names, they were spelled the way the French would spell them. Furthermore, many of the sounds the European explorers heard had no equivalents in their own languages, so the new words usually bore little

---

° **Sovereign Nation:** Native American nations govern themselves and are not subject to the laws of the U.S. government except through treaty or agreement.

The Wind People **65**

A Reading Informational Materials
GRADE-LEVEL STANDARD

❓ Outlining. What is the main idea of this paragraph, and what is the first supporting detail? [*Main idea*—Kaw lands and population shrink. *First supporting detail*—Europeans push west into Kaw lands.]

B Correcting Misconceptions

Tell students that although Mr. Mehojah was the last full-blooded member of the Kaw nation, on his people's tribal rolls there were listed about 2,500 persons in the year 2000. The Kaw, like most Native American peoples, include many members of mixed ancestry.

Monitoring students' progress. Have students create acrostics with the letters in the word *Kansa*, listing facts that they have learned about the Kaw.

[Possible acrostic:

K illed by European diseases.

A cres of land Kaw occupied by early 1800s—twenty million.

N ames for places and animals were changed by French explorers.

S outh wind—Kaw believed they were its people.

A fter 1825, the United States took most of Kaw land.]

Kaw sisters in the early 1900s.

A Kaw dwelling from about 1900.

resemblance to the native words. This is how *U-Moln-Holn* became *Omaha* and *Wi-Tsi-Ta* became *Wichita*. The Kaw (or Kansa) called themselves Koln-Za or Kanza; the names we know them by are the French and English versions of those names.

Winds of Change

The Kaw are also known as the Wind People or the People of the South Wind. They believed that since they could not control the wind, they should try to form a relationship with it. But when the winds of change hit the Kaw, with the westward push of European immigrants, the Kaw were helpless. They saw their lands and their population shrink. The European settlers brought deadly diseases with them—diseases such as influenza and smallpox, to which the Kaw had no immunity. Battles with other Native American peoples further reduced the Kaw's numbers.

The End of the Kaw

The most devastating blow to the Kaw was struck by the U.S. government. Beginning in 1825, other peoples were permitted to occupy Kaw land; the Kaw themselves were confined to two million acres in what is now the Kansas, or Kaw, River valley. In 1872, the federal government moved the nation from the valley to a 100,000-acre reservation in Oklahoma. After the Kaw were removed from their native land, struggles over leadership broke out, dividing and fatally weakening the nation.

By 1995, only four Kaw were left: Mr. Mehojah, his brother, and two nephews. Mr. Mehojah's last surviving nephew died in 1998. By the year 2000, the Kaw were gone.

Social Science

The Kaw. After learning that the Kaw inhabited the central Great Plains and were moved in 1872 to Oklahoma, students may puzzle over references in "Ta-Na-E-Ka" to Mary's home "on the northernmost reaches of the Missouri River." Explain that although numerous Native American peoples were forcibly relocated to Oklahoma in the late 1800s, some group members evaded authorities and remained in their homelands or moved to nearby areas. Rose Creek, where Mary's grandfather was wounded as a boy in 1883, is in South Dakota. Mary's family apparently lives in the Montana-Dakota area. The northern Missouri River begins in Montana, flowing across the state and through the Dakotas.

Reading Informational Materials

Reading Check

1. Review the notes you took as you read this article. Then, use your notes to create an **outline.** For a start, see page 64.

2. List three Kaw names that were modified by the French and English.

3. Where were the Kaw moved to in 1872?

TestPractice

The Wind People

1. The writer probably tells the Kaw creation myth because —
   A it contrasts with what eventually happened to the Kaw
   B it explains why the Kaw died out
   C it predicts what happened to the Kaw
   D it explains how they got the name Kaw

2. Suppose an **outline** of this article lists these main ideas:
   I.   The Kaw creation story
   II.
   III. Winds of change
   IV. The end of the Kaw

   Which **main idea** should be Roman numeral II?
   F Last Kaw dies on April 23, 2000
   G Encounters with European explorers
   H Europeans bring disease
   J Other people allowed to occupy Kaw land

3. French explorers learned Kaw names for local peoples and places by —
   A studying a textbook
   B talking to the Kaw
   C taking part in Kaw rituals
   D looking at maps of the Mississippi Valley

4. Suppose an **outline** of this article has a main heading that reads "Winds of Change." Which of these details do *not* support that main idea?
   F With European immigration, Kaw lands and population shrink.
   G Deadly diseases spread among Kaw.
   H Kaw fight with other Native Americans and reduce population further.
   J French explorers change Kaw names.

Reading Standard 2.4 Clarify an understanding of texts by creating outlines.

The Wind People   **67**

Activity. Have a volunteer locate these place-names on a map.

INDIVIDUAL

Reading Informational Materials

Reading Check

1. See possible outline sample on p. 64.

2. *U-Moln-Holn* became *Omaha*, *Wi-Tsi-Ta* became *Wichita*, and *Koln-Za* or *Kanza* became *Kaw* or *Kansas*.

3. a reservation in Oklahoma

TestPractice

Answers and Model Rationales

1. **A** Students should realize that a group's creation myth is unlikely to predict or explain the group's extinction. The creation myth in the article also does not explain how the Kaw got their name.

2. **G** Students should see from the article's subheads that "Encounters with European explorers" is a main idea.

3. **B** Students should conclude that if the information had been in maps or books, there would have been no need for exploration. It is unlikely that French explorers would be permitted to take part in rituals, which are often sacred and open only to Kaw members.

4. **J** Students should realize that only J refers to information that is not given in the section labeled "Winds of Change."

Test-Taking Tips

Remind students that they can immediately eliminate options that they know are incorrect while they try to determine the correct answer.

Vocabulary Development

Practice 1
Possible Answers

1. ■ Alaska—*alakshak*, "mainland."
   ■ Alabama—*alba amo*, "thicket clearers."
   ■ (North or South) Dakota—*dakóta*, "allies."
   ■ Iowa—*ayúxba*, "sleepy ones."
   ■ Minnesota—*mnísóta*, "whitish water."
   ■ Mississippi—*missisipioui*, "big river."
   ■ Missouri—*ouemessourita*, "those that have big canoes."
   ■ Ohio—*oheo*, "fine river."
   ■ Oklahoma—*okla*, "people" + *homma*, "red."
2. ■ Sioux (City)—"little snake," "enemy."
   ■ Saskatoon—"berry."
   ■ (Lake) Winnebago—"those of the dirty water."
   ■ Tupelo—"tree" + "swamp."

Practice 2

1. moccasins
2. moose, muskrat, opossum or possum, raccoon, skunk, woodchuck
3. hickory, hominy, pecan, persimmon, squash, succotash
4. hickory, pecan, sequoia, persimmon
5. toboggan
6. mackinaw

ASSESSING

Assessment
■ *Progress Assessment of Reading*
  ■ Selection Test, p. 22

Vocabulary Development

Words from Native American Languages
Many rivers, mountains, and other geographical features in the United States were given English versions of Indian names, from the Appalachian Mountains in the East to the Willamette River in the West.

PRACTICE 1

1. The names of more than twenty states come from Native American languages. Can you name five? Use a dictionary to check your guesses and to learn about the origins of the names. Write down the names' original meanings and spellings.
2. If you look at a map or an atlas of the United States, you'll find a variety of place names that come from Native American languages. Choose three, and look up their original meanings in a dictionary.

PRACTICE 2

Many English words come from other languages. The words in the list below come from Native American languages. Use the words to answer the questions that follow. Then, write sentences using the words, or draw pictures to create an illustrated dictionary.

hickory	opossum or possum	squash
hominy	pecan	succotash
mackinaw	persimmon	toboggan
moccasins	raccoon	woodchuck
moose	sequoia	
muskrat	skunk	

Which of the items on the list

1. would you be most likely to put on your feet?
2. are animals?
3. are foods?
4. are types of trees?
5. will carry you down a hill?
6. will carry you across a river or keep you warm?

Reading Standard 1.3 Recognize the origins and meanings of frequently used foreign words in English, and use these words accurately in speaking and writing.

The Bracelet

Literary Focus
Character and Point of View
This story lets you into the mind of its main character, Ruri, who is also the narrator. Ruri uses the **first-person point of view,** speaking as "I." As she tells her story, Ruri reveals the qualities of her character, as well as her thoughts and feelings. Because Ruri is telling the story herself, you won't know for sure what other people are thinking and feeling. You'll know only what Ruri tells you.

Reading Skills
Making Predictions
As you read stories, you make **predictions.** That means you guess what will happen next. You base your guesses on clues the writer gives you and on what you know from your own experience. Making predictions is part of the fun of reading stories. We match wits with the writer, to see if we can guess how all the puzzles and problems will be worked out. Probably we are pleased when we guess correctly, but most of us also love to be surprised.

Make the Connection
Quickwrite ✏
What stories or movies or TV shows can you think of in which painful events are used to teach us never to repeat mistakes? Give at least two examples, and describe the lessons you learned.

Background
Shortly after the United States entered World War II against Japan, more than 110,000 people of Japanese ancestry who were living in the United States were forced to move to guarded camps. Most were American citizens who had been born here and had done nothing wrong. But the U.S. government feared that they might give support to Japan. When they were finally allowed to leave the camps, after the war, many Japanese Americans found that other people had taken over their homes and businesses. In 1989, the U.S. government issued a formal apology to Japanese Americans for the injustice that had been done to them.

Vocabulary Development
Look for these words as you read the story. Notice how **context**, the words near each vocabulary word, helps you guess its meaning.

evacuated (ē·vak′yoō·āt′id) v.: removed from an area. *During the war, Japanese Americans were evacuated from the West Coast. Their removal had tragic consequences.*

interned (in·turnd′) v.: imprisoned or confined. *Ruri's father was interned in a prisoner-of-war camp.*

aliens (āl′yənz) n.: foreigners. *The U.S. government treated Japanese Americans as if they were enemy aliens.*

forsaken (fôr·sā′kən) adj.: abandoned; deserted. *The garden looked as forsaken as Ruri felt when she had to leave home.*

Reading Standard 3.5 Identify the speaker, and recognize first-person narration.

The Bracelet   69

STANDARDS FOCUS, pp. 69–77
(For grade-level and review standards taught in this selection, see citations on Pupil's Edition pages.)

Standard Coming Up in the Next Grade Level
■ Grade 7, Literary Response and Analysis 3.3   **Analyze characterization as delineated through a character's thoughts, words, speech patterns, and actions; the narrator's description; and the thoughts, words, and actions of other characters.**

Reading Skills
■ Make predictions.

Summary *at grade level*

This story is set in 1942, after Japan's attack on Pearl Harbor. Fearing treachery, the U.S. government is rounding up Japanese Americans, such as Ruri and her mother and sister, and sending them to internment camps. Before the family is sent off, Ruri's best friend, Laurie, gives her a bracelet that she vows to wear forever. At the camp, Ruri loses the bracelet, and she becomes distraught. Her mother consoles her by saying that we do not need objects like the bracelet to remember the people we love; they are always with us, in our hearts.

► Resources Reminder
Media
■ *Audio CD Library*
  ■ disc 2
■ *Fine Art Transparencies*
  ■ Transparency 4

Standards Starter

Motivate. Show the *Visual Connections* video segment "War, Internment, and Atonement" (Videocassette A, Segment 2), which is about the U.S. government's internment of Japanese Americans. Ask students if they know any Japanese Americans whose family members lived in the camps. Encourage students to respond to the video and suggest what lessons our country learned from this episode in its history. Then, have students complete the Quickwrite activity.

Preview Vocabulary

After students read the definitions of the Vocabulary words, have partners play "Guess My Word!" The first player chooses a word and gives synonyms until the second player guesses the word. When all four words have been used, players switch roles and play again. Afterward, have students select the best synonym for each word.

1. **evacuated** [Possible synonyms: abandoned, cleared, removed, left.]
2. **interned** [Possible synonyms: imprisoned, confined, detained.]
3. **aliens** [Possible synonyms: outsiders, strangers, foreigners.]
4. **forsaken** [Possible synonyms: abandoned, outcast, deserted.]

Assign the Reading

Read the story aloud to students up to the introduction of Laurie Madison on p. 71. Then, you may want to have on-level students read the rest of the story silently in class while you work with small groups of readers having difficulty. Encourage all students to ask questions about confusing scenes or references. Advanced learners may answer the Focus On questions as homework.

HOMEWORK

The Bracelet

YOSHIKO UCHIDA

"Mama, is it time to go?" I hadn't planned to cry, but the tears came suddenly, and I wiped them away with the back of my hand. I didn't want my older sister to see me crying.

"It's almost time, Ruri," my mother said gently. Her face was filled with a kind of sadness I had never seen before.

I looked around at my empty room. The clothes that Mama always told me to hang up in the closet, the junk piled on my dresser, the old rag doll I could never bear to part with—they were all gone. There was nothing left in my room, and there was nothing left in the rest of the house. The rugs and furniture were gone, the pictures and drapes were down, and the closets and cupboards were empty. The house was like a gift box after the nice thing inside was gone; just a lot of nothingness.

It was almost time to leave our home, but we weren't moving to a nicer house or to a new town. It was April 21, 1942. The United States and Japan were at war, and every Japanese person on the West Coast was being evacuated by the government to a concentration camp. Mama, my sister Keiko, and I were being sent from our home, and out of Berkeley, and eventually out of California.

Vocabulary
evacuated (ē·vak′yoō·āt′id) v.: removed from an area.

70   Chapter 2   Characters: The People You'll Meet

RESOURCES

Vocabulary and Spelling
■ *Vocabulary Development*
  ■ Vocabulary Worksheet, p. 7
■ *Spelling Lessons and Activities*
  ■ Latin Roots, pp. 66–67, 72–75, 78–79

Assessment
■ *Progress Assessment of Reading*
  ■ Selection Test, p. 24
■ *One-Stop Planner* CD-ROM with Test Generator

The doorbell rang, and I ran to answer it before my sister could. I thought maybe by some miracle a messenger from the government might be standing there, tall and proper and buttoned into a uniform, come to tell us it was all a terrible mistake, that we wouldn't have to leave after all. Or maybe the messenger would have a telegram from Papa, who was interned in a prisoner-of-war camp in Montana because he had worked for a Japanese business firm.

The FBI had come to pick up Papa and hundreds of other Japanese community leaders on the very day that Japanese planes had bombed Pearl Harbor. The government thought they were dangerous enemy aliens. If it weren't so sad, it would have been funny. Papa could no more be dangerous than the mayor of our city, and he was every bit as loyal to the United States. He had lived here since 1917.

When I opened the door, it wasn't a messenger from anywhere. It was my best friend, Laurie Madison, from next door. She was holding a package wrapped up like a birthday present, but she wasn't wearing her party dress, and her face drooped like a wilted tulip.

"Hi," she said. "I came to say goodbye."

She thrust the present at me and told me it was something to take to camp. "It's a bracelet," she said before I could open the package. "Put it on so you won't have to pack it." She knew I didn't have one inch of space left in my suitcase. We had been instructed to take only what we could carry into camp, and Mama had told us that we could each take only two suitcases.

"Then how are we ever going to pack the dishes and blankets and sheets they've told us to bring with us?" Keiko worried.

"I don't really know," Mama said, and she simply began packing those big impossible things into an enormous duffel bag—along with umbrellas, boots, a kettle, hot plate, and flashlight.

"Who's going to carry that huge sack?" I asked.

But Mama didn't worry about things like that. "Someone will help us," she said. "Don't worry." So I didn't.

Laurie wanted me to open her package and put on the bracelet before she left. It was a thin gold chain with a heart dangling on it. She helped me put it on, and I told her I'd never take it off, ever.

"Well, goodbye then," Laurie said awkwardly. "Come home soon."

"I will," I said, although I didn't know if I would ever get back to Berkeley again.

I watched Laurie go down the block, her long blond pigtails bouncing as she walked. I wondered who would be sitting in my desk at Lincoln Junior High now that I was gone. Laurie kept turning and waving, even walking backward for a while, until she got to the corner. I didn't want to watch anymore, and I slammed the door shut.

The next time the doorbell rang, it was Mrs. Simpson, our other neighbor. She was going to drive us to the Congregational Church, which was the Civil Control

Vocabulary
interned (in·turnd′) v.: imprisoned or confined, especially during a war.
aliens (āl′yənz) n.: foreigners.

A Literary Focus
GRADE-LEVEL STANDARD
❓ Character and point of view.
When the doorbell rings, what do you learn about Ruri's attitude toward the relocation? [She hasn't entirely accepted that it will happen; she hopes it is a mistake.] **What does this tell you about the kind of person she is?** [Possible response: She hopes for the best.]

B Content-Area Connections
HISTORY
Pearl Harbor. On December 7, 1941, the Japanese launched a surprise air attack on Pearl Harbor, Hawaii, in an attempt to destroy the U.S. Pacific fleet. The brutal attack was successful: 18 ships and more than 180 aircraft were destroyed. About 2,335 military personnel were killed. This motivated the United States to join World War II on the side of the Allies (Great Britain, China, France, and the Soviet Union) against the Axis powers (Germany, Italy, and Japan).

C Literary Focus
GRADE-LEVEL STANDARD
❓ Character and point of view.
Ruri's friend Laurie is not Japanese American. What does this suggest about both girls? [They are not prejudiced against people who come from different ethnic backgrounds.]

D Literary Focus
REVIEW STANDARD
❓ Simile. Have students identify the simile in this paragraph. ["her face drooped like a wilted tulip"] **What does this tell you about Laurie?** [She is unhappy about Ruri's leaving.]

E Literary Focus
GRADE-LEVEL STANDARD
❓ Character and point of view.
How does Ruri's mother react? [She does not complain about what can't be helped; she behaves with dignity and courage.] **What does her statement "Someone will help us" reveal?** [She has faith in human nature.]

DIFFERENTIATING INSTRUCTION

Learners Having Difficulty
Modeling. To help students read "The Bracelet," you may wish to model the process of thinking about character. Explain to students that observing what a character says, does, thinks, and feels can help them figure out the character's personality. Read aloud the first two paragraphs of the story. Then, say: "Ruri's question and her tears show that she is sensitive. Her action of wiping away her tears and her thought about her sister show that she wants to be strong."

Encourage students as they read to ask themselves: "What is Ruri like? What can I learn about her character from her words, actions, thoughts, and feelings?"

▶ Resources Reminder
Reading
■ *Interactive Reading*
   ■ Graphic Organizer: Character Map, p. 69

A Reading Skills

Interpreting. Why is each family given a number? [Possible responses: Numbers make it easier for the government to keep track of the families; numbers dehumanize the families, which makes it easier to treat them unfairly.]

B Literary Focus
GRADE-LEVEL STANDARD

Character and point of view. What do you learn about Ruri's parents from Ruri's memories of the irises? [Possible responses: They love each other very much; they treat each other with kindness and respect.]

Station where all the Japanese of Berkeley were supposed to report.

It was time to go. "Come on, Ruri. Get your things," my sister called to me.

It was a warm day, but I put on a sweater and my coat so I wouldn't have to carry them, and I picked up my two suitcases. Each one had a tag with my name and our family number on it. Every Japanese family had to register and get a number. We were Family Number 13453.

Mama was taking one last look around our house. She was going from room to room, as though she were trying to take a mental picture of the house she had lived in for fifteen years, so she would never forget it.

I saw her take a long last look at the garden that Papa loved. The irises beside the fish pond were just beginning to bloom. If Papa had been home, he would have cut the first iris blossom and brought it inside to Mama. "This one is for you," he would have said. And Mama would have smiled and said, "Thank you, Papa San"° and put it in her favorite cut-glass vase.

But the garden looked shabby and forsaken now that Papa was gone and Mama was too busy to take care of it. It looked the way I felt, sort of empty and lonely and abandoned.

When Mrs. Simpson took us to the Civil Control Station, I felt even worse. I was scared, and for a minute I thought I was going to lose my breakfast right in front of everybody. There must have been over a thousand Japanese people gathered at the church. Some were old and some were

young. Some were talking and laughing, and some were crying. I guess everybody else was scared too. No one knew exactly what was going to happen to us. We just knew we were being taken to the Tanforan Race-tracks, which the army had turned into a camp for the Japanese. There were fourteen other camps like ours along the West Coast.

° **San:** Japanese term added to names to indicate respect.

Vocabulary
forsaken (fôr·sā′kən) *adj.:* abandoned; deserted.

English-Language Learners
Building background. Explain that Ruri and her family were forced to leave their home because of the outbreak of war between Japan and the United States. Point out that Ruri says of her life at that time, "No one knew exactly what was going to happen to us." If there are any students in the class who have been forced to leave their homes because of a war, a

natural catastrophe, or other upheaval, invite them to talk about how it felt. Remember that only those who feel comfortable discussing such issues should be encouraged to share.

Resources Reminder
For lessons designed for both intermediate and advanced English-language learners,

see *Lesson Plans for Language Development,* pp. 30–32, 42, 47.

Special Education Students
For lessons designed for special education students, see *Lesson Plans for Language Development,* pp. 33, 42, 47.

What scared me most were the soldiers standing at the doorway of the church hall. They were carrying guns with mounted bayonets. I wondered if they thought we would try to run away and whether they'd shoot us or come after us with their bayonets if we did.

A long line of buses waited to take us to camp. There were trucks, too, for our baggage. And Mama was right; some men were there to help us load our duffel bag. When it was time to board the buses, I sat with Keiko, and Mama sat behind us. The bus went down Grove Street and passed the small Japanese food store where Mama used to order her bean-curd cakes and pickled radish. The windows were all boarded up, but there was a sign still hanging on the door that read, "We are loyal Americans."

The crazy thing about the whole evacuation was that we were all loyal Americans. Most of us were citizens because we had been born here. But our parents, who had come from Japan, couldn't become citizens because there was a law that prevented any Asian from becoming a citizen. Now everybody with a Japanese face was being shipped off to concentration camps.

"It's stupid," Keiko muttered as we saw the racetrack looming up beside the highway. "If there were any Japanese spies around, they'd have gone back to Japan long ago."

"I'll say," I agreed. My sister was in high school and she ought to know, I thought.

When the bus turned into Tanforan, there were more armed guards at the gate, and I saw barbed wire strung around the entire grounds. I felt as though I were going into a prison, but I hadn't done anything wrong.

We streamed off the buses and poured into a huge room, where doctors looked down our throats and peeled back our eyelids to see if we had any diseases. Then we were given our housing assignments. The man in charge gave Mama a slip of paper. We were in Barrack 16, Apartment 40.

"Mama!" I said. "We're going to live in

C **Vocabulary Development**
GRADE-LEVEL STANDARD
The roots of English. Point out the word *bayonets.* Tell students that a bayonet is a daggerlike steel weapon attached to the muzzle end of a gun and used for stabbing in hand-to-hand combat. Explain that the word comes from the French language and that the weapon was named after the French town of Bayonne, where it was first made and used.

D **Reading Skills**
❓ Identifying cause and effect.
Why are the Japanese Americans being taken from their homes? [The government is afraid of their possible loyalty to Japan and betrayal of the United States during wartime.] **What effect do you think this treatment may have on the Japanese Americans?** [Possible responses: fear and distrust of the government in the future, loss of respect for the United States.]

E **Correcting Misconceptions**
The internment camps are sometimes referred to as "concentration camps" in this story. Explain that this term more commonly refers to the camps where Nazis starved, tortured, and murdered millions of European Jews, Romany, and others. Make sure students understand that the United States did none of these things to the Japanese Americans.

F **Literary Focus**
REVIEW STANDARD
❓ Simile. What effect on readers does Ruri's comparison between the camp and a prison have? [Possible responses: The comparison helps readers feel Ruri's fear; it brings the injustice of the situation to life.]

Advanced Learners
Acceleration. Move advanced learners toward the seventh-grade Literary Response and Analysis Standard 3.3, which requires that they analyze characterization by studying a character's words, thoughts, and actions and by examining other characters' reactions to that character.

Activity. Have students create word webs showing their analysis of Laurie's character. Rays of the web should show the following clues to character traits:
- Laurie's words
- Laurie's actions
- Ruri's description of Laurie

At the ends of the rays, students can give specific examples of each type of clue.

A Literary Focus
GRADE-LEVEL STANDARD

❓ Character and point of view.
What is Ruri's response to the news that the family will live in an apartment? Why does she respond in this way? [She is excited because she associates the word with elegance and exclusiveness.] What does this tell you about her? [Possible responses: She is optimistic; she is naive.]

B Reading Skills

❓ Making predictions. What do you predict the apartment will be like? Why? [Possible response: small, crude, and rough because it is in an internment camp.]

C Literary Focus
GRADE-LEVEL STANDARD

❓ Character and point of view.
What character traits does Mama exhibit when she speaks to Ruri about the lost bracelet? [Possible responses: warmth, wisdom, understanding.]

GUIDED PRACTICE

Monitoring students' progress. Have the class identify the following statements as true or false. Ask students to locate passages in the text that support their answers.

True-False

1. Ruri's father has lived in the United States for a long time. [T]

2. Laurie gives Ruri a bracelet for her birthday. [F]

3. The family is taken from Berkeley, California, to an internment camp. [T]

4. Ruri and her mother whine about their stall at the camp. [F]

5. Laurie comes to visit Ruri at the camp. [F]

(A) an apartment!" The only apartment I had ever seen was the one my piano teacher lived in. It was in an enormous building in San Francisco, with an elevator and thick-carpeted hallways. I thought how wonderful it would be to have our own elevator. A house was all right, but an apartment seemed elegant and special.

(B) We walked down the racetrack, looking for Barrack 16. Mr. Noma, a friend of Papa's, helped us carry our bags. I was so busy looking around I slipped and almost fell on the muddy track. Army barracks had been built everywhere, all around the racetrack and even in the center oval.

Mr. Noma pointed beyond the track toward the horse stables. "I think your barrack is out there."

He was right. We came to a long stable that had once housed the horses of Tanforan, and we climbed up the wide ramp. Each stall had a number painted on it, and when we got to 40, Mr. Noma pushed open the door.

"Well, here it is," he said, "Apartment 40."

The stall was narrow and empty and dark. There were two small windows on each side of the door. Three folded army cots were on the dust-covered floor, and one light bulb dangled from the ceiling. That was all. This was our apartment, and it still smelled of horses.

Mama looked at my sister and then at me. "It won't be so bad when we fix it up," she began. "I'll ask Mrs. Simpson to send me some material for curtains. I could make some cushions too, and . . . well . . ." She stopped. She couldn't think of anything more to say.

Mr. Noma said he'd go get some mattresses for us. "I'd better hurry before they're all gone." He rushed off. I think he wanted to leave so that he wouldn't have to see Mama cry. But he needn't have run off, because Mama didn't cry. She just went out to borrow a broom and began sweeping out the dust and dirt. "Will you girls set up the cots?" she asked.

It was only after we'd put up the last cot that I noticed my bracelet was gone. "I've lost Laurie's bracelet!" I screamed. "My bracelet's gone!"

We looked all over the stall and even down the ramp. I wanted to run back down the track and go over every inch of ground we'd walked on, but it was getting dark and Mama wouldn't let me.

I thought of what I'd promised Laurie. I wasn't ever going to take the bracelet off, not even when I went to take a shower. And now I had lost it on my very first day in camp. I wanted to cry.

I kept looking for it all the time we were in Tanforan. I didn't stop looking until the day we were sent to another camp, called Topaz, in the middle of a desert in Utah. And then I gave up.

(C) But Mama told me never mind. She said I didn't need a bracelet to remember Laurie, just as I didn't need anything to remember Papa or our home in Berkeley or all the people and things we loved and had left behind.

"Those are things we can carry in our hearts and take with us no matter where we are sent," she said.

And I guess she was right. I've never forgotten Laurie, even now.

MINI-LESSON Reading

Developing Word-Attack Skills
On the chalkboard, write these words from the selection. Have volunteers tell if the *c* in each word stands for the sound /k/ or /s/.

face	come	camp
ceiling	city	cut

Have students use these words to make generalizations about when *c* stands for /k/ and when *c* stands for /s/. [*C* stands for /k/ before *a*, *o*, and *u*; *c* stands for /s/ before *e* and *i*; *ce* stands for /s/ at the end of a word.]

Activity. Have volunteers read the words below and tell which of the generalizations explain the sounds of *c* in the words.

1. concentration [*c* before *o*: /k/; before *e*: /s/]

2. bracelet [*c* before *e*: /s/]

3. cicada [*c* before *i*: /s/; before *a*: /k/]

4. gesticulate [*c* before *u*: /k/]

5. circulation [*c* before *i*: /s/; before *u*: /k/]

Yoshiko Uchida

So It Won't Happen Again

Yoshiko Uchida (1921–1992) was in her last year of college when the United States entered World War II. Like most other people of Japanese descent on the West Coast, Uchida and her family were uprooted by the government and forced to go to an internment camp. She and her family lived at Tanforan Racetrack in horse stall 40, answering to Family Number 13453 instead of their own name. Uchida later gave the same family number and "address" to the fictional family in her short story "The Bracelet." Uchida said that in writing about the internment camps, she tried to give readers a sense of the courage and strength that enabled most Japanese Americans to endure this tragedy.

There was another reason that she wrote about the camps:

> I always ask the children why they think I wrote *Journey to Topaz* and *Journey Home*, in which I tell of the wartime experiences of the Japanese Americans. . . . 'To tell how you felt? To tell what happened to the Japanese people?'
>
> 'Yes,' I answer, but I continue the discussion until finally one of them will say, 'You wrote those books so it won't ever happen again.'
>
> And that is why I wrote this book. I wrote it for the young Japanese Americans who seek a sense of continuity with their past. But I wrote it as well for all Americans, with the hope that through knowledge of the past, they will never allow another group of people in America to be sent into desert exile ever again.

For Independent Reading

Uchida's many novels for young people include *Journey to Topaz* and its sequel, *Journey Home*. She also wrote a trilogy about a Japanese American girl called Rinko: *The Jar of Dreams*, *The Best Bad Thing*, and *The Happiest Ending*.

Meet the Writer

Background. In addition to non-fiction and short stories, Yoshiko Uchida also wrote versions of traditional Japanese folk tales. For example, "Momotaro: Boy-of-the-Peach" tells the story of a boy who jumps out of an enormous peach that a woman finds floating down the river where she is washing clothes. She and her husband take care of the boy until he is fifteen, when he goes off to perform a good deed. Uchida first heard this story from her mother.

Uchida started keeping a journal the day she graduated from elementary school. "I was trying to hold on to and somehow preserve the magic as well as the joy and sadness of certain moments in my life," she explains. "I guess that's really what books and writing are all about."

For Independent Reading

If students choose to read Uchida's trilogy, point out that they will learn how the young Japanese American girl Rinko faces racial prejudice.

■ If students would like to read more about the detention of Japanese Americans, they might read *Farewell to Manzanar* by Jeanne W. Houston and James Houston. This true story tells of a family's experiences in an internment camp.

■ Students who like historical fiction such as "The Bracelet" might enjoy Laurence Yep's *Dragonwings*, the story of Moonshadow, who leaves China in 1903 to live in San Francisco with a father he doesn't know. Life isn't easy for them, but they work together to build a flying-dragon machine.

▶ Resources Reminder

Reading

■ *Interactive Reading*

For another selection by Yoshiko Uchida, see "Foreigner in Japan," in *Interactive Reading*, p. 82. You may want to assign this to advanced learners.

Advanced Learners

Enrichment. Have interested students form a small reading group in which to read and discuss *Journey to Topaz*. Students can read the book on their own and then get together to discuss it. *Monitoring tip:* Ask students, "How did reading this book enrich your understanding of 'The Bracelet'?"

SMALL-GROUP

INDEPENDENT PRACTICE

Literary Response and Analysis

Reading Check

1. The United States and Japan are at war, and the United States is sending many Japanese Americans on the West Coast to internment camps.
2. He has been sent to a prisoner-of-war camp in Montana.
3. Possible answer: Laurie gives Ruri a bracelet to remember her by.
4. The barracks were used as horse stables.
5. Ruri never finds the lost bracelet. She accepts her mother's words of consolation that she doesn't need the bracelet because she can carry the memory of Laurie in her heart.

Interpretations

6. Students know from the outset that the family is going to a camp, so their predictions should have focused on what the camp would be like and how the family would cope.
7. Possible answers: the U.S. government; racism; prejudice.
8. Possible answers: Ruri is loving, respectful, and optimistic. She remembers Laurie in spite of losing the bracelet. Ruri's respect for her mother's advice helps her deal with the loss.
9. Possible answers: She is sensible, generous, patient, optimistic; she has an unbreakable faith in the human spirit. Her wise advice will help Ruri deal with her loss and show what she has truly gained.
10. Possible answers: The first-person point of view makes the story more immediate and realistic. Ruri can present the story as an innocent young person. What she does not fully understand and can't explain is the suspicion and prejudice behind the internment and that the internment is unconstitutional.

Literary Response and Analysis

Reading Check

1. Why does Ruri's family have to leave home?
2. What has happened to Ruri's father?
3. Why does Laurie give Ruri a bracelet?
4. What were the barracks used for before Ruri and her family came to live there?
5. The **climax** of the story is the loss of the bracelet. What happens in the story's **resolution**?

Interpretations

6. When you began reading this story, how did you **predict** it would end? How accurate was your prediction?
7. The plot centers on a **conflict,** or problem, that goes far beyond the characters in the story. Ruri and her family are on one side of this conflict. Who or what is on the other side of it?
8. List three qualities, or **character traits,** that Ruri reveals in this story. How do Ruri's qualities affect the story's **resolution** (the way the story ends)?
9. List three **character traits** that Ruri's mother reveals. How does her mother help Ruri accept the situation?
10. Why do you think the writer chose to tell the story from the **first-person point of view**? What can

Ruri tell you that no other character can tell? What things does Ruri *not* know?
11. What is the story's **theme,** or insight about life? Find a passage in the story that supports your statement of theme. Be sure to compare your statement of the story's theme with the themes discovered by your classmates.

Evaluation

12. Does the author succeed in teaching a lesson in this story? Does she do this as well as the authors of the stories and the directors of the movies you listed for the Quickwrite on page 69? Explain.

Writing
Another Point of View

Suppose that Ruri's mother told this story. What might she say about the events that Ruri describes? How might Laurie tell the story? Using a different first-person narrator, retell the events in the story. Be sure to keep the events in chronological order.

Art/Writing
Gone but Not Forgotten

Is there someone in your life whom you'll always carry in your heart? Draw a picture of the person, or make a collage that shows how you feel about him or her. Under the illustration, write a few lines explaining why you will always remember that person.

Reading Standard 3.2 Analyze the effect of the qualities of the character (for example, courage or cowardice, ambition or laziness) on the plot and the resolution of the conflict.

Reading Standard 3.5 Identify the speaker, and recognize first-person narration.

11. Possible answer: The story's theme is that love and dignity overcome injustice. Passages will vary.

Evaluation

12. Possible answers: Yes, the narrator's enduring love for her friend and her

mother's steadfast optimism and dignity teach a powerful lesson that is drawn from real life. No, fictional stories and movies can create scenarios that more dramatically teach about love and respect.

Vocabulary Development

The Roots of English
Many of the words we use today can be traced to Latin or to Old English, the language used in England between the 400s and about 1056.

PRACTICE 1

From the Word Bank, choose the word that correctly completes each of the sentences below. Then, use each word in a sentence that shows you know its meaning.

1. The Old English word *forascan,* meaning "to oppose," is related to the word _____.
2. The Latin word *alienus,* meaning "other," is the root of the word _____.
3. The Latin word *internus,* meaning "inward," is related to the word _____.
4. The Latin verb *vacuare,* meaning "to make empty," is the basis of the word _____.

Word Bank

evacuated
interned
aliens
forsaken

PRACTICE 2

In the twentieth century, a number of words came into English from Japanese, including the words listed below. Use a dictionary to find out what each word means. Then, fill in the blanks in the sentences that follow the word list. Use context clues to find the words that fit best. Can you think of other words from Japanese that have entered the English language?

kimono (kə·mō′nə)   sayonara (sä′yô·nä′rä)
futon (fōō′tän′)   origami (ôr′ə·gä′mē)
karaoke (kar′ē·o′kē)

1. I bought my friend a beautiful silk _____ for her birthday.
2. My cousin enjoyed sleeping on a _____ so much that she said "_____" to her inner-spring mattress.
3. Flocks of _____ cranes cut from red paper decorated each table.
4. My grandfather sang _____ at the party celebrating his ninetieth birthday.

Reading Standard 1.3 Recognize the origins and meanings of frequently used foreign words in English, and use these words accurately in speaking and writing.

The Bracelet   **77**

Vocabulary Development

Practice 1
1. forsaken
   He has forsaken his country.
2. aliens
   I like movies about space aliens.
3. interned
   They were interned in a camp.
4. evacuated
   We evacuated because of the approaching storm.

Practice 2
1. kimono
2. futon, sayonara
3. origami
4. karaoke

Possible other words: sushi, bonsai, tempura.

Resources Reminder
Vocabulary and Spelling
- *Vocabulary Development*
  - Vocabulary Worksheet, p. 7
- *Lesson Plans for Language Development*
  - Vocabulary, p. 47

ASSESSING

Assessment
- *Progress Assessment of Reading*
  - Selection Test, p. 24

RETEACHING

For a lesson reteaching how the qualities of a character affect the plot and its resolution, see **Reteaching,** p. 489B.

DIFFERENTIATING INSTRUCTION

Learners Having Difficulty
Have partners write answers to the Reading Check questions. *Monitoring tip:* If students are unable to work out how Ruri's problem is resolved (question 5), encourage them to recall the conversation between Ruri and her mother at the end of the story.

Advanced Learners
Enrichment. Divide students into small groups to discuss other ways that the U.S. government might have dealt with the fear and suspicion felt toward Japanese Americans during World War II.
Activity. Have students come up with a proposal that would have both respected the rights of Japanese Americans and addressed the security concerns of the time.

STANDARDS FOCUS, pp. 78–85

(For the grade-level and review standards taught in this selection, see citations on Pupil's Edition pages.)

Summary *at grade level*

After the Japanese bombed Pearl Harbor, President Franklin D. Roosevelt authorized the relocation of Japanese Americans living near the West Coast. They were to be moved inland to internment camps. It took almost fifty years for the government to acknowledge the illegality and injustice of that action and to officially apologize to those former internees who were still alive. Along with a letter of apology from the president, each survivor received a check for twenty thousand dollars. The letter acknowledged that no sum of money could compensate for what the Japanese Americans had lost.

Resources Reminder

Media
- *Audio CD Library*
  - disc 2
- *Visual Connections*
  - Videocassette, Segment 2

Wartime Mistakes, Peacetime Apologies

Taking Logical Notes

Research. The word alone is enough to make some people squirm and groan. But if you know how to take logical notes, doing research is no problem.

Get a stack of index cards, and follow these steps:

1. Read through the selection once to find the main ideas.

2. Make a card for each main idea.

3. Take notes in your own words, or use quotation marks around the author's words.

As you read "Wartime Mistakes, Peacetime Apologies," look for the blanks on the model cards, and write down the missing word or words on a piece of paper. Take it one idea at a time.

Government officials registering Japanese Americans at a reception center in Los Angeles, California, 1942.

Reading Standard 2.4
Clarify an understanding of texts by creating logical notes.

78   Chapter 2   Characters: The People You'll Meet

RESOURCES

Planning
- *One-Stop Planner* CD-ROM with Test Generator
- *On Course: Mapping Instruction*

Media
- *Audio CD Library*
  - disc 2
- *Visual Connections*
  - Videocassette, Segment 2

Reading
- *Interactive Reading*
  - Graphic Organizer: Timeline, p. 70

Differentiating Instruction
- *Lesson Plans for Language Development*
  - English-Language Learners, pp. 34, 43, 47
  - Special Education Students, pp. 34, 43, 47

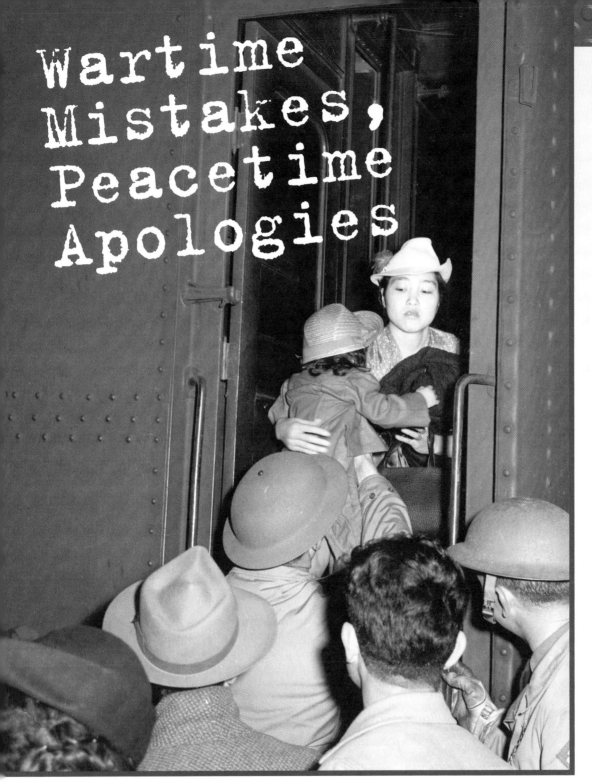

Wartime Mistakes, Peacetime Apologies

PRETEACHING

Standards Starter

Motivate. Ask students to share what they know about the unjust treatment of Japanese Americans during World War II. Invite students to speculate about the meaning of the title "Wartime Mistakes, Peacetime Apologies" and to predict who offered and who received apologies.

Assign the Reading

Invite students to skim through the article, noting the sidebars and note cards throughout. Read aloud the opening paragraph on p. 80 in class; then, assign the rest of the article as homework. In class the next day, model filling in the blanks of the first note card.

HOMEWORK

►Resources Reminder

Reading

■ *Interactive Reading*
  ▪ Graphic Organizer: Timeline, p. 70

Vocabulary and Spelling

■ *Vocabulary Development*
  ▪ Decoding Worksheet, p. 8
  ▪ Cumulative Vocabulary Review, p. 9

Assessment

■ *Progress Assessment of Reading*
  ▪ Selection Test, p. 27
■ *One-Stop Planner* CD-ROM with Test Generator

A Reading Informational Materials
GRADE-LEVEL STANDARD

Taking logical notes. After students have read the selection once and re-read this page, have them identify the main idea of this paragraph. [Imamoto and more than 120,000 other Japanese Americans were unfairly detained by an order issued by President Franklin D. Roosevelt.] **Then, regarding the first note card, ask:**

- When did something happen to Yoshiko Imamoto? [March 13, 1942]
- What happened? [The FBI arrested her with no warning.]
- Why was this unjust? [She had broken no laws.]

B Reading Informational Materials
GRADE-LEVEL STANDARD

Taking logical notes. Ask why the first two notes on the Pearl Harbor note card are important. [They tell what happened at Pearl Harbor, and when.] **Then, have students complete the second two notes.**

- Japanese Americans felt [caught in the middle].
- They were treated [with suspicion by neighbors and co-workers].

C Reading Informational Materials
GRADE-LEVEL STANDARD

Taking logical notes. Tell students to look for the appropriate passages in the text as they fill in the third note card.

- affected [more than 120,000 people of Japanese ancestry]
- issued [on February 19, 1942]
- allowed [the military to relocate people]
- never used [Japanese]
- Only [Japanese Americans] were moved.
- Most were moved [to prisonlike camps].

(A) On March 13, 1942, Yoshiko Imamoto opened her door to face three FBI agents. They let her pack a nightgown and a Bible, then took her to jail while they "checked into a few things." Imamoto had lived in America for twenty-four years. She was a teacher and had done nothing wrong. But a month earlier, President Franklin D. Roosevelt had issued Executive Order 9066, which drastically changed the lives of Imamoto and more than 120,000 other people of Japanese ancestry living in the United States.

(B) When Japan bombed Pearl Harbor on December 7, 1941, Japanese Americans were caught in the middle. They felt like Americans but looked like the enemy. Neighbors and co-workers eyed them suspiciously.

(C) Then Executive Order 9066, issued on February 19, 1942, authorized the exclusion of "any or all persons" from any areas the military chose. The word "Japanese" was never used, but the order was designed to allow the military to force Japanese Americans living near the coast to leave their homes for the duration of the war. Some were allowed to move inland, but most, like Yoshiko Imamoto, were herded into prisonlike camps.

Japanese American children wait for a train to take them to an internment camp.

Yoshiko Imamoto
- On _____ (when?), FBI arrested her with no warning.
- 24-year U.S. resident
- teacher
- had broken no laws

Pearl Harbor
- 12/7/1941
- Japan attacked U.S.
- Japanese Americans felt _____ (how?).
- They were treated _____ (how? by whom?).

Executive Order 9066
- issued by President Franklin D. Roosevelt
- affected _____ (how many?) people
- issued _____ (when?)
- allowed _____ (what?)
- never used _____ (what word?)
- Only _____ (who?) were moved.
- Most were moved _____ (where?).

DIFFERENTIATING INSTRUCTION

English-Language Learners
Explain that all U.S. government documents are written in legalese. Pair students, and have them go over the excerpt from Executive Order 9066 together, looking for the main subject and verbs. [Subject—I. Verbs—authorize, direct.] Then, take each subordinate clause in turn until students understand the whole sentence. Students should understand that Roosevelt's order authorized the military to designate certain areas as sensitive to national security. Within these areas, the military could remove people at will.

 Resources Reminder

For lessons designed for intermediate and advanced English-language learners, see *Lesson Plans for Language Development*, pp. 34, 43, 47.

I hereby authorize and direct the Secretary of War, and the Military Commanders whom he may from time to time designate, whenever he or any designated Commander deems such action necessary or desirable, to prescribe[1] military areas in such places and of such extent as he or the appropriate Military Commander may determine, from which any or all persons may be excluded, and with respect to which, the right of any person to enter, remain in, or leave shall be subject to whatever restrictions the Secretary of War or the appropriate Military Commander may impose in his discretion.[2]

—*President Franklin D. Roosevelt, excerpt from Executive Order 9066, 1942*

After the war, Japanese Americans tried to start over. They had lost their jobs, their property, and their pride. Some used the Japanese American Evacuation Claims Act of 1948 to get compensation[3] for property they had lost. But it was not until the late 1960s that cries for redress—compensation for all they had suffered—began to emerge.

In 1976, Executive Order 9066 was officially ended by President Gerald Ford. Four years later, President Jimmy Carter signed a bill that created the Commission on Wartime Relocation and Internment of Civilians (CWRIC) to investigate the relocation of Japanese Americans. The CWRIC concluded that Executive Order 9066 was "not justified by military necessity" but was the result of "race prejudice, war hysteria,

D

After the War
- Japanese Americans had lost _____ (what?).
- _____ (what?) was used by some Japanese Americans to claim payment for lost property.
- _____ (what?) began in the late 1960s.

E

9066 Ended—Investigation Begun
- _____ (who?) ended 9066 in _____ (when?).
- _____ (who?) authorized CWRIC _____ (to do what?).
- CWRIC recommended _____ (what?).

1. **prescribe** (prē·skrīb′) *v.*: define officially.
2. **in his discretion** (di·skresh′ən): according to his wishes or judgment.
3. **compensation** *n.*: payment given to make up for a loss or injury.

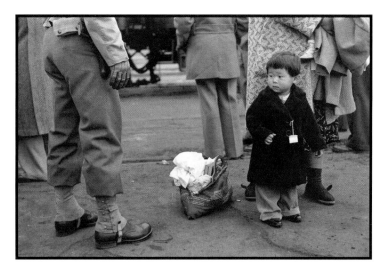

Ⓐ Reading Informational Materials
GRADE-LEVEL STANDARD
❓ Taking logical notes. Have students look at the "Repayment" note card. Why are the points listed on the note card important? [They identify the main supporters of the bill and the main objection to it.] Help students find the following data to fill in the blank on this sample note card.

■ Opponents argued that ["the government had acted legally and appropriately at the time."]

Ⓑ English-Language Learners
Understanding word origins. Point out the word *lobbying*. Ask whether students know what a *lobby* is. Explain that it is an entrance area of a public building and that *lobbying* is the name given to the activity of petitioning a public official because the *lobby* is the place where people can get access to him or her.

Ⓒ Reading Informational Materials
GRADE-LEVEL STANDARD
Taking logical notes. Ask students to summarize the paragraph on the court ruling. [Possible response: Three Japanese Americans won a lawsuit against the government for the relocation orders.] Have students use their summary to complete the first two notes on the card.

■ [Three Japanese Americans] took the government to court.
■ The court decided [the government's actions were illegal].

Then, have students complete the third note.

■ This ruling helped build support for [redress].

and a failure of political leadership." In 1983, the commission recommended to Congress that each surviving Japanese American evacuee be given a payment of twenty thousand dollars and an apology.

Ⓐ Ⓑ   A bill to authorize the payments was introduced in the House of Representatives in 1983 but met resistance. Intensive lobbying[4] by Japanese Americans was met by arguments that the government had acted legally and appropriately at the time.

Ⓒ   Meanwhile, three men who had long since served their jail sentences for refusing to comply with curfew[5] or relocation orders filed suit[6] to challenge the government's actions. The court ruled that the government had had no legal basis for detaining Japanese Americans.

---

4. **lobbying** *v.* used as *n.*: activity aimed at influencing public officials.
5. **curfew** (kur'fyōō') *n.*: Shortly before the relocation began, the head of the Western Defense Command, Lt. Gen. John DeWitt, set a curfew. Between 8:00 P.M. and 6:00 A.M. each day, "all persons of Japanese ancestry" had to remain indoors, off the streets.
6. **filed suit:** went to court in an attempt to recover something.

Repayment
• Bill introduced in House of Representatives in 1983.
• supported by Japanese Americans
• Opponents argued that _____ (what?).

Court Ruling
• _____ (who?) took the government to court.
• The court decided _____ (what?).
• This ruling helped build support for _____ (what?).

CONTENT-AREA CONNECTIONS

History
President Roosevelt. Franklin D. Roosevelt (1882–1945), the person who signed Executive Order 9066, was one of the most effective and controversial presidents in U.S. history. In addition to authorizing Executive Order 9066, he launched the New Deal, a series of ambitious economic initiatives designed to help people hurt by the Great Depression. Many business leaders objected to these initiatives and felt Roosevelt was leading the country toward socialism.

Activity. Invite students to research one of the controversial moves Roosevelt made during his presidency. You might suggest they examine his request to add more justices to the Supreme Court. Have individuals briefly report their findings to the class.

INDIVIDUAL

The rulings increased pressure to provide redress. In 1988, Congress approved the final version of the redress bill, which became known as the Civil Liberties Act. It was signed by President Ronald Reagan on August 10, 1988. Two years later, Congress funded the payments.

In 1990, at the age of ninety-three, Yoshiko Imamoto opened her door not to FBI agents, but to a small brown envelope containing a check for twenty thousand dollars and an apology from President George Bush. It had taken almost fifty years and the actions of four presidents, but the government had made redress and apologized for its mistakes.

—Nancy Day,
from *Cobblestone Magazine*

Add to Repayment card:
- Congress approved repayment bill in 1988.
- called Civil Liberties Act
- signed by _____ (whom?) _____ (when?)
- Payments were sent _____ (when?).

Add to Yoshiko Imamoto card:
- in 1990, received _____ (what?)
- She was 93 years old.
- It had taken _____ (how long?).
- It had taken the work of four presidents.

A monetary sum and words alone cannot restore lost years or erase painful memories; neither can they fully convey our Nation's resolve to rectify[7] injustice and to uphold the rights of individuals. We can never fully right the wrongs of the past. But we can take a clear stand for justice and recognize that serious injustices were done to Japanese Americans during World War II.

—President George Bush,
excerpt from letter accompanying
redress checks, 1990

7. **rectify** *v.*: correct.

D Reading Informational Materials
GRADE-LEVEL STANDARD
Taking logical notes. Ask students to look at the blanks on the top note card and fill in the missing information.
- **signed by** [President Ronald Reagan] [on August 10, 1988]
- **Payments were sent** [two years later in 1990].

E Reading Informational Materials
GRADE-LEVEL STANDARD
Taking logical notes. Point out that the information on the last note card is to be added to the Yoshiko Imamoto card. After students read the last paragraph, have them supply the missing information about Imamoto.
- **in 1990, received** [an apology and a payment of twenty thousand dollars]
- **It had taken** [fifty years].

F Reading Skills
❓ Comparing and contrasting. Have students compare and contrast the excerpt from President Bush's letter with the excerpt from President Roosevelt's Executive Order 9066. How are they different? Why are they different? [Possible responses: The language of the letter is personal, and the sentences are easy to understand. The language of the order is official, and the syntax and vocabulary are difficult. The differences in style exist because of the differences in purpose and audience. The letter was an apology to ordinary people who had suffered, while the 9066 was an official order directed to civil servants and the military.]

FAMILY/COMMUNITY ACTIVITY

Have students and their families discuss the United States' treatment of Japanese Americans during the war. Parents and grandparents can share any memories they have of life in the 1940s and 1950s in the United States. Do they recall instances of prejudice against Japanese Americans? How did they feel about Executive Order 9066? Do students' families feel that something like this might happen again in the United States, perhaps to a different ethnic group? Why or why not? You may wish to use this activity as a springboard to a whole-class discussion in which students can share ideas and opinions. Be sure students get permission before sharing family members' experiences with prejudice.

Reading Informational Materials

INDEPENDENT PRACTICE

Reading Informational Materials

Reading Check

1. The military could exclude anyone from any area.

2. The presidents who helped bring about "peacetime apologies" to Japanese Americans were Ford, Carter, Reagan, and Bush.

3. The CWRIC declared that the relocation of Japanese Americans was an unjust and unnecessary military action caused by racial prejudice, "war hysteria," and poor leadership.

4. The government gave each survivor a letter of apology from President Bush and a check for twenty thousand dollars.

Test Practice

Answers and Model Rationales

1. **A** The answer cannot be B because the article does not mention that Imamoto was a mother. The article says that Imamoto was ninety-three in 1990. In 1942, she would have been forty-five, and the article says she had lived in the United States for twenty-four years at that point. Thus, Imamoto came to the United States when she was around twenty-one.

2. **J** The letter is too formal and dignified to be called "friendly." It is too calm to be called "worried." The letter admits wrong without bitterness or resentment, so it is not "angry." Thus, by a process of elimination, students should see that J is correct.

3. **A** The article states that Japanese Americans lobbied for redress and that those who supported the government's 1942

Reading Check

Use your note cards to answer these questions. Revise your note cards if they don't have enough information.

1. What powers did Executive Order 9066 give the military?

2. Which presidents helped bring about the U.S. government's "peacetime apologies" to Japanese Americans?

3. What were the results of the CWRIC's investigation?

4. What did the government finally do for interned Japanese Americans?

Test Practice

Wartime Mistakes, Peacetime Apologies

1. From information in the article, you can conclude that Yoshiko Imamoto came to the United States when she was —
   A   a young woman
   B   a mother with a young child
   C   a baby
   D   a child

2. What is the **tone** of the letter the government sent with the payments?
   F   Friendly
   G   Angry
   H   Worried
   J   Apologetic

3. Discussion of a redress bill caused **conflict** between —
   A   Japanese Americans and people who felt that the government had done nothing wrong
   B   Japanese American members of Congress and other elected officials
   C   people who had been evacuated and veterans of World War II
   D   Congress and the Supreme Court

4. Which of the following is a **main idea** that could be a heading on a note card?
   F   Yoshiko Imamoto arrested
   G   Japan attacked United States
   H   Compensation ordered
   J   Pearl Harbor

5. Which sentence best **summarizes** Executive Order 9066?
   A   Military commanders must follow the instructions given by the secretary of war.
   B   When an area of any size is put under military control, all civilians in that area must be evacuated.
   C   The military may set aside certain areas and decide who enters, stays, or leaves those areas.
   D   Japanese Americans must leave California.

Reading Standard 2.4
Clarify an understanding of texts by creating logical notes.

policy disagreed with them. Therefore, A is correct.

4. **J** While F, G, and H would likely be notes under different main ideas in the essay, only J qualifies as a main idea.

5. **C** Students should see that A, B, and D all use the word *must*, but Executive Order 9066 left things to the discretion of the military. Thus, C is correct.

Test-Taking Tips

For information on how to answer multiple-choice items, refer students to **Test Smarts**, p. 690.

Vocabulary Development

Excluded People, Excluded Words

Japanese Americans were not the only group to face hostility during World War II. Germany, like Japan, was at war with the United States, and German Americans also experienced prejudice.

Some German Americans responded by changing their names—from Stein to Stone, for example, or from Knoebel to Noble. Some German-sounding street names were changed too. Even everyday words that had German origins or were connected in some way to Germany were replaced in the name of patriotism. Here are some examples:

Original		Replacement
dachshund	→	liberty pup
frankfurter	→	hot dog
German measles	→	liberty measles
German shepherd	→	Alsatian
hamburger	→	Salisbury steak

PRACTICE

With the class, study the words listed above. Which of the replacements are still in use today? Which of the original words have returned to everyday use? Using a good dictionary, try to find the origin of both the original words and the replacements. Which words come from the names of German cities? Why does *ham* appear in a word for ground *beef*?

Wartime Mistakes, Peacetime Apologies **85**

Vocabulary Development

Practice

- Words still in use today: *hot dog, Salisbury steak*
- All of the original words have returned to everyday use.
- Word origins:
  dachshund—Ger. *dachs,* badger + *hund,* dog.
  frankfurter—named after the German city of Frankfurt.
  hamburger—named after the German city and state of Hamburg.
  hot dog—U.S. named for its resemblance to a dachshund.
  liberty pup, liberty measles, and *Salisbury steak*—U.S. names arose during World War I; with the United States at war with Germany, there was a movement to eliminate German words from American vocabulary.
- Words that come from the names of German cities: *frankfurter* (Frankfurt), *hamburger* (Hamburg)
- The word *ham* appears in a word for ground beef because the word *hamburger* comes from the term *Hamburg steak,* and steak is beef.

Resources Reminder

Vocabulary and Spelling
- *Vocabulary Development*
  - Decoding Worksheet, p. 8
  - Cumulative Vocabulary Review, p. 9
- *Lesson Plans for Language Development*
  - Vocabulary, p. 47

ASSESSING

Assessment
- *Progress Assessment of Reading*
  - Selection Test, p. 27

STANDARDS FOCUS, pp. 86–89

(For the grade-level standard taught in this lesson, see citations on Pupil's Edition pages.)

Prerequisite Standard

■ Grade 5, Reading Comprehension 2.3 **Discern main ideas and concepts presented in texts, identifying and assessing evidence that supports those ideas.**

Summary ⬇ *below grade level*

The 442nd Regimental Combat Team, a segregated unit of the U.S. Army that fought in World War II, was made up of soldiers of Japanese descent from Hawaii and the mainland. At first the two groups did not get along, but when the Hawaiians visited an internment camp in Arkansas and saw the shabby way that mainland Japanese Americans were being treated, the two groups came together and dedicated themselves to proving that they were good U.S. soldiers. The 442nd fought on the battlefields of Europe and was among the most highly decorated units in U.S. military history. However, it is the regiment's dedication to and sacrifice for their country, not their medals, that has shone through history.

▶ Resources Reminder

Media
■ *Audio CD Library*
  ▪ disc 2

Go for Broke: The Purple-Heart Team

Creating Summaries to Clarify Understanding

Does this situation sound familiar? You see a friend at lunch and ask, "How was the movie?" And then you hear how it was—scene by scene, word by word, detail by endless detail. You were really asking to hear a summary, which would touch on the important points and leave out all those details. A **summary** is a short restatement of the important events and characters in a narrative or the main ideas in a work of nonfiction. Here's a summary of a story, "The Bracelet" (for the complete story, see page 70):

Summary of a Short Story

"The Bracelet" by Yoshiko Uchida is a short story set on the West Coast during World War II. The main character is a Japanese American girl named Ruri, who, along with her family, is forced to leave her home and live in an internment camp. Before she leaves, Ruri receives a bracelet from Laurie, her best friend. Ruri loses the bracelet at the camp, and for a long time she is upset. She keeps looking for the bracelet but never finds it. She comes to realize that she does not need objects like the bracelet to remember the beloved people and things she had to leave behind.

State title and author.

Name main character and setting (if important). Sum up basic situation.

State problem character faces.

Briefly restate main events.

Describe character's discovery (theme of story).

Reading Standard 2.4 Clarify an understanding of texts by creating summaries.

Japanese American soldiers stationed in Italy during World War II.

86

RESOURCES

Planning
■ *One-Stop Planner* CD-ROM with Test Generator
■ *On Course: Mapping Instruction*

Media
■ *Audio CD Library*
  ▪ disc 2

Reading
■ *Interactive Reading*
  ▪ Graphic Organizer: Notes Organizer, p. 71

Differentiating Instruction
■ *Lesson Plans for Language Development*
  ▪ English-Language Learners, pp. 35, 44, 47
  ▪ Special Education Students, pp. 35, 44, 47

Summarizing an Informational Text

You can summarize any piece of writing, fiction or nonfiction. Creating summaries of informational materials is especially useful if you are doing research from a number of sources. Reviewing your summaries will help you recognize ways one source differs from another.

As you read "Go for Broke: The Purple-Heart Team," the article that follows, make a cluster diagram like the one below. Use it to record the most important ideas in the article. Some of the ideas in the article have been recorded in this cluster diagram.

To find more information for your cluster, stop at the end of each paragraph and retell the main points. Then, put those points in your cluster. When you're finished reading, write down each main idea and circle it. Finally, connect ideas that belong together, and cross out minor points. Which idea in the cluster diagram would you cross out?

The 442nd Regimental Combat Team being honored in November 1944 for their bravery in battle.

Standards Starter

Build prerequisite skills. Remind students that in order to find the main idea of a paragraph they should ask themselves, "Which sentence gives the key information on the topic?" Have students use the following checklist to look over their cluster diagrams:

■ Have I circled the main ideas I want to include in my summary?

■ Have I crossed out minor points?

■ Have I connected ideas that go together?

▶ Resources Reminder

Reading

■ *Interactive Reading*
  ■ Graphic Organizer: Notes Organizer, p. 71

Assessment

■ *Progress Assessment of Reading*
  ■ Selection Test, p. 29
■ *One-Stop Planner* CD-ROM with Test Generator

A Content-Area Connections
HISTORY

The Purple Heart. Tell students that the Purple Heart is a medal given to every U.S. soldier wounded in combat.

B Reading Informational Materials
GRADE-LEVEL STANDARD

❓ Creating summaries. How would you summarize this long paragraph? [Possible response: Once the Hawaiian soldiers of Japanese descent learned about the internment camps, relations between them and the Japanese American soldiers from the mainland became more friendly.]

C Reading Informational Materials
GRADE-LEVEL STANDARD

❓ Creating summaries. How would you connect the ideas of "highly decorated" and "injustice to the families" with other ideas in your cluster diagram? [Connect "highly decorated" to "442nd" circle; connect "injustice to the families" to "men from mainland" circle.]

D Reading Informational Materials
REVIEW STANDARD

Discerning the main idea. Have students restate the main idea of this paragraph. [In spite of the way the U.S. government had treated their families, Japanese American soldiers were among the bravest and most dedicated in U.S. military history.]

E Reading Informational Materials
GRADE-LEVEL STANDARD

❓ Creating summaries. Would you include information from this letter in your summary? Why or why not? [Possible responses: No, because it is simply supporting evidence for the major point made in the previous paragraph. Yes, the letter shows the depth of a soldier's appreciation for his nation.]

Go for Broke
A *The Purple-Heart Team*
by Flo Ota De Lange

The motto of the 442nd Regimental Combat Team was "Go for Broke," a Hawaiian slang phrase that means "Give it your all." And that's what these men did.

The 442nd Regimental Combat Team was a segregated U.S. Army unit that fought in World War II. It was made up of Japanese Americans from the mainland and Hawaii. When these two groups first got together in 1943 at Camp Shelby in Mississippi, they didn't get along. The mainland men thought that the Hawaiians didn't speak English very well; the Hawaiians were B unaware that the families of the men from the mainland had been imprisoned in internment camps set up for Japanese Americans C during the war. So there was a fair amount of conflict between the two groups until both groups visited a detention camp for Japanese Americans in Jerome D Arkansas. There the Hawaiians saw what was troubling the men from the mainland, and problems between the two groups ceased.

During their time at Camp Shelby, the men of the 442nd decided that they would all complete every assignment that came their way. So if they were sent on a twenty-five-mile march and one of the men faltered because of heat stroke, another man would take the sick man's rifle, a second man would take his pack, and, if necessary, still others would pick him up and carry him to their destination so that they could all complete the assignment.

The 442nd Regimental Combat Team was one of the most highly decorated units in U.S. military history. The men of the 442nd, who numbered 4,500 at full strength, earned more than 3,900 decorations. But what made the men of the 442nd special wasn't their medals; it was the bravery and dedication they showed in spite of the injustice that had been done to them and their families. Simply because of their ancestry, Japanese Americans were suspected of being spies. While they were being accused of disloyalty, denied due process, and forced to leave their homes, their sons were serving with distinction in the U.S. Army.

Frank Hachiya, a member of the 442nd, longed to get home to Hood River, Oregon, but before he could leave the battlefields of Europe and join his family in Oregon, he was killed by a sniper. At his funeral, Frank's eighth-grade teacher, Martha Ferguson McKune, read from a letter Frank had written her from overseas:

E *I read where some people stated that they did not fully appreciate their country until they had traveled abroad, and I realize it now. . . . I am not very handy with words. . . . The love of one's country—it is a strange and mystifying thing. When I look back over life . . . and think of the time I have wasted in ignorance of how to live . . . how I did not value time . . . it hurts me now. I am aware of the fact of life as a gift. I shall be grateful for one thing to the war, that is in making me realize life.*

Have students ask military veterans in their families or neighborhoods about their experiences in the service. Did they ever have to serve with soldiers they didn't like? How did being in the military build trust and rapport? Students can compare and contrast the stories they hear with the story of the 442nd.

Reading Informational Materials

Reading Standard 2.4 Clarify an understanding of texts by creating summaries.

Reading Check: Creating a Summary

Write a summary of "Go for Broke." Use the connected ideas in your cluster diagram to decide on the main points you want to include in your summary and the order you want to put them in. Before you start writing, ask yourself, "What is the main idea the author is trying to communicate?"

When you're finished, re-read your summary, or ask someone else to read it. Is the author's message clearly stated? Is there enough information in the summary, or is there too much?

Grammar Link MINI-LESSON

Watch Your *Don't*s and *Doesn't*s

- The words *don't* and *doesn't* are contractions of *do not* and *does not*. Use *don't* with all plural subjects and with the pronouns *I* and *you*.

  I don't [do not] like writing summaries.

  You don't [do not] mind writing summaries.

  Many students don't [do not] know how to write summaries.

- Use *doesn't* with all singular subjects except *I* and *you*.

  Shawn doesn't [does not] like romance novels.

  He doesn't [does not] like poetry either.

  It doesn't [does not] seem important to him.

Tip: If you don't know which contraction to use, try substituting *does not* and *do not,* and see which one sounds right.

  He [does not/do not] like poetry either.

You wouldn't say, "He do not . . . ," so it is *wrong* to say, "He don't [do not] like poetry either."

  It [does not/do not] seem important to him.

You wouldn't say, "It do not . . . ," so it is *wrong* to say, "It don't seem important to him."

PRACTICE

Choose the correct verb for each sentence. If you are unsure, substitute the phrases *do not* and *does not* to see if they sound right.

1. It doesn't/don't seem fair that the 442nd was discriminated against.
2. If Frank Hachiya's letter doesn't/don't move you, you must be coldhearted.
3. Some people doesn't/don't realize how much others suffer from prejudice.
4. My friend doesn't/don't believe what I tell him.

For more help, see Problems in Agreement in the *Holt Handbook*, pages 127–137.

Reading Informational Materials

Reading Check

Suggest to students that they order the article's main points by numbering those parts of the diagram consecutively. This step will help them make sure that their summaries list all of the main points of the article in the correct order. Then, urge students to re-read the article one more time, looking for the central idea or underlying message. [Possible summary: See summary on p. 86.]

Grammar Link

Practice

1. It [doesn't] seem fair that the 442nd was discriminated against.
2. If Frank Hachiya's letter [doesn't] move you, you must be cold-hearted.
3. Some people [don't] realize how much others suffer from prejudice.
4. My friend [doesn't] believe what I tell him.

ASSESSING

Assessment
- *Progress Assessment of Reading*
  - Selection Test, p. 29

STANDARDS FOCUS, pp. 90–107

(For grade-level and review standards taught in this lesson, see citations on Pupil's Edition pages.)

Prerequisite Standard

■ Grade 5, Literary Response and Analysis 3.3 **Contrast the actions, motives (e.g., loyalty, selfishness, conscientiousness), and appearances of characters in a work of fiction, and discuss the importance of the contrasts to the plot or theme.**

Standard Coming Up in the Next Grade Level

■ Grade 7, Literary Response and Analysis 3.3 **Analyze characterization as delineated through a character's thoughts, words, speech patterns, and actions; the narrator's description; and the thoughts, words, and actions of other characters.**

Reading Skills

■ Make inferences.

Summary *at grade level*

In this play the young hero, Juanito, leaves his home to seek his fortune. Walking through a forest, he first encounters a *duende*, a mischievous, magical creature. He then meets a virtuous young woman with magical powers, Blanca Flor, whom the evil Don Ricardo has imprisoned. Juanito tries to win Blanca Flor's freedom but fails at the impossible tasks. She intercedes, performing the tasks, and the two flee, but not before Don Ricardo brings a curse upon them that causes Juanito to forget Blanca Flor. In the end, however, the two are happily reunited.

▶ Resources Reminder

Media

■ *Audio CD Library*
  ■ disc 3
■ *Fine Art Transparencies*
  ■ Transparency 5

Blanca Flor

Literary Focus
Characterization

Making characters come alive is one of the writer's most important and most difficult tasks. How do writers build characters out of words? They

- tell us directly what the character is like (good, evil, kind, sneaky)
- let the character talk
- describe the character's appearance
- show the character in action
- tell us what the character thinks
- show us how others respond to the character

In *Blanca Flor*, for example, the writer tells us directly that Don Ricardo is evil. He also tells us directly about the Duende (dwen'de). To find out what he says, check the list of characters at the beginning of the play.

Reading Skills
Making Inferences About Character

Reading Standard 3.2 Analyze the effect of the qualities of the character (for example, courage or cowardice, ambition or laziness) on the plot.

You can use a graphic organizer like the one on the right to analyze the characters you meet in stories. Fill out a chart like the one at the top of the next column as you read *Blanca Flor* or when you review the play after your first reading. Once you have gathered your clues, look over your chart carefully. Then, write down a word or two naming the most important qualities of each character you have met.

Character [Name]:
Writer's direct comments:
Character's words:
Character's looks:
Character's actions:
Character's thoughts:
Responses of others:

Make the Connection

The play you're about to read, *Blanca Flor*, is based on an old European story. The story's bare-bones plot could be summed up as "boy meets girl, boy loses girl, boy wins girl (or girl wins boy)." What movies and TV shows have you seen recently that can be summed up that way? Do most of these boy-meets-girl or girl-meets-boy plots turn out happily?

Quickwrite ✏

Think of stories you know—children's stories, novels, stories on TV and in the movies. Work with a partner, and see if you can find examples of these popular character types:

- the strong hero or heroine
- the evil villain
- the innocent child
- the person with special powers
- the lovers in danger
- the helpful animal character
- the liar

RESOURCES

Planning
■ *One-Stop Planner* CD-ROM with Test Generator
■ *On Course: Mapping Instruction*

Media
■ *Audio CD Library*
  ■ disc 3
■ *Fine Art Transparencies*
  ■ Transparency 5

Reading
■ *Interactive Reading*
  ■ Graphic Organizer: Story Frame and Character Chart, p. 72

Differentiating Instruction
■ *Lesson Plans for Language Development*
  ■ English-Language Learners, pp. 36–38, 45, 48
  ■ Special Education Students, pp. 39, 45, 48

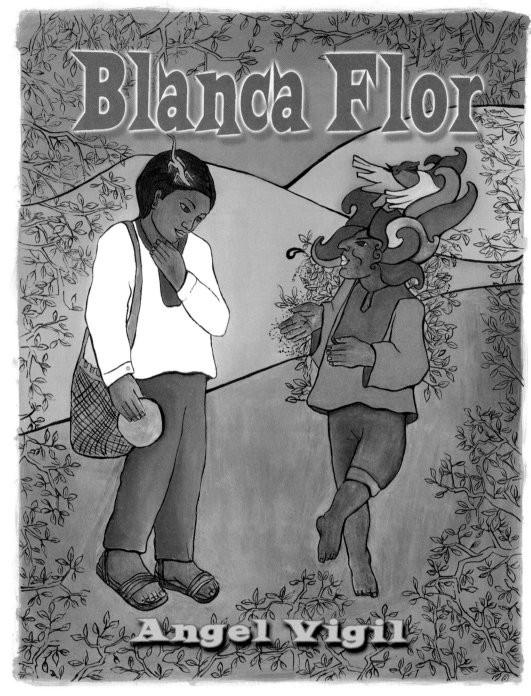

Blanca Flor

Angel Vigil

Standards Starter

Build background. It might interest students to know that the play is based on the folk drama tradition of the Hispanic Southwest, which dates back to the Spanish colonial period in the United States.

Assign the Reading

Assign each of the characters in Scenes 1 and 2 to students who will read aloud while the rest of the class follows along, reading silently. Then, allow most students to continue reading independently. Assign the Focus On questions for Scenes 1–5 (p. 98) and Scenes 6–10 (p. 106) as homework. Meanwhile, work with small groups of students having difficulty.

HOMEWORK

Assessment
- *Progress Assessment of Reading*
  - Selection Test, p. 31
- *One-Stop Planner* CD-ROM with Test Generator

A Vocabulary Development
GRADE-LEVEL STANDARD
Using Spanish words in English.
If you have Spanish-speaking students in your class, ask one to pronounce the names of the characters aloud.

B Literary Focus
GRADE-LEVEL STANDARD
❓ **Characterization.** How does the author reveal what Juanito is like? [He lets us hear Juanito think out loud.]

C Vocabulary Development
GRADE-LEVEL STANDARD
Using Spanish words in English.
Have non-Spanish-speaking students use context clues and cognates to figure out the meaning of the Spanish words *la familia* ("the family") and *mamacita* (an affectionate term for "mother").

D Reading Skills
❓ **Making inferences.** Say, "Oh, and don't forget . . . a dried-out tortilla," in the ironic tone of voice Juanito might use. Then, ask students, "What character trait does Juanito's remark reveal?" [He has a sense of humor.]

Characters
(in order of appearance)

The Narrator

Juanito, a young man

The Duende, a gnomelike, mischievous creature who lives in the forest

Blanca Flor, a young woman

Don[1] Ricardo, an evil man

Don Ramon, the father of Juanito

Doña[2] Arlette, the mother of Juanito

Two Doves, actors in costume

Scene 1.
IN THE FOREST.

The Narrator. *Blanca Flor*, "White Flower." There never was a story with such a beautiful name as this story of Blanca Flor. At the beginning of our story, a young man named Juanito has left home to seek his fortune in the world. With the blessing of his parents to aid and protect him, he has begun what will be a fantastic adventure. At the beginning of his journey, he wanders into a forest and stops by a stream to rest and eat some of the tortillas his mother had packed for his journey.

[JUANITO *enters and walks around the stage as if looking for a comfortable place to rest. He finally decides upon a spot and sits down. He takes out a tortilla from his traveling bag and he begins to talk to himself.*]

---

1. **Don** (dän): Spanish for "Sir" or "Mr."
2. **Doña** (dô'nyä): Spanish for "Lady" or "Madam."

Juanito. Whew! I'm hot. This river looks like a good spot to rest for a while. I'm so tired. Maybe this journey wasn't such a good idea. Right now I could be home with *la familia* eating a good supper that *mamacita* cooked for us. But no, I'm out in the world seeking my fortune. So far I haven't found very much, and all I have to show for my efforts are two worn-out feet and a tired body . . . oh, and don't forget (*holding up a dried tortilla*) a dried-out tortilla . . . (*He quickly looks around as if startled.*) What was that? (*He listens intently and hears a sound again.*) There it is again. I know I heard something . . .

[As JUANITO *is talking*, THE DUENDE *enters, sneaking up behind him.*]

Juanito. Must be my imagination. I've been out in the woods too long. You know, if you're alone too long, your mind starts to play tricks on you. Just look at me. I'm talking to my tortilla and hearing things . . .
The Duende (*in a crackly voice*). Hello.
Juanito. Yikes! Who said that! (*He turns around quickly and is startled to see* THE DUENDE *behind him.*) Who are you?
The Duende (*with a mischievous twinkle in his eye*). Hello.
Juanito. Hello . . . who, who are you? And where did you come from?

[THE DUENDE *grabs the tortilla out of* JUANITO'*s hand and begins to eat it. During the rest of the scene* THE DUENDE *continues to eat tortillas.*]

Juanito. Hey, that's my tortilla.
The Duende (*in a playful manner*). Thank you very much. Thank you very much.
Juanito (*to the audience*). He must be a forest Duende. I've heard of them. They're spirits who live in the wood and play tricks

---

Learners Having Difficulty
Modeling. To help students read *Blanca Flor*, you may wish to model the reading skill of making inferences. This skill can help students recognize the qualities of the characters. Read Juanito's first speech aloud. Then, say: "From what Juanito says and does here, I would guess that he may give up easily when the going gets tough. I'll read on to see if the inference I made

about this character is correct." Then, have students apply the skill as they read *Blanca Flor*. As they read, encourage them to ask themselves, "What qualities of the character might these words and actions suggest?"

 Resources Reminder
Reading
■ *Interactive Reading*

■ Graphic Organizer: Story Frame and Character Chart, p. 72

English-Language Learners
Students whose first language is Spanish can enrich the class's experience of *Blanca Flor* by clarifying elements of Latin American culture in the play. For English-language learners from other cultures, explain that the play comes from the

on humans. I better go along with him or he might hurt me. (*He offers* THE DUENDE *another tortilla.* THE DUENDE *takes the tortilla and begins to eat it, too.*) I hope he's not too hungry. If he eats all my tortillas, I won't have any left, and it'll be days before I get food again. I'll have to eat wild berries like an animal. (*He reaches for the tortilla and* THE DUENDE *hits his hand.*) Ouch, that hurt!

The Duende. Looking for work, eh?

Juanito. Now I know he's a Duende. He can read minds.

The Duende. No work here. Lost in the forest. No work here.

Juanito. I know that. We're in the middle of the forest. But I know there'll be work in the next town.

The Duende. Maybe work right here. Maybe.

Juanito. Really. Where?

[THE DUENDE *points to a path in the forest.* JUANITO *stands up and looks down the path.*]

Juanito. There's nothing down that path. I've been down that path and there is nothing there.

The Duende. Look again. Look again. Be careful. Be careful. (*He begins to walk off, carrying the bag of tortillas with him.*)

Juanito. Hey, don't leave yet. What type of work? And where? Who do I see? Hey, don't leave yet!

The Duende (THE DUENDE *stops and turns*). Be careful. Danger. Danger. (*He exits.*)

Juanito. Hey! That's my bag of tortillas. Oh, this is great. This is really going to sound good when I get back home. My tortillas? . . . Oh, they were stolen by a forest Duende. Not to worry . . . (*He yells in the direction of the departed* DUENDE.) And I'm not lost! . . . This is great. Lost and hungry and

no work. I guess I'm never going to find my fortune in the world. But what did he mean about work . . . and be careful . . . and danger. I've been down that path and there was nothing there . . . I don't think there was anything there. Oh well, there is only one way to find out. It certainly can't get much worse than things are now, and maybe there is work there.

[JUANITO *exits, in the direction of the path* THE DUENDE *indicated.*]

Scene 2.
FARTHER IN THE FOREST.

The Narrator. In spite of the Duende's warning, Juanito continued on the path of danger. As he came into a clearing, he came to a house and saw a young woman coming out of it.

[JUANITO *enters,* BLANCA FLOR *enters from the opposite side of the stage and stops, remaining at the opposite side of the stage.*]

Juanito. Where did this house come from? I was here just yesterday and there was no house here. I must really be lost and turned around. (*He sees the young woman and waves to her.*) Hey! Come here. Over here!

[BLANCA FLOR *runs to* JUANITO.]

Blanca Flor (*with fear in her voice*). How did you find this place? You must leave right away. The owner of this place is gone, but he will return soon. He leaves to do his work in the world, but he will return unexpectedly. If he finds you here, you'll never be able to leave. You must leave right away.

Juanito. Why? I haven't done anything.

Blanca Flor. Please, just leave. And hurry!

Blanca Flor, Scenes 1–5 **93**

Hispanic culture of the Southwest. Then, concentrate on the English in the text.

Special Education Students
For lessons designed for special education students, see *Lesson Plans for Language Development*, pp. 39, 45, 48.

Advanced Learners
Acceleration. Use this activity to move advanced learners toward the seventh-

grade Standard 3.3, which requires that they analyze characterization. Explain that static characters stay the same throughout a story, whereas dynamic characters grow and change as real people do. As students read, have them note any examples of growth in Juanito, Blanca Flor, and Don Ricardo.

DIRECT TEACHING

E Reading Skills

❓ Making inferences. Remind students that earlier in the story, Juanito went along with the Duende out of fear that the Duende might hurt him. How does Juanito seem to feel about the Duende now? [He no longer fears the Duende.] How do you know? [He tries to order the Duende around.]

F Literary Focus
GRADE-LEVEL STANDARD
Characterization. Ask students to cite examples of Juanito's sense of humor. [Possible responses: "Oh, this is great. This is really going to sound good when I get back home"; "Oh, they were stolen by a forest Duende. Not to worry . . ."] Then, ask how his sense of humor helps him. [Possible response: It helps him stay upbeat despite the loss of his food.]

G Literary Focus
REVIEW STANDARD
❓ Cause and effect in plots. Juanito chooses a certain path because the Duende points that way. What effect might Juanito's choice have? [Possible response: He might find trouble, since the Duende is mischievous. (The actual effect, though, is his meeting Blanca Flor, precipitating the rest of the play.)]

H Literary Focus
GRADE-LEVEL STANDARD
Characterization. Everyone but Juanito seems to understand that this is a fairy tale, complete with magic, a villain, a fair maiden, and a potential hero (Juanito himself). Encourage students to notice, as they continue reading, how some characters don't quite fit the standard roles. For example, at this point, Juanito seems a somewhat dim hero.

DIRECT TEACHING

A Reading Skills

❓ Making inferences. What can you infer about Blanca Flor's qualities, based on these words and actions? [She is kind, unselfish, and courageous.]

B Literary Focus
GRADE-LEVEL STANDARD

❓ Characterization. How does the author use Juanito's response to Don Ricardo to emphasize Don Ricardo's "bad guy" nature? [Possible response: Juanito's "gathering all his courage" to answer Don Ricardo emphasizes how intimidating Don Ricardo is.]

C Reading Skills

❓ Making predictions. What do you predict will happen when Juanito tries to do the tasks? [Possible responses: He's the hero and in fairy tales anything is possible; he'll succeed at one of the tasks and free Blanca Flor; he'll fail and be rescued by Blanca Flor or the Duende.]

Juanito. Who are you? And why are you here?

Blanca Flor. I am Blanca Flor. My parents died long ago, and I am kept by this man to pay off their debts to him. I have to work day and night on his farm until I can be free. But he is mean, and he has kept prisoner others who have tried to free me. He makes them work until they die from exhaustion.

Juanito. Who would be so mean?

Blanca Flor. His name is Don Ricardo.

[DON RICARDO *enters, suddenly and with great force.*]

Don Ricardo (*addressing* JUANITO). Why are you here! Didn't she tell you to leave!

Blanca Flor (*scared*). Don't hurt him. He is lost in the forest and got here by mistake. He was just leaving.

Don Ricardo. Let him answer for himself. Then I will decide what to do with him.

Juanito (*gathering all his courage*). Yes, she did tell me to leave. But . . . but I am in the world seeking my fortune and I am looking for work. Is there any work for me to do here?

Don Ricardo. Seeking your fortune! They always say that, don't they, Blanca Flor. Well, I will give you the same chance I have given others. For each of three days, I will give you a job. If in three days you have completed the jobs, then you may leave. If not, then you will work here with me until you are dead. What do you say, fortune-seeker?

Blanca Flor (*pulling* JUANITO *aside*). Do not say yes. You will never leave here alive. Run and try to escape.

Juanito. But what about you? You are more trapped than anybody.

94 Chapter 2 Characters: The People You'll Meet

Blanca Flor. That is not your worry. Just run and try to escape.

Juanito (*suddenly turning back to* DON RICARDO). I will do the work you ask.

Don Ricardo (*laughing*). Blanca Flor, it is always your fault they stay. They all think they will be able to set you free. Well, let's give this one his "fair" chance. (*To* JUANITO) Here is your first job. See that lake over there? Take this thimble (*he gives a thimble to* JUANITO) and use it to carry all the water in the lake to that field over there.

Juanito. You want me to move a lake with a thimble?!

Don Ricardo. You wanted work, fortune-seeker. Well, this is your job. Have it finished by morning or your fate will be the same as all the others who tried to save poor Blanca Flor. (*He exits.*)

Juanito. What type of man is he? I have heard legends of evil men who keep people captive, and in my travels I heard many stories of young men seeking their fortunes who were never seen again, but I always thought they were just stories.

Blanca Flor. You have had the misfortune to get lost in a terrible part of the forest. Didn't anyone warn you to stay away from here?

Juanito. Yes . . . one person did. But I thought he was a forest Duende, and I didn't really believe him.

Blanca Flor. It was a forest Duende. In this part of the forest there are many creatures with magic. But my keeper, his magic is stronger than any of ours.

Juanito. Ours? . . . What do you mean, ours? Are you part of the magic of this forest?

Blanca Flor. Do not ask so many questions. The day is passing by, and soon it will be morning.

Juanito. Morning. I'm supposed to have moved the lake by then. I know this job is impossible, but while God is in his heaven there is a way. I will do this job. And when I am done, I will help you escape from here.

[JUANITO *and* BLANCA FLOR *exit.*]

Scene 3.
THE NEXT MORNING.

JUANITO *and* BLANCA FLOR *enter. As* THE NARRATOR *speaks,* JUANITO *and* BLANCA FLOR *act out the scene as it is described.*

The Narrator. Juanito took the thimble and started to carry the water from the lake. He worked as hard as he could, but soon he began to realize that the job really was an impossible one, and he knew he was doomed. He sat down and began to cry because his luck had abandoned him and because his parents' blessings offered no protection in that evil place. Blanca Flor watched Juanito's valiant effort to move the water. As she watched him crying, her heart was touched, and she decided to use her powers to help him. She knew that it was very dangerous to use her powers to help Juanito and to cross Don Ricardo, but she felt it was finally time to end her own torment. As Juanito cried, Blanca Flor took out her brush and began to brush his hair. She cradled Juanito in her arms and her soothing comfort soon put him to sleep . . .

[*As soon as* JUANITO *is asleep,* BLANCA FLOR *gently puts his head down and leaves, taking the thimble with her.*]

The Narrator. When Juanito awoke, he frantically looked for the thimble and, not finding it, ran to the lake. When he reached the lake, he stood at its banks in amazement.

Blanca Flor, Scenes 1–5 **95**

DIRECT TEACHING

D Literary Focus
REVIEW STANDARD
Archetypal elements: Motif.
Explain that impossible tasks, such as moving a lake with a thimble, are a common fairy tale motif—an element that recurs in tales throughout the world. Ask students what other impossible tasks they know from fairy tales. [Possible response: spinning straw into gold.]

E Reading Skills
? Making inferences. Point out Blanca Flor's comment that "his magic is stronger than any of ours." Ask students what Blanca Flor's use of the word *ours* might imply about her. [Possible response: that she belongs to a group of magical people.] Ask students, "Does Juanito seem to catch that implication? How can you tell?" [Yes, because he asks her, "Are you part of the magic of this forest?"]

F Literary Focus
GRADE-LEVEL STANDARD
? Characterization. What qualities does Juanito show with this speech? [Possible responses: a kind heart; courage.] Point out to students that Juanito's stepping more into the role of hero—he has just vowed to rescue the fair maiden—advances the plot by putting him into direct conflict with the evil Don Ricardo.

G Literary Focus
REVIEW STANDARD
? Comparing characters. How are Juanito and Blanca Flor different from the standard hero and fair maiden? [Unlike the standard hero, Juanito sits down and cries. Unlike the standard fair maiden, Blanca Flor is quite powerful and decides to take matters into her own hands rather than waiting to be rescued.]

DEVELOPING FLUENCY

Activity. Create up to six mixed-ability groups, each with four or more students. Then, read all or part of the play aloud as a class, having each group share one character's role. Encourage group members to devise equitable and comfortable ways to divide up their lines. They may decide that they will take turns in a certain order, that each group member will read a certain number of lines, or that members will use a preset signal when they are ready for the next member to take over. Encourage students to enjoy themselves by hamming it up when they find melodrama in their lines.

MIXED-ABILITY

Ⓐ Literary Focus
GRADE-LEVEL STANDARD

Characterization. Ask students how the stage directions emphasize Don Ricardo's villainy. [He is described as "in full force and very angry"and then as exiting "with a flourish." You can practically see him swirling a cloak and twirling the ends of his moustache.]

Ⓑ Reading Skills

❓ **Making predictions.** What is likely to happen while Juanito is asleep, based on what happened the last time he fell asleep under the spell of Blanca Flor's hairbrush? [Possible response: The rocks will be moved, seeds planted, wheat grown and harvested and then ground and baked into bread.]

Ⓒ Literary Focus
GRADE-LEVEL STANDARD

❓ **Characterization.** How does the author let the reader know the emotions that Juanito and Don Ricardo are feeling? [He uses stage directions for the actors: Juanito is "shaking with fear," and Don Ricardo is "very angry."] How does Don Ricardo's anger advance the plot? [Possible response: It makes him try harder to thwart Juanito.]

Ⓓ Literary Focus
REVIEW STANDARD

❓ **Comparing characters.** Who has the role of rescuer now, and whom is the rescuer planning to save? [Blanca Flor has become the rescuer. She plans to save herself and Juanito.]

All the water was gone. He looked over to the other part of the field, and there stood a lake where before there was nothing. He turned to look for Blanca Flor, but instead there was Don Ricardo.

[DON RICARDO *enters.*]

Ⓐ **Don Ricardo** (*in full force and very angry*). This must be the work of Blanca Flor, or else you have more power than I thought. I know Blanca Flor is too scared to ever use her powers against me, so as a test of your powers, tomorrow your next job will not be so easy. See that barren[3] ground over on the side of the mountain? You are to clear that ground, plant seeds, grow wheat, harvest it, grind it, cook it, and have bread for me to eat before I return. You still have your life now, but I better have bread tomorrow. (*He exits, with a flourish.*)[4]

[JUANITO *exits.*]

Scene 4.
THE NEXT MORNING.

As THE NARRATOR *speaks,* JUANITO *and* BLANCA FLOR *enter and act out the scene as it is described.*

The Narrator. Immediately upon waking the next morning, Juanito tried to move the rocks in the field, but they were impossible to move because of their great size. Once again, Juanito knew that his efforts were useless. He went over to the new lake and fell down in exhaustion. As he lay in the grass by the lake, Ⓑ Blanca Flor came to him once more and began to brush his hair. Soon, Juanito was asleep.

[BLANCA FLOR *exits.*]

---

3. **barren** *adj.:* not producing crops or fruit.
4. **flourish** *n.:* sweeping movement.

The Narrator. As before, when he awoke, Juanito dashed to the field to make one last attempt to do his work. When he got there, he again stopped in amazement. The field was clear of rocks, and the land had been planted and harvested. As he turned around, there stood Blanca Flor.

[BLANCA FLOR *enters.*]

Blanca Flor (*she hands a loaf of bread to* JUANITO). Give this to Don Ricardo.
Juanito. How did you do this?

[DON RICARDO *enters, quickly.*]

Don Ricardo. What do you have?
Juanito (*shaking with fear*). Just . . . just this loaf of bread. (*Giving the bread to* DON Ⓒ RICARDO) Here is the bread you asked for.
Don Ricardo (*very angry*). This is the work of Blanca Flor. This will not happen again. Tomorrow, your third job will be your final job, and even the powers of Blanca Flor will not help you this time! (*He exits.*)
Blanca Flor. Believe me, the third job will be impossible to do. It will be too difficult even for my powers. We must run from here if there is to be any chance of escaping his Ⓓ anger. He will kill you because I have helped you. Tonight I will come for you. Be ready to leave quickly as soon as I call for you.

[JUANITO *and* BLANCA FLOR *exit.*]

Scene 5.
LATER THAT NIGHT.

On one side of the stage, JUANITO *sits waiting. On the other side,* BLANCA FLOR *is in her room grabbing her traveling bag. As she leaves her room, she turns and mimes spitting three times as* THE NARRATOR *describes the action.*

CONTENT-AREA CONNECTIONS

Mathematics
Powers of three. The "powers of three" have often been noted in folklore: three little pigs, three blind mice, three billy goats gruff. Have pairs of students investigate the special mathematical properties of the number three. Among them is the fact that any number, however large, is evenly divisible by three if the sum of its digits is divisible by three.

Activity. Encourage students to find more examples and to create a poster or other display illustrating their findings.

WHOLE-CLASS

The Narrator. Late that night, as Juanito waited for her, Blanca Flor packed her belongings into a bag. Before she left the house, she went to the fireplace and spat three times into it.

[BLANCA FLOR *joins* JUANITO.]

Blanca Flor (*quietly calling*). Juanito . . . Juanito.

Juanito. Blanca Flor, is it time?

Blanca Flor. Yes. We must leave quickly, before he finds out I am gone, or it will be too late.

Juanito. Won't he know you are gone as soon as he calls for you?

Blanca Flor. Not right away. I've used my powers to fool him. But it won't last long. Let's go!

[JUANITO *and* BLANCA FLOR *exit.*]

The Narrator. When Don Ricardo heard the noise of Juanito and Blanca Flor leaving, he called out . . .

Don Ricardo (*from offstage*). Blanca Flor, are you there?

The Narrator. The spit she had left in the fireplace answered.

Blanca Flor (*from offstage*). Yes, I am here.

The Narrator. Later, Don Ricardo called out again.

Don Ricardo (*from offstage*). Blanca Flor, are you there?

The Narrator. For a second time, the spit she had left in the fireplace answered.

Blanca Flor (*from offstage*). Yes, I am here.

The Narrator. Still later, Don Ricardo called out again, a third time.

Don Ricardo (*from offstage*). Blanca Flor, are you there?

The Narrator. By this time, the fire had evaporated Blanca Flor's spit, and there was no answer. Don Ricardo knew that Blanca Flor was gone, and that she had run away with Juanito. He saddled his horse and galloped up the path to catch them before they escaped from his land.

DIRECT TEACHING

E Learners Having Difficulty

Breaking down difficult text/visualizing. Make sure students understand the following important facts about the second part of this scene: (1) Only the Narrator is onstage, (2) the actors playing Don Ricardo and Blanca Flor speak from offstage, (3) from another room, Don Ricardo is checking to find out if Blanca Flor is in her room, and (4) Blanca Flor's spit in the fireplace has magically acquired the power to speak in her voice and thus fool Don Ricardo into thinking she is still in her room. To help students visualize this setup, suggest that they draw a rough sketch of the stage and include speech balloons showing from where the voices are coming.

GUIDED PRACTICE

Monitoring students' progress. Guide students in completing the following sentence starter to summarize Scenes 1–5: *Juanito wanted to seek his fortune, but _____. So _____, and then _____. So_____, and then . . .*

INDEPENDENT PRACTICE

Literary Response and Analysis

Reading Check

1. c
2. a
3. b
4. d

Vocabulary Development

Practice

- Remind students that in dictionaries, word origins appear in brackets either near the beginning or at the end of an entry.
- Foods chosen will depend on students' tastes and on their dictionary skills.
- Names of the suggested foods come from the following languages: pasta (Italian), pizza (Italian), sushi (Japanese), lo mein (Chinese), enchilada (American Spanish), taco (American Spanish), scone (Scottish).

Literary Response and Analysis
Scenes 1–5

Reading Check

The **plot** of a story is made up of a series of causes and their effects. **Effects** are what happens. **Causes** are what makes events happen. A **cause-and-effect chain** is a series of events in which each event causes another one to happen, like dominoes falling in a row.

The events listed in the columns below take place in Scenes 1–5 of *Blanca Flor.* Match each cause in the left-hand column with its effect in the right-hand column.

Cause	Effect
1. The Duende points to a path in the forest.	a. Juanito decides to try to rescue Blanca Flor.
2. Juanito hears Blanca Flor's story.	b. Don Ricardo catches Juanito on his land.
3. Juanito ignores Blanca Flor's warning and refuses to leave.	c. Juanito meets Blanca Flor.
4. Blanca Flor moves the lake for Juanito.	d. Don Ricardo gives Juanito a harder task.

Vocabulary Development

Foreign Words Frequently Used in English: Eat Your Words

Have you ever eaten a *tortilla,* as the Duende does? How about a *croissant* or a *bagel*? The names of these foods come from Spanish, French, and Yiddish. When English speakers began eating these foods, their names came into the English language. After all, *bread* is a good word, but it doesn't capture the specific—and delicious—qualities of tortillas, croissants, and bagels.

Some Words for Your Menu

pasta

pizza

sushi

lo mein

enchilada

taco

scone

PRACTICE

With a partner, create a menu of five or six foods with foreign names. Use a dictionary or the Internet to find out where the name of each food comes from.

DIFFERENTIATING INSTRUCTION

Learners Having Difficulty
Have students complete the Reading Check with partners. Remind them that effects follow causes. Encourage students to read each cause, recall what happens next in the play, and then look for the appropriate effect. *Monitoring tip:* If students have trouble matching causes with effects, remind them to take into account the char-

acters' qualities. You might say, "Juanito is kind. What would he be likely to do after hearing the story of Blanca Flor's imprisonment? Don Ricardo is mean. What would he be likely to do when the impossible task he gave Juanito is completed?"

Advanced Learners
Enrichment. Assign the Reading Check on p. 98 as homework, inviting advanced

learners to change each cause slightly and then to speculate about how the effect would change.

Activity. Have students read another folk tale or fairy tale and create a cause-and-effect chain showing how a series of events moves the plot along.

HOMEWORK

Scene 6.
IN THE FOREST.

JUANITO *and* BLANCA FLOR *enter, running and out of breath.*

Juanito. Blanca Flor, we can rest now. We are free.

Blanca Flor. No, Juanito, we will not be free until we are beyond the borders of Don Ricardo's land. As long as we are on his land, his powers will work on us.

Juanito. How much farther?

Blanca Flor. Remember the river where you met the Duende? That river is the border. Across it we are free.

Juanito. That river is still really far. Let's rest here for a while.

Blanca Flor. No, he is already after us. We must keep going. I can hear the hooves of his horse.

Juanito (*he looks around desperately*). Where? How can that be?

Blanca Flor. He is really close. Juanito, come stand by me. Quickly!

Juanito (*still looking around*). I don't hear anything.

Blanca Flor (*grabbing him and pulling him to her*). Juanito! Now!

[*As* THE NARRATOR *describes the action,* JUANITO *and* BLANCA FLOR *act out the scene.* BLANCA FLOR *does not actually throw a brush. She mimes throwing the brush and the action.*]

The Narrator. Blanca Flor looked behind them and saw that Don Ricardo was getting closer. She reached into her bag, took her brush, and threw it behind her. The brush turned into a church by the side of the road. She then cast a spell on Juanito and turned him into a little old bell ringer. She turned herself into a statue outside the church.

[DON RICARDO *enters, as if riding a horse.*]

Don Ricardo (*addressing the bell ringer* [JUANITO]). Bell ringer, have you seen two young people come this way recently? They would have been in a great hurry and out of breath.

Juanito (*in an old man's voice*). No . . . I don't think so. But maybe last week, two young boys came by. They stopped to pray in the church . . . Or was it two girls. I don't know. I am just an old bell ringer. Not many people actually come by this way at all. You're the first in a long time.

Don Ricardo. Bell ringer, if you are lying to me you will be sorry. (*He goes over to the statue* [BLANCA FLOR], *who is standing very still, as a statue. He examines the statue very closely and then addresses the bell ringer* [JUANITO].) Bell ringer, what saint is this a statue of? The face looks very familiar.

Juanito. I am an old bell ringer. I don't remember the names of all the saints. But I do know that the statue is very old and has been here a long time. Maybe Saint Theresa or Saint Bernadette.

Don Ricardo. Bell ringer, if you are lying, I will be back! (*He exits.*)

Juanito. Adiós, Señor!

[BLANCA FLOR *breaks her pose as a statue and goes to* JUANITO.]

Blanca Flor. Juanito, Juanito. The spell is over.

Juanito. What happened? I did hear the angry hooves of a horse being ridden hard.

Blanca Flor. We are safe for a while. But he will not give up, and we are not free yet.

[JUANITO *and* BLANCA FLOR *exit.*]

A **Literary Focus**
REVIEW STANDARD

Comparing characters. In this section, point out that again it is Blanca Flor who is the strong and competent one. Ask students which aspects of Juanito's behavior seem childlike by comparison. [Possible responses: He is unaware of danger; he begs to rest; he asks, "How much farther?"]

B **Literary Focus**
REVIEW STANDARD

Archetypal elements: Motif. Ask students what motifs, or universally recurring elements, in this sequence they recognize from other fairy tales. [Possible responses: a tense chase scene, magical transformations.]

C **Vocabulary Development**
GRADE-LEVEL STANDARD

Using Spanish words in English. Point out the Spanish phrase *"Adiós, Señor!"* Ask students when they have heard or used one or both of these Spanish words in their daily lives. [Students may have heard them in television programs and commercials, at sports events, and so on.] Point out that these Spanish words are so commonly used that most English speakers understand them.

A Reading Skills

? Making inferences. This time it is Juanito who hears what Blanca Flor does not. What might this change imply about a transformation in Juanito's character? [Possible response: Juanito may be gaining maturity or competence.]

B Learners Having Difficulty

Varying reading rate. Advise students to read this stage direction slowly and carefully in order to imagine the scene.

C Literary Focus
GRADE-LEVEL STANDARD

? Characterization. Which of Don Ricardo's lines sound especially cruel? [Possible responses: "I could hear their scared little voices," "Juanito will pay for this," "Blanca Flor will never have the chance to escape again."] Point out that the emphasis on Don Ricardo's cruelty deepens the conflict: Juanito and Blanca Flor are in imminent danger.

Scene 7. FARTHER INTO THE FOREST.

The Narrator. Blanca Flor and Juanito desperately continued their escape. As they finally stopped for a rest, they had their closest call yet.

[BLANCA FLOR and JUANITO enter.]

Juanito. Blanca Flor, please, let's rest just for a minute.
Blanca Flor. OK. We can rest here. I have not heard the hooves of his horse for a while now.
Juanito. What will he do if he catches us?
Blanca Flor. He will take us back. I will be watched more closely than ever, and you will—
Juanito (sadly). I know. Was there ever a time when you were free? Do you even remember your parents?
Blanca Flor. Yes. I have the most beautiful memories of my mother, our house, and our animals. Every day, my father would saddle the horses and together we would—
Juanito. Blanca Flor . . . I hear something.
Blanca Flor (alarmed). He's close. Very close.

[As THE NARRATOR describes the action, JUANITO and BLANCA FLOR act out the scene. BLANCA FLOR does not actually throw a comb. She mimes throwing the comb and the action.]

The Narrator. Blanca Flor quickly opened her bag and threw her comb behind her. Immediately the comb turned into a field of corn. This time she turned Juanito into a scarecrow, and she turned herself into a stalk of corn beside him.

[DON RICARDO enters, as if riding a horse.]

Don Ricardo. Where did they go? I still think that the bell ringer knew more than he was saying. They were just here. I could hear their scared little voices. Juanito will pay for this, and Blanca Flor will never have the chance to escape again . . . Now where did they go? Perhaps they are in this field of corn. It is strange to see a stalk of corn grow so close to a scarecrow. But this is a day for strange things. (He exits.)
Blanca Flor. Juanito, it is over again. Let's go. The river is not far. We are almost free.

[JUANITO breaks his pose as a scarecrow and stretches and rubs his legs as BLANCA FLOR looks around apprehensively.][5]

Juanito. Blanca Flor, that was close. We have to hurry now. The river is just through these trees. We can make it now for sure if we hurry.
The Narrator. But they spoke too soon. Don Ricardo had gotten suspicious about the field of corn and returned to it. When he saw Juanito and Blanca Flor he raced to catch them.

[DON RICARDO enters suddenly and sees them.]

Don Ricardo. There you are. I knew something was wrong with that field of corn. Now you are mine.

[As THE NARRATOR describes the action, JUANITO and BLANCA FLOR act out the scene. BLANCA FLOR does not actually throw a mirror. She mimes throwing the mirror and the action.]

The Narrator. When Blanca Flor saw Don Ricardo, she reached into her bag and took out a mirror, the final object in the bag. She threw the mirror into the middle of the road.

---
5. **apprehensively** adv.: fearfully; uneasily.

CONTENT-AREA CONNECTIONS

Culture
Gender roles in literature. Historically, in Western civilization and many other cultures, it has been believed that men are more physically capable and more adventurous than women—that men are the rescuers and women the rescued. The motif of maidens in danger and heroes who rescue them is an outgrowth of this assumption. Today this belief is being questioned.

Activity. After students finish reading the play, challenge them to think about the following statement and to find evidence either supporting or opposing it: "In *Blanca Flor* it is not so much the hero who rescues the maiden, but the maiden who rescues the hero." [Possible support: Blanca Flor performs the tasks set by Don Ricardo when Juanito cannot, she magically conceals their escape, and she rescues Juanito from a likely marriage to someone he doesn't love. Possible opposition: Blanca Flor acts as if she needs rescuing, she never tries to escape on her own, and she is lonely when Juanito forgets her.]

INDIVIDUAL

Instantly, the mirror became a large lake, its waters so smooth and still that it looked like a mirror as it reflected the sky and clouds. When Don Ricardo got to the lake, all he saw was two ducks, a male and a female, swimming peacefully in the middle of the lake. Suddenly, the ducks lifted off the lake and flew away. As they flew away, Don Ricardo knew that the ducks were Juanito and Blanca Flor, and that they were beyond his grasp. As they disappeared, he shouted one last curse.

[JUANITO *and* BLANCA FLOR *exit.*]

Don Ricardo. You may have escaped, Blanca Flor, but you will never have his love. I place a curse on both of you. The first person to embrace him will cause him to forget you forever! (*He exits.*)

Scene 8.
NEAR JUANITO'S HOME.

BLANCA FLOR *and* JUANITO *enter.*

The Narrator. Disguised as ducks, Blanca Flor and Juanito flew safely away from that evil land and escaped from Don Ricardo. They finally arrived at Juanito's home, and using Blanca Flor's magical powers, they returned to their human selves.

Juanito. Blanca Flor, we are close to my home. Soon we will be finally safe forever. I will introduce you to my family, and we will begin our new life together . . . Blanca Flor, why do you look so sad? We have escaped the evil Don Ricardo, and soon we will be happy forever.

Blanca Flor. We have not escaped. His final curse will forever be over us.

Juanito. Remember, that curse will work only in his own land. You yourself told me

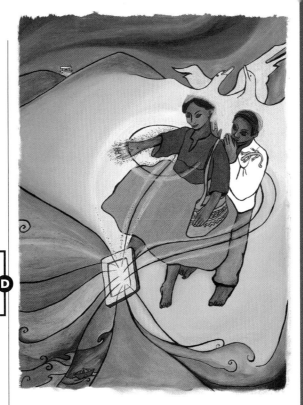

that once we were beyond the borders of his land, his powers would have no hold on us.

Blanca Flor. His powers are very great, Juanito.

Juanito. Blanca Flor, you have never explained to me the source of your own powers. Are your powers also gone?

Blanca Flor. The powers have always been in the women of my family. That is why Don Ricardo would not let me leave. He was afraid that I would use my powers against him. I have never been away from that land, so I do not know about my powers in this new land.

Juanito. You will have no need for your powers here. Soon we will be with my family. Wait outside while I go and tell my family that I have returned from seeking my fortune,

D **Literary Focus**
GRADE-LEVEL STANDARD
❓ **Characterization.** How does Don Ricardo's cruelty keep the conflict going, even after Juanito and Blanca Flor escape him? [Possible response: His curse puts them in danger of losing their love for each other and their happiness.]

E **Literary Focus**
REVIEW STANDARD
❓ **Cause and effect in plots.** What effect do you think Don Ricardo's curse will have when Juanito goes in to meet his family? Encourage students to come up with reasonable guesses. [The actual effect is that his parents' embrace activates the curse.]

A **Literary Focus**
GRADE-LEVEL STANDARD

? Characterization. How does the author show that Juanito values Blanca Flor and love? [Possible responses: He went to seek his fortune and found love rather than riches but says, "All my dreams have come true." He tells Blanca Flor, "I am not afraid of any curse. Not with you here with me."]

B **Literary Focus**
GRADE-LEVEL STANDARD

Characterization. In most fairy tales, parents are either very kind or very cruel. Ask students whether the author portrays Juanito's parents as kind or as cruel. [kind] Then, ask how their conversation shows this. [Possible responses: They talk about their concern for Juanito; they miss Juanito but accept that he needs freedom to grow up.]

C **Literary Focus**
REVIEW STANDARD

? Cause and effect in plots. What is the cause of Juanito's forgetfulness? [Don Ricardo's curse] What do you think the effects of the forgetfulness will be? [Possible responses: Blanca Flor and Juanito will be separated; Juanito will fall in love with someone else.]

---

safe at last. Then I will tell them that the fortune I found was you.

A **Blanca Flor.** Juanito, remember the curse.
Juanito. I am not afraid of any curse. Not with you here with me. All my dreams have come true. Come, let's go meet my family.

[JUANITO and BLANCA FLOR exit.]

Scene 9.
AT JUANITO'S HOME.

DON RAMON and DOÑA ARLETTE are sitting at home passing the time with idle talk.

The Narrator. Juanito's parents had waited patiently for their son to return from seeking his fortune in the world. They did not know that his return home was only the beginning of another chapter of his great adventure.
Doña Arlette. Do you ever think we will hear from Juanito? It has been months since he left to seek his fortune in the world.
Don Ramon. We will hear word soon. I remember when I left home to seek my fortune in the world. Eventually, I found that the best thing to do was return home and make my fortune right here, with my *familia* at my side. Soon he will discover the same thing and you will have your son back.

B **Doña Arlette.** It is easier for a father to know those things. A mother will never stop worrying about her children.
Don Ramon. I worry about the children just as much as you do. But there is no stopping children who want to grow up. He has our blessing and permission to go, and that will be what brings him back safe to us. Soon. You just wait.

[JUANITO enters. His parents are overjoyed to see him.]

Juanito. Mama! Papa! I am home.
Doña Arlette. ¡Mi 'jito![6]
Don Ramon. Juanito!

[Overjoyed with seeing JUANITO, his parents rush and embrace him.]

Doña Arlette. God has answered my prayers. Mi 'jito has returned home safe.
Don Ramon. Juanito, come sit close to us and tell us all about your adventures in the world. What great adventures did you have?
Juanito. I had the greatest adventures. For the longest time I was unlucky and unable to find work but finally I . . . I . . .
Doña Arlette. What is it? Are you OK? Do you need some food?
Juanito. No, I'm OK. It's just that I was going to say something and I forgot what I was going to say.
Don Ramon. Don't worry. If it is truly **C** important, it'll come back.
Juanito. No, I've definitely forgotten what I was going to say. Oh well, it probably wasn't important anyway.
Doña Arlette. Did you meet someone special? Did you bring a young woman back for us to meet?
Juanito. No, I didn't have those kind of adventures. Pretty much nothing happened, and then I finally decided that it was just best to come home.
Don Ramon (to DOÑA ARLETTE). See what I told you? That is exactly what I said would happen.
Doña Arlette. Now that you are home, it is time to settle down and start your own family. You know our neighbor Don Emilio has a younger daughter who would make a

---

6. **mi 'jito** (mē hē'tô): contraction of *mi hijito*, Spanish for "my little son."

MINI-LESSON Reading

Developing Word-Attack Skills
Point out that in English words, the sound /h/ is spelled with the letter *h*. Ask students to identify words in *Blanca Flor* in which the sound /h/ is spelled with an *h*. [Possible responses: hot, home, hears, human, hope, hungry.] Use the character name Juanito to demonstrate that in Spanish the sound /h/ is spelled with the letter *j*. Invite students to name other familiar Spanish words in which the

sound /h/ is spelled with a *j*. [Possible responses: jalapeño, fajita, junta.]
Remind students that in some English words the letter *h* is silent. The list of such words is finite. You can share it with students by writing these words on the chalkboard:

heir   herb   hour
honor   honest

very good wife. Perhaps we should go visit her family this Sunday.

Juanito. You know, that would probably be a good idea. I must admit that I was hoping I would find love on my adventures, but I have come home with no memories of love at all. Perhaps it is best to make my fortune right here, close to home.

Don Ramon (*to* DOÑA ARLETTE). See? That is exactly what I said would happen.

[*All exit.*]

Scene 10. MONTHS LATER AT JUANITO'S HOME.

The Narrator. Blanca Flor had seen the embrace and knew that the evil curse had been fulfilled. Brokenhearted, she traveled to a nearby village and lived there in hopes that one day the curse could be broken.

The people of the village soon got to know Blanca Flor and came to respect her for the good person she was. One day, Blanca Flor heard news that a celebration was being held in honor of Juanito's return home. She immediately knew that this might be her one chance to break the curse. From the times when she had brushed Juanito's hair, she had kept a lock of his hair. She took one strand of his hair and made it into a dove. She then took one strand of her own hair and turned it into another dove. She took these two doves to Juanito's celebration as a present.

[JUANITO *and* DON RAMON *are sitting talking.*]

Don Ramon. Juanito, what was the most fantastic thing that happened on your adventures?

Juanito. Really, Father, nothing much at all happened. Sometimes I begin to have a

Blanca Flor, Scenes 6–10 **103**

DIRECT TEACHING

D Literary Focus
ADVANCED STANDARD
Analyzing characterization.
Point out that the author characterizes Don Ramon and Doña Arlette as stereotypical parents: Doña Arlette promptly offers her son some food and suggests that he get married, while Don Ramon provides general reassurances and keeps saying, "See what I told you?" Ask students why the author might have chosen to introduce two stereotypical characters at this point. [Possible responses: They provide comic relief to offset the tension of Juanito's forgetting Blanca Flor.]

E Reading Skills
? Making inferences. What character traits or emotions do Blanca Flor's actions suggest to you? [Possible responses: She loves Juanito deeply; she is sentimental to have saved a lock of his hair; she thinks ahead.]

F English-Language Learners
? Building background knowledge. Show students a picture of a dove, and say the word aloud. Ask students, "What English words rhyme with *dove*?" [Possible responses: love, above, shove.] Then, ask them, "What English words that have *–ove* at the end do not rhyme with *dove*?" [Possible responses: move, prove, stove, clove.] You might ask students how to say *dove* in their first language. In Spanish it is *paloma*.

The letter *h* is silent at the beginning of these words, and it is also silent when it comes after *ex–* in words like *exhibit* and *exhaust*.
Activity. Write the following sentences on the chalkboard, and have volunteers read each one aloud. Have them explain how they knew the pronunciation of the underlined words.

1. The traveler was hungry and <u>exhausted</u>.
2. He reached the inn at a late <u>hour</u>.
3. The innkeeper took him for an <u>honest</u> man and gave him shelter.
4. He fed him <u>fajitas</u> and pickled <u>jalapeños</u>.
5. The traveler thanked his <u>honorable</u> host.

A Advanced Learners

Enrichment. Tell students that songs are used to advance the plot in some of Shakespeare's plays; one example is "Ariel's Song" in *The Tempest*. Ask students what kind of music they would compose for the magical singing doves.

memory of something, but it never becomes really clear. At night I have these dreams, but when I awake in the morning I cannot remember them. It must be some dream I keep trying to remember . . . or forget.
Don Ramon. I remember when I went into the world to seek my fortune. I was a young man like you . . .

[DOÑA ARLETTE *enters.*]

Doña Arlette. Juanito, there's a young woman here with a present for you.
Juanito. Who is it?
Doña Arlette. I don't really know her. She is the new young woman who just recently came to the village. The women of the church say she is constantly doing good works for the church and that she is a very good person. She has brought you a present to help celebrate your coming home safe.

Juanito. Sure. Let her come in.

[BLANCA FLOR *enters with the* TWO DOVES. *The* DOVES *are actors in costume.*]

Blanca Flor (*speaking to* JUANITO). Thank you for giving me the honor of presenting these doves as gifts to you.
Juanito. No. No. The honor is mine. Thank you. They are very beautiful.
Blanca Flor. They are special doves. They are singing doves.
Doña Arlette. I have never heard of singing doves before. Where did you get them?
A Blanca Flor. They came from a special place. A place where all things have a magic power. There are no other doves like these in the world.
Don Ramon. Juanito, what a gift! Let's hear them sing!

FAMILY/COMMUNITY ACTIVITY

Guide class members in organizing a reader's theater production of *Blanca Flor*, starring students and members of their families. Have students introduce the play to their families by reading favorite scenes aloud at home, then explaining the reader's theater concept and urging family members to volunteer for roles. Hold rehearsals, and schedule one or more performances that other students, families, and community members can attend. If the production is presented during school hours, you might also invite classes from local elementary schools.

Doña Arlette. Yes, let's hear them sing.

Blanca Flor (*to* JUANITO). May they sing to you?

Juanito. Yes, of course. Let's hear their song.

[*Everyone sits to listen to the* DOVES' *song. As the* DOVES *begin to chant, their words begin to have a powerful effect on* JUANITO. *His memory of* BLANCA FLOR *returns to him.*]

Doves. Once there was a faraway land
A land of both good and evil powers.
A river flowed at the edge like a steady
    hand
And it was guarded by a Duende for all the
    hours.
Of all the beautiful things the land
    did hold

The most beautiful with the purest power
Was a young maiden, true and bold
Named Blanca Flor, the White Flower.

Juanito. I remember! The doves' song has made me remember. (*Going to* BLANCA FLOR) Blanca Flor, your love has broken the curse. Now I remember all that was struggling to come out. Mama, Papa, here is Blanca Flor, the love I found when I was seeking my fortune.

[JUANITO *and* BLANCA FLOR *embrace.*]

Don Ramon. This is going to be a really good story!

[*All exit, with* JUANITO *stopping to give* BLANCA FLOR *a big hug.*]

B Literary Focus
REVIEW STANDARD
❓ Cause and effect in plots.
What effect does the doves' singing have on Juanito? [It makes him remember his adventures with Blanca Flor.] In view of that fact, what effect does their singing have on the plot of the play? [Possible response: It makes the happy ending possible.]

GUIDED PRACTICE

Monitoring students' progress.
Guide students in creating a character-traits word web, labeling the center circle "Characters" and writing character names in surrounding circles. Students should then expand the web, adding circles to record traits for each character and more circles to record events influenced by the traits.

Meet the Writer
Background. Angel Vigil is a storyteller, author, and stage director. His book *The Corn Woman: Stories and Legends of the Hispanic Southwest* was named one of the year's best books for teenagers by the New York Public Library in 1995.

For Independent Reading
Encourage students who choose to read *¡Teatro!* to read one of the plays aloud in performance style.

■ Students who enjoyed *Blanca Flor* might enjoy *The Crest and the Hide and Other African Stories of Heroes, Chiefs, Bards, Sorcerers, and Common People* by Harold Courlander, a collection of tales of tasks accomplished by African men.

MEET THE WRITER

Angel Vigil

The Oral Tradition
Angel Vigil (1947–   ) was born in New Mexico and was raised "in a large, traditional Hispanic extended family, with loving grandparents and plenty of aunts and cousins."

Although *Blanca Flor* is based on a traditional European tale, the play also draws on Hispanic folklore. The mischievous little tricksters called *duendes* make trouble for people in stories told throughout the Hispanic Southwest.

For Independent Reading
You can find other plays based on Hispanic stories in Vigil's *¡Teatro! Plays from the Hispanic Culture for Young People.* You might also enjoy reading *The Corn Woman: Stories and Legends of the Hispanic Southwest* and *The Eagle on the Cactus: Traditional Stories from Mexico.*

DIFFERENTIATING INSTRUCTION

Advanced Learners
Collecting folklore. Be sure students understand that stories passed down orally from generation to generation constitute folklore. Point out to students that their own relatives, like Angel Vigil's, are sources of folklore.
Enrichment. Encourage students to interview older family members about stories,

factual and fictional, that they heard and loved as children. These may be fairy tales, stories made up by family members, jokes, or family anecdotes. Tell students to ask family members' permission to take notes or tape the interviews and to share the selected results with the class.

INDEPENDENT PRACTICE

Literary Response and Analysis

Reading Check

1. b
2. a
3. d
4. c

Interpretations

5. Possible answers: *Juanito*—naive (slow to catch on), kind (tries to rescue Blanca Flor), brave (stands up to Don Ricardo). *Blanca Flor*—kind (helps Juanito, does good deeds in the village), powerful (bests Don Ricardo), inventive (uses her magic in creative ways). *Don Ricardo*—cruel (enslaves Blanca Flor, kills others), vindictive (curses Juanito and Blanca Flor).

6. Possible answers: Blanca Flor, because her magic permits escape from Don Ricardo and breaks his curse; Juanito, because his bravery, love, and encouragement inspire Blanca Flor.

7. Possible answers: Don Ricardo plans three tasks for Juanito (Scene 2); Blanca Flor spits three times into the fireplace, and Don Ricardo calls for her three times (Scene 5); she throws three magic objects from her bag (Scenes 6–7).

Evaluation

8. Possible answer: Blanca Flor and Juanito would not have gotten together. Only her assertiveness wins the day.

FOCUS ON

Literary Response and Analysis
Scenes 6–10

Reading Check
Earlier you matched causes and effects in Scenes 1–5. Now, do the same for Scenes 6–10. Match the causes in the left-hand column with their effects in the right-hand column.

Cause	Effect
1. Blanca Flor throws her comb behind her.	a. Don Ricardo puts his curse on Juanito.
2. Blanca Flor and Juanito escape from Don Ricardo's lands.	b. A field of corn appears.
3. Juanito's parents embrace him.	c. Juanito remembers Blanca Flor.
4. Blanca Flor returns to Juanito's house with two doves.	d. Juanito forgets Blanca Flor.

Interpretations

Reading Standard 3.2 Analyze the effect of the qualities of the character (for example, courage or cowardice, ambition or laziness) on the plot and the resolution of the conflict.

5. Choose two of the main characters in the play, and list two or three of each **character's qualities.** (If you choose Blanca Flor, for example, you might list courage and kindness.) Look back at your character chart for ideas. Then, give examples of the characters' actions that illustrate the qualities you listed.

6. Decide which character has the greatest effect on the **plot** and the resolution of the **conflict.**

7. The number three is a common **motif,** an element that appears again and again in literature. Where do things happen in threes in *Blanca Flor*?

Evaluation

8. How would the outcome of this play have been different if Blanca Flor had been less forceful, shyer, and more accepting of her fate? Be sure to compare your responses with those of your classmates.

Writing
A Change of Scenery

Retell the story of *Blanca Flor,* setting it in another time and place. (You might want to set it in your neighborhood today.) Before you start writing, give the characters new names. Think of three impossible tasks for the hero, and decide what items the heroine will throw and what they will turn into. You might want to use the types listed in the Quickwrite as characters.

106 | Chapter 2 | Characters: The People You'll Meet

DIFFERENTIATING INSTRUCTION

Learners Having Difficulty
Have students pair up to complete the Reading Check and Interpretations questions in class. *Monitoring tip:* If students are unable to generalize about characters' traits (question 5), tell them to re-read scenes involving the characters and to ask themselves, "What do this person's actions add up to?" You might provide a list of adjectives for students to draw from, listing words such as *kind, unkind, brave, cowardly, ambitious, lazy, honest, dishonest, innocent,* and *experienced.*

Writing. Guide students in filling out story maps in class, roughing out plot, setting, characters, and action, before they write stories at home.

HOMEWORK

Vocabulary Development

Reading Standard 1.3 Recognize the origins and meanings of frequently used foreign words in English, and use these words accurately in speaking and writing.

Using Spanish Words in English

American English has been borrowing words from Spanish for centuries, especially in the western United States. More Spanish words come into English all the time. Even if you are not a Spanish speaker, you may know the Spanish way to say goodbye to friends: *Adios, amigos.*

You can sometimes figure out the meaning of an unfamiliar Spanish word by thinking of English words that resemble it. (If Spanish is your first language, you can figure out the meanings of some English words in a similar way.)

PRACTICE

Find an English dictionary that tells you the origins of words, including the language they come from. Look up each of the words listed in the first column. In the second column, write down the word's Spanish meaning or the Spanish word it's derived from. (The Spanish word itself may have come from another language.) In the third column, write the English meaning (look in a dictionary, or draw on your own knowledge). In the fourth column, write a sentence that uses the word.

TEN WORDS FROM SPANISH			
Word	Spanish Meaning or Original Spanish	English Meaning	Sentence
tornado	tornar, "to turn"	whirlwind; rapidly rotating column of air	The tornado ripped the roof off.
alligator			
armadillo			
bonanza			
cafeteria			
canyon			
chocolate			
mascara			
patio			
sombrero			
stampede			

Blanca Flor **107**

Advanced Learners

Enrichment. Bring in world folklore collections, and invite students to browse through them, looking for plots, themes, or characters similar to those of *Blanca Flor*. Have students share their findings with the class.

Vocabulary Development

Practice

Etymologies and definitions will vary because dictionaries vary.

- *alligator.* Spanish—*el lagarto,* "the lizard." *English*—a reptile related to the crocodile. *Sentence*—The alligator lurked in the swamp.
- *armadillo. Spanish*—"little armored one." *English*—nocturnal, burrowing mammal with bony plates. *Sentence*—Armadillos hold their breath underwater.
- *bonanza. Spanish*—"fair weather." *English*—rich find. *Sentence*—The gold miners struck a bonanza.
- *cafeteria. Spanish*—"coffee store." *English*—self-service restaurant. *Sentence*—The school cafeteria offers chili.
- *canyon. Spanish*—cañón, "tube, pipe, gorge." *English*—narrow valley between high cliffs. *Sentence*—A wild river wound through the canyon.
- *chocolate. Spanish*—"bitter water." *English*—food made from ground, roasted cacao beans. *Sentence*—Mom loves chocolate.
- *mascara. Spanish*—"mask." *English*—a cosmetic for lashes. *Sentence*—Runny mascara makes one look like a raccoon.
- *patio. Spanish*—"pastureland." *English*—a courtyard. *Sentence*—Let's eat out on the patio.
- *sombrero. Spanish*—"hat, canopy" from *sombra,* "shade." *English*—a broad-brimmed hat. *Sentence*—Here come the cowboys in their sombreros.
- *stampede. Spanish*—estampida, "uproar." *English*—a wild rush of animals. *Sentence*—The free offer caused a customer stampede.

ASSESSING

Assessment
- *Progress Assessment of Reading*
  - Selection Test, p. 31

Reading Informational Materials

STANDARDS FOCUS, pp. 108–109

(For the grade-level standard reviewed in this lesson, see Pupil's Edition, p. 108.)

INTRODUCING THE STANDARDS REVIEW

Use this review to test students' abilities to use outlines and summaries to clarify their understanding of what they read.

DIRECT TEACHING

Ⓐ Reading Informational Materials
GRADE-LEVEL STANDARD

❓ **Outlining.** What main idea do the first two paragraphs suggest? [Possible response: The quinceañera is an important coming-of-age ritual.] How might you outline the information in these two paragraphs? [Possible outline:
I. Key coming-of-age ritual
 A. Marks fifteenth birthday of a Mexican or Mexican American girl
 B. Dates back to Aztec culture
 C. Months of preparation
 D. Formal dress, honor court]

Ⓑ Reading Informational Materials
GRADE-LEVEL STANDARD

❓ **Summary.** Which words in this paragraph signal a main idea? ["The most important part"] Explain why this idea should, or should not, be included in a summary. [It should be included because a summary must state the main ideas.]

Reading Informational Materials

 DIRECTIONS: Read the informational article. Then, read each question, and write the letter of the best response.

Celebrating the Quinceañera
Mara Rockliff

Ⓐ You stand at the back of the church between your parents and godparents, your knees shaking. You feel special, and a bit awkward, in your first formal dress and your tiara. Your honor court has walked up the aisle ahead of you: fourteen girls in pastel dresses, fourteen boys in tuxedos. With you and your escort there are fifteen couples—one for each year of your life. The long months of planning and preparation have finally ended. Your quinceañera has begun.

The quinceañera (kēn′sā·ä·nye′rə, from the Spanish words *quince,* "fifteen," and *años,* "years") is a rite of passage celebrated by Mexicans and Mexican Americans. People believe that the tradition can be traced back to the Aztec culture, in which girls commonly married at the age of fifteen. Today a girl's quinceañera marks her coming-of-age. It means that she is ready to take on adult privileges and responsibilities.

Ⓑ The most important part of your quinceañera is the *misa de acción de gracias,* the thanksgiving Mass. You slowly walk up the aisle to the front of the church. You kneel, placing a bouquet of fifteen roses on the altar to thank the Virgin Mary for bringing you to this important day. A birthstone ring glitters on your finger, and a religious medal hangs from your neck, inscribed with your name and today's date—special gifts from adult relatives or friends of the family. The priest will bless your medal during the Mass.

Next comes a sermon, followed by prayers and readings from the Bible. You recite your speech, and the service ends. Then the photographer rushes over, and you pose for an endless series of photographs with your family and friends.

But the quinceañera celebration has just begun, for the fiesta is still to come. You enter to the sound of music, a traditional mariachi band or a DJ playing current hits. You dance in turn with your father, your grandfathers, your escort. You and your honor court perform a group dance that you have rehearsed. Then everyone joins in the dancing.

Reading Standard 2.4 Clarify an understanding of texts by creating outlines, logical notes, summaries, or reports.

MINI-LESSON Reading

Reviewing Word-Attack Skills
Activity. Write these words on the chalkboard, and have students read each one aloud. Then, have them orally add the suffix *–ation* or *–ion* and say the new word.

1. hibernate [–ion]
2. hesitate [–ion]
3. investigate [–ion]
4. decorate [–ion]
5. realize [–ation]

Activity. Write these sets of words on the chalkboard with the letters underlined as shown. Have volunteers read the words and identify the two words in which the underlined letters stand for the same sounds.

You're almost too excited to eat, but the food is wonderful. There's your favorite—chicken in mole sauce, made from chilies and unsweetened chocolate. The tables are covered with everything from tamales and corn soup to an elaborately decorated cake.

Later, as everyone watches, your father removes the flat shoes you have worn all day and replaces them with a pair of high heels. In your parents' eyes you are no longer a child. They'll treat you differently from now on, and they'll expect you to act more like an adult as well.

Among your many gifts, one stands out: the last doll. It's not a toy for you to play with, of course; it's a symbol of the childhood you're leaving behind. If you have a younger sister, you might present it to her. You look around at the people who have watched you grow up. You see tears in many eyes. The quinceañera is a tradition many centuries old, but for you it will happen only once.

1. A **summary** of this article would —
   A   criticize aspects of the celebration
   B   cover the most important points
   C   discuss the quality of the writing
   D   focus on one part of the article

2. In an **outline** of this article, all of these might be details under a main heading *except* —
   F   girl dances with father and grandfather
   G   honor court performs dance
   H   DJ or mariachi band plays music
   J   what happens at the party

3. If you quoted a phrase or sentence from this article on a note card, you would put the writer's words —
   A   in quotation marks
   B   in capital letters
   C   in parentheses
   D   in a footnote

4. Which sentence best states the **main idea** of this article?
   F   The food is the best part of the quinceañera.
   G   The quinceañera happens only once in a girl's lifetime.
   H   The quinceañera is a girl's rite of passage into adulthood.
   J   Girls who celebrate their quinceañera usually do not appreciate what it represents.

5. If you were taking notes for a **summary** of this article, what event would you cite in the blank below?
   You go to Thanksgiving Mass.

   _____

   Your medal is blessed.
   You give a speech.
   A   Father gives you high heels.
   B   You receive a symbolic doll.
   C   You enjoy a wonderful feast.
   D   You place roses on the altar.

	A	B	C
1.	exhaust	exhibit	inhibit [A, B]
2.	century	contrary	civility [A, C]
3.	jalapeño	injurious	justification [B, C]
4.	heritage	heir	hieroglyphics [A, C]

C **Reading Informational Materials**
GRADE-LEVEL STANDARD
? **Summary.** How would you summarize this paragraph? [Much rich food is served.] Which information from this paragraph would you omit from a summary? [names of specific foods]

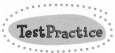

Answers and Model Rationales

1. **B**   The purpose of a summary is not to critique (A and C) or to examine details (D), but to give a broad overview.

2. **J**   F, G, and H all provide specific details. J is the general phrase forming the main heading under which the details would be listed.

3. **A**   C and D may seem to be possible choices, but A is best because quoted material always must be enclosed in quotation marks, regardless of whether it appears in parentheses or in a footnote.

4. **H**   F and G are not the main idea because they reflect only certain portions of the article; J is neither stated nor implied in the article.

5. **D**   The third paragraph gives this detail as preceding both of the other events cited in the question, as well as preceding A, B, and C.

Test-Taking Tips
Remind students that differentiating between main ideas and details is one key to understanding how to take notes and create outlines and summaries. Suggest that students re-read the article, scanning for main ideas before beginning the Test Practice.

For more information on answering multiple-choice items, refer students to **Test Smarts,** p. 690.

Test Practice

Vocabulary Development

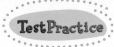

Answers and Model Rationales

1. **C** *Lofty* and *noble* have positive connotations, whereas *weak* (A) has negative connotations, and *old* and *stuffed* (B and D) are neutral.

2. **F** *Shrewd* comes from a word meaning "goblin or evil spirit," so *nice* (G) would not apply. *Angry* and *hungry* (H and J) might describe its temporary states, but only cleverness would be one of its traits.

3. **A** To diet (C) is to eat modestly, the opposite of gorge. To buy (B) and to investigate (D) describe actions unrelated to eating.

4. **G** *Audacity* comes from a Latin word meaning "daring." *Appetite, discomfort,* and *anxiety* (F, H, and J) have nothing to do with daring, but *boldness* does.

5. **B** *Evacuate* comes from a Latin word meaning "to empty the contents from." *Remove* (B) best fits this definition.

6. **H** To be interned in a camp is to be confined there.

7. **A** B and D may seem possible, because people speak of alien aircraft and alien warriors. However, since all four choices are nouns, students should realize that only *foreigner* is synonymous with the noun *alien*.

8. **G** People who are forsaken often feel sad. Of the four options *abandoned* is the state most closely related to sadness.

Vocabulary Development

TestPractice

Synonyms

DIRECTIONS: Choose the word that is closest in meaning to the underlined word.

1. A lofty idea is —
   A   weak
   B   old
   C   noble
   D   stuffed

2. A shrewd person is —
   F   clever
   G   nice
   H   angry
   J   hungry

3. To gorge on food is to —
   A   overeat
   B   buy
   C   diet
   D   investigate

4. If you have audacity, you have —
   F   appetite
   G   boldness
   H   discomfort
   J   anxiety

5. Evacuate means —
   A   mistreat
   B   remove
   C   desert
   D   value

6. If people are interned, they are —
   F   drafted
   G   confronted
   H   confined
   J   reprimanded

7. An alien is —
   A   a foreigner
   B   an aircraft
   C   a politician
   D   a warrior

8. If you are forsaken, you are —
   F   bored
   G   abandoned
   H   dirty
   J   satisfied

Vocabulary Review

Use this activity to assess whether students have retained the chapter Vocabulary.
Activity. Have students select the correct word to complete the sentences.

grimace	alien	shrewd
audacity	evacuate	

1. The dog proved its _____ by stealing our pizza right off the table. [audacity]

2. When Chau offered discounts to repeat customers, we knew she was a _____ businesswoman. [shrewd]

3. Will it be necessary to _____ civilians from the area if war breaks out? [evacuate]

4. The gangster's face twisted into a horrible _____. [grimace]

5. Police in Paris considered him an _____. [alien]

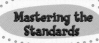

AN EXPLANATION

The Human Seasons: Explaining a Ritual

In "Ta-Na-E-Ka" you read about the coming-of-age ritual of the Kaw. Most cultures have rituals that mark important stages in a person's life or important events in the year—a wedding is a good example of such a ritual. Think of a ritual you're familiar with or one you'd like to learn more about. Gather information about it, using encyclopedias, the Internet, libraries, even interviews with people familiar with the ritual. Write an explanation of how the ritual is carried out. (You could use as a model the article on the quinceañera on pages 108–109.) Before you begin to write, think about the order of the events that make up the ritual—in other words, think about what happens at each stage or in each event in the ritual. Fill out a chart like the following one to be sure you have your main events in the right order:

Preparation	Event 1	Event 2	Event 3	[and so on]

Then, collect details for these parts of the ritual: food, clothing, music, setting, and people who attend. You could call your essay "How to Become a Bar Mitzvah," or "How to Celebrate Kwanzaa," or "How to Celebrate Halloween."

➤ Use "Writing a 'How-to' Explanation," pages 528–544, for help with this assignment.

Another Choice

PERFORMANCE

Onstage with Blanca Flor!

With a small group, rehearse and perform a reading of at least two scenes of the play. Do either a live dramatic reading in front of the class or a taped reading for an imaginary radio broadcast. As you rehearse, be sure to look closely at stage directions that tell you how lines should be spoken. Sometimes the dialogue itself gives you clues to the way the characters feel. Work on using your voice to convey emotions like pride, terror, and nervousness. Your group should pick a director to help actors rehearse their lines. If you do a radio broadcast, you will need someone to work on the sound effects.

Writing Applications **111**

Evaluation Criteria

A good explanatory composition

1. states a thesis or purpose
2. includes enough facts and details to explain the thesis clearly
3. follows an organizational pattern appropriate to content and purpose
4. credits the sources on which it is based

ASSESSING

Assessment

■ *Progress Assessment of Reading*
   ■ Chapter Test, p. 34
■ *Diagnostic and Summative Assessments*
   ■ First-Quarter Test, p. 41

After you have completed Chapters 1 and 2 and all related instruction, you may want your students to take this test.

Using Academic Language

Literary Terms

As part of the review of Literary Response and Analysis Standard 3.2, ask students to look back through the chapter to find the meanings of the terms listed at the right. Then, have students show their grasp of Standard 3.2 by citing passages from a selection in the chapter that illustrate the meanings of the following terms.

Character (pp. 52, 53, 54); **Conflict** (pp. 52, 54); **External Conflict** (p. 54); **Internal Conflict** (p. 54); **First-Person Point of View** (p. 69); **Characterization** (p. 90).

Informational Terms

As part of the review of Reading Comprehension Standard 2.4, ask students to look back through the chapter to find the meaning of the following terms that pertain to Standard 2.4. Then, ask students to explain how they would use the items and techniques listed below to clarify information.

Outlining (p. 64); **Main Ideas and Subheads** (p. 64); **Clarifying Questions** (p. 64); **Taking Notes** (pp. 64, 78); **Summary** (p. 86).

Read On

For Independent Reading

If students enjoyed the themes and topics explored in this chapter, you might recommend these titles for independent reading.

Assessment Options

The following projects can help you evaluate and assess your students' outside reading. Videotapes or audiotapes of completed projects may be included in students' portfolios.

■ **Write to pen pals.** Have students write a letter to a major character in one of the recommended books. They should explain in their letter the approach they would have taken to resolve the character's conflict.

■ **Conduct a news interview.** Have pairs of students take the roles of a book character and a reporter. Ask the pairs to brainstorm at least five questions that the reporter can ask the character, such as "What gave you the idea to . . .?" Videotape the pairs as they perform their interviews.

California Reading List Titles

Because of Winn-Dixie
Skellig
Julie of the Wolves

Fiction

Happy Together

When ten-year-old Opal Buloni moves to a small town in Florida, her life changes for the better. The title of Kate DiCamillo's novel explains why: *Because of Winn-Dixie*. Winn-Dixie is the eccentric but lovable dog Opal adopts upon her arrival. Winn-Dixie helps Opal make some wonderful friends, including a pet-store clerk who plays a mean guitar and a librarian who makes delicious candy. Winn-Dixie also brings Opal closer to her quiet preacher father.

A Mysterious Stranger

In David Almond's *Skellig*, Michael is dealing with a messy new house and an ill baby sister when he comes across Skellig, a strange, decrepit creature residing in Michael's filthy garage. Initially Michael is frightened by Skellig, until he and his new friend Mina order Chinese food for the creature and help lead him out of the darkness. From this relationship Michael discovers the value of compassion and the magic in his own life.

A Member of the Pack

A thirteen-year-old Inuit girl named Miyax runs away from home and gets lost on the Alaskan tundra—a vast, treeless wilderness region—in Jean Craighead George's Newbery Medal–winning novel *Julie of the Wolves*. Miyax is menaced by a host of dangers until a pack of wolves gradually accepts her as one of their own.

A Lack of Communication

Philip Molloy is suspended when he defies school policy by humming along to the national anthem. He *says* he is humming to be patriotic. But that's only part of the story: He really wants to irritate his English teacher, who gave him a D and kept him off the track team. Philip's deception turns a minor infraction into a media circus in Avi's popular novel *Nothing but the Truth*.

This title is available in the HRW Library.

112 Chapter 2 Characters: The People You'll Meet

Toward Reading a Million Words Annually

Estimated Word Counts of Read On Books:

Fiction		Nonfiction	
Because of Winn-Dixie	21,000	*Duke Ellington: Giant of Jazz*	25,000
Skellig	33,000	*Julius Caesar*	10,000
Julie of the Wolves	40,000	*Black Stars: African American*	
Nothing but the Truth	25,0000	Inventors	35,000
Connections to *Nothing but the*		*Changing Places: A Kid's View of*	
Truth	7,500	Shelter Living	2,000

Nonfiction

The Duke

If you're interested in music or African American history, you'll enjoy Wendie C. Old's *Duke Ellington: Giant of Jazz*. Ellington's compositions and performances helped bring jazz into the American mainstream. Old introduces you to Ellington's music and to the members of his band. If you'd like to hear one of Ellington's best albums, try *Ellington at Newport 1956*.

The Leader of an Empire

In this biography, called *Julius Caesar*, Robert Green gives an overview of the Roman dictator's life and career. You'll find out about Caesar's ambition to be Rome's dictator and his brilliance as a military strategist. Green's text includes maps, time lines, and illustrations to help you feel you are there in ancient Rome.

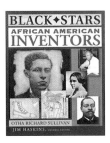

Creative Minds

In *Black Stars: African American Inventors*, Otha Richard Sullivan tells the stories of twenty-five African Americans who overcame prejudice to become important inventors. Their inventions range from a gas mask to a lighting system used in theaters. If you like these stories, you may want to try other books in the *Black Stars* series.

True Stories

Homelessness in America is a problem that can't be ignored. Margie Chalofsky, Glen Finland, and Judy Wallace give eight homeless children a voice in *Changing Places: A Kid's View of Shelter Living*. Some of the children, like twelve-year-old Molly, are hopeful that they will soon find a home of their own. Others, like eight-year-old Anthony, are troubled by self-doubt. All tell stories you will not soon forget.

- **Create an advertisement.** Have students create an advertisement or poster for a book they have read. Their ad or poster should include a drawing and a quotation from the text that reveal something interesting about the main character to "grab" potential readers. Students might also ask classmates or friends who have read the book to provide a favorable critical comment that could be quoted as part of the ad or poster.

- **Design a life map.** Ask students to draw a map showing main events in the life of a memorable character in one of the fiction or nonfiction books. The map should show the person's "path" through life, with small illustrations or icons pointing out each "turning point," "fork in the road," "uphill climb," and so on. For example, a small drawing of a carton of Chinese food might mark the turning point in *Skellig* when Michael and Mina begin to make friends with the creature living in Michael's garage.

 Resources Reminder

Reading

- *Interactive Reading*

For additional readings that relate to the selections in this chapter, see *Interactive Reading*, Chapter 2.

- *The Ancient World:* A Content-Area Reader

DIFFERENTIATING INSTRUCTION

The Read On titles are organized into the following categories:

Below Grade Level ⬇
Because of Winn-Dixie
Skellig
Changing Places: A Kid's View of Shelter Living

At Grade Level ↔
Nothing but the Truth
Julius Caesar

Above Grade Level ⬆
Julie of the Wolves
Duke Ellington: Giant of Jazz
Black Stars: African American Inventors

Chapter 3 The Heart of the Matter: Themes and Conclusions

Program Organization

Holt Literature and Language Arts provides a complete curriculum for standards-based instruction in vocabulary, reading, literature, writing, and speaking and listening. The instructional content of the program is divided into quarters to enable teachers to anticipate and administer the quarterly assessments required by California.

About Chapter 3

Standards-based lesson plans and suggestions for pacing the presentation of Chapter 3 and the related instructional material are provided in *On Course: Mapping Instruction*, Chapter 3.

- Chapter 3 helps students identify and analyze themes conveyed through characters, actions, and images, evaluate an author's evidence, and identify and interpret figurative language in prose.
- The related instructional material for Chapter 3 is shown on the chart. This related instructional material will also be covered in the second quarterly assessment.

Holt Literature and Language Arts

Pupil's Edition

Part 1, Chapter 3

The Heart of the Matter:
Themes and Conclusions, pp. 114–169
- Reading Standards 1.2, 2.6, 3.6
- Writing Application: **Writing a Response to Literature**

Part 2, Workshop 3

Response to Literature
Writing a Short Story Interpretation,
pp. 552–569
- Writing Standard 2.4

Giving and Listening to an Oral
Response to Literature, pp. 570–574
- Listening and Speaking Standard 2.3

Part 2, Mini-Workshop 4

Writing a Movie Review, pp. 673–675
- Writing Standard 2.4

Holt Handbook

Chapter 5

Complements
Written and Oral English-Language Conventions
- Looking Ahead, Gr. 7 Standard 1.3,
  pp. 105–116

Chapter 6

Agreement
Written and Oral English-Language Conventions
- Grade-Level Standard 1.2, pp. 124–140

Which vocabulary, informational reading, and literature standards are taught in Chapter 3?

In this chapter, students will master the following Grade 6 standards. They will also review a standard from Grade 4. Selections or features marked with a ✔ constitute the minimum course of study that provides coverage of all grade-level standards.

Grade 6 Standards

Word Analysis, Fluency, and Systematic Vocabulary Development

1.2 Identify and interpret figurative language.

✔ Using Context Clues to Clarify Meaning, p. 129

✔ Interpreting Figurative Language, p. 129

✔ Figurative Language, p. 134

Identifying Hyperbole, p. 143

Reading Comprehension (Focus on Informational Materials)

2.6 Determine the adequacy and appropriateness of the evidence for an author's conclusions.

"Everybody Is Different, but the Same Too" (interview), pp. 130–133

"Uniform Style" (informational article), pp. 144–147

✔ "One Child's Labor of Love" (interview), pp. 157–161

✔ Standards Review: Reading Informational Materials, pp. 164–165

Literary Response and Analysis

3.6 Identify and analyze features of themes conveyed through characters, actions, and images.

✔ "Theme: The Power of a Story" (standards essay), pp. 116–117

"The All-American Slurp" (short story), pp. 118–128

"The Emperor's New Clothes" (fairy tale), pp. 135–142

✔ "Baucis and Philemon" (myth), pp. 149–155

✔ Standards Review: Literary Response and Analysis, pp. 162–163

Review Standards Grade 4

Vocabulary 1.2 Apply knowledge of idioms to determine the meaning of words and phrases.

Interpreting Idioms, p. 143

Interpreting Idioms, p. 148

Mastering the California Standards CHAPTER 3

Mastering the California Standards CHAPTER 3

Where do I locate lesson plans, additional resources, and other teaching aids?

- This Annotated Teacher's Edition and *On Course: Mapping Instruction* provide direction in planning and implementing a complete California standards–based curriculum. These components include instructions for administering diagnostic, progress, and summative tests; for presenting instruction of the standards; for differentiating instruction to provide universal access; and for locating and using the program's ancillaries.

- The program's resources are referenced at the beginning of each selection, in the bottom margin of this teacher's edition.

- Reminders for using additional resources appear in this teacher's edition at point of use.

- The *One-Stop Planner* CD-ROM with Test Generator contains editable lesson plans and all of the print ancillaries, available in PDF format.

What if I don't have time to teach all of Chapter 3?

- Most standards can be taught with a minimum number of selections and features. In the chart on p. 113B, the core lessons you need in or-der to provide complete coverage of the chapter standards are identified with a ✔.

- Use the Standards Review, pp. 162–165, for a quick review and informal assessment of the grade-level standards covered in Chapter 3.

What provisions have been made for students who have additional class time scheduled in language arts?

- *Interactive Reading* provides for additional direct instruction and practice of the grade-level standards taught in Chapter 3. It can be used as an introduction to instruction or as an opportunity for remediation.

- *Lesson Plans for Language Development,* Chapter 3, provides alternative teaching strategies and additional worksheets designed specifically for English-language learners and special education students. Many of the suggestions and activities in this ancillary will also be helpful to students in the regular classroom who are having difficulty with particular skills.

In addition to vocabulary, reading, and literature, what other language arts are covered in Chapter 3?

Writing Activities in Chapter 3
- Reader's Theater: All-American Scenes, p. 128
- A Fashion Statement, p. 142
- All Is Revealed, p. 155

Writing Applications (p. 167)
- Thinking Theme (short story interpretation)
- Other Choices: How to Give a Party (exposition); Pro or Con (persuasion)

Grammar Links in Chapter 3
- Clear Pronoun References, p. 148
- Pronouns as Objects of Prepositions, p. 156
- The Homophones *Their, There,* and *They're,* p. 161

Universal Access

How do I differentiate instruction to ensure that all my students master the standards?

Holt Literature and Language Arts provides comprehensive, differentiated instruction for all types of students.

- Most of the general instruction and teaching strategies in the Annotated Teacher's Edition are at grade level. These instructions will work well with the majority of your students.

- In Chapter 3, suggestions for advanced learners are provided in the Annotated Teacher's Edition. Point-of-use suggestions for learners having difficulty, English-language learners, and special education students are also provided.

- *Interactive Reading* is designed to anticipate and/or remediate problems that students may experience in achieving mastery of the standards. *Interactive Reading* includes reading-strategy lessons, lower-level practice reads, and worksheets for every informational and literary text in *Holt Literature and Language Arts*, Pupil's Editions. *Interactive Reading* also contains three additional selections for each chapter and suggestions for extension projects, many of which are ideal for advanced learners working on their own. See *Interactive Reading*, Teacher's Edition, for specific information on using the reader to differentiate instruction in Chapter 3.

- *Lesson Plans for Language Development,* Chapter 3, offers teaching strategies and additional worksheets designed specifically for English-language learners and special education students.

Assessment

How do I determine whether or not my students are making progress in mastering the standards?

Progress Assessment

- Use the Standards Review at the end of Chapter 3, pp. 162–165, for an informal assessment of the informational reading and literature standards in Chapter 3.

- Use the Selection Tests for Chapter 3 in the *Progress Assessment of Reading* booklet to test comprehension and progress on mastering the standard(s) taught with a selection.

- Use Chapter Test 3 in the *Progress Assessment of Reading* booklet to test students' cumulative progress in mastering the standards taught in the chapter.

Summative Assessment

The content of *Holt Literature and Language Arts* has been divided into quarters to allow you to administer the four summative tests required by California. Chapters 3 and 4 and related instructional material constitute the second quarter of instruction. At the end of Chapter 4, you may ask students to take the Midyear Test in the *Diagnostic and Summative Assessments* booklet.

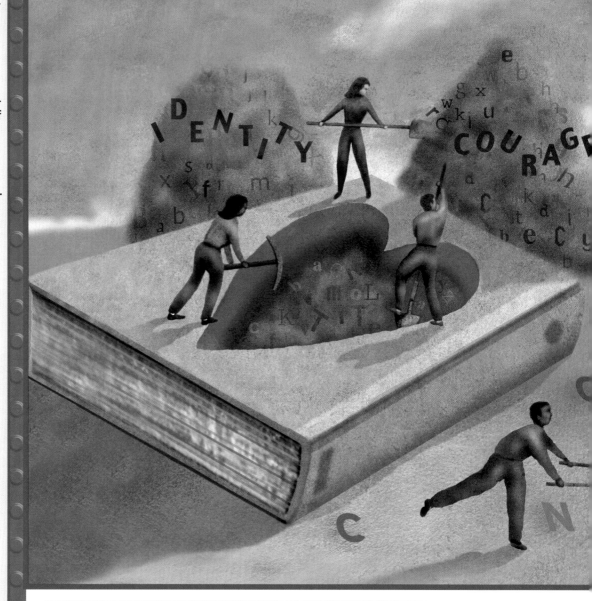

CHAPTER

3 The Heart of the Matter
Themes and Conclusions

Prerequisite Standards

- Grade 5, Vocabulary 1.5 **Understand and explain the fig-urative and metaphorical use of words in context.**

- Grade 5, Reading Comprehension 2.5 **Distinguish facts, supported inferences, and opinions in text.**

- Grade 5, Literary Response and Analysis 3.4 **Understand that** *theme* **refers to the meaning or moral of a selection, and recog-nize themes (whether implied or stated directly) in sample works.**

Standard Coming Up in the Next Grade Level

- Grade 7, Literary Response and Analysis 3.4 **Identify and ana-lyze recurring themes across works (e.g., the value of brav-ery, loyalty, and friendship; the effects of loneliness).**

CHAPTER RESOURCES

Planning
- *One-Stop Planner* CD-ROM with Test Generator
- *On Course: Mapping Instruction*
  - Chapter 3
- *At Home: A Guide to Standards Mastery*
- *At Home: In Five Languages*
- *Supporting Instruction in Five Languages*

Reading
- *Interactive Reading*
  - Chapter 3

Differentiating Instruction
- *Lesson Plans for Language Development*
  - Chapter 3

Vocabulary and Spelling
- *Vocabulary Development*
  - Cumulative Vocabulary Review, p. 12

California Standards

Here are the Grade 6 standards you will study for mastery in Chapter 3. You will also review a standard from an earlier grade.

Reading

Word Analysis, Fluency, and Systematic Vocabulary Development

1.2 Identify and interpret figurative language.

Grade 4 Review
1.2 Apply knowledge of idioms to determine the meaning of words and phrases.

Reading Comprehension (Focus on Informational Materials)

2.6 Determine the adequacy and appropriateness of the evidence for an author's conclusions.

Literary Response and Analysis

3.6 Identify and analyze features of themes conveyed through characters, actions, and images.

go.
hrw
.com

KEYWORD:
HLLA 6-3

California Standards **115**

STANDARDS FOCUS, pp. 116–117

(*For the grade-level standard taught in this lesson, see Pupil's Edition, p. 116.*)

Prerequisite Standard

■ Grade 5, Literary Response and Analysis 3.4 **Understand that** *theme* **refers to the meaning or moral of a selection, and recognize themes (whether implied or stated directly) in sample works.**

Literary Focus: Theme

Remind students that the plot of a story is only what happens in it; the theme is what the story reveals about life. What happens in a story may help readers infer the theme, but the theme goes beyond the specific story to state a truth about real life. Encourage students also to go beyond what is happening in a story when they read and to ask themselves the following questions: "Is this writer trying to urge readers toward a specific point of view? If so, what is it? What does the title of the story signify? Does it point to the story's theme? How does the main character change in the course of the story? What do the word choices and imagery reveal about the theme?"

⟶ Resources Reminder

Reading

■ *Interactive Reading*

Before you teach Chapter 3 of *Holt Literature and Language Arts,* you may want to preteach the literary concept and a related reading strategy.

• To introduce students to the literary concept before they read this essay, assign p. 99 of *Interactive Reading.*

• To introduce students to a reading strategy that will help them grasp the literary concept, assign p. 99 of *Interactive Reading.*

• To give students practice applying the strategy to a short, vocabulary-controlled selection, assign the Practice Read on p. 100 of *Interactive Reading.*

LITERARY RESPONSE AND ANALYSIS

Theme *by Madeline Travers Hovland*
THE POWER OF A STORY

There's a big question we often ask about stories. That big question is "What does it all mean?" When we ask that question, we're asking about theme.

The **theme** of a story is the truth that it reveals about life. Theme gives a story its power.

Writers don't usually state themes directly. They want us to infer themes based on what the characters discover or how they change in the course of a story.

Theme can be supported by the language of a story. For example, writers often include details of violent weather to support a theme having to do with great passion.

"The Golden Touch" is a retelling of an ancient Greek myth about King Midas, a man who could turn everything into gold. What is its theme?

The Golden Touch

Midas was king of a country in Asia Minor. He lived in a beautiful palace surrounded by lush and fragrant gardens. Midas had a little daughter whom he loved dearly. But Midas wasn't a happy king. He never looked out upon his gardens and saw the crocuses come up through the rich soil in spring. He ignored the perfume of the roses in the warm summer. He never saw the snow sparkle on the mountains.

Reading Standard 3.6 Identify and analyze features of themes conveyed through characters, actions, and images.

What Midas loved most was his treasure room, deep down in a chilly stone chamber. He spent whole days amid the cobwebs in the dimly lighted room, counting his gold. He loved letting the shiny gold coins slip through his hands. But no matter how much gold he had, Midas always wanted more.

In the next part of the story, Midas makes some bad decisions. Since we know his character flaws, we are not surprised at the king's selfish actions.

One day, while Midas was sitting counting his gold, he suddenly heard a whizzing sound. Out of nowhere the god Dionysus° appeared before him. Midas was afraid and hid his face.

"Midas," the god said, "you need not fear me. I remember your kindness toward my old servant some months ago. Therefore, I have decided to grant you one wish. What do you want most of all in the world?"

Midas laughed with glee. "Gold!" he roared. "Let everything I touch turn into gold!"

Dionysus shook his head sadly. "That is unwise," the god warned. But Midas was firm. "Your wish is granted," the god said, and he took off as quickly as he had arrived.

———
°Dionysus (dī′ə·nī′səs).

116 Chapter 3 The Heart of the Matter: Themes and Conclusions

---

DIFFERENTIATING INSTRUCTION

Learners Having Difficulty
Theme. To help students discover the theme of a story, remind them that they will need to read between the lines. Tell students to look for clues to a story's theme, such as lessons the characters learn or discoveries they make. Have students think of a well-known story such as "The Boy Who Cried 'Wolf.'" Invite students to tell the story in their own words and explain how the character's experiences help reveal the theme.

Advanced Learners
Acceleration. In order to move advanced learners toward the seventh-grade Standard 3.4, discuss the issue of recurring themes in stories. Point out that different works—books, stories, movies, plays, and television shows—often have similar themes.

Now we wonder what will happen next. What will Midas do with his golden touch? Here are the **complications** in Midas's story. Notice the words the storyteller uses to describe gold. Also notice the words used to describe nature and the king's little daughter.

Just then Midas heard a bell signaling that lunch was ready. As he walked back to the palace, he picked a dewy, fragrant pink rose for his little daughter. Imagine how startled he was when the green stem changed to hard yellow metal—gold! The soft petals hardened and turned bright yellow. The rigid gold flower was so heavy that he dropped it on the ground.

Midas ran into the dining hall, shouting with delight. Everything he touched on the way turned into gold. His robe became gleaming gold. The door became gold. The table changed into gold. Midas's gold frenzy made him very hungry, and he grabbed a loaf of soft bread. But as he bit into it, the smell and taste of metal sickened him. His teeth broke on the hard gold, and his mouth filled with blood. He quickly grabbed a glass of water and tried to drink, but choked and spit out liquid gold.

Then the little princess came running in. Before Midas could stop her, she jumped up for a hug. Even as they embraced, Midas realized that something horrible was happening. He felt his beautiful, warm child stiffening and becoming as cold as death. She too had been transformed into gold.

All night long, Midas wept tears of gold. Holding the rigid gold statue that had been his daughter, he prayed to the gods. With the morning sun, Dionysus appeared. "Please, please, please," Midas begged, "take away this terrible gift, and give me back my daughter."

Dionysus said, "So be it. From now on may you be a better person." Even as the god disappeared, Midas felt a rush of joy and love. He covered his little daughter's face with kisses as she became soft and warm, a flesh-and-blood child again.

From that time on, Midas devoted himself to enjoying the woodlands and meadows of his kingdom.

 Practice

1. The lesson a character learns can often be stated as a **theme.** Always state a theme as a complete sentence. Which of these themes do you think is revealed in the Midas story? (A story may have several themes.)
   - Gold isn't everything.
   - Nothing is as important as love.
   - Do not ignore wise advice.
   - Be careful what you wish for.
2. Find at least three words that describe nature and human beings as full of life and beauty. Then, find other words that describe gold as hard and lifeless. How does this use of language help support one of the story's themes?

Theme: The Power of a Story   **117**

 Practice

1. Some students may choose the first statement as the theme because Midas learns that gold is worthless compared to the living things around him. Others may choose the second statement, noting that it is when Midas almost loses his daughter that his life truly changes. Most students would agree that the last two statements are lessons but not the central themes of the story.
2. Words to describe nature and human beings include *vital, animated, bountiful, dynamic,* and *glorious.* Words to describe gold are *cold, dead, dull, heartless,* and *inert.* The language of these lists supports the theme that gold isn't everything. The words for gold are unappealing, while the words for nature and people are life-affirming.

Apply
Encourage students to choose another well-known story, such as "The Tortoise and the Hare" or "The Emperor's New Clothes," and create possible theme statements for it to share with the class.

 HOMEWORK

▶ **Resources Reminder**
Differentiating Instruction
■ *Lesson Plans for Language Development*

For additional instruction on theme for English-language learners and special education students, see *Lesson Plans for Language Development,* pp. 49–50.

Activity. Have students consider one of the themes revealed in the Midas story, such as "nothing is as important as love." Then, ask students to think about another work that has the same theme. Tell students to consider the images, word choices, and main characters' actions in each work. Encourage students to ask themselves the following questions: "How are the two works similar? How are they different? What do these similarities and differences tell me about the theme of each work?" Invite students to share their thoughts with the class.

Prerequisite Standard

■ Grade 5, Literary Response and Analysis 3.4 **Understand that** *theme* **refers to the meaning or moral of a selection, and recognize themes (whether implied or stated directly) in sample works.**

Reading Skills

■ Summarize a story.

Summary ⬆ *above grade level*

Having recently emigrated from China, the Lin family must adjust to the United States. The narrator, the daughter of the family, describes their embarrassment at the Gleasons' dinner party when the Lins pull the strings off the celery sticks served to them and then realize that everyone is staring at them in surprise. The cultural conflicts ease as the children make friends at school and Mr. Lin begins to succeed at work. Dining at an elegant restaurant to celebrate Mr. Lin's promotion, the family eats soup in the traditional Chinese way—by slurping it—to the amazement of the other diners and the embarrassment of the narrator. After three months the Lins have their own dinner party. They are amused to see that their American guests are as confused by traditional Chinese food as they had been by the raw celery. After dinner the narrator and her friend Meg enjoy chocolate milkshakes, and the narrator is amazed to hear Meg slurp the last of her drink. Meg grins and tells her Chinese friend, "All Americans slurp."

The All-American Slurp

Literary Focus
Subject Versus Theme

A story's theme is different from its subject. The **subject** is what the story is about. You can usually name a subject in a word or two. **Theme** is what the story means. Theme is an idea about life that the story's characters, actions, and images bring home to you.

The chart below illustrates the difference between a subject and a theme:

Subject	Theme
growing up	Growing up means taking responsibility.
nature	Nature can be beautiful but deadly.
love	People sometimes express love through actions, not words.

Always try to connect a story's theme to your own life. Also remember that no two readers will state a theme in exactly the same way.

Reading Skills
Summarizing

When you **summarize** a story, you tell about its main events in your own words. Summarizing is a useful skill because it helps you recall what happens in a story. It also helps you peel a story down to its core, to the events that advance the plot and reveal the theme.

This story is divided into six parts. (Each part is numbered, as you'll see when you start reading.) After you read each part, try to summarize in two or three sentences what happened in that section.

Make the Connection
Quickwrite 🖉

Have you ever been embarrassed because you didn't know how you were supposed to behave in a new situation—at a party, at a new friend's house, in a foreign country? Write a few lines about your experience.

Vocabulary Development

Here are some words that are important to Namioka's story:

lavishly (lav'ish·lē) *adv.:* generously; plentifully. *The table was heaped lavishly with food.*

mortified (môrt'ə·fīd') *v.* used as *adj.:* ashamed; deeply embarrassed. *Mortified by her family's behavior, she fled to the ladies' room.*

spectacle (spek'tə·kəl) *n.:* remarkable sight. *The narrator fears that her noisy brother is making a spectacle of himself.*

etiquette (et'i·kit) *n.:* acceptable manners and behavior. *Slurping is not proper etiquette in a fancy restaurant.*

Reading Standard 3.6 Identify and analyze features of themes conveyed through characters, actions, and images.

RESOURCES

Planning
■ *One-Stop Planner* CD-ROM with Test Generator
■ *On Course: Mapping Instruction*

Media
■ *Audio CD Library*
  ■ disc 4
■ *Visual Connections*
  ■ Videocassette, Segment 3

■ *Fine Art Transparencies*
  ■ Transparency 6

Reading
■ *Interactive Reading*
  ■ Strategy Launch: Most Important Words, p. 99
  ■ Practice Read: "Walk a Mile in Someone Else's Shoes," p. 100
  ■ Graphic Organizer: Pyramid, p. 108

THE ALL-AMERICAN SLURP

Lensey Namioka

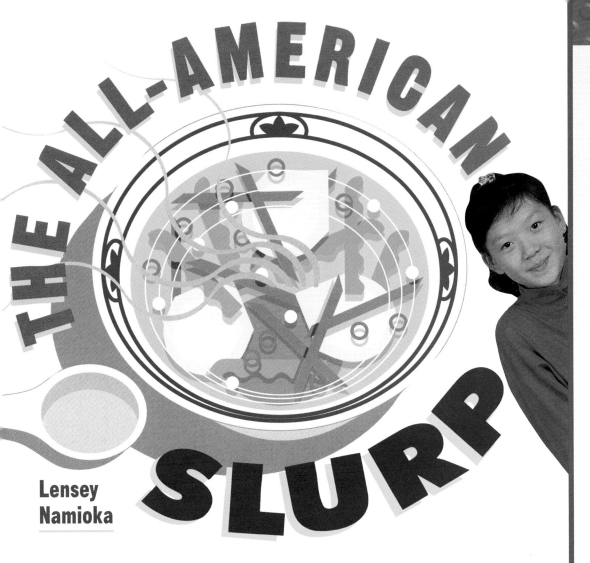

① The first time our family was invited out to dinner in America, we disgraced ourselves while eating celery. We had immigrated to this country from China, and during our early days here we had a hard time with American table manners.

In China we never ate celery raw, or any other kind of vegetable raw. We always had to disinfect the vegetables in boiling water first.

When we were presented with our first relish tray, the raw celery caught us unprepared.

We had been invited to dinner by our neighbors, the Gleasons. After arriving at the house, we shook hands with our hosts and packed ourselves into a sofa. As our family of four sat stiffly in a row, my younger brother and I stole glances at our parents for a clue as to what to do next.

The All-American Slurp **119**

- *Interactive Reading,* Teacher's Edition
  - Transparency 3: Most Important Words

Differentiating Instruction
- *Lesson Plans for Language Development*
  - English-Language Learners, pp. 51–53, 66, 72
  - Special Education Students, pp. 54, 66, 72

Vocabulary and Spelling
- *Vocabulary Development*
  - Vocabulary Worksheet, p. 10

Assessment
- *Progress Assessment of Reading*
  - Selection Test, p. 41
- *One-Stop Planner* CD-ROM with Test Generator

DIRECT TEACHING

▶ Resources Reminder

Media

- *Audio CD Library*
  - disc 4
- *Visual Connections*
  - Videocassette, Segment 3
- *Fine Art Transparencies*
  - Transparency 6

Ⓐ English-Language Learners

Interpreting idioms. Ask students if they are familiar with the expression *to follow suit* (to imitate the actions of others). If they are not, have one of your English-proficient students explain the idiom.

Mrs. Gleason offered the relish tray to Mother. The tray looked pretty, with its tiny red radishes, curly sticks of carrots, and long, slender stalks of pale-green celery. "Do try some of the celery, Mrs. Lin," she said. "It's from a local farmer, and it's sweet."

Ⓐ Mother picked up one of the green stalks, and Father followed suit. Then I picked up a stalk, and my brother did too. So there we sat, each with a stalk of celery in our right hand.

Mrs. Gleason kept smiling. "Would you like to try some of the dip, Mrs. Lin? It's my own recipe: sour cream and onion flakes, with a dash of Tabasco sauce."

Most Chinese don't care for dairy products, and in those days I wasn't even ready to drink fresh milk. Sour cream

sounded perfectly revolting. Our family shook our heads in unison.

Mrs. Gleason went off with the relish tray to the other guests, and we carefully watched to see what they did. Everyone seemed to eat the raw vegetables quite happily.

Mother took a bite of her celery. *Crunch.* "It's not bad!" she whispered.

Father took a bite of his celery. *Crunch.* "Yes, it is good," he said, looking surprised.

I took a bite, and then my brother. *Crunch, crunch.* It was more than good; it was delicious. Raw celery has a slight sparkle, a zingy taste that you don't get in cooked celery. When Mrs. Gleason came around with the relish tray, we each took another stalk of celery, except my brother. He took two.

120

DIFFERENTIATING INSTRUCTION

Learners Having Difficulty
Modeling. Some students may need to read an easier selection before beginning "The All-American Slurp." Use the Practice Read in *Interactive Reading,* p. 100. You can then use the transparency to model the strategy of finding the most important words. This strategy will help students to identify the story's theme. Then, have students apply the strategy to help them read

"The All-American Slurp." As they read, encourage students to ask themselves, "What lessons are the characters learning?"

▶ Resources Reminder
Reading

- *Interactive Reading,* Teacher's Edition
  - Transparency 3: Most Important Words

English-Language Learners
After students have finished their summary of the first section, have them write a question about something in the scene that they do not understand. Perhaps certain students are unfamiliar with "strings" of celery, "radishes," or "dip." Then, have students work in groups to answer each other's questions.

There was only one problem: Long strings ran through the length of the stalk, and they got caught in my teeth. When I help my mother in the kitchen, I always pull the strings out before slicing celery.

I pulled the strings out of my stalk. *Z-z-zip, z-z-zip.* My brother followed suit. *Z-z-zip, z-z-zip, z-z-zip.* To my left, my parents were taking care of their own stalks. *Z-z-zip, z-z-zip, z-z-zip.*

Suddenly I realized that there was dead silence except for our zipping. Looking up, I saw that the eyes of everyone in the room were on our family. Mr. and Mrs. Gleason, their daughter Meg, who was my friend, and their neighbors the Badels—they were all staring at us as we busily pulled the strings of our celery.

"z-z-zip"

That wasn't the end of it. Mrs. Gleason announced that dinner was served and invited us to the dining table. It was lavishly covered with platters of food, but we couldn't see any chairs around the table. So we helpfully carried over some dining chairs and sat down. All the other guests just stood there.

Mrs. Gleason bent down and whispered to us, "This is a buffet dinner. You help yourselves to some food and eat it in the living room."

Our family beat a retreat back to the sofa as if chased by enemy soldiers. For the rest of the evening, too mortified to go back to the dining table, I nursed a bit of potato salad on my plate.

Next day, Meg and I got on the school bus together. I wasn't sure how she would feel about me after the spectacle our family made at the party. But she was just the same as usual, and the only reference she made to the party

was, "Hope you and your folks got enough to eat last night. You certainly didn't take very much. Mom never tries to figure out how much food to prepare. She just puts everything on the table and hopes for the best."

I began to relax. The Gleasons' dinner party wasn't so different from a Chinese meal after all. My mother also puts everything on the table and hopes for the best.

2 Meg was the first friend I had made after we came to America. I eventually got acquainted with a few other kids in school, but Meg was still the only real friend I had. My brother didn't have any problems making friends. He spent all his time with some boys who were teaching him baseball, and in no time he could speak English much faster than I could—not better, but faster.

I worried more about making mistakes, and I spoke carefully, making sure I could say everything right before opening my mouth. At least I had a better accent than my parents, who never really got rid of their Chinese accent, even years later. My parents had both studied English in school before coming to America, but what they had studied was mostly written English, not spoken.

Father's approach to English was a scientific one. Since Chinese verbs have no tense, he was fascinated by the way English verbs

---

Vocabulary

lavishly (lav′ish·lē) *adv.:* generously; plentifully.

mortified (môrt′ə·fīd′) *v.* used as *adj.:* ashamed; deeply embarrassed.

spectacle (spek′tə·kəl) *n.:* strange or remarkable sight.

The All-American Slurp **121**

B Vocabulary Development
GRADE-LEVEL STANDARD

❓ **Understanding figurative language.** The narrator and her family leave the buffet table hastily. To what does the narrator compare their action? [to that of retreating from enemy soldiers] Why is this comparison effective? [It conveys the humiliation the Lins feel coping with intimidating American customs.]

C Reading Skills

❓ **Hypothesizing.** Why does Meg make friendly comments after the party? [Possible responses: Her parents may have been concerned that the Lins did not have a good time. Her mother may have told her to say something nice to the narrator.]

D Literary Focus
GRADE-LEVEL STANDARD

❓ **Theme.** The narrator states one of the themes of the story here. How might students restate this idea in their own words? [Possible response: No matter how great the cultural differences are between people, there are similarities as well.]

E Content-Area Connections
CULTURE

Accents. Inform students that when people learn a second language in adulthood, they often have a hard time losing the accent of the first language. It is much easier when the second language is acquired in childhood.

▶ **Resources Reminder**
For lessons designed for intermediate and advanced English-language learners, see *Lesson Plans for Language Development,* pp. 51–53, 66, 72.

Special Education Students
For lessons designed for special education students, see *Lesson Plans for Language Development,* pp. 54, 66, 72.

Advanced Learners
Enrichment. As students read, invite them to discuss or write about one of these questions: "What are good manners?" or "How should you act when you are hosts so as not to embarrass your guests?"

A **Vocabulary Development**
GRADE-LEVEL STANDARD

? **Using context clues.** What context clues help you to figure out that the word *blurted* means "burst out with"? [Possible response: Clues include the word *hurriedly* and the fact that Mrs. Lin was flustered and had no time to think about what polite phrase she was supposed to say.]

B **Literary Focus**
GRADE-LEVEL STANDARD

? **Theme.** How do the visits between Meg and the narrator reinforce the idea that people from different cultures have a lot in common? [Both girls enjoy borrowing each other's clothes and striking poses in front of the mirror.]

changed form according to whether they were in the present, past, perfect, pluperfect, future, or future perfect tense. He was always making diagrams of verbs and their inflections, and he looked for opportunities to show off his mastery of the pluperfect and future perfect tenses, his two favorites. "I shall have finished my project by Monday," he would say smugly.

Mother's approach was to memorize lists of polite phrases that would cover all possible social situations. She was constantly muttering things like "I'm fine, thank you. And you?" Once she accidentally stepped on someone's **A** foot and hurriedly blurted, "Oh, that's quite all right!" Embarrassed by her slip, she resolved to do better next time. So when someone stepped on *her* foot, she cried, "You're welcome!"

In our own different ways, we made progress in learning English. But I had another worry, and that was my appearance. My brother didn't have to worry, since Mother bought him blue jeans for school, and he dressed like all the other boys. But she insisted that girls had to wear skirts. By the time she saw that Meg and the other girls were wearing jeans, it was too late. My school clothes were bought already, and we didn't have money left to buy new outfits for me. We had too many other things to buy first, like furniture, pots, and pans.

The first time I visited Meg's house, she took me upstairs to her room, and I wound up trying on her clothes. We were pretty much the same size since Meg was shorter and thinner than average. Maybe that's how we became friends in the first place. Wearing Meg's jeans and T-shirt, I looked at myself in the mirror. I could almost pass for an American—from the back, anyway. At least the kids in school wouldn't stop and stare at me in the hallways, which was what they did when they saw me in my white blouse and navy-blue skirt that went a couple of inches below the knees.

B

"shloop"

When Meg came to my house, I invited her to try on my Chinese dresses, the ones with a high collar and slits up the sides. Meg's eyes were bright as she looked at herself in the mirror. She struck several sultry poses, and we nearly fell over laughing.

3 The dinner party at the Gleasons' didn't stop my growing friendship with Meg. Things were getting better for me in other ways too. Mother finally bought me some jeans at the end of the month, when Father got his paycheck. She wasn't in any hurry about buying them at first, until I worked on her. This is what I did. Since we didn't have a car in those days, I often ran down to the neighborhood store to pick up things for her. The groceries cost less at a big supermarket, but the closest one was many blocks away. One day, when she ran out of flour, I offered to borrow a bike from our neighbor's son and buy a ten-pound bag of flour at the big supermarket. I mounted the boy's bike and waved to Mother. "I'll be back in five minutes!"

Before I started pedaling, I heard her voice behind me. "You can't go out in public like that! People can see all the way up to your thighs!"

"I'm sorry," I said innocently. "I thought you were in a hurry to get the flour." For dinner we

CONTENT-AREA CONNECTIONS

Geography
China. Ask students to locate China on a map or globe and to speculate on what method of transportation the narrator's family may have used to travel to the United States. Have them keep in mind that the family is not wealthy. Also, have students locate San Francisco, New York City, and Vancouver, B.C., Canada, three major landing points for Chinese immigrants.

WHOLE-CLASS

were going to have pot stickers (fried Chinese dumplings), and we needed a lot of flour.

"Couldn't you borrow a girl's bicycle?" complained Mother. "That way your skirt won't be pushed up."

"There aren't too many of those around," I said. "Almost all the girls wear jeans while riding a bike, so they don't see any point buying a girl's bike."

We didn't eat pot stickers that evening, and Mother was thoughtful. Next day we took the bus downtown and she bought me a pair of jeans. In the same week, my brother made the baseball team of his junior high school, Father started taking driving lessons, and Mother discovered rummage sales. We

soon got all the furniture we needed, plus a dartboard and a 1,000-piece jigsaw puzzle. (Fourteen hours later, we discovered that it was a 999-piece jigsaw puzzle.) There was hope that the Lins might become a normal American family after all.

4 Then came our dinner at the Lakeview restaurant. The Lakeview was an expensive restaurant, one of those places where a head-waiter dressed in tails conducted you to your seat, and the only light came from candles and flaming desserts. In one corner of the room a lady harpist played tinkling melodies.

Father wanted to celebrate because he had just been promoted. He worked for an

DIRECT TEACHING

C Reading Skills

? Interpreting. How does the incident with the bicycle change Mrs. Lin's attitude toward Americanization? [Possible responses: She has a better understanding of certain aspects of American culture; she is more willing to adapt to American culture.]

D Reading Skills

? Predicting. What do you think will happen at the restaurant? [Possible responses: Some students may predict that the Lins will find themselves in another embarrassing situation. Other students may say that everything will be fine because the Lins have more experience now.]

E English-Language Learners

Interpreting idioms. Explain that the phrase *dressed in tails* means "dressed in a man's formal evening costume with a swallowtail coat." Headwaiters often wear tails.

DEVELOPING FLUENCY

Activity. Have students conduct a random reading of the story. First, ask them to read the story silently, taking notes on the words, phrases, or sentences that they find funny. Next, let students read aloud in random order the parts of the story they have marked. Then, ask them to explain to the class why they chose the passages they did.

WHOLE-CLASS

A Content-Area Connections
CULTURE

Chow mein. It is amusing that the Lins consider chow mein to be Western food while many Americans consider it Chinese food. Tell students that chow mein is actually a dish invented by Chinese immigrant chefs for their non-Chinese customers.

B Reading Skills

Summarizing. Father seems to be prepared for any situation. Ask students to summarize all the steps he has taken to improve things for himself and for his family.

C English-Language Learners

Translating foreign words. If there are any French-speaking students in the class, have them pronounce *pâté en croûte* in unison. Explain that this appetizer consists of a meat paste (often made of goose livers) wrapped in a pastry crust. Then, ask why the narrator is squirming. [She is embarrassed by her father's attempts to translate the menu.]

D Vocabulary Development
GRADE-LEVEL STANDARD

❓ Understanding figurative language. To what does the narrator compare the sound of her family eating soup? [to the sucking sound of a receding tide as it drains water from the tide pools]

---

electronics company, and after his English started improving, his superiors decided to appoint him to a position more suited to his training. The promotion not only brought a higher salary but was also a tremendous boost to his pride.

Up to then we had eaten only in Chinese restaurants. Although my brother and I were becoming fond of hamburgers, my parents **Ⓐ** didn't care much for Western food, other than chow mein.

But this was a special occasion, and Father asked his co-workers to recommend a really elegant restaurant. So there we were at the Lakeview, stumbling after the headwaiter in the murky dining room.

At our table we were handed our menus, and they were so big that to read mine, I almost had to stand up again. But why bother? It was mostly in French, anyway.

Ⓑ Father, being an engineer, was always systematic. He took out a pocket French dictionary. "They told me that most of the items would be in French, so I came prepared." He even had a pocket flashlight the size of a marking pen. While Mother held the flashlight over the menu, he looked up the items that were in French.

Ⓒ "*Pâté en croûte*," he muttered. "Let's see . . . *pâté* is paste . . . *croûte* is crust . . . hmmm . . . a paste in crust."

The waiter stood looking patient. I squirmed and died at least fifty times.

At long last Father gave up. "Why don't we just order four complete dinners at random?" he suggested.

"Isn't that risky?" asked Mother. "The French eat some rather peculiar things, I've heard."

"A Chinese can eat anything a Frenchman can eat," Father declared.

The soup arrived in a plate. How do you get soup up from a plate? I glanced at the other diners, but the ones at the nearby tables were not on their soup course, while the more distant ones were invisible in the darkness.

Fortunately my parents had studied books on Western etiquette before they came to America. "Tilt your plate," whispered my mother. "It's easier to spoon the soup up that way."

She was right. Tilting the plate did the trick. But the etiquette book didn't say anything about what you did after the soup reached your lips. As any respectable Chinese knows, the correct way to eat your soup is to slurp. This helps to cool the liquid and prevent you from burning your lips. It also shows your appreciation.

Ⓓ We showed our appreciation. *Shloop*, went my father. *Shloop*, went my mother. *Shloop*, *shloop*, went my brother, who was the hungriest.

The lady harpist stopped playing to take a rest. And in the silence, our family's consumption of soup suddenly seemed unnaturally loud. You know how it sounds on a rocky beach when the tide goes out and the water drains from all those little pools? They go *shloop, shloop, shloop*. That was the Lin family eating soup.

At the next table a waiter was pouring wine. When a large *shloop* reached him, he froze. The bottle continued to pour, and red wine flooded the table top and into the lap of a customer. Even the customer didn't notice anything at first, being also hypnotized by the *shloop, shloop, shloop*.

Vocabulary
etiquette (et′i·kit) *n.:* acceptable manners and behavior.

MINI-LESSON Reading

Developing Word-Attack Skills

Remind students that the letter *c* before *e* or *i* is a soft *c*, and its sound is the same as the sound of the letter *s*: /s/. As an example, display the word *decide*. Then, write the selection word *delicious* on the chalkboard and read it aloud. Repeat the word, and ask students what sound the letters *ci* stand for here. Help students recognize that the letters *ci* in *delicious* stand for the sound /sh/.

Activity. Display these sentences. Have volunteers read the sentences and tell what sound the letter *c* stands for in the underlined word.

1. <u>Facial</u> expressions reveal a lot. [/sh/]

2. Reading them is not a <u>precise</u> art. [/s/]

3. Expressions can give <u>crucial</u> hints. [/sh/]

4. Paying attention can be <u>beneficial</u>. [/sh/]

5. People don't <u>publicize</u> their feelings. [/s/]

6. Some never comment or <u>criticize</u>. [/s/]

7. They encourage others on <u>principle</u>. [/s/]

8. Some people give <u>precious</u> few hints about what they really think. [/sh/]

It was too much. "I need to go to the toilet," I mumbled, jumping to my feet. A waiter, sensing my urgency, quickly directed me to the ladies' room.

I splashed cold water on my burning face, and as I dried myself with a paper towel, I stared into the mirror. In this perfumed ladies' room, with its pink-and-silver wallpaper and marbled sinks, I looked completely out of place. What was I doing here? What was our family doing in the Lakeview restaurant? In America?

The door to the ladies' room opened. A woman came in and glanced curiously at me. I retreated into one of the toilet cubicles and latched the door.

Time passed—maybe half an hour, maybe an hour. Then I heard the door open again, and my mother's voice. "Are you in there? You're not sick, are you?"

There was real concern in her voice. A girl can't leave her family just because they slurp their soup. Besides, the toilet cubicle had a few drawbacks as a permanent residence. "I'm all right," I said, undoing the latch.

Mother didn't tell me how the rest of the dinner went, and I didn't want to know. In the weeks following, I managed to push the whole thing into the back of my mind, where it jumped out at me only a few times a day. Even now, I turn hot all over when I think of the Lakeview restaurant.

5 But by the time we had been in this country for three months, our family was definitely making progress toward becoming Americanized. I remember my parents' first PTA meeting. Father wore a neat suit and tie, and Mother put on her first pair of high heels. She stumbled only once. They met my homeroom teacher and beamed as she told

them that I would make honor roll soon at the rate I was going. Of course Chinese etiquette forced Father to say that I was a very stupid girl and Mother to protest that the teacher was showing favoritism toward me. But I could tell they were both very proud.

6 The day came when my parents announced that they wanted to give a dinner party. We had invited Chinese friends to eat with us before, but this dinner was going to be different. In addition to a Chinese American family, we were going to invite the Gleasons.

"Gee, I can hardly wait to have dinner at your house," Meg said to me. "I just *love* Chinese food."

That was a relief. Mother was a good cook, but I wasn't sure if people who ate sour cream would also eat chicken gizzards stewed in soy sauce.

Mother decided not to take a chance with chicken gizzards. Since we had Western guests, she set the table with large dinner plates, which we never used in Chinese meals. In fact we didn't use individual plates at all, but picked up food from the platters in the middle of the table and brought it directly to our rice bowls. Following the practice of Chinese American restaurants, Mother also placed large serving spoons on the platters.

The dinner started well. Mrs. Gleason exclaimed at the beautifully arranged dishes of food: the colorful candied fruit in the sweet-and-sour pork dish, the noodle-thin shreds of chicken meat stir-fried with tiny peas, and the glistening pink prawns° in a ginger sauce.

At first I was too busy enjoying my food to notice how the guests were doing. But soon I remembered my duties. Sometimes

---
°**prawns** *n.:* large shrimps.

The All-American Slurp   **125**

E **Reading Skills**

? **Interpreting.** Why does the narrator suddenly leave the table? [She is embarrassed when people in the restaurant notice how loudly her family is slurping their soup.]

F **Literary Focus**
REVIEW STANDARD

External and internal conflict. Ask students to stop at this point to consider what conflicts the narrator is facing. [Possible response: She must adjust to a new environment, the French restaurant (external conflict), as well as deal with the painful feeling of being embarrassed by her own family (internal conflict).]

G **Literary Focus**
GRADE-LEVEL STANDARD

? **Theme.** Why does the narrator decide to rejoin her family? [She realizes that although their ignorance of American customs sometimes embarrasses her, they do care for her. Also, no one would want to live in a toilet stall permanently.]

H **Content-Area Connections**
CULTURE

Chinese etiquette. Traditional Chinese etiquette requires that people respond to compliments by showing modesty, as Mr. and Mrs. Lin do here.

I **Reading Skills**

? **Predicting.** What do you think will happen when the Gleasons have dinner at the Lins' house? [Possible responses: The Gleasons may be as embarrassed as the Lins were when they ate dinner at the Gleasons' house; everything will go fine because the Gleasons won't be so easily embarrassed.]

CONTENT-AREA CONNECTIONS

Culture
Dinnertime around the world. It's a Chinese custom to eat with chopsticks and a U.S. custom to use a fork. In every culture, people have their own ways of eating. Ask students to research the eating utensils, favorite foods, and table manners of a culture other than their own. Suggest that they give a talk on what they find out.

Students might demonstrate some eating customs or draw diagrams of seating arrangements and table settings.

INDIVIDUAL

A Learners Having Difficulty

? Finding details. Ask students to stop and think about how the Gleasons are eating. Is it the proper Chinese way? [no] How do they know? [Possible response: The narrator compares Mrs. Gleason's mixing of foods to mixing concrete and is shocked when she sees Mr. Gleason using his fingers to eat.]

B Literary Focus
GRADE-LEVEL STANDARD

? Theme. Why does the narrator recall celery strings at this point in the story? [Possible response: When she sees the Gleasons making mistakes in Chinese etiquette, she remembers the time when the Lins made a mistake in American etiquette.]

C Reading Skills

? Appreciating wordplay. Bring to students' attention the words that end the story. How do they relate to the title? [The statement "All Americans slurp" recalls the title "The All-American Slurp."]

Monitoring students' progress. Guide the class in answering these comprehension questions. Direct students to locate passages in the text that support their responses.

Short Answer

1. What two mistakes do the Lins make at the Gleasons'? [pulling strings from the celery and placing chairs at the buffet table]

2. Why does the narrator want a pair of jeans? [so she will look like all the other kids at school]

3. What is the narrator's friend's name? [Meg]

4. Why does the narrator hide in the bathroom of the restaurant? [She is ashamed because her family members slurp their soup.]

guests were too polite to help themselves and you had to serve them with more food.

I glanced at Meg to see if she needed more food, and my eyes nearly popped out at the sight of her plate. It was piled with food: The sweet-and-sour meat pushed right against the chicken shreds, and the chicken sauce ran into the prawns. She had been taking food from a second dish before she finished eating her helping from the first!

Horrified, I turned to look at Mrs. Gleason. She was dumping rice out of her bowl and putting it on her dinner plate. Then she ladled prawns and gravy on top of the rice and mixed everything together, the way you mix sand, gravel, and cement to make concrete.

I couldn't bear to look any longer, and I turned to Mr. Gleason. He was chasing a pea around his plate. Several times he got it to the edge, but when he tried to pick it

up with his chopsticks, it rolled back toward the center of the plate again. Finally he put down his chopsticks and picked up the pea with his fingers. He really did! A grown man!

All of us, our family and the Chinese guests, stopped eating to watch the activities of the Gleasons. I wanted to giggle. Then I caught my mother's eyes on me. She frowned and shook her head slightly, and I understood the message: The Gleasons were not used to Chinese ways, and they were just coping the best they could. For some reason I thought of celery strings.

When the main courses were finished, Mother brought out a platter of fruit. "I hope you weren't expecting a sweet dessert," she said. "Since the Chinese don't eat dessert, I didn't think to prepare any."

"Oh, I couldn't possibly eat dessert!" cried Mrs. Gleason. "I'm simply stuffed!"

Meg had different ideas. When the table was cleared, she announced that she and I were going for a walk. "I don't know about you, but I feel like dessert," she told me, when we were outside. "Come on, there's a Dairy Queen down the street. I could use a big chocolate milkshake!"

Although I didn't really want anything more to eat, I insisted on paying for the milkshakes. After all, I was still hostess.

Meg got her large chocolate milkshake and I had a small one. Even so, she was finishing hers while I was only half done. Toward the end she pulled hard on her straws and went *shloop, shloop.*

"Do you always slurp when you eat a milkshake?" I asked, before I could stop myself.

Meg grinned. "Sure. All Americans slurp."

"slurp"

How do immigrants change when they come to the United States? What lessons do they learn? Have students interview family members or friends who have experienced or are familiar with the immigrant experience. Students should brainstorm a list of questions for the interviews, including the basic *5W-How?* questions. Have students carry out the interviews for homework and report back to the class on their findings.

Lensey Namioka

Moving Between Cultures

It's only natural for **Lensey Namioka** (1929–   )
to write about young people trying to cope with
the strange ways of a new culture. She has spent
much of her own life adjusting to new people and
places. Namioka was born in China, where her family moved around
a lot when she was young. "Being on the move meant that I grew up
with almost no toys," she says. "To amuse ourselves, my sister and I
made up stories." When she was a teenager, her family immigrated
to the United States.

Before she began writing for young people, Namioka worked as a
mathematics teacher. Her realistic novels about teenagers today draw
on her Chinese heritage. Her adventure novels set in long-ago Japan
draw on her husband's Japanese heritage.

For Independent Reading

If you liked "The All-American Slurp," you might "shloop"
up Namioka's four novels about a musical family of Chinese
immigrants living in Seattle. The latest one is *Yang the
Eldest and His Odd Jobs*. For a more challenging
novel written for teenagers, try Namioka's
Ties That Bind, Ties That Break.
Set in China and San Francisco,
it tells of a girl who rebels
against the age-old Chinese
tradition of binding girls' feet.

Meet the Writer

Background. Lensey Namioka
moved to the United States when
she was a teenager and now
lives with her husband in Seattle,
Washington. She says, "As an
immigrant, I want my books to
show young readers here that
there are worlds very different
from their own."

For Independent Reading

For students who wish to encounter
other worlds with Namioka, recommend these two titles: *Valley of the
Broken Cherry Trees* and *Village of
the Vampire Cat*.

You also might recommend the
following titles:

- For another story about a
  family who immigrates to the
  United States, recommend
  Lupita Mañana by Patricia
  Beatty. In it a thirteen-year-old
  Mexican girl takes on great
  responsibility to help her family.

- Students who are interested in
  learning more about Chinese culture will enjoy *The Superlative
  Horse* by Jean Merrill. The author
  retells a Taoist tale from 350 B.C.
  about a young boy who earns a
  position of honor in China.

INDEPENDENT PRACTICE

Literary Response and Analysis

Reading Check

1. Possible answers:

   b. Meg and the narrator have fun trying on each other's clothes.

   c. The narrator convinces her mother to buy her a pair of blue jeans.

   d. The narrator is embarrassed by her family's slurping at a fancy restaurant.

   e. At a PTA meeting, the narrator's parents, in the Chinese way, modestly turn aside the teacher's compliments.

Interpretations

2. The Lins are confused by the raw vegetables and the buffet dinner arrangement. The Gleasons have trouble eating with chopsticks, and they mix the Chinese dishes together.

3. Possible answer: When the narrator sees that Americans are unfamiliar with Chinese customs, she becomes more forgiving about the mistakes that she and her family have made.

4. Possible answer: Different cultures are not so different after all.

Evaluation

5. Possible answers: She is not on target. The Lins' misadventures seem mild when compared to the unfriendly behavior and even outright prejudice many immigrants face. She is on target because the awkward and humorous situations the Lins experience ring true to life. Most students should be able to relate an experience on a trip or at a social occasion in which they, like the Lins, were perplexed as to how to behave.

Literary Response and Analysis

Reading Check

1. Sum up what happens in each of the story's six episodes. First, copy the chart below. Then, complete the chart by **summarizing** each part of the plot. (The first and last episodes are summarized for you.) Try to summarize each part in two or three sentences.

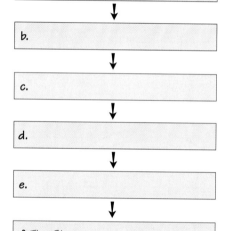

a. The Lins eat at the Gleasons' and make noise with celery, which they've never eaten raw. They aren't sure how to act at a buffet.

b.

c.

d.

e.

Reading Standard 3.6 Identify and analyze features of themes conveyed through characters, actions, and images.

f. The Gleasons eat at the Lins' and make mistakes because they don't know Chinese customs. At the end, Meg shloops from her milkshake, and the narrator discovers that all Americans make noise when they drink milkshakes.

Interpretations

2. What American customs confuse the Lins when they eat at the Gleasons'? What mistakes do the Gleasons make when they eat at the Lins'?

3. Often the way the main character in a story changes or grows gives you a clue to the story's **theme**. What does the narrator learn about Americans that changes the way she feels about herself and her family?

4. Meg's comment that "all Americans slurp" hints at the story's **theme**. What do you think that theme is? State the theme in one or two sentences.

Evaluation

5. You may know people who have come to the United States. Does the author make the immigrant experience sound too easy, or is she on target? Did the story remind you of your own experiences in a new situation? (Check your Quickwrite notes.) Discuss your responses.

Performance

Reader's Theater: All-American Scenes

Work with some classmates to prepare a dramatic reading of one or more of the scenes in this story. Prepare a script for each scene. How many readers will you need? Try splitting up the narrator's part. You may want to use props in your performance. Rehearse your reading; then, perform it in front of an audience.

DIFFERENTIATING INSTRUCTION

Learners Having Difficulty

Have students work in pairs to answer the Reading Check question. *Monitoring tip:* If students have difficulty working out the events of the plot, have them re-read, asking themselves these questions: "What happens first? What happens next? Then what happens?" You also could share with the group the summaries of an advanced learner.

Advanced Learners

Encourage students to gather in small groups to discuss the narrator's tone. Is it amused? sad? upbeat? a bit of all three?

Vocabulary Development

Using Context Clues to Clarify Meaning

PRACTICE 1

Write four sentences about the story, using the words in the Word Bank. You can use another form of a word if you wish—for example, *lavish* instead of *lavishly.* Use **context clues** that will help someone figure out the words' meanings. Here is an example of the use of context clues in the story (page 121): "'This is a buffet dinner. You help yourselves to some food and eat it in the living room.'" What clues tell you what a *buffet* is?

Word Bank

lavishly
mortified
spectacle
etiquette

Interpreting Figurative Language

Figurative language, which is not literally true, compares one thing to something very different. Three common figures of speech are metaphor, simile, and personification.

PRACTICE 2

1. A **metaphor** directly compares two very different things. What is a red face compared to in this sentence?

   Her face blazed with embarrassment.

2. A **simile** compares two very different things but uses a word of comparison, such as *like, as, as if, resembles,* or *seems.*

   Her face was like a blazing fire.

   Make up another simile to describe a red face. Begin with "Her face was like . . ."

3. **Personification** gives human or living characteristics to something that is not human or is not alive. What are these appetizers compared to? (What does this statement make you *see?*)

   Strange appetizers stared up from the tray.

Reading Standard 1.2
Identify and interpret figurative language.

The All-American Slurp   **129**

Vocabulary Development

Practice 1

Possible Answers

- The table was overloaded with a *lavish* display of food.
- Although she was *mortified* by her family some of the time, she was proud of them too.
- The mother worried that her daughter was making a *spectacle* of herself; she wanted her child to be quiet and refined.
- At a buffet, it is proper *etiquette,* or behavior, to take a small amount from each dish on the table.

Practice 2

1. A red face is compared to a blazing fire.
2. Her face was like a plump tomato.
3. The appetizers are compared to people or creatures with eyes. It makes you imagine unappealing blobs of things to eat.

▶ **Resources Reminder**

Vocabulary and Spelling

- *Vocabulary Development*
  - Vocabulary Worksheet, p. 10
- *Lesson Plans for Language Development*
  - Vocabulary, p. 72

ASSESSING

Assessment

- *Progress Assessment of Reading*
  - Selection Test, p. 41

RETEACHING

For a lesson reteaching theme, see **Reteaching,** p. 489M.

STANDARDS FOCUS, pp. 130–134

(For grade-level and review standards taught in this lesson, see citations on Pupil's Edition pages.)

Prerequisite Standard

■ **Grade 5, Reading Comprehension 2.4 Draw inferences, conclusions, or generalizations about text, and support them with textual evidence and prior knowledge.**

Summary ⬌ *at grade level*

A newcomer to the United States, Iranian-born Nilou talks about the difficulties of becoming an American while keeping the culture and traditions of her native country alive. She mentions school clubs and the celebration of holidays as ways to preserve traditions. As Nilou settles into U.S. life, she concludes that America is indeed a "melting pot" of many cultures. Everyone here, she says, "is different, but the same too."

PRETEACHING

Standards Starter

Motivate. Ask students to think about the conflicts that immigrants to the United States face in preserving their cultures and then brainstorm two lists with the titles "What Do Immigrants Leave Behind?" and "What Do Immigrants Gain by Coming to the United States?"

Assign the Reading

Ask a volunteer to read aloud the opening to the article. Then have students read the interview in pairs. One partner reads a paragraph of text and the other, the summary, and then partners reverse roles. Assign the questions on p. 133 as homework.

HOMEWORK

Everybody Is Different, but the Same Too

Texts That Present a Conclusion

Some informative texts are written to present certain conclusions. The writer presents evidence and then draws a conclusion based on that evidence. For example, a writer might present facts and statistics about changing weather conditions and end with the conclusion that we are experiencing the effects of global warming.

Evaluating a Writer's Conclusions

Your job, as a reader, is to evaluate the conclusion.

When you read informational texts, you expect the writer's evidence to add up to a conclusion that makes sense. But don't be fooled—writers aren't perfect. The fact that something looks nice and neat on a printed page doesn't mean it's well thought out. One way to see if a writer's evidence supports a conclusion is to **summarize** the important information—that is, sum up in your own words the writer's evidence. Then, review your summary. Does all the evidence clearly support the writer's conclusion?

In the selection that follows, a young girl from Iran talks about coming to America. Her main points are summarized next to the selection. Do you think they support her conclusion? You'll have a chance to explain at the end of "Everybody Is Different, but the Same Too."

Reading Standard 2.6 Determine the adequacy and appropriateness of the evidence for an author's conclusions.

RESOURCES

Planning
■ *One-Stop Planner* CD-ROM with Test Generator
■ *On Course: Mapping Instruction*

Media
■ *Audio CD Library*
   ■ disc 4

Reading
■ *Interactive Reading*
   ■ Graphic Organizer: Evidence Flow Chart, p. 109

Differentiating Instruction
■ *Lesson Plans for Language Development*
   ■ English-Language Learners, pp. 55, 67, 72

Background

In the following responses to an interviewer, Nilou, an Iranian American girl, talks about fitting into American life. As a Jewish girl living in Iran, Nilou felt out of place. After the monarchy in Iran was overthrown, in 1979, religious freedom was suppressed. Nilou had to go to school on Saturday, the Jewish day of rest and worship. Her family had few freedoms, and they feared for their future. When Nilou was eight years old, her parents decided that the family had to leave the country. They secretly began selling their possessions, even though they worried about being caught and punished—perhaps even killed—for trying to leave. In 1985, Nilou and her family finally managed to leave Iran. They flew to New York and eventually settled in Maryland.

Everybody Is Different, but the Same Too

Summarize (What the Text Says)

↓

Nilou talks about the difficulty of keeping her ties to Iranian culture now that she's living in the United States.

↓

She explains why it would be hard to live in Iran as a woman and why she's happy to be in the United States.

↓

Keeping a culture alive is hard. I think I am partly Iranian, partly American—I don't know. We keep our culture alive by traditions and by the five holidays that we celebrate.

I have changed definitely. In Iran, as a woman, I'd go to school, but universities are very hard to get into. In Iran I would have to get a job after high school and get married when I'm twenty or something. Most women don't work in very high positions, especially because the culture is very sexist. I'm happy to be here. Everybody is trying to be more politically correct here.

▶ Resources Reminder

Media
■ *Audio CD Library*
  ▪ disc 4

Reading
■ *Interactive Reading*
  ▪ Graphic Organizer: Evidence Flow Chart, p. 109

Ⓐ Vocabulary Development
GRADE-LEVEL STANDARD

❓ Using context clues. What context clue helps you to figure out that the phrase *politically correct* means "just and fair to all groups"? [The word *sexist*, which means "biased in favor of one sex" (usually men), is used in opposition to "politically correct."]

▪ Special Education Students, pp. 55, 67, 72

Assessment
■ *Progress Assessment of Reading*
  ▪ Selection Test, p. 44
■ *One-Stop Planner* CD-ROM with Test Generator

A **Reading Informational Materials**
GRADE-LEVEL STANDARD
? **Evaluating conclusions.** Draw students' attention to Nilou's conclusion here that "America is really a melting pot." What evidence does Nilou offer? [She says that schools, buildings, and furniture in America come from different cultures and that you can't look at a group of Americans and identify them as such because they all look different.]

B **Reading Informational Materials**
GRADE-LEVEL STANDARD
? **Evaluating conclusions.** Point out that this closing sentence is the source of the title. It sums up Nilou's conclusion about life in the United States. Do students agree with her? Why or why not? [Some students will point to the diversity in U.S. life and agree. Others will argue that there is a dominant U.S. culture that makes it difficult for minority groups to preserve traditional customs.]

GUIDED PRACTICE

Monitoring students' progress. Have students make a list of the positive and negative aspects of Nilou's life in the United States. Then, ask them how they would best sum up her experience here.

In schools there is a Spanish club, a Chinese club, but I don't know if there is an Iranian club. We are trying to make an Iranian club but I don't know if it will work—there are [only] about eleven or twelve kids.

I think a club is a way of trying to keep the culture alive. In the Hispanic club, every Thursday, they get together and they dance, and on Tuesdays, they have meetings. We also have an international concert that we can go to. [You can] sing if you like, dance, bring food, you know, just whatever you want to do, whatever you want to present of your culture.

A About fitting into American life: When I came to public school, I saw that America is really a melting pot; it borrows things from other cultures—schools, building, furniture, everything from different cultures—and so there is no American way. You can't look at people and say they look like Americans, because America is really borrowing from everything else and everybody is American. And that was when I realized I am American—because all Americans are different.

We should teach that people are people and everybody is the same. They just have different ways of handling their problems and different lifestyles. But we probably have the same goals.

My friends are from all different parts of the world. My American friends are different, my Iranian friends **B** are different, everybody is different, but the same too.

—Nilou, from *Newcomers to America*

> She tells how clubs in school and an international concert help students from different backgrounds stay connected to their culture.

> Nilou sees America as a melting pot—everyone's different, so everyone fits in.

> **Conclusion**
> She concludes that people are all the same, with the same goals.

> **Evaluation**
> Why I think the conclusion does/doesn't add up:
> _____
> _____

DIFFERENTIATING INSTRUCTION

Learners Having Difficulty
Explain that this selection is an interview and that Nilou is responding to a series of questions that are not given. If it helps students, you might provide these implied questions:

• How do you keep your Iranian culture alive?

• How have you changed since you came to the United States?

• How do you fit into U.S. culture?

• What should we teach students about people from different cultures?

Reading Informational Materials

Reading Check

1. What does Nilou think would have happened to her after high school if she had stayed in Iran?

2. What did Nilou learn about fitting into American life when she started public school?

3. What ideas about people would Nilou like to see taught?

Reading Informational Materials

Test Practice

Everybody Is Different, but the Same Too

1. According to Nilou, a major difference between the United States and Iran is that in the United States —

   A women have more opportunities

   B there is more prejudice

   C most people do not appreciate what it means to be free

   D anyone who wants to can go to college

2. Nilou suggests all of these ways of keeping a culture alive *except* —

   F celebrating the holidays of that culture

   G having a club for students of that cultural background

   H following the traditions of that culture

   J refusing to mix with people of different cultures

3. When Nilou says, "America is a melting pot," she is using a **metaphor** that compares America to —

   A a pot of rice

   B a pot in which all kinds of ingredients are melted together

   C a bucket of melted steel, which will harden and become strong

   D different kinds of foods

4. Which statement best expresses Nilou's **conclusion**?

   F The differences between people will always cause trouble.

   G People change a great deal when they move to a new country.

   H We have small differences, but people are all just about the same.

   J You have to work very hard if you want to keep your culture alive.

Reading Standard 2.6 Determine the adequacy and appropriateness of the evidence for an author's conclusions.

Answers and Model Rationales

1. A Nilou specifically mentions A in her interview.

2. J Nilou recommends F, G, and H, so J is correct by a process of elimination.

3. B Students should narrow the choice to A or B because both mention a pot. B is correct because it mentions "all kinds of ingredients," the way the United States contains all kinds of people.

4. H Students should realize that F, G, and J reflect various points Nilou makes in her interview, but that H sums up her final conclusion.

Test-Taking Tips

Point out to students that questions 1–3 focus on specific details in the interview. Question 4 requires students to look at the interview as a whole.

  For more instruction on how to answer multiple-choice questions, refer students to **Test Smarts,** p. 690.

Reading Check

1. Nilou thinks that she would have married early and been unable to continue her education.

2. She learned that much of life in the United States is made up of things borrowed from other cultures and that being different is what many Americans have in common.

3. She would like to see students taught that most people have the same goals, but that they have different ways of handling problems and different lifestyles.

Vocabulary Development

Practice

Possible Answers

1. ■ *Simile*—America is like a stew.
   ■ *Metaphor*—America is a safe harbor.
   ■ *Metaphor*—America is a jig-saw puzzle.

2. ■ *Simile*—A smile to a loved one is like an umbrella on a rainy day.
   ■ *Simile*—My brain functions like a computer.
   ■ *Simile*—Home is as sweet as honey.
   ■ *Metaphor*—Happiness is a slice of the moon.
   ■ *Metaphor*—A computer is a headache.
   ■ *Simile*—Love resembles a lullaby.

3. ■ *Simile*—My hometown im-prisons me like a pound cages in a dog.
   ■ *Simile*—My hometown holds me down like quicksand.
   ■ *Metaphor*—My hometown is a vacuum cleaner that sucks any original thought into its belly.

 Resources Reminder

Differentiating Instruction

■ *Lesson Plans for Language Development*
  ▪ Vocabulary, p. 72

ASSESSING

Assessment

■ *Progress Assessment of Reading*
  ▪ Selection Test, p. 44

Vocabulary Development

Figurative Language

Figurative language is language based on unusual comparisons, and it is not literally true. People who study these things say that there are more than three hundred kinds of figures of speech. Two popular kinds of figurative language are similes and metaphors.

- A **simile** compares two unlike things, using a word of comparison, such as *like, as, than,* or *resembles.*

  America is <u>like</u> a melting pot.

- A **metaphor** compares two unlike things directly, without using a word of comparison.

  America <u>is</u> a melting pot.

PRACTICE

1. In his autobiography, *Barrio Boy,* the writer Ernesto Galarza describes America not as a melting pot but as a griddle, on which his teachers warmed knowledge into their students and roasted racial hatreds out of them. Make up three metaphors or similes that compare America to something else. Be ready to explain your comparisons. (Remember that similes and metaphors must be based on some similarities between the two things being compared; otherwise, they don't make sense.) Open with "America is . . ."

2. Make up at least three metaphors and three similes, each of which compares one of the items listed below to another very different thing (it must be a noun). The first one has been done for you.

   My cat . . .
   My cat Honey is a steam shovel at mealtime.

A smile . . .	Happiness . . .
My brain . . .	A computer . . .
Home . . .	Love . . .

3. Use three similes or metaphors to describe your favorite place or a place you don't like at all.

Reading Standard 1.2
Identify and interpret figurative language.

The Emperor's New Clothes

Literary Focus
Theme: Getting the Message

Writers of stories send messages. A story's message is its **theme,** what it reveals to us about people or life. Theme is different from plot. The **plot** of "The Emperor's New Clothes" is the sequence of events in the story. Theme is what the story means. You infer a theme from what happens in a story, but a theme goes far beyond the story to state a truth about real life. As you read, see what message you get from this story.

Reading Skills
Making Generalizations: Putting It All Together

A **generalization** is a broad, general conclusion drawn from several examples or pieces of evidence. A statement of a story's theme is a kind of generalization. From specific evidence in the story, you make a universal statement about life. To make a statement about the theme of "The Emperor's New Clothes," you have to

- think about the main events and conflicts in the story
- decide what the characters have learned by the end of the story
- state the idea in a general way, so that it applies not just to the story but to real life

Make the Connection
Quickwrite 🖉

The emperor in this story loves clothes. Think about how you would describe your fashion style. Is it classic? wild? preppy? grunge? hip-hop? Why do you love to wear certain clothes—and dislike wearing others? Jot down words that describe the clothes you most like to wear.

Reading Standard 3.6 Identify and analyze features of themes conveyed through characters, actions, and images.

The Emperor's New Clothes **135**

🐻 **STANDARDS FOCUS, pp. 135–143**

(*For grade-level and review standards taught in this selection, see citations on Pupil's Edition pages.*)

Prerequisite Standard
- Grade 5, Literary Response and Analysis 3.4 **Understand that** *theme* **refers to the meaning or moral of a selection, and recognize themes (whether implied or stated directly) in sample works.**

Standard Coming Up in the Next Grade Level
- Grade 7, Literary Response and Analysis 3.4 **Identify and analyze recurring themes across works (e.g., the value of bravery, loyalty, and friendship; the effects of loneliness).**

Reading Skills
- Make generalizations.

Summary ⬇ *below grade level*

The emperor loves new clothes. Two swindlers claim they can make beautiful clothes that are invisible to anyone stupid or unfit for office. The emperor pays the swindlers, who pretend to weave and sew him a magnificent outfit. Afraid of seeming foolish, the emperor's good minister, honest official, courtiers, the emperor himself, and finally the townspeople all claim to see the nonexistent clothes. The charade continues as the emperor parades through town naked, until a child cries, "But he has nothing on at all."

RESOURCES

Planning
- *One-Stop Planner* CD-ROM with Test Generator
- *On Course: Mapping Instruction*

Media
- *Audio CD Library*
  - disc 4
- *Fine Art Transparencies*
  - Transparency 7

Reading
- *Interactive Reading*
  - Graphic Organizer: Character-Word Boxes, p. 110

Differentiating Instruction
- *Lesson Plans for Language Development*
  - English-Language Learners, pp. 56–58, 68, 73

- Special Education Students, pp. 59, 68, 73

Assessment
- *Progress Assessment of Reading*
  - Selection Test, p. 46
- *One-Stop Planner* CD-ROM with Test Generator

Standards Starter

Build background. To help students appreciate the story's ironic theme, have them discuss qualities and deeds of great historical rulers, such as the Roman emperor Augustus, King Asoka of India, or Alexander the Great. If necessary, tell students that the Roman emperor Augustus greatly expanded the Roman empire and brought Rome great wealth. He also often imprisoned or killed those who disagreed with him.

Assign the Reading

Read the first three paragraphs aloud to the class. Then, for students reading at and above grade level, assign the rest of the story as independent reading and the Reading Check questions (p. 142) as homework. Meanwhile, continue working with small groups of students having difficulty.

HOMEWORK

 Resources Reminder

Media

- *Audio CD Library*
  - disc 4
- *Fine Art Transparencies*
  - Transparency 7

136

DIFFERENTIATING INSTRUCTION

Learners Having Difficulty
Modeling. To help students determine the theme of "The Emperor's New Clothes," model how to make a generalization. Point out that a generalization is a broad, general statement drawn from specific evidence. Say: "From the details in the first paragraph you might make this generalization: 'A ruler who is vain about his appearance appears foolish.'" As students read the

story, encourage them to ask themselves, "What does this character's behavior show about life in general?"

 Resources Reminder
- *Interactive Reading*
  - Graphic Organizer: Character-Word Boxes, p. 110

English-Language Learners
Point out that an emperor is the ruler of an empire, a political unit encompassing several nations. Ask students to summarize traditional stories about rulers from their native culture and to identify common elements such as royal characters, loyal assistants, trickster figures, and moral lessons that they might also encounter in "The Emperor's New Clothes."

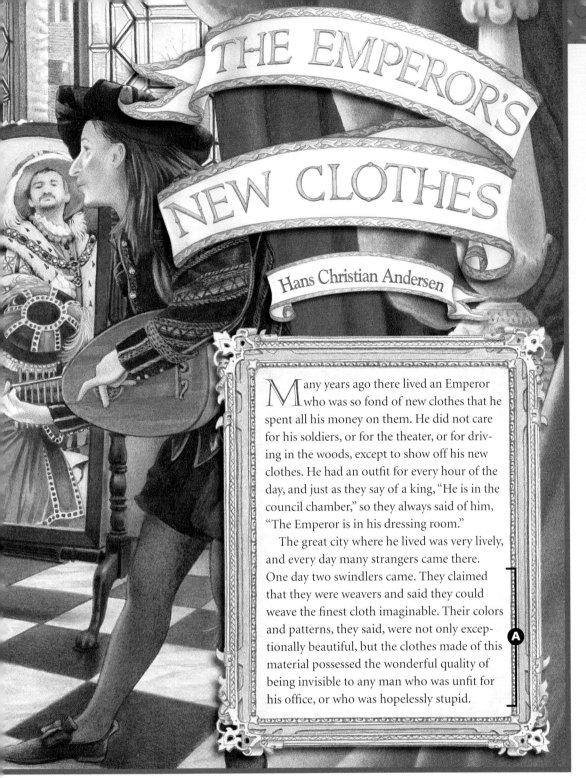

THE EMPEROR'S NEW CLOTHES

Hans Christian Andersen

Many years ago there lived an Emperor who was so fond of new clothes that he spent all his money on them. He did not care for his soldiers, or for the theater, or for driving in the woods, except to show off his new clothes. He had an outfit for every hour of the day, and just as they say of a king, "He is in the council chamber," so they always said of him, "The Emperor is in his dressing room."

The great city where he lived was very lively, and every day many strangers came there. One day two swindlers came. They claimed that they were weavers and said they could weave the finest cloth imaginable. Their colors and patterns, they said, were not only exceptionally beautiful, but the clothes made of this material possessed the wonderful quality of being invisible to any man who was unfit for his office, or who was hopelessly stupid.

DIRECT TEACHING

▶**Resources Reminder**
You might display Fine Art Transparency 7, *Self-Portrait* by Rembrandt van Rijn. Invite students to speculate about the character of the subject and compare him to the emperor in this illustration, who is also sitting for a portrait.

A **English-Language Learners**
❓ **Building background knowledge.** The word *swindler* means "someone who profits by cheating or tricking someone else." What trick are these swindlers playing? [They pretend to be weavers who can make clothes that can't be seen by anyone who is incompetent or stupid.]

▶**Resources Reminder**
For lessons designed for intermediate and advanced English-language learners, see *Lesson Plans for Language Development*, pp. 56–58, 68, 73.

Special Education Students
For lessons designed for special education students, see *Lesson Plans for Language Development*, pp. 59, 68, 73.

Advanced Learners
Acceleration. Use this activity to move advanced learners toward the seventh-grade Standard 3.4, which requires that they identify and analyze recurring themes across works.
Activity. Point out that many stories focus on human weaknesses and their consequences. After their first reading of this

story, ask students to name one major weakness of either the emperor, the good old minister, or the honest official. Then, have students brainstorm lists of other works whose main character shows one of the same weaknesses. Challenge students to compare the consequences of the same human weakness across several works. Are the consequences always negative?

A Reading Skills

? Making generalizations. The emperor quickly pays two weavers a lot of money for clothes that they say will be invisible to some. Based on this specific action of the emperor, what statements might a reader make about emperors in general? [Possible responses: Emperors are headstrong; they are wealthy; they are foolish.]

B Reading Skills

? Making inferences. What do you think is the real reason that the emperor sends someone else to see how the weavers are progressing? What clues in these paragraphs help you figure this out? [The emperor sends someone else because deep down he fears that he may be stupid or unfit for office. Clues: "rather uneasy," "of course," "send somebody else first," "all were anxious to see how bad or stupid their neighbors were."]

C Literary Focus
REVIEW STANDARD

? Character's motive. Why doesn't the minister admit he can't see the cloth? [He fears that he is stupid or inept, and he doesn't want others to discover his "faults."]

D Literary Focus
GRADE-LEVEL STANDARD

? Theme. What lesson about life do these scenes suggest? [Possible response: People will do anything to avoid seeming stupid or inept.] Why do you think the writer chose an emperor and ministers as main characters to reveal this theme? [Possible responses: to show that pride, vanity, and self-doubt can get even the great in trouble; to poke fun at people in high positions.]

A "Those must be wonderful clothes," thought the Emperor. "If I wore them, I should be able to find out which men in my empire were unfit for their posts, and I could tell the clever from the stupid. Yes, I must have this cloth woven for me without delay." So he gave a lot of money to the two swindlers in advance, so that they could set to work at once.

They set up two looms[1] and pretended to be very hard at work, but they had nothing on the looms. They asked for the finest silk and the most precious gold, all of which they put into their own bags, and worked at the empty looms till late into the night.

B "I should very much like to know how they are getting on with the cloth," thought the Emperor. But he felt rather uneasy when he remembered that whoever was not fit for his office could not see it. He believed, of course, that he had nothing to fear for himself, yet he thought he would send somebody else first to see how things were progressing.

Everybody in the town knew what a wonderful property the cloth possessed, and all were anxious to see how bad or stupid their neighbors were.

"I will send my honest old minister to the weavers," thought the Emperor. "He can judge best how the cloth looks, for he is intelligent, and nobody is better fitted for his office than he."

So the good old minister went into the room where the two swindlers sat working at the empty looms. "Heaven help us!" he thought, and opened his eyes wide. "Why, I cannot see anything at all," but he was careful not to say so.

Both swindlers bade him be so good as

to step closer and asked him if he did not admire the exquisite pattern and the beautiful colors. They pointed to the empty looms, and the poor old minister opened his eyes even wider, but he could see nothing, for there was nothing to be seen. "Good Lord!" **C** he thought, "can I be so stupid? I should never have thought so, and nobody must know it! Is it possible that I am not fit for my office? No, no, I must not tell anyone that I couldn't see the cloth."

"Well, have you got nothing to say?" said one, as he wove.

"Oh, it is very pretty—quite enchanting!" said the old minister, peering through his glasses. "What a pattern, and what colors! I shall tell the Emperor that I am very much pleased with it."

"Well, we are glad of that," said both the weavers, and they described the colors to him and explained the curious pattern. The old minister listened carefully, so that he might tell the Emperor what they said.

Now the swindlers asked for more money, more silk, and more gold, which they re- **D** quired for weaving. They kept it all for themselves, and not a thread came near the looms, but they continued, as before, working at the empty looms.

Soon afterward the Emperor sent another honest official to the weavers to see how they were getting on and if the cloth was nearly finished. Like the old minister, he looked and looked but could see nothing, as there was nothing to be seen.

"Is it not a beautiful piece of cloth?" said the two swindlers, showing and explaining the magnificent pattern, which, however, was not there at all.

"I am not stupid," thought the man, "so it must be that I am unfit for my high post. It

---

1. **looms** *n.:* machines used for weaving thread into cloth.

DEVELOPING FLUENCY

Activity. Have student pairs take turns reading and acting out favorite scenes from the story. As one student reads a segment aloud, the other mimes the action. Whichever student will be miming may choose the segment to be read. Encourage students to experiment with several scenes and to present their most successful to the class.

PAIRED

is ludicrous,² but I must not let anyone know it." So he praised the cloth, which he did not see, and expressed his pleasure at the beautiful colors and the fine pattern. "Yes, it is quite enchanting," he said to the Emperor.

Everybody in the whole town was talking about the beautiful cloth. At last the Emperor wished to see it himself while it was still on the loom. With a whole company of chosen courtiers, including the two honest councilors who had already been there, he went to the two clever swindlers, who were now weaving away as hard as they could but without using any thread.

"Is it not magnificent?" said both the honest statesmen. "Look, Your Majesty, what a pattern! What colors!" And they pointed to the empty looms, for they imagined the others could see the cloth.

"What is this?" thought the Emperor. "I do not see anything at all. This is terrible! Am I stupid? Am I unfit to be Emperor? That would indeed be the most dreadful thing that could happen to me!"

---

2. **ludicrous** (loo'di·krəs) *adj.:* ridiculous; laughable.

"Yes, it is very beautiful," said the Emperor. "It has our highest approval," and nodding contentedly, he gazed at the empty loom, for he did not want to say that he could see nothing. All the attendants who were with him looked and looked, and, although they could not see anything more than the others, they said, just like the Emperor, "Yes, it is very fine." They all advised him to wear the new magnificent clothes at a great procession that was soon to take place. "It is magnificent! beautiful, excellent!" went from mouth to mouth, and everybody seemed delighted. The Emperor awarded each of the swindlers the cross of the order of knighthood to be worn in their buttonholes, and the title of Imperial Court Weavers.

Throughout the night preceding the procession, the swindlers were up working, and they had more than sixteen candles burning. People could see how busy they were, getting the Emperor's new clothes ready. They pretended to take the cloth from the loom, they snipped the air with big scissors, they sewed with needles without any thread, and at last said: "Now the Emperor's new clothes are ready!"

A Vocabulary Development
GRADE-LEVEL STANDARD

❓ Figurative language. What is the figurative meaning of the idiomatic statement *That is just the beauty of it*? [Possible response: It means "that is the best thing about it."]

B Literary Focus
ADVANCED STANDARD

Comparing themes. After students have enjoyed the humor of the swindlers' smooth patter and the emperor's putting on imaginary clothes, have them read the brief retelling of Aesop's "The Fox and the Crow" on p. 229. Challenge students to compare themes in "The Fox and the Crow" and "The Emperor's New Clothes." [Both tales show that vanity leads people to be taken advantage of and to behave foolishly.] Students might also find thematic similarities in "The Sneetches" (p. 381), in which a swindler takes advantage of his customers' desire for prestige.

C Reading Skills

❓ Making generalizations. What truth about people's behavior do you see in the emperor's comments and actions? [Possible responses: Some people are so conceited that they do not realize when they are being foolish; people may say or do anything to maintain the appearance of competence and control.]

D Literary Focus
GRADE-LEVEL STANDARD

❓ Theme. Why does the emperor decide to continue with the procession, even though he and everyone else know that he is not wearing any clothes? [Possible responses: He is too proud and vain to admit the truth publicly; he feels that he must maintain his dignity at all costs; a reversal would imply weakness.]

The Emperor, followed by all his noblest courtiers, then came in. Both the swindlers held up one arm as if they held something, and said: "See, here are the trousers! Here is the coat! Here is the cloak!" and so on. "They are all as light as a cobweb! They make one feel as if one had nothing on at all, **Ⓐ** but that is just the beauty of it."

"Yes!" said all the courtiers, but they could not see anything, for there was nothing to see.

"Will it please Your Majesty graciously to take off your clothes?" said the swindlers. "Then we may help Your Majesty into the new clothes before the large mirror!"

Ⓑ The Emperor took off all his clothes, and the swindlers pretended to put on the new clothes, one piece after another. Then the Emperor looked at himself in the glass from every angle.

"Oh, how well they look! How well they fit!" said all. "What a pattern! What colors! Magnificent indeed!"

"They are waiting outside with the canopy which is to be borne over Your Majesty in the procession," announced the master of ceremonies.

Ⓒ "Well, I am quite ready," said the Emperor. "Doesn't my suit fit me beautifully?" And he turned once more to the mirror so that people would think he was admiring his garments.

The chamberlains, who were to carry the train, fumbled with their hands on the ground as if they were lifting up a train. Then they pretended to hold something up in their hands. They didn't dare let people know that they could not see anything.

And so the Emperor marched in the procession under the beautiful canopy, and all who saw him in the street and out of the windows exclaimed: "How marvelous the Emperor's new suit is! What a long train he has! How well it fits him!" Nobody would let the others know that he saw nothing, for then he would have been shown to be unfit for his office or too stupid. None of the Emperor's clothes had ever been such a success.

"But he has nothing on at all," said a little child.

"Good heavens! Hear what the innocent child says!" said the father, and then each whispered to the other what the child said: "He has nothing on—a little child says he has nothing on at all!" "He has nothing on at all," cried all the people at last. And the **Ⓓ** Emperor too was feeling very worried, for it seemed to him that they were right, but he thought to himself, "All the same, I must go through with the procession." And he held himself stiffer than ever, and the chamberlains walked on, holding up the train which was not there at all.

140 Chapter 3   The Heart of the Matter: Themes and Conclusions

---

FAMILY/COMMUNITY ACTIVITY

Instruct students to re-read "The Emperor's New Clothes" with their families. Students might read the story aloud to their families, or they might take turns reading it with other family members. Then, have students invite their families to collaborate on an updated oral version of the story. Idea starters might include "The Boss's New Laptop" (its monitor display is said to be visible only to smart and competent employees) or "The President's New Cell Phone" (said to transmit calls for wise and ethical politicians only). Encourage students to share their families' versions of the story with the class.

Hans Christian Andersen

Portrait of Hans Christian Andersen (1852) by Frederik Ludwig Storch. Oil on canvas.

Hans Christian Andersen Museum, Odense, Denmark.

A Fairy-Tale Life

Once upon a time, **Hans Christian Andersen** (1805–1875), the son of a poor shoemaker, lived in a small town in Denmark called Odense. As a boy, Hans loved the theater, but he couldn't pay for tickets. So he made friends with an usher and got a copy of each program.

> With this I seated myself in a corner and imagined an entire play, according to the name of the piece and the characters in it. That was my first unconscious poetizing.

A fortuneteller predicted a great future for Hans and said his hometown would someday be lighted up in his honor. Hans was only fourteen when he went to Copenhagen to seek his fortune. By age twenty-eight he had failed as a singer, actor, and dancer, though he had had some success as a writer. That year he began writing the fairy tales that soon made him known around the world. Ideas for these tales came from his life, he said.

> [They] lay in my mind like seeds and only needed a gentle touch—the kiss of a sunbeam or drop of malice—to flower.

Almost every year around Christmas until he was sixty-eight, Andersen published new fairy tales. Late in his life his hometown of Odense held a festival for him, and the whole city was lighted up in his honor. It's no wonder that Andersen called his autobiography *The Fairy Tale of My Life*!

For Independent Reading

You can find more tales by Hans Christian Andersen in his collected works. If you haven't read his stories yet, you might want to read them now. Andersen's stories can be read both for entertainment and for their deeper meaning. Here are some favorites: "Thumbelina," "The Ugly Duckling," "The Little Mermaid," "The Steadfast Tin Soldier," "The Snow Queen," and "The Nightingale."

The Emperor's New Clothes   **141**

Meet the Writer

Background. After three years of struggling as a part-time actor in Copenhagen, Denmark, Andersen won a scholarship and was able to begin formal studies. Although his first book was published that same year, he did not really establish himself as a writer until he was twenty-three and had passed his graduation exams. Ten years later, the king of Denmark granted Andersen a lifetime income—a "poet's pension"—which made him financially independent. Although Andersen is best remembered for his fairy tales, he also wrote numerous plays, travel books, and volumes of poetry.

For Independent Reading

Students who read more of Andersen's fairy tales may also want to view a video of the 1952 musical based on the story of Andersen's life. Titled *Hans Christian Andersen*, the musical stars Danny Kaye.

- Students who appreciate the folk-tale elements of "The Emperor's New Clothes" will enjoy Priscilla Jaquith's *Bo Rabbit Smart for True: Folktales from the Gullah,* animal tales in which smug and pompous characters are cleverly defeated.

- If students like medieval settings, suggest *The Door in the Wall* by Marguerite De Angeli. A privileged boy in medieval England learns the value of humility when disasters separate him from his parents and drastically change his life.

- Steer fans of historical fiction toward *The Witch of Blackbird Pond* by Elizabeth George Speare. Kit, with her trunks full of brightly colored dresses, shocks her Puritan relatives when she comes to colonial Connecticut from Barbados. She adopts Puritan clothing but keeps her own integrity as she battles widespread bigotry and fear.

DIFFERENTIATING INSTRUCTION

Advanced Learners

Enrichment. Encourage students to further research Andersen's life and to examine his travel writings, such as *A Poet's Bazaar*, and his memoir *The Fairy Tale of My Life.*

Activity. Challenge students to use their research to evaluate these comments by Poul Borum, a modern critic from Andersen's native Denmark: "Andersen was enormously productive in all literary genres, bad plays, sentimental poems, charming but flawed novels, brilliant journalistic travel sketches and memoirs—all of them about himself. He must have been an impossible person, a hypochondriac and egomaniac, sponging on his noble friends, always whimpering about lack of recognition or boasting of his fame. But his humor, his understanding, and his language are miraculous."

INDEPENDENT PRACTICE

Literary Response and Analysis

Reading Check

1. He spends it all on clothes.
2. They say the cloth is invisible to anyone stupid or incompetent.
3. He wants an easy way to evaluate his staff; he wants to know which of his subjects are smart and which are stupid; he loves beautiful clothes.
4. He asks his honest old minister and another honest official.
5. Nothing; he is naked.
6. A little child reveals the truth.

Interpretations

7. Possible answers: The officials' motives include self-doubt, fear of seeming stupid or inept, and unwillingness to admit they have lied.
8. The emperor emerges as arrogant, vain, and unyielding.
9. Most students will select b, since it is shown most clearly by the two honest advisors and the adults watching the parade.

Evaluation

10. He seems to see children as unhindered by pride or vanity and therefore more honest than adults. Some students may agree that children are more clearsighted than adults; others may point out that they themselves are still young enough to be considered children, yet they are quite capable of false pride, vanity, dishonesty, and similar failings.

BONUS QUESTION

Students may use examples ranging from a boss's devotion to a worthless plan to his or her having spinach stuck on a front tooth.

Literary Response and Analysis

Reading Check

1. On what does the emperor spend all his money?
2. What special quality do the swindlers claim their cloth has?
3. Why is the emperor interested in the swindlers' cloth? List three reasons.
4. Whom does the emperor ask to check the cloth?
5. What does the emperor wear to the procession?
6. Who reveals the truth about the emperor's new clothes?

Interpretations

7. A character's **motives** are the reasons for his or her actions. What motives do the emperor's officials have for not telling the emperor the truth?
8. The emperor continues to march even though everyone knows he's wearing no clothes. What **character traits** does the emperor reveal by his actions?
9. Readers often find different **themes** in the same story. From the following generalizations, choose the one that you think best states the main theme of "The Emperor's New Clothes." Come up with a better statement of the theme if you can.
   a. We should not trust people who use flattery.
   b. People often do not speak the truth to the powerful because they're afraid of looking foolish.
   c. An honest person can be trusted to tell the truth.
   d. Children always tell the truth.

   Explain why you chose the theme you did. Be sure to give examples from the story to support your theme.

Evaluation

10. What do you think is the storyteller's opinion of children? of adults? Explain why you agree or disagree with these opinions.

Writing
A Fashion Statement

In your Quickwrite you jotted down notes on the clothes you like to wear and what they say about you. Refer to your notes, and write a paragraph about yourself and your favorite clothes. You might even include an illustration. Be sure to include a topic statement in your paragraph, either as the first or the last sentence. Your topic statement should sum up the main point you are making about your clothes.

BONUS QUESTION

Describe a real-life situation today in which people might be afraid to tell their boss (or their teacher) the truth.

Reading Standard 3.6 Identify and analyze features of themes conveyed through characters, actions, and images.

DIFFERENTIATING INSTRUCTION

Learners Having Difficulty
Pair students to complete the Literary Response and Analysis questions. If students are unable to select the theme (question 9), have them re-read p. 140, column 2, asking themselves, "Why don't the spectators tell the truth?" Tell them to state the answer as a sentence and then broaden it into a generalization about human nature.
Writing. Guide students in roughing out topic statements. Then, have them complete their paragraphs as homework.

HOMEWORK

Advanced Learners
Use the story as a springboard for a discussion of the word *integrity*. Ask which characters (if any) show integrity. Then, ask what this suggests about Andersen's view of people.

Vocabulary Development

Identifying Hyperbole

Hyperbole (hī·pur'bə·lē) is exaggerated or overstated language. Hyperbole is a type of figurative language and so is not to be taken literally. If you say, "I ate a mountain of food," you're using hyperbole. You want to make a point about how hungry you were.

PRACTICE 1

Find three examples of hyperbole in the sentences below:

"If I've told you once, I've told you a thousand times," the emperor shouted at his officials, so loudly that he could be heard miles away. "Don't tell me about the poor people in this kingdom. Such talk bores me to death. Now help me get ready for my procession."

Interpreting Idioms

An **idiom** (id'ē·əm) is an expression unique to a language. (*Idiom* comes from the Greek word *idios,* meaning "one's own" or "personal.") *Head over heels in love* and *raining cats and dogs* are English idioms. Idioms are difficult because they mean something different from what the words actually say. People who grow up with a language understand its idioms without even thinking about them. If you're learning a new language, however, idioms may give you trouble.

PRACTICE 2

Find at least five idioms in the following paragraph. Working with a partner, see if you can explain what each idiom means.

The weavers pretended to be working their fingers to the bone, but they were pulling the wool over everybody's eyes. The emperor's servants weren't willing to stick their necks out. Things came to a head during the procession. The emperor thought he was dressed to kill. Then a child spilled the beans. "That man has no clothes on," she said. The weavers had made a monkey out of the emperor.

Grade 4 Review Reading Standard 1.2 Apply knowledge of idioms to determine the meaning of words and phrases.

Reading Standard 1.2 Identify and interpret figurative language.

The Emperor's New Clothes **143**

Vocabulary Development

Practice 1

Examples: "If I've told you once, I've told you a thousand times"; "so loudly that he could be heard miles away"; "bores me to death."

Practice 2

Idioms and their meanings are listed below.

- *working their fingers to the bone,* "working very hard"
- *pulling the wool over everybody's eyes,* "tricking everyone"
- *stick out their necks,* "risk anything personal"
- *came to a head,* "reached a crucial point"
- *dressed to kill,* "very well dressed"
- *spilled the beans,* "told the secret"
- *made a monkey out of,* "tricked"

▶ **Resources Reminder**

Differentiating Instruction

- *Lesson Plans for Language Development*
  - Vocabulary, p. 73

ASSESSING

Assessment

- *Progress Assessment of Reading*
  - Selection Test, p. 46

RETEACHING

For a lesson reteaching theme, see **Reteaching,** p. 489M.

STANDARDS FOCUS, pp. 144-148

(For grade-level and review standards taught in this selection, see citations on Pupil's Edition pages.)

Prerequisite Standard

■ Grade 5, Reading Comprehension 2.3 **Discern main ideas and concepts presented in texts, identifying and assessing evidence that supports those ideas.**

Summary *at grade level*

Using quotations and statistics, this article examines controversy over the adoption of uniforms in U.S. public schools and concludes that the idea is worth trying. Opponents maintain that uniforms quash individuality, infringe on civil liberties, and impose financial hardship (though some schools do offer financial aid). Proponents claim that uniforms improve behavior—statistics support this claim—and encourage a serious approach to education. Some students and parents also welcome the freedom from clothing competition.

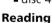 Resources Reminder

Media
■ *Audio CD Library*
  ▪ disc 4

Reading
■ *Interactive Reading*
  ▪ Graphic Organizer: Support Chart, p. 111

Uniform Style

Recognizing and Evaluating Evidence

Writers can cite many kinds of evidence to support a conclusion. When writers deal with emotionally charged issues—like requiring students to wear school uniforms—they usually bring out the heavy artillery: quotations, statistics, case studies.

1. **Quotations** are likely to be comments from people who have something significant to say about the topic. **Direct quotations**—people's exact words—are easy to spot. They're always enclosed in quotation marks.

   According to a sixth-grader at Valley Academy, "Kids are proud of who they are instead of worrying about what they're wearing."

2. **Statistics** are information expressed as numbers (such as percentages or measurements). Sometimes statistics are presented in charts or graphs.

   One principal says that test scores went up 20 percent the first year kids wore uniforms.

Reading Standard 2.6 Determine the adequacy and appropriateness of the evidence for an author's conclusions.

3. **Case studies** are specific examples. Case studies may illustrate the point made in the conclusion.

   A recent study conducted in more than thirty public schools where uniforms are required shows that social and economic conflicts were greatly reduced.

When you read informational materials intended to persuade you to take a certain action or to think in a certain way, be sure to examine the kinds of support the writer has used. Ask yourself, "Does the evidence provide support for the conclusion? Would other kinds of support have worked better? Should the writer have presented *more* evidence—has the conclusion been supported only partially?" When you consider questions like these, you're evaluating the adequacy and appropriateness of the writer's evidence.

RESOURCES

Planning
■ *One-Stop Planner* CD-ROM with Test Generator
■ *On Course: Mapping Instruction*

Media
■ *Audio CD Library*
  ▪ disc 4

Reading
■ *Interactive Reading*
  ▪ Graphic Organizer: Support Chart, p. 111

Differentiating Instruction
■ *Lesson Plans for Language Development*
  ▪ English-Language Learners, pp. 60, 69, 73

Uniform Style

*S*ome claim that it makes students harder working, less violent, and better behaved. Others protest that it takes away students' freedom to think for themselves.

A fiendish plot to control students through brain implants? No—it's the issue of public school students' wearing uniforms.

Why are more and more public schools in the United States considering uniforms? "It's the whole issue of setting a tone for the day," says Mary Marquez, an elementary school principal in Long Beach, California, the first school district in the nation to make uniforms mandatory.[1] "When students are in their uniforms, they know they are going to school to learn, not going outside to play."

If sporting the latest fashions makes kids feel hip and cool, does wearing a school uniform make them feel more like serious students? Many teachers and principals say yes. They believe that uniforms motivate[2] their students to live up to higher standards and that they promote school spirit, discipline, and academic excellence.

---

1. **mandatory** (man′də·tôr′ē) *adj.:* required.
2. **motivate** (mōt′ə·vāt′) *v.:* cause someone to do something or act in a certain way; push or drive.

145

PRETEACHING

Standards Starter

Motivate. Challenge students to design the perfect school clothes. Might they include lots of pockets? pants with zip-off legs for sudden weather changes? hats with built-in video cameras to eliminate note-taking? color-change fabrics for hour-to-hour variety? Elicit a wide range of ideas.

DIRECT TEACHING

A **Reading Informational Materials**
GRADE-LEVEL STANDARD
? **Evaluating evidence.** How does the writer show that Mary Marquez is an appropriate person to quote on the issue of school uniforms? [The writer identifies Marquez as a principal in a school district where uniforms are mandatory.]

- Special Education Students, pp. 60, 69, 73

Vocabulary and Spelling
- *Vocabulary Development*
  - Decoding Worksheet, p. 11
  - Cumulative Vocabulary Review, p. 12

Assessment
- *Progress Assessment of Reading*
  - Selection Test, p. 49
- *One-Stop Planner* CD-ROM with Test Generator

A Reading Informational Materials
GRADE-LEVEL STANDARD

❓ Evaluating evidence. What is the "story"—the conclusion—that these statistics support? [Possible responses: the idea that uniforms make schools safer; the idea that uniforms make students better behaved.] Why do you think the writer mentions that other districts report similar statistics? [Possible response: Statistics from only one school district might not adequately support the conclusion.]

B Reading Informational Materials
REVIEW STANDARD

❓ Main idea. Does the writer seem to support or oppose the mandating of school uniforms? [to support it] How can you tell? [Although she writes that "the jury is still out" on the question, her final paragraph mentions "possible benefits," and her closing words are "Why not give uniforms a try?"]

GUIDED PRACTICE

Guide the class in answering these comprehension questions. Direct students to locate passages in the text that support their responses.

True-False

1. All schools nationwide are considering school uniforms. [F]

2. Some teachers and principals believe that uniforms promote discipline and academic excellence. [T]

3. Civil liberties experts are concerned that uniforms will limit an individual's rights. [T]

4. School crime in Long Beach has risen since students began wearing uniforms. [F]

But what about the right to individuality, creativity, self-expression? That's what civil liberties experts are concerned about, and many students and parents agree. Some have even gone so far as to bring lawsuits against schools that won't let students wear what they like.

Still, many parents, tired of shelling out money month after month to buy trendy clothing for their children, are only too pleased to have uniforms settle the question once and for all. Many students also welcome an end to clothing competition. "I don't worry about what I wear in the morning," says twelve-year-old uniform wearer Hortencia Llanas. "I just slip on the clothes." Students from wealthy families no longer show off their expensive clothes at school, and students who can't afford them no longer face ridicule for the way they dress. (Of course, buying school uniforms can be hard on the pocketbook as well. A number of schools have started programs to help parents pay for them.)

Some of the statements made by supporters of uniforms may seem exaggerated—for example, how could requiring students to dress alike make public schools safer? But there are logical arguments to back up this claim. Fights are less likely to break out over a leather jacket or a $150 pair of sneakers if no one is wearing such items to school. Those who don't belong on school grounds stand out among students wearing school uniforms.

In Long Beach, statistics tell the story: School crime went down 36 percent after students began wearing uniforms. Fighting dropped 51 percent and vandalism 18 percent. Other districts that began requiring uniforms report similar improvements.

In public school districts across the country, the jury is still out on the question of school uniforms. But with so many possible benefits, many ask: Why not give uniforms a try?

—Mara Rockliff

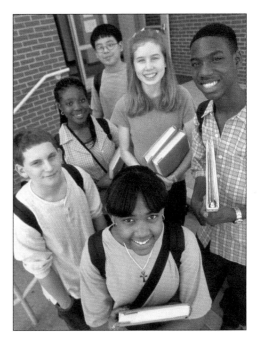

DIFFERENTIATING INSTRUCTION

Learners Having Difficulty
Modeling. Write the words *quotations, examples,* and *statistics* on the chalkboard, and remind students that these are the kinds of evidence that writers use to back up their opinions. In the first paragraph, call students' attention to the quotation by a school principal who has had extensive experience in the use of school uniforms. Next, help students identify in the second paragraph the examples

given of the positive effects of uniforms. Then, point out the statistics cited in the next-to-last paragraph. As they read the article, encourage students to ask themselves, "What evidence supports the writer's opinion?"

▶ **Resources Reminder**

■ *Interactive Reading*
  ■ Graphic Organizer: Support Chart, p. 111

Reading Informational Materials

Reading Informational Materials

Reading Check

1. What people are **quoted** in this article? What point does each one make?

2. What is civil liberties experts' concern about school uniforms?

3. Give three **statistics** cited by the writer in support of school uniforms.

4. Do you believe the writer has provided strong **support** for her final statement? Explain why or why not.

TestPractice

Uniform Style

1. Which statement best expresses the writer's **conclusion**?

   A Requiring students to wear uniforms solves all of their schools' problems.

   B Since uniforms offer many benefits, schools should give them a try.

   C School uniforms keep students from being creative.

   D School uniforms have proved to be a bad idea.

2. Why does the writer mention the concerns of civil liberties experts?

   F To prove that students who wear uniforms are less violent than students who wear street clothes to school

   G To remind readers that everyone should be concerned about students' test scores

   H To show that some people oppose school uniforms

   J To show how expensive kids' clothes are

3. Which of the following **conclusions** is supported in the article?

   A Students' ability to focus on their schoolwork improves when they aren't thinking about being fashionable.

   B Wearing uniforms makes kids feel hip and cool.

   C A family has no right to bring a lawsuit against a public school.

   D Schools that require students to wear uniforms should pay for them.

4. What **support** does the writer give for the idea that requiring students to wear uniforms instead of street clothes can prevent violence?

   F Statements by civil liberties experts

   G Statistics from Long Beach

   H A quotation from a school superintendent

   J A quotation from Hortencia Llanas

Reading Standard 2.6 Determine the adequacy and appropriateness of the evidence for an author's conclusions.

Uniform Style **147**

TestPractice

Answers and Model Rationales

1. **B** Explain that B is a paraphrase of the author's final sentence. A is not stated or implied. C gives views of experts, not the author. D does not support the writer's conclusion.

2. **H** The concerns of civil liberties experts are cited to present the opponents' point of view on the issue. Point out that expert opinion is a kind of evidence that can support an idea.

3. **A** Explain that the quote from Mary Marquez supports this idea.

4. **G** Point out that F and H refer to material not found in the article, and J to a quotation supporting a different idea.

Test-Taking Tips

Remind students to read all the choices before selecting one. Sometimes the first or second choice will seem workable, but another one will be even better.

For more instruction on answering multiple-choice questions, refer students to **Test Smarts,** p. 690.

Reading Check

1. Principal Mary Marquez of Long Beach, California, the first school district in the nation to mandate uniforms, says that uniforms set a more serious, academic tone. Student Hortencia Llanas says that because of uniforms she doesn't have to worry about what to wear.

2. They think that uniforms represent a loss of individual freedoms.

3. After Long Beach adopted uniforms, school crime decreased by 36 percent, fighting by 51 percent, and vandalism by 18 percent.

4. Possible answer: Yes, the writer states that many teachers believe uniforms motivate academic achievement, that parents spend lots of money on trendy clothing, and that wearing uniforms helps make schools safer.

Vocabulary Development

Practice
Possible Answers

1. If Leroy lives up to his teachers' expectations, he'll be a famous musician one day. [behave in accord with]

2. How much did you shell out for the used computer? [pay]

3. Daily fast-food snacks can be hard on the pocketbook. [expensive]

4. The jury is still out on whether Mimi will get to keep the iguana. [The decision has not yet been made.]

 Resources Reminder

Vocabulary and Spelling

■ *Vocabulary Development*
  ■ Decoding Worksheet, p. 11
  ■ Cumulative Vocabulary Review, p. 12

■ *Lesson Plans for Language Development*
  ■ Vocabulary, p. 73

Grammar Link

Practice

1. When Tracy and her mother saw the uniform, Tracy said she didn't like it.

2. When Kim was choosing a uniform, she called Norma.

3. Roberto talked to Henry and then called Trong. Roberto would not change his mind.

 ASSESSING

Assessment

■ *Progress Assessment of Reading*
  ■ Selection Test, p. 49

FOCUS ON

Vocabulary Development

Grade 4 Review Reading Standard 1.2 Apply knowledge of idioms to determine the meaning of words and phrases.

Interpreting Idioms

When your friend says she's going to hit the books, you don't expect her to start punching her math book. *Hitting the books* is an **idiom,** an expression whose meaning differs from the literal meaning of the words. An idiom's meaning is unique to a particular language, so it may be hard for someone learning the language to understand.

PRACTICE

How would you explain the following idioms from "Uniform Style" to someone? Use each idiom in a sentence, and then write a definition of it.

1. live up to
2. shell out
3. hard on the pocketbook
4. jury is still out

Grammar Link MINI-LESSON

Clear Pronoun References

Pronouns always refer to a noun or to another pronoun. The word the pronoun refers to is called its **antecedent** (an'tə·sēd''nt). To avoid confusion, make sure each pronoun you use clearly refers to its antecedent.

CONFUSING **Ralph talked to Miguel about the dress code. He did not agree with it.**

Who did not agree with the dress code, Ralph or Miguel? It is not clear because *He* could refer to either boy. Replace *He* with the correct name.

CLEAR **Ralph talked to Miguel about the dress code. Miguel did not agree with it.**

PRACTICE

Rewrite each sentence so that the antecedent of each pronoun is clear.

1. When Tracy and her mother saw the uniform, she said she didn't like it.

2. Kim called Norma when she was choosing a uniform.

3. Roberto talked to Henry and then called Trong. He would not change his mind.

For more help, see Agreement of Pronoun and Antecedent in the *Holt Handbook,* pages 137–142.

148 Chapter 3 The Heart of the Matter: Themes and Conclusions

---

Baucis and Philemon

Literary Focus
Universal Themes: Ties That Bind

Whenever you read literature—whether it's an African folk tale first told hundreds of years ago or a novel set in New York City today—you're likely to run into familiar character types, plots, and themes. Why are there so many similarities between stories from different places and periods? No one knows for sure. But the similarities suggest that people who lived long ago had many of the same fears and wishes that we have today. The similarities also suggest that people from different parts of the world can agree on what is important in life.

   As you read the ancient Greek myth "Baucis and Philemon," look for similarities between this story from long ago and real life today. In particular, think about **theme,** the message of the myth. Does that message still apply today?

Metamorphosis: Shifting Shapes

A **metamorphosis** (met′ə·môr′fə·sis) is a total change in shape or form. A larva's transformation into a butterfly is a metamorphosis. The wormlike larva undergoes a dramatic change in form to become a beautiful butterfly. A tadpole goes through a metamorphosis to become a frog. Metamorphosis is important in mythology. "Baucis and Philemon" begins with a metamorphosis in which the gods Zeus and Hermes change into humans. In myths, gods can transform anyone or anything into any form they choose.

As you read this myth, look for another amazing metamorphosis.

Reading Skills
Recognizing Connections

Myths speak in a universal language—that's why you still see so many references to them today, on television and in newspapers as well as in stories. As you read "Baucis and Philemon," be on the lookout for **connections** wherever you encounter the little open-book sign.

- What kind of behavior does the story encourage? What qualities in people are rewarded? Are qualities like these rewarded today?
- How are people today tested for the depth of their concern for others?
- Is the **theme** of this old story still important to us today?

Make the Connection
Quickwrite ✏️

Suppose you were traveling centuries ago, long before the days of motels and campgrounds. Hungry and tired, you would have to find shelter as night approached. If you stopped at a house, you could be fairly certain that you'd be welcomed and given a meal and a bed for the night. Hospitality, or generosity to guests, was a sacred duty in many parts of the ancient world, especially ancient Greece. People were expected to share what they had, even with strangers. Freewrite about the way we treat strangers today.

Reading Standard 3.6 Identify and analyze features of themes conveyed through characters, actions, and images.

Baucis and Philemon 149

STANDARDS FOCUS, pp. 149–156

(For grade-level and review standards taught in this selection, see citations on Pupil's Edition pages.)

Prerequisite Standard
- Grade 5, Literary Response and Analysis 3.6 **Evaluate the meaning of archetypal patterns and symbols that are found in myth and tradition by using literature from different eras and cultures.**

Standard Coming Up in the Next Grade Level
- Grade 7, Literary Response and Analysis 3.4 **Identify and analyze recurring themes across works (e.g., the value of bravery, loyalty, and friendship; the effects of loneliness).**

Reading Skills
- Recognize connections.

Summary ↔ *at grade level*

In this Greek myth, the gods Zeus and Hermes, disguised as humans, are refused hospitality by everyone but a poor old couple, Baucis and Philemon. To reward the couple for their generosity toward strangers, the gods grant them two wishes. Philemon asks only that their humble cottage become a temple for the gods and that he and his wife die at the same time. Years later, on their usual evening walk, the two generous, loving people are transformed into two tall trees with intertwined branches.

RESOURCES

Planning
- *One-Stop Planner* CD-ROM with Test Generator
- *On Course: Mapping Instruction*

Media
- *Audio CD Library*
  - disc 4

Reading
- *Interactive Reading*
  - Graphic Organizer: Theme Chart, p. 112

Differentiating Instruction
- *Lesson Plans for Language Development*
  - English-Language Learners, pp. 61–63, 70, 74

- Special Education Students, pp. 64, 70, 74

Assessment
- *Progress Assessment of Reading*
  - Selection Test, p. 51
- *One-Stop Planner* CD-ROM with Test Generator

Standards Starter

Build background knowledge.
Remind students that myths are stories usually involving gods and often have timeless themes. Students can identify Greek myths by the presence (and often interference) of any number of powerful and passionate Greek gods, including Zeus, ruler of the gods, and his messenger, Hermes.

Assign the Reading

This selection is short enough to have students read it aloud in class. You may wish to have less-advanced students listen to the recording of the story from the *Audio CD Library,* disc 4, track 6, and then read the selection at home to reinforce their understanding. All students can read the Meet the Writer page at home.

HOMEWORK

VIEWING THE ART

Michelangelo Merisi, known as **Caravaggio** (1573–1610), created paintings of extraordinary naturalism, evident in the realistic details of this still life. Although Caravaggio closely studied the work of the great Renaissance master Michelangelo, he insisted that nature was his only teacher.

Activity. Have students identify the realistic elements in this painting, such as the wormholes in the apple.

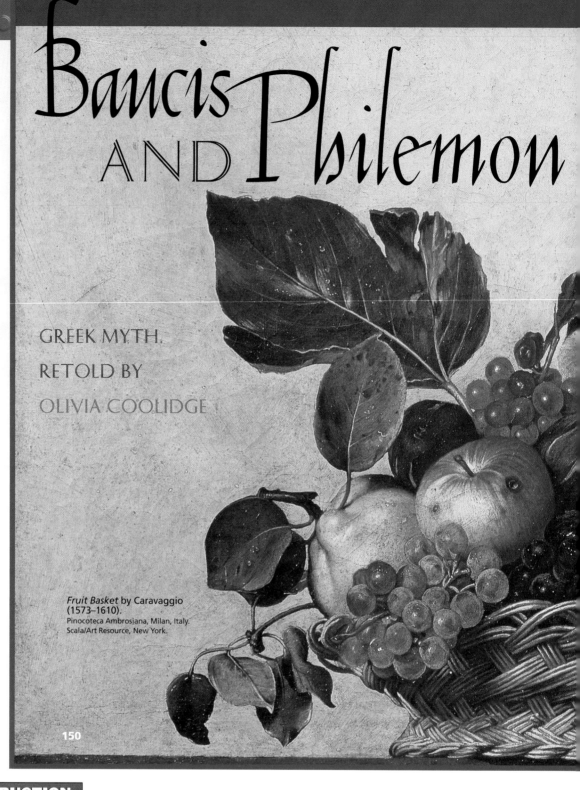

Baucis AND Philemon

GREEK MYTH,
RETOLD BY
OLIVIA COOLIDGE

Fruit Basket by Caravaggio (1573–1610).
Pinocoteca Ambrosiana, Milan, Italy.
Scala/Art Resource, New York.

150

DIFFERENTIATING INSTRUCTION

Learners Having Difficulty
Modeling. To help students see that the themes of "Baucis and Philemon" relate to life today, model the reading skill of recognizing connections. Read the story aloud through the first two sentences of the second paragraph. Then, say: "This reminds me of what often happens in our own world. Many people turn away when a homeless person asks for help. A few people,

though, are as generous as the characters in the myth and offer real support to people in need." As they read, have students ask themselves this question: "How are the qualities and feelings of these characters like those of people today?"

▶ **Resources Reminder**

■ *Interactive Reading*
  ■ Graphic Organizer: Theme Chart, p. 112

English-Language Learners
Students may need help with understanding details about the Greek household mentioned in the story. Encourage them to ask classmates for explanations of words such as *wineskin* or processes such as curing bacon or pickling cherries.

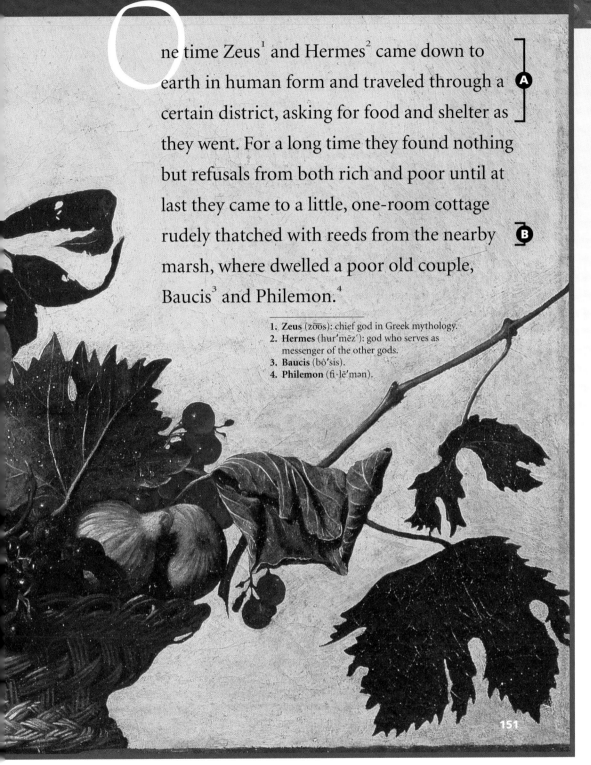

One time Zeus[1] and Hermes[2] came down to earth in human form and traveled through a certain district, asking for food and shelter as they went. For a long time they found nothing but refusals from both rich and poor until at last they came to a little, one-room cottage rudely thatched with reeds from the nearby marsh, where dwelled a poor old couple, Baucis[3] and Philemon.[4]

---

1. **Zeus** (zo͞os): chief god in Greek mythology.
2. **Hermes** (hur′mēz′): god who serves as messenger of the other gods.
3. **Baucis** (bô′sis).
4. **Philemon** (fi·lē′mən).

151

A Literary Focus
REVIEW STANDARD
? Patterns in myths: Metamorphosis. What metamorphosis occurs at the beginning of the story? [Zeus and Hermes transform themselves into humans.] How does this metamorphosis help you identify the story as a Greek myth? [Metamorphoses usually occur in fantasy stories or myths. Because Zeus and Hermes are Greek gods, a story involving their metamorphosis must be a Greek myth.]

B English-Language Learners
Understanding multiple-meaning words. Students may not know the meaning of *rudely* as it is used here. Tell them that besides "inconsiderately," *rudely* can also mean "crudely" or "poorly." In other words, the cottage roof is not well made.

▶**Resources Reminder**
For lessons designed for intermediate and advanced English-language learners, see *Lesson Plans for Language Development,* pp. 61–63, 70, 74.

Special Education Students
For lessons designed for special education students, see *Lesson Plans for Language Development,* pp. 64, 70, 74.

Advanced Learners
Acceleration. The following activity can test advanced learners' mastery of the seventh-grade Standard 3.4, which requires that they identify and analyze recurring themes.
Activity. Have students write a paragraph comparing a theme or themes from this story with another story they are familiar with, such as the "Parable of the Good Samaritan," that has a similar theme or themes.

A **Literary Focus**
ADVANCED STANDARD

? **Universal themes.** How do Baucis and Philemon treat the strangers? [They graciously welcome the strangers and give them food and shelter.] **What other stories can you recall that begin in this way?** [Many myths and folk tales from various cultures begin with humble people offering hospitality to strangers. Others, such as "Nail Soup" from Sweden, build lessons around characters that fail to offer such help.]

B **Reading Skills**

Making connections. Remind students that people read literature to gain insight into their own lives.

[Possible response to question 1: Students may describe friends or relatives who join organizations to welcome newcomers to a community or who volunteer in soup kitchens to feed transients or the homeless.]

C **Literary Focus**
ADVANCED STANDARD

? **Universal themes.** What character traits does Philemon reveal in this speech? [Philemon's speech shows that the couple are pious and humble.] **What other tales do you know that promote these virtues?** [Students may mention religious stories from various traditions or folk tales such as "Cinderella."]

The two had little to offer, since they lived entirely from the produce of their plot of land and a few goats, fowl, and pigs. Nevertheless, they were prompt to ask the strangers in and to set their best before them. The couch that they pulled forward for their guests was roughly put together from willow boughs, and the cushions on it were stuffed with straw. One table leg had to be propped up with a piece of broken pot, but Baucis scrubbed the top with fragrant mint and set some water on **A** the fire. Meanwhile Philemon ran out into the garden to fetch a cabbage and then lifted down a piece of home-cured bacon from the blackened beam where it hung. While these were cooking, Baucis set out her best delicacies on the table. There were ripe olives, sour cherries pickled in wine, fresh onions and radishes, cream cheese, and eggs baked in the ashes of the fire. There was a big earthenware bowl in the midst of the table to mix their crude, homemade wine with water.

The second course had **B** to be fruit, but there were nuts, figs, dried dates, plums, grapes, and apples, for this was their best season of the year. Philemon had even had it in mind to kill their only goose for dinner, and there was a great squawking and cackling that went on for a long time. Poor old Philemon wore himself out trying to catch

> **MAKING CONNECTIONS**
> 1. Do Baucis and Philemon act like people you know?

that goose, but somehow the animal always got away from him until the guests bade him let it be, for they were well served as it was. It was a good meal, and the old couple kept pressing their guests to eat and drink, caring nothing that they were now consuming in one day what would ordinarily last them a week.

At last the wine sank low in the mixing bowl, and Philemon rose to fetch some more. But to his astonishment as he lifted the wineskin to pour, he found the bowl was full again as though it had not been touched at all. Then he knew the two strangers must be gods, and he and Baucis were awed and afraid. But the gods smiled kindly at them, and the younger, who seemed to do most of the talking, said, "Philemon, you have welcomed us beneath your roof this day when richer men refused us shelter. Be sure those shall be punished who would not help the wandering stranger, but you shall have whatever reward you choose. Tell us what you will have."

C The old man thought for a little with his eyes bent on the ground, and then he said: "We have lived together here for many years, happy even though the times have been hard. But never yet did we see fit to turn a stranger from our gate or to seek a reward for entertaining him. To have spoken with the immortals[5] face to face is a thing few

---
5. **immortals** *n.:* ancient Greek gods.

MINI-LESSON **Reading**

Developing Word-Attack Skills
Write these words from the selection on the chalkboard: *through, bough, though, thought,* and *rough.* Point out that each of the words is spelled with the letters *ough,* but the letters stand for a different sound in each word. Read the words one by one, and help students identify the sound *ough* stands for in each word.

- In *through, ough* stands for /o͞o/.
- In *bough, ough* stands for /ou/.
- In *though, ough* stands for /ō/.
- In *thought, ough* stands for /au/, that is /ô/.
- In *rough, ough* stands for /uf/.

Activity. Display these sentences. Have volunteers read them aloud. Then, have the class identify the word on the chalkboard

that contains the same *ough* sound as the underlined word. (Some sounds appear more than once.)

1. The gods <u>sought</u> food and shelter. [thought]

2. The couple provided more than <u>enough</u>. [rough]

men can boast of. In this small cottage, humble though it is, the gods have sat at meat. It is as unworthy of the honor as we are. If, therefore, you will do something for us, turn this cottage into a temple where the gods may always be served and where we may live out the remainder of our days in worship of them."

"You have spoken well," said Hermes, "and you shall have your wish. Yet is there not anything that you would desire for yourselves?"

Philemon thought again at this, stroking his straggly beard, and he glanced over at old Baucis with her thin, gray hair and her rough hands as she served at the table, her feet bare on the floor of trodden earth. "We have lived together for many years," he said again, "and in all that time there has never been a word of anger between us. Now, at last, we are growing old and our long companionship is coming to an end. It is the only thing that has helped us in the bad times and the source of our joy in the good. Grant us this one request, that when we come to die, we may perish in the same hour and neither of us be left without the other."

He looked at Baucis and she nodded in

<kbd>MAKING CONNECTIONS</kbd>
2. What does Philemon's request show about the things he and his wife value? Do you know anyone with the same values?

approval, so the old couple turned their eyes on the gods.

"It shall be as you desire," said Hermes. "Few men would have made such a good and moderate request."

<kbd>MAKING CONNECTIONS</kbd>
3. What requests of the gods might more selfish people make?

Thereafter the house became a temple, and the neighbors, amazed at the change, came often to worship and left offerings for the support of the aged priest and priestess there. For many years Baucis and Philemon lived in peace, passing from old to extreme old age. At last, they were so old and bowed that it seemed they could only walk at all if they clutched one another. But still every evening they would shuffle a little way down the path that they might turn and look together at the beautiful little temple and praise the gods for the honor bestowed on them. One evening it took them longer than ever to reach the usual spot, and there they turned arm in arm to look back, thinking perhaps that it was the last time their limbs would support them so far. There as they stood, each one felt the other stiffen and change and only had time to turn and say once, "Farewell," before they disappeared. In their place stood two tall trees growing closely side by side with branches interlaced. They seemed to nod and whisper to each other in the passing breeze.

Baucis and Philemon **153**

3. They served bread made from dough. [though]

4. The gods were able to slough off their weariness. [rough]

5. Such kindness ought to be rewarded. [thought]

Monitoring students' progress.
Guide the class in answering these comprehension questions. Direct students to locate passages in the text that support their responses.

True-False

1. Baucis and Philemon are gods who come to earth as humans. [F]

2. Zeus and Hermes enjoy Baucis and Philemon's hospitality. [T]

3. Baucis and Philemon wish to die together when their time comes. [T]

4. Baucis and Philemon's cottage metamorphoses into a mansion. [F]

5. Baucis and Philemon metamorphose into birds. [F]

Meet the Writer

Background. Olivia Coolidge is well known for her extensive writing on ancient Greek and Roman themes in books such as *The Golden Days of Greece, Lives of Famous Romans, The Trojan War, Caesar's Gallic War* (the story of Caesar's campaign in Gaul as related by a fictitious first-person narrator), and *Roman People*. Her work about ancient Greece, *Men of Athens*, was named a Newbery Honor Book.

For Independent Reading

If students want to read another myth with a strong message about humility and pride, recommend "Arachne" from Coolidge's book *Greek Myths*.

▶ Resources Reminder

Reading

■ *Interactive Reading*

For other Greek myths and related readings, see *Interactive Reading*, p. 114.

Olivia Coolidge

A Twist of Fate

Olivia Coolidge (1908–   ) was enjoying a perfectly normal childhood in London with a perfectly normal dislike for Greek literature (which her father was urging her to read) when she twisted her ankle. For three months the cruel sprain kept her from going outside to play, and so she read—and read. Pretty soon she was even reading Greek poetry, and she made a shocking discovery. She loved it!

As happens sometimes in Greek myths, the young woman gladly accepted her fate: a lifelong love of the classics. (The word *classics* refers to Greek myths and other timeless works.) Her interest led her to Oxford University, where she continued her studies in the classics. Later, reflecting on why her own stories often spring from the classics, Olivia Coolidge noted:

> ❝ I write about history, biography, and ancient legends for teens because I am more interested in values that always have been of concern to people than I am in the form we express them in at this moment. Distant places and past ages show that these values are not expressed better in the United States in the twentieth century, but merely differently. My general purpose therefore is to give a picture of life. ❞

For Independent Reading

If you'd like to read other myths retold by Olivia Coolidge, look for *Greek Myths*. To learn more about the ancient world from which these myths come, see Coolidge's book *The Golden Days of Greece*.

FAMILY/COMMUNITY ACTIVITY

Encourage students to read this story together with family members. After everyone has read the story, they can discuss family traditions of hospitality. Suggest they talk about what they would serve Zeus and Hermes if the gods showed up at their door. This would also be a good opportunity for families to discuss guidelines for dealing with strangers who arrive unexpectedly.

Literary Response and Analysis

Reading Check

1. Why do the two gods come down to earth?
2. When do Baucis and Philemon realize that the strangers are gods?
3. How do the old couple please the gods?
4. What reward does Hermes offer?
5. What are Philemon's two wishes? In what ways do they come true?

Interpretations

6. In a myth a **metamorphosis** can be a reward, a punishment, or just a disguise. Which types of metamorphoses occur in this myth? What purpose does each transformation serve? You might organize your ideas in a chart like this one:

Metamorphosis	Type and Purpose
Zeus and Hermes become humans.	The gods disguise themselves. Their purpose is . . .

7. The ancient myths were meant to teach lessons about how to behave. What lessons do you think the Greeks learned from this story? Are those lessons still important today? Why or why not?

8. Look at your notes for the Quickwrite on page 149. How do we treat strangers today? Why do you think we treat them this way? (How do you think Zeus and Hermes would be treated if they arrived in your neighborhood today?)

9. Do you know people like Baucis and Philemon? Who are they, and how are they similar to this good couple from the ancient world?

Writing

All Is Revealed

A **theme** is an idea about life that is revealed in a work of literature. These are some of the themes of "Baucis and Philemon":

- Generous people are rewarded.
- You do not need to be wealthy to be generous.
- Always be kind to strangers, as there's no telling who they might be.

Choose one of these themes to write about in a paragraph or two. Use details from the myth to show how the story expresses this theme.

BONUS QUESTION

What does the myth tell you about what the ancient Greeks had for dinner?

Reading Standard 3.6 Identify and analyze features of themes conveyed through characters, actions, and images.

Baucis and Philemon 155

Literary Response and Analysis

Interpretations

6. Students' charts should also address the transformation of the cottage and the metamorphosis of Baucis and Philemon at the story's end.

7. The Greeks learned that it is important to share what they have and to be generous to everyone, even to strangers. Most students will feel that these lessons are still important.

8. Students may say that the gods would not be invited into someone's home today because our society no longer expects that kind of hospitality or because inviting strangers into one's home can be dangerous.

9. Answers will vary.

BONUS QUESTION

The myth says that the ancient Greeks ate cabbage, bacon, olives, sour cherries pickled in wine, fresh onions and radishes, cream cheese, eggs, nuts, figs, dried dates, plums, grapes, apples, and goose. They drank wine and perhaps goat's milk.

Reading Check

1. The gods come down to earth to see if people show hospitality to others, especially to strangers.
2. They realize the strangers are gods when the bowl of wine refills itself.
3. They are generous, even though they are poor and have little to share.
4. The god offers them any reward they wish.
5. Philemon asks the gods to turn the couple's home into a temple and to let him and Baucis die together. Their home is turned into a temple, and at the moment of death, the two old people metamorphose into two trees with intertwining branches.

Vocabulary Development

Practice

- *Mars*—planet, candy bar
- *Venus*—planet
- *Saturn*—planet, car
- *Apollo*—space missions
- *Mercury*—planet, element
- *Jupiter*—planet
- *Vulcan*—alien race in *Star Trek*
- *Poseidon*—ship's name in a movie

 Resources Reminder

Differentiating Instruction

- *Lesson Plans for Language Development*
  - Vocabulary, p. 74

Grammar Link

Practice

1. Baucis was in the kitchen when the gods decided to test Philemon and <u>her</u>.

2. The gods gave <u>him</u> and <u>her</u> a choice.

3. Between you and <u>me</u>, I would not have passed that test.

4. Was turning into trees a happy ending for Philemon and <u>her</u>?

ASSESSING

Assessment

- *Progress Assessment of Reading*
  - Selection Test, p. 51

RETEACHING

For a lesson reteaching theme, see **Reteaching,** p. 489M.

Vocabulary Development

Reading Standard 1.3 Recognize the origins and meanings of frequently used foreign words in English.

Words from Mythology

The Greek and Roman names for the gods are still used in modern life. For instance, Pluto, the name of the god of the underworld, is now the name of a planet and a cartoon character.

PRACTICE

How have these mythological names been used in the modern world? Are some of the names used for more than one thing?

Mars	Saturn	Mercury	Vulcan
Venus	Apollo	Jupiter	Poseidon

Grammar Link MINI-LESSON

Pronouns as Objects of Prepositions

A **prepositional phrase** begins with a preposition and ends with a noun or pronoun, which is called the **object of the preposition.**

to Baucis	about Philemon
without her	for him
after her	between him and her

When a pronoun is the object of the preposition, it must be in the objective form. Choosing the correct form of the pronoun isn't difficult when the object of a preposition is a single pronoun. The trouble comes when a preposition has two objects:

The myth appealed to Lila and I/me.

To figure out the correct choice, try out the sentence with just one pronoun at a time. (You wouldn't say, "The myth appealed to I.")

CORRECT **The myth appealed to Lila and <u>me</u>.**

PRACTICE

For each sentence, decide which of the underlined pronouns is correct.

1. Baucis was in the kitchen when the gods decided to test Philemon and <u>she/her</u>.

2. The gods gave <u>he/him</u> and <u>she/her</u> a choice.

3. Between you and <u>I/me</u>, I would not have passed that test.

4. Was turning into trees a happy ending for Philemon and <u>she/her</u>?

For more help, see Using Pronouns Correctly in the *Holt Handbook*, page 187–188.

One Child's Labor of Love

Evaluating Evidence

"Hey, our new coach is great!" exclaims Tam.

"How do you know?" you ask.

"I just know. Take my word for it."

Tam has drawn a conclusion (our new coach is great!), and you want to know how he has reached his conclusion. By asking your question, you're trying to decide two things: First, does Tam have enough information to form a reliable conclusion? Second, does Tam have evidence to support his conclusion? Here's Tam's evidence: "I just know." This reply gives no evidence at all. Tam just says, "Take my word for it."

Since Tam's evidence doesn't convince you, you keep digging. "Not good enough, Tam. Tell me more."

"She looks like this other really cool coach I used to know."

Looking like someone else does not make a "great" coach! Dig on. "So what? What else do you know?"

"Her teams have won almost all of their games for the last five years."

That is certainly adequate and appropriate evidence for deciding whether a coach is good. But does a winning average automatically make a great coach?

"She showed me how to fix a problem I've been having with my jump shot. I've been struggling with that shot for a year, but she knew what I was doing wrong just from watching me play once."

This is certainly reliable evidence. It shows that the coach is knowledgeable.

Judging evidence is easy. **Inappropriate evidence** makes you think, "What does that have to do with anything?" If you have to trust the person instead of relying on facts, it's **inadequate evidence.** Evidence is adequate when you've been given enough information to draw your own conclusion. So what do you think? Is she a great coach or not?

Distinguishing Between Fact and Opinion

Appropriate evidence is based on facts. **Facts** are pieces of information that can be proved true. In the discussion about the coach, Tam cites facts about the coach's winning average. In contrast, **opinions** are personal beliefs or attitudes. Tam states a few of those, such as "I just know" (definitely inappropriate evidence). A **valid opinion** is a belief or judgment supported by facts. Valid opinions can provide strong support for a conclusion. Be on the lookout for facts and valid opinions in "One Child's Labor of Love."

Reading Standard 2.6 Determine the adequacy and appropriateness of the evidence for an author's conclusions.

Craig Kielburger at right, in Manila, Philippines, in 1998.

One Child's Labor of Love **157**

STANDARDS FOCUS, pp. 157-161

(For grade-level and review standards taught in this selection, see citations on Pupil's Edition pages.)

Prerequisite Standard

■ Grade 5, Reading Comprehension 2.5 **Distinguish facts, supported inferences, and opinions in text.**

Summary *at grade level*

Sixteen-year-old Craig Kielburger first got passionate about child labor when he was twelve. That's when he founded Free the Children, an organization that works to end child labor around the world. Craig began his group after reading about Iqbal Masih, a Pakistani boy who was killed for speaking out against child labor. The facts show that Craig has been successful in getting his message out. Free the Children now has chapters in twenty-five countries and more than five thousand members worldwide. In 1998, Craig was awarded the prestigious Franklin and Eleanor Roosevelt Medal of Freedom. In his fight against child labor, Craig has traveled through Asia and met many political leaders, but this young activist says that it's the poor children, generous and helpful despite hardship, who impress him the most.

▶ Resources Reminder

Media
■ *Audio CD Library*
  ▪ disc 4

Reading
■ *Interactive Reading*
  ▪ Graphic Organizer: Evidence Cards, p. 113

RESOURCES

Planning
■ *One-Stop Planner* CD-ROM with Test Generator
■ *On Course: Mapping Instruction*

Media
■ *Audio CD Library*
  ▪ disc 4

Reading
■ *Interactive Reading*
  ▪ Graphic Organizer: Evidence Cards, p. 113

Differentiating Instruction
■ *Lesson Plans for Language Development*
  ▪ English-Language Learners, pp. 65, 71, 74
  ▪ Special Education Students, pp. 65, 71, 74

Assessment
■ *Progress Assessment of Reading*
  ▪ Selection Test, p. 54
■ *One-Stop Planner* CD-ROM with Test Generator

Motivate. Invite students to imagine themselves having to rise at dawn, hungry and cold, to work in a factory for twelve hours. Then, assign the reading in class.

DIRECT TEACHING

A Reading Informational Materials
GRADE-LEVEL STANDARD

Evaluating evidence. Point out to students that the introduction to the transcript calls Craig Kielburger an activist who possesses a "passionate intolerance for child labor and slavery." As they read the text, ask students to look for and evaluate evidence that supports this claim.

B Reading Informational Materials
REVIEW STANDARD

❓ Distinguishing fact and opinion. What two facts are presented here that support the idea that Craig is an activist? [He has met with important leaders, and he has won a prestigious award.]

C Reading Skills

❓ Drawing conclusions. What conclusions about child labor can you draw from the facts presented about Iqbal Masih? [Possible responses: Child labor is horrible and inhumane; it is dangerous for child laborers to protest their enslavement.]

D Reading Informational Materials
GRADE-LEVEL STANDARD

❓ Evaluating evidence. What evidence is presented here to support the claim that Craig is an activist? [Craig started a group called Free the Children and traveled to Asia to document child labor.] Is this evidence adequate and appropriate? [Yes. The facts show that Craig is actively fighting against child labor.]

One Child's Labor of Love

A CBS, NEW YORK—Tuesday, October 5, 1999, 6:14 P.M.—When *60 Minutes* correspondent Ed Bradley first met Craig Kielburger three years ago, the 13-year-old possessed a passionate intolerance for child labor and slavery.

Now 16, Craig has met with some of the most important political and religious leaders of his time. And last **B** year, he joined the ranks of John F. Kennedy, Harry Truman, Elie Wiesel, and Desmond Tutu as he took home the prestigious[1] Franklin and Eleanor Roosevelt Medal of Freedom. Bradley recently revisited Craig to track his progress.

To understand how a teenager from Toronto became the inspiration for a 5,000-member organization called Free the Children, with chapters in 25 countries, consider what Craig had to say at age 13: "Basically, we're told slavery [was] abolished," Craig explained. "But it was really shocking, because . . . I was just reading through the different research that I got, and you find the worst type of slavery still exists today—slavery of children."

C When Craig was age 12, he read a newspaper article about a boy his age in Pakistan, Iqbal Masih. Iqbal's parents, like so many others, had offered their son's labor at age 4 in exchange for a small loan. Iqbal spent the next six years chained to a rug loom, working 12-hour days for pennies, until he finally escaped and joined a crusade against child labor. But after Iqbal won worldwide recognition, his life was cut short when, at age 12, he was shot dead in the streets of his village. No one has been convicted of the murder, and Craig vowed to keep his cause alive. . . .

Craig started a group called Free the Children. The board of directors meet Saturdays in Craig's den, which has become the command center. They are in daily contact, by phone or fax, with a host of international human rights groups.

D Having always done his homework to keep up on the issue, Craig soon felt that homework isn't enough. He had to meet the children he was trying to help. . . . This prompted him to take a trip to Asia—a trip his parents were wholeheartedly against. . . . Craig's parents eventually found his cause so convincing that they . . . bought his plane ticket to travel halfway around the world. Chaperoned at each stop by local human rights advocates[2] and armed with a video camera, Craig went from Bangladesh to Thailand, and then to India, Nepal, and Pakistan.

Craig Kielburger with children in Manila, Philippines, in 1998.

---

1. **prestigious** (pres·tij′əs) *adj.:* much admired and sought after.
2. **advocates** (ad′və·kits) *n.:* supporters; defenders.

DIFFERENTIATING INSTRUCTION

Learners Having Difficulty
Modeling. Since the events in this article are not described in chronological order, some students may have difficulty understanding what happened when. Have these students go back and look for signal words and phrases, such as "three years ago" or "last year," that can help them place the events in chronological order. Suggest they list the events in the article in the order in which they happened. [Possible list: Craig reads about Iqbal Masih; Craig founds Free the Children; Craig takes a trip to Asia; Craig wins a Medal of Freedom award.]

English-Language Learners
Some students may not know how to pronounce many of the unfamiliar names in this article. Discuss as a class the pronunciation

"The perception that I had was that child labor is all in the deep, dark back alleys, [where] no one can see it, beyond public scrutiny.[3] But the truth is, it's practiced in the open," Craig says. . . .

"One shop that I went into, I met one 8-year-old girl . . . [who] was just pulling apart syringes and needles, piece by piece, and putting them in buckets for their plastics. She wore no gloves, literally had no shoes. . . . All she was doing was squatting on the ground, surrounded by a pile of needles. They were from hospitals, from the street, from the garbage. We asked her, 'Don't you worry about AIDS and other diseases like that?' We got no response. She didn't know what they were." . . .

Craig spends a great deal of his time on the road, often alone. He is part of an individualized program that allows him to travel and keep up with his class work. . . . "I plan on going all the way through my Ph.D., so I'm going to be in school till I'm 40 or something," Craig says. "I hope to . . . study international conflict mediation.[4] I've had the chance to travel to Bosnia quite a bit . . . and areas of armed conflict . . . to see what war does. I want to be involved in helping stop wars before they begin." . . .

Craig has met his share of political leaders. . . . "It's great meeting with them. . . . They're all incredibly interesting people. I enjoyed meeting all of them, but they're still not the people who impress me the most." . . .

So who does impress this teenager?

"In Thailand, there was a young street girl, [to whom] I handed an orange. And she automatically took the orange, and she peeled it, and she broke it, and she shared it with her friends," Craig says. "Or a child I saw in India. He was crippled, so his friends were carrying him from place to place so he wouldn't be left behind. And to this day I'm convinced that if you took these children and put them in those positions of power, we would see this world truly be a different place."

—from *60 Minutes*

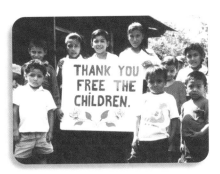

(Top) Craig Kielburger with the Dalai Lama in Stockholm, Sweden, in 2000.
(Above) Students at a school in Nicaragua that is sponsored by Free the Children.

---
3. **scrutiny** (skrōot'′n·ē) *n.*: close examination or study.
4. **mediation** (mē'·dē·ā'shən) *n.*: attempt to settle disputes by stepping in and trying to help.

One Child's Labor of Love   **159**

One Child's Labor of Love   **159**

Reading Informational Materials

Reading Check

1. Possible answers: Craig founded Free the Children; Craig worked hard to keep up on the issue of child labor; Craig traveled to Asia to document and fight against child labor.

2. Possible answers: Craig calls the existence of child slavery "shocking"; Craig vowed to keep Iqbal Masih's cause alive; Craig is extremely impressed by the poor children he met in Asia.

Answers and Model Rationales

1. **D** A is addressed in the story but not the article; B is addressed in the article but not the story; C is addressed in neither; both the story and the article address D.

2. **H** F and G are verifiable facts. J is an intention. H states Craig's belief and is thus an opinion.

3. **C** Details in the article do not support A, B, or D as conclusions. There are, however, adequate details to support C.

4. **J** No details in the article support J, but details can be found that support F, G, and H.

Test-Taking Tips

If students are unsure of the answer to a multiple-choice question, remind them to strategize by eliminating as many choices as possible and then reviewing the wording of both the question and any remaining answers.

For more instruction on answering multiple-choice questions, refer students to **Test Smarts,** p. 690.

Reading Informational Materials

Reading Check

1. The writer concludes that Craig Kielburger is intolerant of child labor and slavery, that he refuses to allow these wrongs to exist unchallenged. Find three examples of **appropriate evidence** that support this conclusion.

2. The author concludes that Craig Kielburger is "passionate" about his beliefs. Find three examples of **evidence** that support this conclusion about Craig's strong feelings.

One Child's Labor of Love

1. What **theme** is addressed in both "Baucis and Philemon" and "One Child's Labor of Love"?
   A Generous people are rewarded.
   B Slavery must be abolished worldwide.
   C Good always triumphs over evil.
   D People should try to help those in need.

2. Which of the following statements is an **opinion**?
   F "I've had the chance to travel to Bosnia quite a bit . . . to see what war does."
   G "He was crippled, so his friends were carrying him from place to place so he wouldn't be left behind."
   H "I'm convinced that if you took these children and put them in those positions of power, we would see this world truly be a different place."
   J "I plan on going all the way through my Ph.D. . . ."

3. There is **adequate evidence** for the reader to conclude that Craig meets with political leaders to —
   A talk with the people who have impressed or inspired him most
   B complete an assignment for school
   C bring the issue of children's rights to their attention
   D have his picture taken with them

4. The author provides **adequate evidence** to support all of the following conclusions *except* —
   F Craig Kielburger cares deeply about the rights of children
   G Craig Kielburger is intolerant of child labor and slavery
   H one teenager's actions can make a big difference in the world
   J Craig Kielburger hopes to become famous and win awards

Reading Standard 2.6 Determine the adequacy and appropriateness of the evidence for an author's conclusions.

Grammar Link MINI-LESSON

The Homophones *Their, There,* and *They're*

Are you confused about when to use *their, there,* and *they're*? There are good reasons for mixing these words up. They're homophones (häm'ə·fōnz')—words that are pronounced the same although their meanings are different.

their	there	they're
a pronoun— the possessive form of *they*	an adverb that means "in that place"	a contraction of *they are*
At first the directors held their meetings in Craig's den.	There in Bosnia he saw what war does.	"They're all incredibly interesting people."
	or	
	a word used with forms of the verb *to be,* usually at the beginning of a sentence	
	"In Thailand, there was a young street girl...."	

PRACTICE

Copy the following sentences, and write the correct word— *their, there,* or *they're*—in each blank. If you have trouble, see if the words *they are* (for *they're*) fit. If they don't make sense, you know that *they're* is incorrect.

Then, ask yourself if the word is a possessive: Does it signify ownership? If it doesn't, you know that *their* is incorrect.

1. I enjoyed meeting all of them _____, but _____ not the ones who impress me the most.
2. I thought it was _____ in the dark back alleys.
3. _____ were several kids having _____ pictures taken with Craig.

For more help, see Glossary of Usage in the *Holt Handbook,* pages 229–230.

One Child's Labor of Love **161**

Grammar Link

Practice

1. I enjoyed meeting all of them there, but they're not the ones who impressed me the most.
2. I thought it was there in the dark back alleys.
3. There were several kids having their pictures taken with Craig.

Assessment

■ *Progress Assessment of Reading*
  ■ Selection Test, p. 54

Literary Response and Analysis

STANDARDS FOCUS, pp. 162–163

(For the grade-level standard reviewed in this lesson, see Pupil's Edition, p. 162.)

INTRODUCING THE STANDARDS REVIEW

Use this review to assess students' grasp of the features of themes and the way theme is conveyed.

DIRECT TEACHING

A **Literary Focus**
GRADE-LEVEL STANDARD
❓ **Characters and theme.**
Would you characterize Siksik and Mikmik as strong and brave or meek and fearful? [They are meek and fearful, as they address the hyena as "sir," passively answer his questions, and tell him they fear him.] **What happens to them?** [They are eaten.]

B **Literary Focus**
GRADE-LEVEL STANDARD
❓ **Characters and theme.** How is Jureybon different in looks and personality from his brothers? [Jureybon's nickname suggests that he is small and unhealthy looking in comparison to his brothers, but he behaves more bravely than they do.] **How does Jureybon's personality save him?** [He bravely challenges the hyena and intimidates him, causing him to run away.]

C **Literary Focus**
GRADE-LEVEL STANDARD
❓ **Characters and theme.** What lessons about fear and courage might the actions of the three goats suggest? [Possible responses: Don't let fear rule you; courage can make up for physical weakness.]

Literary Response and Analysis

 DIRECTIONS: Read the following selection. Then, read each question, and write the letter of the best response.

Little Mangy One

Lebanese folk tale, retold by Inea Bushnaq

Once upon a time three little goats were grazing on the side of a stony hill. Their names were Siksik, Mikmik, and Jureybon, the Little Mangy One. Soon a hyena scented them and loped up. "Siksik!" called the hyena. "Yes sir!" answered the goat. "What are those points sticking out of your head?" "Those are my little horns, sir," said the goat. "What is that patch on your back?" continued the hyena. "That is my hair, sir," replied the goat. "Why are you shivering?" roared the hyena. "Because I am afraid of you, sir," said the goat. At this the hyena sprang and gobbled him right up. Next the hyena turned to Mikmik, who answered like his brother, and he too was quickly devoured.

Then the hyena approached Jureybon, the Little Mangy One. Before the hyena came within earshot, Jureybon began to snort. As the hyena

drew nearer, Jureybon bellowed, "May a plague lay low your back, O cursed one! What have you come for?" "I wish to know what the two points on your head are," said the hyena. "Those? Why, those are my trusty sabers!" said the goat. "And the patch on your back, what is that?" said the hyena. "My sturdy shield, of course!" sneered the goat. "Then why are you shivering?" asked the hyena. "Shivering? I'm trembling with rage! I'm shaking with impatience, for I cannot wait to throttle you and squeeze your very soul till it starts out of your eye sockets!" snarled the goat, and began to advance on the hyena.

The hyena's heart stopped beating for an instant; then he turned and ran for his life. But Jureybon sprang after him over the rocks and gored him with his sharp little horns, slitting open his belly and freeing his two little brothers inside.

Reading Standard 3.6 Identify and analyze features of themes conveyed through characters, actions, and images.

MINI-LESSON **Reading**

Reviewing Word-Attack Skills
Activity. Display these sets of words. Have volunteers identify the two words in which the letters *ci* stand for the same sound or sounds. Answers are underlined.

1. appreciate   <u>cinder</u>   <u>publicity</u>
2. <u>spacious</u>   <u>social</u>   science
3. <u>special</u>   decide   <u>delicious</u>
4. <u>placid</u>   <u>city</u>   precious
5. <u>official</u>   <u>facial</u>   specific

Activity. Display these sets of words. Have volunteers identify the two words in which the letters *ough* stand for the same sounds. If they're not sure, have them consult a dictionary. Answers are underlined.

1. though   <u>cough</u>   <u>trough</u>

1. Unlike Siksik and Mikmik, Jureybon responds to the hyena by —
   A running away
   B refusing to talk to him
   C attacking him
   D answering all of his questions

2. The words Jureybon uses to describe his horns and the patch on his back suggest images of —
   F strength
   G anger
   H hunger
   J fear

3. What is the **conflict** in this story?
   A A hyena tries to eat three goats.
   B Three goats are arguing among themselves.
   C Three goats try to kill a hyena.
   D A hyena is trying to find his way home.

4. One of the **themes** of this story could be stated as —
   F never challenge a bully
   G cleverness can help the weak
   H be kind to strangers
   J there's strength in numbers

5. The first paragraph contains a context clue you can use to figure out the meaning of <u>devoured</u>. Which group of words helps you understand *devoured*?
   A "gobbled him right up"
   B "the hyena sprang"
   C "I am afraid of you"
   D "turned to Mikmik"

Standards Review **163**

Answers and Model Rationales

1. **C** Students should realize that Jureybon does not run away (A) or refuse to talk to the hyena (B). All three goats answer the hyena's questions, so D is not correct. Unlike his brothers, Jureybon attacks the hyena, so C is the correct answer.

2. **F** Hunger (H) is projected by the hyena, not by the goats. J is suggested by Siksik's and Mikmik's words, not by Jureybon's. F is better than G because Jureybon's descriptions, "sturdy shield" and "trusty sabers," suggest strong self-defense.

3. **A** The hungry hyena interrupts the grazing goats.

4. **G** After reading the last paragraph, students should see that standing up to danger and hiding fear (G) let Jureybon kill the marauding hyena and rescue his brothers as well.

5. **A** Students should recognize that *devoured* is a contextual restatement of the phrase "gobbled him right up"(A).

Test-Taking Tips

Tell students that if they draw a complete blank on a question, they should skip it and go back to it after responding to other questions. The other questions may jog their memories.

For more information on answering multiple-choice questions, refer students to **Test Smarts,** p. 690.

2. bough   bought   fought
3. <u>rough</u>   tough   cough
4. through   ought   bought
5. <u>slough</u> (off)   <u>enough</u>   bough

Literary Terms
As part of the review of Literary Response and Analysis Standard 3.6, ask students to look back through the chapter to find the meanings of the terms at right. Then, have students show their grasp of Standard 3.6 by citing passages from two or three selections in the chapter that illustrate the meanings of the following terms.
Subject (p. 118); **Theme** (pp. 118, 135, 149); **Plot** (p. 135); **Universal Themes** (p. 149).

Standards Review

Reading Informational Materials

STANDARDS FOCUS, pp. 164–165

(For the grade-level standard reviewed in this lesson, see Pupil's Edition, p. 164.)

INTRODUCING THE STANDARDS REVIEW

Use this review to assess students' grasp of the effectiveness of supporting evidence. Use these annotations only if you want to conduct this review orally.

DIRECT TEACHING

A **Reading Informational Materials**
GRADE-LEVEL STANDARD

❓ **Evaluating evidence.** What statistics does the author present in this paragraph? [percentages of overweight U.S. children in three consecutive decades] What trend do these statistics show? [The percentage of overweight U.S. children is increasing rapidly.]

B **Reading Informational Materials**
GRADE-LEVEL STANDARD

❓ **Evaluating evidence.** What kinds of support does the author use here? [experts' opinions, quotations, and information deriving from studies] How can readers decide whether Doctors Crespo and Andersen are appropriate sources of support for the author's conclusion? [In the previous paragraph, the author identifies them as medical school professors specializing in health, fitness, and weight management.]

Reading Informational Materials

TestPractice

DIRECTIONS: Read the article. Then, read each question, and write the letter of the best response.

Too Much TV Can Equal Too Much Weight

by Jamie Rodgers, 12 years old
Children's Express

A In 1970, only 10 percent of kids in America were overweight. In the 1980s, it was 30 percent, and in the 1990s, it was 60 percent. Studies show that obesity is linked to watching TV and using the Internet.

Children's Express interviewed two professors from Johns Hopkins University School of Medicine about the link. Ross Andersen, M.D., is with the weight management center, and Carlos Crespo, M.D., is an assistant professor of health and fitness.

B "Dr. Crespo and I have published a study that appeared in the *Journal of the American Medical Association*. We looked at how fat kids were in relation to the number of hours of television they watch per day," said Andersen. "We found that kids who are low TV watchers were much leaner. The kids who were the fattest were those who watched a lot of TV. We defined a lot as four or more hours per day. Roughly, one in three kids in America is watching four or more hours per day. I would estimate sitting in front of a computer would be just as great a risk factor for being overweight."

Andersen and Crespo say the blame is not just on the parents. Sometimes it's a lack of places to play.

"[It's a] lack of facilities, services for the children to be able to go out and play basketball or go to a swimming pool. The community should have open spaces and safe spaces for girls and boys to be active," said Crespo.

"The thing is not that it's bad to watch TV; it's just that you need to have a balance. There [is] a certain number of hours in the day you're supposed to sleep, do your homework, . . . [and] go to school, and then there is a certain [number] of hours that you're free to do whatever you want. If you spend that time watching TV, then you spend less time doing physical activity.". . .

"Kids and parents need to look for opportunities to remain physically active. So instead of sitting down to watch *Who Wants to Be a Millionaire*, it may be that the whole family could get up and go for a walk.". . .

Reading Standard 2.6 Determine the adequacy and appropriateness of the evidence for an author's conclusions.

164 Chapter 3 The Heart of the Matter: Themes and Conclusions

---

Using Academic Language

Informational Terms
As part of the review of Reading Comprehension Standard 2.6, ask students to look back through the chapter to find the meaning of the terms and phrases at the right and, using these words, to explain Standard 2.6:

Summarize (p. 130); **Conclusion** (p. 130); **Evidence** (p. 144); **Quotations** (p. 144); **Direct Quotations** (p. 144); **Statistics** (p. 144); **Case Studies** (p. 144); **Inappropriate Evidence** (p. 157); **Inadequate Evidence** (p. 157); **Facts** (p. 157); **Opinions** (p. 157); **Valid Opinion** (p. 157).

1. What percentage of American children were overweight during the 1990s?
   A 10
   B 20
   C 40
   D 60

2. Studies show that obesity is linked to watching TV and —
   F going for walks
   G doing homework
   H using the Internet
   J taking long naps

3. Which of the following statements is *not* true?
   A The author uses quotations to support her conclusions.
   B The author uses statistics to support her conclusions.
   C The author uses experts' opinions to support her conclusions.
   D The author does not provide adequate support for her conclusions.

4. The doctors define "a lot of TV" as —
   F one or more hours per day
   G two or more hours per day
   H three or more hours per day
   J four or more hours per day

5. Andersen and Crespo place part of the blame for overweight in children on —
   A lack of playgrounds
   B poor health education
   C lack of medical attention
   D fast foods

6. The doctors believe that children and parents should —
   F prepare meals together
   G remain physically active
   H watch TV together
   J surf the Internet

7. The *best* statement of the writer's **conclusion** is that —
   A the whole family should go on a diet
   B obesity in children is linked to watching TV
   C parents must take blame for children's obesity
   D we need to stop watching TV

Answers and Model Rationales

1. **D** This statistic appears in the first paragraph of the selection.

2. **H** Students should immediately eliminate F because walking is active. Homework (G) is sedentary, but most students spend far less time on homework than on TV or Internet use. Naps (J) are not mentioned in the selection.

3. **D** The author uses quotations, statistics, and expert opinions to support her conclusions.

4. **J** This information is at the end of the third paragraph.

5. **A** The article does not mention B, C, or D, but it refers specifically to a lack of places to play (A) in the fourth paragraph.

6. **G** Students should recognize this choice from the first sentence of the last paragraph. No mention of the ideas in H and J appears in the article. While diet is an important issue, the author doesn't mention families preparing meals together.

7. **B** The article does not mention A or D, and it clearly states the blame is not just on the parents.

Test-Taking Tips

Remind students that if they're not sure of an answer, they should take their best guess rather than leave the item blank.

For more information on answering multiple-choice questions, refer students to **Test Smarts,** p. 690.

Test Practice

Vocabulary Development

Context Clues

Modeling. Model the thought process for answering item 1 by saying, "The context gives me an example of *audacity*—coming to class very late when someone has told you to be prompt. So I'm looking for a word whose meaning can be negative. Too much *boldness* can be negative, so *boldness* must mean *audacity*."

Answers and Model Rationales

1. **B** See rationale above.

2. **H** Splitting a seam in one's pants would cause embarrassment. *Embarrassed* is closest in meaning to *mortified*.

3. **A** Students should notice that *devastating* is used in conjunction with "cause quite a bit of damage." Only *destructive* (A) carries that meaning.

4. **F** The context sets Jack's stinginess with his rent money in opposition to his lavish spending on friends. *Generously* (F) is an antonym for *stingily*, so *generously* must be nearest in meaning to *lavishly*.

5. **B** The context example describes clothing that would create an eye-catching display.

6. **J** The context example describes a response to a parade in honor of a rare achievement. F and G are unlikely responses to such an event. H could also apply to an unpleasant event, so J is the best choice.

7. **C** Proper behavior at the table is a matter of manners (C).

8. **H** The standard response to a fire alarm is to get out of the building, removing oneself from danger (H).

Vocabulary Development

Test Practice

Context Clues

DIRECTIONS: Use **context clues** to determine the meaning of the underlined words in each of the following sentences.

1. I can't believe you have the audacity to show up fifteen minutes late when I asked you to be on time. And you're eating an ice-cream cone! *Audacity* means —
   A decency
   B boldness
   C willpower
   D intelligence

2. Joe was mortified when his pants split as he sat down. *Mortified* means —
   F pleased
   G offended
   H embarrassed
   J frightened

3. I've seen earthquakes cause quite a bit of damage, but this one was truly devastating. *Devastating* means —
   A destructive
   B interesting
   C fulfilling
   D disappointing

4. Jack claims he can't pay his rent, yet he spends money lavishly on expensive gifts for his friends. *Lavishly* means —
   F generously
   G unhappily
   H foolishly
   J intelligently

5. Since he was wearing his velvet cape and neon jumpsuit, I assumed James wished to make a spectacle of himself. *Spectacle* means —
   A warrior
   B display
   C mockery
   D mannequin

6. Our school doesn't win state championships too often, so I'm really going to savor the victory parade. *Savor* means —
   F ruin
   G ignore
   H remember
   J enjoy

7. The fact that he started eating before everyone had been served shows that he's not concerned about etiquette. *Etiquette* means —
   A clothing
   B criticism
   C manners
   D regulations

8. After the fire alarm sounded, the residents were evacuated from the building. *Evacuated* means —
   F cared for
   G forgotten
   H removed
   J misplaced

166 Chapter 3 The Heart of the Matter: Themes and Conclusions

Vocabulary Review

Use this activity to assess whether students have retained the chapter Vocabulary.
Activity. Have students select the correct word to complete the following sentences.

mortified	devastating	lavishly
spectacle	etiquette	

1. My mother was _____ when the cat jumped up on the table and ate a bite of turkey from our guest's plate. [mortified]

2. Writing thank-you notes is considered proper _____. [etiquette]

3. The drum major with the flaming baton created quite a _____ at halftime. [spectacle]

4. The movie star was _____ supplied with a roomful of beautiful costumes. [lavishly]

5. Losing the first playoff game had a _____ effect on our team's morale. [devastating]

RESPONSE TO LITERATURE

Thinking Theme

Mastering the
Standards

In a brief essay, discuss the **theme** that you found revealed in one of the stories in this chapter. To refresh your memory, skim the story before you begin to gather your details. Then, think about the main events in the story and the discoveries the main character has made by the end of the action. Look for key passages that seem to point to the story's theme. You may want to fill in a chart like this one:

Open your essay by stating the title and author of your story. Then, state the theme as you see it. Briefly describe the events and character changes or discoveries that support the theme. Finally, describe the way you feel about the story's theme.

> Use "Writing a Short-Story Interpretation," pages 552–569, for help with this assignment.

Story Title and Author:
Main events:
Discoveries made by the main character:
Key passages:

Mastering the
Standards

Evaluation Criteria

A good interpretation of theme

1. exhibits careful reading, understanding, and insight
2. makes a clear interpretive claim
3. organizes the interpretation around several clear ideas, premises, or images
4. develops and justifies the interpretation through sustained use of examples and textual evidence

ASSESSING

Assessment

■ *Progress Assessment of Reading*
  ■ Chapter Test, p. 56

Other Choices

EXPOSITION

1 **How to Give a Party**

In "The All-American Slurp" the Lins feel uncomfortable at the Gleasons' dinner party because they are unsure about American customs. Have you ever been to a party and not known what to do—when to dance or how to eat the food? Write a **how-to paper** on planning and hosting a party where everyone feels great and has fun. Brainstorm a to-do list that will help make your party a success. Include details explaining *how, when,* and *why,* if necessary.

> Use "Writing a 'How-to' Explanation," pages 528–544, for help with this assignment.

PERSUASION

2 **Pro or Con?**

The essay "Uniform Style" discusses school uniforms. Where do you stand on the issue? Explain your opinion in a **persuasive essay.** Give at least three reasons to support your position, and include evidence (facts, examples, statistics) to back up your reasons. You may want to end your paper by briefly explaining why you think this issue is important and what you think should be done about it.

> Use "Writing a Persuasive Essay," pages 618–635, for help with this assignment.

Writing Applications   **167**

Read On

For Independent Reading

If students enjoyed the themes and topics explored in this chapter, you might recommend these titles for independent reading.

Assessment Options

The following projects can help you evaluate and assess your students' outside reading. Videotapes or audiotapes of completed projects may be included in students' portfolios.

- **Present a slide show.** Ask students to create a slide show of original drawings of images from one of the selections. Encourage students to include images related to the selection's theme. If possible, provide samples of slide shows. Have students choose appropriate background music and narration for their presentations.

- **Develop a travel brochure.** Suggest that students create a travel brochure advertising a tour through a place important to the theme of one of the Read On selections. Brochures might show significant settings, landmarks, and local events. Bring in sample travel brochures for students to use as models. Students may use drawings, magazine illustrations, or artwork created with computer graphics programs. Have students share their brochures with the class.

California Reading List Titles

The Pigman
Adaline Falling Star
City: A Story of Roman Planning and Construction

Fiction

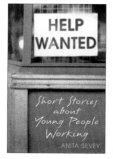

Windows of Opportunity

Have you ever wondered what your first job will be like? Maybe you've had a few odd jobs already. If so, you may see yourself in *Help Wanted*, a collection of twelve quirky short stories about young people at work. In this anthology, compiled by Anita Silvey, you'll meet a former child actress who finds truth in the La Brea Tar Pits, a young secretary whose typewriter has a mind of its own, and a teen who gets a little help in the fast-food business from her aunt Edna.

"How Glad I Am to Be Alive!"

In Paul Zindel's novel *The Pigman*, John and Lorraine befriend Mr. Pignati, a lonely widower with a weakness for bad jokes and miniature pigs and a passion for life. This unlikely hero becomes a model of joy, freedom, and courage for John and Lorraine. Then tragedy tears the Pigman away. In the sequel, *The Pigman's Legacy*, John and Lorraine are drawn back to the Pigman's abandoned house and are shaken when they discover another lonely older man living there. For the true story of the year the teenage Zindel met his own "pigman," try *The Pigman and Me*.

This title is available in the HRW Library.

Fight to the Finish

After conquering Troy, Ulysses angers the gods, who determine that his voyage home will last ten years. On his odyssey he meets the one-eyed Cyclops; the sorceress Circe, who turns men into pigs; and the monsters Scylla and Charybdis. *The Adventures of Ulysses*, retold by Bernard Evslin, recounts the story of a hero's struggle to return and reclaim his home.

The Open Road

When her father, the legendary Kit Carson, goes searching for adventure, Adaline Falling Star is left with her mother's relatives in St. Louis. They are offended by her bold personality, so she decides to leave and head into the wilderness. In Mary Pope Osborne's novel *Adaline Falling Star*, Adaline searches for her father and discovers herself along the way.

Toward Reading a Million Words Annually

Estimated Word Counts of Read On Books:

Fiction		Nonfiction	
Help Wanted: Short Stories About Young People Working	59,000	City: A Story of Roman Planning and Construction	14,000
The Pigman	38,000	Bad Guys	6,300
Connections to The Pigman	10,000	Prehistoric Life	26,000
The Adventures of Ulysses	35,000	The Stars	45,000
Adaline Falling Star	27,100		

Nonfiction

Glory Days

Did you know that the ancient Romans were skilled city planners? David Macaulay goes back to 26 B.C. in *City: A Story of Roman Planning and Construction* to describe the way the Romans built their cities. Drawing on his knowledge of hundreds of ancient Roman cities, he shows how planners might have created an imaginary city called Verbonia. Macaulay's illustrations show aqueducts, a forum, a house, a central market, and storehouses. He also draws a comparison between ancient cities and cities of today.

Larger Than Life

American outlaws like Jesse James and Belle Starr capture our imaginations. But are the stories about their lives fact or fiction? In *Bad Guys*, Andrew Glass looks at eight of these mysterious figures and uncovers the truth behind the legends. You'll find that many of these desperadoes preferred the stories told about them to the facts.

Walking with the Dinosaurs

Using stunning photographs and imaginative design, *Prehistoric Life* by William Lindsay transports you to the distant past, where you'll step into some pretty big footprints. You can watch the past unfold in the accompanying *Eyewitness Video* series.

Twinkle, Twinkle

When you gaze at the night sky, what do you see? You'll know what you're looking at after you read *The Stars* by H. A. Rey. Using clear graphics and easy-to-read text, Rey shows you a fun, exciting new way of looking at the constellations. You'll never get lost in the dark again!

Read On   **169**

- **Compare a book and a story.** Have students write an essay in which they compare the characters, events, and themes of one of the books suggested here and one of the selections they have read in this chapter. Encourage students to present their essays to the class or to submit the essays for publication in a school newspaper or magazine.

- **Compose a song.** Invite students to write songs reflecting the experiences of characters in the Read On selections that they choose. Tell students to express the themes of the selections by mentioning what a character learns or how the character changes. Students may choose familiar melodies for their songs, or they may compose their own music. Encourage students to perform their songs for the class.

Resources Reminder

Reading

- *Interactive Reading*

For additional readings that relate to the selections in this chapter, see *Interactive Reading*, Chapter 3.

- *The Ancient World:* A Content-Area Reader

The Read On titles are categorized as shown below:

Below Grade Level
Adaline Falling Star
Bad Guys

At Grade Level ↔
Help Wanted: Short Stories About Young People Working

The Adventures of Ulysses
Prehistoric Life
The Stars

Above Grade Level ↑
The Pigman
City: A Story of Roman Planning and Construction

Chapter 4 Forms and Patterns: Stories and Explanations

Program Organization

Holt Literature and Language Arts provides a complete curriculum for standards-based instruction in vocabulary, reading, literature, writing, and speaking and listening. The instructional content of the program is divided into quarters to enable teachers to anticipate and administer the quarterly assessments required by California.

About Chapter 4

Standards-based lesson plans and suggestions for pacing the presentation of Chapter 4 and the related instructional material are provided in *On Course: Mapping Instruction,* Chapter 4.

- Chapter 4 helps students identify and describe the major characteristics of forms of fiction, analyze text that uses comparison-and-contrast organization, and identify and interpret words with multiple meanings.

- The related instructional material for Chapter 4 is shown on the chart. This related instructional material will also be covered in the second quarterly assessment.

Holt Literature and Language Arts

Pupil's Edition

Part 1, Chapter 4

Forms and Patterns: Stories and Explanations, pp. 170–239
- Reading Standards 1.2, 2.2, 3.1
- Writing Application **Writing a Comparison-Contrast Essay**

Part 2, Mini-Workshop 1

Writing a Comparison-Contrast Essay, pp. 660–664
- Writing Standard 2.2

Holt Handbook

Chapter 7

Using Verbs Correctly
Written and Oral English-Language Conventions
- Grade-Level Standard 1.2, pp. 160–164

Chapter 8

Using Pronouns Correctly
Written and Oral English-Language Conventions
- Review, Gr. 5 Standard 1.2, pp. 177–191

Diagnostic and Summative Assessments: Midyear Test

Which vocabulary, informational reading, and literature standards are taught in Chapter 4?

In this chapter, students will master the following Grade 6 standards. Selections or features marked with a ✔ constitute the minimum course of study that provides coverage of all grade-level standards.

Grade 6 Standards

Word Analysis, Fluency, and Systematic Vocabulary Development

1.2 Identify and interpret words with multiple meanings.

Synonyms and Antonyms, p. 188

Words with Multiple Meanings, p. 188

✔ Words with Multiple Meanings, p. 202

Words with Multiple Meanings, p. 207

Clarifying Word Meanings, p. 223

Words with Multiple Meanings, p. 233

Reading Comprehension (Focus on Informational Materials)

2.2 Analyze text that uses the compare-and-contrast organizational pattern.

"Separate but Never Equal" (informational article), pp. 189–192

✔ "Goodbye Records, Hello CDs" (informational article), pp. 203–206

✔ Standards Review: Reading Informational Materials, pp. 234–235

Literary Response and Analysis

3.1 Identify the forms of fiction, and describe the major characteristics of each form.

✔ "Forms of Fiction: It's All a Story" (standards essay), pp. 172–173

The Gold Cadillac (novella), pp. 174–187

"La Bamba" (short story), pp. 193–201

"Medusa's Head" (myth) and "Perseus and the Gorgon's Head" (cartoon), pp. 208–222

"He Lion, Bruh Bear, and Bruh Rabbit" (folk tale), "The Fox and the Crow" (reader's theater), and "The Wolf and the House Dog" (reader's theater), pp. 224–232

Where do I locate lesson plans, additional resources, and other teaching aids?

- This Annotated Teacher's Edition and *On Course: Mapping Instruction* provide direction in planning and implementing a complete California standards–based curriculum. These components include instructions for administering diagnostic, progress, and summative tests; for presenting instruction of the standards; for differentiating instruction to provide universal access; and for locating and using the program's ancillaries.

- The program's resources are referenced at the beginning of each selection, in the bottom margin of this teacher's edition.

- Reminders for using additional resources appear in this teacher's edition at point of use.

- The *One-Stop Planner* CD-ROM with Test Generator contains editable lesson plans and all of the print ancillaries, available in PDF format.

What if I don't have time to teach all of Chapter 4?

- Most standards can be taught with a minimum number of selections and features. In the chart on p. 169B, the core lessons you need in order to provide complete coverage of the chapter standards are identified with a ✔.

- Use the Standards Review, pp. 234–235, for a quick review and informal assessment of the grade-level standards covered in Chapter 4.

What provisions have been made for students who have additional class time scheduled in language arts?

- *Interactive Reading* provides for additional direct instruction and practice of the grade-level standards taught in Chapter 4. It can be used as an introduction to instruction or as an opportunity for remediation.

- *Lesson Plans for Language Development,* Chapter 4, provides alternative teaching strategies and additional worksheets designed specifically for English-language learners and special education students. Many of the suggestions and activities in this ancillary will also be helpful to students in the regular classroom who are having difficulty with particular skills.

In addition to vocabulary, reading, and literature, what other language arts are covered in Chapter 4?

Writing Activities in Chapter 4
- Narrating an Experience, p. 187
- The Show Must Go On (make a list of tips to handle stage fright), p. 201
- Writing a Story, p. 222
- A Fable for Our Time (writing a story about animals), p. 232

Writing Applications (p. 237)
- M and M (comparison and contrast)
- Other Choices: Perseus Revisited, Telling Tales (narrative writing)

Grammar Links in Chapter 4
- Pronoun and Contraction Mix-ups, p. 223
- Understanding Homophones: *To, Too,* and *Two*, p. 233

Universal Access

How do I differentiate instruction to ensure that all my students master the standards?

Holt Literature and Language Arts provides comprehensive, differentiated instruction for all types of students.

- Most of the general instruction and teaching strategies in the Annotated Teacher's Edition are at grade level. These instructions will work well with the majority of your students.

- In Chapter 4, suggestions for advanced learners are provided in the Annotated Teacher's Edition. Point-of-use suggestions for learners having difficulty, English-language learners, and special education students are also provided.

- *Interactive Reading* is designed to anticipate and/or remediate problems that students may experience in achieving mastery of the standards. *Interactive Reading* includes

reading-strategy lessons, lower-level practice reads, and worksheets for every informational and literary text in *Holt Literature and Language Arts,* Pupil's Editions. *Interactive Reading* also contains three additional selections for each chapter and suggestions for extension projects, many of which are ideal for advanced learners working on their own. See *Interactive Reading,* Teacher's Edition, for specific information on using the reader to differentiate instruction in Chapter 4.

- *Lesson Plans for Language Development,* Chapter 4, offers teaching strategies and additional worksheets designed specifically for English-language learners and special education students.

Assessment

How do I determine whether or not my students are making progress in mastering the standards?

Progress Assessment

- Use the Standards Review at the end of Chapter 4, pp. 234–235, for an informal assessment of the informational reading and literature standards in Chapter 4.

- Use the Selection Tests for Chapter 4 in the *Progress Assessment of Reading* booklet to test comprehension and progress on mastering the standard(s) taught with a selection.

- Use Chapter Test 4 in the *Progress Assessment of Reading* booklet to test students' cumulative progress in mastering the standards taught in the chapter.

Summative Assessment

At the end of this chapter, you may ask students to take the Midyear Test in the *Diagnostic and Summative Assessments* booklet. This test covers *Holt Literature and Language Arts,* Chapters 3 and 4, Workshop 3, and Mini-Workshops 1, "Writing a Comparison-Contrast Essay" and 2, "Writing a Movie Review," as well as the *Holt Handbook,* Chapters 5–8.

Forms and Patterns
Stories and Explanations

STANDARDS FOCUS

(*For grade-level and review standards taught in this chapter, see Pupil's Edition, p. 171.*)

Prerequisite Standards

■ Grade 5, Vocabulary 1.3 **Understand and explain frequently used synonyms, antonyms, and homographs.**

■ Grade 5, Reading Comprehension 2.4 **Draw inferences, conclusions, or generalizations about text, and support them with textual evidence and prior knowledge.**

Standards Coming Up in the Next Grade Level

■ Grade 7, Vocabulary 1.3 **Clarify word meanings through the use of definition, example, restatement, or contrast.**

■ Grade 7, Reading Comprehension 2.4 **Identify and trace the development of an author's argument, point of view, or perspective in text.**

■ Grade 7, Literary Response and Analysis 3.1 **Articulate the expressed purposes and characteristics of different forms of prose (e.g., short story, novel, novella, essay).**

CHAPTER RESOURCES

Planning
■ *One-Stop Planner* CD-ROM with Test Generator
■ *On Course: Mapping Instruction*
  ■ Chapter 4
■ *At Home: A Guide to Standards Mastery*
■ *At Home: In Five Languages*
■ *Supporting Instruction in Five Languages*

Reading
■ *Interactive Reading*
  ■ Chapter 4

Differentiating Instruction
■ *Lesson Plans for Language Development*
  ■ Chapter 4

Vocabulary and Spelling
■ *Vocabulary Development*
  ■ Cumulative Vocabulary Review, p. 16

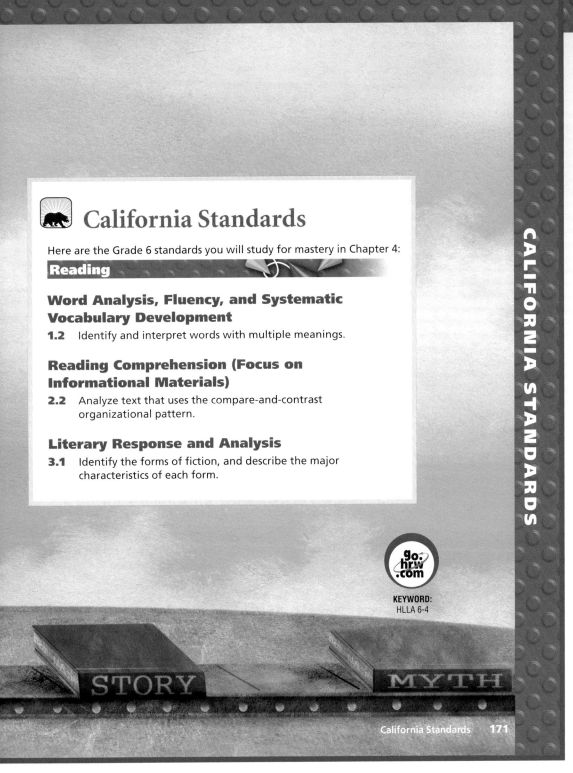

California Standards

Here are the Grade 6 standards you will study for mastery in Chapter 4:

Reading

Word Analysis, Fluency, and Systematic Vocabulary Development

1.2 Identify and interpret words with multiple meanings.

Reading Comprehension (Focus on Informational Materials)

2.2 Analyze text that uses the compare-and-contrast organizational pattern.

Literary Response and Analysis

3.1 Identify the forms of fiction, and describe the major characteristics of each form.

KEYWORD:
HLLA 6-4

STORY   MYTH

California Standards **171**

INTRODUCING THE CHAPTER

This chapter introduces several forms of fiction to readers, including short stories, fables, and a folk tale. As students read these various forms of fiction, they will realize that although fiction comes in many shapes and sizes, it always has the same basic characteristics. With each selection, students can focus on some of these characteristics, such as theme or character. Interspersed with the fiction are informational essays that use a compare-and-contrast structure. The chapter ends with an opportunity for students to use this to develop and write comparison-and-contrast essays based on the literature.

▶ Resources Reminder

Planning
- *At Home: A Guide to Standards Mastery*

You may want to send students home with selected parent letters from this resource. Translations of these letters are available in *At Home: In Five Languages*. *Supporting Instruction in Five Languages* provides translations of the selection summaries.

Reading
- *Interactive Reading*
  - Reading Log

The California framework requires students to read materials apart from in-class assignments. Additional reading suggestions are included on the Read On pages and on selected pages in the Pupil's and Teacher's Editions. You may want to use the Reading Log to help students track their progress.

Grammar
- *Holt Handbook*
  - Forms of Personal Pronouns, pp. 177–188
  - Contractions, pp. 304–307

Assessment
- *Progress Assessment of Reading*
  - Chapter Test, p. 81

- *Diagnostic and Summative Assessments*
  - Midyear Test, p. 60

Internet
go.hrw.com
Keyword: HLLA 6-4

California Standards **171**

STANDARDS FOCUS, pp. 172–173

(For the grade level standard taught in this lesson, see Pupil's Editon, p. 172.)

Prerequisite Standard

■ Grade 4, Literary Response and Analysis 3.1 **Describe the structural differences of various imaginative forms of literature, including fantasies, fables, myths, legends, and fairy tales.**

Literary Focus: Forms of Fiction

Point out to students that fiction is a category of literature and that, within the category, there are many varieties. Write the category "Sports" on the chalkboard, and have students come up with a list of different kinds of sports, such as ball sports, water sports, etc. Then, ask them to come up with a set of characteristics that defines the category. Point out that although there are many different kinds of sports, they share some basic characteristics, which is what allows us to define them as sports. The same is true of fiction.

► Resources Reminder

Reading

■ *Interactive Reading*

Before you teach Chapter 4 of *Holt Literature and Language Arts,* you may want to preteach the literary concept and a related reading strategy.

• To introduce students to the literary concept before they read this essay, assign p. 141 of *Interactive Reading.*

• To introduce students to a reading strategy that will help them grasp the literary concept, assign p. 141 of *Interactive Reading.*

• To give students practice applying the strategy to a short, vocabulary-controlled selection, assign the Practice Read on p. 142 of *Interactive Reading.*

Forms of Fiction *by* Mara Rockliff

IT'S ALL A STORY

Why do we love to read stories we know are pure products of the imagination? Maybe it's because a good story seems as if it *could* have happened. Maybe we feel that it *should* have happened. Whether it's the latest in Bruce Coville's Alien Adventures series or J.R.R. Tolkien's *The Lord of the Rings* trilogy, we just can't get enough of **fiction,** the made-up stories that fill our lives.

Good fiction shows us something important about life. It may not be factual, but we know that what it reveals is *true.*

Myths: Our First Stories?

Probably the first stories people ever told were **myths**—stories about gods and heroes that people told to give human shape to the world around them. Myths often address very basic questions: Where does fire come from? What makes the seasons change? Why do people die? Although myths differ greatly in their details, most were connected at some time with a culture's religious beliefs. These stories were passed on orally from generation to generation long before they were written down.

Myths are central to human experience. In the Western world the best-known myths are from ancient Greece and Rome. (*Myth* comes from the Greek word *mythos,* meaning "story.") These myths have been written down for more than two thousand years. But the myths of Greece and Rome are only a small part of the body of myths. There are thousands of cultures, and myths are central to every one of them.

Some people believe that scientific explanations have taken the place of myths. But myths also answer questions well beyond the scope of science: Who are we? Where are we going? How should we live? What is courage? What is love? Who are our heroes? What is the difference between right and wrong?

Fables: Teaching Stories

Another very old type of story is the short teaching story called the **fable.** Fables are told by people all over the world—from Africa to India to America. The most famous fables in the Western world were told by Aesop (ē′səp), a man held in slavery in ancient Greece. The boy who cried wolf, the goose that laid the golden eggs, the slow but steady tortoise who outraced the speedy hare—references to Aesop's fables, with their practical morals, can still be heard in everyday conversation today, 2,600 years later. (You'll find two of Aesop's fables, retold as reader's theater, on pages 229–231.)

Legends: Stories Based on History

People tell stories about historical events too. As these stories are told and retold,

Reading Standard 3.1 Identify the forms of fiction, and describe the major characteristics of each form.

DIFFERENTIATING INSTRUCTION

Learners Having Difficulty
Forms of fiction. Help students distinguish between myths, fables, legends, and folk tales by highlighting the following definitions:

• *myth*—a story involving gods and other superhuman beings

• *fable*—a brief story that teaches a moral

• *legend*—a story believed to have a historical basis that has been passed down from one generation to the next

• *folk tale*—an entertaining or meaningful story that does not involve gods or religious beliefs and is passed down from one generation to the next

English-Language Learners
Forms of fiction. To help students create definitions of the different forms of fiction, suggest that they first come up with one or two adjectives for each form. For instance, adventure fiction can be described as

they often become less and less accurate. Heroes become superhuman, enemies become more villainous, victories become more fantastic. These exaggerated stories about historic events are called **legends.** We still read legends about the Trojan War, for instance. These legends are partly true (there really was a war in Troy around 1200 B.C.) and partly imaginary (a serpent probably did *not* rise out of the sea and strangle one of the Trojans). American history has also been the source of legends, such as the ones about the frontiersman Davy Crockett. Crockett did fight at the Alamo, but he probably did *not* wade across the Mississippi or ride a streak of lightning.

Folk Tales: Traveling Stories

A **folk tale** is a story that has been passed down over the years by word of mouth. Generations of storytellers have passed on tales of genies and flying carpets, giants and elves and princesses, talking animals and magical wishes that come in threes.

Folk tales tend to travel from one culture to another. Folk tales with similar story lines often turn up in cultures thousands of miles apart. Whose evil stepmother makes her do all the work and won't let her go to the big party? Who goes anyway and loses her slipper? In Europe the answer is Cinderella; in China it's Yeh-Shen. West Africans, Egyptians, Koreans, Americans from the Appalachian Mountains—all have their own versions of this folk tale.

Fiction: Stories Today

The word **fiction** usually refers to short stories and novels. Fiction can be an adventure, a mystery, or a romance. Fiction can be fantasy, science fiction, or historical fiction. "Formula fiction" satisfies us by following a formula—"boy meets girl" or "the good guy wins" or "crime doesn't pay." Today most writers of good fiction try to be original. They move beyond the old plot formulas to bring us new, surprising forms of stories (like a murder mystery written by forty-five people and published on the Internet). That's the magic of fiction: In stories as in life, you never know what will happen next.

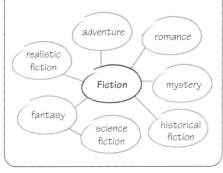

Copy this cluster diagram, showing types of fiction popular today. Then, think of an example of each type of fiction, and write the title in the bubble. Add a sentence or two defining that type of fiction. You might work with a group on this project and create a large display for the class bulletin board.

Forms of Fiction: It's All a Story **173**

Story titles for the cluster diagram will vary. The following sentences are some sample definitions of the different types of fiction:

Adventure—Adventure stories are always exciting. They usually contain a plot, setting, and conflict involving the outdoors.

Romance—Romance stories usually involve two main characters that meet and fall in love. The complications that ensue make up the plot.

Mystery—Mysteries revolve around a central crime. They usually contain at least two important characters: the person who commits the crime and the person who solves it.

Historical fiction—Historical fiction brings real people and events together with a made-up plot and characters.

Science fiction—Science fiction stories are imaginative stories based on scientific ideas.

Fantasy—Fantasy stories are imaginative stories that could not possibly happen in real life.

Realistic fiction—Realistic fiction tells about things that can and do happen in real life.

Apply

Ask students to peruse novels in the library, in the classroom, or at home, looking at the titles, the front-cover illustrations, and the back-cover blurbs. Have them use this information to try and identify what forms of fiction their novels are. Students should make a list of the novels they peruse and the forms they assign them.

HOMEWORK

"exciting and dangerous," while mysteries might be "suspenseful." Working in a group, students can use these adjectives to craft definitions for the cluster diagram.

Advanced Learners

Forms of fiction. Advanced learners can discuss and find examples of hybrid forms of fiction, such as historical romances or science fiction mysteries. Suggest that these students

each come up with one or two story titles that do not easily fit into one category. Have students figure out a way to modify the design of the cluster diagram so that they can include their titles.

▶ Resources Reminder

Differentiating Instruction

- *Lesson Plans for Language Development*

For additional instruction on forms of fiction for English-language learners and special education students, see *Lesson Plans for Language Development,* pp. 75–76.

The Gold Cadillac

STANDARDS FOCUS, pp. 174–188

(For grade-level and review standards taught in this selection, see citations on Pupil's Edition pages.)

Prerequisite Standard

■ Grade 5, Literary Response and Analysis 3.1 **Identify and analyze the characteristics of poetry, drama, fiction, and nonfiction, and explain the appropriateness of the literary forms chosen by an author for a specific purpose.**

Standard Coming Up in the Next Grade Level

■ Grade 7, Literary Response and Analysis 3.1 **Articulate the expressed purposes and characteristics of different forms of prose (e.g., short story, novel, novella, essay).**

Reading Skills

■ Make and adjust predictions.

Summary ⬌ *at grade level*

This story, set in 1950, is narrated by a young African American girl. 'Lois is baffled when her mother, Dee, refuses to ride in the new gold Cadillac bought by 'lois's father, Wilbert. The father announces his plan to drive the Cadillac from the family's Ohio home to his parents' Mississippi farm, and Dee insists that she and the children go along. In the South, 'lois is upset by signs reading "White Only." A white police officer assumes the car is stolen and jails Wilbert. The night of his release, the family must park on a rural road to rest. 'Lois is terrified. The next day the family turns back to borrow a cousin's Chevrolet. During their week in Mississippi, Wilbert talks with 'lois about racism and his hopes for change. At home, Dee urges him to keep the Cadillac, but he sells it. 'Lois never forgets the trip south.

Literary Focus

The Novella

A novel, a novella, and a short story are all members of the family of fiction. They resemble each other too. They have plot, characters, setting, and theme—all the elements you studied in Chapters 1–3. If they were lined up by size for a family photo, the novel would be the tall one at one end. The short story would, of course, be the short one at the other end, and the novella would be in the middle. In other words, a **novella** is a story that's shorter than a novel but longer than a short story.

A novella is small enough to be published with other stories yet long enough to be published by itself. *The Gold Cadillac* is a novella; it was first published as a short book.

Reading Skills 📖

Making and Adjusting Predictions

When we read, we make **predictions** by combining new information with our prior knowledge. When we get more information, we often **adjust** these predictions.

As you read this story, you'll notice little open-book signs. When you see a sign, make a prediction in response to the question next to it.

Reading Standard 3.1 Identify the forms of fiction, and describe the major characteristics of each form.

Make the Connection

Did you know that at one time there were

- separate drinking fountains and restrooms for whites and African Americans?
- restaurants in which African Americans were not allowed to eat?

These things used to be a reality, right here in the United States. The civil rights movement of the 1950s and 1960s ended most forms of segregation, but this story takes place earlier.

Quickwrite ✏️

Write down your thoughts on the conditions described above. What can people do to prevent this kind of injustice today?

Vocabulary Development

You'll learn these words as you read the story:

evident (ev'ə·dənt) *adj.*: obvious. *It's evident to everyone that Dee is angry.*

rural (roor'əl) *adj.*: having to do with country life. *The narrator's grandparents live in a rural area, on a big farm.*

heedful (hēd'fəl) *adj.*: attentive; keeping in mind. *Heedful of her parents' warnings, she watches carefully.*

ignorance (ig'nə·rəns) *n.*: lack of knowledge. *Her father says that people sometimes pass unfair laws out of ignorance.*

174 | Chapter 4 | Forms and Patterns: Stories and Explanations

---

RESOURCES

Planning

■ *One-Stop Planner* CD-ROM with Test Generator
■ *On Course: Mapping Instruction*

Media

■ *Audio CD Library*
  ■ disc 5

Reading

■ *Interactive Reading*
  ■ Strategy Launch: From Form to Prediction, p. 141
  ■ Practice Read: "The Cellar," p. 142
  ■ Graphic Organizer: Form-Analysis Map, p. 149

The Gold Cadillac

Mildred D. Taylor

Standards Starter

Motivate. Invite students to describe their favorite kinds of cars. Encourage them to speculate about what they might do if a parent or guardian came home tonight in the car students covet the most.

Preview Vocabulary

Discuss the Vocabulary words and their definitions. Then, use this activity to build students' familiarity with the words.

1. Identify one thing that is evident in the classroom.
2. What would you expect to see and hear in a rural setting?
3. Should cyclists be heedful of the traffic around them? Why or why not?
4. Would you give a ticket to a speeder who claimed ignorance of the speed limit? Why or why not?

Assign the Reading

Have students listen and follow along silently in their textbooks as you play the audio CD in class. Stop after the first seven paragraphs of the novella, and have students write their answers to the first prediction question. Then, continue playing the CD through the part where Dee walks the girls to church (p. 178), and ask students to make any necessary adjustments in their predictions. For students reading at or above grade level, assign the rest of the novella, the prediction questions, and the Reading Check questions (p. 187) as homework. Meanwhile, continue working with small groups of students who are having difficulty.

HOMEWORK

▶ Resources Reminder

Media
- *Audio CD Library*
  - disc 5

- *Interactive Reading,* Teacher's Edition
  - Transparency 4: From Form to Prediction

Differentiating Instruction

- *Lesson Plans for Language Development*
  - English-Language Learners, pp. 77–79, 98, 107
  - Special Education Students, pp. 80, 98, 107

Vocabulary and Spelling

- *Vocabulary Development*
  - Vocabulary Worksheet, p. 13
- *Spelling Lessons and Activities,* pp. 18–19

Assessment

- *Progress Assessment of Reading*
  - Selection Test, p. 64
- *One-Stop Planner* CD-ROM with Test Generator

Resources Reminder

Reading

- *Interactive Reading*
  - Strategy Launch: From Form to Prediction, p. 141
  - Practice Read: "The Cellar," p. 142
  - Graphic Organizer: Form-Analysis Map, p. 149

A Reading Skills

Making and adjusting predictions. Remind students to base their predictions on clues in the story plus their own knowledge of human feelings and behavior. Ask them to explain which details in the story helped them make their predictions.

[Possible responses to question 1: The girls' joy, the father's pleasure, and the neighbors' interest suggest that the mother will be delighted with the new car. The fact that the mother did not share in the decision to make this expensive purchase suggests that she will be upset.]

My sister and I were playing out on the front lawn when the gold Cadillac rolled up and my father stepped from behind the wheel. We ran to him, our eyes filled with wonder. "Daddy, whose Cadillac?" I asked.

And Wilma demanded, "Where's our Mercury?"

My father grinned. "Go get your mother and I'll tell you all about it."

"Is it ours?" I cried. "Daddy, is it ours?"

"Get your mother!" he laughed. "And tell her to hurry!"

Wilma and I ran off to obey, as Mr. Pondexter next door came from his house to see what this new Cadillac was all about. We threw open the front door, ran through the downstairs front parlor and straight through the house to the kitchen, where my mother was cooking and one of my aunts was helping her. "Come on, Mother-Dear!" we cried together. "Daddy say come on out and see this new car!"

A "What?" said my mother, her face showing her surprise. "What're you talking about?"

"A Cadillac!" I cried.

"He said hurry up!" relayed Wilma.

And then we took off again, up the back stairs to the second floor of the duplex. Running down the hall, we banged on all the apartment doors. My uncles and their wives stepped to the doors. It was good it was a Saturday morning. Everybody was home.

"We got us a Cadillac! We got us a Cadillac!" Wilma and I proclaimed in unison.[1]

 PREDICTING

1. How do you predict 'lois's mother will react to the new car?

---
1. **in unison:** in chorus; in the same words, spoken at the same time.

We had decided that the Cadillac had to be ours if our father was driving it and holding on to the keys. "Come on see!" Then we raced on, through the upstairs sunroom, down the front steps, through the downstairs sunroom, and out to the Cadillac. Mr. Pondexter was still there. Mr. LeRoy and Mr. Courtland from down the street were there too, and all were admiring the Cadillac as my father stood proudly by, pointing out the various features.

"Brand-new 1950 Coupe deVille!" I heard one of the men saying.

"Just off the showroom floor!" my father said. "I just couldn't resist it."

My sister and I eased up to the car and peeked in. It was all gold inside. Gold leather seats. Gold carpeting. Gold dashboard. It was like no car we had owned before. It looked like a car for rich folks.

"Daddy, are we rich?" I asked. My father laughed.

"Daddy, it's ours, isn't it?" asked Wilma, who was older and more practical than I. She didn't intend to give her heart too quickly to something that wasn't hers.

"You like it?"

"Oh, Daddy, yes!"

He looked at me. "What 'bout you, 'lois?"

"Yes, sir!"

My father laughed again. "Then I expect I can't much disappoint my girls, can I? It's ours, all right!"

Wilma and I hugged our father with our joy. My uncles came from the house, and my aunts, carrying their babies, came out too. Everybody surrounded the car and owwed and ahhed. Nobody could believe it.

Then my mother came out.

Everybody stood back grinning as she approached the car. There was no smile on

---

DIFFERENTIATING INSTRUCTION

Learners Having Difficulty
Modeling. Some students may need to read an easier selection before beginning *The Gold Cadillac.* Use the Practice Read in *Interactive Reading*, p. 142. You can then use the transparency to model the strategy called "From Form to Prediction." This strategy will help students to develop an awareness of the characteristics of the novella form with its plot and subplots.

Then, have students apply the strategy to help them read *The Gold Cadillac.* As they read, encourage students to ask themselves, "What might this conflict lead to?"

Resources Reminder

Reading

- *Interactive Reading,* Teacher's Edition, Transparency 4: From Form to Prediction

English-Language Learners
Be sure students are aware of the legalized discrimination that African Americans faced before the civil rights movement of the 1950s and 1960s. Explain that racial segregation was the law in many southern states. Also explain that in 1950, Cadillacs were the United States' premier luxury cars, symbols of wealth and status.

---

her face. We all waited for her to speak. She stared at the car, then looked at my father, standing there as proud as he could be. Finally she said, "You didn't buy this car, did you, Wilbert?"

"Gotta admit I did. Couldn't resist it."

"But . . . but what about our Mercury? It was perfectly good!"

"Don't you like the Cadillac, Dee?"

"That Mercury wasn't even a year old!"

My father nodded. "And I'm sure whoever buys it is going to get themselves a good car. But we've got ourselves a better one. Now stop frowning, honey, and let's take ourselves a ride in our brand-new Cadillac!"

My mother shook her head. "I've got food on the stove," she said and, turning away, walked back to the house.

There was an awkward silence, and then my father said, "You know Dee never did much like surprises. Guess this here Cadillac was a bit too much for her. I best go smooth things out with her."

Everybody watched as he went after my mother. But when he came back, he was alone.

"Well, what she say?" asked one of my uncles.

My father shrugged and smiled. "Told me I bought this Cadillac alone, I could just ride in it alone."

Another uncle laughed. "Uh-oh! Guess she told you!"

"Oh, she'll come around," said one of my aunts. "Any woman would be proud to ride in this car."

"That's what I'm banking on," said my father as he went around to the street side of the car and opened the door. "All right! Who's for a ride?"

"We are!" Wilma and I cried.

All three of my uncles and one of my aunts, still holding her baby, and Mr. Pondexter climbed in with us, and we took off for the first ride in the gold Cadillac. It was a glorious ride, and we drove all through the city of Toledo. We rode past the church and past the school. We rode through Ottawa Hills,

> **My father told our Detroit relatives that he was in the doghouse with my mother about buying the Cadillac.**

where the rich folks lived, and on into Walbridge Park and past the zoo, then along the Maumee River. But none of us had had enough of the car, so my father put the car on the road and we drove all the way to Detroit. We had plenty of family there, and everybody was just as pleased as could be about the Cadillac. My father told our Detroit relatives that he was in the doghouse with my mother about buying the Cadillac. My uncles told them she wouldn't ride in the car. All the Detroit family thought that was funny, and everybody, including my father, laughed about it and said my mother would come around.

It was early evening by the time we got back home, and I could see from my mother's face she had not come around.

The Gold Cadillac   **177**

B **Literary Focus**
GRADE-LEVEL STANDARD
? **Forms of fiction: Novella.** Explain to students that the conflict that is developing here introduces a subplot of the novella. What is the conflict? ['Lois's father is proud of the car, but her mother is displeased.] Tell students to be aware of this subplot as they continue to read. Explain that the subplot will ultimately flow into the novella's main plot and deepen it.

C **Literary Focus**
GRADE-LEVEL STANDARD
? **Forms of fiction: Novella.** In the subplot, how is the conflict between Dee and Wilbert becoming more intense? [Despite Wilbert's attempt to "smooth things out," Dee now refuses to ride in the Cadillac.]

D **English-Language Learners**
Interpreting idioms. Call attention to the idiom *in the doghouse,* and explain that it means "in trouble." Ask students to speculate on the origin of the idiom. [Possible response: A dog might be confined to a doghouse as punishment.]

E **Vocabulary Development**
GRADE-LEVEL STANDARD
Multiple meanings. Remind students that the adjective *funny* can mean either "humorous" or "strange." Ask students which meaning the context of this sentence suggests. [The words *laughed about it* suggest that *funny* means "humorous."]

▶ Resources Reminder
For lessons designed for both intermediate and advanced English-language learners, see *Lesson Plans for Language Development,* pp. 77–79, 98, 107.

Special Education Students
For lessons designed for special education students, see *Lesson Plans for Language Development,* pp. 80, 98, 107.

Advanced Learners
Acceleration. Use this activity to move advanced learners toward seventh-grade Standard 3.1, which requires that they articulate the purposes and characteristics of different forms of prose. First, explain to students that authors choose different forms for different purposes. An essay states the author's ideas directly and clearly. A novel reveals complex ideas gradually and indirectly

through characters' experiences. A short story is brief and may focus on only one idea or character, but it can be intense and extremely memorable. A novella combines a short story's intensity with some of a novel's complexity.

After students' first reading of *The Gold Cadillac,* encourage them to speculate about what might have been omitted if it were cast as a short story and what might have been added if it were cast as a novel.

The Gold Cadillac   **177**

A Literary Focus
GRADE-LEVEL STANDARD
? Forms of fiction: Novella.
In this subplot, how does 'lois respond to her mother's attitude toward the car? [Possible responses: She is confused by it; she disapproves of it.]

B Literary Focus
GRADE-LEVEL STANDARD
Forms of fiction: Novella. Tell students that a novella may present in-depth portraits of several characters. Ask students what insight this exchange provides about Dee and the reasons for her anger. [She and Wilbert had agreed to save money for a house in a better area, and now she feels betrayed.]

C Reading Skills
? Drawing conclusions. How would you describe 'lois's life, based on the details in this paragraph? [Possible responses: happy, interesting, fun, prosperous, secure, contented, full of togetherness.]

A She was angry now not only about the car, but that we had been gone so long. I didn't understand that, since my father had called her as soon as we reached Detroit to let her know where we were. I had heard him myself. I didn't understand either why she did not like that fine Cadillac and thought she was being terribly disagreeable with my father. That night, as she tucked Wilma and me in bed, I told her that too.

"Is this your business?" she asked.

"Well, I just think you ought to be nice to Daddy. I think you ought to ride in that car with him! It'd sure make him happy."

"I think you ought to go to sleep," she said and turned out the light.

B Later I heard her arguing with my father. "We're supposed to be saving for a house!" she said.

"We've already got a house!" said my father.

"But you said you wanted a house in a better neighborhood. I thought that's what we both said!"

"I haven't changed my mind."

"Well, you have a mighty funny way of saving for it, then. Your brothers are saving for houses of their own, and you don't see them out buying new cars every year!"

"We'll still get the house, Dee. That's a promise!"

"Not with new Cadillacs we won't!" said my mother, and then she said a very loud good night, and all was quiet.

The next day was Sunday, and everybody figured that my mother would be sure to give in and ride in the Cadillac. After all, the family always went to church together on Sunday. But she didn't give in. What was worse, she wouldn't let Wilma and me ride in the Cadillac either. She took us each by

the hand, walked past the Cadillac where my father stood waiting, and headed on toward the church three blocks away. I was really mad at her now. I had been looking forward to driving up to the church in that gold Cadillac and having everybody see.

C On most Sunday afternoons during the summertime, my mother, my father, Wilma, and I would go for a ride. Sometimes we just rode around the city and visited friends and family. Sometimes we made short trips over to Chicago or Peoria or Detroit to see relatives there or to Cleveland, where we had relatives too, but we could also see the Cleveland Indians play. Sometimes we joined our aunts and uncles and drove in a caravan[2] out to the park or to the beach. At the park or the beach, Wilma and I would run and play. My mother and my aunts would spread a picnic, and my father and my uncles would shine their cars.

But on this Sunday afternoon, my mother refused to ride anywhere. She told Wilma and me that we could go. So we left her alone in the big, empty house, and the family cars, led by the gold Cadillac, headed for the park. For a while I played and had a good time, but then I stopped playing and went to sit with my father. Despite his laughter he seemed sad to me. I think he was missing my mother as much as I was.

That evening, my father took my mother to dinner down at the corner cafe. They walked. Wilma and I stayed at the house, chasing fireflies in the backyard. My aunts and uncles sat in the yard and on the porch, talking and laughing about the day and watching us. It was a soft summer's evening, the kind that came every day and was expected. The smell of charcoal and of

---

2. **caravan** *n.:* group of cars traveling together.

Developing Word-Attack Skills
Write the selection word *unison* on the chalkboard. Discuss its meaning, and identify the two root words that make up the word: *uni,* "one," and *son,* "sound." Compare the pronunciation of the letters *uni* in *unison* with the pronunciation of the same letters in the word *unimpressed.* The initial *u* in *unison* has a long sound, whereas the initial *u* in *unimpressed* has a short

sound. Discuss how the letters *uni* in *unison* form a prefix that means "one," but in *unimpressed,* they are a combination of the prefix *un–* with the first letter of the base word *impressed.*
Activity. Display these sentences. Have volunteers read the sentences and tell if the initial *u* in the underlined word has a long or short sound.

1. The girls answered in <u>unison</u>. [long]
2. The uncles were <u>united</u> in their opinion. [long]
3. The girls' mother was <u>unimpressed</u>. [short]
4. Wilbert had made a <u>unilateral</u> decision. [long]
5. It broke the family <u>unity</u>. [long]

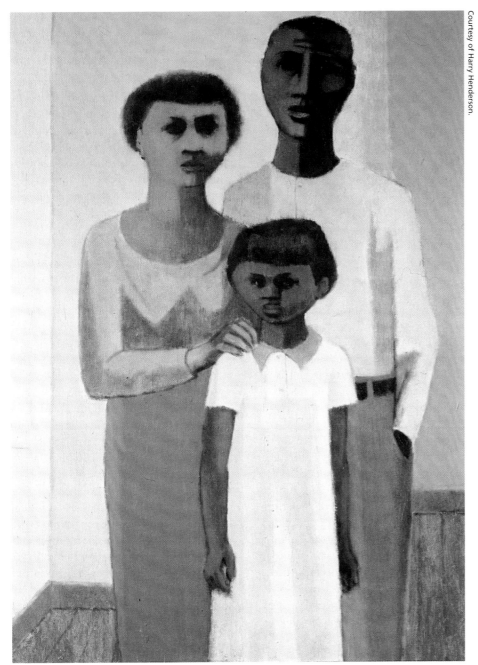

Courtesy of Harry Henderson.

Family No. 9 (1968) by Charles Alston.

VIEWING THE ART

Charles Alston (1907–1977) was an accomplished painter, sculptor, graphic artist, illustrator, and educator. During the Depression, Alston became a muralist for the Federal Arts program of the WPA (Works Progress Administration) and lobbied for the inclusion of other African American artists. His murals appear in New York City's Metropolitan Museum of Art, Harlem Hospital, and New York City's Abraham Lincoln High School and Harriet Tubman High School. In an interview, Alston once said he believed that the black experience was also an American experience and that he did not believe there was such a thing as "black art."

Activity. Have students speculate what families 1 through 8 in Alston's series might look like. Have students describe exactly what they see in this painting, including colors and shapes (note the triangles formed by the girl's collar and the mother's blouse). Be sure they compare their descriptions in class.

CONTENT-AREA CONNECTIONS

Culture and Math
Prices in the '50s. In 1950, the median annual family income was $3,319. In 2000, by contrast, it had soared to more than fifty thousand dollars. Of course, prices in 1950 were also much lower than they are today. A gallon of gas, for example, sold for around twenty-seven cents, and the median price of a new house was eleven thousand dollars. Cadillacs were the undisputed U.S. luxury cars. A new Cadillac Coupe de Ville, like the one 'lois's father bought, cost $3,995. This was a staggering sum at the time, more than a year's income for many families.

Activity. Have students calculate the cost of the 1950 Coupe de Ville and the cost of a new house as a percentage or fraction of the 1950 median annual income. You might ask students to show the results in bar graph format. Encourage them to discuss what their figures suggest about the relative prosperity of 'lois's family.

WHOLE-CLASS

A **Vocabulary Development**
GRADE-LEVEL STANDARD

❓ **Multiple meanings.** The word *still* can be used as an adjective that means "quiet" or "motionless" (e.g., the air is still) or as an adverb that means "yet" or "without having stopped" (e.g., the dance is still going on). How can the context of this sentence help you decide the meaning of *still*? [Possible response: Since the girls are chasing something, *still* can't mean "motionless," but it can mean "yet" or "without having stopped."]

B **Literary Focus**
GRADE-LEVEL STANDARD

❓ **Forms of fiction: Novella.** Another subplot is introduced as Wilbert enters a new conflict. With whom is he in conflict here? [He is in conflict with his relatives and neighbors.] What are the two sides of the conflict? [Wilbert believes he has a right to drive his car anywhere he wishes, but his relatives and neighbors worry about the danger he may face from racists in the rural South if they see him driving a luxury car.]

barbecue drifting from up the block, the sound of laughter and music and talk drifting from yard to yard were all a part of it. Soon one of my uncles joined Wilma and **A** me in our chase of fireflies, and when my mother and father came home, we were at it still. My mother and father watched us for a while, while everybody else watched them to see if my father would take out the Cadillac and if my mother would slide in beside him to take a ride. But it soon became evident that the dinner had not changed my mother's mind. She still refused to ride in the Cadillac. I just couldn't understand her objection to it.

Though my mother didn't like the Cadillac, everybody else in the neighborhood certainly did. That meant quite a few folks too, since we lived on a very busy block. On one corner was a grocery store, a cleaner's, and a gas station. Across the street was a beauty shop and a fish market, and down the street was a bar, another grocery store, the Dixie Theater, the cafe, and a drugstore. There were always people strolling to or from one of these places, and because our house was right in the middle of the block, just about everybody had to pass our house and the gold Cadillac. Sometimes people took in the Cadillac as they walked, their heads turning for a longer look as they passed. Then there were people who just outright stopped and took a good look before continuing on their way. I was proud to say that car belonged to my family. I felt mighty important as people called to me as I ran down the street. "'Ey, 'lois! How's that Cadillac, girl? Riding fine?" I told my mother how much everybody liked that car. She was not impressed and made no comment.

Since just about everybody on the block

knew everybody else, most folks knew that my mother wouldn't ride in the Cadillac. Because of that, my father took a lot of good-natured kidding from the men. My mother got kidded too, as the women said if she didn't ride in that car, maybe some other woman would. And everybody laughed about it and began to bet on who would give in first, my mother or my father. But then my father said he was going to drive the car south into Mississippi to visit my grandparents, and everybody stopped laughing.

My uncles stopped.

So did my aunts.

Everybody.

"Look here, Wilbert," said one of my uncles, "it's too dangerous. It's like putting a loaded gun to your head."

"I paid good money for that car," said my father. "That gives me a right to drive it where I please. Even down to Mississippi."

My uncles argued with him and tried to talk him out of driving the car south. So did **B** my aunts, and so did the neighbors, Mr. LeRoy, Mr. Courtland, and Mr. Pondexter. They said it was a dangerous thing, a mighty dangerous thing, for a black man to drive an expensive car into the rural South.

"Not much those folks hate more'n to see a northern Negro coming down there in a fine car," said Mr. Pondexter. "They see those Ohio license plates, they'll figure you coming down uppity, trying to lord your fine car over them!"

I listened, but I didn't understand. I didn't understand why they didn't want my father to drive that car south. It was his.

Vocabulary
evident (ev′ə·dənt) *adj.:* easily seen or understood; obvious.
rural (rōōr′əl) *adj.:* having to do with the country or country life.

CONTENT-AREA CONNECTIONS

History
Racism in the United States. After the Civil War, the Thirteenth, Fourteenth, and Fifteenth Amendments to the U.S. Constitution abolished slavery and made the recently freed slaves full citizens. However, after 1877, the states of the old Confederacy passed laws to deny African Americans their freedom. These came to be known as Jim Crow laws, from the name of an act in min-

strel shows that was derogatory to African Americans. Jim Crow laws enforced racial segregation in public places, including schools, restaurants, movie theaters, parks, and public transportation. In the South, "separate but equal" facilities for African Americans and whites became the norm. Of course, these facilities were rarely equal.

In the North and West, many African American students also attended segregated

schools. The 1954 U.S. Supreme Court ruling in *Brown* v. *Board of Education of Topeka* (which overturned the doctrine of school segregation) dealt a blow to legalized racism. Most other Jim Crow laws were abolished in 1964 with the passage of the Civil Rights Act. Some schools in the South and the North were not integrated until the late 1970s.

"Listen to Pondexter, Wilbert!" cried another uncle. "We might've fought a war to free people overseas, but we're not free here! Man, those white folks down south'll lynch[3] you soon's look at you. You know that!"

PREDICTING

2. From Mr. Pondexter and the uncles' warnings, what do you predict will happen on the trip?

Wilma and I looked at each other. Neither one of us knew what *lynch*[3] meant, but the word sent a shiver through us. We held each other's hand.

My father was silent, then he said: "All my life I've had to be <u>heedful</u> of what white folks thought. Well, I'm tired of that. I worked hard for everything I got. Got it honest, too. Now I got that Cadillac because I liked it and because it meant something to me that somebody like me from Mississippi

"It's my car, I paid for it, and I'm driving it south."

could go and buy it. It's my car, I paid for it, and I'm driving it south."

My mother, who had said nothing through all this, now stood. "Then the girls and I'll be going too," she said.

"No!" said my father.

My mother only looked at him and went off to the kitchen.

My father shook his head. It seemed he didn't want us to go. My uncles looked at

each other, then at my father. "You set on doing this, we'll all go," they said. "That way we can watch out for each other." My father took a moment and nodded. Then my aunts got up and went off to their kitchens too.

All the next day, my aunts and my mother cooked and the house was filled with delicious smells. They fried chicken and baked hams and cakes and sweet potato pies and mixed potato salad. They filled jugs with water and punch and coffee. Then they packed everything in huge picnic baskets, along with bread and boiled eggs, oranges and apples, plates and napkins, spoons and forks and cups. They placed all that food on the back seats of the cars. It was like a grand, grand picnic we were going on, and Wilma and I were mighty excited. We could hardly wait to start.

My father, my mother, Wilma, and I got into the Cadillac. My uncles, my aunts, my cousins got into the Ford, the Buick, and the Chevrolet, and we rolled off in our caravan headed south. Though my mother was finally riding in the Cadillac, she had no praise for it. In fact, she said nothing about it at all. She still seemed upset, and since she still seemed to feel the same about the car, I wondered why she had insisted upon making this trip with my father.

We left the city of Toledo behind, drove through Bowling Green and down through the Ohio countryside of farms and small towns, through Dayton and Cincinnati, and across the Ohio River into Kentucky. On the other side of the river, my father stopped the car and looked back at Wilma and me and said, "Now from here on, whenever we stop

---

3. **lynch** *v.*: kill a person without legal authority, usually by hanging. Lynchings are committed by violent mobs that have taken the law into their own hands.

Vocabulary
heedful (hēd′fəl) *adj.*: attentive; keeping in mind.

The Gold Cadillac **181**

C Reading Skills

Making and adjusting predictions. You may want to have students write and save their predictions, adjusting them as they read more of the story.

[Possible responses to question 2: Feeling that the dire warnings of neighbors and relatives foreshadow trouble or that current incidents involving race indicate the pervasiveness of racism in the United States, some students may predict that Wilbert will be attacked. Other students may predict that the trip will be uneventful, since dire warnings don't always mean trouble.]

D Literary Focus
GRADE-LEVEL STANDARD

❷ **Forms of fiction: Novella.** Wilbert is an important character in the novella. What insights into his character do his words provide? Why are the Cadillac and the trip south so important to him? [They are assertions of his freedom, his sense of accomplishment, his rights as an American; they are a protest against racism.]

E Literary Focus
REVIEW STANDARD

❷ **Character.** What character traits does Dee possess based on this paragraph? [Possible responses: She is independent, stubborn, and highly principled. She is quietly courageous. She is loving and protective of her husband and family.]

DEVELOPING FLUENCY

Activity. After your students have finished a first reading of the novella, invite eleventh-grade U.S. history students to visit your classroom as guests. Place the older students in small groups with your students. In each group, have your students orally summarize the novella for their guests. Next, have each group of students and guests read a given section of the novella aloud in a round robin. Explain that group members may read as much or as little as is comfortable for them, but they must continue taking turns until they have finished their assigned section. Then, bring everyone together to discuss the novella. Encourage the guests to tell which parts of the reading they found surprising or memorable and to share what they know about the 1950s.

SMALL-GROUP

A Literary Focus
ADVANCED STANDARD

? Acceleration. Halfway through the novella, the theme of racism begins to emerge through dialogue. How does this contrast with the way the main point of an essay about racism would be presented? [An essay's main point would be clearly and directly stated near the beginning.]

B Content-Area Connections
HISTORY

Signs of segregation. Some students may wonder if the description of the signs is exaggerated. Explain that at this time racial segregation was common in the United States. Throughout the South, signs like these were posted and enforced everywhere, from laundromats to lunch counters.

C Literary Focus
REVIEW STANDARD

? Conflict. What has 'lois understood about the picnic basket? [Her mother packed the picnic basket not for a pleasant family outing, but because the family will not be allowed in "white only" restaurants in the South.] What is 'lois experiencing for the first time in her life? [racism]

D Reading Skills

Making and adjusting predictions. [Possible responses to question 3: The police will be angry that he is driving a fine car; they will falsely accuse him of a violation; they will threaten or hurt him.]

E English-Language Learners

Understanding connotations. Make sure students understand that it is an insult for a white police officer to call an African American man "boy."

A and there're white people around, I don't want either one of you to say a word. *Not one word!* Your mother and I'll do the talking. That understood?"

"Yes, sir," Wilma and I both said, though we didn't truly understand why.

My father nodded, looked at my mother, and started the car again. We rolled on, down Highway 25 and through the blue-**B** grass hills of Kentucky. Soon we began to see signs. Signs that read: "White Only, Colored Not Allowed." Hours later, we left the Bluegrass State and crossed into Tennessee. Now we saw even more of the signs saying: "White Only, Colored Not Allowed." We saw the signs above water fountains and in restaurant windows. We saw them in ice cream parlors and at hamburger stands. We saw them in front of hotels and motels, and on the restroom doors of filling stations. I didn't like the signs. I felt as if I were in a foreign land.

I couldn't understand why the signs were there, and I asked my father what the signs meant. He said they meant we couldn't drink from the water fountains. He said they meant we couldn't stop to sleep in the motels. He said they meant we couldn't stop to eat in the **C** restaurants. I looked at the grand picnic basket I had been enjoying so much. Now I understood why my mother had packed it. Suddenly the picnic did not seem so grand.

Finally we reached Memphis. We got there at a bad time. Traffic was heavy and we got separated from the rest of the family. We tried to find them but it was no use. We had to go on alone. We reached the Mississippi state line, and soon after, we heard a police siren. A police car came up behind us. My father slowed the Cadillac, then stopped. Two white policemen got out of their car.

They eyeballed the Cadillac and told my **D** father to get out.

E "Whose car is this, boy?" they asked.

I saw anger in my father's eyes. "It's mine," he said.

"You're a liar," said one of the policemen. "You stole this car."

"Turn around, put your hands on top of that car, and spread-eagle," said the other policeman.

My father did as he was told. They searched him and I didn't understand why. I didn't understand either why they had called my father a liar and didn't believe that the Cadillac was his. I wanted to ask, but I remembered my father's warning not to say a word, and I obeyed that warning.

The policemen told my father to get in the back of the police car. My father did. One policeman got back into the police car. The other policeman slid behind the wheel of our Cadillac. The police car started off. The Cadillac followed. Wilma and I looked at each other and at our mother. We didn't know what to think. We were scared.

The Cadillac followed the police car into a small town and stopped in front of the police station. The policeman stepped out of our Cadillac and took the keys. The other policeman took my father into the police station.

"Mother-Dear!" Wilma and I cried. "What're they going to do to our daddy? They going to hurt him?"

"He'll be all right," said my mother. "He'll be all right." But she didn't sound so sure of that. She seemed worried.

We waited. More than three hours we waited. Finally my father came out of the police station. We had lots of questions to

> **📖 PREDICTING**
> **3.** What do you think the police will do to 'lois's father?

CONTENT-AREA CONNECTIONS

History

Southern roots. In 1910, only one in ten African Americans lived outside the South. During and after World War I and World War II, however, tens of thousands of African Americans left the South for other regions, finding work in rapidly expanding factories and mills. For example, in just ten years, from 1940 to 1950, the number of African Americans in the western states more than tripled. By 2000, more than half of all African Americans lived outside the South. However, many African Americans living in other regions maintain strong ties with the South through relatives who still live there. This was true of Mildred D. Taylor's family; she remembers, "There were two sides of the South I saw. The one of racism, of oppression and segregation, filled me with fear and anger. But the other

Open Road, from the series *Landscape of the Apocalypse* (1972) by Martin Hoffman.
Acrylic on canvas (60" × 80").

ask him. He said the police had given him a ticket for speeding and locked him up. But then the judge had come. My father had paid the ticket and they had let him go.

He started the Cadillac and drove slowly out of the town, below the speed limit. The police car followed us. People standing on steps and sitting on porches and in front of stores stared at us as we passed. Finally we were out of the town. The police car still followed. Dusk was falling. The night grew black, and finally the police car turned around and left us.

We drove and drove. But my father was tired now and my grandparents' farm was still far away. My father said he had to get some sleep, and since my mother didn't

drive, he pulled into a grove of trees at the side of the road and stopped.

"I'll keep watch," said my mother.

"Wake me if you see anybody," said my father.

"Just rest," said my mother.

So my father slept. But that bothered me. I needed him awake. I was afraid of the dark and of the woods and of whatever lurked there. My father was the one who kept us safe, he and my uncles. But already the police had taken my father away from us once today, and my uncles were lost.

"Go to sleep, baby," said my mother. "Go to sleep."

But I was afraid to sleep until my father

The Gold Cadillac **183**

VIEWING THE ART

Martin Hoffman (1935–), a Florida-born artist, creates paintings that appear simple but have complex implications. Also an accomplished drummer, Hoffman went on musical tours to Cuba, the Dominican Republic, and cities in the United States in the early 1950s.

Activity. Have students read the title. *Open Road* is part of the series *Landscape of the Apocalypse*. *Apocalypse* often refers to a prophecy revealing the end of the world. Ask students if *Open Road* suggests to them the end of something or the start of something. How does an open road connect with the story?

F English-Language Learners
Building background knowledge. If necessary, explain to students that the word *ticket* can mean "a piece of paper specifying a sum of money to be paid as punishment for a driving infraction."

G Reading Skills
❷ Drawing conclusions. Why does the police car follow the family's car for so long? [Possible responses: The police want to intimidate the family; they want to be sure the family really leaves the region.]

H Literary Focus
REVIEW STANDARD
❷ Conflict. 'Lois's first responses to racism are confusion and distaste. What is she feeling now? [She is afraid.] What causes her to feel this way? [Possible responses: the darkness, the lonely woods and "whatever lurked there," the way the police have treated her father, the fact that her uncles have disappeared, and the "White Only" signs she has been seeing all day—the racism that she now sees lurking everywhere.]

South, a South of family and of community, filled with warmth and love, opened to me a sense of history and filled me with pride."
Activity. Place students of differing abilities in groups of three or four, and ask each group to research a southern state that 'lois's family drives through. Have each group create a poster in the shape of its state. Posters should have words and images

to show key facts about the states and events in the states' histories.

MIXED-ABILITY

A Literary Focus
GRADE-LEVEL STANDARD

Forms of fiction: Novella. This night of terror, when 'lois's fear peaks and the family is in danger, marks the climax of the plot. As students finish the novella, tell them to pay attention to how the conflicts in the plot and subplots are resolved.

B Reading Skills

Making and adjusting predictions. [Possible responses to question 4: Wilbert's determination and his reassurances to 'lois suggest that the family will continue south. His recognition of 'lois's terror suggests that he will turn back.]

C Literary Focus
REVIEW STANDARD

❓ Theme. When Wilbert turns back to switch cars, he has made a decision about priorities. How would you describe his priorities? [Possible responses: He still opposes racism, but he is placing his family and their safety first. His love for his family is more important to him than his pride in driving a beautiful car.]

D Learners Having Difficulty

Paraphrasing. Explain that the phrase *golden splendor* refers to the gold Cadillac. It suggests a golden carriage or the chariot of the sun. Then, have students paraphrase the sentence. [Possible paraphrase: Instead of driving through Mississippi in our impressive-looking car, we drove through it in our cousin's average-looking car.]

E Literary Focus
REVIEW STANDARD

❓ Theme. How does 'lois try to overcome her fears about racism? [She learns about her father's outlook on racism and his hopes for change in the future.]

---

woke. I had to help my mother keep watch. I figured I had to help protect us too, in case the police came back and tried to take my father away again. There was a long, sharp knife in the picnic basket, and I took hold of it, clutching it tightly in my hand. Ready to strike, I sat there in the back of the car, eyes wide, searching the blackness outside the Cadillac. Wilma, for a while, searched the night too, then she fell asleep. I didn't want to sleep, but soon I found I couldn't help myself as an unwelcome drowsiness came over me. I had an uneasy sleep, and when I woke, it was dawn and my father was gently shaking me. I woke with a start and my hand went up, but the knife wasn't there. My mother had it.

My father took my hand. "Why were you holding the knife, 'lois?" he asked.

I looked at him and at my mother. "I—I was scared," I said.

My father was thoughtful. "No need to be scared now, sugar," he said. "Daddy's here and so is Mother-Dear." 📖

> 📖 **PREDICTING**
> 4. Will the family keep going south, or will they turn back?

Then after a glance at my mother, he got out of the car, walked to the road, looked down it one way, then the other. When he came back and started the motor, he turned the Cadillac north, not south.

"What're you doing?" asked my mother.

"Heading back to Memphis," said my father. "Cousin Halton's there. We'll leave the Cadillac and get his car. Driving this car any farther south with you and the girls in the car, it's just not worth the risk."

And so that's what we did. Instead of driving through Mississippi in golden splendor, we traveled its streets and roads and highways in Cousin Halton's solid, yet not so splendid, four-year-old Chevy. When we reached my grandparents' farm, my uncles and aunts were already there. Everybody was glad to see us. They had been worried. They asked about the Cadillac. My father told them what had happened, and they nodded and said he had done the best thing.

We stayed one week in Mississippi. During that week I often saw my father, looking deep in thought, walk off alone across the family land. I saw my mother watching him. One day I ran after my father, took his hand, and walked the land with him. I asked him all the questions that were on my mind. I asked him why the policemen had treated him the way they had and why people didn't want us to eat in the restaurants or drink from the water fountains or sleep in the hotels. I told him I just didn't understand all that.

My father looked at me and said that it all was a difficult thing to understand and he didn't really understand it himself. He said it all had to do with the fact that black people had once been forced to be slaves. He said it had to do with our skins being colored. He said it had to do with stupidity and ignorance. He said it had to do with the law, the law that said we could be treated like this here in the South. And for that matter, he added, any other place in these United States where folks thought the same as so many folks did here in the South. But he also said, "I'm hoping one day though we can drive that long road down here and there won't be any signs. I'm hoping one day the police won't stop us just because of the color of our skins

---

Vocabulary
ignorance (ig′nə·rəns) *n.*: lack of knowledge.

---

and we're riding in a gold Cadillac with northern plates."

When the week ended, we said a sad good-bye to my grandparents and all the Mississippi family and headed in a caravan back toward Memphis. In Memphis, we returned Cousin Halton's car and got our Cadillac. Once we were home, my father put the Cadillac in the garage and didn't drive it. I didn't hear my mother say any more about the Cadillac. I didn't hear my father speak of it either.

📖 **PREDICTING**

5. What do you predict the family will do with the Cadillac?

F

Some days passed, and then on a bright Saturday afternoon while Wilma and I were playing in the backyard, I saw my father go into the garage. He opened the garage doors wide so the sunshine streamed in and began to shine the Cadillac. I saw my mother at the kitchen window staring out across the yard at my father. For a long time, she stood there watching my father shine his car. Then she came out and crossed the yard to the garage, and I heard her say, "Wilbert, you keep the car."

G

He looked at her as if he had not heard.

"You keep it," she repeated and turned and walked back to the house.

My father watched her until the back door had shut behind her. Then he went on shining the car and soon began to sing. About an hour later he got into the car and drove away. That evening when he came back, he was walking. The Cadillac was nowhere in sight.

"Daddy, where's our new Cadillac?" I demanded to know. So did Wilma.

He smiled and put his hand on my head. "Sold it," he said as my mother came into the room.

"But how come?" I asked. "We poor now?"

"No, sugar. We've got more money towards our new house now, and we're all together. I figure that makes us about the richest folks in the world." He smiled at my mother, and she smiled too and came into his arms.

I heard her say, "Wilbert, you keep the car."

After that, we drove around in an old 1930s Model A Ford my father had. He said he'd factory-ordered us another Mercury, this time with my mother's approval. Despite that, most folks on the block figured we had fallen on hard times after such a splashy showing of good times, and some folks even laughed at us as the Ford rattled around the city. I must admit that at first I was pretty much embarrassed to be riding around in that old Ford after the splendor of the Cadillac. But my father said to hold my head high. We and the family knew the truth. As fine as the Cadillac had been, he said, it had pulled us apart for a while. Now, as ragged and noisy as that old Ford was, we all rode in it together, and we were a family again. So I held my head high.

Still, though, I thought often of that Cadillac. We had had the Cadillac only a little more than a month, but I wouldn't soon forget its splendor or how I'd felt riding around inside it. I wouldn't soon forget either the ride we had taken south in it. I wouldn't soon forget the signs, the policemen, or my fear. I would remember that ride and the gold Cadillac all my life.

H

The Gold Cadillac **185**

DIRECT TEACHING

F **Reading Skills**

Making and adjusting predictions. [Possible responses to question 5: The family will keep the car because it symbolizes Wilbert's pride; they will sell it because it has caused trouble, because they can use the money, or because Wilbert's priorities have changed.]

G **Literary Focus**
GRADE-LEVEL STANDARD
❓ **Forms of fiction: Novella.** Why do you think Dee changes her mind about the Cadillac? [Possible responses: She understands what the car means to her husband; she doesn't want to give in to racists.]

H **Literary Focus**
REVIEW STANDARD
❓ **Theme.** What does 'lois learn from her experiences with the gold Cadillac? [Possible responses: She learns that family unity is more important than the judgment of outsiders, that racism can threaten her and her family, that the world can be unfair, that it is possible to stand up to injustice, and that the goal is to oppose injustice without compromising important values.]

GUIDED PRACTICE

Monitoring students' progress. Guide students in responding to these comprehension questions.

Short Answer

1. Who disapproves of the new gold Cadillac? ['lois's mother]
2. When does Dee first ride in the Cadillac? [on the trip south]
3. Why does Wilbert trade the Cadillac for a cousin's Chevrolet? [to protect his family]
4. Why is Wilbert proud of the Model A Ford? [It unites the family.]

FAMILY/COMMUNITY ACTIVITY

Invite a local historical society member, a history teacher, or another community expert to speak to students about segregation in the United States before the Civil Rights Act of 1964. Prior to the speaker's visit, have students prepare questions for him or her, based on what they have read in *The Gold Cadillac*. Direct students to take notes during the speaker's presentation and to ask their questions at the appropriate time.

Afterward, have students create "news reports" about the presentation, using their notes and interviewing each other for commentary. Students might then collaborate on creating one composite article to submit to the school newspaper, to send to the speaker, or both.

Meet the Writer

Background. Mildred D. Taylor comes from a long line of story-tellers, and her work is influenced by their oral tradition. "I wanted to include the teachings of my own childhood," she says of her work, "the values and principles upon which I and so many other black children were reared. I wanted to show a family united by love and self-respect, as parents strong and sensitive attempted to guide their children successfully, without harming their spirits, through the hazardous maze of living in a dis-criminatory society. I wanted to show happy, loved children, about whom other children of all colors, or of all cultures, could say, 'I really like them. I feel what they feel.'"

Tell students that besides working as an author, Mildred D. Taylor taught for many years and served in the Peace Corps in Ethiopia. She has won many honors, including a New York Times Notable Book citation and a Christopher Award for *The Gold Cadillac*.

For Independent Reading

■ Let students know that *Roll of Thunder, Hear My Cry* and *Let the Circle Be Unbroken* are his-torical fiction set in Mississippi during the 1930s.

■ For the tale of a boy's quiet tri-umph over racism and despair, introduce students to William H. Armstrong's *Sounder.*

■ Fans of fantasy and science fic-tion may enjoy Belinda Hurmence's *A Girl Called Boy.* In this novel, a modern African American girl time-travels into her family's past in the U.S. South of the 1850s.

Mildred D. Taylor

Weaving Memories into Fiction

Mildred D. Taylor (1943–   ) tells about the memories behind *The Gold Cadillac:*

"For a few years when I was a child, I lived in a big house on a busy street with my mother, my father, my sister, and many aunts and uncles and cousins. We were originally a Mississippi family who had migrated to the industrial North during and after World War II. My father was the first of the family to go to the North and that was when I was only three weeks old. When I was three months old, my mother, my older sister, and I followed. A year after our arrival, my parents bought the big house on the busy street. During the next nine years, aunts and uncles and cousins from both sides of the family arrived yearly from Mississippi and stayed in that big house with us until they had earned enough to rent another place or buy houses of their own.

I loved those years. There were always cousins to play with. There was always an aunt or uncle to talk to when my parents were busy, and there seemed always to be fun things to do and plenty of people to do them with. On the weekends the whole houseful of family often did things together. Because my father, my uncles, and my older male cousins all loved cars, we often rode in caravan out to the park, where the men would park their cars in a long, impressive row and shine them in the shade of the trees while the women spread a picnic and chatted, and my sister, younger cousins, and I ran and played. Sometimes we traveled to nearby cities to watch a baseball game. And sometimes we took even longer trips, down country highways into the land called the South.

I have many good memories of those years, including the year my father brought home a brand-new Cadillac. I also have memories of those years that long troubled me. I have woven some of those memories into this story of fiction called *The Gold Cadillac.*"

For Independent Reading

If you'd like to read more fiction woven from Taylor's memories, check out *Song of the Trees* and *Roll of Thunder, Hear My Cry,* winner of the Newbery Medal for distinguished American literature for children. *Let the Circle Be Unbroken* is the sequel to *Roll of Thunder, Hear My Cry.*

DIFFERENTIATING INSTRUCTION

Learners Having Difficulty
Pair students to complete the Interpre-tations questions on p. 187. *Monitoring tip:* If students are unable to identify a subplot (question 7), have them re-read pages 177–178, asking themselves questions such as "Who is in conflict with whom?" and "How is this conflict worked out in the story?"

Writing. Guide students in filling out their planning charts in class. Then, have them complete their narratives as homework.

HOMEWORK

Advanced Learners
Enrichment. Point out that the gold Cadillac takes 'lois, her father, and her

mother each on a different inner "journey" of understanding. Direct students to chart each character's journey by listing how the character responds to the car at first, what the character experiences as a result of the car, and how the character changes. Have students illustrate one memorable moment from each character's journey.

Literary Response and Analysis

Reading Check

1. Why doesn't 'lois's mother like the new Cadillac?

2. How does the rest of the family feel about the car?

3. What state is the family from? What state do they travel to?

4. What do the police accuse 'lois's father of?

5. What does the father do with the Cadillac at the end of the story?

Interpretations

6. How would you describe the main **conflict** in this story? (Who or what threatens the family on their journey?)

7. Longer works of fiction sometimes contain **subplots** that are related to the main conflict but are less important. Describe a second **conflict** in this story, and tell how it is resolved. (Hint: Think about the mother's reaction to the Cadillac.)

8. How do you think the journey south changes 'lois? How does it change her father?

9. Go back to the **predictions** you made as you read. At which points did you adjust your predictions?

10. Near the end of the story, 'lois asks if her family is poor. What does her father mean when he says they may be "the richest folks in the world"?

11. In one or two words, state what you think the **subject** of this story is.

Then, in a complete sentence, state what you see as the story's **theme.** Find at least one passage in the story that supports the theme.

Evaluation

12. Describe your opinions and feelings about Taylor's story. To organize your thoughts, try answering these questions:

   • How believable is the story?

   • Did the events described in the story make you feel uncomfortable, or did they make you feel another way?

   • Do you have any questions you would like to ask the author?

Writing
Narrating an Experience

Have you ever met with an injustice that changed your view of the world? Describe your experience in a short narrative. Organize your details in a chart like this one:

Place:
What happened:
How it ended:
My feelings:

BONUS QUESTION

In the 1950s, a Cadillac was a sign of wealth and status. What qualifies as a status symbol today?

Reading Standard 3.1 Identify the forms of fiction, and describe the major characteristics of each form.

Reading Check

1. Her husband bought it without consulting her, with savings that they had agreed to use for buying a better house.
2. They love it.
3. The family lives in Ohio and travels to Mississippi.
4. They accuse him of lying and of having stolen the car.
5. He sells it.

BONUS QUESTION

Students may list clothing, electronic equipment, jewelry, or expensive cars.

Literary Response and Analysis
Interpretations

6. Possible answer: The family is threatened by racist laws and attitudes in the South.

7. Possible answers: When Wilbert buys a new Cadillac, Dee is hurt and angry. She thinks the luxury car is far too expensive, while Wilbert feels he deserves it. The conflict is resolved when Wilbert sells the car to keep the family together.

8. She has a better understanding of the obstacles her parents have overcome and the battles she will have to fight. Her father is now more interested in having his family safe and together.

9. Students can track their predictions on a chart like this:

Prediction	Adjustment	Outcome

10. He means the family is rich because they have each other.

11. Possible answers: *Subject*—racism; family unity. *Theme*—Preserving family unity is an important way to fight racism; when fighting racism, you should compromise but not give up when your family might be harmed. Possible passage: "As fine as the Cadillac had been, he said, it had pulled us apart for a while. Now as ragged and noisy as that old Ford was, we all rode in it together, and we were a family again. So I held my head high."

Evaluation

12. Students should recognize that the story is historically accurate. Some may find the narrator unrealistically naive or the happy ending unrealistic. They may have felt indifference, discomfort, shock, or anger. Students may want to ask Taylor more about the era, her family, or her experiences.

Vocabulary Development

Practice 1

- *rural. Synonym*—country. *Antonym*—urban. *Sentence*—The farm children went to a rural school.

- *heedful. Synonym*—attentive. *Antonym*—indifferent. *Sentence*—Heedful of the dog's pain, the veterinarian gently bandaged its sore paw.

- *ignorance. Synonym*—unaware-ness. *Antonym*—knowledge. *Sentence*—Tran's ignorance of French traffic laws made it dangerous for him to drive in Paris.

Practice 2

1. ■ *smooth. Definition*—remove difficulties. *Part of speech*—verb.
   ■ *smooth. Definition*—even. *Part of speech*—adjective.

2. ■ *mind. Definition*—thoughts. *Part of speech*—noun.
   ■ *mind. Definition*—look after. *Part of speech*—verb.
   ■ *mind. Definition*—object to. *Part of speech*—verb.

 Resources Reminder

Vocabulary and Spelling

- *Vocabulary Development*
  - Vocabulary Worksheets, p. 13
- *Lesson Plans for Language Development*
  - Vocabulary, p. 107

 ASSESSING

Assessment

- *Progress Assessment of Reading*
  - Selection Test, p. 64

 RETEACHING

For a lesson reteaching forms of fiction, see **Reteaching,** p. 489G.

FOCUS ON

Vocabulary Development

Synonyms and Antonyms

PRACTICE 1

Semantic mapping can help you clarify a word's meaning. Using the cluster opposite as a model, map the three other words listed in the Word Bank. At the center of the map, write a Word Bank word. Then, write down a synonym and an antonym, and write a sentence using the word.

Remember that **synonyms** are words with similar meanings. **Antonyms** are words that are opposite or nearly opposite in meaning.

Word Bank

evident
rural
heedful
ignorance

```
        evident

antonym       synonym
unclear       obvious

        sentence
    Her confidence
    was evident.
```

Words with Multiple Meanings

A **multiple-meaning word** is like a fork in the road: Each road, and each definition, will take you in a different direction. To make things even more complicated, many multiple-meaning words can function as different parts of speech.

> **Dad came back to the car.** [Here, *back* is an adverb meaning "toward an earlier position."]
>
> **Mother decided to back Dad's plan.** [Here, *back* is a verb meaning "support."]

To decide on the correct meaning of a multiple-meaning word, decide what part of speech it is and look at its context, the words and sentences around it. Then, check your definition against the original sentence to see if it makes sense.

PRACTICE 2

Define the underlined multiple-meaning word in each set of sentences, and tell what part of speech it is.

Reading Standard 1.2
Identify and interpret words with multiple meanings.

1. Tired of arguing, he decided to <u>smooth</u> things out with his wife.
   I kept slipping on the <u>smooth</u> floor.

2. I finally asked the question that had been on my <u>mind</u>.
   <u>Mind</u> your little sister while I go to the store.
   Would you <u>mind</u> closing that door?

188 Chapter 4 Forms and Patterns: Stories and Explanations

Separate but Never Equal

Text Structures: Compare and Contrast

People make sense of the world by noting ways in which people, places, and ideas are similar (**comparing**) and different (**contrasting**). The next time you're with your friends, notice how often they use a comparison or a contrast.

> "Sue's party was like a rock concert."
> "It was more like a zoo."
> "Is a zoo a bad thing?"
> "Brenda's party was ten times better."
> "But Sue had great food."

Try to go a whole day without making a comparison or a contrast, and challenge a friend to do the same thing. Afterward, compare notes: Could you do it?

The article that follows is about segregation in the United States before 1954. Until then, segregation was legal as long as "separate but equal" facilities were provided for whites and African Americans. To help us understand what segregation was like, the writer compares life for blacks and for whites under segregation.

Every American should know about the two cases mentioned in this article: *Plessy* v. *Ferguson* and *Brown* v. *Board of Education of Topeka, Kansas.*

Background

Legal cases are given names that usually indicate who is arguing against whom. *Plessy* v. *Ferguson* is the name of a case that involved someone named Plessy arguing against someone named Ferguson. The *v.* in the name stands for

versus, a word from Latin that means "against." (It's like *vs.* in *Mets vs. Yankees* or *San Diego vs. Atlanta*.)

Plessy was an African American man who, in 1892, was forced to leave a train car that was reserved for whites. In a Louisiana court he challenged the state law requiring separate train cars for blacks and whites. Ferguson was John H. Ferguson, the judge who heard the case and decided against Plessy. The case eventually reached the U.S. Supreme Court. There Plessy argued that the Louisiana law violated the U.S. Constitution.

Plessy lost his case in the Supreme Court: The majority held that requiring "separate but equal" facilities for blacks and whites was lawful.

Brown v. *Board of Education of Topeka, Kansas* is the name of a suit brought in 1951 by Oliver Brown on behalf of his daughter Linda. The Browns lived in Topeka, Kansas, where the schools were segregated, and Linda attended an all-black elementary school. Brown sued the Topeka Board of Education and lost the case.

Some months later Brown and the NAACP (National Association for the Advancement of Colored People) appealed to the U.S. Supreme Court, which combined their case with other school segregation cases, from Virginia, South Carolina, and Delaware. In 1954, the Court ruled in favor of Brown. *Brown* v. *Board of Education* was one of the most important cases brought before the Supreme Court in the twentieth century.

Reading Standard 2.2 Analyze text that uses the compare-and-contrast organizational pattern.

Separate but Never Equal   **189**

STANDARDS FOCUS, pp. 189–192

(For grade-level and review standards taught in this selection, see citations on Pupil's Edition pages.)

Summary ⬄ *at grade level*

This essay uses comparison and contrast to illustrate the injustice of legalized segregation in the United States. Segregation became legal as a result of the *Plessy* v. *Ferguson* case, when the 1896 U.S. Supreme Court ruled in favor of "separate but equal" public facilities. Federally sanctioned segregation became illegal in 1954, with *Brown* v. *Board of Education of Topeka,* when the U.S. Supreme Court ruled against segregated public schools. The essay provides a quotation and numerous examples, including an item-by-item comparison and contrast of black public schools and white ones, showing that racially segregated public facilities were always unequal.

 Resources Reminder

Media
- *Audio CD Library*
  - disc 5

Reading
- *Interactive Reading*
  - Graphic Organizer: Venn Diagram, p. 150

Planning
- *One-Stop Planner* CD-ROM with Test Generator
- *On Course: Mapping Instruction*

Media
- *Audio CD Library*
  - disc 5

Reading
- *Interactive Reading*
  - Graphic Organizer: Venn Diagram, p. 150

Differentiating Instruction
- *Lesson Plans for Language Development*
  - English-Language Learners, pp. 81, 99, 107

- Special Education Students, pp. 81, 99, 107

Assessment
- *Progress Assessment of Reading*
  - Selection Test, p. 67
- *One-Stop Planner* CD-ROM with Test Generator

Standards Starter

Motivate. Write on the chalk-board the following statement by British philosopher Herbert Spencer (1820–1903): "No one can be perfectly free till all are free." Ask students to discuss and interpret the statement. Encourage them to provide examples from their own knowledge and experiences.

Assign the Reading

Play the audio CD recording of the words by Congressman John Lewis. Then, assign advanced learners to read the selection and do the Focus On page as homework. Monitor other students as they read in pairs or groups.

HOMEWORK

DIRECT TEACHING

A **Reading Informational Materials**
GRADE-LEVEL STANDARD
? **Comparison-and-contrast pattern.** What general difference was there, according to John Lewis, between the facilities marked "White" and those marked "Colored"? [Facilities marked "Colored" were generally inferior.]

B **Content-Area Connections**
HISTORY

Protesting segregation. John R. Lewis (1940–   ) organized sit-ins and other nonviolent protests at segregated lunch counters and other facilities in the South during the early 1960s. These demonstrations helped to raise public awareness of the injustice of segregation, leading to the passage of the Civil Rights Act of 1964. Lewis, from Alabama, was elected to the U.S. House of Representatives in 1986.

Separate
but Never Equal

A *When I was a boy, I would go downtown . . . , and I'd see the signs saying "White" and "Colored" on the water fountains. There'd be a beautiful, shining water fountain in one corner of the store marked "White," and in another corner was just a little spigot marked "Colored." I saw the signs saying "White Men," "Colored Men," and "White Women," "Colored Women." And at the theater we had to go upstairs to go to a movie. You bought your ticket at the same window that the white people did, but they could sit downstairs, and you had to go upstairs.*

B *—U.S. Congressman and civil rights leader John Lewis*

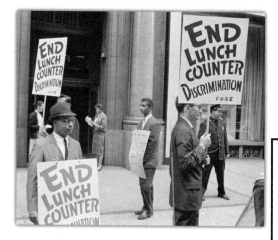
Lunch-counter segregation protest in 1960.

❶ In 1896, in a famous case known as *Plessy* v. *Ferguson*, the U.S. Supreme Court ruled that states could enact laws separating people by skin color as long as the facilities for African Americans were equivalent to those for whites. This "separate but equal" decision stood for more than half a century, supporting a system of racial segregation in states throughout the South.

❷ In reality, separate was never equal. Take buses, for example. The fare was the same for all passengers, regardless of race. But if the "white section" at the front of the bus filled up, the invisible line separating it from the "colored section" simply moved back. Black people had to stand up so that white people could sit.

❸ Consider shopping. An African American woman could buy the same dress as a white woman, but she wasn't allowed to try it on in the store—and if she found that it didn't fit, she couldn't return it. Or restaurants. Some white-owned restaurants filled orders for blacks only at their takeout window. Others wouldn't serve them at all.

❹ Perhaps most separate, and most unequal, were the public schools. If you attended a "colored school," you might walk eight miles to school every morning, while buses full of white children drove past on their way to schools closer by. The schools attended by white children would be modern and well

DIFFERENTIATING INSTRUCTION

English-Language Learners
Be sure students know that the U.S. Supreme Court is the country's highest judicial body and that its decisions overrule those of all other judges and courts in the nation. Also, tell students that the noun *suit* can mean "an argument brought to court" and that the verb *sue* means "to take someone to court."

▶Resources Reminder
For lessons designed for intermediate and advanced English-language learners, see *Lesson Plans for Language Development,* pp. 81, 99, 107.

Special Education Students
For lessons designed for special education students, see *Lesson Plans for Language Development,* pp. 81, 99, 107.

Students attending a segregated school in the 1890s.

maintained, while yours would be old and run-down. White students would have up-to-date books and materials, while you **C** might be forced to share a twenty-year-old textbook with three other students.

❺ In 1949, several African American parents sued their school district over the inequalities between the local white elementary school and the school their children were forced to attend. Two years earlier the district had built a brand-new school for white students while leaving the black students' school in disrepair. Unlike the all-black school, the all-white school had an auditorium, a kindergarten, a part-time music teacher, a well-equipped playground, and a lunch program. The all-white school had a teacher and a separate room for each grade; the all-black school had only two teachers and two classrooms for all eight grades.

❻ Finally, in 1954, the U.S. Supreme Court ruled in *Brown* v. *Board of Education* that segregated schools were by their very nature unequal. No longer would the highest court in the land support the myth of *Plessy* v. *Ferguson*. Separate could never be equal.

—Mara Rockliff

Separate but Never Equal   **191**

DIRECT TEACHING

C **Reading Informational Materials**
GRADE-LEVEL STANDARD
❓ **Comparison-and-contrast pattern.** Does the author focus more on similarities or on differences in this paragraph? [differences] How does this focus support the topic sentence of the paragraph? [The topic sentence states that public school systems were "most unequal," and the focus on differences shows what the inequalities were.]

GUIDED PRACTICE

Monitoring students' progress. Guide students in using the information in the essay to compare and contrast conditions for whites and blacks in the segregated South.
   On the chalkboard, draw a two-column chart, labeling one column "White" and the other "Black." Have students fill in details about drinking fountains, movie theaters, buses, shopping, and restaurants. (In the Independent Practice questions, students will contrast conditions in the schools.)

Advanced Learners
Enrichment. Point out that Homer Plessy, Oliver Brown, and John Lewis risked their lives to oppose racism. Have students form small groups, and have each group list other people who have fought injustice and briefly describe the efforts of those individuals. [Possibilities range from Rosa Parks and Martin Luther King, Jr., to Mohandas K. Gandhi, Nelson Mandela, and Aung San Suu Kyi.]

Have groups compare their lists, verify any entries that another group questions, and take note of persons who appeared on more than one list. Students may want to display their lists for other students to read.

INDEPENDENT PRACTICE

Reading Informational Materials

Reading Check

1. Lewis compares "White" and "Colored" water fountains and movie theater seating.

2. It was an 1896 U.S. Supreme Court ruling that legalized racial segregation if facilities were "separate but equal."

3. The district built a new school for whites but ignored the run-down, inadequate school for blacks.

4. The Supreme Court ruled five years later.

5. *All-white school*—new building, auditorium, kindergarten, music teacher, playground, lunch program, one room and one teacher for each grade. *All-black school*—run-down building, no auditorium, no kindergarten, no music teacher, no playground, no lunch program, two rooms and two teachers for all grades.

Answers and Model Rationales

1. **D** Point out that A contradicts the essay's main idea and B is a factual error. C is true, but does not go far enough, so D is the best answer.

2. **F** G reflects only part of the essay, and H is too general. J contradicts the main idea. Only F gets at the heart of the article.

3. **B** C can be eliminated because the essay describes conditions in the South; D, because a map won't show conditions. B is a better answer than A because the essay focuses on history.

Reading Informational Materials

Reading Check

1. In the opening quote, John Lewis makes three **comparisons.** What are they?

2. What is *Plessy* v. *Ferguson*?

3. Why did some African American parents sue their school district in 1949?

4. How long after that did it take for the Supreme Court to rule that separate schools were unequal?

5. In paragraph 5, the writer **contrasts** the schools attended by black children with those attended by white children. Draw an outline of two school buildings. Label one *All-White School* and one *All-Black School.* In each, list the contrasting points made in the essay.

Test Practice

Separate but Never Equal

1. In *Brown* v. *Board of Education* the Supreme Court ruled that segregated schools are —
   A similar
   B legal
   C unequal
   D illegal

2. "Separate but Never Equal" works as a **title** for this article because the article —
   F shows why the *Plessy* v. *Ferguson* ruling was unfair
   G examines the conditions in public schools
   H shows that things change over time
   J justifies segregation

3. To learn more about the conditions described in this essay, you should —
   A ask your principal
   B talk to your history teacher
   C read about conditions in northern schools
   D study a map of the South

4. In which of these situations would reading a **compare-and-contrast** article be most helpful?
   F You need to find out how life in China today differs from life in the United States.
   G You need to do research on *Brown* v. *Board of Education.*
   H You need to find out how many books Mildred Taylor has written.
   J You want to learn how the Supreme Court works.

Reading Standard 2.2 Analyze text that uses the compare-and-contrast organizational pattern.

4. **F** F is correct because choosing between two brands requires understanding of similarities and differences.

Test-Taking Tips

For information on how to answer multiple-choice items, refer students to **Test Smarts,** p. 690.

ASSESSING

Assessment

■ *Progress Assessment of Reading*
   ■ Selection Test, p. 67

La Bamba

Literary Focus
The Short Story

Some forms of fiction have existed for centuries, but the short story is a newcomer. It became popular in the United States during the nineteenth century. At that time, magazines were beginning to be published, and new stories appeared in each issue. People gobbled them up, and a new form of fiction was born.

A **short story** is a fictional prose narrative that generally runs from five to twenty pages. A fictional narrative is one that's made up, invented by the writer.

Story and Structure

From the time they first appeared, short stories have been built the same way. You can use a chart like this one to map the structure of most stories:

These building blocks are also found in novels and novellas, but the short story is, well, short. A short story usually has just one or two main characters and one

conflict. It usually has no subplots.

Most short stories can be read in about an hour, in one sitting. Good short stories deliver an emotional punch, and they deliver fast. Maybe that's why the short story is so popular in our fast-paced age.

Reading Skills
Sequencing: What Happened When?

Most narratives are written in **chronological** order—the writer relates events in the order in which they happen. As you read a story, you'll find **time clues,** such as *later, next morning, three days earlier.* These clues tell you when events occur.

When you review a story, ask yourself these questions:

- What are the story's key events?
- When did each event happen?
- What happened before that event?
- What happened afterward?
- Did one event cause another event to happen?

As you read "La Bamba," look for a **flashback** to an earlier time—to an incident involving a flashlight.

Make the Connection
Quickwrite 🖉

Jot down some notes about a time when you had to perform in front of an audience. What do you remember about the experience? Did your mouth go dry? Did your voice shake? Did you forget your lines?

Reading Standard 3.1 Identify the forms of fiction, and describe the major characteristics of each form.

STANDARDS FOCUS, pp. 193–202

(*For grade-level and review standards taught in this selection, see citations on Pupil's Edition pages.*)

Standard Coming Up in the Next Grade Level

- Grade 7, Literary Response and Analysis 3.1 **Articulate the expressed purposes and characteristics of different forms of prose (e.g., short story, novel, novella, essay).**

Reading Skills

- Determine sequence.

Summary ⬆ *above grade level*

For his school talent show, Manuel decides to pantomime a recording of Ritchie Valens's "La Bamba." During the rehearsal, however, the record gets damaged, but Manuel doesn't realize it. Coping with stage fright at the talent show, Manuel goes onstage and begins his act. When the record sticks, Manuel pantomimes the same words over and over, while the audience laughs and applauds. On the verge of tears after the show, Manuel is surprised when people congratulate him on his cleverness and sense of humor. Now, in the coveted limelight, he realizes that he has risen to the occasion. In bed that night, Manuel thinks that next year he won't volunteer for the show—probably.

RESOURCES

Planning
- *One-Stop Planner* CD-ROM with Test Generator
- *On Course: Mapping Instruction*

Media
- *Audio CD Library*
  - disc 5

Reading
- *Interactive Reading*
  - Graphic Organizer: Short-Story Map, p. 151

Differentiating Instruction
- *Lesson Plans for Language Development*
  - English-Language Learners, pp. 82–84, 100, 108

- Special Education Students, pp. 85, 100, 108

Assessment
- *Progress Assessment of Reading*
  - Selection Test, p. 69
- *One-Stop Planner* CD-ROM with Test Generator

Standards Starter

Build background. It might be necessary to describe records and record players to students who are only familiar with CDs and mini-discs. Be sure to explain what a forty-five looks like and discuss the problems of skipping and sticking that often plague record players.

Assign the Reading

You may want to ask a Spanish-speaking volunteer to provide the pronunciations of the Spanish words and phrases in the selection. Students will enjoy listening to the audio CD recording of the selection's first page. Then, assign advanced learners to read the selection independently while you monitor other students as they read aloud in small reading groups.

 Resources Reminder

Media

- *Audio CD Library*
  - disc 5

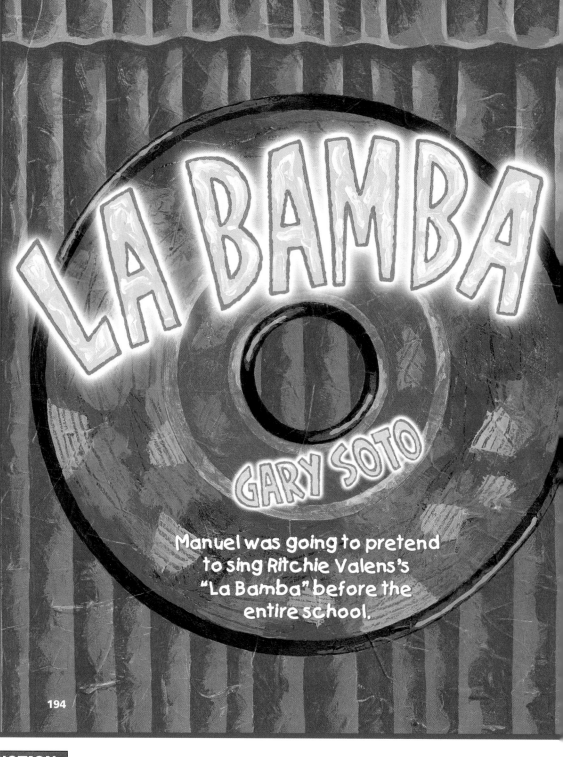

LA BAMBA

GARY SOTO

Manuel was going to pretend to sing Ritchie Valens's "La Bamba" before the entire school.

194

DIFFERENTIATING INSTRUCTION

Learners Having Difficulty

Some students may need help determining the sequence of events that make up the plot. Tell students that the story basically follows the structure of a school day. As students read, have them look for clues such as *when he got to school, during lunch, during rehearsal, that night, the next morning.*

 Resources Reminder

Reading

- *Interactive Reading*
  - Graphic Organizer: Short-Story Map, p. 151

English-Language Learners

Draw an outline of a boy on the chalkboard, and label it *Manuel.* As students read the story, have each one think of a word or phrase that describes Manuel— how he looks, how he sounds, how he feels, what his thoughts are. Write the words and phrases inside the outline.

Resources Reminder

For lessons designed for intermediate and advanced English-language learners, see *Lesson Plans for Language Development,* pp. 82–84, 100, 108.

Manuel was the fourth of seven children and looked like a lot of kids in his neighborhood: black hair, brown face, and skinny legs scuffed from summer play. But summer was giving way to fall: The trees were turning red, the lawns brown, and the pomegranate trees were heavy with fruit. Manuel walked to school in the frosty morning, kicking leaves and thinking of tomorrow's talent show. He was still amazed that he had volunteered. He was going to pretend to sing Ritchie Valens's[1] "La Bamba" before the entire school.

Why did I raise my hand? he asked himself, but in his heart he knew the answer. He yearned for the limelight. He wanted applause as loud as a thunderstorm and to hear his friends say, "Man, that was bad!" And he wanted to impress the girls, especially Petra Lopez, the second-prettiest girl in his class. The prettiest was already taken by his friend Ernie. Manuel knew he should be reasonable since he himself was not great-looking, just average.

Manuel kicked through the fresh-fallen leaves. When he got to school, he realized he had forgotten his math workbook. If the teacher found out, he would have to stay after school and miss practice for the talent show. But fortunately for him, they did drills that morning.

During lunch Manuel hung around with Benny, who was also in the talent show. Benny was going to play the trumpet in spite of the fat lip he had gotten playing football.

"How do I look?" Manuel asked. He cleared his throat and started moving his lips in pantomime. No words came out, just a hiss that sounded like a snake. Manuel tried to look emotional, flailing his arms on the high notes and opening his eyes and mouth as wide as he could when he came to "Para bailar la baaaaammmba."[2]

After Manuel finished, Benny said it looked all right but suggested Manuel dance while he sang. Manuel thought for a moment and decided it was a good idea.

"Yeah, just think you're like Michael Jackson or someone like that," Benny suggested. "But don't get carried away."

During rehearsal, Mr. Roybal, nervous about his debut as the school's talent co-ordinator, cursed under his breath when the lever that controlled the speed on the record player jammed.

"Darn," he growled, trying to force the lever. "What's wrong with you?"

"Is it broken?" Manuel asked, bending over for a closer look. It looked all right to him.

Mr. Roybal assured Manuel that he would have a good record player at the talent show, even if it meant bringing his own stereo from home.

---

1. **Ritchie Valens** (1941–1959), the professional singer mentioned in the story, was the first Mexican American rock star. In 1959, when he was only seventeen, Valens was killed in a plane crash.

2. **para bailar la bamba** (pä′rä bī′lär lä bäm′bä): Spanish for "to dance the bamba."

Ⓐ Content-Area Connections
HISTORY

Ritchie Valens. Rock-and-roll pioneer Ritchie Valens (1941–1959) recorded his first hit song, "Come On, Let's Go," when he was only seventeen years old. Soon afterward, he had an even bigger hit with "Donna," a love ballad dedicated to his ex-girlfriend. Valens's Mexican American background prompted his biggest hit, a rock version of the Mexican folk song "La Bamba," which became a party staple. Almost thirty years after Valens perished in the tragic plane crash that also claimed the lives of his fellow rock stars Buddy Holly and the Big Bopper, the popular Los Angeles–based Latin rock group Los Lobos did a new hit version of "La Bamba" for a film biography of Valens's life.

Ⓑ Reading Skills

❓ Making predictions. Based on this conversation between Manuel and Mr. Roybal, what do you think will happen at the talent show? [Many students will predict that the record player will break or something else will go wrong.]

Special Education Students
For lessons designed for special education students, see *Lesson Plans for Language Development,* pp. 85, 100, 108.

Advanced Learners
Acceleration. Use the following activity with advanced learners to move them toward the seventh-grade Standard 3.1, which requires that they articulate the purposes and characteristics of different forms of prose.

Activity. Suggest that students use the following questions to help them distinguish between short stories, novellas, novels, autobiographies, biographies, and essays.
• How long is the work?
• Is it a true story or a fictional account?

• How complicated is the plot? How many subplots appear?
• What is the purpose of the work?

A Literary Focus
GRADE-LEVEL STANDARD
❓ Forms of fiction: The short story. Remind students that a short story is a relatively brief work of fiction that involves a main character who wants something. Who is the main character here, and what does he want? [The main character, Manuel, wants to impress Petra Lopez, the second-prettiest girl in his class, and his family and friends by performing well in the talent show.]

B Learners Having Difficulty
❓ Finding details. While Benny is playing the trumpet, what event occurs that might affect Manuel's chances in the talent show? [He drops the record, and it rolls across the floor.]

C Reading Skills
Sequencing. Ask students when this embarrassing moment with the dead battery and the lightbulb actually occurred. [in first grade] Be sure students realize that Manuel is recalling this incident while lying in bed the night before the talent show.

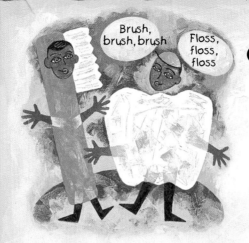

Manuel sat in a folding chair, twirling his record on his thumb. He watched a skit about personal hygiene, a mother-and-daughter violin duo, five first-grade girls jumping rope, a karate kid breaking boards, three girls singing "Like a Virgin," and a skit about the pilgrims. If the record player hadn't been broken, he would have gone after the karate kid, an easy act to follow, he told himself.

As he twirled his forty-five record, Manuel thought they had a great talent show. The entire school would be amazed. His mother and father would be proud, and his brothers and sisters would be jealous and pout. It would be a night to remember.

Benny walked onto the stage, raised his trumpet to his mouth, and waited for his cue. Mr. Roybal raised his hand like a symphony conductor and let it fall dramatically. Benny inhaled and blew so loud that Manuel dropped his record, which rolled across the cafeteria floor until it hit a wall.

Manuel raced after it, picked it up, and wiped it clean.

"Boy, I'm glad it didn't break," he said with a sigh.

That night Manuel had to do the dishes and a lot of homework, so he could only practice in the shower. In bed he prayed that he wouldn't mess up. He prayed that it wouldn't be like when he was a first-grader. For Science Week he had wired together a C battery and a bulb and told everyone he had discovered how a flashlight worked. He was so pleased with himself that he practiced for hours pressing the wire to the battery, making the bulb wink a dim, orangish light. He showed it to so many kids in his neighborhood that when it was time to show his class how a flashlight worked, the battery was dead. He pressed the wire to the battery, but the bulb didn't respond. He pressed until his thumb hurt and some kids in the back started snickering.

But Manuel fell asleep confident that nothing would go wrong this time.

The next morning his father and mother beamed at him. They were proud that he was going to be in the talent show.

"I wish you would tell us what you're doing," his mother said. His father, a pharmacist who wore a blue smock with his name on a plastic rectangle, looked up from the newspaper and sided with his wife. "Yes, what are you doing in the talent show?"

"You'll see," Manuel said, with his mouth full of Cheerios.

MINI-LESSON Reading

Developing Word-Attack Skills
Why did Manuel volunteer for the talent show? Perhaps because all year, he had yearned for the limelight. Write the selection words *year* and *yearned* on the chalkboard. Have students read the words aloud. Point out that the letters that spell *year* are part of the word *yearned,* but the vowel sounds are different. In *year,* the sound is /ir/. In *yearned,* the sound is /ûr/. Do a simi-

lar comparison with the selection words *hear* and *rehearsal.*
Activity. Write *year* and *yearned* as column heads on the chalkboard. Then, one at a time, display these words. Have students read the word aloud. Ask a volunteer to decide if the vowel sound in the word is the same as the vowel sound in *year* or *yearned* and write the word in the appropriate column.

cleared [year]
heard [yearned]
hurt [yearned]
deer [year]
dirty [yearned]
here [year]
pearl [yearned]
fear [year]
appear [year]

learn [yearned]
germs [yearned]
cursed [yearned]
cheer [year]
worse [yearned]
weird [year]
learn [yearned]
fierce [year]
mere [year]

The day whizzed by, and so did his afternoon chores and dinner. Suddenly he was dressed in his best clothes and standing next to Benny backstage, listening to the commotion as the cafeteria filled with school kids and parents. The lights dimmed, and Mr. Roybal, sweaty in a tight suit and a necktie with a large knot, wet his lips and parted the stage curtains.

"Good evening, everyone," the kids behind the curtain heard him say. "Good evening to you," some of the smart-alecky kids said back to him.

"Tonight we bring you the best John Burroughs Elementary has to offer, and I'm sure that you'll be both pleased and amazed that our little school houses so much talent. And now, without further ado, let's get on with the show." He turned and, with a swish of his hand, commanded, "Part the curtain." The curtains parted in jerks. A girl dressed as a toothbrush and a boy dressed as a dirty gray tooth walked onto the stage and sang:

Brush, brush, brush
Floss, floss, floss
Gargle the germs away—hey! hey! hey!
After they finished singing, they turned to Mr. Roybal, who dropped his hand. The toothbrush dashed around the stage after the dirty tooth, which was laughing and having a great time until it slipped and nearly rolled off the stage.

Mr. Roybal jumped out and caught it just in time. "Are you OK?"

The dirty tooth answered, "Ask my dentist," which drew laughter and applause from the audience.

The violin duo played next, and except for one time when the girl got lost, they sounded fine. People applauded, and some even stood up. Then the first-grade girls maneuvered onto the stage while jumping rope. They were all smiles and bouncing ponytails as a hundred cameras flashed at once. Mothers "awhed" and fathers sat up proudly.

The karate kid was next. He did a few kicks, yells, and chops, and finally, when his father held up a board, punched it in two. The audience clapped and looked at each other, wide-eyed with respect. The boy bowed to the audience, and father and son ran off the stage.

Manuel remained behind the stage, shivering with fear. He mouthed the words to "La Bamba" and swayed left to right. Why did he raise his hand and volunteer? Why couldn't he have just sat there like the rest of the kids and not said anything? While the karate kid was onstage, Mr. Roybal, more sweaty than

La Bamba **197**

D **Vocabulary Development**
GRADE-LEVEL STANDARD
❓ **Interpreting multiple-meaning words.** The word *part,* in this context, is a verb that means "to separate." What other meanings does this word have? [a portion of something, not the whole thing]

E **Reading Skills**
❓ **Sequencing.** Remind students that authors use time clues such as *today, at noon,* and *at last* to make the sequence of events clear. What time clues appear in this account of the talent show? [*next, then, next,* and *finally*]

❓ Speculating. How do you think Manuel feels as he notices his brother thumb-wrestling and the other kids walking toward the drinking fountain? [Possible responses: Their inattention adds to his stage fright. It makes him feel nervous, angry, dismayed, and insulted.]

B Literary Focus
GRADE-LEVEL STANDARD

❓ Figurative language. What two things are being compared here? [the audience watching Manuel and visitors watching a monkey at a zoo] How does this simile convey Manuel's emotions? [It reveals Manuel's acute embarrassment that the audience is not appreciating or "getting into" his performance.]

C Reading Skills

❓ Identifying cause and effect. Why does the record get stuck despite the fact that Mr. Roybal brought a new record player to the talent show? [Manuel dropped the record earlier and probably scratched it.]

D Reading Skills

Sequencing. Have students stop here and review the sequence of events that resulted in this excruciatingly embarrassing moment. They should ask themselves, "What happened first?" "What happened as a result?" and "What happened next?"

---

before, took Manuel's forty-five record and placed it on a new record player.

"You ready?" Mr. Roybal asked.

"Yeah . . ."

Mr. Roybal walked back on stage and announced that Manuel Gomez, a fifth-grader in Mrs. Knight's class, was going to pantomime Ritchie Valens's classic hit "La Bamba."

The cafeteria roared with applause. Manuel was nervous but loved the noisy crowd. He pictured his mother and father applauding loudly and his brothers and sister also clapping, though not as energetically.

Manuel walked on stage and the song started immediately. Glassy-eyed from the shock of being in front of so many people, Manuel moved his lips and swayed in a made-up dance step. He couldn't see his parents, but he could see his brother Mario, who was a year younger, thumb-wrestling with a friend. Mario was wearing Manuel's favorite shirt; he would deal with Mario later. He saw some other kids get up and head for the drinking fountain, and a baby sitting in the middle of an aisle sucking her thumb and watching him intently.

What am I doing here? thought Manuel. This is no fun at all. Everyone was just sitting there. Some people were moving to the beat, but most were just watching him, like they would a monkey at the zoo.

But when Manuel did a fancy dance step, there was a burst of applause and some girls screamed. Manuel tried another dance step. He heard more applause and screams and started getting into the groove

as he shivered and snaked like Michael Jackson around the stage. But the record got stuck, and he had to sing

Para bailar la bamba
Para bailar la bamba
Para bailar la bamba
Para bailar la bamba

again and again.

Manuel couldn't believe his bad luck. The audience began to laugh and stand up in their chairs. Manuel remembered how the forty-five record had dropped from his hand and rolled across the cafeteria floor. It probably got scratched, he thought, and now it was stuck, and he was stuck dancing and moving his lips to the same words over and over. He had never been so embarrassed. He would have to ask his parents to move the family out of town.

After Mr. Roybal ripped the needle across the record, Manuel slowed his dance steps to a halt. He didn't know what to do except bow to the audience, which applauded wildly, and scoot off the stage, on the verge of tears. This was worse than the homemade flashlight. At least no one laughed then; they just snickered.

Manuel stood alone, trying hard to hold back the tears as Benny, center stage, played his trumpet. Manuel was jealous because he sounded great, then mad as he recalled that it was Benny's loud trumpet playing that made the forty-five record fly out of his hands. But when the entire cast lined up for a curtain call, Manuel received a burst of applause that was so loud it shook the walls of the cafeteria. Later, as he mingled with the kids and parents, everyone

---

FAMILY/COMMUNITY ACTIVITY

Assign students the task of finding out from family and friends which songs, if any, they performed while they were in school. Students should return to class and compile a class list of the songs.

patted him on the shoulder and told him, "Way to go. You were really funny."

Funny? Manuel thought. Did he do something funny?

Funny. Crazy. Hilarious. These were the words people said to him. He was confused but beyond caring. All he knew was that people were paying attention to him, and his brother and sisters looked at him with a mixture of jealousy and awe. He was going to pull Mario aside and punch him in the arm for wearing his shirt, but he cooled it. He was enjoying the limelight. A teacher brought him cookies and punch, and the popular kids who had never before given him the time of day now clustered around him. Ricardo, the editor of the school bulletin, asked him how he made the needle stick.

"It just happened," Manuel said, crunching on a star-shaped cookie.

At home that night his father, eager to undo the buttons on his shirt and ease into his La-Z-Boy recliner, asked Manuel the same thing, how he managed to make the song stick on the words "Para bailar la bamba."

Manuel thought quickly and reached for scientific jargon he had read in magazines. "Easy, Dad. I used laser tracking with high optics and low functional decibels per channel." His proud but confused father told him to be quiet and go to bed.

"Ah, que niños tan truchas,"[3] he said as he walked to the kitchen for a glass of milk. "I don't know how you kids nowadays get so smart."

Manuel, feeling happy, went to his bedroom, undressed, and slipped into his pajamas. He looked in the mirror and began to pantomime "La Bamba," but stopped because he was tired of the song. He crawled into bed. The sheets were as cold as the moon that stood over the peach tree in their backyard.

He was relieved that the day was over. Next year, when they asked for volunteers for the talent show, he wouldn't raise his hand. Probably.

---

3. **que niños tan truchas** (kā nēn'yōs tän troo'chäs): Spanish for "what smart kids."

E Literary Focus
GRADE-LEVEL STANDARD
? Characterization. Point out that both Ricardo and Manuel's father ask Manuel how he got the record to stick. How does Manuel respond? [He tells Ricardo that it just happened. He tells his father that he used laser tracking to stop the needle.] **Why does Manuel change his answer?** [Possible response: He wants to impress his father.]

F Literary Focus
GRADE-LEVEL STANDARD
? Characterization. What does the ending of the story reveal about Manuel's character? [Possible response: It shows that he realizes things turned out better for him than perhaps he deserved.] **What questions about Manuel does the ending leave unanswered?** [Will he skip the talent show next year because he knows his success was a fluke, or will he enter it because he has gained self-confidence and enjoys the limelight?]

G Literary Focus
GRADE-LEVEL STANDARD
Forms of fiction: The short story. Remind students that a short story can be read in one sitting and has one or two main characters, one conflict, no subplots, and a single theme. Have students enumerate the ways in which "La Bamba" fits these criteria. [It is four and a half pages long. It has one main character, Manuel; one conflict, the talent show; no subplots; and a single theme, "sometimes things turn out better than one could possibly hope."]

Meet the Writer

Background. Gary Soto's books are often about the experiences and feelings of youngsters growing up as Mexican Americans. He has written fiction, poetry, essays, and autobiographical recollections and has produced short films for Spanish-speaking children.

For Independent Reading

For a look at Gary Soto's own world, recommend *A Summer Life,* a collection of autobiographical sketches.

Gary Soto

"My Friends . . . Jump Up and Down on the Page"

Like Manuel in "La Bamba," **Gary Soto** (1952–) grew up in a Mexican American family in California's San Joaquin Valley. He remembers being competitive:

> I was a playground kid. I jumped at every chance to play. The game didn't matter. It could be kickball or baseball, or chess or Chinese checkers—anything that allowed me to compete.

He also says that he was not a very good student until he went to college and discovered poetry. Soon he yearned to be a writer himself— to win recognition by recapturing the world of his childhood in words. Of his early days as a writer, Soto remembers this:

> I was a poet before I was a prose writer. As a poet, I needed only a sheaf of paper, a pen, a table, some quiet, and, of course, a narrative and spurts of image. I liked those years because the writing life was tidy. When I first started writing recollections and short stories, however, I needed more. I needed full-fledged stories and the patience of a monk. I needed to recall the narrative, characters, small moments, dates, places, etc. I was responsible for my writing, and, thus, it was tremendous work to keep it all in order. When I was writing *Living up the Street,* I clacked away on my typewriter with a bottle of white-out within view. I wrote, rewrote, and rewrote the rewrite, so that my friends would jump up and down on the page.

For Independent Reading

To meet more of Gary Soto's lively friends, check out *Baseball in April* and *Local News.*

DIFFERENTIATING INSTRUCTION

Advanced Learners
Tell students that Soto has produced a number of short films for young viewers.
Activity. Have students imagine that they are in charge of publicity for an upcoming film of "La Bamba." Have students work in small groups to create an advertising campaign with posters and newspaper ads for the film.

SMALL-GROUP

Literary Response and Analysis

Reading Check

1. Make a sequence chart like the one below, showing the order of the **main events** in "La Bamba."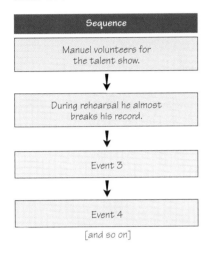

Sequence
Manuel volunteers for the talent show.
↓
During rehearsal he almost breaks his record.
↓
Event 3
↓
Event 4

[and so on]

Interpretations

2. Manuel remembers his attempt to show how a flashlight works. What does this memory tell you about Manuel's **character**?

3. Gary Soto loves to use unusual comparisons, such as similes. A **simile** is a comparison between two unlike things, using a word such as *like, as,* or *resembles*. What simile does Soto use to describe the way the audience members watch Manuel? Find two other similes in the story.

4. How are Manuel's moments onstage different from what he imagined? Does the audience agree with Manuel that his performance is a disaster?

Evaluation

5. Do you think Soto's descriptions of Manuel's experiences and of the talent show are funny? If so, tell which moments or descriptions struck you as humorous. If not, explain why you didn't laugh.

6. How believable are Manuel's experiences and feelings? Review your Quickwrite notes, and compare Manuel's stage debut with your own experiences in front of an audience.

Writing
The Show Must Go On

How would you help someone handle stage fright? Put together a list of tips called "How to Deal with Stage Fright." You can find advice in an article or a book on public speaking. You might even interview someone who does a lot of speaking or performing (maybe the PTA president or a soloist in a choir). Collect as many tips as you can.

Reading Standard 3.1 Identify the forms of fiction, and describe the major characteristics of each form.

La Bamba **201**

Literary Response and Analysis

Reading Check

1. *Event 3*—Manuel is nearly overcome by stage fright when it is his turn to perform. *Event 4*—During his performance, the record sticks, and he has to pantomime the same line over and over. *Event 5*—The audience likes his act, thinking that he did it on purpose to be funny. *Event 6*—At home, Manuel realizes that he has changed.

Interpretations

2. Soto probably includes this memory to show readers why Manuel wants so much to be a success in the show.

3. Manuel says that people looked at him the way people look at a monkey in a zoo. Other similes might include: "a hiss that sounded like a snake" to describe a sound or Manuel "shivered and snaked like Michael Jackson."

4. Manuel thought that he would enjoy his time on the stage; instead, he is embarrassed and convinced that he has failed. In fact, the audience loves him and believes that he is trying to be funny on purpose.

Evaluation

5. Possible answers: Many students will think they are funny. Humorous moments include the incidents with the lightbulb and Manuel's onstage response to the stuck record. Others may argue that they felt too sorry for Manuel to laugh.

6. Many students will sympathize with Manuel's stage fright, finding it very believable. However, some may feel that the ending is unbelievable. Many students will recall humiliations from their own elementary-school days.

The Arts
Talent in the classroom. Discussing Manuel's experiences in the talent show may bring up the subject of students' own talents. Have students raise their hands in response to these questions: "Who plays a musical instrument?" "Who sings?" "Who dances?" "Who draws or paints or works with clay?" and "Who likes to act?"

Activity. Hold a mini-talent show to give students a chance to perform for their peers. Each act should last no longer than a few minutes.

WHOLE-CLASS

Vocabulary Development

Practice

Possible Answers

- *cast.* The day after the ski trip she hobbled to school with her leg in a <u>cast</u>. In the class play she was <u>cast</u> in the role of the wicked queen.

- *fall.* The deep reds and golds of the leaves make <u>fall</u> my favorite season of the year. I was looking up at the blue sky and the white puffy clouds when I slipped and took a bad <u>fall</u> on the slick leaves.

- *sign.* The <u>sign</u> on the fence in front of him was clear: "No trespassers allowed." He started to talk to her, but then realized that her silence was a <u>sign</u> that she wanted to be alone.

- *stage.* At this <u>stage</u> of the year, it is clear that some students in the class are doing very well indeed. Her parents were concerned about her decision to become an actress and go on the <u>stage</u>.

Students' illustrations must make the difference in meaning clear.

▶ Resources Reminder

Differentiating Instruction

- *Lesson Plans for Language Development*
  - Vocabulary, p. 108

ASSESSING

Assessment

- *Progress Assessment of Reading*
  - Selection Test, p. 69

RETEACHING

For a lesson reteaching forms of fiction, see **Reteaching,** p. 489G.

Vocabulary Development

Words with Multiple Meanings

Multiple-meaning words are words with more than one meaning. When you look up a multiple-meaning word in a dictionary, you'll find a numbered list of definitions, as in this example:

> **shower** (shou'ər) *n.* **1.** a brief rainfall **2.** a party at which someone is honored and given gifts **3.** a bath in which water pours down on the body —*v.* **1.** to spray **2.** to pour forth like a shower **3.** to take a shower

If you come across a multiple-meaning word and you're not sure which meaning is the one intended, figure out what part of speech it is. Then, look at its **context,** the words around it. If you're still confused, look at the definitions listed in a dictionary. Then, choose the one that fits best in the sentence.

Here is a sentence from "La Bamba." Which definition of *shower* fits best in the context?

> **"That night Manuel had to do the dishes and a lot of homework, so he could only practice in the <u>shower</u>."**

PRACTICE

The following multiple-meaning words are from "La Bamba." Think about the different meanings of each word. Then, choose four of the words. For each of your words, write *two* sentences that show *two* distinct meanings. If you can't think of more than one meaning for a word, look in a dictionary.

cast   fall   wire   sign   battery   stage   time

Choose one of the pairs of sentences you've written, and illustrate them with pictures that show the difference in meaning.

Reading Standard 1.2 Identify and interpret words with multiple meanings.

Goodbye Records, Hello CDs

Text Structures: Compare and Contrast

Writers who want to present two sides of an issue often organize their material in a comparison-and-contrast pattern. This is a good way to show how two or more things are different and also how they're alike. When writers **compare** things, they look for similarities. When they **contrast** things, they look for differences.

When writers compare and contrast, they generally arrange their ideas according to one of two organizational patterns: the **point-by-point pattern** and the **block pattern.**

A writer using the point-by-point pattern moves back and forth between the subjects being compared, discussing one feature at a time. See the chart below on the left for an example of a point-by-point comparison.

A writer using the block pattern covers all the points of comparison for the first subject, then all the points of comparison for the second subject, and so on. See the chart below on the right for a comparison organized according to the block pattern.

STANDARDS FOCUS, pp. 203–207

(For grade-level and review standards taught in this selection, see citations on Pupil's Edition pages.)

Summary ⬆ *above grade level*

This essay uses the block method to compare and contrast records and CDs. The author first discusses the invention, technological development, and advantages and disadvantages of record players and vinyl records. The author explains that the first sound recording was made by Thomas Edison in 1877 on a cylinder covered with tinfoil. A hand-cranked machine with a metal needle created dents and grooves in the tinfoil, and these corresponded to the sound waves made by Edison's voice. Eventually vinyl records emerged, using this analog technology to provide high-quality sound. Unfortunately, however, records could easily become scratched or warped.

In the next stage of the comparison, the author examines the invention, technological development, and advantages and disadvantages of CD players and CDs. This technology involves dividing every second of sound into frames that are assigned digital codes. This digital technology captures sound waves with amazing accuracy. In addition, because CDs are read with a laser, they don't get worn with repeated play as records do.

Comparing Records and CDs: Point-by-Point Pattern	
Point of comparison 1: how they're made	• **records:** vibrations produced by sound waves cut a groove on a disc • **CDs:** computers translate sound waves into electronic information
Point of comparison 2: how they sound	• **records:** somewhat inaccurate • **CDs:** nearly perfect

Comparing Records and CDs: Block Pattern	
Subject 1: records	• **Feature 1:** how they're made • **Feature 2:** how they sound
Subject 2: CDs	• **Feature 1:** how they're made • **Feature 2:** how they sound

Reading Standard 2.2 Analyze text that uses the compare-and-contrast organizational pattern.

RESOURCES

Planning
- *One-Stop Planner* CD-ROM with Test Generator
- *On Course: Mapping Instruction*

Media
- *Audio CD Library*
  - disc 5
- *Visual Connections*
  - Videocassette, Segment 4

Reading
- *Interactive Reading*
  - Graphic Organizer: Compare-and-Contrast Frame, p. 152

Differentiating Instruction
- *Lesson Plans for Language Development*
  - English-Language Learners, pp. 86, 101, 108

- Special Education Students, pp. 86, 101, 108

Assessment
- *Progress Assessment of Reading*
  - Selection Test, p. 73
- *One-Stop Planner* CD-ROM with Test Generator

Standards Starter
Build prerequisite skills.
Remind students that to compare, they should ask, "How are these things alike?" and to contrast, they should ask, "How are these things different?"

Assign the Reading
Draw readers' attention to the side notes. Have advanced learners create a chart showing the author's pattern of organization. Guide less-advanced learners in identifying each point of comparison and contrast.

►Resources Reminder
Media
- *Audio CD Library*
  - disc 5
- *Visual Connections*
  - Videocassette, Segment 4

Ⓐ Reading Informational Materials
GRADE-LEVEL STANDARD
Compare-and-contrast pattern.
Draw students' attention to the fact that the title and the first two sentences clearly state what two things are going to be compared and contrasted in the essay. [records and CDs]

Ⓑ Reading Informational Materials
GRADE-LEVEL STANDARD
❓ Figurative language. What are records being compared to here? [dinosaurs] Why is this a good comparison? [Possible response: Dinosaurs are extinct, and records are obsolete.]

GOOD BYE RECORDS, Hello CDs

Ⓐ

The writer introduces the topic.

Twenty years ago every music lover in America had a turntable for playing vinyl records. Then, in 1983, the CD player arrived on the scene. It quickly became the fastest-selling machine in home-electronics history. Record stores couldn't order the new CDs fast enough to keep up with demand. Soon CDs were everywhere, and record players had gone the way of the dinosaurs. What happened?

Ⓑ

THE FIRST "RECORD"

She describes the invention of sound recording.

It all goes way back to 1877, when the inventor Thomas Edison made the first sound recording ever. The "record" was a cylinder covered with tinfoil, and the recorder was a hand-cranked machine with a metal **stylus,** or needle. "Mary had a little lamb," Edison said into the machine, and as he turned the crank, the vibrations of his voice made the stylus wiggle, carving grooves and dents in the foil.

Subject 1: RECORDS The writer describes the first record player.

Edison called his new machine a **phonograph.** The word comes from the Greek roots *–phono–,* meaning "sound," and *–graph–,* meaning "write." The stylus had "written" the sounds of his words on the foil, and it could "read" them back over and over. The dents made the stylus vibrate, and the vibrations came out through a horn as a scratchy, croaking version of Edison's voice—at least until the foil wore out, as it did after about five playings.

She tells how record players changed.

A century later, sound recording had come a long way. Edison's tinfoil cylinders and hand-cranked phonograph were ancient history, replaced by long-playing vinyl records that were played on high-

---

DIFFERENTIATING INSTRUCTION

Learners Having Difficulty
If students have difficulty seeing the pattern that the writer is following, provide some help by asking them the following questions: What are records? When were they invented? How do they work? What are their advantages and disadvantages? Then, repeat the same questions for CDs.

►Resources Reminder
Reading
- *Interactive Reader*
  - Graphic Organizer: Compare-and-Contrast Frame, p. 152

fidelity electronic stereo systems. Country music, disco, rock—whatever you liked, you could slide a record album out of its cardboard cover, drop it on your turntable, set the needle in the groove, and settle back to listen to some pretty good sounds.

What had *not* changed was the basic technology. It was still **analog,** meaning that each squiggly groove cut in the surface of a record corresponded to the sound wave it captured. And analog technology had certain problems. In a live performance the volume of the music can range from extremely soft to extremely loud. But to fit in a groove that a stylus could follow, the range of volume in any one recording had to be narrowed. Then there were playback problems, such as "wow" and "flutter" (changes in pitch caused by slight variations in the turntable's speed) and "rumble" (noise picked up from the turntable's motor).

Even records that sounded good at first could eventually warp or wear out. Records also got scratched easily—often by a slip of the same stylus that read the grooves—and a scratch could ruin a record, making the same bit of music play over and over and over: "*Para bailar la bamba, para bailar la bamba, para bailar la bamba . . .*"

THE CD REVOLUTION

Enter the compact disc, or CD. Sound is recorded on a CD not by a needle cutting a groove on a disk but by a computer translating sound waves into electronic information. The computer divides each second of sound into 44,100 units, each of which gets its own digital code. The code represents one of 65,536 possible sound values. This wide range of sound values allows tiny variations in sound to be captured with amazing accuracy. That's why the sound of a CD is true to life. Imagine that you're trying to match a particular shade of paint to a color in a picture. If you have 65,536 shades to choose from, you have a good chance of finding one that's almost exactly like the color you're looking for.

At first the CD sometimes sounded *too* perfect. Early CDs reproduced even the squeak of a violinist's fingers on an instrument's string, something a live concert audience would probably never hear—or want to. Some music lovers found the sound of CDs cold and artificial in its computerized perfection.

Then listeners came to appreciate the benefits of CDs. Not only is their sound better than that of records, but they're more durable, thanks to the new technology. Sound is recorded on the surface of a CD in the form of tiny pits and smooth areas. The surface is then covered with layers of aluminum and acrylic. Thus, the laser in a CD player never actually touches the surface on which the music is recorded. Unlike a phonograph needle, which can scratch or wear out a record, the laser will not damage or wear out a CD.

Best of all, unlike record players, which cost more the better the sound quality, all CD systems use lasers and digital technology. So even the cheapest CD player offers music lovers excellent sound. Edison would be amazed.

—Mara Rockliff

The writer describes problems with records and record players.

She explains how records can be damaged.

Subject 2: CDs The writer explains how CDs work.

She describes some of the advantages of CDs.

The writer ends with a final point of contrast.

English-Language Learners
Some students may find this comparison of analog and digital technology difficult. To explain analog technology, use a magnifying glass to show students the grooves in an LP recording that are produced by a needle that transmits sound vibrations to the vinyl. A playback system reproduces those vibrations. In digital recording, sound is converted by a computer into a stream of numbers—zeros and ones—which become indentations in the CD surface. The playback system converts these numbers into sound.

Resources Reminder
For lesson plans for English-language learners, see *Lesson Plans for Language Development,* pp. 86, 101, 108.

C **Reading Informational Materials**
GRADE-LEVEL STANDARD
Compare-and-contrast pattern. After discussing the invention and development of records and record players, the author turns to the problems with their technology. What are these? [Possible responses: narrow range of volume; playback problems caused by variations in the turntable speed or noise vibrations from the turntable's motor.]

D **Vocabulary Development**
GRADE-LEVEL STANDARD
Interpreting multiple-meaning words. This sentence contains a number of words with multiple meanings: *wow, flutter, rumble.* Ask volunteers to imitate a recording affected by these audio problems.

E **Reading Informational Materials**
GRADE-LEVEL STANDARD
Compare-and-contrast pattern. Point out the heading that signals the beginning of the second block in this compare-and-contrast essay. The writer begins this section by describing the technology behind CDs. How does this echo the structure of the first half of the essay? [She covers the technological development of CDs, just as she covered the technological development of records earlier.]

GUIDED PRACTICE

Monitoring students' progress. Have students make a list of the pros and cons of records and CDs as discussed in the essay. Then, ask them to add their own opinions.

INDEPENDENT PRACTICE

Reading Informational Materials

Reading Check

1. The block pattern.
Possible chart:
Records. Feature 1—invention [first sound recording in 1877]. *Feature 2*—technology [analog; grooves on surface correspond to sound waves]. *Feature 3*—pros and cons [good sound; narrow range; can warp or be scratched]. *CDs. Feature 1*—invention [one hundred years later]. *Feature 2*—technology [digital; sound divided into units and each unit coded]. *Feature 3*—pros and cons [accurate sound; durable; "cold" sound].

2. Each groove cut into the surface of a record corresponds to the sound wave it captures.

3. Possible answers: Problems include a narrow range of volume and easily damaged records. CD recording technology allows for a wide range of possible sound values, and since the surface on which the music is recorded is protected and never actually touched, the discs will not be damaged through use.

4. Possible answers: *Similarities*—Both records and CDs provide true-to-life sound and are easy to store. *Differences*—Records use analog technology to turn sound waves into grooves, while CDs use digital technology to turn sound waves into electronic information. Records can be damaged through use, while CDs are more durable.

Answers and Model Rationales

1. **A**   A is a detail about CDs in the essay. B and C are true for records, not CDs. D is not supported in the essay.

Reading Informational Materials

Reading Check

1. What overall pattern of organization does the writer use: **point by point** or **block**? To check your answer, make a chart showing how the essay is organized. (You can use the charts on page 203 as a model.)

2. How is **analog** technology defined?

3. What are some of the problems with analog technology? How are these problems avoided with the technology used to make CDs?

4. **Compare** and **contrast** records and CDs by naming two ways in which they're similar and two ways in which they're different.

TestPractice

GOODBYE RECORDS, Hello CDs

1. Which of the following statements is true of CDs?
   A They do not wear out easily.
   B They're made by cutting a groove on a disc.
   C They're played on a turntable.
   D Their sound is not true to life.

2. This article was written mainly to —
   F persuade people to buy records
   G explain the differences between CDs and records
   H prove that live music is best
   J describe the life of Thomas Edison

3. In the word telegraph the Greek root *–graph–* means —
   A write
   B draw
   C speak
   D picture

4. In the first paragraph of the essay, the writer says that "record players had gone the way of the dinosaurs." She uses the expression "gone the way of the dinosaurs" to show that record players —
   F take up too much room
   G are disliked by consumers
   H are easier to operate than CD players
   J are no longer in use

5. According to the article, another word for stylus is —
   A flutter
   B needle
   C groove
   D turntable

Reading Standard 2.2
Analyze text that uses the compare-and-contrast organizational pattern.

2. **G**   Students should realize that G is the only answer to reflect the article's purpose.

3. **A**   Students should use the information about the roots of the word *phonograph* in the essay to answer this question.

4. **J**   F, G, and H are not mentioned in the essay; J is the only answer that makes sense here.

5. **B**   This detail appears in the second paragraph of the essay.

Test-Taking Tips

For more instruction on how to answer multiple-choice items, refer students to **Test Smarts,** p. 690.

Vocabulary Development

Words with Multiple Meanings

PRACTICE

The quotations below are taken from "Goodbye Records, Hello CDs." Write a sentence about each of the subjects listed below each quotation, using the underlined word. You may be able to think of several meanings for some of the words. Use any form of the words you like.

1. "Every music lover in America had a turntable for playing vinyl <u>records</u>." Use the word *records* in sentences about a —
   - trial
   - dance contest
2. "The vibrations came out through a <u>horn</u> as a scratchy, croaking version of Edison's voice. . . ." Use the word *horn* in sentences about a —
   - zoo
   - concert
3. "Country music, disco, <u>rock</u>—whatever you liked, you could . . . settle back to listen to some pretty good sounds." Use the word *rock* in sentences about a —
   - forest
   - fishing trip
4. "Changes in <u>pitch</u> caused by slight variations in the turntable's speed . . ." Use the word *pitch* in sentences about a —
   - song
   - baseball game
5. "Sound is recorded . . . by a computer translating sound <u>waves</u> into electronic information." Use the word *waves* in sentences about —
   - the ocean
   - a farewell party

Reading Standard 1.2
Identify and interpret words with multiple meanings.

Goodbye Records, Hello CDs **207**

Vocabulary Development

Practice
Possible Answers

1. During the trial the press discovered that the witness had a criminal <u>record</u>. Luckily the disc jockeys had extra <u>records</u> for the dance contest.
2. At the zoo we were impressed by the rhino with the large <u>horn</u>. The loudest instruments in the band were the <u>horns</u>.
3. In the forest we came to a one hundred-foot-tall <u>rock</u> cliff. We had to be careful not to <u>rock</u> our unstable canoes.
4. The singer's closing note was right on <u>pitch</u>—not sharp or flat. The first <u>pitch</u> of the baseball season was a strike.
5. We sailed our boat over ten-foot-tall <u>waves</u>. At the school dance the rock band made <u>waves</u> of loud noise.

ASSESSING

Assessment
■ *Progress Assessment of Reading*
   ■ Selection Test, p. 73

STANDARDS FOCUS, pp. 208–223

(For grade-level and review standards taught in this selection, see citations on Pupil's Edition pages.)

Reading Skills
■ Dialogue with the text.

Summary ⬆ *above grade level*

An oracle tells King Acrisios of Argos that his only daughter, Danae, will bear a child who will kill him. Trying to alter fate, the hard-hearted king imprisons Danae, but the god Zeus appears to the girl and fathers a son, Perseus. Acrisios puts his daughter and her baby in a wooden chest and throws it into the sea. The chest washes up on an island ruled by Polydectes, who falls in love with Danae but whom she refuses. When Perseus grows up, Polydectes decides to get him out of the way so that he can force Danae to marry him. He orders the young man to bring back the head of the monster Medusa, one of the three Gorgons, whose gaze turns people to stone. The goddess Athene helps Perseus, giving him a shield and telling him how to get winged sandals, a hat of invisibility, and a sack that will hold Medusa's head. The god Hermes also gives him a diamond sword. Perseus sets off and eventually reaches the Gorgons. Gazing at Medusa's reflection in his shield, he severs her head and escapes her two fearsome sisters. On the way home he rescues Andromeda, princess of Ethiopia, from a sea monster and then marries her. Back on the island, Perseus finds Polydectes persecuting Danae, and turns him to stone. Perseus then goes to Argos to find his grandfather, but Acrisios flees in terror to Larissa, where an athletic contest is being held. Perseus takes part and unwittingly kills his grandfather, sitting in the audience, during the discus throw. The oracle's prophecy is fulfilled at last, and Perseus becomes king of Argos.

Medusa's Head *and* Perseus and the Gorgon's Head

Literary Focus
Mythic Heroes

What characters can fly, become invisible, and call on other magical powers in the fight against evil? You'll probably think of modern comic-book characters, such as Batman or Superman. In "Medusa's Head" you'll meet an ancient mythic hero, Perseus, who can do all these things—and more.

In the world of **myth,** heroes do things we wish we could do and things we're glad we don't have to do. Heroes in myths represent the hopes and fears of the people who created them.

Heroes in myths are often helped by gods. Sometimes they are gods themselves. These superheroes usually have magical powers, and they always face great difficulties and challenges (like slaying a monster). Often a mythic hero saves a whole society from ruin.

Reading Skills 📖
Dialogue with the Text

As you read this story, jot down your responses to it. Ask questions about unfamiliar words, and try to predict what will happen next.

Make the Connection
Talk It Over

Reading Standard 3.1 Identify the forms of fiction, and describe the major characteristics of each form.

The idea of fate is important in this Greek myth. *Fate* refers to a power that is believed to decide the future no matter what we do. You learn right away in this story that a king has received bad news

from an oracle (ôr′ə·kəl)—a priest or priestess who can foretell the future. He has learned that one day he will be killed by his own grandson.

Think about this situation for a few minutes. Then, with several classmates, discuss what it would be like to know what will happen in the future.

Vocabulary Development

These are the words you'll learn as you read "Medusa's Head":

descended (dē·send′id) *v.:* moved to a lower place; came down. *Out of pity, Zeus, king of the Greek gods, descended to the imprisoned girl.*

perplexity (pər·plek′sə·tē) *n.:* bewilderment; confusion. *In his perplexity, Perseus turned to Athene.*

perpetual (pər·pech′oo·əl) *adj.:* permanent; constant. *Medusa's sisters live in a place of perpetual twilight, where there is neither day nor night.*

recesses (rē′ses·əz) *n.:* inner places. *The sisters scrambled to the recesses of the cave after Perseus stole their sight.*

hovered (huv′ərd) *v.:* remained suspended in the air. *Wearing the winged sandals, Perseus hovered high above the rocks.*

208 Chapter 4 Forms and Patterns: Stories and Explanations

RESOURCES

Planning
■ *One-Stop Planner* CD-ROM with Test Generator
■ *On Course: Mapping Instruction*

Media
■ *Audio CD Library*
  ■ disc 6

Reading
■ *Interactive Reading*
  ■ Graphic Organizer: Myth Chart, p. 153

Differentiating Instruction
■ *Lesson Plans for Language Development*
  ■ English-Language Learners, pp. 87–89, 91, 102–103, 109
  ■ Special Education Students, pp. 90, 102–103, 109

Characters and Places

King Acrisios (ə·crē′sē·ōs′) **of Argos** (är′gäs′): Argos was an ancient city and kingdom in southern Greece. Also spelled Acrisius.

Proitos (prō·ē′tōs): brother of King Acrisios.

Danae (dan′ā·ē′): daughter of King Acrisios. She bears Zeus's son Perseus.

Apollo: Greek god of light, medicine, poetry, and prophecy. The oracle of Apollo was a priest or priestess through whom the god was believed to speak.

Zeus (zoōs): king of the Greek gods.

Dictys (dic′tis): fisherman, brother of Polydectes. He and Polydectes live on the island of Seriphos. Also spelled Seriphus.

Polydectes (päl′ē·dek′tēz): king of Seriphos.

Perseus (pʉr′sē·əs): son of Danae and Zeus.

Gorgons: three fearsome sisters with brass hands, gold wings, and serpentlike scales. Medusa, the youngest Gorgon, has snakes for hair and a face so terrible that it turns to stone anyone who looks at it.

Athene (ə·thē′nē): Greek goddess of crafts, war, and wisdom. Her name is also spelled *Athena*.

Phorcides (fôr′sə·dēz): three sisters who live in a cave and have only one eye and one tooth between them.

Hermes (hʉr′mēz′): messenger of the gods.

Cepheus (sē′fē·əs): king of Ethiopia.

Cassiopeia (kas′ē·ō·pē′ə): queen of Ethiopia.

Andromeda (an·dräm′ə·də): daughter of King Cepheus and Queen Cassiopeia. She has been chained to a rock near the sea to calm the anger of the god Poseidon.

Nereus (nir′ē·əs): a minor sea god.

Poseidon (pō·sī′dən): god of the sea.

Medusa's Head / Perseus and the Gorgon's Head **209**

Standards Starter

Build background. The characters are listed on p. 209 in order of their appearance. To help students become familiar with them, ask students to classify the characters by using the following questions.

■ Which characters are gods? [Apollo, Zeus, Hermes, Nereus, Poseidon]

■ Which character is a goddess? [Athene]

■ Which characters are kings? [Acrisios, Polydectes, Cepheus]

■ Which character is a queen? [Cassiopeia]

■ Which characters are princesses? [Danae, Andromeda]

■ Which characters are brothers of kings? [Proitos, Dictys]

■ Which character is the child of a human and a god? [Perseus]

■ Which characters are groups of sisters? [Gorgons, Phorcides]

Preview Vocabulary

Have students use context clues to identify the best Vocabulary word for each blank.

1. Never stopping, the planets are in _____ orbit around the sun. [perpetual]

2. As the day ended, the sun _____ toward the western horizon. [descended]

3. Peering into the dark _____ of the cave, we saw sleeping bats. [recesses]

4. The rabbit's vanishing left the magician's audience in a state of _____. [perplexity]

5. The kite _____ high in the air, buoyed by the breeze. [hovered]

Assign the Reading

Play the audio recording of this selection as students follow along in their textbooks. Stop at the point where Perseus reaches the stone gorge where the Gorgons lie sleeping. Students reading at grade level can finish the selection as homework or in class while you work with small groups of students having difficulty with the text. You may want to keep one book open to the cartoon "Perseus and the Gorgon's Head" (pp. 218–221) to help struggling students follow the plot details and characters in "Medusa's Head." Students reading above grade level can read the remainder of the selection and answer the Focus On questions (p. 222) as homework.

HOMEWORK

▶ **Resources Reminder**

Reading

■ *Interactive Reading*
  ■ Graphic Organizer: Myth Chart, p. 153

The Head of Medusa by Peter Paul Rubens (1577–1640). Oil on canvas.
Kunsthistorisches Museum, Gemaeldegalerie, Vienna, Austria.

MEDUSA'S HEAD

GREEK MYTH, RETOLD BY *Olivia Coolidge*

210 Chapter 4 Forms and Patterns: Stories and Explanations

DIFFERENTIATING INSTRUCTION

Learners Having Difficulty
Modeling. To help students read "Medusa's Head" and "Perseus and the Gorgon's Head," model the reading skill of having a dialogue with the text. Say: "As I read, I'll jot down my questions and thoughts about what's happening in the story. I'll also make notes about unfamiliar words and try to predict what will happen next in the story." Encourage students, as they read, to ask themselves: "What questions occur to me as I'm reading? What's my response to what I just read? What do I think is likely to happen next?"

English-Language Learners
Learners having difficulty may benefit from reading the cartoon strip "Perseus and the

King Acrisios of Argos was a hard, selfish man. He hated his brother, Proitos, who later drove him from his kingdom, and he cared nothing for his daughter, Danae. His whole heart was set on having a son who should succeed him, but since many years went by and still he had only the one daughter, he sent a message to the oracle of Apollo to ask whether he should have more children of his own. The answer of the oracle was terrible. Acrisios should have no son, but his daughter, Danae, would bear him a grandchild who should grow up to kill him. At these words Acrisios was beside himself with fear and rage. Swearing that Danae should never have a child to murder him, he had a room built underground and lined all through with brass. Thither he conducted Danae and shut her up, bidding her spend the rest of her life alone.

It is possible to thwart the plans of mortal men, but never those of the gods. Zeus himself looked with pity on the unfortunate girl, and it is said he descended to her through the tiny hole that gave light and air to her chamber, pouring himself down into her lap in the form of a shower of gold.

When word came to the king from those who brought food and drink to his daughter that the girl was with child, Acrisios was angry and afraid. He would have liked best to murder both Danae and her infant son, Perseus, but he did not dare for fear of the gods' anger at so hideous a crime. He made, therefore, a great chest of wood with bands of brass about it. Shutting up the girl and her baby inside, he cast them into the sea, thinking that they would either drown or starve.

Again the gods came to the help of Danae, for they caused the planks of the chest to swell until they fitted tightly and let no water in.

The chest floated for some days and was cast up at last on an island. There Dictys, a fisherman, found it and took Danae to his brother, Polydectes, who was king of the island. Danae was made a servant in the palace, yet before many years had passed, both Dictys and Polydectes had fallen in love with the silent, golden-haired girl. She in her heart preferred Dictys, yet since his brother was king, she did not dare to make her choice. Therefore she hung always over Perseus, pretending that mother love left her no room for any other, and year after year a silent frown would cross Polydectes' face as he saw her caress the child.

At last, Perseus became a young man, handsome and strong beyond the common and a leader among the youths of the island, though he was but the son of a poor servant. Then it seemed to Polydectes that if he could once get rid of Perseus, he could force Danae to become his wife, whether she would or not. Meanwhile, in order to lull the young man's suspicions, he pretended that he intended to marry a certain noble maiden and would collect a wedding gift for her. Now the custom was that this gift of the bridegroom to the bride was in part his own and in part put together from the marriage presents of his friends and relatives. All the young men, therefore, brought Polydectes a present, excepting Perseus, who was his servant's son and possessed nothing to bring. Then Polydectes said to the others, "This young man owes me more than any of you, since I took him in and brought him

---

Vocabulary

descended (dē·send'id) v.: moved to a lower place; came down.

Medusa's Head **211**

Gorgon's Head" on pp. 218–221 before reading this selection. The informal language of the cartoon can minimize problems with the highly formal language of "Medusa's Head," and the drawings can help students identify the numerous characters and the complicated plot events.

HOMEWORK

▶ **Resources Reminder**
For lessons designed for both intermediate and advanced English-language learners, see *Lesson Plans for Language Development,* pp. 87–89, 91, 102–103, 109.

Special Education Students
For lessons designed for special education students, see *Lesson Plans for Language Development,* pp. 90, 102–103, 109.

DIRECT TEACHING

▶ **Resources Reminder**

Media
- *Audio CD Library*
  - disc 6

A **Content-Area Connections**
CULTURE

Primogeniture. In kingdoms such as Argos, a ruler's eldest male child would succeed the ruler. To have no son was to have no successor. This line of succession was part of the system of *primogeniture,* in which the eldest son was sole legal heir to his parents' estate. Traces of the system still remain in modern European monarchies where the monarch's eldest son inherits the throne. Today, however, the eldest daughter can usually succeed to the throne if there are no sons.

B **Literary Focus**
GRADE-LEVEL STANDARD
❓ **Forms of fiction: Myths.** In this myth, what powers does the god Zeus have? [He can see everything in the lives of mortals; he can change into different shapes and materials, such as a "shower of gold."]

C **Reading Skills**
❓ **Dialogue with the text.** What questions occur to you as you read this section of the story? [Possible responses: Why does Acrisios hate his brother? What is an oracle? Where is Danae's mother? Why doesn't Danae's mother protect her? Couldn't the king and his wife adopt? What kind of person is Danae? What will happen to her and the baby?]

D **Literary Focus**
GRADE-LEVEL STANDARD
❓ **Mythic heroes.** What qualities does the young Perseus already have in common with mythic heroes? [He is the son of a god and a human; he is unusually strong and handsome; others look to him as a leader.]

Medusa's Head **211**

A Reading Skills

? Dialogue with the text. What do you think Polydectes might ask Perseus to bring him? Why? [Possible response: Polydectes will probably ask for something dangerous or impossible to get, since he wants to get rid of Perseus.]

B Learners Having Difficulty

? Identifying sequence. What steps must Perseus take in order to slay the Gorgon? [First, he must go to the sisters Phorcides. Then, he must find the nymphs, who will provide a hat of darkness, winged sandals, and a knapsack. Next, he will receive a shield from Athene and a sword from Hermes. Finally, when Perseus is near the Gorgon, he must turn his eyes away and use her reflection in the shield to guide his sword.]

C Literary Focus
GRADE-LEVEL STANDARD

? Forms of fiction: Myths. How do gods and goddesses help Perseus? [Athene gives him advice, promises him a shield, and says she will be with him on his quest. Hermes will give him a magical sword.]

VIEWING THE ART

Michelangelo Merisi, known as Caravaggio (1573–1610), was a master of realism and naturalism. He used ordinary people as models and employed extreme contrasts of light and dark, known as *chiaroscuro,* to give his paintings an intense, dramatic quality. **Activity.** Ask students to describe the features of the painting that seem faithful to the description of Medusa. Ask them how they picture Medusa.

Medusa by Michelangelo Caravaggio (1573–1610). Uffizi, Florence, Italy. Scala/Art Resource, New York.

up in my own house, and yet he gives me nothing."

Perseus answered in anger at the injustice of the charge, "I have nothing of my own, Polydectes, yet ask me what you will, and I will fetch it, for I owe you my life."

At this Polydectes smiled, for it was what he had intended, and he answered, "Fetch me, if this is your boast, the Gorgon's head."

Now the Gorgons, who lived far off on the shores of the ocean, were three fearful sisters with hands of brass, wings of gold, and scales like a serpent. Two of them had scaly heads and tusks like the wild boar, but the third, Medusa, had the face of a beautiful woman with hair of writhing serpents, and so terrible was her expression that all who looked on it were immediately turned to stone. This much Perseus knew of the Gorgons, but of how to find or kill them, he had no idea. Nevertheless, he had given his promise, and though he saw now the satisfaction of King Polydectes, he was bound to keep his word. In his perplexity, he prayed to the wise goddess Athene, who came to him

in a vision and promised him her aid.

"First, you must go," she said, "to the sisters Phorcides, who will tell you the way to the nymphs who guard the hat of darkness, the winged sandals, and the knapsack which can hold the Gorgon's head. Then I will give you a shield, and my brother Hermes will give you a sword, which shall be made of adamant, the hardest rock. For nothing else can kill the Gorgon, since so venomous is her blood that a mortal sword, when plunged in it, is eaten away. But when you come to the Gorgons, invisible in your hat of darkness, turn your eyes away from them and look only on their reflection in your gleaming shield. Thus you may kill the monster without yourself being turned to stone. Pass her sisters by, for they are immortal, but smite off the head of Medusa with the hair of writhing snakes. Then put it in your knapsack and return, and I will be with you."

The vision ended, and with the aid of Athene, Perseus set out on the long journey to seek the Phorcides. These live in a dim cavern in the far north, where nights and days are one and where the whole earth is overspread with perpetual twilight. There sat the three old women mumbling to one another, crouched in a dim heap together, for they had but one eye and one tooth between them, which they passed from hand to hand. Perseus came quietly behind them, and as they fumbled for the eye, he put his strong, brown hand next to one of the long,

Vocabulary

perplexity (pər·plek′sə·tē) *n.:* bewilderment; confusion.

perpetual (pər·pech′oo·əl) *adj.:* permanent; constant.

CONTENT-AREA CONNECTIONS

Science

Resources: Minerals. Students may consider Hermes's gift to Perseus even more impressive when they learn that *adamant* is an old name for diamond. Athene accurately describes adamant as "the hardest rock": Diamond is the only material rated ten on the Mohs scale, used for evaluating the relative hardness of minerals. The Mohs scale classifies minerals by determining which other minerals can scratch them.

Activity. Group students to research additional properties (color, weight, cleavage) of diamond and two of the other hard minerals familiar as gemstones. Have students use their findings to create illustrated descriptions of swords that could be made from each of the minerals they have investigated.

SMALL-GROUP

yellow ones, so that the old crone thought that it was her sister's and put the eye into it. There was a high scream of anger when they discovered the theft, and much clawing and groping in the dim recesses of the cavern. But they were helpless in their blindness and Perseus could laugh at them. At length, for the price of their eye, they told him how to reach the nymphs, and Perseus, laying the eye quickly in the hand of the nearest sister, fled as fast as he could before she could use it.

Again it was a far journey to the garden of the nymphs, where it is always sunshine and the trees bear golden apples. But the nymphs are friends of the wise gods and hate the monsters of darkness and the spirits of anger and despair. Therefore, they received Perseus with rejoicing and put the hat of darkness on his head, while on his feet they bound the golden, winged sandals, which are those Hermes wears when he runs down the slanting sunbeams or races along the pathways of the wind. Next, Perseus put on his back the silver sack with the gleaming tassels of gold, and flung across his shoulder the black-sheathed sword that was the gift of Hermes. On his left arm he fitted the shield that Athene gave, a gleaming silver shield like a mirror, plain without any marking. Then he sprang into the air and ran, invisible like the rushing wind, far out over the white-capped sea, across the yellow sands of the eastern desert, over strange streams and towering mountains, until at last he came to the shores of the distant ocean which flowed round all the world.

There was a gray gorge of stone by the ocean's edge, where lay Medusa and her

Vocabulary
recesses (rē′ses·əz) *n.:* inner places.

Medusa. Mosaic.   The Athens Museum.

Medusa's Head   213

D Literary Focus
GRADE-LEVEL STANDARD
❷ Mythic heroes. Athene doesn't tell Perseus how to get the information he needs from the Phorcides. How do his actions show that he has unusual abilities befitting a mythic hero? [Possible responses: He quickly sizes up the situation, cleverly seizes the advantage, boldly demands what he wants, and laughs at the horrific sisters.]

E Reading Skills
❷ Dialogue with the text. Characters in myths do things we wish we could do, as well as things we're glad we don't have to do. What can Perseus do that you wish you could do? [Possible responses: run in the air, be invisible.] What does he do that you're glad you don't have to do? [Possible responses: handle the Phorcides' eye; track down and kill a monster; risk being turned to stone.]

DEVELOPING FLUENCY

Activity. Guide students in presenting an oral retelling of "Medusa's Head." First, divide the myth into four parts: (1) from the beginning through Perseus's young manhood; (2) from Polydectes's challenge through Perseus's visit to the Phorcides; (3) from Perseus's visit to the nymphs through his slaying of Medusa; and (4) Perseus's journey home and the accidental killing of his grandfather. Then, place students in groups of four, and assign each member one part of the myth. Remind students to focus on action that will appeal to younger listeners. Lastly, invite a group of younger students to hear the retelling and discuss which parts of the myth they found most memorable and why.

CROSS-AGE

VIEWING THE ART

This Greek sculpture appears on a building in Selinunte, an early Greek settlement on the southern coast of Sicily. This is a *relief sculpture,* which means that it has figures that project from surrounding plane surfaces. Many of the figures in ancient Greek sculpture wear what is called the "archaic smile," a mysterious small smile that does not always fit either the figure or the situation.

Activity. First, have students identify the two figures on the right. [Perseus, Medusa] (The third figure is a man turned to stone.) Then, ask how the figure of Medusa differs from her description in the myth. [The myth says her face is beautiful but has a horrifying expression. Her face in this relief is anything but beautiful.] Finally, have students compare the figure of Medusa in this relief with the figure on p. 210.

Galleria Nazionale, Palermo, Italy Scala/Art Resource, New York.

Perseus beheading the Gorgon Medusa, from a temple in Selinunte, an ancient Greek colony in Sicily.

sisters sleeping in the dim depths of the rock. All up and down the cleft, the stones took fantastic shapes of trees, beasts, birds, or serpents. Here and there, a man who had looked on the terrible Medusa stood forever with horror on his face. Far over the twilit gorge Perseus hovered invisible, while he loosened the pale, strange sword from its black sheath. Then, with his face turned away and eyes on the silver shield, he dropped, slow and silent as a falling leaf, down through the rocky cleft, twisting and turning past countless strange gray shapes, down from the bright sunlight into a chill, dim shadow echoing and reechoing with the dashing of waves on the tumbled rocks beneath. There on the heaped stones lay the Gorgons sleeping together in the dimness, and even as he looked on them in the shield, Perseus felt stiff with horror at the sight.

Two of the Gorgons lay sprawled together,

Vocabulary
hovered (huv'ərd) *v.:* remained suspended in the air.

Geography

The world of the ancient Greeks. Perseus begins traveling almost as soon as he is born, and he visits many places in the course of his quest for Medusa's head. The places mentioned in the myth reflect the ancient Greeks' geographic knowledge of Africa and the Middle East, as well as the Mediterranean region. Have students consult the map on p. 209 and use it to trace Perseus's travels, beginning with his voyage in the chest from Argos to Seriphos.

Activity. Direct students to create picture postcards depicting places Perseus sees on his quest for Medusa's head. On the backs of the postcards, have students write notes that Perseus might have sent to Danae, telling what happened in those places.

INDIVIDUAL

shaped like women, yet scaled from head to foot as serpents are. Instead of hands they had gleaming claws like eagles, and their feet were dragons' feet. Skinny metallic wings like bats' wings hung from their shoulders. Their faces were neither snake nor woman, but part both, like faces in a nightmare. These two lay arm in arm and never stirred. Only the blue snakes still hissed and writhed round the pale, set face of Medusa, as though even in sleep she were troubled by an evil dream. She lay by herself, arms outstretched, face upwards, more beautiful and terrible than living man may bear. All the crimes and madnesses of the world rushed into Perseus' mind as he gazed at her image in the shield. Horror stiffened his arm as he hovered over her with his sword uplifted. Then he shut his eyes to the vision and in the darkness struck.

There was a great cry and a hissing. Perseus groped for the head and seized it by the limp and snaky hair. Somehow he put it in his knapsack and was up and off, for at the dreadful scream the sister Gorgons had awakened. Now they were after him, their sharp claws grating against his silver shield. Perseus strained forward on the pathway of the wind like a runner, and behind him the two sisters came, smelling out the prey they could not see. Snakes darted from their girdles,° foam flew from their tusks, and the great wings beat the air. Yet the winged sandals were even swifter than they, and Perseus fled like the hunted deer with the speed of desperation. Presently the horrible noise grew faint behind him, the hissing of snakes and the sound of the bat wings died away. At last the Gorgons could smell him no longer and returned home unavenged.

° **girdles** *n.*: belts or sashes.

By now, Perseus was over the Libyan desert, and as the blood from the horrible head touched the sand, it changed to serpents, from which the snakes of Africa are descended.

The storms of the Libyan desert blew against Perseus in clouds of eddying sand, until not even the divine sandals could hold him on his course. Far out to sea he was blown, and then north. Finally, whirled around the heavens like a cloud of mist, he alighted in the distant west, where the giant Atlas held up on his shoulders the heavens from the earth. There the weary giant, crushed under the load of centuries, begged Perseus to show him Medusa's head. Perseus uncovered for him the dreadful thing, and Atlas was changed to the mighty mountain whose rocks rear up to reach the sky near the gateway to the Atlantic. Perseus himself, returning eastwards and still battling with the wind, was driven south to the land of Ethiopia, where King Cepheus reigned with his wife, Cassiopeia.

As Perseus came wheeling in like a gull from the ocean, he saw a strange sight. Far out to sea the water was troubled, seething and boiling as though stirred by a great force moving in its depths. Huge, sullen waves were starting far out and washing inland over sunken trees and flooded houses. Many miles of land were under water, and as he sped over them, he saw the muddy sea lapping around the foot of a black, upstanding rock. Here on a ledge above the water's edge stood a young girl chained by the arms, lips parted, eyes open and staring, face white as her linen garment. She might have been a statue, so still she stood, while the light breeze fluttered her dress and stirred her loosened hair. As Perseus looked at her and

A Learners Having Difficulty

❓ **Identifying details.** Which details tell you that this is a damsel in distress? [Her arms are chained to a ledge; her staring eyes, open mouth, and extreme pallor show that she is terrified.]

B Literary Focus
REVIEW STANDARD

❓ **Archetypal patterns.** A water monster is an *archetype,* an image or character that recurs in tales around the world. What other tales involving water monsters do you know? [Possible responses: Students might mention the Old Testament story of Jonah and the mighty whale or tales of the Loch Ness monster. You might also tell students about the Norse myths of the Midgard serpent, Gilgamesh's loss of his prize to a great serpent in a spring, and Krishna's battle with a serpent in a lake.]

C Reading Skills

❓ **Dialogue with the text.** What is your initial reaction to Andromeda and her situation? Why? [Some students may think she will endanger Perseus; others may sympathize with her and be eager for Perseus to rescue her.]

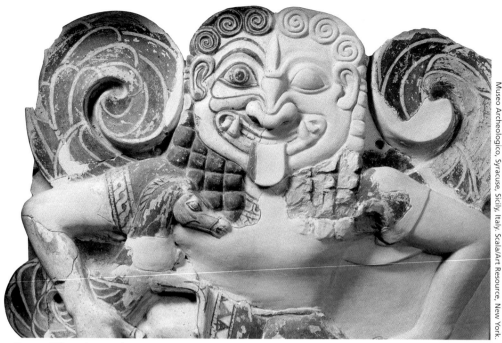

Gorgon (6th century B.C.).

Museo Archeologico, Syracuse, Sicily, Italy. Scala/Art Resource, New York.

looked at the sea, the water began to boil again, and miles out a long gray scaly back of vast length lifted itself above the flood. At that, there was a shriek from a distant knoll where he could dimly see the forms of people, but the girl shrank a little and said nothing. Then Perseus, taking off the hat of darkness, alighted near the maiden to talk to her, and she, though nearly mad with terror, found words at last to tell him her tale.

Her name was Andromeda, and she was the only child of the king and of his wife, Cassiopeia. Queen Cassiopeia was exceedingly beautiful, so that all people marveled at her. She herself was proud of her dark eyes, her white, slender fingers, and her long black hair, so proud that she had been heard to boast that she was fairer even than the sea nymphs, who are daughters of Nereus. At this, Nereus in wrath stirred up Poseidon, who came flooding in over the land, covering it far and wide. Not content with this, he sent a vast monster from the dark depths of the bottomless sea to ravage the whole coast of Ethiopia. When the unfortunate king and queen had sought the advice of the oracle on how to appease the god, they had been ordered to sacrifice their only daughter to the sea monster Poseidon had sent. Not daring for their people's sake to disobey, they had chained her to this rock, where she now awaited the beast who should devour her.

Perseus comforted Andromeda as he stood by her on the rock, and she shrank closer against him while the great gray back writhed its half-mile length slowly towards the land. Then, bidding Andromeda hide her face, Perseus sprang once more into the air, unveiling the dreadful head of dead Medusa to the monster, which reared its dripping jaws yards high into the air. The mighty tail stiffened all of a sudden, the boiling of the water ceased, and only the gentle waves of the receding ocean lapped around a long, gray ridge of stone. Then Perseus freed Andromeda and restored her to her father and beautiful mother. Thereafter, with their consent, he married her amid scenes of tremendous rejoicing, and with his bride set sail at last for the kingdom of Polydectes.

Polydectes had lost no time on the departure of Perseus. First he had begged Danae to become his wife, and then he had threatened her. Undoubtedly, he would have got his way by force if Danae had not fled in terror to Dictys. The two took refuge at the altar of a temple whence Polydectes did not dare drag them away. So matters stood when Perseus returned. Polydectes was enraged to see him, for he had hoped at least that Danae's most powerful protector would never return. But now, seeing him famous and with a king's daughter to wife, he could not contain himself. Openly he laughed at the tale of Perseus, saying that the hero had never killed the Gorgon, only pretended to, and that now he was claiming an honor he did not deserve. At this, Perseus, enraged by the insult and by reports of his mother's persecution, said to him, "You asked me for the Gorgon's head. Behold it!" And with that he lifted it high, and Polydectes became stone.

Then Perseus left Dictys to be king of that island, but he himself went back to the Grecian mainland to seek out his grandfather, Acrisios, who was once again king of Argos.

First, however, he gave back to the gods the gifts they had given him. Hermes took back the golden sandals and the hat of darkness, for both are his. But Athene took Medusa's head, and she hung it on a fleece around her neck as part of her battle equipment, where it may be seen in statues and portraits of the warlike goddess.

Perseus took ship for Greece, but his fame had gone before him, and King Acrisios fled secretly from Argos in terror, since he remembered the prophecy and feared that Perseus had come to avenge the wrongs of Danae. The trembling old Acrisios took refuge in Larissa, where it happened the king was holding a great athletic contest in honor of his dead father.

Heroes from all over Greece, among whom was Perseus, came to the games. As Perseus was competing at the discus throwing, he threw high into the air and far beyond the rest. A strong wind caught the discus as it spun, so that it left the course marked out for it and was carried into the stands. People scrambled away to right and left. Only Acrisios was not nimble enough. The heavy weight fell full on his foot and crushed his toes, and at that, the feeble old man, already weakened by his terrors, died from the shock. Thus the prophecy of Apollo was fulfilled at last; Acrisios was killed by his grandson. Then Perseus came into his kingdom, where he reigned with Andromeda long and happily.

To read about Olivia Coolidge, see Meet the Writer on page 154.

Medusa's Head **217**

To read about Olivia Coolidge, see Meet the Writer on page 154.

Resources Reminder

Media

- *Audio CD Library*
  - disc 6

A Reading Skills

? Dialogue with the text. What appeals most to you about the beginning of this cartoon strip? [Possible responses: funny animal characters; sarcastic; informal; a little like slapstick; witty; in color.]

B Literary Focus
REVIEW STANDARD

? Archetypal patterns. What other tales do you know in which a young hero floats in a chest, basket, or other unlikely container? [Possible responses: Moses in his basket on the Nile; Osiris imprisoned in a chest by Seth, floating across the ocean; Japan's legendary Momotaro, found floating downriver inside a peach.]

C Literary Focus
GRADE-LEVEL STANDARD

? Mythic heroes. In this cartoon version of the myth, which details suggest that young Perseus may be a mythic hero? [He survives the voyage in the wooden chest; he's strong and handsome; he's confident and brave.]

D English-Language Learners

Slang. Let students know that *drip* is a derogatory slang term meaning "undesirable person."

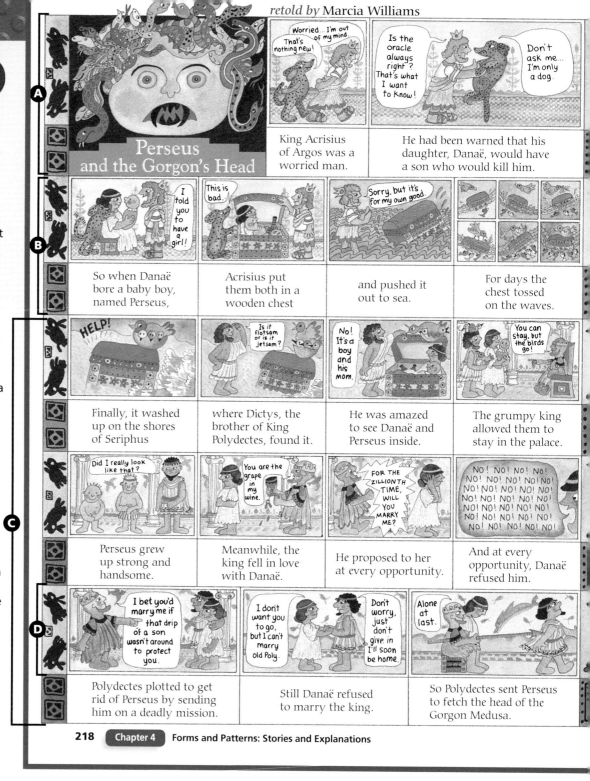

retold by Marcia Williams

Perseus and the Gorgon's Head

King Acrisius of Argos was a worried man.

He had been warned that his daughter, Danaë, would have a son who would kill him.

So when Danaë bore a baby boy, named Perseus,

Acrisius put them both in a wooden chest

and pushed it out to sea.

For days the chest tossed on the waves.

Finally, it washed up on the shores of Seriphus

where Dictys, the brother of King Polydectes, found it.

He was amazed to see Danaë and Perseus inside.

The grumpy king allowed them to stay in the palace.

Perseus grew up strong and handsome.

Meanwhile, the king fell in love with Danaë.

He proposed to her at every opportunity.

And at every opportunity, Danaë refused him.

Polydectes plotted to get rid of Perseus by sending him on a deadly mission.

Still Danaë refused to marry the king.

So Polydectes sent Perseus to fetch the head of the Gorgon Medusa.

DIFFERENTIATING INSTRUCTION

Learners Having Difficulty
Dramatization. Encourage students to prepare and perform "Perseus and the Gorgon's Head" as a brief play, using the cartoon as their script. The performance should run about five to ten minutes. Remind students to include sound effects, background music, simple props/costumes, and appropriate actions, gestures, and body language.

Encourage students to capture the playful spirit of the cartoon.

(Pages 218–221) *Perseus and the Gorgon's Head* from the book *Greek Myths for Young Children* copyright ©1991 by Marcia Williams.

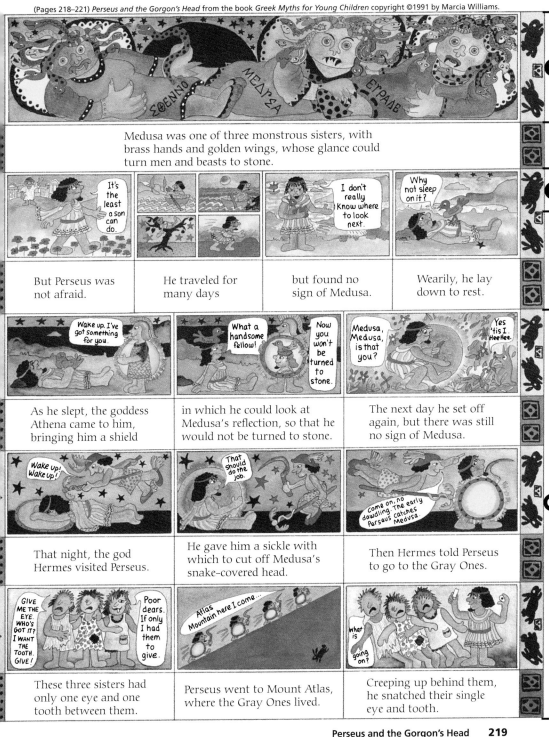

E Reading Skills

? Dialogue with the text.
What information does this cartoon give you about the Gorgons? [Possible responses: It shows them as so big they can barely fit in the panel; it shows them all as ugly and fierce, with tusks or fangs and with snakes for hair; it shows their names in Greek, printed on their clothes.]

F English-Language Learners

? Interpreting idioms. The "it" that the bird tells Perseus to "sleep on" is a decision: He needs to decide where to look next. *Sleep on it* means "wait until morning to decide." How do the pictures make this meaning clear? [The pictures show Perseus pausing to sleep and think about his next action.]

G Literary Focus
GRADE-LEVEL STANDARD

? Mythic heroes. Does Perseus seem heroic in this version of the myth? Why or why not? [Possible responses: Yes, because he shows great bravery, is helped by the gods, and performs superhuman deeds; no, because he is comical.]

Perseus and the Gorgon's Head   219

A English-Language Learners

❓ Building background knowledge. In this cartoon, the nymphs give Perseus a bag in which to put Medusa's head. In "Medusa's Head," they give him a knapsack—a specific kind of bag also called a *backpack, satchel,* or *bookbag.* As the pictures here show, a bag is carried in the hand. How do you think a knapsack, or backpack, is carried? [on the back]

B Literary Focus
GRADE-LEVEL STANDARD
❓ Forms of fiction: Myths. What great dangers does Perseus face in these scenes from the myth? [He might be killed or turned to stone.] What might happen to others if he fails? [His mother might be forced to marry a man she detests.]

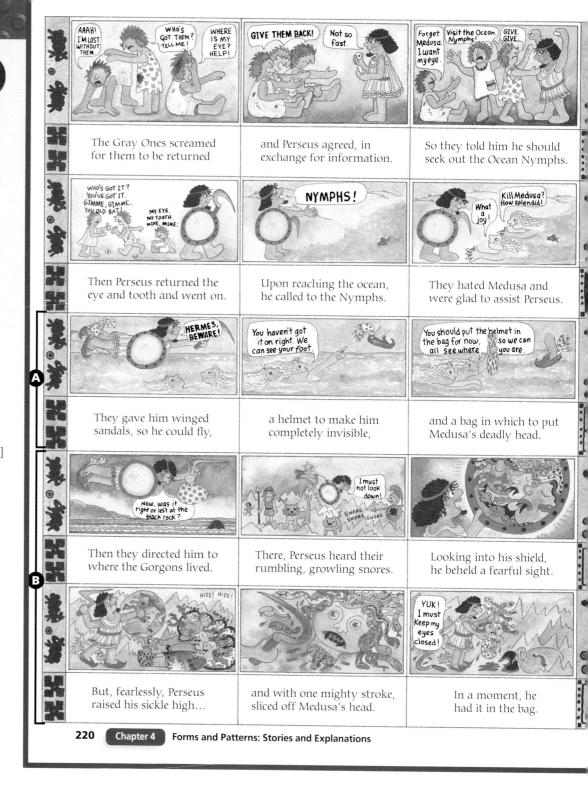

220 | Chapter 4 | Forms and Patterns: Stories and Explanations

As he leapt into the air, Medusa's sisters woke.

Quickly, Perseus donned the helmet and instantly vanished from their sight.

His journey home was not an easy one.

But, after a year, he arrived at Seriphus.

Perseus found his mother hiding from King Polydectes in the temple.

So he went on to the palace.

Polydectes was convinced that Perseus had long since been turned to stone.

The king was horrified to see him alive.

But before he could speak, Perseus pulled out Medusa's head.

Its gaze immediately turned the king to stone.

Perseus then rescued his mother and, before leaving the island, crowned Dictys the new King of Seriphus.

They sailed for Argos where, later, Perseus accidentally killed King Acrisius, as the oracle had predicted.

Perseus and the Gorgon's Head 221

C Advanced Learners

Puns. Ask if any students can explain the humor in the right-hand frame. If necessary, tell them that *Fanged if I know* is a pun on *Hanged if I know*, a slang expression for "I don't know." Ask students to identify the visual element to the pun. [The Gorgons have fangs.]

D Reading Skills

? Dialogue with the text. What do you think of the humor in this cartoon version of the myth? [Some students will enjoy the wordplay, burlesque action, and irreverent comments; others may find the humor corny. Encourage students to point out examples that support their opinions.]

E Literary Focus
GRADE-LEVEL STANDARD
? Forms of fiction: Myths. Which ancient Greek belief is emphasized by the final panel? [The belief that fate is beyond human control.]

Monitoring students' progress. Have students summarize the differences between the story of Perseus told in this cartoon and the story told in "Medusa's Head."

Have each student choose an episode from the myth that corresponds to an episode in the cartoon strip. Direct students to read the myth episode aloud at home to a parent or guardian, and then to show the corresponding part of the cartoon strip. Have students and adults discuss what they like most, and least, about each version. Afterward, with the adults' permission, have students report in class on their responses.

INDEPENDENT PRACTICE

Literary Response and Analysis

Reading Check

1. b. Acrisios locks Danae in an underground chamber.

e. Danae and Perseus are found by Dictys and made servants to King Polydectes. Both men fall in love with Danae.

g. Athene tells Perseus how to get Medusa's head.

i. Perseus forces the Phorcides to tell him how to reach the nymphs.

k. The nymphs give Perseus tools to help him conquer Medusa.

m. Perseus cuts off Medusa's head and shows it to Atlas, who turns to stone.

o. Perseus rescues Andromeda.

q. Perseus goes to find Acrisios.

Interpretations

2. Possible answer: Perseus is heroic, predictable, too idealized to identify with. Some students may say we have no real-life superheroes who literally fly or kill monsters; others may point out that astronauts fly; scientists kill monstrous viruses; humanitarians rescue people; and artists, athletes, and performers accomplish other wonders.

3. Perseus is part god, son of Zeus. He is bold, brave, strong, and handsome. The gods aid him on his quest, he kills a monster, and he helps many people.

4. In this myth, fate is inevitable, even for a king. Some students may say we can control our own destinies; others may counter that some events are beyond human control.

5. Students should cite specific films or television shows and explain which mythic elements their choices share with the story of Perseus.

Literary Response and Analysis

Reading Check

1. Fill in the missing events in this **summary** of Perseus's story.

a. Acrisios is told that he will be killed by his grandson.

b. _____

c. Zeus visits Danae as a shower of gold.

d. Perseus and his mother are cast out to sea.

e. _____

f. King Polydectes orders Perseus to bring back Medusa's head.

g. _____

h. Perseus finds the sisters Phorcides.

i. _____

j. Perseus visits the nymphs.

k. _____

l. Perseus finds Medusa.

m. _____

n. Perseus sees Andromeda chained to a rock.

o. _____

p. Perseus turns Polydectes to stone.

q. _____

r. Perseus kills Acrisios with a discus.

Reading Standard 3.1 Identify the forms of fiction, and describe the major characteristics of each form.

Interpretations

2. What do you think of Perseus? Do we have heroes like him today? Refer to your reading notes for your responses to the story.

3. Why is Perseus a good example of a **mythic hero**? (Think about how he handles the challenges on his **quest** and how the gods help him.)

4. How does this **myth** illustrate the idea that no one can escape fate? What do you think of the ancient Greek belief that everything is decided in advance by fate?

5. Modern stories of action heroes often resemble ancient myths. What movies or TV shows remind you of the story of Perseus? Think about these elements in the myth:

a. the hero threatened at birth

b. the beautiful woman in danger

c. the awful monster

d. the role played by magic

e. the perils faced by the hero

f. the people who help the hero

g. the triumph of good over evil

Writing
Writing a Story

Make up a story about a character who has the power to become invisible. Jot down some ideas about the following points:

• the way the character becomes invisible

• things an invisible character can do that any visible character cannot do

• the dangers an invisible character might face

If you wish, tell your story in the form of a cartoon.

222 Chapter 4 Forms and Patterns: Stories and Explanations

DIFFERENTIATING INSTRUCTION

Learners Having Difficulty

Work with students on questions 3 and 4 especially. *Monitoring tip:* If students are unable to explain how Perseus fits the role of mythic hero (question 3), have them re-read p. 212, asking themselves "How is Perseus different from other youths?"
Writing. Have students recall movies that feature invisible characters such as *Ghost*

Dad or *The Sixth Sense.* What difficulties do these characters face?

HOMEWORK

Vocabulary Development

Clarifying Word Meanings

PRACTICE

1. Use the words *descended* and *hovered* to explain how Perseus captures Medusa's head.
2. Use the word *perplexity* to explain how Perseus feels when he's told to fetch the Gorgon's head.
3. Use the word *perpetual* to explain what Atlas's job is.
4. Use the word *recesses* to describe the den of the Gorgons.

Word Bank

descended
perplexity
perpetual
recesses
hovered

Grammar Link MINI-LESSON

Pronoun and Contraction Mix-ups

Contraction	Possessive Pronoun
it's (it is/has)	its
they're (they are)	their
you're (you are)	your
who's (who is/has)	whose

1. Use an apostrophe to show where letters are missing in a **contraction** (a shortened form of a word or group of words):

   Who's [Who is] the man holding the Gorgon's head?

2. Don't use an apostrophe with a **possessive personal pronoun.**

   They're [They are] sleeping on the rocks near their sister, Medusa.

   Andromeda, you're [you are] free, and your future looks bright.

   Whose head is that? Who's [Who is] asking?

   It's [It is] a hat of darkness that protects its owner.

PRACTICE

Write a short dialogue between Perseus and Andromeda in which Perseus explains how he killed Medusa. Use *it's* and *its*, *your* and *you're*, *their* and *they're*, and *whose* and *who's* in your dialogue.

For more help, see The Forms of Personal Pronouns, pages 177–188, and Contractions, pages 304–307, in the *Holt Handbook.*

Medusa's Head / Perseus and the Gorgon's Head   **223**

ASSESSING

Assessment
- *Progress Assessment of Reading*
  - Selection Test, p. 75

RETEACHING

For a lesson reteaching forms of fiction, see **Reteaching**, p. 489G.

Vocabulary Development

Practice
Possible Answers

1. Perseus hovered above Medusa as she slept. Then, he descended and cut off her head.
2. Perseus is filled with perplexity because he does not know how to find the Gorgons.
3. Atlas never gets a break from the perpetual task of holding up the sky.
4. The Gorgons lurk in the dim recesses of a rocky gorge by the ocean.

➤ **Resources Reminder**

Vocabulary and Spelling
- *Vocabulary Development*
  - Vocabulary Worksheet, p. 14
  - Decoding Worksheet, p. 15
  - Cumulative Vocabulary Review, p. 16
- *Spelling Lessons and Activities*
For additional practice with homophones, see pp. 18, 19.
- *Lesson Plans for Language Development*
  - Vocabulary, p. 109

Grammar Link

Practice
Possible Dialogue

Perseus. I found the Gorgons in their lair. They're pretty gruesome.

Andromeda. I'll bet it's hard to kill a monster like that.

Perseus. The trick is to look at its reflection, not at its face.

Andromeda. Whose idea was it for you to kill Medusa, anyway?

Perseus. It was a promise I made to this guy who's a king—like your father, only mean.

Andromeda. How noble! Oh, Perseus, you're my hero.

STANDARDS FOCUS, pp. 224–233

(For grade-level and review standards taught in this selection, see citations on Pupil's Edition pages.)

Prerequisite Standard

- Grade 4, Literary Response and Analysis 3.1 **Describe the structural differences of various imaginative forms of literature, including fantasies, fables, myths, legends, and fairy tales.**

Standard Coming Up in the Next Grade Level

- Grade 7, Literary Response and Analysis 3.1 **Articulate the expressed purposes and characteristics of different forms of prose (e.g., short story, novel, novella, essay).**

Reading Skills

- Identify cause and effect.

Summary *at grade level*

In the folk tale "He Lion, Bruh Bear, and Bruh Rabbit," a lion feels that as king of the forest, he is entitled to scare other animals with his boastful roar of "ME AND MYSELF." The animals ask for help from Bruh Bear and Bruh Rabbit, who tell he Lion that Man is really king of the forest and talk he Lion into going to find Man. As the rabbit and bear hide nearby, he Lion meets a hunter who shoots at him. He Lion learns his lesson and tones down his roar. In the fable "The Fox and the Crow," a trickster fox appeals to a crow's vanity to make her drop her food, which the fox then gobbles up. In the fable "The Wolf and the House Dog," a dog almost talks a hungry wolf into trading freedom for a job as a domestic animal.

He Lion, Bruh Bear, and Bruh Rabbit *and* The Fox and the Crow *and* The Wolf and the House Dog

Literary Focus
Folk Tales and Fables

Folk tales and fables have been around for thousands of years, much, much longer than novels, novellas, and short stories. Both folk tales and fables are stories that were told aloud for hundreds of years before they were written down.

The first folk tale that follows comes from Africa. On the surface, stories like this one seem to be entertaining tales about big, mean animals and small, crafty ones. But if you read between the lines, you often find that the point the storyteller is making has to do with people, not animals.

The Trickster Hero

Reading Standard 3.1 Identify the forms of fiction, and describe the major characteristics of each form.

The heroes of many folk tales are **tricksters.** They're underdogs, like the cartoon characters Mighty Mouse, Tweety the Canary, and Roadrunner. Their enemies may be big and powerful, but tricksters win every time because they're so clever—though they sometimes seem silly, even stupid. What's more, their tricks often teach important lessons. Don Coyote, Anansi the Spider, Raven—tricksters like these show up time and again in folk tales from all over the world. Brer Rabbit, who is called Bruh (Brother) Rabbit in this story, is one of the trickiest.

Reading Skills
Cause and Effect

A story's **plot** is made up of a series of related events. One event in a plot **causes** something else to happen, which is called an **effect.** The effect in turn becomes the cause of other events.

In each of the next three selections, a plot moves through a simple chain of causes and effects to its conclusion. Use a graphic organizer, such as a flowchart, to record the chain of events.

```
┌─────────┐
│ Event 1 │
└─────────┘
     ↓
┌─────────┐
│ Event 2 │
└─────────┘
     ↓
┌───────────┐
│ and so on │
└───────────┘
```

Make the Connection
Quickwrite

Would you choose to be the strongest person in the world, the smartest, or the most self-confident? Would you choose freedom over safety and comfort? Write two or three sentences explaining your choices.

RESOURCES

Planning
- *One-Stop Planner* CD-ROM with Test Generator
- *On Course: Mapping Instruction*

Media
- *Audio CD Library*
  - disc 6
- *Visual Connections*
  - Videocassette, Segments 5, 6

- *Fine Art Transparencies*
  - Transparency 8

Reading
- *Interactive Reading*
  - Graphic Organizers: Folk Tale Grid (for "He Lion..."), p. 154; Fable Chart (for Aesop fables), p. 155

He Lion, Bruh Bear, and Bruh Rabbit

African American folk tale, retold by **Virginia Hamilton**

Say that he Lion would get up each and every mornin. Stretch and walk around. He'd roar, "ME AND MYSELF. ME AND MYSELF," like that. Scare all the little animals so they were afraid to come outside in the sunshine. Afraid to go huntin or fishin or whatever the little animals wanted to do.

"What we gone do about it?" they asked one another. Squirrel leapin from branch to branch, just scared. Possum playin dead, couldn't hardly move him.

He Lion just went on, stickin out his chest and roarin, "ME AND MYSELF. ME AND MYSELF."

The little animals held a sit-down talk, and one by one and two by two and all by all, they decide to go see Bruh Bear and Bruh Rabbit. For they know that Bruh Bear been around. And Bruh Rabbit say he has, too.

So they went to Bruh Bear and Bruh Rabbit. Said, "We have some trouble. Old he Lion, him scarin everybody, roarin every mornin and all day, 'ME AND MYSELF. ME AND MYSELF,' like that."

He Lion, Bruh Bear, and Bruh Rabbit **225**

PRETEACHING

Standards Starter

Motivate. Ask students to name cartoon characters popular when they were younger. Invite students to tell which ones they liked best and which of the characters' traits appealed to them. Then, assign the Quickwrite.

Assign the Reading

For students reading at or above grade level, assign the folk tale and fables as homework or independent reading. Meanwhile, continue working with small groups of students having difficulty. After everyone has read the selections, have the class read them aloud, taking parts.

HOMEWORK

DIRECT TEACHING

➤ Resources Reminder

Media
■ *Audio CD Library*
  ■ disc 6

Reading
■ *Interactive Reading*
  ■ Graphic Organizers: Folk Tale Grid (for "He Lion..."), p. 154; Fables Chart (for Aesop fables), p. 155

A Literary Focus
GRADE-LEVEL STANDARD
❓ Forms of fiction: Folk tale.
What are some features of the dialect used in this folk tale? [The final *g* is dropped from -*ing* words (*mornin, huntin, fishin*); sentence fragments are used ("Stretch and walk around").]

B English-Language Learners
Interpreting idioms. Tell students that the idiom *been around* means to have experience and that *he Lion* is an idiomatic term for a male lion.

Differentiating Instruction
■ *Lesson Plans for Language Development*
  ■ English-Language Learners, pp. 92–94, 96, 97, 104–106, 110
  ■ Special Education Students, pp. 95–97, 104–106, 110

Vocabulary and Spelling
■ *Spelling Lessons and Activities*, pp. 18, 19

Assessment
■ *Progress Assessment of Reading*
  ■ Selection Test, p. 78
■ *One-Stop Planner* CD-ROM with Test Generator

He Lion, Bruh Bear, and Bruh Rabbit **225**

A Reading Skills

❓ Making inferences. From these sentences, what can you figure out about the character of Bruh Rabbit? [Possible responses: He's "seen enough to know not to be afraid," so he's experienced and brave; he knows "how to handle" lions, so he's smart.]

B Literary Focus
GRADE-LEVEL STANDARD

❓ Forms of fiction: Folk tale. What has Bruh Rabbit seen that Bruh Bear has not? [He has seen Man.] In this folk tale, what makes Bruh Rabbit seem a more likely trickster than Bruh Bear? [Possible responses: Bruh Rabbit seems smarter, bolder, more experienced, and more confident. He seems to have a plan for dealing with he Lion.]

"Why he Lion want to do that?" Bruh Bear said.

"Is that all he Lion have to say?" Bruh Rabbit asked.

"We don't know why, but that's all he Lion can tell us and we didn't ask him to tell us that," said the little animals. "And him scarin the children with it. And we wish him to stop it."

"Well, I'll go see him, talk to him. I've known he Lion a long kind of time," Bruh Bear said.

"I'll go with you," said Bruh Rabbit. "I've known he Lion most long as you."

That bear and that rabbit went off through the forest. They kept hearin somethin. Mumble, mumble. Couldn't make it out. They got farther in the forest. They heard it plain now. "ME AND MYSELF. ME AND MYSELF."

"Well, well, well," said Bruh Bear. He wasn't scared. He'd been around the whole forest, seen a lot.

A "My, my, my," said Bruh Rabbit. He'd seen enough to know not to be afraid of an old he lion. Now old he lions could be dangerous, but you had to know how to handle them.

The bear and the rabbit climbed up and up the cliff where he Lion had his lair.[1] They found him. Kept their distance. He watchin them and they watchin him. Everybody actin cordial.[2]

"Hear tell you are scarin everybody, all the little animals, with your roarin all the time," Bruh Rabbit said.

"I roars when I pleases," he Lion said.

"Well, might could you leave off the noise first thing in the mornin, so the little animals

can get what they want to eat and drink?" asked Bruh Bear.

"Listen," said he Lion, and then he roared: "ME AND MYSELF. ME AND MYSELF. Nobody tell me what not to do," he said. "I'm the king of the forest, *me and myself.*"

"Better had let me tell you somethin," Bruh Rabbit said, "for I've seen Man, and I know him the real king of the forest."

He Lion was quiet awhile. He looked straight through that scrawny lil Rabbit like he was nothin atall. He looked at Bruh Bear and figured he'd talk to him.

"You, Bear, you been around," he Lion said.

"That's true," said old Bruh Bear. "I been about everywhere. I've been around the whole forest."

"Then you must know somethin," he Lion said.

"I know lots," said Bruh Bear, slow and quiet-like.

"Tell me what you know about Man," he Lion said. "He think him the king of the forest?"

"Well, now, I'll tell you," said Bruh Bear, "I been around, but I haven't ever come across Man that I know of. Couldn't tell you nothin about him."

B So he Lion had to turn back to Bruh Rabbit. He didn't want to but he had to. "So what?" he said to that lil scrawny hare.

"Well, you got to come down from there if you want to see Man," Bruh Rabbit said. "Come down from there and I'll show you him."

He Lion thought a minute, an hour, and a whole day. Then, the next day, he came on down.

He roared just once, "ME AND MYSELF. ME AND MYSELF. Now," he said, "come show me Man."

1. **lair** *n.*: home of a wild animal; den.
2. **cordial** (kôr′jəl) *adj.*: warm and friendly.

DIFFERENTIATING INSTRUCTION

Learners Having Difficulty
Modeling. To help students read "He Lion, Bruh Bear, and Bruh Rabbit," model the reading skill of recognizing cause and effect. Say: "Suppose you read that the lion's roar scares the other animals. You can tell that the lion's roar is the cause and the animals' fear is the effect. Then, you read that because the animals were afraid, they had a talk. Their fear is the cause, and the

talk is an effect. So one cause had an effect and that effect became the cause of something else." Encourage students as they read to ask "What causes this effect?" and "How does this effect turn into a cause of a new effect?"

English-Language Learners
Students may find the dialect of this folk tale easier to understand if they read the

tale aloud. Students will also benefit from listening to the CD recording of the tale.

▶ Resources Reminder
For lessons designed for both intermediate and advanced English-language learners, see *Lesson Plans for Language Development,* pp. 92–94, 96, 97, 104–106, 110.

So they set out. He Lion, Bruh Bear, and Bruh Rabbit. They go along and they go along, rangin the forest. Pretty soon, they come to a clearin. And playin in it is a little fellow about nine years old.

"Is that there Man?" asked he Lion.

"Why no, that one is called Will Be, but it sure is not Man," said Bruh Rabbit.

So they went along and they went along. Pretty soon, they come upon a shade tree. And sleepin under it is an old, olden fellow, about ninety years olden.

"There must lie Man," spoke he Lion. "I knew him wasn't gone be much."

"That's not Man," said Bruh Rabbit. "That fellow is Was Once. You'll know it when you see Man."

So they went on along. He Lion is gettin tired of strollin. So he roars, "ME AND MY-SELF. ME AND MYSELF." Upsets Bear so that Bear doubles over and runs and climbs a tree.

"Come down from there," Bruh Rabbit tellin him. So after a while Bear comes down. He keepin his distance from he Lion, anyhow. And they set out some more. Goin along quiet and slow.

In a little while they come to a road. And comin on way down the road, Bruh Rabbit sees Man comin. Man about twenty-one years old. Big and strong, with a big gun over his shoulder.

"There!" Bruh Rabbit says. "See there, he Lion? There's Man. You better go meet him."

"I will," says he Lion. And he sticks out his chest and he roars, "ME AND MYSELF. ME AND MYSELF." All the way to Man he's roarin proud, "ME AND MYSELF, ME AND MYSELF!"

"Come on, Bruh Bear, let's go!" Bruh Rabbit says.

"What for?" Bruh Bear wants to know.

"You better come on!" And Bruh Rabbit takes ahold of Bruh Bear and half drags him to a thicket. And there he makin the Bear hide with him.

For here comes Man. He sees old he Lion real good now. He drops to one knee and he takes aim with his big gun.

Old he Lion is roarin his head off: "ME AND MYSELF! ME AND MYSELF!"

The big gun goes off: PA-LOOOM!

C Learners Having Difficulty

Re-reading. Ask students to re-read to find the ages of Will Be and Was Once. [nine and ninety] Explain that *Man* in this tale is used to mean a male at the most vigorous stage of life.

D Literary Focus
GRADE-LEVEL STANDARD
❓ Forms of fiction: Folk tale. How do you now know that Bruh Rabbit, not Bruh Bear, is the trickster? [Possible responses: Bruh Bear is afraid of he Lion, but Bruh Rabbit is not; Bruh Rabbit is in charge.]

E Reading Skills
❓ Cause and effect. How might he Lion's behavior cause the hunter to shoot? [Possible response: The hunter might think he Lion is about to attack since the lion is striding straight up to him and roaring.]

Special Education Students
For lessons designed for special education students, see *Lesson Plans for Language Development,* pp. 95–97, 104–106, 110.

Advanced Learners
Acceleration. Use this activity to move advanced learners toward the seventh-grade Standard 3.1, which requires that they articulate the purposes and characteristics of different forms of prose. Assign a one-page essay, with the moral of either of the two fables as its thesis statement. Ask students to read their essays aloud and then to present brief, informal talks in which they compare their essays and the corresponding fables as prose forms. They might consider purpose, structure, clarity, and entertainment value.

A Literary Focus
GRADE-LEVEL STANDARD
? Forms of fiction: Folk tale.
Humor is an element of many folk tales. What humor do you find in this scene? [Possible responses: There is a slapstick quality to the images of he Lion bouncing back onto his tail and then flying through the air into a thicket; the onomatopoeia of the lion's roar and the gun's "PA-LOOOM" create humor; after he Lion has nearly been killed by Man, Bruh Bear's dry question is humorously ironic.]

B Literary Focus
GRADE-LEVEL STANDARD
? Forms of fiction: Folk tale. If you read between the lines of this folk tale, what do you think the teller is really talking about? What lesson does the tale teach? [Possible responses: No matter how strong you think you are, there is always someone who can humble you; it is important to be considerate of others.]

Meet the Writer

Virginia Hamilton

Background. Hamilton says, "I'm sure if anyone saw me working, they would see somebody who appeared to be in a trance, because it's that deep concentration you have to have to really go into yourself, which feels as if you're going out into the paper that you're writing on. . . . It's a very inward kind of working which is outward bound at the same time."

For Independent Reading

Students reading *The House of Dies Drear* will be interested to know that Virginia Hamilton grew up in a village that was once a station on the Underground Railroad.

■ For fans of humorous folk-tales, suggest *The Jack Tales,* collected in Appalachia and retold by Richard Chase.

A He Lion falls back hard on his tail. The gun goes off again. PA-LOOOM! He Lion is flyin through the air. He lands in the thicket.

"Well, did you see Man?" asked Bruh Bear.

"I seen him," said he Lion. "Man spoken to me unkind, and got a great long stick him keepin on his shoulder. Then Man taken that stick down and him speakin real mean. Thunderin at me and lightnin comin from that stick, awful bad. Made me sick. I had to turn around. And Man pointin that stick again and thunderin at me some more. So I come in here, cause it seem like him throwed some stickers at me each time it thunder, too."

"So you've met Man, and you know zactly what that kind of him is," says Bruh Rabbit.

"I surely do know that," he Lion said back.

Awhile after he Lion met Man, things were some better in the forest. Bruh Bear knew what Man looked like so he could keep out of his way. That rabbit always did know to keep out of Man's way. The little animals could go out in the mornin because he Lion **B** was more peaceable. He didn't walk around roarin at the top of his voice all the time. And when he Lion did lift that voice of his, it was like, "Me and Myself and Man. Me and Myself and Man." Like that.

Wasn't too loud at all.

MEET THE WRITER

Virginia Hamilton

Telling Tales
For most of her life, **Virginia Hamilton** (1936–   ) has lived in the place where she was born and raised, Yellow Springs, Ohio. It's where her grandfather settled after he escaped from slavery in pre–Civil War days. Virginia was named for the state where he lived before his escape.

About her family and Yellow Springs, the place she calls home, Hamilton says:

" My mother's 'people' were warm-hearted, tight with money, generous to the sick and landless, closemouthed, and fond of telling tales and gossip about one another and even their ancestors. They were a part of me from the time I understood that I belonged to all of them. My uncle King told the best tall tales; my aunt Leanna sang the finest sorrowful songs. My own mother could take a slice of fiction floating around the family and polish it into a saga. "

For Independent Reading
You'll find more folk tales in Hamilton's collection *The People Could Fly.* If you like animal tales, check out her collection *A Ring of Tricksters.*

▶ **Resources Reminder**

Reading

For other selections by Virginia Hamilton, see "Telling Tales," p. 166, and "Papa John's Tall Tale," p. 173, in Interactive Reading. You may want to assign these to advanced learners.

The Fox and the Crow

Aesop

Greek fable, dramatized by **Mara Rockliff**

Narrator. One fine morning a Fox was wandering through the woods, enjoying the lovely spring weather.

Fox. Lovely spring weather is all very well, but a fox can't live on sunshine and fresh air. I could use some breakfast right about now.

Narrator. Suddenly he noticed a Crow sitting on the branch of a tree above him. The Fox didn't think much of crows as a rule, but this particular Crow had something very interesting in her beak.

Fox. Cheese. Mmm. A nice big yellow chunk of cheese. I would love that cheese. I deserve that cheese. But how can I get that cheese?

Narrator. The Fox thought awhile, and then he called up to the Crow.

Fox. Good morning, you fabulous bird.

Narrator. The Crow looked at him suspiciously. But she kept her beak closed tightly on the cheese and said nothing.

Fox. What beautiful beady eyes you have! And you certainly look great in black feathers. I've seen a lot of birds in my time, but you outbird them all. A bird with your good looks must have a voice to match. Oh, if only I could hear you sing just one song. Then I would know you were truly the Greatest Bird on Earth.

Narrator. Listening to all this flattery, the Crow forgot her suspicion of the Fox. She forgot her cheese, too. All she could think of was impressing the Fox with a song. So she opened her beak wide and let out a loud "Caw!" Down fell the cheese, right into the Fox's open mouth.

Fox. Thanks! That tasted every bit as good as it looked. Well, now I know you have a voice—and I hope I never have to hear it again. But where are your brains?

All Together. If you let flattery go to your head, you'll pay the price.

The Fox and the Crow **229**

A Reading Skills

? Cause and effect. What is causing the wolf to be so hungry? [Every time she tries to steal some food, watchdogs alert their owners, who chase her off.]

B English-Language Learners

Interpreting idioms. Explain to students that a "dog on a bun" refers to the food called a "hot dog" or "frankfurter." The writer uses the idiomatic phrase here to create humor.

C Reading Skills

? Cause and effect. What causes the wolf to try to conceal her real thoughts from the dog? [Possible responses: He looks much stronger than she is; she's too weak to eat him.] **What effect do her compliments have on the dog?** [He begins to offer her advice.]

The Wolf and the House Dog

Aesop

Greek fable, dramatized by **Mara Rockliff**

A **Narrator.** Once there was a Wolf who never got enough to eat. Her mouth watered when she looked at the fat geese and chickens kept by the people of the village. But every time she tried to steal one, the watchful village dogs would bark and warn their owners.

Wolf. Really, I'm nothing but skin and bones. It makes me sad just thinking about it.

Narrator. One night the Wolf met up with a House Dog who had wandered a little too far from home. The Wolf would gladly have eaten him right then and there.

B **Wolf.** Dog stew . . . cold dog pie . . . or maybe just dog on a bun, with plenty of mustard and ketchup . . .

Narrator. But the House Dog looked too big and strong for the Wolf, who was weak from hunger. So the Wolf spoke to him very humbly and politely.

C **Wolf.** How handsome you are! You look so healthy and well fed and delicious—I mean, uh, terrific. You look terrific. Really.

FAMILY/COMMUNITY ACTIVITY

Assign students to read either the folk tale or one of the two fables to their families. Then, have students ask family members to tell them another fable or folk tale, preferably one that the family members heard as children. Have students take notes, if necessary, and share their family members' tales with the class.

House Dog. Well, you look terrible. I don't know why you live out here in these miserable woods, where you have to fight so hard for every crummy little scrap of food. You should come live in the village like me. You could eat like a king there.

Wolf. What do I have to do?

House Dog. Hardly anything. Chase kids on bicycles. Bark at the mailman every now and then. Lie around the house letting people pet you. Just for that they'll feed you till you burst—enormous steak bones with fat hanging off them, pizza crusts, bits of chicken, leftovers like you wouldn't believe.

Narrator. The Wolf nearly cried with happiness as she imagined how wonderful her new life was going to be. But then she noticed a strange ring around the Dog's neck where the hair had been rubbed off.

Wolf. What happened to your neck?

House Dog. Oh . . . ah . . . nothing. It's nothing, really.

Wolf. I've never seen anything like it. Is it a disease?

House Dog. Don't be silly. It's just the mark of the collar that they fasten my chain to.

Wolf. A chain! You mean you can't go wherever you like?

House Dog. Well, not always. But what's the difference?

Wolf. What's the difference? Are you kidding? I wouldn't give up my freedom for the biggest, juiciest steak in the world. Never mind a few lousy bones.

Narrator. The Wolf ran away, back to the woods. She never went near the village again, no matter how hungry she got.

All Together. Nothing is worth more than freedom.

Aesop

Fables for Freedom

Not much is known about **Aesop** (sixth century B.C.). According to the ancient Greek historian Herodotus, he came from Africa and was held in slavery in Greece. The fables credited to Aesop may have originally come from ancient India. Aesop's fables were used to make points about politics. Aesop eventually won his freedom, but he met a violent death, perhaps because his fables offended someone powerful.

Aesop, with figures from his fables. Printed in Augsburg, Bavaria, in 1498 by Johann Schonsperger.

The Wolf and the House Dog **231**

D **Literary Focus**
GRADE-LEVEL STANDARD

? **Forms of fiction: Fable.** In this fable, how does the wolf's behavior show that she is a trickster? [Possible responses: The wolf tries to steal food; she speaks deceptively to the dog; she is weak but wily; her quick thinking lets her keep what she values most.]

Meet the Writer

Aesop

Background. Aesop is in part a legendary figure. Some sources say that he was granted freedom after several years of slavery; others say that he spoke unclearly, perhaps with an accent. This has suggested to scholars that he may have arrived in Greece as a captive from another country.

For Independent Reading

Students reading more of Aesop's fables might enjoy the rhymed versions by the seventeenth-century French poet Jean de La Fontaine.

■ Animal fables over two thousand years old, originating in India, are gathered in *Jataka Tales,* edited by Nancy DeRoin.

Advanced Learners
Enrichment. Tell students that Virginia Hamilton values music almost as much as she values writing. As a young woman, she performed as a singer. Her father was a professional musician; she describes him as "a superb mandolinist" and recalls the comforting sound of his music when she lay awake in the darkness as a child.

Activity. Play for students "Le festin d'Ésope" ("The Feast of Aesop"), no. 12 in Études for Piano, op. 39, by Charles-Valentin Alkan. Invite students to discuss how the music captures the spirit of the folk tale and fables they have read. Encourage students to identify specific segments of the composition that relate to elements of folk tale and fable, such as humor, animal characters, and a concluding lesson or moral.

Literary Response and Analysis

Reading Check

1. *Events in "He Lion . . ."*—he Lion's intimidating roaring, the small animals' request for help, Bruh Rabbit and Bruh Bear's talk with he Lion, the trek to see Man, the encounters with Will Be and Was Once, the meeting with Man and his gun, he Lion's comments, and his changed behavior. *Events in "The Fox and the Crow"*—the fox's walk in the woods, his sighting the crow with the cheese, the fox's flattery, the crow's opening her beak to sing, her dropping the cheese, and the fox's response and comments. *Events in "The Wolf and the House Dog"*—the hungry wolf's meeting with the dog, the wolf's flattery and the dog's response and advice, the wolf's noticing the collar marks, and her running away.

2. *"He Lion . . ."*—Bruh Rabbit. *"The Fox and the Crow"*—the fox. *"The Wolf and the House Dog"*—the wolf.

3. He Lion thinks he's strongest, but Man turns out to be strongest.

4. The crow is singing to show the fox that she is the greatest bird on earth. The fox gets her cheese.

5. The dog encourages the wolf to take a job as a house dog. The wolf values freedom above all.

Interpretations

6. Possible answers: They are small, quick, crafty, and agile.

7. Possible answers: Bullies and arrogant people are like he Lion; vain and self-centered people are like the crow.

8. Possible answers: *"He Lion..."*— Be considerate of others. *"The Fox and the Crow"*—Beware of people who are too flattering

---

Reading Check

1. Review the flowcharts you made to track the events of each selection. Compare your flowcharts in class. Did you include all the **causes** and **effects**?

2. Who is the **trickster** in each story?

3. In "He Lion, Bruh Bear, and Bruh Rabbit," which animal thinks he's the strongest? Who turns out to be the strongest?

4. In "The Fox and the Crow," why does the crow open her beak? What does the fox get from the crow?

5. In "The Wolf and the House Dog," what does the house dog encourage the wolf to do? What does the wolf value above everything else?

Interpretations

6. What qualities do rabbits and foxes have that make people think they'd be good **tricksters**?

7. The animals in folk tales and fables often talk and act like people. What people remind you of the lion and the crow?

8. Unlike short stories, folk tales and fables teach **morals,** or **practical lessons** about how to behave and get along in the world. What lesson do you find in each of these stories? (The lessons are stated directly at the end of Aesop's fables.) How do you feel about each lesson? Is it useful? Is it a good or wise lesson? Explain your responses. (Be sure to check your Quickwrite notes.)

Reading Standard 3.1 Identify the forms of fiction, and describe the major characteristics of each form.

Writing
A Fable for Our Time

Write a short short animal story that teaches one of these lessons:

- Kindness is never wasted.
- Slow and steady wins the race.
- It's best not to want what you can't have.

You might first jot down some ideas in a chart like this one:

Moral:
Animal characters:
Their problem:
What happens:

Performance
Places, Everyone!

Get together with a group of classmates interested in presenting "He Lion . . ." or one of the fables by Aesop. You can either do a live performance with props and costumes or tape your reading. If you decide on "He Lion . . . ," break the story into scenes. Decide if you need a narrator to provide details not supplied in the dialogue. Write out each character's lines. You may want to get together with groups who have prepared the two other stories and present them to the class in sequence. Assign another group of students to act as your critics.

▶ Use "Presenting and Listening to an Oral Narrative," pages 519–524, for help with this assignment.

---

because they may get the better of you. *"The Wolf and the House Dog"*— Freedom is our most valuable possession. The students' feelings and opinions of each lesson will vary; however, encourage them to apply the lessons to their own lives.

Vocabulary Development

Reading Standard 1.2
Identify and interpret words with multiple meanings.

Words with Multiple Meanings

Multiple-meaning words can be confusing. A multiple-meaning word is always spelled the same way, but it means different things in different **contexts.** To find the correct meaning, figure out what part of speech the word is; then, examine its context. Finally, decide which meaning best fits the sentence.

PRACTICE

Choose the correct meaning of each underlined word.

1. Does a fox know the difference between right and wrong?

    a. opposite of left   **b.** what is just and proper

2. He broke every rule in the forest.

    a. law   **b.** line

3. He Lion went flying through the air.

    a. tune   **b.** sky

4. "I surely do know that," he Lion answered back.

    a. in return   **b.** part of a chair

Grammar Link MINI-LESSON

Understanding Homophones:
To, Too, and *Two*

To, too, and *two* are **homophones** (häm′ə·fōnz′)—words that sound alike but are spelled differently and have different meanings. Don't let trickster words like *to, too,* and *two* fool you. Remembering what each word means will help you use it correctly.

- **to:** toward; in the direction of (*to* is also part of the infinitive form of a verb)

- **too:** also; more than enough

- **two:** a number—one plus one

PRACTICE

Choose the correct word in the underlined pair in each sentence.

The little animals go to/two see Bruh Bear and Bruh Rabbit because he Lion is making too/to much noise. He Lion doesn't like talking too/to Bruh Rabbit. He Lion's roar is too/to loud for Bruh Bear. He Lion wants two/to see Man. After seeing Man, he Lion is no longer two/too loud.

Three Fables   **233**

Vocabulary Development

Practice

1. b. "wrong" is the clue.

2. a. "broke" is the clue.

3. b. "flying" is the clue.

4. a. "answered" is the clue.

Grammar Link

Practice

1. to

2. too

3. to

4. too

5. to

6. too

▶ **Resources Reminder**

Vocabulary and Spelling

- *Spelling Lessons and Activities*

For additional practice with homophones, see pp. 18–19.

- *Lesson Plans for Language Development*
  - Vocabulary, p. 110

ASSESSING

Assessment

- *Progress Assessment of Reading*
  - Selection Test, p. 78

RETEACHING

For a lesson reteaching forms of fiction, see **Reteaching,** p. 489G.

Standards Review

Reading Informational Materials

STANDARDS FOCUS, pp. 234–235

(*For the grade-level standard reviewed in this lesson, see Pupil's Edition, p. 234.*)

INTRODUCING THE STANDARDS REVIEW

Use this review to test students' understanding of the use of the compare-and-contrast organizational pattern. Use these annotations only if you want to conduct this review orally.

DIRECT TEACHING

Ⓐ Reading Informational Materials
GRADE-LEVEL STANDARD

❓ Compare-and-contrast pattern. Which words show that the writer is introducing a new subject and a contrast? ["Now a different view of this scene."] What method is used to organize this compare-and-contrast essay? [the block method]

Ⓑ Reading Informational Materials
GRADE-LEVEL STANDARD

❓ Compare-and-contrast pattern. How is the spider's reaction similar to the reaction of the neighbor? [Possible responses: Both are alarmed and disoriented; both have an exaggerated idea of what they have encountered; both have a "pressing question," though the questions differ.]

Reading Informational Materials

TestPractice   DIRECTIONS: Read the following essay. Then, read each question, and write the letter of the best response.

from All I Really Need to Know I Learned in Kindergarten
Robert Fulghum

This is my neighbor. Nice lady. Coming out her front door, on her way to work and in her "looking good" mode. She's locking the door now and picking up her daily luggage: purse, lunch bag, gym bag for aerobics, and the garbage bucket to take out. She turns, sees me, gives me the big, smiling Hello, and takes three steps across her front porch. And goes "AAAAAAAAGGGGGGGGG-HHHHHHHHH!!!!" (*That's a direct quote.*) At about the level of a fire engine at full cry. Spider web! She has walked full force into a spider web. And the pressing question, of course: Just where is the spider *now?*

She flings her baggage in all directions. And at the same time does a high-kick, jitter-bug sort of dance—like a mating stork in crazed heat. Clutches at her face and hair and goes "AAAAAAAAGG-GGGGGGHHHHHHHHHHH!!!!!" at a new level of intensity. Tries opening the front door without unlocking it. Tries again. Breaks key in the lock. Runs around the house headed for the back door. Doppler effect° of "AAAAAGGGHHHHaaggh . . ."

Now a different view of this scene. Here is the spider. Rather ordinary, medium gray, middle-aged lady spider. She's been up since before dawn working on her web, and all is well. Nice day, no wind, dew point just right to keep things sticky. She's out checking the moorings and thinking about the little gnats she'd like for breakfast. Feeling good. Ready for action. All of a sudden everything breaks loose—earthquake, tornado, volcano. The web is torn loose and is wrapped around a frenzied moving haystack, and a huge piece of raw-but-painted meat is making a sound the spider never heard before: "AAAAAAAAGGGGGGGGGHHHHHH-HHHH!!!!!!" It's too big to wrap up and eat later, and it's moving too much to hold down. Jump for it? Hang on and hope? Dig in?

___

° **Doppler effect:** change in the pitch of a sound, produced when the source of the sound moves toward or away from the listener.

Reading Standard 2.2 Analyze text that uses the compare-and-contrast organizational pattern.

MINI-LESSON   **Reading**

Reviewing Word-Attack Skills
Activity. Display these sets of words. Have students identify the word in which the initial *u* stands for the long *u* sound. Answers are underlined.

1. unintended   understand   <u>unison</u>
2. <u>unicorn</u>   unidentified   unformed
3. uninvited   <u>universe</u>   unusual
4. uneven   unequal   <u>unique</u>
5. unable   <u>unit</u>   unaware

Activity. Display these sets of words with the /ir/ or /ûr/ sound. Have students identify the two words in each set that rhyme. Answers are underlined.

1. <u>here</u>   <u>year</u>   wear
2. <u>heard</u>   <u>word</u>   feared

Human being. She has caught a human being. And the pressing question is, of course: Where is it going, and what will it do when it gets there?

The neighbor lady thinks the spider is about the size of a lobster and has big rubber lips and poisonous fangs. The neighbor lady will probably strip to the skin and take a full shower and sham-poo just to make sure it's gone—and then put on a whole new outfit to make certain she is not inhabited.

The spider? Well, if she survives all this, she will really have something to talk about—the one that got away that was THIS BIG. "And you should have seen the JAWS on the thing!"

1. What does the writer **compare** and **contrast** in this essay?
   A A jitterbug and a stork
   B People and spiders
   C A spider web and a front porch
   D Breakfast foods

2. What **pattern** does the writer use to organize his essay?
   F Block method
   G Point-by-point method
   H Chronological order
   J Cause-and-effect pattern

3. Both the human and the spider start out feeling —
   A scared
   B hungry
   C good
   D sleepy

4. The human and the spider are both —
   F very old
   G male
   H very young
   J female

5. The spider —
   A thinks of the human as a piece of raw but painted meat
   B thinks of the human as a friend
   C wants to go in and shower
   D bites the human

6. The human —
   F thinks of the spider as a piece of raw but painted meat
   G thinks of the spider as having rubber lips and poisonous fangs
   H doesn't think anything of the spider at all
   J thinks the spider is cute

7. After the encounter the human will —
   A take a shower and put on a new outfit
   B kill the spider
   C call the exterminator
   D let the spider rebuild her web

8. After the encounter the spider will —
   F crawl into a hole and die
   G talk about the one that got away
   H repair her web
   J go after the human

Answers and Model Rationales

1. **B** Students should quickly eliminate A, C, and D as things that are mentioned in the essay but not compared. B is the only possible answer because it applies to the whole essay.

2. **F** Since this review focuses on the compare-and-contrast pattern, students should eliminate H and J. F is correct, not G, because the writer's first two paragraphs provide a block of information about the lady, and the next two provide a block of information about the spider.

3. **C** The essay describes the spider as "feeling good," and students can infer that the lady feels good because she is "in her 'looking good' mode" and gives the narrator "the big, smiling Hello." The essay does not say that the neighbor is hungry (B). Neither the neighbor nor the spider starts out feeling scared (A) or sleepy (D).

4. **J** Knowing the spider is middle-aged eliminates F and H. The only choice is J, female.

5. **A** The essay suggests that it is the human who wants to do C. The spider neither bites the human nor sees her as a friend. A correctly describes the spider's idea of the human.

6. **G** F is thought by the spider. The description in J is opposite to the human's thoughts. Only G matches the human's thoughts.

7. **A** B, C, and D are all possible actions the human could take after her encounter. Only A, the desire to take a shower and put on a new outfit, is predicted in the essay.

8. **G** H is likely, but the essay doesn't mention it. The essay does not suggest that the spider is dying (F) or vengeful (J). G accurately describes her probable intention.

3. curse   hears   worse
4. hurt   heart   flirt
5. worn   learn   burn

Test-Taking Tips

Remind students that the compare-and-contrast pattern is a way of organizing based on similarities and differences. Encourage students to skim the essay again, noticing how the neighbor and the spider are alike and different, before answering the Test Practice items.

For more information on answering multiple-choice items, refer students to **Test Smarts,** p. 690.

Test Practice

Vocabulary Development

Synonyms

Modeling. Model the thought process of a good reader getting the answer to item 1 by saying, "I remember that an awkward move is the opposite of a graceful one. So *clumsy* and *silly* are two likely choices. An awkward move doesn't have to be silly, though, so *clumsy* is the best choice."

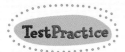

Answers and Model Rationales

1. **C** See rationale above.
2. **F** Serving (J) may be part of savoring, but only F is correct.
3. **B** When something is evident, it can be noticed. B, *clear,* is nearest in meaning.
4. **H** Tolerance is like acceptance, so F and G are incorrect. H, *accepting,* is the better of the two remaining choices.
5. **C** *Rural* means the country. *Agricultural* is closest in meaning.
6. **H** H, *aware,* is nearest in meaning to *heedful.*
7. **C** *Audacity* means "daring," so A and D are incorrect. Audacity has more to do with boldness (C) than with humor (B), so C is the best choice.
8. **G** To *ponder* is to think deeply, so F can be eliminated. H is the word's opposite, and J is irrelevant. This leaves G.
9. **A** Ignorance is related to a lack of knowledge (A).
10. **J** *Devastated* is close in meaning to *destroyed.* G and H are unrelated to this idea. F, *robbed,* might lead to devastation, but need not. J, *destroyed,* is closest in meaning.

Vocabulary Development

TestPractice

Synonyms

DIRECTIONS: Choose the word or group of words that is closest in meaning to the under-lined word.

1. Someone who is awkward is —
   A quiet
   B silly
   C clumsy
   D shocking

2. To savor is to —
   F enjoy
   G forget
   H save
   J serve

3. Something that is evident is —
   A sad
   B clear
   C possible
   D strange

4. To be tolerant is to be —
   F angry
   G frightened
   H accepting
   J content

5. A rural place is —
   A warm
   B mountainous
   C agricultural
   D crowded

6. To be heedful is to be —
   F helpful
   G angry
   H aware
   J courageous

7. Audacity is —
   A loyalty
   B humor
   C boldness
   D kindness

8. To ponder something is to —
   F predict it
   G consider it
   H ignore it
   J celebrate it

9. Ignorance is —
   A lack of knowledge
   B lack of wealth
   C lack of opportunity
   D lack of ability

10. Something that is devastated is —
    F robbed
    G painted
    H occupied
    J destroyed

Vocabulary Review

Use this activity to assess whether students have retained the chapter Vocabulary.
Activity. Have students select the correct word from the box to complete the sentences.

| rural | evident | ignorance | heedful |

1. He Lion's loud roar made it _____ that he was nearby. [evident]
2. Should 'lois's father have been more _____ of his relatives' warnings? [heedful]
3. The dog lives in a _____ village, where people keep geese and chickens. [rural]
4. Manuel kept his family in _____ about what his talent-show act would be. [ignorance]

COMPARISON AND CONTRAST

M and M

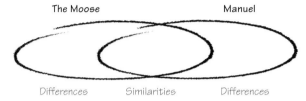
Mastering the Standards

Write a composition comparing and contrasting two characters from the short stories "Just Once" (page 7) and "La Bamba" (page 194). Both the Moose in "Just Once" and Manuel in "La Bamba" find themselves in front of a roaring crowd. In what other ways are the boys alike? Focus on the feelings they experience. In what important ways are they different? (Hint: Think about the way each story ends.) Before you begin writing, use a Venn diagram like this one to organize your ideas:

The Moose   Manuel

Differences   Similarities   Differences

▶ Use "Writing a Comparison-Contrast Essay," pages 660–664, for help with this assignment.

Other Choices

NARRATIVE WRITING

1 Perseus Revisited

Rewrite the story of Perseus, setting it in the year 2010. Before you write, decide on answers to these questions:

- Where and when is your story set?
- Who is your hero? (You might make the hero a woman.)
- What is be the purpose of the hero's quest?
- What kind of job does your modern-day Polydectes have?
- What is the monster like?
- How is the hero rewarded?

▶ Use "Writing a Short Story," pages 500–518, for help with this assignment.

NARRATIVE WRITING

2 Telling Tales

Create a trickster to use as the main character in a story. Trickster characters are often animals; you may want to model your trickster on Bruh Rabbit in Virginia Hamilton's "He Lion, Bruh Bear, and Bruh Rabbit." You might tell how the trickster outwits a character who is much stronger, uses a trick to teach someone a lesson, or plays a trick that backfires. First, think of an animal that would make a good trickster. Then, think of his or her opponent, who is much larger and stronger but not as clever. If you are artistic, tell your story in a series of cartoon panels.

Mastering the Standards

Evaluation Criteria

A good comparison-and-contrast composition

1. states the thesis or purpose
2. discusses how the subjects being compared are similar and different
3. organizes ideas clearly using the point-by-point or block pattern
4. links ideas with appropriate transitional words
5. offers persuasive evidence to validate arguments and conclusions

ASSESSING

Assessment

- *Progress Assessment of Reading*
  - Chapter Test, p. 81
- *Diagnostic and Summative Assessments*
  - Midyear Test, p. 60

After you have completed chapters 3 and 4 and Writing Workshops 3 and 4, you may want your students to take this test.

Using Academic Language

Literary Terms

As part of the review of Literary Response and Analysis Standard 3.1, ask students to look back through the chapter to find the meanings of the terms listed at right. Then, have students demonstrate their understanding of Standard 3.1 by citing passages from a story in the chapter that illustrate

the meanings of the following terms. **Novella** (p. 174); **Short Story** (p. 193); **Mythic Hero** (p. 208); **Myth** (p. 208); **Fate** (p. 208); **Folk Tales and Fables** (p. 224); **Trickster Hero** (p. 224).

Informational Terms

As part of the review of Reading Comprehension Standard 2.2, ask students

to look back through the chapter to find the meaning of the following terms and phrases, and using the words below, to explain Standard 2.2.
Compare and Contrast (pp. 189, 203); **Comparisons** (p. 203); **Contrasts** (p. 203); **Point-by-point pattern** (p. 203); **Block pattern** (p. 203).

Read On

For Independent Reading

If students enjoyed the various forms of fiction explored in this chapter, you might recommend the following titles for independent reading.

Assessment Options

The following projects can help you evaluate and assess your students' outside reading. Videotapes or audiotapes of completed projects may be included in students' portfolios.

■ **Compare and contrast folk tales.** Have students form small discussion groups and compare and contrast the African American folk tales in Richard and Judy Dockrey Young's book to Virginia Hamilton's "He Lion, Bruh Bear, and Bruh Rabbit." Encourage students to focus attention on literary elements such as style (especially the presence or absence of dialect), humor, imagery (evoking either fantasy or reality), and theme.

■ **Give a dramatic retelling.** Have students choose a favorite story from *The Ch'i-Lin Purse: A Collection of Ancient Chinese Stories* and practice a dramatic retelling of it. Remind students that facial expressions, tone of voice, and hand gestures are all important features of a lively and engaging dramatic retelling.

■ **Write a scene.** Have students work in pairs to write a scene, including dialogue, in which a father and his son discuss their experiences during the years that the father was away from home.

California Reading List Titles

Forty Acres and Maybe a Mule
Sounder
Ashanti to Zulu: African Traditions

Fiction

A Gold Mine of Stories

Richard and Judy Dockrey Young introduce readers to a rich tradition of storytelling in *African-American Folktales for Young Readers.* You'll meet larger-than-life characters like Annie Christmas and the mysterious Fling-a-Mile and learn about the origins of these timeless stories, described by people who still tell them today.

Expect the Unexpected

Linda Fang has collected her favorite ancient Chinese stories in *The Ch'i-Lin Purse.* Some of the stories come from Chinese novels and operas; others are inspired by actual historical events. All include twists and turns that will keep you on your toes. The stories are accompanied by lively illustrations.

Not Quite Free

At the end of the Civil War, Pascal's brother Gideon tells Pascal and his friend Nelly that families once held in slavery have a chance to claim forty acres of land. What the young friends don't know is that finding this land will be difficult and keeping it nearly impossible. Harriette Gillem Robinet tells a tale of tragedy and injustice in *Forty Acres and Maybe a Mule.*

Family Ties

In his novel *Sounder,* William H. Armstrong tells the story of an African American share-cropper who is arrested for stealing food for his starving family. His son spends years searching for him; then one day the young man and Sounder, the family's hunting dog, hear footsteps approaching the house.

This title is available in the HRW Library.

Toward Reading a Million Words Annually

Estimated Word Counts of Read On Books:

Fiction		Nonfiction	
African-American Folktales for Young Readers	40,000	The Mexican American Family Album	78,000
The Ch'i-Lin Purse: A Collection of Ancient Chinese Stories	25,000	Mississippi Challenge	44,000
Forty Acres and Maybe a Mule	32,000	Making Sense: Animal Perception and Communication	18,000
Sounder	24,000	Ashanti to Zulu: African Traditions	2,100
Connections to Sounder	9,800		

Nonfiction

Hardship and Achievement

In *The Mexican American Family Album*, Dorothy and Thomas Hoobler tell about some of the historical events that have shaped the lives of Mexican Americans. The book contains photographs and firsthand accounts of generations of Mexicans who immigrated to the United States.

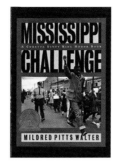

People Power

Mildred Pitts Walter chronicles the African American struggle for equal rights in Mississippi in *Mississippi Challenge*, a Coretta Scott King Honor book. The state's explosive political climate during the 1960s forms the backdrop for the protests held by people determined to end racial discrimination. Their courageous actions eventually broke down the walls of segregation.

Just a Fable?

In *Making Sense: Animal Perception and Communication*, Bruce Brooks explores the ways animals communicate. Brooks explains how animals "talk" to one another in ways you've probably never noticed.

From A to Z

Margaret Musgrove introduces you to the cultures of twenty-six African peoples in *Ashanti to Zulu: African Traditions*. Accompanying the text are Leo and Diane Dillon's illustrations depicting life among these peoples.

- **Create a mural.** Have students work in a group to design and create a mural inspired by *The Mexican American Family Album*. Students may choose to depict some of the historic events or people that the book features. The group should present its mural to the class, explaining the events and people depicted on it.
- **Make a bulletin board.** Students can work in a group to create a bulletin board based on Bruce Brooks's book. Suggest that students look in magazines or other sources for pictures of some of the animals discussed. The group can then post these images on the bulletin board, together with information on how each of the animals communicates.
- **Annotate a map.** Students who read *Ashanti to Zulu: African Traditions* can work together to annotate a map of Africa, identifying and labeling the location of the African tribes and cultures discussed in the book. Suggest that they create illustrative icons, based on information from the book, to accompany each label.

 Resources Reminder

Reading
- *Interactive Reading*

For additional readings that relate to the selections in this chapter, see *Interactive Reading,* Chapter 4.
- *The Ancient World:* A Content-Area Reader

DIFFERENTIATING INSTRUCTION

The titles are categorized as follows:

Below Grade Level ⬇
Forty Acres and Maybe a Mule
Ashanti to Zulu: African Traditions

At Grade Level ⬌
The Ch'i-Lin Purse: A Collection of Ancient Chinese Stories

Sounder
The Mexican American Family Album

Above Grade Level ⬆
African-American Folktales for Young Readers
Mississippi Challenge
Making Sense: Animal Perception and Communication

Chapter 5 Biography and Autobiography: Looking at Lives

Program Organization

Holt Literature and Language Arts provides a complete curriculum for standards-based instruction in vocabulary, reading, literature, writing, and speaking and listening. The instructional content of the program is divided into quarters to enable teachers to anticipate and administer the quarterly assessments required by California.

About Chapter 5

Standards-based lesson plans and suggestions for pacing the presentation of Chapter 5 and the related instructional material are provided in *On Course: Mapping Instruction,* Chapter 5.

- Chapter 5 helps students identify the speaker and identify the difference between first- and third-person narration, connect and clarify main ideas by identifying their relationship to other sources and topics, monitor expository text for unknown words, and use context clues to determine their meaning.

- The related instructional material for Chapter 5 is shown on the chart. This related instructional material will also be covered in the third quarterly assessment.

Holt Literature and Language Arts

Pupil's Edition

Part 1, Chapter 5

Biography and Autobiography: Looking at Lives, pp. 240–325
- Reading Standards 1.4, 2.3, 3.5
- Writing Application **Writing a Research Report**

Part 2, Workshop 4

Research: Writing a Research Report, pp. 578–603
- Writing Standard 2.3

Giving and Evaluating a Research Presentation, pp. 604–608
- Listening and Speaking Standard 2.2

Using Electronic Texts to Locate Information, pp. 609–614
- Writing Standard 1.4

Part 2, Mini-Workshop 8

Creating Graphics, pp. 686–687
- Listening and Speaking Standard 1.6

Holt Handbook

Chapter 9

Using Modifiers Correctly
Written and Oral English-Language Conventions
- Looking Ahead, Gr. 7 Standard 1.1, pp. 211–215
- Review, Gr. 5 Standard 1.2, pp. 197–215

Chapter 10

A Glossary of Usage
Written and Oral English-Language Conventions
- Grade-Level Standards 1.0, 1.5, pp. 221–234

Which vocabulary, informational reading, and literature standards are taught in Chapter 5?

In this chapter, students will master the following Grade 6 standards. They will also review a standard from Grade 5. Selections or features marked with a ✔ constitute the minimum course of study that provides coverage of all grade-level standards.

Grade 6 Standards

Word Analysis, Fluency, and Systematic Vocabulary Development

1.4 Monitor expository text for unknown words or words with novel meanings by using word, sentence, and paragraph clues to determine meaning.

   Prefixes, p. 253
✔ Context Clues, p. 261
✔ Context Clues, p. 285
   Clarifying Word Meanings, p. 299
   Related Words: Word Trees Increase Your Vocabulary, p. 306
   Multiple-Meaning Words, p. 307

Reading Comprehension (Focus on Informational Materials)

2.3 Connect and clarify main ideas by identifying their relationships to other sources and related topics.

✔ "Bringing Tang Home" (magazine article) and "Where the Heart Is" (informational article), pp. 254–260
   "The Brother I Never Had" (student essay), pp. 269–272
   "All Aboard with Thomas Garrett" (magazine article)
   from *Harriet Tubman: The Moses of Her People* (biography) } pp. 300–306, 308–314
   from *The Harriet Tubman Series* (fine art)
✔ Standards Review: Reading Informational Materials, pp. 320–321

Literary Response and Analysis

3.5 Identify the speaker and recognize the difference between first- and third-person narration (e.g., autobiography compared with biography).

✔ "First- and Third-Person Narration: Look Who's Talking" (standards essay), pp. 242–243
   "Storm" from *Woodsong* (autobiography), pp. 244–252
   "Brother" from *I Know Why the Caged Bird Sings* (autobiography), pp. 262–267
   from *The Land I Lost* (essay), pp. 274–284
✔ "A Glory over Everything" from *Harriet Tubman: Conductor on the Underground Railroad* (biography), pp. 286–298
✔ Standards Review: Literary Response and Analysis, pp. 315–319

Review Standards Grade 5

Reading 1.3   Understand and explain frequently used synonyms, antonyms, and homographs.

           Antonyms: Reversing Meaning, p. 268

           Finding Synonyms: Thesaurus Rex to the Rescue, p. 268

Mastering the California Standards CHAPTER 5

Where do I locate lesson plans, additional resources, and other teaching aids?

- This Annotated Teacher's Edition and *On Course: Mapping Instruction* provide direction in planning and implementing a complete California standards–based curriculum. These components include instructions for administering diagnostic, progress, and summative tests; for presenting instruction of the standards; for differentiating instruction to provide universal access; and for locating and using the program's ancillaries.

- The program's resources are referenced at the beginning of each selection, in the bottom margin of this teacher's edition.

- Reminders for using additional resources appear in this teacher's edition at point of use.

- The *One-Stop Planner* CD-ROM with Test Generator contains editable lesson plans and all of the print ancillaries, available in PDF format.

What if I don't have time to teach all of Chapter 5?

- Most standards can be taught with a minimum number of selections and features. In the chart on p. 239B, the core lessons you need in order to provide complete coverage of the chapter standards are identified with a ✔.

- Use the Standards Review, pp. 315–321, for a quick review and informal assessment of the grade-level standards covered in Chapter 5.

What provisions have been made for students who have additional class time scheduled in language arts?

- *Interactive Reading* provides for additional direct instruction and practice of the grade-level standards taught in Chapter 5. It can be used as an introduction to instruction or as an opportunity for remediation.

- *Lesson Plans for Language Development,* Chapter 5, provides alternative teaching strategies and additional worksheets designed specifically for English-language learners and special education students. Many of the suggestions and activities in this ancillary will also be helpful to students in the regular classroom who are having difficulty with particular skills.

In addition to vocabulary, reading, and literature, what other language arts are covered in Chapter 5?

Writing Activities in Chapter 5
- Straight from the Dog's Mouth (point of view exercise), p. 252
- My Greatest Person (character sketch), p. 267
- The Main Events (summation of story), p. 284
- Through Other Eyes: Speaker and Point of View (poetry exercise), p. 297

Writing Applications (p. 323)
- What Matters (research report)

- Other Choices: Taking a Stand (persuasive essay); Calling All Paws (how-to explanation)

Grammar Links in Chapter 5
- Using *Good* and *Well* Correctly, p. 253
- Comparing with Adjectives, p. 273
- Modifiers: Don't Misplace Them, p. 273
- Don't Use *Bad* and *Badly* Badly, p. 299

Universal Access

How do I differentiate instruction to ensure that all my students master the standards?

Holt Literature and Language Arts provides comprehensive, differentiated instruction for all types of students.

- Most of the general instruction and teaching strategies in the Annotated Teacher's Edition are at grade level. These instructions will work well with the majority of your students.

- In Chapter 5, suggestions for advanced learners are provided in the Annotated Teacher's Edition. Point-of-use suggestions for learners having difficulty, English-language learners, and special education students are also provided.

- *Interactive Reading* is designed to anticipate and/or remediate problems that students may experience in achieving mastery of the standards. *Interactive Reading* includes reading-strategy lessons, lower-level practice reads, and worksheets for every informational and literary text in *Holt Literature and Language Arts,* Pupil's Editions. *Interactive Reading* also contains three additional selections for each chapter and suggestions for extension projects, many of which are ideal for advanced learners working on their own. See *Interactive Reading,* Teacher's Edition, for specific information on using the reader to differentiate instruction in Chapter 5.

- *Lesson Plans for Language Development,* Chapter 5, offers teaching strategies and additional worksheets designed specifically for English-language learners and special education students.

Assessment

How do I determine whether or not my students are making progress in mastering the standards?

Progress Assessment

- Use the Standards Review at the end of Chapter 5, pp. 315–321, for an informal assessment of the informational reading and literature standards in Chapter 5.

- Use the Selection Tests for Chapter 5 in the *Progress Assessment of Reading* booklet to test comprehension and progress on mastering the standard(s) taught with a selection.

- Use Chapter Test 5 in the *Progress Assessment of Reading* booklet to test students' cumulative progress in mastering the standards taught in the chapter.

Summative Assessment

The content of *Holt Literature and Language Arts* has been divided into quarters to allow you to administer the four summative tests required by California. Chapters 5 and 6 and related instructional material constitute the third quarter of instruction. At the end of Chapter 6, you may ask students to take the Third-Quarter Test in the *Diagnostic and Summative Assessments* booklet.

Mastering the California Standards CHAPTER 5

CHAPTER

STANDARDS FOCUS

(For grade-level and review standards taught in this chapter, see Pupil's Edition, p. 241.)

Prerequisite Standards

- Grade 4, Vocabulary 1.4 **Know common roots and affixes derived from Greek and Latin, and use this knowledge to analyze the meaning of complex words (e.g., *international*).**

- Grade 4, Vocabulary 1.5 **Use a thesaurus to determine related words and concepts.**

- Grade 5, Reading Comprehension 2.3 **Discern main ideas and concepts presented in texts, identifying and assessing evidence that supports those ideas.**

- Grade 5, Literary Response and Analysis 3.1 **Identify and analyze the characteristics of poetry, drama, fiction, and nonfiction, and explain the appropriateness of the literary forms chosen by an author for a specific purpose.**

Standard Coming Up in the Next Grade Level

- Grade 7, Literary Response and Analysis 3.5 **Contrast points of view (e.g., first and third person, limited and omniscient, subjective and objective) in narrative text, and explain how they affect the overall theme of the work.**

5 | Biography and Autobiography
Looking at Lives

CHAPTER RESOURCES

Planning

- *One-Stop Planner* CD-ROM with Test Generator
- *On Course: Mapping Instruction*
  - Chapter 5
- *At Home: A Guide to Standards Mastery*
- *At Home: In Five Languages*
- *Supporting Instruction in Five Languages*

Reading

- *Interactive Reading*
  - Chapter 5

Differentiating Instruction

- *Lesson Plans for Language Development*
  - Chapter 5

Vocabulary and Spelling

- *Vocabulary Development*
  - Cumulative Vocabulary Review, p. 25

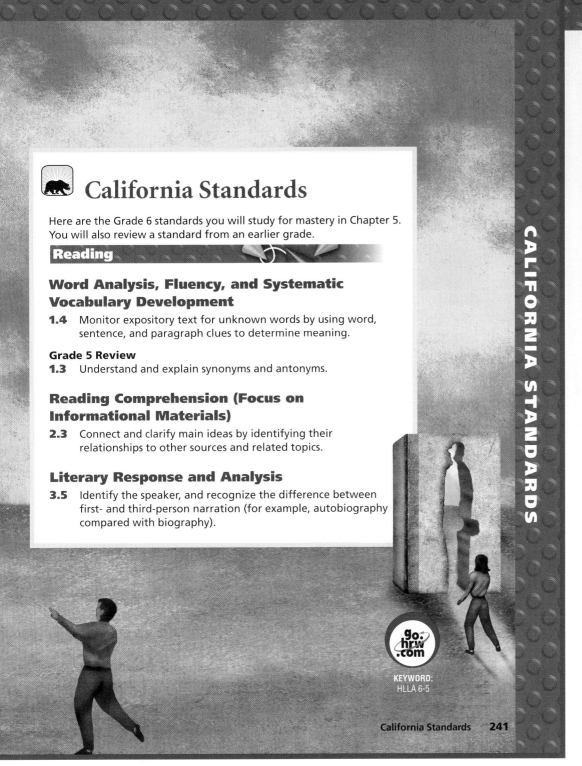

California Standards

Here are the Grade 6 standards you will study for mastery in Chapter 5. You will also review a standard from an earlier grade.

Reading

Word Analysis, Fluency, and Systematic Vocabulary Development

1.4 Monitor expository text for unknown words by using word, sentence, and paragraph clues to determine meaning.

Grade 5 Review
1.3 Understand and explain synonyms and antonyms.

Reading Comprehension (Focus on Informational Materials)

2.3 Connect and clarify main ideas by identifying their relationships to other sources and related topics.

Literary Response and Analysis

3.5 Identify the speaker, and recognize the difference between first- and third-person narration (for example, autobiography compared with biography).

go.hrw.com

KEYWORD:
HLLA 6-5

California Standards **241**

INTRODUCING THE CHAPTER

This chapter's gripping autobiographical and biographical writings open windows into other times, places, and lives. The concepts of first-person and third-person narration are introduced, with different aspects of first- and third-person point of view explored for each selection. Thematically related informational materials following each literary selection encourage broad-range thinking, and lessons guide students in connecting and comparing main ideas across texts. To lead students into synthesizing and applying these reading skills, the chapter culminates with guidelines for writing brief research reports, using autobiographical and biographical materials as sources.

▶ Resources Reminder

Planning
- *At Home: A Guide to Standards Mastery*

You may want to send students home with selected parent letters from this resource. Translations of these letters are available in *At Home: In Five Languages. Supporting Instruction in Five Languages* provides translations of the selection summaries.

Reading
- *Interactive Reading*
  - Reading Log

The California framework requires students to read materials apart from in-class assignments. Additional reading suggestions are included on the Read On pages and on selected pages in the Pupil's and Teacher's Editions. You may want to use the Reading Log to help students track their progress.

- *Spelling Lessons and Activities*
  - Root Words and Affixes, pp. 40–47, 52, 60–63, 68–75

Grammar
- *Holt Handbook*
  - Special Problems in Using Modifiers, pp. 204–205

- Using Modifiers Correctly, pp. 199–201, 211–214
- A Glossary of Usage, p. 223

Assessment
- *Progress Assessment of Reading*
  - Chapter Test, p. 105
- *One-Stop Planner* CD-ROM with Test Generator

Internet
- go.hrw.com
  Keyword: HLLA 6-5

STANDARDS FOCUS, pp. 242–243

(*For the grade-level standard taught in this lesson, see Pupil's Edition, p. 242.*)

Standard Coming Up in the Next Grade Level

■ Grade 7, Literary Response and Analysis 3.5 **Contrast points of view** (e.g., first and third person, limited and omniscient, subjective and objective) in narrative text, and explain how they affect the overall theme of the work.

Literary Focus: First- and Third-Person Narration

Bring in and read to students a short newspaper article about an event (the more amusing or surprising, the better) involving a well-known political, entertainment, or sports figure. Explain that the article is written in the third person, and that a version of it might appear in a biography of the figure. Then, invite volunteers to take the role of the well-known figure and retell the event from his or her own point of view, using the pronouns *I, me,* and so on.

   Explain that the volunteers are speaking in the first person, and ask how the first-person and third-person accounts differ. Point out that the first-person account might appear in an autobiography.

Resources Reminder

Reading

■ *Interactive Reading*

Before you teach Chapter 5 of *Holt Literature and Language Arts,* you may want to preteach the literary concept and a related reading strategy.

• To introduce students to the literary concept before they read this essay, assign p. 179 of *Interactive Reading.*

• To introduce students to a reading strategy that will help them grasp the literary concept, assign p. 179 of *Interactive Reading.*

• To give students practice applying the strategy to a short, vocabulary-controlled selection, assign the Practice Read on p. 180 of *Interactive Reading.*

First- and Third-Person Narration *by* Madeline Travers Hovland

LOOK WHO'S TALKING

"How'd It Go Today?"

If you were a middle-school student named Michael, you might answer this way:

"Well, I missed the bus and had to walk to school. So I got there late and had to check in at the principal's office. After that bad scene, I went to first-period math. Just my luck—the kids were already taking a test, so I was sent to the library. I had to give up study period to make up the test. But the rest of my day was great! Guess what? I made the soccer team!"

When you tell someone about your day, you're telling a true story. You're the narrator, so you tell the story in the **first person.** That means you use first-person pronouns—*I, me, us, our, my, mine*. You look at things one way—your way. You reveal only your own thoughts and feelings. After all, only you can know what's going on inside your own head.

Autobiography: "Self-Written Life"

Nonfiction is "not fiction"—it is writing based on fact. The subjects of nonfiction can vary as much as the

Reading Standard 3.5
Identify the speaker, and recognize the difference between first- and third-person narration (for example, autobiography compared with biography).

world itself. The most personal kind of nonfiction is autobiographical writing. When you describe something that happened to you, you're telling an autobiographical story. An **autobiography** is a writer's account of his or her own life, written from the first-person point of view.

   The word *autobiography* is made up of three parts. The prefix *auto*– means "self," the word root *–bio*– means "life," and the suffix *–graphy* means "writing." So an autobiography is a person's written account of his or her own life. Gary Paulsen's *Woodsong* (page 245) is a good example of autobiographical writing.

Biography: "Written Life"

A **biography** is the story of a person's life written by another person. Biographers write from the **third-person point of view.** They do not write from the "I" point of view because they are not the subject of the life story. Instead, they write about their subject using third-person pronouns—*his, her, their, he, she, they, them.*

   A biographer writing an account of Michael's school day might begin this way:

DIFFERENTIATING INSTRUCTION

Learners Having Difficulty

Help clarify the meaning of *autobiography* for students. Ask students if they have ever kept a diary. Explain that they have probably written about their own thoughts, feelings, and activities in a diary, so they have already done a form of autobiographical writing.

English-Language Learners

Review with students the English first-person singular pronouns *I, me, my,* and *mine* and the first-person plural pronouns *we, us, our,* and *ours.* Model using each pronoun correctly in a sentence. Then, ask students to make up their own sentences using the pronouns.

Michael missed the bus, so he had to walk to school. He wasn't surprised—and neither was the vice-principal—when he got there late, again.

Biographers spend a lot of time—sometimes many years—finding out as much as they can about their subject. They interview people who knew the person. They read firsthand accounts, such as letters and journals. They dig up newspaper and magazine articles that mention the person. If they're writing about a person who lived long ago, they read historical accounts of the time so that they understand the world the subject lived in.

What a biographer chooses to leave out of a biography is as important as what he or she puts in. According to Russell Freedman, author of "The Mysterious Mr. Lincoln":

"The most difficult part of writing, whether it's biography or fiction, is deciding what to leave out. You want the reader to bring his or her own imagination to the piece. In biography, you are leaving out most things. Lincoln lived twenty-four hours a day for his whole life. It's the biographer's job to pick out the most significant details, the ones that tell something about the man or woman."

Practice

Draw a time line of your life. Label the left end "Birth" and the right end "Now." Above the line, write two or three major events that have happened in your life. Then, pick one of the events on your time line. (It's OK to choose "Birth" or "Now.") Write a paragraph about the event from the first-person point of view, as if you were writing an autobiography. Then, write about the same event from the third-person point of view, as if you were writing a biography.

Birth | We move to California. | My sister is born. | I start school. | Now

First- and Third-Person Narration: Look Who's Talking   **243**

Other milestones that students might list include meeting a best friend, getting a pet, taking a memorable trip, or starting music or sports lessons.

Possible first-person paragraph—When I was eight, my aunt gave me a puppy. I had been begging for a dog since I was three. I named him Jump and loved how he played tug-of-war with my clothes, leaped into the bathtub with me, and howled in harmony when I practiced my trumpet. My parents were less enthusiastic about him than I was.

Possible third-person paragraph—When Eileen was eight, her aunt gave her a puppy. Eileen had been begging for a dog since she was three. She named him Jump. He was overactive, noisy, and hard to train. He destroyed her clothing and upset her daily routines. Still, her parents patiently put up with the creature.

Apply

Assign students to find a brief magazine article written in the third person. Then, ask them to rewrite it using the first-person point of view.

HOMEWORK

▶ **Resources Reminder**

Differentiating Instruction

■ *Lesson Plans for Language Development*

For additional instruction on first- and third-person narration for English-language learners and special education students, see *Lesson Plans for Language Development,* pp. 111–112.

Advanced Learners
Acceleration. Use this activity to move students toward the seventh-grade Standard 3.5, which requires that they contrast different points of view and learn how point of view affects theme. First, introduce the term *omniscient.* Define it as "all-knowing," from the Latin *omni–,* "all," and *sciens,* "knowing." Explain that an *omniscient* third-person narrator explains what goes on in the minds of several characters. A *limited* third-person narrator, by contrast, writes from the viewpoint of only one character and does not explain what goes on in the minds of any other characters.
Activity. Have students skim their favorite literary works and bring in brief examples showing the third-person limited point of view and the third-person omniscient point of view.

HOMEWORK

STANDARDS FOCUS, pp. 244–253

(For grade-level and review standards taught in this selection, see citations on Pupil's Edition pages.)

Prerequisite Standard

- Grade 4, Vocabulary 1.4 **Know common roots and affixes derived from Greek and Latin, and use this knowledge to analyze the meaning of complex words (e.g., *international*).**

Standard Coming Up in the Next Grade Level

- Grade 7, Literary Response and Analysis 3.5 **Contrast points of view (e.g., first and third person, limited and omniscient, subjective and objective) in narrative text, and explain how they affect the overall theme of the work.**

Reading Skills

- Find the main idea.

Summary ⟷ *at grade level*

In this autobiographical essay, Paulsen brings readers into the world of dog-sledding, where a dog named Storm stands out for his strength, sense of humor, and ability to communicate. Storm watches with "scale eyes" while the sled is loaded and growls in disapproval at loads that look too heavy. On sled runs, Storm lets Paulsen know that all is well by carrying a stick in his mouth. If Paulsen ignores the dogs' needs, however, Storm drops the stick. To Paulsen, Storm is a true friend who has taught him important lessons about life.

Storm

Literary Focus
First-Person Point of View

Everything you read is told from a particular point of view. In a story told from the **first-person point of view**, a character in the story is speaking to you. This person is called the **narrator**, which means "storyteller." It's easy to recognize a first-person narration because throughout the story the storyteller speaks of himself or herself using first-person pronouns—*I, me, we, us, mine, ours.* In this episode from a true adventure story, Gary Paulsen, the narrator, speaks as "I."

Reading Skills
Finding the Main Idea

The **main idea** is the most important idea in a nonfiction piece. To figure out the main idea, follow these steps:

- Look at the **key details** or **events.** What ideas do they support?
- Look for a major idea stated several times in slightly different words.
- Look for **key passages** near the end of the selection. Is the writer summing up a main idea?

Answering the questions near the little open-book logos will help you identify Paulsen's main idea.

Reading Standard 3.5 Identify the speaker, and recognize first-person narration.

Make the Connection
Think-Pair-Share

What can you learn about a pet or a wild animal from your own observations?

Make a two-column chart like the one below. In one column, list examples of behavior you have noticed in different animals. In the other column, write what you think each action shows about the animal. ✏️

The Animal's Actions	What They Tell Me
A big dog lies down when my dog gets near.	The big dog is showing that he's friendly.
Blue jays divebomb my cat Fern.	They want to scare her.

Background

"Storm" is taken from *Woodsong,* Gary Paulsen's account of his adventures in northern Minnesota. There he ran a team of sled dogs. Paulsen later ran the Iditarod (i·dit′ə·räd), a 1,180-mile dog-sled race across Alaska.

Vocabulary Development

Don't get snowed under by new words when you're reading the story. Learn them now!

disengage (dis′in·gāj′) *v.:* unfasten. *Before I disengage the leash, I get the dog under control.*

regain (ri·gān′) *v.:* recover. *I stopped to let the dog rest and regain her strength.*

emit (ē·mit′) *v.:* give out; send forth. *Dogs emit quick breaths when they pant.*

RESOURCES

Planning
- *One-Stop Planner* CD-ROM with Test Generator
- *On Course: Mapping Instruction*

Media
- *Audio CD Library*
  - disc 7

Reading
- *Interactive Reading*
  - Strategy Launch: Say Something, p. 179
  - Practice Read: "The Picture," p. 180
  - Graphic Organizer: Point of View Questionnaire, p. 188
- *Interactive Reading,* Teacher's Edition
  - Transparency 5: Say Something

Courtesy of The Greenwich Workshop, Inc.
© 1994 Scott Kennedy, © The Greenwich Workshop®, Inc. Shelton, Connecticut.

STORM

from *Woodsong* Gary Paulsen

It is always possible to learn from dogs, and in fact the longer I'm with them, the more I understand how little I know. But there was one dog who taught me the most. Just one dog. Storm. First dog. . . .

Joy, loyalty, toughness, peacefulness—all of these were part of Storm. Lessons about life and, finally, lessons about death came from him.

 FINDING THE MAIN IDEA
1. What important idea does Paulsen express in this paragraph?

A

Storm   245

Standards Starter

Motivate. Ask students how animals show their personalities. Invite students to share stories of animals they have known or observed, such as the friendliest, laziest, or craziest. Then, assign the Think-Pair-Share activity.

Preview Vocabulary

Point out that all three Vocabulary words are verbs. Remind students that verbs express action. Then, pair students to mime the actions of these verbs. Use the following ideas, or have students devise their own.

1. Stand on one foot facing your partner. Mirror each other's actions as you begin to lose your balance and then <u>regain</u> it.
2. Link arms with your partner. Now show how you can <u>disengage</u>.
3. Working together, <u>emit</u> the sounds of a car needing a tuneup.

▶ Resources Reminder

Media
- *Audio CD Library*
  - disc 7

Reading
- *Interactive Reading*
  - Strategy Launch: Say Something, p. 179
  - Graphic Organizer: Point of View Questionnaire, p. 188

DIRECT TEACHING

A **Reading Skills**
Finding the main idea. [Possible response to question 1: He has learned a lot from dogs, particularly from his first dog, Storm.]

Differentiating Instruction
- *Lesson Plans for Language Development*
  - English-Language Learners, pp. 113–115, 134, 143
  - Special Education Students, pp. 116, 134, 143

Vocabulary and Spelling
- *Vocabulary Development*
  - Vocabulary Worksheet, p. 17

- Decoding Worksheet, p. 18
- *Spelling Lessons and Activities*
  - Prefixes, pp. 44–47, 52, 62–63, 70–71

Assessment
- *Progress Assessment of Reading*
  - Selection Test, p. 88
- *One-Stop Planner* CD-ROM with Test Generator

Eager to Run by Scott Kennedy.

A **Reading Skills**

? Finding the main idea. What idea about Storm might these details suggest? [Possible responses: that he is playful; that he is unusual; that he is mischievous.]

B **Literary Focus**
GRADE-LEVEL STANDARD

? First-person point of view. Which pronouns in this section make it clear that the narrator is using the first-person point of view? [me, I]

C **English-Language Learners**

Building background knowledge. Explain that a bootie is a small, soft shoe. Many owners of sled dogs use booties to protect the dogs' paws from sharp ice, stones, and other hazards.

D **Vocabulary Development**
REVIEW STANDARD

? Roots and affixes. The word *disappear* starts with the same prefix as one of the Vocabulary words for this selection. What is the prefix? [*dis–*] How does adding the prefix change the meaning of the word *appear*? [Possible response: *Appear* means "to become visible"; adding the prefix *dis–* reverses the meaning, so that *disappear* means "to vanish."]

He had a bear's ears. He was brindle colored[1] and built like a truck, and his ears were rounded when we got him, so that they looked like bear cub ears. They gave him a comical look when he was young that somehow hung on to him even when he grew old. He had a sense of humor to match his ears, and when he grew truly old, he somehow resembled George Burns.[2]

At peak, he was a mighty dog. He pulled like a machine. Until we retired him and used him only for training puppies, until we let him loose to enjoy his age, he pulled, his back over in the power curve, so that nothing could stop the sled.

A In his fourth or fifth year as a puller, he started doing tricks. First he would play jokes on the dog pulling next to him. On long runs he would become bored, and when we least expected it, he would reach across the gang line and snort wind into the ear of the dog next to him. I ran him with many different dogs and he did it to all of them—chuckling when the dog jumped and shook his or her head—but I never saw a single dog get mad at him for it. Oh, there was once a dog named Fonzie who nearly took his head off, but Fonzie wasn't really **B** mad at him so much as surprised. Fonzie once nailed me through the wrist for waking him up too suddenly when he was sleeping. I'd reached down and touched him before whispering his name.

Small jokes. Gentle jokes, Storm played. He took to hiding things from me. At first I couldn't understand where things were going. **C** I would put a bootie down while working on **D** a dog, and it would disappear. I lost a small ladle[3] I used for watering each dog, a cloth glove liner I took off while working on a dog's feet, a roll of tape, and finally, a hat.

He was so clever.

When I lost the hat, it was a hot day and I had taken the hat off while I worked on a dog's harness. The dog was just ahead of Storm, and when I knelt to work on the

---

1. **brindle colored:** gray or brown and streaked or spotted with a dark color.
2. **George Burns** (1896–1996): American comedian and actor with large ears.

3. **ladle** *n.:* cup-shaped spoon with a long handle for dipping out liquids.

DIFFERENTIATING INSTRUCTION

Learners Having Difficulty
Modeling. If students need to read an easier selection before reading "Storm," use the Practice Read in *Interactive Reading,* p. 180. Then, use the transparency to model the strategy of Say Something. This strategy can help students identify the narrator of a text. Have students apply the strategy to help them read "Storm." As they read, encourage students to engage in a dialogue with the narrator, pausing often to make a comment or form a question about a passage.

 Resources Reminder

Reading

- *Interactive Reading,* Teacher's Edition
  - Transparency 5: Say Something

© 1987 Scott Kennedy, © The Greenwich Workshop®, Inc. Courtesy of The Greenwich Workshop, Inc., Shelton, Connecticut.

harness—he'd chewed almost through the side of it while running—I put the hat down on the snow near Storm.

Or thought I had. When I had changed the dog's harness, I turned and the hat was gone. I looked around, moved the dogs, looked under them, then shrugged. At first I was sure I'd put the hat down; then, when I couldn't find it, I became less sure, and at last I thought perhaps I had left it at home or dropped it somewhere on the run.

Storm sat quietly, looking ahead down the trail, not showing anything at all.

I went back to the sled, reached down to disengage the hook, and when I did, the dogs exploded forward. I was not quite on the sled when they took off, so I was knocked slightly off balance. I leaned over to the right to regain myself, and when I did, I accidentally dragged the hook through the snow.

And pulled up my hat.

It had been buried off to the side of the trail in the snow, buried neatly with the snow smoothed over the top, so that it was completely hidden. Had the snow hook not scraped down four or five inches, I never would have found it.

I stopped the sled and set the hook once more. While knocking the snow out of the hat and putting it back on my head, I studied where it had happened.

Right next to Storm.

He had taken the hat, quickly dug a hole, buried the hat and smoothed the snow over it, then gone back to sitting, staring ahead, looking completely innocent.

When I stopped the sled and picked up the hat, he looked back, saw me put the hat on my head, and—I swear—smiled. Then he shook his head once and went back to work pulling.

Along with the jokes, Storm had scale eyes. He watched as the sled was loaded, carefully calculated the weight of each item, and let his disapproval be known if it went too far.

One winter a friend gave us a parlor stove with nickel trim. It was not an enormous stove, but it had some weight to it and some

> 📖 **FINDING THE MAIN IDEA**
> 2. What lesson does Paulsen learn from Storm's tricks?

Vocabulary
disengage (dis′in·gāj′) v.: unfasten.
regain (ri·gān′) v.: recover.

Storm **247**

Never Alone (detail) by Scott Kennedy.

DIRECT TEACHING

VIEWING THE ART

Scott Kennedy grew up in Colorado Springs, where camping and hiking trips with his father inspired Kennedy's love of the wilderness. He says that hiking and fishing help him "slow down" and that through his painting, he tries to give others "a breath of fresh air."

Activity. Ask students to describe the sensations that Kennedy's paintings (pp. 245–250) arouse. Invite them to describe how Kennedy uses color and light to convey a cold, wintry feeling or mood.

A Reading Skills

❓ **Finding the main idea.** What ideas about Storm does Paulsen develop by relating this event? [Possible responses: Storm is intelligent; he knows by the size of its load that the sled will be very heavy. Storm is independent of the team; he sits facing the sled and does not move when they do. Storm is a skilled communicator; he shows his anger by growling at the stove. Storm is loyal; despite his disapproval, he helps to pull the sled.]

bulk. This friend lived twelve miles away—twelve miles over two fair hills followed by about eight miles on an old, abandoned railroad grade.[4] We needed the stove badly (our old barrel stove had started to burn through), so I took off with the team to pick it up. I left early in the morning because I wanted to get back that same day. It had snowed four or five inches, so the dogs would have to break trail. By the time we had done the hills and the railroad grade, pushing in new snow all the time, they were ready for a rest. I ran them the last two miles to where the stove was and unhooked their tugs so they could rest while I had coffee.

We stopped for an hour at least, the dogs sleeping quietly. When it was time to go, my friend and I carried the stove outside and put it in the sled. The dogs didn't move.

---

4. **railroad grade:** rise or elevation in a railroad track.

Except for Storm.

He raised his head, opened one eye, did a perfect double take—both eyes opening wide—and sat up. He had been facing the front. Now he turned around to face the sled—so he was facing away from the direction we had to travel when we left—and watched us load the sled.

It took some time, as the stove barely fit on the sled and had to be jiggled and shuffled around to get it down between the side rails.

Through it all, Storm sat and watched us, his face a study in interest. He did not get up but sat on his back end, and when I was done and ready to go, I hooked all the dogs back in harness—which involved hooking the tugs to the rear ties on their harnesses. The dogs knew this meant we were going to head home, so they got up and started slamming against the tugs, trying to get the sled to move.

CONTENT-AREA CONNECTIONS

Science

Ecology. A biome similar to that in which Paulsen and Storm do their sledding exists on Baffin Island, a remote region of northeastern Canada. This island of 183,810 square miles is mostly tundra, or treeless land, with permanently frozen subsoil (permafrost) and temperatures usually below freezing.

Scientists observed a group of five adult wolves and seven pups functioning as a family there. The group occupied a series of dens that were halfway between the summer and winter grounds of the wolves' main prey, caribou, or large deer. The wolves used division of labor to cope with the challenges of tundra life. While one

wolf went out in search of food, another stayed behind to shelter and care for the pups. When the "designated hunter" returned, doling out meat to the hungry pups and preparing for a long nap, another adult would set out on the cold, wearying journey across the tundra in search of more meat.

© 1993 Scott Kennedy. © The Greenwich Workshop® Inc. Courtesy of The Greenwich Workshop, Inc., Shelton, Connecticut.

All of them, that is, but Storm.

Storm sat backward, the tug hooked up but hanging down. The other dogs were screaming to run, but Storm sat and stared at the stove.

Not at me, not at the sled, but at the stove itself. Then he raised his lips, bared his teeth, and growled at the stove.

When he was finished growling, he snorted twice, stood, turned away from the stove, and started to pull. But each time we stopped at the tops of the hills to let the dogs catch their breath after pulling the sled and stove up the steep incline, Storm turned and growled at the stove.

The enemy.

The weight on the sled.

I do not know how many miles Storm and I ran together. Eight, ten, perhaps twelve thousand miles. He was one of the first dogs and taught me the most, and as we worked

B

together, he came to know me better than perhaps even my own family. He could look once at my shoulders and tell how I was feeling, tell how far we were to run, how fast we had to run—knew it all.

FINDING THE MAIN IDEA
3. What important idea does Paulsen repeat in this paragraph? **C**

When I started to run long, moved from running a work team, a trap line team, to training for the Iditarod, Storm took it in stride, changed the pace down to the long trot, matched what was needed, and settled in for the long haul. **D**

He did get bored, however, and one day while we were running a long run, he started doing a thing that would stay with him—with us—until the end. We had gone forty or fifty miles on a calm, even day with no bad wind. The temperature was a perfect ten below zero. The sun was bright, everything was moving well, and the dogs had settled into the rhythm that could take them a hundred or a thousand miles. **E**

And Storm got bored.

At a curve in the trail, a small branch came out over the path we were running, and as Storm passed beneath the limb, he jumped up and grabbed it, broke a short piece off—about a foot long—and kept it in his mouth.

All day.

And into the night. He ran, carrying the stick like a toy, and when we stopped to feed or rest, he would put the stick down, eat, then pick it up again. He would put the stick down carefully in front of him, or across his paws, and sleep, and when he awakened, he would pick up the stick, and it soon became a thing between us, the stick.

He would show it to me, making a contact, a connection between us, each time

Storm **249**

DIRECT TEACHING

B **Literary Focus**
GRADE-LEVEL STANDARD
? **First-person point of view.** What makes Paulsen feel that Storm knows more about him than his own family does? [Possible responses: Storm and he have run thousands of miles together; they communicate without words; Storm shares a very important part of his life that his family may know little about.]

C **Reading Skills**
Finding the main idea. [Possible response to question 3: Paulsen has learned a lot from Storm about dog sledding and about himself, and Storm has learned a lot about Paulsen.]

D **Content-Area Connections**
CULTURE
Iditarod. The Iditarod is a dog-sled race from Anchorage to Nome, Alaska, held in mid-March each year. Dog teams cross almost 1,200 miles of snow and ice.

E **Literary Focus**
REVIEW STANDARD
? **Character.** Paulsen describes the cold weather by using such words as "calm, even," "a perfect ten below zero," and "bright." He uses the phrases "moving well" and "settled into the rhythm" to describe training for the Iditarod. What do these word choices suggest about Paulsen's feelings for the weather and the task? [Possible responses: He likes the cold and the task; he sees the conditions as ideal; he feels everything is going well; he is used to extreme cold; he is content.]

MINI-LESSON **Reading**

Developing Word-Attack Skills
Write the selection word *temperature* on the chalkboard. Have students identify the consonant in the word that does not have its usual sound: *t* /ch/. Point out that there are a number of words in which the letter *t* stands for /ch/ when it comes before *u* in a middle or final syllable. Share these examples: *nature, feature, statue.*
Activity. Display these pairs of words without underlines. Ask volunteers to read them

aloud and identify the word in which *t* stands for /ch/.

1. posture	poster	**7.** future	futile
2. creator	creature	**8.** captive	capture
3. cultivate	culture	**9.** gesture	jester
4. fortune	retune	**10.** picture	pictorial
5. statue	status	**11.** factor	factual
6. actor	actual	**12.** nature	native

DIRECT TEACHING

A Literary Focus
GRADE-LEVEL STANDARD

First-person point of view.
What does Paulsen show us by enclosing "examine" in quotation marks? [Possible responses: that he is pretending to examine the stick for the dog's benefit; that he is joining in the dog's game.]

B Reading Skills

Finding the main idea. What does the ritual with the stick show you about the relationship between Storm and Paulsen? [Possible responses: It shows that they communicate closely with each other; that they depend on each other; that they respect each other.]

C Literary Focus
REVIEW STANDARD

Character. Storm's refusal to pick up the stick displays an aspect of his personality. What quality do you think he is showing? [Possible responses: intelligence, dignity, perseverance, stubbornness, skill at communicating.]

D Reading Skills

Finding the main idea.
[Possible responses to question 4: that winning is not always the most important thing; that a sled driver should put the team's well-being first; that Storm is very smart.]

Never Alone (detail) by Scott Kennedy.

we stopped. I would pet him on top of the head and take the stick from him—he would emit a low, gentle growl when I took the stick. I'd "examine" it closely, nod and seem to approve of it, and hand it back to him.

Each day we ran, he would pick a different stick. And each time I would have to approve of it, and after a time, after weeks and months, I realized that he was using the sticks as a way to communicate with me, to tell me that everything was all right, that I was doing the right thing.

Once, when I pushed them too hard during a pre-Iditarod race—when I thought it was important to compete and win (a feeling that didn't last long)—I walked up to Storm, and as I came close to him, he pointedly dropped the stick. I picked it up and held it out, but he wouldn't take it. He turned his face away. I put the stick against his lips and tried to make him take it, but he let it fall to the ground. When I realized what he was

doing, I stopped and fed and rested the team, sat on the sled, and thought about what I was doing wrong. After four hours or so of sitting—watching other teams pass me—I fed them another snack, got ready to go, and was gratified to see Storm pick up the stick. From that time forward I looked for the stick always, knew when I saw it out to the sides of his head that I was doing the right thing. And it was always there.

Through storms and cold weather, on the long runs, the long, long runs where there isn't an end to it, where only the sled and the winter around the sled and the wind are there, Storm had the stick to tell me it was right, all things were right.

> **FINDING THE MAIN IDEA**
> 4. What does Storm's behavior with the stick teach Paulsen?

Vocabulary
emit (ē·mit') *v.:* give out; send forth.

DIFFERENTIATING INSTRUCTION

Advanced Learners
Enrichment. Working in small groups, have students discuss the nature of intelligence and to come up with their own definition of it. Have them discuss questions like these: In what different ways are humans intelligent? Can nonhuman animals be considered intelligent? Are there situations in which an animal such as a dog

might have more intelligence or knowledge than a person? What might dogs "know" that humans do not?

Learners Having Difficulty
Pair students to complete the Literary Response and Analysis questions on p. 252. *Monitoring tip:* If students are unable to identify the main idea (question 6), have them re-read the first and last pages of the

essay, asking themselves "What opening statements does Paulsen make about Storm?" and "How does Paulsen sum up his relationship with Storm?"
Writing. Have students write the first paragraph in class, using first-person pronouns and point of view. Then, have them complete their stories as homework.

HOMEWORK

Gary Paulsen

Good Cooking

The son of an army officer who moved his family with each new assignment, **Gary Paulsen** (1939–   ) lived all over the United States when he was a boy. Because he was always moving, Paulsen had no real friends when he was growing up. One winter day he wandered into a public library to keep warm, and the librarian offered him a library card. He remembers:

> When she handed me the card, she handed me the world.... It was as though I had been dying of thirst and the librarian had handed me a five-gallon bucket of water. I drank and drank.

This passion for reading eventually led to an interest in writing. Paulsen left his engineering job and became editor of a magazine, an experience he has called "the best of all possible ways to learn about writing." His first book was a collection of interviews with Vietnam War veterans. Since then he has written more than forty books, along with hundreds of magazine articles and short stories. Writing means the world to him:

> I have not done anything else in my life that gives me the personal satisfaction that writing does. It pleases me to write—in the very literal sense of the word. When I have done well with it, and 'cooked' for a day so that it felt good when I put it down—it flowed and worked right. When all that is right, I go to sleep with an immense feeling of personal satisfaction.

For Independent Reading

Paulsen has cooked up a feast of adventure stories for young adults. If you're interested in wilderness-survival tales, try the novels *Dogsong* and *Hatchet*. Both were named Newbery Honor Books by the American Library Association.

Meet the Writer

Background. Besides being a professional writer, Paulsen has worked as a teacher, an engineer, a magazine editor, an actor, a professional archer, a singer, a truck driver, a migrant farm worker, and a sergeant in the United States Army. His stories for young adults usually feature teenagers who learn something about themselves through an experience with nature. Paulsen writes from his personal experiences with nature as a hunter and trapper and as a dog-sled racer in the Iditarod. He prefers writing for young people rather than adults because "Adults created the mess which we are struggling to outlive. Adults have their minds set." He believes that young people, on the other hand, "know the score," and when he asks questions in his stories, Paulsen believes "that young people have the answers."

For Independent Reading

If students choose to read *Dogsong,* tell them that Paulsen wrote most of it by firelight, in the camps he made while training for the Iditarod.

- Students interested in animal intelligence might enjoy *The Story of Nim,* by Anna Michel, the true story of a chimp trained to use sign language.
- *Rascal,* by Sterling North, tells of an orphaned raccoon that the author raises. Wildlife fans will be hooked.
- For a classic dog story, introduce students to *Lassie Come Home,* by Eric Knight.

Advanced Learners

Enrichment. Tell students that Gary Paulsen competed in the Iditarod twice before health problems forced him to retire from racing. He feels that his many years and experiences in the northern wilderness opened his mind and changed his life.

Activity. Suggest that students find out more about the Iditarod and Paulsen's experiences with it. They might explore the history of the race, find out which years Paulsen competed, and read about issues and controversies affecting the race before, during, and after those years.

INDEPENDENT PRACTICE

Literary Response and Analysis

Reading Check

1. The narrator is Gary Paulsen.
2. first person
3. *Anecdote* 1—Storm and the hat. *Anecdote* 2—Storm and the stove. *Anecdote* 3—Storm and the stick.

Interpretations

4. Possible answers: Respecting others is more important than winning; a friend will tell you when you're wrong; it's important to play and enjoy life even when you're working; communication can help to solve problems; teamwork requires loyalty and trust.
5. Possible answers: dedicated; caring; humorous; observant; tough yet gentle.
6. Possible answers: Friendship with an animal can be as meaningful as friendship with a human; being true to yourself and to your friends is the most important thing; contentment comes from doing your best at what you love.

Evaluation

7. Written responses will vary.
8. Possible answers: Paulsen knows dogs well and is a careful observer, so he's not likely to misinterpret or exaggerate. He may be misinterpreting (how could he know why Storm carried the stick?) or exaggerating (a dog wouldn't smooth snow over a place where he'd buried something) to make a better story. It's not possible to tell the complete truth, since writers may overlook some things, and they must shape their work to make coherent points. Nonfiction writers should at least try for complete truth

Literary Response and Analysis

Reading Check

1. Who is the narrator of these stories about Storm?
2. From what **point of view** is "Storm" told—first person or third person?
3. The graphic below shows how "Storm" is structured:

An **anecdote** (an′ik·dōt′) is a brief story told to make a point. Fill in a graphic like the one above to show the structure of Paulsen's text.

Interpretations

4. In your own words, **sum up** what Storm teaches the narrator.
5. When Paulsen describes Storm, he also gives clues to his own **character.** What kind of person do you think Paulsen is?
6. Is this piece only about dogs, or is it about something else also? In one

or two sentences, state what you see as Paulsen's **main idea.**

Evaluation

7. Paulsen describes Storm as the "dog who taught me the most." Think of something you have learned from an animal. Compare what you learned with what Paulsen learns from Storm.
8. Writers of biographies and auto-biographies are sometimes criticized for stretching the truth to make their accounts more interesting. What do you think of the way Paulsen interprets Storm's jokes and tricks? Do you think he is exaggerating? Should writers of nonfiction stories always try to be completely truthful? Is that possible? Give your opinion on these questions, and support it with two good reasons.

Writing

Straight from the Dog's Mouth

Imagine that Storm decides to tell the world a few things about Paulsen and that Storm's so smart he can write his own stories about his human pal. How would Storm tell the story of hauling the heavy stove? Use the personal pronoun *I* to retell the story from Storm's **point of view.** (Did Paulsen interpret Storm's actions correctly?)

Reading Standard 3.5
Identify the speaker, and recognize first-person narration.

because *nonfiction* means "truth," and anything less betrays readers' trust.

Vocabulary Development

Prefixes

Each word in the Word Bank has a **prefix**—a letter or group of letters added to the beginning of a word to change its meaning. Knowing the meaning of a few prefixes can help you figure out the meaning of many unfamiliar words.

PRACTICE

Make a chart like the one below for the prefixes of the words in the Word Bank: *dis–*, *re–*, and *e–*.

Prefix	Meaning	Examples
anti–	against	antislavery antibiotic antifreeze

> **Word Bank**
> disengage
> regain
> emit

Grammar Link MINI-LESSON   **PRACTICE**

Using *Good* and *Well* Correctly

The word *good* should be used to modify nouns and pronouns. The word *well* should generally be used to modify verbs.

> Storm's funny face always looked **good** to Paulsen. [*Good* modifies the noun *face*.]
> Storm worked **well** with the team. [*Well* modifies the verb *worked*.]

Do not use *good* to modify a verb.

NONSTANDARD	Storm works good even when he is tired.
STANDARD	Storm works well even when he is tired.

Note that *feel good* and *feel well* mean different things. *Feel good* means "feel happy or pleased." *Feel well* means "feel healthy."

> Even if he didn't **feel well** [healthy], Paulsen felt **good** [happy] when he saw Storm.

Complete each of the following sentences by choosing the correct word from the underlined pair.

1. Storm ate good/well today.
2. The team looked good/well.

Hint: Circle the words *good* and *well* wherever they appear in your writing. Then, draw an arrow from the circled word to the word it modifies. If the arrow points to a noun or a pronoun, be sure you've used an adjective. If the arrow points to a verb, an adjective, or an adverb, be sure you've used an adverb.

For more help, see Special Problems in Using Modifiers in the *Holt Handbook*, pages 204–206.

Storm   **253**

Vocabulary Development

Practice

Students' examples will vary.

- *dis–*. Meaning—away, opposing. *Examples*—disease, disrepair, disagree, discourage, distaste.
- *re–*. Meaning—again, anew, back. *Examples*—reconsider, rewrite, replace, research.
- *e–*. Meaning—out. *Examples*—emigrate, emerge, erupt, eject.

Resources Reminder

Vocabulary and Spelling

- *Vocabulary Development*
  - Vocabulary Worksheet, p. 17
  - Decoding Worksheet, p. 18
- *Lesson Plans for Language Development*
  - Vocabulary, p. 143
- *Spelling Lessons and Activities,* pp. 44–47, 52, 62–63, 70–71

Grammar Link

Practice

1. well
2. good

ASSESSING

Assessment

- *Progress Assessment of Reading*
  - Selection Test, p. 88

RETEACHING

For a lesson reteaching first-person narration, see **Reteaching,** p. 489A.

STANDARDS FOCUS, pp. 254–261

(For grade-level and review standards taught in this selection, see citations on Pupil's Editions pages.)

Prerequisite Standard
Grade 5, Reading Comprehension **2.3 Discern main ideas and concepts presented in texts, identifying and assessing evidence that supports those ideas.**

Summary ⬌ *at grade level*

> Two articles show the powerful bonds that can develop between animals and humans. "Bringing Tang Home" describes a volunteer's efforts to help feral cats. Tang, a wild orange kitten, is captured and will be sent to a good home.
>
> "Where the Heart Is" discusses the amazing journeys that some pets have taken out of devotion to their owners. Bobby, a dog lost on a vacation, treks three thousand miles to find his owner seven months later. Sugar, a cat adopted by neighbors when his owner moves to another state, travels fifteen hundred miles to appear at his owner's new farm fourteen months later. Research suggests that animals have extra senses that allow them to "home in" on those they love and trust. How they do it remains a mystery, but for these remarkable pets it seems certain that it was their emotional connection to their owners that propelled their remarkable journeys.

🔺 Resources Reminder

Media
- *Audio CD Library*
  - disc 7
- *Visual Connections*
  - Videocassette, Segment 7

Reading
- *Interactive Reading*
  - Graphic Organizer: Main-Idea Web, p. 189

Connecting and Clarifying Main Ideas
Storm *and*
Bringing Tang Home *and*
Where the Heart Is

Linking Across Selections

The subject of a piece of writing can usually be stated in just a word or two: *love, dogs, growing up.* The **main idea** is the most important thing a writer has to say *about* the subject. The main idea answers the question "What about it?"— what about love or dogs or growing up?

In "Storm," Gary Paulsen gives us a subject that's easy to identify: his dog Storm. But what does Paulsen want to say *about* Storm? By telling us about Storm, what is he saying about dogs in general?

Finding a main idea takes some practice. Sometimes there's more than one main idea in a piece of nonfiction, just as there can be more than one theme to a story. Copy the chart below, which shows four main ideas you might have found in "Storm."

Possible Main Ideas

Humans and animals have a special bond.	There are many things about animals that humans can't explain.
Animals may understand humans better than humans understand animals.	Humans can learn from their animal friends.

Reading Standard 2.3 Connect and clarify main ideas by identifying their relationships to other sources.

Now, write "Storm" under each main idea that you think Paulsen's story best illustrates or supports. (You may decide to write "Storm" under all the ideas.)

The two selections that follow have animals as their subject. After you read each selection, go back to your chart. Write the selection titles ("Bringing Tang Home" and "Where the Heart Is") under the main ideas they illustrate or support. When you've finished filling in the chart, notice how some of the main ideas connect to all three selections.

Vocabulary Development

These are the words you'll be learning as you read "Bringing Tang Home":

furtive (fur′tiv) *adj.:* done in a sneaky or secretive way. *The kitten made a furtive movement toward the food.*

formidable (fôr′mə·də·bəl) *adj.:* fearsome. *The cat let out a formidable yowl.*

feral (fir′əl) *adj.:* untamed; wild. *The feral cat finally let me touch her.*

lure (loor) *v.:* tempt; attract. *They used food to lure the wild cats to safety.*

controversial (kän′trə·vur′shəl) *adj.:* debatable; tending to stir up argument. *His method of rescuing wild cats is controversial.*

254 Chapter 5 Biography and Autobiography: Looking at Lives

RESOURCES

Planning
- *One-Stop Planner* CD-ROM with Test Generator
- *On Course: Mapping Instruction*

Media
- *Audio CD Library*
  - disc 7

- *Visual Connections*
  - Videocassette, Segment 7

Reading
- *Interactive Reading*
  - Graphic Organizer: Main-Idea Web, p. 189

Bringing Tang Home

In the warm half-light at the end of a summer day, the woods near my home fall quiet as if holding their breath waiting for the wild creatures of the night. Twilight is nature's shift change: In an hour's time the day will be gone and night will be filled with the furtive rustlings of animals who'd rather their comings and goings be unnoticed by the residents of the nearby houses.

I let my own breath out slowly, quietly, for I am also waiting, as is the woman beside me. The night creatures we wait for, though, aren't meant to be wild: We are waiting for cats.

Among the Wild Things

The opossum, the raccoon, and the skunk steal food from their human neighbors on the other side of the river levee but want nothing in the way of affection. They flee from the sound of footsteps and bare formidable teeth if cornered. "Approach at your peril!" they snarl before melting into the shadows.

But the cats aren't quite so anxious to run. Perhaps this is because their kind and ours have been linked for countless generations, or perhaps it is because, among all the animals, cats alone chose the path of their own domestication and remember it still. Whatever the reason, in the heart of **A**

Vocabulary
furtive (fʉr′tiv) *adj.:* done in a sneaky or secretive way.
formidable (fôr′mə·də·bəl) *adj.:* fearsome.

Bringing Tang Home **255**

A **Reading Informational Materials**
GRADE-LEVEL STANDARD
❓ Clarifying the main idea.
What is the narrator's companion doing? [She is helping feral cats.] Why is she doing this? [Possible responses: She cares about the cats; she wants to provide them the security of living as pets.]

B **English-Language Learners**
Building background knowledge. Tell students that the trap being used is a wire cage with a spring-loaded door, designed not to injure the animal.

C **Reading Informational Materials**
GRADE-LEVEL STANDARD
❓ Clarifying the main idea.
Does the narrator favor killing feral cats or rescuing them? [She favors rescuing them.] Which words show you this? [Possible responses: She calls the rescuers' work a "labor of love"; she finds the thought of the rescuers' success "pleasant to contemplate."]

D **Advanced Learners**
❓ Enrichment. How does the author personify nature at the beginning and end of the essay? [She writes that that the woods grow silent "as if holding their breath" and that "the summer night hugs me in a warm embrace."] (The literary term *personification* will be taught later in the program.)

these cats—of every cat gone feral—remains a memory of how pleasant is the company of a human, or how sweet is the feel of a hand swept warmly from just behind the ears and along the supple spine to the end of the tail.

My companion tonight is one of those people who work to return the wild ones to a life of such pleasures. The cats in these woods belong to her, as much as they belong to anyone. She traps the older ones and has them fixed and vaccinated before releasing them to these woods again, for they are too wild to be good pets. The kittens—for despite all the spaying and neutering, there are always new cats, and so, new kittens—she traps, and tames, and finds homes for.

We are after the last of the spring kittens this night, a pale orange tabby male she has named Tang (as in orange Tang). The older cats know what the trap is about, and only the most desperate starvation would lure them inside again. The kittens aren't so worldly-wise. The appeal of canned food is enough for them, and all but Tang have already been enticed inside for the first step on their journey back to domestication.

The Task of Taming

In the dimming light we can barely see the half-grown kitten move inside. The trap slams shut with a crack that scatters the cats—all but the young tabby, who now cannot flee. He hurls himself against the sides of his cage, yowls in fear, and hisses in anger.

The sound beside me is no less explosive. "Yes!" cries my companion. "We got him!"

Tang doesn't yet know it, but he is on his way home. After a few weeks of gentle and

gradual socialization, he'll be placed with someone who'll love him. A better fate, surely, than the one he faced as one of the ferals, whose short lives are full of desperation—and often end brutally.

Despite the dangers that claim so many, wild cats are everywhere on the edges of our lives, from the alleys of our cities and the parks of our suburbs to the wild areas and farmland that fill in the gaps between. And in many of those places are people like Tang's captor, quietly pursuing a labor of love that can be as thankless as it often is controversial. Some people would rather see the ferals killed, but these volunteers see another way.

One kitten, one summer evening at a time, they are making a difference. Few thoughts are as pleasant to contemplate as the summer night hugs me in a warm embrace.

—Gina Spadafori

Vocabulary
feral (fir′əl) *adj.:* untamed, wild.
lure (loor) *v.:* tempt; attract.
controversial (kän′trə·vur′shəl) *adj.:* debatable; tending to stir up argument.

DIFFERENTIATING INSTRUCTION

Learners Having Difficulty
To help students identify the main ideas of these articles, ask them to preview the titles, subheads, and illustrations to determine the articles' subjects. [The subjects are taming and finding a home for a wild cat and the journeys of various animals to find their owners.] Make sure students understand that the main ideas are what the writer says about the subject.

▶ Resources Reminder

Reading
■ *Interactive Reading*
  ▪ Graphic Organizer: Main-Idea Web, p. 189

English-Language Learners
These students will benefit from hearing "Bringing Tang Home" re-read aloud as they follow along silently. For lessons

designed for intermediate and advanced English-Language learners, see *Lesson Plans for Language Development*, pp. 117–118, 135–136, 143.

Where the Heart Is

Two-year-old Bobby, partly English sheepdog but mostly collie, had become separated from Frank Brazier while on vacation in Indiana.

On a cold February evening in 1924, a gaunt dog limped up to a farmhouse in Silverton, Oregon, where he had once lived with his family as a pup. But the house was silent, the family long departed. Since August, the dog's lonely journey had taken him across Illinois and Iowa. He had swum rivers, including the dangerous and icy Missouri; he had crossed the great Rocky Mountains in the middle of winter. He had caught squirrels and rabbits for food. At times he had been helped by strangers:

E English-Language Learners

Understanding idioms. Explain to students that the title "Where the Heart Is" is a fragment of the common English idiom *home is where the heart is.* Ask students whether this information provides them with new insight as to what the article will be about.

Special Education Students

For lessons designed for special education students, see *Lesson Plans for Language Development,* pp. 117–118, 135–136, 143.

Advanced Learners

Acceleration. Use this activity to move students toward the eighth-grade Standard 2.3, which requires that they analyze similarities and differences between texts. Have them compare and contrast "Bringing Tang Home" and "Where the Heart Is" in terms of their treatment and organization of ideas. Have them answer these questions:

• How do both articles use examples to make a point?

• In what ways are the openings and endings of the articles similar or different?

A **Reading Informational Materials**
GRADE-LEVEL STANDARD
❓ **Clarifying the main idea.**
What is Bobby's remarkable feat? [He treks over 3,000 miles home to find his family.] What motivates him? [Possible responses: devotion, love, loyalty.]

B **Reading Informational Materials**
GRADE-LEVEL STANDARD
❓ **Clarifying the main idea.**
Informational texts often pose questions, and then give answers to the questions. The questions and their answers are usually key to the article's main idea: What question does the writer ask here? [How did the cat find its owner?] Point out the related questions that follow about remarkable achievements by animals.

C **Reading Informational Materials**
GRADE-LEVEL STANDARD
❓ **Clarifying the main idea.**
The text poses a possible answer to the questions it has raised. What is that answer? [Possible responses: Animals may have senses that people lack; animals may have ESP.]

He had eaten stew with hobos and Thanksgiving dinner with a family who sheltered him for several weeks. But once he had regained his strength, the dog traveled on, always heading west. The dog lay down to rest for the night at the empty farmhouse. In the morning, on paws with pads worn almost to bone, he made his way slowly into town, into the restaurant where his family now lived, and climbed upstairs to a bedroom, to lick the face of the man he had walked some three thousand miles to find. Bobby had come home.

Two-year-old Bobby, partly English sheepdog but mostly collie, had become separated from Frank Brazier while on vacation in Indiana. When word got out about Bobby's remarkable journey, the president of the Oregon Humane Society decided to document the facts and find the people who had seen or helped Bobby along the way. Bobby eventually became one of the most honored heroes in dog history, recognized with numerous medals and awards for his courage, devotion, and perseverance.

How did Bobby find his way home? Nobody knows for sure. We do know that Bobby's story is unusual but not unique. For centuries there have been reports of animals performing mystifying and wonderful feats like Bobby's. There are stories of other animals who tracked their families, sometimes over thousands of miles, to places where the animals themselves had never been, over routes the owners had never traveled. The story of Sugar may be the longest recorded trip of this kind.

Stacy Woods, a high school principal, planned to move from Anderson, California, to a farm in Gage, Oklahoma, 1,500 miles away. She couldn't take her cat Sugar, because he was terrified of riding in the car. So a neighbor agreed to adopt him. Fourteen months later, as Stacy Woods was milking a cow in her Oklahoma barn, Sugar jumped through an open window onto her shoulder. The astonished Woods family later learned that Sugar had disappeared three weeks after they had left him with the neighbor. Proving that the cat was really Sugar was easy because Sugar had an unusual hip deformity. But the main question remains unanswered today: How did Sugar find his owner? Similar questions have been raised about many other animals. How did Hugh Brady Perkins's homing pigeon find his way to Hugh's hospital window, 120 miles from his home, after the boy was rushed to the hospital in the middle of the night? How do some pets know when their favorite family members are coming home unexpectedly? How do some pets know from great distances when their family members are hurt or ill or in trouble?

In recent decades, researchers have studied questions like these. They have pondered the possibility that animals draw on information picked up in some way other

Fourteen months later, as Stacy Woods was milking a cow in her Oklahoma barn, Sugar jumped through an open window onto her shoulder.

than through the five well-known senses (sight, hearing, smell, taste, and touch).

Researchers have found that some animals have senses humans lack, like bats' ability to detect objects from echoes and certain snakes' ability to sense tiny temperature differences through special organs. Some people theorize that animals have a form of ESP (extrasensory perception). At Duke University, Joseph Banks Rhine collected more than five hundred stories of unexplainable animal feats that seem to support this theory. Rhine devoted his life to researching these events. Studies conducted at the Research Institute at Rockland State

Hospital in New York also support the notion of an extrasensory connection between animals and humans, particularly humans the animals know well and trust.

Of course, whatever our theories say, we don't really know what goes on in the heart and mind of an animal. Perhaps the question of *how* they find us is not the most important one. A better question to ponder may be *why* they find us, even when faced with overwhelming difficulties. It has been said that home is where the heart is. It's clear that for Bobby and Sugar and countless others, home is where one particular heart is.

—Sheri Henderson

DIRECT TEACHING

D Learners Having Difficulty

Breaking down difficult text.
This sentence has a long subject ("Studies . . . in New York") and a long predicate ("support the notion . . . between animals and humans"), with a qualifying phrase at the end ("particularly . . . trust") that modifies the predicate. Provide starters to help students break the sentence into simpler parts:

- Studies support the notion of . . .
- The findings were made at . . .
- The connection may be particularly strong with . . .

E Reading Informational Materials
GRADE-LEVEL STANDARD
❓ Clarifying the main idea.
What does the narrator consider the most important question about the amazing animal feats she has described? [Why do animals find us?] What does she think the answer is? [Possible responses: because they love us; because their hearts tell them where home is.]

GUIDED PRACTICE

Monitoring students' progress.
Have students make two columns, headed "Humans Devoted to Animals" and "Animals Devoted to Humans." Guide students in listing characters from the selections in the appropriate columns.

FAMILY/COMMUNITY ACTIVITY

Invite adult volunteers from the community to visit classes and read aloud to students. Ask volunteers to choose selections that focus on the theme of bonds between humans and animals. Hold a brief orientation meeting for volunteers beforehand during which you can make introductions, provide background on your school and students, and review volunteers' selections if desired. Have them read for twenty to thirty minutes and share ways that reading has enhanced their lives. On the day of the Read-In, select student guides to escort the volunteers to classrooms. You might recruit volunteers from local service clubs (Rotary, Kiwanis, Lions), community businesses, and relatives of students and faculty.

Reading Informational Materials

INDEPENDENT PRACTICE

Reading Informational Materials

Reading Check

1. Possible answers: Both articles might appear under "Humans and animals have a special bond" and "There are many things about animals that humans can't explain."

2. Possible answer: "Humans and animals have a special bond." Examples: "Storm"—"he came to know me better than perhaps even my own family"; "Bringing Tang Home"—"their kind and ours have been linked for countless generations"; "Where the Heart Is"—"support the notion of an extrasensory connection between animals and humans."

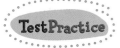

Answers and Model Rationales

1. **B** Point out the key words *all three selections,* and explain that the writer of "Bringing Tang Home" would not agree with C, the writer of "Where the Heart Is" would not agree with D, and the writer of "Storm" would not agree with A.

2. **G** Point out the key word *not* in the question, and remind students that only Tang, a feral kitten, has no relationship with humans.

3. **A** Remind students that "Where the Heart Is" mentions scientific research, whereas "Storm" and "Bringing Tang Home" include only anecdotes and personal commentary.

4. **G** Explain that in "Storm" and "Bringing Tang Home," the narrators use the first-person point of view, referring to themselves

Reading Check

1. Go back to the chart of possible main ideas that you made before you read "Bringing Tang Home" and "Where the Heart Is" (page 254). Write the titles of these two selections under the main ideas that they best illustrate or support.

2. Which of the main ideas applies to "Storm," "Bringing Tang Home," and "Where the Heart Is"? Support your answer with examples from each selection.

Reading Standard 2.3 Connect and clarify main ideas by identifying their relationships to other sources.

TestPractice

Storm / Bringing Tang Home / Where the Heart Is

1. The writers of all three selections would probably agree that —
   A dogs and cats are not intelligent
   B relationships between animals and people benefit both
   C abandoned and lost animals should be left to survive on their own
   D dogs and cats stay with humans only because humans feed them

2. If you were writing an essay on close relationships between people and animals, which of the following animals would *not* be a good example to use?
   F Storm
   G Tang
   H Bobby
   J Sugar

3. In which selections are scientific **facts** as well as **anecdotes** (very brief stories told to make a point) used to support the main idea?
   A "Where the Heart Is"
   B "Storm"
   C "Bringing Tang Home"
   D All of the above

4. Which statement about the **point of view** of these selections is accurate?
   F All selections are written from the first-person point of view.
   G The stories of Tang and Storm are told from the first-person point of view.
   H The story of Tang and "Where the Heart Is" are told from the first-person point of view.
   J All three selections are told from the third-person point of view.

as *I.* In "Where the Heart Is," the words *I* and *me* do not appear; that selection is written from the third-person point of view.

Test-Taking Tips

Tell students to check questions for key words and phrases such as *not* or *of all three selections* and to choose answers accordingly.

For more instruction on answering multiple-choice questions, refer students to **Test Smarts,** p. 690.

Vocabulary Development

Context Clues

You can often figure out the meaning of a new word by looking at its **context**—the words or sentences surrounding it. For example, in "Bringing Tang Home," Gina Spadafori writes, "In the dimming light we can barely see the half-grown kitten move inside." You may not know the meaning of *dimming,* but you do know that you need light to see. Since it is nightfall and Spadafori can barely see the kitten, you can figure out that *dimming* means "fading."

> **Word Bank**
> furtive
> formidable
> feral
> lure
> controversial

PRACTICE

Read each of the quotations below, using context to help you choose the correct meaning of the underlined word.

1. "In an hour's time the day will be gone and night will be filled with the furtive rustlings of animals who'd rather their comings and goings be unnoticed by the residents of the nearby houses."

   a. playful   **b.** secretive   **c.** noisy   **d.** foolish

2. "They flee from the sound of footsteps and bare formidable teeth if cornered. 'Approach at your peril!' they snarl before melting into the shadows."

   a. surprising   **b.** playful   **c.** fearsome   **d.** weak

3. "The night creatures we wait for . . . aren't meant to be wild: We are waiting for cats. . . . In the heart of these cats— of every cat gone feral—remains a memory of how pleasant is the company of a human. . . ."

   a. tame   **b.** fierce   **c.** insane   **d.** wild

4. "The older cats know what the trap is about, and only the most desperate starvation would lure them inside again."

   a. yank   **b.** want   **c.** tempt   **d.** shove

5. "And in many of those places are people like Tang's captor, quietly pursuing a labor of love that can be as thankless as it often is controversial. Some people would rather see the ferals killed, but these volunteers see another way."

   a. debatable   **b.** fair   **c.** humorous   **d.** persuasive

Reading Standard 1.4 Monitor expository text for unknown words by using word and sentence clues to determine meaning.

Vocabulary Development

Practice

Possible Answers

1. **b**   The animals want to be unnoticed, so their sounds would be secretive (b), not play- ful, noisy, or foolish (a, c, or d).

2. **c**   The animals snarl "Approach at your peril!" so their teeth would not appear playful or weak (b or d). For a cornered wild animal to bare its teeth would not be surprising (a). *Fearsome* (c) is the best choice.

3. **d**   The cats are described as *wild,* so students can guess that *wild* (d) is a synonym for *feral.*

4. **c**   Starvation is inanimate; it could not yank or shove an ani- mal (a or d) or want anything (b). But the feeling of starvation could tempt (c) an animal to enter a trap baited with food.

5. **a**   *Controversial* contains much of the word *controversy,* which can be a synonym for *debate,* so *debatable* (a) is the best option.

▶ Resources Reminder

Vocabulary and Spelling
■ *Vocabulary Development*
  ▪ Vocabulary Worksheet, p. 19
■ *Lesson Plans for Language Development*
  ▪ Vocabulary, p. 143

ASSESSING

Assessment
■ *Progress Assessment of Reading*
  ▪ Selection Test, p. 91

STANDARDS FOCUS, pp. 262–268

(For grade-level and review standards taught in this selection, see citations on Pupil's Edition pages.)

Prerequisite Standard

■ Grade 4, Vocabulary 1.5 Use a thesaurus to determine related words and concepts.

Standard Coming Up in the Next Grade Level

■ Grade 7, Literary Response and Analysis 3.5 Contrast points of view (e.g., first and third person, limited and omniscient, subjective and objective) in narrative text, and explain how they affect the overall theme of the work.

Reading Skills

■ Infer the main idea.

Summary ⟷ *at grade level*

Set in the 1930s in Arkansas, this is a loving sketch of Angelou's beloved only brother, Bailey. Angelou portrays him as graceful, mischievous, daring, clever, full of life, and protective of her. Descriptions of tricks and games he played reinforce this characterization.

PRETEACHING

Standards Starter

Build prerequisite skills. As they begin to read, remind students to look for clue words such as *I, me, my, we,* and *us* to establish the point of view.

Preview Vocabulary

To review the Vocabulary words on p. 262, ask students which word might be used in each situation:

1. hearing a car alarm [grating]
2. honoring a teacher [lauded]
3. seeing a disaster [aghast]
4. timing a race [precision]

Brother

Literary Focus
Autobiography

When you write in a diary or journal about something that happened to you, you're writing a true story about yourself. An **autobiography** is the true story of a person's life written by that person.

Autobiographies are written from the **first-person point of view.** That means that the writer speaks in the first person, using pronouns like *I, we, me, us, mine,* and *ours.* Reading an autobiography puts us inside the writer's mind and heart. It lets us see the world through another person's eyes.

Description

Description is writing that helps us imagine someone or something, usually by appealing to our sense of sight. In this selection, Maya Angelou paints a portrait in words of her brother, Bailey, as a boy. He's "small, graceful, and smooth," with "velvet-black skin" and "black curls." As you can tell from these details, description can also help us *feel* something (the velvet skin). It can appeal to our senses of smell, taste, and hearing as well.

Description is used in all kinds of writing—in fiction and poetry, of course, but also in historical accounts, science writing, newspaper articles, even personal letters and journals.

Reading Standard 3.5 Identify the speaker, and recognize first-person narration.

Reading Skills 📖
Inferring the Main Idea

Some writers state the **main idea** of a piece of writing directly. Others leave it up to you to figure out the main idea. This means that you have to use details in the text to **infer,** or guess, the larger idea the writer is getting at. Read this text twice; the second time, list key details and important passages that you think reveal Angelou's main idea.

Make the Connection
Quickwrite ✏️

In her autobiography, Maya Angelou says simply that her brother, Bailey, was "the greatest person in my world." Who is the greatest person in your world? Your choice could be someone you know or a public figure you admire. Write a few sentences identifying the person and explaining why he or she is "the greatest."

Vocabulary Development

Here are the words you'll learn as you read Maya Angelou's description of her brother:

grating (grāt′iŋ) *adj.:* irritating. *The visitors found Maya's manner grating.*

lauded (lôd′id) *v.:* praised highly. *They lauded Bailey for his looks and insulted me.*

aghast (ə·gast′) *adj.:* shocked; horrified. *Momma was aghast at our behavior.*

precision (prē·sizh′ən) *n.:* exactness; accuracy. *Bailey moved with grace and precision.*

RESOURCES

Planning
■ *One-Stop Planner* CD-ROM with Test Generator
■ *On Course: Mapping Instruction*

Media
■ *Audio CD Library*
  ■ disc 7

■ *Fine Art Transparencies*
  ■ Transparency 9

Reading
■ *Interactive Reading*
  ■ Graphic Organizer: Description Chart, p. 190

Brother

FROM *I Know Why the Caged Bird Sings*

MAYA ANGELOU

Boy by the Sea (1995) by Jonathan Green, Naples, Florida. Oil on canvas (18" × 17").

Photograph by Tim Stamm.

Brother **263**

? **Finding the main idea.** What details reveal Angelou's feelings for her brother? [Possible responses: She is grateful he is her only sibling; she admires his beauty and grace; she is glad he loves her.]

B **Literary Focus**
REVIEW STANDARD

? **Description.** The narrator describes her hair as "black steel wool." Based on this detail, how do you think she sees herself? [Possible responses: as scratchy, abrasive, unattractive.]

C **Literary Focus**
REVIEW STANDARD

? **Description.** What senses do words in this description appeal to? [Possible responses: sight and touch—"clean streams down his ashy legs," "pockets full of loot," "laughing eyes"; smell—"like a vinegar barrel or a sour angel."] What attitude toward Bailey does this description express? [Possible responses: delight, admiration.]

Bailey was the greatest person in my world. And the fact that he was my brother, my only brother, and I had no sisters to share him with, was such good fortune that it made me want to live a Christian life just to show God that I was grateful. Where I was big, elbowy, and grating, he was small, graceful, and smooth. . . . He was lauded for his velvet-black skin. His hair fell down in black curls, and my head was covered with black steel wool. And yet he loved me.

When our elders said unkind things about my features (my family was handsome to a point of pain for me), Bailey would wink at me from across the room, and I knew that it was a matter of time before he would take revenge. He would allow the old ladies to finish wondering how on earth I came about, then he would ask, in a voice like cooling bacon grease, "Oh Mizeriz[1] Coleman, how is your son? I saw him the other day, and he looked sick enough to die."

Aghast, the ladies would ask, "Die? From what? He ain't sick."

And in a voice oilier than the one before, he'd answer with a straight face, "From the Uglies."

I would hold my laugh, bite my tongue, grit my teeth, and very seriously erase even the touch of a smile from my face. Later, behind the house by the black-walnut tree, we'd laugh and laugh and howl.

Bailey could count on very few punishments for his consistently outrageous behavior, for he was the pride of the Henderson/Johnson family.

1. **Mizeriz:** dialect term for "Mrs."

His movements, as he was later to describe those of an acquaintance, were activated with oiled precision. He was also able to find more hours in the day than I thought existed. He finished chores, homework, read more books than I, and played the group games on the side of the hill with the best of them. He could even pray out loud in church and was apt at stealing pickles from the barrel that sat under the fruit counter and Uncle Willie's nose.

Once when the Store was full of lunchtime customers, he dipped the strainer, which we also used to sift weevils[2] from meal and flour, into the barrel and fished for two fat pickles. He caught them and hooked the strainer onto the side of the barrel, where they dripped until he was ready for them. When the last school bell rang, he picked the nearly dry pickles out of the strainer, jammed them into his pockets, and threw the strainer behind the oranges. We ran out of the Store. It was summer and his pants were short, so the pickle juice made clean streams down his ashy legs, and he jumped with his pockets full of loot and his eyes laughing a "How about that?" He smelled like a vinegar barrel or a sour angel.

After our early chores were done, while Uncle Willie or Momma minded the Store,

2. **weevils** *n.:* small beetles that feed on grains, cotton, and other crops.

Vocabulary
grating (grāt'iŋ) *adj.:* irritating; annoying.
lauded (lôd'id) *v.:* praised highly.
aghast (ə·gast') *adj.:* shocked; highly horrified.
precision (prē·sizh'ən) *n.:* exactness; accuracy.

264 **Chapter 5** **Biography and Autobiography: Looking at Lives**

Learners Having Difficulty
To help students infer the main idea of "Brother," encourage them as they read to pay special attention to how Angelou feels about her brother and what he means to her.

English-Language Learners
For lessons designed for intermediate and advanced English-language learners, see

Lesson Plans for Language Development, pp. 119–121, 137, 144.

Special Education Students
For lessons designed for special education students, see *Lesson Plans for Language Development,* pp. 122, 137, 144.

Advanced Learners
Acceleration. This activity can help to move students toward the seventh-grade

Standard 3.5, which requires that they contrast points of view.
Activity. Have students form small groups and rewrite the first paragraph of "Brother" in the third person, and then discuss the difference point of view makes. From which point of view are Angelou's feelings for her brother more clearly expressed?

Fishing on the Trail (1990) by Jonathan Green, Naples, Florida. Oil on canvas (47" × 79").

Photograph by Tim Stamm.

we were free to play the children's games as long as we stayed within yelling distance. Playing hide-and-seek, his voice was easily identified, singing, "Last night, night before, twenty-four robbers at my door. Who all is hid? Ask me to let them in, hit 'em in the head with a rolling pin. Who all is hid?" In follow the leader, naturally he was the one who created the most daring and interesting things to do. And when he was on the tail of

D

the pop the whip, he would twirl off the end like a top, spinning, falling, laughing, finally stopping just before my heart beat its last, and then he was back in the game, still laughing.

Of all the needs (there are none imaginary) a lonely child has, the one that must be satisfied, if there is going to be hope and a hope of wholeness, is the unshaking need for an unshakable God. My pretty black brother was my Kingdom Come.

E

Brother **265**

D **English-Language Learners**

? **Build background knowledge.** The games hide-and-seek, follow the leader, and pop the whip may be unfamiliar to some students. Ask volunteers to explain the games and chant the rhyme.

E **Literary Focus**
GRADE-LEVEL STANDARD

? **Autobiography.** How has the first-person point of view allowed readers into Angelou's mind and heart? [Possible response: Angelou allows readers to see how she thinks and feels about Bailey.]

VIEWING THE ART

Jonathan Green. For biographical information, see p. 263.

Activity. Ask students why they think this painting was chosen to accompany "Brother." [Possible responses: In the painting, two children are playing together, just as Angelou and Bailey do. The joyful, innocent mood of the painting echoes the tone of Angelou's reminiscences.]

GUIDED PRACTICE

Monitoring students' progress. Guide the class in answering these comprehension questions.

Short Answer

1. What does Bailey look like? [He is small and graceful and has velvet-black skin and black curls.]
2. What does Bailey steal from the store? [pickles]
3. Name two games the children play. [follow the leader, hide-and-seek, pop the whip.]
4. Who is the most daring when playing games? [Bailey]

FAMILY/COMMUNITY ACTIVITY

Encourage students to share with family members this excerpt from Maya Angelou's autobiography. After reading the story, the family may want to discuss the close bond between Angelou and Bailey and answer questions like these: "How do members of our family stick up for one other? What makes family relationships special or different from the

relationships we have with other people?" You might send a note home to parents, explaining the activity and the benefits to students of reading at home.

Meet the Writer

Background. Maya Angelou, who attended high school in San Francisco, California, says that her time there might have been lost but for the influence of one particular teacher. "Miss Kirwin was that rare educator who was in love with information. I will always believe that her love of teaching came not so much from her liking for students but from her desire to make sure that some of the things she knew would find repositories so that they could be shared again." Two important chances for Angelou to share her art with the world came in the 1990s when she read some of her poetry aloud at President Clinton's inauguration in 1993 and at the Million Man March in Washington, D.C., in 1995.

For Independent Reading

Students may also enjoy reading other memoirs and autobiographies. You might recommend the following titles:

■ If students want to read another author's autobiography, they can try *A Girl from Yamhill: A Memoir* by acclaimed children's writer Beverly Cleary.

■ Interested students can read about an artist's life in the autobiography *Self-Portrait* by Trina Hyman.

▶ Resources Reminder

Reading

■ *Interactive Reading*

For other selections by and about Maya Angelou, see *Interactive Reading*, p. 195. You may want to assign these to advanced learners.

Maya Angelou

"The Power of the Word"

Maya Angelou's remarkable career has taken her far from the time when she was Bailey's lonely, gawky sister. Angelou (1928–   ) has worked hard all her life—as a streetcar conductor, a waitress, a singer, a dancer, an actress, a civil rights worker, a college professor, a TV producer, and above all, a writer. In 1993, Maya Angelou read to the nation the poem President Clinton had asked her to compose and deliver at his inauguration.

In an interview, Angelou talks about how she has triumphed, both as a person and as a writer, over obstacles in her path:

> I believe all things are possible for a human being, and I don't think there's anything in the world I can't do. Of course, I can't be five feet four because I'm six feet tall. I can't be a man because I'm a woman. The physical gifts are given to me, just like having two arms is a gift. In my creative source, wherever that is, I don't see why I can't sculpt. Why shouldn't I? Human beings sculpt. I'm a human being. . . .
>
> All my work, my life, everything is about survival. All my work is meant to say 'You may encounter many defeats, but you must not be defeated.' In fact, the encountering may be the very experience which creates the vitality and the power to endure.

For Independent Reading

For more of Angelou's ideas about life, read her poem "Life Doesn't Frighten Me."

DIFFERENTIATING INSTRUCTION

Advanced Learners
Enrichment. Tell students that Maya Angelou grew up in the pre–Civil Rights South, when it was still segregated. When she was only three and her brother Bailey was only four, their parents separated and sent them by train to live with their grandmother in the small, segregated town of Stamps, Arkansas. This period of Angelou's life forms the backdrop for "Brother." Her experience of segregation, as well as her participation in the Civil Rights movement, had a profound influence on Angelou and her work.
Activity. Have students research Maya Angelou and the Civil Rights movement. They can enter *Maya Angelou* or *Civil Rights* as keywords in a search engine to see what information they can discover.

Learners Having Difficulty
In class, have students write answers to the Reading Check and Interpretations questions. *Monitoring tip:* If students have difficulty filling in the chart for question 7, have them re-read the story, looking for examples of description. After they locate these examples, they should ask themselves: From this description of Bailey, what image of him do I see in my imagination?

Literary Response and Analysis

Reading Check

1. From which **point of view** is this description of Bailey told—first person or third person? How do you know?

2. How is the writer different in appearance from other members of her family?

3. How does Bailey stick up for his sister when people say unkind things about her?

4. Why is Bailey rarely punished for his behavior?

5. List three things Bailey is good at.

6. According to the writer, what does a lonely child need most?

Interpretations

7. Divide a piece of paper into two columns. In the left-hand column, quote three or four **descriptions** from "Brother" that helped you picture Bailey. In the right-hand column, write your response to each quotation.

8. What words would *you* use to describe Bailey's personality? How did you feel about him?

9. Were you surprised by anything in the last paragraph of "Brother"? What does this paragraph tell you about Angelou?

10. Angelou says that she was not as handsome as Bailey was. How important do you think physical appearance is in making someone lovable?

Writing

My Greatest Person

Look back at your Quickwrite notes, and review what you wrote about the greatest person in your world. Now, write a character sketch describing that person. Help your readers see what the person looks like. Describe an action taken by the person that reveals his or her character or personality. (Now that you've read Angelou's description, you may want to write about someone other than the person you first chose.) Be sure to explain how you feel about the person—why is he or she "the greatest"? ✏

What's the Main Idea?

Check your reading notes, and write a few sentences stating what you think Angelou's **main idea** is. Sometimes the main idea of a passage is summed up in the first or last paragraph. Which details in the first and last paragraphs help you understand what Angelou's brother means to her?

Reading Standard 3.5 Identify the speaker, and recognize the difference between first- and third-person narration.

Literary Response and Analysis

Reading Check

1. Words such as *my, I, me,* and *we* signal that the account is told in the first person.

2. She is plain while the rest of her family was handsome.

3. Bailey sticks up for his sister by insulting and making fun of the person who criticizes her.

4. He is seldom punished because his family is so proud of him.

5. He is good at defending his sister, playing games, stealing pickles, and praying aloud.

6. A lonely child most needs "an unshakable God."

Interpretations

7. Possible answers:
   - *Description*—"in a voice like cooling bacon grease." *Response*—He'd be a good defender—he's smooth.
   - *Description*—"He jumped with his pockets full of loot and his eyes laughing." *Response*—He's very active and alive.
   - *Description*—"He would twirl off the end like a top, spinning, falling, laughing." *Response*—He's a daredevil; he's athletic.

8. Possible answers: loving, loyal, daring, clever, sly, energetic. Students may like Bailey because he is smart, fun, and a good leader; some may feel he is too fresh and bossy.

9. Possible answers: that Angelou was a lonely child; that she says lonely children need a faith in an enduring God; that Bailey gave her the kind of security faith gives us. Possible answer: The paragraph tells readers that Angelou is perceptive.

10. Possible answers: Appearance has little or nothing to do with being lovable; a handsome person attracts attention and admiration and may seem easier to love.

How does this image make me feel about Bailey's personality?

Writing. You may wish to help students create character webs with descriptive words and phrases about their subject before they begin writing their paragraphs at home.

HOMEWORK

Advanced Learners
Enrichment. In discussing point of view, have students think about the fact that no two people participating in an event ever experience it or tell about it in exactly the same way. How each of us perceives the world is individual and unique.

Activity. Ask students to write diary entries from Bailey's point of view, in which he describes his own and his sister's activities on the days of the events that Angelou refers to. Have students share and compare their entries.

Vocabulary Development

Practice 1

1. The guard's <u>precision</u> lost the game for us.
2. That bully <u>lauded</u> my best friend.
3. Jack has a <u>grating</u> voice.
4. Max was <u>aghast</u> at the mean remarks.

Practice 2

Possible Answers

- *grate*—abrade, irritate, annoy
- *laud*—praise, honor, extoll, compliment, commend
- *aghast*—surprised, shocked, astonished
- *precision*—accuracy, correctness, exactness

Resources Reminder

Vocabulary and Spelling

- *Vocabulary Development*
  - Vocabulary Worksheet, p. 20
- *Lesson Plans for Language Development*
  - Vocabulary, p. 144

ASSESSING

Assessment

- *Progress Assessment of Reading*
  - Selection Test, p. 92

RETEACHING

For a lesson reteaching narrative point of view, see **Reteaching,** p. 489A.

FOCUS ON

Vocabulary Development

Antonyms: Reversing Meaning

Antonyms (an'tə·nimz') are words that are opposite in meaning. For example, the words *graceful* and *clumsy* are antonyms; they have opposite meanings.

> **Word Bank**
>
> grating
> lauded
> aghast
> precision

PRACTICE 1

Find a Word Bank word that is an **antonym** of the underlined word in each sentence. Then, rewrite the sentence, using the Word Bank word in place of the underlined word.

1. The guard's <u>sloppiness</u> lost the game for us.
2. That bully <u>insulted</u> my best friend.
3. Jack has a <u>soothing</u> voice.
4. Max was <u>untroubled</u> by the mean remarks.

Finding Synonyms: Thesaurus Rex to the Rescue

Synonyms (sin'ə·nimz) are words with the same or nearly the same meanings. A **thesaurus** (from a Greek word meaning "treasure") contains lists of synonyms for certain words. If you look up *aghast* in a thesaurus, you'll find synonyms like *thunderstruck, surprised, shocked,* and *astonished.*

PRACTICE 2

In a thesaurus, look up the four words listed in the Word Bank, and list the synonyms you find for each word. (Look up *grate*, not *grating*, and *laud*, not *lauded*.) Then, go back to the text, and substitute some of your synonyms for Angelou's original choices. Do all the synonyms work?

Grade 5 Review Reading Standard 1.3 Understand and explain synonyms and antonyms.

BORN LOSER reprinted by permission of Newspaper Enterprise Association, Inc.

Connecting and Clarifying Main Ideas

Brother *and*
The Brother I Never Had

Review: Finding a Main Idea

When you have to identify the **main idea** of a piece of nonfiction, ask yourself, "What's the subject?" (Remember that the subject can often be summed up in one word or phrase.) Sometimes the **title** tells you what the subject is. What was the title of the last selection? "Brother." That's your subject. Now ask yourself, "What about it?" What *about* a brother? Your answer to that question is your main idea.

On a sheet of paper, write one sentence summing up Maya Angelou's main idea about her brother. (If you think there's more than one, write a sentence for each.) Don't get caught in the details. If you find yourself starting on your second sheet of paper, you've lost your focus. Look at the big picture, and try again. Ask yourself, "What's the most important thing Angelou says about her brother?"

Review: Comparing Main Ideas

The next selection is called "The Brother I Never Had." (Do you see a pattern here?) After you read this selection, write a sentence stating its main idea.

Then, compare the main ideas of the two selections. In what ways are they connected? In what ways are they different from each other? (You may want to collect your main ideas in a chart like the one on page 254.)

(continued)

Reading Standard 2.3
Connect and clarify main ideas by identifying their relationships to other sources and related topics.

Prerequisite Standard

■ Grade 5, Reading Comprehension 2.3 Discern main ideas and concepts presented in texts, identifying and assessing evidence that supports those ideas.

Summary ⬇ *below grade level*

The narrator describes a walk he once took with Joe, a strong and caring cousin whom the narrator regarded as an older brother. They stopped at Mila's Diner and at the Jamaica Fish Market. The narrator's experience with Joe has influenced his own behavior toward his two younger brothers.

▶ Resources Reminder

Media
■ *Audio CD Library*
  ▪ disc 7
Reading
■ *Interactive Reading*
  ▪ Graphic Organizer: Main-Idea Chart, p. 191

RESOURCES

Planning
■ *One-Stop Planner* CD-ROM with Test Generator
■ *On Course: Mapping Instruction*

Media
■ *Audio CD Library*
  ▪ disc 7

Reading
■ *Interactive Reading*
  ▪ Graphic Organizer: Main-Idea Chart, p. 191

Differentiating Instruction
■ *Lesson Plans for Language Development*
  ▪ English-Language Learners, pp. 123, 138, 144

■ Special Education Students, pp. 123, 138, 144

Assessment
■ *Progress Assessment of Reading*
  ▪ Selection Test, p. 95
■ *One-Stop Planner* CD-ROM with Test Generator

Standards Starter

Motivate. Ask students to think about what it means to be someone's brother or sister. What qualities make someone a sibling? What qualities could turn a friend or relative into a "brother" or "sister"?

Assign the Reading

The selection is short enough to have students read it first at home and then again aloud as a class. Have volunteers take turns reading paragraphs aloud.

HOMEWORK

Thinking About Related Topics

Think back to the work you did as you read "Storm" (page 245), "Bringing Tang Home" (page 255), and "Where the Heart Is" (page 257). The subject of all three selections is animals, and all three deal with the relationships between animals and people. If you are interested in connections, you will think about other topics related to animals and their special relationships to humans. You might think about how pets improve your health, how animals are used in rescue work, and how to listen to your pet. You might even think about animal brains and how they are different from human brains.

Now, think about the subject of brothers, which is also very broad. On your paper, jot down a few topics related to the subject of brothers. Make a cluster diagram like the one below. Put the **main idea** you discovered in "Brother" in the circle under "Main Idea." Put each of your related topics in other circles in a cluster.

Why is all of this important? It's important because ideas are interconnected. Seeing how one idea relates to another broadens your understanding of our rich and complex world. You'll find this skill especially useful whenever you do research. Some people think that finding connections between ideas should be a lifelong quest!

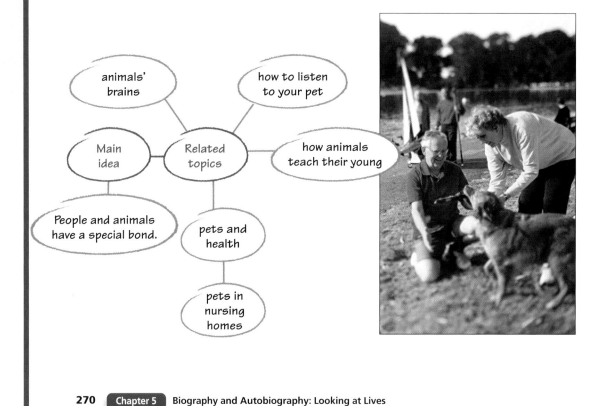

270 | Chapter 5 | Biography and Autobiography: Looking at Lives

---

Learners Having Difficulty
Students may have trouble understanding when the events of the selection actually happened. Help them see that the narrator is looking back on events that happened five years earlier.

English-Language Learners
Some students may be confused by the reference to Jamaica (p. 271, first paragraph).

Explain that here Jamaica refers to an area in the borough of Queens in New York City, not to the Caribbean country.

▶ Resources Reminder
For lessons designed for intermediate and advanced English-language learners, see *Lesson Plans for Language Development,* pp. 123, 138, 144.

Special Education Students
For lessons designed for special education students, see *Lesson Plans for Language Development,* pp. 123, 138, 144.

Advanced Learners
Enrichment. Invite students to analyze Joe's character by making inferences about him based on his actions. The narrator describes Joe as "strong, kind, and caring."

The Brother I Never Had

That day stood clear in my mind. My cousin Joe and I were taking a stroll in the Jamaica area of New York. We had left my uncle's office at about three o'clock and walked to Mila's Diner down the street. I had always thought of Joe as my older brother, and today's experience reaffirmed it.

We walked into that neat little diner and ordered onion rings and Coke. Those onion rings were the best I had ever eaten. Joe introduced me to all the regulars at the diner, and then we sat with them for about an hour. They talked and I listened. They talked about college, work, girls, and life. My cousin kept trying to get me into the conversation, but I refused to speak.

After some time we walked over to the Jamaica Fish Market and looked at all the strange fish they had brought in that day. I tried to pick up a crab out of a basket full of crabs and got pinched. I tried to get some sympathy from Joe, but all he did was smile—not laugh, just smile.

We left the store and headed back to Mila's Diner. We hadn't talked much, just walked. I never had an older brother, and Joe was the only person that was like me and the only one I would consider as my older brother. I wanted to be just like him. He was strong, kind, and caring, and most of all, he loved me.

Now five years later I'm the older brother of two little people. I try to be the same person Joe was for me. He cared for me, as I care for my brothers. He watched out for me, as I watch out for my brothers. Joe is now in college and I guess we've gotten a bit farther apart. That's what getting older does to a person. Every once in a while, though, I think about that walk, and I always wonder if we can ever do it again.

—Gim George
Holy Spirit Regional School
Huntsville, Alabama

The Brother I Never Had   **271**

Do the details the narrator shares support that assertion? Have students create a character web for Joe.

DIRECT TEACHING

Ⓐ Reading Informational Materials
GRADE-LEVEL STANDARD
❓ Autobiography. From what point of view is this selection narrated? [the first person] **How do you know?** [The opening sentences contain the signal words *my, I,* and *we*.]

Ⓑ Reading Informational Materials
GRADE-LEVEL STANDARD
Clarifying the main idea. Ask students to locate, in the fourth paragraph, the author's statement of the main idea. ["Joe was the only person that was like me and the only one I would consider as my older brother. I wanted to be just like him. He was strong, kind, and caring, and most of all, he loved me."]

Ⓒ Reading Informational Materials
GRADE-LEVEL STANDARD
❓ Connecting and clarifying main ideas. How are the narrator's feelings about Joe similar to Angelou's feelings about Bailey in "Brother"? [Possible response: Both look up to their "brothers" and are comforted by them.]

GUIDED PRACTICE

Monitoring students' progress. Ask students to connect and clarify the main ideas from "Brother" and "The Brother I Never Had."

Short Answer

1. How are Bailey and Joe alike? [Both are role models.]

2. What similar feelings about their "brothers" do the narrators express? [love and respect]

3. What important idea about brothers do the selections share? [The presence of an older brother can have a beneficial effect.]

4. How are Bailey and Joe different? [Joe is quiet; Bailey is not.]

The Brother I Never Had   **271**

Reading Informational Materials

INDEPENDENT
PRACTICE

Reading Informational Materials

Test Practice

Answers and Model Rationales

1. **A** Point out that the brothers make the narrators' lives less stressful, calmer, and more satisfying, so B, C, and D are incorrect.

2. **G** The ideas expressed in F and J are present in only one of the selections, and the idea expressed in H is not addressed in either selection.

3. **D** The other choices all refer to details from only one of the two selections and therefore could not fit both.

4. **F** G, H, and J all deal with the topic of siblings and are therefore related to the selections about brothers. Only F does not deal with siblings.

Test-Taking Tips

The wording of multiple-choice questions can be tricky. Remind students to read each multiple-choice question carefully before choosing an answer. Suggest that they pay particular attention to such key words as *without, both,* and *except* in the Test Practice questions. Encourage students to go back and re-read the question after they have read through all the possible answers but before they have chosen one.

For more instruction, refer students to **Test Smarts,** p. 690.

Test Practice

Brother / The Brother I Never Had

These questions will test your skill at connecting and clarifying the **main ideas** in "Brother" (page 263) and "The Brother I Never Had" (page 271).

1. The reader can **infer** that without their "brothers," life for these two writers would be —
   A lonelier
   B easier
   C calmer
   D more satisfying

2. Which **main idea** is presented in *both* selections?
   F Brothers and sisters can be best friends.
   G Someone close to you, like a brother or cousin, can show you how to live.
   H Brothers and sisters often compete.
   J A person doesn't have to be your parents' child to be a brother to you.

3. Which of these **titles** could be used for *both* selections?
   A "A Cousin, a Brother, a Friend"
   B "A Walk to Remember"
   C "The Sour Angel"
   D "My Brother, My Hero"

4. All the titles below could be considered **related topics** to "Brother" and "The Brother I Never Had" *except* —
   F "The Childless Household: A New Study"
   G "I'm a Twin and Proud of It!"
   H "Sibling Rivalry: What Happens When Brothers and Sisters Don't Get Along?"
   J "Are Siblings Better Off in Life Than Only Children?"

Reading Standard 2.3
Connect and clarify main ideas by identifying their relationships to other sources and related topics.

Grammar Link MINI-LESSON

Modifiers: Comparing with Adjectives

A **comparative** is an adjective or adverb used to compare two things. A **superlative** is an adjective or adverb used to compare three or more things. Watch out for these two common mistakes:

- Don't use a superlative to compare only two people or things.

                                   sharper
Mrs. Coleman was sharp, but Bailey was ~~sharpest~~.

                     more
Of the two children, Bailey was ~~most~~ daring.

- Don't use both *more* and *–er* to form a comparative. Don't use both *most* and *–est* to form a superlative.

Bailey's work was ~~more~~ better than the other children's.

Bailey is the most graceful~~est~~ person I've ever seen.

Modifiers: Don't Misplace Them

To work well, modifiers have to be in the right place. Here's an example of a **misplaced modifier:**

Maya and Bailey would play after they finished their chores with their friends.

Did Bailey and Maya do their chores with their friends? No, the phrase *with their friends* has been misplaced in the sentence. To fix the sentence, place the modifier as close as possible to the word it modifies—*play*.

Maya and Bailey would play <u>with their friends</u> after they finished their chores.

For more help, see Using Modifiers Correctly in the *Holt Handbook,* pages 199–202 and 211–214.

PRACTICE 1

Correct these comparisons:

1. I cannot imagine anyone more sweeter than Bailey.
2. Between Bailey and his sister, I liked Bailey best.
3. Sometimes I think Mrs. Coleman is the most meanest person I've ever known.
4. Bailey was the most beautifullest person in Maya's world.
5. Some of her poems are more easier than others.
6. Angelou is one of the most strongest women I know.

PRACTICE 2

Move the misplaced modifier in each sentence to the right place. If you are uncertain of the correct placement, draw an arrow from the modifier to the word it modifies. Then, place the modifier next to that word.

1. Bailey was not punished when he misbehaved by his parents.
2. In front of their relatives, Maya admired Bailey's fearlessness.
3. I almost understood every word in the story.

Grammar Link

Practice 1

1. I cannot imagine anyone sweeter than Bailey.
2. Between Bailey and his sister, I liked Bailey better.
3. Sometimes I think Mrs. Coleman is the meanest person I've ever known.
4. Bailey was the most beautiful person in Maya's world.
5. Some of her poems are easier than others.
6. Angelou is one of the strongest women I know.

Practice 2

1. Bailey was not punished by his parents when he misbehaved.
2. Maya admired Bailey's fearlessness in front of their relatives.
3. I understood almost every word in the story.

ASSESSING

Assessment
- *Progress Assessment of Reading*
  - Selection Test, p. 95

STANDARDS FOCUS, pp. 274–285

(For grade-level and review standards taught in this selection, see citations on Pupil's Edition pages.)

Standard Coming Up in the Next Grade Level

- Grade 7, Literary Response and Analysis 3.5 **Contrast points of view (e.g., first and third person, limited and omniscient, subjective and objective) in narrative text, and explain how they affect the overall theme of the work.**

Reading Skills

- Summarize.

Summary ⬆ *above grade level*

In this autobiographical excerpt, the author describes the events surrounding the marriage of Lan and Trung, young neighbors in his village in Vietnam. When their mothers see that they are in love, wedding plans are made. After the ceremony, Lan goes to the river to bathe and is snatched from behind by a crocodile. Trung's relatives conclude that the young bride is dead. However, Trung insists that he hears Lan calling him, even though his friends and family think that he is hallucinating. Finally, he sees Lan waving at him from an island, and the villagers discover that she has escaped the old crocodile by playing dead. Because it seems as though she has returned from the dead, the couple's mothers hold a second wedding celebration.

▶ Resources Reminder

Media
- *Audio CD Library*
  - disc 7

Reading
- *Interactive Reading*
  - Graphic Organizer: Narration-Example Chart, p. 192

---

from The Land I Lost

Literary Focus
Narrators: First Person and Third Person

This excerpt from an **autobiography** starts with **first-person narration.** The writer, Huynh Quang Nhuong (hoon kwaŋ' nyoon), uses the pronoun *I* to tell about his boyhood in Vietnam. This autobiography is the story of more than one person, though. As the narrative progresses, Nhuong switches to the **third person.** You'll notice that when he tells the story of Lan and Trung, "So Close," Nhuong describes the thoughts and feelings of many of the characters. He tells his story from the point of view of someone outside it.

Reading Skills
Summarizing

When you **summarize** a narrative, you describe the **main events** and **key details** in your own words. Summarizing is a useful skill because it helps you recall the main characters and events of a story. After you read "So Close," map out the framework of the story in an organizer like this one:

Reading Standard 3.5 Identify the speaker, and recognize the difference between first- and third-person narration (for example, autobiography.)

Setting:
Main Characters:
Conflict or Problem:
Sequence of Main Events:
1. Trung and Lan get married.
2. That night, Lan goes to the river to bathe.
[Etc.]
Resolution:

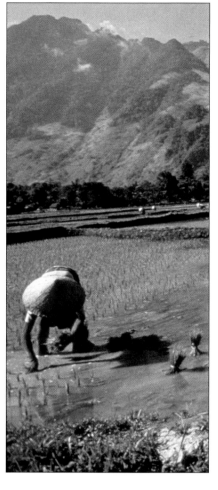

Make the Connection
Quickwrite ✏

Take a good look at the crocodile on page 276. Then, make a cluster diagram showing all the things you associate with crocodiles.

274 Chapter 5 Biography and Autobiography: Looking at Lives

RESOURCES

Planning
- *One-Stop Planner* CD-ROM with Test Generator
- *On Course: Mapping Instruction*

Media
- *Audio CD Library*
  - disc 7

Reading
- *Interactive Reading*

- Graphic Organizer: Narration-Example Chart, p. 192

Differentiating Instruction
- *Lesson Plans for Language Development*
  - English-Language Learners, pp. 124–126, 139, 145
  - Special Education Students, pp. 127, 139, 145

Background

One place where you're likely to meet up with a crocodile is Vietnam, a tropical country in Southeast Asia with many warm, muddy rivers and swamps. Vietnam is about the size of New Mexico, and as you can see on the map, it extends south from China in a long, narrow S-curve.

Most Americans probably still associate Vietnam with war. In this excerpt from his **autobiography,** Huynh Quang Nhuong recalls a more peaceful time in his beautiful country. He shows us a place where people visit with neighbors, fall in love, and work together to solve problems, just as people do all over the world.

Vocabulary Development

Learning these words will help you read the story:

infested (in·fest'id) *v.:* inhabited in large numbers (said of something harmful). *Crocodiles infested the river.*

wily (wī'lē) *adj.:* sly; clever in a sneaky way. *A crocodile becomes more wily with age.*

hallucination (hə·loo'si·nā'shən) *n.:* sight or sound of something that isn't really there. *Trung's relatives think that the voice he heard was a hallucination.*

placate (plā'kāt') *v.:* calm or soothe (someone who is angry). *Some people believe that Lan is trying to placate the crocodile.*

avenge (ə·venj') *v.:* get even for; get revenge for. *Trung vows to avenge Lan's death.*

Standards Starter

Build background. Tell students that Vietnam's history is more than two thousand years old. Although the country was controlled by China until A.D. 939, it enjoyed relative freedom after that time until the arrival of the French in the 1800s. At the time this selection takes place, in the middle of this century, Vietnam's society was mainly agricultural. Most people lived in villages and farmed the land. They were loyal to family above all else, and extended families often lived together.

Preview Vocabulary

Ask students to work together to choose the single best synonym for each Vocabulary word in the following exercise.

1. infested (overrun, visited, enjoyed) [overrun]
2. wily (intelligent, trustworthy, tricky) [tricky]
3. hallucination (memory, vision, thought) [vision]
4. placate (excite, befriend, calm) [calm]
5. avenge (apologize, get even, report) [get even]

Assign the Reading

You may want to have students read the Before You Read pages and the introductory part of the selection (up to the bottom of p. 277) at home. Then, students can read "So Close" in class. Advanced learners can read the entire selection on their own if they wish.

HOMEWORK

Vocabulary and Spelling

■ *Vocabulary Development*
  ■ Vocabulary Worksheet, p. 21
  ■ Decoding Worksheet, p. 22

Assessment

■ *Progress Assessment of Reading*
  ■ Selection Test, p. 97
■ *One-Stop Planner* CD-ROM with Test Generator

A Literary Focus
GRADE-LEVEL STANDARD

Narrator. Point out that in the opening of this excerpt the author uses first-person narration. The author, using the personal pronoun "I," tells his story.

from

The Land I Lost

Huynh Quang Nhuong

I was born on the central highlands of Vietnam in a small hamlet on a riverbank that had a deep jungle on one side and a chain of high mountains on the other. Across the river, rice fields stretched to the slopes of another chain of mountains.

There were fifty houses in our hamlet, scattered along the river or propped against the mountainsides. The houses were made of bamboo and covered with coconut leaves, and each was surrounded by a deep trench to protect it from wild animals or thieves. The only way to enter a house was to walk across a "monkey bridge"—a single bamboo stick that spanned the trench. At night we pulled the bridges into our houses and were safe.

There were no shops or marketplaces in our hamlet. If we needed supplies—medicine, cloth, soaps, or candles—we

---

DIFFERENTIATING INSTRUCTION

Learners Having Difficulty
Make sure students understand that on pp. 276–277 Huynh Quang Nhuong is recalling his own childhood and that in "So Close," on pp. 277–282, he is telling a story about two other people, Trung and Lan. Point out that the narrator begins to tell the story of Trung and Lan directly in the third paragraph on p. 278. From that point on, the narration switches from first person to third person, and "I" appears mainly in quoted dialogue.

Encourage students to practice the reading skill of summarizing as they read "So Close." Have them map out the framework of the story by copying and completing the chart on p. 274 of their books. Suggest that they ask themselves as they read, "What is the next important event?"

English-Language Learners
Students may become confused about who is telling Trung and Lan's story. Point out that Nhuong begins his memoir using first-person narration, but switches to third-person for the story of Lan and Trung. Help students find key phrases in the story, such as "Later in the evening" and "then at dawn," that signal important story events. Students can record these details in their organizers.

had to cross over the mountains and travel to a town nearby. We used the river mainly for traveling to distant hamlets, but it also provided us with plenty of fish.

During the six-month rainy season, nearly all of us helped plant and cultivate fields of rice, sweet potatoes, Indian mustard, eggplant, tomatoes, hot peppers, and corn. But during the dry season, we became hunters and turned to the jungle.

Wild animals played a very large part in our lives. There were four animals we feared the most: the tiger, the lone wild hog, the crocodile, and the horse snake. Tigers were always trying to steal cattle. Sometimes, however, when a tiger became old and slow it became a man-eater. But a lone wild hog was even more dangerous than a tiger. It attacked every creature in sight, even when it had no need for food. Or it did crazy things, such as charging into the hamlet in broad daylight, ready to kill or to be killed.

The river had different dangers: crocodiles. But of all the animals, the most hated and feared was the huge horse snake. It was sneaky and attacked people and cattle just for the joy of killing. It would either crush its victim to death or poison it with a bite.

Like all farmers' children in the hamlet, I started working at the age of six. My seven sisters helped by working in the kitchen, weeding the garden, gathering eggs, or taking water to the cattle. I looked after the family herd of water buffaloes. Someone always had to be with the herd because no matter how carefully a water buffalo was trained, it always was ready to nibble young rice plants when no one was looking. Sometimes, too, I fished for the family while I guarded the herd, for

there were plenty of fish in the flooded rice fields during the rainy season.

I was twelve years old when I made my first trip to the jungle with my father. I learned how to track game, how to recognize useful roots, how to distinguish edible mushrooms from poisonous ones. I learned that if birds, raccoons, squirrels, or monkeys had eaten the fruits of certain trees, then those fruits were not poisonous. Often they were not delicious, but they could calm a man's hunger and thirst.

My father, like most of the villagers, was a farmer and a hunter, depending upon the season. But he also had a college education, so in the evenings he helped to teach other children in our hamlet, for it was too small to afford a professional schoolteacher.

My mother managed the house, but during the harvest season she could be found in the fields, helping my father get the crops home; and as the wife of a hunter, she knew how to dress and nurse a wound and took good care of her husband and his hunting dogs.

I went to the lowlands to study for a while because I wanted to follow my father as a teacher when I grew up. I always planned to return to my hamlet to live the rest of my life there. But war disrupted my dreams. The land I love was lost to me forever.

These stories are my memories. . . .

SO CLOSE

My grandmother was very fond of cookies made of banana, egg, and coconut, so my mother and I always stopped at Mrs. Hong's house to buy these cookies for her on our way back from the marketplace. My mother also

B Vocabulary Development
GRADE-LEVEL STANDARD
❓ **Context clues.** Which words in the second paragraph provide clues to the meaning of *cultivate*? How would you define this word? [Possible response: The word *plant* and the list of vegetables following *cultivate* show that the author is talking about planting and growing vegetables. So *cultivate* must mean "grow."]

C Reading Skills

Building background. After describing daily life in his Vietnamese hamlet, the author says, "The land I love was lost to me forever." Before students read on, have them read the Meet the Writer feature on p. 283 to find out why this occurred.

▶ **Resources Reminder**
For lessons designed for intermediate and advanced English-language learners, see *Lesson Plans for Language Development,* pp. 124–126, 139, 145.

Special Education Students
For lessons designed for special education students, see *Lesson Plans for Language Development,* pp. 127, 139, 145.

Advanced Learners
Enrichment. As students read, have them generate questions about Vietnamese society and customs. When they have finished, have them work in pairs to select the questions they find the most important or interesting. Students can then write these questions in the center of large sheets of paper, build webs around them by listing ways of finding answers, and share their webs with the class.

A Literary Focus
GRADE-LEVEL STANDARD
? Narrator. What happens to the point of view here? [The narrator is no longer speaking in the first person. The story of Lan and Trung is told in the third person, by an omniscient narrator who knows about all the characters and can tell about their past, present, and future.]

B Learners Having Difficulty
? Making inferences. What clues help you determine how the fish gets on the windowsill? [Possible responses: The phrases "Trung was a skillful fisherman," "smile to herself," and "Finally, she decided that Trung was a fine young man" lead students to realize that Trung puts the fish there.]

C Reading Skills
? Interpreting. Why does Trung wish that nobody would move the chair? [Possible responses: He can more easily picture her sitting in the chair if no one moves it; in his mind something of Lan remains in the chair as long as no one touches it.]

D Reading Skills
Summarizing. Have students summarize the events and information in the Trung and Lan story so far. [Lan and Trung were inseparable playmates and are now attracted to each other. Lan is popular and pretty, and Trung is a skillful fisherman. When Trung's mother hears him call Lan's name in his sleep, she and Lan's mother agree that the couple should be married. The mothers agree to the terms of the marriage and announce the engagement.]

E Learners Having Difficulty
? Finding sequence of events. What words in this paragraph help you understand the order of events? [First, then]

liked to see Mrs. Hong because they had been very good friends since grade-school days. While my mother talked with her friend, I talked with Mrs. Hong's daughter, Lan. Most of the time Lan asked me about my older sister, who was married to a teacher and lived in a nearby town. Lan, too, was going to get married—to a young man living next door, Trung.

Trung and Lan had been inseparable playmates until the day tradition did not allow them to be alone together anymore. Besides, I think they felt a little shy with each other after realizing that they were man and woman.

A Lan was a lively, pretty girl, who attracted the attention of all the young men of our hamlet. Trung was a skillful fisherman who successfully plied[1] his trade on the river in front of their houses. Whenever Lan's mother found a big fish on the kitchen windowsill, she **B** would smile to herself. Finally, she decided that Trung was a fine young man and would make a good husband for her daughter.

Trung's mother did not like the idea of her son giving good fish away, but she liked the cookies Lan brought her from time to time. Besides, the girl was very helpful; whenever she was not busy at her house, Lan would come over in the evening and help Trung's mother repair her son's fishing net.

Trung was happiest when Lan was helping his mother. They did not talk to each other, but they could look at each other when his mother was busy with her work. Each time **C** Lan went home, Trung looked at the chair Lan had just left and secretly wished that nobody would move it.

One day when Trung's mother heard her son call Lan's name in his sleep, she decided it

---

1. **plied** *v.*: worked at.

was time to speak to the girl's mother about marriage. Lan's mother agreed they should be married and even waived[2] the custom whereby the bridegroom had to give the bride's family a fat hog, six chickens, six ducks, three bottles of wine, and thirty kilos[3] of fine rice, for the two families had known each other for a long time and were good neighbors.

The two widowed mothers quickly set the dates for the engagement announcement and for the wedding ceremony. Since their decision was immediately made known to relatives and friends, Trung and Lan could **D** now see each other often. . . .

At last it was the day of their wedding. Friends and relatives arrived early in the morning to help them celebrate. They brought gifts of ducks, chickens, baskets filled with fruits, rice wine, and colorful fabrics. Even though the two houses were next to each other, the two mothers observed all the proper wedding day traditions.

First, Trung and his friends and relatives came to Lan's house. Lan and he prayed at her **E** ancestors' altars and asked for their blessing. Then they joined everyone for a luncheon.

After lunch there was a farewell ceremony for the bride. Lan stepped out of her house and joined the greeting party that was to accompany her to Trung's home. Tradition called for her to cry and to express her sorrow at leaving her parents behind and forever becoming the daughter of her husband's family. In some villages the bride was even supposed to cling so tightly to her mother that it would take several friends to pull her away from her home. But instead of crying,

---

2. **waived** *v.*: gave up voluntarily.
3. **kilos** *n.*: kilograms, about 2.2 pounds each.

MINI-LESSON Reading

Developing Word-Attack Skills
Ask students if they know this rhyme:
When two vowels go a-walking,
The first one does the talking.
Explain that the rhyme is a mnemonic device that helps them remember how to decode a vowel *digraph*—two vowels that stand for one-vowel sound. Review with students the vowel pairs that this rhyme applies to:

ai for /ā/, as in *wait*
ea and *ei* for /ē/, as in *eat* and *seize*
ie for /ī/, as in *lie*
oa for /ō/, as in *coat*
ui and *ue* for /ū/, as in *fruit* and *blue*
Point out that in these combinations the first vowel does the talking by, in effect, saying its own name, since the long sounds of the vowels sound the same or almost the same as the letter names.

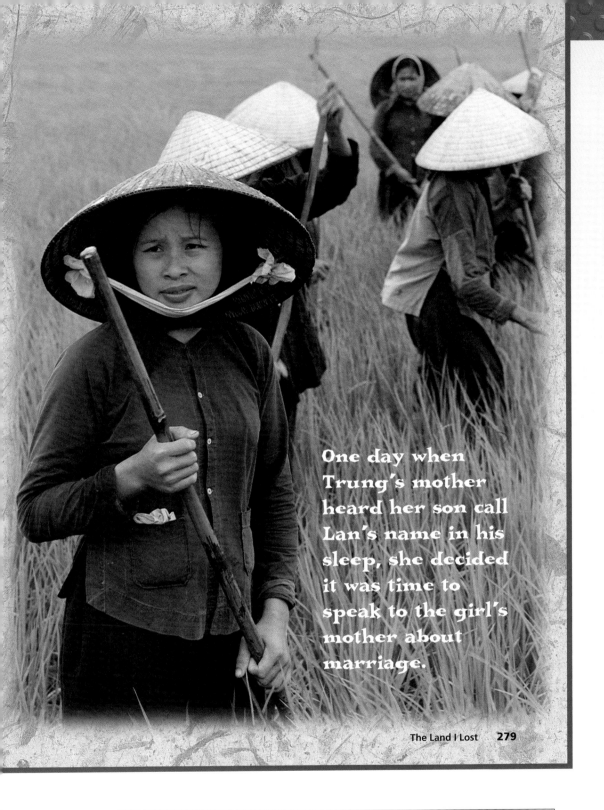

One day when Trung's mother heard her son call Lan's name in his sleep, she decided it was time to speak to the girl's mother about marriage.

Then, explore with students some exceptions to the "two-vowel rule": *ai* stands for /e/ in *again*; *ea* stands for /e/ in *head* and /ēə/ in *idea*; *ei* stands for /ā/ in *vein*; *ie* stands for /īə/ in *fiery*, /ē/ in *belief*, and /e/ in *friend*; and *ui* stands for /i/ in *build*.

Activity. Have students look for words in the selection with the following two-vowel spellings: *ai, ea, ei, ie, oa, ui*. List the words they find on the board. Read each word aloud, and decide whether or not the rule about two vowels that "go a-walking" applies.

A Literary Focus
REVIEW STANDARD

❓ Character. What does Lan's not crying suggest about her? [Possible responses: She is an independent thinker; she is less concerned about tradition than some other people; she is too happy to be marrying Trung to worry about tradition.]

B Content-Area Connections
CULTURE

Wedding customs. Invite students to compare the traditions the narrator describes with the wedding customs they are most familiar with.

C Reading Skills

❓ Analyzing word choice. How would the impact and meaning of the sentence change if the author had written "lived in" instead of "infested"? [Possible responses: *Lived in* carries no bad connotations; the sentence would become a simple statement of fact that arouses no alarm in the mind of the reader. *Infested* carries negative connotations: Rats infest houses; fleas infest dogs and cats; and lice *infest* people. The author's use of *infested* provides a hint that something bad will happen involving crocodiles.]

D Reading Skills

❓ Making predictions. Is the voice Trung hears real, or is he imagining things? Is there some other explanation for the "sound of Lan calling his name"? Ask students to write down a prediction of how they think the story will turn out. When they have finished reading the story, they can check the accuracy of their predictions.

E Reading Skills

Summarizing. Have students summarize the events in this passage and the emotions Trung feels as these events unfold.

A Lan smiled. She asked herself, why should she cry? The two houses were separated by only a garden; she could run home and see her mother anytime she wanted to. So Lan willingly followed Trung and prayed at his **B** ancestors' altars before joining everyone in the big welcome dinner at Trung's house that ended the day's celebrations.

Later in the evening of the wedding night, Lan went to the river to take a bath. Because crocodiles <u>infested</u> the river, people of our **C** hamlet who lived along the riverbank chopped down trees and put them in the river to form barriers and protect places where they washed their clothes, did their dishes, or took a bath. This evening, a <u>wily</u> crocodile had avoided the barrier by crawling up the riverbank and sneaked up behind Lan. The crocodile grabbed her and went back to the river by the same route that it had come.

Trung became worried when Lan did not return. He went to the place where she was supposed to bathe, only to find that her clothes were there, but she had disappeared. Panic-stricken, he yelled for his relatives. They all rushed to the riverbank with lighted torches. In the flickering light they found traces of water and crocodile claw-prints on the wet soil. Now they knew that a crocodile had grabbed the young bride and dragged her into the river.

Since no one could do anything for the girl, all of Trung's relatives returned to the house, urging the bridegroom to do the same. But the young man refused to leave the place; he just stood there, crying and staring at the clothes of his bride.

D Suddenly the wind brought him the sound of Lan calling his name. He was very frightened, for according to an old belief, a crocodile's victim must lure a new victim to his master; if not, the first victim's soul must stay with the beast forever.

Trung rushed back to the house and woke all his relatives. Nobody doubted he thought he had heard her call, but they all believed that he was the victim of a hallucination. Everyone pleaded with him and tried to convince him that nobody could survive when snapped up by a crocodile and dragged into the river to be drowned and eaten by the animal.

The young man brushed aside all their arguments and rushed back to the river. Once again, he heard the voice of his bride in the wind, calling his name. Again he rushed back and woke his relatives. Again they tried to persuade him that it was a hallucination, although some of the old folks **E** suggested that maybe the ghost of the young girl was having to dance and sing to <u>placate</u> the angry crocodile because she failed to bring it a new victim.

No one could persuade Trung to stay inside. His friends wanted to go back to the river with him, but he said no. He resented them for not believing him that there were desperate cries in the wind.

Trung stood in front of the deep river alone in the darkness. He listened to the sound of the wind and clutched the clothes Lan had left behind. The wind became stronger and stronger and often changed direction as the night progressed, but he did not hear any more calls. Still he had no doubt

---

Vocabulary

infested (in·fest′id) *v.:* inhabited in large numbers (said of something harmful).

wily (wī′lē) *adj.:* sly; clever in a sneaky way.

hallucination (hə·loo̅′si·nā′shən) *n.:* perception of something that isn't really there.

placate (plā′kāt′) *v.:* calm or soothe (someone who is angry).

CONTENT-AREA CONNECTIONS

Culture
Vietnamese weddings. Some students might want to learn more about traditional Vietnamese weddings. Explain that the bride wears a pink or red *ao dai,* and the groom, a blue one. An *ao dai* is a long tight-fitting garment split up the sides and worn over pants. On their wedding day, the bride and groom bind their hands together with pink thread as a symbol of happiness and eat a piece of ginseng dipped in salt as a symbol of the difficulties they may face in their future. The celebration always ends with a wedding feast at the groom's house.

Science
Crocodiles. Do students know that in Africa crocodiles kill more people each year than any other meat-eating animal?

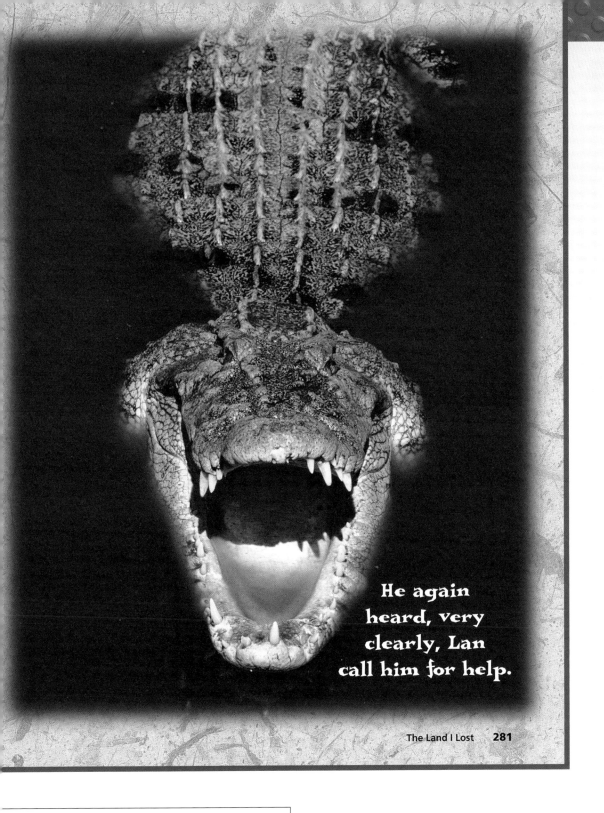

He again heard, very clearly, Lan call him for help.

Activity. Have a small group of interested students research some specific facts about crocodiles. How large do they grow? How long do they live? On which continents are they found? How many species exist? Have students present their findings to the class.

SMALL-GROUP

A Literary Focus
REVIEW STANDARD

❓ **Character.** What does Lan do to escape the crocodile? [She feigns death and then climbs a nearby tree.] What qualities does this act reveal? [Possible responses: bravery, intelligence, quick-wittedness, remarkable self-control.]

B Literary Focus
GRADE-LEVEL STANDARD

❓ **Narrator.** With what kind of narration does the story end, first-person or third-person? How can you tell? [The story closes with third-person narration. Readers can tell because there is no "I" mentioned; instead events are described by an omniscient narrator.]

GUIDED PRACTICE

Monitoring student's progress. Guide the class in answering these comprehension questions. Direct students to locate passages in the text that support their responses.

Short Answer

1. What does Lan's mother find on the windowsill, and who left it there? [Lan's mother finds fish left by Trung.]

2. What does Lan do for Trung's mother? [Lan gives her cookies and helps her fix Trung's fishing net.]

3. Why does Lan's mother ignore the custom of the groom's giving gifts to the bride's family? [The families have been friends and neighbors for years.]

4. What happens to Lan as she bathes on her wedding night? [She is taken away by a crocodile.]

5. How does Trung know that Lan is not dead? [He hears Lan crying for help, and he sees her waving to him from an island.]

---

that the voice he had heard earlier was absolutely real. Then at dawn, when the wind died down, he again heard, very clearly, Lan call him for help.

Her voice came from an island about six hundred meters away. Trung wept and prayed: "You were a good girl when you were still alive, now be a good soul. Please protect me so that I can find a way to kill the beast in order to free you from its spell and avenge your tragic death." Suddenly, while wiping away his tears, he saw a little tree moving on the island. The tree was jumping up and down. He squinted to see better. The tree had two hands that were waving at him. And it was calling his name.

Trung became hysterical and yelled for help. He woke all his relatives and they all rushed to his side again. At first they thought that Trung had become stark mad. They tried to lead him back to his house, but he fiercely resisted their attempt. He talked to them incoherently[4] and pointed his finger at the strange tree on the island. Finally his relatives saw the waving tree. They quickly put a small boat into the river, and Trung got into the boat along with two other men. They paddled to the island and discovered that the moving tree was, in fact, Lan. She had covered herself with leaves because she had no clothes on.

At first nobody knew what had really happened because Lan clung to Trung and cried and cried. Finally, when Lan could talk, they pieced together her story.

Lan had fainted when the crocodile snapped her up. Had she not fainted, the crocodile surely would have drowned her before carrying her off to the island. Lan did not know how many times the crocodile had

tossed her in the air and smashed her against the ground, but at one point, while being tossed in the air and falling back onto the crocodile's jaw, she regained consciousness. The crocodile smashed her against the ground a few more times, but Lan played dead. Luckily the crocodile became thirsty and returned to the river to drink. At that moment Lan got up and ran to a nearby tree and climbed up it. The tree was very small.

Lan stayed very still for fear that the snorting, angry crocodile, roaming around trying to catch her again, would find her and shake her out of the tree. Lan stayed in this frozen position for a long time until the crocodile gave up searching for her and went back to the river. Then she started calling Trung to come rescue her.

Lan's body was covered with bruises, for crocodiles soften up big prey before swallowing it. They will smash it against the ground or against a tree, or keep tossing it into the air. But fortunately Lan had no broken bones or serious cuts. It was possible that this crocodile was very old and had lost most of its teeth. Nevertheless, the older the crocodile, the more intelligent it usually was. That was how it knew to avoid the log barrier in the river and to snap up the girl from behind.

Trung carried his exhausted bride into the boat and paddled home. Lan slept for hours and hours. At times she would sit up with a start and cry out for help, but within three days she was almost completely recovered.

Lan's mother and Trung's mother decided to celebrate their children's wedding a second time because Lan had come back from the dead.

---

4. **incoherently** *adv.:* not clearly.

Vocabulary
avenge (ə·venj′) *v.:* get revenge for; get even for.

FAMILY/COMMUNITY ACTIVITY

Some students may have a family member or family acquaintance who comes from Vietnam or who has spent time there. As a class, brainstorm a list of questions whose answers would provide a new perspective on the country. Students can use the questions to interview the person and then relate the information to the class. You may want to send students home with a letter explaining this activity to families. Review the interview questions in advance and be sure to have students get permission from their interview subjects before sharing potentially sensitive information with the class. Remind interviewers that they are not required to share their interviews with the class if they do not want to.

Huynh Quang Nhuong

To Make People Happy

Huynh Quang Nhuong (1946–   ) was born in a small village in Vietnam between a deep jungle and a chain of high mountains. At the age of six, Huynh learned to tend his family's herd of water buffaloes. His favorite, named Tank, takes part in many of the adventures described in *The Land I Lost*.

Nhuong left his village to study chemistry at the University of Saigon. When war broke out, "the land I love was lost to me forever," he recalls. Nhuong was drafted into the army of South Vietnam. One day on the battlefield he was shot and paralyzed.

In 1969, Nhuong left Vietnam to receive special medical treatment in the United States. He stayed, earned degrees in literature and French, and settled in Columbia, Missouri. His writing is a link between his two lands. He says:

> **I hope that my books will make people from different countries happy, regardless of their political adherences, creeds, and ages.**

For Independent Reading

If you'd like to learn more about Nhuong's youth in Vietnam, read *Water Buffalo Days*.

Meet the Writer

Background. In *The Land I Lost,* Nhuong describes events in the lives of the villagers in his native Mytho—a man who teaches monkeys to pick tea leaves and hunt squirrels, a bridegroom who is killed by a snake on his wedding night, a bloody battle that breaks out between the villagers and a wild hog.

Make sure students understand that when Nhuong refers to the war in his country, he is talking about the conflict that broke out in 1957 between North Vietnam and South Vietnam. The South Vietnamese army, supported to varying degrees by the direct and indirect involvement of the United States, was defeated by the North Vietnamese forces in 1975.

For Independent Reading

Students who are interested in traditional Vietnamese tales will enjoy *Vietnamese Legends* by Le Huy Hap and *Vietnamese Folktales* by Lan Nguyen.

DIFFERENTIATING INSTRUCTION

Advanced Learners

This excerpt from Huynh Quang Nhuong's autobiography briefly describes Vietnamese wedding customs, religion, clothing, food, fishing, and farming.

Enrichment. Invite students to give a short oral report about some aspect of Vietnamese culture that interests them— perhaps the duties of the *chan trau,* or "buffalo boys," who take care of farmers' water buffaloes, or the function of *non la,* the traditional cone-shaped straw hats worn by farmers.

Literary Response and Analysis

Literary Response and Analysis

Literary Response and Analysis

Reading Check

1. Answers will vary. Sample facts include the following: no shops or markets in the hamlet; a six-month rainy season; danger from lone wild hogs, tigers, and horse snakes.

2. The bride and groom are not allowed to be alone together before the ceremony; they give gifts anonymously to each other's family; the families give gifts to each other; tradition calls for the bride to express sorrow at leaving her parents behind.

3. They carry their prey off, drown it, and soften it up before eating it; they become more wily as they grow older.

4. Answers will vary. Students should recognize that since the mothers thought that Lan was dead, her rescue was like having her come back from the dead.

Interpretations

5. Many students will say that they also value love, family, courage, and intelligence.

6. The switch from first-person narration to third-person narration occurs in the third paragraph of the section "So Close," beginning "Lan was a lively, pretty girl." The writer may have known Lan or heard about her experience from someone else.

7. Answers will vary. Many students will note that their lists did not contain facts about the culture and traditions of Vietnam before the war.

Evaluation

8. Answers will vary. Most students will recognize that the title has to do with both the closeness of Lan and Trung and the close escape Lan had from death.

Reading Check

1. Name at least three **facts** you learned about life in the writer's hamlet.

2. What did you learn about marriage customs in the Vietnamese highlands?

3. What did you learn about crocodiles?

4. Why do the mothers feel that Lan has come back from the dead?

Interpretations

5. This selection is about a faraway land where customs are very different from those in the United States. What values and feelings do you share with Nhuong's people?

6. Where does the writer shift from **first-person narration** to **third-person narration**? How do you think the writer learned all these details of Lan's terrifying experience?

7. Look at the diagram you made for the Quickwrite before you began reading. Now that you've read this account, what changes would you make to your diagram?

Evaluation

8. What do you think of the **title** "So Close" for the story of Lan and Trung? What do you think it means?

Reading Standard 3.5 Identify the speaker, and recognize the difference between first- and third-person narration (for example, autobiography).

Writing

The Main Events

Writing a **summary** is a way of summing up the most important events in a story. Refer to the organizer you filled in as you read "So Close," the story of Lan and Trung. Then, write a summary of the story. Use words like *then, after,* and *there* to show your readers when and where events happened. Use words and phrases like *because* and *as a result* to show cause-and-effect connections between events.

Describing a Place

In the first section of his **autobiography,** Nhuong describes life in his village. Write a description of everyday life in your own city, town, or village. Write as if you were going to publish your description in a different country where little is known about customs in the United States—where people live, what they eat, how they make a living.

Open your description with the words *I was born in* or *I live in*. End your description with a statement telling how you feel about your hometown.

Vocabulary Development

Context Clues

PRACTICE 1

Go back and locate the passage in the story where each word in the Word Bank is used. Try to find clues in the passage that help explain the word's meaning. Put the context clues for the Word Bank words in a cluster diagram like this one, which contains clues for the word *infested:*

Word Bank
infested
wily
hallucination
placate
avenge

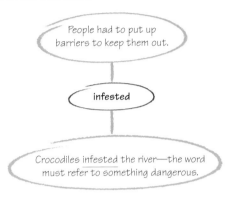

People had to put up barriers to keep them out.

infested

Crocodiles infested the river—the word must refer to something dangerous.

PRACTICE 2

Answer these questions about other context clues in the selection.

1. Find the word *hamlet* in the first paragraph. Which words in the first three paragraphs provide clues to the meaning of *hamlet*? How would you define the word?

2. Find the term *monkey bridge* in the second paragraph. Where does the writer provide a definition of this term right in the context?

3. Find the passage where the word *edible* is used (page 277). What context clues tell you that this word means "fit to be eaten"?

4. Find the word *disrupted* at the very end of the first section (page 277). Use context clues to guess the meaning of *disrupted.*

Reading Standard 1.4 Monitor expository text for unknown words by using word, sentence, and paragraph clues to determine meaning.

The Land I Lost **285**

Practice 1

Possible Answers

- *wily*—The crocodile avoids the barrier, so he must be clever; the crocodile sneaks up behind Lan, so he is sneaky.

- *hallucination*—Everyone believes that Trung thought he heard a call, but they know it could not be real; they believe he is the victim of a trick.

- *placate*—The relatives try to persuade Trung that the call was not real; they want to calm him into acceptance.

- *avenge*—Trung says that he wants to find a way to kill the beast to get even for Lan's death; killing the crocodile would free Lan from a spell.

Vocabulary Development

Answers to Practice 1 are at the bottom of this page.

Practice 2
Possible Answers

1. Clues include the bamboo houses on the river, which suggest a rural area, and the fact that there were no shops or marketplaces, which suggests a small community. The definition of *hamlet* must be a small town or community in a rural area.

2. The definition of *monkey bridge,* "a single bamboo stick that spanned the trench," is in the same sentence with the word.

3. Context clues for *edible* include *edible* mushrooms being distinguished from poisonous mushrooms, so *edible* must mean "safe to eat."

4. The context clue for *disrupted* is that the writer planned to live in his hamlet all his life, but the war changed his life forever. *Disrupted* must mean "interrupted" or "broke apart."

▶ **Resources Reminder**

Vocabulary and Spelling
- *Vocabulary Development*
  - Vocabulary Worksheet, p. 21
  - Decoding Worksheet, p. 22
- *Lesson Plans for Language Development*
  - Vocabulary, p. 145

Assessment
- *Progress Assessment of Reading*
  - Selection Test, p. 97

For a lesson reteaching first-person and third-person narration, see **Reteaching,** p. 489A.

STANDARDS FOCUS, pp. 286–299

(For grade-level and review standards taught in this selection, see citations on Pupil's Edition pages.)

Standard Coming Up in the Next Grade Level

■ Grade 7, Literary Response and Analysis 3.5 **Contrast points of view** (e.g., first and third person, limited and omniscient, subjective and objective) in narrative text, and explain how they affect the overall theme of the work.

Reading Skills

■ Sequence.

Summary ⬆ *above grade level*

On a plantation in Maryland in 1849, Harriet Tubman persuades three of her brothers to run away with her to keep from being sold to a chain gang. Their escape is thwarted by her brothers' fear, and the four runaways turn back. Soon afterward, however, Tubman decides to start out on her own, despite the fact that she suffers from sudden sleeping seizures. She sings a spiritual about being "bound for the promised land" to let her sister know that she is leaving. A white woman who had previously offered help gives Tubman the names of two people on the Underground Railroad. With the aid of abolitionists, who conceal her, feed her, and help transport her, Tubman travels ninety miles to reach the free state of Pennsylvania.

A Glory over Everything

Literary Focus
Third-Person Point of View

"A Glory over Everything" is taken from a **biography,** the true story of a person's life written by another person. Ann Petry tells the story of Harriet Tubman, who escaped from slavery and led many others to freedom. Petry uses the **third-person point of view.** In other words, she writes from the standpoint of someone *outside* the story, not from the standpoint of a character in the story. Using third-person pronouns such as *he, she, they,* and *it,* Petry describes the characters' thoughts and feelings as she imagines them.

Reading Skills 📖
Following the Sequence

Sequence is the order of events in a story. Writers often use words like *first, then,* and *when* to indicate the order of events and the amount of time that has passed. Track Tubman's journey to freedom by completing a chart like the one below. Include six events in your chart, and use time-order words that indicate the sequence of events.

Reading Standard 3.5 Identify the speaker, and recognize the difference between first- and third-person narration.

Sequence Chart
1. **That night,** Harriet prepared to leave.
2. **As** she worked, she heard John stir in his sleep.
3. **When** she was done, she headed for the woods.

Make the Connection

"A Glory over Everything" takes place during the mid-1800s, when slavery was still legal in most southern states. The horror of slavery began in the United States in 1619, when the first Africans arrived in the stinking holds of Dutch slave ships. Slavery was not abolished in the United States until 1865.

What would people feel who were held in slavery—"owned" body and soul by another person? What would they be unable to do? What sorrows would they face? What would they risk if they tried to escape?

Discussion. Share your thoughts with a small group of classmates. Then, choose a group member to summarize for the rest of the class the ideas your group discussed.

Quickwrite ✏️

Write about what you felt and learned during your group discussion. What questions do you have about slavery?

Background

In 1849, when the following portion of Harriet Tubman's **biography** takes place, runaway slaves were free once they crossed into a free state. But after the Fugitive Slave Law was passed in 1850, runaways were not safe until they reached Canada. The Underground Railroad was an operation set up by opponents of slavery to help runaways make their way to freedom. The Underground Railroad wasn't a railroad,

◀ Resources Reminder

Media
■ *Audio CD Library*
  ■ disc 7
■ *Visual Connections*
  ■ Videocassette, Segment 8
■ *Fine Art Transparencies*
  ■ Transparency 10

Harriet's Route to Freedom
Free States ■
Slave states □

PENNSYLVANIA
Philadelphia
Wilmington
NEW JERSEY
Camden
MARYLAND
Baltimore
WASHINGTON D.C.
VIRGINIA
Brodas Plantation

and it didn't run underground. It was made up of people from both the North and the South who offered food, shelter, and protection to people escaping to freedom in the North. To keep the route secret, the organization used railroad terms, such as *stations* for the houses along the way and *conductors* for the people who offered help.

Harriet Tubman, who had escaped from slavery, became one of the most famous conductors on the railroad. She helped more than three hundred men, women, and children along the perilous road to freedom.

In this excerpt from her biography, we meet Harriet Tubman when she is a field hand at the Brodas Plantation in Maryland.

Vocabulary Development

Don't let these words elude you when you read about Harriet Tubman:

elude (ē·lōōd′) v.: escape the notice of; avoid detection by. *A runaway must elude the patrol.*

inexplicable (in·eks′pli·kə·bəl) adj.: not explainable. *Tubman's inexplicable seizures put her at risk.*

legitimate (lə·jit′ə·mət) adj.: here, reasonable; justified. *Runaways had a legitimate reason to fear capture.*

defiant (dē·fī′ənt) adj.: disobedient; boldly resisting. *Harriet's defiant manner disturbed Dr. Thompson.*

sinewy (sin′yōō·ē) adj.: strong; tough. *Her arms were sinewy from hard work.*

A Glory over Everything   **287**

Differentiating Instruction
■ *Lesson Plans for Language Development*
   ■ English-Language Learners, pp. 128–130, 140, 146
   ■ Special Education Students, pp. 131, 140, 146

Vocabulary and Spelling
■ *Vocabulary Development*
   ■ Vocabulary Worksheet, p. 23

Assessment
■ *Progress Assessment of Reading*
   ■ Selection Test, p. 100
■ *One-Stop Planner* CD-ROM with Test Generator

Standards Starter

Build background. Every year from 1840 to 1860 a few thousand people successfully escaped from slavery with the help of the Underground Railroad. Those who helped them included free blacks, white people, and slaves on plantations. The Railroad was not a centralized national organization, but a loosely connected network of people who broke the law to help enslaved people reach freedom. If students need more background information, show the class the *Visual Connections* video segment titled "Freedom's Conductor: Harriet Tubman."

Preview Vocabulary

Have students choose the Vocabulary word that best fits with each of the sentences below.

1. In a game of hide-and-seek, the goal is to _____ your opponent. [elude]
2. The winning runner's legs were long and _____. [sinewy]
3. I can't say why the best team lost; the reason is _____. [inexplicable]
4. The player who is _____ and breaks the rules can be thrown out of a game. [defiant]
5. Everyone on the team had a _____ reason to be in the gym after school. [legitimate]

Assign the Reading

Have members of the class read the biography aloud up through the paragraph on p. 289 in which Tubman hears that her sisters have been sold. Pause to discuss the common practice of breaking up slave families during this era, and then have advanced learners finish the selection independently.

HOMEWORK

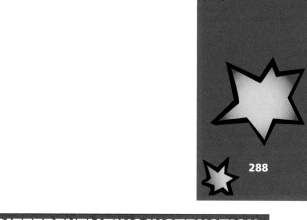

DIRECT TEACHING

▶ **Resources Reminder**

Reading

■ *Interactive Reading*

　■ Graphic Organizer: Biography Chart, p. 193

Ⓐ Reading Skills

Sequencing. Ask students to identify the words and phrases in this passage that signal the order of events. List the words on the chalkboard, numbered in sequence and leaving a space after each entry. [(1) One day in 1849; (2) Then; (3) After that; (4) Then one day] **Next,** call on volunteers to summarize the event that each of these time-order words signals. Have the volunteers write the summaries after the numbered items on the chalkboard. [Possible summaries: (1) One day in 1849 a white woman stopped and watched Tubman. (2) Then she asked Tubman her name. (3) After that the woman told Tubman where she lived. (4) Then one day the woman offered Tubman help.]

When Harriet heard of the sale of her sisters, she knew that the time had finally come when she must leave the plantation.

A GLORY OVER EVERYTHING

Ann Petry

from **Harriet Tubman:**

Conductor on the

Underground Railroad

Ⓐ

One day in 1849, when Harriet was working in the fields near the edge of the road, a white woman wearing a faded sunbonnet went past, driving a wagon. She stopped the wagon and watched Harriet for a few minutes. Then she spoke to her, asked her what her name was, and how she had acquired the deep scar on her forehead.

Harriet told her the story of the blow she had received when she was a girl. After that, whenever the woman saw her in the fields, she stopped to talk to her. She told Harriet that she lived on a farm near Bucktown. Then one day she said, not looking at Harriet but looking instead at the overseer[1] far off at the edge of the fields, "If you ever need any help, Harriet, ever need any help, why, you let me know."

---

1. **overseer** *n.:* person who supervises workers; in this case, a slave driver.

288

DIFFERENTIATING INSTRUCTION

Learners Having Difficulty
Modeling. Explain to students that the sequence chart on p. 286 is tracking events that begin on p. 292, just before Tubman's journey to freedom. You may wish to model how to follow the sequence of events by charting the beginning of the selection. Have students read the first three pages. Then, write the first main event on the chalkboard: "In 1849, when the master starts selling slaves, Harriet tries to escape with her brothers." Call on volunteers to help formulate the next major event: "That night Tubman's brothers force her to turn back." Point out that the chart includes time-order words and lists only the most important events. Encourage students to stop and ask themselves as they read, "What happens next? What follows that?"

English-Language Learners
Use the terms *Underground Railroad* and *runaway* to introduce compound words. Point out that knowing the meanings of the small, simple words that form these terms can help readers define the compound terms. Ask students to try to find other compound words in the text, such as *underbrush* or *handbill*.

That same year the young heir to the Brodas estate[2] died. Harriet mentioned the fact of his death to the white woman in the faded sunbonnet the next time she saw her. She told her of the panic-stricken talk in the quarter, told her that the slaves were afraid that the master, Dr. Thompson, would start selling them. She said that Doc Thompson no longer permitted any of them to hire their time.[3] The woman nodded her head, clucked to the horse, and drove off, murmuring, "If you ever need any help—"

The slaves were right about Dr. Thompson's intention. He began selling slaves almost immediately. Among the first ones sold were two of Harriet Tubman's sisters. They went south with the chain gang[4] on a Saturday.

When Harriet heard of the sale of her sisters, she knew that the time had finally come when she must leave the plantation. She was reluctant to attempt the long trip north alone, not because of John Tubman's threat to betray her[5] but because she was afraid she might

"On a night like this, with all the stars out, it's not black dark."

fall asleep somewhere along the way and so would be caught immediately.

She persuaded three of her brothers to go with her. Having made certain that John was asleep, she left the cabin quietly and met her brothers at the edge of the plantation. They agreed that she was to lead the way, for she was more familiar with the woods than the others.

The three men followed her, crashing through the underbrush, frightening themselves, stopping constantly to say, "What was that?" or "Someone's coming."

She thought of Ben[6] and how he had said, "Any old body can go through a woods crashing and mashing things down like a cow." She said sharply, "Can't you boys go quieter? Watch where you're going!"

One of them grumbled, "Can't see in the dark. Ain't got cat's eyes like you."

"You don't need cat's eyes," she retorted. "On a night like this, with all the stars out, it's not black dark. Use your own eyes."

She supposed they were doing the best they could, but they moved very slowly. She kept getting so far ahead of them that she had to stop and wait for them to catch up with her, lest they lose their way. Their progress was slow, uncertain. Their feet got tangled in every vine. They tripped over fallen logs, and once one of them fell flat on his face. They jumped, startled, at the most ordinary sounds: the murmur of the

---

2. **Brodas estate:** Edward Brodas, the previous owner of the plantation, died in 1849 and left his property to his heir, who was not yet old enough to manage it. In the meantime the plantation was placed in the hands of the boy's guardian, Dr. Thompson.

3. **hire their time:** Some slaveholders allowed the people they held in slavery to hire themselves out for pay to other plantation owners who needed extra help. In such cases the workers were permitted to keep their earnings.

4. **chain gang** *n.:* group of prisoners chained together.

5. Harriet's husband, John Tubman, was a free man who was content with his life. He violently disapproved of his wife's plan to escape and threatened to tell the master if she carried it out.

6. **Ben:** Harriet Tubman's father. Her mother is called Old Rit.

A Glory over Everything   289

DIRECT TEACHING

B Learners Having Difficulty

Questioning. Ask students what questions came to mind as they read this paragraph. [Possible responses: What difference does it make if the heir died? Who is Dr. Thompson? Why would he start selling the slaves?] Tell students that they may find answers to their questions in the footnotes, which provide crucial background information. Explain that the footnotes will help them understand the changes taking place on the estate—changes that give the slaves additional incentive to escape.

C Reading Skills

❓ Making predictions. How do you predict Tubman will try to escape the plantation? [Possible responses: She will go at night; she will go on foot; she will hide in the white woman's wagon as she leaves the plantation.]

D Literary Focus
GRADE-LEVEL STANDARD

❓ Point of view. Remind students that the third-person narrator is writing from outside the story—and can reveal the feelings and actions of all of the characters in the story. Whose thoughts are revealed here? [Tubman's and her brother's]

Resources Reminder

For lessons designed for intermediate and advanced English-language learners, see *Lesson Plans for Language Development,* pp. 128–130, 140, 146.

Special Education Students

For lessons designed for special education students, see *Lesson Plans for Language Development,* pp. 131, 140, 146.

Advanced Learners

Acceleration. Use the following activity with advanced learners to move them toward the seventh-grade Standard 3.5, which requires that they contrast points of view, including first-person and third-person limited.

Activity. Have a group of students present a retelling of Tubman's first escape attempt

using the first-person point of view. Then, have another group present a second retelling, using the limited third-person point of view of only one of Tubman's brothers. Make sure students can see the differences between a first-person account and a third-person limited account. Have the groups work together to identify the differences between the points of view.

A Glory over Everything   **289**

A Reading Skills

❓ **Summarizing.** What kinds of dangers and obstacles did escaping slaves face? [Possible responses: Someone might recognize and report them; handbills were circulated advertising that they were missing and encouraging people to capture them; patrols and bloodhounds searched for them; if they were returned to their masters they faced terrible punishments.]

B Reading Skills

Sequencing. This is a good place to remind students to update their sequence charts. Invite two or more volunteers to read their sequence charts aloud.

wind in the branches of the trees, the twittering of a bird. They kept turning around, looking back.

They had not gone more than a mile when she became aware that they had stopped. She turned and went back to them. She could hear them whispering. One of them called out, "Hat!"

"What's the matter? We haven't got time to keep stopping like this."

"We're going back."

"No," she said firmly. "We've got a good start. If we move fast and move quiet—"

Then all three spoke at once. They said the same thing, over and over, in frantic hurried whispers, all talking at once:

A They told her that they had changed their minds. Running away was too dangerous. Someone would surely see them and recognize them. By morning the master would know they had "took off." Then the handbills advertising them would be posted all over Dorchester County. The patterollers[7] would search for them. Even if they were lucky enough to elude the patrol, they could not possibly hide from the bloodhounds. The hounds would be baying after them, snuffing through the swamps and the underbrush, zigzagging through the deepest woods. The bloodhounds would surely find them. And everyone knew what happened to a runaway who was caught and brought back alive.

She argued with them. Didn't they know that if they went back they would be sold, if

---

7. **patterollers** *n.*: patrollers.

not tomorrow, then the next day, or the next? Sold south. They had seen the chain gangs. Was that what they wanted? Were they going to be slaves for the rest of their lives? Didn't freedom mean anything to them?

"You're afraid," she said, trying to shame them into action. "Go on back. I'm going north alone."

Instead of being ashamed, they became angry. They shouted at her, telling her that she was a fool and they would make her go back to the plantation with them. Suddenly they surrounded her, three men, her own brothers, jostling her, pushing her along, pinioning[8] her arms behind her. She fought against them, wasting her strength, exhausting herself in a furious struggle.

She was no match for three strong men. She said, panting, "All right. We'll go back. I'll go with you."

She led the way, moving slowly. Her thoughts were bitter. Not one of them was willing to take a small risk in order to be free. It had all seemed so perfect, so simple, to have her brothers go with her, sharing the dangers of the trip together, just as a family should. Now if she ever went north, she would have to go alone.

B Two days later, a slave working beside Harriet in the fields motioned to her. She bent

---

8. **pinioning** (pin′yən·iŋ) *v.* used as *adj.*: pinning.

Vocabulary
elude (ē·lōōd′) *v.*: escape the notice of; avoid detection by.

> Harriet went on working but she knew a moment of panic.

CONTENT-AREA CONNECTIONS

Social Studies
Researching the era. Have students work in pairs to prepare a poster presentation on one of the following historical events or figures related to Tubman or slavery in general: the Underground Railroad; Sojourner Truth; Frederick Douglass; the Dred Scott decision; the Emancipation Proclamation. Presentations should include the major facts, human interest stories, and pictures.

PAIRED

Comparing Tubman and Pittman. Have students watch the *Autobiography of Miss Jane Pittman,* a film about a woman who reflects on her life, including her years in slavery. Then, have students create a visual display that depicts episodes from the lives of both Harriet Tubman and Jane Pittman, showing something that the two women have in common.

INDIVIDUAL

The Harriet Tubman Series (1939–1940), No. 7, by Jacob Lawrence.

Harriet Tubman worked as water girl to field hands. She also worked at plowing, carting, and hauling logs.

toward him, listening. He said the water boy had just brought news to the field hands, and it had been passed from one to the other until it reached him. The news was that Harriet and her brothers had been sold to the Georgia trader and that they were to be sent south with the chain gang that very night.

Harriet went on working but she knew a moment of panic. She would have to go

D C

A Glory over Everything   **291**

VIEWING THE ART

Jacob Lawrence (1917–2000), an American painter and educator, first discovered his artistic talent while attending free art classes for children in the Harlem section of New York City. Over a long career, Lawrence created several series of pictures that focused on historical figures or events important to African Americans. Abolitionists John Brown and Frederick Douglass are the subjects of two series. Another, *The Migration Series,* consists of sixty panels that tell the story of African Americans migrating in great numbers to cities in the North from the rural South between the early 1900s and the 1940s. *The Harriet Tubman Series* consists of thirty-one panels and is among Lawrence's most famous works.

Activity. Call students' attention to the fact that this selection is accompanied by several paintings in the series on Harriet Tubman. Invite them to look at the paintings, here and on pp. 310–313, and speculate about events in Tubman's life that might be the subject of other panels in the series.

C Reading Skills

? Making predictions. How do you think this news will affect Tubman? [Possible responses: It will upset her. It will force her to escape immediately, without adequate planning.]

D Content-Area Connections
HISTORY

Chain gangs. Explain that a chain gang, in this context, does not refer to a group of convicts on work detail but instead refers to a group of slaves chained to each other at the ankle. When slaves were moved from place to place, they were often chained together to prevent escapes.

A Glory over Everything   **291**

A Vocabulary Development
GRADE-LEVEL STANDARD
Using context clues. Ask students to try to figure out the meaning of the word *quarter*. [Possible responses: the area of the plantation reserved for field hands; the slaves' place of residence.] Have students identify clues in the context that suggest the meaning of *quarter*. [Possible responses: Tubman "turned aside" from the direction in which she had been heading, which was "toward the house," because Dr. Thompson saw her. As a "field hand" Tubman "had no legitimate reason" for going to the Big House, so when she turned and "went toward the quarter," she was going to a place where she belonged.]

B Literary Focus
GRADE-LEVEL STANDARD
❓ Point of view. Whose thoughts and feelings are revealed in Tubman's chance meeting with Dr. Thompson? [Tubman's and Dr. Thompson's] What does this tell you about the narrator? [Possible response: The narrator stands outside the story and knows everything.]

C Reading Skills
❓ Interpreting. What is Tubman's purpose in singing the song? [Possible responses: to tell her sister she is running away; to express defiance toward Dr. Thompson; to communicate her desire to see her family again at some point in the future.]

D Content-Area Connections
CULTURE
Ash cake was a kind of cake or bread that the slaves baked in the ashes of a fireplace. Salt was used to preserve meats and fish, such as herring.

---

north alone. She would have to start as soon as it was dark. She could not go with the chain gang. She might die on the way because of those inexplicable sleeping seizures. But then she—how could she run away? She might fall asleep in plain view along the road.

But even if she fell asleep, she thought, the Lord would take care of her. She murmured a prayer, "Lord, I'm going to hold steady on to You, and You've got to see me through."

Afterward, she explained her decision to run the risk of going north alone in these words: "I had reasoned this out in my mind; there was one of two things I had a *right* to, liberty or death; if I could not have one, I would have the other; for no man should take me alive; I should fight for my liberty as long as my strength lasted, and when the time came for me to go, the Lord would let them take me."

At dusk, when the work in the fields was over, she started toward the Big House.[9] She had to let someone know that she was going north, someone she could trust. She no longer trusted John Tubman and it gave her a lost, lonesome feeling. Her sister Mary worked in the Big House, and she planned to tell Mary that she was going to run away, so someone would know.

As she went toward the house, she saw the master, Doc Thompson, riding up the drive on his horse. She turned aside and went toward the quarter. A field hand had no legitimate reason for entering the kitchen of the Big House—and yet—there must be some way she could leave word so that afterward someone would think about it and know that she had left a message.

As she went toward the quarter, she began to sing. Dr. Thompson reined in his horse, turned around, and looked at her. It was not the beauty of her voice that made him turn and watch her, frowning; it was the words of the song that she was singing and something defiant in her manner that disturbed and puzzled him.

> *When that old chariot comes,*
>   *I'm going to leave you,*
> *I'm bound for the promised land,*
>   *Friends, I'm going to leave you.*
>
> *I'm sorry, friends, to leave you,*
>   *Farewell! Oh, farewell!*
> *But I'll meet you in the morning,*
>   *Farewell! Oh, farewell!*
>
> *I'll meet you in the morning,*
>   *When I reach the promised land;*
> *On the other side of Jordan,*
>   *For I'm bound for the promised land.*

That night when John Tubman was asleep and the fire had died down in the cabin, she took the ash cake that had been baked for their breakfast and a good-sized piece of salt herring and tied them together in an old bandanna. By hoarding this small stock of food, she could make it last a long time, and with the berries and edible roots she could find in the woods, she wouldn't starve.

Vocabulary

inexplicable (in·eks′pli·kə·bəl) *adj.*: not explainable.

legitimate (lə·jit′ə·mət) *adj.*: here, reasonable; justified.

defiant (dē·fī′ənt) *adj.*: disobedient; openly and boldly resisting.

---

9. **Big House:** plantation owner's house.

CONTENT-AREA CONNECTIONS

Culture
African American spirituals. Arising in the days of slavery, African American spirituals had their roots in the complex rhythms and harmonies of African music. They expressed a deep faith in Christianity, but they also served as an indirect means for the slaves to communicate their discontent. The "promised land," for example, might signify "freedom" or "the free states."
Activity. Have students listen to one or more

spirituals after reading the selection. Some popular spirituals of that period include "Follow the Drinking Gourd," "Go Down, Moses," and "Swing Low, Sweet Chariot," Tubman's favorite song. Ask students to copy the lyrics onto sheets of paper and provide a key to some of the coded phrases in the spirituals. You may wish to display the lyrics in the classroom.

WHOLE-CLASS

She decided that she would take the quilt[10] with her, too. Her hands lingered over it. It felt soft and warm to her touch. Even in the dark, she thought she could tell one color from another because she knew its pattern and design so well.

Then John stirred in his sleep, and she left the cabin quickly, carrying the quilt carefully folded under her arm.

Once she was off the plantation, she took to the woods, not following the North Star, not even looking for it, going instead toward Bucktown. She needed help. She was going to ask the white woman who had stopped to talk to her so often if she would help her. Perhaps she wouldn't. But she would soon find out.

When she came to the farmhouse where the woman lived, she approached it cautiously, circling around it. It was so quiet. There was no sound at all, not even a dog barking or the sound of voices. Nothing.

She tapped on the door, gently. A voice said, "Who's there?" She answered, "Harriet, from Dr. Thompson's place."

When the woman opened the door, she did not seem at all surprised to see her. She glanced at the little bundle that Harriet was carrying, at the quilt, and invited her in. Then she sat down at the kitchen table and wrote two names on a slip of paper and handed the paper to Harriet.

She said that those were the next places where it was safe for Harriet to stop. The

> **She tapped on the door, gently. A voice said, "Who's there?"**

first place was a farm where there was a gate with big white posts and round knobs on top of them. The people there would feed her, and when they thought it was safe for her to go on, they would tell her how to get to the next house or take her there.

For these were the first two stops on the Underground Railroad—going north, from the eastern shore of Maryland.

Thus Harriet learned that the Underground Railroad that ran straight to the North was not a railroad at all. Neither did it run underground. It was composed of a loosely organized group of people who offered food and shelter, or a place of concealment, to fugitives who had set out on the long road to the North and freedom.

Harriet wanted to pay this woman who had befriended her. But she had no money. She gave her the patchwork quilt, the only beautiful object she had ever owned.

That night she made her way through the woods, crouching in the underbrush whenever she heard the sound of horses' hoofs, staying there until the riders passed. Each time, she wondered if they were already hunting for her. It would be so easy to describe her, the deep scar on her forehead like a dent, the old scars on the back of her neck, the husky speaking voice, the lack of height, scarcely five feet tall. The master would say she was wearing rough clothes when she ran away, that she had a bandanna on her head, that she was muscular and strong.

She knew how accurately he would describe her. One of the slaves who could

---

10. **the quilt:** Tubman had painstakingly stitched together a quilt before her wedding.

A Glory over Everything **293**

A Glory over Everything **293**

A **Content-Area Connections**
SOCIAL STUDIES

Explain that in 1849 many people, regardless of race, could not read. The little running figure on the handbill alerted those who could not read that the poster described a runaway. These handbills provided a specific description of the escaped slave and often offered a reward for capturing the runaway. Point out the handbill description that appears under Lawrence's painting on p. 295.

B **Vocabulary Development**
GRADE-LEVEL STANDARD

Multiple meanings. Ask a volunteer to tell how *produce* is pronounced in this context and to explain its meaning and part of speech. [It is pronounced prō′dōōs′, it means "vegetables and fruits," and it is a noun.] Then, call on a second volunteer to tell how *produce* can be pronounced differently and have a different meaning and part of speech. [Stress on the word's second syllable indicates a verb that means "to bring into being" or "to make."] Have students discuss clues in the context that indicate which meaning of the word is intended. [Possible responses: A farmer would load fruits and vegetables; the preposition *with* requires a noun.]

C **Reading Skills**

? **Making judgments.** Was Tubman right to trust the man driving the wagon? Why or why not? [Possible responses: Yes, because her friend had referred her to him; yes, because his wife had already helped her; no, because it is dangerous for a runaway to trust anyone.]

D **Learners Having Difficulty**

Using graphic aids. Refer students to the map on p. 287, and have them trace Tubman's route from Dorchester County, Maryland, to the Pennsylvania border.

A read used to tell the others what it said on those handbills that were nailed up on the trees along the edge of the roads. It was easy to recognize the handbills that advertised runaways because there was always a picture in one corner, a picture of a black man, a little running figure with a stick over his shoulder and a bundle tied on the end of the stick.

Whenever she thought of the handbills, she walked faster. Sometimes she stumbled over old grapevines, gnarled and twisted, thick as a man's wrist, or became entangled in the tough <u>sinewy</u> vine of the honeysuckle. But she kept going.

In the morning she came to the house where her friend had said she was to stop. She showed the slip of paper that she carried to the woman who answered her knock at the back door of the farmhouse. The woman fed her and then handed her a broom and told her to sweep the yard.

Harriet hesitated, suddenly suspicious. Then she decided that with a broom in her hand, working in the yard, she would look as though she belonged on the place; certainly no one would suspect that she was a runaway.

B That night the woman's husband, a farmer, loaded a wagon with produce. Harriet climbed in. He threw some blankets over her, and the wagon started.

It was dark under the blankets and not exactly comfortable. But Harriet decided that riding was better than walking. She was surprised at her own lack of fear, wondered **C** how it was that she so readily trusted these strangers who might betray her. For all she knew, the man driving the wagon might be taking her straight back to the master.

She thought of those other rides in wagons, when she was a child, the same

clop-clop of the horses' feet, creak of the wagon, and the feeling of being lost because she did not know where she was going. She did not know her destination this time either, but she was not alarmed. She thought of John Tubman. By this time he must have told the master that she was gone. Then she thought of the plantation and how the land rolled gently down toward the river, thought of Ben and Old Rit, and that Old Rit would be inconsolable because her favorite daughter was missing. "Lord," she prayed, "I'm going to hold steady onto You. You've got to see me through." Then she went to sleep.

The next morning, when the stars were still visible in the sky, the farmer stopped the wagon. Harriet was instantly awake.

He told her to follow the river, to keep following it to reach the next place where people would take her in and feed her. He said that she must travel only at night and she must stay off the roads because the patrol would be hunting for her. Harriet climbed out of the wagon. "Thank you," she said simply, thinking how amazing it was that there should be white people who were willing to go to such lengths to help a slave get to the North.

D When she finally arrived in Pennsylvania, she had traveled roughly ninety miles from Dorchester County. She had slept on the ground outdoors at night. She had been rowed for miles up the Choptank River by a man she had never seen before. She had been concealed in a haycock[11] and had, at one point, spent a week hidden in a potato

---

11. **haycock** *n.:* pile of hay in a field.

Vocabulary
sinewy (sin′yōō·ē) *adj.:* strong; firm; tough.

MINI-LESSON **Reading**

Developing Word-Attack Skills
Write the words *immediately* and *familiar* (from p. 289) on the chalkboard, and read them aloud. Explain that in some words two vowels together stand for two different sounds. Underline the two vowels that appear together in each word, *ia,* and help students recognize that in *immediately,* the *i* stands for long *e* and the *a* is an unstressed vowel sound. In *familiar,* the *i* has the conso-

nant sound /y/ and the *a* is an unstressed vowel sound. In a similar way, explore the sounds represented by the vowels that appear together in *Harriet, quiet, pinioning.*
Activity. Display these sentences. Have volunteers read them aloud and identify the word in each sentence that has two vowels together that stand for two sounds.

1. Harriet raised her voice to sing. [Harriet]
2. Her manner was defiant. [defiant]

The Harriet Tubman Series (1939–1940), No. 11, by Jacob Lawrence.

"$500 Reward! Runaway from subscriber of Thursday night, the 4th inst., from the neighborhood of Cambridge, my negro girl, Harriet, sometimes called Minty. Is dark chestnut color, rather stout build, but bright and handsome. Speaks rather deep and has a scar over the left temple. She wore a brown plaid shawl. I will give the above reward captured outside the county, and $300 if captured inside the county, in either case to be lodged in the Cambridge, Maryland, jail.

(signed) George Carter,
Broadacres, near Cambridge, Maryland,
September 24th, 1849"

hole in a cabin which belonged to a family of free Negroes. She had been hidden in the attic of the home of a Quaker. She had been befriended by stout German farmers, whose guttural[12] speech surprised her and whose well-kept farms astonished her. She had never before seen barns and fences, farmhouses and outbuildings, so carefully painted. The cattle and horses were so clean they looked as though they had been scrubbed.

When she crossed the line into the free state of Pennsylvania, the sun was coming up. She said, "I looked at my hands to see if I was the same person now I was free. There was such a glory over everything, the sun came like gold through the trees and over the fields, and I felt like I was in heaven."

E

---

12. **guttural** *adj.:* harsh; rasping.

3. She sang about leaving in a chariot. [chariot]

4. She would make the trip without a companion. [companion]

5. She had no reliable friend to go with her. [reliable]

FAMILY/COMMUNITY ACTIVITY

Conductors and stationmasters on the Underground Railroad often spoke in code. For instance, a stationmaster who received a message to expect "four large kegs of dark ale and one small one" would know to look for four adults and one child. To learn more about the Underground Railroad, have students research ex-slave narratives on the Internet with family members.

Hampton University Museum, Hampton, Virginia.

DIRECT TEACHING

VIEWING THE ART

Jacob Lawrence wrote and illustrated a 1968 children's book, *Harriet and the Promised Land,* which tells Harriet Tubman's story in verse.

Activity. Ask students to pretend that they are in the landscape of this Jacob Lawrence painting. Have them jot down their impressions of their surroundings. Suggest that they use their notes to write a poem.

E Literary Focus
GRADE-LEVEL STANDARD

❓ **Point of view.** How is the first-person point of view used here? [Tubman is being quoted word for word.] Explain that direct quotations using the first person can appear within a third-person narrative.

GUIDED PRACTICE

Monitoring student's progress. Guide the class in answering these true-false questions. Direct students to locate passages in the text that support their responses.

True-False

1. Harriet Tubman's first escape attempt was a failure. [T]

2. Tubman turns back because she is afraid. [F]

3. Tubman sings a song hoping to alert her sister that she is running away. [T]

4. The people on the Underground Railroad help Tubman because they know her well. [F]

5. At the time of the story, slavery is legal in the state of Maryland. [T]

Meet the Writer

Background. Ann Petry began her adult life as a certified pharmacist, working in her family's drugstore in Old Saybrook, Connecticut. Later, in New York City, she was a journalist, a teacher, and an actress in the American Negro Theatre. Her first book for children, *The Drugstore Cat* (1949), tells the story of a kitten named Buzzie who lives in a drugstore very much like the one from Petry's youth.

Petry's best-known work for adults is her first novel, *The Street* (1946), a realistic story of a woman living with her young son in Harlem.

Speaking about her two celebrated subjects in books for young adults, Petry said of Harriet Tubman and Tituba of the Salem witch trials, "These women were slaves. I hoped that I had made them come alive, turned them into real people. I tried to make history speak across the centuries in the voices of people—young, old, good, evil, beautiful, ugly."

For Independent Reading

For students who are interested in reading more on this topic, recommend *The Underground Man* by Milton Meltzer, which is based on the life of Calvin Fairbanks, or *Who Comes with Cannons* by Patricia Beatty, about a Quaker family's station on the Underground Railroad.

Ann Petry

"Remember Them"

Ann Petry (1908–1997) is best known for her biography of Harriet Tubman. In a speech at the New York Public Library, Petry told of meeting a girl who had just read the biography. The meeting made Petry think about what she wanted the book to say to her readers.

" As I was about to leave, a little girl came in to return a book of mine, a book I wrote about Harriet Tubman. She was carrying it hugged close to her chest. She laid it down on the table, and the librarian said to her, 'You know, this is Mrs. Petry, the author of the book you are returning.'

I must confess that I was dismayed; . . . though I have had children tell me they enjoyed something I had written, I had never had a face-to-face encounter with a young reader who was actually holding one of my books. The child looked at me, and I looked at her—and she didn't say anything and neither did I. I didn't know what to say. Neither did she. Finally she reached out and touched my arm, ever so gently, and then drew her hand back as though she were embarrassed. I copied her gesture, touching her gently on the arm, because I felt it would serve to indicate that I approved her gesture.

Then I left the library, but I left it thinking to myself: What have I said to this child in this book? . . . Of course, I have been saying: Let's take a look at slavery. I said it in *Harriet Tubman* and again in *Tituba of Salem Village* [another book by Petry].

But what else was I saying? Over and over again, I have said: These are people. Look at them, listen to them, . . . remember them. Remember for what a long, long time black people have been in this country, have been a part of America: a sturdy, indestructible, wonderful part of America, woven into its heart and into its soul. "

DIFFERENTIATING INSTRUCTION

Advanced Learners

Enrichment. Encourage students to imagine being a historical figure fighting for freedom. Possibilities include Frederick Douglass, William Wallace, or Barbara Frietchie, but allow students to choose any freedom fighter they wish. Then, ask them to write a response from that person's point of view to Tubman's quotation in Interpretations question 7.

Learners Having Difficulty

Monitoring tip: If students are unable to work out the sequence of events in the plot for the Reading Check on p. 297, re-read the biography with them, looking for signal words like *next, then, now, later.* Then, help them place the events in the appropriate sequence.

Literary Response and Analysis

Reading Check

1. Imagine that you're a reporter for a secret newspaper put out by the Underground Railroad. Record information for a news story on Tubman's escape. Refer to your **sequence chart** to order the events. Use details in the story to answer the questions *who? what? when? where? why?* and *how?*

Interpretations

2. Think about the discussion of slavery you had before you began reading the biography, and think about your notes for the Quickwrite on page 286. Did any of your feelings or ideas change after you read this biography? Did it raise more questions for you? Explain.

3. What **inferences** can you make about the **character traits** that enabled Tubman to reach freedom? What makes her a hero?

4. Many Africans held in slavery used songs to communicate forbidden messages. When Harriet Tubman sang about leaving on the chariot, what message was she trying to send her sister?

5. In the Bible the Israelites escaping slavery in Egypt eventually cross the Jordan River and enter the land they believe was promised to them by God. What was Tubman's Jordan? What was her promised land?

6. Re-read the paragraph on page 292 that begins "As she went toward the quarter, she began to sing." Explain why this paragraph could appear in a **biography** but not in an **autobiography.** Choose another paragraph of at least five lines, and rewrite it as if it were autobiography. (You'll have to switch from the **third-person point of view** to the **first-person point of view.**)

7. Tubman said that "there was one of two things I had a *right* to, liberty or death; if I could not have one, I would have the other; for no man should take me alive." What other people do you know of, from history or living today, who have risked death to be free?

Evaluation

8. Ann Petry, the author of this biography, never knew Harriet Tubman personally, yet she describes Tubman's thoughts and feelings during her escape. Explain why you think it is or isn't right for a biographer to include such details in someone's life story.

Writing

Through Other Eyes: Speaker and Point of View

Every poem has a **speaker,** a voice that talks to us. The writer and the speaker are not always the same. It's best to think

(continued)

Reading Standard 3.5 Identify the speaker, and recognize the difference between first- and third-person narration (for example, autobiography compared with biography).

A Glory over Everything **297**

Reading Check

1. The correct sequence includes Tubman's first attempt to escape with her brothers; their return to the plantation; the news of her upcoming sale; her immediate need to escape; her singing the spiritual in an effort to alert her sister that she means to escape; her seeking help from the woman in Bucktown; her journey through the woods at night; her stopping at the farmhouse of a white couple; her night jour-

ney in the farmer's wagon; and her long and dangerous journey along the river to Pennsylvania. Possible questions to answer include: "*Who* helped her and who hindered her?" "*What* was the Underground Railroad?" "*When* did Harriet Tubman decide she had to escape?" "*Where* did Tubman end her journey to freedom?" "*Why* did some white people help runaway slaves?" "*How* did Tubman make her way to freedom?"

Literary Response and Analysis

Interpretations

2. Students may say that the biography helped them better understand how the slaves actually felt, increased their admiration of the daring, determined people who escaped slavery, or increased their respect for the white people who took risks to help runaway slaves. Students may have more questions about how other slaves made it to freedom or about what Harriet Tubman did after her escape.

3. Possible answer: Tubman is determined, courageous, and intelligent. Her determination to be free and her bravery in the face of countless dangers make her a hero.

4. Tubman was going to attempt an escape.

5. Tubman's Jordan River is the border between Maryland and Pennsylvania, between the slave states and the free states. Her promised land is the free state of Pennsylvania.

6. In this paragraph, readers know the thoughts of another character, Dr. Thompson, who listens to Tubman's song. In an autobiography of Harriet Tubman there would be no way of knowing precisely what Thompson thought about her singing. Rewrites will vary.

7. Possible answers: soldiers, past and present, who risk their lives for their countries' freedom; volunteers in the civil rights movement in the 1950s and 1960s; fighters in the Warsaw ghetto in 1943, and other anti-Nazi resistance fighters.

Evaluation

8. Possible answers: It is right if it makes the story more interesting without falsifying the historical facts. It is wrong if it distorts history.

A **Literary Focus**
GRADE-LEVEL STANDARD

❓ Point of view. What point of view is the poem told from? [It is told from the first-person point of view. The "I" in the poem is one of Harriet Tubman's fugitives. Notice that the speaker doesn't know why Harriet has lost consciousness. He can tell us only what he sees and feels, which is terror.] What does the speaker mean when he says in the next-to-last line: "this isn't the red sea"? [Moses led the Israelites through the Red Sea when the waters parted miraculously. The frightened fugitive knows that the wide river before him is not going to be parted.]

of the voice in the poem as belonging to a character the poet has created. (For more on poetry, see Chapter 7.)

In "harriet: the leaving," the speaker is a frightened man fleeing slavery with Harriet Tubman. He's *inside* the poem, telling just what *he* observes from his **first-person point of view.** This unnamed man reveals only his own thoughts and feelings. Notice that the man speaks as "I." The "leaving" in the title refers to Tubman's sudden "sleeping seizures."

harriet: the leaving

my lord   she gone again
we's in the middle
of pitch black sky

moon sees us only
we pray   starin back
from the murky river

A

thirteen of us   i think
slave runaways crossin
wide water with no ripple

all cold and shiver
she gone again   my lord
why here? this isn't the red sea
where she go when she go?

—Quraysh Ali Lansana

Write a poem of your own in which the speaker is someone from Tubman's history: Tubman herself, the white woman in the sunbonnet, Tubman's sisters or brothers, her husband, her mother or father, the woman who told her to sweep the yard. You might even speak as Harriet's quilt, the only beautiful

thing she ever owned, which she gave to a woman who helped her. Your speaker will use the first-person pronoun *I*.

The Big Picture
With a few classmates, paint a mural about Tubman's escape. Use a long strip of paper that you can post on the wall when you've finished. With your partners, decide on three or four incidents that you want to picture. Also decide on the places you'll show in your mural. Before you start painting, make sketches, decide on the materials and colors you'll use, and discuss ways to make the painting interesting.

When you're done, write captions identifying the events depicted in your mural. You might want to use as models the captions that accompany Jacob Lawrence's *The Harriet Tubman Series* (see pages 291, 295, and 310–313).

Courtesy of Michigan State University Museum.

Oak-leaf-pattern quilt block from about 1860, said to have been made by a slave held in Alabama.

298   Chapter 5   Biography and Autobiography: Looking at Lives

CONTENT-AREA CONNECTIONS

Culture
African American code quilts. Recent research by Jacqueline L. Tobin and Raymond G. Dobard in *Hidden in Plain View* (1999) suggests that the patterns in quilts created by slaves contained coded messages. The Monkey Wrench pattern, for example, one of ten patterns that the authors identify as making up the "Underground Railroad Quilt Code," signaled that slaves were to

begin collecting tools and belongings in preparation for escape.
Activity. Have students look up and illustrate other code patterns, such as "Flying Geese" or "Drunkard's Path." What were these patterns communicating to slaves hoping to escape?

INDIVIDUAL

Vocabulary Development

Clarifying Word Meanings

PRACTICE

Imagine that you're a newspaper reporter writing about Harriet Tubman.

1. Explain how Tubman managed to elude her pursuers.
2. Mention an inexplicable event that happened to Tubman.
3. Explain why Tubman had a legitimate reason to be defiant.
4. To illustrate your story, draw a picture of the sinewy vines Tubman encountered on her flight.

Word Bank

elude
inexplicable
legitimate
defiant
sinewy

Grammar Link MINI-LESSON

Don't Use *Bad* and *Badly* Badly

Follow these rules when you're deciding between *bad* and *badly*:

- Use *bad* to modify a noun or a pronoun.
- Use *badly* to modify an adjective or a verb.

> **Tubman worried that she would have a bad fall.**
> [*Bad* modifies the noun *fall*.]

> **Tubman wanted her freedom badly.**
> [*Badly* modifies the verb *wanted*.]

The word *bad* should never be used to modify a verb.

NONSTANDARD   **Mr. Thompson treated runaways bad.**

STANDARD   **Mr. Thompson treated runaways badly.**

Note that the expression *feel badly* has become acceptable, though it is ungrammatical, informal English.

INFORMAL   **Tubman felt badly about leaving Old Rit.**

FORMAL   **Tubman felt bad about leaving Old Rit.**

PRACTICE

Act as an editor. Decide which underlined word in each pair is grammatically correct.

1. Tubman felt bad/badly that her brothers gave up their attempt to escape.
2. The situation looked bad/badly to Tubman.
3. If Tubman were caught, she would be beaten bad/badly.
4. She wanted to escape bad/badly.

For more help, see A Glossary of Usage in the *Holt Handbook*, page 223.

A Glory over Everything   **299**

DIFFERENTIATING INSTRUCTION

English-Language Learners
Have groups of students take turns acting out Tubman's journey to freedom. Assign a passage from the excerpt to each group. Have the group choose a reader to be the narrator and others in the group to act out roles, to direct, or to find props. After groups have planned and rehearsed, call on them, according to the sequence of events in the selection, to present their passages.

Advanced Learners
Enrichment. Have students find out more about conductors on the Underground Railroad. Suggest that they enter *Underground Railroad* as keywords in a search engine and continue from there. They might also search for material on Calvin Fairbanks, who spent seventeen years in jail for his activities, or John P. Parker, who wrote an autobiography titled *His Promised Land* (1996).

Vocabulary Development

Practice
Possible Answers

1. Tubman managed to elude her pursuers with the help of the Underground Railroad.
2. Tubman feared traveling alone because, for some inexplicable reason, she might suddenly fall asleep.
3. Tubman had a very legitimate reason to be defiant of her owner; no one has the right to enslave another human being.
4. Students' pictures should include ropy, tough vines.

Grammar Link

Practice
1. bad
2. bad
3. badly
4. badly

▶ **Resources Reminder**

Vocabulary and Spelling
- *Vocabulary Development*
  - Vocabulary Worksheet, p. 23
- *Lesson Plans for Language Development*
  - Vocabulary, p. 146

ASSESSING

Assessment
- *Progress Assessment of Reading*
  - Selection Test, p. 100

RETEACHING

For a lesson reteaching point of view, see **Reteaching,** p. 489A.

STANDARDS FOCUS, pp. 300–314

(For grade-level and review standards taught in this selection, see citations on Pupil's Edition pages.)

Prerequisite Standard

■ Grade 5, Reading Comprehension 2.3 **Discern main ideas and concepts presented in texts, identifying and assessing evidence that supports those ideas.**

Summary *at grade level*

These selections present information from three different sources, each related to the life of Harriet Tubman.

The first, "All Aboard with Thomas Garrett," focuses on the activities of the renowned Delaware abolitionist, who became Tubman's friend. The article describes Garrett's helping Tubman escape across the Delaware-Pennsylvania border, his work assisting thousands of other fugitive slaves, and his passionate defense of his beliefs in a federal circuit courtroom.

The second selection is from a biography of Tubman by Sarah Bradford. In this excerpt, Bradford recounts Tubman's words upon crossing the Pennsylvania border into freedom.

The third and final selection consists of four paintings from Jacob Lawrence's *Harriet Tubman Series*. The pictures and captions vividly depict the experiences Tubman faced escorting fugitive slaves along the Underground Railroad.

►Resources Reminder

Media
■ *Audio CD Library*
  ▪ disc 7

Connecting and Clarifying Main Ideas: Three Readings on Harriet Tubman

All Aboard with Thomas Garrett *and*
from Harriet Tubman: The Moses of Her People *and*
from The Harriet Tubman Series

Connecting Main Ideas Across Texts

If you read "A Glory over Everything," you already know a lot about Harriet Tubman. Here are three more sources on Tubman:

- an article on Thomas Garrett, who sheltered more than 2,700 people fleeing slavery and was a lifelong friend of Tubman's (page 302)
- a long quotation from an 1886 biography of Tubman (page 308)
- four paintings from Jacob Lawrence's *The Harriet Tubman Series*, accompanied by captions telling about Tubman's life (page 310)

Read the materials once for pleasure. Then, read them a second time, keeping a piece of paper handy. Copy the chart of main ideas on the next page, and fill it in by writing down evidence and support from the three pieces.

Look for more **main ideas** to add to the chart as you read. (Remember, there is often more than one main idea in a piece of nonfiction.) Add boxes to your chart if you need them. You don't have to fill in every idea box for every selection; some main ideas will apply to only one or two of the pieces.

Reading Standard 2.3 Connect and clarify main ideas by identifying their relationships to other sources and related topics.

Vocabulary Development

Here are the words you'll be learning as you read "All Aboard with Thomas Garrett":

prudent (prōō′dənt) *adj.:* wise; sensible. *The runaways stayed with Garrett until he felt it was prudent to send them on.*

hazardous (haz′ər·dəs) *adj.:* dangerous; risky. *The Underground Railroad helped runaways make the hazardous journey north.*

diligence (dil′ə·jəns) *n.:* steady effort. *Garrett promised to double his diligence in helping people escape from slavery.*

servitude (sur′və·tōōd′) *n.:* condition of being under another person's control. *The Fifteenth Amendment stated that no citizen should be denied the vote simply because of previous servitude.*

jubilant (jōō′bə·lənt) *adj.:* joyful. *Crowds of jubilant people celebrated the passage of the amendment.*

(Opposite) Quilt made about 1862 by Kissie Gary when she was held in slavery as a child on a South Carolina plantation. According to Gary's granddaughter, Kissie took the quilt with her when she left the plantation as a reminder of "the place of her childhood."
Courtesy of Anacostia Museum, branch of Smithsonian Institution.

300 Chapter 5 Biography and Autobiography: Looking at Lives

RESOURCES

Planning
■ *One-Stop Planner* CD-ROM with Test Generator
■ *On Course: Mapping Instruction*

Media
■ *Audio CD Library*
  ▪ disc 7

Reading
■ *Interactive Reading*
  ▪ Graphic Organizer: Making Connections Chart, p. 194

Differentiating Instruction
■ *Lesson Plans for Language Development*
  ▪ English-Language Learners, pp. 132–133, 141, 142, 146

Connecting Main Ideas in Different Sources

Three Readings on Harriet Tubman

Main Ideas	Idea 1: It was important for free people to help those who were enslaved.	Idea 2: People fleeing slavery were in constant danger.	Idea 3: Freeing people from slavery required hard work and sacrifice.	Idea 4:
Evidence and Support from Readings				
"All Aboard with Thomas Garrett"	No runaway was ever turned away from his door.	"Slave catchers" searched the streets of Wilmington for runaways.		
Harriet Tubman: The Moses of Her People	"I was free, and they should be free. . . ."	"I was a stranger in a strange land. . . ."	"I would make a home for them in the North, and, the Lord helping me, I would bring them all there."	
The Harriet Tubman Series			She traveled at night and hid during the day. She climbed mountains and crossed rivers.	

Related topics: *The Frederick Douglass Series* by Jacob Lawrence; work of Quakers in antislavery movement; Virginia Hamilton's novel *House of Dies Drear* (about Underground Railroad).

- Special Education Students, pp. 132–133, 141, 142, 146

Vocabulary and Spelling
- *Vocabulary Development*
  - Vocabulary Worksheet, p. 24
- *Spelling Lessons and Activities*
  - Root Words and Affixes, pp. 40–47, 52, 60–63, 68–75

Assessment
- *Progress Assessment of Reading*
  - Selection Test, p. 103
- *One-Stop Planner* CD-ROM with Test Generator

Standards Starter
Build prerequisite skills. Tell students that when they read a few different texts on a single topic it is useful to pause between texts to reflect on what they've learned. Have students discuss what they learned about Harriet Tubman's life from reading "A Glory over Everything." Ask them to name some of the main ideas that were presented in that text.

Preview Vocabulary
After students review the Vocabulary words on p. 300, have them answer the following questions:

1. Do you think bungee jumping is prudent behavior? Explain.
2. Name a condition that can make driving hazardous.
3. Describe a time when you exercised diligence.
4. Why would you not want to be in servitude to someone else?
5. When was the last time you felt jubilant?

Assign the Reading
After students read "All Aboard with Thomas Garrett" in class, you may wish to assign the Reading Check and the Vocabulary activities as homework. You might lead an in-class examination of the Jacob Lawrence paintings, as well as a discussion that connects ideas about Tubman and the Underground Railroad from multiple sources.

HOMEWORK

Resources Reminder
Reading
- *Interactive Reading*
  - Graphic Organizer: Making Connections Chart, p. 194

A Reading Skills

? Speculating. Who do you think this couple is? [Possible response: Since the article is about Thomas Garrett and the Underground Railroad, the man may be Garrett. The couple may be abolitionists helping fugitive slaves or disguised slaves trying to reach freedom.] **Why might they ride slowly and then speed up?** [Possible responses: They may drive slowly in the city to avoid attracting attention and then speed up as they near freedom.]

All Aboard with Thomas Garrett

Alice P. Miller

Nineteenth-century map showing the route of the Underground Railroad in southeastern Pennsylvania.

The Granger Collection, New York.

The elderly couple walked sedately down the stairs of the red brick house, every detail of their costumes proclaiming their respectability. The small lady was wearing an ankle-length gray gown, a snowy-white lawn kerchief, and a pleated gray silk bonnet, draped with a veil. The tall white-haired gentleman wore the wide-brimmed beaver hat and the long black waistcoat that was customary among Quakers.

When they reached the sidewalk, he assisted her into the four-wheeled barouche[1] that stood at the curb. Then he climbed into the barouche himself. The driver drove the horses away at a leisurely pace. Not until they were beyond the city limits did he allow the horses to prance along at a brisk pace across the few miles that separated Wilmington, Delaware, from the free state of Pennsylvania.

That tall white-haired gentleman was Thomas Garrett, a white man who

___

1. **barouche** (bə·rōōsh') *n.:* type of horse-drawn carriage.

Learners Having Difficulty
The events in "All Aboard with Thomas Garrett" are not related in chronological order. The selection begins with Garrett's journey with Harriet Tubman, moves back in time to discuss his early life, and then moves ahead to describe his later years. If students have difficulty following the sequence of events, suggest that they construct a time line, using the dates provided, to put events in order.

English-Language Learners
Students who grew up in other countries may not understand many of the geographic references in the text. Use reference materials to help these students visualize the journey made by fugitives and the places mentioned in the selection. On a map of the United States, have students locate the cities of Wilmington and New Castle, and point out the Pennsylvania-Delaware border, or

Mason-Dixon line that divided free states from slave states.

Resources Reminder
For lessons designed for intermediate and advanced English-language learners, see *Lesson Plans for Language Development,* pp. 132–133, 141–142, 146.

had for many years been breaking the law by sheltering runaway slaves. And the little lady at his side was runaway slave Harriet Tubman, clad in clothes donated by his wife. On the preceding night Harriet had slept in a small room secreted behind one wall of Garrett's shoe store, a room that never remained unoccupied for very long. It was Harriet's first visit to Garrett, but she would be returning many times in the future.

Runaway slaves remained with Garrett for one night or two or three until such time as Garrett considered it prudent to send them along to the next station on the Underground Railroad. He provided them with clothing and outfitted them with new shoes from his shoe store. He fed them hearty meals and dressed their wounds. He also forged passes for them so that any slave stopped by a slave catcher would have evidence that he or she was on a legitimate errand.

Some of the money he needed to cover the cost of his hospitality came out of his own pocket, but he was not a rich man. He could not have taken care of so many fugitives were it not for donations made by fellow abolitionists in the North as well as from supporters in foreign countries. There was never quite enough money, but no fugitive was ever turned away from his door. He would have gone without food himself before he would have refused food to a hungry slave.

Garrett, who was born in Upper Darby, Pennsylvania, in 1789, had been helping runaway slaves ever since 1822, when he rescued a young black woman who was trying to escape from her master. At that time he vowed to devote the rest of his life to helping fugitives, and he remained faithful to that vow.

Of all the stations on the Underground Railroad his was probably the most efficiently run and the one most frequently used. The fact that Wilmington was so close to Pennsylvania made it the most hazardous stop on the route. Slave catchers prowled the streets of Wilmington, on the alert for any indication that a black person might be a

Vocabulary
prudent (prōo′dənt) *adj.*: wise; sensible.
hazardous (haz′ər·dəs) *adj.*: dangerous; risky.

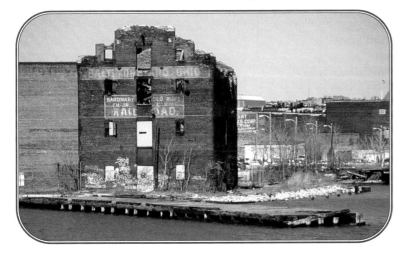
An old building in Baltimore, Maryland, once used as a stop on the Underground Railroad.

All Aboard with Thomas Garrett **303**

DIRECT TEACHING

B **Reading Informational Materials**
GRADE-LEVEL STANDARD
? **Connecting and clarifying main ideas.** What idea from "A Glory over Everything" is reinforced by this information? [Possible response: Abolitionists were willing to take great risks to help slaves along in the Underground Railroad.]

C **Reading Informational Materials**
GRADE-LEVEL STANDARD
? **Connecting and clarifying main ideas.** Consider the methods Tubman uses here to avoid detection and those described in "A Glory over Everything." What main idea do both articles present about what people had to do to escape from slavery? [Possible responses: Both selections describe complicated methods—disguises, hidden rooms, river journeys. People fleeing to the North had to use elaborate measures and exercise extreme caution in order to avoid detection.]

D **Reading Skills**
? **Making generalizations.** Judging from the description provided here, what kind of person was Thomas Garrett? [Possible response: Garrett was generous, welcoming, committed, wise, and willing to take risks.]

E **Reading Informational Materials**
GRADE-LEVEL STANDARD
? **Connecting and clarifying main ideas.** Have students recall that Tubman first escaped to freedom in 1849. What can students conclude from the fact that Garrett first began to help runaways in 1822? [The movement to help people flee slavery had been going on for many years.]

DEVELOPING FLUENCY

Some students, particularly those who are learning English, may be unfamiliar with some of the vocabulary in the article, such as *sedately, proclaiming,* and *customary.* Multiple-meaning words such as *station, sharp, suit, court, addressed, license, fine,* and *bands,* and the homographs *wound* and *close* may also cause confusion.
Activity. Pair students with peer tutors. Ask the partners to read the article together,

pausing at points where the tutor needs to explain the pronunciation and meaning of difficult or confusing words. Then, have the two choose a passage to read and re-read aloud until each can read it with the ease, clarity, and intonation that communicates the meaning of the words.

PEER-TUTORING

A Reading Informational Materials
GRADE-LEVEL STANDARD

Connecting and clarifying main ideas. Suggest that students pause at this juncture to add information to their connecting ideas charts.

B Reading Skills

❓ **Summarizing.** How did Garrett manage to avoid detection for so long? [Possible response: He was extremely clever, used a wide variety of methods to transport fugitive slaves to freedom, and had trustworthy friends who helped.]

C Reading Informational Materials
GRADE-LEVEL STANDARD

❓ **Connecting and clarifying main ideas.** Considering the slave owners' actions here and those described in "A Glory over Everything," what can you conclude about their determination to keep slaves from escaping? [Possible response: The slave owners' actions—including the use of handbills, patrollers, bloodhounds, and the court system—indicate a group of people extremely determined to halt the flow of fugitives.]

The Underground Railroad (1893) by Charles T. Weber.

The Granger Collection, New York.

A runaway. They kept a sharp eye on all roads leading north from Wilmington.

For many years Garrett managed to get away with his illegal activities because he was a clever man and knew ways to avoid detection by the slave catchers. Sometimes he disguised a slave, as he had done with **B** Harriet. Sometimes he dressed a man in a woman's clothing or a woman in a man's clothing or showed a young person how to appear like one bent over with age. Another reason for his success was that he had many friends who admired what he was doing and who could be trusted to help him. They might, for example, conceal slaves under a wagonload of vegetables or in a secret compartment in a wagon.

The slave catchers were aware of what he was doing, but they had a hard time finding the kind of evidence that would **C** stand up in court. At last, in 1848, he was sued by two Maryland slave owners who hoped to bring a stop to his activities by ruining him financially.

The suit was brought into the federal circuit court of New Castle under a 1793 federal law that allowed slave owners to recover penalties from any person who harbored

304   Chapter 5   Biography and Autobiography: Looking at Lives

a runaway slave. The case was heard by Willard Hall, United States District Judge, and by Roger B. Taney, Chief Justice of the United States Supreme Court. Bringing in a verdict in favor of the slave owners, the jurors decided that the slave owners were entitled to $5,400 in fines.

Garrett didn't have anywhere near that much money, but he stood up and addressed the court and the spectators in these words:

"I have assisted fourteen hundred slaves in the past twenty-five years on their way to the North. I now consider this penalty imposed upon me as a license for the remainder of my life. I am now past sixty and have not a dollar to my name, but be that as it may, if anyone knows of a poor slave who needs shelter and a breakfast, send him to me, as I now publicly pledge myself to double my diligence and never neglect an opportunity to assist a slave to obtain freedom, so help me God!"

As he continued to speak for more than an hour, some of the spectators hissed while others cheered. When he finished, one juror leaped across the benches and pumped Garrett's hand. With tears in his eyes, he said, "I beg your forgiveness, Mr. Garrett."

After the trial Garrett's furniture was auctioned off to help pay the heavy fine. But he managed to borrow money from friends and eventually repaid those loans, rebuilt his business, and became prosperous. Meanwhile he went on sheltering slaves for many more years. By the time President Lincoln issued the Emancipation Proclamation[2] in 1863, Garrett's records showed that he had sheltered more than 2,700 runaways.

---

2. **Emancipation Proclamation:** presidential order abolishing slavery in the South.

During those years he had many encounters with Harriet Tubman, as she kept returning to the South and coming back north with bands of slaves. Much of what we know about Harriet today is based on letters that he sent to her or wrote about her. A portion of one of those letters reads thus:

"I may begin by saying, living as I have in a slave State, and the laws being very severe where any proof could be made of anyone aiding slaves on their way to freedom, I have not felt at liberty to keep any written word of Harriet's labors as I otherwise could, and now would be glad to do; for in truth I never met with any person, of any color, who had more confidence in the voice of God, as spoken direct to her soul. . . . She felt no more fear of being arrested by her former master, or any other person, when in his immediate neighborhood, than she did in the State of New York or Canada, for she said she ventured only where God sent her, and her faith in the Supreme Power truly was great."

In April, 1870, the black people of Wilmington held a huge celebration upon the passage of the fifteenth amendment to the Constitution of the United States. That amendment provided that the right of citizens to vote should not be denied or abridged by the United States or by any state on account of race, color, or previous condition of servitude.

Jubilant blacks drew Garrett through the streets in an open carriage on one side of which were inscribed the words "Our Moses."

Vocabulary

diligence (dil'ə·jəns) *n.:* steady effort.

servitude (sur'və·tōōd') *n.:* condition of being under another person's control.

jubilant (jōō'bə·lənt) *adj.:* joyful.

All Aboard with Thomas Garrett   **305**

GUIDED PRACTICE

Monitoring students' progress.
To assess students' understanding of the article, have them create a chart for Thomas Garrett, listing his occupation, talents, beliefs, and personality traits.

INDEPENDENT PRACTICE

Reading Informational Materials

Reading Check

1. Garrett gave food and shelter; clothing; medical attention; safe havens; forged passes and disguises; and transportation.

2. Slave owners sued Garrett, hoping to stop his activities by ruining him financially.

3. Garrett responded by defiantly promising to continue helping people flee slavery.

4. They celebrated the passage of the fifteenth amendment.

5. His speech outlines his fierce devotion to the Underground Railroad. Garrett's letter describes Tubman as determined, fearless, and religious.

6. In the Bible, Moses led the Israelites to freedom, just as Garrett did for slaves.

Vocabulary Development

Practice 1
Possible Answers
- *hazardous*—hazard, hazardously
- *diligence*—diligent, diligently
- *servitude*—service, servant
- *jubilant*—jubilation, jubilee

Reading Informational Materials

Reading Check
1. In what ways did Thomas Garrett help people fleeing slavery?
2. Why was Thomas Garrett brought to trial?
3. How did Garrett respond to the jury's verdict?
4. What did African Americans in Wilmington celebrate in April 1870?
5. What does Garrett's speech tell you about his devotion to his cause? What does his letter add to your knowledge of Harriet Tubman's character?
6. What is the meaning of the last line of this biographical article—that Garrett was called "Our Moses"?

Vocabulary Development

Related Words: Word Trees Increase Your Vocabulary
You can easily add to your vocabulary by checking a dictionary for words related to each new word you look up. Try it right now with *prudent*. In your dictionary you can find *prude, prudence, prudential, prudery,* and *prudish.* All these words are related: They all come from the Latin root *prudentia,* meaning "foresight."

A family tree for *prudentia* appears on the right.

> ### PRACTICE 1
> Do a dictionary search for the other Word Bank words. See how many family trees you can make with your discoveries. Share your trees in class.

Word Bank
prudent
hazardous
diligence
servitude
jubilant

prudentia,
"foresight"

 Resources Reminder

Vocabulary and Spelling
- *Spelling Lessons and Activities*

For a wide range of lessons related to root words and affixes, see pp. 40–47, 52, 60–63, 68–75.

Multiple-Meaning Words

PRACTICE 2

When you come across a word that means more than one thing, you can often use **context** to decide on the correct meaning. Each of the passages below contains an underlined word. Several definition choices for that word follow. All the definitions are correct in one context or another, but only one of the definitions fits in the sentence. Choose the definition that fits best. Then, identify the words in the sentence that helped you make your choice. Item 1 has been completed for you.

1. "The small lady was wearing an ankle-length gray gown, a snowy-white lawn kerchief, and a pleated gray silk bonnet, draped with a veil. The tall white-haired gentleman wore the wide-brimmed beaver hat and the long black waistcoat that was customary among Quakers."

   a. little
   b. selfish
   c. unimportant

Answer: The definition that works best in this context is "little." There is no indication that the woman is selfish or unimportant, and in the next sentence the man is described as *tall*, which means the opposite of *little*. Choice **a** seems like the best answer.

2. "On the preceding night Harriet had slept in a small room secreted behind one wall of Garrett's shoe store, a room that never remained unoccupied for very long."

   a. shop
   b. gather or accumulate
   c. stockpile of provisions

3. "He fed them hearty meals and dressed their wounds."

   a. decorated
   b. applied medication to
   c. clothed

4. "At that time he vowed to devote the rest of his life to helping fugitives, and he remained faithful to that vow."

   a. sleep
   b. remainder
   c. relax

Blocks from a quilt made by Harriet Powers after the Civil War. Powers was born into slavery in Georgia in 1837.
THE BIBLE by Harriet Powers, Smithsonian Institution.

Reading Standard 1.4 Monitor expository text for unknown words by using word clues to determine meaning.

Practice 2

2. **a** Since *Garrett's shoe* precedes *store*, a noun is needed, so b can be eliminated. Since the store has a secret room, it must be a building, not a collection of goods. So a is a better choice than c.

3. **b** Wounds need medical attention—not decoration or clothes—so b is the best choice.

4. **b** The context requires a noun so c can be eliminated. Since the *sleep of his life* would not be useful to fugitives, b is clearly the best answer.

▶ Resources Reminder

Vocabulary and Spelling
- *Vocabulary Development*
  - Vocabulary Worksheet, p. 24
  - Cumulative Vocabulary Review, p. 25
- *Lesson Plans for Language Development*
  - Vocabulary, p. 146

ASSESSING

Assessment
- *Progress Assessment of Reading*
  - Selection Test, p. 103

Ⓐ Reading Informational Materials
GRADE-LEVEL STANDARD
❷ Connecting and clarifying main ideas. Have students note Bradford's actions and recall the aid that Garrett received after his conviction. What can students conclude about abolitionists, their principles, and their willingness to help one another? [Possible response: People who worked to fight slavery often put their principles above their own financial well-being, yet when they found themselves in need fellow abolitionists could be counted on to provide assistance.]

Background

During the Civil War, Harriet Tubman worked for the Union Army as a spy, scout, and nurse. She refused payment for her services because she felt that in this way she would set an example of self-sufficiency and independence. When she returned to her home in Auburn, New York, after the war, she discovered that she was about to lose her house because she couldn't pay for it. To help Tubman,
Ⓐ *the abolitionist Sarah Bradford wrote a biography of her in 1869; she revised it in 1886. Bradford turned over to Tubman the earnings from both editions. This part of Bradford's biography starts where Petry's "A Glory over Everything" ends.*

from

Harriet Tubman
The Moses of Her People

Sarah Bradford

After many long and weary days of travel, she found that she had passed the magic line, which then divided the land of bondage from the land of freedom. But where were the lovely white ladies whom in her visions she had seen, who, with arms outstretched, welcomed her to their hearts and homes. All these visions proved deceitful: She was more alone than ever; but she had crossed the line; no one could take her now, and she would never call her man "Master" more.

"I looked at my hands," she said, "to see if I was the same person now I was free. There was such a glory over everything, the sun came like gold through the trees and over the fields, and I felt like I was in heaven." But then came the bitter drop in the cup of joy. She was alone, and her kindred were in slavery, and not one of them had the courage to dare what she had dared. Unless she made the effort to liberate them, she would never see them more, or even know their fate.

"I knew of a man," she said, "who was sent to the State Prison for twenty-five years. All these years he was always thinking of his home, and counting by years, months, and days, the time till he should be free, and see his family and friends once more. The years roll on, the time of imprisonment is over, the man is free. He leaves the prison gates, he makes his way to his old home, but his old home is not there. The house in which he had dwelt in his childhood had been torn down, and a new one had been put up in its place; his family were gone, their very name was forgotten, there was no one to take him by the hand to welcome him back to life."

"So it was with me," said Harriet; "I had crossed the line of which I had so long been dreaming. I was free; but there was no one there to welcome me to the land

Harriet Tubman (1951) by Robert Savon Pious.

National Portrait Gallery, Smithsonian Institution, Washington, D.C./Art Resource, New York.

of freedom, I was a stranger in a strange land, and my home after all was down in the old cabin quarter, with the old folks and my brothers and sisters. But to this solemn resolution I came: I was free, and they should be free also; I would make a home for them in the North, and, the Lord helping me, I would bring them all there. Oh, how I prayed then, lying all alone on the cold, damp ground. "Oh, dear Lord," I said, "I haven't got a friend but you. Come to my help, Lord, for I'm in trouble!"

B

C

B **Reading Informational Materials**
GRADE-LEVEL STANDARD
? **Connecting and clarifying main ideas.** How does this account of Tubman's thoughts and feelings upon reaching freedom expand upon the one presented in "A Glory over Everything"? [Possible response: In "A Glory over Everything," Tubman describes herself as being "in heaven." Here, she describes a more complex set of thoughts and feelings. She is indeed free, but she is also alone. She realizes that many difficulties lie ahead.]

C **Reading Informational Materials**
GRADE-LEVEL STANDARD
? **Connecting and clarifying main ideas.** What main ideas are contained in this quotation? Have students use their responses to continue filling in their connecting ideas charts.

VIEWING THE ART

Jacob Lawrence moved to New York at the age of thirteen. As a teenager growing up in Harlem, he learned about historical figures such as Harriet Tubman, John Brown, Frederick Douglass, and Toussaint L'Ouverture. Lawrence created his historical series about these figures because he felt that their stories were too complex to be captured in single paintings.

Activity. Have students comment on the relationship between the background sky and the four huddled figures staring at the moon. [Possible responses: The dark sky seems to dominate the very small figures. Lawrence may be trying to emphasize that Tubman and her companions are all alone in the middle of a long and uncertain journey. To maintain their determination, they focus on the star that they hope will lead them to freedom.]

Background

Jacob Lawrence (1917–2000) created The Harriet Tubman Series *of thirty-one paintings between 1939 and 1940. The series is a visual biography that depicts Tubman's work with the Underground Railroad and her service in the Civil War. The series is one of Lawrence's most famous works.*

Lawrence wrote long captions to go with the paintings because at the time he created the series most people knew little about Tubman's life. Much of the information in the captions comes from Sarah Bradford's biographies of Tubman.

from The *Harriet Tubman* Series

Jacob Lawrence

Hampton University Museum, Hampton, Virginia.

The Harriet Tubman Series (1939–1940), No. 15, by Jacob Lawrence.

In the North, Harriet Tubman worked hard. All her wages she laid away for the one purpose of liberating her people, and as soon as a sufficient amount was secured, she disappeared from her Northern home, and as mysteriously appeared one dark night at the door of one of the cabins on the plantation, where a group of trembling fugitives was waiting. Then she piloted them North, traveling by night, hiding by day, scaling the mountains, wading the rivers, threading the forests—she, carrying the babies, drugged with paregoric. So she went, nineteen times liberating over three hundred pieces of living, breathing "property."

The Harriet Tubman Series (1939–1940), No. 19, by Jacob Lawrence.

Hampton University Museum, Hampton, Virginia.

Such a terror did she become to the slave-holders that a reward of forty thousand dollars was offered for her head, she was so bold, daring, and elusive.

VIEWING THE ART

Jacob Lawrence created many of his best-known paintings while still a very young man. He was only twenty-three when he completed *The Migration Series,* sixty paintings that chronicled the movement of African Americans from the rural South to the urban North. Half of these paintings were purchased by New York's Museum of Modern Art, an event that helped to break the art world's "color line." Lawrence's were the first paintings by an African American to enter that museum's prestigious collection.

Activity. Have students examine the action depicted in the painting. Who are the figures in the foreground? What are they doing? [Possible response: They are slave owners examining a handbill offering a reward for Tubman.] Who does the fist represent? What action is it taking? [Possible response: The fist may represent Tubman, whisking away a fleeing slave.] What main idea does this painting and its caption share with information presented in "A Glory over Everything" and "All Aboard with Thomas Garrett"? [Possible responses: Slave owners were determined to stop those who were helping slaves flee to the North, but they never completely succeeded.]

VIEWING THE ART

During the 1930s, **Jacob Lawrence** was employed by the Works Progress Administration, or WPA. The WPA, one of President Franklin Roosevelt's New Deal programs during the Great Depression, provided jobs for millions of Americans, including many in the arts. Playwright Eugene O'Neill, painter Jackson Pollock, and writers Zora Neale Hurston and Claude McKay were just a few of the thousands of artists who participated in WPA projects.

Activity. Focus students' attention on the posture and expressions of Tubman and her fellow fugitives. How do they appear? How does the journey seem to have affected them? [Possible response: They appear worn down mentally and physically by the difficulties they have experienced while in flight.] What ideas from the related readings does this painting and its caption reinforce? [Possible responses: Fleeing slavery was a dangerous and spiritually taxing experience; the participation of people like Garrett in assisting fugitives was essential if they were to succeed in achieving freedom.]

Hampton University Museum, Hampton, Virginia.

The Harriet Tubman Series (1939–1940), No. 22, by Jacob Lawrence.

Harriet Tubman, after a very trying trip North in which she had hidden her cargo by day and had traveled by boat, wagon, and foot at night, reached Wilmington, where she met Thomas Garrett, a Quaker who operated an Underground Railroad station. Here, she and the fugitives were fed and clothed and sent on their way.

Hampton University Museum, Hampton, Virginia.

The Harriet Tubman Series (1939–1940), No. 20, by Jacob Lawrence.

In 1850, the Fugitive Slave Law was passed, which bound the people north of the Mason and Dixon Line to return to bondage any fugitives found in their territories—forcing Harriet Tubman to lead her escaped slaves into Canada.

VIEWING THE ART

Jacob Lawrence painted for almost seven decades, his style remaining unaffected by changing currents in the world of art. Said Lawrence, "The so-called art movements usually come after the fact. If you're unfortunate enough to get swept up in a movement, then you'll find yourself following yourself."

Activity. Have students fill in their connecting ideas charts using information and ideas they have obtained by looking at the art and by reading the captions.

The Harriet Tubman Series **313**

INDEPENDENT PRACTICE

Reading Informational Materials

Reading Check

1. Possible answers: "There are both good people and bad people in the world"; "Beauty is more than skin deep"; "You can do anything you put your mind to"; "Just do it."

2. Answers will vary. One possible answer supporting the idea "There are both good people and bad people in the world" is (from "All Aboard with Thomas Garrett") "As he continued to speak, some of the spectators hissed while others cheered."

3. Possible related topics: the Abolitionist movement; the Fugitive Slave Act.

Answers and Model Rationales

1. **A**   In this question, *all* is the keyword. B and C are ideas presented only in the Garrett reading. Tubman's loneliness is described only in the biography excerpt. A encompasses an idea present in *all* the selections.

2. **H**   Only H specifically connects to Tubman's commitment to free slaves after she had gained her own freedom.

3. **C**   Only C expresses a viewpoint that would likely be shared by *all* three writers.

4. **H**   F and J can be eliminated since we have no information about the life of the writer of "All Aboard with Thomas Garrett." G is close but we can't be sure of Bradford's view of Garrett. Each reading displays a sympathetic view toward those fleeing slavery so H is the best choice.

Reading Informational Materials

Reading Check

1. Go back to the chart you made for the readings on Harriet Tubman (see page 301). Add at least two **main ideas** to the chart so that you have six ideas across the top.

2. Fill in the idea boxes with evidence and support from the readings on Harriet Tubman. (Remember that you don't have to fill in every idea box for each reading. Some main ideas will apply to only one or two of the selections.)

3. Think of at least one more **related topic,** and add it to the box at the bottom of the chart.

TestPractice

All Aboard with Thomas Garrett /
from Harriet Tubman: The Moses of Her People / *from* The Harriet Tubman Series

1. Which **main idea** is presented in all three Tubman readings?
   A   Runaways were always in danger of being returned to slaveholders.
   B   Thomas Garrett sheltered hundreds of runaways.
   C   African Americans celebrated the passage of the Fifteenth Amendment.
   D   Harriet Tubman was overcome by loneliness once she was free.

2. Which of the following **main ideas** does the statement "I was free, and they should be free also" connect to?
   F   Thomas Garrett gave runaways large sums of money.
   G   Runaways often faced harsh conditions when they headed north.
   H   Harriet Tubman would not rest until she had helped many more people escape from slavery.
   J   Harriet Tubman feared being returned to a slaveholder.

3. The writers of all three readings would probably agree that —
   A   runaways felt no obligation toward the people they left behind
   B   African Americans were able to enjoy the benefits of freedom as soon as they reached the North
   C   freeing people from slavery required hard work on the part of many people
   D   most of the people she met helped Harriet Tubman

4. From the readings you can **infer** that all three writers —
   F   were friendly with Harriet Tubman
   G   admire Thomas Garrett
   H   sympathize with the fugitives
   J   grew up under harsh conditions

Reading Standard 2.3 Connect and clarify main ideas by identifying their relationships to other sources and related topics.

Test-Taking Tips

Remind students to use all available time when taking a standardized test. Suggest that if time remains after they answer all questions, they should return to those they found difficult and double-check their work.
   For more information on how to answer multiple choice questions, refer students to **Test Smarts,** p. 690.

ASSESSING

Assessment
■ *Progress Assessment of Reading*
   ■ Selection Test, p. 103

Literary Response and Analysis

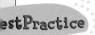

DIRECTIONS: Read the following two selections. Then, read each question on page 319, and write the letter of the best response.

John Brown (1800–1859) was an abolitionist, someone working to end slavery in the United States. The first selection that follows is from Gwen Everett's biography of John Brown. Everett writes from the point of view of Brown's daughter Annie. In this selection, Annie recalls her father's fateful raid on a federal arsenal in Harpers Ferry, Virginia, in 1859. Brown had planned to march south with his "liberation army," freeing people from slavery, enlisting volunteers, and eventually bringing slavery to an end. He raided the arsenal in search of weapons.

from John Brown: One Man Against Slavery

Gwen Everett

We listened carefully to Father's reasons for wanting to end slavery. None of us questioned his sincerity, for we knew he believed God created everyone equal, regardless of skin color. He taught us as his father had taught him: To own another person as property—like furniture or cattle—is a sin. When Father was twelve years old, he witnessed the cruel treatment of black men, women, and children held in bondage and he vowed, then and there, that one day he would put an end to the inhumanity.

"I once considered starting a school where free blacks could learn to read and write, since laws in the South forbid their education," he told us. "And, when we moved to North Elba, New York, we proved that black and white people could live together in peace and brotherhood."

"One person—one family—can make a difference," he said firmly.

"Slavery won't end by itself. It is up to us to fight it."

Father called us by name: Mary, John, Jason, Owen, and Annie (me). He asked us to say a prayer and swear an oath that we, too, would work to end slavery forever. Then he told us his plan.

He would lead a small group of experienced fighting men into a state that allowed slavery. They would hide in the mountains and valleys during daylight. And, under the cover of night, members of his "liberation army" would sneak onto nearby plantations and help the slaves escape.

Freed slaves who wished to join Father's army would learn how to use rifles and pikes—spear-shaped weapons. Then, plantation by plantation, Father's liberation army would move deeper south—growing larger and stronger—eventually freeing all the slaves.

Reading Standard 3.5 Identify the speaker, and recognize the difference between first- and third-person narration (for example, autobiography compared with biography).

Standards Review **315**

Literary Response and Analysis

 STANDARDS FOCUS, pp. 315–319

(For the grade-level and review standards reviewed in this lesson, see Pupil's Edition, p. 315.)

INTRODUCING THE STANDARDS REVIEW

Use this review to assess students' grasp of the literary standards taught in this chapter. If necessary, you can use the annotations to guide students in their reading before they answer the questions.

DIRECT TEACHING

A Literary Focus
GRADE-LEVEL STANDARD
? Comparing points of view.
Ask students to look for clues that indicate first-person narration in this passage. What pronouns are used? [We, us] Whose thoughts are given? [the writer's and her siblings']

MINI-LESSON Reading

Reviewing Word-Attack Skills
Activity. Display these sets of words. Have volunteers read the words and identify the word in which the letter *t* stands for the sound /ch/.

1. feather   feature   feast

2. punctual   function   junction

3. lecture   election   lectern

4. situate   institute   citation

5. vital   virtue   volunteer

Activity. Display these words. Have volunteers underline the two vowel letters that appear together and tell if the letters stand for one sound or two.

1. quiet [two]   **6.** create [two]

2. friend [one]   **7.** said [one]

3. riot [two]   **8.** defiant [two]

4. voice [one]   **9.** immediate [two]

5. thread [one]   **10.** dial [two]

STANDARDS REVIEW

DIRECT TEACHING

A Literary Focus
GRADE-LEVEL STANDARD
❓ Comparing points of view.
In what ways would third-person narration change the impact of Annie's statements about her father? [Possible response: Because third-person narration is less personal, it would detract from the emotional impact of her statements.] How do Annie's feelings for her father affect her portrayal of him? [Possible responses: Most students will say that she loves and admires her father and thinks his actions were right. Some students may feel that this makes her portrayal biased.]

Father's idea sounded so simple. Yet my brothers and I knew this was a dangerous idea. It was illegal for black people to handle firearms and for whites to show them how. It was also against the law to steal someone else's property; and, in effect, Father was doing this by encouraging slaves to leave their masters.

The fateful night of Sunday, October 16, 1859, Father and eighteen of his men marched into Harpers Ferry. They succeeded in seizing the arsenal and several buildings without firing a single shot. By morning the townspeople discovered the raiders and began to fight back. Then a company of marines led by Lieutenant Colonel Robert E. Lee arrived to reinforce the local troops.

The fighting lasted almost two days. When it was over, Father was wounded and four townspeople and ten of Father's men were dead. Newspapers across the country reported every detail of the trial, which was held during the last two weeks of October in Charles Town, Virginia. On October 31, the jury took only forty-five minutes to reach its decision. They found Father guilty of treason against the Commonwealth of Virginia, conspiring with slaves to rebel, and murder.

On December 1, my mother visited him in jail, where they talked and prayed together for several hours. I wished I could have been there to tell Father how courageous I thought he was.

He was executed the next morning.

Father's raid did not end slavery. But historians said that it was one of the most important events leading to the Civil War, which began in April 1861. The war destroyed slavery forever in our country, but it also took 619,000 lives and ruined millions of dollars' worth of property. My father must have known this would come to pass, for the day he was hanged, he wrote: "I, John Brown, am now quite certain that the crimes of this guilty land will never be purged away but with Blood."

Years after Father's death, I still had sleepless nights. Sometimes I recalled our conversations. Other times I found comfort in the verse of a song that Union soldiers sang about Father when they marched into battle.

His sacrifice we share! Our sword will victory crown!
For freedom and the right remember old John Brown!
His soul is marching on.

Yes indeed, I think to myself, one man against slavery did make a difference.

In 1850, Congress passed the Fugitive Slave Law. This law required federal officials to arrest people fleeing slavery and return them to their "owners." Here, Harriet Tubman comes to the aid of a runaway who has been captured and is in danger of being returned to slavery.

from Harriet Tubman: Conductor on the Underground Railroad

Ann Petry

On April 27, 1860, [Harriet Tubman] was in Troy, New York. She had spent the night there and was going on to Boston to attend an antislavery meeting. That morning she was on her way to the railroad station. She walked along the street slowly. She never bothered to find out when a train was due; she simply sat in the station and waited until a train came which was going in the direction she desired.

It was cold in Troy even though it was the spring of the year. A northeast wind kept blowing the ruffle on her bonnet away from her face. She thought of Maryland and how green the trees would be. Here they were only lightly touched with green, not yet in full leaf. Suddenly she longed for a sight of the Eastern Shore with its coves and creeks, thought of the years that had elapsed since she first ran away from there.

She stopped walking to watch a crowd of people in front of the courthouse, a pushing, shoving, shouting crowd. She wondered what had happened. A fight? An accident? She went nearer, listened to the loud excited voices. "He got away." "He didn't." "They've got him handcuffed." Then there was an eruptive movement, people pushing forward, other people pushing back.

Harriet started working her way through the crowd, elbowing a man, nudging a woman. Now and then she asked a question. She learned that a runaway slave named Charles Nalle had been arrested and was being taken inside the courthouse to be tried.

When she finally got close enough to see the runaway's face, a handsome frightened face, his guards had forced him up the courthouse steps. They were trying to get through the door but people blocked the way.

She knew a kind of fury against the system, against the men who would force this man back into slavery when they themselves were free. The Lord did not intend that people should be slaves, she thought. Then without even thinking, she went up the steps, forced her way through the crowd, until she stood next to Nalle.

B

C

B **Literary Focus**
GRADE-LEVEL STANDARD
❓ Comparing points of view.
This is a classic third-person narration by an omniscient narrator. An omniscient, or all-knowing, narrator can take us into a character's mind and heart. What details in this section tell us what Tubman is thinking and feeling? [In the second paragraph we are told that Tubman thought of Maryland and the green of the trees. She "longed" for a sight of the Eastern shore with its coves and creeks. She thought of the years that had elapsed since she had run away.] **How do you think the biographer knew that these were Tubman's thoughts?** [Possible response: she might have imagined the thoughts; she might have figured, based on her own experience, that people get homesick for the place where their family lives. She might also have had access to Tubman's own journals, or to the journals of people who knew Tubman and knew she occasionally got homesick for Maryland. A biographer wrote Tubman's story in 1869, when Tubman was still alive. (See p. 309.) Petry might have found these details there.]

C **Literary Focus**
GRADE-LEVEL STANDARD
❓ Comparing points of view.
How does the point of view of this biography differ from that of the excerpt about John Brown? [The narrator in this biography is not someone who relates her own experiences but someone who reports from outside the story.]

DIRECT TEACHING

Ⓐ Literary Focus
GRADE-LEVEL STANDARD
❓ Comparing points of view.
How might this event be different
if it were narrated by the boy?
[Possible response: The boy would use
the pronoun *I* and might describe how
excited, nervous, and puzzled he was
to have a strange woman suddenly
telling him to yell "fire."]

Ⓑ Literary Focus
GRADE-LEVEL STANDARD
❓ Comparing points of view.
The speaker's point of view has
an impact on the details that are
reported. Someone in the story
might not see the same things that
someone outside the story sees.
What details about Harriet Tubman
might be different in the policeman's narration of the events?
[Possible response: He would see her
as just an old woman who clumsily
knocked him down.]

Ⓐ There was a small boy standing near her, mouth open, eyes wide with curiosity. She grabbed him by the collar and whispered to him fiercely, "You go out in the street and holler 'Fire, fire' as loud as you can."

The crowd kept increasing and she gave a nod of satisfaction. That little boy must have got out there in the street and must still be hollering that there's a fire. She bent over, making her shoulders droop, bending her back in the posture of an old woman. She pulled her sunbonnet way down, so that it shadowed her face. Just in time, too.

Ⓑ One of the policemen said, "Old woman, you'll have to get out of here. You're liable to get knocked down when we take him through the door."

Harriet moved away from Nalle, mumbling to herself. She heard church bells ringing somewhere in the distance, and more and more people came running. The entire street was blocked. She edged back toward Nalle. Suddenly she shouted, "Don't let them take him! Don't let them take him!"

She attacked the nearest policeman so suddenly that she knocked him down. She wanted to laugh at the look of surprise on his face when he realized that the mumbling old woman who had stood so close to him had suddenly turned into a creature of vigor and violence. Grabbing Nalle by the arm, she pulled him along with her, forcing her way down the steps, ignoring the blows she received, not really feeling them, taking pleasure in the fact that in all these months of inactivity she had lost none of her strength.

When they reached the street, they were both knocked down. Harriet snatched off her bonnet and tied it on Nalle's head. When they stood up, it was impossible to pick him out of the crowd. People in the street cleared a path for them, helped hold back the police. As they turned off the main street, they met a man driving a horse and wagon. He reined in the horse. "What goes on here?" he asked.

Harriet, out of breath, hastily explained the situation. The man got out of the wagon. "Here," he said, "use my horse and wagon. I don't care if I ever get it back just so that man gets to safety."

Nalle was rapidly driven to Schenectady and from there he went on to the West—and safety.

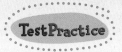

Answers and Model Rationales

1. The account called *John Brown: One Man Against Slavery* was written —
   A in the third person
   B in the first person
   C by Harriet Tubman
   D by John Brown himself

2. Which of the following statements would John Brown and Harriet Tubman be most likely to agree with?
   F One person fighting against slavery could make a difference.
   G The Fugitive Slave Law was fair and just.
   H Slavery could be ended without violence.
   J People should not involve family members in attempts to end slavery.

3. Which of the following sentences is an example of **first-person narration**?
   A "Harriet started working her way through the crowd. . . ."
   B "Years after Father's death, I still had sleepless nights."
   C "She knew a kind of fury against the system. . . ."
   D "People in the street cleared a path for them. . . ."

4. *Harriet Tubman: Conductor on the Underground Railroad* is —
   F a biography
   G an autobiography
   H an essay
   J a short story

5. Which of these titles seems most likely to be the title of an **autobiography**?
   A *The Civil War: 1861–1865*
   B *How I Gained My Freedom*
   C *Work Songs and Field Hollers*
   D *The Story of the Underground Railroad*

6. One difference between Ann Petry's account and Gwen Everett's account is that —
   F Gwen Everett writes in the first person
   G Ann Petry writes in the first person about someone she knew
   H Ann Petry has written an autobiography and Gwen Everett has written a biography
   J Gwen Everett did not know the person she wrote about

1. **B** The account is told by an "I," so it is written in the first person. Therefore A is wrong. It is not about Harriet Tubman and not told by her, so C is wrong. Nor is it by John Brown himself, since he is spoken of as "he," so D is wrong.

2. **F** Students can eliminate G immediately. Only F is true for both Brown and Tubman. There is evidence in the text that Brown believed violence to be inevitable and that he encouraged the involvement of his family; therefore choices H and J are incorrect.

3. **B** Students should recognize B as the only one that uses the first-person pronoun "I." The other answers are examples of third-person narration.

4. **F** Students should realize that this is the story of a person, told by another person, and thus a biography. It is not told by the person herself, G; it is not fiction, J; and it does not examine a subject, issue, or topic, H.

5. **B** A would suit a history text, and C and D sound like titles for nonfiction books. B, which uses the first-person pronoun "I," is the answer.

6. **F** F is the only correct answer. Ann Petry did not write in the first person, so G is wrong. Ann Petry did not write an autobiography, so H is wrong. Gwen Everett wrote about her father, someone she knew, so J is wrong.

Test-Taking Tips

When test items involve two passages, tell students to read the second passage looking for ways it differs from the first.

For more information on how to answer multiple-choice questions, refer students to **Test Smarts** on p. 690.

Standards Review **319**

Standards Review

Reading Informational Materials

 STANDARDS FOCUS, pp. 320–321

(For the grade-level and review standards reviewed in this lesson, see Pupil's Edition, p. 320.)

INTRODUCING THE STANDARDS REVIEW

Use this review to test students' ability to examine different but related sources and to clarify a main idea. Use these annotations only if you want to conduct this review orally.

DIRECT TEACHING

A **Reading Informational Materials**
GRADE-LEVEL STANDARD
❓ **Clarifying the main idea.**
Point out to students that the fourth sentence in this passage states the main idea. "Max is my... gentle giant with a soft meow." How does the author support this idea? [Possible response: She provides facts about Max's strength and gentleness that support and explain the statement that Max is a gentle giant.]

B **Reading Informational Materials**
GRADE-LEVEL STANDARD
❓ **Clarifying the main idea.**
What facts support the main idea that the writer's dog helps him feel more independent? [Possible response: Rita tells the writer when she hears important sounds, such as the ringing of an alarm clock or the telephone. She is his ears as well as his friend and hero.]

Reading Informational Materials

 TestPractice DIRECTIONS: Read the following passages. Then, read each question, and choose the best response.

Pet Heroes

We got Max from a group that traps wild kittens and tames them. When Max came to us, he was scrawny and little. Now he's a broad-shouldered, sun-yellow cat, the biggest cat in the 'hood. Max is my hero because he's a gentle giant with a soft meow. Yet he's kept some of his wild ways. He runs from everybody except me and my parents. He insists on his freedom to roam outside, especially on moonlit nights. He won't eat cat food unless he's really, really hungry. He prefers the mice and rats he catches on his own. Max knows we don't want him to catch birds, so he just watches them. He's kind to other cats—as long as they show him respect. He hates being pounced on. He loves curling up next to the sweet-smelling lavender plants in our yard, jumping from high places, cuddling at night, and getting stroked and scratched while giving me a cat massage with his big paws. I used to worry when he took off for a few days, but he always comes back. Max is my golden boy. He has a little voice but a big heart.

—Lynn

Rita is a small, shaggy, sandy-brown fluff ball. She's what some people call a mix—some poodle, some terrier, and a bit of something else. Rita is my hero because she's my hearing-ear dog. A woman from a place that trains dogs for deaf people found Rita in an animal shelter. Rita had been there for weeks, and nobody had claimed her. She went through five months of training. Then I got lucky. I was chosen to be the one who got to take her home.

I get along well by using American Sign Language, but having Rita tell me when she hears sounds like the ringing of an alarm clock or a telephone makes me feel even more independent. I love Rita. She is my special friend.

—Alex and Rita

Before I got Mopsy, I didn't know a bunny could be so much fun. Mopsy likes to play jokes on our cat. She creeps up behind him and nibbles his tail. She follows me around like a hopping shadow. Sometimes, to get attention, she jumps straight up in the air. Then, when she gets tired, she flops

 Reading Standard 2.3 Connect and clarify main ideas by identifying their relationships to other sources and related topics.

DIFFERENTIATING INSTRUCTION

Advanced Learners
Activity. Challenge advanced learners to create their own Standards Review test on connecting and clarifying main ideas. Invite them to find or write three short but related passages and then compose test items based on these passages. These test items should involve the implied main ideas that appear in all three passages. You might volunteer to take students' tests and see how well you perform on them.

down and takes a power nap. Mopsy loves to play, and she's never mean. My mom says that Mopsy must have learned her playful ways from her mother, who was a classroom rabbit.

Once a week we take Mopsy to visit my great-grandfather at his nursing home. He and his friends love to see her. Mopsy gets to sit on their laps and on their beds. She is quiet and never bites. That's why she's my hero.

—Michael

1. Which **title** fits all three paragraphs?
   A "Giving Humans a Helping Hand"
   B "My Pet Is My Hero"
   C "Courageous Critters"
   D "Keeping Animals Safe"

2. Which of the following **main ideas** is found in all three paragraphs?
   F To be considered a hero, an animal must show great courage.
   G Animals make better use of their time than humans do.
   H People can learn a great deal from their animal friends.
   J People should spend more time with their pets.

3. All of the following titles describe articles that probably deal with topics related to these readings *except* —
   A "Tips on Caring for Your Dog"
   B "Can Pets Make People Happy?"
   C "My Iguana Is a Good Friend"
   D "When Rover Made My Day"

4. What word *best* describes the **tone** of all three paragraphs?
   F sarcastic
   G critical
   H sincere
   J mocking

5. Which of the following statements about pets is *not* a **fact**?
   A Cats make better pets than dogs.
   B Dogs can be trained to help deaf people.
   C Some cats like to hunt for their own food.
   D Mopsy visits a nursing home every week.

Test-Taking Tips

Point out that the main idea of a passage is sometimes stated directly by the writer. Encourage students to look for a statement of the main idea in each passage before answering the Test Practice items that ask them to relate these ideas.

For more information on how to answer multiple-choice questions, refer students to **Test Smarts**, p. 690.

DIRECT TEACHING

C Reading Informational Materials
GRADE-LEVEL STANDARD
? Clarifying the main idea. Ask students to respond to the humorous but affectionate tone of this passage. What implied main idea does this tone suggest? [Possible response: Mopsy—just by being the playful bunny she is—can make people happy.]

TestPractice

Answers and Model Rationales

1. **B** The pets in the three passages are not especially courageous or brave (C); there are no facts about keeping them safe (D); and Max did not help Lynn in any purposeful or intentional way (A). Therefore, B is correct.

2. **H** F is not supported in the essays. G and J may be implied by all three essays, but only H reflects the main idea of all three passages.

3. **A** All answers except A are reasonable titles for related readings; pet care is the only topic that is not covered in any of the passages.

4. **H** Students should recognize that F, G, and J are too negative. H, *sincere,* is the only answer that describes the writers' affection for their pets.

5. **A** The word *better* provides a clue that A expresses a value judgment or opinion about cats and dogs as pets. B, C, and D are all verifiable statements from the passages.

Vocabulary Development

Multiple-Meaning Words

Modeling. Use the rationale for answer 1, below, to model the thought process of a good reader.

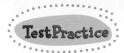

Answers and Model Rationales

1. **C** In the model sentence and C, the word *set* means "ready." In A *set* means "to arrange"; in B it means "theater scenery"; and in D it means "to program an alarm clock."

2. **G** In the model sentence and G, the word *call* means a "plea" or an "appeal for action." In F and H, *call* means "to contact someone"; and in J *call* is a state of readiness.

3. **C** In the model sentence and C, the word *deep* suggests strength or intensity of feeling. In A, B, and D *deep* indicates a physical amount.

4. **J** In the model sentence and J, *fill* means "to suffuse or permeate." In F *fill* is a noun indicating a state of satisfaction; in H *fill* means "to complete by supplying information"; and in G it means "to assume the responsibilities of a position."

5. **B** In the model sentence and B, *return* means "to go back." In A, a tax return is an official document; in C *return* means "to exchange"; and in D, it means "opposite direction."

Vocabulary Development

Test Practice

Multiple-Meaning Words

DIRECTIONS: Read each of the following sentences. Then, choose the answer in which the underlined word is used in the same way.

1. After much preparation, the men were set for their journey.

   In which sentence does the word *set* have the same meaning as in the sentence above?

   A Mom set the plates on the table.

   B The stage crew had to construct a set for the play.

   C The coach said her team was set to play.

   D I set the alarm for 6:00 A.M.

2. Thomas Garrett made a call for the end of slavery.

   In which sentence does the word *call* have the same meaning as in the sentence above?

   F Call me on the cell phone.

   G The task force considered making a call for volunteers.

   H Harry was ready to call the family for dinner.

   J The doctor was on call during the night.

3. It's obvious that Thomas Garrett felt deep sympathy for enslaved people.

   In which sentence does the word *deep* have the same meaning as in the sentence above?

   A The swimming pool is eight feet deep.

   B Mr. Jones took a deep breath.

   C Mrs. Lopez feels deep affection for her husband.

   D Harriet hid deep in the woods.

4. Harriet Tubman's heroism would fill her friends with admiration.

   In which sentence does the word *fill* have the same meaning as in the sentence above?

   F I had my fill of turkey.

   G I think she can fill the position of class president.

   H Could you fill out this form?

   J A sunny day can fill me with joy.

5. Harriet Tubman would return to the South to free more people.

   In which sentence does the word *return* have the same meaning as in the sentence above?

   A Send in your tax return by April 15.

   B Ms. Jones will be happy when she can return to work after her illness.

   C Bill will return the favor someday.

   D The return trip seemed much longer.

Vocabulary Review

Use the following activity to find out whether your students have retained the Vocabulary taught in this chapter.
Activity. Have students select the correct word from the box to complete the following sentences.

lauded	placate	precarious
aghast	prudent	

1. The hero sat quietly as he was _____ for his bravery. [lauded]

2. The audience was _____ when the set collapsed onto the stage. [aghast]

3. Fugitive slaves were in a _____ or dangerous position. [precarious]

4. A more _____ person would have packed food and water before setting off into the desert. [prudent]

5. In order to _____ the irate customer, the shopkeeper apologized profusely. [placate]

Writing Applications

Mastering the Standards

RESEARCH REPORT

What Matters

Harriet Tubman's escape from slavery was probably the most important event in her life. Suppose you were writing a report about a historical figure you admire. Use history books, encyclopedia articles, biographies, and online sources to research the person's life. What do you think was the most important event or experience in that person's life? (Try to imagine how your subject would answer that question.) Start by giving some background on the person. Then, describe the key event in the person's life, and explain why it was so important to your subject.

► Use "Writing a Research Report," pages 578–603, for help with this assignment.

Other Choices

PERSUASIVE WRITING

1 Taking a Stand

In this chapter you read about the special relationship between humans and animals. This special bond has inspired many people to fight for humane treatment and protection of animals. Think of an issue you care deeply about, perhaps one involving animals. For example, you may feel that stronger laws should be passed to protect whales. You may believe that city parks should have more space set aside in which dogs can run free. Write a letter expressing your point of view on an issue you care about. Address it to a local, state, or U.S. government official—whichever is appropriate for the issue. Include facts, statistics, examples, and quotations from experts to support your position.

► Use "Writing a Persuasive Essay," pages 618–635, for help with this assignment.

HOW-TO PAPER

2 Calling All Paws

Make a "pawbook" (handbook) on the care and raising of dogs, cats, ferrets, fish, or other animals. Begin by deciding what to include in your pawbook. Here are some ideas for a book on dogs:

- picking a pooch—information on choosing the right dog
- basic training—training techniques and tips on getting through the training period
- dogspeak—information on the ways dogs communicate—body language, barking, growling

You might want to illustrate your pawbook.

► Use "Writing a 'How-to' Explanation," pages 528–544, for help with this assignment.

Mastering the Standards

Evaluation Criteria

A good research report

1. poses relevant questions
2. narrows the topic appropriately
3. supports the main idea with facts, details, examples, and explanations from multiple authoritative sources
4. includes a bibliography

ASSESSING

Assessment

■ *Progress Assessment of Reading*
   ■ Chapter Test, p. 105

Using Academic Language

Literary Terms
As part of the review of Literary Response and Analysis Standard 3.5, ask students to look back through the chapter to find the meanings of the terms listed at right. Then, have students demonstrate their understanding of Standard 3.5 by citing passages from a story in the chapter that illustrate

the meanings of the following terms. **First-Person Point of View** (pp. 244, 262); **Narrator** (p. 244); **Autobiography** (p. 262); **Biography** (p. 286); **Third-Person Point of View** (p. 286).

Informational Terms
As part of the review of Reading

Comprehension Standard 2.3, ask students to look back through the chapter to find the meanings of the terms listed below and, using those terms, to explain Standard 2.3. **Main Idea** (pp. 254, 269, 300); **Title** (p. 269).

Read On

If students enjoyed the themes and topics explored in this chapter, you might recommend these titles for independent reading.

Assessment Options

The following projects can help you evaluate and assess your students' outside reading. Videotapes or audiotapes of completed projects may be included in students' portfolios.

- **Conduct an interview.** Have pairs of students act as Lionel Magee and a magazine reporter. Ask the pairs to brainstorm questions the reporter can ask the character from *Maniac Magee,* such as "How does it feel to be homeless?" "What was going through your mind when you met . . . ?" Videotape the pairs as they perform their interviews.

- **Write a letter.** Invite students to compose a letter that Harriet Jacobs might have written to either Harriet Tubman or Dr. James Norcom, her owner's father. If they choose Harriet Tubman, tell them to incorporate facts from "A Glory over Everything" in their fictionalized letter.

- **Write a scene.** Have students work in pairs to write a scene, including dialogue, in which the characters from *The Watsons Go to Birmingham—1963* discuss their experiences on the trip.

California Reading List Titles

Maniac Magee
The Watsons Go to Birmingham— 1963
Shipwreck at the Bottom of the World

Fiction

Not Your Average Family

The adventures of the family in William Sleator's *Oddballs* are simply hilarious. Wild ideas flow nonstop out of such kooky characters as Jack, the budding hypnotist; Vicky, who likes to dye herself purple; and Bill, mastermind of the odd "pituh-plays." Mischievous and witty, the characters in this collection of stories set a style of their own as they cope with growing up.

A Modern-Day Myth

In Jerry Spinelli's Newbery Award– winning novel *Maniac Magee,* twelve-year-old Lionel Magee captures the imagination of the residents of Two Mills, Pennsylvania. His athletic feats surprise and impress his classmates—you won't believe how many touchdowns he scores! His most amazing accomplishment is something that anyone with a kind heart is capable of.

A Life Imagined

Harriet Jacobs's life story is truly inspirational. Jacobs escaped from slavery and an abusive owner by hiding in her grandmother's attic for seven years and then making her way north to freedom. Mary E. Lyons's *Letters from a Slave Girl* is a fictionalized account of Jacobs's ordeal told in the form of letters.

Traveling On

In Christopher Paul Curtis's novel *The Watsons Go to Birmingham—1963,* ten- year-old Kenny's brother Byron keeps getting into trouble. Kenny's parents decide to head south from their home in Flint, Michigan, to visit Grandma Sands in Alabama, hoping she'll bring Byron into line. The trip takes a terrifying turn when racial tensions explode.

This title is available in the HRW Library.

Toward Reading a Million Words Annually

Estimated Word Counts of Read On Books:

Fiction		Nonfiction	
Oddballs	31,000	Harriet Tubman: The Moses	
Maniac Magee	38,000	of Her People	33,000
Letters from a Slave Girl	26,000	Orphan Train Rider	32,000
The Watsons Go to Birmingham—1963	50,000	Shipwreck at the Bottom of the World	38,000
Connections to *The Watsons Go to Birmingham—1963*	6,600	Zlata's Diary	39,000

Nonfiction

She Gave All She Had

Sarah Bradford's biography *Harriet Tubman: The Moses of Her People* is a firsthand account of the woman who did so much to free African Americans from slavery. Bradford tells of Tubman's many sacrifices and heroic acts during the Civil War period.

A Long Ride

For many reasons, hundreds of American children were sent west by train to new homes and families during the late nineteenth and early twentieth century. Lee Nailling was one such child. Andrea Warren recounts Nailling's early experiences and eventual happiness in *Orphan Train Rider*. Warren also presents an overview of the history of these trains and describes the problems the children faced with their new families.

Endurance

Jennifer Armstrong's *Shipwreck at the Bottom of the World* tells the story of Ernest Shackleton, who tried to cross Antarctica with his crew of twenty-seven explorers. On the journey his ship broke up in icebound waters. Shackleton and five of his men lived for several months on ice floes and eventually had to navigate a tiny boat through the perilous South Atlantic Ocean to search for help. (We won't tell you how the story ends!)

Surrounded by Horror

Zlata Filipović began keeping a diary in September 1991. Soon after, war broke out in her home country, Bosnia and Herzegovina. In *Zlata's Diary* she describes her family's struggle to survive amid the violence and tells how the war came between her and many of her friends. In the end, Zlata remains hopeful that her life will change for the better.

Read On   **325**

- **Design a time line.** Have students work together to create a time line for the major events in Harriet Tubman's life. Students can make additional entries about important historical events that occurred during the time period.
- **Mount a photo display.** Most children sent west on orphan trains were destitute youngsters from the slums of New York City. Ask students to mount a photo display comparing and contrasting tenement life and rural life using photocopies of pictures in *Orphan Train Rider* and photocopies of photographs of slum children taken by Lewis Hines, Jacob Riis, and others of the period.
- **Illustrate a diary.** Zlata illustrated her diary with hand-drawn sketches and doodles such as peace signs. She also used pictures cut out from magazines. Ask students to choose an entry from Zlata's diary and illustrate it in her style. Encourage them to relate their illustrations to the content of the entry.

 Resources Reminder

Reading

- *Interactive Reading*

For additional readings that relate to the selections in this chapter, see Interactive Reading, Chapter 5.

- *The Ancient World:* A Content-Area Reader

Chapter 6 Looking at Texts: Uses of the Imagination

Program Organization

Holt Literature and Language Arts provides a complete curriculum for standards-based instruction in vocabulary, reading, literature, writing, and speaking and listening. The instructional content of the program is divided into quarters to enable teachers to anticipate and administer the quarterly assessments required by California.

About Chapter 6

Standards-based lesson plans and suggestions for pacing the presentation of Chapter 6 and the related instructional material are provided in *On Course: Mapping Instruction,* Chapter 6.

- Chapter 6 helps students explain the effects of common literary devices in fiction and nonfiction, make assertions about text based on accurate supporting evidence, and explain "shades of meaning" in related words.

- The related instructional material for Chapter 6 is shown on the chart. This related instructional material will also be covered in the third quarterly assessment.

Holt Literature and Language Arts

Pupil's Edition

Part 1, Chapter 6

Looking at Texts:
Uses of the Imagination, pp. 326–375
- Reading Standards 1.2, 2.8, 3.4
- Writing Application **Writing a Descriptive Essay**

Part 2, Mini-Workshop 2

Writing a Descriptive Essay, pp. 665–670
- Writing Standard 2.2

Holt Handbook

Chapter 11

Capital Letters
Written and Oral English-Language Conventions
- Grade-Level Standard 1.4, pp. 239–257

Chapter 12

Punctuation: End Marks,
Commas, Semicolons, Colons
Written and Oral English-Language Conventions
- Grade-Level Standard 1.3, pp. 268–282

Diagnostic and Summative Assessments: Third-Quarter Test

Which vocabulary, informational reading, and literature standards are taught in Chapter 6?

In this chapter, students will master the following Grade 6 standards. They will also review standards from Grade 5. Selections or features marked with a ✔ constitute the minimum course of study that provides coverage of all grade-level standards.

Grade 6 Standards
Word Analysis, Fluency, and Systematic Vocabulary Development
1.5 Understand and explain "shades of meaning" in related words (e.g., *softly* and *quietly*).
Finding Synonyms, p. 337
✔ Connotations and Denotations: Shades of Meaning, p. 362
✔ Connotations: Words Are Loaded with Feelings, p. 369

Reading Comprehension (Focus on Informational Materials)
2.7 Make reasonable assertions about a text through accurate, supporting citations.
"Lincoln's Humor" (essay), pp. 338–340
✔ "Getting Leftovers Back on the Table" (essay), pp. 359–361
✔ Standards Review: Reading Informational Materials, pp. 370–371

Literary Response and Analysis
3.7 Explain the effects of common literary devices (e.g., symbolism, imagery, metaphor) in a variety of fictional and nonfictional texts.
✔ "Literary Devices: Using Your Imagination" (standards essay), pp. 328–329
"The Mysterious Mr. Lincoln" (biography), pp. 330–336
✔ "What Do Fish Have to Do with Anything?" (short story), pp. 347–357
"Eleven" (short story), pp. 363–368

Review Standards Grade 5
Vocabulary
1.3 Understand and explain frequently used synonyms, antonyms, and homographs.
Antonyms, p. 341
Identifying Antonyms, p. 358

Reading
2.1 Understand how text features (e.g., format, graphics, sequence, diagrams, illustrations, charts, maps) make information accessible and usable.
"A Civil War Thanksgiving" (article), pp. 343–346

Where do I locate lesson plans, additional resources, and other teaching aids?

- This Annotated Teacher's Edition and *On Course: Mapping Instruction* provide direction in planning and implementing a complete California standards–based curriculum. These components include instructions for administering diagnostic, progress, and summative tests; for presenting instruction of the standards; for differentiating instruction to provide universal access; and for locating and using the program's ancillaries.

- The program's resources are referenced at the beginning of each selection, in the bottom margin of this teacher's edition.

- Reminders for using additional resources appear in this teacher's edition at point of use.

- The *One-Stop Planner* CD-ROM with Test Generator contains editable lesson plans and all of the print ancillaries, available in PDF format.

What if I don't have time to teach all of Chapter 6?

- Most standards can be taught with a minimum number of selections and features. In the chart on page 325B, the core lessons you need in order to provide complete coverage of the chapter standards are identified with a ✔.

- Use the Standards Review, pp. 370–371, for a quick review and informal assessment of the grade-level standards covered in Chapter 6.

What provisions have been made for students who have additional class time scheduled in language arts?

- *Interactive Reading* provides for additional direct instruction and practice of the grade-level standards taught in Chapter 6. It can be used as an introduction to instruction or as an opportunity for remediation.

- *Lesson Plans for Language Development*, Chapter 6, provides alternative teaching strategies and additional worksheets designed specifically for English-language learners and special education students. Many of the suggestions and activities in this ancillary will also be helpful to students in the regular classroom who are having difficulty with particular skills.

In addition to vocabulary, reading, and literature, what other language arts are covered in Chapter 6?

Writing Activities in Chapter 6
- It Depends on Your Point of View (rewrite a story using a different first-person narrator), p. 368

Writing Applications (p. 373)
- Make It Alive (descriptive essay)

- Another Choice: Thinking About Theme (response to literature)

Grammar Links in Chapter 6
- Direct and Indirect Quotations, p. 358
- Punctuating Dialogue, p. 369

Universal Access

How do I differentiate instruction to ensure that all my students master the standards?

Holt Literature and Language Arts provides comprehensive, differentiated instruction for all types of students.

- Most of the general instruction and teaching strategies in the Annotated Teacher's Edition are at grade level. These instructions will work well with the majority of your students.

- In Chapter 6, suggestions for advanced learners are provided in the Annotated Teacher's Edition. Point-of-use suggestions for learners having difficulty, English-language learners, and special education students are also provided.

- *Interactive Reading* is designed to anticipate and/or remediate problems that students may experience in achieving mastery of the standards. *Interactive Reading* includes reading-strategy lessons, lower-level practice reads, and worksheets for every informational and literary text in *Holt Literature and Language Arts,* Pupil's Editions. *Interactive Reading* also contains three additional selections for each chapter and suggestions for extension projects, many of which are ideal for advanced learners working on their own. See *Interactive Reading,* Teacher's Edition, for specific information on using the reader to differentiate instruction in Chapter 6.

- *Lesson Plans for Language Development,* Chapter 6, offers teaching strategies and additional worksheets designed specifically for English-language learners and special education students.

Assessment

How do I determine whether or not my students are making progress in mastering the standards?

Progress Assessment

- Use the Standards Review at the end of Chapter 6, pp. 370–371, for an informal assessment of the informational reading and literature standards in Chapter 6.

- Use the Selection Tests for Chapter 6 in the *Progress Assessment of Reading* booklet to test comprehension and progress on mastering the standard(s) taught with a selection.

- Use Chapter Test 6 from the *Progress Assessment of Reading* booklet to test students' cumulative progress in mastering the standards taught in the chapter.

Summative Assessment

At the end of this chapter, you may ask students to take the Third-Quarter Test in the *Diagnostic and Summative Assessment* booklet. This test covers *Holt Literature and Language Arts,* Chapters 5 and 6, Workshop 4, and Mini-Workshop 8, "Creating Graphics," as well as the *Holt Handbook,* Chapters 9–12.

STANDARDS FOCUS

(For grade-level and review standards taught in this chapter, see Pupil's Edition, p. 327.)

Prerequisite Standards

- Grade 4, Literary Response and Analysis 3.5 **Define figurative language (e.g., simile, metaphor, hyperbole, personification), and identify its use in literary works.**
- Grade 5, Reading Comprehension 2.4 **Draw inferences, conclusions, or generalizations about text, and support them with textual evidence and prior knowledge.**
- Grade 5, Reading Comprehension 2.5 **Distinguish facts, supported inferences, and opinions in text.**
- Grade 5, Literary Response and Analysis 3.5 **Describe the function and effect of common literary devices (e.g., imagery, metaphor, symbolism).**

Standards Coming Up in the Next Grade Levels

- Grade 7, Vocabulary 1.3 **Clarify word meanings through the use of definition, example, restatement, or contrast.**
- Grade 7, Reading Comprehension 2.6 **Assess the adequacy, accuracy, and appropriateness of the author's evidence to support claims or assertions, noting instances of bias or stereotyping.**
- Grade 7, Literary Response and Analysis 3.6 **Analyze a range of responses to a literary work, and determine the extent to which the literary elements in the work shaped those responses.**
- Grade 8, Literary Response and Analysis 3.6 **Identify significant literary devices (e.g., metaphor, symbolism, dialect, irony) that define a writer's style, and use those elements to interpret the work.**

6 | Looking at Texts
Uses of the Imagination

CHAPTER RESOURCES

Planning
- *One-Stop Planner* CD-ROM with Test Generator
- *On Course: Mapping Instruction*
  - Chapter 6
- *At Home: A Guide to Standards Mastery*
- *At Home: In Five Languages*
- *Supporting Instruction in Five Languages*

Reading
- *Interactive Reading*
  - Chapter 6

Differentiating Instruction
- *Lesson Plans for Language Development*
  - Chapter 6

Vocabulary and Spelling
- *Vocabulary Development*
  - Cumulative Vocabulary Review, p. 28

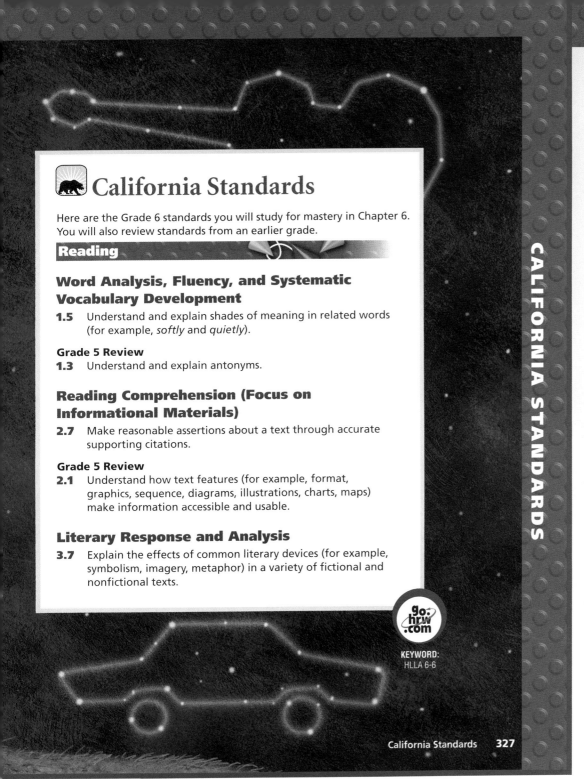

California Standards

Here are the Grade 6 standards you will study for mastery in Chapter 6. You will also review standards from an earlier grade.

Reading

Word Analysis, Fluency, and Systematic Vocabulary Development

1.5 Understand and explain shades of meaning in related words (for example, *softly* and *quietly*).

Grade 5 Review

1.3 Understand and explain antonyms.

Reading Comprehension (Focus on Informational Materials)

2.7 Make reasonable assertions about a text through accurate supporting citations.

Grade 5 Review

2.1 Understand how text features (for example, format, graphics, sequence, diagrams, illustrations, charts, maps) make information accessible and usable.

Literary Response and Analysis

3.7 Explain the effects of common literary devices (for example, symbolism, imagery, metaphor) in a variety of fictional and nonfictional texts.

go.hrw.com

KEYWORD:
HLLA 6-6

California Standards **327**

INTRODUCING THE CHAPTER

The stories coming up in this chapter demonstrate how literary devices are used by writers to get readers to sit up and take notice. These tools—imagery, similes and metaphors, personification, and symbols—are discussed as they appear in selections that range from a biography of President Abraham Lincoln to a short story about just one day in the life of an eleven-year-old girl. Students will come away from the chapter with an understanding of the tools available for making good writing even better.

Informational essays follow specific works and are intended not only to help students recognize adequately supported assertions made in a text but also to encourage students to make their own well-supported claims about that text. At the end of the chapter students will use these writing tools to create a description.

Resources Reminder

Planning

■ *At Home: A Guide to Standards Mastery*

You may want to send home with students selected parent letters from this resource. Translations of these letters are available in *At Home: In Five Languages*. *Supporting Instruction in Five Languages* provides translations of the selection summaries.

Reading

■ *Interactive Reading*
  ▪ Reading Log

The California framework requires students to read materials apart from in-class assignments. Additional reading suggestions are included on the Read On pages and on selected pages in the Pupil's and Teacher's Editions. You may want to use the Reading Log to help students track their progress.

Grammar

■ *Holt Handbook*
  ▪ Direct and Indirect Quotations, pp. 292–299
  ▪ Punctuating Dialogue, pp. 292–299

Assessment

■ *Progress Assessment of Reading*
  ▪ Chapter Test, p. 126

■ *Diagnostic and Summative Assessments*
  ▪ Third-Quarter Test, p. 79

■ *One-Stop Planner* CD-ROM with Test Generator

Internet

■ go.hrw.com
  Keyword: HLLA 6-6

STANDARDS FOCUS, pp. 328–329

(For the grade-level standard taught in this lesson, see Pupil's Edition, p. 328.)

Prerequisite Standards

- Grade 4, Literary Response and Analysis 3.5 **Define figurative language (e.g., simile, metaphor, hyperbole, personification), and identify its use in literary works.**
- Grade 5, Literary Response and Analysis 3.5 **Describe the function and effect of common literary devices (e.g., imagery, metaphor, symbolism).**

Literary Focus: Literary Devices

Encourage students to think of good writers as having a talent for seeing things in a special way. Good writers might describe something in a way that appeals to one of the senses, or they might compare one thing to another thing in a way that makes the first object seem clear or real.

Review the literary devices in the essay using the examples to point out how each of them works to stimulate readers' imaginations.

◤ Resources Reminder

Reading

- *Interactive Reading*

Before you teach Chapter 6 of *Holt Literature and Language Arts,* you may want to preteach the literary concept and a related reading strategy.

- To introduce students to the literary concept before they read this essay, assign p. 223 of *Interactive Reading.*
- To introduce students to a reading strategy that will help them grasp the literary concept, assign p. 223 of *Interactive Reading.*
- To give students practice applying the strategy to a short, vocabulary-controlled selection, assign the Practice Read on p. 224 of *Interactive Reading.*

Literary Devices *by* John Leggett

USING YOUR IMAGINATION

Fiction is a way we communicate our feelings. In fact, some people say that fiction works only when it does just that. If your feelings are asleep when you read a story, the story is probably a failure. Here are some of the ways writers use words to awaken our feelings as well as our imaginations.

Making Us Feel

Let's say that Charlie is on his way to an important job interview when he finds that he's coming down with a cold. (Maybe that sounds pretty unimportant to you, but it makes a conflict, and it increases our interest in Charlie. Most of us know what it feels like to have a cold coming on.)

Rather than just saying Charlie is coming down with a cold, a good writer will make us *feel* the way Charlie feels, which isn't very good:

> Charlie saw how the rain was spattering the high shine on his shoes and turned up his coat collar against the cold. Then he felt a little prickling at the back of his throat, the place where he believed two holes led upward into his nose. A tingling within these channels announced a sneeze. Out it came. *Kachooo!* Charlie's ears now felt too warm, his spine felt chilly, and ice water seemed to be seeping through his toes. He recognized these as sure signs of a cold.

> The worst of it, though, was the misery. It didn't matter anymore if he found a nice girlfriend, or lived to a splendid old age, or ever had a better job. Nothing mattered at all—except whether the stupid bus would ever come and deliver him from this miserable street corner.

If you shared Charlie's misery—if you thought, "I know exactly how he feels"—then the writer was successful. Here are three of the many ways writers use words to affect our feelings and appeal to our imagination.

Imagery: Words That Create Pictures

Imagery is language that creates pictures. Imagery can also reach our other senses. It can help us not only to see something but also to smell or taste it, hear it, and feel its textures and temperatures.

> The first stroke of the young violinist's bow produced a piercing whine, so unintended that the artist's eyes rolled in sympathy with his audience.

This image helps you picture a concert scene, hear a piercing sound, and then see the artist roll his eyes. (The image might make you laugh as well.)

Reading Standard 3.7 Explain the effects of common literary devices (for example, symbolism, imagery, metaphor) in a variety of fictional and nonfictional texts.

DIFFERENTIATING INSTRUCTION

Learners Having Difficulty

To help students respond to item 1 in the Practice, ask a talented art student to draw on the chalkboard an object in the room that they like and then an object that they want to escape. Then, use these drawings to help students write an evocative description of each object.

English-Language Learners

Students who are just learning English might have difficulty understanding that imagery refers to pictures and sounds, and sometimes also to smells, tastes, and sensations. To help them grasp this concept, have students describe an object to a partner as precisely as possible without actually naming it. Encourage them to use phrases such as

Simile and Metaphor: Making Comparisons

In a **simile** a writer describes something by comparing it to something else—something very different. A simile makes its comparison with words such as *like, as, than,* and *resembles.*

By the time we took the meatloaf out of the oven, it resembled a chunk of coal.

The sea was as smooth as glass.

In a **metaphor** a writer compares two different things directly, without using words such as *like, as, than,* or *resembles.*

The sea was a sheet of glass.

By the time we took it out of the oven, the meatloaf was a chunk of coal.

Personification: Making the World Human

In **personification** something non-human is spoken of as if it were human. Personification can also occur when something that is not living is spoken of as if it were alive.

The sea sang a song of peace.

The meatloaf looked at me sadly.

Symbolism: Ripples of Meaning

Some symbols are public; we all agree on what they stand for. A blindfolded woman holding a scale symbolizes justice. A red rose symbolizes love. In literature a **symbol** is a person, place, or thing that stands for itself and for something beyond itself as well.

In the Genesis account in the Bible, the apple that Eve hands to Adam is an apple, but it also symbolizes many things to many people. That apple could stand for temptation, knowledge, even sin.

Practice

1. **Images.** Choose an object in the room, and describe it in a way that makes it seem appealing. Now, describe the same object in a way that makes us want to get out of the room. Use words that help us see the object—perhaps smell it, hear it, taste it, feel it.

2. **Figurative language.** The general term for similes, metaphors, personification, and symbols is ***figurative language.*** (The word *figurative* suggests that these uses of language are not meant to be taken literally. That meatloaf did not literally stare at you. It has no eyes.) Use these starters to create your own figures of speech:

   Love is . . .   The world is . . .
   Happiness is . . .   Ice is . . .
   Security is . . .   Fire is . . .

3. **Symbol.** Draw an animal that could symbolize a human quality (courage, greed, laziness). Underneath your picture, identify the quality your creature represents.

Practice

1. Possible images: *Appealing*—the chalkboard is smooth, it smells like the first day of school, it's clean and shiny and ready for use, it looks like an empty canvas waiting to be filled, and it is fresh and expectant. *Unappealing*—the chalkboard is cold and institutional, it smells of old chalk and sends out a gray cloud of chalk dust that gags us, it has a medicinal smell, it never looks clean, and it blocks off the light from the window.

2. Possible comparisons:

   Love is like a kitten; love is a river.

   Happiness is like a balloon; happiness is a chocolate cake.

   Security is as warm as flannel pajamas; security is a fairy godmother.

   The world is as colorful as a garden; the world is a round, swirling marble.

   Ice is like a cold look; ice is a piece of glass.

   Fire is like a sword; fire is a sunflower.

3. Illustrations will vary. You should be able to tell what human quality is being represented without seeing the caption.

Apply

Have students choose a pet or favorite animal and brainstorm several figures of speech describing it. Students can share their work with the rest of the class, who might suggest words or phrases to add to the descriptions.

"looks like a _____," "smells as if it were _____," and "_____ to the touch."

Advanced Learners

Have students choose a paragraph from a story or essay in this textbook or from their independent reading and identify the literary devices used in it. Students should then meet in a group to read the paragraphs aloud and discuss these questions: How do these tools help me with the meaning of the paragraph? What effect do they have on the mood, the tone, the message?

▶ Resources Reminder

Differentiating Instruction

■ *Lesson Plans for Language Development*

For additional instruction on literary devices for English-language learners and special education students, see *Lesson Plans for Language Development*, pp. 147–148.

STANDARDS FOCUS, pp. 330–337

(For grade-level and review standards taught in this selection, see citations on Pupil's Edition pages.)

Prerequisite Standard

■ Grade 5, Literary Response and Analysis 3.5 **Describe the function and effect of common literary devices (e.g., imagery, metaphor, symbolism).**

Standard Coming Up in the Next Grade Levels

■ Grade 8, Literary Response and Analysis 3.6 **Identify significant literary devices (e.g., metaphor, symbolism, dialect, irony) that define a writer's style, and use those elements to interpret the work.**

Reading Skills

■ Use prior knowledge.

Summary *above grade level*

This chapter of Russell Freedman's Newbery Medal–winning photobiography presents details, metaphors, and anecdotes that personalize the familiar figure of Abraham Lincoln. Lincoln's gawky height, folksy humor, homespun speech, and superstitious beliefs are contrasted with his ambition, sadness, skill in argument, and eloquence as a speaker and a writer.

▶ Resources Reminder

Media

■ *Audio CD Library*
  ■ disc 8
■ *Visual Connections*
  ■ Videocassette, Segment 9

Reading

■ *Interactive Reading*
  ■ Strategy Launch: What and Why?, p. 223
  ■ Practice Read: "Who Was Cleopatra?," p. 224
  ■ Graphic Organizer: Metaphor Matching Map, p. 229

The Mysterious Mr. Lincoln

Literary Focus
Metaphor

When you say, "My cell phone is my lifeline," you're using a metaphor. A **metaphor** is an imaginative comparison between two things that seem to have little in common. A metaphor says that something *is* something else: not "His hand is *like* a wet fish" but "His hand *is* a wet fish."

Metaphors are often used in poetry. You could even call metaphor *the soul of poetry* (that's a metaphor). Writers use metaphors to stir our imagination, to help us see ordinary things in new and fresh ways. A metaphor can sometimes make a point as well as hundreds of words can.

Reading Standard 3.7 Explain the effects of metaphor in nonfictional texts.

Reading Skills
Using Prior Knowledge

Preview "The Mysterious Mr. Lincoln" by surveying the text and the photographs and captions. This process will help you recall what you already know about Lincoln and will suggest questions to you. Afterward, record facts you know and questions about the man who, in 1861, became our sixteenth president. Use the K and W columns of the KWL chart below.

K What I Know	W What I Want to Know	L What I Learned
Lincoln was president during the Civil War.	Why is Lincoln "mysterious"?	

Make the Connection
Quickwrite ✏️

What does it take to be a good leader? List the qualities, and describe the background, experience, and education you think a president should have.

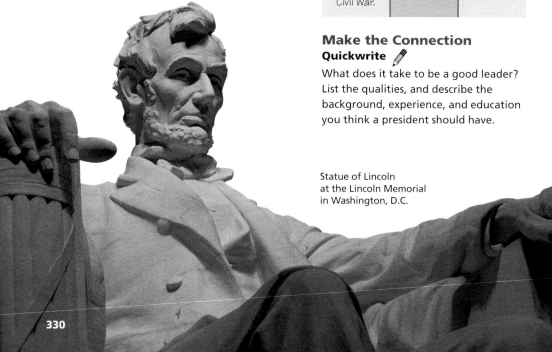

Statue of Lincoln at the Lincoln Memorial in Washington, D.C.

330

RESOURCES

Planning
■ *One-Stop Planner* CD-ROM with Test Generator
■ *On Course: Mapping Instruction*

Media
■ *Audio CD Library*
  ■ disc 8
■ *Visual Connections*
  ■ Videocassette, Segment 9

Reading
■ *Interactive Reading*
  ■ Strategy Launch: What and Why?, p. 223
  ■ Practice Read: "Who Was Cleopatra?," p. 224
  ■ Graphic Organizer: Metaphor Matching Map, p. 229

Vocabulary Development

As you read about Lincoln, you'll be learning these words:

gawky (gô′kē) *adj.*: clumsy; awkward. *As a youth, Lincoln was tall and gawky.*

repose (ri·pōz′) *n.*: state of rest or inactivity. *He sometimes looked sad in repose.*

listless (list′lis) *adj.*: lifeless; lacking in interest or energy. *When he was silent, he seemed gloomy and listless.*

animation (an′i·mā′shən) *n.*: liveliness. *Although he was often quiet, Lincoln spoke with animation.*

defy (dē·fī′) *v.*: resist; oppose. *Lincoln's appearance seemed to defy description.*

reticent (ret′ə·sənt) *adj.*: reserved; tending to speak little. *Lincoln's law partner described him as secretive and reticent.*

melancholy (mel′ən·käl′ē) *adj.*: mournful; gloomy. *Although he loved telling stories and jokes, at heart Lincoln was a melancholy man.*

omens (ō′mənz) *n.*: things believed to be signs of future events. *Although he had a logical mind, Lincoln had a superstitious belief in omens.*

paramount (par′ə·mount′) *adj.*: main; most important. *Preserving the Union was his paramount concern.*

crusade (krōō·sād′) *n.*: struggle for a cause. *The war became a crusade for both sides.*

The Mysterious Mr. Lincoln

Russell Freedman

Abraham Lincoln wasn't the sort of man who could lose himself in a crowd. After all, he stood six feet four inches tall, and to top it off, he wore a high silk hat.

His height was mostly in his long, bony legs. When he sat in a chair, he seemed no taller than anyone else. It was only when he stood up that he towered above other men.

At first glance most people thought he was homely. Lincoln thought so too, referring once to his "poor, lean, lank face." As a young man he was sensitive about his gawky looks, but in time, he learned to laugh at himself. When a rival called him "two-faced" during political debate, Lincoln replied: "I leave it to my audience. If I had another face, do you think I'd wear this one?"

According to those who knew him, Lincoln was a man of many faces. In repose he often seemed sad and gloomy. But when he began to speak, his expression changed.

Vocabulary
gawky (gô′kē) *adj.*: clumsy; awkward.
repose (ri·pōz′) *n.*: state of rest or inactivity.

The Mysterious Mr. Lincoln **331**

- *Interactive Reading*, Teacher's Edition
  - Transparency 6: What and Why?

Differentiating Instruction

- *Lesson Plans for Language Development*
  - English-Language Learners, pp. 149–151, 164, 170
  - Special Education Students, pp. 152, 164, 170

Vocabulary and Spelling

- *Vocabulary Development*
  - Vocabulary Worksheet, p. 26

Assessment

- *Progress Assessment of Reading*
  - Selection Test, p. 111
- *One-Stop Planner* CD-ROM with Test Generator

PRETEACHING

Standards Starter

Build prerequisite skills. Reinforce students' understanding of metaphor as a way to reveal character by having them come up with metaphors for themselves. Model the task by saying the following: "I am a packrat because I never throw anything out."

Preview Vocabulary

Write the Vocabulary words from this page on the board and discuss their meanings. Then, ask students to replace the underlined words in these sentences with Vocabulary words.

1. Tired, Rosa Parks sought <u>rest</u> in a seat on the bus and refused to get up for a white person. [repose]
2. Her action began a <u>struggle</u> for civil rights that became one of the <u>most important</u> events of the 1960s. [crusade; paramount]
3. The <u>dejected</u> parishioners were roused to their feet by the minister's call to demonstrate. [listless]
4. Never <u>reserved</u> about injustice, Martin Luther King, Jr., broke out of his <u>sad</u> mood and spoke to the people with <u>vigor</u>. [reticent; melancholy; animation]
5. I recall one <u>awkward</u> teenager joining the fight to <u>resist</u> unjust laws. [gawky; defy]
6. Threats against Dr. King were <u>signs</u> that he would not live long. [omens]

DIRECT TEACHING

A **Literary Focus**
GRADE-LEVEL STANDARD
❓ Character. Point out the passage in which a rival insults Lincoln by calling him "two-faced," meaning "double-dealing." What does Lincoln's response to this insult reveal about him? [Possible responses: He is a fast thinker and is skilled at playing with words; he has a keen sense of humor; he is a masterful politician who deflects his opponent's criticism.]

A Content-Area Connections
HISTORY

The daguerreotype. Tell students that two Frenchmen, painter Louis Daguerre and scientist Joseph Niepce, invented the daguerreotype, one of the earliest forms of photography, in the 1830s. Though this process required the subject to remain absolutely still for several minutes, it quickly became popular. Explain that the invention of photography changed people's perceptions of themselves and the world. It allowed them for the first time to witness events and people many miles away, and it enabled them to keep a pictorial record of their own lives. Invite students to speculate about how life today would be different if there were no cameras.

B Literary Focus
GRADE-LEVEL STANDARD

❓ **Character.** What does this paragraph tell you about Lincoln's character? [He did not talk about his inner thoughts and feelings; he was reticent.] How does the author make this trait of Lincoln's seem believable? [Possible response: The author quotes Lincoln's law partner, who described Lincoln as "secretive" and "shut-mouthed."]

(Log cabin) The Granger Collection, New York.

President Lincoln's first Home in Illinois.

"The dull, listless features dropped like a mask," said a Chicago newspaperman. "The eyes began to sparkle, the mouth to smile; the whole countenance[1] was wreathed in animation, so that a stranger would have said, 'Why, this man, so angular and solemn a moment ago, is really handsome!'"

Lincoln was the most photographed man of his time, but his friends insisted that no photo ever did him justice. It's no wonder. Back then, cameras required long exposures. The person being photographed had to "freeze" as the seconds ticked by. If he blinked an eye, the picture would be blurred. That's why Lincoln looks so stiff and formal in his photos. We never see him laughing or joking.

Artists and writers tried to capture the "real"

Lincoln that the camera missed, but something about the man always escaped them. His changeable features, his tones, gestures, and expressions, seemed to defy description.

Today it's hard to imagine Lincoln as he really was. And he never cared to reveal much about himself. In company he was witty and talkative, but he rarely betrayed his inner feelings. According to William Herndon, his law partner, he was "the most secretive—reticent—shut-mouthed man that ever lived."

In his own time, Lincoln was never fully

1. **countenance** (koun'tə·nəns) *n.:* face.

Vocabulary

listless (list'lis) *adj.:* lifeless; lacking in interest or energy.

animation (an'i·mā'shən) *n.:* liveliness; life.

defy (dē·fī') *v.:* resist; oppose.

reticent (ret'ə·sənt) *adj.:* reserved; tending to speak little.

DIFFERENTIATING INSTRUCTION

Learners Having Difficulty
Modeling. Some students may need to read an easier selection before beginning "The Mysterious Mr. Lincoln." Use the Practice Read in *Interactive Reading*, p. 224. Then, use the transparency to model the strategy of What and Why? This strategy will help students to appreciate the use of literary devices, such as metaphor. Have students apply the strategy to help them read

"The Mysterious Mr. Lincoln." Encourage students to ask themselves as they read, "What two things are being compared? Why did the writer choose this metaphor?"

 Resources Reminder

Reading
■ *Interactive Reading*, Teacher's Edition
  ■ Transparency 6: What and Why?

■ *Interactive Reading*
  ■ Graphic Organizer: Metaphor Matching Map, p. 229

English-Language Learners
For these students, you may want to preview such idioms as *do him justice,* meaning "portray or show to full advantage"; *ring in our ears,* meaning "are famous or memorable"; and *whistle down sadness,*

understood even by his closest friends. Since then, his life story has been told and retold so many times he has become as much a legend as a flesh-and-blood human being. While the legend is based on truth, it is only partly true. And it hides the man behind it like a disguise.

The legendary Lincoln is known as Honest Abe, a humble man of the people who rose from a log cabin to the White House. There's no doubt that Lincoln was a poor boy who made good. And it's true that he carried his folksy manners and homespun speech to the White House with him. He said "howdy" to visitors and invited them to "stay a spell." He greeted diplomats while wearing carpet slippers, called his wife "mother" at receptions, and told bawdy[2] jokes at cabinet meetings.

Lincoln may have seemed like a common man, but he wasn't. His friends agreed that he was one of the most ambitious people they had ever known. Lincoln struggled hard to rise above his log-cabin origins, and he was proud of his achievements. By the time he ran for president he was a wealthy man, earning a large income from his law practice and his many investments. As for the nickname Abe, he hated it. No one who knew him well ever called him Abe to his face. They addressed him as Lincoln or Mr. Lincoln.

Lincoln is often described as a sloppy dresser, careless about his appearance. In fact, he patronized the best tailor in Springfield, Illinois, buying two suits a year. That was at a time when many men lived, died, and were buried in the same suit.

It's true that Lincoln had little formal

Abraham Lincoln and his son Tad (1865).

"eddication," as he would have pronounced it. Almost everything he "larned" he taught himself. All his life he said "thar" for *there,* "git" for *get,* "kin" for *can.* Even so, he became an eloquent public speaker who could hold a vast audience spellbound and a great writer whose finest phrases still ring in our ears. He was known to sit up late into the night, discussing Shakespeare's plays with White House visitors.

He was certainly a humorous man, famous for his rollicking stories. But he was also moody and melancholy, tormented by long and frequent bouts of depression. Humor was his therapy. He relied on his yarns,[3] a friend observed, to "whistle down sadness."

---

3. **yarns** *n.*: entertaining stories filled with exaggeration. Storytellers like Lincoln could be said to "spin" yarns.

Vocabulary
melancholy (mel′ən·käl′ē) *adj.*: mournful; gloomy.

---

2. **bawdy** *adj.*: humorous but crude.

The Mysterious Mr. Lincoln   **333**

VIEWING THE ART

Mathew Brady (c. 1823–1896) documented the battlefields of the Civil War, hiring teams of photographers to help him take more than six thousand pictures. These photographs have profoundly influenced our understanding of the Civil War. Brady's portraits of Lincoln, along with his photographs of the battles of Bull Run and Gettysburg, remain his most famous works.

C English-Language Learners
Reading dialect. Tell students that *howdy* is a greeting meaning "How do you do?" or "Hello" and that *stay a spell* is an expression welcoming someone or inviting him or her to stay for a short, indefinite period of time. Explain that these are regional terms or expressions that people used in the area where Lincoln grew up. You might ask these students to share words used to greet visitors in their native languages.

D English-Language Learners
Reading dialect. Point out that the words "eddication" and "larned" are misspellings of the words "education" and "learned" and that the misspellings are intended to show readers how Lincoln and others from his region would have pronounced these words.

meaning "act or pretend to be happy to fend off or overcome sadness."

▶ **Resources Reminder**
For lessons designed for intermediate and advanced English-language learners, see *Lesson Plans for Language Development,* pp. 149–151, 164, 170.

Special Education Learners
For lessons designed for special education students, see *Lesson Plans for Language Development,* pp. 152, 164, 170.

Advanced Learners
Acceleration. The following activity can help you move students toward a fuller understanding of the seventh-grade Standard 3.6, which requires that they ana-

lyze how a work's literary elements affect their responses to it.
Activity. Have small groups discuss whether or not "The Mysterious Mr. Lincoln" would be as interesting to read without the use of metaphor that Russell Freedman employs. How do the metaphors help the character of Abraham Lincoln come alive for readers?

A Reading Skills

Using prior knowledge. This is a good point to remind students to look back at their KWL charts, fill in new things they have learned, and write down additional things they would like to learn from the selection. Encourage students to share what they have learned by reading their chart entries aloud.

B Literary Focus
GRADE-LEVEL STANDARD

❓ Metaphor. Lincoln's critics referred to him as a "stupid baboon." What does this metaphor mean? [Possible responses: His critics were claiming he was no smarter than a monkey.]

C Reading Skills

Using prior knowledge. Elicit students' prior knowledge of Frederick Douglass to help them understand the importance of his comments. Students should add their knowledge of Douglass to their KWL charts. If necessary, supply the following information: Douglass (1817–1895) was born into slavery in Maryland. As a young man in 1838, he escaped to Massachusetts and became a leader in the anti-slavery and later civil rights movements. His autobiography, first published in 1845, is an American classic.

D Literary Focus
GRADE-LEVEL STANDARD

❓ Character. What have you learned about Lincoln that might have made Douglass change his mind? [Students may point to Lincoln's perception of the war as a moral crusade to end slavery.]

He had a cool, logical mind, trained in the courtroom, and a practical, commonsense approach to problems. Yet he was deeply superstitious, a believer in dreams, omens, and visions.

We admire Lincoln today as an American folk hero. During the Civil War, however, he was the most unpopular president the nation had ever known. His critics called him a tyrant, a hick,[4] a stupid baboon who was unfit for his office. As commander in chief of the armed forces, he was denounced as a bungling amateur who meddled in military affairs he knew nothing about. But he also had his supporters. They praised him as a farsighted statesman, a military mastermind who engineered the Union victory.

Lincoln is best known as the Great Emancipator, the man who freed the slaves. Yet he

---

4. **hick** *n.:* awkward, inexperienced person from the country.

did not enter the war with that idea in mind. "My paramount object in this struggle *is* to save the Union," he said in 1862, "and is *not* either to save or destroy slavery." As the war continued, Lincoln's attitude changed. Eventually he came to regard the conflict as a moral crusade to wipe out the sin of slavery.

No black leader was more critical of Lincoln than the fiery abolitionist[5] writer and editor Frederick Douglass. Douglass had grown up as a slave. He had won his freedom by escaping to the North. Early in the war, impatient with Lincoln's cautious leadership, Douglass called him "preeminently the white man's president, entirely devoted to the welfare of white men." Later, Douglass changed his mind and came to admire Lincoln. Several years after the war, he said this about the sixteenth president:

"His greatest mission was to accomplish two things: first, to save his country from dismemberment[6] and ruin; and second, to free his country from the great crime of slavery. . . . Taking him for all in all, measuring the tremendous magnitude of the work before him, considering the necessary means to ends, and surveying the end from the beginning, infinite wisdom has seldom sent any man into the world better fitted for his mission than Abraham Lincoln."

---

5. **abolitionist** *n.:* person who supported abolishing, or ending, slavery in the United States.
6. **dismemberment** *n.:* separation into parts; division.

Vocabulary
omens (ō′mənz) *n.:* things believed to be signs of future events.
paramount (par′ə·mount′) *adj.:* main; most important.
crusade (krōō·sād′) *n.:* struggle for a cause or belief.

CONTENT-AREA CONNECTIONS

History
Lincoln's personal tragedies. Lincoln's time in the White House was full of sadness. One cause for concern was his wife, Mary Todd Lincoln, who was disliked by much of the public. Because Mrs. Lincoln had strong family ties to the Confederacy, many in Washington secretly accused her of being a Confederate sympathizer. Lincoln's greatest personal tragedy, however, was the death of his beloved younger son Willie from typhoid fever. Neither Lincoln nor his wife ever truly recovered from this terrible blow.

Russell Freedman

"I Know Lincoln Better Than I Know Some of My Friends"

Russell Freedman (1929–) has written more than thirty nonfiction books for children and young adults. His book *Lincoln: A Photobiography*, which includes "The Mysterious Mr. Lincoln," won the Newbery Medal for the most distinguished contribution to children's literature in 1988. Freedman had this to say about writing a biography of the famous sixteenth president:

> The Lincoln I grew up with was a cardboard figure, too good to believe. As an adult, I read a couple of books that indicated he was just like everyone else—someone subject to depression, someone who had trouble making up his mind—and that intrigued me. When I had some inkling he was a complicated person in his own right, I decided I wanted to know more about him.
>
> I got to know Lincoln the way I'd try to know anyone in real life. How do you understand people? You observe them, discover their memories, find out their thoughts, their ideas of right and wrong. Once you do that, they become somebody's you know. I'd say I know Lincoln better than I know some of my friends because I've studied him more closely.

For Independent Reading

You may enjoy Freedman's books about other personalities he's studied closely. His biographies include *Eleanor Roosevelt: A Life of Discovery; Babe Didrikson Zaharias: The Making of a Champion; Teenagers Who Made History; The Life and Death of Crazy Horse;* and *The Wright Brothers: How They Invented the Airplane.*

The Mysterious Mr. Lincoln   **335**

INDEPENDENT PRACTICE

Literary Response and Analysis

Reading Check

Partial Outline:

I. *Appearance*—He was tall and gawky.

  A. "He stood six feet four inches tall."

  B. "poor, lean, lank face"

II. *Personality*—He was witty but not very open and given to bouts of depression.

  A. "In company he was witty and talkative, but he rarely betrayed his inner feelings."

  B. "But he was also moody and melancholy."

III. *The legend versus the reality*—The legend is that he was Honest Abe, a common man who made good. The reality is that he was an ambitious man who made good.

  A. "The legendary Lincoln is known as Honest Abe, a humble man of the people."

  B. "Lincoln may have seemed like a common man, but he wasn't."

  C. "By the time he ran for president he was a wealthy man."

Interpretations

1. Possible answers: He feels that the real Lincoln was someone that few people really knew; Lincoln's life has become shrouded in legend.

2. Students may say that they were surprised that Lincoln was ambitious and became wealthy, that he was superstitious, or that he did not at first want to destroy slavery. Possible answer: These facts are not part of his popular image.

3. The metaphors tell readers that Lincoln was very tall and had many sides to his personality.

4. Being "two-faced" means acting or saying different things around

Literary Response and Analysis

Reading Check

Creating an outline is a good way to review a nonfiction work. Listed below are the **main topics** discussed in this piece on Lincoln. Complete the outline by summing up the **main idea** of each numbered section and listing **supporting details.** (List supporting details as A, B, C, and so on.) For help in making an outline, see page 64.

  I. Appearance

  II. Personality

  III. The legend versus the reality

  IV. Education

  V. Humor and beliefs

  VI. Reputation during presidency

  VII. Position on slavery

Interpretations

1. Why does the writer call Lincoln "mysterious"?

2. Go back to the KWL chart you made before you started reading. Correct any inaccurate statements in the K column. Then, in the L column, list three facts you learned about Lincoln. What was the most surprising thing you learned about Lincoln from this selection? Why did it surprise you?

3. We usually associate metaphors with poetry, but metaphors are used in all kinds of writing and speaking. Freedman uses **metaphor** when he says that Lincoln "towered above other men" and that he was "a

Reading Standard 3.7
Explain the effects of metaphor in nonfictional texts.

man of many faces." Explain these comparisons—what do they tell you about Lincoln?

4. Using another **metaphor,** a rival called Lincoln "two-faced." What does this commonly used metaphor mean?

5. Frederick Douglass used a **metaphor** when he stated that Lincoln's first great mission was to "save his country from dismemberment." What does *dismemberment* mean? What is Douglass comparing the country to by using this term?

6. Review your Quickwrite notes. Does Lincoln have the qualifications for president that you listed? Do you think he would win if he ran for president in our next election? Explain why or why not. ✏

Listening and Speaking
Picks and Pans

Read Russell Freedman's *Lincoln: A Photobiography* and another book or article on Lincoln. Team up with a classmate who has read the same two books, and discuss the strengths and weaknesses of each. Then, present the books to the class as if you were a pair of reviewers on TV. Explain why you would—or wouldn't—recommend each book to readers your age. Use a scale like this one:

Forget it!   0   1   2   3   4   Read it!

different people. It implies double dealing or dishonesty.

5. *Dismemberment* means taking apart or cutting into pieces. By using this metaphor, Douglass is comparing the country to a body whose limbs, or members, are being removed violently.

6. Answers will vary, depending upon the criteria listed. If sense of humor or vision were qualities students listed, most

students would predict that Lincoln would win.

Listening and Speaking

Before students begin reading, remind them that a good biography must make the subject come alive. It also must be accurate, interesting, and reflect both primary and secondary sources.

Vocabulary Development

Finding Synonyms

A **thesaurus** (from the Greek for "treasure") is a reference book containing lists of synonyms. (You can find a thesaurus online or in a library.) **Synonyms** (sin′ə·nimz) are words that are similar in meaning. If you look up *gawky* in a thesaurus, you'll find synonyms like *awkward, ungainly, clumsy, graceless,* and *inelegant.*

The meanings of synonyms are related but slightly different. Try replacing a word in a sentence with one of its synonyms. You'll find that the meaning may change slightly.

PRACTICE

Below the Word Bank is another list of words. Go through the list, and find one or two synonyms for each Word Bank word. Next, go back to the text, and replace each Word Bank word with its synonym. Then, read each sentence. Has the meaning remained the same, or has it changed slightly? Set up your sentences this way:

> "As a young man he was sensitive about his gawky/clumsy looks."

Clumsy is not the same as *gawky.* It refers to the way someone moves rather than the way someone looks.

LARGE, GREAT, HUGE, CONSIDERABLE, BULKY, VOLUMINOUS, AMPLE, MASSIVE, CAPACIOUS, SPACIOUS, MIGHTY, TOWERING, MONSTROUS...

ROGET'S BRONTOSAURUS

From *The New Yorker Cartoon Album 1975–1985.*

Word Bank

gawky
repose
listless
animation
defy
reticent
melancholy
omens
paramount
crusade

Synonyms

campaign
clumsy
disobey
gloomy
inactivity
lifeless
liveliness
main
principal
reserved
resist
rest
sad
signs
silent

Reading Standard 1.5 Understand and explain shades of meaning in related words.

The Mysterious Mr. Lincoln **337**

Vocabulary Development

Practice

1. "In repose/inactivity/rest he often seemed sad and gloomy." Neither synonym fits as well as *repose.*

2. "The dull, listless/lifeless features dropped like a mask." The synonym fits the meaning of the sentence well.

3. "The eyes began to sparkle, the mouth to smile; the whole countenance was wreathed in animation/liveliness." *Liveliness* is an acceptable synonym.

4. "His changeable features, his tones, gestures, and expressions, seemed to defy/resist/disobey description." *Resist* fits, but *disobey* doesn't.

5. "He was 'the most secretive— reticent/reserved/silent—shut-mouthed man that ever lived.'" *Silent* fits, but *reserved* doesn't.

6. "But he was also melancholy/sad/gloomy, tormented by long and frequent bouts of depression." *Gloomy* fits, but *sad* is too mild.

7. "Yet he was deeply superstitious, a believer in dreams, omens/signs, and visions." The synonym fits the meaning of the sentence well.

8. "My paramount/main/principal object in this struggle *is* to save the Union." The synonyms fit the meaning of the sentence well.

9. "Eventually he came to regard the conflict as a moral crusade/campaign to wipe out the sin of slavery." The synonym fits the sentence reasonably well.

▶ Resources Reminder

Vocabulary and Spelling

- *Vocabulary Development*
  - Vocabulary Worksheet, p. 26
- *Lesson Plans for Language Development*
  - Vocabulary, p. 170

ASSESSING

Assessment

- *Progress Assessment of Reading*
  - Selection Test, p. 111

RETEACHING

For a lesson reteaching literary devices used in nonfiction, see **Reteaching**, p. 489N.

(For grade-level and review standards taught in this selection, see citations on Pupil's Edition pages.)

Prerequisite Standard

- Grade 5, Reading Comprehension 2.4 **Draw inferences, conclusions, or generalizations about text, and support them with textual evidence and prior knowledge.**

Summary at grade level

> The writer asserts that Lincoln was the best humorist ever to occupy the White House. To support this assertion, the writer describes how Lincoln, as both a lawyer and a politician, used his humor to achieve his goals and how the president's opponents feared his jabs. To make his case, the writer provides three examples of Lincoln's use of humor.

PRETEACHING

Standards Starter

Motivate. Write the following statement on the chalkboard, and invite students to discuss it: "Humor is a very powerful weapon." How can humor be used to wield power or control situations?

Assign the Reading

The selection is short enough to have students read it first at home and then again aloud as a class. Have volunteers take turns reading the humorous anecdotes aloud.

▶ Resources Reminder

Reading
- *Interactive Reading*
  - Graphic Organizer: Assertion Chart, p. 230

Lincoln's Humor

Making and Supporting Assertions

An **assertion** is a statement or claim. In his biography of Abraham Lincoln, Russell Freedman makes several assertions about Lincoln. For example, he claims that Lincoln was "mysterious." Freedman is careful to back up his statements about Lincoln with **citations,** or evidence. Citations give weight to an assertion and help make it believable.

Look at the following chart to see how Freedman supported some of his assertions. What evidence does Freedman offer for the third assertion? Flip back through "The Mysterious Mr. Lincoln" to find out.

Read the next article, and see if the writer supports his assertions about Lincoln's sense of humor.

Reading Standard 2.7 Make reasonable assertions about a text through accurate supporting citations.

"The Mysterious Mr. Lincoln"	
Assertion (Claim)	**Citation (Proof)**
1. "Lincoln was a man of many faces."	• He was sad and gloomy in repose. • He was smiling and animated when speaking.
2. People think of Lincoln as a "man of the people," but in many ways he wasn't.	• He was highly ambitious. • Although he had little formal education, he was an accomplished speaker and writer. • He was wealthy.
3. Lincoln is sometimes thought of as a careless dresser, but he actually cared a great deal about his appearance.	[You find the evidence.]

The Granger Collection, New York.

Long Abraham Lincoln a Little Longer.

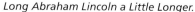

RESOURCES

Planning
- *One-Stop Planner* CD-ROM with Test Generator
- *On Course: Mapping Instruction*

Media
- *Audio CD Library*
  - disc 8

Reading
- *Interactive Reading*
  - Graphic Organizer: Assertion Chart, p. 230

Differentiating Instruction
- *Lesson Plans for Language Development*
  - English-Language Learners, pp. 153, 165, 170

LINCOLN'S HUMOR

It is puzzling how Lincoln could laugh, joke, and tell stories, despite his terrible burdens as president during the Civil War. Lincoln was the first and the best humorist ever to occupy the White House. A friend said, "He could make a cat laugh."

Lincoln called laughter "the joyous, beautiful, universal evergreen of life." For Lincoln laughter relieved life's pressures and soothed its disappointments. Both as a lawyer and as a politician, he used amusing stories to make important points clear to his listeners. Storytelling put people at ease or nudged them from an unwanted topic or point of view. It also pleasantly brought an interview to a close and a visitor's welcome departure from the president's office.

Political opponents feared Lincoln's humorous jabs, which often destroyed their best arguments. Stephen A. Douglas, Lincoln's opponent in a Senate race, said, "Every one of his stories seems like a whack upon my back. . . . When he begins to tell a story, I feel that I am to be overmatched."

Lincoln's words got extra force from his facial expressions and gestures—a shrug of his shoulders, raised eyebrows, a turned-down mouth, a comically twisted face—which made his audiences roar with laughter.

Here is a sampling of Lincoln's humor and the uses he made of it:

- As a young lawyer, Lincoln once defended a farmer who had been attacked by his neighbor's dog. To fend off the dog, the farmer had poked it with a pitchfork, wounding it. The dog's owner then took the case to court to recover damages. His lawyer argued that the farmer should have struck the dog with the handle end of the pitchfork to avoid causing it serious harm. In the farmer's defense, Lincoln exclaimed that the dog should have avoided frightening the farmer by approaching him with *its* other end.

- As president, Lincoln was besieged with visitors seeking jobs and favors. One day while a visitor was pressing his demands, Lincoln's doctor entered the room. Lincoln, holding out his hands, asked him, "Doctor, what are those blotches?" "They're a mild smallpox," the doctor replied. "They're all over me," said Lincoln. "It's contagious, I believe." "Very contagious," said the doctor as the visitor hastily departed. "There is one good thing about this," said Lincoln to his doctor after the caller had left. "I now have something I can give to everybody."

- Impatient with his Civil War generals, who were slow to engage their forces in battle, Lincoln began requiring frequent reports of their progress. An irritated general sent this telegram to the White House: "We have just captured six cows. What shall we do with them?" Lincoln replied, "Milk them."

—Louis W. Koenig

- Special Education Students, pp. 153, 165, 170

Assessment
- *Progress Assessment of Reading*
  - Selection Test, p. 114
- *One-Stop Planner* CD-ROM with Test Generator

Resources Reminder

Media
- *Audio CD Library*
  - disc 8

A Reading Skills

? Interpreting. Since cats don't laugh, what do you think Lincoln's friend means? [Lincoln was so funny that he could make laugh even a person who, like a cat, never laughs.]

B Reading Informational Materials
GRADE-LEVEL STANDARD

? Making and supporting reasonable assertions. What assertion does the author make here? [He claims that Lincoln's political opponents feared his humor.] How does he support this assertion? [He quotes from Stephen A. Douglas, a political opponent of Lincoln's.]

C Reading Informational Materials
GRADE-LEVEL STANDARD

? Making and supporting reasonable assertions. What assertion in the text do these examples of Lincoln's humor help to support? [Possible responses: "Lincoln was the first and best humorist ever to occupy the White House"; "Both as a lawyer and as a politician, he used amusing stories to make important points clear to his listeners."]

GUIDED PRACTICE

Monitoring students' progress. Have students make charts like the one on the Before You Read page for "Lincoln's Humor." Suggest that they go through the selection paragraph by paragraph to identify all the assertions the author makes and the evidence he uses to support them.

INDEPENDENT PRACTICE

Reading Informational Materials

Reading Check

1. He makes the assertion that "Lincoln was the first and best humorist ever to occupy the White House."

2. He offers examples of how Lincoln's humor helped him to intimidate political opponents, win cases, get rid of bothersome job seekers, and keep his generals in line.

Answers and Model Rationales

1. **A** Evidence is given to support assertion A.

2. **H** H identifies a quotation from the selection that directly supports the assertion.

3. **C** C applies because the author supplies many details that describe Lincoln's sense of humor.

4. **G** G is supported by the information in the essay.

5. **B** The author cites many examples that support assertion B. A is contradicted by the essay, and C and D may have been true but were not Lincoln's primary reasons for using humor.

Test-Taking Tips

Tell students that some test items are incomplete sentences. Students should use each answer to complete the sentence and select the answer supported by the text.

For more instruction on how to answer multiple-choice items, refer students to **Test Smarts,** p. 690.

Reading Informational Materials

Reading Check

1. What **assertion** about Lincoln does the writer make in the first paragraph?

2. How does the writer **support** his assertion that Lincoln's sense of humor helped him?

LINCOLN'S HUMOR

1. The information in this article supports the **assertion** that —
   A Lincoln used humor to cope with the difficulties of being president
   B Lincoln should have appeared more serious to the public
   C Lincoln was the most popular president ever
   D Lincoln worried about his health

2. What **evidence** from the article suggests that Lincoln would do well in a debate if he were a candidate today?
   F Lincoln was handsome, so he would look good on television.
   G Lincoln always seemed more intelligent than his opponents.
   H The quotation by Stephen A. Douglas shows that Lincoln used humor effectively to defeat debating opponents.
   J Lincoln's plain speaking appealed to people all over the country.

3. We can reasonably **assert** that this essay was written mainly to —
   A persuade people to like Lincoln
   B persuade people to laugh more
   C describe Lincoln's sense of humor
   D criticize Lincoln's character

4. The information in this essay supports the **assertion** that —
   F Lincoln disliked the military
   G Lincoln used humor and amusing stories throughout his career
   H Lincoln did not get impatient during the Civil War
   J Lincoln told funny stories only when he was a lawyer

5. The three samples of Lincoln's humor at the end of this article support the **assertion** that —
   A Lincoln told jokes for no reason at all
   B Lincoln used humor to cope with problems
   C Lincoln used humor to hurt people
   D Lincoln's humor went over the heads of most people

Reading Standard 2.7 Make reasonable assertions about a text through accurate supporting citations.

DIFFERENTIATING INSTRUCTION

Learners Having Difficulty
Modeling. Help students increase their understanding of this selection by having them work with partners to restate some of the more difficult or confusing sentences and paragraphs. Begin by modeling this process for them. The sentence "Lincoln was the first and best humorist ever to occupy the White House," for example, could be restated more simply as "Lincoln was the funniest president we have ever had."

English-Language Learners
Humor often differs from culture to culture. To help English-language learners to fully appreciate Lincoln's humor, suggest that they team up with fluent English speakers who can explain that Lincoln creates humor by being sarcastic in the first anecdote, purposefully untruthful in the second anecdote, and literal in the third.

Vocabulary Development

Antonyms

An **antonym** (an′tə·nim′) is a word that is opposite or nearly opposite in meaning to another word. In the selection you just read, you learned that Lincoln's opponents feared his humor. Some antonyms for *opponents* are *colleagues, allies,* and *companions.* Learning antonyms of unfamiliar words can broaden your vocabulary. (You can sometimes find antonyms in dictionary and thesaurus entries.)

PRACTICE

Read each of the sentences below. Then, choose the **antonym,** or opposite, of the underlined word.

1. Lincoln called laughter "the joyous, beautiful, universal evergreen of life." An antonym of *joyous* is —

a. sad   **b.** ugly   **c.** peaceful   **d.** happy

2. Lincoln used humorous stories to ease visitors' departure from his office. An antonym of *departure* is —

a. rush   **b.** leaving   **c.** arrival   **d.** exit

3. Lincoln felt that laughter soothed life's disappointments. An antonym of *soothed* is —

a. worsened   **b.** smoothed   **c.** corrected   **d.** helped

4. Lincoln grew impatient with generals who were slow to engage their forces in battle. An antonym of *engage* is —

a. marry   **b.** rally   **c.** withdraw   **d.** employ

5. As a young lawyer, Lincoln once defended a farmer who had been threatened by a dog. An antonym of *defended* is —

a. attacked   **b.** freed   **c.** supported   **d.** protected

Grade 5 Review Reading Standard 1.3 Understand and explain antonyms.

Lincoln's Humor   **341**

Vocabulary Development

Practice

1. a

2. c

3. a

4. c

5. a

Resources Reminder

Differentiating Instruction

■ *Lesson Plans for Language Development*
- Vocabulary, p. 170

Assessment

■ *Progress Assessment of Reading*
- Selection Test, p. 114

For a lesson reteaching how citations support assertions, see **Reteaching,** p. 489F.

STANDARDS FOCUS, pp. 342–346

(For grade-level and review standards taught in this selection, see citations on Pupil's Edition pages.)

Summary ⬆ *above grade level*

This article uses illustrations from the period as it recounts the journalist Sarah Josepha Hale's crusade to make Thanksgiving a national holiday. The article also explains the reasons for President Lincoln's decision to do so.

 Resources Reminder

Media
- *Audio CD Library*
  - disc 8

Reading
- *Interactive Reading*
  - Graphic Organizer: Text/Graphic Features Chart, p. 231

PRETEACHING

Standards Starter

Motivate. Invite students to share descriptions of Thanksgiving traditions in their households. If students do not celebrate Thanksgiving, invite them to describe a holiday they celebrate in which food plays an important role.

Assign the Reading

Have students read the article first at home and then go over it again in class, paying particular attention to the quotations.

HOMEWORK

A Civil War Thanksgiving

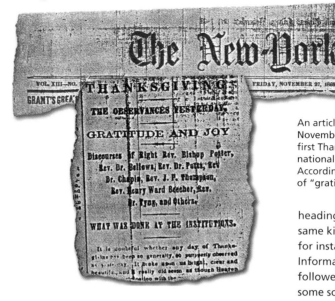

An article in *The New York Times* of November 27, 1863, describes the first Thanksgiving celebrated as a national holiday in the United States. According to the headline, it was a day of "gratitude and joy."

Grade 5 Review Reading Standard 2.1 Understand how text features (for example, format, graphics, sequence, diagrams, illustrations, charts, maps) make information accessible and usable.

Understanding Text Features

Informational materials like textbooks, newspapers, and magazines often include **text features** designed to help you get the information you need. The textbook page you're looking at right now has several of those special features, including headings, a logo, an illustration and caption, color, and boldface type. Other features that help you read informational materials include maps, charts, and tables.

Look at Headings

A **heading** is a kind of title. Headings are words or phrases used to break up a text into sections. They're usually printed in a color or size meant to attract your attention. A repeated heading is always followed by the same kind of material. In this textbook, for instance, the heading "Reading Informational Materials" is always followed by an informative text of some sort.

Use Graphic Features

Graphic features include color, boldface type, and logos (tiny pictures). Graphic features help you find what you're looking for quickly. For example, a bear logo like the one on this page appears every time information about a California standard is presented.

Maps, charts, tables, and **illustrations** (often accompanied by **captions**) are other kinds of graphic features. They are often used to help you picture something described in the text. They can convey a lot of information in a small space. A **caption** is the text accompanying a graphic feature that explains what you are looking at. Be sure to read captions for maps, charts, tables, and illustrations carefully.

RESOURCES

Planning
- *One-Stop Planner* CD-ROM with Test Generator
- *On Course: Mapping Instruction*

Media
- *Audio CD Library*
  - disc 8

Reading
- *Interactive Reading*
  - Graphic Organizer: Text/Graphic Features Chart, p. 231

Differentiating Instruction
- *Lesson Plans for Language Development*
  - English-Language Learners, pp. 154, 166, 170

A Civil War Thanksgiving

In the cause of unity, President Lincoln makes the holiday official.

The newsboys on the street cried out the news: General Grant's Union troops had won a smashing victory in Tennessee, and the Rebels were in full retreat! To thankful Northerners, the timing seemed too good to be true. It was November 26, 1863, the day Thanksgiving made its debut as a legal U.S. holiday.

There were no pro football games that day. Americans' attention, North and South, was on the field of battle of the Civil War (1861–1865). But in other ways—turkey and all the trimmings, for example—it was a Thanksgiving we could recognize today.

(Above) Journalist Sarah Josepha Hale crusaded to make Thanksgiving a national day of unity. On September 28, 1863, Hale wrote a letter (left) to President Lincoln, asking him to make Thanksgiving a "National and fixed Union Festival."

The Granger Collection, New York.

A English-Language Learners

Building background knowledge. Some students may not get this reference to pro football games. If necessary, explain that it has become a tradition to have an afternoon pro football game on television on Thanksgiving. For many families, watching the game is part of their Thanksgiving ritual.

B Reading Informational Materials
REVIEW STANDARD
? Understanding text features. What two text features does this caption explain? [It identifies the woman in the photograph as Sarah Josepha Hale and explains the hand-written letter fragment.]

- Special Education Students, pp. 154, 166, 170

Assessment
- *Progress Assessment of Reading*
  - Selection Test, p. 116
- *One-Stop Planner* CD-ROM with Test Generator

A **Content-Area Connections**
HISTORY

The first Thanksgiving. If necessary, remind students of the history of the Pilgrims' first Thanksgiving at Plymouth Colony. Explain that the Pilgrims, who arrived in Plymouth in December 1620, endured a very long and hard winter. In fact, half the group died from disease, exposure, and starvation. The Wampanoags, Native Americans in the area, helped the survivors get through until spring. The following fall, when the Pilgrims had finished bringing in their first crops, they decided to celebrate with the Native Americans and give thanks for the bountiful harvest. Invite students with knowledge of the first Thanksgiving to share what they know.

B **Reading Informational Materials**
REVIEW STANDARD

❷ Understanding text features. How are the quotations in this selection set off as text features? [They are set off from the regular text with extra space and set in color.] Why might quotations be set off this way in a text? [Possible responses: to highlight their importance; to make sure that readers recognize them as quotations.]

A Every schoolchild learns that Thanksgiving dates to the harvest feast Pilgrim settlers at Plymouth Colony, Massachusetts, had shared with Native Americans in 1621. But few know that it took the Civil War, and a long crusade by a magazine editor named Sarah Josepha Hale, to make the holiday truly national.

Born in New Hampshire in 1788, Hale became a prominent journalist at a time when rigid custom kept most women at home. Widowed at an early age, she turned to writing to support her five children. She wrote the famous nursery rhyme that begins, "Mary had a little lamb . . ."

Hale loved Thanksgiving, already a tradition in New England. Her 1827 novel *Northwood* has a Thanksgiving dinner description you probably shouldn't read if you're hungry:

B The roasted turkey took precedence[1] on this occasion, being placed at the head of the table; and well did it become its lordly station, sending forth the rich odor of its savory stuffing, and finely covered with the frost of the basting. At the foot of the board a surloin [sirloin] of beef, flanked on either side by a leg of pork and a joint of mutton, seemed placed as a bastion[2] to defend innumerable bowls of gravy and plates of vegetables disposed in that quarter. A goose and a pair of ducklings occupied side stations on the table. . . . There was a huge plumb [plum] pudding, custards, and pies of every name and description ever known in Yankee land; yet the pumpkin pie occupied the most distinguished niche.[3]

1. **precedence** (pres′ə·dəns) *n.:* first rank.
2. **bastion** *n.:* structure built for defense.
3. **niche** (nich) *n.:* position.

But however sumptuous, Thanksgiving in the early 19th century wasn't a legal holiday, was still held on different dates in different places, and was ignored altogether in much of the nation. Hale favored adoption of a uniform national holiday, and saw Thanksgiving not only as a day to be grateful for divine blessings, but also as a way to unite the country and promote pride in its freedom. She wrote:

We have too few holidays. Thanksgiving, like the Fourth of July, should be considered a national festival and observed by all our people . . . as an exponent[4] of our republican institutions.

When Hale became editor of a popular women's magazine called *Godey's Lady's Book,* she used it to press for an official national Thanksgiving. One editorial page asked that

from this year, 1847, henceforth and forever, as long as the Union endures, the *last Thursday in November* be the day set apart by every State for its annual Thanksgiving.

She wrote such an editorial every year for 16 years, and peppered Presidents with letters pleading her cause.

What finally established Hale's unifying holiday was the war that tore the Union apart. In 1863, by one account, she visited President Abraham Lincoln in the White House. Historians aren't sure about that, but they know her editorial that year called for making Thanksgiving national by presidential proclamation—and that is just what Lincoln promptly did.

4. **exponent** (ek·spōn′ənt) *n.:* symbol.

DIFFERENTIATING INSTRUCTION

Learners Having Difficulty
Have students work in small groups to identify the text features of "A Civil War Thanksgiving," such as the title, subheading, illustrations, captions, and quotations set in color. Then, have them discuss how these features increase their understanding of the article or their interest in reading it.

English-Language Learners
References to American history and popular culture in this selection may prove to be stumbling blocks for these students. Invite students to a special workshop where you go over the following list of references from the selection: Pilgrims and Plymouth colony; "Mary had a little lamb . . ."; New England; General Ulysses S. Grant; Missionary Ridge; *The New York Times;* Rebels; Union.

An illustration showing Thanksgiving as it might have been celebrated in the late 1800s.

Eager to grasp any tool to promote national unity, Lincoln proclaimed the last Thursday in November a day of "thanksgiving and prayer," noting that

In the midst of a civil war of unequaled magnitude and severity ... order has been maintained, the laws have been respected and obeyed, and harmony has prevailed[5] everywhere, except in the theater of military conflict, while that theater has been greatly contracted[6] by the advancing armies and navies of the Union.

The holiday brought news of those armies. General Ulysses S. Grant's troops had stormed Tennessee's Missionary Ridge—without having been ordered to do so. In New York City, people cheered the news, then packed into churches to hear Thanksgiving sermons. *The New York Times* wrote:

Everybody wore a holiday face. In the afternoon all the places of amusement were crowded to overflowing ... The war news so opportunely[7] arriving gave renewed zest to the thankfulness and enjoyment ...

It took another 17 months to end the Civil War and restore the Union. And Congress later moved the holiday to the fourth, not the last, Thursday in November. But Thanksgiving had taken hold, and would be an enduring tradition, North and South.

—Timothy Kelley, from *The New York Times Upfront*

---

5. **prevailed** *v.*: triumphed; came into effect.
6. **contracted** *v.*: reduced; shrunk.

7. **opportunely** *adv.*: at a favorable time.

A Civil War Thanksgiving **345**

Advanced Learners
As this article shows, the Thanksgiving holiday has always had great social and political influence in America.
Enrichment. Have students discuss the symbolism of Thanksgiving as a national holiday. Why does our society celebrate the Pilgrims' harvest feast? What are the pros and cons of having a uniquely American, nonreligious holiday?

A Civil War Thanksgiving **345**

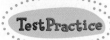

INDEPENDENT PRACTICE

TestPractice

Answers and Model Rationales

1. **B** No evidence is given to support A. While C may have been an underlying wish of Lincoln's, it is not the reason expressed in the article. D is mentioned in the article as one of Hale's arguments for the holiday but is not mentioned by Lincoln.

2. **H** The quotations are not in boldface (F), or italics (G), and have no headings (J). Therefore the answer is H.

3. **A** Captions are the text that appears under or beside graphic features and tells what the features are about. B, C, and D refer to other types of graphic features that do not explain illustrations.

4. **H** There is no evidence to support assertions F and J. Assertion G is contradicted by the fact that Hale worked as a magazine editor and wrote editorials and novels. Assertion H is supported by the fact that her campaign was long.

5. **D** There are illustrations of A, B, and C in the selection but no illustration of D.

6. **G** Only G can be correct since the quotations are from three sources—Hale, Lincoln, and *The New York Times*.

7. **D** The other choices are opinions, while D is an actual fact.

Test-Taking Tips

Remind students to read a multiple-choice question carefully before looking at the possible answers. Sometimes the wording of the question will make it easy to eliminate one or more possible answers.

For more instruction on how to answer multiple-choice items, refer students to **Test Smarts**, p. 690.

Reading Informational Materials

TestPractice

A Civil War Thanksgiving

1. According to the article, Lincoln made Thanksgiving a national holiday to —
   A honor the Pilgrims
   B promote national unity
   C help bring an end to the Civil War
   D increase the number of national holidays

2. In this article, which **graphic feature** helps you locate the long quotations in the text?
   F Boldface
   G Italics
   H Color
   J Headings

3. Which **graphic feature** explains what is shown in the illustrations?
   A Captions
   B Charts
   C Diagrams
   D Headings

4. The information in the article supports the **assertion** that Sarah Hale —
   F objected to the Civil War
   G felt that women should not work outside the home
   H refused to give up on a cause she believed in
   J was interested in Thanksgiving only because she came from New England

5. The illustrations for this article include all of the following items *except* —
   A a newspaper clipping from 1863
   B a portrait of Sarah Hale
   C a reproduction of a letter
   D a map of Missionary Ridge

6. The long quotations in this article are —
   F all from Hale's novel *Northwood*
   G from several sources
   H all from Lincoln's Thanksgiving proclamation
   J all from *Godey's Lady's Book*

7. Which of the following statements from this article is a **fact**?
   A "We have too few holidays."
   B "Everybody wore a holiday face."
   C "Every schoolchild learns that Thanksgiving dates to the harvest feast Pilgrim settlers . . . had shared with Native Americans in 1621."
   D "Thanksgiving in the early 19th century wasn't a legal holiday. . . ."

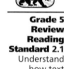

Grade 5 Review Reading Standard 2.1 Understand how text features (for example, format, graphics, illustrations) make information accessible and usable.

346 Chapter 6 Looking at Texts: Uses of the Imagination

ASSESSING

Assessment
- *Progress Assessment of Reading*
  - Selection Test, p. 116

What Do Fish Have to Do with Anything?

Literary Focus
Symbolism

A **symbol** is a person, place, thing, or action that has meaning in itself and that stands for something else as well. Many symbols are traditional. They're easily understood because people have agreed on their meaning. A dove, for example, often symbolizes peace. Uncle Sam is a symbol of the United States. Peter Pan is a symbol of everlasting childhood.

Symbolism, the use of symbols, adds another layer of meaning to all kinds of texts, from poetry to fiction and nonfiction. In this story the writer uses things, like cave-dwelling fish and a poundcake, to mean what they are—and much more.

Reading Skills
Making Inferences

Writers rarely come right out and explain what their symbols mean. You have to find the symbols and figure out their meaning on your own. You do this by **making inferences.** You use details to **infer,** or guess at, the larger ideas the writer is trying to convey.

As you read, you'll see little open-book signs at certain points in the story. Stop at those points, and answer the questions.

Make the Connection
What's Your Opinion?

Rate the following ideas about life, all of which are expressed in the story. Use this scale to rate the statements:

1 = disagree, 2 = no opinion,
3 = agree.

1. "Parents need to protect their children."

2. "Questions that have no answers shouldn't be asked."

3. "Money will cure a lot of unhappiness."

4. "People are ashamed of being unhappy."

Quickwrite

From the list, choose a statement that you agree or disagree with. Explain why you feel the way you do.

Vocabulary Development

Look for and learn these words as you read the story:

vaguely (vāg'lē) *adv.:* not clearly or definitely; in a general way. *She answered vaguely because she felt uncomfortable telling the whole story.*

urgency (ur'jən·sē) *n.:* pressure; insistence. *Hearing the urgency in her voice, Willie quickly turned around.*

contemplated (kän'təm·plāt'id) *v.:* studied carefully. *Willie contemplated his food before eating it.*

intently (in·tent'lē) *adv.:* with close attention. *Willie gazed intently at the man.*

Reading Standard 3.7 Explain the effects of symbolism in fictional texts.

What Do Fish Have to Do with Anything? **347**

STANDARDS FOCUS, pp. 347–358

(For grade-level and review standards taught in this selection, see citations on Pupil's Edition pages.)

Prerequisite Standards

- Grade 5, Vocabulary 1.3 **Understand and explain frequently used synonyms, antonyms, and homographs.**
- Grade 5, Literary Response and Analysis 3.5 **Describe the function and effect of common literary devices (e.g., imagery, metaphor, symbolism).**

Standard Coming Up in the Next Grade Levels

- Grade 8, Literary Response and Analysis 3.6 **Identify significant literary devices (e.g., metaphor, symbolism, dialect, irony) that define a writer's style, and use those elements to interpret the work.**

Reading Skills

- Make inferences.

Summary ⟷ *at grade level*

On a walk home from school with his mother, Willie asks about a beggar they pass, but his mother is unwilling to talk about him. At home, Willie has a snack and does his homework, all the time wondering about the beggar. For a few days, Willie visits the beggar, giving him nickels and cake. Willie asks about unhappiness, hoping to help his mother, who has been sad since his father left. The man shares his cure for unhappiness: "What a person needs is always more than they say." Then, the beggar disappears, and Willie learns that his mother had the police remove him. Willie tells her that she is like the fish that live in dark, underwater caves and cannot see.

Standards Starter

Build prerequisite skills.
Remind students that in stories the main character often changes and grows as a result of the events. The writer doesn't usually tell the reader directly that a character has changed, but lets the character's actions show the reader what is going on. As students read this story, have them look for change in the main character.

Bear in mind that there may be students in class who have been directly or indirectly affected by homelessness. Before students read the story, you might discuss with the class the possible reasons why anyone could find themselves without a permanent place to live. Natural disasters such as a fire, flood, or tornado could be a place to begin.

Preview Vocabulary

Have students work in pairs to read the Vocabulary words and their definitions on p. 347. Then, have partners take turns pantomiming the meanings of the words while the other partner guesses which words are being suggested. For example, a student might

- gaze around the room <u>vaguely</u>
- search with <u>urgency</u> for something lost or mislaid
- <u>contemplate</u> artwork or a poster on the wall
- stare <u>intently</u> at someone or something

Assign the Reading

You may want to have average readers work with partners to read the story and answer the inferential questions. Advanced readers can work independently and answer the questions as homework.

HOMEWORK

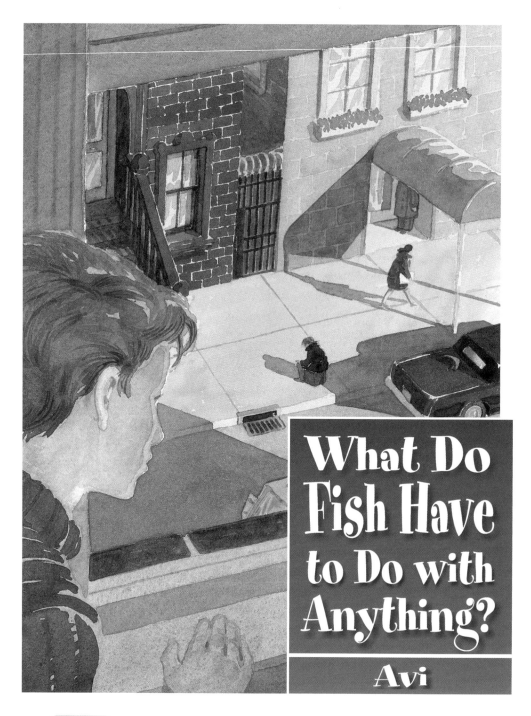

What Do Fish Have to Do with Anything?

Avi

RESOURCES

Vocabulary and Spelling
- *Vocabulary Development*
  - Vocabulary Worksheet, p. 27
  - Cumulative Vocabulary Review, p. 28

Assessment
- *Progress Assessment of Reading*
  - Selection Test, p. 118
- *One-Stop Planner* CD-ROM with Test Generator

DIFFERENTIATING INSTRUCTION

Learners Having Difficulty
Modeling. To help students read "What Do Fish Have to Do with Anything?," model the reading skill of making inferences about symbols. Have students read the story up through the sixth paragraph on p. 350. Point out that Mrs. Markham speaks of money as a cure for unhappiness. Say: "To different people, money might stand for security or abundance or greed. For Mrs. Markham, money is a symbol of happiness."

Every day Mrs. Markham waited for her son, Willie, to come out of school when it was over. They walked home together. If asked why, Mrs. Markham would say, "Parents need to protect their children."

One Monday afternoon as they approached their apartment building, she suddenly tugged at Willie. "Don't look that way," she said.

"Where?"

"At that man over there."

As they walked, Willie stole a look back over his shoulder. A man Willie had never seen before was sitting on a red plastic milk crate near the curb. His matted, streaky gray hair hung like a ragged curtain over a dirty face. His shoes were torn. Rough hands lay upon his knees. One hand was palm up.

"What's the matter with him?" Willie asked.

Keeping her eyes straight ahead, Mrs. Markham said, "He's sick." She pulled Willie around. "Don't stare. It's rude."

"What kind of sick?"

Mrs. Markham searched for an answer. "He's unhappy," she said.

"What's he doing?"

"Come on, Willie; you know. He's begging."

"Did anyone give him anything?"

"I don't know. Now come on, don't look."

"Why don't you give him anything?"

"We have nothing to spare."

When they got home, Mrs. Markham removed a white cardboard box from the refrigerator. It contained poundcake. Using her thumb as a measure, she carefully cut a half-inch-thick piece of cake and gave it to Willie on a clean plate. The plate lay on a plastic mat decorated by images of roses with diamondlike dewdrops. She also gave

him a glass of milk and a folded napkin.

Willie said, "Can I have a bigger piece of cake?"

Mrs. Markham picked up the cake box and ran a manicured pink fingernail along the nutrition information panel. "A half-inch piece is a portion, and a portion contains the following nutrients. Do you want to hear them?"

"No."

"It's on the box, so you can accept what it says. Scientists study people and then write these things. If you're smart enough, you could become a scientist. Like this." Mrs. Markham tapped the box. "It pays well."

Willie ate his cake and drank the milk. When he was done, he took care to wipe the crumbs off his face as well as to blot the milk moustache with the napkin.

His mother said, "Now go on and do your homework. You're in fifth grade. It's important."

Willie gathered up his books that lay on the empty third chair. At the kitchen entrance he paused. "What *kind* of unhappiness does he have?"

"Who's that?"

"That man."

Mrs. Markham looked puzzled.

"The begging man. The one on the street."

"Could be anything," his mother said, vaguely. "A person can be unhappy for many reasons."

"Like what?"

"Willie . . ."

"Is it a doctor kind of sickness? A sickness you can cure?"

"I wish you wouldn't ask such questions."

Vocabulary

vaguely (vāg′lē) *adv.*: not clearly or definitely; in a general way.

What Do Fish Have to Do with Anything? **349**

▶ **Resources Reminder**

Media
- Audio CD Library
  - disc 8
- *Fine Art Transparencies*
  - Transparency 11

A **Reading Skills**

❓ **Evaluating.** Do you think Mrs. Markham is telling the truth when she says that they can't afford to give the beggar anything? Why or why not? [Possible responses: Yes, it seems they live in a poor neighborhood, and so it is unlikely that they can afford to be generous; no, she is just stingy or uncaring or doesn't want to encourage beggars.]

B **Literary Focus**
REVIEW STANDARD

❓ **Character.** What can you infer about Mrs. Markham from her comment? [Possible responses: She accepts things at face value; she doesn't like to look below the surface or question too deeply.]

Encourage students as they read to ask themselves: "What special meaning does this idea or object have for the character?"

▶ **Resources Reminder**

Reading
- *Interactive Reading*
  - Graphic Organizer: Symbol Chart, p. 232

English-Language Learners
Students may wonder why homeless people exist in our wealthy nation. Explain that the United States has a welfare system, but that many people do not qualify for assistance; others have no access to the system or have mental or physical problems that prevent them from seeking aid.

▶ **Resources Reminder**

For lessons designed for intermediate and advanced English-language learners, see *Lesson Plans for Language Development*, pp. 155–157, 167, 171.

Special Education Students
For lessons designed for special education students, see *Lesson Plans for Language Development*, pp. 158, 167, 171.

What Do Fish Have to Do with Anything? **349**

A Reading Skills

Making inferences. Remind students that making an inference means putting clues from the story together with what they know. Ask students to identify clues that hint at Mrs. Markham's attitude toward money. [Possible responses: She remembers the words of the salesperson and wants Willie to remember them; she seems to believe that money can cure unhappiness; earlier, she said that being a scientist "pays well" and she refused to spare any money for the beggar.]

[Possible response to question 1: She has little money herself and must work late hours to earn it.]

B English-Language Learners

Interpreting idioms. Students who are learning English may not be familiar with the terms *convenience store* and *night shift.* Explain that a convenience store is a small neighborhood store that may be open twenty-four hours a day and that carries a limited selection of packaged foods and household items. The night shift is the late-night work period, often the hours from 11:00 P.M. to 7:00 A.M.

C Literary Focus
REVIEW STANDARD

❓ Character. What does Willie learn from the dog? Why does he grin? [Willie learns that dogs, like people, sometimes do the opposite of what they are told to do. Willie grins because he recognizes his own behavior in the dog's actions.]

D Learners Having Difficulty

Questioning. Students may be puzzled about why Willie wonders "how much happiness you could rent for a nickel." Have them recall Mrs. Markham's saying that the man was begging because money will "cure" unhappiness and her quoting the salesperson's remark about renting happiness.

"Why?"

"Questions that have no answers shouldn't be asked."

"Can I go out?"

"Homework first."

Willie turned to go.

"Money," Mrs. Markham suddenly said. "Money will cure a lot of unhappiness. That's why that man was begging. A salesperson once said to me, 'Maybe you can't buy happiness, but you can rent a lot of it.' You should remember that."

> **🕮 MAKING INFERENCES**
>
> 1. Why do you think Mrs. Markham is so concerned about money?

The apartment had three rooms. The walls were painted mint green. Willie walked down the hallway to his room, which was at the front of the building. By climbing up on the windowsill and pressing against the glass, he could see the sidewalk five stories below. The man was still there.

It was almost five when he went to tell his mother he had finished his school assignments. She was not there. He found her in her bedroom, sleeping. Since she had begun working the night shift at a convenience store—two weeks now—she took naps in the late afternoon.

For a while Willie stood on the threshold,[1] hoping his mother would wake up. When she didn't, he went to the front room and looked down on the street again. The begging man had not moved.

Willie returned to his mother's room.

"I'm going out," he announced softly.

Willie waited a decent interval[2] for his mother to waken. When she did not, Willie

---

1. **threshold** (thresh′ōld′) *n.:* entrance.
2. **interval** *n.:* period of time between two events.

---

made sure his keys were in his pocket. Then he left the apartment.

Standing just outside his door, he could keep his eyes on the man. It appeared as if he had still not moved. Willie wondered how anyone could go on without moving for so long in the chilly October air. Was staying in one place part of the man's sickness?

During the twenty minutes that Willie watched, no one who passed looked in the beggar's direction. Willie wondered if they even saw the man. Certainly no one put any money into his open hand.

A lady leading a dog by a leash went by. The dog strained in the direction of the man sitting on the crate. The dog's tail wagged. The lady pulled the dog away. "Heel!" she commanded.

The dog—tail between its legs—scampered to the lady's side. Even so, the dog twisted around to look back at the beggar.

Willie grinned. The dog had done exactly what he had done when his mother told him not to stare.

Pressing deep into his pocket, Willie found a nickel. It was warm and slippery. He wondered how much happiness you could rent for a nickel.

Squeezing the nickel between his fingers, Willie walked slowly toward the man. When he came before him, he stopped, suddenly nervous. The man, who appeared to be looking at the ground, did not move his eyes. He smelled bad.

"Here." Willie stretched forward and dropped the coin into the man's open right hand.

"Bless you," the man said hoarsely, as he folded his fingers over the coin. His eyes, like high beams on a car, flashed

---

DIFFERENTIATING INSTRUCTION

Advanced Learners

Acceleration. Use this activity to move advanced learners toward the eighth-grade Standard 3.6, which requires that they consider symbolism in interpreting a work.

Activity. Ask students to identify the symbols in the story and what each stands for. Then, have students discuss these questions:

- What themes do the symbols convey?
- Is the homeless man a symbol of a group in our society?
- How would you interpret Avi's message about the homeless?

up at Willie, then dropped.

Willie waited for a moment, then went back up to his room. From his front room he looked down on the street. He thought he saw the coin in the man's hand but was not sure.

After supper Mrs. Markham got ready to go to work. She kissed Willie good night. Then, as she did every night, she said, "If you have regular problems, call Mrs. Murphy downstairs. What's her number?"

"274–8676," Willie said.

"Extra bad problems, call Grandma."

"369–6754."

"Super-special problems, you can call me."

"962–6743."

"Emergency, the police."

"911."

"Don't let anyone in the door."

"I won't."

"No television past nine."

"I know."

"But you can read late."

"You're the one who's going to be late," Willie said.

"I'm leaving," Mrs. Markham said.

After she went, Willie stood for a long while in the hallway. The empty apartment felt like a cave that lay deep below the earth. That day in school Willie's teacher had told them about a kind of fish that lived in caves. These fish could not see. They had no eyes. The teacher had said it was living in the dark cave that made them like that.

Before he went to bed, Willie took another look out the window. In the pool of light cast by the street lamp, Willie saw the man.

On Tuesday morning when Willie went to school, the man was gone. But when he came home from school with his mother, he was there again.

"*Please* don't look at him," his mother whispered with some urgency.

During his snack Willie said, "Why shouldn't I look?"

"What are you talking about?"

"That man. On the street. Begging."

"I told you. He's sick. It's better to act as if you never saw them. When people are that way, they don't wish to be looked at."

"Why not?"

Mrs. Markham thought for a while. "People are ashamed of being unhappy."

"Are you sure he's unhappy?"

"You don't have to ask if people are unhappy. They tell you all the time."

"Is that part of the sickness?"

"Oh, Willie, I don't know. It's just the way they are."

Willie contemplated the half-inch slice of cake his mother had just given him. He said, "Ever since Dad left, you've been unhappy. Are you ashamed?"

Mrs. Markham closed her eyes. "I wish you wouldn't ask that."

Willie said, "Are you?"

"Willie . . ."

"Think he might come back?"

"It's more than likely," Mrs. Markham said, but Willie wondered if that was what she really thought. He did not think so. "Do you think Dad is unhappy?"

"Where do you get such questions?"

"They're in my mind."

"There's much in the mind that need not be paid attention to."

Vocabulary

urgency (ur′jən·sē) *n.:* pressure; insistence.

contemplated (kän′təm·plāt′id) *v.:* studied carefully.

What Do Fish Have to Do with Anything? **351**

A Reading Skills

Making inferences. To help students answer question 2, you might ask why Willie brings up the sightless fish at this point in the conversation. [Possible responses: When Willie's mother tries to make the situation go away by ignoring it, Willie is reminded of the fish that "live in caves" and "forget to see." Willie may realize that his mother is trying to shut her eyes to reality.]

[Possible responses to question 2: The fish might stand for people who are isolated or who stay in a very narrow routine. The lack of eyes might stand for people's lack of curiosity or "blindness" in not noticing what's around them. The darkness might stand for ignorance or fear or their lack of understanding.]

B Learners Having Difficulty

❓ **Questioning.** Who is the man referring to when he says, "A man has the right to remain silent"? [He may be referring either to himself or to Willie. Neither the man nor Willie wants to share his inner thoughts about unhappiness.]

C Vocabulary Development
REVIEW STANDARD

❓ **Identifying antonyms.** Antonyms are words that are opposites. What would be an antonym for the word *certain* as it is used here? [Possible responses: uncertain, doubtful, unsure.]

D Reading Skills

❓ **Making inferences.** What does the homeless man's answer suggest about his feelings? [It suggests that he really is unhappy and is ashamed or embarrassed to admit this to others.] Why is the man now more willing to talk to Willie? [because Willie is now willing to share something about his own feelings]

"Fish that live in caves have no eyes."

"What are you talking about?"

"My teacher said it's all that darkness. The fish forget to see. So they lose their eyes."

"I doubt she said that."

"She did."

"Willie, you have too much imagination."

After his mother went to work, Willie gazed down onto the street. The man was there. Willie thought of going down, but he knew he was not supposed to leave the building when his mother worked at night. He decided to speak to the man tomorrow.

Next afternoon—Wednesday—Willie said to the man, "I don't have any money. Can I still talk to you?"

The man's eyes focused on Willie. They were gray eyes with folds of dirty skin beneath them. He needed a shave.

"My mother said you were unhappy. Is that true?"

"Could be," the man said.

"What are you unhappy about?"

The man's eyes narrowed as he studied Willie intently. He said, "How come you want to know?"

Willie shrugged.

"I think you should go home, kid."

"I am home." Willie gestured toward the apartment. "I live right here. Fifth floor. Where do you live?"

"Around."

"*Are* you unhappy?" Willie persisted.

The man ran a tongue over his lips. His Adam's apple bobbed.

Willie said, "I'm trying to learn about unhappiness."

> **MAKING INFERENCES**
> 2. What might the fish stand for? What might the missing eyes and the darkness symbolize?

"Why?"

"I don't think I want to say."

"A man has the right to remain silent," the man said and closed his eyes.

Willie remained standing on the pavement for a while before walking back to his apartment. Once inside his own room, he looked down from the window. The man was still there. At one moment Willie was certain he was looking at the apartment building and the floor on which Willie lived.

The next day—Thursday—after dropping a nickel in the man's palm, Willie said, "I've decided to tell you why I want to learn about unhappiness."

The man gave a grunt.

"See, I've never seen anyone look so unhappy as you do. So I figure you must know a lot about it."

The man took a deep breath. "Well, yeah, maybe."

Willie said, "And I need to find a cure for it."

"A *what*?"

"A cure for unhappiness."

The man pursed his lips and blew a silent whistle. Then he said, "Why?"

"My mother is unhappy."

"Why's that?"

"My dad left."

"How come?"

"I don't know. But she's unhappy all the time. So if I found a cure for unhappiness, it would be a good thing, wouldn't it?"

"I suppose."

Willie said, "Would you like some cake?"

"What kind?"

Vocabulary
intently (in·tent'lē) *adv.:* with close attention.

DEVELOPING FLUENCY

This story contains scenes of important dialogue between Willie and his mother and between Willie and the homeless man. The dialogue moves the plot along and provides insights into the three characters.

Activity. Have students work in pairs reading portions of the dialogue aloud. First, students should look in the text for clues to the tone and phrasing the characters might use.

Then, they should practice speaking. Next, have students read the dialogue aloud for the class and be prepared to explain their interpretations.

PAIRED

"I don't know. Cake."

"Depends on the cake."

On Friday Willie said to the man, "I found out what kind of cake it is."

"Yeah?"

"Poundcake. But I don't know why it's called that."

"Probably doesn't matter."

For a moment neither said anything. Then Willie said, "In school my teacher said there are fish that live in caves and the caves are dark, so the fish don't have eyes. What do you think? Do you believe that?"

"Sure."

"You do? How come?"

"Because you said so."

"You mean, just because someone *said* it you believe it?"

"Not someone. You."

Willie said, "But, well, maybe it *isn't* true."

The man grunted.

"Hey, do you believe it?"

Willie nodded.

"Well, you're not just anyone. You got eyes. You see. You ain't no fish."

"Oh."

"What's your name?"

"Willie."

"That's a boy's name. What's your grown-up name?"

Willie thought for a moment. "William, I guess."

"And that means another thing."

"What?"

> 🐟 **MAKING INFERENCES**
>
> 3. What does the man mean when he tells Willie, "You ain't no fish"?

> 🐟 **MAKING INFERENCES**
>
> 4. Why does the man ask Willie what his "grown-up" name is?

"I'll take some of that cake."

Willie smiled. "You will?"

"Just said it, didn't I?"

"I'll get it."

Willie ran to the apartment. He took the box from the refrigerator as well as a knife, then hurried back down to the street. "I'll cut you a piece," he said.

As the man looked on, Willie opened the box, then held his thumb against the cake to make sure the portion was the right size. With a poke of the knife he made a small mark for the proper width.

Just as he was about to cut, the man said, "Hold it!"

Willie looked up. "What?"

"What were you doing with your thumb there?"

"I was measuring the right size. The right portion. One portion is what a person is supposed to get."

"Where'd you learn that?"

ⓔ Reading Skills

Making inferences. [Possible response to question 3: The man means that Willie is aware of the world around him. He notices, for example, the unhappiness of his mother, and he sees the homeless man as an individual who has value.]

ⓕ Reading Skills

Making inferences. [Possible response to question 4: The homeless man is treating Willie as if he were an adult. In the man's opinion, Willie is grown-up and mature.]

A Literary Focus
REVIEW STANDARD

? Character. What does Willie learn from the homeless man? [Possible responses: He learns to think for himself; he learns to be generous; he learns that each person is an individual and has his or her own needs— no one is average.]

B Advanced Learners

? Acceleration. The theme of a story is an idea about life that is revealed in the work. Encourage students to interpret the words of the homeless man and express them as a theme. What does the homeless man mean? What is his message or idea about life? [Possible responses: People are individuals with individual needs; having basic survival needs met is not enough; our needs can be psychological as well as physical; a person cannot always articulate what he or she needs.]

C Reading Skills

Making inferences. [Possible response to question 5: He gives the man both pieces of cake to show he understands that people need more than they usually will admit. The cake may symbolize what a person needs, such as goodness or sweetness or the generosity of another person.]

"It says so on the box. You can see for yourself." He held out the box.

The man studied the box, then handed it back to Willie. "That's just lies," he said.

"How do you know?"

"William, how can a box say how much a person needs?"

"But it does. The scientists say so. They measured, so they know. Then they put it there."

"Lies," the man repeated.

Willie studied the man. His eyes seemed bleary.[3] "Then how much should I cut?" he asked.

The man said, "You have to look at me, then at the cake, and then you're going to have to decide for yourself."

"Oh." Willie looked at the cake. The piece was about three inches wide. Willie looked up at the man. After a moment he cut the cake into two pieces, each an inch and a half wide. He gave one piece to the man and kept the other.

"Bless you," the man said, as he took the piece and laid it in his left hand. He began to break off pieces with his right hand and one by one put them into his mouth. Each piece was chewed thoughtfully. Willie watched him piece by piece.

When the man was done, he dusted his hands of crumbs.

"Now I'll give you something," the man said.

"What?" Willie said, surprised.

"The cure for unhappiness."

"You know it?" Willie asked, eyes wide.

The man nodded.

"What is it?"

---

3. **bleary** *adj.:* dim or blurred, as from lack of rest.

"It's this: What a person needs is always more than they say."

Willie thought for a while. "Who's *they*?" he asked.

The man pointed to the cake box. "The people on the box," he said.

Willie thought for a moment; then he gave the man the other piece of cake.

The man took it, saying, "Good man," and then ate it.

The next day was Saturday. Willie did not go to school. All morning he kept looking down from his window for the man, but it was raining and he did not appear. Willie wondered where he was but could not imagine it.

Willie's mother woke about noon. Willie sat with her while she ate the breakfast he had made. "I found the cure for unhappiness," he announced.

"Did you?" his mother said. She was reading a memo from the convenience store's owner.

"It's, 'What a person needs is always more than they say.'"

His mother put her papers down. "That's nonsense. Where did you hear that?"

"That man."

"What man?"

"On the street. The one who was begging. You said he was unhappy. So I asked him."

"Willie, I told you I didn't want you to even look at that man."

"He's a nice man . . ."

"How do you know?"

"I've talked to him."

"When? How much?"

Willie shrank down. "I did, that's all."

> **MAKING INFERENCES**
>
> 5. Why does Willie give the man both pieces of cake? What might the cake symbolize?

"Willie, I forbid you to talk to him. Do you understand me? Do you? Answer me!"

"Yes," Willie said, but in his mind he decided he would talk to the man one more time. He needed to explain why he could not talk to him anymore.

On Sunday, however, the man was not there. Nor was he there on Monday.

"That man is gone," Willie said to his mother as they walked home from school.

"I saw. I'm not blind."

"Where do you think he went?"

"I couldn't care less. And you might as well know, I arranged for him to be gone."

Willie stopped short. "What do you mean?"

"I called the police. We don't need a nuisance like that around here. Pestering kids."

"He wasn't pestering me."

"Of course he was."

"How do you know?"

"Willie, I have eyes. I can see."

Willie stared at his mother. "No, you can't. You're a fish. You live in a cave."

 MAKING INFERENCES

6. Is Willie being fair when he tells his mother that she's a fish living in a cave? Why or why not? **E**

"Willie, don't talk nonsense."

"My name isn't Willie. It's William." Turning, he walked back to the school playground. **F**

Mrs. Markham watched him go. "Fish," she wondered to herself; "what do fish have to do with anything?"

What Do Fish Have to Do with Anything?   **355**

D Reading Skills

? Speculating. Why do you think Mrs. Markham is so upset with Willie? [Possible responses: She is afraid that the homeless man will hurt Willie; she is angry that Willie disobeyed her; she does not like the idea that the homeless man has put into Willie's head.]

E Reading Skills

Making inferences. [Possible response to question 6: Willie is being fair—he compares his mother to a blind fish living in a cave because of her refusal to respect the homeless man as a human being, and the fish symbolizes her blindness.]

F Literary Focus
GRADE-LEVEL STANDARD

? Symbol. The boy turns away from his mother and calls himself William. What does the name stand for? [The name symbolizes his becoming more independent and adult, his facing life on his own.]

GUIDED PRACTICE

Monitoring students' progress. Have students answer the questions.

Short Answer

1. In the afternoon, Willie eats a snack of _____. [pound cake]

2. Willie's mother tells him not to talk to the _____. [homeless man]

3. Mrs. Markham works at a _____. [convenience store]

4. Mrs. Markham thinks _____ can cure unhappiness. [money]

5. The homeless man is taken away by the _____. [police]

FAMILY/COMMUNITY ACTIVITY

As a class, brainstorm a list of questions to ask family and community members about how they think the homeless are treated in the community. Be sensitive to the possibility that some students may have family members that are homeless or have been homeless themselves in the past. Students should take notes on the answers and do some research of their own about the facilities for the homeless in the area. Students may report their results to the class.

Background. Avi (pronounced "Ah-vee") says that when he visits schools, "I always ask to speak to the learning-disabled kids. They come in slowly, waiting for yet another pep talk. . . . Eyes cast down, they won't even look at me. . . . I don't say a thing. I lay out pages of my own copyedited manuscripts, which are covered with red marks. 'Look here,' I say, 'see that spelling mistake. There, another spelling mistake. Looks like I forgot to put a capital letter there. Oops! Letter reversal.' Their eyes lift. They are listening. And I am among friends."

For Independent Reading

For more about the trials of growing up, recommend *Nobody's Family Is Going to Change* by Louise Fitzhugh.

MEET THE WRITER

Avi

"Don't Be Satisfied with Answers Others Give You"

Avi (1937–   ) says he became a writer out of sheer stubbornness. In elementary school and high school, he failed many subjects, not knowing at the time that he had a serious learning disability. Still, he was determined to prove to everyone that he could write if he just set his mind to it. First he tried to write plays, then novels for adults, but he had little success. He didn't discover his true audience until he became a father and began taking an interest in writing for children and young adults.

> Only when my own kids came into my life did I start to write for young people. I was to find what I did best. Writing for kids has been at the center of my life ever since.

Avi offers the following advice to young people thinking of becoming writers:

> Listen and watch the world around you. Try to understand why things happen. Don't be satisfied with answers others give you. Don't assume that because everyone believes a thing, it is right *or* wrong. Reason things out for yourself. Work to get answers on your own.

For Independent Reading

Avi has written many novels about strong-willed young people making tough decisions in challenging or dangerous situations. These include *Wolf Rider: A Tale of Terror; Windcatcher;* and *The True Confessions of Charlotte Doyle,* a Newbery Honor Book and the winner of the Boston Globe–Horn Book Award for fiction in 1991 (this title is available in the HRW Library).

DIFFERENTIATING INSTRUCTION

Advanced Learners
Enrichment. Tell students that children are the fastest growing segment of homeless people. Although statistics on the homeless vary, at least 100,000 children in the United States are without shelter every day. That's enough children to fill all the seats in three football stadiums. Most of these children are under five years old.

Activity. Have students find out more about the problem of homeless children in this country. Suggest that they use the Internet for their research and that they be prepared to present their findings to the class.

Literary Response and Analysis

Reading Check

1. What does Willie do when Mrs. Markham tells him not to look at the homeless man?

2. Why does Mrs. Markham refuse to give the man money?

3. According to Willie's teacher, why did the fish in the cave lose their eyes?

4. What does Willie give the man?

5. What happens to the man at the end of the story?

Interpretations

6. Summarize the conversation Willie has with the homeless man about the right amount of cake to serve a person. What do you think the man is trying to say to Willie?

7. Look back at the statements you rated earlier. Where are they expressed in the story? How has reading the story affected the way you look at the statements? 🖉

8. Avi mentions the fish four times in this story. Why does he refer to them so frequently? What do the fish **symbolize,** or stand for, in the story? (Think about the **inferences** you made as you read the story.) 📚

9. Who says, "What do fish have to do with anything?" Explain why you think the quotation does or doesn't make a good title for this story. How does the title relate to the story's **theme**?

Evaluation

10. What do you think of the character of Mrs. Markham? What kind of person is she? Notice that both Willie and the homeless man seem wiser than Willie's mother. How do you feel about this? Is the writer being fair to Willie's mother? Explain your evaluations.

11. On page 356, Avi says, "Don't be satisfied with answers others give you. Don't assume that because everyone believes a thing, it is right or wrong. Reason things out for yourself. Work to get answers on your own." Evaluate these statements. Is Avi's advice good, or could it lead to trouble?

Listening and Speaking
Pros and Cons

In some cities, people can be arrested for begging on the street. Do you think this is fair? Why or why not? With a few classmates, hold a debate on these questions. First, come up with a statement that answers the questions. Then, form two teams: one to argue for and one to argue against the position expressed in the statement. Do research on the Internet with your team to find evidence supporting your point of view.

Reading Standard 3.7 Explain the effects of symbolism in fictional texts.

What Do Fish Have to Do with Anything?   **357**

Literary Response and Analysis

Interpretations

6. Willie says that the portion size is noted on the box, but the man says Willie should look at him and then decide the amount. The man tells Willie the cure for unhappiness: People always need more than they say. The man is telling Willie to think for himself and to treat each person as an individual.

7. Statement 1 can be found on p. 349, 2 and 3 on p. 350, and 4 on p. 351. Students are likely to have changed some of their opinions.

8. The blind fish symbolize people who close themselves off from reality. The fish contrast with Willie's own awareness of and openness to the world around him.

9. Willie's mother asks this at the end of the story. Possible response: It is a good title because it focuses on her inability to see the relationship between herself and the fish. The title emphasizes the theme that refusing to face reality keeps a person locked in unhappiness.

Evaluation

10. Mrs. Markham is serious, rigid, and unimaginative. Some students may say that Avi is fair because he also portrays her as a deeply unhappy person who is doing what she thinks is best to protect and care for her son. Others may say that Avi is unfair because the story is told from the viewpoint of a child who might not understand all of the reasons for his mother's behavior.

11. Possible answer: Avi's advice is good because it encourages aspiring writers to think creatively and independently.

Reading Check

1. Willie looks back over his shoulder at the man.

2. She says they have no money to spare.

3. The fish lost their eyes because they lived in a dark cave and didn't use them.

4. Twice, Willie gives the beggar a nickel; later, he gives the man two pieces of cake.

5. The police take him away.

Listening and Speaking

Students from rural and suburban areas may have little firsthand familiarity with the problem of homelessness. To help them form opinions on the subject, you might show photographs of homeless city people from news articles.

Vocabulary Development

Practice

1. vaguely
2. contemplated
3. intently
4. urgency

 Resources Reminder

Vocabulary and Spelling

- *Vocabulary Development*
  - Vocabulary Worksheet, p. 27
  - Cumulative Vocabulary Review, p. 28

Grammar Link

Practice

1. Possible answers: *Direct*— "What's the matter with him?" Willie asked. *Indirect*—Willie asked what was wrong with him. *Direct*—Willie said, "Can I have a bigger piece of cake?" *Indirect*—Willie asked for a bigger piece of cake. *Direct*—"Are you unhappy?" Willie persisted. *Indirect*—Willie kept asking the man if he was unhappy.

2. That day in school, Willie's teacher had said, "There is a kind of fish that lives in caves. These fish cannot see. They have no eyes. Living in a dark cave has made them like that."

 ASSESSING

Assessment

- *Progress Assessment of Reading*
  - Selection Test, p. 118

 RETEACHING

For a lesson reteaching symbolism, see **Reteaching**, p. 489N.

Vocabulary Development

Grade 5
Review
Reading
Standard 1.3
Understand and explain antonyms.

Identifying Antonyms

Antonyms are words with opposite meanings. *Hot* and *cold* are antonyms; so are *kind* and *cruel, generous* and *selfish, wisely* and *foolishly.* Thinking of a word's antonyms can sometimes help you pinpoint its meaning.

PRACTICE

Complete each of the following sentences with the word from the Word Bank that is the antonym of the underlined word.

1. Someone who speaks clearly is not speaking _____.
2. Someone who ignored an issue would be the opposite of someone who _____ it.
3. If you spoke carelessly or lightly about your plans, you would be the opposite of someone who spoke _____ about them.
4. The opposite of *indifference* or *unconcern* is _____.

Word Bank

vaguely
urgency
contemplated
intently

Grammar Link MINI-LESSON

Direct and Indirect Quotations

In the story, Willie has several conversations with his mother and with the homeless man. The exact words of those talks, called **direct quotations,** are put in quotation marks.

> Willie said, "Would you like some cake?"

Sometimes, instead of quoting someone's exact words, Avi summarizes what the person said. These summaries, called **indirect quotations,** are not placed in quotation marks.

> That day in school Willie's teacher had told them about a kind of fish that lived in caves. These fish could not see. They had no eyes. The teacher had said it was living in the dark cave that made them like that.

PRACTICE

1. Find three direct quotations in the story, and rewrite them as indirect quotations.

2. Look at the indirect quotation at the left. Rewrite it as a direct quotation, using the exact words Willie's teacher might have used. Remember to put her words in quotation marks.

For more help, see Quotation Marks in the *Holt Handbook,* pages 292–299.

358 Chapter 6 Looking at Texts: Uses of the Imagination

Getting Leftovers Back on the Table

Making Assertions About a Text

An **assertion** is a statement or claim. **Citations** are items of evidence used to back up an assertion. Making assertions about a text is easy if you follow these steps:

- Think about the facts presented in the text.
- Put the information together, and think about what it all means.
- Use evidence from the text to make an assertion.
- Evaluate your assertion by asking yourself how well evidence from the text supports it.

The article you're about to read tells what a Florida student named David Levitt did to fight hunger. After you read the article, make a graphic organizer like the one below, showing your assertions about the text and the citations you used to support them.

"Getting Leftovers Back on the Table"

Citation
Twenty percent of the food produced in the United States goes to waste.

Citation
Millions of Americans go to sleep hungry.

Assertion
David Levitt was troubled by two big problems.

Reading Standard 2.7 Make reasonable assertions about a text through accurate supporting citations.

Prerequisite Standard

- Grade 5, Reading Comprehension 2.4 **Draw inferences, conclusions, or generalizations about text and support them with textual evidence and prior knowledge.**

Summary ⬌ *at grade level*

In many cafeterias, supermarkets, bakeries, and restaurants, leftover food is thrown out. About twenty percent of the nation's food is wasted while millions of people go hungry. In Florida, a sixth-grader named David Levitt crusaded against such waste. He suggested donating leftovers from his school cafeteria to the homeless, but the idea was rejected because of school rules. David persisted and found a way to satisfy the school's requirements. He also persuaded manufacturers to provide the food containers they needed to meet the state's health regulations. After two years of work, his program provided needy people with 250,000 pounds of food. David was honored at the White House for his efforts.

PRETEACHING

Standards Starter

Build prerequisite skills.
Remind students that an assertion is a claim or a statement and that a citation backs up or supports an assertion. You may wish to offer an example of a citation and ask volunteers for an assertion that the citation could support. [Example: *Citation*—A German shepherd leads rescue workers to a person buried alive under the debris of an earthquake. *Possible assertion*—A dog is a person's best friend.]

RESOURCES

Planning
- *One-Stop Planner* CD-ROM with Test Generator
- *On Course: Mapping Instruction*

Media
- *Audio CD Library*
  - disc 8

Reading
- *Interactive Reading*
  - Graphic Organizer: Assertion Web, p. 233

Differentiating Instruction
- *Lesson Plans for Language Development*
  - English-Language Learners, pp. 159, 168, 171
  - Special Education Students, pp. 159, 168, 171

Assessment
- *Progress Assessment of Reading*
  - Selection Test, p. 121
- *One-Stop Planner* CD-ROM with Test Generator

DIRECT TEACHING

▶ Resources Reminder

Media
- *Audio CD Library*
  - disc 8

Ⓐ Reading Informational Materials
GRADE-LEVEL STANDARD

❓ Making and supporting assertions. What evidence backs up the assertion that a lot of food is wasted? [Evidence includes the fact that every day giant bins fill with discarded food and the statistic that twenty percent of the nation's food is wasted.]

Ⓑ Reading Informational Materials
GRADE-LEVEL STANDARD

❓ Making and supporting assertions. What fact mentioned here would support an assertion that the problem of wasted food can be solved? [A successful program was carried out in Kentucky.]

Ⓒ Reading Informational Materials
GRADE-LEVEL STANDARD

❓ Making and supporting assertions. At this point, what evidence in the article would support an assertion that the problem is not a simple one? [After overcoming one obstacle, David was faced with another: the state health department rules.]

Getting Leftovers Back on the Table

Ⓐ When you're standing in line in the school cafeteria, do you ever wonder what happens to all the food that doesn't get served? Every day, giant bins behind the cafeterias—and supermarkets, restaurants, and bakeries—fill up with discarded food. As much as 20 percent of the food produced in the United States goes to waste. Yet every night millions of Americans go to sleep hungry.

Too big a problem for one kid to tackle? A sixth-grader named David Levitt didn't think so. He started small, in the halls of his own Florida middle school. By the time he was in his first year of high school, his crusade against hunger had taken him all the way to the White House.

Getting Started

David's journey began the day he noticed how much food was thrown out in his school cafeteria. He stopped the principal in the hallway and asked why the school couldn't donate leftover lunches to local homeless shelters and soup kitchens.

The principal told him that several parents had had the same idea. School rules prohibited serving the same food twice, however, so uneaten lunches had to be thrown away.

Overcoming Odds

Ⓑ David wasn't discouraged. He did research on a group in Kentucky that picked up leftovers from restaurants and donated them to charities. He used what he learned to draw up a plan for his own program.

Then he presented it at a meeting of the county school board. The board approved David's plan—not just for his school, but for all ninety-two schools in the county. "It just took a kid to make them see this matters," David says.

Solving New Problems

Ⓒ The battle wasn't over yet. Conditions set by the state department of health had to be met. For example, donated food had to be packed in special containers—which the schools didn't have the money to buy. So David wrote to manufacturers and asked for donations. Soon cases of the containers arrived at his doorstep, and David, now in seventh grade, was able to make his first delivery to a local food bank. "That," he says, "was satisfaction."

Success at Last

David went on to enlist the support of restaurants, supermarkets, and caterers. After two years his program had brought a quarter of a million pounds of food to hungry people in his area. By the time he started high school, David and his older sister were at work on a proposal to be presented to their state legislature. Under the plan similar programs would be set up to bring leftover food to hungry people all over Florida.

That spring, David went to Washington, D.C., to receive an award for his efforts. As the First Lady presented him with his medal, he asked her, "What do you do with the White House leftovers?"

—by Mara Rockliff

DIFFERENTIATING INSTRUCTION

Learners Having Difficulty
Some students may be put off by the idea that citations are often facts and statistics. To reassure them, point out that the statistics and facts in the article are a way to represent what they can easily see for themselves—some people waste food; others do not get enough. As students read the article, have them pause at factual or statistical citations. Encourage them to relate the facts cited to what they themselves have observed or learned about.

English-Language Learners
The article offers an opportunity to explain compound words to students and help them see how these words are formed from two smaller words. You may wish to point out and analyze these words from the article: *leftover, supermarkets, overflow, nationwide, hallway, homeless,* *doorstep.* Encourage students to look for and list other compound words that they encounter in their reading.

▶ Resources Reminder

For lessons designed for intermediate and advanced English language learners, see *Lesson Plans for Language Development,* pp. 159, 168, 171.

Reading Informational Materials

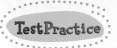
Reading Check

1. What plan did David present to the school board?

2. Describe two problems David faced in putting his plan into effect.

3. What did David ask the First Lady when she gave him his medal?

4. Make two or three **assertions** about the information in this text. Fill out a graphic organizer like the one on page 359 for each assertion.

Reading Informational Materials

Test Practice

Answers and Model Rationales

1. **B** Students should realize that B is the only option that reflects an assertion supported by the article. D is incorrect since researching did help David with his plan. A and C may be true statements, but they are not supported in the article.

2. **J** J may be a true statement, but it is not a fact in the article. The facts in F, G, and H are all found in the article.

3. **A** There is no information in the article about whether things go easily for David or about his popularity or grades (B, C, and D). Only A—that he does not give up—is supported.

4. **J** All answers are true except J. David worked on a proposal for the Florida state legislature, not Congress.

Test-Taking Tips

Remind students to read each question carefully and be alert for any words such as *not* and *except* (questions 2 and 4) that change the nature of the question.

For more information on how to answer multiple-choice questions, refer students to **Test Smarts,** p. 690.

Test Practice

Getting Leftovers Back on the Table

1. The information in this article supports the **assertion** that —
   A   it is impossible to solve the problem of hunger
   B   one person can make a big difference
   C   it is difficult to persuade a school board to take action
   D   researching other programs won't help you plan your own

2. Which of the following **facts** is *not* mentioned in the article?
   F   Twenty percent of food produced in the United States goes to waste.
   G   Millions of Americans go to sleep hungry.
   H   The Florida state health department has established rules for donating food.
   J   In some countries, hunger is an even bigger problem than in the United States.

3. We can reasonably **assert** that —
   A   David Levitt isn't easily discouraged
   B   things always go easy for David Levitt
   C   David Levitt is popular at school
   D   David Levitt gets good grades

4. After David's plan was approved by the school board, he did all of the following things *except* —
   F   persuade manufacturers to donate containers
   G   learn how to donate food in accordance with the state health department's guidelines
   H   ask restaurants and supermarkets for help
   J   send a proposal to Congress

Reading Standard 2.7 Make reasonable assertions about a text through accurate supporting citations.

Reading Check

1. David presented a plan about donating leftovers from the school cafeteria to charities.

2. School rules did not allow serving the same food twice. State health rules required that certain containers be used.

3. David asked what she did with leftovers at the White House.

4. Possible answers: *Assertion*—Many hungry people could be fed if food were not wasted. *Citations*—Restaurants, cafeterias, and bakeries throw away food every day. Twenty percent of the nation's food is wasted. *Assertion*—David's persistence solved the problem. *Citations*—After the principal rejected the idea, David researched and presented a plan that the school board approved. When the state required containers that the school could not afford, David got donations from manufacturers.

Vocabulary Development

Practice 1
Possible Answers

1. slender, slight, slim, thin

2. plump, portly, robust, rounded, sturdy, voluptuous, well-fed

3. antique, experienced, mature, senior

4. aromatic, fragrant, perfumed, redolent, scented, spicy

5. bargain, inexpensive, reasonable, reduced

Practice 2
Possible Answers

1. money, jewels, shine, yellow, metal

2. grass, fresh, health, dollars, emerald, spring

3. animal, power, dog ancestor, fierceness, hunter

4. wool, mildness, warmth, softness, young

5. constitution, rules, campaign, lawmaker, government

6. charity, good, service, willingness, helpfulness

 Resources Reminder

Differentiating Instruction

- *Lesson Plans for Language Development*
  - Vocabulary, p. 171

 ASSESSING

Assessment

- *Progress Assessment of Reading*
  - Selection Test, p. 121

 RETEACHING

For a lesson reteaching how citations support assertions, see **Reteaching,** p. 489F.

Vocabulary Development

Connotations and Denotations: Shades of Meaning

Why do we call the president's wife the *First Lady* instead of the *First Woman*? *Woman* and *lady* have similar **denotations,** or dictionary meanings, but different connotations.

Connotations are the feelings and ideas that have become attached to certain words. Both *woman* and *lady* refer to a female adult, but *lady* suggests one who is in a high position (as in *First Lady*) or one who is refined and well-mannered.

A word's connotations can be positive or negative. A word with positive connotations calls up good associations; a word with negative connotations calls up bad associations.

"I am careful; you are thrifty; he is stingy": This old saying shows how words with related meanings can have very different connotations.

PRACTICE 1

Listed below are five words with negative connotations. For each one, think of another word with the same general meaning but with more positive connotations. You may want to use a dictionary or a thesaurus.

1. scrawny 3. old 5. cheap
2. fat 4. smelly

PRACTICE 2

Reading Standard 1.5 Understand and explain shades of meaning in related words.

Usually people agree on a word's **connotations,** but sometimes words suggest different things to different people. Look at the six words listed below. Name at least two things you associate with each word. Then, compare your list with your classmates' lists. Which do you agree on? Which do you disagree on?

1. gold 3. wolf 5. politician
2. green 4. lamb 6. volunteer

Eleven

Literary Focus
Imagery:
It Appeals to Your Senses
Imagery is language that appeals to the senses: sight, hearing, smell, taste, and touch. Writers use images to create pictures of things they've experienced or imagined. They search for just the right words to create the same pictures in our minds. In "Eleven," Sandra Cisneros creates an image of a red sweater that is hard to forget.

Reading Skills
Making Inferences
An **inference** is a kind of guess. When you **make inferences** as you read, you look for clues; then you guess what will happen next and what it all means. You base your inferences on your own experiences and combine that information with clues you find in the story. See what inferences you make as you read this story. (This is one guessing game you can't lose, since you're an expert at being eleven.)

Make the Connection
We all have different opinions about what is embarrassing. With a group, make a list of embarrassing situations you've faced, seen on television, or read about in a story. Then, rank each situation on a scale from 1 to 4, 1 being slightly embarrassing and 4 being "crawl under a rock" embarrassing.

Quickwrite 🖉
Jot down answers to the following questions:
- What do you do when you're embarrassed?
- Have you ever seen anybody get embarrassed in front of a group of people?

Reading Standard 3.7 Explain the effects of imagery in fictional texts.

Eleven **363**

STANDARDS FOCUS, pp. 363–369

(For grade-level and review standards taught in this selection, see citations on Pupil's Edition pages.)

Prerequisite Standard
■ Grade 5, Literary Response and Analysis 3.5 **Describe the function and effect of common literary devices (e.g., imagery, metaphor, symbolism).**

Standard Coming Up in the Next Grade Levels
■ Grade 8, Literary Response and Analysis 3.6 **Identify significant literary devices (e.g., metaphor, symbolism, dialect, irony) that define a writer's style, and use those elements to interpret the work.**

Reading Skills
■ Make inferences.

Summary ⟷ *at grade level*

This realistic, first-person story is told by a girl named Rachel on her eleventh birthday. It's a confusing time for Rachel, and the day grows worse when her teacher, Mrs. Price, insists that an ugly red sweater she has found belongs to Rachel. Although Rachel protests, Mrs. Price insists that Rachel wear the sweater. In agony, Rachel puts on the hated sweater and begins weeping. Soon, another girl remembers that the sweater is hers. Although Mrs. Price tries to gloss over the incident, Rachel feels her birthday has been spoiled by the injustice.

▶ Resources Reminder

Media
■ *Audio CD Library*
  ■ disc 8
■ *Fine Art Transparencies*
  ■ Transparency 12

RESOURCES

Reading
■ *Interactive Reading*
  ■ Graphic Organizer: Imagery Grid, p. 234
Differentiating Instruction
■ *Lesson Plans for Language Development*
  ■ English-Language Learners, pp. 160–162, 169, 172

■ Special Education Students, pp. 163, 169, 172
Assessment
■ *Progress Assessment*, Part 1
  ■ Selection Test, p. 123
■ *One-Stop Planner* CD-ROM with Test Generator

Build prerequisite skills. Tell students that this story is told from the first-person point of view, and elicit from them that a first-person narrator is a character who refers to himself or herself as *I*. Explain that in this story they will "hear" the thoughts of a girl and learn a great deal about her feelings.

DIRECT TEACHING

Ⓐ Reading Skills

❓ Making inferences. Ask students to find a clue in the narrator's words that helps them understand how she feels about turning eleven. [Possible response: "You feel like you're still ten."] **What feelings might her words reflect?** [Possible response: She is worried about her approaching birthday and about maturing; she is concerned that she won't feel older or be able to handle life better.]

Ⓑ Literary Focus
GRADE-LEVEL STANDARD

Imagery. Remind students that images can capture the emotions we feel by appealing to one or more of our senses. The images here create pictures that describe Rachel's complex feelings about what growing older is like.

Eleven

Sandra Cisneros

Ⓐ What they don't understand about birthdays and what they never tell you is that when you're eleven, you're also ten, and nine, and eight, and seven, and six, and five, and four, and three, and two, and one. And when you wake up on your eleventh birthday you expect to feel eleven, but you don't. You open your eyes and everything's just like yesterday, only it's today. And you don't feel eleven at all. You feel like you're still ten. And you are—underneath the year that makes you eleven.

Like some days you might say something stupid, and that's the part of you that's still ten. Or maybe some days you might need to sit on your mama's lap because you're scared, and that's the part of you that's five. And maybe one day when you're all grown up maybe you will need to cry like if you're three, and that's okay. That's what I tell Mama when she's sad and needs to cry. Maybe she's feeling three.

Ⓑ Because the way you grow old is kind of like an onion or like the rings inside a tree trunk or like my little wooden dolls that fit one inside the other, each year inside the next one. That's how being eleven years old is.

You don't feel eleven. Not right away. It takes a few days, weeks even, sometimes even months before you say Eleven when they ask you. And you don't feel smart eleven, not until you're almost twelve. That's the way it is.

Only today I wish I didn't have only eleven years rattling inside me like pennies in a tin Band-Aid box. Today I wish I was one hundred and two instead of eleven because if I was one hundred and two I'd have known what to say when Mrs. Price put the red sweater on my desk. I would've known how to tell her it wasn't mine instead of just sitting there with that look on my face and nothing coming out of my mouth.

"Whose is this?" Mrs. Price says, and she holds the red sweater up in the air for all the class to see. "Whose? It's been sitting in the coatroom for a month."

"Not mine," says everybody. "Not me."

"It has to belong to somebody," Mrs. Price keeps saying, but nobody can remember. It's an ugly sweater with red plastic buttons and

DIFFERENTIATING INSTRUCTION

Learners Having Difficulty
Modeling. To help students read "Eleven," model the reading skill of making inferences. Read the story aloud through the first sentence of the fifth paragraph. Then, say: "Rachel is describing how she feels inside: her eleven years are like pennies rattling around in a tin box. From my experience I can imagine the sound of those pennies as being tinny and hollow.

That gives me a clue that, inside, Rachel feels empty and inadequate." Encourage students as they read to ask themselves: "How can I relate this clue in the story to my own experience?"

English-Language Learners
As students read, have them create a word map of the narrator by surrounding the word *Rachel* with words that describe her.

▶ Resources Reminder

For lessons designed for intermediate and advanced English-language learners, see *Lesson Plans for Language Development*, pp. 160–162, 169, 172.

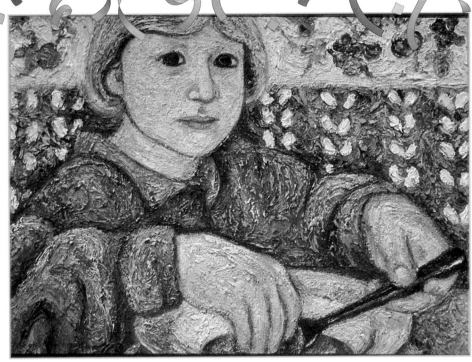

Girl Seated at Table by Rosa Ibarra.

a collar and sleeves all stretched out like you could use it for a jump-rope. It's maybe a thousand years old and even if it belonged to me I wouldn't say so.

Maybe because I'm skinny, maybe because she doesn't like me, that stupid Sylvia Saldívar says, "I think it belongs to Rachel." An ugly sweater like that, all raggedy and old, but Mrs. Price believes her. Mrs. Price takes the sweater and puts it right on my desk, but when I open my mouth nothing comes out.

"That's not, I don't, you're not . . . Not mine," I finally say in a little voice that was maybe me when I was four.

"Of course it's yours," Mrs. Price says.

"I remember you wearing it once." Because she's older and the teacher, she's right and I'm not.

Not mine, not mine, not mine, but Mrs. Price is already turning to page thirty-two, and math problem number four. I don't know why but all of a sudden I'm feeling sick inside, like the part of me that's three wants to come out of my eyes, only I squeeze them shut tight and bite down on my teeth real hard and try to remember today I am eleven, eleven. Mama is making a cake for me for tonight, and when Papa comes home everybody will sing Happy birthday, happy birthday to you.

Eleven   365

VIEWING THE ART

The Puerto Rican artist **Rosa Ibarra** often uses her children as models. Her paintings concentrate on the human figure and employ strong colors. Ibarra uses a style called impasto, in which the paint is applied to the canvas in thick layers, producing an almost sculptural effect.

Activity. Ask students to point out similarities and differences between the girl in the painting and Rachel in the story. [Possible responses: They are similar in age and in their quietness. Rachel seems less confident and more fearful than does the girl in the painting.]

C Literary Focus
GRADE-LEVEL STANDARD
❷ **Imagery.** How do the images here help you "see" the sweater as Rachel sees it? [They describe the color and shape and plastic buttons; they exaggerate its age ("maybe a thousand years old") and condition ("all stretched out," "you could use it for a jump-rope") to help readers understand how old and decrepit the sweater seems to Rachel.]

D Reading Skills
❷ **Making inferences.** Why doesn't Rachel assert herself and refuse to accept the sweater? [Possible responses: She is frightened of Mrs. Price; she doesn't think that she has the right to contradict a teacher or person in authority; she doesn't want to make a fool of herself in front of the class.]

Special Education Students
For lessons designed for special education students, see *Lesson Plans for Language Development*, pp. 163, 169, 172.

Advanced Learners
Acceleration. Use the following activity to move advanced learners toward the eighth-grade Standard 3.6, for which they interpret symbols.

Activity. Have students interpret the symbolic meaning of the red sweater by discussing questions like these: How would you describe the red sweater? How is it the opposite of what Rachel might want for her birthday? How does Rachel feel when she is forced to wear it? What does the sweater symbolize?

Eleven   365

DIRECT TEACHING

A Learners Having Difficulty

❓ Drawing conclusions. How can you tell that Rachel doesn't want to come into contact with the sweater? [She moves it with her ruler so she won't have to touch it. She moves her things and chair away from it.]

B Advanced Learners

❓ Acceleration. What do you think putting on the red sweater means to Rachel? [Possible response: It means that she is taking on the identity of the despised, ugly, old, discarded, worthless sweater.]

C Reading Skills

❓ Making inferences. Why does Rachel wish she were invisible? [Possible responses: She wants to escape Mrs. Price's insensitive treatment; she is embarrassed to be seen crying.]

D Literary Focus
GRADE-LEVEL STANDARD

❓ Imagery. How does the image of the vanishing balloon help you understand Rachel's feelings? [Possible response: It helps readers understand how far from this experience Rachel wishes she were and thus how painful it is for her.]

A But when the sick feeling goes away and I open my eyes, the red sweater's still sitting there like a big red mountain. I move the red sweater to the corner of my desk with my ruler. I move my pencil and books and eraser as far from it as possible. I even move my chair a little to the right. Not mine, not mine, not mine.

In my head I'm thinking how long till lunchtime, how long till I can take the red sweater and throw it over the schoolyard fence, or leave it hanging on a parking meter, or bunch it up into a little ball and toss it in the alley. Except when math period ends Mrs. Price says loud and in front of everybody, "Now, Rachel, that's enough," because she sees I've shoved the red sweater to the tippy-tip corner of my desk and it's hanging all over the edge like a waterfall, but I don't care.

"Rachel," Mrs. Price says. She says it like she's getting mad. "You put that sweater on right now and no more nonsense."

"But it's not—"

"Now!" Mrs. Price says.

B This is when I wish I wasn't eleven, because all the years inside of me—ten, nine, eight, seven, six, five, four, three, two, and one—are pushing at the back of my eyes when I put one arm through one sleeve of the sweater that smells like cottage cheese, and then the other arm through the other and stand there with my arms apart like if the sweater hurts me and it does, all itchy and full of germs that aren't even mine.

C That's when everything I've been holding in since this morning, since when Mrs. Price put the sweater on my desk, finally lets go, and all of a sudden I'm crying in front of everybody. I wish I was invisible but I'm not. I'm eleven and it's my birthday today and I'm crying like I'm three in front of everybody. I put my head down on the desk and bury my face in my stupid clown-sweater arms. My face all hot and spit coming out of my mouth because I can't stop the little animal noises from coming out of me, until there aren't any more tears left in my eyes, and it's just my body shaking like when you have the hiccups and my whole head hurts like when you drink milk too fast.

But the worst part is right before the bell rings for lunch. That stupid Phyllis Lopez, who is even dumber than Sylvia Saldívar, says she remembers the red sweater is hers! I take it off right away and give it to her, only Mrs. Price pretends like everything's okay.

Today I'm eleven. There's a cake Mama's making for tonight, and when Papa comes home from work we'll eat it. There'll be candles and presents and everybody will sing Happy birthday, happy birthday to you, Rachel, only it's too late.

D I'm eleven today. I'm eleven, ten, nine, eight, seven, six, five, four, three, two, and one, but I wish I was one hundred and two. I wish I was anything but eleven, because I want today to be far away already, far away like a runaway balloon, like a tiny *o* in the sky, so tiny-tiny you have to close your eyes to see it.

Developing Word-Attack Skills
Remind students that in many words the letters *ea* stand for long *e*. Share some examples of words with *ea* for a long *e*, and invite students to suggest others. Write all the words on the chalkboard. Then, write these sentences on the board:
  I love to read.
  I have read every book on this shelf.
Have students read the sentences and com-

pare the pronunciations of *read*. Help them recognize that in the first sentence, the present-tense *read* has the long *e* sound; in the second sentence, the past-tense *read* has the short *e* sound. Point out that although *ea* most often stands for long *e*, in some words it stands for short *e*.
Activity. Display these sentences. Have volunteers underline the words with *ea* and tell if the letters stand for long *e* or short *e*.

1. No one wanted the <u>dreadful</u> <u>sweater</u>. [short *e*]
2. It wasn't <u>clean</u> and <u>neat</u>. [long *e*]
3. I would not <u>reach</u> for it in cold <u>weather</u>. [long *e*; short *e*]
4. I would rather get a <u>head</u> cold <u>instead</u>. [short *e*]
5. And I care about my <u>health</u>! [short *e*]

Sandra Cisneros

"Inside I'm Eleven"

Sandra Cisneros (1954–   ) was born in Chicago and grew up speaking Spanish and English. Although she sometimes had a hard time in school, she eventually became a teacher and a highly acclaimed writer. Her childhood experiences, her family, and her Mexican American heritage all find a place in her writing.

In much of her writing, Cisneros explores the feeling of being shy and out of place.

> What would my teachers say if they knew I was a writer? Who would've guessed it? I wasn't a very bright student. I didn't much like school because we moved so much and I was always new and funny-looking. . . . At home I was fine, but at school I never opened my mouth except when the teacher called on me, the first time I'd speak all day.
>
> When I think how I see myself, I would have to be at age eleven. I know I'm older on the outside, but inside I'm eleven. I'm the girl in the picture with skinny arms and a crumpled shirt and crooked hair. I didn't like school because all they saw was the outside of me.

For Independent Reading

Another memorable Cisneros character narrates the novel *The House on Mango Street*. Esperanza is a young girl who wishes for a lot of things in her life, including a new name: Zeze the X.

Eleven 367

DIFFERENTIATING INSTRUCTION

Advanced Learners

Tell students that Sandra Cisneros often writes vignettes. Explain that vignettes are brief sketches or portraits that focus on one person or one day or even one moment in the life of a character.

Enrichment. Have students find vignettes written by Cisneros to read aloud to the class.

GUIDED PRACTICE

Monitoring students' progress. Guide the class in answering these questions.

Short Answer

1. The story takes place on Rachel's _____ birthday. [eleventh]
2. The color of the sweater is _____. [red]
3. Rachel hates the sweater because it is _____. [old and ugly]
4. Mrs. Price thinks that the sweater belongs to _____. [Rachel]
5. The sweater really belongs to _____. [Phyllis Lopez]

Meet the Writer

Background. Sandra Cisneros says that she didn't have a "normal" childhood. She explains that her idea of what was "normal" came from the images projected from a television set in the 1960s—images from popular situation comedies like *Ozzie and Harriet* and *Father Knows Best,* in which the families lived in big houses with lawns and picket fences. Her family moved often from Mexico City to Chicago and back again, and Cisneros didn't have the time to settle in one place before it was time to move again. In addition to the frequent moves, Cisneros felt lonely because she had six brothers but no sisters. As a result, she sought refuge in books.

▶ Resources Reminder

Reading

■ *Interactive Reading*

For another selection by Sandra Cisneros, see "Three Wise Guys" in *Interactive Reading,* p. 236. You may want to assign this to advanced learners.

Literary Response and Analysis

Reading Check

1. She has just turned eleven. She wants to be 102 because then she'd know what to say to Mrs. Price.
2. A girl named Sylvia says that the sweater belongs to Rachel. Mrs. Price believes her and forces Rachel to take the sweater. Rachel is humiliated. Mrs. Price makes Rachel put the sweater on, and Rachel begins to cry. Later, someone else claims the sweater. Mrs. Price does not apologize.

Interpretations

3. Rachel means that we often still feel the way we did when we were younger. She means we are the sum of our experiences.
4. Mrs. Price assumes that Rachel would own an ugly red sweater and not admit it.
5. Students can infer that Rachel is sensitive and cannot overcome her feelings about this unpleasant incident. The humiliation has ruined her birthday.
6. Some students would feel bad for Rachel; some might think she is overreacting or not understand why she is upset. Some students might say they would have told the teacher that she had hurt Rachel's feelings or they would have tried to comfort Rachel; others might say they would have done nothing because it was not their place to intercede or because they would not risk angering Mrs. Price.
7. Some students might have refused to put the sweater on; others might have asked friends for help in revealing the truth. Be sure students understand that when Rachel puts on the despised sweater she is revealing that she feels three years old; she sees the teacher as older and

Literary Response and Analysis

Reading Check

1. How old is Rachel in this story? Why does she say she wants to be 102?
2. Briefly describe what happens to Rachel after Mrs. Price asks, "Whose is this?"

Interpretations

3. Rachel says that "when you're eleven, you're also ten, and nine," and so on (page 364). What does she mean?
4. What assumptions does Mrs. Price seem to make about Rachel?
5. At the end of the story, Rachel says that "everybody will sing Happy birthday, . . . only it's too late" (page 366). What **inference** can you make about her from this statement?
6. How did you react to the scene in which Rachel begins to cry in class (page 366)? If you were in her class, would you have done anything? Why or why not?
7. If you were Rachel, what would you have done when Mrs. Price said, "You put that sweater on right now"? Be sure to look back at the notes you made for the Quickwrite on page 363.
8. Find the **images** and **metaphors** that Cisneros uses to describe getting older—rings in a tree trunk, layers of an onion, pennies in a box, wooden dolls fitting inside one another. Which do you think are the most interesting or accurate descriptions

Reading Standard 3.7 Explain the effects of imagery in fictional texts.

of growing up? Do you think any of these images are not effective?

9. List all the **images** in the story that help you see—and even smell and feel—the hated red sweater. Did Cisneros succeed in making the sweater seem *real*? Why or why not?
10. Cisneros uses **imagery** to create word pictures that appeal to one or more of our five senses. Here's one example: "My face all hot and spit coming out of my mouth because I can't stop the little animal noises from coming out of me." It's a striking image that appeals to our senses of sight, touch, taste, and hearing. Find another example of an image in the story that appeals to two or more senses. Which image makes the strongest impression on you?

Writing
It All Depends on Your Point of View

"Eleven" is told from the **first-person point of view,** with Rachel as the narrator. She uses the words *I, me,* and *mine* as she describes her humiliating experience with the red sweater. What might Mrs. Price say about the incident if she, rather than Rachel, were the narrator? How might another student in the class describe it? Rewrite the story, using a different first-person narrator. Try to include **images** in your retelling. Is the red sweater as ugly as Rachel thinks it is?

therefore powerful; she is shy and has little self-esteem.

8. The images are in paragraphs 3–5. Possible answers: The nesting dolls image is effective because a doll is an image of a person; the images of tree rings and an onion are compelling because they suggest layers of experience hidden from the outside world.
9. Images include: "an ugly sweater with red plastic buttons"; "sleeves all

stretched out like you could use it for a jump-rope"; "maybe a thousand years old"; "smells like cottage cheese"; "all itchy and full of germs"; "clown-sweater arms." Cisneros's detailed sensory imagery makes the sweater seem vividly real.

10. Possible answers: "rattling inside me like pennies in a tin Band-Aid box" (sight, sound); "the part of me that's three wants to come out of my eyes, only I squeeze them shut tight" (sight, touch).

Vocabulary Development

Reading Standard 1.5
Understand and explain shades of meaning in related words.

Connotations: Words Are Loaded with Feelings

A word's **connotations** are the feelings and associations that have come to be attached to the word. For example, Rachel calls the red sweater "ugly." Someone who didn't hate the sweater so much might just say it was "unattractive" or "plain." *Ugly* is a strong word with extremely negative connotations.

PRACTICE

Think about *skinny,* a word Rachel uses to describe herself. The words in the box at the right mean more or less the same thing as *skinny.* Which words have positive connotations? Which have negative connotations? Put the words in order, starting with the one whose connotations seem the most negative and ending with the one whose connotations seem the most positive.

> slim
> slender
> bony
> scrawny
> lean

Grammar Link MINI-LESSON

Punctuating Dialogue

Follow these tips when you write dialogue:

- Put quotation marks before and after a **direct quotation**— a person's exact words.

    "Whose is this?" said Mrs. Price.

- A **speaker tag** is a phrase, such as *he said,* that identifies the speaker. If a speaker tag comes before a quotation, put a comma after the tag. If a speaker tag interrupts a sentence, put commas before and after the tag.

    Mrs. Price said, "Put it on now."

    "Rachel," she said, "put it on now."

- If a speaker tag follows a quotation, insert a comma, question mark, or exclamation point before the ending quotation mark. Never use a period before a speaker tag.

    "Whose sweater is this?" she asked.

    "Not mine," said everyone.

- Always begin a quotation with a capital letter.

    Mrs. Price said, "Put it on now."

PRACTICE

Find a piece of your own writing that contains dialogue, and check the punctuation. If you've made mistakes punctuating the dialogue, copy the example sentences at the left. Refer to them when you proofread your writing.

For more help, see Quotation Marks in the *Holt Handbook,* pages 292–299.

Eleven **369**

Vocabulary Development

Practice

scrawny, bony, lean, slim, slender

Grammar Link

Practice

Have students select a piece of writing from their portfolios that contains dialogue. You may wish to have partners exchange papers and check the punctuation for mistakes.

▶ Resources Reminder

Differentiating Instruction

- *Lesson Plans for Language Development*
  - Vocabulary, p.172

ASSESSING

Assessment

- *Progress Assessment of Reading*
  - Selection Test, p. 123

RETEACHING

For a lesson reteaching imagery, see **Reteaching,** p. 489N.

Learners Having Difficulty

Have students revise the following dialogue by adding commas, end marks, and quotation marks where necessary.

1. I think the sweater belongs to Rachel said Sylvia ["I think the sweater belongs to Rachel," said Sylvia.]

2. That sweater Rachel said is too big for me ["That sweater," Rachel said, "is too big for me."]

3. Mrs. Price said Rachel stop crying [Mrs. Price said, "Rachel, stop crying."]

4. I can't Rachel answered I wish I could ["I can't," Rachel answered. "I wish I could."]

5. Rachel moaned My birthday is ruined [Rachel moaned, "My birthday is ruined."]

Standards Review

STANDARDS REVIEW

STANDARDS FOCUS, pp. 370–371

(For the grade-level standard reviewed in this lesson, see Pupil's Edition, p. 370.)

Prerequisite Standard

■ Grade 5, Reading Comprehension 2.5 **Distinguish facts, supported inferences, and opinions in text.**

INTRODUCING THE STANDARDS REVIEW

Use this review to test students' ability to assess whether assertions are reasonable and supporting citations accurate. Use these annotations only if you want to conduct this review orally.

DIRECT TEACHING

A **Reading Informational Materials**
GRADE-LEVEL STANDARD
❓ **Making and supporting reasonable assertions.** What assertion about Sharma is made in the first paragraph? [Sharma has enabled many Indian girls to attend school.]

Reading Informational Materials

 DIRECTIONS: Read the article. Then, read each question, and write the letter of the best response.

His Gift to Girls

A taxi driver funds a school in India.

Ritu Upadhyay

A Hundreds of little girls in the tiny Indian village of Doobher Kishanpur wake up and go to school each day. Sure, in America girls do the same thing. But in Doobher Kishanpur (dōō′ bʉr kish′ən·pōōr), it's nearly a miracle. Thanks to a generous cab driver, many of these students are the first girls in their family to read and write.

Om Dutta Sharma has spent the past 20 years driving a yellow taxicab in New York City for 80 hours a week. After saving all his extra cash, Sharma used it to open the Ram Kali School for Girls in 1997. The school is named for his mother, who—like many poor women in India—never learned to read or write.

Before the school opened, the girls in this village had no chance to learn. Their parents, who are very poor, could not afford to send them to schools in the neighboring towns where the boys study.

An Unlikely Hero
Sharma, 65, came to the U.S. 25 years ago with one goal: to make money. A

trained lawyer in India, Sharma was frustrated to learn that he would not be able to practice law in the U.S. unless he went back to school. As he stood on the street, cars whizzing by, the idea of driving a taxi struck him: "I love to drive, so why not get paid?"

Sharma never wanted money for himself. He felt he had a debt to repay to the poor farming community where he grew up. "If I can help somebody be on the right path, then the purpose of living is achieved," says Sharma.

By American standards, Sharma's salary is not much. But in India, it goes a long way. Each month his dollars pay

Reading Standard 2.7 Make reasonable assertions about a text through accurate supporting citations.

MINI-LESSON Reading

Reviewing Word-Attack Skills
Activity. Display these words. Have volunteers read each word, tell the number of syllables, and identify the syllable in which the sound /ô/ is heard.

1. audience [3]
2. withdrawn [2]
3. applause [2]
4. cautiously [3]

5. jigsaw [2]
6. undaunted [3]
7. installment [3]
8. awesome [2]

9. coverall [3]
10. haunted [2]
11. nautical [3]
12. mawkish [2]

13. cauliflower [4]
14. caustic [2]
15. auction [2]
16. plausible [3]

Activity. Display these sets of words. Have volunteers identify the two words in each set that have the same vowel sound. Answers are underlined.

1. health	heal	help
2. breath	teeth	wreath
3. dread	red	greed
4. seal	wealth	well
5. bread	breed	bred
6. heap	hedge	head
7. stead	steep	step
8. sheath	sheep	shed

four teachers ($58 each), a local pharmacist ($100) for medicine, and a physician ($100) to keep all the schoolchildren healthy. He also donates the earnings from a mango grove he inherited in India to the school. That pays for the students' books and school uniforms.

A Driver's Work Is Never Done

Sharma says he will retire only when he has enough money to open up four more schools, as well as free health clinics. For now, he's happy saving his money and meeting passengers. "I learn so much when they open up their hearts and minds to me."

1. Om Dutta Sharma wanted to give something back to the village where he grew up. What did he do?
   A He came to the United States and worked as a taxi driver.
   B He opened a school for boys in a neighboring town.
   C He came to the United States to study law.
   D He opened a school for girls in Doobher Kishanpur.

2. The information in the article supports the **assertion** that —
   F all children in India attend school
   G not all children in India attend school
   H all schools in India are financed by the government
   J in India, boys and girls attend classes together

3. Which statement is an **opinion**?
   A Om Dutta Sharma pays the salaries of four teachers.
   B Sharma pays for the girls' books and uniforms.
   C Sharma's mother never learned to read or write.
   D Sharma wouldn't have liked being a lawyer in the United States.

4. Which **assertion** would Sharma probably agree with?
   F Few children deserve an education.
   G Helping people gives meaning to life.
   H It's important to leave the past behind you.
   J Success is measured by the kind of job you have.

5. We can reasonably **assert** that this article was written to —
   A persuade people to like Sharma
   B show the value of education
   C explain the benefits of driving a cab
   D show that it doesn't take millions to make a difference

Standards Review **371**

Test-Taking Tips

Remind students to re-read the multiple-choice questions after they look at the possible answers but before they choose one.

For more instruction on how to answer multiple-choice questions, refer students to **Test Smarts**, p. 690.

B Reading Informational Materials
GRADE-LEVEL STANDARD
❓ **Making and supporting reasonable assertions.** What evidence supports the assertion that Sharma funds the school? [The article cites what he pays for teachers, uniforms, books, and so on.]

C Reading Informational Materials
GRADE-LEVEL STANDARD
❓ **Making and supporting reasonable assertions.** What assertion could you make about Sharma that is supported by evidence? [Possible response: Sharma is generous and dedicated to helping people.]

Answers and Model Rationales

1. **D** While A is true, it doesn't tell how Sharma gave back to the village. There is no evidence of B in the article, and C is incorrect. Only D explains how Sharma gave something back to his native village.

2. **G** Evidence in the article contradicts F, H, and J, so these assertions are unreasonable. There is evidence to support G.

3. **D** A, B, and C are all facts. They are cited in the text. D is an opinion and is not cited in the text.

4. **G** A quote from Sharma in the article supports the idea that Sharma would agree with this assertion. Facts in the article contradict assertions H and J.

5. **D** While A might be an outcome of reading the article, it is not the article's main purpose. This article does not cite any evidence to support B or C. However, Sharma's story does support D.

Test Practice

Vocabulary Development

Context Clues

Modeling. Model the thought process of a good reader getting the answer to item 1 by saying: "If you substitute either *struggle* or *solution* for *crusade,* the sentence makes no sense, so C and D can't be right. The players want to win 'for their beloved coach,' so they don't need an excuse, A. You can serve a cause that fits the meaning here, so B is correct."

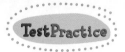

Answers and Model Rationales

1. B See rationale above.

2. F A period of rest, or repose, enables us to work, so F is correct.

3. B Actions that create mystery hinder understanding, so A and C are not correct. To *stop* understanding, D, relates to this idea, but to *resist*, B, is the best choice in the context.

4. G The phrase "leaped up" describes a physical activity. F, H, and J describe an attitude. *Liveliness*, G, is a physical state that fits the context.

5. C If everything else is secondary, then her goal must be primary. Choices A, B, and D are unrelated to this meaning. The best choice is C, *main*.

6. H Richard feels "ill at ease," so looking *awkward*, H, makes perfect sense.

7. D The sentence suggests that the two friends are opposites in nature. A, B, and C are different from "outgoing" in meaning; but only D, *reserved*, has the opposite meaning.

8. F The image of the sky is sad and dreary. The only choice that matches that description is F, *gloomy*.

Vocabulary Development

TestPractice

Context Clues

DIRECTIONS: Use **context clues** to determine the meaning of the underlined word in each of the following sentences.

1. For the team the new season became a <u>crusade</u> to win the state championship for their beloved coach. *Crusade* means —

   A excuse
   B cause
   C struggle
   D solution

2. Lounging on the couch, Ali enjoyed a few moments of <u>repose</u> before beginning his work. *Repose* means —

   F rest
   G anxiety
   H confusion
   J cleanliness

3. Their mysterious actions <u>defy</u> understanding. *Defy* means —

   A observe
   B resist
   C dare
   D stop

4. At the word "walk," the dog leapt up, full of <u>animation</u>. *Animation* means —

   F hostility
   G liveliness
   H anger
   J respect

5. Her <u>paramount</u> goal is to finish the project on time; everything else is secondary. *Paramount* means —

   A poor
   B hilly
   C main
   D good

6. Next to his small, graceful mother, Richard seemed <u>gawky</u> and ill at ease. *Gawky* means —

   F handsome
   G shocking
   H awkward
   J charming

7. It's hard to believe they're best friends: Lauren is outgoing and talkative, and Jane is shy and <u>reticent</u>. *Reticent* means —

   A mischievous
   B content
   C foolish
   D reserved

8. The gray, overcast sky seemed to mirror David's <u>melancholy</u> mood. *Melancholy* means —

   F gloomy
   G odd
   H angry
   J baffled

Vocabulary Review

Use this activity to assess whether students have retained the chapter Vocabulary.
Activity. Have students write their answers to the questions. Possible answers are given.

1. What would you do if your friend Jill was feeling <u>melancholy</u>? [try to talk Jill out of her sadness]

2. What kind of <u>omen</u> might cause Mrs. Davis to cancel her trip? [The airline company she's flying on has a plane crash a week before her trip.]

3. Why would it be difficult to follow directions that were described <u>vaguely</u>? [They wouldn't contain enough information.]

4. What kind of telephone call would have a sense of <u>urgency</u>? [a call to 911]

5. What might someone stare at <u>intently</u>? [a puzzle, a work of art]

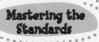

Mastering the Standards

DESCRIPTIVE ESSAY

Make It Alive

In descriptive writing you want your reader to imagine a person, a place, or a thing. You want to use words that will help readers use their senses: sight, hearing, smell, taste, and touch. Russell Freedman helps you see Abraham Lincoln when he describes his "long, bony legs" and his "lean, lank face." The narrator in "Eleven" helps us imagine the odor of the repulsive red sweater when she says that it "smells like cottage cheese." Sarah Hale helps us imagine smelling and tasting a Thanksgiving dinner in the description on page 344. Write a descriptive essay about someone or something you know well. It could be someone you see at home or in school. It could be the place you love best. It could be a favorite meal. Before you write, gather your details in a chart like this:

Senses	Descriptive Details
Sights	
Sounds	
Smells	
Tastes	
Textures or temperatures	

▶ Use "Writing a Descriptive Essay," pages 665–670, for help with this assignment.

Another Choice

RESPONSE TO LITERATURE

Thinking About Theme

Theme is the *meaning* of a story. To find a story's theme, think about what the main characters learn in the story and what *you* learned as you shared their experiences.

In a paragraph or two, discuss the theme of "Eleven" (page 364). First,

skim the story; then, think about the main events and the discoveries the main character has made by the end of the story. Think about what *you* have discovered about childhood hurts. Look for key passages that seem to point to the story's theme.

▶ Use "Writing a Short-Story Interpretation," pages 552–569, for help with this assignment.

Writing Applications **373**

Mastering the Standards

Evaluation Criteria

A good descriptive essay

1. states the writer's feelings about the subject
2. establishes the setting
3. describes the subject, using sensory details
4. follows an appropriate organizational pattern

ASSESSING

Assessment

■ *Progress Assessment of Reading*
  ■ Chapter Test, p. 126
■ *Diagnostic and Summative Assessments*
  ■ Third-Quarter Test, p. 79

After you have completed Chapters 5 and 6 and all related instruction, you may want your students to take this test.

Using Academic Language

Literary Terms
As part of the review of Literary Response and Analysis Standard 3.7, ask students to look back through the chapter to find the meanings of the terms listed at right. Then, have students demonstrate their understanding of Standard 3.7 by citing passages from stories in the chapter that illustrate the meanings of the following terms.

Metaphor (p. 330); **Symbol** (p. 347); **Symbolism** (p. 347); **Imagery** (p. 363).

Informational Terms
As part of the review of Reading Comprehension Standard 2.7, ask students to look back through the chapter to find the meanings of the terms listed below and, using the terms, to explain Standard 2.7.
Assertion (p. 359); **Citations** (p. 359).

Read On

For Independent Reading

If students enjoyed the themes and topics shared in this chapter, you might recommend these titles for independent reading.

Assessment Options

The following projects can help you evaluate and assess your students' outside reading. Videotapes or audiotapes of completed projects may be included in students' portfolios.

- **Write a book review.** Students can write their own book reviews of *Darnell Rock Reporting.* They might imagine that they are writing their reviews for a newspaper like the *Oakdale Gazette.* Remind them to include both their opinion of the book and commentary on its message.

- **Have a debate.** Have a group of students debate about Jody's decision in *The Yearling.* Would students have decided as Jody did? The groups should work together to come up with a debate question and assign members to the two debate sides. Each side should be given time to prepare their arguments before the debate is held.

- **Create book illustrations.** Readers respond in very personal ways to poetry. Invite students to create their own illustrations for one of the poems in *Talking to the Sun.* Have them compare and contrast their illustrations with those found in the book.

California Reading List Titles

The Yearling

Fiction and Poetry

The Power of the Press

Darnell Rock, a staff writer at the *Oakdale Gazette,* doesn't think people will care about anything he writes—so why should he bother writing? Then Darnell meets Sweeby Jones, a homeless man whose troubles capture his interest. Soon, thanks to an article by Darnell, Sweeby Jones is on the minds of students, teachers, and community leaders. In Walter Dean Myers's *Darnell Rock Reporting,* a young man finds that writing about serious issues can make a difference.

A Boy and His Fawn

Have you ever seen a baby animal in the wild and wanted to bring it home and raise it? Jody Baxter does just that in *The Yearling*—but in the end he must decide his tamed fawn's fate. Marjorie Kinnan Rawlings won a Pulitzer Prize in 1939 for this novel, set near her home in rural Florida.

This title is available in the HRW Library.

A Path to Discovery

Kira fears that her village will reject her now that she's lost her parents. She doesn't realize how much the Council of Guardians values her amazing talent for embroidery. While Kira is decorating a ceremonial robe for the annual Ruin Song Gathering, she learns about her family and her village's mysterious history. In *Gathering Blue,* Lois Lowry celebrates an artist's ability to reveal the truth.

Magic in the Arts

Is there a relationship between painting and poetry? They may be linked more closely than you think. In *Talking to the Sun,* Kenneth Koch and Kate Farrell have compiled a diverse collection of poems, each of which is accompanied by a work of art. This book will stir your imagination.

374 Chapter 6 Looking at Texts: Uses of the Imagination

Toward Reading a Million Words Annually

Estimated Word Counts of Read On Books:

Fiction		Nonfiction	
Darnell Rock Reporting	31,000	*Frank O. Gehry: Outside In*	8,300
The Yearling	135,000	*Lincoln: In His Own Words*	60,000
Connections to *The Yearling*	17,000	*Escape from Slavery:*	
Gathering Blue	50,000	*The Boyhood of Frederick*	
Talking to the Sun	24,000	*Douglass in His Own Words*	18,000
		Black Women Leaders	
		of the Civil Rights Movement	39,000

Nonfiction

A Pioneer in His Field

Frank O. Gehry's playful, imaginative designs have taken architecture in a totally new direction. Gehry's designs include a building shaped like binoculars and a pair of towers inspired by the 1930s dance team of Fred Astaire and Ginger Rogers. His pathbreaking design for the Guggenheim Museum in Bilbao, Spain, invigorated that city. In *Frank O. Gehry: Outside In,* Jan Greenberg and Sandra Jordan explore the life of the man behind these innovative ideas.

The Man Who Was the Sixteenth President

Abraham Lincoln was known as a brilliant writer and speaker. Through words he could stir people's emotions and influence their thinking. For *Lincoln: In His Own Words*, Milton Meltzer has selected speeches and writings from different periods of Lincoln's life.

Young and Brave

In *Escape from Slavery: The Boyhood of Frederick Douglass in His Own Words,* you'll learn about one of the most important figures in America's history. Like Lincoln, Douglass was a great writer and speaker, though he never went to school. In this book, Douglass describes the struggles of his early years, which paved the way for his lifelong battle against racism. According to Coretta Scott King, Douglass's accounts provide "one of the best firsthand descriptions of slavery ever written."

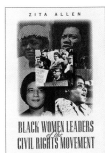

Unsung Heroes

Zita Allen has long felt that an important part of the civil rights movement is underrepresented in history books: the contributions of women. In *Black Women Leaders of the Civil Rights Movement*, Allen looks at the achievements of figures like Mary McLeod Bethune and Ella Baker and explains their importance in the fight for equality.

Read On   375

- ■ **Design an object.** Students who read *Frank O. Gehry: Outside In* can use the book as inspiration for a design of their own. Tell students that when designing they should keep in mind an object's form and function. Point out that good designs don't sacrifice function for form or vice versa. A good design makes an object both attractive and easy to use.

- ■ **Give a speech.** Many people consider oratory an art form. Certainly the ability to give a good speech is a valuable asset for anyone in public life. Both Abraham Lincoln and Frederick Douglass were known for their flair for public speaking. Invite students to choose one of Lincoln's speeches or a section from Douglass's book to present orally. Give them a chance to practice speaking effectively. Remind them that tone of voice, pauses between words and sentences, and gestures can all contribute to the effectiveness of a speech.

- ■ **Create a poster.** Have students work in a group to design and create a poster inspired by *Black Women Leaders of the Civil Rights Movement*. Students should represent every woman discussed in the book on the poster. Remind them that the most interesting posters contain both words and illustrations.

▶ Resources Reminder

Reading
- ■ *Interactive Reading*

For additional readings that relate to the selections in this chapter, see *Interactive Reading*, Chapter 6.
- ■ *The Ancient World:* A Content-Area Reader

DIFFERENTIATING INSTRUCTION

The Read On titles are categorized as shown below.

Below Grade Level ⬇
Darnell Rock Reporting
Gathering Blue
Frank O. Gehry: Outside In

At Grade Level ↔
The Yearling
Escape from Slavery: The Boyhood of Frederick Douglass in His Own Words

Above Grade Level ⬆
Talking to the Sun
Lincoln: In His Own Words
Black Women Leaders of the Civil Rights Movement

Chapter 7 Rhyme and Reason

Program Organization

Holt Literature and Language Arts provides a complete curriculum for standards-based instruction in vocabulary, reading, literature, writing, and speaking and listening. The instructional content of the program is divided into quarters to enable teachers to anticipate and administer the quarterly assessments required by California.

About Chapter 7

Standards-based lesson plans and suggestions for pacing the presentation of Chapter 7 and the related instructional material are provided in *On Course: Mapping Instruction,* Chapter 7.

- Chapter 7 helps students define how tone or meaning is conveyed in poetry, note instances of fallacious reasoning, and identify and interpret figurative language.

- The related instructional material for Chapter 7 is shown on the chart. This related instructional material will also be covered in the fourth quarterly assessment.

Holt Literature and Language Arts

Pupil's Edition

Part 1, Chapter 7

Rhyme and Reason, pp. 376–425
- Reading Standards 1.2, 2.8, 3.4
- Writing Application **Writing a Problem-Solution Essay**

Part 2, Mini-Workshop 6

Writing a Problem-Solution Explanation, pp. 678–680
- Writing Standard 2.2

Part 2, Mini-Workshop 7

Giving and Listening to a Problem-Solution Explanation, pp. 681–685
- Listening and Speaking Standard 2.5

Holt Handbook

Chapter 13

Punctuation: Underlining (Italics), Quotation Marks, Apostrophes, Hyphens, Parentheses
Written and Oral English-Language Conventions
- Looking Ahead, Gr. 7 Standard 1.5, pp. 308–312
- Review, Gr. 5 Standard 1.3, pp. 292–298

Which vocabulary, informational reading, and literature standards are taught in Chapter 7?

In this chapter, students will master the following Grade 6 standards. Selections or features marked with a ✔ constitute the minimum course of study that provides coverage of all grade-level standards.

Grade 6 Standards

Word Analysis, Fluency, and Systematic Vocabulary Development

1.2 Identify and interpret figurative language and words with multiple meanings.

✔ Identifying and Interpreting Figurative Language, p. 410

Reading Comprehension (Focus on Informational Materials)

2.8 Note instances of unsupported inferences, fallacious reasoning, persuasion, and propaganda in text.

✔ Recognizing Persuasive Techniques, pp. 412–414
✔ Recognizing Propaganda Techniques, pp. 415–418
✔ Standards Review: Reading Informational Materials, p. 419

Literary Response and Analysis

3.4 Define how tone or meaning is conveyed in poetry through word choice, figurative language, sentence structure, line length, punctuation, rhythm, repetition, and rhyme.

✔ "Poetry: Sound Effects" (standards essay), pp. 378–379
    "The Sneetches" (poem), pp. 380–386
✔ "Poetry: Seeing Likenesses" (essay), pp. 387–388
✔ "Ode to Mi Gato" (poem)
    "In a Neighborhood in Los Angeles" (poem) } pp. 389–394
    "Hard on the Gas" (poem)
    "An old silent pond" (haiku)
    "Winter rain" (haiku) } pp. 395–398
    "Bad-tempered, I got back" (haiku)
    "A balmy spring wind" (haiku)
    "How to Read (and Own) a Poem" (essay), p. 399
    "Poem" (poem) and "Motto" (poem), pp. 400–403
    "John Henry" (poem), pp. 404–409
✔ Standards Review: Literary Response and Analysis, pp. 420–421

Where do I locate lesson plans, additional resources, and other teaching aids?

- This Annotated Teacher's Edition and *On Course: Mapping Instruction* provide direction in planning and implementing a complete California standards–based curriculum. These components include instructions for administering diagnostic, progress, and summative tests; for presenting instruction of the standards; for differentiating instruction to provide universal access; and for locating and using the program's ancillaries.

- The program's resources are referenced at the beginning of each selection, in the bottom margin of this teacher's edition.

- Reminders for using additional resources appear in this teacher's edition at point of use.

- The *One-Stop Planner* CD-ROM with Test Generator contains editable lesson plans and all of the print ancillaries, available in PDF format.

What if I don't have time to teach all of Chapter 7?

- Most standards can be taught with a minimum number of selections and features. In the chart on p. 375B, the core lessons you need in order to provide complete coverage of the chapter standards are identified with a ✔.

- Use the Standards Review, pp. 419–421, for a quick review and informal assessment of the grade-level standards covered in Chapter 7.

What provisions have been made for students who have additional class time scheduled in language arts?

- *Interactive Reading* provides for additional direct instruction and practice of the grade-level standards taught in Chapter 7. It can be used as an introduction to instruction or as an opportunity for remediation.

- *Lesson Plans for Language Development,* Chapter 7, provides alternative teaching strategies and additional worksheets designed specifically for English-language learners and special education students. Many of the suggestions and activities in this ancillary will also be helpful to students in the regular classroom who are having difficulty with particular skills.

In addition to vocabulary, reading, and literature, what other language arts are covered in Chapter 7?

Writing Activities in Chapter 7
- Wordplay, p. 386
- Odes Aloud, p. 394
- Haiku by You, p. 398
- Human Versus Machine (write a song), p. 409

Listening and Speaking
- A Two-Tone Reading, p. 403

Writing Applications (p. 423)
- Solve it Your Way (problem-solution essay)
- Another Choice: Calling All Cats (research report)

Grammar Links in Chapter 7
- End All End-Mark Errors, p. 411

Universal Access

How do I differentiate instruction to ensure that all my students master the standards?

Holt Literature and Language Arts provides comprehensive, differentiated instruction for all types of students.

- Most of the general instruction and teaching strategies in the Annotated Teacher's Edition are at grade level. These instructions will work well with the majority of your students.

- In Chapter 7, suggestions for advanced learners are provided in the Annotated Teacher's Edition. Point-of-use suggestions for learners having difficulty, English-language learners, and special education students are also provided.

- *Interactive Reading* is designed to anticipate and/or remediate problems that students may experience in achieving mastery of the standards. *Interactive Reading* includes

reading-strategy lessons, lower-level practice reads, and worksheets for every informational and literary text in *Holt Literature and Language Arts,* Pupil's Editions. *Interactive Reading* also contains three additional selections for each chapter and suggestions for extension projects, many of which are ideal for advanced learners working on their own. See *Interactive Reading,* Teacher's Edition, for specific information on using the reader to differentiate instruction in Chapter 7.

- *Lesson Plans for Language Development,* Chapter 7, offers teaching strategies and additional worksheets designed specifically for English-language learners and special education students.

Assessment

How do I determine whether or not my students are making progress in mastering the standards?

Progress Assessment

- Use the Standards Review at the end of Chapter 7, pp. 419–421, for an informal assessment of the informational reading and literature standards in Chapter 7.

- Use the Selection Tests for Chapter 7 in the *Progress Assessment of Reading* booklet to test comprehension and progress on mastering the standard(s) taught with a selection.

- Use Chapter Test 7 in the *Progress Assessment of Reading* booklet to test students' cumulative progress in mastering the standards taught in the chapter.

Summative Assessment

The content of *Holt Literature and Language Arts* has been divided into quarters to allow you to administer the four summative tests required by California. Chapters 7 and 8 and related instructional material constitute the fourth quarter of instruction. At the end of Chapter 8, you may ask students to take the End-of-Year Test in the *Diagnostic and Summative Assessments* booklet.

STANDARDS FOCUS

(For grade-level and review standards taught in this chapter, see Pupil's Edition, p. 377.)

Prerequisite Standards

■ Grade 5, Vocabulary 1.5 **Understand and explain the figurative and metaphorical use of words in context.**

■ Grade 5, Reading Comprehension 2.5 **Distinguish facts, supported inferences, and opinions in text.**

■ Grade 5, Literary Response and Analysis 3.5 **Describe the function and effect of common literary devices (e.g., imagery, metaphor, symbolism).**

Standards Coming Up in the Next Grade Level

■ Grade 7, Vocabulary 1.1 **Identify idioms, analogies, metaphors, and similes in prose and poetry.**

■ Grade 7, Reading Comprehension 2.6 **Assess the adequacy, accuracy, and appropriateness of the author's evidence to support claims and assertions, noting instances of bias and stereotyping.**

CHAPTER

7 Rhyme and Reason

Planning
■ *One-Stop Planner* CD-ROM with Test Generator
■ *On Course: Mapping Instruction*
   ■ Chapter 7
■ *At Home: A Guide to Standards Mastery*
■ *At Home: In Five Languages*
■ *Supporting Instruction in Five Languages*

Reading
■ *Interactive Reading*
   ■ Chapter 7

Differentiating Instruction
■ *Lesson Plans for Language Development*
   ■ Chapter 7

Grammar
■ *Holt Handbook*
   ■ End Marks, pp. 263–267

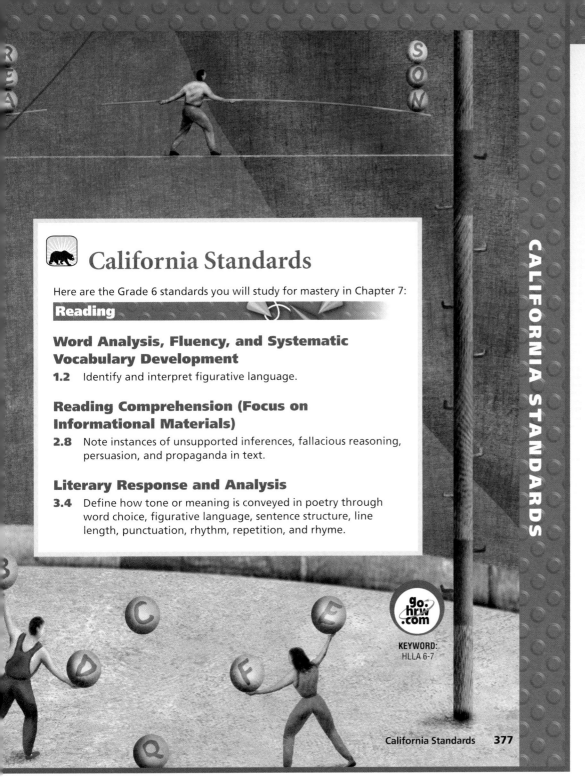

California Standards

Here are the Grade 6 standards you will study for mastery in Chapter 7:

Reading

Word Analysis, Fluency, and Systematic Vocabulary Development

1.2 Identify and interpret figurative language.

Reading Comprehension (Focus on Informational Materials)

2.8 Note instances of unsupported inferences, fallacious reasoning, persuasion, and propaganda in text.

Literary Response and Analysis

3.4 Define how tone or meaning is conveyed in poetry through word choice, figurative language, sentence structure, line length, punctuation, rhythm, repetition, and rhyme.

go.hrw.com

KEYWORD:
HLLA 6-7

California Standards **377**

Assessment
- *Progress Assessment of Reading*
  - Chapter Test, p. 146
- *One-Stop Planner* CD-ROM with Test Generator

Internet
- go.hrw.com
  Keyword: HLLA 6-7

INTRODUCING THE CHAPTER

This chapter introduces poetry that resonates with the reader long after the book has been closed. Using forms ranging from simple to complex, the poets presented here use the musicality of language to enact unique responses to the human condition. Various elements of poetry, including sound effects, figurative language, and structure, are discussed with each selection so that students develop a heightened understanding of what makes a poem a poem. In the second segment of the chapter, students read informational essays and practice analyzing persuasive writing for faulty reasoning, unsupported inferences, and propaganda techniques. The chapter culminates in an opportunity for students to write their own problem-solution essays on topics that concern them.

▶ Resources Reminder

Planning
- *At Home: A Guide to Standards Mastery*

You may want to send home with students selected parent letters from this resource. Translations of these letters are available in *At Home: In Five Languages. Supporting Instruction in Five Languages* provides translations of the selection summaries.

Reading
- *Interactive Reading*
  - Reading Log

The California framework requires students to read materials apart from in-class assignments. Additional reading suggestions are included on the Read On pages and on selected pages in the Pupil's and Teacher's Editions. You may want to use the Reading Log to help students track their progress.

STANDARDS FOCUS, pp. 378–379

(For the grade-level standard taught in this lesson, see Pupil's Edition, p. 378.)

Prerequisite Standard

■ Grade 5, Literary Response and Analysis 3.1 **Identify and analyze the characteristics of poetry, drama, fiction, and nonfiction, and explain the appropriateness of the literary form chosen by an author for a specific purpose.**

Standard Coming Up in the Next Grade Levels

■ Grade 8, Literary Response and Analysis 3.1 **Determine and articulate the relationship between the purposes and characteristics of different forms of poetry (e.g., ballad, lyric, couplet, epic, elegy, ode, sonnet).**

Literary Focus: Sound Effects

Bring in and play a well-known and fairly simple song, such as "My Country 'Tis of Thee" or "I've Been Working on the Railroad." Then, use the following activities to start students thinking about elements of poetry:

■ Invite students to tap out the beat, or rhythm, of the song. They may find that this task is not as simple as it seems, since rhythms include variations. Point out that variations help to make the music interesting.

■ Point out the first rhymed words in the song, and invite students to identify others. Challenge students to suggest more words that rhyme with those they have identified.

■ Point out an example of repetition in the song—a word, phrase, or refrain—and ask students to identify others.

Poetry *by John Malcolm Brinnin*
SOUND EFFECTS

Rhyme: Chiming Sounds

We all love **rhyme.** Rhyme can be as simple as the pairing of *moth* with *cloth* or a bit more complicated, like *antelope* matched with *cantaloupe.* Most rhymes are made by pairing the last word in one line with the last word in another line. Rhymes formed in this way are called **end rhymes.** Sometimes the last word in a line will be echoed by a word placed at the beginning or in the middle of the following line. A rhyme formed in this way is called an **internal rhyme.**

Rhyme makes the music in poetry, and it helps you to memorize lines, or stanzas, or even whole poems. Here is a stanza by a famous poet who uses rhymes and other sound effects to make even an invasion of rats seem funny.

And out of the houses the rats came
    tumbling;
Great rats, small rats, lean rats,
    brawny rats,
Brown rats, black rats, gray rats,
    tawny rats,
Grave old plodders, gay young friskers,
Cocking tails and pricking whiskers . . .

— Robert Browning, from
    "The Pied Piper of Hamelin"

Alliteration: Repeating a Sound

Alliteration is the repetition of a single consonant sound in words that are close together (for example, *p* in "Peter Piper picked a peck of pickled peppers"). Alliteration is one of the simplest forms of repetition a poet can use. Read aloud "Cynthia in the Snow" so you can hear how the repeated faint hissing of *s* and *sh* sounds imitates the snow falling.

Cynthia in the Snow

It SHUSHES.
It hushes
The loudness in the road.
It flitter-twitters,
And laughs away from me.
It laughs a lovely whiteness,
And whitely whirs away,
To be
Some otherwhere,
Still white as milk or shirts.
So beautiful it hurts.
        —Gwendolyn Brooks

Meter: The Beat of a Poem

When poets are ready to put their ideas and feelings into words, they have to make a choice. They must ask themselves, "Should I express this idea in lines regulated by a beat that sounds like *ta-dum, ta-dum, ta-dum*? Would it

Reading Standard 3.4
Define how tone or meaning is conveyed in poetry through rhythm, repetition, and rhyme.

DIFFERENTIATING INSTRUCTION

Learners Having Difficulty
Modeling. These students may benefit from practice before reading the essay and the poems it includes. On the chalkboard, write a limerick such as the following one: "There was a young lady of Niger / Who smiled as she rode on a tiger. / They returned from the ride / With the lady inside / And the smile on the face of the tiger."

Tell students that you are going to read the limerick aloud, and you want them to

fill in the rhyming word each time you pause at the end of a line. Pause at the ends of ll. 2, 4, and 5. Next, model tapping out the meter of the limerick's first line. As you tap, say, "Ta-dum, ta-ta-ta-dum, ta-ta-dum." Then, have students tap out the rest of the lines with you.

English-Language Learners
Before students read the essay, read aloud the poems by Robert Browning and

be expressed better in lines that sound like ordinary conversation, such as 'Of course. You're right. I never thought of that'?" If they decide on a regular beat, all the lines they write will be more or less the same length and have the same beat. This beat is called **meter**—a regular pattern of accented and unaccented syllables. Robert Browning's lines on the rat invasion (see page 378) are written in meter. Read them aloud. You can't miss that beat.

Poets may decide to ignore meter and write in loose groupings of words and phrases, known as **free verse.** Like conversation, free verse does not have a regular beat. Free verse is simply poetry written to sound like regular conversation.

How do you decide whether to write in meter or free verse? When you write a poem, you must trust yourself. Say what comes from your heart, in the form most natural to you.

Here is a poem in free verse on what may seem like an unpoetic subject. Read the poem aloud. Use the sense of the lines to decide when to pause and when to read straight through to the next line.

Good Hot Dogs

for Kiki

Fifty cents apiece
To eat our lunch
We'd run
Straight from school
Instead of home
Two blocks
Then the store
That smelled like steam
You ordered
Because you had the money
Two hot dogs and two pops for here
Everything on the hot dogs
Except pickle lily
Dash those hot dogs
Into buns and splash on
All that good stuff
Yellow mustard and onions
And french fries piled on top all
Rolled up in a piece of wax
Paper for us to hold hot
In our hands
Quarters on the counter
Sit down
Good hot dogs
We'd eat
Fast till there was nothing left
But salt and poppy seeds even
The little burnt tips
Of french fries
We'd eat
You humming
And me swinging my legs
———Sandra Cisneros

Have each student choose a poem to read aloud in class. Students can choose any poem they like: a familiar nursery rhyme, a limerick, or a poem they have discovered in independent reading. If possible, bring in poetry anthologies for students to look through.

Have each student read his or her poem aloud as the rest of the class listens. Have the class identify end rhymes, internal rhymes, alliteration, meter, and free verse. Encourage students to give their opinions on how well each poet used these elements to create tone or meaning in his or her poem.

▶ **Resources Reminder**

Reading
■ *Interactive Reading*

Before you teach Chapter 7 of *Holt Literature and Language Arts*, you may want to preteach the literary concept and a related reading strategy.

• To introduce students to the literary concept, assign p. 263 of *Interactive Reading*.
• To introduce students to a reading strategy that will help them grasp the literary concept, assign p. 263 of *Interactive Reading*.
• To give students practice applying the strategy to a short, vocabulary-controlled selection, assign the Practice Read "The Just Us Club" on p. 264 of *Interactive Reading*.

Gwendolyn Brooks. Hearing the poems will help students to recognize the rhyme, alliteration, and meter they study in the essay.

▶ **Resources Reminder**
For lessons on poetry designed for intermediate and advanced English-language learners and special education students, see *Lesson Plans for Language Development,* pp. 173–174.

Advanced Learners
Acceleration. Use this activity to move students toward the eighth-grade Standard 3.1, which requires that they explore the characteristics of different forms of poetry. Introduce the concept of a couplet by offering this example:
   A truth that's told with bad intent
   Beats all the lies you can invent.
   —William Blake

Explain that two lines of poetry working together as a unit are known as a couplet. **Activity.** Have students write their own couplets expressing truths they have learned. Tell them to keep the lines similar in meter, to use end rhymes, and to experiment with internal rhyme and alliteration.

STANDARDS FOCUS, pp. 380–386

(For grade-level and review standards taught in this selection, see citations on Pupil's Edition pages.)

Prerequisite Standard

■ Grade 5, Literary Response and Analysis 3.4 **Understand that** *theme* **refers to the meaning or moral of a selection, and recognize themes (whether implied or stated directly) in sample works.**

Summary ⇨ *at grade level*

Inventive rhymes and a galloping rhythm set a humorous tone in this poem about Sneetches—the snobbish Star-Bellies and the hapless Plain-Bellies. A traveling con artist, Sylvester McMonkey McBean, exploits the Plain-Bellies' envy and sells them belly stars. The Sneetches with the original stars promptly pay McBean to remove their stars. The newly starred Sneetches do likewise. A wild race ensues ("Off again! On again!") until no one knows who "should" and "shouldn't" have a star. Once McBean has collected all their money, he leaves, and the Sneetches declare all Sneetches equal.

PRETEACHING

Standards Starter

Motive. Bring in an advertisement that plays on people's desire to be part of a group. Invite students to discuss the message and the ways that in-groups often discriminate against others.

The Sneetches

Literary Focus
Rhymes: *Sneetches* and *Eaches*

Everyone knows what a **rhyme** is: two words that have the same chiming sounds, like *nose* and *rose*. When he was asked, "What is rhyme?" Dr. Seuss replied, "A rhyme is something without which I would probably be in the dry-cleaning business." To keep his poems galloping along with catchy rhymes, Dr. Seuss often invented words to rhyme with real words. For instance, throughout "The Sneetches" he rhymes the real word *stars* with the made-up word *thars*. For that matter, who ever heard of Sneetches before Dr. Seuss invented them?

Mark That Rhyme; Scan That Rhythm

Poets often use a pattern of rhymes, called a **rhyme scheme,** in a poem. To find a poem's rhyme scheme, mark the first line and all the lines that rhyme with it *a;* mark the second line and all the lines that rhyme with it *b;* and so on.

To find a poem's **meter,** you read the poem aloud. Mark each stressed syllable you hear with the symbol **'** and each unstressed syllable with the symbol ˘. This marking is called **scanning.**

Here are the first four lines of "The Sneetches," with the rhyme scheme and meter marked:

Reading Standard 3.4 Define how tone or meaning is conveyed in poetry through rhythm and rhyme.

Now, the Star-Belly Sneetches	a
Had bellies with stars	b
The Plain-Belly Sneetches	a
Had none upon thars.	b

In poems with a strong, regular beat, variation is important. Reading a poem with an unchanging pattern of beats is as exciting as listening to the *ticktock, ticktock* of a clock. Read "The Sneetches" aloud, and notice how Dr. Seuss varies the pattern of syllables in the poem.

Make the Connection
Talk It Over

Like many of Dr. Seuss's poems, "The Sneetches" is meant for both children and adults. Underneath the clever wordplay and lively rhythms of the poems there's usually a serious message. As you read this poem, think about the point Dr. Seuss is making about people and the way they treat one another.

Quickwrite ✏️

Before you begin, join a small group and make a list of injustices you are aware of. Discuss events you've read about in newspapers or seen on TV. List some of the reasons people are treated unfairly. (Reasons may be as simple as the clothes people wear or as complex as their personal beliefs.)

RESOURCES

Planning
■ *One-Stop Planner* CD-ROM with Test Generator
■ *On Course: Mapping Instruction*

Media
■ *Audio CD Library*
  ■ disc 9

Reading
■ *Interactive Reading*
  ■ Strategy Launch: Text Reformulation, p. 263
  ■ Practice Read: "The Just Us Club," p. 264
  ■ Graphic Organizer: Rhyme Alliance Chart, p. 270

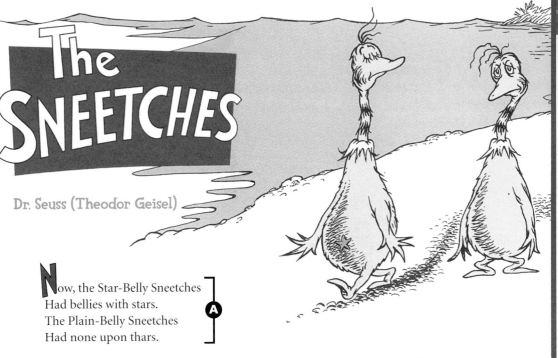

The SNEETCHES

Dr. Seuss (Theodor Geisel)

Now, the Star-Belly Sneetches
Had bellies with stars.
The Plain-Belly Sneetches
Had none upon thars.

5   Those stars weren't so big. They were really so small
    You might think such a thing wouldn't matter at all.

    But, because they had stars, all the Star-Belly Sneetches
    Would brag, "We're the best kind of Sneetch on the beaches."
    With their snoots in the air, they would sniff and they'd snort
10 "We'll have nothing to do with the Plain-Belly sort!"
    And whenever they met some, when they were out walking,
    They'd hike right on past them without even talking.

    When the Star-Belly children went out to play ball,
    Could a Plain Belly get in the game . . . ? Not at all.
15 You only could play if your bellies had stars
    And the Plain-Belly children had none upon thars.

    When the Star-Belly Sneetches had frankfurter roasts
    Or picnics or parties or marshmallow toasts,
    They never invited the Plain-Belly Sneetches.
20 They left them out cold, in the dark of the beaches.
    They kept them away. Never let them come near.
    And that's how they treated them year after year.

The Sneetches   381

■ *Interactive Reading*, Teacher's Edition
    ■ Transparency 7: Text Reformulation
Differentiating Instruction
■ *Lesson Plans for Language Development*
    ■ English-Language Learners,
      pp. 175–177, 193, 198
    ■ Special Education Students,
      pp. 178, 193, 198

Assessment
■ *Progress Assessment of Reading*
    ■ Selection Test, p. 133
■ *One-Stop Planner* CD-ROM with Test
  Generator

Assign the Reading
Start by having the class read the poem aloud. Next, go over p. 380 as a class. Then, for students reading at or above grade level, assign a second reading of the poem and questions 1–7 on p. 386 as homework, and continue to work with small groups of students having difficulty.

HOMEWORK

▶ Resources Reminder
Reading
■ *Interactive Reading*
    ■ Strategy Launch: Text Reformulation, p. 263
    ■ Graphic Organizer: Rhyme Alliance Chart, p. 270

DIRECT TEACHING

Ⓐ Literary Focus
GRADE-LEVEL STANDARD
❓ Rhyme and rhythm. What real word does the invented word *thars* replace? [*theirs*] Why doesn't the author use *theirs*? [It doesn't rhyme, and it isn't funny.]

Ⓑ Literary Focus
GRADE-LEVEL STANDARD
❓ Rhyme and rhythm. Alliteration is the repetition of a single consonant sound in words that are close together. Which words in this line show alliteration? [*snoots, sniff, snort*] What effects does it create here? [Possible responses: It makes the line flow smoothly; it emphasizes the Star-Bellies' "snootiness."]

Ⓒ English-Language Learners
Building background knowledge. Explain to students that frankfurters (or hot dogs—you might show the photo on p. 379) and marshmallows are often put on sticks and roasted over a grill at outdoor parties or picnics.

A Literary Focus
GRADE-LEVEL STANDARD

❓ Rhyme and rhythm. Which words in this stanza show end rhyme? [*Sneetches, beaches, stars, cars*] What is the stanza's rhyme scheme? [*aabb*] What effects do you think this rhyme scheme creates? [Possible response: The pairs of rhymed lines are humorous, bouncy, and rhythmic.]

B Literary Focus
GRADE-LEVEL STANDARD

❓ Rhyme and rhythm. Rhymes that occur within the same line are called internal rhymes. Which word does Dr. Seuss make up to create an internal rhyme with *moping*? [*doping*]

C Advanced Learners

❓ Forms of poetry. What is the rhyme scheme of this stanza? [*aabbccc*] Three lines of poetry, usually rhyming, that function as a unit are called a triplet. What effect do you think the triplet creates here after many sets of rhymed couplets? [Possible responses: The triplet reinforces McBean's sales pitch; it varies the poem's sound.]

D Reading Skills

❓ Analyzing motives. What do you think are McBean's motives? [Possible answer: He wants to make money from the Sneetches' prejudice, not help them resolve their differences.]

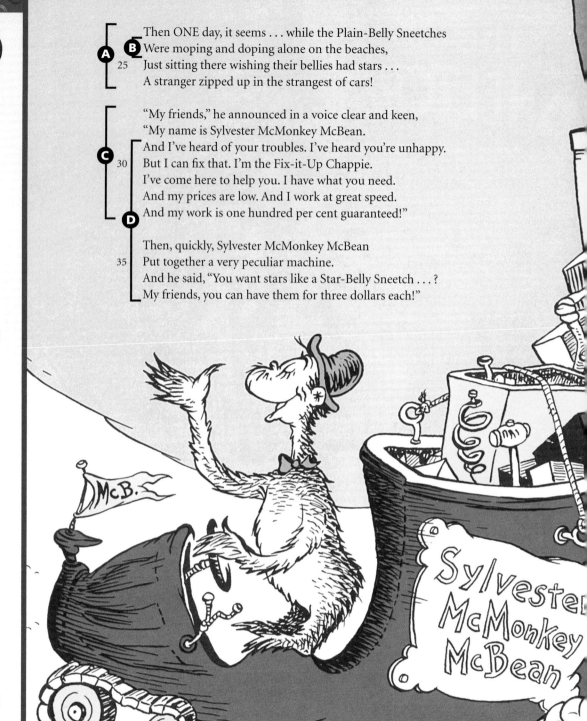

A B Then ONE day, it seems . . . while the Plain-Belly Sneetches
Were moping and doping alone on the beaches,
25 Just sitting there wishing their bellies had stars . . .
A stranger zipped up in the strangest of cars!

C "My friends," he announced in a voice clear and keen,
"My name is Sylvester McMonkey McBean.
And I've heard of your troubles. I've heard you're unhappy.
30 But I can fix that. I'm the Fix-it-Up Chappie.
I've come here to help you. I have what you need.
And my prices are low. And I work at great speed.
D And my work is one hundred per cent guaranteed!"

Then, quickly, Sylvester McMonkey McBean
35 Put together a very peculiar machine.
And he said, "You want stars like a Star-Belly Sneetch . . .?
My friends, you can have them for three dollars each!"

Learners Having Difficulty
Modeling. If students need to read an easier selection before beginning "The Sneetches," use the Practice Read "The Just Us Club" in *Interactive Reading*, p. 265. Then, use the transparency to model the strategy of text reformulation. This strategy will help students to understand the meaning of a poem. Have students apply the strategy to help them read "The Sneetches."

As they read, encourage students to ask themselves, "How would I express the meaning of these lines in my own words?"

▶ Resources Reminder 🖥
Reading
- *Interactive Reading*, Teacher's Edition
  - Transparency 7: Text Reformulation

English-Language Learners
Be sure students understand that *Sneetch* is a made-up word. Then, familiarize them with the following words, which may seem made up but are not: *snoots* (noses); *chappie* (little man); *clambered* (climbed); *snooty* (snobbish); *contraption* (gadget).

▶ Resources Reminder
For lessons designed for intermediate and

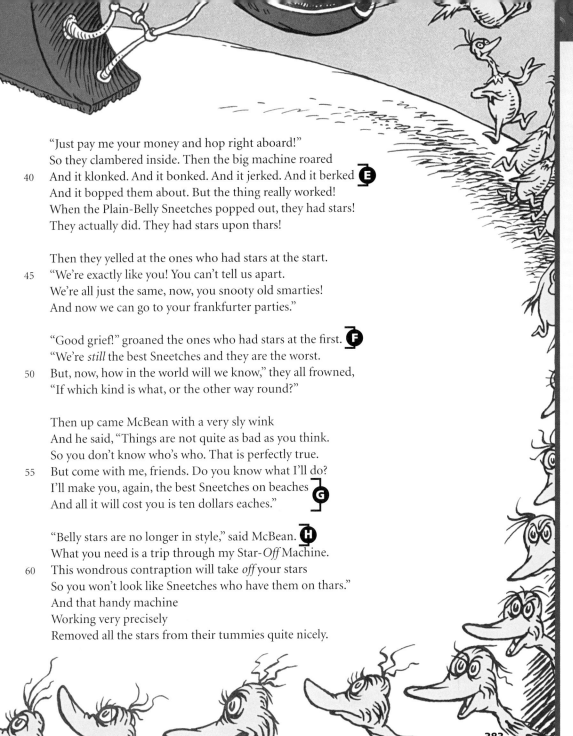

"Just pay me your money and hop right aboard!"
So they clambered inside. Then the big machine roared
40 And it klonked. And it bonked. And it jerked. And it berked **E**
And it bopped them about. But the thing really worked!
When the Plain-Belly Sneetches popped out, they had stars!
They actually did. They had stars upon thars!

Then they yelled at the ones who had stars at the start.
45 "We're exactly like you! You can't tell us apart.
We're all just the same, now, you snooty old smarties!
And now we can go to your frankfurter parties."

"Good grief!" groaned the ones who had stars at the first. **F**
"We're *still* the best Sneetches and they are the worst.
50 But, now, how in the world will we know," they all frowned,
"If which kind is what, or the other way round?"

Then up came McBean with a very sly wink
And he said, "Things are not quite as bad as you think.
So you don't know who's who. That is perfectly true.
55 But come with me, friends. Do you know what I'll do?
I'll make you, again, the best Sneetches on beaches **G**
And all it will cost you is ten dollars eaches."

"Belly stars are no longer in style," said McBean. **H**
What you need is a trip through my Star-*Off* Machine.
60 This wondrous contraption will take *off* your stars
So you won't look like Sneetches who have them on thars."
And that handy machine
Working very precisely
Removed all the stars from their tummies quite nicely.

383

DIRECT TEACHING

E Literary Focus
REVIEW STANDARD
? Onomatopoeia.
Onomatopoeia is the use of a word whose sound imitates or suggests its meaning. Onomatopoeic words sound like the things they refer to. Words like *boom*, *growled*, and *plunked* are examples of ono-matopoeia. What onomatopoeic words does Dr. Seuss use in this line? [*klonked, bonked, jerked,* and *berked*]

F English-Language Learners
Understanding idioms. Tell students that "Good grief!" is an idiomatic expression of dismay.

G Literary Focus
GRADE-LEVEL STANDARD
? Rhyme and rhythm. What internal rhyme do you find in this line? [*Sneetches/beaches*] Notice how the internal rhyme sets read-ers up for the rhyme with the humorous, made-up word *eaches* at the end of the next line.

H Literary Focus
REVIEW STANDARD
? Theme. Have students name some examples of fashion styles that have been popular one day and outdated the next. (Encourage students to recall last year's fashion fads.) Ask them why they think people follow these fads. [Possible responses: They want to feel accepted, to look up-to-date, to be popular, to look as if they belong to a special group.]

advanced English-language learners, see *Lesson Plans for Language Development,* pp. 175–177, 193, 198.

Special Education Students
For lessons designed for special education students, see *Lesson Plans for Language Development*, pp. 178, 193, 198.

Advanced Learners
Acceleration. Use this activity to move students toward the eighth-grade Standard 3.1, which requires that they explore vari-ous forms of poetry. Tell students that two lines of poetry that usually rhyme are called a couplet; three lines of poetry that usually rhyme are called a triplet; and four lines, usually with alternate rhymes (*abab, abba, abcb*), are called a quatrain. Point out ll. 5–6 as an example of a couplet.
Activity. Have students find two places in the poem where there are three consec-utive rhymed lines and one place where there are four. [ll. 31–33, 80–82; ll. 89–92] Then, challenge students to decide whether the sets function as units and can be classi-fied as triplets or quatrains. Have them give reasons for their decisions based on the poem's content as well as its form.

VIEWING THE ART

Theodor Seuss Geisel (1904–1991) wrote and illustrated forty-seven books, which have been translated into eighteen languages. In 1984, Seuss won a Pulitzer Prize for a lifetime contribution to education and entertainment.

Activity. Have students point out details Seuss uses in his illustrations to show the Sneetches' humanlike traits. [Possible responses: Their facial expressions, gestures, and the hats they wear make them seem human.]

Ⓐ Literary Focus
GRADE-LEVEL STANDARD
❓ Rhyme and rhythm. How does the rhyme scheme change in this stanza? [After many stanzas comprised mainly of rhymed couplets (*aabb*), this stanza's rhyme scheme is *aaaa*.] What effect do you think the change in rhyme scheme creates? [Possible response: The new rhyme scheme emphasizes the ironic twist in the story; it heightens the Sneetches' excitement.]

Ⓑ Literary Focus
GRADE-LEVEL STANDARD
❓ Rhyme and rhythm. Which words rhyme in this stanza? [*beaches/Sneetches; two/through/knew/who*] What variations in rhyme and rhythm do you notice here? [Possible responses: The rhyme scheme is not *aabb*, but *aabbbcccdc*. The rhythm is varied by the two short lines.]

Ⓒ Reading Skills
❓ Drawing conclusions. Why does McBean leave? [He has taken all the Sneetches' money, and that's what he was after in the first place.]

Ⓓ Literary Focus
REVIEW STANDARD
❓ Theme. What have the Sneetches learned? [That appearances aren't important; that they are all equal.]

65 [Then, with snoots in the air, they paraded about
Ⓐ And they opened their beaks and they let out a shout,
"We know who is who! Now there isn't a doubt.
The best kind of Sneetches are Sneetches without!"

Then, of course, those with stars all got frightfully mad.
70 To be wearing a star now was frightfully bad.
Then, of course, old Sylvester McMonkey McBean
Invited *them* into his Star-Off Machine.

Then, of course from THEN on, as you probably guess,
Things really got into a horrible mess.

75 [All the rest of that day, on those wild screaming beaches,
The Fix-it-Up Chappie kept fixing up Sneetches.
Off again! On again!
In again! Out again!
Ⓑ Through the machines they raced round and about again,
80 Changing their stars every minute or two.
They kept paying money. They kept running through
Until neither the Plain nor the Star-Bellies knew
Whether this one was that one . . . or that one was this one
Or which one was what one . . . or what one was who.

85 [Then, when every last cent
Ⓒ Of their money was spent,
The Fix-it-Up Chappie packed up
And he went.

And he laughed as he drove
90 In his car up the beach,
"They never will learn.
No. You can't teach a Sneetch!"

[But McBean was quite wrong. I'm quite happy to say
That the Sneetches got really quite smart on that day,
95 The day they decided that Sneetches are Sneetches
Ⓓ And no kind of Sneetch is the best on the beaches.
That day, all the Sneetches forgot about stars
And whether they had one, or not, upon thars.

MINI-LESSON Reading

Developing Word-Attack Skills
Use rhyming word pairs from the poem to explore different spellings for the vowel plus *r* sound /ʉr/. Have students brainstorm for other words that rhyme with *berked* and *worked*. [*clerked, lurked, perked, shirked, smirked*] Write the words on the chalkboard, underlining the letters that would form the sound /ʉr/. Repeat the activity with the rhyming words *first* and *worst*. [*burst, cursed,* *immersed, thirst, wurst*] Together, make a list of the spellings for the sound /ʉr/.
Activity. Introduce this rhyming word pair from the poem: *true/do.* Have students work with partners to brainstorm for words that rhyme with *true* and *do.* Have students read their completed lists, and create a master list of rhyming words on the chalkboard. You may want to organize this list by the different spellings of the vowel sound /o͞o/.

Theodor Seuss Geisel

© 2001 Bill Nelson.

Creature Feature

Dr. Seuss is the pen name of **Theodor Seuss Geisel** (1904–1991), who began drawing fantastic animal cartoons while he was still a child. (His father ran the local zoo.) An art teacher told him that he would never learn to draw, and twenty-seven publishers rejected his first children's book, *And to Think That I Saw It on Mulberry Street* (1937). Even so, Dr. Seuss went on to write and illustrate more than forty children's classics, full of nonsense rhymes, wacky creatures, and his special brand of wisdom.

Judging by the number of books Dr. Seuss has sold—at least 200 million copies—he is one of the most popular writers in history. As he did in "The Sneetches," Dr. Seuss often used his zany characters to look at serious issues as if "through the wrong end of a telescope."

Dr. Seuss explained how he decided on his pen name:

> The 'Dr. Seuss' name is a combination of my middle name and the fact that I had been studying for my doctorate when I decided to quit to become a cartoonist. My father had always wanted to see a Dr. in front of my name, so I attached it. I figured by doing that, I saved him about ten thousand dollars.

For Independent Reading

Books by Dr. Seuss that use wacky-looking creatures to convey a serious message include *The Lorax* (about protecting the environment) and *The Butter Battle Book* (about war).

Meet the Writer

Background. The May 1954 issue of *Life* magazine claimed that children were having difficulty learning to read because their books were boring. This sparked Geisel's publisher, Bennet Cerf, to present Geisel with a list of 400 words that first-graders should know, to be used as the basis for an elementary reader. Nine months later, Geisel had used 220 of the words to create *The Cat in the Hat,* an instant success. Six years later, Cerf bet Geisel fifty dollars that he couldn't write an entire book using only fifty words. Geisel won the bet with *Green Eggs and Ham.*

Where did Dr. Seuss get all his wild ideas? Tongue firmly in cheek, he once claimed, "I get all my ideas in Switzerland near the Forka Pass. There is a little town called Gletch, and two thousand feet up above Gletch there is a small hamlet called Uber Gletch. I go there on the fourth of August every summer to get my cuckoo clock repaired. While the cuckoo is in the hospital, I wander around and talk to the people in the streets. They are very strange people, and I get my ideas from them."

For Independent Reading

Students reading *The Lorax* and *The Butter Battle Book* might also enjoy viewing the videos.

- For fans of lighthearted and energetic poetry, suggest Shel Silverstein's *A Light in the Attic.*
- Students will find wacky, humorous prose, with quirky illustrations by the author, in James Thurber's *My Life and Hard Times.*

▶ Resources Reminder

Reading

- *Interactive Reading*

For other poems by Theodor Seuss Geisel, see "Vrooms," "If We Didn't Have Birthdays," and "Too Many Daves" in *Interactive Reading*, pp. 276–278. You may want to assign these to the whole class.

Possible list:

o	oo	ue	ew	ough
do	boo	blue	dew	through
to	too	due	few	

INDEPENDENT PRACTICE

Literary Response and Analysis

Reading Check

1. Star-Bellies snub Plain-Bellies because the Plain-Bellies lack belly stars. The Star-Bellies exclude the Plain-Bellies from the Star-Bellies' activities.

2. He offers to put stars on the Plain-Bellies for three dollars each and to take off the Star-Bellies' stars for ten dollars each.

3. He leaves when he gets all the Sneetches' money. The Sneetches decide that stars don't matter.

Interpretations

4. Possible answers: *Star-Bellies*—snobbish, proud. *Plain-Bellies*—envious, insecure.

5. He thinks they are stupid and can't learn, but he's wrong: They do learn to get along.

6. Possible answer: They can't tell which Sneetches originally did or didn't have stars.

7. Made-up words—*thars, berked, eaches, Sneetches.* Internal rhymes—*moping/ doping, klonked/bonked.*

8. The rhythm races, showing how frantically the Sneetches run about. The shorter lines show the abruptness of McBean's leaving, and their simple rhythm suggests he is not frantic, but cool and calculating.

9. Possible rhyme scheme, first three stanzas: *abab cc aaddee.* The first stanza is different. Possible answer: Students may say rhymed couplets in the second and third stanzas make the longer lines clearer or funnier.

10. Possible scansion for second stanza: Thŏse stárs wĕren't sŏ bíg. Thĕy wĕre réallŷ sŏ smáll / Yŏu míght thínk sŭch ă thíng wŏuldn't máttĕr ăt áll. The meter varies in many stanzas; ll. 34–37 and 44–47 are two more examples of different meter.

Literary Response and Analysis

Reading Check

1. Why do one group of Sneetches think they're better than the other group? How do they treat that group?

2. What offer does McBean make to the Plain-Bellies? What offer does he then make to the Star-Bellies?

3. When does McBean finally leave? What happens afterward?

Interpretations

4. What one word might describe the Star-Bellies? the Plain-Bellies?

5. What opinion does McBean have of the Sneetches in general? Do you think he is right or wrong? Why?

6. Why do the Sneetches finally change their behavior?

7. What words has Dr. Seuss made up to keep lines **rhymed**? Can you find at least one **internal rhyme**—two or more rhyming words *within* a line?

8. Read lines 75–88 aloud. Feel the beat as you say the words. How does the **rhythm** suggest the way the Sneetches feel? What does the change in rhythm and in line length suggest about McBean?

9. Working with a partner, mark the **rhyme scheme** of at least three stanzas of "The Sneetches." Use the letter code you learned earlier (see page 380). Which stanzas are different? Do the differences "make a difference"? Why or why not?

10. Read a few stanzas of this poem aloud; then, copy two stanzas onto

Reading Standard 3.4 Define how tone or meaning is conveyed in poetry through rhythm and rhyme.

a piece of paper. Scan them, marking stressed and unstressed syllables in each line (see page 380). Is the meter identical in every line?

11. What do you think is the **moral,** or lesson, of this poem? Can you think of anyone in real life who behaves like the characters in "The Sneetches"? (For ideas, look back at your Quickwrite notes.) ✏

12. If someone tells you, "I don't like your tone of voice," you know the person is talking about your attitude. In literature, **tone** refers to the writer's attitude toward a subject. The tone of a work can be serious, playful, sarcastic, bitter, and so on. What tone do you detect underneath the funny nonsense rhymes and bouncy rhythms?

Writing
Wordplay

To make his lines rhyme and to add to the fun, Dr. Seuss sometimes changes a spelling, adds a new ending sound, or even invents a word. Find the funny words invented by Dr. Seuss in lines 4, 40, and 57. What word does each made-up word rhyme with?

Write a line of poetry to rhyme with the following line. (Since no word in English rhymes with *orange*, you'll have to invent a rhyming word.)

Eva was eating an orange

---

11. Possible answer: Don't judge others by their appearance. Students may cite snobs, bigots, or political figures that act like Sneetches or McBean.

12. Possible answer: Underneath the humorous rhymes and rhythms, there is a serious tone condemning bigotry.

ASSESSING

Assessment

■ *Progress Assessment of Reading*
  ■ Selection Test, p. 133

Poetry *by John Malcolm Brinnin*

SEEING LIKENESSES

Poetry lives and breathes because poets make especially imaginative comparisons—they have a special talent for seeing one thing in terms of something else, something very different. We call these comparisons between unlike things **figures of speech.** There are three main figures of speech: metaphors, similes, and personification.

Metaphors and Similes

"My baby sister's a doll," you might say, comparing your sister's size and sweetness to the perfection of a doll. At another time you might say, "My brother is a rat," comparing your poor brother to the nastiest little creature you can think of. In both cases you would be making a kind of comparison called a **metaphor**—a form of comparison that directly compares two unlike things. A metaphor wastes no time in getting to the point.

On the other hand, if you said, "My sister is *like* a doll," or, with a sudden change of heart, "My brother's as good as gold," you would in each case be making a **simile**—a form of comparison in which one thing is compared to another unlike thing by using specific words of comparison, such as *like, as,* and *resembles.*

Poets try to find unusual metaphors and similes. Christina Rossetti, when she was in love, used a simile and wrote, "My heart is like a singing bird." If she had made a metaphor, she would have written, "My heart *is* a singing bird." Emily Dickinson, thinking about the problems fame can bring, said, "Fame is a bee." If she had made a simile, she would have said, "Fame is *like* a bee."

Personification: Making the World Human

One of the most familiar kinds of comparison is **personification**—that is, speaking of something that is not human as if it had human abilities and human reactions.

"The sky wept buckets all day long." In this example of personification, a

(continued)

Peanuts reprinted by permission of United Feature Syndicate, Inc.

Reading Standard 3.4 Define how tone or meaning is conveyed in poetry through figurative language.

Poetry: Seeing Likenesses **387**

STANDARDS FOCUS, pp. 387–388

(For the grade-level standard taught in this lesson, see Pupil's Edition, p. 387.)

Prerequisite Standard

■ Grade 4, Literary Response and Analysis 3.5 **Define figurative language (e.g., simile, metaphor, hyperbole, personification), and identify its use in literary works.**

Standard Coming Up in the Next Grade Level

■ Grade 7, Literary Response and Analysis 3.6 **Analyze a range of responses to a literary work, and determine the extent to which the literary elements in the work shaped those responses.**

Literary Focus: Figurative Language

Remind students that music lyrics, like poetry, use a lot of figurative language, including similes, metaphors, and personification. Go over a few examples of your own with the class, such as the metaphors in Paul Simon's famous ballad "Bridge Over Troubled Water." Then, invite students to share the lyrics from some of their favorite songs. Have them identify and explain any figurative language that the lyrics contain.

DIFFERENTIATING INSTRUCTION

Learners Having Difficulty

Have students examine the cartoon on p. 387. How does Lucy's comparison in the second panel help students understand what kind of hitter the batter usually is? How does the third panel create an ironic and humorous contradiction of this comparison? [Lucy's grandmother can throw her purse with force.]

Advanced Learners

Acceleration. Use this activity to move students toward the seventh-grade Standard 3.6, which requires that they determine how elements in a literary work shape readers' responses.

Activity. Have students discuss Edward Lueders's poem "Your Poem, Man . . . " and determine its main point. [Figures of speech

have the power to help us see the world in fresh, new ways; they help us to see how things in the world are connected.] Then, have students discuss the impact of the poem's figures of speech. Would the poem be as effective without these comparisons?

Apply

Present students with the following figures of speech. Have volunteers identify each figure of speech as a metaphor, a simile, or personification and explain what is being compared.

1. Icicles are cold daggers. [*Figure of speech*—metaphor. *Comparison*—Icicles are being compared to cold daggers.]

2. Don't touch those! Those paints are like precious jewels to Miranda. [*Figure of speech*—simile. *Comparison*—Paints are compared to precious jewels.]

3. His bangs were a curtain, shielding his eyes. [*Figure of speech*—metaphor. *Comparison*—Hair is compared to a curtain.]

4. Abraham Lincoln said, "The world will little note nor long remember what we say here, but it can never forget what they did here." [*Figure of speech*—personification. *Comparison*—The world is given human attributes of remembering and forgetting.]

5. "But they that wait upon the Lord shall renew their strength; they shall mount up with wings as eagles" comes from Isaiah 40:31. [*Figure of speech*—simile. *Comparison*—They are compared to eagles using the word *as*.]

natural, nonhuman thing—the sky—is spoken of as though it had human abilities and human feelings. This description is much more visual than a plain statement of fact, such as "Yesterday it rained for hours."

Any of us can turn almost anything into imaginative language. After all, each of us has "a touch of the poet." This is partly what makes us human—the ability to see connections between different parts of our world.

Your Poem, Man . . .

unless there's one thing seen
suddenly against another—a parsnip
sprouting for a President, or
hailstones melting in an ashtray—
nothing really happens. It takes
surprise and wild connections,
doesn't it? A walrus chewing
on a ballpoint pen. Two blue tail-
lights on Tyrannosaurus Rex. Green
cheese teeth. Maybe what we wanted
least. Or most. Some unexpected
pleats. Words that never knew
each other till right now. Plug us
into the wrong socket and see
what blows—or what lights up.
Try
     untried
          circuitry,
new
     fuses.
Tell it like it never really was,
man,
and maybe we can see it
like it is.

          —Edward Lueders

Ode to Mi Gato *and* In a Neighborhood in Los Angeles *and* Hard on the Gas

Literary Focus

Tone: The Speaker's Feelings

Tone refers to the way a speaker is feeling. When you listen to people, you can often tell from their voices and facial expressions how they feel. You can usually tell if they're serious, happy, worried, or angry. When you read a poem, however, you have to depend on words alone to learn how the speaker (the voice talking to you in the poem) is feeling.

Ode: A Poem of Praise

An **ode** is a poem written to honor someone or something of great importance to the speaker. When people hear the word *ode,* they usually think of a poem written in a grand, dignified style. Gary Soto brings the ode down to earth. He uses ordinary language and the rhythms of everyday speech as he celebrates his *gato,* or cat.

Make the Connection

Quickwrite ✏️

Think about the love songs you hear on the radio. Love has also inspired thousands of poems. In two of the next three poems, the speaker lovingly recalls a relative. The speaker of the first poem celebrates a pet.

Think of someone or something special you'd like to celebrate or remember. Then, draw a gift diagram like the one below. Fill it with words, phrases, and memories telling the person or thing what he, she, or it has done for you.

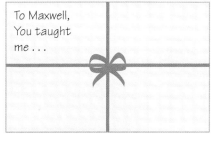

To Maxwell,
You taught
me . . .

Reading Standard 3.4 Define how tone or meaning is conveyed in poetry through figurative language.

STANDARDS FOCUS, pp. 389–394

(For grade-level and review standards taught in this selection, see citations on Pupil's Edition pages.)

Standard Coming Up in the Next Grade Levels

- Grade 8, Literary Response and Analysis 3.1 **Determine and articulate the relationship between the purposes and characteristics of different forms of poetry (e.g., ballad, lyric, couplet, epic, elegy, ode, sonnet).**

Summary ⬆ *above grade level*

Each of the three poems in this grouping uses figurative language to celebrate its subject. Each has a loving, affectionate tone.

"Ode to Mi Gato" is a free-verse poem praising the speaker's cat.

"In a Neighborhood in Los Angeles" celebrates the speaker's grandmother, who cared for him when he was a child and whom he will always remember.

"Hard on the Gas" pays tribute to the speaker's grandfather through an extended metaphor that compares how he drives a car to how he lives his life.

▶ Resources Reminder

Media

- *Audio CD Library*
  - disc 9

RESOURCES

Planning

- *One-Stop Planner* CD-ROM with Test Generator
- *On Course: Mapping Instruction*

Media

- *Audio CD Library*
  - disc 9

Reading

- *Interactive Reading*
  - Graphic Organizer: Comparative Elements Chart, p. 271

Differentiating Instruction

- *Lesson Plans for Language Development*
  - English-Language Learners, pp. 179–181, 194, 199

- Special Education Students, pp. 182, 194, 199

Assessment

- *Progress Assessment of Reading*
  - Selection Test, p. 136
- *One-Stop Planner* CD-ROM with Test Generator

Standards Starter

Motivate. The people we remember are not just those we see on TV or read about in a newspaper. More often they are people who have been there for us when we've needed them. Ask students to think of a person or pet that has been there for them—made them laugh, comforted them. Then, urge students to preview these poems by looking at the accompanying artwork and photographs.

Assign the Reading

Allow students to choose the order in which they will read these poems. Urge them to look for points of comparison among the poems.

▶ Resources Reminder

Reading
- *Interactive Reading*
  - Graphic Organizer: Comparative Elements Chart, p. 271

VIEWING THE ART

This is an eighteenth-century copy of *Spring Play in a T'ang Garden*, a painting done during the great Ming dynasty in China (1384–1644). The title refers to the T'ang dynasty, an earlier dynasty (618–907) which was a golden age for the arts and culture. This charming painting is part of a handscroll. A handscroll usually consists of a series of connected scenes painted on a roll of thin material—in this case, silk—which the viewer unrolls to admire the scenes one at a time.

DIFFERENTIATING INSTRUCTION

Learners Having Difficulty

Ask students what images they see as they read these poems. Which of these images would be fun to illustrate—the cat decked out in a hat and cape for Halloween or the grandmother with her braids and moon-covered dresses? Have students choose a medium such as watercolors, colored pencils, markers, poster paints, photography, collage, or modeling clay to create their favorite image.

English-Language Learners

Although the vocabulary in "Ode to Mi Gato" is not difficult, English-language learners may not comprehend some of Soto's figurative language. Ask them to sketch or explain in other words what is meant by each of the following figures of speech:

- nuggets *raining* into a bowl (ll. 15–16)
- a meow *like the rusty latch* (ll. 31–32)

- the *loop* of the speaker's arms (ll. 34–35)
- jump *like a splash of milk* (ll. 55–57)

▶ Resources Reminder

For lessons designed for intermediate and advanced English-language learners, see *Lesson Plans for Language Development*, pp. 179–181, 193, 199.

Ode to Mi Gato 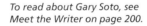 Gary Soto

He's white
As spilled milk,
My cat who sleeps
With his belly
5   Turned toward
The summer sky.
He loves the sun,
Its warmth like a hand.
He loves tuna cans
10   And milk cartons
With their dribble
Of milk. He loves
Mom when she rattles
The bag of cat food,
15   The brown nuggets
Raining into his bowl.
And my cat loves
Me, because I saved
Him from a dog,
20   Because I dressed him
In a hat and a cape
For Halloween,
Because I dangled
A sock of chicken skin
25   As he stood on his
Hind legs. I love mi gato,
Porque I found
Him on the fender
Of an abandoned car.
30   He was a kitten,

With a meow
Like the rusty latch
On a gate. I carried
Him home in the loop
35   Of my arms.
I poured milk
Into him, let him
Lick chunks of
Cheese from my palms,
40   And cooked huevo
After huevo
Until his purring
Engine kicked in
And he cuddled
45   Up to my father's slippers.
That was last year.
This spring,
He's excellent at sleeping
And no good
50   At hunting. At night
All the other cats
In the neighborhood
Can see him slink
Around the corner,
55   Or jump from the tree
Like a splash of
Milk. We lap up
His love and
He laps up his welcome.

To read about Gary Soto, see Meet the Writer on page 200.

(Opposite) *Spring Play in a T'ang Garden* (detail) (18th century). Copy of a painting attributed to Hsuan Tsung (Ming dynasty). Handscroll; colors on silk.

Ode to Mi Gato   **391**

A English-Language Learners

Reading Spanish words. Ask Spanish-speaking students to pronounce and define these Spanish words from the title and the body of the poem for the class: in the title, *mi gato* [mē gä′tō, "my cat"]; in l. 27, *porque* [pôr·kā′, "because"]; in l. 41, *huevo* [wā′vō, "egg"].

B Literary Focus
GRADE-LEVEL STANDARD
❓ Interpreting figurative language. What two things does Soto compare in this simile? [He compares the warmth of the sun on the cat's belly to the warmth of a human hand.] **Point out that the simile implies that the cat enjoys being petted the way he enjoys the sun on his belly.**

C Literary Focus
ADVANCED STANDARD
❓ Ode. Remind students that an ode pays tribute to something or someone that the speaker cherishes. In this ode, what does the speaker give the cat? [The speaker gives the cat a home, food, protection, and love.] **What does the cat give the speaker?** [He gives the speaker love, amusement, responsive meows, and appreciative purring.]

Special Education Students
For lessons designed for special education students, see *Lesson Plans for Language Development*, pp. 182, 194, 199.

Advanced Learners
Enrichment. Both "In a Neighborhood in Los Angeles" and "Hard on the Gas" use images that bring to life the people being celebrated. They do this, however, without using specific details of their personal appearances. Have students write a paragraph describing the way they think either the grandma ("In a Neighborhood in Los Angeles") or the grandfather ("Hard on the Gas") looks.

A **Literary Focus**
GRADE-LEVEL STANDARD

? Tone. What tone is set in the first stanza? [Possible responses: The informal word *grandma* sets an affectionate tone. Also, by giving his grandma credit for teaching him Spanish, the speaker sets a tone of gratitude.]

B **Learners Having Difficulty**

Punctuation. Students may be confused by the lack of punctuation in this poem. Explain that in prose "*mijito* / don't cry" would normally appear in quotation marks. The grandmother would say this to soothe the speaker.

C **Advanced Learners**

? Speculating. Why do you think the speaker's grandma sings and dances with the chairs? [Possible responses: She is trying to cheer up her grandson; she is feeling happy; she is feeling lonely herself.]

D **Literary Focus**
GRADE-LEVEL STANDARD

? Interpreting figurative language. How can the speaker's grandma wear Mexico's mountains, deserts, and ocean in her eyes? [Possible responses: The poet is using figurative language to say that the grandmother's memories of her home show in her eyes; her Mexican heritage is part of her personality.]

E **Literary Focus**
GRADE-LEVEL STANDARD

? Tone. How do the words of these closing lines help you understand the speaker's feelings toward his grandmother and the tone of the poem? [Possible responses: The speaker says he still feels his grandmother with him, whispering "mijito." This whispered endearment conveys their closeness. The tone is one of fondness and gratitude.]

IN A NEIGHBORHOOD IN LOS ANGELES

FRANCISCO X. ALARCÓN

A
I learned
Spanish
from my grandma

B
mijito°
5 don't cry
she'd tell me

on the mornings
my parents
would leave

10 to work
at the fish
canneries

C
my grandma
would chat
15 with chairs

sing them
old
songs

dance
20 waltzes with them
in the kitchen

when she'd say
niño barrigón°
she'd laugh

25 with my grandma
I learned
to count clouds

to point out
in flowerpots
30 mint leaves

my grandma
wore moons
on her dress

Mexico's mountains
35 deserts
ocean

in her eyes
I'd see them
in her braids

D
40 I'd touch them
in her voice
smell them

one day
I was told:
45 she went far away

E
but still
I feel her
with me

whispering
50 in my ear
mijito

—*translated by*
Francisco Aragon

4. **mijito** (mē·hē′tô): contraction of *mi hijito*, Spanish for "my little child."

23. **niño barrigón** (nēn′yô bä′rē·gôn′): Spanish for "potbellied boy."

CONTENT-AREA CONNECTIONS

Geography

Mexico. The speaker in this poem saw Mexico in his grandmother's eyes. Mexico is a land of varied geography: Volcanoes, mountain chains, beaches, jungles, and deserts can all be found in this southern neighbor of the United States. Mountains cover two thirds of the country to the east and west, with high plateaus of flat land in between, where many Mexicans live. The coastal plains separate the mountains from the surrounding oceans.

Activity. Encourage interested students to use an atlas to find Mexico's mountain chains and the bodies of water that surround the country. [*Mountain chains*—Sierra Madre Occidental, Sierra Madre Oriental, Sierra Madre del Sur. *Bodies of water*—Pacific Ocean, Gulf of California, Gulf of Mexico, Caribbean Sea.]

INDIVIDUAL

HARD ON THE GAS

Janet S. Wong

My grandfather taught himself to drive
rough, the way he learned to live,

push the pedal, hard on the gas,
rush up to 50,
coast a bit,

rush, rest, rush, rest— **G**

When you clutch the bar above your right shoulder
he shoots you a look that asks,
Who said the ride would be smooth?

F

H

Francisco X. Alarcón
Janet S. Wong

"Poetry Is, in a Way, Like Shouting"

Francisco X. Alarcón (1954–   ), who grew up both in the United States and in Mexico, says that his family has been binational for four generations. Alarcón's roots are important to him; he regularly visits the Mexican village his ancestors came from.

Alarcón was brought up mainly in Los Angeles by his grandmother, the woman he celebrates in his poem "In a Neighborhood in Los Angeles." His career as a poet began when he was thirteen years old and started writing down his grandmother's songs.

Janet Wong (1962–   ) bases many of her poems on her experiences growing up Asian American. Wong decided to become a poet after working as a lawyer for several years.

> " Poetry is, in a way, like shouting. Since you can't yell at the top of your lungs for a long time, you have to decide what you really need to say, and say it quickly. "

Activity. Students should be given the chance to appreciate the rhythmic qualities of poetry. Group students in pairs for echo readings. First, one partner should read a section of a poem aloud, then the other partner should repeat what the first student has read. Have different students experiment by pausing at different points in the poem. After students have read a poem a few times in this way, have them discuss how the rhythmic qualities of the poem affected their readings.

PAIRED

F **Reading Skills**

? **Interpreting.** Based on this comparison between how the grandfather drives and how he lives, what do you think his life has been like? [Possible responses: He has suffered ups and downs; he plows into things head on and then has to retreat and take it easy.]

G **Literary Focus**
GRADE-LEVEL STANDARD
? **Word choice and tone.** How does reading the line *"rush, rest, rush, rest—"* aloud help you to envision the grandfather's life? [Possible responses: The word *rush* explodes from the mouth and then *rest* lingers on the tongue. There is a natural pause after the first pair of words, and then the pattern is repeated, reinforcing the pattern of the grandfather's life.]

H **Reading Skills**

? **Interpreting.** Why does the speaker clutch the bar? [Possible response: to keep her balance because the ride is bumpy.] What do you think "the ride" represents? [Possible response: life.]

Monitoring students' progress. Guide the class in answering these true-false questions.

True-False

1. The speaker in "Ode to Mi Gato" rescued the cat at the local animal shelter. [F]

2. The cat in "Ode to Mi Gato" is not much of a hunter. [T]

3. The grandmother in "In a Neighborhood in Los Angeles" cared for the speaker when he was young. [T]

4. The grandfather in "Hard on the Gas" is teaching the speaker a lesson about life. [T]

INDEPENDENT PRACTICE

Literary Response and Analysis

Interpretations

1. *"In a Neighborhood in Los Angeles."* Subject—grandmother. *Subject Celebrated For*—caring for and teaching the speaker when he was a child. *Speaker's Tone*—respectful; fond remembrance.

   "Ode to Mi Gato." Subject—pet cat. *Subject Celebrated For*—its love; the fun it brings the speaker. *Speaker's Tone*—humorous; affectionate.

   "Hard on the Gas." Subject—grandfather. *Subject Celebrated For*—the tough way he lived his life. *Speaker's Tone*—fond; humorous.

2. The cat in "Ode to Mi Gato" is as white as spilled milk. Later, the way the cat jumps from a tree is compared to a splash of milk.

3. In ll. 13–20 of "In a Neighborhood in Los Angeles," the grandma chats with the chairs, sings them songs, and waltzes with them.

4. In ll. 57–58, the speaker says that they "lap up" the love of the cat; the family is portrayed as if it were the cat drinking milk.

5. Possible answers: A life that is "hard on the gas" would be one that is stressful, is full of ups and downs, moves rapidly, and is full of risks. A life that is "rush, rest, rush, rest" would be one with stops and starts, triumphs and setbacks.

Evaluation

6. Students may appreciate the use of Spanish words and feel that they add authenticity and color to the poems.

Literary Response and Analysis

Interpretations

1. Compare these three poems by filling out a chart like the one at the bottom of this page. First, identify the subject of each poem—the person or thing it's about. Next, state what the subject in each poem is loved, celebrated, or remembered for. Then, find a word or two that describes the speaker's **tone,** the way he or she feels about the subject.

2. At the beginning of "Ode to Mi Gato," the speaker uses a **simile** comparing a cat to spilled milk. How is the cat like spilled milk? Find another simile comparing the cat to milk.

3. The grandmother in the poem "In a Neighborhood in Los Angeles" **personifies** chairs. Which lines show that she sees her chairs as people?

4. Gary Soto uses a kind of reverse **personification** at the end of his poem, where he compares his family to a cat. Find the lines in which he makes this comparison.

5. An **extended metaphor** carries a comparison through a whole poem. In "Hard on the Gas" the poet uses an extended metaphor to compare a way of driving to a way of living. What kind of life would be "hard on the gas"? What kind of life could be described as "rush, rest, rush, rest"?

Evaluation

6. Spanish words are used in Gary Soto's poem and in the translation of Alarcón's poem. What do you think of this technique? What effect does the use of Spanish words have on the poems?

Writing
Odes Aloud

What special person or thing (a friend, a pet, even a computer) would you like to celebrate in an **ode**? Look back at your Quickwrite for ideas. Before you write, list a few details of your subject to help readers understand why you feel so strongly about it. Try to include a figure of speech or two in your ode.

Reading Standard 3.4 Define how tone or meaning is conveyed in poetry through figurative language.

Poem	Subject	What the Subject Is Loved, Celebrated, or Remembered For	Speaker's Tone
"In a Neighborhood in Los Angeles"			
"Ode to Mi Gato"			
"Hard on the Gas"			

ASSESSING

Assessment
- *Progress Assessment of Reading*
  - Selection Test, p. 136

RETEACHING

Reteaching
For a lesson reteaching how tone or meaning is conveyed through poetic elements, see **Reteaching,** pp. 489J–489K.

Haiku

Literary Focus
Word Choice

In poetry every word counts, because a poet must pack a lot of meaning into just a few phrases. When choosing their words, poets consider what words mean, how they sound, and what they suggest.

Haiku

Haiku (hī'kōō') is the most widely known form of Japanese poetry. In haiku every word must be chosen with special care because haiku have a strictly defined form. A haiku in Japanese consists of three lines and a total of seventeen syllables: five syllables each in lines 1 and 3 and seven syllables in line 2. (The number of syllables may vary in English translations.)

Here are some of the rules that haiku poets generally follow.

1. A haiku is about a moment in daily life.

2. A haiku describes particular things, often two contrasting things.

3. A haiku records a moment of enlightenment—a sudden discovery about life.

4. A haiku is usually about a season of the year. Often a haiku contains a *kigo*, a "season" word, like *frog* for summer or *willow* for spring.

A haiku is like a painting in which the artist uses just a few brush strokes to suggest a subject, leaving the rest to your imagination.

Make the Connection
Quickwrite ✏️

Think of an outdoor scene you've observed. Try to picture it clearly and even hear some sounds. Freewrite for a minute or two about what you see and hear.

Snow at Night by Ando Hiroshige. Japanese engraving.

The Art Archive/Oriental Art Museum, Genoa/Dagli Orti (A).

Reading Standard 3.4 Define how tone or meaning is conveyed in poetry through word choice.

STANDARDS FOCUS, pp. 395–398

(For grade-level and review standards taught in this selection, see citations on Pupil's Edition pages.)

Prerequisite Standard
■ Grade 5, Literary Response and Analysis 3.5 Describe the function and effect of common literary devices (e.g., imagery, metaphor, symbolism).

Standard Coming Up in the Next Grade Levels
■ Grade 8, Literary Response and Analysis 3.1 Determine and articulate the purposes and characteristics of different forms of poetry (e.g., ballad, lyric, couplet, epic, elegy, ode, sonnet).

Summary ↔ *at grade level*

Each haiku captures a brief, vivid moment through careful word choice and imagery. In "An old silent pond" the sudden splash of a frog disturbs the peaceful silence of a pond. "Winter rain" presents an image of a warmly lighted farmhouse as seen from the outside through winter rain. "Bad-tempered, I got back" suggests that the poet's mood improves when he sees the willow tree in his yard. In "A balmy spring wind" an indistinct memory is brought back to the poet by the caress of a warm spring breeze.

Haiku **395**

RESOURCES

Planning
■ *One-Stop Planner* CD-ROM with Test Generator
■ *On Course: Mapping Instruction*

Media
■ *Audio CD Library*
  ▪ disc 9

Reading
■ *Interactive Reading*
  ▪ Graphic Organizer: Balance Scale Diagrams, p. 272

Differentiating Instruction
■ *Lesson Plans for Language Development*
  ▪ English-Language Learners, pp. 183, 185, 195, 200

■ Special Education Students, pp. 184, 186, 195, 200

Assessment
■ *Progress Assessment of Reading*
  ▪ Selection Test, p. 139
■ *One-Stop Planner* CD-ROM with Test Generator

Standards Starter

Build prerequisite skills. Explain that haiku illuminate connections between the natural world and the world of human emotions. In haiku, precise word choices create images that resonate with meaning. These images evoke emotional associations in the reader.

DIRECT TEACHING

A Literary Focus
ADVANCED STANDARD

❓ Haiku. Most traditional haiku poets follow the rule of three lines with five, seven, and five syllables per line, respectively. How many syllables are in each line of this haiku? [five, seven, five]

B Literary Focus
REVIEW STANDARD

❓ Imagery. What two contrasting images has the poet created in this haiku? [The cold rain contrasts with the warm, inviting light in the window.]

C Literary Focus
REVIEW STANDARD

❓ Symbolism. In this haiku the willow is the *kigo,* or season word, for spring. What else do you think the willow tree might stand for? [peacefulness, security] Explain that in traditional Japanese society the willow tree also symbolized patience and endurance, perhaps because a willow bends with the wind and so endures.

D Literary Focus
GRADE-LEVEL STANDARD

❓ Word choice and tone. What does the word *balmy* suggest to you? [Possible response: gentle, calm, comforting.] What tone does it create? [a soothing tone]

A
An old silent pond . . .
A frog jumps into the pond,
splash! Silence again.

—Matsuo Bashō

B
Winter rain:
A farmhouse piled with firewood,
A light in the window.

—Nozawa Bonchō

C
Bad-tempered, I got back:
Then, in the garden,
The willow tree.

—Ōshima Ryōta

D
A balmy spring wind
Reminding me of something
I cannot recall

—Richard Wright

Sudden Shower at Atake (1857) by Ando Hiroshige. Japanese woodcut.

DIFFERENTIATING INSTRUCTION

Learners Having Difficulty
Point out that in three of the four haiku, the first line consists of a lone image from nature ("An old silent pond," "Winter rain," "A balmy spring wind"). Have students jot down associations these images evoke for them and compare these associations with what is described in the haiku. Were they surprised by the haiku's insight or discovery about life? Why or why not?

English-Language Learners
For lessons designed for intermediate and advanced English-language learners, see *Lesson Plans for Language Development,* pp. 183, 185, 195, 200.

Special Education Students
For lessons designed for special education students, see *Lesson Plans for Language Development,* pp. 184, 186, 195, 200.

Matsuo Bashō
Nozawa Bonchō
Ōshima Ryōta
Richard Wright

The True Nature of Things

Matsuo Bashō (1644–1694) is one of Japan's most famous poets. Bashō was born into a wealthy family and grew up in a village in western Japan. He began writing verses when he was nine. By the time Bashō was thirty, he was traveling around Japan and working as a professional poetry teacher. **Nozawa Bonchō** (16?? –1714) was one of his students.

Many of the haiku written by Bashō and his students were inspired by nature. Bashō urged his students to look for the "true nature of things." He insisted that haiku should be written in simple language and deal with everyday life. He took his pen name from a banana tree (*bashō* in Japanese) that he planted in his yard.

Ōshima Ryōta (1707–1787) incorporated Zen ideas into his haiku and his painting. (Zen is a form of Buddhism that emphasizes meditation.)

Modern poets in many countries have written haiku. **Richard Wright** (1908–1960), an African American writer famous for his autobiography *Black Boy*, composed more than four thousand haiku in the two years before his death. Wright called them hoku.

Meet the Writers

Background. Matsuo Bashō is considered the inventor of the haiku form as we know it today. He was a deeply spiritual man who became a Zen monk in his later years. His haiku showed a zest for life and an awareness that all things are related. He believed that nature's inner beauty could illuminate the meaning of life.

Richard Wright is one of America's most important writers. He was born in Mississippi, the son of a sharecropper and a mother who was unable to take care of him for much of his childhood. He spent some time in orphanages and was brought up for the most part by relatives. Wright is best known for his prose works exploring the effects of racism, but many of the haiku poems he wrote right before his death give a human face to nature.

For Independent Reading

For students who are interested in reading more haiku, recommend *Cricket Songs: Japanese Haiku* and *More Cricket Songs: Japanese Haiku,* both edited by Harry Behn.

VIEWING THE ART

Three woodblock prints by Japanese artists illustrate these haiku. *Snow at Night* and *Sudden Shower at Atake*, on pp. 395–396, were designed by Ando Hiroshige (1797–1858). *The Great Wave off Kanagawa*, on p. 398, was designed by Katsushika Hokusai (1760–1849). Point out to students that the perspectives of these prints are compressed. Distant objects seem to be on almost the same plane as nearby objects. This distortion of perspective and the innovative use of colors and shapes shown in Japanese prints of this period would later have a strong influence on Impressionist painters in Europe.

Activity. People can be seen in two of the prints. Have students describe their feelings as they face the forces of nature.

Advanced Learners

Enrichment. Provide students with the following short history of the haiku: Examples of short verses similar to haiku have been found in thirteenth- or fourteenth-century Japanese literature. However, the art of haiku was not perfected until the seventeenth century when the greatest of the classical haiku poets, Bashō, lived. While English authors were composing long, intricate poems, Bashō and his pupils were writing pure, compressed verses. In the centuries since Bashō, the haiku form has been adopted by poets all over the world.

Activity. Encourage students to research the modern haiku and formulate two generalizations about the differences between classical and contemporary haiku.

INDEPENDENT PRACTICE

Literary Response and Analysis

Interpretations

1. Possible answers: "*An old silent pond*"—summer. "*Winter rain*"—winter. "*Bad-tempered, I got back*"—spring. "*A balmy spring wind*"—spring.

2. Possible answers: *See*—the light in the window and the piled-up firewood in "Winter rain"; the willow tree in "Bad-tempered, I got back"; the still pond in "An old silent pond." *Hear*—the splash of the frog and the silence restored in "An old silent pond."

3. "Winter rain" presents the contrasting images of cold winter rain outside and the cozy warm farmhouse inside; "An old silent pond" presents the contrasting images of the still silence of the pond broken by the splash of the frog; "Bad-tempered, I got back" presents the contrasting image of the foul-humored poet and the comforting willow tree.

4. Possible answers: In "An old silent pond" the poet notices the contrast between the splash of the frog and the silence before and after; nature, which can be both loud and silent, restores itself. In "Winter rain" the poet notices the difference between the cold rain outside and the warm light within; nature can be harsh. In "Bad-tempered, I got back" the poet discovers the peace of the garden and the willow tree; nature can soothe and give one the strength to persevere. In "A balmy spring wind" the poet discovers that the feel of the wind triggers an indistinct memory; nature sometimes can inspire us to try to recall a lost memory.

5. Possible answer: In "A balmy spring wind" the nostalgic, gentle tone is created by words like *balmy, spring, reminding,* and *recall.*

Literary Response and Analysis

Interpretations

1. Which season do you think each haiku describes? (Remember that a frog is often used to suggest summer and a willow tree to suggest spring.)

2. List three or four **images** in these haiku that help you **see** something and two **images** that help you **hear** sounds.

3. Which haiku present **contrasting images**?

4. In each haiku, what exactly does the poet notice or discover? What part does nature play in each discovery?

5. Choose one haiku, and describe its **tone**—the speaker's attitude toward the subject. Which words suggest that tone?

6. Choose one haiku, and state its **message** in your own words.

7. Find two haiku that contain five syllables in the first and last lines and seven syllables in the middle line.

Evaluation

8. In Japan, poetry-writing contests are held every year in which judges award prizes for the best haiku. Suppose you're one of the judges, and you're considering these four haiku. Which would you award the prize for? Why?

The Great Wave off Kanagawa (c. 1831–1833) by Katsushika Hokusai.
The Metropolitan Museum of Art, H. O. Havemeyer Collection, Bequest of Mrs. H. O. Havemeyer, 1929.

Reading Standard 3.4 Define how tone or meaning is conveyed in poetry through word choice.

Writing
Haiku by You

Haiku are fun to write. Before you write, review the rules for writing haiku on page 395. (If you wish, you can skip the rule about the seventeen syllables.) Then, keep filling out charts like the one below until you've found images and a feeling that you think will work. You might try to open with a word naming your season. Try to list some contrasting images in your chart. One important rule: Your poem should consist of three lines.

Haiku Ideas
Season:
Sight images:
Sound images:
Touch images:
Smell images:
Taste images:
Feeling or discovery:

6. Possible answers: "*An old silent pond*"—silence disrupted can be restored. "*Winter rain*"—A warm, well-lit home can provide a refuge from the harshness of winter weather. "*Bad-tempered, I got back*"—one's own garden provides respite from the cares of the world. "*A balmy spring wind*"—the feel of something, like the wind, can stir memories in our subconscious mind.

7. The two haiku that follow the syllable rule are "An old silent pond" and "A balmy spring wind."

Evaluation

8. Answers will vary. Students should support their decisions by pointing out parts of the poems that appeal to them.

How to Read (and Own) a Poem

Don't let this happen to you:

There once was a man in our nation
Who suffered a bad situation.
    The poem he read
    Made no sense in his head
Because he ignored punctuation.

Seven Easy Steps to Reading Poetry

Punctuation is just one thing to look for when you're reading a poem. Follow these guidelines, and poetry will come alive for you:

1 Read the poem aloud at least once. You'll find it easier to make sense of a poem if you hear how it sounds.

2 Pay attention to **punctuation.** Pause briefly at commas and semicolons, and longer after periods. If you see dashes, expect sudden shifts in thought. If you see no punctuation at the end of a line, don't pause.

3 Feel the poem's **rhythm.** Poetry has a special rhythmic sound, like music.

4 Poets pay special attention to **word choice.** Use context clues to figure out the meanings of unfamiliar words. (Use a dictionary if you're stuck.) Do any of the words have more than one meaning?

5 Poets use **comparisons.** If you're reading a poem in which snowflakes are described as if they were insects, let the comparison create a picture in your mind. Think about why the poet chose *this* comparison. How does it make you feel?

6 Think about the poem's meaning. What does the poem say to *you*? Does it relate to your life in any way? Does it offer you a new way of looking at something?

7 If you like the poem, memorize it. Now it's yours.

Reading Standard 3.4 Define how meaning is conveyed in poetry through word choice, figurative language, sentence structure, line length, punctuation, rhythm, repetition, and rhyme.

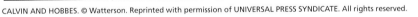

A QUANDARY

MOM ONCE SAID SHE LOVED ME JUST THE WAY I AM, SO I WONDER WHAT WOULD HAPPEN IF I BECAME A CLAM.

if HER SON WAS GRAY AND GRIMY SLIPPERY AND SLIMY, AN OVERSIZED HORS D'OEUVRE, WOULD MOM STILL HAVE THE NERVE?

GOOD POETRY GIVES ME GOOSEBUMPS.

CALVIN AND HOBBES. © Watterson. Reprinted with permission of UNIVERSAL PRESS SYNDICATE. All rights reserved.

How to Read (and Own) a Poem **399**

STANDARDS FOCUS, p. 399

(For the grade-level standard taught in this lesson, see Pupil's Edition, p. 399.)

Reading Skills: How to Read (and Own) a Poem

Ask students if they have ever spoken aloud, thought about the meaning of, or memorized the lyrics to a song they like. Point out that these approaches to song lyrics are exactly how readers should approach poetry. Then, go over the seven steps to owning a poem with students. Be sure they see that the process of learning song lyrics and reading poetry is the same, except that with poetry students must watch for punctuation.

Apply

Invite students to practice owning a poem. Have them choose poems, either from the textbook or from independent reading. Students should apply each of the seven steps to their poems. After they finish this activity, have them write brief paragraphs evaluating these steps. Which step enriched their understanding of the poem the most?

HOMEWORK

DIFFERENTIATING INSTRUCTION

Learners Having Difficulty

As students go over this page, have them concentrate on step 6. How does making connections to their own lives help them appreciate poetry? How does it affect their opinions about or interest in the poems? Encourage students to talk about why they like poems they can relate to their own lives.

English-Language Learners

These students should pay special attention to steps 2, 4, and 5. Encourage them to ask fluent classmates for help in deciphering punctuation and figuring out word meanings and comparisons. Then, suggest that each student select a poem he or she likes and commit it to memory (step 7) to recite later in front of the entire class.

STANDARDS FOCUS, pp. 400–403

(For grade-level and review standards taught in this selection, see citations on Pupil's Edition pages.)

Standard Coming Up in the Next Grade Level

■ Grade 7, Literary Response and Analysis 3.6 **Analyze a range of responses to a literary work, and determine the extent to which the literary elements in the work shaped those responses.**

Summary ⬇ *below grade level*

In "Poem," Hughes's tone is sad and wistful as he mourns the loss of a friend. In "Motto," Hughes adopts a hipster tone and jazz-style rhythms to create a motto for life.

PRETEACHING

Standards Starter

Build prerequisite skills.
Remind students that it is often easier to identify a poem's tone if they read the poem aloud.

DIRECT TEACHING

Ⓐ **Literary Focus**
GRADE-LEVEL STANDARD
❓ Tone. What is the tone of this poem? [Possible responses: sad, poignant, resigned.] How does the repetition of the poem's first line help to convey this tone? [Possible response: The repetition of the first line in the last line emphasizes the speaker's love for his friend, making the fact that the friend has left even more sad.]

Poem *and* Motto

Literary Focus
Tone: An Attitude

Tone is the attitude a speaker takes toward a subject. We express tones all the time: Our words and voices can express joy, sadness, confusion, anger—and many other feelings. You might think that a poet would always express the same tone in his or her works, but that is not the case. Two poems by the same poet can express totally different tones, as in these poems by Langston Hughes.

Make the Connection
Speaking

Try this experiment with tones: With one or more partners, take turns saying these three sentences aloud. Use your voice to express the tones named in parentheses. Notice how punctuation helps suggest the different tones.

I *won!* (joy)
I *won?* (doubt)
I *won?* (sarcasm)

Reading Standard 3.4 Define how tone or meaning is conveyed in poetry through word choice, sentence structure, line length, and punctuation.

Witness (1987) by Hughie Lee-Smith.
Courtesy, June Kelly Gallery, New York.

Poem
Langston Hughes

I loved my friend.
He went away from me.
Ⓐ There's nothing more to say.
The poem ends,
Soft as it began—
I loved my friend.

RESOURCES

Media
■ *Audio CD Library*
  ▪ disc 9

Reading
■ *Interactive Reading*
  ▪ Graphic Organizer: Tone Webs, p. 273

Differentiating Instruction
■ *Lesson Plans for Language Development*
  ▪ English-Language Learners, pp. 187, 196, 201
  ▪ Special Education Students, pp. 188, 196, 201

Assessment
■ *Progress Assessment of Reading*
  ▪ Selection Test, p. 142

Motto
Langston Hughes

I play it cool
And dig all jive.
That's the reason
I stay alive.

My motto,
As I live and learn,
            is:
*Dig And Be Dug
In Return.*

Carolina Shout by Romare Bearden.
Mint Museum of Art, Charlotte, North Carolina. Museum Purchase: National Endowment for the Arts Matching Fund and the Charlotte Debutante Club Fund. Romare Bearden Foundation/Licensed by VAGA, New York.

Motto   **401**

B Literary Focus
REVIEW STANDARD

? **Rhythm.** How would you describe the rhythm of the first stanza? [Students should recognize that the first stanza has a regular rhythm and that the rhythm is fast, with staccato-like beats.]

C Literary Focus
GRADE-LEVEL STANDARD

? **Tone.** How does the speaker's choice of words help to reveal his tone, or attitude? [Possible responses: The speaker uses a lot of slang, which makes him sound cool and hip; he is saying he's learned not to "mess with" other people.]

D Literary Focus
GRADE-LEVEL STANDARD

? **Tone.** How do line length and punctuation in this stanza help to reveal the poem's tone? [Possible responses: The short line, "is," and the colon both emphasize the speaker's motto and his hip, aloof attitude. They also force the reader to pause, adding emphasis to the final two lines.]

GUIDED PRACTICE

Monitoring students' progress. Have small groups of students make charts with the headings "Word Choice," "Sentence Structure," "Line Length," and "Punctuation." Then, have the groups go over the two poems, filling in the appropriate information under each heading. They can use the charts to compare and contrast the tones of the two poems.

DIFFERENTIATING INSTRUCTION

Learners Having Difficulty
If students need help understanding what is meant by tone, have them use facial expressions and body language to mime different feelings, such as sadness, regret, delight, sarcasm, or a sense of wonder. Explain that just as they use their body language to convey attitude, poets use words, rhymes, and rhythm to express attitude or "tone."

▶ Resources Reminder
Reading
■ *Interactive Reading*
   ■ Graphic Organizer: Tone Webs, p. 273

English-Language Learners
Students may have trouble with the slang terms found in "Motto," particularly as some of them are no longer current. Suggest that these students pair up with fluent partners

and consult a dictionary of slang to discover the definitions for each term. Once they know the meaning of the slang, students can re-read the poem on their own.

▶ Resources Reminder
For lessons designed for intermediate and advanced English-language learners, see *Lesson Plans for Language Development*, pp. 187, 196, 201.

Meet the Writer

Background. Langston Hughes lived in six different American cities before he was twelve years old. Before he began writing for a living, he held jobs as a truck driver, a farmer, a cook, a waiter, a sailor, and a doorman at a Paris nightclub. Hughes began his writing career as a poet and then became a short story writer, novelist, playwright, song lyricist, radio writer, children's book author, and columnist. While working as a columnist, he used humor to express his opinions about the social injustice African Americans were facing in the United States. His poems, which often incorporate jazz and blues rhythms and simple rhymes, express both the jazzed-up excitement and weary blues of African American life in his era.

For Independent Reading

Remind students to use the seven steps for reading (and owning) a poem as they read *The Dream Keeper*. You also might recommend the following titles:

- If students want more of Hughes's poetry, they might consider *Don't You Turn Back,* a collection of Langston Hughes protest poems.
- Langston Hughes's legacy continues in *Black Out Loud,* a collection of modern African American poetry edited by Arnold Adoff.

VIEWING THE ART

Romare Bearden (1914–1988) was born in New York City and lived there throughout the Harlem Renaissance. He often used collage to depict the rollicking musical scene of the times.

Activity. What mood does *Jazz* on p. 403 convey? [a mood of celebration]

Langston Hughes

The Dream Keeper

Langston Hughes (1902–1967) was lonely as a child until he found a home in the world of books.

> Books began to happen to me, and I began to believe in nothing but books and the wonderful world of books—where if people suffered they suffered in beautiful language and not in monosyllables, as we did in Kansas.

Hughes wrote his first poem in elementary school—but only *after* his classmates had elected him class poet.

> [My class] had elected all the class officers, but there was no one in our class who looked like a poet, or had ever written a poem. . . . The day I was elected, I went home and wondered what I should write. Since we had eight teachers in our school, I thought there should be one verse for each teacher, with an especially good one for my favorite teacher. I felt the class should have eight, too. So my first poem was about the longest poem I ever wrote—sixteen verses, which were later cut down. In the first half of the poem, I said that our school had the finest teachers there ever were. And in the latter half, I said our class was the greatest class ever graduated. So at graduation when I read the poem, naturally everybody applauded loudly. That was the way I began to write poetry.

Hughes later settled in New York City, where he became a leading figure in the cultural movement known as the Harlem Renaissance. His poems often echo the rhythms of blues and jazz.

For Independent Reading

Hughes is most celebrated for his poems. You can sample some of his best poems in a collection called *The Dream Keeper and Other Poems.*

Portrait of Langston Hughes (c. 1925) by Winold Reiss.

National Portrait Gallery, Smithsonian Institution, Washington, D.C./ Art Resource, New York.

DIFFERENTIATING INSTRUCTION

Advanced Learners

Musical influences on Hughes. Music had a defining influence on Langston Hughes's poetry. After students read the poems, ask advanced learners to borrow Ken Burns's documentary on jazz from the library and select relevant portions of it to present to the class as background for "Motto."

Activity. Have students present additional poems from Hughes's work and explain how they are influenced by either blues or jazz. Possibilities include poems from *Ask Your Mama* (jazz poems) and poems such as "Blues Montage" or "The Weary Blues."

Literary Response and Analysis

Interpretations

1. Think about the "I" in "Poem." What do you know about this **speaker**?

2. Think about the "I" in "Motto." What do you know about this **speaker**? (What does he have to do to stay alive?)

3. Hughes used the slang of jazz musicians in many of his poems. You may know what the speaker in "Motto" means when he says, "I play it cool." What are the slang meanings of *dig* and *jive*? (Use a good dictionary if you need to.) How would you state the speaker's motto in your own words?

4. **Tone** is a speaker's feeling or attitude toward a subject. Here is a list of tones. Which would you match with "Poem"? with "Motto"? Be ready to defend your choices. (Which tones do not apply to either poem?)

sad	wistful
upbeat	sorrowful
sarcastic	defiant
bitter	boastful
desperate	joyful

5. Try rephrasing "Motto," substituting **different words** for *cool, dig,* and *jive*. What happens to the **tone** of the poem?

Listening and Speaking
A Two-Tone Reading

Prepare the two poems for an oral presentation. Before your reading, make a script for each poem. Look carefully at the **punctuation,** and mark points where you'll pause. Decide which lines or words to emphasize (watch for **short lines** and **long lines**). Also decide what **tone,** or attitude, you want to convey in your readings.

Another possibility is setting the poems to music. What kind of musical setting would suit each poem?

BONUS QUESTION

What's your motto?

Reading Standard 3.4
Define how tone or meaning is conveyed in poetry through word choice, sentence structure, line length, and punctuation.

Jazz (1979) by Romare Bearden.
Sheldon Memorial Art Gallery and Sculpture Garden. University of Nebraska–Lincoln. F. M. Hall Collection.

Poem / Motto   **403**

STANDARDS FOCUS, pp. 404–411

(For grade-level and review standards taught in this selection, see citations on Pupil's Edition pages.)

Prerequisite Standard

■ Grade 4, Literary Response and Analysis 3.2 **Identify the main events of the plot, their causes, and the influence of each event on future actions.**

Summary ⬌ *at grade level*

This song tells the story of the folk hero John Henry. Its refrain, "Lord, Lord," creates a tone of pride and sorrow. The repetition of lines at the end of each stanza emphasizes John Henry's strength and courage.

As a baby, John Henry predicts that a hammer will cause his death. As an adult he hammers through rock, digging railroad tunnels. When the captain plans to replace John Henry's labor with a steam-powered drill, John Henry races the drill. He cuts through fifteen feet of rock, compared with the steam drill's nine feet—but the effort kills him. John Henry becomes a legend, and his ringing hammer strokes can still be heard for miles around.

John Henry

Literary Focus
Repetition

Repetition is repeating something—a word, a phrase, a stanza, a sound, a pattern. Repetition helps give poetry its music. Poets also use repetition to emphasize important ideas, to create a mood, even to build suspense.

One of the simplest kinds of repetition used in poetry, songs, and speeches is the refrain. A **refrain** is a word, phrase, line, or group of lines repeated at intervals. (The wording of a refrain may change slightly from time to time.) Most songs you hear or sing have a refrain. "The Star-Spangled Banner" includes a refrain at the end of each verse: "Oh! say, does that star-spangled banner yet wave / O'er the land of the free and the home of the brave?" Martin Luther King, Jr.'s most famous speech is built on the refrain "I have a dream."

Make the Connection
Talk It Over 🖉

"John Henry" is a ballad about a contest between a man and a machine. What can machines do better than people? What can people do better than machines? Working with a few classmates, list some answers to these questions. Then, make a chart like the one that follows, and fill it in with the best items from your list. Write down two items in each column.

Reading Standard 3.4
Define how tone or meaning is conveyed in poetry through repetition.

Contests People Would Win	Contests Machines Would Win
song writing	clothes washing

Background

Nobody knows whether John Henry, the hero of this song, was a real person, but people began singing about him in the early 1870s. He is said to have been an African American laborer in the crew constructing the Big Bend Tunnel of the Chesapeake and Ohio Railroad. According to the legend, someone set up a contest between John Henry and a steam drill. If you can, listen to a recording of the song "John Henry."

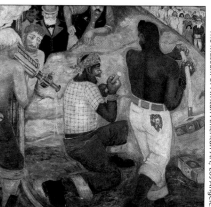

John Henry on the Right, Steam Drill on the Left (detail) (1944–1947) by Palmer C. Hayden.

The Museum of African American Art, Los Angeles.

John Henry

When John Henry Was a Baby (1944–1947) by Palmer C. Hayden.

The Museum of African American Art, Los Angeles.

A N O N Y M O U S   A F R I C A N   A M E R I C A N

Standards Starter

Motivate. List machines you have used this morning (e.g., alarm clock, hair dryer, TV, microwave, car, calculator, computer), and ask students to add to the list. Have students discuss the advantages and disadvantages of a morning with no machines. Then, assign the Talk It Over activity.

Assign the Reading

You might go over the Before You Read page as a class. Then, for students reading at and above grade level, assign the song and the Reading Check questions as homework. Meanwhile, continue working with small groups of students having difficulty. After all students have completed a first reading of the song, have the class read it aloud.

HOMEWORK

 Resources Reminder

Media
- *Audio CD Library*
  - disc 9
- *Fine Art Transparencies*
  - Transparency 13

Reading
- *Interactive Reading*
  - Graphic Organizer: Refrain Reformulation Pyramid, p. 274

DIFFERENTIATING INSTRUCTION

Learners Having Difficulty
These students may benefit from hearing the song played as they follow along in their books. Encourage students to listen for lines and phrases that are repeated, including those with slight variations.

English-Language Learners
Point out to students that this song includes features of dialect, such as the shortening of *–ing* to *–in'* (*sittin'*, *buryin'*), the use of *gonna* for going to, and the use of the nonstandard negative *ain't*. Pronounce these terms for students, and explain what they mean.

Resources Reminder

For lessons designed for intermediate and advanced English-language learners, see *Lesson Plans for Language Development*, pp. 189, 191, 197, 202.

Special Education Students
For lessons designed for special education students, see *Lesson Plans for Language Development*, pp. 191, 197, 202.

A **Literary Focus**
GRADE-LEVEL STANDARD

? **Repetition.** Which line is repeated in this verse? [the fourth] What do you think the repetition emphasizes? [Possible responses: the surprising fact that this three-day-old baby can talk; his ominous prediction that a hammer will kill him.]

B **Literary Focus**
REVIEW STANDARD

Poetry. Be sure students know that a group of lines that would be called a stanza in a poem is called a verse in a song.

C **Reading Skills**

? **Interpreting.** What do you think John Henry means in this verse? [Possible response: He admits that a person is no match for a machine, but he is determined to try to beat the machine or die trying.]

D **Literary Focus**
GRADE-LEVEL STANDARD

? **Repetition.** What pattern of repetition does each verse show? [The fifth line of each verse repeats the fourth; "Lord, Lord" ends the fourth line of every verse.]

E **English-Language Learners**

Dialect. Tell students that *ain't* is a nonstandard negative that can mean "isn't," "don't," "haven't," or "hasn't." *Ain't* is used in informal speech.

A
John Henry was about three days old
Sittin' on his papa's knee.
He picked up a hammer and a little piece of steel
Said, "Hammer's gonna be the death of me, Lord, Lord!
5   Hammer's gonna be the death of me."

B
The captain said to John Henry,
"Gonna bring that steam drill 'round
Gonna bring that steam drill out on the job
Gonna whop that steel on down, Lord, Lord!
10   Whop that steel on down."

C
John Henry told his captain,
"A man ain't nothin' but a man
But before I let your steam drill beat me down
I'd die with a hammer in my hand, Lord, Lord!
15   I'd die with a hammer in my hand."

John Henry said to his shaker,°
"Shaker, why don't you sing?
I'm throwing thirty pounds from my hips on down
D Just listen to that cold steel ring, Lord, Lord!
20   Listen to that cold steel ring."

John Henry said to his shaker,
"Shaker, you'd better pray
'Cause if I miss that little piece of steel
Tomorrow be your buryin' day, Lord, Lord!
25   Tomorrow be your buryin' day."

The shaker said to John Henry,
"I think this mountain's cavin' in!"
John Henry said to his shaker, "Man,
E That ain't nothin' but my hammer suckin' wind,
        Lord, Lord!
30   Nothin' but my hammer suckin' wind."

---

16. **shaker** *n.:* worker who holds the drill.

DIFFERENTIATING INSTRUCTION

Advanced Learners
Acceleration. Use this activity to move students toward the eighth-grade Standard 3.1, which requires that they explore purposes and characteristics of different forms of poetry. First, tell students that "John Henry" is a ballad, a song that tells a story and has a refrain.
Activity. Challenge students to add more verses to the ballad, filling in some of the gaps in the story. For example, John Henry grows from babyhood to adulthood between the first two verses. What happens to him during that time? Tell students to maintain the rhyme scheme and meter of the original ballad in their verses. Encourage students to read their work aloud to classmates.

John Henry on the Right, Steam Drill on the Left (1944–1947) by Palmer C. Hayden.

The Museum of African American Art, Los Angeles.

The man that invented the steam drill
Thought he was mighty fine
But John Henry made fifteen feet
The steam drill only made nine, Lord, Lord! **F**
35   The steam drill only made nine.

John Henry hammered in the mountain
His hammer was striking fire
But he worked so hard, he broke his poor heart **G**
He laid down his hammer and he died, Lord, Lord!
40   He laid down his hammer and he died.

John Henry had a little woman
Her name was Polly Ann
John Henry took sick and went to his bed
Polly Ann drove steel like a man, Lord, Lord! **H**
45   Polly Ann drove steel like a man.

John Henry 407

DIRECT TEACHING

F Reading Skills

❷ Analyzing character. Why is John Henry able to win the race? [Possible response: He has qualities that the steam drill does not have—a will to win, courage, determination, pride.]

G Learners Having Difficulty

❷ Identifying the conflict. Like all ballads, this song tells a story. What is the main conflict in the story? [Possible responses: John Henry battles a mechanical steam drill; John Henry is trying to resist the trend toward machinery replacing human workers.] How is the conflict resolved? [John Henry races the steam drill and wins, but he dies in the process.]

H Learners Having Difficulty

Understanding comparisons. The expression "like a man" suggests that Polly Ann is unusually strong. Her ability to do the work of a man (who is assumed to be stronger than she is) echoes John Henry's ability to do the work of a machine (which is assumed to be stronger than he is).

CONTENT-AREA CONNECTIONS

History
Railroad workers. The railroad industry was the largest employer of African American men after the Civil War. Chinese and Irish immigrants also contributed greatly to the construction of the railroads. These workers laid rails, set ties, and performed jobs for lower wages than anyone else would accept. Most of the Irish railroad workers had immigrated to the United States to escape Ireland's potato famine (1845–1849). They worked the rails from the East Coast to Utah, and they were famous for being hard workers. Chinese immigrants labored almost every day of the month for about half the pay of the Irish workers. They volunteered for the most dangerous jobs, which involved working with explosives.

A Vocabulary
Development
GRADE-LEVEL STANDARD

? Figurative language.
Personification is a kind of figurative language that involves giving human traits to nonhuman things. What human trait is given to the locomotive? [It speaks.]

B Literary Focus
GRADE-LEVEL STANDARD

? Repetition. How is this verse different from all the others in the song? [It has a three-line refrain instead of a two-line refrain.] Why do you think it is like this? [Possible responses: It echoes the perpetual ring of John Henry's hammer; it marks the end of the song; it creates a feeling of triumph rather than tragedy, because John Henry's legend endures.]

VIEWING THE ART

Palmer C. Hayden (1893–1973) was born in Wide Water, Virginia. Hayden painted African American subjects, and his work shows strong influences from African motifs and designs. While some critics admired his portrayal of African Americans, others were disturbed by his exaggeration of African physical features because it seemed to echo the tradition of stereotypical portrayals of black people by white artists. Hayden always denied that the exaggerations were intended to demean his subjects. The paintings illustrating this selection are from a series of twelve canvases depicting the legend of John Henry.

Activity. Point out that just as the song includes a refrain, the paintings include recurring images. Encourage students to identify some of these images. [birds, hammers, circles (wheels, rings), bandannas]

The Museum of African American Art, Los Angeles.

He Laid Down His Hammer and Cried (1944–1947)
by Palmer C. Hayden.

John Henry had a little baby
You could hold him in the palm of your hand
The last words I heard that poor boy say,
"My daddy was a steel-driving man, Lord, Lord!
50   My daddy was a steel-driving man."

They took John Henry to the graveyard
And they buried him in the sand
A And every locomotive comes a-roaring by
Says, "There lies a steel-driving man, Lord, Lord!
55   There lies a steel-driving man."

Well, every Monday morning
When the bluebirds begin to sing
B You can hear John Henry a mile or more
You can hear John Henry's hammer ring, Lord, Lord!
60   You can hear John Henry's hammer ring.

FAMILY/COMMUNITY ACTIVITY

Encourage students to read "John Henry" aloud to parents or guardians at home. Afterward, have students ask the adults about other versions of the legend of John Henry that they might have heard. Students and adults might also discuss whether the replacement of human workers with machines is still a problem today. With the adults' permission, ask students to write summaries of their discussions. Invite volunteers to read their summaries aloud in class.

Literary Response and Analysis

Reading Check

1. Review the main events of John Henry's story; then, complete a **sequence chart** like the one below. Add as many boxes as you need.

> **a.** When John Henry was three days old, he picked up a hammer and made a prediction.

> **b.** When he grew up, he told his captain he'd rather die than be outdone by a steam drill.

> **c.**

2. Who do you think eventually wins the contest between John Henry and the steam drill? Use lines from the song to support your answer.

3. **Folk heroes** are superheroes, people with qualities admired by those who give them lasting fame. How does John Henry show that he is a superhero, even as a baby?

4. How does Polly Ann show that she's a superhero too?

5. Who or what keeps John Henry's name alive?

Interpretations

6. Which lines are repeated in each stanza? Which words are a **refrain** for the whole poem? How could the refrain be sung differently each time to suggest different feelings?

7. What is the **tone** of this song—is it mournful, defiant, proud, angry? Be ready to read John Henry's story aloud to express the tone you've named.

Writing

Human Versus Machine

Write a song or story for the twenty-first century about a person who challenges a machine. Where does your story take place? What is the machine? How has it challenged your hero? Who wins the contest—the human or the machine? For ideas, look back at the lists you made for Make the Connection on page 404.

Reading Standard 3.4 Define how tone or meaning is conveyed in poetry through repetition.

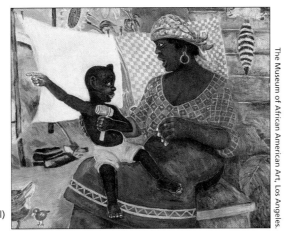

When John Henry Was a Baby (detail) (1944–1947) by Palmer C. Hayden.

The Museum of African American Art, Los Angeles.

Literary Response and Analysis

Reading Check

1. Possible sequence chart entries: (c) John Henry raced the steam drill and was winning. (d) Inside a mountain, his heart gave out. (e) His wife Polly Ann took over his job. (f) His baby son called him "a steel-driving man." (g) John Henry was buried. (h) Passing trains and the sound of his hammer kept his name alive.

2. Possible answer: Lines 33–35 show that John Henry outperforms the steam drill and wins the contest.

3. John Henry has great physical strength, and he faces near-impossible odds with courage and determination. As a baby, he lifts a hammer, speaks, and foretells the future.

4. She does the job of superhero John Henry, and she does it well.

5. The passing locomotives and the sound of John Henry's hammer keep his name alive.

Interpretations

6. The fourth line, minus the phrase "Lord, Lord," is repeated in each stanza. The phrase "Lord, Lord" is a refrain throughout the poem. Students' ideas for singing the words "Lord, Lord" will vary.

7. Possible answer: The tone is proud and sad. The refrain "Lord, Lord" sounds mournful; the repeated phrase *steel-driving man* and the many references to the ringing of hammer and steel create images of strength and pride.

Advanced Learners

Enrichment. Play for students a musical version of "John Henry," such as the recording by Harry Belafonte. Explain that this is a work song—a song laborers sing to maintain the rhythm of their repetitive tasks and to make the time pass.

Activity. Bring in or have students bring in more examples of traditional work songs, such as "I've Been Working on the Railroad," "The Song of the Volga Boatmen," sea chanteys, "Sixteen Tons," "I Ride an Old Paint," and so on. Encourage students to identify refrains and other examples of repetition in the songs.

Vocabulary Development

Practice

1. The person loved by the speaker in the poem is being compared to a red rose. A beloved person and a red rose are both beautiful. Simile.
2. The speaker in the poem is being compared to a cloud. Both the speaker and the cloud are alone, and both move over the earth in isolation. Simile.
3. The Lord is being compared to a shepherd. The Lord and a shepherd both provide protection from want. Metaphor.
4. Lightning is being compared to a table fork. Both lightning and a table fork are pronged and sharp. Metaphor.
5. The sea is being compared to a huge dog. Both the sea and the dog are hungry, restless, and gray, and both roll on the beach all day. Metaphor.
6. America is being compared to a singer. Both America and a singer can sing "varied carols." Personification.
7. The soul of the speaker in the poem is being compared to rivers. The speaker's soul and the river both have become deep. Simile.
8. Hope is being compared to a bird. Both hope and a bird can take flight. Metaphor.
9. The wind is being compared to a person. Both rise, shout, whistle, and kick leaves around. Personification.
10. A person's face is being compared to a garden. The face has beauty in it like a garden. Metaphor.

Vocabulary Development

Identifying and Interpreting Figurative Language

Figurative language is based on comparisons; it is not meant to be understood literally. There are hundreds of types of figurative language, or figures of speech; three of the most commonly used are **similes**, **metaphors**, and **personification.**

PRACTICE

For each of the following quotations, identify the two things being compared, explain how they're alike, and identify the figure of speech being used: simile, metaphor, or personification.

1. "O my Love is like a red, red rose . . ."   —Robert Burns
2. "I wandered lonely as a cloud
   That floats on high o'er vales and hills . . ."
                                    —William Wordsworth
3. "The Lord is my shepherd; I shall not want."
                                    —from Psalm 23
4. "The Lightning is a yellow Fork
   From Tables in the sky . . ."   —Emily Dickinson
5. "The sea is a hungry dog,
   Giant and gray.
   He rolls on the beach all day."   —James Reeves
6. "I hear America singing, the varied carols I hear . . ."
                                    —Walt Whitman
7. "My soul has grown deep like the rivers . . ."
                                    —Langston Hughes
8. "'Hope' is the thing with feathers—
   That perches in the soul—"   —Emily Dickinson
9. "The wind stood up, and gave a shout;
   He whistled on his fingers, and
   Kicked the withered leaves about . . ."
                                    —James Stephens
10. "There is a garden in her face,
    Where roses and white lilies grow . . ."
                                    —Thomas Campion

Reading Standard 1.2 Identify and interpret figurative language.

A Box of Figures of Speech

simile: comparison between two unlike things in which *like, a[s], than, resembles,* or a similar word is used (f[or] example, *life is like a flowing river*)

metaphor: compariso[n] between two unlike things in which a word such as *like, as, than, [or] resembles* is not used (for example, *life is a flowing river*)

personification: figu[re] of speech in which human traits are given to nonhuman things, such as animals or forc[es] of nature (for exampl[e,] *the river sang a song of triumph*)

MINI-LESSON   Reading

Developing Word-Attack Skills
Use the song to reinforce students' awareness of direct sound-letter correspondences. Write this line from the song on the chalkboard: *Gonna whop that steel on down.* Discuss the words *gonna* and *whop.* Point out that using *gonna* for "going to" reflects natural, informal speech, and that *whop* is an onomatopoeic word—the sound of the word imitates an actual sound. Explain that when writers want to represent language

exactly as it is heard, they use the most regular sound-letter correspondences and try to spell the words exactly as they sound. In *gonna,* the *o* stands for a short *o.* To make sure the *o* is read as short, there are two *n*'s after it. Similarly, the pronunciation of *whop* is clear: The *o* is short, and the word rhymes with *hop* and *top.*
Activity. Display these lines of dialogue, which include examples of vernacular language. Have volunteers use their knowledge

Grammar Link MINI-LESSON

End All End-Mark Errors

The punctuation at the end of a sentence is called an **end mark.** Like stop signs, end marks prevent collisions. Read the following lines aloud. Can you tell where each sentence starts and where it ends?

> **When the reporter resorted to name-calling, I realized I was reading propaganda from now on I'll read his articles carefully**

Three kinds of end marks are used in English: periods (.), question marks (?), and exclamation points (!). Read the following examples aloud to see how changing the end mark can affect the meaning of a sentence.

> **John's reasoning is faulty.**
> **John's reasoning is faulty?**
> **John's reasoning is faulty!**

The use of end marks may differ from language to language. In Spanish, for example, a question mark or exclamation point appears both before and after a question or exclamation. (Punctuation marks at the beginning of a question or exclamation are *inverted*, or set upside down.)

> **¿Qué pasa?** [What's happening?]
> **¡Qué lastima!** [What a shame!]

PRACTICE 1

Copy the paragraph below. Then, revise it by adding six end marks and capitalizing as needed.

> Was Terry excited you bet the soccer match was about to begin the first game of the year is always the most exciting Terry had practiced hard for six weeks she was sure her efforts would pay off tonight

PRACTICE 2

As you proofread your own writing, highlight all your end marks. Then, check them: Ask yourself where each thought ends—really ends. Put an end mark at that point to show that the next word marks the beginning of a whole new thought.

For more help, see End Marks in the *Holt Handbook*, pages 263–267.

PEANUTS reprinted by permission of United Feature Syndicate, Inc.

John Henry   **411**

Grammar Link

Practice 1

Was Terry excited? You bet! The soccer match was about to begin. The first game of the year is always the most exciting. Terry had practiced hard for six weeks. She was sure her efforts would pay off tonight.

Practice 2

Encourage students to read their work aloud while proofreading the placement of end marks.

ASSESSING

- *Progress Assessment of Reading*
  - Selection Test, p. 144

RETEACHING

For a lesson reteaching repetition in poetry, see **Reteaching,** pp. 489J–489K.

---

of direct sound-letter correspondences to decode the words and read the sentences aloud.

1. "It's gettin' late. I gotta go."
2. "I wanna get home before dark."
3. "Gimme my book first."
4. "Fuh-nee. Ya oughta let me read it."
5. "When ya gonna finish it?"
6. "I dunno. It's takin' longer'n I thought."

STANDARDS FOCUS, pp. 412–414

(For grade-level and review standards taught in this selection, see citations on Pupil's Edition pages.)

Prerequisite Standard

■ Grade 5, Reading Comprehension 2.5 **Distinguish facts, supported inferences, and opinions in text.**

Standard Coming Up in the Next Grade Level

■ Grade 7, Reading Comprehension 2.6 **Assess the adequacy, accuracy, and appropriateness of the author's evidence to support claims and assertions, noting instances of bias and stereotyping.**

PRETEACHING

▶ **Resources Reminder**

Differentiating Instruction

■ *Lesson Plans for Language Development*

For additional instruction for English-language learners and special education students on recognizing persuasive techniques, see *Lesson Plans for Language Development,* p. 192.

Becoming a Critical Reader
Recognizing Persuasive Techniques

Persuasion is everywhere. Advertisements urge us to buy things; politicians ask for our votes; editorial writers try to influence our thinking on issues. **Persuasion** is the use of language or of visual images to get us to *believe* or *do* something. Skillful persuaders use a number of techniques to get us to see things their way.

Logical Appeals

Logic is correct reasoning. You're using logic when you put facts together and conclude that "if this is true, then that must be true." A logical persuasive argument is built on opinion supported by **reasons** and **evidence.**

Whenever someone tries to persuade you, ask yourself, "*How* is this person trying to convince me?" Be alert to common kinds of fallacious, or faulty, reasoning. When you see the word *fallacious* (fə·lā'shəs), think of the word *false*. **Fallacious reasoning** is false reasoning. On the surface the person's arguments make sense, but if you look closely, you'll find flaws in the reasoning.

Reading Standard 2.8 Note instances of fallacious reasoning and persuasion in text.

DIFFERENTIATING INSTRUCTION

Learners Having Difficulty
These students may benefit from a brief concept review before reading the essay. Ask students to define *persuasion.* [attempts to convince others to change their actions or their thinking] Then, remind students that some persuasive techniques are appeals to emotion, while others are appeals to reason. Have students imagine trying to talk their parents into allowing them to see a controversial movie. Guide students in formulating examples of both kinds of appeal.

English-Language Learners
Before students read the essay on faulty or fallacious reasoning, introduce the related word *fallacy,* meaning "false idea" or "mistake in reasoning."

Fallacious Reasoning: Two Plus Two Isn't Three

Here are three kinds of fallacious reasoning:

1 **Hasty generalizations. A gener-alization** is a broad statement that tells about something "in general." Valid generalizations are based on solid evidence. For example, someone who has experience with cats might say, "Most cats love milk." Valid generaliza-tions, like that one, usually include **qualifying words**—*most, some, generally*. Qualifying words allow for exceptions to a generalization (here, cats that don't like milk).

A **hasty generalization** is one that is based on incomplete evidence.

HASTY GENERALIZATION

Jane Goes Overboard

Jane and I went to the Dinner Diner for lunch the other day. Jane ordered a cheeseburger, and it was horrible! She says that she'll never eat in a diner again.

EXPLANATION

Maybe the Dinner Diner's cheese-burgers do taste like shoe leather, but that doesn't mean *every* diner serves a bad cheeseburger. Jane is making a hasty generalization about *all* diners from a single bad experience.

Circular reasoning.

2 **Circular reasoning. Circular reasoning** goes around and around without ever getting anywhere. It says the same thing over and over again, each time using slightly different words.

CIRCULAR REASONING

Too Long Is Too Long Is Too Long

We should cancel these play practices because they are too long. Sometimes they last three hours. We don't need to spend so much time practicing. Three-hour practices are too long.

EXPLANATION

This argument presents no reasons to back up the opinion. At first glance it seems to offer support, but if you look closely, you'll see that the same idea is repeated three times!

Reading Informational Materials: Recognizing Fallacious Reasoning

You might wish to write the following humorous fallacious reasoning on the chalkboard:

- Eggplants have no hair.
- Great-uncle Ebenezer has no hair.
- Therefore, Great-uncle Ebenezer is an eggplant.

Ask students to explain the weak-nesses in this reasoning. [Just because two things share one charac-teristic doesn't mean they are the same.] Then, point out that though this example is obviously fallacious, many instances of fallacious rea-soning seem sound at first glance. In fact, students may have to read a persuasive argument twice to be able to evaluate its reasoning.

Advanced Learners

Acceleration. Use this activity to move students toward the seventh-grade Standard 2.6, which requires that they assess the adequacy of evidence that supports assertions.

Activity. Show students the following report:

"For one week, the twenty-five students in Mr. Pike's class stopped playing video games. That week, Mr. Pike's students had 10 percent fewer playground fights and arguments than they had had the week before. This proves that if kids don't play video games, playground violence will decrease."

Ask students to identify the type of fallacy the report represents. [hasty generalization] Then, ask students to suggest ways to support the generalization adequately. [Possible responses: Redo the study with a larger and more varied group; run the study for a longer time; include control groups; include data from other relevant studies.]

Reading Information Materials

Identifying Fallacious Reasoning

Practice 1

Possible Answers

1. Circular reasoning: Each sentence says the same thing, with no data to back up the assertion.

2. Only-cause fallacy: There are many possible causes for Ross's good grades.

3. Hasty generalization: Because one person enjoys wearing a school uniform, it does not necessarily follow that everyone should wear one.

4. Only-cause fallacy: There are many possible reasons for attendance to be higher in the springtime than in the winter.

5. Circular reasoning: Both sentences say the same thing, and there is no evidence to back up the assertion.

Practice 2

Possible Answers

1. Jim's three-year-old brother loves monster movies, so when our club volunteers at the preschool, it would be a great idea to show a monster movie to all the three-year-olds.

2. When Governor Noah Vail was in office, students' test scores rose throughout the state, so re-electing Governor Vail will improve students' performance even more.

3. Two hours of homework each night is too much. That is far too long a time for kids to spend on homework. Expecting kids to do two hours of homework is excessive.

3 **Only-cause fallacy.** In the **only-cause fallacy** a situation is seen as the result of only one cause. Situations often have many causes.

ONLY-CAUSE FALLACY

Todd Drops the Ball
Our team lost the game tonight because Todd didn't play well. Todd is usually our best player, but he missed lots of shots and didn't get many rebounds. The blame for this loss lies squarely on Todd's shoulders.

EXPLANATION

Can you see the fallacy in this reasoning? Todd is only one player on a team of many, so his poor playing couldn't be the *only* reason his team lost. Maybe other players on the team didn't play well, either. Maybe the opposing team put their best defender on Todd. Maybe the winning team played a better game.

"We would have won if Todd had gotten that rebound in the first quarter."

Identifying Fallacious Reasoning

PRACTICE 1

All of the following items illustrate fallacious reasoning. Identify the kind of faulty reasoning in each—**hasty generalization, circular reasoning,** or **only-cause fallacy.** Then, explain why the reasoning is faulty.

1. Students should wear uniforms because they're cheaper than regular clothes. Regular clothes are too expensive. Wearing uniforms means that you don't have to spend lots of money on new clothes.

2. Since Ross started to wear a uniform, he's been getting good grades. He's always studied really hard, and he was on the honor roll three times last year.

3. I love my school uniform. Everyone should wear one.

4. We started wearing uniforms at my school right after spring break. Attendance is much better than it was during the winter.

5. Wearing uniforms will help keep kids from acting up in class and in the halls. Uniforms will make kids behave better.

PRACTICE 2

With a partner or on your own, write one example of each of the following types of fallacious reasoning. Then, read your examples to the class. Can the class identify the fallacy in each one?

1. hasty generalization
2. only-cause fallacy
3. circular reasoning

Apply

Encourage students to bring in examples of hasty generalizations, only-cause fallacy, and circular reasoning that they notice in political campaign materials, editorials, and advertisements.

Becoming a Critical Reader
Recognizing Propaganda Techniques

Propaganda is a kind of persuasion designed to keep us from thinking for ourselves. Propaganda relies on appeals to our emotions rather than logical arguments and reasoning. Much propaganda consists of one-sided arguments.

Not all propaganda is bad, however. Most people would agree that a doctor who uses emotional appeals to discourage kids from smoking is using "good propaganda."

Here are several techniques used in propaganda. You'll probably recognize some of them.

1 Bandwagon appeals. A **bandwagon appeal** urges you to do something because everyone else is doing it. (The word *bandwagon* refers to a decorated wagon used in a parade. A bandwagon carried—yes—the band. Kids would often jump on the bandwagon for an exciting ride.) A person using a bandwagon appeal takes advantage of our desire to be part of a group. It's the "don't be the last person on your block to have one" technique, and it is often used by advertisers.

A BANDWAGON APPEAL

Eight out of ten people in your area have already signed up for this long-distance service. Time is running out, so hurry! Everyone knows what a bargain this is. Shouldn't you save money too?

EXPLANATION

The fact that "everyone is doing it" is not a convincing reason for *you* to do it (or to jump on the bandwagon).

STANDARDS FOCUS, pp. 415–418

(For grade-level and review standards taught in this selection, see citations on Pupil's Edition pages.)

Prerequisite Standard
- Grade 5, Reading Comprehension 2.5 **Distinguish facts, supported inferences, and opinions in text.**

Standard Coming Up in the Next Grade Level
- Grade 7, Reading Comprehension 2.6 **Assess the adequacy, accuracy, and appropriateness of the author's evidence to support claims and assertions, noting instances of bias and stereotyping.**

PRETEACHING

Assign the Reading
Read the essay with students and discuss how the illustrations relate to the various propaganda techniques.

Reading Standard 2.8 Note instances of propaganda in text.

Becoming a Critical Reader: Recognizing Propaganda Techniques **415**

DIFFERENTIATING INSTRUCTION

Learners Having Difficulty
Facilitate initial success for these students by guiding them in recalling what they already know about two familiar practices—name-calling and stereotyping—before they read the essay. First, ask volunteers to offer their own definitions of name-calling (giving negative labels to someone or something) and stereotyping (assuming that all members of a group have the same traits). Point out that both practices affect people emotionally. Explain that both practices are sometimes used in persuasion, and tell students that persuasive techniques affecting people's emotions are called propaganda. Then, direct students to read the essay, looking for discussions of stereotyping, name-calling, and three other propaganda techniques.

Reading Informational Materials: Recognizing Propaganda Techniques

On one side of the board, write *fleshy, furred drupes;* on the other, write *juicy, sweet peaches.* Ask students which they would rather eat. If no one guesses the catch, tell students that both phrases describe the same fruit. Point out that one phrase has a more positive emotional effect than the other. Then, explain that propaganda techniques, like those two descriptions, play on people's emotions. The goal of propaganda is to get people to make decisions on the basis of "knee-jerk" emotional responses, without taking time to think things through.

2 **Use of stereotypes.** A **stereotype** is a fixed idea about all the members of a group, one that doesn't allow for individual differences. Stereotyping leads to prejudice—evaluating people on the basis of their membership in a group rather than on their individual characteristics.

USE OF A STEREOTYPE

You just can't trust politicians—they'll do anything to get elected.

EXPLANATION

This sentence unfairly lumps all politicians together. As a group, politicians aren't always popular, but not all are untrustworthy.

3 **Name-calling. Name-calling** is using labels to arouse negative feelings toward someone instead of giving reasons and evidence to support an argument.

USE OF NAME-CALLING

Only a liberal tree-hugger would fail to see the importance of building the new supermall. Who needs that rat-infested park, anyway? Let's pave it over!

EXPLANATION

No convincing reasons for building the mall are given. Instead, the person making this argument dismisses any opponents by calling them names.

4 **Snob appeal.** Advertisers use **snob appeal** when they associate their product with wealth, glamour, or membership in a select society. The message they're sending is that using their product sets you apart from the crowd.

USE OF SNOB APPEAL

The average person thinks that any old hair-care product will do. But you know better. Ultra Turbo Hair is designed for people who insist on quality—people like you.

EXPLANATION

This advertisement makes an appeal to people's desire to feel special. It offers no information about the product itself.

DIFFERENTIATING INSTRUCTION

English-Language Learners
Before students read the essay, you might familiarize them with the derogatory terms *snob* (someone who thinks himself or herself superior to others) and *liberal tree-hugger* (someone who wants to sacrifice human luxury and convenience in order to protect the environment).

Resources Reminder
For lessons designed for intermediate and advanced English-language learners, see *Lesson Plans for Language Development,* p. 192.

Special Education Students
For lessons designed for special education students, see *Lesson Plans for Language Development,* p. 192.

5 **Testimonial.** When a football star recommends a breakfast cereal, he's making an emotional appeal to his fans. The message is that you can be just like him if you eat the same cereal. Famous people who recommend a product or a candidate for office are using glamour, talent, and fame to persuade you to part with your money or your vote.

USE OF A TESTIMONIAL

Hello. I'm not a politician, but I play one on television. I'm here today to urge you to vote for Richard Richards as governor of our great state.

EXPLANATION

In this situation a respected state senator or representative would provide a more trustworthy testimonial than an actor who plays a politician on TV.

Ⓐ **Reading Informational Materials**
GRADE-LEVEL STANDARD
Testimonials. Challenge students to name stars who endorse various products and to assess their qualifications for the role.

Becoming a Critical Reader: Recognizing Propaganda Techniques **417**

Advanced Learners
Acceleration. Use this activity to move students toward the seventh-grade Standard 2.6, which requires that they assess evidence supporting claims and assertions, noting instances of bias and stereotyping.
Activity. Lead students in a discussion of various bases for stereotyping: gender, race, age, religion, socioeconomic class, profession, appearance, speech mannerisms, and so on. Then, have students work in small groups to analyze the views of both sides in a current world conflict (such as a civil war or a clash between countries), looking for examples of stereotyping. Ask each group to report its findings to the class.

Reading Informational Materials

Identifying Propaganda

Practice 1

1. snob appeal
2. bandwagon appeal
3. stereotyping
4. testimonial
5. name-calling
6. name-calling
7. bandwagon appeal

Practice 2
Possible Answers

1. Everyone's flocking to Splash-O-Rama Water Park. Don't be left out of all the fun—come on out to Splash-O-Rama this weekend!

2. The coach who made Shaun run laps is just like all adults. They overreact to minor mistakes, and they have no sense of humor.

3. Only fools could overlook how pathetic the mayor is. Let's get rid of that immoral crook.

4. The chancellor of that elite university, Wotsamatta U, drives a Snazzmobile. It's just the car for an intelligent and prestigious person like you.

5. Space shuttle astronaut Barbara Blastoff says, "My favorite soft drink is Rocket Root Beer. Try it for an out-of-this-world energy blast!"

Practice 3

Have students share and discuss examples of propaganda techniques that they notice in television commercials, direct-mail circulars, newspaper and magazine advertisements, and political campaign materials.

HOMEWORK

Identifying Propaganda

PRACTICE 1

Identify the type of propaganda used in each of the following statements.

1. Women with the finest fashion sense wear Stirrup Earrings.

2. Don't be left out in the cold. Order the vest worn by ninety percent of all ski instructors—the SupraDown hooded vest.

3. The people who want to build the mall are businessmen. All businessmen are selfish and care only about making money.

4. Hi. I'm Dan Nulty, the Olympic gold medalist. I invest all my money with Dansforth Funds. I suggest you go with a winner too!

5. Don't hire Oliver. He's a lazy whiner.

6. Senator Axman is a bleeding-heart liberal and a hypocrite. Vote for Mary Michaels.

7. Come to the protest. Almost everyone will be cutting classes tomorrow to join the march.

PRACTICE 2

With a partner, make up one example of each of the following types of propaganda. Then, read the example to the class, and see if they can identify the kind of propaganda you've used.

1. bandwagon appeal
2. stereotype
3. name-calling
4. snob appeal
5. testimonial

PRACTICE 3

The type of persuasive writing that you come across most often is advertising. Advertisers try to get you to buy their products by using pictures, words, and music. Look through several magazines, and listen critically to advertisements you see and hear on television and the radio. Bring to class advertisements that appeal to your emotions. Try to find advertisements that use some of the techniques discussed in this chapter.

Also look for examples of "good propaganda"—advertisements that urge you to do something positive. You might find advertisements from charitable organizations asking you to make a donation, for example. Bring these to class too.

Take notes on the advertisements you bring to class, and discuss the propaganda techniques used in each.

Reading Informational Materials

TestPractice

Identifying Faulty Reasoning

DIRECTIONS: Match each item on the left with the type of fallacious reasoning or propaganda it defines or represents on the right. Write the letter of the correct answer on the line next to the number.

___ 1. a famous person's promotion of a product

    2. an argument that says the same thing over and over

___ 3. a statement that encourages you to do something because everyone else is doing it

    4. persuasion that appeals to people's desire to feel special

___ 5. an argument claiming that a situation is the result of a single cause

    6. a judgment about someone made solely on the basis of his or her membership in a group

___ 7. a conclusion based on incomplete evidence

    8. the use of labels to stir up negative feelings about someone

a. bandwagon appeal

b. stereotype

c. name-calling

d. snob appeal

e. testimonial

f. hasty generalization

g. circular reasoning

h. only-cause fallacy

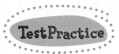

Reading Standard 2.8 Note instances of fallacious reasoning and propaganda in text.

Standards Review   419

Reading Informational Materials

STANDARDS FOCUS, p. 419

(*For the grade-level standard reviewed in this lesson, see Pupil's Edition, p. 419.*)

INTRODUCING THE STANDARDS REVIEW

Explain that this review on types of fallacies consists of a matching item exercise.

TestPractice

Answers and Model Rationales

1. **e**   Students should note the use of the word *famous* in the item. A testimonial by a famous person would appeal to the consumer's desire to succeed.

2. **g**   Students should pick up the clue "same thing over and over" in the item and recognize that this repetition is a type of circular reasoning.

3. **a**   Students should reason that an appeal to do something because everyone else is doing it is an appeal to the need to be part of a group, to be on the bandwagon.

4. **d**   Something that makes people feel special is an example of snob appeal.

5. **h**   The phrase "result of only one cause" identifies this as an only-cause fallacy.

6. **b**   An argument that excludes or ignores individual differences is a stereotype.

7. **f**   A conclusion made with inadequate evidence is a hasty generalization.

8. **c**   Using a label that stirs up negative feelings is the same thing as name-calling.

DIFFERENTIATING INSTRUCTION

Advanced Learners
Enrichment. Many students are already familiar with unsupported inferences, fallacious reasoning, and propaganda from their own reading and television viewing.
Activity. Have students find and display examples of these persuasive techniques.

Test-Taking Tips
Since there are eight items and eight answers and the instructions do not say that answers can be used more than once, remind students to eliminate choices as soon as they have used them.

Literary Response and Analysis

**STANDARDS
FOCUS, pp. 420–421**

*(For the grade-level standard
taught in this lesson, see Pupil's
Edition, p. 420.)*

INTRODUCING THE
STANDARDS REVIEW

Use this review to assess students'
grasp of the standard taught in
this chapter. If necessary, you can
use the annotations to guide students in their reading before they
answer the questions.

DIRECT TEACHING

A **Literary Focus**
GRADE-LEVEL STANDARD

❓ Figurative language. How
are Jordan's eyes like two radar
screens? Why is this metaphor an
especially apt one? [Possible
responses: They track the action as
radar does. The metaphor suggests
the laser accuracy of Jordan's shot; it
suggests Jordan has the ability to "see
through" other players to get a shot.]

B **Literary Focus**
GRADE-LEVEL STANDARD

❓ Word choice. Why is *chaos* an
effective word choice in this line?
[Possible responses: it describes the
scene on the floor in one word; it
includes the other players, the crowd's
cheering, and the confusion that
reigns in the final minutes of play.]

 DIRECTIONS: Read the following poem. Then, read each question,
and write the letter of the best response.

*This poem describes a moment in the 1998 National Basketball Association Finals game
between the Chicago Bulls and the Utah Jazz. The Bulls superstar Michael Jordan scored
the winning shot with just 5.2 seconds left in the game. This victory brought the team their
sixth NBA title. The game, which took place on June 14, 1998, in Salt Lake City, Utah, was
Jordan's last; he retired from basketball a few months later.*

Forty-one Seconds on a Sunday in June,
in Salt Lake City, Utah   *for Michael Jordan*
Quincy Troupe

rising up in time, michael jordan hangs like an icon,° suspended in space,
cocks his right arm, fires a jump shot for two, the title game on the line,
A his eyes two radar screens screwed like nails into the mask of his face

bore in on the basket, gaze focused, a thing of beauty, no shadow, or trace,
5   no hint of fear, in this, his showplace, his ultimate place to shine,
rising up in time michael jordan hangs like an icon, suspended in space,

after he has moved from baseline to baseline, sideline to sideline, his coal-face
B shining, wagging his tongue, he dribbles through chaos, snaking serpentine,°
his eyes two radar screens screwed like nails into the mask of his face,

10   he bolts a flash up the court, takes off, floats in for two more in this race
for glory, it is his time, what he was put on earth for, he can see the headline,
rising up in time, michael jordan hangs like an icon, suspended in space,

inside his imagination, he feels the moment he will embrace, knows his place
is written here, inside this quickening pace of nerves, he will define,
15   his eyes two radar screens screwed like nails into the mask of his face,

**Reading
Standard 3.4**
Define how
tone or
meaning
is conveyed in
poetry through
word choice,
figurative
language,
sentence
structure,
line length,
punctuation,
rhythm,
repetition,
and rhyme.

1. **icon** (ī′kän′) *n.:* image; also, person or thing regarded with great respect and admiration.
8. **serpentine** (sur′pən·tīn′) *adj.* used as *adv.:* in a snakelike way.

MINI-LESSON   Reading

Reviewing Word-Attack Skills
Activity. Display these sets of words, and
have students identify the two words in
each set that rhyme.

1. through   clue   rough
[through/clue]

2. third   word   tired
[third/word]

3. cursed   pierced   first
[cursed/first]

4. beach   screech   sketch
[beach/screech]

5. tuned   frowned   hound
[frowned/hound]

6. bored   gourd   soured
[bored/gourd]

7. machine   incline   unseen
[machine/unseen]

8. stars   Mars   mares
[stars/Mars]

inside this moment he will rule on his own terms, quick as a cat he interfaces° time, victory & glory, as he crosses over his dribble he is king of this shrine,° rising up in time, michael jordan hangs like an icon, suspended in space, his eyes two radar screens screwed like nails into the mask of his face

---

16. **interfaces** *v.*: brings together; joins.
17. **shrine** *n.*: place held in high honor because of its association with an event, a person, or a holy figure.

---

1. Which of the following phrases from the poem contains a **simile**?
   A "he bolts a flash up the court"
   B "fires a jump shot for two, the title game on the line"
   C "he feels the moment he will embrace"
   D "rising up in time, michael jordan hangs like an icon"

2. "Quick as a cat" (line 16) is an example of —
   F metaphor
   G simile
   H personification
   J alliteration

3. Which of the following statements describes the poem's structure?
   A The first and third lines of each stanza rhyme.
   B Each stanza begins with the same line.
   C Each line has the same number of words.
   D The first and second lines of each stanza rhyme.

4. Which of the following phrases is repeated four times in the poem?
   F "he bolts a flash up the court, floats in for two more in this race"
   G "he bolts a flash up the court, takes off, floats in for two more in this race"
   H "michael jordan hangs like an icon, suspended in space"
   J "it is his time, what he was put on earth for, he can see the headline"

5. Which word best describes the speaker's **tone** in this poem?
   A Dazed
   B Admiring
   C Loving
   D Envious

6. Which of the following phrases is an example of alliteration?
   F "inside this quickening pace of nerves"
   G "suspended in space"
   H "the title game on the line"
   J "he bolts a flash up the court"

Standards Review   **421**

C Literary Focus
GRADE-LEVEL STANDARD
? Word choice. Which words in these lines convey the idea that Jordan is the best—better than anyone else? [rule, victory, glory, king]

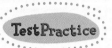

Answers and Model Rationales

1. **D** The phrase in D is a simile because it uses the word *like* to make a comparison between two unlike things—Michael Jordan and an icon. Students should eliminate A, which makes a comparison but does not use the words *like* or *as,* and B and C, which do not make comparisons.

2. **G** The phrase is a simile because it makes a comparison between two unlike things using the word *as.* All other choices can be eliminated since the phrase does not fit the definition of a metaphor (a comparison made without the use of *like* or *as*), personification (a nonhuman object talked about as if it were human), or alliteration (the repetition of a sound in words close together).

3. **A** Students should immediately eliminate all choices but A.

4. **H** The phrase in H is repeated in ll. 1, 6, 12, and 18. The phrase quoted in F is inaccurate; the phrases in G and J are not repeated.

5. **B** B is the best answer because the speaker's tone is one of deeply felt admiration.

6. **G** Students should be able to eliminate all choices but G, which repeats the sound of the letter *s* in words that are close together.

---

9. stretch   reach   leech
   [reach/leech]
10. hoot   suit   foot
   [hoot/suit]
11. sew   few   go
   [sew/go]
12. teeth   wreath   breath
   [teeth/wreath]

Activity. Ask students to use their knowledge of sound-letter correspondences to decode these vernacular expressions.
1. gonna [going to]
2. gimme [give me]
3. ya [you]
4. dunno [don't know]

Vocabulary Development (Review)

Synonyms

Modeling. Model the thought process of a good reader getting the answer to item 1 by saying: "Two words are synonyms if they mean the same or nearly the same thing. Therefore, I need to look at the answers to find another word that has the same meaning as *mortified*. First, I know that *mortified* means 'embarrassed' or 'ashamed.' A means neither of those. B and C don't either. But answer D is *ashamed.* I already know that *ashamed* means the same thing as *mortified,* so D is correct."

Answers and Model Rationales

1. **D** See rationale above.
2. **G** *Etiquette* means "proper behavior," which is the same thing as *manners.*
3. **A** To savor is to taste with pleasure, or enjoy.
4. **J** Another word for *shrewd* is *clever.*
5. **C** *Audacity* means "boldness" or "daring," so C is correct.
6. **G** If a building is evacuated, the people are taken out of it, leaving it empty. Therefore, *emptied* is correct.
7. **D** One meaning of *intern* is "to work for free." Since *employ* means "to hire for money," A is incorrect. Another meaning of *intern* is "to detain or jail." Therefore, D is correct.
8. **J** *Tolerance* means "patience," so a synonym for *tolerant* would be *patient* or *accepting.*
9. **C** Another word for *lavish* is *plentiful.* Therefore, C, *plentifully,* is correct.

Vocabulary Development (Review)

This Test Practice reviews vocabulary words that you have studied in earlier chapters.

TestPractice

Synonyms

DIRECTIONS: Write the letter of the word or group of words that is closest in meaning to the underlined word.

1. Someone who is <u>mortified</u> is —
   A frightened
   B ill
   C impressed
   D ashamed

2. <u>Etiquette</u> means —
   F sewing
   G manners
   H accessories
   J ideas

3. If you <u>savor</u> something, you —
   A enjoy it
   B buy it
   C dislike it
   D ignore it

4. The <u>shrewdest</u> competitor is the most —
   F talented
   G energetic
   H attentive
   J clever

5. <u>Audacity</u> means —
   A kindness
   B fear
   C daring
   D loudness

6. If a building is <u>evacuated</u>, it is —
   F damaged
   G emptied
   H decorated
   J sold

7. <u>Interned</u> means —
   A employed
   B discouraged
   C relieved
   D imprisoned

8. A <u>tolerant</u> person is —
   F eloquent
   G helpful
   H exciting
   J accepting

9. <u>Lavishly</u> means —
   A dutifully
   B cautiously
   C plentifully
   D shyly

10. A <u>spectacle</u> is a sight that is —
    F remarkable
    G frightening
    H overwhelming
    J boring

10. **F** A spectacle is a remarkable sight. It can but does not have to be frightening, G, or overwhelming, H. It is never a boring sight, J.

▶ Resources Reminder

Vocabulary and Spelling

■ *Lesson Plans for Language Development*
   ■ Vocabulary, pp. 198–202

PROBLEM-SOLUTION ESSAY

Solve It Your Way

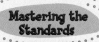
Mastering the
Standards

When you write a problem-solution essay, you zero in on a problem and develop and present your own solution. Good problem-solution writing addresses problems that concern people everywhere. That doesn't mean you have to write about global issues, like war or energy shortages. You can find good ideas for problem-solution writing by thinking about problems you've read about or experienced. For example, you could write about problems caused by people's tendency to band together and form groups, as the Sneetches did. Think of groups that have formed in either your community or your school. Have you noticed any conflicts between in-groups and outsiders?

List a few problems you're concerned about. Then, write down ideas for resolving one of these conflicts. Think about how readers might respond to your ideas. What details could you include to help them see the problem clearly? What objections might they make to your ideas? How could you answer their arguments? Try making a flowchart like the one below to organize your thoughts before you begin writing.

▶ Use "Writing a Problem-Solution Explanation," pages 678–680, for help with this assignment.

Another Choice

RESEARCH REPORT

Calling All Cats

"Ode to Mi Gato" (page 391) gives you glimpses of the behavior of cats. If you were preparing a brief research report on cats, what topics would you explore? Think about questions like these:

- How many breeds of cats are there?
- How are house cats related to wild cats, such as cougars and lynxes?

- What special role did cats play in ancient Egypt?

Then, choose a topic, and narrow it down so that you can cover it in several paragraphs. Gather information on the topic from books, magazines, encyclopedias, and the Internet.

▶ Use "Writing a Research Report," pages 578–603, for help with this assignment.

Mastering the
Standards

Evaluation Criteria

A good problem-solution essay

1. examines the problem
2. presents one or more solutions and shows how each one would work
3. follows a clear organizational pattern, such as listing solutions from least to most practical, and so on
4. anticipates and answers readers' arguments
5. offers persuasive evidence to validate arguments and conclusions as needed

ASSESSING

Assessment

■ *Progress Assessment of Reading*
  ■ Chapter Test, p. 146

Using Academic Language

Literary Terms
As part of the review of Literary Response and Analysis Standard 3.4, ask students to look back through the chapter to find the meanings of the terms listed below. Then, have students show their grasp of Standard 3.4 by citing lines from poems in the chapter that illustrate the meanings of the following terms.
Rhyme (p. 380); **Rhyme Scheme** (p. 380);

Meter (p. 380); **Scanning** (p. 380); **Tone** (pp. 389, 400); **Ode** (p. 389); **Haiku** (p. 395); **Repetition** (p. 404); **Refrain** (p. 404).

Informational Terms
As part of the review of Reading Comprehension Standard 2.8, ask students to look back through the chapter to find the meanings of the terms and phrases listed at right and to use the terms to explain Standard 2.8.

Persuasion (p. 412); **Logical Appeals** (p. 412); **Logic** (p. 412); **Reasons** (p. 412); **Evidence** (p. 412); **Fallacious Reasoning** (p. 412); **Generalizations** (p. 413); **Qualifying Words** (p. 413); **Hasty Generalizations** (p. 413); **Circular Reasoning** (p. 413); **Only-Cause Fallacy** (p. 414); **Propaganda** (p. 415); **Bandwagon Appeals** (p. 415); **Stereotypes** (p. 416); **Name-Calling** (p. 416); **Snob Appeal** (p. 416); **Testimonial** (p. 417).

Read On

For Independent Reading

Encourage students to choose their independent reading from both the poetry titles and the nonfiction titles on life in the ancient world.

Assessment Options

The following projects can help you evaluate and assess your students' outside reading. Videotapes or audiotapes of completed projects may be included in students' portfolios.

■ **Make word illustrations.** Encourage students to find their own clever and imaginative ways to illustrate the words within words from Richard Wilbur's book. Collect all the illustrations to make a companion book to *The Pig in the Spigot.*

■ **Hold a poetry reading.** Have interested students sign up to give readings of their favorite poems from these collections. Allow them time to practice reading their poems aloud. Then, set aside a "poetry afternoon" for the readings. Encourage the rest of the class to ask questions about the poems they hear.

California Reading List Titles

Salting the Ocean
I'm Nobody! Who Are You?
Science in Ancient Mesopotamia

Poetry

Poems by Students

During her years as a teacher, Naomi Shihab Nye assembled an enormous collection of her students' poetry. In *Salting the Ocean* she presents some of her favorites. Nye's students write with passion about subjects like a hometown, a beloved family member, even a spelling bee.

A Great American Talent

Emily Dickinson was one of the world's greatest poets. During her lifetime, however, she was anything but famous. More than seventeen hundred poems were discovered after her death in 1886, but only seven had been published while she was alive. *I'm Nobody! Who Are You?* includes poems with a special appeal for young people. Dickinson's poems are short but rich in meaning.

A Dependable Pen

Have you ever thought you'd see an *ape* on a *trapeze*? or an *elf* in a *belfry*? You never know what you'll find—or where you'll find it— in Richard Wilbur's collection *The Pig in the Spigot.* Read it to discover the magic of words within words.

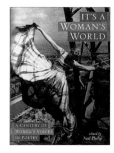

Poems by Women

During the twentieth century, women poets have become more and more visible. Neil Philip collects some of their finest work in *It's a Woman's World.* Philip includes works by poets you may recognize as well as a generous selection of works by new poets.

Toward Reading a Million Words Annually

Estimated Word Counts of Read On Books:

Poetry		Nonfiction	
Salting the Ocean	9,200	*Science in Ancient Mesopotamia*	8,900
I'm Nobody! Who Are You?	3,100	*The Stone Age News*	14,000
The Pig in the Spigot	1,400	*Street Smart! Cities of the Ancient World*	16,000
It's a Woman's World	12,000	*The Mystery of the Mammoth Bones*	23,000

Nonfiction
Connections to Social Studies and Science

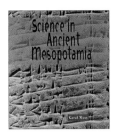

A Running Start

The people of ancient Mesopotamia (now Syria, Turkey, and Iraq), who established the first civilization in 5000 B.C., were naturally curious about how the world works. *Science in Ancient Mesopotamia* looks at their discoveries in mathematics, medicine, and astronomy. Carol Moss shows you that Mesopotamians were far ahead of their time.

Extra! Extra!

The Stone Age News is an imaginary prehistoric newspaper created by Alison Roberts and Fiona MacDonald. In it you'll find stories about hunters, advice on making a cave feel like a home, advertisements for footwear, even a weather forecast. The illustrations offer glimpses of everyday life in prehistoric times. In this book you'll also learn about the features of a newspaper.

First Steps

Have you ever wondered what city life was like long ago? In *Street Smart! Cities of the Ancient World*, you'll learn about the marble buildings of ancient Greek city-states and the grand temples built by the ancient Egyptians. You may not realize it, but most modern cities are constructed according to ideas first put into practice in ancient Rome, Mesopotamia, and other early cultures.

Rebuilding the Past

In 1801, Charles Willson Peale went to look at a set of huge bones that had been discovered in New York. He couldn't tell whether they had belonged to an elephant, a mammoth, or another mammal. He had to assemble a crew, risk flooding and cave-ins at digging sites, and reconstruct the creature's skeleton to find out for certain. In *The Mystery of the Mammoth Bones,* James Cross Giblin tells about Peale's quest and his scientific discovery, whose impact is still felt today.

■ **Hold a science conference.** Invite students to prepare presentations based on topics from *Science in Ancient Mesopotamia, Street Smart! Cities of the Ancient World,* or *The Mystery of the Mammoth Bones.* Their presentations should include an oral summary of their topic, supplemented by visuals such as posters. Set aside class time to hold a "science conference" in which these students get to give their presentations to the rest of the class.

■ **Make a model.** Interested students can make models based on the buildings discussed in *Street Smart! Cities of the Ancient World.* Students can display their models in the classroom. Remind them to include a card with each model, identifying the building's function and the city and time period where and when it was built.

▶ **Resources Reminder**

Reading

■ *Interactive Reading*

For additional readings that relate to the selections in this chapter, see *Interactive Reading,* Chapter 7.

■ *The Ancient World:* A Content-Area Reader

DIFFERENTIATING INSTRUCTION

The Read On titles are categorized as shown below.

I'm Nobody! Who Are You?
Science in Ancient Mesopotamia

Below Grade Level ⬇
The Pig in the Spigot
The Stone Age News

Above Grade Level ⬆
It's a Woman's World
Street Smart! Cities of the Ancient World
The Mystery of the Mammoth Bones

At Grade Level ↔
Salting the Ocean

Holt Literature and Language Arts: Mastering the California Standards
Chapter 8 You the Critic

Program Organization

Holt Literature and Language Arts provides a complete curriculum for standards-based instruction in vocabulary, reading, literature, writing, and speaking and listening. The instructional content of the program is divided into quarters to enable teachers to anticipate and administer the quarterly assessments required by California.

About Chapter 8

Standards-based lesson plans and suggestions for pacing the presentation of Chapter 8 and the related instructional material are provided in *On Course: Mapping Instruction,* Chapter 8.

- Chapter 8 helps students critique the credibility of plot and characterization and follow multistep instructions.
- The related instructional material for Chapter 8 is shown on the chart. This related instructional material will also be covered on the fourth quarterly assessment.

Holt Literature and Language Arts

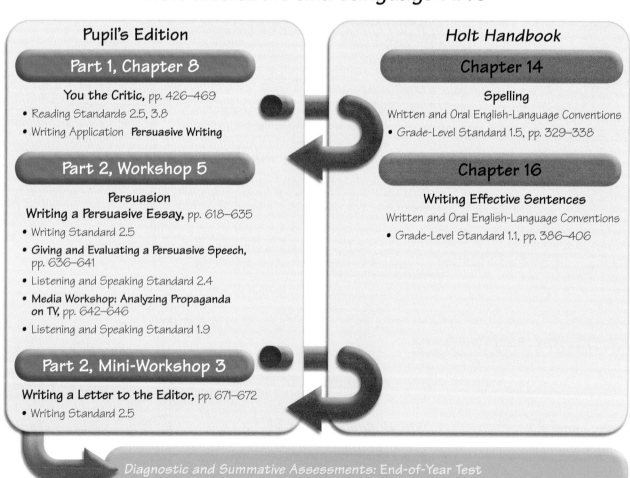

Pupil's Edition

Part 1, Chapter 8

You the Critic, pp. 426–469
- Reading Standards 2.5, 3.8
- Writing Application **Persuasive Writing**

Part 2, Workshop 5

Persuasion
Writing a Persuasive Essay, pp. 618–635
- Writing Standard 2.5
- **Giving and Evaluating a Persuasive Speech,** pp. 636–641
- Listening and Speaking Standard 2.4
- **Media Workshop: Analyzing Propaganda on TV,** pp. 642–646
- Listening and Speaking Standard 1.9

Part 2, Mini-Workshop 3

Writing a Letter to the Editor, pp. 671–672
- Writing Standard 2.5

Holt Handbook

Chapter 14

Spelling
Written and Oral English-Language Conventions
- Grade-Level Standard 1.5, pp. 329–338

Chapter 16

Writing Effective Sentences
Written and Oral English-Language Conventions
- Grade-Level Standard 1.1, pp. 386–406

Diagnostic and Summative Assessments: End-of-Year Test

Which vocabulary, informational reading, and literature standards are taught in Chapter 8?

In this chapter, students will master the following Grade 6 standards. They will also review a standard from Grade 4. Selections or features marked with a ✔ constitute the minimum course of study that provides coverage of all grade-level standards.

Grade 6 Standards

Reading Comprehension (Focus on Informational Materials)

2.5 Follow multiple-step instructions for preparing applications (e.g., for a public library card, bank savings account, sports club, league membership).

✔ Pompeii Museum Application for Volunteer Work (application form), pp. 447–449

Pet Adoption Application (application form), pp. 461–463

Standards Review: Reading Informational Materials, pp. 464–465

Literary Response and Analysis

3.8 Critique the credibility of characterization and the degree to which plot is contrived or realistic (e.g., compare use of fact and fantasy in historical fiction).

✔ "Literary Criticism: Finding the Right Words" (standards essay), pp. 428–429

✔ "The Dog of Pompeii" (short story), pp. 430–441

✔ "Pompeii" (history), pp. 442–445

"Zlateh the Goat" (short story), pp. 450–456

"Trial by Fire" (article), pp. 457–458

Review Standard Grade 4

Vocabulary

1.4 Know common roots and affixes derived from Greek and Latin, and use this knowledge to analyze the meaning of complex words (e.g., *international*).

Using Word Parts to Build Meanings: Prefixes, p. 446

Using Word Parts to Build Meanings: Suffixes, p. 459

Where do I locate lesson plans, additional resources, and other teaching aids?

- This Annotated Teacher's Edition and *On Course: Mapping Instruction* provide direction in planning and implementing a complete California standards–based curriculum. These components include instructions for administering diagnostic, progress, and summative tests; for presenting instruction of the standards; for differentiating instruction to provide universal access; and for locating and using the program's ancillaries.

- The program's resources are referenced at the beginning of each selection, in the bottom margin of this teacher's edition.

- Reminders for using additional resources appear in this teacher's edition at point of use.

- The *One-Stop Planner* CD-ROM with Test Generator contains editable lesson plans and all of the print ancillaries, available in PDF format.

What if I don't have time to teach all of Chapter 8?

- Most standards can be taught with a minimum number of selections and features. In the chart on p. 425B, the core lessons you need in order to provide complete coverage of the chapter standards are identified with a ✔.

- Use the Standards Review, pp. 464–465, for a quick review and informal assessment of the grade-level standards covered in Chapter 8.

What provisions have been made for students who have additional class time scheduled in language arts?

- *Interactive Reading* provides for additional direct instruction and practice of the grade-level standards taught in Chapter 8. It can be used as an introduction to instruction or as an opportunity for remediation.

- *Lesson Plans for Language Development*, Chapter 8, provides alternative teaching strategies and additional worksheets designed specifically for English-language learners and special education students. Many of the suggestions and activities in this ancillary will also be helpful to students in the regular classroom who are having difficulty with particular skills.

In addition to vocabulary, reading, and literature, what other language arts are covered in Chapter 8?

Writing Activities in Chapter 8
- Comparing Stories, p. 458

Writing Applications (p. 467)
- Taking a Stand (persuasive essay)
- Other Choices: It's a Dog's Life (comparison and contrast); Historical Fiction (short story)

Grammar Links in Chapter 8
- Pronouns and Antecedents Should Always Agree, p. 460

Universal Access

How do I differentiate instruction to ensure that all my students master the standards?

Holt Literature and Language Arts provides comprehensive, differentiated instruction for all types of students.

- Most of the general instruction and teaching strategies in the Annotated Teacher's Edition are at grade level. These instructions will work well with the majority of your students.

- In Chapter 8, suggestions for advanced learners are provided in the Annotated Teacher's Edition. Point-of-use suggestions for learners having difficulty, English-language learners, and special education students are also provided.

- *Interactive Reading* is designed to anticipate and/or remediate problems that students may experience in achieving mastery of the standards. *Interactive Reading* includes reading-strategy lessons, lower-level practice reads, and worksheets for every informational and literary text in *Holt Literature and Language Arts,* Pupil's Editions. *Interactive Reading* also contains three additional selections for each chapter and suggestions for extension projects, many of which are ideal for advanced learners working on their own. See *Interactive Reading,* Teacher's Edition, for specific information on using the reader to differentiate instruction in Chapter 8.

- *Lesson Plans for Language Development,* Chapter 8, offers teaching strategies and additional worksheets designed specifically for English-language learners and special education students.

Assessment

How do I determine whether or not my students are making progress in mastering the standards?

Progress Assessment

- Use the Standards Review at the end of Chapter 8, pp. 464–465, for an informal assessment of the informational reading and literature standards in Chapter 8.

- Use the Selection Tests for Chapter 8 from the *Progress Assessment of Reading* booklet to test comprehension and progress on mastering the standard(s) taught with a selection.

- Use Chapter Test 8 in the *Progress Assessment of Reading* booklet to test students' cumulative progress in mastering the standards taught in the chapter.

Summative Assessment

At the end of this chapter, you may ask students to take the End-of-Year Test in the *Diagnostic and Summative Assessments* booklet. This test covers *Holt Literature and Language Arts,* Chapters 7 and 8, Workshop 5 on Persuasion, and Mini-Workshops 3, "Writing a Letter to the Editor," 6, "Writing a Problem-Solution Explanation," and 7, "Giving and Listening to a Problem-Solution Explanation," as well as the *Holt Handbook,* Chapters 13–15.

8 You the Critic

(For grade-level and review standards taught in this chapter, see Pupil's Edition, p. 427.)

Prerequisite Standard

■ Grade 5, Literary Response and Analysis 3.7 **Evaluate the author's use of various techniques (e.g., appeal of characters in a picture book, logic and credibility of plots and settings, use of figurative language) to influence readers' perspectives.**

Standards Coming Up in the Next Grade Level

■ Grade 7, Literary Response and Analysis 3.2 **Identify events that advance the plot, and determine how each event explains past or present action(s) or foreshadows future action(s).**

■ Grade 7, Literary Response and Analysis 3.6 **Analyze a range of responses to a literary work, and determine the extent to which the literary elements in the work shaped those responses.**

CHAPTER RESOURCES

Planning

■ *One-Stop Planner* CD-ROM with Test Generator
■ *On Course: Mapping Instruction*
  ■ Chapter 8
■ *At Home: A Guide to Standards Mastery*
■ *At Home: In Five Languages*
■ *Supporting Instruction in Five Languages*

Reading

■ *Interactive Reading*
  ■ Chapter 8

Differentiating Instruction

■ *Lesson Plans for Language Development*
  ■ Chapter 8

Vocabulary and Spelling

■ *Vocabulary Development*
  ■ Cumulative Vocabulary Review, p. 31

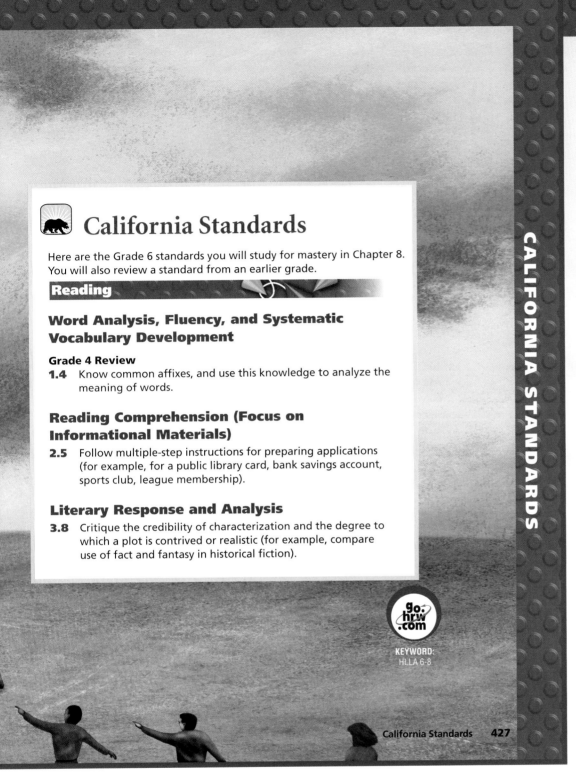

California Standards

Here are the Grade 6 standards you will study for mastery in Chapter 8. You will also review a standard from an earlier grade.

Reading

Word Analysis, Fluency, and Systematic Vocabulary Development

Grade 4 Review

1.4 Know common affixes, and use this knowledge to analyze the meaning of words.

Reading Comprehension (Focus on Informational Materials)

2.5 Follow multiple-step instructions for preparing applications (for example, for a public library card, bank savings account, sports club, league membership).

Literary Response and Analysis

3.8 Critique the credibility of characterization and the degree to which a plot is contrived or realistic (for example, compare use of fact and fantasy in historical fiction).

go.hrw.com
KEYWORD:
HLLA 6-8

California Standards **427**

California Standards **427**

INTRODUCING THE CHAPTER

In this chapter two tales of devoted animals tug at the heart. One story is set in ancient Pompeii. The other is set many years ago in a small Polish village. A lively piece of nonfiction follows each work, the first a history of Pompeii and the second a true story of a cat that rescued her kittens from a fire. As students read, they practice critiquing the credibility of the plot and characters and distinguishing factual and fictional elements in both the stories and the nonfiction works. Next, students learn to fill out application forms, practicing with an application for a volunteer job at the Pompeii Museum and an application for adopting a pet. Finally, students are invited to write their own persuasive letter about an issue they care about, using skills they have developed while working with the selections in the chapter.

► Resources Reminder

Planning
■ *At Home: A Guide to Standards Mastery*

You may want to send home with students selected parent letters from this resource. Translations of these letters are available in *At Home: In Five Languages. Supporting Instruction in Five Languages* provides translations of the selection summaries.

Reading
■ *Interactive Reading*
  ▪ Reading Log

The California framework requires students to read materials apart from in-class assignments. Additional reading suggestions are included on the Read On pages and on selected pages in the Pupil's and Teacher's Editions. You may want to use the Reading Log to help students track their progress.

(For the grade-level standard taught in this lesson, see Pupil's Edition, p. 428.)

Prerequisite Standard

- Grade 5, Literary Response and Analysis 3.7 **Evaluate the author's use of various techniques (e.g., appeal of characters in a picture book, logic and credibility of plots and settings, use of figurative language) to influence readers' perspectives.**

Literary Focus: Literary Criticism

You might bring in brief book and film reviews found in newspapers, newsmagazines, young people's magazines, or on the Web. Select reviews of works that are currently popular with your students. Point out the parts of the reviews that deal with character and plot, and invite students to look for any words that are listed in the literary criticism glossary in this essay.

 Resources Reminder

Reading

- *Interactive Reading*

Before you teach Chapter 8 of *Holt Literature and Language Arts,* you may want to preteach the literary concept and a related reading strategy.

- To introduce students to the literary concept before they read this essay, assign p. 293 of *Interactive Reading.*

- To introduce students to a reading strategy that will help them grasp the literary concept, assign p. 293 of *Interactive Reading.*

- To give students practice applying the strategy to a short, vocabulary-controlled selection, assign the Practice Read on p. 294 of *Interactive Reading.*

Literary Criticism *by* Kylene Beers

FINDING THE RIGHT WORDS

Your language arts teacher asks you whether you liked a story you've just read. You tell her you didn't. She asks why not. How are you most likely to respond?

1. "I don't know."
2. "It was boring."
3. "The characters were not believable; they did things real people would never do. The plot didn't seem believable either—not realistic at all."
4. "I just didn't like it."

Which response explains why you didn't like the story? It's easy to see that that would be statement 3.

You've certainly answered your teacher's question with statements 1, 2, and 4, but you haven't given specific information on what you didn't like.

Beyond "It's Boring" or "I Really Like It"

Here are some responses to Christopher Paul Curtis's novel *Bud, Not Buddy.* Which statements offer opinions that are supported with specific, detailed explanations?

Reading Standard 3.8 Critique the credibility of characterization and the degree to which a plot is contrived or realistic (for example, compare use of fact and fantasy in historical fiction).

1. "I liked this book a lot. It was really good. Other people will like it too."
2. "This is a great book. It is fun in parts and sad in parts, and the plot has a lot of good action."
3. "I didn't like this book too much. It wasn't good, and so I didn't like it."

4. "I didn't like this book. I didn't think it was realistic that a little kid would travel all over the country. And the ending was disappointing—he doesn't find his real dad."

If you picked statements 2 and 4, you picked the best answers. Statements 1 and 3 certainly offer opinions, but those opinions have no support.

Good literary critics know how to explain what they like or don't like about a text. They go beyond "It's really good" or "It's boring" to offer specifics. But what are those specifics? How can you discuss a text in a convincing way?

The chart on page 429 shows some of the words and phrases critics use when they talk about the characters and plot of a work of fiction. Using these words will help you move from vagueness to specifics.

Evaluating Characters: Believable or Not?

One of the most important words on these lists is *credible. Credible* means "believable." The opposite of *credible* is *incredible,* meaning "not believable." When we read fiction, we expect, above all, that the characters will be credible, that they will act the way real people do. Even if we're reading science fiction with Martians as characters, we still want to believe in the characters.

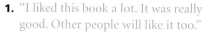 DIFFERENTIATING INSTRUCTION

Learners Having Difficulty

These students may need a brief review of plot and character before reading the essay. Point out that plots involve conflicts—clashes of opposing forces—which build to a climax, or a high point of excitement or tension when the conflict is usually resolved. This tension is what makes a plot suspenseful, as opposed to plodding or predictable. Then, remind students that authors create characterization through direct description

and indirectly, as well, by showing the characters in action and by showing how others react to them.

English-Language Learners

Be sure students grasp the difference between the general term *criticism,* which usually means "making negative comments," and the term *literary criticism,* which means "analyzing elements of a literary work." Explain that literary criticism

To decide whether characters are credible, ask yourself these questions:

- Do the characters have weaknesses as well as strengths? Is a character too good to be true? too strong? too unselfish? too evil?
- Do the characters talk and act like real people?
- Do the characters grow and change as a result of the events in the story?

Evaluating Plot: Believable or Not?

One word critics often use in talking about plot is *contrived.*

A contrived plot includes events that are not believable. A contrived plot may contain too many coincidences, like chance meetings. In a contrived plot major obstacles are quickly overcome. If you read a story in which two lovers on a sinking ship struggle through icy water up to their waists, hack through chains holding the hero captive, kill a gunman, leap onto an ice floe, and survive, you know you're dealing with a contrived plot.

To test the credibility of a plot, ask yourself questions like these:

- Do the events in the plot grow naturally out of the decisions and actions of the characters?
- Do many of the events result from chance or luck, or are there believable causes and effects?
- Do events unfold the way they would in real life?

LITERARY CRITICISM: A GLOSSARY	
Words and Phrases Used to Describe Plot	
Positive	**Negative**
realistic *or* credible	unrealistic *or* not credible
well-paced	plodding
suspenseful	predictable
satisfying ending	disappointing ending
subplots tied together well	confusing subplots
Words and Phrases Used to Describe Characters	
Positive	**Negative**
original	stereotyped
believable *or* credible *or* convincing	unbelievable *or* unconvincing
well-rounded	flat
dynamic—*refers to characters who change and grow and make discoveries about themselves and about life*	static—*refers to characters who remain the same throughout a story*

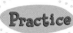

With a partner, choose a work of fiction you've read or a movie you've seen recently. Jot down notes on the credibility of the plot and the characters. Try to come up with two comments about the characters and two comments about the plot. Give the story or movie a thumbs-up or thumbs-down rating, using the words from the lists to support your rating. Then, share your ratings in class.

Now you're talking like a real critic.

Literary Criticism: Finding the Right Words   **429**

Students' comments on plot and characters will vary but should touch on the following key points: *Characters*—Are they one-sided, or do they have both virtues and faults? Do they grow and change as real people do? Do their speech and actions seem believable? Key terms that students might use include *credible, incredible, original, stereotyped, well rounded, flat, dynamic,* and *static.*
Plot—Does the action reasonably follow from characters' deeds and decisions? Are outcomes plausible, or are they implausibly unlucky, lucky, coincidental, or miraculous? Key terms that students might use include *credible, contrived, believable, well paced, plodding, suspenseful, predictable, satisfying,* and *disappointing.*

Apply

Ask each student to prepare a brief (one-paragraph) review of the most recent episode of his or her favorite television show. Students should critique the credibility of the show's main characters and of the episode's plot.

HOMEWORK

▶ Resources Reminder

Differentiating Instruction

- *Lesson Plans for Language Development*

For additional instruction for English-language learners and special education students on literary criticism, see *Lesson Plans for Language Development,* pp. 203–204.

---

involves comments on strengths as well as weaknesses; in fact, some pieces of literary criticism are entirely positive.

Advanced Learners

Acceleration. Use this activity to move students toward the seventh-grade Standard 3.6, which requires that they analyze a range of responses to a literary work and determine the extent to which literary elements in the work shaped those responses.

Activity. Have students pair up and use the Internet to gather between two and four reviews of one book. Direct students to compare the reviewers' comments on characterization and plot. On what do the reviewers agree or disagree? Have each student pair share its findings with the class. If any students have read the books, encourage them to add their own critiques of plot and characters.

STANDARDS FOCUS, pp. 430–446

(For grade-level and review standards taught in this selection, see citations on Pupil's Edition pages.)

Prerequisite Standard

■ Grade 5, Literary Response and Analysis 3.7 **Evaluate the author's use of various techniques (e.g., appeal of characters in a picture book, logic and credibility of plots and settings, use of figurative language) to influence readers' perspectives.**

Standard Coming Up in the Next Grade Level

■ Grade 7, Literary Response and Analysis 3.6 **Analyze a range of responses to a literary work, and determine the extent to which the literary elements in the work shaped those responses.**

Reading Skills

■ Make inferences.

Summary ⬆ *above grade level*

This short story takes place in ancient Pompeii. A blind orphan named Tito and his dog, Bimbo, live in the streets, and Bimbo trots off briefly each day to get food for his master. Tito's favorite food is raisin cake. One day, Tito overhears people discussing whether Mount Vesuvius is giving warnings of an eruption. He is awakened that night by Bimbo: The eruption has begun. Bimbo saves the dazed and disoriented Tito, leading him to the sea. Just before Tito is taken into a boat, Bimbo mysteriously vanishes. Eighteen hundred years later, in the ruins of a Pompeii bakery, archaeologists find the skeleton of a dog with a petrified raisin cake in his mouth.

The Dog of Pompeii *and* Pompeii

Literary Focus
Credible Characters: We Believe They're Real

First they spring out of a writer's mind; then they live in a reader's imagination, as if they were real. Who are they? They're **credible** (kred′ə·bəl) **characters**—people in stories who seem as real as the flesh-and-blood people we know.

Even in fantasies, where the laws of nature don't always operate, characters can be so credible, or true to life, that we find ourselves caring deeply about them.

Blanca Flor (see page 91) is a good example. The play about her is a fantasy; things happen that we know could never occur in real life. But Blanca Flor is such a credible character that we can almost picture her sitting next to us.

Reading Skills
Making Inferences

As you read, you make **inferences**, or guesses. You guess what will happen next. You guess about things the writer has deliberately left out. You base your guesses on details in the story and on your own experiences. When you make inferences as you read, you're using your imagination, just as the writer is using his or hers. You may end up supplying hundreds of details that the storyteller just couldn't fit in. In a way, you become a storyteller too!

Reading Standard 3.8 Critique the credibility of characterization and the degree to which a plot is contrived or realistic (for example, compare use of fact and fantasy in historical fiction).

Make the Connection
Quickwrite ✏

Jot down any facts you know about the city of Pompeii (päm·pā′ē), in Italy, and the eruption of the volcano Vesuvius (və·sōō′vē·əs) that took place there almost two thousand years ago. If you don't know anything about the subject, look at the pictures that illustrate the story. Write down any questions that come to mind.

RESOURCES

Planning
■ *One-Stop Planner* CD-ROM with Test Generator
■ *On Course: Mapping Instruction*

Media
■ *Audio CD Library*
  ■ disc 10
■ *Visual Connections*
  ■ Videocassette, Segment 10

■ *Fine Art Transparencies*
  ■ Transparency 14

Reading
■ *Interactive Reading*
  ■ Strategy Launch: "Save the Last Word for Me," p. 293
  ■ Practice Read: "My Field Trip to Pompeii," p. 294
  ■ Graphic Organizer: Chain of Events Chart, p. 301

Background

"The Dog of Pompeii" is **historical fiction.** Louis Untermeyer combined a fictional story with facts about actual historical events. The story's setting is Pompeii, an ancient Roman city that was buried by a volcanic eruption in A.D. 79.

The volcano that destroyed the city of Pompeii also preserved it. Excavations there began in the eighteenth century. Archaeologists brought the past to life as they uncovered buildings, furniture, food, paintings, and tools. They found rock-hard loaves of bread. They also found about two thousand hollow forms of humans, dogs, and other animals that had been frozen in place by the ash that buried them. Perhaps Louis Untermeyer was inspired to write this story when he saw the forms of the dogs that had been buried by ash in Pompeii.

An Italian archaeologist named Giuseppe Fiorelli found a way to make molds of the bodies, by pumping plaster into the hollows they had left in the ashes. When the plaster within one of the hollows hardened, the ash around it was chipped off. What remained was a plaster cast in the shape of the body.

Today three quarters of old Pompeii has been unearthed. You can visit Pompeii as a tourist; no time machine is necessary. You can walk the same streets, look at the same buildings, and gaze at the same volcano, sleeping for now, that the unsuspecting residents of Pompeii saw for the last time on that day nearly two thousand years ago.

Vocabulary Development

Here are the words you'll learn as you read the story:

ambitious (am·bish′əs) *adj.:* eager to succeed. *The ambitious citizens of Pompeii hoped to make their city famous.*

proverb (präv′ərb) *n.:* short traditional saying that expresses a truth. *"Haste makes waste" is a proverb.*

revived (ri·vīvd′) *v.:* awakened; brought back to life. *The splashing water revived him, and he sat up.*

Cave Canem (Beware the Dog). Ancient Roman floor mosaic from Pompeii.

The Dog of Pompeii   **431**

Standards Starter

Motivate. Use the *Visual Connections* segment titled "Molten Mountains," Videocassette Segment 10, to pique students' interest in volcanic eruptions.

Preview Vocabulary

To build students' familiarity with the Vocabulary words, use the following brief exercise. First, discuss the three words and their meanings. Then, have students match words and definitions from the two columns below.

1. ambitious [c]	**a.**	traditional saying
2. proverb [a]	**b.**	awakened
3. revived [b]	**c.**	eager for success

Assign the Reading

You might read the first third of the story as a class, up to "'I tell you,' rumbled a voice which Tito recognized as bath master Rufus's . . .'" on p. 435. Then, for students reading at or above grade level, assign the rest of the story as homework. Meanwhile, continue reading aloud with small groups of students having difficulty.

HOMEWORK

▶ Resources Reminder

Media
- *Audio CD Library*
  - disc 10
- *Visual Connections*
  - Videocassette, Segment 10
- *Fine Art Transparencies*
  - Transparency 14

Reading
- *Interactive Reading*
  - Strategy Launch: "Save the Last Word for Me," p. 293
  - Graphic Organizer: Chain of Events Chart, p. 301

- *Interactive Reading,* Teacher's Edition
  - Transparency 8: "Save the Last Word for Me"

Differentiating Instruction
- *Lesson Plans for Language Development*
  - English-Language Learners, pp. 205–207, 215, 219
  - Special Education Students, pp. 208, 215, 219

Vocabulary and Spelling
- *Vocabulary Development*
  - Vocabulary Worksheet, p. 29

Assessment
- *Progress Assessment of Reading*
  - Selection Test, p. 153
- *One-Stop Planner* CD-ROM with Test Generator

Explain to students that in the illustrations for this selection, the artist has superimposed drawings of characters in ancient Roman costume over images of the present-day ruins of Pompeii.

Activity. Ask students to discuss the impact of juxtaposing fictional characters and actual images of Pompeii. How does the art add to—or detract from—the credibility of the characters in the story?

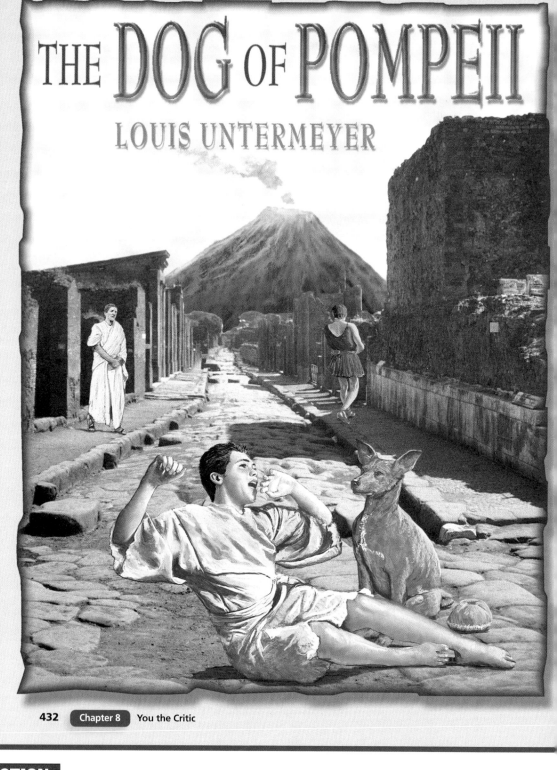

THE DOG OF POMPEII
LOUIS UNTERMEYER

DIFFERENTIATING INSTRUCTION

Learners Having Difficulty
Modeling. Some students may need to read an easier selection before beginning "The Dog of Pompeii." Use the Practice Read in *Interactive Reading*, p. 294. You can then use the transparency to model the strategy of Save the Last Word for Me. This strategy will help students to express their opinions about the credibility of the characters and the degree to which the plot is realistic or contrived. Have students apply

the strategy to "The Dog of Pompeii." As they read, encourage them to ask themselves, "Do the characters behave as real people do?" and "Do the events have believable causes and effects?"

 Resources Reminder

Reading
- *Interactive Reading*, Teacher's Edition
  - Transparency 8: "Save the Last Word for Me"

English-Language Learners
Help students locate Pompeii on a map of modern Italy (about a dozen miles south of Naples). Show the fine art transparency of Mt. Vesuvius and tell students that the volcano has erupted many more times since A.D. 79, notably in 472, 512, 1631, 1872, 1906, and 1944.

Tito and his dog Bimbo lived (if you could call it living) under the wall where it joined the inner gate. They really didn't live there; they just slept there. They lived anywhere. Pompeii was one of the gayest of the old Latin towns, but although Tito was never an unhappy boy, he was not exactly a merry one. The streets were always lively with shining chariots and bright red trappings; the open-air theaters rocked with laughing crowds; sham[1] battles and athletic sports were free for the asking in the great stadium. Once a year the Caesar[2] visited the pleasure city and the fireworks lasted for days; the sacrifices[3] in the forum were better than a show.

But Tito saw none of these things. He was blind—had been blind from birth. He was known to everyone in the poorer quarters. But no one could say how old he was, no one remembered his parents, no one could tell where he came from. Bimbo was another mystery. As long as people could remember seeing Tito—about twelve or thirteen years—they had seen Bimbo. Bimbo had never left his side. He was not only dog but nurse, pillow, playmate, mother, and father to Tito.

Did I say Bimbo never left his master? (Perhaps I had better say comrade, for if anyone was the master, it was Bimbo.) I was wrong. Bimbo did trust Tito alone exactly three times a day. It was a fixed routine, a custom understood between boy and dog since the beginning of their friendship, and the way it worked was this: Early in the morning,

shortly after dawn, while Tito was still dreaming, Bimbo would disappear. When Tito awoke, Bimbo would be sitting quietly at his side, his ears cocked, his stump of a tail tapping the ground, and a fresh-baked bread—more like a large round roll—at his feet. Tito would stretch himself; Bimbo would yawn; then they would breakfast. At noon, no matter where they happened to be, Bimbo would put his paw on Tito's knee and the two of them would return to the inner gate. Tito would curl up in the corner (almost like a dog) and go to sleep, while Bimbo, looking quite important (almost like a boy), would disappear again. In half an hour he'd be back with their lunch. Sometimes it would be a piece of fruit or a scrap of meat, often it was nothing but a dry crust. But sometimes there would be one of those flat rich cakes, sprinkled with raisins and sugar, that Tito liked so much. At suppertime the same thing happened, although there was a little less of everything, for things were hard to snatch in the evening, with the streets full of people. Besides, Bimbo didn't approve of too much food before going to sleep. A heavy supper made boys too restless and dogs too stodgy[4]—and it was the business of a dog to sleep lightly with one ear open and muscles ready for action.

But, whether there was much or little, hot or cold, fresh or dry, food was always there. Tito never asked where it came from and Bimbo never told him. There was plenty of rainwater in the hollows of soft stones; the old egg woman at the corner sometimes gave him a cupful of strong goat's milk; in the grape season the fat winemaker let him have drippings of the mild juice. So there

1. **sham** *adj.:* make-believe.
2. **Caesar** (sē′zər) *n.:* Roman emperor. The word *Caesar* comes from the family name of Julius Caesar, a great general who ruled Rome as dictator from 49 to 44 B.C.
3. **sacrifices** *n.:* offerings (especially of slaughtered animals) to the gods.

4. **stodgy** (stä′jē) *adj.:* heavy and slow in movement.

A Literary Focus
GRADE-LEVEL STANDARD

❓ **Historical fiction: Fact versus fantasy.** Which parts of this description are historical fact, and which are fictional? [The descriptions of Pompeii are historical fact; the descriptions of Tito and Bimbo are fictional.] Point out that the historical accuracy of the setting lends credibility to the characters.

B Reading Skills

❓ **Making inferences.** From these details, what might you infer about Tito's family, economic level, and earlier years? [Possible responses: He has no family to care for him; he is poor; he has been homeless since he was very young.]

C Literary Focus
GRADE-LEVEL STANDARD

❓ **Critiquing characterization.** Have students read this passage with and without the sections in parentheses. Do these additional phrases make Tito and Bimbo seem more credible? [Possible responses: Yes, because they emphasize the bond between the boy and the dog; no, because a human and a dog wouldn't really switch roles, as the phrases suggest.]

▶ **Resources Reminder**

For lessons designed for intermediate and advanced English-language learners, see *Lesson Plans for Language Development*, pp. 205–207, 215, 219.

Special Education Students

For lessons designed for special education students, see *Lesson Plans for Language Development*, pp. 208, 215, 219.

Advanced Learners
Acceleration. Use this activity to move students toward the seventh-grade Standard 3.6, which requires that they analyze a range of responses to a literary work and determine the extent to which literary elements in the work shaped those responses.
Activity. As the class reads "The Dog of Pompeii," have students survey classmates to learn (1) how much they like the story and (2) how credible they consider Tito and

Bimbo. Survey questions might ask respondents to rate their enjoyment of the story and the credibility of the characters on a scale of 1 (low) to 10 (high). Then, direct students to analyze the results of their surveys, looking for the correlation between respondents' enjoyment of the story and their assessment of the credibility of its characters. You might have students display their results as charts or graphs accompanied by brief explanations.

A Reading Skills

❓ Making inferences. The writer does not explain what these games are. How might you infer how the games are played? [Possible response: Readers could base inferences on the names of the games and on memories of games that they themselves have played.]

B Literary Focus
GRADE-LEVEL STANDARD

❓ Historical fiction: Fact versus fantasy. What are some details that you learn about Roman life from this passage? [Possible responses: the food served at a feast, how clothes were kept moth-free, how fevers were treated, the different foods found in a market.]

C Reading Skills

Making inferences. [Possible response to question 1: There will probably be tasty leftovers from the "grand dinner," and Bimbo will try to get some for Tito and himself.]

D English-Language Learners

❓ Building background knowledge. Explain that in ancient Roman towns, the forum was the most important public area. Ask students which places in modern towns serve the function of the forum, as described in this paragraph. [Possible responses: civic centers, town squares, malls, shopping centers, marketplaces.]

---

was no danger of going hungry or thirsty. There was plenty of everything in Pompeii—if you knew where to find it—and if you had a dog like Bimbo.

As I said before, Tito was not the merriest boy in Pompeii. He could not romp with the **A** other youngsters and play "hare and hounds" and "I spy" and "follow your master" and "ball against the building" and "jackstones" and "kings and robbers" with them. But that did not make him sorry for himself. If he could not see the sights that delighted the lads of Pompeii, he could hear and smell things they never noticed. He could really see more with his ears and nose than they could with their eyes. When he and Bimbo went out walking, he knew just where they were going and exactly what was happening.

"Ah," he'd sniff and say, as they passed a handsome villa,[5] "Glaucus Pansa is giving a grand dinner tonight. They're going to have three kinds of bread, and roast pigling, and stuffed goose, and a great stew—I think bear stew— and a fig pie." And Bimbo **C** would note that this would be a good place to visit tomorrow.

> 🐾 **MAKING INFERENCES**
> 1. Why would this villa be a good place to visit tomorrow?

B Or, "H'm," Tito would murmur, half through his lips, half through his nostrils. "The wife of Marcus Lucretius is expecting her mother. She's shaking out every piece of goods in the house; she's going to use the best clothes—the ones she's been keeping in pine needles and camphor[6]—and there's an extra girl in the kitchen. Come, Bimbo, let's get out of the dust!"

---
5. **villa** *n.:* large house.
6. **camphor** (kam′fər) *n.:* strong-smelling substance used to keep moths away from clothing. Camphor is still used for this purpose.

Or, as they passed a small but elegant dwelling opposite the public baths, "Too bad! The tragic poet is ill again. It must be a bad fever this time, for they're trying smoke fumes instead of medicine. Whew! I'm glad I'm not a tragic poet!"

Or, as they neared the forum, "Mm-m! What good things they have in the macellum[7] today!" (It really was a sort of butcher-grocer-marketplace, but Tito didn't know any better. He called it the macellum.) "Dates from Africa, and salt oysters from sea caves, and cuttlefish, and new honey, and sweet onions, and—ugh!—water-buffalo steaks. Come, let's see what's what in the forum." And Bimbo, just as curious as his comrade, hurried on. Being a dog, he trusted his ears and nose (like Tito) more than his eyes. And so the two of them entered the center of Pompeii.

D The forum was the part of the town to which everybody came at least once during the day. It was the central square, and everything happened here. There were no private houses; all was public—the chief temples, the gold and red bazaars, the silk shops, the town hall, the booths belonging to the weavers and jewel merchants, the wealthy woolen market, the shrine of the household gods. Everything glittered here. The buildings looked as if they were new—which, in a sense, they were. The earthquake of twelve years ago had brought down all the old structures and, since the citizens of Pompeii were ambitious to rival Naples and even Rome, they had seized the opportunity to rebuild the whole town. And

---
7. **macellum** (mə′sel·əm) *n.:* market, especially a meat market.

Vocabulary
ambitious (am·bish′əs) *adj.:* eager to succeed or to achieve something.

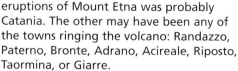

Geography
Roman Italy. Provide the following background material on the geography of southern Italy under the Roman Empire: The city of Naples, on the Italian mainland near Pompeii and Mount Vesuvius, was founded as a Greek colony and captured by Romans in the fourth century B.C. To the south, Mount Etna, at more than ten thousand feet, dominates the eastern coast of the island of Sicily. One of the "two towns . . . ruined" by the

eruptions of Mount Etna was probably Catania. The other may have been any of the towns ringing the volcano: Randazzo, Paterno, Bronte, Adrano, Acireale, Riposto, Taormina, or Giarre.
Activity. Pair students, and ask them to locate Rome, Naples, Pompeii, Mount Vesuvius, Sicily, Mount Etna, and Catania on a map of Italy.

PAIRED

they had done it all within a dozen years. There was scarcely a building that was older than Tito.

Tito had heard a great deal about the earthquake, though being about a year old at the time, he could scarcely remember it. This particular quake had been a light one—as earthquakes go. The weaker houses had been shaken down, parts of the outworn wall had been wrecked; but there was little loss of life, and the brilliant new Pompeii had taken the place of the old. No one knew what caused these earthquakes. Records showed they had happened in the neighborhood since the beginning of time. Sailors said that it was to teach the lazy city folk a lesson and make them appreciate those who risked the dangers of the sea to bring them luxuries and protect their town from invaders. The priests said that the gods took this way of showing their anger to those who refused to worship properly and who failed to bring enough sacrifices to the altars and (though they didn't say it in so many words) presents to the priests. The tradesmen said that the foreign merchants had corrupted the ground and it was no longer safe to traffic in imported goods that came from strange places and carried a curse with them. Everyone had a different explanation and everyone's explanation was louder and sillier than his neighbor's.

They were talking about it this afternoon as Tito and Bimbo came out of the side street into the public square. The forum was the favorite promenade[8] for rich and poor.

What with the priests arguing with the politicians, servants doing the day's shopping, tradesmen crying their wares, women displaying the latest fashions from Greece and Egypt, children playing hide-and-seek among the marble columns, knots of soldiers, sailors, peasants from the provinces[9]—to say nothing of those who merely came to lounge and look on—the square was crowded to its last inch. His ears even more than his nose guided Tito to the place where the talk was loudest. It was in front of the shrine of the household gods that, naturally enough, the householders were arguing.

"I tell you," rumbled a voice which Tito recognized as bath master Rufus's, "there won't be another earthquake in my lifetime or yours. There may be a tremble or two, but

🔖 **MAKING INFERENCES**
2. What didn't people at this time understand about earthquakes?

---
8. **promenade** (präm'ə·nād') *n.*: public place where people stroll.

9. **provinces** *n.*: places far from the capital, under Roman control.

The Dog of Pompeii   435

Ⓐ Literary Focus
GRADE-LEVEL STANDARD

❓ Historical fiction: Fact versus fantasy. One technique of historical fiction is to put dialogue about historical fact in the mouths of fictional characters. What makes the dialogue between the locals and the stranger seem credible? [Possible responses: They use informal language such as "I tell you" and "how about"; it's believable that some people would predict disaster and others would dismiss the predictions.]

Ⓑ Literary Focus
GRADE-LEVEL STANDARD
Critiquing characterization.
Writers of historical fiction sometimes make their characters seem real by highlighting similarities between the historical characters and modern people. The resentment expressed by citizens of the small town of Pompeii toward the nearby big city of Naples mirrors the sometimes troubled relations between many of today's big cities and their suburbs.

Ⓒ English-Language Learners

Idioms. Point out the idiom *mind their own business,* and tell students that it means "stop meddling in others' lives."

---

earthquakes, like lightnings, never strike twice in the same place."

Ⓐ "Do they not?" asked a thin voice Tito had never heard. It had a high, sharp ring to it and Tito knew it as the accent of a stranger. "How about the two towns of Sicily that have been ruined three times within fifteen years by the eruptions of Mount Etna? And were they not warned? And does that column of smoke above Vesuvius mean nothing?"

"That?" Tito could hear the grunt with which one question answered another. "That's always there. We use it for our weather guide. When the smoke stands up straight, we know we'll have fair weather; when it flattens out, it's sure to be foggy; when it drifts to the east—"

"Yes, yes," cut in the edged voice. "I've heard about your mountain barometer.[10]

---

10. **barometer** (bə·räm′ət·ər) *n.:* instrument for measuring atmospheric pressure. Barometers are used in forecasting changes in the weather.

But the column of smoke seems hundreds of feet higher than usual and it's thickening and spreading like a shadowy tree. They say in Naples—"

Ⓑ "Oh, Naples!" Tito knew this voice by the little squeak that went with it. It was Attilio the cameo cutter.[11] "They talk while we suffer. Little help we got from them last time. Naples commits the crimes and Pompeii pays the price. It's become a proverb with us. Ⓒ Let them mind their own business."

"Yes," grumbled Rufus, "and others', too."

"Very well, my confident friends," responded the thin voice, which now sounded curiously flat. "We also have a proverb— and it is this: *Those who will not listen to*

---

11. **cameo cutter:** artist who carves small, delicate pictures on gems or shells.

Vocabulary
proverb (präv′ərb) *n.:* short traditional saying that expresses a truth.

MINI-LESSON   Reading

Developing Word-Attack Skills
Write the selection word *explanation* on the chalkboard, and read it aloud. Underline the suffix *–tion,* and have students pronounce it. [/shən/] Point out that in the suffix *–tion, t* before *i* stands for the consonant sound /sh/. Invite students to suggest other words that end with the sound /shən/. Their suggestions may include words that end with *–sion,* such as *tension* and *mansion,* and words with *–ion*

after *sh,* such as *cushion* and the selection word *fashion.* Write students' suggestions on the chalkboard, underlining the letters that stand for the sound /sh/ in each word.

Next, write the selection word *appreciate* on the chalkboard. Read the word aloud, and have a volunteer identify the spelling for the /sh/ sound in the word. Help students recognize that *c* stands for /sh/ in *appreciate.* In a similar way, have students identify the letters

---

men must be taught by the gods. I say no more. But I leave a last warning. Remember the holy ones. Look to your temples. And when the smoke tree above Vesuvius grows to the shape of an umbrella pine, look to your lives."

Tito could hear the air whistle as the speaker drew his toga about him, and the quick shuffle of feet told him the stranger had gone.

> **MAKING INFERENCES**
> 3. What do you think will happen to Pompeii?

"Now what," said the cameo cutter, "did he mean by that?"

"I wonder," grunted Rufus. "I wonder."

Tito wondered, too. And Bimbo, his head at a thoughtful angle, looked as if he had been doing a heavy piece of pondering. By nightfall the argument had been forgotten. If the smoke had increased, no one saw it in the dark. Besides, it was Caesar's birthday and the town was in a holiday mood. Tito and Bimbo were among the merrymakers, dodging the charioteers who shouted at them. A dozen times they almost upset baskets of sweets and jars of Vesuvian wine, said to be as fiery as the streams inside the volcano, and a dozen times they were cursed and cuffed. But Tito never missed his footing. He was thankful for his keen ears and quick instinct—most thankful of all for Bimbo.

They visited the uncovered theater, and though Tito could not see the faces of the actors, he could follow the play better than most of the audience, for their attention wandered—they were distracted by the scenery, the costumes, the byplay,[12] even by themselves—while Tito's whole attention was

centered in what he heard. Then to the city walls, where the people of Pompeii watched a mock naval battle in which the city was attacked by the sea and saved after thousands of flaming arrows had been exchanged and countless colored torches had been burned. Though the thrill of flaring ships and lighted skies was lost to Tito, the shouts and cheers excited him as much as any, and he cried out with the loudest of them.

The next morning there were two of the beloved raisin-and-sugar cakes for his breakfast. Bimbo was unusually active and thumped his bit of a tail until Tito was afraid he would wear it out. The boy could not imagine whether Bimbo was urging him to some sort of game or was trying to tell him something. After a while, he ceased to notice Bimbo. He felt drowsy. Last night's late hours had tired him. Besides, there was a heavy mist in the air—no, a thick fog rather than a mist—a fog that got into his throat and scraped it and made him cough. He walked as far as the marine gate[13] to get a breath of the sea. But the blanket of haze had spread all over the bay and even the salt air seemed smoky.

> **MAKING INFERENCES**
> 4. What do you think Bimbo wants to tell Tito? What inference can you make about the smoke?

He went to bed before dusk and slept. But he did not sleep well. He had too many dreams—dreams of ships lurching in the forum, of losing his way in a screaming crowd, of armies marching across his chest, of being pulled over every rough pavement of Pompeii.

He woke early. Or, rather, he was pulled awake. Bimbo was doing the pulling. The

---

12. **byplay** *n.:* action taking place outside the main action of a play.

13. **marine gate:** gate in a city wall leading to the sea.

The Dog of Pompeii   **437**

D Reading Skills

Making inferences. Students might base responses to question 3 on the stranger's apparent knowledge of other eruptions and on the growth of the smoke plume over Mount Vesuvius.

[Possible responses to question 3: Pompeii will experience a deadly eruption; Pompeii will be destroyed by the eruption of Mount Vesuvius.]

E Literary Focus
GRADE-LEVEL STANDARD
❓ Critiquing characterization.
The birthday of the Caesar, or Roman emperor, is like a Fourth of July celebration or carnival. Do you find Tito's behavior during this festival believable? Why or why not? [Possible responses: Yes, because most young people would want to experience the festivities; no, because a blind person would not really be able to avoid all the unusual obstacles.]

F Literary Focus
GRADE-LEVEL STANDARD
❓ Critiquing characterization.
True-to-life characters are not perfect. Like real people, they sometimes show poor judgment. What judgment errors does Tito make on this day? [Possible responses: He fails to connect the smoky air with the stranger's warning of a growing smoke cloud over Mount Vesuvius; he dismisses Bimbo's unusual behavior.]

G Reading Skills

Making inferences. You might tell students that scientists have recorded many instances of animals behaving in unusual ways just before natural disasters.

[Possible responses to question 4: Bimbo senses disaster and wants to warn Tito; the haze and smoke are from Mount Vesuvius; a deadly eruption is about to start, as the stranger warned.]

---

that stand for the sound /sh/ in the selection word *politicians*. [ci]
Activity. Display the following sentences. Have volunteers identify the words with the /sh/ sound and the letter or letters that spell /sh/.

1. A volcanic eruption destroyed Pompeii. [erup_tion]

2. Its destruction was also its preservation. [destruc_tion, preserva_tion]

3. Cinders buried its mansions. [man_sions]

4. Its statues and decorations are preserved. [decora_tions]

5. There have been excavations of Pompeii. [excava_tions]

6. They reveal the spacious public forum. [spa_cious]

A **Literary Focus**
REVIEW STANDARD

? Using figurative language.
Untermeyer uses figurative language to describe the sounds of the impending eruption as Tito hears them. What might Tito feel as he hears these sounds? [Possible responses: dread, panic, despair.]

B **Reading Skills**

Making inferences. [Possible responses to question 5: The water is hot because of geothermal activity associated with the eruption of Mount Vesuvius; magma rising in Mount Vesuvius is heating the underground source of the fountain's water.]

C **Reading Skills**

Making inferences. [Possible response to question 6: The volcano is erupting with a huge explosion—part of the mountain is being blown away; the blast may be leveling forests on the slopes of Mount Vesuvius.]

D **Literary Focus**
GRADE-LEVEL STANDARD

? Critiquing plot. How credible do you find Tito's "miraculous" escape? [Possible responses: Very, since Bimbo is his guide and animals have an instinct for survival; not very, since he is slower than others and would be more likely to be trapped.]

E **Reading Skills**

Making inferences. [Possible response to question 7: The fumes and smoke may be poisonous.] After students have read Robert Silverberg's article "Pompeii" (p. 442), they will understand that Tito's drowsiness is caused by carbon monoxide poisoning from the gas released by the eruption.

---

dog had dragged Tito to his feet and was urging the boy along. Somewhere. Where, Tito did not know. His feet stumbled uncertainly; he was still half asleep. For a while he noticed nothing except the fact that it was hard to breathe. The air was hot. And heavy. So heavy that he could taste it. The air, it seemed, had turned to powder—a warm powder that stung his nostrils and burned his sightless eyes.

Then he began to hear sounds. Peculiar sounds. Like animals under the earth. Hissings and groanings and muffled cries that a dying creature might make dislodging the stones of his underground cave. There was no doubt of it now. The noises came from underneath. He not only heard them—he could feel them. The earth twitched; the twitching changed to an uneven shrugging of the soil. Then, as Bimbo half pulled, half coaxed him across, the ground jerked away from his feet and he was thrown against a stone fountain.

The water—hot water—splashing in his face revived him. He got to his feet, Bimbo steadying him, helping him on again. The noises grew louder; they came closer. The cries were even more animal-like than before, but now they came from human throats. A few people, quicker of foot and more hurried by fear, began to rush by. A family or two—then a section—then, it seemed, an army broken out of bounds. Tito, bewildered though he was, could recognize Rufus as he bellowed past him, like a water buffalo gone mad. Time was lost in a nightmare.

It was then the crashing began. First a sharp crackling, like a monstrous snapping of twigs; then a roar like the fall of a whole

> **MAKING INFERENCES**
> 5. Why do you suppose the water is hot?

forest of trees; then an explosion that tore earth and sky. The heavens, though Tito could not see them, were shot through with continual flickerings of fire. Lightnings above were answered by thunders beneath. A house fell. Then another. By a miracle the two companions had escaped the dangerous side streets and were in a more open space. It was the forum. They rested here awhile—how long, he did not know.

Tito had no idea of the time of day. He could feel it was black—an unnatural blackness. Something inside—perhaps the lack of breakfast and lunch—told him it was past noon. But it didn't matter. Nothing seemed to matter. He was getting drowsy, too drowsy to walk. But walk he must. He knew it. And Bimbo knew it; the sharp tugs told him so. Nor was it a moment too soon. The sacred ground of the forum was safe no longer. It was beginning to rock, then to pitch, then to split. As they stumbled out of the square, the earth wriggled like a caught snake and all the columns of the temple of Jupiter[14] came down. It was the end of the world—or so it seemed. To walk was not enough now. They must run. Tito was too frightened to know what to do or where to go. He had lost all

> **MAKING INFERENCES**
> 6. Tito doesn't know what is going on. What is happening right now with the volcano?

> **MAKING INFERENCES**
> 7. Why is Tito drowsy?

---

14. **Jupiter:** the supreme god in the religion of the Romans.

Vocabulary
revived (ri·vīvd′) v.: brought back to life or to a waking state.

CONTENT-AREA CONNECTIONS

History
Roman leaders. Titus was the emperor whose birthday was being feted just before the eruption of Mount Vesuvius. Although Titus had been a military leader and had destroyed Jerusalem in A.D. 70, his brief reign as emperor (A.D. 79–81) was peaceful. Among his major accomplishments was finishing the great Coliseum in Rome, which hosted sham naval battles and gladiator fights.

Culture
Guide dogs. Bimbo's behavior resembles that of modern guide dogs, which are trained to assist the visually impaired. The first school for guide dogs was established in Germany after World War I to help visually impaired veterans. In the United States, Seeing Eye, Inc., was founded in 1929.

sense of direction. He started to go back to the inner gate; but Bimbo, straining his back to the last inch, almost pulled his clothes from him. What did the creature want? Had the dog gone mad?

Then suddenly he understood. Bimbo was telling him the way out—urging him there. The sea gate, of course. The sea gate—and then the sea. Far from falling buildings, heaving ground. He turned, Bimbo guiding him across open pits and dangerous pools of bubbling mud, away from buildings that had caught fire and were dropping their burning beams. Tito could no longer tell whether the noises were made by the shrieking sky or the agonized people. He and Bimbo ran on— the only silent beings in a howling world.

New dangers threatened. All Pompeii seemed to be thronging toward the marine gate and, squeezing among the crowds, there was the chance of being trampled to death. But the chance had to be taken. It was growing harder and harder to breathe. What air there was choked him. It was all dust now—dust and pebbles, pebbles as large as beans. They fell on his head, his hands—pumice stones from the black heart of Vesuvius. The mountain was turning itself inside out. Tito remembered a phrase that the stranger had said in the forum two days ago: "Those who will not listen to men must be taught by the gods." The people of Pompeii had refused to heed the warnings; they were being taught now—if it was not too late.

Suddenly it seemed too late for Tito. The red-hot ashes blistered his skin, the stinging vapors tore his throat. He could not go on. He staggered toward a small tree at the side of the road and fell. In a moment

Bimbo was beside him. He coaxed. But there was no answer. He licked Tito's hands, his feet, his face. The boy did not stir. Then Bimbo did the last thing he could—the last thing he wanted to do. He bit his comrade, bit him deep in the arm. With a cry of pain, Tito jumped to his feet, Bimbo after him. Tito was in despair, but Bimbo was determined. He drove the boy on, snapping at his heels, worrying his way through the crowd, barking, baring his teeth, heedless of kicks or falling stones. Sick with hunger, half dead with fear and sulfur fumes, Tito pounded on, pursued by Bimbo. How long, he never knew. At last he staggered through the marine gate and felt soft sand under him. Then Tito fainted. . . .

Someone was dashing seawater over him. Someone was carrying him toward a boat.

"Bimbo," he called. And then louder, "Bimbo!" But Bimbo had disappeared.

Voices jarred against each other. "Hurry—hurry!" "To the boats!" "Can't you see the child's frightened and starving!" "He keeps calling for someone!" "Poor boy, he's out of his mind." "Here, child—take this!"

They tucked him in among them. The oarlocks creaked; the oars splashed; the boat rode over toppling waves. Tito was safe. But he wept continually.

"Bimbo!" he wailed. "Bimbo! Bimbo!" He could not be comforted.

Eighteen hundred years passed. Scientists were restoring the ancient city; excavators[15] were working their way through the stones and trash that had buried the entire town. Much had already been brought to light—

15. **excavators** (eks′kə·vāt′ərz) *n.*: diggers; here, archaeologists.

The Dog of Pompeii   439

DIRECT TEACHING

F **Literary Focus**
GRADE-LEVEL STANDARD
❓ **Critiquing characters.**
Believable characters are three-dimensional: They grow, learn, and change. What has Tito just learned? [Possible responses: that the key to survival is getting to the harbor; that Bimbo has a reasonable plan of escape.]

G **Reading Skills**
❓ **Making inferences.** What lesson does Tito probably think the people are being taught? [Possible responses: to take precautions; to heed the warnings of the wise; to respect nature.]

H **Literary Focus**
GRADE-LEVEL STANDARD
❓ **Critiquing plot.** What makes Bimbo bite Tito? [Possible responses: Bimbo knows that if Tito doesn't keep going, he will die; Bimbo loves Tito and will do anything to save his life.]
Do you find this action believable? [Possible responses: Yes, many dogs look after young children; no, a dog would panic before or during an eruption.]

DEVELOPING FLUENCY

Activity. Invite a guide dog expert to speak to the class about the training and skills of guide dogs or other assistance dogs. Tell the speaker that students will have some questions based on a story they have read. Then, direct students to prepare questions that will help them analyze the credibility of Bimbo's behavior. Have students scan "The Dog of Pompeii" for passages that describe Bimbo's behavior. Tell each student to mark passages relating to his or her question. After the visitor's presentation when students ask their prepared questions, have them read aloud the related passages to provide background for the visitor. Make it clear that students may also ask other questions about the information that the visitor has presented.

WHOLE-CLASS

CONTENT-AREA CONNECTIONS

Science

Volcanic eruptions. Details about the 1980 eruption of Mount Saint Helens in Washington State may shed light on what happened when Mount Vesuvius erupted. For several weeks before Mount Saint Helens erupted, it emitted smoke and steam. A bulge grew on one side of the mountain as magma forced its way toward the surface. The eruption began with an earthquake, a landslide, and a ten-minute explosion that tore away part of the mountain. The rising magma had heated subterranean water to the boiling point and beyond. Now, superheated steam and shattered rock blasted out, leveling forests for 150 square miles. Then, the mountain began spewing pumice and ash. Ashes blanketed Yakima, eighty miles away, and lightning in the ash cloud ignited forest fires. Pumice heated to one thousand degrees Fahrenheit flowed down the mountain, reaching one hundred miles per hour.

In Pompeii, after the eruption of Mount Vesuvius in A.D. 79, the ash, pumice, cinders, and small stones lay so deep and had been packed so tightly by the torrents of rain that followed the explosion that only the rooftops of the houses peeped out of what seemed like solid ground.

statues, bronze instruments, bright mosaics,[16] household articles; even delicate paintings had been preserved by the fall of ashes that had taken over two thousand lives. Columns were dug up, and the forum was beginning to emerge.

It was at a place where the ruins lay deepest that the director paused.

"Come here," he called to his assistant. "I think we've discovered the remains of a building in good shape. Here are four huge millstones that were most likely turned by slaves or mules—and here is a whole wall standing with shelves inside it. Why! It must have been a bakery. And here's a cu-

---

16. **mosaics** (mō·zā'iks) *n.:* pictures or designs made by inlaying small bits of stone, glass, tile, or other materials in mortar.

---

rious thing. What do you think I found under this heap where the ashes were thickest? The skeleton of a dog!"

"Amazing!" gasped his assistant. "You'd think a dog would have had sense enough to run away at the time. And what is that flat thing he's holding between his teeth? It can't be a stone."

"No. It must have come from this bakery. You know it looks to me like some sort of cake hardened with the years. And, bless me, if those little black pebbles aren't raisins. A raisin cake almost two thousand years old! I wonder what made him want it at such a moment."

📖 **MAKING INFERENCES**

8. What is the answer to the director's question?

"I wonder," murmured the assistant.

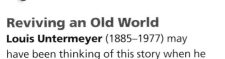

MEET THE WRITER

Louis Untermeyer

Reviving an Old World

Louis Untermeyer (1885–1977) may have been thinking of this story when he described the writer's job as the "struggle somehow to revive an old world, or create a new one."

As a child, Untermeyer loved to read, but he disliked school, especially math. His parents expected him to go to college, but he dropped out of high school when he was sixteen. For the next twenty-two years he worked in his family's jewelry business. He says he did

not become serious about working or writing until he met the poet Robert Frost in 1915. Frost became Untermeyer's lifelong friend. It was Frost who encouraged Untermeyer to quit his day job and become a full-time writer.

Today Untermeyer is best known not for his own writing but for the very popular collections of poetry he put together, some for children and some for adults. In his autobiography *From Another World* he describes himself as a friend to three generations of poets.

The Dog of Pompeii   441

CONTENT-AREA CONNECTIONS

History

Roman bakeries. Much of the bread that the people of Pompeii ate came from bakeries that milled their own flour. As the text notes, slaves were used to turn huge mortar-like grinders that crushed grain into flour. The dough made from the flour was then shaped into flat loaves and baked in closed ovens or open hearths.

Activity. Encourage students to share recipes for various types of raisin breads.

WHOLE-CLASS

DIRECT TEACHING

A ▶ **Reading Skills**

❓ **Making inferences.** Untermeyer's narrative advances almost two thousand years in one bold sentence. What details does he leave to readers' imagination? [Possible response: what happens to Tito after he escapes.]

B ▶ **Reading Skills**

Making inferences. [Possible response to question 8: The dog was Bimbo, and he was stealing the cake for Tito.]

GUIDED PRACTICE

Monitoring students' progress. Guide students in responding to these true-false comprehension questions.

True-False

1. Pompeii was a city in the ancient Roman Empire. [T]
2. Tito was a patrician, or member of the upper classes. [F]
3. Pompeii was destroyed by a flood in A.D. 79. [F]
4. Tito and Bimbo were killed when Pompeii was destroyed. [F]
5. The reader last sees Bimbo with a raisin cake in his mouth. [T]

Meet the Writer

Background. In addition to writing or editing more than one hundred books, Untermeyer worked as a lecturer, a consultant in English poetry at the Library of Congress, and a popular panelist on the 1950s television game show *What's My Line?* Although best remembered for his poetry anthologies, Untermeyer said his favorite type of fiction was "a combination of historical reconstruction and poetic fantasy."

Connections

Summary *at grade level*

This piece of historical writing recounts the destruction of Pompeii in A.D. 79. Its research is based on the human and animal remains unearthed by archaeologists in the ruins of Pompeii and on reports by Romans living at the time of the eruption of Vesuvius. To enliven the history, the author creates believable stories about the experiences of the people and animals whose remains have been discovered during the ongoing excavation of Pompeii.

CONNECTIONS / The Historical Account

"The Dog of Pompeii" is historical fiction, a mix of historical facts and fictional events and characters.

The historical event that is central to the story took place in A.D. 79: the eruption of Mount Vesuvius, a volcano fifteen miles south of Naples, Italy. The eruption killed about two thousand people in the seaside towns of Pompeii and Herculaneum and buried them under twenty feet of ashes and rubble.

In his nonfiction book *Lost Cities and Vanished Civilizations*, Robert Silverberg describes Pompeii in A.D. 79 and tells about the eruption of Mount Vesuvius. In writing his book, Silverberg drew on the findings of archaeologists who conducted excavations of Pompeii and Herculaneum.

As you read this excerpt from Silverberg's book, take notes on details that appear both there and in Untermeyer's story. Your purpose in reading this excerpt is to evaluate the accuracy of the short story. You may find it helpful to use sticky notes as you read the excerpt. When you come across a fact that's used in the short story, stick a note next to it. On the note, identify the place in the short story where the detail occurs.

Pompeii as it looks today.

POMPEII
ROBERT SILVERBERG

The people of Pompeii knew that doom was on hand, now. Their fears were doubled when an enormous rain of hot ashes began to fall on them, along with more lapilli.[1] Pelted with stones, half smothered by ashes, the Pompeiians cried to the gods for mercy. The wooden roofs of some of the houses began to catch fire as the heat of the ashes reached them. Other buildings were collapsing under the weight of the pumice stones that had fallen on them.

In those first few hours, only the quick-witted managed to escape. Vesonius Primus, the wealthy wool merchant, called his family together and piled jewelry and

---

1. **lapilli** (lə·pil'ī') *n.*: small pieces of hardened lava.

RESOURCES

Media
- *Audio CD Library*
  - disc 10
- *Visual Connections*
  - Videocassette, Segment 10
- *Fine Art Transparencies*
  - Transparency 14

Reading
- *Interactive Reading*
  - Graphic Organizer: Parallel Events Chart, p. 302

Assessment
- *Progress Assessment of Reading*
  - Selection Test, p. 156

money into a sack. Lighting a torch, Vesonius led his little band out into the nightmare of the streets. Overlooked in the confusion was Vesonius' black watchdog, chained in the courtyard. The terrified dog barked wildly as lapilli struck and drifting white ash settled around him. The animal struggled with his chain, battling fiercely to get free, but the chain held, and no one heard the dog's cries. The humans were too busy saving themselves.

Many hundreds of Pompeiians fled in those first few dark hours. Stumbling in the darkness, they made their way to the city gates, then out, down to the harbor. They boarded boats and got away, living to tell the tale of their city's destruction. Others preferred to remain within the city, huddling inside the temples, or in the public baths, or in the cellars of their homes. They still hoped that the nightmare would end—that the tranquility of a few hours ago would return. . . .

It was evening, now. And new woe was in store for Pompeii. The earth trembled and quaked! Roofs that had somehow withstood the rain of lapilli went crashing in ruin, burying hundreds who had hoped to survive the eruption. In the forum, tall columns toppled as they had in 63.[2] Those who remembered that great earthquake screamed in new terror as the entire city seemed to shake in the grip of a giant fist.

2. There had been an earthquake in Pompeii sixteen years before Vesuvius erupted.

Mount Vesuvius erupting in 1944.

Three feet of lapilli now covered the ground. Ash floated in the air. Gusts of poisonous gas came drifting from the belching crater, though people could still breathe. Roofs were collapsing everywhere. Rushing throngs, blinded by the darkness and the smoke, hurtled madly up one street and down the next, trampling the fallen in a crazy, fruitless dash toward safety. Dozens of people plunged into dead-end streets and found themselves trapped by crashing buildings. They waited there, too frightened to run farther, expecting the end.

The rich man Diomedes was another of those who decided not to flee at the first sign of alarm. Rather than risk being crushed by

Pompeii   443

A Content-Area Connections
HISTORY
The destruction of Pompeii. The events and timetable of the A.D. 79 eruption of Mount Vesuvius, and even the names of Pompeiian citizens, are details that could have come from eyewitness accounts and from the memoirs of survivors. One witness to the eruption was the Roman historian Pliny the Younger, who described it in two letters to another historian, Tacitus.

B Reading Informational Materials
GRADE-LEVEL STANDARD
? Historical writing: Fact versus fiction. On what might Silverberg have based this account of the behavior of one specific dog? [Possible response: Archaeologists might have found a dog's remains along with a chain in a courtyard, and Silverberg might have made inferences about the dog's behavior based on his knowledge of dogs.] Notice that by including made-up but credible details, Silverberg makes the history both understandable and entertaining.

DIFFERENTIATING INSTRUCTION

Advanced Learners
Enrichment. Tell students that for people living today, the eruption of Mount Vesuvius is probably the best-known event of A.D. 79. However, most people in the world at that time were unaware of the catastrophe. News media did not exist, and numerous other things were happening throughout the ancient world to catch the locals' attention.

Activity. Have groups of students find out about other important events in the world between A.D. 50 and 100. They might use the Internet or the library or both to investigate what else was going on in the Roman Empire, as well as events in China, Japan, India, the Middle East, non-Roman Africa, and the Americas. Then, direct groups to design the front page of a newspaper that includes at least one story from

each area. (Stories may report on broad developments as well as specific events.) The newspaper should have an appropriate masthead and illustrations. Stories may be continued on subsequent pages if necessary.

A Reading Skills

? Comparing and contrasting.
What similar evidence of poisonous vapors do you recall from "The Dog of Pompeii"? [Possible response: Tito, like Diomedes' daughter, coughs and struggles to breathe.]

B English-Language Learners

Verb tenses. Point out that Silverberg switches from past tense to present when discussing the effects of carbon monoxide poisoning. Explain the reason for the shift: The author uses the past tense to narrate historical events (events that ended in the past) and the present tense to explain scientific fact (something that continues to be true in the present).

C Reading Skills

? Historical writing: Fact versus fiction. Which details in this paragraph do you think represent details learned by archaeologists and historians, and which details were probably invented by the author? [Possible response: The remains of the people in the blind alley, of the beggar, and of the goat could have been discovered by archaeologists; the sound of the goat's bell and the fact that the goat belonged to the beggar could have been inferred by the author.]

---

the screaming mobs, Diomedes calmly led the members of his household into the solidly built basement of his villa. Sixteen people altogether, as well as his daughter's dog and her beloved little goat. They took enough food and water to last for several days.

But for all his shrewdness and foresight, Diomedes was undone anyway. Poison gas was creeping slowly into the underground shelter! He watched his daughter begin to cough and struggle for breath. Vesuvius was giving off vast quantities of deadly carbon monoxide that was now settling like a blanket over the dying city.

"We can't stay here!" Diomedes gasped. Better to risk the uncertainties outside than to remain here and suffocate. "I'll open the door," he told them. "Wait for me here."

Accompanied only by an old and faithful servant, who carried a lantern to light Diomedes' way in the inky blackness, the nobleman stumbled toward the door. He held the silver key in his hand. Another few steps and he would have been at the door, he could have opened it, they could have fled into the air—but a shroud of gas swooped down on him. He fell, still clutching the key, dying within minutes. Beneath the porch, fourteen people waited hopefully for him, their lives ticking away with each second. Diomedes did not return. At the last moment, all fourteen embraced each other, servants and masters alike, as death took them.

The poison gas thickened as the terrible night continued. It was possible to hide from the lapilli, but not from the gas, and Pompeiians died by the hundreds. Carbon monoxide gas keeps the body from absorbing oxygen. Victims of carbon monoxide poisoning get sleepier and sleepier, until

they lose consciousness, never to regain it. All over Pompeii, people lay down in the beds of lapilli, overwhelmed by the gas, and death came quietly to them. Even those who had made their way outside the city now fell victim to the spreading clouds of gas. It covered the entire countryside.

In a lane near the forum, a hundred people were trapped by a blind-alley wall. Others hid in the stoutly built public bathhouses, protected against collapsing roofs but not against the deadly gas. Near the house of Diomedes, a beggar and his little goat sought shelter. The man fell dead a few feet from Diomedes' door; the faithful goat remained by his side, its silver bell tinkling, until its turn came.

All through the endless night, Pompeiians wandered about the streets or crouched in their ruined homes or clustered in the temples to pray. By morning, few remained alive. Not once had Vesuvius stopped hurling lapilli and ash into the air, and the streets of Pompeii were filling quickly. At midday on August 25, exactly twenty-four hours after the beginning of the holocaust,[3] a second eruption racked the volcano. A second cloud of ashes rose above Vesuvius' summit. The wind blew ash as far as Rome and Egypt. But most of the new ashes descended on Pompeii.

The deadly shower of stone and ashes went unslackening into its second day. But it no longer mattered to Pompeii whether the eruption continued another day or another year. For by midday on August 25, Pompeii was a city of the dead.

---

3. **holocaust** *n.*: great destruction of life.

CONNECTING AND COMPARING TEXTS

"Pompeii" and "The Dog of Pompeii" describe the same historical event from two different standpoints: The former is nonfiction, and the latter is historical fiction. Silverberg's primary purpose in "Pompeii" is to inform the reader about the eruption, whereas Untermeyer's primary purpose in "The Dog of Pompeii" is to entertain the reader. To achieve his purpose, each author combines techniques of narrative and informative writing; each incorporates careful research on the facts of the eruption, gleaned from archaeological evidence and other primary sources; and each uses credible characters—human and animal—whose individual dramas give special life to the story of the eruption. In "The Dog of Pompeii," however, the characters are central to the work and are involved in an invented plot, whereas in "Pompeii," they merely illustrate historical events.

Literary Response and Analysis

Reading Check

1. Why does Tito depend on Bimbo for food?

2. What sign does the volcano give before it erupts? How do some people explain the sign?

3. Where does Bimbo take Tito during the volcano's eruption?

4. What happens to Bimbo in the end?

5. Why are scientists surprised to find a dog buried in the ruins?

Interpretations

6. Where are we taken at the end of the story? What question is answered there?

7. How would you answer the director's question about the raisin cake?

8. In this story, **setting** plays an important role; it is the setting that creates the problem for the characters. How does the setting threaten the lives of the people (and animals) of Pompeii?

Evaluation

9. Many people read historical fiction for its **settings,** to learn about history. What did you learn about the way people lived in Pompeii—their religious beliefs, leisure activities, diet, attitudes toward nature? If you had questions before you started reading, how were they answered?

10. Are Tito and Bimbo **credible characters**—that is, do they behave like real boys and real dogs you've met or you know of? Give one example of something you found credible *or* incredible in the characterization of Tito. Then, do the same for Bimbo.

11. Could the events in this story really have happened, or does the plot seem **contrived** and unconvincing? Be prepared to discuss your evaluation of the story's plot. Have details ready to defend your responses.

Discussion

Evaluating Texts: Is It True?

In class or a small group, discuss the details in "The Dog of Pompeii" that are confirmed by Silverberg's nonfiction account. You should have found at least three details that appear in both the story and the article. In your discussion, consider this question: How did Silverberg find out what happened to these people and animals?

- Vesonius Primus, his family, and his dog
- Diomedes
- the beggar and his goat

Reading Standard 3.8 Critique the credibility of characterization and the degree to which a plot is contrived or realistic (for example, compare use of fact and fantasy in historical fiction).

The Dog of Pompeii / Pompeii   **445**

Literary Response and Analysis

Evaluation

9. The story mentions festivals, plays, stadium events, children's games, and parties; it lists foods in bakeries, markets, and homes; it describes clothing, medical practices, and religious ceremonies; it shows characters citing natural phenomena as acts of the gods. Answers to students' questions will vary.

10. Possible answers: *Incredible*— that Tito is bright and capable, although he has been raised only by a dog; that Bimbo fetches food rather than eating it himself. *Credible*—that Tito likes sweets and festivities; that Bimbo is agitated before the eruption.

11. Possible answers: Tito's escape is contrived given the odds; the dog's skeleton with the raisin cake is contrived (if the dog's body decomposed, so would the cake); the plot is not contrived, since in real life people beat the odds and flukes happen.

Discussion

Details in both selections—rains of stones and ash; people escaping in boats; people hiding in the public baths; people trapped in dead-end side streets; earthquakes; columns toppling; deadly fumes; panicked throngs; houses collapsing. *Discussion question*—Silverberg made inferences based on the remains of people and animals, on objects found nearby, and on survivors' accounts.

Reading Check

1. Tito is a homeless, blind orphan.

2. The volcano's smoke thickens and spreads. Some people see this as a warning of the gods' displeasure.

3. Bimbo takes Tito to the sea.

4. Bimbo dies trying to bring a raisin cake to Tito.

5. They feel that an unchained dog could have escaped.

Interpretations

6. At a twentieth-century archaeological dig, the mystery of Bimbo's disappearance is answered.

7. Possible answer: The dog loved its master so much (or was so bound by habit) that it risked death to fetch the cake.

8. Possible answer: An erupting volcano subjects the characters to deadly fumes, earthquakes, and rains of stones and ash.

Vocabulary Development

Practice 1
Possible Answers

1. No, an owner's ambition would not help. The dog would need talent to be a star.

2. A dog is a boy's best friend; A dog makes so many friends because it can wag its tail but not its tongue.

3. You might remind people of the threats to the species' survival. Lots of cute pictures of the species might help.

Practice 2

1. ■ *discomfort. Prefix— dis–. Prefix meaning—"opposing." Word meaning—"lack of comfort."*

   ■ *incapable. Prefix— in–. Prefix meaning—"not." Word meaning—"not capable."*

   ■ *nonstop. Prefix— non–. Prefix meaning—"not." Word meaning—"without stopping."*

   ■ *unhappy. Prefix— un–. Prefix meaning—"not." Word meaning—"not happy."*

2. Possible answers: The rain of ashes brought great <u>discomfort</u> to Tito and Bimbo. The gases made Tito so sleepy, he was <u>incapable</u> of moving on. Bimbo tried <u>nonstop</u> to keep Tito moving toward the sea. Tito was very <u>unhappy</u> to be saved without Bimbo.

▶ Resources Reminder

Vocabulary and Spelling
■ *Vocabulary Development*
  ▪ Vocabulary Worksheet, p. 29
■ *Lesson Plans for Language Development*
  ▪ Vocabulary, p. 219
■ *Spelling Lessons and Activities*
  ▪ Prefixes, pp. 62–63, 70–71

Vocabulary Development

Clarifying Word Meanings

> **PRACTICE 1**
>
> Show your mastery of the words in the Word Bank by answering the following questions.
> 1. Do you think that an <u>ambitious</u> owner could make any dog a star?
> 2. Write a <u>proverb</u> that expresses a truth about animals.
> 3. How would you <u>revive</u> interest in saving an endangered species?

Word Bank
ambitious
proverb
revived

Using Word Parts to Build Meanings: Prefixes

> **PRACTICE 2**
>
> Sometimes you can figure out the meaning of an unfamiliar word if you analyze the meanings of its parts. The more prefixes you know, the more words you'll be able to figure out.
> A **prefix** is a word part added to the beginning of a word or root. The chart below lists common prefixes.
> 1. Identify the **prefix** in each of the words listed just below. In the chart, find the meaning of the prefix; then, define the whole word.
>
>   discomfort   incapable   nonstop   unhappy
> 2. Use each word from item 1 in a sentence or two about Bimbo and Tito.

Grade 4 Review Reading Standard 1.4 Know common affixes, and use this knowledge to analyze the meaning of words.

Common Prefixes		
Prefix	**Meaning**	**Examples**
dis–	opposing; away	dishonor, dislike
in–	not	incomplete, incorrect
non–	not	nonhuman, nonprofit
un–	not	unwise

ASSESSING

Assessment
■ *Progress Assessment of Reading*
  ▪ Selection Tests, pp. 153, 156

RETEACHING

For a lesson on critiquing the credibility of plot and character, see **Reteaching**, pp. 489O–489P.

Preparing an Application

Applications: How to Fill in the Blanks

Chances are, if you want to get a part-time job or work as a volunteer, you'll be asked to fill out an application. The more carefully you prepare your application, the better your chances of getting a positive response are.

Imagine that you're applying to work as a volunteer guide at the Pompeii Museum. Follow these steps when you fill out your application:

1. Don't pick up your pen until you **read the application all the way through.**

2. If the application includes a question that requires more than a quick answer, **write down or type your response before you write it on the application** itself. Write in complete sentences. When you're done, ask an adult to review what you've written. Then, copy your answer, **along with any revisions,** onto the application.

3. **Answer questions truthfully.** If the application asks whether you have experience with animals, don't say yes just because you once saw a snake on a Boy Scout camping trip. You might instead point out how learning to work as part of a team in the Scouts will help you to be an effective volunteer.

4. **Print or type** information carefully, with no crossouts.

5. **Fill in** all the blanks. Write *n/a* (for "not applicable") in response to questions that don't apply to you.

6. Check your **spelling.**

7. **Sign and date** your application.

You may be asked to give references on an application. A **reference** is someone the person reviewing your application can call to get information about you. (Anyone you list as a reference should be an adult.) For example, on a job application you might be asked for references the employer could call to find out whether you're a good worker. Be sure to ask permission before you list someone as a reference. Your reference will then expect the call and will have a chance to prepare detailed and useful information about you.

Reading Standard 2.5
Follow multiple-step instructions for preparing applications.

Preparing an Application **447**

RESOURCES

Planning
- *One-Stop Planner* CD-ROM with Test Generator
- *On Course: Mapping Instruction*

Differentiating Instruction
- *Lesson Plans for Language Development*
  - English-Language Learners, pp. 209, 216, 219
- Special Education Students, pp. 209, 216, 219

Assessment
- *Progress Assessment of Reading*
  - Selection Test, p. 158
- *One-Stop Planner* CD-ROM with Test Generator

STANDARDS FOCUS, 447–449

(For grade-level and review standards taught in this selection, see citations on Pupil's Edition pages.)

Summary ↔ *at grade level*

> This selection is an application form for volunteers who wish to serve as children's guides at a fictional museum. It includes a job description and instructions for filling in and submitting the application. It asks for standard personal data as well as information about the applicant's qualifications and motivation.

PRETEACHING

Standards Starter

Motivate. Have students re-examine the illustrations for "The Dog of Pompeii," on pp. 432, 435, 436, and 440. Point out that the characters are imaginary, but the background shows accurate views of the ruins of Pompeii. Explain that the town is so well preserved that archaeologists found eighteen hundred-year-old graffiti still on the walls. Today the excavated ruins are a town-sized museum. Ask students to imagine that they have been whisked to Italy for the summer, to a village just outside Pompeii. Then, assign p. 447.

Assign the Reading

You may wish to have advanced learners read and fill out the application on p. 448 and answer the Reading Check questions as homework. Monitor other students as they read the application form, drawing their attention to the sidenotes.

HOMEWORK

Ⓐ Reading Informational Materials
GRADE-LEVEL STANDARD

❓ Preparing an application.
What should you do even before you pick up a pen to fill in your name on the first line? [Read the application all the way through.]

Ⓑ Reading Informational Materials
GRADE-LEVEL STANDARD

❓ Preparing an application.
What do you think you should do if you don't have e-mail? [Write "n/a."] Why shouldn't you just leave that space blank? [The employer might think you overlooked the question.]

Ⓒ Reading Informational Materials
GRADE-LEVEL STANDARD

❓ Preparing an application.
What are three steps you should take before you fill in your answers to questions 6–8? [Possible response: Write your responses on a separate sheet of paper, ask an adult to review them, and make any needed revisions.]

Ⓓ Reading Informational Materials
GRADE-LEVEL STANDARD

Preparing an application. "No later than June 10" means that the application must be in the museum office on or before June 10—the earlier, the better. If you were mailing it from nearby, you would put it in the mail at least a week before the deadline.

Pompeii Museum
Application for Volunteer Work

> Be neat and complete.

General Information

Ⓐ 1. Name: _____

> Print all information.

2. Parent's or guardian's name: _____

3. Address: _____
   Street   City   State and zip code

> Make sure that any names, addresses, and telephone numbers you give are accurate.

4. Phone number: _____   Ⓑ E-mail address: _____

5. School name: _____   Teacher's name: _____

School address: _____

Work Information

This volunteer work involves leading small groups of children in grades 1–3 on informative tours of the museum. Volunteers must be able to learn information about the museum and convey it in a way that interests young children. Please answer the following questions in your own handwriting.

> Carefully follow all directions for filling out and returning the application.

6. What experience do you have that you think would help you work with young children?_____

Ⓒ 7. What made you interested in working as a volunteer in this museum? _____

8. What do you think are some good ways to interest children in a topic? _____

> Answer questions like these in complete sentences.

9. Do you have dependable transportation to and from the museum?_____

Ⓓ 10. Please return this application no later than June 10. With your application, please enclose a letter of recommendation from an adult (not a family member) who is familiar with your work habits and your ability to work with children.

Signature _____   Date _____

DIFFERENTIATING INSTRUCTION

Learners Having Difficulty
Tell students that the way an application is filled out can make the difference between getting and not getting a job. Explain that being able to follow directions is an important skill for a prospective employee. If students need help, have them meet in small groups that you monitor. Make sure the groups review the steps on p. 447 and read the application all the way through before they begin to write. Have students work through each question together.

Special Education Students
For lessons designed for special education students, see *Lesson Plans for Language Development*, pp. 209, 216, 219.

Reading Informational Materials

Reading Check

1. What are the volunteers' main duties?

2. Take out a sheet of paper, and number it from 1 to 10. Write down your answers to each of the application questions. Next to number 10, write down the name of the person you would choose to write the letter of recommendation.

3. Why isn't it a good idea to type your answers on the form?

4. Why shouldn't you ask your best friend, who's in the seventh grade, to write the letter of recommendation?

TestPractice

Pompeii Museum
Application for Volunteer Work

1. The museum director's purpose in asking questions 6–8 is to find out —

  A where you live

  B where you go to school

  C whether you have transportation to and from the museum

  D about you and your interest in the job

2. You could enclose a letter of recommendation from any of the following people *except* —

  F your teacher

  G your soccer coach

  H your aunt

  J a neighbor you've done babysitting for

3. The best time to mail your application would be —

  A as soon as possible

  B on June 10

  C on June 9

  D on June 15

4. The purpose of question 9 is to find out whether —

  F you'll be able to get to work every day

  G you like to walk

  H you live in the neighborhood

  J you own a bicycle

5. When you sign the application form, you're telling the museum that you —

  A are the best person for the position

  B have answered the questions truthfully

  C really want the job

  D are under no obligation to accept the position

Reading Standard 2.5
Follow multiple-step instructions for preparing applications.

Preparing an Application   **449**

Reading Informational Materials

TestPractice

Answers and Model Rationales

1. D This item focuses on the main purpose of the "Work Information" section of the application. A and B apply to the "General Information" section. C applies to question 9.

2. H Point out the word *except,* and remind students that the instructions for question 10 specify that the letter not be from a family member.

3. A The application must arrive at the museum office by June 10, so B and D are too late; C is still too risky.

4. F An employer is primarily interested in whether an employee will be at work when expected, F. The question does not ask about the prospective employee's preferences, G; place of residence, H; or possessions, J.

5. B A signature does not indicate whether one is qualified or truly wants the job (A and C). An applicant is never obligated to accept a position, D. A signature attests to the truth of what one has written, B.

Test-Taking Tips

For more information on how to answer multiple-choice questions, refer students to **Test Smarts,** p. 690.

Reading Check

1. The main duties are leading small groups of young children on museum tours and presenting information about the museum to them in an engaging way.

2. Students' answers to the application questions will vary.

3. The instructions under "Work Information" say to answer in your own handwriting.

4. The instructions for question 10 say an adult must provide the reference.

STANDARDS FOCUS, pp. 450–460

(For grade-level and review standards taught in this selection, see citations on Pupil's Edition pages.)

Prerequisite Standard

■ Grade 5, Literary Response and Analysis 3.7 **Evaluate the author's use of various techniques (e.g., appeal of characters in a picture book, logic and credibility of plots and settings, use of figurative language) to influence readers' perspectives.**

Standard Coming Up in the Next Grade Level

■ Grade 7, Literary Response and Analysis 3.2 **Identify events that advance the plot, and determine how each event explains past or present action(s) or foreshadows future action(s).**

Reading Skills

■ Make predictions.

Summary ⬆ *above grade level*

> In a Polish village many years ago, twelve-year-old Aaron must sell the family's beloved goat, Zlateh, to the town butcher. Aaron sets out sadly with the goat, but their progress is halted by a blizzard. In order to survive, they burrow into a snow-covered haystack. Aaron tells stories to Zlateh, who provides Aaron with milk. The snow stops three days later. They return home, the family's financial situation improves, and no one again mentions selling Zlateh.

▶ Resources Reminder

Reading

■ *Interactive Reading*
  • Graphic Organizer: Plot Map, p. 303

Zlateh the Goat

Literary Focus
Suspense: What Happens Next?

Isaac Bashevis Singer, the author of "Zlateh the Goat," liked reading stories that kept him wondering what would happen next. "From my childhood I have always loved tension in a story," he wrote. Singer is talking about **suspense**—that feeling of anxious curiosity about what will happen next in a story.

At first glance, "Zlateh the Goat" seems to be just a story about a family living in a small village and a boy who is sent to market with the family's goat. But Zlateh is an unusually appealing animal, and this account of her trip to the butcher could change your attitude toward goatdom. That's because a sudden change in the weather transforms this simple tale into a suspenseful page turner.

Reading Skills 📖
Making Predictions

When we read a suspenseful story, we often find ourselves predicting what will happen next. If we predict correctly, we're pleased. If the writer surprises us, we're even happier. We like to be surprised by what happens in stories—just as we enjoy being surprised by things that happen in real life.

Reading Standard 3.8
Critique the credibility of characterization and the degree to which a plot is contrived or realistic.

Make the Connection

Think-pair-share. What messages have animals sent you lately? Think of a time when you realized an animal was telling you something or showing you how it felt. Share your story with a classmate.

Background

"Zlateh the Goat" takes place around Hanukkah (кнä'noo·kä'), a Jewish religious festival usually observed in December. Hanukkah celebrates the rededication of the Temple in Jerusalem in 165 B.C., following the victory of Jewish fighters over a huge Syrian army. The Temple, which had been taken over by Antiochus, ruler of the Syrians, had been violated and damaged. While the Jews were purifying and repairing the Temple, a miracle occurred. A tiny bit of oil for the holy lamp—barely enough for one day—lasted eight days. Do you see a miracle in Zlateh's story as well?

Vocabulary Development

Be sure you know these words as you read the story:

penetrated (pen'i·trāt'id) *v.:* pierced; made a way through. *Sunlight penetrated the clouds.*

cleft (kleft) *adj.:* split; divided. *Goats have cleft hooves.*

chaos (kā'äs) *n.:* total confusion or disorder. *The storm created chaos outside Aaron's shelter.*

exuded (eg·zyood'id) *v.:* gave off. *The hay exuded warmth.*

450 Chapter 8 **You the Critic**

RESOURCES

Planning
■ *One-Stop Planner* CD-ROM with Test Generator
■ *On Course: Mapping Instruction*

Media
■ *Audio CD Library*
  • disc 10

■ *Fine Art Transparencies*
  • Transparency 15

Reading
■ *Interactive Reading*
  • Graphic Organizer: Plot Map, p. 303

ISAAC BASHEVIS SINGER
Zlateh THE GOAT

*A*t Hanukkah time the road from the village to the town is usually covered with snow, but this year the winter had been a mild one. Hanukkah had almost come, yet little snow had fallen. The sun shone most of the time. The peasants complained that because of the dry weather there would be a poor harvest of winter grain. New grass sprouted, and the peasants sent their cattle out to pasture.

For Reuven the furrier[1] it was a bad year, and after long hesitation he decided to sell Zlateh the goat. She was old and gave little milk. Feyvel the town butcher had offered eight gulden[2] for her. Such a sum would buy

---

1. **furrier** (fûr′ē·ər) *n.:* someone who makes and repairs fur garments.
2. **gulden** (gŏŏl′dən) *n.:* coins formerly used in several European countries.

Hanukkah candles, potatoes and oil for pancakes, gifts for the children, and other holiday necessaries for the house. Reuven told his oldest boy, Aaron, to take the goat to town.

Aaron understood what taking the goat to Feyvel meant, but he had to obey his father. Leah, his mother, wiped the tears from her eyes when she heard the news. Aaron's younger sisters, Anna and Miriam, cried loudly. Aaron put on his quilted jacket and a cap with earmuffs, bound a rope around Zlateh's neck, and took along two slices of bread with cheese to eat on the road. Aaron was supposed to deliver the goat by evening, spend the night at the butcher's, and return the next day with the money.

Zlateh the Goat **451**

A **Literary Focus**
ADVANCED STANDARD

❓ **Dramatic irony.** Tell students that dramatic irony occurs when the reader knows something a character does not know. What do you know that Zlateh does not know? [Readers know that this time Zlateh should not be so trusting; she is going to be slaughtered.]

B **Literary Focus**
ADVANCED STANDARD

❓ **Suspense.** The family expects the trip to take Aaron and Zlateh all day. What do you wonder when the weather changes? [Possible responses: Students may wonder how severe the storm will be, if someone will get hurt, or if they will even make it to town.]

C **Reading Skills**

❓ **Making predictions.** What do you predict will happen now? [Possible response: Since Aaron can no longer see, he and Zlateh could easily become lost.]

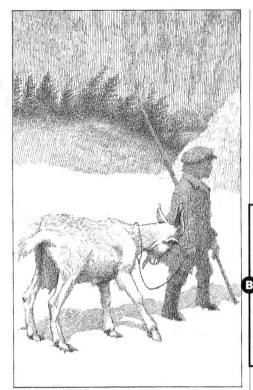

When Aaron brought her out on the road to town, she seemed somewhat astonished. She'd never been led in that direction before.

While the family said goodbye to the goat, and Aaron placed the rope around her neck, Zlateh stood as patiently and good-naturedly as ever. She licked Reuven's hand. **A** She shook her small white beard. Zlateh trusted human beings. She knew that they always fed her and never did her any harm.

When Aaron brought her out on the road to town, she seemed somewhat astonished. She'd never been led in that direction before. She looked back at him questioningly, as if to say, "Where are you taking me?" But after a while she seemed to come to the conclusion that a goat shouldn't ask questions. Still, the road was different. They passed new fields, pastures, and huts with thatched roofs. Here and there a dog barked and came running after them, but Aaron chased it away with his stick.

B The sun was shining when Aaron left the village. Suddenly the weather changed. A large black cloud with a bluish center appeared in the east and spread itself rapidly over the sky. A cold wind blew in with it. The crows flew low, croaking. At first it looked as if it would rain, but instead it began to hail as in summer. It was early in the day, but it became dark as dusk. After a while the hail turned to snow.

In his twelve years Aaron had seen all kinds of weather, but he had never experienced a snow like this one. It was so dense it shut out the light of the day. In a short time their path was completely covered. The wind became as cold as ice. The road to town was narrow and winding. Aaron no longer knew where **C** he was. He could not see through the snow. The cold soon penetrated his quilted jacket.

At first Zlateh didn't seem to mind the change in weather. She too was twelve years old and knew what winter meant. But when her legs sank deeper and deeper into the snow, she began to turn her head and look at Aaron in wonderment. Her mild eyes seemed

Vocabulary
penetrated (pen'i·trāt'id) v.: pierced; made a way through.

DIFFERENTIATING INSTRUCTION

Learners Having Difficulty
Modeling. To help students read "Zlateh the Goat," model how to make predictions. Read the story aloud to students through the second paragraph of the second column on p. 452. Then, say: "I predict that this sudden change in the weather will keep Aaron and Zlateh from completing their journey to town." Encourage students to ask themselves as they read on, "What might happen next? Why?"

English-Language Learners
The storm presents a variety of vocabulary words useful for describing cold weather. Words such as *snowflake, blizzard, hail,* and *frost* may be new to some English-language learners. Ask students to jot down these and related words. Later, have them discuss the meanings of the words.

▶ **Resources Reminder**

For lessons designed for intermediate and advanced English-language learners, see *Lesson Plans for Language Development,* pp. 212–214, 219, 222.

Special Education Students
For lessons designed for special education students, see *Lesson Plans for Language Development,* pp. 213, 217, 220.

to ask, "Why are we out in such a storm?" Aaron hoped that a peasant would come along with his cart, but no one passed by.

The snow grew thicker, falling to the ground in large, whirling flakes. Beneath it Aaron's boots touched the softness of a plowed field. He realized that he was no longer on the road. He had gone astray. He could no longer figure out which was east or west, which way was the village, the town. The wind whistled, howled, whirled the snow about in eddies. It looked as if white imps were playing tag on the fields. A white dust rose above the ground. Zlateh stopped. She could walk no longer. Stubbornly she anchored her cleft hooves in the earth and bleated as if pleading to be taken home. Icicles hung from her white beard, and her horns were glazed with frost.

Aaron did not want to admit the danger, but he knew just the same that if they did not find shelter, they would freeze to death. This was no ordinary storm. It was a mighty blizzard. The snowfall had reached his knees. His hands were numb, and he could no longer feel his toes. He choked when he breathed. His nose felt like wood, and he rubbed it with snow. Zlateh's bleating began to sound like crying. Those humans in whom she had so much confidence had dragged her into a trap. Aaron began to pray to God for himself and for the innocent animal.

Suddenly he made out the shape of a hill. He wondered what it could be. Who had piled snow into such a huge heap? He moved toward it, dragging Zlateh after him. When he came near it, he realized that it was a large haystack which the snow had blanketed.

Aaron realized immediately that they were saved. With great effort he dug his way through the snow. He was a village boy and knew what to do. When he reached the hay, he hollowed out a nest for himself and the goat. No matter how cold it may be outside, in the hay it is always warm. And hay was food for Zlateh. The moment she smelled it, she became contented and began to eat. Outside, the snow continued to fall. It quickly covered the passageway Aaron had dug. But a boy and an animal need to breathe, and there was hardly any air in their hide-out. Aaron bored a kind of a window through the hay and snow and carefully kept the passage clear.

Zlateh, having eaten her fill, sat down on her hind legs and seemed to have regained her confidence in man. Aaron ate his two slices of bread and cheese, but after the difficult journey he was still hungry. He looked at Zlateh and noticed her udders were full. He lay down next to her, placing himself so that when he milked her, he could squirt the milk into his mouth. It was rich and sweet. Zlateh was not accustomed to being milked that way, but she did not resist. On the contrary, she seemed eager to reward Aaron for bringing her to a shelter whose very walls, floor, and ceiling were made of food.

Through the window Aaron could catch a glimpse of the chaos outside. The wind carried before it whole drifts of snow. It was completely dark, and he did not know whether night had already come or whether it was the darkness of the storm. Thank God that in the hay it was not cold. The dried hay, grass, and field flowers exuded the warmth of the summer sun. Zlateh ate frequently; she nibbled from above, below,

Vocabulary

cleft (kleft) *adj.:* split; divided.
chaos (kā′äs′) *n.:* total confusion or disorder.
exuded (eg·zyo͞od′id) *v.:* gave off.

Zlateh the Goat   453

Zlateh the Goat   453

DIRECT TEACHING

D Literary Focus
GRADE-LEVEL STANDARD
❷ Critiquing characterization and plot. Does this turn of the plot seem realistic? Could such a frightful snowstorm happen so suddenly and cause such extreme conditions? [Possible responses: The storm is possible, since people in a rural village years ago had no access to weather forecasts and terrible storms do sometimes strike without warning. The storm seems contrived because it is so alarming.]

E Literary Focus
ADVANCED STANDARD
❷ Suspense. How does this passage increase the story's suspense? [Aaron cannot turn around and go home because he can no longer figure out directions; he and Zlateh might freeze to death.]

F English-Language Learners
Increasing vocabulary. Help students pronounce the word *icicles* and relate it to the word *ice*. If they are unfamiliar with icy weather, help them visualize Zlateh's appearance.

G Reading Skills
❷ Making predictions. How do you think the story will turn out? Write down your prediction, and come back to it later to compare it with the actual outcome of the story. [Predictions will vary. Some students might fear that Aaron and Zlateh will die.]

H Literary Focus
ADVANCED STANDARD
Dramatic irony. Remind students that dramatic irony occurs when readers know something a character does not know. Ask them to explain why Zlateh's distrust at this point is an example of dramatic irony. [Earlier, when Zlateh suspected nothing, Aaron was leading her to the butcher. Now he is trying to help her.]

Advanced Learners
Acceleration. Use this activity with advanced learners to move them toward the seventh-grade Standard 3.2, which requires them to determine how events explain or foreshadow other actions.

Activity. After students have read the story and completed the Reading Check, have them make a presentation to the class, using a graphic chart as an aid, that shows how each event explains a prior event or foreshadows a future action.

A Reading Skills

? Making predictions. How will Aaron and Zlateh help keep each other alive? [Possible responses: They will give each other warmth; Zlateh will provide milk; they will give each other companionship and comfort.]

B Literary Focus
ADVANCED STANDARD

? Suspense. Is this passage effective in building tension about what might happen next? Why or why not? [Possible responses: Yes, the darkness and the worry about whether Aaron can clear the window passage build anxiety about what will happen to the characters. No, the matter is resolved so quickly that readers hardly have time to worry.]

C Literary Focus
GRADE-LEVEL STANDARD

? Critiquing characterization and plot. Aaron believes that the wind has "the sound of devilish laughter" and that Zlateh is communicating an acceptance of "all that God gives us." Do you agree that this is what Zlateh means by "Maaaa"? [Possible responses: Aaron is reading his own thoughts into the sound of the wind and Zlateh's "Maaaa." Aaron is interpreting Zlateh's gentle "Maaaa" to mean an acceptance of reality.]

"Zlateh, what do you think about what has happened to us?"

from the left and right. Her body gave forth an animal warmth, and Aaron cuddled up to her. He had always loved Zlateh, but now she was like a sister. He was alone, cut off from his family, and wanted to talk. He began to talk to Zlateh. "Zlateh, what do you think about what has happened to us?" he asked.

"Maaaa," Zlateh answered.

"If we hadn't found this stack of hay, we would both be frozen stiff by now," Aaron said.

"Maaaa," was the goat's reply.

"If the snow keeps on falling like this, we may have to stay here for days," Aaron explained.

"Maaaa," Zlateh bleated.

"What does 'Maaaa' mean?" Aaron asked. "You'd better speak up clearly."

"Maaaa. Maaaa," Zlateh tried.

"Well, let it be 'Maaaa' then," Aaron said patiently. "You can't speak, but I know you understand. I need you and you need me. Isn't that right?"

"Maaaa."

Aaron became sleepy. He made a pillow out of some hay, leaned his head on it, and dozed off. Zlateh too fell asleep.

When Aaron opened his eyes, he didn't know whether it was morning or night. The snow had blocked up his window. He tried to clear it, but when he had bored through to the length of his arm, he still hadn't reached the outside. Luckily he had his stick with him and was able to break through to the open air. It was still dark outside. The snow continued to fall and the wind wailed, first with one voice and then with many. Sometimes it had the sound of devilish laughter. Zlateh too awoke, and when Aaron greeted her, she answered, "Maaaa." Yes, Zlateh's language consisted of only one word, but it meant many things. Now she was saying, "We must accept all that God gives us—heat, cold, hunger, satisfaction, light, and darkness."

Aaron had awakened hungry. He had eaten up his food, but Zlateh had plenty of milk.

For three days Aaron and Zlateh stayed in

Developing Word-Attack Skills

Remind students that vowel, consonant, then *e* is a common spelling for long vowel sounds. Use these one-syllable words as examples: *late, mete, line, note.* Explain that the same vowel, consonant, and *e* clue that helps them recognize long vowels in one-syllable words can help them recognize syllables with long vowels in multisyllable words. Display these words: *penetrate,*

realize, indicate. Have students identify the syllable in each word that is spelled with vowel, consonant, and *e.*

Activity. Display these words without underlines. Have students underline the syllables in which a long vowel sound is spelled with vowel, consonant, and *e.*

1. indic<u>ate</u>
2. comm<u>ute</u>
3. notar<u>ize</u>
4. inciner<u>ate</u>
5. paras<u>ite</u>
6. reciproc<u>ate</u>
7. domestic<u>ate</u>
8. coll<u>ide</u>
9. categor<u>ize</u>
10. horo<u>scope</u>
11. antagon<u>ize</u>
12. rec<u>ede</u>

the haystack. Aaron had always loved Zlateh, but in these three days he loved her more and more. She fed him with her milk and helped him keep warm. She comforted him with her patience. He told her many stories, and she always cocked her ears and listened. When he patted her, she licked his hand and his face. Then she said, "Maaaa," and he knew it meant, I love you too.

The snow fell for three days, though after the first day it was not as thick and the wind quieted down. Sometimes Aaron felt that there could never have been a summer, that the snow had always fallen, ever since he could remember. He, Aaron, never had a father or mother or sisters. He was a snow child, born of the snow, and so was Zlateh. It was so quiet in the hay that his ears rang in the stillness. Aaron and Zlateh slept all night and a good part of the day. As for Aaron's dreams, they were all about warm weather. He dreamed of green fields, trees covered with blossoms, clear brooks, and singing birds. By the third night the snow had stopped, but Aaron did not dare to find his way home in the darkness. The sky became clear and the moon shone, casting silvery nets on the snow. Aaron dug his way out and looked at the world. It was all white, quiet, dreaming dreams of heavenly splendor. The stars were large and close. The moon swam in the sky as in a sea.

On the morning of the fourth day, Aaron heard the ringing of sleigh bells. The haystack was not far from the road. The peasant who drove the sleigh pointed out the way to him—not to the town and Feyvel the butcher, but home to the village. Aaron had decided in the haystack that he would never part with Zlateh.

Aaron's family and their neighbors had searched for the boy and the goat but had found no trace of them during the storm. They feared they were lost. Aaron's mother and sisters cried for him; his father remained silent and gloomy. Suddenly one of the neighbors came running to their house with the news that Aaron and Zlateh were coming up the road.

There was great joy in the family. Aaron told them how he had found the stack of hay and how Zlateh had fed him with her milk. Aaron's sisters kissed and hugged Zlateh and gave her a special treat of chopped carrots and potato peels, which Zlateh gobbled up hungrily.

Nobody ever again thought of selling Zlateh, and now that the cold weather had finally set in, the villagers needed the services of Reuven the furrier once more. When Hanukkah came, Aaron's mother was able to fry pancakes every evening, and Zlateh got her portion too. Even though Zlateh had her own pen, she often came to the kitchen, knocking on the door with her horns to indicate that she was ready to visit, and she was always admitted. In the evening, Aaron, Miriam, and Anna played dreidel.[3] Zlateh sat near the stove, watching the children and the flickering of the Hanukkah candles.

Once in a while Aaron would ask her, "Zlateh, do you remember the three days we spent together?"

And Zlateh would scratch her neck with a horn, shake her white bearded head, and come out with the single sound which expressed all her thoughts, and all her love.

---

3. **dreidel** (drā′dəl): spinning top played with at Hanukkah. Its four sides display Hebrew letters that stand for "A great miracle happened there."

Meet the Writer

Background. Educated at a rabbinical seminary in Poland, Isaac Bashevis Singer chose to celebrate his Jewish heritage as a writer rather than as a rabbi. He also chose to write in Yiddish, the language then spoken by Eastern European Jews who lived in villages like the one in "Zlateh the Goat." Even after he immigrated to the United States in 1935, where he became a naturalized citizen, Singer continued to write in Yiddish. However, he often translated his own work into English or supervised its translation by others. He won the National Book Award for a children's book, *A Day of Pleasure: Stories of a Boy Growing Up in Warsaw,* and the 1978 Nobel Prize in literature for his "impassioned narrative art."

For Independent Reading

Students who wish to read more of Singer's stories will find them in these collections: *Zlateh the Goat and Other Stories* and *Naftali the Storyteller and His Horse, Sus.*

- You might also recommend a gripping story about a boy in conflict with an adult over the survival of a beloved animal: *The Midnight Fox* by Betsy Byars.
- Another heartwarming story about pets and survival in the wild is *The Incredible Journey* by Sheila Burnford. In this novel two dogs and a cat travel almost three hundred miles across wilderness to find their way home.

▶ Resources Reminder

Reading

- *Interactive Reading*

For another selection by Isaac Bashevis Singer, see "Utzel and His Daughter, Poverty" in *Interactive Reading,* p. 305. You may want to assign this to advanced learners.

Isaac Bashevis Singer

"Time Does Not Vanish"

Isaac Bashevis Singer (1904–1991) was born in a village like the one in this story and grew up in Warsaw, Poland, where his father was a rabbi. As a boy he read constantly and was curious about everything. Both of Singer's parents were skilled storytellers.

Singer listened and watched carefully, storing in his memory scenes, people, and incidents he would write about later in his life. His stories won him the Nobel Prize for Literature in 1978.

In "Zlateh the Goat" and many other stories, Singer recalls a way of life that no longer exists. He wrote:

> Children are as puzzled by passing time as grown-ups. What happens to a day once it is gone? Where are all our yesterdays with their joys and sorrows? Literature helps us remember the past with its many moods. To the storyteller yesterday is still here as are the years and the decades gone by.
>
> In stories time does not vanish. Neither do men and animals. For the writer and his readers all creatures go on living forever. What happened long ago is still present. …
>
> I dedicate this book to the many children who had no chance to grow up because of stupid wars and cruel persecutions which devastated cities and destroyed innocent families. I hope that when the readers of these stories become men and women they will love not only their own children but all good children everywhere.

For Independent Reading

If you liked "Zlateh the Goat," try reading *The Fools of Chelm and Their History* or *A Day of Pleasure: Stories of a Boy Growing Up in Warsaw.*

DIFFERENTIATING INSTRUCTION

Advanced Learners
Enrichment. Tell students that Singer drew much of his material from real life—from his own boyhood and from stories told to him by others; stories that were sometimes strange or even fantastic but true. Singer loved hearing these stories because they taught him something new about human nature.

Activity. Have students find out more about Singer's unusual stories. Where did he find the ideas? Where do they often take place?

CONNECTIONS

A True Story

Trial by Fire

After battling a blaze in an abandoned auto shop on March 29 last year, New York City firefighters were startled to hear meowing. There, amid the smoke, sat three crying kittens; across the street were two more. Within moments, their mother, a badly injured calico,° was found nearby. "She had done her job and pulled them out one by one," says firefighter David Giannelli, who placed the animals in a box. "Her eyes were burnt shut, but she touched every one of those babies with the tip of her nose."

A

°**calico** (kal′i·kō′) *n.:* cat with spots and markings of several colors.

Dr. Larry Cohen and David Giannelli are happy that Scarlett and her kittens are on the road to recovery.

Karen Wellen holds her newly adopted cat, Scarlett.

Taken to Long Island's North Shore Animal League, the kittens and their mother—named Scarlett at the shelter—were treated for smoke inhalation and burns. "The instinct to save your young is very strong," says Dr. Bonnie Brown, North Shore's medical director. "This was just an extraordinary example." Sifting through 2,000 adoption applications, administrators finally sent Scarlett home with Karen Wellen, a New York City writer, and her parents. (One kitten died from a viral infection; the others were placed in area homes.) Now three times a day, Scarlett—a plump 15 pounds—receives eye cream to counter damage to her lids but otherwise is healthy and loving. Karen can't believe her own luck: "This cat risked her life to save her kittens. To come out of it with such a sweet personality is amazing."

B

—from *People Magazine*, July 14, 1997

Zlateh the Goat   457

CONNECTING AND COMPARING TEXTS

The two texts tell similar stories about animals who escape death and rescue loved ones. In the short story "Zlateh the Goat," the patient, motherlike goat Zlateh saves Aaron from freezing and starvation. In the article "Trial by Fire," a mother cat rescues her five kittens from a blaze. "Zlateh the Goat" builds suspense by allowing the reader to know what the boy and the goat are thinking during their ordeal. In "Trial by Fire," the reader must rely on facts and quotations from eyewitnesses to learn about Scarlett's remarkable feat. In each case, the narrative techniques of fiction and nonfiction tell a satisfying story that ends happily for the animals involved.

Connections

Summary ⬄ *at grade level*

> This one-page article focuses on a mother cat who suffered serious burns when she saved her five kittens from a fire in an abandoned auto shop in New York City. The mother cat—later named Scarlett—and her kittens were treated at Long Island's North Shore Animal League. One kitten died. Good homes were found for Scarlett, however, and for the other four kittens. Scarlett is now a happy, healthy, loving cat.

DIRECT TEACHING

▶ Resources Reminder

Media
- *Audio CD Library*
  - disc 10

Reading
- *Interactive Reading*
  - Graphic Organizer: Venn Diagram, p. 304

Assessment
- *Progress Assessment of Reading*
  - Selection Test, p. 163

A Reading Skills

❓ **Finding the main idea.** What amazing feat does the mother cat perform? [She saves her five kittens from a fire, even though her own eyes are burned shut in the process.]

B Reading Skills

❓ **Comparing and contrasting.** How is Scarlett like Zlateh in the story "Zlateh the Goat"? [Possible responses: She helps others survive; she is not concerned about just herself; she is loving and accepting.] What qualities does Scarlett have that we usually associate with human beings? [Possible responses: motherly love, great courage.]

INDEPENDENT PRACTICE

Literary Response and Analysis

Reading Check

1. Possible story map:

Characters—Aaron, the oldest son; Zlateh, the family's beloved goat

Setting—a Polish village many years ago

Problem—In a mild winter a furrier's family needs money, so Aaron must take Zlateh to town to be sold to the butcher for slaughter.

Main Events—A. On the trip to town, a sudden snowstorm arises. B. Aaron and Zlateh take shelter in a haystack. C. After three days, the storm ends, and Aaron and Zlateh go home.

Resolution—The family now values Zlateh too much to sell her.

Interpretations

2. Suspenseful moments: the onset of the snowstorm; Aaron loses his way; he realizes they must find shelter or freeze to death. Outcomes of students' predictions will vary.

3. Zlateh is saved from death; Aaron and Zlateh nearly die in the storm but help each other survive; Aaron's family believes he is dead, but he and Zlateh return. Students may say that the story shows that love can overcome death.

4. Zlateh's patience, trust, devotion, and generosity are examples to Aaron. He and his family learn that humans and animals can depend on each other for survival and friendship.

Literary Response and Analysis

Reading Check

1. Review the story's **plot** by filling in a story map like the one below.

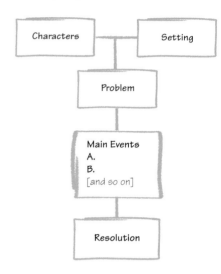

Interpretations

2. List at least two points in the story where you felt **suspense**—where you worried about what would happen next. Did the next event in the plot happen as you predicted it would, or were you surprised? Explain.

3. Hanukkah celebrates a rebirth: the rededication of the Temple in Jerusalem. Why do you suppose Singer set "Zlateh the Goat" during Hanukkah? What does the story say to you about the power of love?

4. Singer, who was a dedicated vegetarian, once said, "I love birds and all animals, and I believe men can learn a lot from God's creatures." In this story, what does Aaron learn from Zlateh? What does Aaron's family learn?

Evaluation

5. Where in the story does Zlateh express her thoughts and feelings? Did you find Zlateh's methods of communication **credible,** or believable? Why or why not?

6. Is the **plot** of this story **credible**—that is, could these events happen in real life—or are parts of the plot not believable, according to your own experience? Back up your evaluation of the plot with details from the story and from the true story "Trial by Fire" (see page 457).

Writing
Comparing Stories

"The Dog of Pompeii" (page 432) and "Zlateh the Goat" have many similarities, even though one story takes place in an ancient Roman city and the other takes place in an eastern European village many centuries later. Write a brief essay comparing the two stories. Focus on the stories' plots, characters, and themes.

➤ Use "Writing a Comparison-Contrast Essay," pages 660–664, for help with this assignment.

Reading Standard 3.8 Critique the credibility of characterization and the degree to which a plot is contrived or realistic.

Evaluation

5. Zlateh expresses herself through her patient following of Aaron's lead, with her "Maaaas" in the haystack, and by asking admittance to the house. Students who are familiar with animals may find her methods of communication credible.

6. Most students will recognize that the story takes place in a remote time and place but is still believable. Those who have little understanding of snowstorms, poverty, or farming may have difficulty with such things as survival in a haystack or a goat in the house. To back up their assessment of the plot, students will cite Scarlett's ability to save her kittens—though her "eyes were burnt shut"—as evidence that animals can demonstrate amazing acts of courage and love.

Vocabulary Development

Vocabulary Development

PRACTICE 1

Show your mastery of the Word Bank words by answering the following questions.

1. Describe three scenes of chaos.
2. Draw a picture of a cleft hoof. Describe the way a cleft in a rock would look.
3. What might you use to penetrate the darkness at night?
4. Name three plants that exude strong odors.

Word Bank

penetrated
cleft
chaos
exuded

Using Word Parts to Build Meanings: Suffixes

PRACTICE 2

Sometimes you can figure out the meaning of an unfamiliar word if you analyze the meaning of its parts. The more suffixes you know, the more words you'll be able to figure out.

A **suffix** is a word part added to the end of a word or root. The chart below lists common suffixes.

1. Identify the **suffix** in each of the words listed just below. In the chart, find the meaning of the suffix; then, define the whole word.

   fearful   frighten   hopeless   lonely   troublesome

2. Use each word from item 1 in a sentence or two about Aaron and Zlateh.

Common Suffixes

Suffix	Meaning	Examples
–able	capable of being	likable, laughable
–en	make	deepen, lengthen
–ful	full of	stressful, doubtful
–ion	act or condition of	inspection, reaction
–less	without	penniless, hopeless
–ly	in a certain way	quickly, smoothly
–ness	quality of being	shyness, happiness
–some	like; tending to be	tiresome, lonesome
–ous	characterized by	luxurious, dangerous

Grade 4 Review Reading Standard 1.4 Know common affixes, and use this knowledge to analyze the meaning of words.

Zlateh the Goat **459**

Vocabulary Development

Practice 1

1. Possible answers: an airport with many delays; a street with fallen wires and trees after a hurricane or tornado; a highway during rush hour.
2. Students' drawings should show a hoof with a split in the middle. A cleft in a rock would look like a partial split.
3. Possible answers: a flashlight, a candle, a lantern.
4. Possible answers: roses, lilies, hyacinths.

Practice 2

1. ■ *fearful. Suffix— –ful. Suffix meaning*—"full of." *Word meaning*—"full of fear."

   ■ *frighten. Suffix— –en. Suffix meaning*—"make." *Word meaning*—"make afraid."

   ■ *hopeless. Suffix— –less. Suffix meaning*—"without." *Word meaning*—"without hope."

   ■ *stormy. Suffix— –y. Suffix meaning*—"in a certain way." *Word meaning*—"to behave like a storm."

   ■ *troublesome. Suffix— –some. Suffix meaning*—"full of." *Word meaning*—"full of trouble."

2. Possible answers: Aaron and Zlateh were fearful when they could no longer find their way. The howling wind frightened them. Aaron's situation would have been hopeless without Zlateh to feed him milk. Aaron and Zlateh comforted each other through three lonely troublesome days.

▶ Resources Reminder

Vocabulary and Spelling

■ *Vocabulary Development*
  ▪ Vocabulary Worksheet, p. 30
  ▪ Cumulative Vocabulary Review, p. 31

■ *Lesson Plans for Language Development*
  ▪ Vocabulary, p. 220

Grammar Link

Practice

Anyone who loves animals will find his or her interest grabbed by "Zlateh the Goat." It would be hard for someone to take an animal he or she loves to be butchered. No one likes to lose something he or she loves.

VIEWING THE ART

Marc Chagall (1887–1985) was born in Russia and lived in France. An imaginative artist of the surreal, Chagall painted people and objects so that they often seem to defy the laws of gravity, floating serenely above the landscape. His work often reflects his memories of the Russian-Jewish village where he grew up and is filled with folklore, fantasy, humor, and biblical themes.

Activity. Ask students which elements of the painting seem realistic [the wooden tub, the houses at background right] and which seem especially fanciful [the goat and the bird]. How does the painting connect with "Zlateh the Goat"? [Possible response: It's almost as if it is a painting of Aaron's village and Zlateh herself.]

ASSESSING

Assessment
■ *Progress Assessment of Reading*
  ■ Selection Tests, pp. 160, 163

RETEACHING

For a lesson reteaching critiquing characterization and plot, see **Reteaching**, pp. 489O–489P.

Grammar Link MINI-LESSON

Pronouns and Antecedents Should Always Agree

A pronoun usually refers to a noun or another pronoun, called its **antecedent.** Whenever you use a pronoun, make sure it agrees with its antecedent in number and gender. Doing this is usually easy, except when you use certain pronouns as antecedents.

Use a singular pronoun to refer to *each, either, neither, one, everyone, everybody, no one, anyone, someone,* or *somebody.*

> Nobody would be happy about bringing <u>his or her</u> animal to a butcher.

Nobody is singular, so you use the singular pronouns *his* and *her.* You need both *his* and *her* because the gender of *nobody* can be either masculine or feminine.

> Aaron's mother and sisters were upset about Zlateh; <u>everyone</u> had tears in <u>her</u> eyes.

Everyone is singular, so you use the singular pronoun *her.* You use *her* (rather than *his or her*) because *everyone* refers to Aaron's mother and sisters.

> **PRACTICE**

Act as an editor: Correct the use of antecedents in the following paragraph about "Zlateh the Goat." Rewrite the sentences if you wish.

Anyone who loves animals will find their interest grabbed by "Zlateh the Goat." It would be hard for someone to take an animal they love to be butchered. No one likes to lose something they love.

For more help, see Agreement of Pronoun and Antecedent in the *Holt Handbook,* pages 137–142.

The Village (1973) by Marc Chagall.
©1999 Artists Rights Society (ARS), New York / ADAGP, Paris.

DIFFERENTIATING INSTRUCTION

Learners Having Difficulty

If you wish to give students additional practice with this skill, have them revise the following sentences so that the pronouns agree with their antecedents.

1. Anyone who wants to sell their pet should think twice before they do it. [Anyone who wants to sell his or her pet should think twice before he or she does it *or* People who want to sell their pets should think twice before they do it.]

2. Everyone loves to see their pet. [Everyone loves to see his or her pet *or* All people love to see their pets.]

3. Each student has to do their own work. [Each student has to do his or her own work *or* All students have to do their own work.]

4. Nobody has ever lost their coat before. [Nobody has ever lost his or her coat before.]

Pet Adoption Application

Application Advice

"Trial by Fire" tells the true story of a heroic cat who saved her kittens' lives by carrying them out of a burning building.

Animal shelters give new life to hundreds of cats and dogs every day. Volunteers and veterinarians nurse abandoned animals back to health, in the hope that each one will find a good home.

Taking care of a pet is a serious commitment. Shelter staff try to make sure every adopter is a responsible person who will love and care for the animal. They require anyone seeking to adopt to fill out an application that asks for important personal information. The staff members use the information to determine whether the person would be a good pet owner.

Before you begin filling out any application—whether it's for pet adoption, a job, or admission to college—read it first. You can often learn a great deal about whatever you're applying for by reading through the application. For example, after looking through a shelter application, you may realize you're not really ready to bring Rover or Frisky into your home to live.

Here are some other tips for filling out an application:

- Don't leave any line blank. If a question doesn't apply to you, just write *n/a*, which means "not applicable."

- If the form requires a signature, be sure to sign and date it.

- Take your time, and write as neatly as you can.

- After you fill out the application, read it through carefully to make sure you didn't miss anything.

Reading Standard 2.5 Follow multiple-step instructions for preparing applications.

Pet Adoption Application **461**

STANDARDS FOCUS, pp. 461–463

(For grade-level and review standards taught in this selection, see citations on Pupil's Edition pages.)

Summary ↔ *at grade level*

> This selection is an application for someone wishing to adopt a pet. In addition to requesting personal data, the form includes a series of questions about the applicant's lifestyle and residence.

PRETEACHING

Standards Starter

Motivate. Invite pet owners to tell how they came to have pets. Ask if any pets were adopted from an animal shelter and, if so, what that experience involved.

Assign the Reading

Advanced learners can read the application and answer the Focus On questions independently while you monitor groups of students who need help.

RESOURCES

Planning
- *One-Stop Planner* CD-ROM with Test Generator
- *On Course: Mapping Instruction*

Differentiating Instruction
- *Lesson Plans for Language Development*
    - English-Language Learners, pp. 218, 220
    - Special Education Students, pp. 218, 220

Assessment
- *One-Stop Planner* CD-ROM with Test Generator

A Reading Informational Materials
GRADE-LEVEL STANDARD

? Following multiple-step instructions. What basic information is required on the top right-hand side of the application? [the type of animal wanted for adoption; the name, address, and telephone number of the applicant]

B Reading Informational Materials
GRADE-LEVEL STANDARD

Following multiple-step instructions. Encourage students who have pets now or who once had pets to locate the place on the application where they would list details about their pet. [Section 4] Ask students to identify the question that is asked of both former and present pet owners. [How long did you have the pet?] Why is this an important question? [Possible response: It might indicate whether the owner took good care of the pet.]

GUIDED PRACTICE

Monitoring students' progress. Have students explain why people who want to adopt pets must fill out application forms carefully.

INSTRUCTIONS: **Adopter,** print carefully in **UNSHADED AREAS ONLY**—do not write in shaded areas.

Pet Adoption Application ☐ Puppy ☐ Kitten ☐ Dog ☐ Cat

Date / /	Single Adoption	Double Adoption	Age
Day	Time ☐AM ☐PM	Breed	Color
			Sex
Voluntary Contribution	Size: S___ M___ L___	Spay/Neuter
Cash $	☐Pure	☐Mix	Vaccine Type
Check $	Pet's Name	Vaccine Date
D V M A circle one $	ASC Int. No.	Rabies Tag
Credit A/R ($)		Rabies Date
Total Voluntary Contribution $_____		Wormed
X_____		Med. Given

Program — H T D O L R G (circle one)
MTA MTD — 1 2
Adoption Number

☐MR. ☐MRS. ☐MS. ☐MISS ☐MR. & MRS.
☐Adopter's Last Name   First Name

Street Address   Apt. #

City   State Zip Code

Home Phone   Business Phone
( ) -   ( ) -

NMR Tech. App.

Name of Reference	Address	City	State	Telephone	ID Source
				( )	☐Yes ☐No
				( )	D V ☐Yes / M A ☐No
				( )	

1. WHOM IS THE PET FOR? Self____ Gift____ For whom?_____ Adopter's age:____

2. IF YOU'RE SINGLE: Do you live alone? Yes   No   Do you live with family? Yes   No
   Do you work? Yes   No   What are your hours?

   IF YOU'RE MARRIED: Do both work? Yes   No   Husband's hours: Wife's hours:
   How many children at home?   Ages: , , ,
   Who will be responsible for the pet? Husband   Wife   Children   Other

3. DO YOU: OWN ☐ RENT ☐ (CHECK ONE)   HOUSE ☐ APT. ☐ (CHECK ONE) Floor #   Elevator in the building? Yes   No
   If renting, does your lease allow pets? Yes____ No____ Are you moving? Yes____ No____ When?____
   Do you have use of a private yard? Yes____ No____ Is it fenced? Yes___ No___ Fence height:_____
   Where will your pet be kept?____ DAYTIME /____ NIGHTTIME   Any allergy to pets? Yes____ No____

4. DO YOU HAVE OTHER PETS NOW? Yes   No   Breed:
   Where did you get the pet?   How long have you had it?

   HAVE YOU EVER HAD A PET BEFORE? Yes   No   Breed:
   How long did you have the pet?   What happened to the pet?
   Have you ever adopted from this shelter? Yes   No   Where is the pet now?

5. YOUR OCCUPATION:_____ Business Phone: ( )_____
   Company:_____ Supervisor's Name:_____

VET'S NAME	CITY, STATE	ZIP CODE

Adopter's Signature:

DIFFERENTIATING INSTRUCTION

Learners Having Difficulty
Complicated applications may intimidate some students. Provide them with simpler examples, or break down the material requested into smaller parts. Emphasize that most applications ask basic questions about the applicant, which are followed by more specific questions. Ask students to think about what information is needed on an application and why it is needed.

English-Language Learners
Point out that many applications are produced in two languages. Students may want to locate or create an application written in English and in their native language.

Advanced Learners
Students may design and write their own applications, deciding first what the application is for and then what information will be required of the applicants.

Reading Informational Materials

Reading Check

1. A **reference** is a person who can provide information about you. Why would the adoption shelter want references for an adopter?

2. Why is it important for the adoption shelter to know whether you rent or own your home?

3. What information do you think the shelter is really looking for when it asks what pets you have now?

TestPractice

Pet Adoption Application

1. Which of the following people would not be a suitable reference?
   - **A** A teacher
   - **B** A parent
   - **C** A classmate
   - **D** An aunt

2. The main thing the shelter wants to know about an applicant is —
   - **F** whether the applicant will feed the animal the right food
   - **G** whether the applicant plans to let the dog or cat run free through the neighborhood
   - **H** whether the applicant will always keep the pet's best interests in mind
   - **J** what kind of dog or cat the applicant wants

3. The abbreviation *n/a* stands for "not applicable." What does the term *not applicable* mean?
   - **A** None of your business
   - **B** Does not apply to me
   - **C** Not again
   - **D** No answer

4. The application asks for your veterinarian's name. What would be the best thing to do if you didn't already have a vet?
   - **F** Just leave the space blank.
   - **G** Write *n/a*.
   - **H** Ask the shelter to recommend one.
   - **J** Make up a name.

Reading Standard 2.5 Follow multiple-step instructions for preparing applications.

Pet Adoption Application **463**

Reading Check

1. Possible answers: A shelter would want to check with people who know the applicant to be sure that he or she is honest and responsible and will feed and care for the pet and not abuse it.

2. Possible answers: A shelter would want to be sure that a pet will have a secure and loving home and will never be abandoned. Some renters' leases don't allow pets.

3. Possible answers: The shelter may be checking that there are not too many pets in a household and that the new pet would be compatible with an older pet. They may believe that people who already have pets would make good owners.

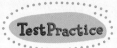

INDEPENDENT PRACTICE

Reading Informational Materials

TestPractice

Answers and Model Rationales

1. **C** A classmate might be considered too young for a reference. A teacher, A, who knows the applicant's level of responsibility would be an excellent reference. A reference from a parent, B, or an aunt, D, would assure the shelter that the family supports the decision to adopt.

2. **H** The shelter's main concern is that all the applicants be committed to their pets' best interests. F and G are not addressed in the application. Only after an applicant has been accepted is the kind of pet considered, J.

3. **B** B is the only correct choice, since *not applicable* means "does not apply to me."

4. **G** Since the applicant has no vet, the only choice is G. If you leave the space blank (F), it looks like you forgot to respond. H would apply once the applicant has been accepted. Making up a name, J, is the same as telling an untruth and would make you seem unreliable and dishonest.

Test-Taking Tips

For more information on how to answer multiple-choice questions, refer students to **Test Smarts,** p. 690.

Standards Review

Reading Informational Materials

STANDARDS FOCUS, pp. 464–465

(For the grade-level standard reviewed in this lesson, see Pupil's Edition, p. 464.)

INTRODUCING THE STANDARDS REVIEW

Use this review to test students' ability to follow instructions when completing an application. Use these annotations only if you want to conduct this review orally.

DIRECT TEACHING

Ⓐ Reading Informational Materials
GRADE-LEVEL STANDARD
❓ Following multiple-step instructions. What information is asked for in Section 1? [the applicant's name, address, home telephone number, e-mail address, Social Security number, and age]

Ⓑ Reading Informational Materials
GRADE-LEVEL STANDARD
❓ Following multiple-step instructions. What kinds of things might you put for special skills or training in Section 3? [Possible responses: hobbies; arts and crafts skills or classes; knowledge of museum-related subjects, such as dinosaurs, mammals, or rocks.]

Reading Informational Materials

 DIRECTIONS: Read the following application form. Then, read each question, and write the letter of the best response.

Natural History Museum Volunteer Application

Ⓐ 1. Name: _____
Address: _____ City, State, Zip code: _____
Home telephone: _____ E-mail: _____
Social Security number: _____ Age: ☐ Under 18 ☐ Over 18

2. Education School most recently attended: _____

3. Employment If a résumé is available, please submit it along with your application.
(Please check *Past* or *Present*.)
☐ Past ☐ Present Volunteer work: _____

Ⓑ Special skills or training: _____
Computer skills: _____
Fluency in other languages (please specify): _____

4. Is there a specific department or program at the museum in which you would like to work if a volunteer job is available? _____
Why do you want to volunteer at the Natural History Museum? _____
_____

5. Availability Please check the times you are available to volunteer.

	Mon.	Tues.	Wed.	Thurs.	Fri.	Sat.	Sun.
9:00 A.M.–1:00 P.M.							
1:00 P.M.–5:00 P.M.							
5:00 P.M.–8:30 P.M.							

When can you start? _____
A minimum commitment of one year is required. Can you meet this requirement? _____

Reading Standard 2.5 Follow multiple-step instructions for preparing applications.

I HAVE READ AND AM IN POSSESSION OF A COPY OF THE "VOLUNTEER REGULATIONS AND PROCEDURES."
Signature _____ Date _____

MINI-LESSON Reading

Reviewing Word-Attack Skills
Activity. Display these words, and have students identify the letters that stand for the sound /sh/.

1. partial [ti]
2. special [ci]
3. ambitious [ti]
4. nutritious [ti]
5. malicious [ci]
6. suspicion [ci]
7. installation [ti]
8. habitation [ti]
9. pension [si]
10. cautious [ti]
11. obnoxious [xi]
12. infectious [ti]
13. pretentious [ti]
14. competition [ti]
15. delicious [ci]
16. gracious [ci]
17. precious [ci]
18. contentious [ti]
19. facetious [ti]
20. pronunciation [ti]

1. In what section should you indicate that you speak more than one language?

   A 1
   B 2
   C 3
   D 4

2. The purpose of section 5 is to find out —

   F what hours you're available to work
   G what work experience you have
   H where you live
   J what your educational background is

3. For what department is the museum hiring?

   A Tours
   B Research
   C Sales
   D The application doesn't say.

4. Which of the following statements belongs in section 4?

   F I can design Web sites.
   G I've always been interested in dinosaurs.
   H I can start working immediately.
   J I am a skilled scuba diver.

5. For how long must you agree to work if you take the job?

   A Six months
   B One year
   C Two years
   D Three months

Answers and Model Rationales

1. **C** A space to indicate fluency in other languages and to specify which languages appears in Section 3. This serves as a reminder to read the entire application before filling it out. Point out that an applicant who is rushing might indicate fluency in a foreign language in the space allotted for special skills or training and then realize that this information belongs in a different place.

2. **F** Section 5 asks when the applicant is available to work. Students should recognize that Section 1 asks for the information in H; Section 2, for the information in J; and Section 3, for the information in G.

3. **D** Nowhere on the application does it say which departments are looking for volunteers, though Section 4 asks applicants to name a department or program that interests them.

4. **G** G answers the question "Why do you want to volunteer at The Museum of Natural History?" F and J belong in Section 3, while H belongs in Section 5.

5. **B** In Section 5, the application states, "A minimum commitment of one year is required. Can you meet this requirement?"

Test-Taking Tips

Remind students to look over the entire application before answering the questions. Suggest that they make a list of the general categories of information asked for in each section.

For more instruction on how to answer multiple-choice items, refer students to **Test Smarts,** p. 690.

Activity. Display the following words. For each word, have students underline the syllable or syllables that contain a long vowel sound.

1. criticize [cize]
2. complete [plete]
3. parasite [site]
4. capitalize [ize]
5. estimate [mate (as v.)]
6. envelope [lope]
7. rampage [page]
8. advertise [tise]
9. translate [late]
10. intimidate [date]
11. explode [plode]
12. assimilate [late]
13. duplicate [du and cate (as v.)]
14. anecdote [dote]
15. institute [tute]
16. instigate [gate]
17. consolidate [date]
18. columbine [bine]
19. costume [tume]
20. proliferate [pro and ate]

Vocabulary
Development
Context Clues

Modeling. Model the thought process of a good reader getting the answer to item 1 by saying: "Bimbo brought fresh, or newly made, food to Tito. In the same way, a cake from the pastry shop would taste newly made. In A, *fresh* means 'pure and clear,' in C, 'original,' and in D, 'new.' Therefore, B is correct."

Answers and Model Rationales

1. **B**   See rationale above.

2. **F**   In the example sentence, *pitch* is used as a verb meaning "move up and down," so F, in which *pitch* also means "move up and down," is correct. In G, *pitch* is used as a noun, meaning "a thrown ball"; in H, as a verb meaning "help," and in J, as a verb meaning "throw."

3. **B**   In the example sentence, *mass* is an adjective meaning "large." Only in B is *mass* an adjective with the same meaning. In A and C, *mass* is a noun. In D, *mass* is a verb.

4. **H**   In the example sentence and in H, *public* is used as an adjective meaning "open to anyone." In F, *public* is used as an adjective meaning "known to most people"; in G, as a noun meaning "a group of people"; and in J, as a noun meaning "a place where all may come."

Vocabulary Development

TestPractice

Context Clues

DIRECTIONS: Read each of the following sentences. Then, choose the answer in which the underlined word is used in the same way.

1. Bimbo brought fresh food to Tito. In which sentence does the word *fresh* have the same meaning as in the sentence above?

   A   There was a cool, fresh breeze blowing.

   B   The cake tasted fresh.

   C   The fall fashions included many new, fresh designs.

   D   After a bad day at work, John vowed to make a fresh start tomorrow.

2. The ground—the very world, it seemed—began to pitch and shake. In which sentence does the word *pitch* have the same meaning as in the sentence above?

   F   The choppy waves caused the boat to pitch wildly.

   G   The first pitch of the game was a curveball.

   H   If everyone would pitch in, we could finish the job a lot sooner.

   J   I asked Tony to pitch me the can off the shelf.

3. A mass panic set in as people began fleeing for their lives. In which sentence does the word *mass* have the same meaning as in the sentence above?

   A   By the end of the football game, Barry was a mass of bruises.

   B   I joined a mass demonstration at City Hall.

   C   We measured the rock's mass.

   D   The students began to mass in front of the school.

4. People gathered at the public square to gossip and share news. In which sentence does the word *public* have the same meaning as in the sentence above?

   F   The newly elected senator has been a public figure for years.

   G   The movie-going public does not consider him a star.

   H   Joey liked to meet his friends at the public park.

   J   Before their debate, the two candidates would not meet in public.

Vocabulary Review

Use this activity to assess whether students have retained the chapter Vocabulary. **Activity.** Have students select the correct words from the box to complete the following sentences.

penetrated	cleft	chaos	revived
ambitious	proverb	exuded	

1. In the midst of _____, Jane spoke quietly and _____calm. [chaos, exuded]

2. The wisdom of that simple _____ made a deep impression as it _____ my mind. [proverb, penetrated]

3. After breathing toxic fumes, he fainted and had to be _____. [revived]

4. Deer have _____ hooves. [cleft]

5. Because she was talented and _____, she was quickly promoted. [ambitious]

PERSUASIVE WRITING

Taking a Stand

Mastering the Standards

Both "The Dog of Pompeii" and "Zlateh the Goat" deal with the special relationship between animals and people. This bond has inspired many people to fight for the protection and humane treatment of animals. Think of an issue you care deeply about, perhaps one involving animals. For example, you may feel that stronger laws should be passed to protect whales. You may believe that cities should set aside more space in which dogs can run free. Write a persuasive letter or essay expressing your view on the issue you choose. Address it to a local, state, or U.S. government official—whichever is appropriate for the issue. Include facts, statistics, examples, and quotations from experts to support your position. Use the framework below to organize your letter.

> **Framework for a Persuasive Essay**
> **Introduction** (statement of the issue, the pros and cons of different positions on the issue, and your position): _____
> **Reason 1** with two supporting details (facts, examples, and personal experiences): _____
> **Reason 2** with two supporting details: _____
> **Conclusion** (restatement of your opinion and a call to action): _____

➤ Use "Writing a Persuasive Essay," pages 618–635, for help with this assignment.

Other Choices

COMPARISON AND CONTRAST

1 **It's a Dog's Life**

Writers know that people are interested in animals, and they often use animal characters to reveal something to us about ourselves. Compare the dog in "Storm" (page 245) with Bimbo, the dog of Pompeii. Do you think the writer of each story is saying something about how *people* should live and act?

➤ Use "Writing a Comparison-Contrast Essay," pages 660–664, for help with this assignment.

SHORT STORY

2 **Historical Fiction**

"The Dog of Pompeii" is **historical fiction,** fiction based on events that actually happened in the past. Think of another historical event or period, and write a story about an imaginary person who was there. Possibilities include the building of the Pyramids, life in the ancient Greek city of Sparta or Athens, and the first Thanksgiving at Plymouth. To make your story authentic, do research in a library or on the Internet.

➤ Use "Writing a Short Story," pages 500–518, for help with this assignment.

Mastering the Standards

Evaluation Criteria

A good persuasive essay

1. states a clear point of view on an issue of concern

2. anticipates and addresses reader concerns and the pros and cons of different positions on the issue

3. supports the position with reasons and such details as facts, statistics, examples, and quotations from experts

ASSESSING

Assessment

- *Progress Assessment of Reading*
  - Chapter Test, p. 165
- *Diagnostic and Summative Assessments*
  - End-of-Year Test, p. 98

After you have completed Chapters 7 and 8 and all related instruction, you may want your students to take this test.

Using Academic Language

Literary Terms

As part of the review of Literary Response and Analysis Standard 3.8, ask students to look back through the chapter to find the meanings of the terms at right. Then, have students demonstrate their understanding of Standard 3.8 by citing passages from stories in the chapter that illustrate the meanings of the following terms.

Credible Characters (p. 430); **Suspense** (p. 450).

Informational Terms

As part of the review of Reading Comprehension Standard 2.5, ask students to look back through the chapter to find the meaning of the following term and to use it to explain Standard 2.5.
Reference (p. 447).

Read On

For Independent Reading

If students enjoyed the themes and topics explored in this chapter, you might recommend these titles for independent reading.

Assessment Options

The following projects can help you evaluate and assess your students' outside reading. Video-tapes or audiotapes of completed projects may be included in students' portfolios.

- **Create a dramatic monologue.** Have students create and present dramatic monologues as either Beric from *Outcast*, Charlotte Doyle from *The True Confessions of Charlotte Doyle,* or Sarah Bishop from *Sarah Bishop.* The monologues should recount some of the character's adventures as well as his or her thoughts and feelings about events that occurred in the book. Give students time to rehearse before presenting their monologues.

- **Make a mural.** Have students design and create murals based on images from any or all of the books. Students can work in any medium they choose: crayons, paint, colored pencils, or chalk. Students who have read the same book may want to work together to create images.

- **Give a presentation.** Have small groups work together to prepare presentations about volcanoes based on information found in *The Buried City of Pompeii* and *Volcano: The Eruption and Healing of Mount St. Helens* and on additional research. Groups should use graphics, such as charts and diagrams, as well as photographs, to explain volcanic eruptions and to show their power.

California Reading List Title

The True Confessions of Charlotte Doyle
Sarah Bishop
My Life in Dog Years

Fiction

An Orphan's Adventure

When a Roman trading ship is destroyed, Beric is the only survivor. A British tribe takes Beric in and raises him as one of their own. As Beric reaches manhood, the tribe suffers through bad times. Beric is blamed for their troubles and banished from his home. In Rosemary Sutcliff's *Outcast*, Beric lives in fear of his life until he finds a home at last.

Chaotic Waters

When she boards an English ship bound for Rhode Island, Charlotte Doyle has no idea that she'll be the only female passenger on board. She soon finds herself caught up in the conflict between a power-mad captain and his bitter, rebellious crew. Then, Charlotte is given an unusual gift, and events take a shocking turn in Avi's *The True Confessions of Charlotte Doyle.*

This title is available in the HRW Library.

Fighting for Independence

The American Revolution turns the members of Sarah's family against one another, and Sarah is left on her own. Then the British Army accuses her of setting fire to a militia building, and she finds herself friendless and on the run. She must call on all her wits and instincts to survive in Scott O'Dell's gripping novel *Sarah Bishop.*

What It Was Like

The eruption of Mount Vesuvius and destruction of Pompeii continue to intrigue people centuries later. In *The Buried City of Pompeii*, Shelly Tanaka looks at the disaster through the eyes of Eros, a steward. Following Eros's tale, Tanaka presents a scientific explanation for the eruption of the volcano.

Toward Reading a Million Words Annually

Estimated Word Counts of Read On Books:

Fiction		Nonfiction	
Outcast	81,000	Blizzard!	32,000
The True Confessions of Charlotte Doyle	53,000	My Life in Dog Years	22,000
		Ancient Rome	15,000
Connections to The True Confessions of Charlotte Doyle	6,800	Volcano: The Eruption and Healing of Mount St. Helens	6,500
Sarah Bishop	42,000		
The Buried City of Pompeii	14,000		

Nonfiction

Whiteout

On March 12, 1888, New York City residents were overwhelmed by a huge blizzard. Rich and poor alike struggled to find food and water, and thousands lost their lives to the fierce winds and freezing temperatures. In his book *Blizzard!*, Jim Murphy shows us how a force of nature can completely disrupt everyday life. The book's photographs and illustrations of the storm will freeze your toes.

The Best of Friends

Have you ever had a dog? The writer Gary Paulsen has had dozens over the years. One of his dogs scared off bullies when Paulsen was a boy. Another saved his life. In *My Life in Dog Years*, Paulsen tells about the special animals that have been a constant source of companionship and happiness for him.

Stay Awhile!

In *Ancient Rome*, Simon James takes you on a tour of Rome in the days of the empire. James shows you what Roman forts, theaters, and town houses looked like, and his transparent cutaways give you a glimpse of what went on inside. You'll also learn about structures like forums and aqueducts. If you enjoy this book, you may want to read other titles in the *See Through History* series.

A Time of Terror

In this chapter you read about a devastating volcanic eruption that took place hundreds of years ago. Patricia Lauber examines a recent eruption in *Volcano: The Eruption and Healing of Mount St. Helens*. Lauber's text, accompanied by stunning photographs, gives you an up-close look at the eruption and the destruction it caused, as well as the recovery period that followed.

Read On   469

- **Produce a skit.** Have students work to create and put on skits based on the stories in *My Life in Dog Years*. Give students time to rehearse their skits, gather props, and create sets before setting aside time for the class to view the productions.

- **Write a review.** Have students write book reviews of either *Blizzard!* or *Ancient Rome*. Remind them that a good book review gives some details from the book and discusses its strong and weak points, as well as relating the reviewer's opinion of the book.

 Resources Reminder

Reading

- *Interactive Reading*

For additional readings that relate to the selections in this chapter, see *Interactive Reading*, Chapter 8.

- *The Ancient World*: A Content-Area Reader

DIFFERENTIATING INSTRUCTION

The Read On titles are categorized as shown below:

Below Grade Level ⬇
Sarah Bishop
Volcano: The Eruption and Healing of Mount St. Helens

At Grade Level ↔
The True Confessions of Charlotte Doyle

The Buried City of Pompeii
My Life in Dog Years
Ancient Rome

Above Grade Level ⬆
Outcast
Blizzard!

Using Reading Matters

Reading Matters is a handbook of eight Strategy Lessons designed specifically because reading *does* matter. Students can use the lessons to master various Grade 6 reading standards for informational and literary texts. The first seven Strategy Lessons are designed for use with the corresponding chapters in Part 1. The final Strategy lesson (Lesson 8) focuses on reading fluency and can be used with all Part 1 chapters. Each lesson offers a particular strategy that can be used as a preteaching, reteaching, or review tool.

Reading Matters Strategy Lessons appear at the end of Part 1. Students should view the information here much as they would view the information in a handbook: Information in handbooks can be accessed at any point, read in any order, and revisited as many times as needed. That's the underlying philosophy of Reading Matters. As you look through these lessons, you'll find that the strategies presented in each lesson can be used with many selections in *Holt Literature and Language Arts.* Furthermore, these lessons can help students read a variety of literary and informational materials, not just the materials in this book.

Using Reading Matters with the Pupil's Edition

As you look through Reading Matters, note that each lesson is addressed directly to your students. Students can turn to this section on an as-needed basis. That means you should

- preview Reading Matters with students early in the year
- make sure students understand that part of being a proficient reader means knowing how to get through difficult reading on their own
- check that students understand that Chapters 1–7 in Part 1 have accompanying lessons in Reading Matters
- remind students to refer to the Fluency Chart on p. 488 and the Reading-Rate Chart on p. 489, and have them assess their fluency and reading throughout the year

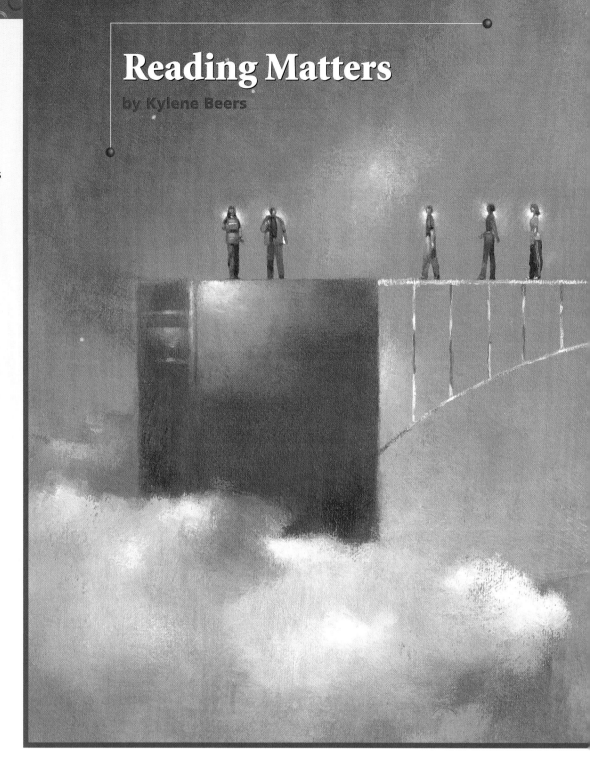

Reading Matters
by Kylene Beers

- remind students often that these lessons can help them with all types of texts, informational as well as literary

As you plan your instruction for each standard, examine the corresponding Strategy Lesson in Reading Matters prior to instruction. See if the strategy presented is one you want to offer as *preteaching instruction* for the chapter. If you prefer, save this Strategy Lesson for students who need *remediation.* Because *reteaching* and *review* are an important part of the instructional cycle, you can also save the Strategy Lessons for use toward the end of a chapter or even as you've moved into the next chapter.

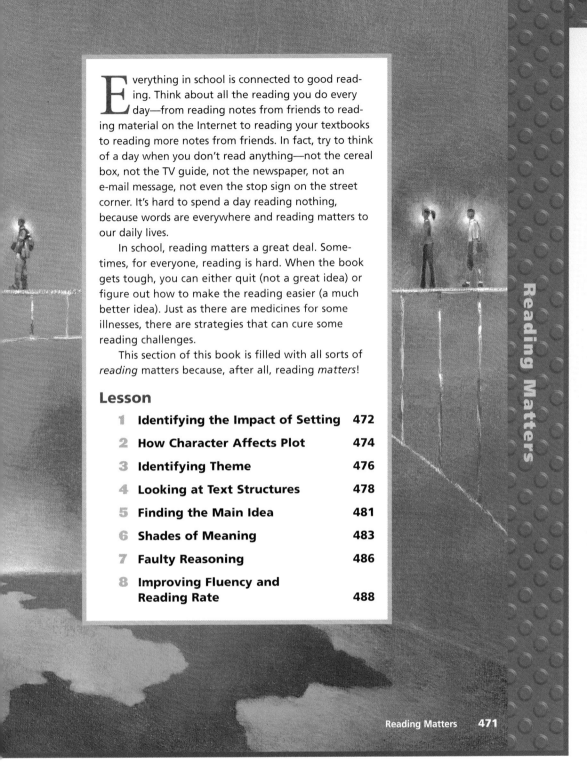

Everything in school is connected to good reading. Think about all the reading you do every day—from reading notes from friends to reading material on the Internet to reading your textbooks to reading more notes from friends. In fact, try to think of a day when you don't read anything—not the cereal box, not the TV guide, not the newspaper, not an e-mail message, not even the stop sign on the street corner. It's hard to spend a day reading nothing, because words are everywhere and reading matters to our daily lives.

In school, reading matters a great deal. Sometimes, for everyone, reading is hard. When the book gets tough, you can either quit (not a great idea) or figure out how to make the reading easier (a much better idea). Just as there are medicines for some illnesses, there are strategies that can cure some reading challenges.

This section of this book is filled with all sorts of *reading* matters because, after all, reading *matters*!

Lesson

Reading Matters

Using Reading Matters with *Interactive Reading*

Mastering the standards isn't about students' learning how to do something in one particular text; standards mastery is about students' mastering reading skills and applying those skills in a variety of situations. That's why we give students lots of opportunities to practice the skills they are learning, both in *Holt Literature and Language Arts* and in ancillary materials, especially in the consumable student book called *Interactive Reading*. Just check the table of contents of *Interactive Reading* to find the pages that use the Reading Matters strategies. Note that the Fluency Chart in Strategy Lesson 8 should be referred to as students read aloud in *Interactive Reading* and work to improve their fluency and reading rate.

Reading Matters **471**

Reading Strategies

Use this Strategy Lesson with the stories in Chapter 1, where students must identify how setting affects plot. This strategy will also be useful with "The Dog of Pompeii" and "Zlateh the Goat," both in Chapter 8.

Strategy Lesson 1

Identifying the Impact of Setting

Somebody Wanted But So

I asked my students to think about how the folk tale "Goldilocks and the Three Bears" would be different if it had taken place underwater instead of in the forest. One student said, "They'd all get wet." Someone else said that the bears would be fish. Another said that Goldilocks would be a mermaid. Then someone said, "The bears, which would be fish, wouldn't have gone out for a walk but instead would have gone to school!" She paused, then asked, "Get it? School . . . fish . . . fish travel in schools!" Everyone moaned, but they got it. Then they came up with all sorts of other ways in which the story would be different if it were set underwater (beds would be clam beds; porridge would be seaweed soup; fish wouldn't walk to school but would ride seahorses).

Reading Standard 3.3
Analyze the influence of setting on the problem and its resolution.

Change Setting, Change Story

Those students understood that changing the **setting**—when and where the story takes place—affects other elements of the story.

Characters, action, even the story's resolution can be affected by the story's setting. In fact, writers often make events happen *where* they happen and *when* they happen for specific reasons. Try this:

Think about . . .	and change the setting . . .
the Narnia books	from England to the United States
The Watsons Go to Birmingham—1963	from 1963 to 1863 and then to 1993
The Flintstones	from prehistoric times to the year 2000

Somebody Wanted But So . . .

Just how much of an impact does setting have on a story's problem and its resolution? To figure this out, you can use a strategy called **Somebody Wanted But So** (SWBS). Jot down those words on your paper, like this:

Somebody	Wanted	But	So

Next, think of an old story you are familiar with. Under "Somebody," name the "somebody" in the story. Under "Wanted," state what he or she wanted. In the "But" column, describe the problem that arose. Finally, under "So," explain how the problem was resolved. When you're done, your SWBS chart will look something like this:

Somebody	Wanted	But	So
Goldilocks	food and a place to rest in the forest since night was coming on,	there was no one in the lonely house she found,	she entered and ate the food on the table and ruined some things, then got scared when the bears came home from work.

PRACTICE 1

1. What happens in the "Wanted" column if the location of the story changes? (Set the story in a place other than the forest, and see what happens.)

2. What happens in the "Wanted" column if the time of the story is changed (to early morning, for example)?

3. How might changing that column affect the "But" and "So" columns?

4. How much of a difference do the changes in setting make to the outcome of the story?

PRACTICE 2

In the story "All Summer in a Day" (page 18), setting is especially important. Make an SWBS chart for several of the characters in that story. Next, think about what changes would occur in the "Wanted," "But," and "So" columns if the story were set in the Sahara, rather than on Venus. Are the changes in the outcome column—the "So" column—significant?

Somebody	Wanted	But	So
Margot			
The children			
The teacher			

Identifying the Impact of Setting **473**

Reading Strategies

Use this strategy with the stories in Chapter 2, where students analyze the effect of character on both plot and the resolution of the conflict. You can also refer students to this strategy when they read "The Gold Cadillac" in Chapter 4 and "Eleven" in Chapter 6.

Strategy Lesson 2

How Character Affects Plot

If . . . Then . . .

Take a Close Look!

Is the runner in this picture

- **confident or fearful?**
- **strong or weak?**

The outcome of this runner's leap depends on how you interpret the drawing. Without any information about the character, it's hard to know what he is going to do. In the same way, knowing something about a character helps you understand the development of a story's plot and the resolution of the conflict.

Remember

Plot is the series of related events that make up a story.

Conflicts are the problems faced by the characters.

The **resolution** is the final part of the story, in which the conflicts are resolved and the story ends.

Characters are the people or animals that are the actors in the plot.

Reading Standard 3.2
Analyze the effect of the qualities of the character (for example, courage or cowardice, ambition or laziness) on the plot and the resolution of the conflict.

If . . . Then . . .

It's not difficult to identify the characters in a story or describe the events of the plot, but sometimes it's hard to explain how a character's qualities affect the outcome of the plot. To do this, use the **If . . . Then . . .** strategy.

If . . . Then . . . at Work: "Three Little Pigs"

If Pig Number Three is smart and hardworking, *then* he'll live in a brick house, outwit the wolf when the wolf comes knocking at his door, and live happily ever after. But *if* Pig Number Three is as careless and lazy as his brothers, *then* he'll live in a house made of flimsy materials, be outwitted by the wolf, and find himself the wolf's next meal.

After you read "Ta-Na-E-Ka" (page 55), think about the main character, Mary. Look at the list of character traits on the right, and find the four qualities that best describe Mary.

Then, think about how the story would be different if Mary had the opposite qualities. How would the plot be different? How would the conflict be resolved? How would the story end?

Set up your exercise like this:

If	Then
Mary had been . . .	[this would probably have happened.]

Sometimes characters surprise us. A weak character who is put to the test becomes extraordinarily brave. An honest character who faces a difficult situation cheats. That is one of the joys of reading: In a well-written story, people can surprise us—just as they do in real life.

The "If" column of the chart below presents three versions of a character named Sam. In the "Then" column, write a few lines describing what would happen if each "Sam" were faced with the following situation:

Sam has just found a wallet with two hundred dollars inside. There is no identification in the wallet. What will Sam do?

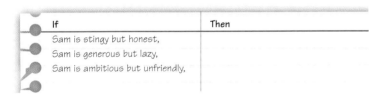

If	Then
Sam is stingy but honest,	
Sam is generous but lazy,	
Sam is ambitious but unfriendly,	

Character Traits

bold/shy
brave/cowardly
careful/careless
eager/reluctant
expert/unskilled
fair/unfair
faithful/disloyal
friendly/unfriendly
gentle/fierce
genuine/fake
happy/sad
hardworking/lazy
honest/sneaky
kind/cruel
obedient/disobedient
patient/impatient
powerful/weak
reliable/unreliable
respectful/rude
wise/foolish

Reading Matters

How Character Affects Plot   **475**

Reading Strategies

Use this strategy with the stories in Chapter 3, where students identify how theme is revealed through characters, actions, and images. be sure that students think about how their most important word relates to each of these story elements. You will be surprised at how quickly they make the connections.

Strategy Lesson 3

Identifying Theme

Most Important Word

If finding the **theme** of a story or novel is as difficult for you as finding a needle in a haystack, read on!

Theme Isn't Topic or Plot

Theme—what a story reveals about life—emerges as you read the story or novel. Don't confuse theme with topic or plot.

- The **topic** of the poem "Casey at the Bat" is a baseball game.

- The **plot** involves a mighty baseball player who tries to save a game but instead strikes out.

- Some might say the **theme** shows us that in life many things are uncertain; others might say the theme shows us that even the mightiest sometimes meet with failure.

In other words, the same story or novel might reveal different themes to different people.

Most Important Word

To find the theme of a piece of literature, try a strategy called **Most Important Word.** Ask yourself what the most important word in a story is, and *why* that word is so important. Thinking about these questions will help you focus on the theme of the work. After you decide on the word, consider how it relates to the setting, characters, plot, and conflict of the story.

Reading Standard 3.6 Identify and analyze features of themes conveyed through characters, actions, and images.

Most Important Word

How does this word relate to the **setting**?

How does this word relate to the **characters**?

How does this word relate to the **plot**?

How does this word relate to the **conflict**?

After reading "The All-American Slurp" (page 119), one student stated the theme as "Embarrassing things sometimes happen to all people." She decided that that was the theme after choosing *embarrassed* as the most important word and thinking about how the idea of being embarrassed related to the characters, plot, setting, and conflict of the story.

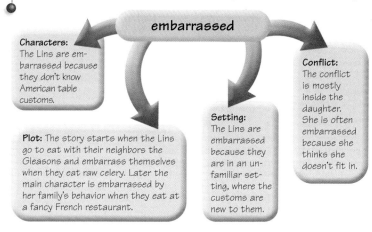

embarrassed

Characters: The Lins are embarrassed because they don't know American table customs.

Plot: The story starts when the Lins go to eat with their neighbors the Gleasons and embarrass themselves when they eat raw celery. Later the main character is embarrassed by her family's behavior when they eat at a fancy French restaurant.

Setting: The Lins are embarrassed because they are in an unfamiliar setting, where the customs are new to them.

Conflict: The conflict is mostly inside the daughter. She is often embarrassed because she thinks she doesn't fit in.

How would the information in these boxes change if you thought the most important word in "The All-American Slurp" was *family* or *American* or even *slurp*?

After you read "The Emperor's New Clothes" (page 137), choose the most important word from the three listed just below (or choose a word of your own). Then, complete the chart. Use the information in the chart to figure out the story's theme. (You can usually state a story's theme in one sentence.)

innocent
foolish
insecure

Most Important Word

| Character | Setting | Plot | Conflict |

Reading Matters

Looking at Text Structures

Reading Strategies

Use this strategy with the informational texts in Chapter 4, where students identify techniques of comparison and contrast. See "Separate But Equal" and Goodbye Records, Hello CDs." You could also refer students to this lesson when they are assigned to write their own comparison-contrast essay (see pp. 237 and 660–664).

> **Study these two pictures. Find at least five ways in which the two pictures differ. Then, with a partner, compare your findings.**

Think about how you went about comparing those two pictures. You probably compared part of one picture with a similar part in the other picture. In this way, you found contrasts between the two pictures.

You can do something similar when you read a text. You can compare characters, ideas, settings, and events by looking at one part of a text and comparing it with another part. Sometimes writers help us by using a text structure called **comparison and contrast.**

Comparison and Contrast

When writers point out ways in which things are alike, they are making a **comparison.** When they point out ways in which things are different, they are making a **contrast.** Here are some words and phrases that signal comparisons and contrasts:

Grade 4 Review Reading Standard 2.1 Identify structural patterns found in informational text (for example, cause and effect).

Grade 5 Review Reading Standard 2.2 Analyze text that is organized in sequential or chronological order.

Reading Standard 2.2 Analyze text that uses the compare-and-contrast organizational pattern.

Comparison:	Contrast:
additionally, also, by the same token, equally, in the same manner, just as, like, likewise, similarly, too	although, but, by contrast, different from, however, in spite of, nevertheless, on the contrary, on the other hand, though, unlike, yet

Writers of informational texts often use comparison and contrast. Such texts might be organized by the **point-by-point method** or by the **block method.** You'll find models of these organizational structures on page 203.

Sequencing and Chronological Order

Writers use a **sequence structure** when the order of events is important. *Sequence* refers to the order in which events occur. **Chronological order,** the time order in which events occur, is one kind of sequence structure.

Which of these would you write using a sequence structure?

1. a description of what you did at school yesterday

2. an essay explaining why you believe the age for getting a driver's license should be lowered or raised

3. instructions for dealing with a flash fire in your area

4. instructions for making pizza at home

If you aren't sure which of these require a sequence structure, try discussing each topic without using words like *first, second, third, next, later, after, then,* and *finally.* If you find that you don't need these words, the sequence, or order of events, probably isn't important.

Informational texts in which sequencing is often used include science articles, history texts, and instruction manuals.

Cause and Effect

Another text structure writers use is called **cause and effect.** This structure is often used in informational texts, such as social studies books, which focus on the causes and effects of wars or discoveries or political movements. The following sentences illustrate the cause-and-effect structure:

1. Because the temperature fell below thirty-two degrees, the water froze.

2. Jonas stopped smiling when he got braces on his teeth.

3. The dinosaurs were wiped out when a huge meteorite smashed into the earth.

4. The wind from the volcanic eruption carried rocks that flattened whole forests of 180-foot trees.

Here's how that information might be presented in a cause-and-effect chart:

Cause	Effect
Temperature fell below thirty-two degrees.	The water froze.
Jonas got braces.	Jonas stopped smiling.
Meteorite smashed into the earth.	Dinosaurs disappeared.
Wind carried rocks as big as cars.	Rocks flattened forests.

Looking at Text Structures   **479**

When you read a text that discusses cause and effect, keep track of **causal relationships** (causes and effects) by making a chart like the one on page 479. As you read, ask yourself what caused various outcomes. Give it a try with this passage. (Hint: Two of the sentences don't contain a causal relationship.)

(1) In 1803, the United States bought the Louisiana Territory from the French dictator Napoleon. (2) Settlers moved into the Louisiana Territory, forcing American Indians off the land. (3) The Indians responded by fighting for what they believed was theirs. (4) Most settlers saw no need to ask the Indians to share the land or sell the land to them.

PRACTICE

What text structure (**comparison and contrast, sequencing, or cause and effect**) is used in each of the following sentences?

1. Blood that travels to the heart through veins carries carbon dioxide; blood that travels from the heart through arteries carries oxygen.

2. After blood passes through the lungs, it returns to the heart through the pulmonary veins.

3. If the heart's mitral valve is blocked, blood can't flow from the upper left chamber of the heart to the lower left chamber. If it can't flow to that chamber, it can't get to the aorta, and problems arise.

4. The heart moves blood through the circulatory system the way a tire pump forces air through a hose.

5. Exercise helps strengthen the heart.

6. People who eat right and exercise help their hearts stay healthy; people who eat a lot of fatty foods and get little exercise generally have less healthy hearts.

Finding the Main Idea

Using a Little TLC

Reading Strategies
Use this strategy with the informational texts in Chapter 5, where students must identify main ideas. Finding the main idea is one of the most common questions on reading tests.

Look at the "text" below. Then, answer these questions:

XXXXXXXXX

xxxxxx

xx xxxxx xxxxx xx xxxx xxx xxxx xxx **1)** xxxxx xx xxxxxxx xx xx **2)** xxxx xxxxx xxxxx xxxxxxx xx xxxxxxxx xxxx xxxxx xxxx

xxxxxx

xxxxxx xxxxx xxxxxx xxxxxx xxx xxxxx xxxx xxxx xxxxxxx xxxx x xxx **xxxxxx** xxxxx xxx xxx xxxxxxx xxxxxx xxxxx xxxxxx xxxxx xxx xxxxx xxxxx xxxxx xxxx xxx xxx xxxxxxxx xxxxx xxxxx xxxxx xxxxx xxxxx xxxxx xxxx xx xxxx xxxx x xxxx xxx.

1. Is the "text" fiction or nonfiction?

2. Does it have a title?

3. How many topics does it cover? At which point does the topic change?

4. What do the numbers in the first paragraph indicate?

5. Why is one of the "words" in the second paragraph set in boldface?

Now, look at the "text" again. Even though you can't read it, you can still figure out a number of things about it. You may have guessed that it is nonfiction (fiction doesn't usually include numbered lists, as this text does). You may have noticed that it deals with two topics and that the first paragraph includes a list of two items. You may have spotted a boldface term in the second paragraph (another feature rarely seen in fiction). That's a lot to learn from a "text" that's made up of *X*'s!

Previewing the Text

Experienced readers can get information from a text even before they begin to read it. For instance, when you pick up a novel, you know you'll be reading a story that has characters trying to resolve a conflict. When you pick up an informational text—like a textbook, a magazine, or a computer manual—you know you'll be looking at topics and main ideas.

Reading Standard 2.3 Connect and clarify main ideas by identifying their relationships to other sources and related topics.

Cracking the Code

Identifying the characters in a novel or story is easy—they're the people taking part in the action. Identifying the main idea in an informational text can be a bit trickier.

Finding the Main Idea **481**

Tips for Finding the Main Idea

Here are some tips to keep in mind as you look for the main idea in an informational text:

1. Remember that the topic and the main idea are not the same. The **topic** is what the text is all about. The **main idea** is the most important thing said about that topic.

2. Remember that writers sometimes state the main idea directly, often near the beginning or the end of the text.

3. Keep in mind that if the main idea isn't stated directly, you must **infer** it from the information in the text. As you read, ask yourself, "What's the most important point being made about the topic of this text?"

4. Try using a little **TLC.** *TLC* in another context means "tender loving care." Here it means find the **T**opic; **L**ook for the *least* important sentences, and set them aside; **C**onnect the other ideas to the topic to come up with the main idea.

PRACTICE

Read the following paragraph. Identify the topic; then, use the **TLC strategy** to identify the main idea. The questions below will help you apply the strategy.

> Most texts do not state the main idea directly. It's up to you to figure out the main idea yourself. As you read a text, think about its topic. Then, decide which details of this topic are the most important. Once you've done that, ask yourself, "What do these details say about the topic?" Using this method will help you find the main idea of the text.

1. What is the topic of this paragraph?

2. Which sentence or sentences are the *least* important in explaining that topic?

3. Which sentence or sentences are the *most* important in explaining that topic?

4. Restate the most important sentences in your own words to come up with the main idea.

Find the Topic. → Look for the least important sentences, and set them aside. → Connect the other ideas in the remaining sentences to the topic.

Shades of Meaning

Becoming Word-Wise

Reading Strategies

Use this key strategy with the informational text in Chapter 6 called "Getting Leftovers Back on the Table" and with the story "Eleven." This strategy could also be used with the poems in Chapter 7.

Your best friend whispers to you, "That is the coolest thing, don't you think?" Later, another friend says, "Did you hear what she said to him? That was so cold." When you're angry about something, another friend tells you, "Chill."

Cool, cold, chill—three words that are usually weather related but in these conversations are not. Words often mean different things in different contexts. Using the right word at the right time is important if you want to make a point. If you don't believe that, the next time you want to say, "That is so cool," instead say, "That is so chill!" You'll get a strange look and a quick lesson on the importance of using the right word at the right time.

OK . . .

• Your mom says, "How was your day?" You say, "OK."

• A teacher asks, "How'd you do on the test?" You answer, "OK."

• Your friend says, "You wanna go to the mall?" You say, "OK!"

1. In which situation do you think *OK* really means "great"?

2. What might it mean in the other situations?

3. Why do people use a word like *OK* in situations in which they don't really mean *OK*?

Your answer to the third question may have been that it's simply easier to say "OK." Using the same word over and over takes very little effort. But using the right word can help you communicate your thoughts clearly.

Reading Standard 1.5 Understand and explain shades of meaning in related words (for example, *softly* and *quietly*).

Shades of Meaning **483**

Get Specific

Read these two sentences, and discuss the differences between them:

- Ben walked quietly down the hallway.

- Ben walked softly down the hallway.

Even though both sentences tell you that Ben isn't making much noise as he walks down the hallway, there is a difference. The first sentence suggests that Ben is walking quietly by simply not talking. The second sentence creates a picture of Ben carefully placing one foot in front of the other so that he makes as little noise as possible. *Quietly* and *softly* are related—both have to do with noise level—but their meanings are slightly different.

Recognizing shades of difference between words helps you pick the right word when you're writing. It also helps you understand exactly what a writer means when you're reading.

PRACTICE 1

Read each of the following pairs of words. Then, ask yourself how the words in each pair are related and how they differ.

stop/pause	annoyed/angry	forgetful/neglectful
grimace/frown	shrink/shrivel	hot/scalding
sad/depressing	complex/hard	happy/overjoyed

Working with a partner, make a diagram for each pair to show how the words are both alike and different in meaning. Here is an example for *stop* and *pause:*

Read each of the following sentences. Choose a word from the underlined pair to complete each sentence. Be prepared to explain why you chose that word. (You may find that in some sentences either word could be used, depending on what is meant.)

1. After the rain stopped, we suddenly/quickly ran to the car.

2. The grimace/frown on her face told me that she was not only disappointed but also in pain.

3. My watch stopped/paused after it fell into the bathtub.

4. The mechanism of the watch, with all its tiny moving parts, was very hard/complex.

5. After sitting in the hot sun for a week, the plums looked as shriveled/shrunken as raisins.

6. When he took the shirt out of the dryer, Jay saw that it had shriveled/shrunk.

Becoming Word-Wise

You can increase your word-wisdom by remembering **FDR**—not President Franklin Delano Roosevelt, but the other FDR: **F**ocus, **D**ouble-check, **R**e-read!

FDR

Focus on the verbs you use in your writing. Don't write *said* if you mean *shouted*. Don't write *ran* if *skipped* is more accurate.

Double-check your adjectives and adverbs in a thesaurus to be sure you're using the most accurate descriptive words.

Re-read texts to find words that stand out. Ask yourself why the writers chose those words. Your word-wisdom will increase as you think about writers' word choices.

Shades of Meaning   **485**

Faulty Reasoning

Bandwagon Appeal

Have you ever used one of these arguments in hopes of getting your way?

- "But everybody else is going."
- "Everyone has one but me."
- "Nobody else has to do that."

You may have gotten a response like "Well, you aren't everyone" or "If everybody jumped off a bridge, would you jump too?" or "Just who is everybody?" If you were asked to name "everybody," you may have realized that you had only five or six names—or even fewer. Your argument—the "everyone else is doing it" argument—suddenly fell apart, revealed as what it really is: an argument with no valid support.

This argument, called the **bandwagon appeal,** is a type of faulty reasoning. Card stacking, testimonial, and faulty generalization are three others.

Card Stacking

This kind of argument presents only one side of an issue, leaving out any information favorable to the other side. Here is an illustration of card stacking: A student tries to explain a bad grade to her parents by claiming that the teacher is too tough, the test covered too much material, and everyone in the class did poorly. She doesn't mention that she skipped the teacher's after-school review sessions, waited until the night before the test to study, and didn't keep up with the homework. Another example is an advertisement stating, "Summit Outerwear's double-stitched seams, titanium zippers and snaps, and breathable nylon-composite shell offer comfort and protection. Try finding these features in our competitors' products; you'll be looking for a long time." (What desirable features of the competition *aren't* we told about?)

Reading Standard 2.8
Note instances of unsupported inferences, fallacious reasoning, persuasion, and propaganda in text.

Testimonial

When advertisers use a testimonial, they try to persuade you to do something by using a respected or popular person to endorse their message. They might pay a famous athlete a lot of money to say something nice about their product. A testimonial might proclaim, "Golf great Don Kelley wears these running shoes. Shouldn't you?" or "You may know me as the commander of the space shuttle, but on weekends you'll find me at the wheel of the Gopher 200 riding mower. Great for doing the big jobs right here on earth." Endorsement by a famous person doesn't mean that a product is right for you.

Faulty Generalization

Faulty generalizations are false or unsound, or do not apply in all cases. A person who says, "Since all teenagers are careless drivers, the driving age should be raised to twenty-one" is using a faulty generalization. Every teenager is *not* a careless driver.

PRACTICE

Choose one of the five scenarios listed below. Prepare an argument, using one or more of the techniques discussed above. Then, exchange responses with a classmate, and see if you can spot the faulty reasoning in your partner's argument.

1. You need to explain why you didn't make the honor roll.

2. You want your parents to buy you an expensive new computer game.

3. You want your own phone and phone line.

4. You're trying to persuade your neighbors to buy candy you're selling for your school.

5. You want your parents to let you get an after-school job.

PEANUTS reprinted by permission of United Features Syndicate, Inc.

Faulty Reasoning **487**

This lesson does not relate specifi-cally to Chapter 8 in Part 1 but should be referred to frequently as you work with students' fluency and reading rates throughout the year. In each chapter of *Interactive Reading,* you will find passages of selections highlighted for students' fluency practice. Strategy Lesson 8 can be referred to as students practice reading to improve fluency and reading rates.

Strategy Lesson 8

Improving Fluency and Reading Rate

Did you know that people sometimes get tickets for driving too *slowly*?

It's also possible to read too slowly. If people read too quickly, they may miss important informa-tion; if they read too slowly, they may have trouble making sense of what they're reading.

How Can I Improve?

Reading fluency (how easily and well you read) and **reading rate** (how fast you read) are related. If you are a fluent reader, you

- read with expression
- know when to pause
- read by phrases or thought groups instead of word by word
- know when you don't under-stand what you've read
- know how to adjust your rate to what you are reading

If you think you need to improve your fluency, practice reading aloud, either alone (use a tape recorder so that you can lis-ten to yourself) or with a buddy.

Choose a passage or para-graph that's 150–200 words long. Read it to yourself silently a few times; then, read it aloud. Afterward, fill out the checklist above.

Keep practicing; you'll soon see that your score is going down—which means that your fluency is going up.

| Name _____ |
| Date _____ |
| Listener's Name _____ |

Oral Fluency	Often	Some-times	Never
	5 points	3 points	0 points
Reads word by word			
Stops and starts			
Re-reads words or sentences			
Ignores			
• periods			
• commas			
• question marks			
• quotation marks			
Reads too fast			
Reads too slow			
Slurs words			
Reads too loudly			
Reads too softly			
Guesses at pronunciations			
Seems nervous			
Loses place in text			

Final Score: _____

Reading Standard 1.1
Read aloud narrative and expository text fluently and accurately and with appropriate pacing, intonation, and expression.

What's My Reading Rate?

If fluency is tied to reading rate, then what rate is right? Remember that different rates are right for different kinds of texts. You might zip through a comic book, but you need to move more slowly through your social studies textbook. In other words, your reading rate depends on what you're reading and why you're reading it.

If you think you read too slowly all the time, you can improve your reading rate. Follow these steps:

1. Choose something you want to read. (Don't choose something that's too easy.)
2. Ask a friend to time you as you read aloud for one minute.
3. Count the words you read in that one minute.
4. Repeat this process two more times, with different passages.
5. Add the three numbers, and divide the total by three.

That number is your oral reading rate.

The chart at the right shows average reading rates for students in grades 3–6.

If you think your rate is too low, practice reading aloud every week or so, having someone time you as you read for one minute. Use the *same* passages to practice fluency. Use *new* passages to check your reading rate.

Grade Level	Average Words per Minute
3	110
4	140
5	160
6	180

Don't Forget . . .

If you don't understand what you read, you aren't reading fluently. As you read, keep asking yourself if what you're reading makes sense. If you get confused at any point, stop and re-read. From time to time, pause and think about what you've read. Sum up the main events or ideas. Be sure you understand what causes events to happen. Compare what actually happens with what you expected. If you still don't understand what you're reading, try reading more slowly.

Improving Fluency and Reading Rate 489

Reading Matters

Reteaching Lessons

Plot

Objective: To understand plot as the pattern of related events in a story.

Direct Teaching: Use the following information to introduce the lesson to students:

A plot is the pattern of events in a story. Every plot involves characters in conflict—struggling with some problem. The climax of a story comes when the struggle reaches the most exciting point. The problem may or may not be solved; either way the story ends with a resolution, winding things up and showing how events turn out.

Guided Practice: Plot chain. Have students re-read the first pages of "Ta-Na-E-Ka" (p. 55). Remind students of Mary's main conflict, or problem: She doesn't want to go through the ritual survival ordeal, but her family wants her to. Explain that in the first part of the story, she struggles with the problem of how to avoid the ordeal. This struggle is like a miniplot. Then, draw the following plot chain on the chalkboard:

Have volunteers complete this chain by listing what else Mary does to make it possible to spend her Ta-Na-E-Ka at Ernie's cafe. Tell students to add more event boxes and a climax box. Be sure that they list only events relating to the stated problem: Mary's scheme for avoiding the survival ordeal.

Independent Practice: Plot chain. Assign students to fill in another chain based on Mary's second problem: facing her grandfather and other family members when she returns home. Tell students to make as many boxes as necessary. Have students use time-order words, such as *first, next, then,* and *after,* to mark transitions between events. When students bring their completed graphics to class, have them put the two chains together to reveal the entire plot of the story.

[Possible answer:
Conflict—First, Mary walks home, feeling nervous about facing her family.
Event—Then, her family welcomes her, and she sees Roger exhausted and moaning.
Event—Soon her family notices what good shape she is in, and her grandfather asks how she stayed so well fed.
Event—She tells the truth, daring to add that she doubts Grandfather ever tasted the bitter berries they were supposed to live on.
Climax—Grandfather laughs and admits she's right.
Resolution—Roger says Mary is smart. Grandfather scolds her for not following tradition but says he thinks she is wiser than he about surviving "in a world that wasn't made for Indians."]

Characterization

Objective: To understand characterization as the way a writer reveals traits of characters.

Direct Teaching: Introduce the lesson to the students with the following information:

A story's characters are the actors in the story. The way a writer describes a character is called characterization. Writers may describe characters directly, by stating how the character looks and what the character's traits are (selfish, generous, heroic, and so on). Writers most often present characters indirectly, by telling us how the character behaves and what the character says and thinks. The writer also shows us how the character affects other people.

Guided Practice: Character chart. Have students read Avi's story "What Do Fish Have to Do with Anything?" (p. 348). Explain that Avi, like most writers, uses indirect characterization to help us understand Mrs. Markham and her son. Put the following character chart on the chalkboard. Point out that two character traits are supported by details from the story. Have students find passages that support the other character traits.

Character: Mrs. Markham

Trait	Characterization
concerned and caring toward son	Indirect: every day waits for her son to come out of school
	Indirect: says, "Parents need to protect their children."
not very caring toward beggar	Indirect: tells her son not to look at beggar
a little stingy	
uptight, not generous	
concerned about appearance	
concerned about money	
hardworking	

[Possible answers:
• *a little stingy.* Characterization—Indirect: carefully cuts cake.
• *uptight, not generous.* Characterization—Indirect: doesn't like Willie's questions, makes Willie repeat phone numbers.
• *concerned about appearance.* Characterization—Indirect: doesn't want Willie to look at beggar.
• *concerned about money.* Characterization—Indirect: wants Willie to be a scientist because "It pays well."
• *hardworking.* Characterization—Indirect: works nights.]

Independent Practice: Character chart. Have students create a second chart for Willie. They should list at least four of Willie's character traits, such as *curious* and *kind,* and cite passages from the story that reveal those traits. When students have completed their charts, have them use both charts to compare the characters of mother and son.

[Possible answers:
Character: Willie
• *curious.* Characterization—Indirect: asks a lot of questions about beggar.
• *kind.* Characterization—Indirect: wants mother to give beggar money.
• *worries about things.* Characterization— Indirect: wants to know why beggar is unhappy; wants to make his mother happy; asks if his dad is unhappy.
• *generous.* Characterization—Indirect: gives beggar a nickel.
• *imaginative.* Characterization—Indirect: Mother says, "Willie, you have too much imagination."
• *stands up for what is right.* Characterization— talks to the man and gives him cake even though his mother forbids it.]

Reading Standard 1.2
Identify and interpret figurative language and words with multiple meanings.

Figurative Language

Objective: To identify and interpret figurative language and words with multiple meanings.

Direct Teaching: Share the following thoughts with students:

> One of the amazing things about words is that their meanings change and grow as people use words in different ways. Before 1950, for example, the word *cool* just meant "something cold; the opposite of warm." Then, when jazz musicians and beatniks started using *cool* as a slang term meaning "great" or "interesting," the dictionary definition expanded to include that use of the word.
>
> One of the ways in which language often changes is through the use of figurative language, or figures of speech. *Figurative language* is language that describes one thing in terms of something else, although the description is not literally true. When your friend says, "Hey, that shirt is cool," she doesn't mean that your shirt has a low temperature. Instead, she is comparing the stylishness of your shirt with the hip but aloof style of a well-dressed model.
>
> There are many different kinds of figurative language. Two of the most common kinds are similes and metaphors. A *simile* compares two unlike things by using a word such as *like, as, than,* or *resembles*. If I say that the clouds are *like* cotton candy, I have captured the fluffiness of the clouds with a simile that compares it to the fluffiness of cotton candy. A *metaphor* compares one thing to something different by saying that it *is* that other thing. For instance, if I say that the homework assignment *is* a piece of cake, I am using a metaphor to compare the ease and fun of completing the assignment to the ease and fun of eating cake. An *implied metaphor* is a comparison between two unlike things that suggests that one thing is another. For example, if I say that someone *wormed* his way into my class, I am implying a comparison between his or her actions and the wriggling movement of a worm.

Guided Practice: Figurative-language football. Have students review the story "Just Once" (p. 7). Explain that even this straightforward story about a football game is full of figurative language, especially metaphors and similes. Divide the class into two teams. Have one team make the "kickoff" by reading one of the following passages from the story aloud. Ask the other team to identify the kinds of figurative language being used in the passage and to interpret what two things are being compared. If the team answers correctly, they may search through the story for another example of the same use of figurative language. If they find another example, they score a touchdown. If they can't find another correct example in two minutes, the other team gets to receive the kickoff.

- "For sure, the Moose was not the first interior lineman in the history of football, or even the history of Bedford City High, who banged heads up front and wore bruises like badges of honor. . . ."
  [*Like badges of honor* is a simile that uses *like* to compare the linemen's pride in their bruises to the display of a medal or a badge of honor.]

- "And so these linemen, or most of them, go back to banging heads without saying the first word about the dream that flickered through their minds."
  [*The dream that flickered through their minds* contains an implied metaphor comparing the brief, fleeting hope of the linemen to the flickering of a candle's flame.]

- "When the Moose was called on to open a hole in the line for one of the Bears' runners, the hole more often than not resembled an open garage door."
  [*The hole more often than not resembled an open garage door* is a simile that uses *resembled* to compare the width of the hole the Moose's blocking creates on the field to the width of an open garage door.]

Figurative Language **489D**

Shades of Meaning

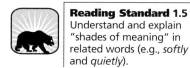

Reading Standard 1.5
Understand and explain "shades of meaning" in related words (e.g., *softly* and *quietly*).

> **Objective:** To understand and explain "shades of meaning" in related words (e.g., *softly* and *quietly*).

Direct Teaching: Share the following information with students:

> **What is the difference between a *plan* and a *scheme*? What is the difference between *caution* and *wariness*? Although dictionary definitions, or *denotations*, of the words in each pair are the same, each word suggests very different feelings and associations. The feelings and associations suggested by a word make up its *connotations*. When you read either fiction or nonfiction, you should be sensitive to connotations as well as denotations. Often connotations are the key to the writer's attitude toward the subject matter. Connotations may be positive or negative, active or passive, subjective or objective, and so on. They put a spin on words, giving them a "shade of meaning" that goes beyond their literal sense.**

Guided Practice: In-class activity. Have students review Gary Soto's poem "Ode to Mi Gato" (p. 391). Then, display the following altered lines from the poem. For each line, ask students to identify the word that has been changed and to write a precise statement that explains how the new word's connotations differ from the original word. Finally, ask students to write a statement that explores why Soto used the original word in question and how it contributes to the overall tone and meaning of the poem.

1. He's pale / As spilled milk

   [Possible answer: *Pale,* as opposed to *white,* has negative, unhealthy connotations and might suggest a cat that is more mysterious, difficult, or frightening than the speaker's cat. Soto probably chose *white* because it suggests the simple, clear, friendly character of the cat.]

2. Because I flaunted / A sock of chicken skin

3. With a meow / Like the oxidized latch / On a gate.

4. I poured milk / Into him, let him / Lick pieces of / Cheese from my palms

5. Until his purring / Engine switched on

6. And he squeezed / Up to my father's slippers.

7. This spring, / He's excellent at snoozing

8. And no good / At stalking.

9. All the other cats / In the neighborhood / Can see him sneak / Around the corner

10. Or jump from the tree / Like a slop of / Milk.

11. We lap up / His devotion and

12. He laps up his reception.

Reteaching the Standards

Reasonable Assertions

Reading Standard 2.7
Make reasonable asser-
tions about a text through
accurate, supporting
citations.

Objective: To make reasonable assertions about a text through accurate, supporting citations.

Direct Teaching: Share the following information with students:

> Being a good reader means more than just soaking up information like a sponge. Skillful readers analyze texts as they read; they determine what conclusions they can reasonably draw from the information presented, and they support these conclusions with specific evidence from the text. As a critical reader, you should always ask yourself, "What message is the author trying to communicate here? How does the author back up that message with logical arguments, facts, quotations, statistics, and other information?"

Guided Practice: In-class activity. Have students review the article "Go for Broke" (p. 88), taking turns reading each paragraph aloud. Then, have them find partners and complete the following activity. Display the following assertions regarding "Go for Broke," and have students copy them down. For each assertion, have students write (1) whether or not the assertion is reasonable, based on the information in the text, and (2) which details, facts, statistics, and other information in the text support the claim.

Assertions:

- The 442nd Regimental Combat Team was the most-decorated unit in military history.
  [Not reasonable; the article only says it was one of the most decorated in U.S. military history.]

- The Japanese American soldiers were more patriotic than most Americans.
  [Not reasonable; there is no mention of how patriotic most Americans were.]

- Out of the 4,500 soldiers in the 442nd, 3,900 earned decorations.
  [Not reasonable; many soldiers probably won more than one medal.]

- Adversity and persecution often make people strive harder to prove that they can succeed.
  [Reasonable; students might cite the unusual number of decorations the 442nd received, along with the suspicion, discrimination, and internment hardships that Japanese Americans faced during the war.]

- The Hawaiian and mainland soldiers didn't get along until they were held prisoner in an internment camp in Arkansas.
  [Not reasonable; simply false—they only visited the camp.]

- The members of the 442nd rejected the competitive principle of "each man for himself."
  [Reasonable; students might cite the group's decision to make sure all soldiers in the 442nd completed every assignment.]

- Frank Hachiya was glad that the war was being fought.
  [Not reasonable; Hachiya says only that he is grateful because the war made him appreciate life more.]

- The initial friction between the two groups of soldiers was a result of ignorance and prejudice.
  [Reasonable; students might point out the prejudice in dismissing anyone who doesn't speak perfect English and note the ignorance on the part of the Hawaiian soldiers about the hardships suffered by the mainland Japanese American families.]

Independent Practice: Generating reasonable assertions. When students finish, have the partners generate three more reasonable assertions about the article and support them with specific citations from the text. Then, have the students make three reasonable, supported assertions about another text you have read in the class. Have partners share their assertions with the rest of the class.

Reteaching the Standards

Reading Standard 3.1
Identify the forms of
fiction, and describe the
major characteristics of
each form.

Forms of Fiction

Objective: To identify the forms of fiction, and describe the major characteristics of each form.

Direct Teaching: Share the following thoughts with students:

> When people say something is "pure fiction," they usually mean that something is made up or not based on factual reality. Technically speaking, though, fiction today refers to two forms of prose writing—novels and short stories. While poems and plays often have made-up characters and events, they constitute different genres of literature in themselves. As an experienced reader, you should learn to recognize the characteristics of short stories and novels and to understand the powers and limitations of each form.

Guided Practice: Literary analysis charts. Display the following chart on the chalkboard, and have students copy it on a sheet of paper.

Form of Fiction: Short Story

Length: *ten to twenty book pages*

Plot Elements: *one or two conflicts*

Characters: *a few central characters*

Settings: *only a few different settings*

Objective: *to capture a particular moment or event in life*

Explain that the chart identifies the characteristics of a short story. To summarize, a short story is usually ten to twenty book pages long and is typically built around one or two main conflicts. A short story has only one or two main characters and a limited number of total characters. Also, it usually has only a few different settings because the author's objective is to capture one particular moment or event in life. Once you are sure students grasp these characteristics, have them copy and fill in the chart below for the novel.

Form of Fiction: Novel

Length:

Plot Elements:

Characters:

Settings:

Objective:

In what ways does a novel differ from a short story? Help students to understand that a novel usually stretches from one hundred to eight hundred book pages in length. It has more plot complications, more conflicts, and even subplots involving characters other than the hero. The novel often introduces multiple settings and explores broader themes. The objective of a novel is not to illuminate a single moment but to create a universe, capturing the entire life of a person, a town, or an era.

Independent Practice: Research and reading. As an ongoing homework assignment, have each student select a novel that interests him or her from the Read On feature at the end of each chapter in Part 1. After students read a novel, have them complete a chart for the work, filling in the various conflicts and subplots, the cast of characters, the multiple settings, and the broad objective of the author. Point out that this chart might fill a page or two.

Reteaching the Standards

Character and Plot

Reading Standard 3.2
Analyze the effect of the qualities of the character (e.g., courage or cowardice, ambition or laziness) on the plot and the resolution of the conflict.

Objective: To analyze the effect of the qualities of character (e.g., courage or cowardice, ambition or laziness) on the plot and the resolution of the conflict.

Direct Teaching: Share the following information with students:

After watching the latest Bruce Willis movie or reading a comic book, you might think that the conflicts in a story can be resolved only through physical action. The hero disconnects the villain's time bomb or wins the horse race or saves someone's life. In great literature (and in real life), however, the plot and the central conflict of a story are often resolved through the qualities of people's characters rather than a decisive punch or leap. In fact, the most crucial moments of growing up or achieving success or falling in love are those that reveal qualities of character. Literature helps us understand ourselves and our world by showing us how situations are resolved through the simple but powerful qualities that make us who we are.

Guided Practice: Character / Plot chart. Explain to students that they are about to read an early example of a story in which qualities of character are the decisive factors in the resolution of the plot. Then, have students take turns reading the myth "Baucis and Philemon" (p. 150) aloud. When students have finished, display the categories for the following chart, and have them copy it down on their own sheets of paper. Have students brainstorm a few items for each column and then complete the chart in small groups. Possible responses are provided in brackets.

Plot / Conflict	Character Qualities	Resolution
[The gods visit the world in disguise and become angry that people show so little kindness to strangers.]	[Baucis and Philemon are generous and self-sacrificing.]	[Impressed by Baucis and Philemon's noble characters, the gods reveal themselves and offer their hosts a reward.]
[Rich citizens with plenty to spare refuse to help the wandering gods.]	[Although poor, Baucis and Philemon show kindness without knowing they will get anything in return.]	
[Baucis and Philemon are content with their lives and can't think of what to ask of the gods.]		

Independent Practice: Character / Plot chart. Remind students that many familiar stories feature conflicts that are resolved through crucial qualities of character. Then, assign the following exercise as homework.

Step 1. Choose a classic fairy tale or myth that most people know well, such as "Goldilocks and the Three Bears," "Pinocchio," or "The Three Billy Goats Gruff," and jot down some notes summarizing the central conflict and how the plot is resolved.

Step 2. Take notes about the important qualities of the central characters in the story. Are they selfish or generous, honest or deceitful, careful or reckless? Support these qualities with details from the story.

Step 3. Decide which quality of character is most important in the story you have selected, the quality that determines how the story is resolved. Then, create a chart like the one above, with a title such as "Greed in Goldilocks and the Three Bears" or "Honesty in Pinocchio." Be sure the completed chart explains the role this quality plays in the story's plot.

Reading Standard 3.3
Analyze the influence of setting on the problem and its resolution.

Setting and Plot

Reteaching the Standards

> **Objective:** To analyze the influence of setting on the problem and its resolution.

Direct Teaching: Share the following thoughts with students:

> The setting of a story is more than just the time and place in which a story unfolds. Effective writers structure their narratives so that the setting influences the central problems in the story and often plays an important role in resolving them. By setting a scene in an ancient forest that is described as wild and wicked, a writer can highlight a violent conflict between two characters. By placing a character on a desert island, an author can set up a conflict between the character and nature or a conflict within the character between sanity and insane loneliness. As you read, watch for how setting can both symbolize and reinforce certain ideas in a story and also how it can play an active role in determining the story's outcome.

Guided Practice: Charting setting's influence. Have students form groups of four or five and read aloud the short story "All Summer in a Day" (p. 18). As students are reviewing the story, display on the chalkboard the following passage from the story's climax:

> They stood in the doorway of the underground for a moment until it was raining hard. Then they closed the door and heard the gigantic sound of the rain falling in tons and avalanches, everywhere and forever.
>
> "Will it be seven more years?"
>
> "Yes. Seven."
>
> Then one of them gave a little cry.
>
> "Margot!"
>
> "What?"
>
> "She's still in the closet where we locked her."
>
> "Margot."

> They stood as if someone had driven them, like so many stakes, into the floor. They looked at each other and then looked away. They glanced out at the world that was raining now and raining and raining steadily. They could not meet each other's glances. Their faces were solemn and pale. They looked at their hands and feet, their faces down.

Have the members of each group analyze the role of setting in this passage and how it contributes to the resolution of the central problems of the story. Have them create a chart like the one below, which traces the influence of setting on the problem. Remind students to state the central problem or conflict in a complete sentence and to use specific examples to show how setting influences it.

Central Problem / Conflict	Influence of Setting	Outcome
[Margot's memory of the sun and Earth make her different from the other children, and it leads them to exclude her, torment her, and lock her in a closet before the sun comes out.]	[The other children experience the joy of playing in the sun and the sorrow of watching it disappear for another seven years.]	[The children have a better understanding of what life on Venus is like for Margot; they feel ashamed of their mistreatment of her and let her out of the closet.]

Independent Practice: Charting setting's influence. Once students have completed their charts, have them choose another story from this textbook or from their own reading and chart the setting's influence on the conflict and the resolution. You might suggest that they look at stories in the adventure genre, in which setting often plays a big role in the conflict.

Tone and Meaning

Reading Standard 3.4
Define how tone or meaning is conveyed in poetry through word choice, figurative language, sentence structure, line length, punctuation, rhythm, repetition, and rhyme.

Objective: To define how tone or meaning is conveyed in poetry through word choice, figurative language, sentence structure, line length, punctuation, rhythm, repetition, and rhyme.

Direct Teaching: Share the following thoughts with students:

Unlike a news story or a grocery list, a poem doesn't use words just to provide information. Instead, a poem conveys meaning and tone by drawing attention to its original *use* of words and language. A poem forces us to look at more than just what the words say and to ask ourselves *why* the poet made particular choices about the language and structure of the poem. When you read a poem, consider the following questions:

- What feelings or ideas does the poet's choice of particular words convey?

- How do the images, metaphors, similes, and other figurative uses of language in the poem create a particular tone or suggest a particular meaning?

- How is this tone or meaning reinforced by the length of lines in the poem, by the punctuation, or by the repetition of certain words?

- Do the rhythm and the rhyme scheme of the poem convey a particular tone or produce meaningful sound effects?

Remember: A poem is a highly structured and compressed use of language that is rich in meaning. You shouldn't expect to grasp fully on your first reading all that a poem is saying. Instead, you should return to a poem again and again, deepening your understanding with new perspectives and new questions.

Guided Practice: In-class activity. Have students read aloud the haiku on p. 396. Remind students that haiku is one of the most condensed and tightly structured forms of poetry, but also one of the most powerful and full of feeling. The spare three lines of haiku suggest a layered web of meanings, scenes, images, and feelings. Have students study the haiku in pairs, discuss their reactions, and complete the following assignment.

Step 1. First, partners should construct a statement that they think captures either the meaning or the tone of the haiku. For instance, for the first haiku, beginning "An old silent pond . . . ," students might write:

> **Theme**—This haiku makes the reader appreciate how nature moves in circular patterns, shifting from peaceful calm to random interruptions, which are themselves swallowed up again by calm.

Step 2. Partners should then select three different features of the poem and explain how they effectively convey the meaning or tone the students identified in the statement they wrote for Step 1. Students may focus on word choice, figurative language, sentence structure, line length, punctuation, rhythm, repetition, or rhyme. For the first haiku, students might come up with the following answer:

a. **Punctuation**—The ellipses in the first line convey a sense of the ongoing peace of the "old silent pond." The exclamation point in the third line emphasizes the interruption of the quiet pond by the loud splash of the jumping frog. The period in the third line closes the poem, emphasizing nature's peaceful continuity that's reported in the two-word statement "Silence again."

b. **Repetition**—The repetition of "silent" in the first line and then "Silence" in the third line reinforces the sense that the pond has come full circle. The repetition of "pond" in the first and second lines builds a sense of calmness and continuity—which is ruptured by the "splash!" in the third line.

c. **Rhythm**—The rhythm of the haiku mimics the cycle of nature in the scene it describes. The steady, quiet beat of the syllables in the first two lines is interrupted by the one sharp syllable "splash!" which suggests a pause before the poem goes back to the steady rhythm of "Silence again."

Independent Practice: Creative rewriting. To help students further understand how tone and meaning are conveyed through the structure and style of a poem, have them complete the following assignment as homework. Have each student select one of the haiku on p. 396 and rewrite it by altering two elements of its structure and style so as to convey a different effect. For example, by altering word choice and punctuation in the first haiku, students might change the whole tone and meaning of the poem.

An ancient stagnant bog.

A creature lurches into the waters!

Burbling—swallowed by silence.

Have students share their creative rewriting with the class.

Speakers

Reading Standard 3.5
Identify the speaker, and recognize the difference between first- and third-person narration (e.g., autobiography compared with biography).

Objective: To identify the speaker, and recognize the difference between first- and third-person narration (e.g., autobiography compared with biography).

Direct Teaching: Introduce the lesson to the students with the following information:

The speaker in a narrative is your tour guide through the text. The speaker can take part in the action or float above it with a godlike viewpoint. A speaker can be opinionated and subjective about the characters and events or can take a neutral, objective, and distanced point of view. One important clue that will help you identify the speaker of a work is whether the speaker talks in the first person, using pronouns like *I, me,* and *mine,* or whether the speaker talks in the third person, referring only to *he, she, his,* and *its.* A first-person speaker is often a participant in the narrative, as in an autobiography, where a person writes about "my life." A third-person speaker more often offers an "invisible" point of view on the subject matter, as in a biography, where a writer tells the story of someone else's life but generally says little about himself or herself.

Guided Practice: Comparing and contrasting speakers. Write the following two passages on the board:

According to those who knew him, Lincoln was a man of many faces. In repose he often seemed sad and gloomy. But when he began to speak, his expression changed. "The dull, listless features dropped like a mask," said a Chicago newspaperman. "The eyes began to sparkle, the mouth to smile; the whole countenance was wreathed in animation, so that a stranger would have said, 'Why, this man, so angular and solemn a moment ago, is really handsome!'"

Bailey was the greatest person in my world. And the fact that he was my brother, my only brother, and I had no sisters to share him with, was such

good fortune that it made me want to live a Christian life just to show God that I was grateful. Where I was big, elbowy, and grating, he was small, graceful, and smooth. . . . He was lauded for his velvet-black skin. His hair fell down in black curls, and my head was covered with black steel wool. And yet he loved me.

Have a volunteer read the passages aloud. Then, have students discuss the speaker of each passage and determine whether each passage is told from a first- or third-person point of view. Have students write down three or four characteristics of each speaker. Is the speaker neutral and distanced or opinionated and involved in the narrative? Does the speaker remain "invisible" behind the subject matter, or does the speaker include a self-portrait in the narrative? Have volunteers share their conclusions. Then, ask students how they can tell that the first passage is in the third person. [The narrator is not in the story but stands above it, describing Lincoln and those around him from a distance and using only third-person pronouns like *he* and *his.*] Then, have students explain how they can tell that the second passage was in the first person. [The speaker uses first-person pronouns like *I* and *my* and has a subjective, active role in the story.] Have students take a guess about what form of literature each passage belongs to. [The first passage is an example of biography; the second is an example of autobiography.]

Independent Practice: Biography versus autobiography. As homework, have students select a biography and an autobiography from the library and analyze both kinds of speakers. Is the speaker in each book neutral and objective or biased and subjective? Is the speaker involved in the story or above it all?

Reading Standard 3.6
Identify and analyze features of themes conveyed through characters, actions, and images.

Theme

Reteaching the Standards

Objective: To identify and analyze features of themes conveyed through characters, actions, and images.

Direct Teaching: Share the following information with students:

> The theme of a story is its basic message or idea. Keep in mind, however, that most authors don't simply come out and *tell* their readers, "The theme of this work is . . . " Instead, they *show* the theme through the characters they create; through the actions these characters take; and through the images used to describe events, people, and places. As you read, you should be asking yourself questions like, "What does this character suggest about people in general?" "How might this character's actions represent something that most people do?" and "What broader idea might this image stand for or symbolize?" Questions like these will help you understand how an author uses a work to communicate a theme.

Guided Practice: Discussion. Have students re-read the story "Just Once" (p. 7). Then, write the following themes or messages on the chalkboard, and discuss whether or not they think any of these statements capture some of the themes of the story.

1. Beware of getting what you want.

2. It's sometimes best to quit while you are ahead.

3. If you keep pursuing your goals and don't get discouraged by what other people think, you can achieve almost anything.

Independent Practice: Writing about theme. After students discuss these statements as possible themes of the story, have them brainstorm ideas for two more possible themes in the story. Display these additional statements, and have students copy them down. Then, have students break into groups of two or three to discuss how these new themes are conveyed through the characters, actions, and images of the story. How do the actions of the Moose, his coach, and the cheering crowd help convey each of these messages? How do the vivid physical images of the football game express the new themes? Have students take notes on their group discussions and then write a paragraph explaining how one new theme is communicated through the characters, actions, and images of the story. Remind students to be specific and to cite page numbers to support their interpretations. Have students who wrote on the same theme compare their paragraphs.

Literary Devices

Reading Standard 3.7
Explain the effects of common literary devices (e.g., symbolism, imagery, metaphor) in a variety of fictional and nonfictional texts.

Objective: To explain the effects of common literary devices (e.g., imagery) in a variety of fictional and nonfictional texts.

Direct Teaching: Share the following with students:

Great literature doesn't just make us think—it can create a whole world of sights, sounds, smells, tastes, and sensations. Good writing will not only contain powerful ideas, but will also include *imagery,* language that appeals to the senses. Imagery can remind us how it feels to swim in the ocean, or it can make us hungry for chili. Most often an author will use imagery to paint a picture of a particular place or setting.

Guided Practice: Images. Have volunteers read aloud these excerpts from "All Summer in a Day" (p. 18) and "Solar System Bodies: Venus" (p. 38) to find four powerful images.

The children lay out, laughing, on the jungle mattress and heard it sigh and squeak under them, resilient and alive. They ran among the trees, they slipped and fell, they pushed each other, they played hide-and-seek and tag, but most of all they squinted at the sun until tears ran down their faces; they put their hands up to that yellowness and that amazing blueness and they breathed of the fresh, fresh air and listened and listened to the silence which suspended them in a blessed sea of no sound and no motion. They looked at everything and savored everything. Then, wildly, like animals escaped from their caves, they ran and ran in shouting circles. They ran for an hour and did not stop running.

Venus, second planet from the sun, has sometimes been called Earth's sister planet because the two are so similar in size and mass. But there the similarities end. Venus is covered by thick, rapidly spinning clouds that trap surface heat, creating a scorched greenhouselike world with temperatures hot enough to melt lead, and pressure so

intense that standing on Venus would feel like the pressure felt 900 m (3,000 ft.) deep in Earth's oceans. . . . Much of the surface is covered by vast lava flows. In the north, an elevated region named Ishtar Terra is a lava-filled basin larger than the continental United States. Near the equator, the Aphrodite Terra highlands, more than half the size of Africa, extend for almost 10,000 km (6,200 mi.). Volcanic flows have also produced long, sinuous channels extending for hundreds of miles.

Independent Practice: Cluster diagram. Ask students to create a cluster diagram for each image they noted above. Each diagram should include the image in the center and bubbles that identify the sense or senses (sight, sound, smell, taste, touch) that the image evokes. Explain that imagery has both an immediate effect on a reader and a broader effect on the passage in which it appears. For instance, an image of wheat fields "extending in all directions like an ocean" might remind a particular reader of her parents' farm and emphasize the isolation of the characters in the story. For each image that students noted, have them identify the personal effect the image had and the effect on the paragraph. Here is a model based on the Bradbury excerpt.

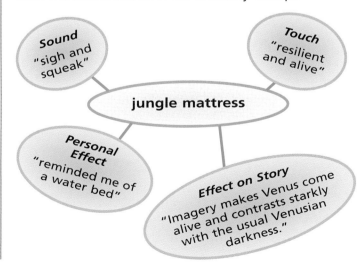

Reteaching the Standards

Critique of Credibility

Reading Standard 3.8
Critique the credibility of characterization and the degree to which a plot is contrived or realistic (e.g., compare use of fact and fantasy in historical fiction).

Objective: To critique the credibility of characterization and the degree to which a plot is contrived or realistic (e.g., compare use of fact and fantasy in historical fiction).

Reteaching the Standards

Direct Teaching: Introduce the lesson to students with the following information:

> Good readers are also critical readers. When you approach a literary text, you should ask yourself whether or not you find the characters and plot convincing and why. Does the author create vivid characters that are as complicated, startling, and moving as living, breathing human beings? Do they resemble cardboard cutouts, all-good or all-bad, with predictable emotions and characteristics? Does the plot reflect the intricate patterns of cause and effect and chance that shape events in the real world? Does the story's conflict have emotional power and depth? Does the plot surprise you with its twists and turns, or does it bore you with predictable problems and easy, convenient solutions? These are just some of the questions you should ask as a critical reader.

Guided Practice: Critical discussion. Review the plot of Gary Soto's story "La Bamba" (p. 194). Then, read aloud the following passage from the story:

> Manuel stood alone, trying hard to hold back the tears as Benny, center stage, played his trumpet. Manuel was jealous because he sounded great, then mad as he recalled that it was Benny's loud trumpet playing that made the forty-five record fly out of his hands. But when the entire cast lined up for a curtain call, Manuel received a burst of applause that was so loud it shook the walls of the cafeteria. Later, as he mingled with the kids and parents, everyone patted him on the shoulder and told him, "Way to go. You were really funny."
>
> Funny? Manuel thought. Did he do something funny?
>
> Funny. Crazy. Hilarious. These were the words people said to him. He was confused but beyond caring. All he knew was that people were paying attention to him, and his brother and sisters looked at him with a mixture of jealousy and awe. He was going to pull Mario aside and punch him in the arm for wearing his shirt, but he cooled it. He was enjoying the limelight. A teacher brought him cookies and punch, and the popular kids who had never before given him the time of day now clustered around him. Ricardo, the editor of the school bulletin, asked him how he made the needle stick.
>
> "It just happened," Manuel said, crunching on a star-shaped cookie.

Ask students to discuss how credible they find the characters and plot in this passage and the story as a whole. Do they find Manuel's quick shifts from tears to jealousy to anger to pride and happiness convincing? Do they believe that the popular kids would really be impressed by the talent-show performance, or does this seem like an easy way for Soto to provide a happy ending? Would the audience truly respond to Manuel's performance by shaking the walls of the cafeteria with their applause? Have students ever had a similar experience, in which an event they thought was a disaster (like the needle sticking on the record) turned into a triumph? Have they ever done something that they thought was embarrassing but that struck other people as entertaining or impressive? Have students formulate a critique of the story, using their answers to these questions as a starting point. Remind them that a critique doesn't have to be negative. It just needs to be a judgment about the story that is supported by information from the story, personal knowledge, and their own reasoning. Suggest that students fill in a chart like the one that follows to organize their critique.

| Information from story | + | Personal knowledge | + | My reasoning | = | My judgment |

Have students share their critiques with the rest of the class and discuss whether or not each critique is fair and logical. Remind students that a story doesn't have to be realistic to be convincing, but that if a story departs from reality, it should do so for a reason—for instance, to bring out an important meaning or truth.

Independent Practice: Class critiques. After students have presented their critiques orally, have them revise the critiques, drawing on their own work and the ideas presented to the class. Then, publish the evaluations in a class booklet titled *"La Bamba"—bueno o no?*

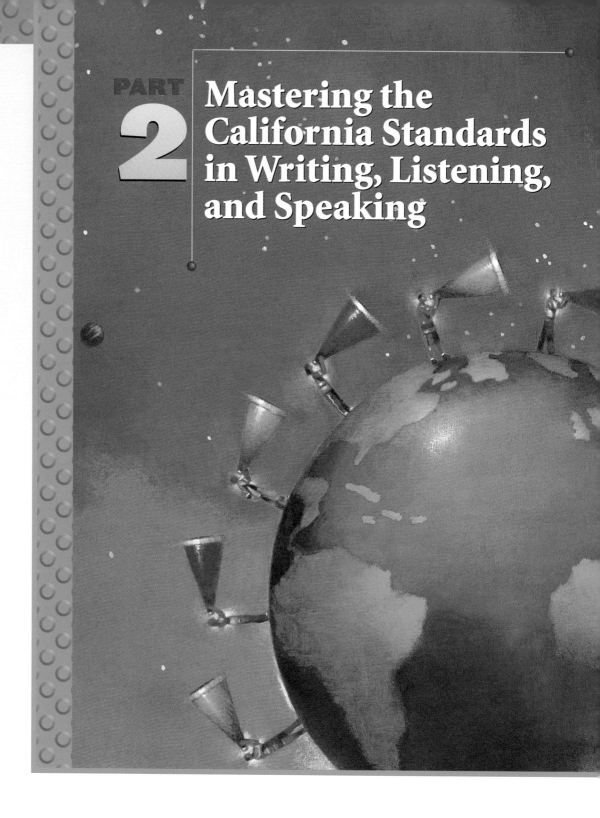

Mastering the California Standards in Writing, Listening, and Speaking

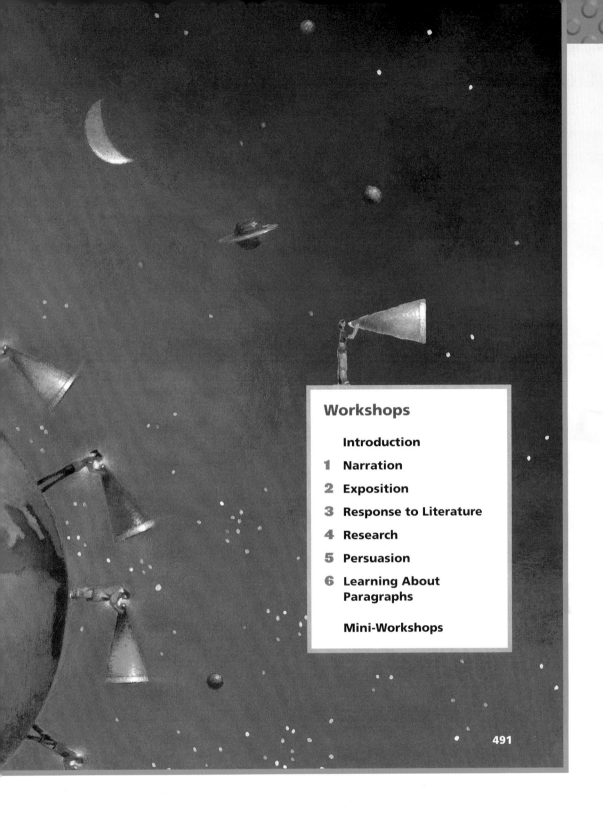

Workshops

491

Introduction The Writing Process

Program Organization

Holt Literature and Language Arts provides a complete curriculum for standards-based instruction in vocabulary, reading, literature, writing, speaking and listening, and media. The instructional content of the program is divided into quarters to enable teachers to anticipate and administer the quarterly assessments required by California.

Teaching the Introduction will acquaint students with some of the fundamental concepts of the writing process. It will provide a foundation for writing as students go through the other workshops.

Language Arts Content

This introduction uses the writing strategies to enable students to master successfully the writing application.

What standards are taught in the Introduction?

In the Introduction, students will master the following Grade 6 standards:

Writing Strategies

1.0 Students write clear, coherent, and focused essays. The writing exhibits students' awareness of the audience and purpose. Students progress through the stages of the writing process as needed.

1.1 Choose the form of writing (e.g., letter to the editor) that best suits the intended purpose.

1.5 Compose documents with appropriate formatting by using word-processing skills and principles of design (e.g., margins, spacing, columns).

Writing Application

2.0 Students write narrative, expository, persuasive, and descriptive texts of at least 500 to 700 words in each genre. Student writing demonstrates a command of standard American English and the organizational and drafting strategies outlined in Writing Standard 1.0

Instructional Planning and Support

Where do I locate lesson plans, additional resources, and other teaching aids?

- The Annotated Teacher's Edition and *On Course: Mapping Instruction* provide direction in planning and implementing a complete California standards–based curriculum. These components include instructions for administering diagnostic, progress, and summative tests; for presenting instruction of the standards; for differentiating instruction to provide universal access; and for locating and using the program's ancillaries.

- The program's resources are referenced at the beginning of each workshop in the bottom margin of this teacher's edition.

- Reminders for using additional resources appear in this teacher's edition at point of use.

- The *One-Stop Planner* CD-ROM contains editable lesson plans and all print ancillaries, available in PDF format.

Universal Access

How do I differentiate instruction to ensure that all my students master the standards?

Holt Literature and Language Arts provides comprehensive, differentiated instruction for all types of students.

- Most of the general instruction and teaching strategies in the Annotated Teacher's Edition are at grade level. These instructions will work well with the majority of your students.

- Advanced students have at least one activity for each workshop. The suggested activities are found in this teacher's edition at point of instruction.

- *Universal Access: Writing, Listening, & Speaking,* Introduction, opens with Teaching Notes that suggest which worksheets and transparencies are appropriate for each of three levels of learners.

- *Universal Access: Lesson Plans for Language Development,* Introduction, offers teaching strategies and additional worksheets designed specifically for English-language learners and special education students.

- *Daily Language Activities Transparencies* and *Spelling: Lessons & Activities* provide ongoing review of and additional practice in a range of language arts skills.

- For every workshop, preselected Web sites and activities are available to provide enrichment, independent practice, and enhanced instructional opportunities.

Introduction

STANDARDS FOCUS

Writing

Prerequisite Standard

Grade 5

■ 1.4 Create simple documents by using electronic media and employing organizational features (e.g., passwords, entry and pull-down menus, word searches, the thesaurus, spell checks).

Standard Coming Up in the Next Level

Grade 7

■ 1.6 Create documents by using word-processing skills and publishing programs; develop simple databases and spreadsheets to manage information and prepare reports.

WHAT'S AHEAD?

In this section you will learn how effective writers

■ identify a purpose and audience

■ choose an appropriate form

■ read professional models

■ create think sheets and summaries

■ format and proofread manuscripts

GO TO: go.hrw.com
KEYWORD: HLLA

Introduction

Writing is like mastering a sport or making a new friend—a **process** that passes through many stages before it is complete. This introduction will prepare you for the remaining workshops in this book by introducing you to the writing process. You will also practice these language arts standards.

California Standards

Writing

1.0 The writing exhibits students' awareness of the audience and purpose. Students progress through the stages of the writing process as needed.

1.1 Choose the form of writing (e.g., personal letter, letter to the editor, review, poem, report, narrative) that best suits the intended purpose.

1.5 Compose documents with appropriate formatting by using word-processing skills and principles of design (e.g., margins, spacing, page orientation).

2.0 Student writing demonstrates a command of standard American English.

The Writing Process

Last night you wrote a story in just half an hour. When your friends read it, though, they had trouble following the plot. Chances are, you did not give yourself enough time to make your ideas clear. Writing is a process made up of many steps, and each step takes time. The chart on the next page lists the steps of the writing process and strategies used to complete each step.

Writing 1.0 Students progress through the stages of the writing process as needed.

INTRODUCTION RESOURCES

California Standards and Correlations

■ *Writing, Listening, & Speaking*, pp. xiv–xvi (Shows this workbook's correlations to the CA standards)

Reinforcement

■ *Writing, Listening, & Speaking*, pp. xvii–xxv, TPs. 1–4

■ *Daily Language Activities*

Internet

■ go.hrw.com (keyword: HLLA)

UNDERSTANDING THE WRITING PROCESS

Steps	Strategies Used to Complete the Step
Prewriting	• Identify your **purpose** and **audience**. • Choose a topic and a **form** for your writing. • Read a **professional model** of your chosen form. • Draft a sentence that expresses your **main idea**. • **Gather information** about the topic. • Begin to **organize** the information.
Writing	• Draft an **introduction**. • Provide **background information**. • Follow a **plan** for putting your ideas in order. • State your **supporting points** and **elaborate** on them. • Wrap things up with a **conclusion**.
Revising	• **Evaluate** your draft or ask a **peer** to evaluate it. • **Revise** to improve content, organization, and style.
Publishing	• **Proofread** to find and correct spelling, punctuation, and grammar errors. • Use correct **manuscript style**. (See Tip.) • **Share** your finished writing with readers. • **Reflect** on your writing experience.

TIP Here are some basic **guidelines for manuscript style**.

- use only one side of the paper
- place the page so that it is taller than it is wide (unless you have a large graphic that will only fit if you turn the page sideways)
- double-space or skip lines
- leave a one-inch margin at the top, bottom, and sides of the paper
- number pages in the top, right-hand corner; do not number the first page

Choose a Form

Writers present their ideas in many different **forms**—such as poems, essays, or short stories. How does a writer choose a form?

Purpose and Audience Most of the time, your teacher will assign a form for your writing. **When you choose the form, however, make sure it fits your purpose and audience.**

◁ KEY CONCEPT

- **Purpose** Your general purpose will be to express yourself, to entertain, to explain, or to persuade. Chances are, though, you will also have a more specific purpose in mind—for example, to express the emotions you felt when you moved to another country. Identifying your specific purpose is the first key to selecting the right form. The chart on the next page shows which forms are commonly used for which purposes.

Writing 1.1 Choose the form of writing (e.g., personal letter, letter to the editor, review, poem, report, narrative) that best suits the intended purpose. 1.5 Compose documents with appropriate formatting by using word-processing skills and principles of design (e.g., margins, spacing, page orientation).

Choose a Form **493**

Standards Starter

Motivate. Ask students to think of something they do well, such as shoot a basketball, play guitar, or ride a skateboard. Have volunteers describe to the class all the steps that go into performing their activity. You may want to write the volunteers' comments on the chalkboard. After students have shared the secrets to their successes, point out to the class that writing is also an activity that requires carefully completing a number of steps.

TECHNOLOGY TIP

REVIEW STANDARD
The following suggestion is a review of the 5th-grade **Writing Standard 1.4.**

You may need to provide students with instruction on how to use a word-processing program with the writing process. Make sure students are familiar with creating new files to begin drafting, saving their work, and opening existing files. They may use pull-down menus, toolbar icons, or keyboard shortcuts to accomplish these tasks. The commands will vary according to the word-processing programs students use.

EXAMPLES OF WRITING FORMS BY PURPOSE

to express	to entertain	to inform or explain	to persuade
autobiography	autobiography	book review	advertisement
journal entry	humorous essay	business letter	business letter
poem	poem	comparison-contrast essay	editorial
narrative	play	how-to essay	letter to the editor
personal letter	short story	news story	persuasive essay
reflective essay	song	research or book report	political cartoon

■ **Audience** The form you choose will also depend on your audience. For instance, suppose you want to share your thoughts about a book you have read. If you have a close relationship with your audience, you can choose an informal form such as a personal letter. However, for an audience of readers you don't know well, you should choose a less personal form, such as a book report. Use the steps below to choose the best form for your writing.

THINKING IT THROUGH — Choosing a Form

▶ **STEP 1** Define your purpose. Ask yourself: *Why am I writing?*

I want to explain why a book that I like is so meaningful to me.

▶ **STEP 2** Define your audience. Ask yourself: *Who are my readers, and how well do I know them? How much does my audience already know about the topic? What background information will they need?*

My teacher and my classmates will be my audience. Because I don't know some classmates very well, I should choose a less personal form, such as a book report. They haven't all read the book so I will need to summarize it for them.

▶ **STEP 3** Choose the best form. (Look at the chart above.) Ask yourself: *What form will help me achieve my purpose with this audience?*

A book report will help me achieve my purpose. I can discuss the book using literary terms. I can also include my own thoughts and feelings about the book.

Writing 1.0 The writing exhibits students' awareness of the audience and purpose.

Choosing a Form

Offer students other ways to choose a form:

1. Explore a topic through freewriting.

   Tell students that freewriting can help them identify what they most want to say about a topic, which in turn can help them find the best way to say it.

2. Discuss the topic with a classmate or teacher.

   Tell students that a classmate or teacher might suggest a useful form that might not have occurred to them.

Use the steps in the Thinking It Through on page 494 to choose the form that you think best fits each of the following situations.

- You want to capture the feelings and sensations of your hike in the woods last fall.
- You want to explain to elementary school students what to expect on their first day of middle school.

Reading—Part of the Process

Once you have chosen a form for your writing, read a professional model of that form. For example, to write a book review, read at least one published book review. Reading professional models is especially helpful if you create *think sheets* or *summaries* of selections you read.

Create a Think Sheet   To organize your thoughts and deepen your understanding when reading a model, create a think sheet. A **think sheet** is a record of your questions and comments about a reading selection. Think sheets help you plan responses to selections you have read. They can also help you find writing topics and identify effective writing techniques.

HOW TO CREATE A THINK SHEET

1. Write the title and author of the selection at the top of a sheet of notebook paper. Then, draw a vertical line down the center of the sheet. Label the left-hand column "text" and the right-hand column "responses."

2. As you read the selection, in the left-hand column of your paper, note words or brief passages that catch your interest or seem important.

3. Next to each word or passage, jot down your response in the right-hand column. Responses may include notes on any of the following.
   - use of language
   - organization of information, such as comparison-contrast structure
   - strategies for developing ideas and elaborating, such as using stories

4. When you have finished reading, add to your response column any related ideas or answers you have found to earlier questions.

Reading—Part of the Process   **495**

Choose a Form   W1.1

Suggest these additional situations that students can use to practice selecting forms.

- You want to persuade people to buy the new product you have invented. [advertisement; business letter]
- You want to inform members of the community of a local event. [news story]
- You want to investigate your own ideas and feelings on becoming a teenager. [reflective essay; journal entry]
- You want to entertain someone with an account based on a funny experience you once had. [humorous essay; short story]

Guided and Independent Practice

Answers

Work through the first situation together with the class. Then, assign the remaining situations as independent practice. The following forms are possible answers for each situation.

- capturing feelings and sensations: *poem, journal entry, reflective essay*
- explaining: *comparison-contrast essay, news story*

Create a Think Sheet

A sample think sheet might look like the following.

Text	Responses

How to Create a Summary

Because summarizing is an important standard coming up in grade seven, you may want to begin preparing students to use this skill as part of the prewriting process. Tell students that summarizing is a skill that will help them focus on the organization and development of the models they read. Using a newspaper article, lead students through the steps to create a summary. Display a copy of the article on an overhead projector, or provide students with copies on which they can write. Perform each step and discuss it with students. Then, have students make suggestions as you create the summary from your section notes.

PRACTICE & APPLY 2

Guided and Independent Practice

Answer

After students have read the selection, work through step #2 together as a class. Then, have students complete the assignment as independent practice. The following paragraph is a sample summary of "A Glory over Everything."

One day in 1849, Harriet Tubman, a slave, met a white woman who told Harriet to come to her if Harriet ever needed help. When Harriet's sisters were sold, Harriet decided to escape north with her brothers, but her brothers were too frightened, and so Harriet had to escape alone. She went to the house of the white woman and was immediately started along the Underground Railroad, a loose-knit group of people who harbored and aided escaped slaves. With the help of these people, Harriet Tubman finally reached the free state of Pennsylvania, ninety miles from where she started.

TIP For an example of a **summary**, see page 86.

Write a Summary Summarizing uses your skills as both a reader and a writer. A **summary** is a shortened account of a reading selection. Writing a summary does more than help you understand the content of a selection. It also helps you see how a published author organized his or her ideas. In this way, summarizing others' writing can help you organize your own writing. For example, you might organize your ideas about a book in the same order used by the author of a published book review.

Quick guide

HOW TO CREATE A SUMMARY

1. First, read the selection carefully.

2. Then, skim the selection looking for sections. Sometimes, each section begins with a heading. If a selection has no headings, consider each paragraph a section. On a sheet of paper, list a phrase that identifies the general topic of each section.

3. Under each phrase listed on your paper, write in your own words a sentence identifying the most important ideas included in that section. Make note of the section's main idea and most important supporting points. These will be the points for which the writer provides the most evidence.

4. Combine your section summaries into a paragraph, linking the ideas with transitions. (For more on using transitions, see page 653.)

In your own writing process, remember to use reading selections as models to plan and write your drafts. Keep in mind these strategies for creating think sheets and summaries—you use these strategies in each of the Writing Workshops in this book.

PRACTICE & APPLY 2 **Create a Think Sheet and a Summary**

- First, read "A Glory over Everything," by Ann Petry, which can be found on pages 288–295.

- As you read, use the guidelines on page 495 to create a think sheet.

- Then, write a summary of the selection, using the steps in the chart above.

Using the Writing Process

The Writing Workshops and Writing Mini-Workshops in this book will walk you through the process of writing in a variety of forms. In the final stages of the process, follow the guidelines below to make sure that all your writing is free of common errors. The page numbers in the chart below refer to the *Holt Handbook*.

GUIDELINES FOR PROOFREADING

1. Is every sentence a complete sentence? (See pages 346–351.)

2. Does every sentence begin with a capital letter and end with the correct punctuation mark? (See pages 262–267.)

3. Do singular subjects have singular verbs? Do all plural subjects have plural verbs? (See pages 122–137.)

4. Are verb forms and tenses used correctly? (See pages 146–175.)

5. Are the forms of personal pronouns used correctly? (See pages 176–195.)

6. Are all words spelled correctly? (See pages 316–345.)

When you are editing and proofreading, indicate any changes by using the symbols in the chart below.

SYMBOLS FOR EDITING AND PROOFREADING

Symbol	Example	Meaning of Symbol
≡	I will see you on saturday morning.	Capitalize a lowercase letter.
/	My Dog's name is Spot.	Lowercase a capital letter.
∧	Do not walk away from me.	Insert a missing word, letter, or punctuation mark.
ℓ	After you go go home, give me a call.	Leave out a word, letter, or punctuation mark.
∩	peice	Change the order of letters.
¶	¶ The next day we woke up very early.	Begin a new paragraph.
⊙	Dr. Chavez	Add a period.

Writing 2.0 Student writing demonstrates a command of standard American English.

Workshop 1 Narration

Program Organization

Holt Literature and Language Arts provides a complete curriculum for standards-based instruction in vocabulary, reading, literature, writing, speaking and listening, and media. The instructional content of the program is divided into quarters to enable teachers to anticipate and administer the quarterly assessments required by California.

About Workshop 1

Standards-based lesson plans and suggestions for linking instruction with Workshop 1 and the related instructional material are provided in *On Course: Mapping Instruction*.

- Before beginning Workshop 1, give the Entry-Level Diagnostic Test, *Diagnostic & Summative Assessments.* This test will help you determine whether or not your students need additional instruction and intervention.

- Workshop 1 focuses on narrative structure in writing, listening, and speaking. Chapter 1 connects to this workshop by focusing on narrative structures in both literature and informational readings.

- The related instructional material for Workshop 1 is shown on the chart. This related instructional material will also be covered in the first quarterly assessment. Specific teaching suggestions for the related material are found in Part 1 of this book and in the *Holt Handbook*.

Holt Literature and Language Arts

Pupil's Edition

Part 1, Chapter 1

Structures:
Building Blocks of Meaning, pp. 2–49
- Reading Standards 1.4, 2.1, 3.3
- Writing Application **Writing a Short Story**

Part 2, Workshop 1

Narration: Writing a Short Story,
pp. 500–518
- Writing Standard 2.1

Presenting and Listening to an
Oral Narrative, pp. 519–524
- Listening and Speaking Standard 2.1

Part 2, Mini-Workshop 5

Writing a Personal Narrative, pp. 676–677
- Writing Standard 2.0

Holt Handbook

Chapter 1

Parts of the Sentence
- Written and Oral English-Language Conventions Standard 1.1, pp. 4–16

Chapter 2

Parts of Speech Overview:
Noun, Pronoun, Adjective
- Written and Oral English-Language Conventions Standard 1.2, pp. 34–35; 1.4, pp. 26–28
- Looking Ahead, Gr. 7 Standard 1.3, pp. 25–42

Language Arts Content

This workshop uses the writing and listening and speaking strategies to enable students to master successfully the writing and speaking applications.

What standards are taught in Workshop 1?

In this workshop, students will master the following Grade 6 standards. They will also review several standards from an earlier grade.

Writing Strategies

1.0 Students write clear, coherent, and focused essays. The writing exhibits students' awareness of the audience and purpose. Students progress through the stages of the writing process as needed.

1.1 Choose the form of writing that best suits the intended purpose.

1.2 Create multiple-paragraph compositions.

1.3 Use a variety of effective and coherent organizational patterns, including climactic order.

1.6 Revise writing to improve the organization and consistency of ideas within and between paragraphs.

Writing Applications

2.0 Students write narrative texts of at least 500 to 700 words. Student writing demonstrates a command of standard American English and the organizational and drafting strategies outlined in Writing Standard 1.0.

2.1 Write narratives.

Listening and Speaking Strategies

1.0 Students deliver focused, coherent presentations that convey ideas clearly and relate to the background and interests of the audience. They evaluate the content of oral communication.

1.1 Relate the speaker's verbal communication to the nonverbal message.

1.2 Identify the tone, mood, and emotion conveyed in the oral communication.

1.4 Select an organizational structure and a point of view, matching the purpose, message, occasion, and vocal modulation to the audience.

1.7 Use effective rate, volume, pitch, and tone, and align nonverbal elements to sustain audience interest and attention.

1.8 Analyze the use of rhetorical devices for intent and effect.

Speaking Applications

2.0 Students deliver well-organized formal presentations employing traditional rhetorical strategies. Student speaking demonstrates a command of standard American English and the organizational and delivery strategies outlined in Listening and Speaking Standard 1.0.

2.1 Deliver narrative presentations.

Review Standards, Grade 5

Writing

1.1 Create multiple-paragraph narrative compositions.

2.1 Write narratives.

Listening and Speaking

2.1 Deliver narrative presentations.

Instructional Planning and Support

Where do I locate lesson plans, additional resources, and other teaching aids?

- The Annotated Teacher's Edition and *On Course: Mapping Instruction* provide direction in planning and implementing a complete California standards–based curriculum. These components include instructions for administering diagnostic, progress, and summative tests; for presenting instruction of the standards; for differentiating instruction to provide universal access; and for locating and using the program's ancillaries.

- The program's resources are referenced at the beginning of each workshop in the bottom margin of this teacher's edition: Writing a Short Story and Presenting and Listening to an Oral Narrative.

- Reminders for using additional resources appear in this teacher's edition at point of use.

- The *One-Stop Planner* CD-ROM contains editable lesson plans and all print ancillaries, available in PDF format.

What if I don't have time to teach all of Workshop 1?

- Within this workshop, complete coverage of the application standards is provided by the following instructional features in the Pupil's Edition:
  - Find a Story Idea
  - Think About Purpose and Audience
  - A Writer's Framework
  - Evaluate and Revise Content, Organization, and Style
  - Plan Your Presentation
  - Listen to an Oral Narrative
  - Make Delivery Notes
  - Rhetorical Devices

- Use Standards Practice and Review for a quick assessment and review of workshop standards.

What provisions have been made for students who have additional class time scheduled in language arts?

- *Universal Access: Writing, Listening, & Speaking,* Workshop 1, contains worksheets and transparencies that provide practice, reteaching, and extension of Workshop 1 standards. Each Practice and Apply exercise is supported by graphic organizers or practice activities for on-level learners, advanced learners, and learners having difficulty.

- *Universal Access: Lesson Plans for Language Development,* Workshop 1, provides alternative teaching strategies and additional worksheets designed specifically for English-language learners and special education students. Many of the suggestions and activities in this ancillary will also be helpful to students in the regular classroom who are having difficulty with particular skills.

Mastering the California Standards WORKSHOP 1

Universal Access

How do I differentiate instruction to ensure that all my students master the standards?

Holt Literature and Language Arts provides comprehensive, differentiated instruction for all types of students.

- Most of the general instruction and teaching strategies in the Annotated Teacher's Edition are at grade level. These instructions will work well with the majority of your students.

- Advanced students have at least one activity for each workshop. The suggested activities are found in this teacher's edition at point of instruction. Point-of-use suggestions for learners having difficulty, English-language learners, and special education students are provided.

- *Universal Access: Writing, Listening, & Speaking,* Workshop 1, opens with Teaching Notes that suggest which worksheets and transparencies are appropriate for each of three levels of learners.

- *Universal Access: Lesson Plans for Language Development,* Workshop 1, offers teaching strategies and additional worksheets designed specifically for English-language learners and special education students.

- *Daily Language Activities Transparencies* and *Spelling: Lessons & Activities* provide ongoing review of and additional practice in a range of language arts skills.

- For every workshop, preselected Web sites and activities are available to provide enrichment, independent practice, and enhanced instructional opportunities.

Assessment

How do I determine whether or not my students are making progress in mastering the standards?

Progress Assessment

- Use the Standards Review at the end of Workshop 1 for an informal assessment of the writing, listening, and speaking standards taught in Workshop 1.

- Use Workshop 1 in *Progress Assessment of Writing, Listening, & Speaking* to test students' cumulative progress in mastering the standards taught in the workshop.

Summative Assessment

The content in *Holt Literature and Language Arts* has been divided into four quarters to allow you to administer the four summative tests required by California. Workshop 1 will be assessed in the first quarter of instruction. At the end of Workshop 1, you may ask students to take the First-Quarter Test in the *Diagnostic & Summative Assessments* booklet.

STANDARDS FOCUS

Writing

Prerequisite Standards

Grade 5

■ 1.1 Create multiple-paragraph narrative compositions:

a. Establish and develop a situation or plot.

b. Describe the setting.

c. Present an ending.

■ 2.1 Write narratives:

a. Establish a plot, point of view, setting, and conflict.

b. Show, rather than tell, the events of the story.

Standards Coming Up in the Next Level

Grade 7

■ 2.1 Write fictional or autobiographical narratives:

a. Develop a standard plot line (having a beginning, conflict, rising action, climax, and denouement) and point of view.

b. Develop complex major and minor characters and a definite setting.

c. Use a range of appropriate strategies (e.g., dialogue; suspense; naming of specific narrative action, including movement, gestures, and expressions).

Narration

From grandparents to children, from writer to reader, from people of one nationality to another—everyone likes to share stories. One way for you to participate in sharing stories is by reading the stories of others and then creating your own. In this workshop you will write a short story. You will also prepare and listen to an oral narrative. In the process you will practice these language arts content standards.

WRITING WORKSHOP

Writing a Short Story Page 500

LISTENING AND SPEAKING WORKSHOP

Presenting and Listening to an Oral Narrative Page 519

GO TO: go.hrw.com
KEYWORD: HLLA6 W-1
FOR: Models, Writer's Guides, and Reference Sources

 California Standards

Writing

1.0 Students write clear, coherent, and focused essays [short stories]. The writing exhibits students' awareness of the audience and purpose. Students progress through the stages of the writing process as needed.

1.1 Choose the form of writing (e.g., personal letter, narrative) that best suits the intended purpose.

1.2 Create multiple-paragraph compositions:

b. Develop the topic with supporting details and precise verbs to paint a visual image in the mind of the reader.

1.3 Use a variety of effective and coherent organizational patterns, including arrangement by climactic order.

1.6 Revise writing to improve the organization and consistency of ideas within and between paragraphs.

2.0 Students write narrative texts of at least 500 to 700 words in each genre. Student writing demonstrates a command of standard American English and the organizational and drafting strategies outlined in Writing Standard 1.0.

2.1 Write narratives:

a. Establish and develop a plot and setting and present a point of view that is appropriate to the stories.

b. Include sensory details and concrete language to develop plot and character.

c. Use a range of narrative devices (e.g., dialogue, suspense).

Listening and Speaking

1.0 Students deliver focused, coherent presentations that convey ideas clearly and relate to the background and interests of the audience. They evaluate the content of oral communication.

1.1 Relate the speaker's verbal communication (e.g., pitch, feeling, tone) to the nonverbal message (e.g., posture, gesture).

1.2 Identify the tone, mood, and emotion conveyed in the oral communication.

1.4 Select an organizational structure and a point of view, matching the purpose, message, occasion, and vocal modulation to the audience.

1.7 Use effective rate, volume, pitch, and tone and align nonverbal elements to sustain audience interest and attention.

1.8 Analyze the use of rhetorical devices (e.g., cadence, repetitive patterns, use of onomatopoeia) for intent and effect.

2.0 Students deliver well-organized formal presentations employing traditional rhetorical strategies (e.g., narration, description). Student speaking demonstrates a command of standard American English and the organizational and delivery strategies outlined in Listening and Speaking Standard 1.0.

2.1 Deliver narrative presentations:

a. Establish a context, plot, and point of view.

b. Include sensory details and concrete language to develop the plot and character.

c. Use a range of narrative devices (e.g., dialogue, tension, or suspense).

Listening and Speaking

Prerequisite Standards

Grade 5

■ 2.1 Deliver narrative presentations:

a. Establish a situation, plot, point of view, and setting with descriptive words and phrases.

b. Show, rather than tell, the listener what happens.

Standards Coming Up in the Next Level

Grade 7

■ 2.1 Deliver narrative presentations:

a. Establish a context, standard plot line (having a beginning, conflict, rising action, climax, and denouement), and point of view.

b. Describe complex major and minor characters and a definite setting.

c. Use a range of appropriate strategies, including dialogue, suspense, and naming of specific narrative action (e.g., movement, gestures, expressions).

Writing Workshop

Standards Starter

Motivate. Conduct a brief game of charades in which students try to guess the following titles: "Jack and the Beanstalk," "The Boy Who Cried Wolf," "Mary Had a Little Lamb," "Beauty and the Beast," or other titles. After the game, ask students what these titles have in common. Once they determine that all tell stories, ask them to think of different forms that stories can take, for example, fairy tales, poems, folk tales, nursery rhymes, legends, songs, plays, and so on. Ask students how their lives are enriched by stories.

Introducing the Workshop. To introduce the workshop, use the Journal Warm-up, Transparency 5, in *Writing, Listening, & Speaking*.

Quotation for the Day

"You're a human being, with a unique story to tell. . . . If you speak with passion, many of us will listen. We need stories to live, all of us. We live by story. Yours enlarges the circle."

(Richard Rhodes, 1937–   ,
Pulitzer Prize–winning author of
The Making of the Atomic Bomb)

Pose the question *How do we live by story?* You may suggest that people often communicate through stories—newspapers and magazines carry stories. Ask students if they have ever learned from a story. Are they aware of any stories that preserve history? Are stories that entertain us a necessary part of life? Why or why not?

WHAT'S AHEAD?

In this workshop you will write a short story. You will also learn how to

- create characters, setting, and plot
- arrange events in climactic order
- use sensory details and concrete language
- capitalize proper nouns

| DO THIS

Reference Note
For information on **think sheets**, see page 495.

Writing a Short Story

On the first day of school, you are given your first assignment: *Tell the class what you did this past summer.* "Oh, great," you think, "my summer was soooo boring. I don't have anything to write about." Now imagine that you do not have to write about what actually happened. You can create a summer full of amazing, incredible events.

When you want to create something entirely new, instead of just describing an ordinary and familiar experience, you might write a short fictional **narrative,** or story. Writing a **short story** gives you the chance to use creative writing to explore a whole new world full of people, places, and events that you alone invent.

Professional Model: A Short Story

How will you create excitement for your readers? You could start by imitating professional writers whose works you have enjoyed reading. On the following pages, you will read Cynthia Rylant's short story "Boar Out There," about a young girl who searches for a mysterious beast.

As you read, create a **think sheet** to take note of any questions or comments you have as you read. Also, note what message about life you think the writer reveals in the story. On your think sheet, answer the analysis questions that appear beside the text.

Writing 1.2 Create multiple-paragraph compositions. **2.1** Write narratives.

WORKSHOP RESOURCES

Writing Workshop
Planning
- *On Course: Mapping Instruction*
- *One-Stop Planner* CD-ROM
- *At Home: A Guide to Standards Mastery,* p. 17
- *At Home: In Five Languages*

- *Writing, Listening, & Speaking,* Teaching Notes, p. 1

Differentiating Instruction
- *Lesson Plans for Language Development,* pp. 223–224
- *Supporting Instruction in Five Languages*

Practice
- *Writing, Listening, & Speaking,* Wkshp. 1

Boar Out There

by Cynthia Rylant

Everyone in Glen Morgan knew there was a wild boar in the woods over by the Miller farm. The boar was out beyond the splintery rail fence and past the old black Dodge that somehow had ended up in the woods and was missing most of its parts.

1. Where does the short story take place?

Jenny would hook her chin over the top rail of the fence, twirl a long green blade of grass in her teeth and whisper, "Boar out there."

And there were times she was sure she heard him. She imagined him running heavily through the trees, ignoring the sharp thorns and briars that raked his back and sprang away trembling.

She thought he might have a golden horn on his terrible head. The boar would run deep into the woods, then rise up on his rear hooves, throw his head toward the stars and cry a long, clear, sure note into the air. The note would glide through the night and spear the heart of the moon. The boar had no fear of the moon, Jenny knew, as she lay in bed, listening.

2. What does Jenny think the boar looks like? Why does she think this?

One hot summer day she went to find the boar. No one in Glen Morgan had ever gone past the old black Dodge and beyond, as far as she knew. But the boar was there somewhere, between those awful trees, and his dark green eyes waited for someone.

3. Why do you think Jenny goes looking for the boar?

Jenny felt it was she.

Moving slowly over damp brown leaves, Jenny could sense her ears tingle and fan out as she listened for thick breathing from the trees. She stopped to pick a teaberry leaf to chew, stood a minute, then went on.

Deep in the woods she kept her eyes to the sky. She needed to be reminded that there was a world above and apart from the trees—a world of space and air, air that didn't linger all about her, didn't press deep into her skin, as forest air did.

Answer

The writer's message about life may be that in reality some things are not as they might seem to be. Everyone in the place called Glen Morgan thinks the boar is a fierce creature. However, Jenny discovers that the boar is in fact a ragged being that scares easily.

DIRECT TEACHING

Professional Model

Explain to students that using think sheets to summarize their notes from a reading serves two purposes. First, creating think sheets allows students to place their thoughts, observations, and questions on paper, which, in turn, helps increase reading comprehension. The process of creating think sheets also provides students with ideas for their own writing.

Professional Model Questions

Answers

1. The story takes place in the woods near a place called Glen Morgan.
2. Jenny thinks the boar has a golden horn on its frightening head. She imagines the boar like a mythical horned creature because he is strange and mystical.
3. Jenny thinks the boar is waiting for someone, for her. She also wants to see the legendary boar and test her own bravery.

Reinforcement

- *Daily Language Activities*
- *Spelling*

Evaluation and Assessment

- *Test Generator (One-Stop Planner* CD-ROM)
- *Progress Assessment of Writing, Listening, & Speaking,* Wkshp. 1

- *Diagnostic & Summative Assessments,* First-Quarter Test

Internet

- go.hrw.com (keyword: HLLA6 W-1)

Answers continued

4. The boar is large and gray-black, with a scarred and glistening back, thick legs, and torn and bloody ears.

5. The yell of a bluejay scares the boar away.

6. Jenny is wiser but sad because she knows her mythical, horned boar does not exist. The boar that people fear is actually afraid of many things.

DIRECT TEACHING

Professional Model

You may ask students to identify the purpose and audience for the short story "Boar Out There." Students should explain their answers. [Possible purposes: to entertain, to teach a lesson, or to describe an experience. Intended audience: probably children or young adults, as the story is written from a young girl's perspective.]

Finally, leaning against a tree to rest, she heard him for the first time. She forgot to breathe, standing there listening to the stamping of hooves, and she choked and coughed.

Coughed!

And now the pounding was horrible, too loud and confusing for Jenny. Horrible. She stood stiff with wet eyes and knew she could always pray, but for some reason didn't.

He came through the trees so fast that she had no time to scream or run. And he was there before her.

His large gray-black body shivered as he waited just beyond the shadow of the tree she held for support. His nostrils glistened, and his eyes; but astonishingly, he was silent. He shivered and glistened and was absolutely silent.

4. What does the boar really look like?

Jenny matched his silence, and her body was rigid[1], but not her eyes. They traveled along his scarred, bristling back to his thick hind legs. Tears spilling and flooding her face, Jenny stared at the boar's ragged ears, caked with blood. Her tears dropped to the leaves, and the only sound between them was his slow breathing.

Then the boar snorted and jerked. But Jenny did not move.

High in the trees a bluejay yelled, and, suddenly, it was over. Jenny stood like a rock as the boar wildly flung his head and in terror bolted[2] past her.

Past her. . . .

5. What scares the boar away?

And now, since that summer, Jenny still hooks her chin over the old rail fence, and she still whispers, "Boar out there." But when she leans on the fence, looking into the trees, her eyes are full and she leaves wet patches on the splintery wood. She is sorry for the torn ears of the boar and sorry that he has no golden horn.

6. How has Jenny changed from the experience?

But mostly she is sorry that he lives in fear of bluejays and little girls, when everyone in Glen Morgan lives in fear of him.

---

1. rigid: stiff, unmoving.
2. bolted: suddenly ran quickly away.

502   Workshop 1   **Narration:** Writing a Short Story

Working with a partner, discuss the following questions and write down your responses.

1. **When and where do you think the story takes place? What words tell you this?**

2. **Where does the writer let you know what problem Jenny faces? What words tell you that this is a problem?**

3. **What makes Jenny a realistic character?**

4. **Sometimes the events in a story lead up to an exciting point. List the events of "Boar Out There" on a time line. Then, circle the point where you most wanted to continue reading.**

Prewriting

Find a Story Idea

To start planning a story, you might begin by thinking about interesting people or problems. Have you ever seen a person dressed in a clown's costume driving along the highway? Where might the clown be going and why? Have you even seen a race in which one runner trips near the finish line? What story could be invented about that incident? Look around you. You will discover great ideas for stories. In fact, you might consider recording your ideas in a journal.

Starting with People Your short story has to start somewhere, and many writers start first with characters that will appear in their stories. Maybe your short story will focus on an original character that you have imagined, such as a superhero or an alien. Maybe you will choose a character (either real or fictional) that you have read about in a novel or seen in a film or on the news. For example, you could develop a story about what happens to the character after the novel, film, or news story is over.

Real people can also provide a good beginning for stories. Notice the people around you—the kind-hearted janitor at your school, your friendly neighbor who collects cuckoo clocks, or your energetic and loud six-year-old cousin. What makes them interesting?

TIP Think about the characters in "Boar Out There." You might consider writing the story from the boar's point of view instead of Jenny's, or you might write another story with Jenny coming back as an adult to look for the boar. You could even write a **prequel,** a story that comes before another, explaining why Jenny comes to the woods to look for the boar.

Writing 1.0 Students write focused short stories. Students progress through the stages of the writing process as needed.

Answers

Possible responses are suggested below.

1. The story takes place in the summer, probably not too long ago, in the woods. The author describes the hot summer day and the deep woods. The old Dodge may help prove that the story took place not too long ago. [setting]

2. In the second paragraph, Jenny whispers to the wild boar, almost longingly, like she wants to find him. Words that tell me this is a problem occur in the third and fourth paragraphs: "she was sure she heard him" and "she imagined him." [conflict]

3. Jenny seems real because she is imaginative and curious, as a young girl might be. [character]

4. The following events are listed in order of appearance:
   - Jenny imagines she hears and sees the boar.
   - Jenny goes to find the boar.
   - She hears the boar.
   - The boar emerges from the trees.
   - The two look at each other.
   - The boar runs past Jenny.
   - Jenny feels sorry for the boar.

   Jenny's decision to find the boar seems dangerous and exciting and encourages further reading. [suspense, climax]

Integrating with Grammar, Usage, and Mechanics

As students start their narrative writing, you may want to review verbs and punctuating quotations because these are concepts with which students often have trouble. See the Parts of Speech Overview and Punctuation chapters in the *Holt Handbook*.

Starting with Problems

To help students better understand the difference between internal and external conflicts, you might have students list examples of both or identify conflicts you give them as either external or internal.

The People-Problem Connection

You might provide students with another strategy to match characters with problems. Have students list possible characters and possible problems in a T chart. For example, possible characters may include a young camper, a hungry cat, an ashamed thief, a very large clown, or a kind-hearted janitor. Possible problems may include a big storm, a talking bird, a stolen bicycle, a flat tire, a missing aunt, or a runaway bus. Then, ask students to mix and match characters and problems until they find a combination about which they would like to write.

TIP Characters can face *internal* or *external* conflicts. An **internal conflict** is a problem that is within a character's mind. For example, a character may have to struggle with a decision to lie. An **external conflict** is an outside force that a character must overcome, such as climbing a mountain or fighting a villain.

Starting with Problems   Although you are developing a fictional world for your characters, it cannot be a world that is free of problems. As in real life, problems, or **conflicts,** give short stories drama, interest, and action. To begin thinking about possible problems for your story, listen to friends, family, or people on the news talk about the interesting or unfortunate things that have happened to them—their real-life problems. To plan a story, imagine characters in a short story having these very same problems. Then, ask yourself: *What could a character in a short story do in a situation similar to the real-life one? What other actions might these characters take?*

The People-Problem Connection   Putting characters with problems is the beginning of writing a short story. The steps below can help you match characters with problems.

THINKING IT THROUGH   **Finding a Story Idea**

To find a story idea, make a two-column chart. List possible characters on one side and possible problems on the other. Then, follow the steps below.

▶ **STEP 1** Choose a character and a problem that seem to match for a story idea.

I think I will pick a clever middle school boy and have him discover that his aunt is missing.

▶ **STEP 2** Write a brief description of your character.

I will name the boy Tyrel. He will be a regular visitor to his aunt's house. I want to show his imagination and quick thinking.

▶ **STEP 3** Write a brief explanation of your problem.

A missing aunt would give Tyrel a chance to solve a problem. I could make the problem interesting if the reason for the missing aunt is extraordinary, like a space monster's visit.

TIP Keep in mind that your short story will be 500 to 700 words long, so choose a character and problem that will maintain your readers' interest throughout a story of that length.

▶ **STEP 4** Write a brief description of how your character and problem are related.

I want to show that Tyrel can get his aunt out of a strange situation by doing something ordinary. I want Tyrel to be a hero, even though he is just in middle school.

Writing   2.0 Students write narrative texts of at least 500 to 700 words.

Brainstorm a list of possible characters. Then, brainstorm a separate list of possible problems. Use the steps in the Thinking It Through on page 504 to match a problem with a character or characters. You will use the characters and the problem you have chosen to develop a short story as you work through the activities in this workshop.

Mini-Workshop

If you would like to tell a true story about yourself in the form of a personal letter, see **Writing a Personal Narrative** on pages 676–677.

Think About Purpose and Audience

Let Me Entertain You When you write a story, one **purpose,** or reason for writing, is to be creative. Another purpose is to entertain your audience, the people who will read your story. You may entertain with humor, suspense, tragedy, romance, or adventure. For example, young children might enjoy a funny story about talking birds. Maybe one group of your friends loves adventure stories while another group is entertained by scary stories.

Keeping your audience in mind as you develop your story will ensure that you write stories that entertain your readers. Jot down an audience you think will read your story. Then, identify what kind of story your audience will find entertaining.

← DO THIS

Plan Your Story's Elements

Spotlight a Star Part of planning your story is spotlighting the stars of the story—your characters. Take, for example, the kind-hearted janitor from your school. Maybe you like his friendly personality and quick smile, but your story might be more interesting if he were a spy or fluent in Russian. As the creator of your story, you can describe a character any way you like to fit your story. Jot down answers to the following questions to bring your characters to life.

- How do the characters act?
- How do they look?
- What do the characters think?
- What do they say?
- What do others say about the characters?
- How do others act around them or react to them?

Writing **1.0** The writing exhibits students' awareness of the audience and purpose. **1.1** Choose the form of writing (e.g., personal letter, narrative) that best suits the intended purpose.

Plan Your Story's Elements **505**

Guided and Independent Practice

Monitor students' progress by checking to see that they have developed a list with a minimum of five characters and a list of five problems. Then, instruct students to complete **Practice and Apply 1** by choosing a character or characters and a problem about which they would like to develop a short story.

DIRECT TEACHING

Think About Purpose and Audience

You may want to remind students that there is more than one form in which to present a story. Some forms may be more appropriate depending on students' purpose and audience. For example, a play might be an appropriate form to present information to an audience that seeks entertainment. If the audience is a teacher, a written narrative is probably the most appropriate form for presenting the story.

DIFFERENTIATING INSTRUCTION

Advanced Learners

Acceleration. Use the following activity with students to move them toward the 7th-grade **Writing Standard 2.1b.**

One way to help students create more complex characters is to have them flesh out a character beyond the boundaries of the story. Students can create brief biographies of the characters, develop family trees for the characters, or answer questions such as *What are my character's favorite foods, music, books, hobbies, or school subjects?* The information may not appear in the story, but it can add depth to the narrative by making the character more real to the writer.

RESOURCES

Practice & Apply 1

Guided Practice
- *Writing, Listening, & Speaking*, WS. p. 2

Reteaching and Modeling
- *Writing, Listening, & Speaking*, TP. 6

Reinforcement
- *Writing, Listening, & Speaking*, WS. p. 3

As you answer the questions on page 505, **remember that *sensory details* and *concrete language* will help your readers form a mental picture of your characters. Sensory details** describe what you can see, hear, taste, feel, and smell. **Concrete language** consists of words and phrases that are precise and specific. Adding **dialogue**—the exact words of your characters—is an effective way to add concrete language to your short story. When writing dialogue, try to make it sound natural, just as people actually talk. For example, use short phrases when characters are giving answers to questions instead of writing complete sentences. Use contractions such as "don't" instead of "do not." You can even use slang if you are sure your audience will understand it.

To make your characters seem real, first imagine them. Then, describe to the reader what you see in your mind's eye. In the following chart, one student listed sensory details and concrete language to describe a monster character.

Sensory Details	Concrete Language
Sight: big, scary, lots of eyes, weird body shape, quick moving	Two fangs, five eyes, covered in blue slime
Smell: strong odor came from the monster	Rotting garbage
Sound: weird roaring noises	Roars in anger; in response, Tyrel shouts, "Take this, Stinky!"

Set the Scene The **setting** is the time and place of your story. A setting provides the background for your story and can also help create a problem or a mood. If, for example, you set your story inside a burning building, your setting would be part of your story's problem. If you set your story in a dark cave during a storm, your setting would add a mood of fear or dread. Your setting can also be more ordinary, such as a school sports field.

Whether the setting is dramatic or ordinary, it needs to tie in with your story's characters and problems and be vivid for your readers. To plan your setting, answer the following questions.

- Where will my story take place? inside a house or a bus? outside in a city or on a farm? in outer space or beneath the sea?
- When will my story take place? What time? What season? In the present day, the past, or the future?

Writing **1.2b** Develop the topic with supporting details. **2.1a** Establish and develop a setting. **2.1b** Include sensory details and concrete language to develop character. **2.1c** Use a range of narrative devices (e.g., dialogue).

506 Workshop 1 **Narration:** Writing a Short Story

DIFFERENTIATING INSTRUCTION

English-Language Learners

Using a small-group or partner format with exercises and activities in this chapter has two distinct advantages, especially for the English-language learner. When students can talk with each other, they have more opportunities to practice English, in areas of both comprehension and composition. In addition, when English-language learners use English in discussions with English-proficient speakers, they may work harder to be understood.

▶ Resources Reminder

For more help with English-Language Learners, see *Lesson Plans for Language Development.*

CORRECTING MISCONCEPTIONS

Students sometimes forget that setting is not only a place, but also a time. Time can be as specific as a particular day of the week or a certain time of day. Time also means period in history. Encourage students to provide hints in their stories about the time of the setting. Have cars been invented, or do people rely on horses or futuristic vehicles for transportation? What songs do characters hear on radios or hum as they work? These types of details can help establish the time of the setting.

Who's Doing the Talking?   All short stories have a narrator who tells the story. The narrator tells the story from a certain perspective, or angle, called the **point of view.** A point of view for a short story is either *first person* or *third person.*

First-person Point of View A story in which a character describes the events as happening to him or her has a **first-person point of view.** This point of view (that uses the first-person pronoun *I*) allows a character to describe events, other characters, and feelings from his or her own perspective. The reader knows only what the character sees, hears, knows, and believes. If another character keeps a secret from the narrator, the reader is left wondering what the secret is, too. In this example, notice that "I" has seen actions of other characters but doesn't know what prompted those actions.

> *I saw Ana walk sadly toward her locker. I had seen her arguing with Kirsten, and I wondered what Kirsten had said this time.*

Third-person Point of View When the narrator is not a character in the story but describes all the events and characters in the story, the story has a **third-person point of view** and uses third-person pronouns (such as *she, they,* and *him*). The narrator is like a reporter who is not part of the story's action but tells what he or she sees.

Sometimes the narrator may focus on just one character's thoughts or feelings. Notice that the following passage focuses only on Ana's feelings.

> *Ana walked sadly toward her locker. Kirsten's words rang in her head. Ana couldn't believe Kirsten could be so cruel.*

Other times the narrator may share the thoughts, feelings, and actions of all the characterss in a story. Notice in the following passage that the reader knows the emotions of both Ana and Kurt.

> *Ana walked away, hurt and confused, while Kurt watched her with sympathy. He knew Kirsten could be cruel. What he didn't know was just how ashamed Kirsten was over hurting Ana's feelings.*

When you choose a point of view for your story, be **consistent.** If you choose a first-person point of view, your narrator should not suddenly describe another character's thoughts. If you choose a third-person point of view, your narrator should not use *I* or *me* to describe the story's events, except when a character is speaking dialogue.

 Writing   2.1a Present a point of view that is appropriate to the stories.

Guided and Independent Practice

Monitor students' progress by making sure that their descriptive paragraphs about characters and setting are detailed enough to develop into stories.

Make sure that students have chosen only one point of view for their narrators. If a student has completed a sentence for both first person and third person, you will need to clarify what each point of view is and have the student select only one.

DIRECT TEACHING

What's Happening?

As an alternative to the chart that students will be asked to create for **Practice and Apply 3,** you may provide a time line, stair step, or plot chain graphic for students to use as they develop the series of events for their stories. The purpose of the graphic is to help students be selective when choosing events and to help them avoid writing long "then... then" sentences.

On a sheet of paper, write two paragraphs, one listing and describing your characters and one describing your setting. Then, decide on your point of view by completing the following sentences.

My story will use a _____ (first-person or third-person) narrator.

If my story uses a first-person narrator, it will be told through the eyes, or perspective, of _____.

If my story uses a third-person narrator, it will share the thoughts of _____ (one character or all of the characters).

Explore Plot

What's Happening? Between friends, a standard answer to the question "What's happening?" is often "Not much." In short stories, however, the answer has to be "Lots!" All stories have *plots* for the unfolding story. A **plot** tells what happens and can be divided into parts called **plot elements:**

- A **problem,** or **conflict:** A problem sets the story in motion. How characters deal with the problem is the basis of the story.

- A **series of events:** Usually, each of the events in a story is more surprising or dramatic than the last, building toward a **climax,** or a point of intense drama. This dramatic arrangement of events is called **climactic order.** Climactic order usually means that the events occur in **time order. As you plan your story, arrange events in** *climactic order* **so that the climax delivers the biggest emotional punch.** Readers of fiction expect a climax, so using this type of order will give your story **coherence.** That is, the events of the story will hang together in a way that makes sense.

- **Suspense:** If your readers can predict the high point or if they lose interest while reading, your story may lack *suspense.* **Suspense** keeps the reader wondering what will happen next. You can create suspense with a fast-moving plot that keeps readers guessing. Just make sure your story events develop in a believable way.

- An **outcome:** The **outcome,** or conclusion, of a story, explains what happens after the story's problem is settled. It shows how everything works out. The outcome is also sometimes called the *denouement* (dā´noo män´).

KEY CONCEPT →

TIP To create **suspense** in your story, save some important details to reveal right before your high point, or scatter hints along in your story, to keep your reader curious about what happens next.

 Writing **1.0** Students write clear, coherent short stories. **1.3** Use a variety of effective and coherent organizational patterns, including arrangement by climactic order. **2.1a** Establish and develop a plot. **2.1c** Use a range of narrative devices (e.g., suspense).

508 Workshop 1 **Narration:** Writing a Short Story

Practice and Apply 2

Guided Practice

- *Writing, Listening, & Speaking,* WS. p. 4

Practice and Apply 3

Guided Practice

- *Writing, Listening, & Speaking,* WS. p. 5

For more practice on creating a short story, look at "Boar Out There" on pages 501–502. Re-read the story, and outline the plot elements. Write a brief summary of its climactic order to help you organize your own story.

DO THIS

A Living, Breathing Plot The basic plot of your story can probably be summarized in a few sentences or drawn on a time line. A summary or time line, however, lacks excitement and pizzazz. A good plot comes alive with *sensory details* and *concrete language* as you *show*, not tell, your readers what is happening.

For example, instead of writing, "Gabrielle got scared," which *tells* Gabrielle's actions, use **sensory details** to *show* what she did. For example, "Gabrielle's face turned bright red and she screamed in fear as the reckless driver sped past her." Use **concrete language** to make the plot events vivid. For example, "The driver had been talking on a cell phone and had barely missed Gabrielle as she stood in the crosswalk."

Here is how one student added sensory details and concrete language to the elements of plot.

Plot Element	Concrete Language	Sensory Details
1. Problem: Tyrel can't find his aunt Bernice.	knocks on the door; opens the door; begins to worry	hears a weird roaring noise; yells, "Aunt Bernice!"
2. One event in a series: Tyrel sees and hears his aunt.	Aunt Bernice inside a glass jar, yelling and jumping	aunt screams in a tiny voice like a cartoon character's
3. High point: Tyrel rescues his aunt.	throws soapy water on the monster; squashes the bug	monster roars and its eyes pop out
4. Outcome: Aunt Bernice shares her relief with Tyrel.	aunt whispers	aunt's trembly voice

PRACTICE & APPLY 3 **Explore Plot**

List the problem, series of events, high point, and outcome of your story in a chart in climactic order. Then, describe each element with sensory details and concrete language. In the example above, only one event in the series is listed. Your chart should include every event.

 Writing 2.1b Include sensory details and concrete language to develop plot.

DO THIS

Answers

Plot elements for "Boar Out There" include:

- **Problem:** Jenny wants to find the boar that everyone fears.
- **Events:** Jenny decides to look for the boar and finds him. The two stare at each other for a while as she notes his appearance. The boar is scared away by a blue-jay's call. Jenny continues to think about the boar after her encounter with him.
- **High point:** The climax of the story occurs as Jenny hears the boar running toward her in the forest.
- **Outcome:** Jenny is sad that the boar is afraid of bluejays and is so ragged in appearance.

For a summary of the story's climactic order, see answer 4 in the sidewrap feature **Think About the Model: Answers** on p. 503.

PRACTICE & APPLY 3

As an alternative to **Practice and Apply 3,** students can make plot chains using different colors for events leading to the climax, the climax, and the outcome. Students can then read each other's chains.

Guided and Independent Practice

Monitor students' progress by first checking that they have created a chart similar to the one illustrated on this page. Student charts, however, should contain all the events that compose the body of the student's story. You may also spot-check to see that students have listed sensory details in the final column.

DIFFERENTIATING INSTRUCTION

Learners Having Difficulty

Some students may find writing dialogue to be an intimidating task. Briefly review "Boar Out There." Then, have students pick one of the following two situations and imagine the words the characters might say to each other. Situation 1: Jenny takes a friend into the woods with her and they are together when the boar runs toward them. What do they say to each other? Situation 2: At school the next day, Jenny tells her best friend about her experience. What do Jenny and her friend say to each other? Remind students to start a new paragraph each time the speaker changes.

PRACTICE & APPLY 4

Guided and Independent Practice

Before students complete **Practice and Apply 4** for independent practice, guide them through the framework using a sample idea. You may have students notate their first drafts in the margins to show how each paragraph of their draft corresponds to a step of the framework. You can use students' marginal notations to help you monitor their progress.

Writing

A Writer's Framework

Short Story

Beginning

- Setting and main character
- Problem, or conflict

Middle

- Series of plot events arranged in climactic order (with sensory details, concrete language, and dialogue)
- High point, or climax

End

- Outcome

To begin your short story, use one of these techniques.

- Set the mood by describing the setting.
- Start with action that shows readers what kind of person the main character is.
- Start with **dialogue** that makes readers curious and hints at the problem.

To keep your readers in **suspense**, write the events in **time order**, building toward a **climax**. Keep events and characters lively by using **sensory details** and **concrete language**.

Make the story realistic by using **dialogue**. In the following story, Tyrel yells, "Aunt Bernice? Aunt Bernice!" This dialogue increases the reader's curiosity about the empty house, and the punctuation (*?* and *!*) hints at the problem of Tyrel's missing aunt.

Resolve the story's **problem**, or **conflict**, and tie up any loose ends. Make sure the outcome is believable and satisfies your readers' curiosity.

PRACTICE & APPLY 4 **Draft Your Short Story**

Now it is your turn to write a short story. As you write, refer to the framework above and the Writer's Model on the next page.

Writing 1.2 Create multiple-paragraph compositions. 2.0 Student writing demonstrates the organizational and drafting strategies outlined in Writing Standard 1.0. 2.1c Use a range of narrative devices (e.g., dialogue, suspense).

RESOURCES

Practice and Apply 4

Think Sheet

- *Writing, Listening, & Speaking*, WS. p. 6

Template

- *Writing, Listening, & Speaking*, WS. p. 7

The final draft below closely follows the framework for a short story on the previous page.

Soap to the Rescue

After school Tyrel went to his Aunt Bernice's house. He went there every Tuesday to see if she needed anything. She was his favorite relative. He was especially interested to see her today, because last week they had watched a movie together about space aliens, and just last night he thought he had seen a bright object in the sky, circling over the neighborhood. When he knocked on the door, he heard a weird roaring noise. He opened the door and looked around. He didn't see Aunt Bernice anywhere.

"Aunt Bernice? Aunt Bernice!" Tyrel yelled as he began to worry. Aunt Bernice never missed her favorite soap opera at 3:00. The TV was on in the living room, but Aunt Bernice was not sitting in her overstuffed green chair.

As Tyrel turned toward the kitchen, he noticed three enormous blue footprints leading to the kitchen. He crept down the hall and saw a huge, fierce-looking monster standing in the kitchen. The monster had five gigantic eyes that popped out of its head and were waving frantically in every direction. Two fangs were sticking out of the monster's drooling mouth. Its body was covered in blue slime, and it smelled like rotting

Title

BEGINNING
Characters and Setting
Third-person limited point of view

Problem, or Conflict

MIDDLE
Event 1/Suspense
Character

Event 2/Sensory details
Concrete language

Concrete language

Sensory details

GO TO: go.hrw.com
KEYWORD: HLLA6 W-1
FOR: A Student Model

(continued)

DIRECT TEACHING

A Writer's Model W2.0

You may remind students to include plenty of events in their short stories in order to meet the 500–700 word criteria for paper length. Point out to students that **A Writer's Model** successfully includes a number of events to meet this standard.

	garbage. To Tyrel's growing horror, the monster looked just like the space alien from the movie they had seen.
Event 3	Tyrel was about to run for help. Then suddenly one of the monster's eyes shot out, peering in Tyrel's direction. Tyrel
Dialogue	shouted, "Yi! Yi! Yi!" The monster jumped into the air and zoomed to the other side of the kitchen near the table. Tyrel
Event 4	then noticed a little glass jar on the table. Aunt Bernice was inside it!
Dialogue	"Help me, Tyrel!" she screamed in a tiny voice that sounded like a cartoon character's. Every time she screamed, she tried
Event 5	to jump out of the jar. The jar fell over and began to roll off the table.
Suspense	The monster reached for the jar, but his giant hands couldn't grab it. The jar rolled closer to the edge of the table. Tyrel
Event 6	knew this was his only chance. Just before the jar rolled off the table, Tyrel grabbed it.
Event 7	The monster roared in anger and began to chase Tyrel
Concrete language	around the table. Despite his size, the monster was fast on his feet, and Tyrel couldn't outrun the monster to the door. Then, Tyrel noticed the window and realized the monster would never fit through it.
Event 8	Tyrel edged closer to the wall and leaped out the kitchen window, holding on tightly to the jar. He put Aunt Bernice on the ground. She was safe for now, but he had to figure out how to get rid of the monster for good.
	He remembered that in the old science fiction movie he and Aunt Bernice had seen, a scientist killed a space monster with soap. Soap didn't seem like a very good weapon, but Tyrel was
Event 9	out of options. He found a bucket near an outside faucet. Grabbing it, he ran back inside the house. Silently, he slipped
Event 10	into the bathroom and squirted the liquid soap into the bucket and poured in some water. Armed and ready, Tyrel headed toward the kitchen.
High point, or climax	The monster was roaring, and blue slime was all over the kitchen. Tyrel yelled, "Take this, Stinky!" He threw the soapy water onto the monster. It roared even louder, and all its eyes popped out. Then it shrank to the size of a bug. When Tyrel

turned to go get the glass jar, he saw Aunt Bernice standing behind him, back to her normal size. Tyrel spun back around to see the bug squirming on its back. Raising his knee to his chest, he gave a little hop as he brought his foot down hard, squashing the creature. A drop of blue slime squirted from underneath his shoe.

"Tyrel," whispered Aunt Bernice in a trembly voice, "Let's not tell anybody about this. They'd never believe us. And no more science fiction movies for us—ever!"

END
Outcome

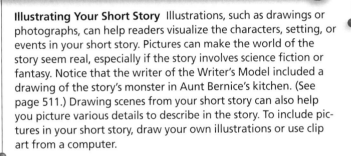

Designing Your Writing

Illustrating Your Short Story Illustrations, such as drawings or photographs, can help readers visualize the characters, setting, or events in your short story. Pictures can make the world of the story seem real, especially if the story involves science fiction or fantasy. Notice that the writer of the Writer's Model included a drawing of the story's monster in Aunt Bernice's kitchen. (See page 511.) Drawing scenes from your short story can also help you picture various details to describe in the story. To include pictures in your short story, draw your own illustrations or use clip art from a computer.

A Writer's Model **513**

Illustrating Your Short Story

Lead a discussion about the cover illustrations on books and the actors who portray book characters in movies. Are students ever disappointed that the characters are not as students imagined them to be while reading the book? Share with students the information that sometimes illustrators of book jackets have not read the book. However, students should pay attention to details in their stories as they create illustrations.

Explain to students that they should take care in revising and proofreading their writing. Just as the product belongs to the writer, so does the responsibility to make that product as good as it can be. Revising is one process by which this goal is met.

DIRECT TEACHING

First Reading: Content and Organization

Explain to students that when reviewing a classmate's story they should not make the changes suggested in the right-hand column of the **Content and Organization Guidelines** on this page. Instead, students should indicate to the writer where and when a revision may be necessary.

REVIEW STANDARD

Elaboration

The following item is a review of the 5th-grade **Writing Standard 2.1b.**

To help students elaborate on their stories, have them use analogies. Specifically, suggest that they create original similes to help write more vivid descriptions. For example, a kitten's cry may be as insistent as that of a hungry baby. A smell may be as foul as forgotten, dirty socks in the bottom of a gym locker.

Revising

Evaluate and Revise Content, Organization, and Style

Take Two   When you are ready to evaluate your story or a classmate's, you should read the story twice. In the first reading, look at the story's **content** (the ideas in the story) and **organization** (the order of the ideas), using the guidelines below. In the second reading, focus on **style,** or the wording of the ideas, using the Focus on Word Choice on page 516.

▶ **First Reading: Content and Organization** Use the following chart to evaluate and revise your short story, making sure it is entertaining and coherent.

Short Story: Content and Organization Guidelines

Evaluation Questions	Tips	Revision Techniques
1 Is the setting clear?	▶ **Put a check mark** next to details about the setting.	▶ If needed, **add** details about place, time of day, and time of year.
2 Do the characters seem real?	▶ Use a colored marker to **highlight** character details, description, and dialogue.	▶ **Elaborate** on characters as needed by adding sensory details, concrete language, and dialogue.
3 Does the character have a problem to overcome?	▶ **Underline** the problem, or conflict.	▶ If necessary, **add** sentences that describe the problem.
4 Are plot events in time order and clearly connected? Does the plot keep the reader in suspense?	▶ **Number** each event. Check that the first event that happens is number 1, the second is number 2, and so on. Check that as the numbers increase, the suspense increases.	▶ **Rearrange** plot events in order. **Add** details that coherently tie events together. **Cut** or **rearrange** details that lessen suspense by revealing plot developments too early in the story.
5 Is the point of view clear and consistent throughout the story?	▶ **Circle** pronouns, such as *I* or *he,* or other details that establish the point of view in the first two paragraphs.	▶ **Cut** pronouns or details that shift from the first-person to the third-person point of view, or vice versa.
6 Is the conflict resolved? Does the story outcome make sense?	▶ **Underline** with a colored pencil the story's high point and outcome.	▶ **Add** a high point, in which the conflict is settled. **Add** details to show how everything works out.

Writing 1.6 Revise writing to improve the organization and consistency of ideas within and between paragraphs.

ONE WRITER'S REVISIONS This revision is an early draft of the short story on pages 511–513.

> The monster was roaring, and blue slime was all over
> *He threw the soapy water onto the monster.* add
> the kitchen. Tyrel yelled, "Take this, Stinky!"It roared even
> *shrank to the size of a bug* replace
> louder, and all its eyes popped out. Then it got very small.
>
> When Tyrel turned to go get the glass jar, he saw Aunt
>
> Bernice standing behind him, back to her normal size.
>
> Tyrel spun back around to see the bug squirming on its
>
> back. Raising his knee to his chest, he gave a little hop as
> *A drop of* add
> he brought his foot down hard, squashing the creature.
> *blue slime squirted from underneath his shoe.*

Responding to the Revision Process

1. Why do you think the writer added a sentence?
2. Why do you think the writer replaced the phrase *got very small?*
3. Why do you think the writer added a final sentence to this paragraph?

> **Second Reading: Style** You have revised your short story so that it is well organized and complete. Now, you will check that you have written the story using the best possible word choice. One way to improve your word choice is to use **concrete language,** words that are specific, such as *exact verbs.* **Exact verbs** make your writing better because they accurately express a specific action. Look at the following guidelines to see if you need more exact verbs in your story.

Style Guidelines

Evaluation Question	▶ Tip	▶ Revision Technique
Does the story include verbs that accurately describe specific actions?	▶ **Draw a box** around exact verbs in the story.	▶ If a paragraph contains only one or two boxed verbs, **replace** some dull verbs with more descriptive ones.

Writing **1.2b** Develop the topic with precise verbs to paint a visual image in the mind of the reader. **2.1b** Include concrete language to develop plot and character.

Evaluate and Revise Content, Organization, and Style **515**

TECHNOLOGY TIP

W1.5
If students typed their stories into a word-processing program, they will need to be able to navigate within the documents as they begin to revise their stories.

To move among pages, students can use the mouse to move the pointer along the scroll bar on the side of the screen. Students can then move freely within the document by clicking and dragging the place marker, by clicking and holding the scroll button, or by clicking on the button for the previous page or the next page.

Students can move within a single page by moving the pointer and clicking or by using arrow keys to reposition the cursor. Text—once it is highlighted—can be copied, moved, modified, or deleted.

PEER REVIEW

As you read your classmate's story, ask yourself these questions.

- Could the writer add dialogue to elaborate on an event? If so, where?
- Is the story's ending satisfying and complete? Why or why not?

GUIDED PRACTICE

Responding to the Revision Process

Answers

1. The sentence was added to establish a cause-and-effect relationship between what Tyrel says and how the monster responds. This helps the story by creating suspense and by adding details about how a character acts.

2. The original phrase was probably replaced to make the monster's appearance after the soaping more clear and vivid.

3. The final sentence lets the reader know that the conflict has been resolved. Tyrel conquered the monster.

REVIEW STANDARD

Concrete Language: Exact Verbs

The following activity is a review of the 5th-grade **Writing Standard 2.1b.**

Write this sentence on the chalkboard: *Kelly _____ up to the front door.* Then, explain to students that you are going to describe different scenarios, and they should suggest exact verbs for filling in the blank in the sentence. For example, offer this scenario: Kelly has just received a report card with excellent grades. In this scenario, exact verbs may include *skipped, bounded,* or *flew.* Other scenarios might include the following: Kelly has a note of concern from the teacher, Kelly is expecting a phone call from a good friend, or Kelly had a hard workout in athletics.

GUIDED PRACTICE

Responding to the Revision Process

Answer

Adding exact verbs makes the story more interesting because readers can visualize the action.

PRACTICE & APPLY 5

Independent Practice

Students should revise their stories in three specific areas: content and organization, verb choice, and peer comments. Students should revise from a hard copy as this will keep them from inadvertently losing material. This will also enable the students and the teacher to see actual revisions and document each story's improvement.

Focus on — Word Choice

Concrete Language: Exact Verbs

Stories are meant to entertain readers. The more you can help readers visualize the action, the more entertaining your story will be. **Concrete language** shows, rather than tells, the reader an event and paints a picture in the reader's mind. **Exact verbs** can help you make the action of the story's events vivid and precise. Look at the following examples. Notice how exact verbs make the action come alive.

Dull Verbs	Exact Verbs
Jesse *ate* his dinner.	Jesse *gobbled down* his dinner.
Natalie *said,* "I'm leaving!"	Natalie *screamed,* "I'm leaving!"
Brian *went* to the store.	Brian *raced* to the store.
Eli *looked* at the phone.	Eli *stared* at the phone.
Mia *wrote* a note.	Mia *scribbled* a note.

COMPUTER TIP

You can use the thesaurus function in a word-processing program to replace dull verbs with exact verbs. Highlight the verb you want to replace, and the thesaurus will list other verbs with the same or similar meanings. From the list, you can choose the exact verb that accurately describes the action.

ONE WRITER'S REVISIONS

> The monster ~~rose~~ and ~~moved quickly~~ to the other side of the kitchen near the table.
> *(jumped into the air)* *(zoomed)*

Responding to the Revision Process

How did replacing dull verbs with exact verbs improve this sentence?

PRACTICE & APPLY 5

Evaluate and Revise Your Short Story

- First, evaluate and revise the content and organization of your story, using the guidelines on page 514.
- Next, use the Focus on Word Choice above to see if you need to replace dull verbs with exact verbs.
- If a peer evaluated your story, think carefully about his or her comments as you revise.

Writing 1.2b Develop the topic with precise verbs to paint a visual image in the mind of the reader. 2.1b Include concrete language to develop plot and character.

RESOURCES

Focus on Word Choice
Independent Practice
- *Writing, Listening, & Speaking*, WS. p. 8. You may choose to assign this independent practice as homework.

HOMEWORK

Practice and Apply 5
Think Sheet
- *Writing, Listening, & Speaking*, WS. p. 9
Independent Practice
- *Writing, Listening, & Speaking*, WS. p. 11
Extension
- *Writing, Listening, & Speaking*, WS. p. 10

Publishing

Proofread Your Short Story

Correctness Counts   Errors in your final draft will be distract-ing to your readers. If you have another person proofread your story, you will be less likely to overlook mistakes. Find and correct any mistakes in spelling, punctuation, capitalization, and grammar before you create your final draft.

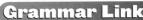

Grammar Link

Capitalizing Proper Nouns

As you write your short story, you will use **nouns**—words that name people, places, things, and ideas. There are two kinds of nouns: *common* and *proper*. A **common noun** names any one of a group of persons, places, things, or ideas. A **proper noun** names a par-ticular person, place, thing, or idea, and begins with a capital letter.

Here are some examples of common and proper nouns.

Common Nouns	Proper Nouns
city	Boston
religion	Judaism
basketball player	Michael Jordan
teacher	Ms. Nguyen

Notice that the title *Ms.* is capitalized in the example above. Capitalize a title that comes *immediately* before the person's name.

Example:

Washington, D.C., was named after President George Washington.

Most titles are not capitalized when they are not immediately followed by a name.

 Writing 2.0 Student writing demonstrates a command of standard American English.

Example:

The first president was George Washington.

PRACTICE

Capitalize the proper nouns in the following sentences.

1. Erica's vacation to visit aunt sue in eng-land was exciting.

    1. aunt sue   Aunt Sue
       england   England

1. Erica spent the entire month of july living in london.

2. The first week she visited the tower of lon-don and buckingham palace.

3. She loved riding on a boat down the thames river with her aunt.

4. She was hoping to see prince william, but he was in scotland with his father.

5. It took over ten hours for her to travel from london's gatwick airport to george bush intercontinental airport.

Reference Note

For more information and practice on **capitalizing proper nouns,** see page 241 in the *Holt Handbook.*

Quotation for the Day

"If you do not write for publication there is little point in writing at all."

(Bernard Shaw, 1856–1950, playwright, critic, and social reformer)

Discuss whether students agree or disagree with Shaw's statement. Those who disagree may feel that the act of writing itself is enjoy-able and therapeutic.

DIRECT TEACHING

Integrating with Grammar, Usage, and Mechanics

If students make mistakes with verbs and punctuating quotations, send them to the Parts of Speech Overview and Punctuation chap-ters in the *Holt Handbook.*

▶ **Resources Reminder**

For help with writing assessment, see 6 Traits—Plus 1 in the "General Scales and Sample Papers" section of *Progress Assessment of Writing, Listening, & Speaking.*

Grammar Link

Guided Practice

(For independent practice, see Proofreading Practice below.)

Answers

1. July, London

2. Tower of London, Buckingham Palace

3. Thames River

4. Prince William, Scotland

5. London's Gatwick Airport, George Bush Intercontinental Airport

Publish Your Short Story
W1.5

You might advise students who have not yet entered their short stories into a word-processing document to do so before publishing their stories. Remind students to include drawings or clip art with their stories, as mentioned in **Designing Your Writing** on Pupil's Edition p. 513, and to replace dull verbs by using the computer's thesaurus as mentioned in **Computer Tip** on p. 516.

Reflect on Your Short Story

Sample responses to the reflection questions in the Pupil's Edition follow.

- Deciding on a character and a problem was the most difficult because there are many combinations of people and problems from which to choose. The easy part was revising the story. Once it was on paper, I found it easier to check for problems with setting, characters, and plot.

- Next time I write a story I will try to use a different point of view.

- The plot of a story may be compared to the order of "events" in an essay. Thinking about the order before writing will probably make my essay organized and effective.

PRACTICE & APPLY 6

Independent Practice

Before students begin proofreading, remind them that they cannot rely solely on a spellcheck program when proofreading for spelling errors. Have students exchange papers for a human spellcheck.

You may wish to provide a standard format for students to use when responding to their own writing, and you may have students place their responses in a portfolio.

Publish Your Short Story

Story Hour   You are finally ready to share your short story with others. After all, that is the purpose of writing a short story. How do you go about getting an audience to read your story?

- Have a story hour in the school library, and read the story aloud to other students.

- Collect stories that would appeal to elementary school students. Put the stories together in a booklet, and distribute it to local elementary schools.

- With a few of your classmates, present your short story as a play. Create your setting by using props, and have the actors wear costumes.

- Distribute your short story to the community by placing copies in pediatricians' offices, dentists' offices, and even the mayor's office.

Reflect on Your Short Story

Building Your Portfolio   Your short story is finally written and published. Now, take the time to think about *what* you wrote and *how* you wrote. Reflecting on work that you have completed will make you a better writer in the future.

- What did you find difficult about writing a story? What did you find easy?

- What would you do differently the next time you write a story?

- Think back on all the steps you took before you actually began writing your short story. Which of these steps would also help you write an essay?

PRACTICE & APPLY 6 **Proofread, Publish, and Reflect on Your Short Story**

Wrap up your experience of writing a short story by following these steps.

- Find and correct any spelling, punctuation, capitalization, or grammar errors in your story.

- Publish your short story using one of the suggestions above.

- Answer the Reflect on Your Short Story questions above. Include your responses in your portfolio.

RESOURCES

Writing Workshop

Assessment

- *Progress Assessment of Writing, Listening, & Speaking,* pp. 2–4, 28–30, 77–85

Presenting and Listening to an Oral Narrative

Talk **Listen**

You are in your sleeping bag inside a tent. You want to sleep, but you toss and turn instead. You and your friends have been telling scary stories around a campfire. You continue to think about the way your friend used her voice and gestures to make you all nearly jump out of your skins. You are impressed by the powerful story, or **oral narrative,** your friend created.

Some oral narratives belong to an oral tradition. That is, they are handed down orally from one generation to the next. Others are made up on the spot. This workshop will help you effectively deliver an oral narrative based on the story you wrote for the Writing Workshop or on a story you have heard before. You will also have the opportunity to listen to stories told by your classmates.

Choose a Narrative

To choose an oral narrative, first consider your **audience, purpose,** and **occasion.** Ask yourself

- *Who will listen to my narrative?*
- *What effect do I want to have on my audience?*
- *When and where will I present my narrative?*

Answering these questions will help you choose the right **message.** For example, if your purpose is to scare your classmates, you might choose to tell a ghost story. If your purpose is to amuse young

WHAT'S AHEAD?

In this workshop you will deliver an oral narrative and listen to your classmates' narratives. You will also learn how to

- **choose a narrative**
- **identify the tone, mood, and emotion of an oral communication**
- **use verbal and nonverbal elements**
- **listen for rhetorical devices**

Listening and Speaking 1.4 Select an organizational structure, matching the purpose, message, and occasion to the audience. **2.1** Deliver narrative presentations.

Choose a Narrative **519**

Listening and Speaking Workshop

WORKSHOP RESOURCES

Listening and Speaking Workshop
Planning
- *On Course: Mapping Instruction*
- *One-Stop Planner* CD-ROM
- *At Home: A Guide to Standards Mastery,* p. 15
- *At Home: In Five Languages*

- *Writing, Listening, & Speaking*
  —Teaching Notes, pp. 13–15
  —Project-Planning Guide, WS. p. 16

Differentiating Instruction
- *Writing, Listening, & Speaking,* TP. 7
- *Lesson Plans for Language Development,* p. 225
- *Supporting Instruction in Five Languages*

Think Sheet
- *Writing, Listening, & Speaking,* WS. pp. 17, 20

Independent Practice
- *Writing, Listening, & Speaking,* WS. p. 18

(continued on p. 520)

Plan Your Presentation

The following tip is a review of the 5th-grade **Listening and Speaking Standard 2.1b.**

Explain to students that by choosing words that show rather than tell, they are more likely to keep their audience's interest and achieve their purpose: to entertain. Students may need to choose words their audience will understand or explain words that may be unfamiliar to their audience. For example, a student telling a story about snowboarding to classmates in Florida may have to "show" what snowboarding is.

MODELING AND DEMONSTRATION

Setting the Scene

On the chalkboard, write this phrase: *telling a really cool story.* Explain to students that this is a mnemonic device, or memory aid, to help them remember the information they must include when setting the scene for their narratives. The first letter in each word signals the first letter in the words they must remember: *t*=title, *a*=author, *r*=reasons for choosing, *c*=context, and *s*=setting. Have students demonstrate that they have a firm grasp of these elements by repeating them back to you with a short description of each element.

---

children, then you might choose a very different narrative, such as the tale of the three little pigs.

Once you have chosen an appropriate story, jot down the basic **plot** events in a **time line.** The **organizational structure** of most stories will be in **time order.** However, your audience, purpose, and occasion may determine how you arrange events and what elements you choose to include in your oral narrative. For example, in telling a scary story, you should include hints about upcoming events that build **suspense** without giving away the ending. In telling a story to a younger audience, you should include plenty of **dialogue,** characters' own words spoken in distinctive voices.

TIP If you choose to retell an old story, feel free to put your own spin on it—adding details and dialogue— even if you originally read the story in a book.

Plan Your Presentation

Setting the Scene When you go to a play, looking at the set can tell you a lot about the play before a word is even spoken. If the set shows an outdoor scene with a stagecoach, for example, you would know the story is not set in modern times. You can help your listeners in the same way by including in your oral narrative an introduction that sets the scene. Your introduction helps prepare listeners to understand your oral narrative. In your introduction, do the following.

- Make a **connection** between your listeners and the story. Use what you know about your audience to ask them a question or mention a common experience that relates to the subject of the story.
- Explain your **reasons** for choosing the narrative you are presenting.
- Establish the **context** of the narrative, telling listeners any important information about the **setting** and identifying the **point of view** from which you will tell the story (for example, a narrator may tell the story or the story may be told by one of its characters).

Here is one student's brief, attention-getting introduction to the folk tale "He Lion, Bruh Bear, and Bruh Rabbit" that begins on page 225.

> Do you remember any stories your family told you as you were growing up? Many families pass down "trickster" stories—stories about animals who talk and play tricks on each other. As a little kid, I always enjoyed the trickster story of He Lion, Bruh Bear, and Bruh Rabbit. Because I have an older brother, I like the fact that, in this story, a smaller animal plays a trick on a bigger one. I chose this story because it shows that it is better to be smart than strong.

Listening and Speaking 1.0 Students deliver focused, coherent presentations that convey ideas clearly and relate to the background and interests of the audience. 1.4 Select a point of view. 2.1a Establish a context, plot, and point of view. 2.1c Use a range of narrative devices (e.g., dialogue, tension, or suspense).

520 Workshop 1 **Narration:** Presenting and Listening to an Oral Narrative

---

(continued from p. 519)

Evaluation and Assessment

- *Writing, Listening, & Speaking*, WS. p. 19
- *Progress Assessment of Writing, Listening, & Speaking*, pp. 31–33
- *Diagnostic & Summative Assessments,* First-Quarter Test

Extension

- *Writing, Listening, & Speaking,* Videocassette, Segment 1

Making Every Word Count   To plan how to tell the story you have chosen, first think about the events that make up the plot and about the characters. Then, consider these techniques for telling about the events and characters in a vivid, entertaining way.

Sensory Details and Concrete Language   As you did in your written short story, you should use **descriptive strategies** to bring the characters and events in your oral narrative to life. These strategies include using *sensory details* and *concrete language*. **Sensory details** appeal to the senses—describing sights, sounds, smells, tastes, or sensations. **Concrete language** uses specific words to give readers an exact mental image of what you are describing.

Reference Note

For more on **sensory details** and **concrete language,** see page 506.

Rhetorical Devices   Rhetorical devices can add to your presentation's impact on listeners and make it more memorable. Think about where you might add some of the rhetorical devices in the following chart to the story you have chosen. The examples below come from Virginia Hamilton's retelling of the folk tale "He Lion, Bruh Bear, and Bruh Rabbit," which appears in Part 1 of this book.

TYPES OF RHETORICAL DEVICES

Rhetorical Device	Effect	Example
Rhythm (Cadence): the beat of the words, created through the words' stressed syllables, their arrangement, and sentence length	Creates mood and can build suspense	*The little animals held a sit-down talk, and one by one and two by two and all by all, they decide to go see Bruh Bear and Bruh Rabbit.*
Onomatopoeia: a word whose sound imitates its meaning	Helps listeners to hear the sounds you are describing	*They kept hearin somethin. Mumble, mumble.*
Repetition: repeating key words, phrases, or sounds	Emphasizes important ideas or events, can add humor, provides coherence	*He'd roar, "ME AND MYSELF. ME AND MYSELF."*

Use a Special Voice   Delivering an oral narrative means more than just talking. When you present **dialogue** from a story, you adjust your own voice to re-create the characters' speech and communicate a different personality for each character. You can also use your voice to keep listeners involved in the narrative by communicating *tone, mood,* and *emotion.*

Listening and Speaking   **1.8** Analyze the use of rhetorical devices (e.g., cadence, repetitive patterns, use of onomatopoeia) for intent and effect.   **2.0** Students deliver well-organized formal presentations employing traditional rhetorical strategies (e.g., narration, description).   **2.1b** Include sensory details and concrete language to develop the plot and character.

Special Education Students

Since the focus of this section is on preparing an oral narrative and not on writing, special education students could use photocopies of their narratives to mark deletions and make notations. If an enlarging copier is available, make large print copies to allow for note-taking space.

▶ **Resources Reminder**

For more help with Special Education Students, see *Lesson Plans for Language Development.*

DIRECT TEACHING

Rhetorical Devices

An audio version of "He Lion, Bruh Bear, and Bruh Rabbit" is available in the *Audio CD Library.* By listening to the audio CD, students can get a better idea of how a story is told out loud.

- **Tone** is the overall feeling of an oral communication. The sound of your voice and your choice of words will indicate the tone of the **message** to your listeners. To identify the tone of a narrative, think about how the story makes you feel. Then, think about how you would share that feeling. For example, a retelling of "He Lion, Bruh Bear, and Bruh Rabbit" would probably have a humorous tone. The storyteller could laugh, use his voice to emphasize funny events, and gesture excitedly.

- **Mood** is the general emotional state of a particular character or speaker. For example, in "He Lion, Bruh Bear, and Bruh Rabbit," the lion's general mood is that of a smug bully. A storyteller might communicate that mood by talking loudly, strutting around with his nose in the air, and gesturing threateningly.

- **Emotion** is a speaker's or character's feeling about a particular thing or event. For example, in "He Lion, Bruh Bear, and Bruh Rabbit," when He Lion finally meets Man, he becomes so frightened that the experience forever changes the way he treats other animals. A storyteller could show this emotion by dropping He Lion's voice from a roar to a whisper and speaking slowly with eyes wide.

Make Delivery Notes

To give an effective presentation, you have to remember a lot of information. In addition to the basic story and characters you will share, you also need to remember

- your introduction
- the sensory details and concrete language you will use to describe the plot and characters
- rhetorical devices that will make your narrative memorable
- narrative devices, such as dialogue and suspense
- the ways in which you will express tone, mood, and emotion

To help you remember all of the elements of your oral narrative, add delivery notes to your time line. Imagine yourself telling your story to an audience, and jot down ideas about the items above and about *verbal* and *nonverbal elements* you want to include. **Verbal elements** include **rate, volume,** and **vocal modulation,** or **pitch**—the high or low sounds of your voice. **Nonverbal elements** include **gestures, facial expressions, posture,** and **eye contact.** The delivery notes one student made on his time line are shown on the next page.

TIP Although the story "He Lion, Bruh Bear, and Bruh Rabbit" appears in this book, the student who made the time line on the next page will retell the story in his own words, just as you should do with the story you choose.

Listening and Speaking 1.4 Match the message and vocal modulation to the audience. 1.7 Use effective rate, volume, pitch, and tone and align nonverbal elements to sustain audience interest and attention. 2.0 Student speaking demonstrates a command of organizational and delivery strategies outlined in Listening and Speaking Standard 1.0.

beginning

Lion roars all the time.	loud voice, stomp around
Animals go see Bruh Bear and Bruh Rabbit.	<u>cadence</u>—narrator: "He stomps and stomps and roars and roars."
Bruh Bear and Bruh Rabbit visit Lion.	use different gestures and facial expressions for each character
Lion says he's king of forest, but Bruh Rabbit says Man is.	<u>repetition</u>—"No, he's the king." "No, I'm the king."
Rabbit takes Lion to see Man; they see little boy, then old man.	use voice to build suspense as they go further into forest and see each person
Lion sees young man with gun; Rabbit and Bear hide.	use voice and gestures to show Rabbit's fear of Man
Lion roars, and Man shoots at Lion.	<u>onomatopoeia</u>—"Roar!" "Ka-boom!"
Lion treats other animals better from then on.	show change in Lion's personality with voice and posture

end

Rehearse and Present

An entertaining oral narrative doesn't just happen—it takes lots of practice. Follow these guidelines.

- Practice the gestures and facial expressions you will use. Use your body and your voice to show the characters in distinctive ways.
- Practice speaking slowly, clearly, and loudly enough so that someone in the back of the classroom will be able to understand you.
- If possible, record your practice session on audiotape or videotape. Then, carefully evaluate it. Make any necessary changes. If you do not have access to a tape recorder or a video camera, practice in front of a mirror.

When you feel comfortable with all of the elements of your presentation, present your oral narrative to the class.

TIP Use **standard American English,** language that is grammatically correct, when telling your story. Use informal English, such as slang, only when a character speaks and you are sure your audience will understand it.

 Listening and Speaking 2.0 Students deliver well-organized formal presentations employing traditional rhetorical strategies (e.g., narration, description). Student speaking demonstrates a command of standard American English. **2.1** Deliver narrative presentations.

Rehearse and Present **523**

Guided and Independent Practice

Monitor students as they mark their narratives for presentation. Particularly note if the text is too crowded to be read easily. Also point out where students may be over-marking. Encourage them to use a simple set of symbols and notes for marking text. After they have finished marking their texts, have them independently practice their presentations.

DIRECT TEACHING

Listen to an Oral Narrative

Write the following acronym on the chalkboard: *LEAN.* Explain to students that these four letters represent four things to keep in mind while listening to other students' presentations: *L*=Lean toward the speaker, don't lounge in your chair; *E*=Eye contact, keep your eyes on the presenter; *A*=Acknowledge, respond as appropriate by using verbal or nonverbal signs; *N*=Notes, take notes during the presentation.

PRACTICE & APPLY **8**

Guided and Independent Practice

Before students present narratives, write on the chalkboard the four questions for judging a presenter's effectiveness. Instruct students to take notes on the presentations in response to the four questions.

Reference Note

For more on **tone, mood,** and **emotion,** see page 522. For more on **rhythm, onomatopoeia,** and **repetition,** see page 521.

Rehearse and Present Your Oral Narrative

- First, choose a narrative and write the events of the narrative on a time line.
- Next, plan your presentation by writing an introduction and adding sensory details, concrete language, rhetorical devices, and delivery notes to your time line.
- Then, practice your presentation, using the information in the bulleted list on page 523, and present your narrative to your class.

Listen to an Oral Narrative

What's That You Say? When you listen to an oral narrative consider the **verbal elements**—*volume, pitch,* and *rate*—of the presentation. Notice also the speaker's use of **nonverbal elements**—*gestures, posture, eye contact,* and *facial expressions.* Watch to see whether the verbal and nonverbal elements match. For example, the speaker may gesture and raise his or her voice at the same time to emphasize an important event. To evaluate a narrative and provide feedback to the speaker, make notes in response to these questions as you listen.

- What is the overall **tone** of the oral narrative? Is it funny, sad, or serious? Explain how the words and the voice and gestures the speaker used to communicate those words helped you figure out the tone.
- What is the general **mood** of each character? What verbal and nonverbal elements helped communicate each character's mood?
- What specific **feelings,** or **emotions,** can you identify in the narrative? What verbal and nonverbal elements helped you identify each emotion?
- Where and why does the speaker use rhetorical devices such as **rhythm, onomatopoeia,** or **repetition?** How effective is each device?

Listen to an Oral Narrative

Using the questions above, listen to two or three of your classmates' oral narratives and make notes to evaluate the presentations for impact, effectiveness, and interest. Discuss your notes with each speaker once he or she has finished presenting.

Listening and Speaking 1.0 They evaluate the content of oral communication. **1.1** Relate the speaker's verbal communication (e.g., pitch, feeling, tone) to the nonverbal message (e.g., posture, gesture). **1.2** Identify the tone, mood, and emotion conveyed in the oral communication. **1.8** Analyze the use of rhetorical devices (e.g., cadence, repetitive patterns, use of onomatopoeia) for intent and effect.

DIRECTIONS: Read the following paragraph from a student's short story. Then, read the questions below it. Choose the best answer, and mark your answers on your own paper.

Flat Out of Luck

Mrs. Fiona McNulty was late. She smashed her wig onto her head, pulled up the suspenders on her overalls, crammed her feet into the openings of her oversized shoes, grabbed her bag of tricks, and raced out the door to her small car. "Oops," she thought to herself, "I should have had that tire checked. It looks low. I don't have time to check it now. I'll do it on the way home from the birthday party." Fifteen minutes later, in the middle of the five o'clock rush-hour traffic jam, Mrs. McNulty felt the tire go flat. She braced herself and moved as quickly as she could to the side of the road. She turned off the motor and climbed out of her car. "Great! What do I do now?" she thought. Mrs. McNulty was already late for her appearance at a child's birthday party as JoJo the Juggling Clown.

1. What words did the writer use to establish the setting?
   A "crammed her feet into the openings of her oversized shoes"
   B "in the middle of the five o'clock rush-hour traffic jam"
   C "braced herself and moved as quickly as she could"
   D "should have had that tire checked"

2. If the writer wanted to add sensory details to the story, which of the following sentences would be appropriate?
   F The birthday party was at a house across town.
   G She had to hurry if she wanted to be on time.
   H She couldn't call anyone because she had left her cell phone at home.
   J Passers-by stared at the clown in a red wig, baggy overalls, and oversized shoes.

3. Why did the student put the sentence, "Great! What do I do now?" in quotation marks?

   A because the sentence is dialogue
   B because it is the title of the story
   C because it is the problem of the story
   D because the sentence creates suspense

4. Imagine you were asked to present this story as an oral narrative. Which of the following gestures would be appropriate to make when saying, "Great! What do I do now?"
   F winking at the audience
   G giving the "thumbs up" sign
   H throwing your arms up in the air
   J running in place while looking behind you

5. If you were listening to an oral narrative of this story, you would expect the tone to be
   A joyous
   B frustrated
   C romantic
   D sad

Narration

Assessment
- *Progress Assessment of Writing, Listening, & Speaking,* Wkshp. 1
- *Diagnostic & Summative Assessments,* First-Quarter Test

Extension
- *Writing, Listening, & Speaking,* p. 21

Standards Practice and Review

(Standards reviewed on this page: W 2.1, L&S 1.1., 1.2. To read the complete standards, see pp. 498–499.)

Answers

1. B
2. J
3. A
4. H
5. B

APPLICATION

Open Mic

If space and time allow, help students set up a "coffee house," or writer's salon. Prior to the event, have students sign up for a turn at the microphone. Instruct them to select passages from their original stories or their oral narratives to present. Passages should be no more than a minute and a half in length, including a brief introduction.

Dim the lights and have students sit informally. Then, allow them to take turns at the microphone. Invite special guests to perform the readings, or hold a contest for the best presentation, complete with a prize presentation. If judges are used in a contest, share with them beforehand the criteria for evaluating oral presentations on p. 524 in the Pupil's Edition.

EXTENSION

Storyboard

For homework, have students survey family members to find out their favorite stories. Students may then create posters that include the titles of the stories, authors, brief explanations of why each story is a favorite, and perhaps pictures from magazines or original artwork to represent each story. Students' posters may then be displayed in   HOMEWORK
the classroom.

Workshop 2 Exposition

Program Organization

Holt Literature and Language Arts provides a complete curriculum for standards-based instruction in vocabulary, reading, literature, writing, speaking and listening, and media. The instructional content of the program is divided into quarters to enable teachers to anticipate and administer the quarterly assessments required by California.

About Workshop 2

Standards-based lesson plans and suggestions for linking instruction with Workshop 2 and the related instructional material are provided in *On Course: Mapping Instruction*.

- Workshop 2 focuses on expository writing and the listening skills needed to follow oral instructions and directions. Chapter 2 connects to this workshop by focusing on character analysis in both literature and informational readings.

- The related instructional material for Workshop 2 is shown on the chart. This related instructional material will also be covered in the first quarterly assessment. Specific teaching suggestions for the related material are found in Part 1 of this book and in the *Holt Handbook*.

Holt Literature and Language Arts

Pupil's Edition

Part 1, Chapter 2

Characters: The People
You'll Meet, pp. 50–113
- Reading Standards 1.3, 2.4, 3.2
- Writing Application **Writing an Explanation**

Part 2, Workshop 2

Exposition
Writing a "How-To"
Explanation, pp. 528–544
- Writing Standard 2.2

Following Oral Instructions and
Directions, pp. 545–548
- Listening and Speaking Standard 2.2

Holt Handbook

Chapter 3

Parts of Speech Overview: Verb, Adverb,
Preposition, Conjunction, Interjection
- Written and Oral English-Language Conventions Standard 1.1 pp. 49–54
- Looking Ahead, Gr. 7 Standard 1.3, pp. 66–67

Chapter 4

The Phrase and the Clause
- Written and Oral English-Language Conventions Standards 1.1, 1.3, pp. 89–100

Diagnostic and Summative Assessments: First-Quarter Test

Language Arts Content

This workshop uses the writing and listening and speaking strategies to enable students to master successfully the writing and speaking applications.

What standards are taught in Workshop 2?

In this workshop, students will master the following Grade 6 standards. They will also review several standards from an earlier grade.

Writing Strategies

1.0 Students write clear, coherent, and focused essays. The writing exhibits students' awareness of the audience and purpose. Students progress through the stages of the writing process as needed.

1.2 Create multiple-paragraph compositions.

1.3 Use a variety of effective and coherent organizational patterns, including climactic order.

1.5 Compose documents with appropriate formatting by using word-processing skills and principles of design (e.g., margins, spacing, columns).

1.6 Revise writing to improve the organization and consistency of ideas within and between paragraphs.

Writing Applications

2.0 Students write expository texts of at least 500 to 700 words. Student writing demonstrates a command of standard American English and the organizational and drafting strategies outlined in Writing Standard 1.0.

2.2 Write expository compositions (e.g., explanation).

Listening and Speaking Strategies

1.3 Restate and execute multiple-step oral instructions and directions.

Review Standards, Grade 5

Writing

1.2 Create multiple-paragraph expository compositions.

Listening and Speaking

1.5 Clarify and support spoken ideas with evidence and examples.

2.2 Deliver informative presentations about an important idea, issue, or event.

Where do I locate lesson plans, additional resources, and other teaching aids?

- The Annotated Teacher's Edition and *On Course: Mapping Instruction* provide direction in planning and implementing a complete California standards–based curriculum. These components include instructions for administering diagnostic, progress, and summative tests; for presenting instruction of the standards, for differentiating instruction to provide universal access; and for locating and using the program's ancillaries.

- The program's resources are referenced at the beginning of each workshop in the bottom margin of this teacher's edition: Writing a "How-to" Explanation and Following Oral Instructions and Directions.

- Reminders for using additional resources appear in this teacher's edition at point of use.

- The *One-Stop Planner* CD-ROM contains editable lesson plans and all print ancillaries, available in PDF format.

What if I don't have time to teach all of Workshop 2?

- Within this workshop, complete coverage of the application standards is provided by the following instructional features in the Pupil's Edition:
  - Writing a "How-to" Explanation
  - Prewriting

- Think About Purpose and Audience
- Plan Your Explanation
- A Writer's Framework
- Proofread Your Explanation

- Use Standards Practice and Review for a quick assessment and review of workshop standards.

What provisions have been made for students who have additional class time scheduled in language arts?

- *Universal Access: Writing, Listening, & Speaking*, Workshop 2 contains worksheets and transparencies that provide practice, reteaching, and extension of Workshop 2 standards. Each Practice and Apply exercise is supported by graphic organizers or practice activities for on-level learners, advanced learners, and learners having difficulty.

- *Universal Access: Lesson Plans for Language Development*, Workshop 2, provides alternative teaching strategies and additional worksheets designed specifically for English-language learners and special education students. Many of the suggestions and activities in this ancillary will also be helpful to students in the regular classroom who are having difficulty with particular skills.

Universal Access

How do I differentiate instruction to ensure that all my students master the standards?

Holt Literature and Language Arts provides comprehensive, differentiated instruction for all types of students.

- Most of the general instruction and teaching strategies in the Annotated Teacher's Edition are at grade level. These instructions will work well with the majority of your students.

- Advanced students have at least one activity for each workshop. The suggested activities are found in this teacher's edition at point of instruction.

- *Universal Access: Writing, Listening, & Speaking,* Workshop 2, opens with Teaching Notes that suggest which worksheets and transparencies are appropriate for each of three levels of learners.

- *Universal Access: Lesson Plans for Language Development,* Workshop 2, offers teaching strategies and additional worksheets designed specifically for English-language learners and special education students.

- *Daily Language Activities Transparencies* and *Spelling: Lessons & Activities* provide ongoing review of and additional practice in a range of language arts skills.

- For every workshop, preselected Web sites and activities are available to provide enrichment, independent practice, and enhanced instructional opportunities.

Assessment

How do I determine whether or not my students are making progress in mastering the standards?

Progress Assessment

- Use the Standards Review at the end of Workshop 2 for an informal assessment of the writing and listening standards taught in Workshop 2.

- Use Workshop 2 in *Progress Assessment of Writing, Listening, & Speaking* to test students' cumulative progress in mastering the standards taught in the workshop.

Summative Assessment

The content in *Holt Literature and Language Arts* has been divided into four quarters to allow you to administer the four summative tests required by California. Workshop 2 will be assessed in the first quarter of instruction. At the end of Workshop 2, you may ask students to take the First-Quarter Test in the *Diagnostic & Summative Assessments* booklet.

Exposition

STANDARDS FOCUS

Writing

Prerequisite Standards

Grade 5

■ 1.2 Create multiple-paragraph expository compositions:
  a. Establish a topic, important ideas, or events in sequence or chronological order.
  b. Provide details and transitional expressions that link one paragraph to another in a clear line of thought.
  c. Offer a concluding paragraph that summarizes important ideas and details.

Standards Coming Up in the Next Level

Grade 7

■ 1.1 Create an organizational structure that balances all aspects of the composition and uses effective transitions between sentences to unify important ideas.

■ 1.2 Support all statements and claims with anecdotes, descriptions, facts and statistics, and specific examples.

WRITING WORKSHOP

Writing a "How-to" Explanation Page 528

LISTENING WORKSHOP

Following Oral Instructions and Directions Page 545

H ere is a riddle for you: How are you and a computer alike? Computers follow a set of instructions to perform a function, and so do you. Think about it.

■ In math class, for example, you learn how to turn an improper fraction into a mixed number.
■ Flip through the channels on TV, and you can see how to increase your physical strength through exercise.
■ This evening, you may heat up a frozen dinner by following the instructions on the box.

The instructions you listen to, view, and read are all designed to teach you to complete a process.

Once you know how a process is done, you can share that knowledge by giving an explanation. In this workshop you will share your knowledge of how to make something by writing a "how-to" explanation. Your paper will be **expository,** or informative. You will also practice the listening skills needed to follow oral instructions and directions. In the process you will practice the following language arts standards.

California Standards

Writing

1.0 Students write clear, coherent, and focused essays. The writing exhibits students' awareness of the audience and purpose. Essays contain formal introductions, supporting evidence, and conclusions. Students progress through the stages of the writing process as needed.

1.2 Create multiple-paragraph expository compositions:
  a. Engage the interest of the reader and state a clear purpose.
  b. Develop the topic with supporting details and precise verbs, nouns, and adjectives to paint a visual image in the mind of the reader.
  c. Conclude with a detailed summary linked to the purpose of the composition.

GO TO: go.hrw.com
KEYWORD: HLLA6 W-2
FOR: Models, Writer's Guides, and Reference Sources

1.3 Use a variety of effective and coherent organizational patterns.

1.5 Compose documents with appropriate formatting by using word-processing skills and principles of design (e.g., margins, spacing, columns).

1.6 Revise writing to improve the organization and consistency of ideas within and between paragraphs.

2.0 Students write expository texts of at least 500 to 700 words. Student writing demonstrates a command of standard American English and the organizational and drafting strategies outlined in Writing Standard 1.0.

2.2 Write expository compositions (e.g. explanation):

    a. State the thesis or purpose.

    b. Explain the situation.

    c. Follow an organizational pattern appropriate to the type of composition.

Listening and Speaking

1.3 Restate and execute multiple-step oral instructions and directions.

Listening and Speaking

Prerequisite Standards

Grade 5

- 1.1 Ask questions that seek information not already discussed.
- 1.2 Interpret a speaker's verbal and nonverbal messages, purposes, and perspectives.

Standards Coming Up in the Next Level

Grade 7

- 1.1 Ask probing questions to elicit information, including evidence to support the speaker's claims and conclusions.

CALIFORNIA STANDARDS

PRETEACHING

Standards Starter

Motivate. Have students think about a simple product that they know how to make, such as a sandwich or a paper airplane. Ask volunteers to explain to the class each step involved in making their products. Tell students that in this workshop, they will learn more about describing the steps in making a product and about writing a "how-to" explanation.

Introducing the Workshop. To introduce the workshop, use the Journal Warm-up, Transparency 8, in *Writing, Listening, & Speaking.*

Quotation for the Day

"So before writing, learn to think."

(Nicolas Boileau-Despréaux, 1636–1711, French critic and poet)

Write the quotation on the chalkboard, and ask students to consider how the quotation applies to a writer who explains a process in a "how-to" article. Guide students to understand how thinking through a process and visualizing each of the steps might help a writer compose a clear and complete "how-to" explanation.

WHAT'S AHEAD?

In this workshop you will write a "how-to" explanation. You will also learn how to

- **consider your audience**
- **plan your instructions**
- **write with precise verbs, nouns, and adjectives**
- **connect ideas by using transitional words and phrases**
- **use commas in a series**

| DO THIS → |

Reference Note
For more on **think sheets,** see page 495.

Writing a "How-to" Explanation

"Mmm, mmm. No one makes a smoothie as well as you do!" Everyone knows how to make something, whether it is a simple product such as a delicious fruit smoothie or a more complicated one such as a two-level treehouse. Whether the process is easy or difficult, making things takes knowledge and talent. What special skills do you have?

In this workshop you will have an opportunity to share your knowledge with others by writing a "how-to" explanation. You will use specific details and **transitional words,** words that connect one idea to another, to give exact instructions for making a product.

Professional Model: A "How-to" Article

Can you think of something that you have learned how to do by reading a book or magazine article? Maybe you have learned to program a VCR to videotape your favorite program by reading the owner's manual. You may have learned how to fix a flat tire on your bike by reading a bicycle repair book. People often share their talents and special knowledge with the public by publishing.

To help you decide what to write about or to find a model for what details to include in your instructions, start by looking at professionally written "how-to" articles such as "Making a Flying Fish," which begins on the next page. Create a **think sheet** as you read the article, making notes on how the flying fish is made and how the writer makes sure her instructions are clear. On your think sheet, you can also answer the numbered analysis questions that appear in the margins.

 Writing 2.2 Write expository compositions (e.g. explanation).

WORKSHOP RESOURCES

Writing Workshop
Planning
- *On Course: Mapping Instruction*
- *One-Stop Planner* CD-ROM
- *At Home: A Guide to Standards Mastery,* p. 19
- *At Home: In Five Languages*

- *Writing, Listening, & Speaking,* —Teaching Notes, p. 22

Differentiating Instruction
- *Lesson Plans for Language Development,* pp. 226–227
- *Supporting Instruction in Five Languages*

Practice
- *Writing, Listening, & Speaking,* Wkshp. 2

Making a Flying Fish

by Paula Morrow
from FACES

Japanese boys and girls have their own special day each year on May 5. It is called Children's Day and is a national holiday. This is a time for families to celebrate having children by telling stories, feasting, going on picnics, or visiting grandparents. Many years ago, May 5 was Boys' Day, and girls had their own holiday on March 3. In modern Japan, all children are honored on the same day.

A special feature of Children's Day is the *koinobori* (koi•nō´bô•ri) that families display in their yards—one for each child in the family. A tall pole is placed in the garden. . . . Fish made of cloth or strong paper are attached to the pole.

> **1. What is a koinobori? What is it used for?**

Each fish has a hoop in its mouth to catch the wind. The largest fish is for the oldest child, and the smallest is for the youngest.

These fish represent a kind of carp known as a strong fighter. These carp battle their way upstream against strong currents. When the *koinobori* dance in the wind, they remind children of carp leaping up a waterfall. This is supposed to inspire children to be equally brave and strong.

You can make your own *koinobori* and fly it from a pole or hang it from your window on May 5. In that way, you can share Children's Day with the boys and girls of Japan.

> **2. Why would you want to make a flying fish?**

You need an 18- by 30-inch piece of lightweight cloth (cotton, rayon, or nylon), fabric paints or felt-tip markers, a needle and thread, scissors, a narrow plastic headband, and string.

> **3. What materials does the writer list?**

DIRECT TEACHING

Professional Model

Explain to students that using think sheets to summarize their notes from a reading serves two purposes. First, creating think sheets allows students to place their thoughts, observations, and questions on paper, which, in turn, helps increase reading comprehension. Second, the process of creating think sheets provides students with ideas for their own writing.

Professional Model Questions

Answers

1. A *koinobori* is a cloth or paper fish that is displayed on a pole in front of a Japanese house on Children's Day. Each *koinobori* represents one of the children living in the house.

2. Making a flying fish would allow one to participate in the Japanese holiday of Children's Day.

3. an 18- by 30-inch piece of lightweight cloth, fabric paints or felt-tip markers, a needle and thread, scissors, a narrow plastic headband, and string

Reinforcement
■ *Daily Language Activities*
■ *Spelling*

Evaluation and Assessment
■ *Test Generator (One-Stop Planner* CD-ROM)
■ *Progress Assessment of Writing, Listening, & Speaking,* Wkshp. 2

■ *Diagnostic and Summative Assessments,* First-Quarter Test

Internet
■ go.hrw.com (keyword: HLLA6 W-2)

4. The first step is to choose a cloth with a bright pattern, or decorate a piece of cloth, and sew it into a sleeve. The first step is introduced by the word *First.*

5. The instruction to "make cuts 5 inches deep" indicates that the fringe will be 5 inches long.

6. The word *Finally* signals the last step in the process.

DIRECT TEACHING

Professional Model

After students read the model, ask them to identify its purpose and audience. [The purpose of the Professional Model is to explain how to make a *koinobori,* or flying fish. Students will probably say that the model is written for a young adult audience. The topic, Children's Day, and the vocabulary and sentence structure seem appropriate for a young audience.]

First, choose a piece of cloth with a bright, colorful pattern or decorate it yourself with felt-tip markers. Fold the fabric in half lengthwise, with the bright side on the inside. Sew a seam ½ inch from the long (30-inch) edge, making a sleeve.

On one end of the sleeve, make a 1-inch-wide hem by turning the right side of the fabric over the wrong side. Then, sew the hem, leaving three 1-inch-wide openings about 5 inches apart. [See the illustration below.]

Make cuts 5 inches deep and 1 inch apart all around the unhemmed end of the sleeve to form a fringe. This is the fish's tail.

Next, turn the sleeve right side out. With fabric paints or a felt-tip marker, add eyes near the hemmed (head) end (away from the fringed tail).

Thread the narrow plastic headband into the head through one of the openings. Continue threading it until the open part of the headband is hidden.

Then, tie a 12-inch-long piece of string to the headband at each of the three openings. Tie the loose ends of the strings together.

Finally, hang your windsock from the strings on a tree limb, a clothes pole, or the eaves of your house. On windy days, it will dance like a carp swimming upstream against a waterfall!

> **4. What is the first step? How do you know?**

> **5. How do you know how long the fringe will be?**

> **6. What word lets you know this is the last step?**

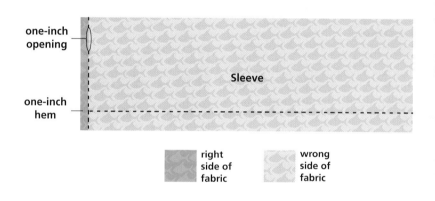

one-inch opening

one-inch hem

Sleeve

right side of fabric

wrong side of fabric

In a small group, discuss the following questions. Then, present your group's responses orally to the class.

1. Do you think the writer's instructions were clear? Why or why not?

2. What sort of specific details did the writer include to help you picture the steps for making a *koinobori*?

3. How did the writer make sure that you followed the correct order of steps for creating the flying fish?

4. Make a graphic organizer, such as a time line, to show the order of the steps for making a flying fish.

Reference Note
For more information on making a **time line**, see page 533.

Prewriting

Choose a Topic

I Know, I Know   To choose a topic for your "how-to" explanation, follow the rule successful writers live by: *Write about what you know*. Brainstorm a list of products that you have successfully made before. Consider the following questions as you create your list.

- Look around your home. What have you built or made?
- What school projects have you made in the past?
- What is your favorite recipe to make?
- What handicrafts do you know how to make?
- Look back at the Professional Model on pages 529–530. Does it remind you of anything you know how to make?

How Do I Decide?   Once you have listed several products, you will need to evaluate them to choose the best one to write about. The best topic will be one that you know well and one that you can write about in a 500- to 700-word paper. The chart on the next page shows how one student first listed several topics and then focused on one of the topics by asking specific questions.

Writing   **1.0** Students write focused essays. Students progress through the stages of the writing process as needed.   **2.0** Students write expository texts of at least 500 to 700 words.

Choose a Topic   **531**

Think About the Model
Answers
Possible responses are given below.

1. The writer's instructions were very clear. They included specific details, precise words, and an illustration.

2. Specific details such as "the bright side" of the fabric and the "hemmed end" help the reader picture each step.

3. The writer used time-sequence words such as *First, Next, Then,* and *Finally* to make the correct order of steps clear.

4. Students' graphic organizers should include the following steps.
   - Choose a piece of cloth or decorate one.
   - Fold the fabric and sew a seam.
   - Make and sew a hem.
   - Form a fringe.
   - Add eyes.
   - Thread the headband through one of the openings in the hem.
   - Tie strings to each of the openings on the headband, and tie the strings together.
   - Hang the windsock.

DIRECT TEACHING

Integrating with Grammar, Usage, and Mechanics

As students begin writing their "how-to" explanations, you may want to stop and review common usage problems and the use of colons with lists because these are concepts with which students often have trouble. See A Glossary of Usage and the punctuation chapters in the *Holt Handbook*.

Topic	Have I made this product before, and do I know the process well?	Does this process have a manageable number of steps (between three and five)?
Paper swan	yes	no—it has over five steps
Snowman decoration ✓	yes	yes—it has about five steps
Soapbox car	not really—I helped my big brother make it	no—this probably takes more than five steps

After evaluating each of his topics, the student whose chart appears above chose the topic that had the most *yes* answers. His explanation will tell others how to make a snowman decoration.

Think About Purpose and Audience

Consider This Your **purpose** for writing an explanation is to teach someone how to make something. **You should begin your explanation by stating your purpose in a sentence.** For instance, the writer of the Writer's Model on page 537 makes this statement of purpose: "This explanation will tell you how to make your own snowman." Use your statement of purpose as a starting point for your introduction.

You will also want to consider what information your **audience,** the people reading your explanation, will need. To do that, use the steps in the Thinking It Through below.

KEY CONCEPT

TIP It is important to **explain the situation** in which your explanation might be used. For example, a fourth-grader might use an explanation of how to make a snowman out of foam balls to make decorations for his or her home for the winter.

THINKING IT THROUGH **Considering Your Audience**

▶ **STEP 1 Identify your audience.**   Fourth-graders

▶ **STEP 2 What words should you define so your audience can understand the process?**   The snowman decoration has a muffler. Fourth-graders may not know that a muffler is a scarf.

▶ **STEP 3 Ask yourself, "What steps caused me trouble?" How can you make those steps clearer?**   I had a problem keeping the sequin eyes in place. I used straight pins to hold them until the glue dried.

Writing 1.0 The writing exhibits students' awareness of the audience and purpose.   **1.2a** State a clear purpose.   **2.2a** State the thesis or purpose.   **2.2b** Explain the situation.

- Brainstorm a list of products that you have made. Then, make a chart like the one on page 532, and evaluate each product. Choose the product that has the most "yes" answers in the chart.

- Once you have a topic, choose an audience. Write a sentence that states a purpose for your explanation and explains a situation in which your product might be used. Then, think about the information your audience will need by completing the steps in the Thinking It Through on page 532.

Plan Your Explanation

As Easy as 1, 2, 3 Imagine the frustration of trying to build a model car if the explanation described painting the model before the car was even put together. Putting the **details,** or steps, in the correct order gives the explanation *coherence.* In a **coherent** paper, all the parts fit together in an organizational pattern that makes sense to the reader. **Most "how-to" papers are written in *chronological order,* or time order.**

KEY CONCEPT

To think of the steps in chronological order, imagine yourself making the product. As you perform each step, write it on a time line. Then, look over your steps and add anything you left out.

Steps to make a snowman decoration:

1	2	3	4 / 3	5 / 4
assemble face and let dry	make middle and let dry	make stand	put snowman together	make muffler

Next, brainstorm the materials you need to make the product. Think carefully about everything you need. If you forget to list a material, your reader will not be able to make the product.

TIP Look over your time line for steps that may distract the reader. Ask yourself, "Does my audience already know how to do this step?" If the answer is "yes," then you do not need that step.

PRACTICE & APPLY 2 **Plan Your Explanation**

Write the steps for making your product in chronological order on a time line. Then, list the needed materials.

Writing **1.0** Students write clear, coherent essays. Essays contain supporting evidence. **1.2b** Develop the topic with supporting details. **1.3** Use a variety of effective and coherent organizational patterns. **2.0** Student writing demonstrates the organizational strategies outlined in Writing Standard 1.0. **2.2c** Follow an organizational pattern appropriate to the type of composition.

Plan Your Explanation **533**

MINI-LESSON THE WRITER'S LANGUAGE

Precision and Coherence

Suppose that the writer of "Making a Flying Fish" had given you the following instructions. Could you follow them?

FLYING FISH WINDSOCK

Sew a sleeve from some cloth. Attach plastic to the sleeve. Put some string on the plastic, and hang up your windsock.

Reading the steps, you might have asked yourself several questions. *What kind of cloth do I use? What kind of plastic? Where do I put the string on the plastic, and how much string do I need?* The directions are too vague. That is, they are too general and sketchy to be useful.

What Exactly Do You Mean? When you explain a process, you must be *precise.* **Precise verbs, nouns,** and **adjectives** paint a clear picture in the reader's mind. They help answer questions such as *Which one? What kind? How?* and *How many?*

Look at the following table. The left-hand column of the table lists vague words that the writer might have used in an early draft of "Making a Flying Fish." The middle column lists the questions the words leave unanswered. The right-hand column shows precise replacements for the words—specific adjectives, nouns, and verbs.

ASKING QUESTIONS TO REPLACE VAGUE WORDS

Vague Words	Questions	Precise Words
cloth	What kind?	**lightweight** cloth [precise adjective]
Add eyes near the end.	Which one?	Add eyes near the **hemmed** end (away from the **fringed tail**). [precise adjectives and nouns]
plastic	What kind?	**narrow,** plastic **headband** [precise adjective and noun]
Put some string on the plastic.	How? How much?	**Tie** a **12-inch-long piece** of string to the **headband.** [precise verb and adjective]

Writing 1.2b Develop the topic with precise verbs, nouns, and adjectives to paint a visual image in the mind of the reader.

Stay the Same Precise language is also *consistent*. In one sense, being **consistent** means always using the same word to refer to the same item. The writer of "Making a Flying Fish" uses the same words, or key terms, to describe the parts of the windsock at each step. For example, once the cloth is sewn on one side, she calls it a *sleeve*. Only after the headband and string are added does she call the sleeve a *windsock*. The writer takes care to use the same term at each stage of the project.

Clear and Connected Another way to make your writing clear is to create *coherence*. In **coherent** writing, one idea flows logically into the next. You can improve coherence by using *transitions*. A **transition** is a word or phrase that shows how ideas fit together. The transitions most often used in "how-to" explanations are *chronological transitions* and *spatial transitions*. **Chronological transitions** answer the question *In what order?* **Spatial transitions** answer the question *Where?*

Here are some examples of transitional words and phrases.

- **Chronological transitions:** *first, second, after, next, then, finally, last*
- **Spatial transitions:** *inside, outside, above, below, into, out of*

When you write directions, you must be clear about the order in which the steps should be completed. If your paper is not clear, your readers may become confused. Precise language and transitions make each step in "Making a Flying Fish" clear and easy to follow.

PRACTICE

Re-read "Making a Flying Fish" on pages 529–530. As you read, jot down the examples that you find of precise verbs, nouns, and adjectives, key terms used consistently, and transitions. You may want to create a table like the one below to help you organize your findings. The first several entries have been done for you.

Precise Words	Consistent Key Terms	Transitions
lightweight cloth (paragraph 5)	cloth (paragraphs 5 and 6)	First (chronological, paragraph 6)
fabric paints (paragraph 5)		inside (spatial, paragraph 6)

 Writing 1.0 Students write clear, coherent essays. **1.6** Revise writing to improve the consistency of ideas within and between paragraphs.

Mini-Lesson: The Writer's Language **535**

RESOURCES

The Writer's Language
Independent Practice
- *Writing, Listening, & Speaking,* WS. p. 27

 MINI-LESSON ········ **THE WRITER'S LANGUAGE**

Guided Practice
(For independent practice see Resources below.)

Answers
Students could fill in a three-column chart using headings and content similar to the sample below.

Precise Words
lightweight cloth (paragraph 5)
fabric paints (paragraph 5)
felt-tip markers (paragraph 5)
narrow plastic headband (paragraph 5)
bright, colorful pattern (paragraph 6)
decorate (paragraph 6)
Fold the fabric in half lengthwise (paragraph 6)
1-inch-wide hem (paragraph 7)
unhemmed end of the sleeve (paragraph 8)
Thread (paragraph 10)
12-inch-long piece of string (paragraph 11)

Consistent Key Terms
cloth (paragraphs 5 and 6)
sleeve (paragraphs 6, 7, 8, and 9)
hem (paragraph 7)
openings (paragraphs 7, 10, and 11)
headband (paragraphs 10 and 11)

Transitions
First (chronological, paragraph 6)
inside (spatial, paragraph 6)
from (spatial, paragraph 6)
Then (chronological, paragraphs 7 and 11)
all around (spatial, paragraph 8)
Next (chronological, paragraph 9)
into (spatial, paragraph 10)
Finally (chronological, paragraph 12)

DIFFERENTIATING INSTRUCTION

English-Language Learners

Some students might be uncertain about how to catch an audience's attention in English. You may want to offer examples of attention-grabbing introductions from students' writing and explain how these introductions catch a reader's attention. These examples may also be useful:

Have you ever wanted to make your own greeting cards?

If you love to work with your hands and don't mind getting messy, then this is a project for you.

I never thought I could . . . until I did this project.

▶ **Resources Reminder**

For more help with English-Language Learners, see *Lesson Plans for Language Development*.

PRACTICE & APPLY 3

Guided and Independent Practice

If you wish to assign a length to students' writing assignments, 500 to 700 words is appropriate. To help you monitor students' understanding of how to organize their "how-to" papers, you may wish to have students use the framework on this page as a model to make an outline of their papers. Then, have students complete **Practice and Apply 3** for independent practice.

A Writer's Framework

"How-to" Explanation

Introduction
- Attention-grabbing opener
- Situation or reason for making the product
- Purpose

Grab your readers' attention before telling what your explanation will help them make. Consider appealing directly to them with a question. Set the scene by **explaining** or **describing a situation** in which the product might be used. **Give the audience a reason** to read on by letting the readers know there is a fun or interesting use for the product.

Body
- List of materials
- Step 1 (with precise language)
- Step 2 (with precise language)
- Step 3 (with precise language) and so on

In the first body paragraph, **list the materials your reader needs** to make the product. One way to list the materials is to put them in the order in which your readers will use them. Another way is to group similar types of materials together. Then, write the steps in the correct **chronological order.** As you write, you should
- place each step in a **separate paragraph**
- elaborate on each step with **precise language**
- include **transitions** to add **coherence**

(For more on **precise language** and **transitions,** see pages 534–535.)

Conclusion
- Summary of the steps
- Restatement of reason

Briefly **summarize the steps** needed to make the product. Then, **restate the reason** for making it. You can also suggest ways to use or display the product. (For more information on writing **introductions** and **conclusions,** see pages 655–656.)

PRACTICE & APPLY 3 Draft Your "How-to" Explanation

Now it is your turn to draft a "how-to" paper. As you write, refer to the framework above and the Writer's Model on the next page.

Writing 1.0 Essays contain formal introductions, supporting evidence, and conclusions. **1.2** Create multiple-paragraph expository compositions. **1.2a** Engage the interest of the reader. **1.2c** Conclude with a detailed summary linked to the purpose of the composition. **2.0** Student writing demonstrates the organizational and drafting strategies outlined in Writing Standard 1.0.

RESOURCES

Practice and Apply 3

Think Sheet
- *Writing, Listening, & Speaking,* WS. p. 28

Template
- *Writing, Listening, & Speaking,* WS. p. 29

A Writer's Model

The final draft below closely follows the framework for a "how-to" explanation on the previous page. Notice the highlighted transitions the writer uses to show chronological order.

A Snowman of Style

Do you want to beat the winter blahs? Decorate your home for the season! This explanation will tell you how to make your own snowman. You can make one without snow.

Picture a plump snowman with bright shiny eyes, a muffler, and a black hat. You can make the same winter wonder with these materials, which you can find at many hobby and craft stores:

> a 5-inch foam ball
> a 4-inch foam ball
> a 3-inch foam ball
> two 12-inch black pipe cleaners
> one 1-inch orange pipe cleaner
> a 2-inch piece of black yarn
> three medium-size buttons
> two medium-size sequins
> a 1- × 15-inch piece of bright cloth
> an 8½- × 11-inch piece of black paper
> a 2-inch black pompom
> three straight pins
> scissors
> glue

The first step is making the snowman's face and hat. The orange pipe cleaner will be the nose. Push the pipe cleaner into the center of the smallest foam ball until it sticks out about ½ inch. Next, use the black yarn to make the mouth. Happy snowmen wear smiles. Confused snowmen have mouths like a series of mountain peaks. Choose an emotion for your snowman, and glue the black yarn down to match the feeling you are trying to create. To make the eyes, glue down the two sequins. Use the straight pins to pin the eyes in place while they dry. Snowmen often wear hats. You can make one by

(continued)

INTRODUCTION
Attention-grabber

Situation/Reason

Purpose

List of materials

BODY
Step one

GO TO: go.hrw.com
KEYWORD: HLLA6 W-2
FOR: A Student Model

A Writer's Model   **537**

MODELING AND DEMONSTRATION

A Writer's Model
Have students read **A Writer's Model** while paying attention to the writer's use of precise language. Point out examples of numbers, exact verbs, comparisons, transitions, and descriptive words in the model. ["12-inch"; "Cut"; "mouths like a series of mountain peaks"; "Next"; "circle of black paper"] Then, have students working in small groups look for other examples. Have groups demonstrate their understanding by sharing their findings with the class.

TECHNOLOGY TIP

If students are using a computer to draft their papers, remind them to save their drafts frequently by using the "save as" feature and renaming the document each time they revise a draft (for example, *Miranda's How-to Draft 1, Miranda's How-to Draft 2,* and so on). This technique will make it easier for students to find passages that were deleted or to recover wording and organization from past drafts.

CRITICAL THINKING

To "test" the content and organization of **A Writer's Model,** spread the materials for the project on a table in the classroom. (Materials for this project can be purchased at craft stores.) Separate the class into randomly selected groups of six students. Then, have groups take turns using the materials to follow the directions in the model. While one group is working with the materials, the other groups could make lists of questions they have about the steps or write ideas for how to improve the model. After each group has tested the model, ask students to discuss the importance of clear writing in a "how-to" explanation and how they could apply what they have learned to their own writing.

(continued)

cutting a 3-inch circle of black paper. Pin the circle to the top of the snowman's head. Glue the black pompom to the center of the paper, and set the head aside to dry.

Step two

Next, you will use the 4-inch foam ball to make the snowman's middle. Cut one of the black pipe cleaners in half to make the arms. Shape each pipe cleaner like a tree branch or jagged line. Then, push each arm in place on the sides of the ball. The three black buttons will make the snowman's shirt. Glue them down the front of the ball. Set the middle aside to dry.

Step three

While you are waiting for the face and middle to dry, you can make a stand to keep your snowman from falling over. Cut a 1- × 5-inch piece of black paper. Form it into a ring by gluing the ends together.

Step four

When everything is dry, you are ready to put the snowman's body together. Take your last black pipe cleaner and cut four 2-inch pieces. Push two of the pipe cleaners in the top of the 4-inch foam ball 1 inch apart. Push the other two pipe cleaners in the bottom of the 4-inch ball 1 inch apart. Make sure you use two pipe cleaners because they will keep the snowman from wobbling. Then, push the snowman's head on top of the pipe cleaners to attach it to the 4-inch ball. Push the 5-inch ball on the bottom pipe cleaners to finish making the snowman's body.

Step five

The final step is making a muffler for your snowman. A muffler is a long fringed scarf that wraps around the neck. The strip of cloth will make the muffler. Create fringe by making cuts into each end of the fabric. Once that is done, tie the muffler around the snowman's neck.

CONCLUSION
Summary of steps

Creating a snowman is simple. Just make the face and hat, the middle, and a stand. Then, you are ready to put the snowman together and tie on a muffler. Put your snowman on a table or shelf, where everyone can see your winter decoration. You might also want to place your snowman in front of a window so your neighbors can see him, too.

Restatement of reason

Suggestions for use/display

Designing Your Writing

Formatting Your Writing   **Formatting** is how text is arranged. Formatting can make a big difference in how your explanation looks and how easy it is to follow. Try arranging your information in different ways by adjusting *spacing, margins,* and *columns.*

- **Spacing** is the distance between lines of text. In **single-spaced text,** the lines are close together. Books, newspapers, and magazines are typically single-spaced. **Double-spaced text** has a full space between lines of text. Double-spacing your classroom papers allows you to make corrections or your teacher to write comments on the page more easily.

- **Margins** are the spaces above, below, to the left, and to the right of the text on the page. Most word-processing programs automatically set the margins of a new page, but they will allow you to set each margin separately. Pages with very small margins, like the following example on the left, can be difficult to read and nearly impossible to write comments on. Pages with larger margins, like the following example on the right, look better and are easier to read. On an 8½- x 11-inch piece of paper, a standard margin is about an inch on each side of the text.

- **Columns** are the sections of text that run vertically, side-by-side on a page. Most word-processing programs allow you to format your text in columns. Two-column text takes up less space than single-column text. If you wanted to publish a class set of "how-to" explanations on saving natural resources, you might use double columns to save paper, as shown in the example on the right.

Writing 1.5 Compose documents with appropriate formatting by using word-processing skills and principles of design (e.g., margins, spacing, columns).

Designing Your Writing   **539**

DIRECT TEACHING

Formatting Your Writing   **W1.5**

Help students explore other word-processing functions. Direct students to use the bullet function to make bulleted lists of the materials that will be needed to complete the processes explained in their papers. Students might also use the border function to "box" the list of materials. Setting apart the list of materials with bullets and borders will make students' processes easier to follow.

"If [the audience is] satisfied with your poor performance, you will not easily make it better.**"**

(Ralph Waldo Emerson, 1803–1882, American author)

Write the quotation on the chalkboard, and ask students how the audience in the quotation relates to the role of peer editor in the classroom. [If the peer editor does not identify unclear writing, the author may not revise it. An awareness of weaknesses in writing will help the author to identify and correct errors in the future.]

DIRECT TEACHING

REVIEW STANDARD

Elaboration

The following activity is a review of the 5th-grade **Writing Standard 1.2b.**

To help students elaborate in the body of their papers by adding precise language, ask them to close their eyes and visualize the steps in the process. Then, ask students to add to their instructions sensory words and details that help them better picture in their minds each of the steps in the process. Remind students that such details are essential for the reader to follow the line of thought in their papers.

Revising

Evaluate and Revise Content, Organization, and Style

Two Is Better Than One   When revising your paper or a peer's, look at the content and organization first, using the guidelines below. The second time you read, concentrate on the sentences, using the Focus on Sentences on page 542.

▶ **First Reading: Content and Organization** Use the chart below on your first reading. It will help you revise the content and organization of a "how-to" explanation.

"How-to" Explanation: Content and Organization Guidelines

Evaluation Questions	▶ Tips	▶ Revision Techniques
❶ Does the introduction state a clear purpose? Does it explain the situation or state the reason for making the product?	▶ **Put brackets** around the statement of purpose. **Put an asterisk** next to the explanation of the situation or the statement of the reason.	▶ If needed, **add** a statement of purpose. **Add** an explanation of the situation or a statement of the reason.
❷ Does the body list all the materials needed to make the product?	▶ **Circle** all the supplies needed to make the product.	▶ **Add** any supplies that have been left out.
❸ Are the steps of the process in the correct chronological order? Is each step in a separate paragraph?	▶ **Write a number** next to each step in the margin of the paper.	▶ To improve coherence, **rearrange** the steps so they are in the correct order and so that each step is in its own paragraph, as needed.
❹ Is each step described with precise language?	▶ **Underline** precise verbs, nouns, and adjectives.	▶ If necessary, **elaborate** on the steps by adding precise words.
❺ Does your explanation use consistent language?	▶ **Highlight** all the words that refer to the same action or item. Use a different color for each action or item.	▶ If needed, **replace** words so that the same word always refers to the same action or item.
❻ Does the conclusion summarize the steps needed? Does it restate the situation or the reason for making the product?	▶ **Draw a wavy line** under the summary of the steps. **Put a star** beside the sentence that restates the situation or the reason.	▶ If needed, **add** a summary of the steps. **Add** a sentence that restates the situation or the reason.

Writing 1.6 Revise writing to improve the organization and consistency of ideas within and between paragraphs.

ONE WRITER'S REVISIONS Here is an early draft of the "how-to" explanation on pages 537–538.

> Next, you will use the 4-inch foam ball to make the snowman's middle. Cut one of the black pipe cleaners in half to make the arms. *Shape each pipe cleaner like a tree branch or jagged line.* Then, push each arm in place on the sides of the ball. The three black buttons will make the snowman's shirt. Glue them down the front of the ball. Set the middle aside to dry. ¶ While you are waiting for the face and middle to dry, you can make a stand to keep your snowman from falling over. Cut a 1- x 5-inch piece of black paper. Form it into a ring by gluing the ends together.

elaborate

rearrange

Responding to the Revision Process

1. How does adding a sentence improve this part of the instructions?
2. How does breaking the one paragraph into two paragraphs make the instructions clearer?

PEER REVIEW

When looking over a peer's paper, ask yourself these questions.

- Would I be able to make this product? Why or why not?
- What parts of the explanation are vague or unclear?

▶ **Second Reading: Style**   You have improved the content and organization of your paper. Now you will concentrate on the style of your sentences. One way to improve your style is to use *transitional words*, such as *first, next,* and *finally.* **Transitional words** connect one idea to another. The following guidelines will help you.

Style Guidelines

Evaluation Question	▶ Tip	▶ Revision Technique
Do transitional words connect one step to another, creating coherence?	▶ **Highlight** each transitional word.	▶ **Add** transitional words to paragraphs that need them.

Writing 1.0 Students write clear, coherent essays.

Responding to the Revision Process

Answers

1. The sentence adds precise language comparing the shape of the pipe cleaner to a tree branch or a jagged line to help readers visualize what to do.

2. The writer broke the paragraph into two so that each main step of the process would have its own paragraph, making it easier for readers to follow the directions.

DIFFERENTIATING INSTRUCTION

Learners Having Difficulty

Some students may benefit from reading their papers aloud before they begin to revise. Doing so will help them find problems with sentence structure, transitional expressions, and so on.

REVIEW STANDARD

Transitional Words

The following activity is a review of the 5th-grade **Writing Standard 1.2b.**

Before students read the **Focus on Sentences,** write the model paragraph from this page on the chalkboard, omitting the underlined transitional words. Read the paragraph aloud, and ask students if the order of the steps is clear. Mention that transitional words such as *first, then,* and *finally* make directions easier to follow because they signal chronological order. Call on volunteers to suggest possible transitional words that would make the connections between steps clearer, and then add them to the paragraph. Finally, have a volunteer read the model paragraph on this page aloud, pointing out the writer's use of transitional words.

GUIDED PRACTICE

Responding to the Revision Process

Answer

The addition of the transitional word *next* makes the paragraph easier to read and understand and makes the order of the steps clearer.

PRACTICE & APPLY 4

Independent Practice

To assess students' mastery, you may want to check their drafts against their revised copies to see that they have made the necessary changes in content and organization and have added transitional words.

Focus on Sentences

Transitional Words

A reader should be able to follow your ideas as easily as a driver follows road signs. Adding **transitional words** between your thoughts will add **coherence,** steering the reader in the right direction. Notice how the underlined transitional words make this paragraph easy to read and understand.

TIP Listed below are common transitional words for chronological order, the order used to explain a process.

after	next
before	often
finally	then
first	when

> To make a tie-dyed shirt, <u>first</u> you will need to wrap rubber bands around several parts of a T-shirt. <u>Next</u>, fill a tub or sink with dye. <u>Then</u>, dunk the shirt into the dye. Rinse the shirt with water and hang to dry. <u>Finally</u>, take off the rubber bands when the shirt is completely dry.

ONE WRITER'S REVISIONS

> The orange pipe cleaner will be the nose. Push the pipe cleaner into the center of the smallest foam ball until it sticks out about ½ inch. *Next,* You will use the black yarn to make the mouth.

Responding to the Revision Process

How did adding a transitional word make this part of the instructions clearer?

PRACTICE & APPLY 4 — Evaluate and Revise Your "How-to" Explanation

Now, take the time to evaluate and revise your paper. First, improve content and organization using the guidelines on page 540. Then, use the Focus on Sentences above to add transitional words to your paper. If a peer evaluated your paper, consider his or her suggestions as you revise.

Writing 1.0 Students write clear, coherent essays.

542 Workshop 2 **Exposition:** Writing a "How-to" Explanation

RESOURCES

Focus on Sentences
Independent Practice
- *Writing, Listening, & Speaking,* WS. p. 33 You may choose to assign this independent practice as homework.

HOMEWORK

Practice and Apply 4
Think Sheet
- *Writing, Listening, & Speaking,* WS. p. 30
Independent Practice
- *Writing, Listening, & Speaking,* WS. p. 32
Extension
- *Writing, Listening, & Speaking,* WS. p. 31

Proofread Your Explanation

Clear the Path   Reading a paper full of errors is like running an obstacle course: Progress is often slow. If you *and* a peer proofread your paper, you are more likely to catch distracting mistakes.

Using Commas in a Series

When you write a "how-to" explanation, you may list materials or give directions in a series. A series consists of three or more items written one after the other.

Use commas to separate three or more items in a series.

Incorrect   Get out a pen, and paper.

Correct   Get out a pen, a ruler, and paper.

To make the meaning of a sentence clear, use a comma before the *and* or *or* in a series.

Unclear   Lori's favorite sandwiches are turkey, ham and cheese. [Does Lori have two or three favorite sandwiches?]

Clear   Lori's favorite sandwiches are turkey, ham, and cheese.

Do not use commas if *all* of the items are joined by *and* or *or*.

Incorrect   You can throw, or roll, or bounce the ball.

Correct   You can throw or roll or bounce the ball.

PRACTICE

Some of the sentences below need commas. Refer to the rules to the left to decide when to use commas. If a sentence needs commas, rewrite the sentence, adding commas where they are needed. If a sentence is correct, write C.

Example:

1. Your snow woman could have long hair a lace collar and earrings.

1. *Your snow woman could have long hair, a lace collar, and earrings.*

1. Glue the eyes hold them with a pin and allow them to dry.

2. My snowman has green eyes a red scarf and blue buttons.

3. Miguel gave his snow teen a headset a T-shirt and a book bag.

4. A snow baby has a bib cap or bow.

5. You can place your snowman on a shelf or a table or a countertop.

Reference Note

For more information and practice on using **commas,** see page 268 in the *Holt Handbook.*

 Writing 2.0 Student writing demonstrates a command of standard American English.

Grammar Link   **543**

RESOURCES

Grammar Link

Proofreading Practice

■ *Writing, Listening, & Speaking,* WS. p. 34
You may choose to assign this proofreading practice as homework.

HOMEWORK

Publish Your Explanation   W1.5

Have students publish their papers using a word processor. Remind them to apply what they learned in **Designing Your Writing** (p. 539) about spacing, margins, and columns. You might also refer them to the **Computer Tip** on this page.

PRACTICE & APPLY 5

Guided and Independent Practice

To monitor students' progress, ask them to look over their revisions and to make a chart of their paper's strengths and weaknesses. Next, direct them to brainstorm ways in which they can correct the paper's weaknesses and capitalize on the paper's strengths to reach the right audience. Answer any questions students might have. Then, assign **Practice and Apply 5** for independent practice.

Resources Reminder

For help with writing assessment, see 6 Traits—Plus 1 in the "General Scales and Sample Papers" section of *Progress Assessment of Writing, Listening, & Speaking.*

Mini-Workshop

Another type of explanation you may write is one that explains problems and solutions. For more information on writing a **problem-solution explanation,** see page 678.

COMPUTER TIP

If you have access to a word processor, use its features to check spelling and grammar when you edit your paper. However, a spellchecker cannot check homonyms such as *its* (showing possession) and *it's* (it is). Similarly, a grammar checker may suggest unnecessary changes, such as writing each item in your list of materials in a separate sentence.

Publish Your Explanation

Tell Them How It Is Done   Since you are the expert, you can share your explanation with others. How do you get your paper to your audience? Use the following suggestions to get people to read your "how-to" explanation.

- If you wrote your "how-to" explanation for a younger audience, make copies of your explanation and give them to an elementary teacher. If your audience is your classmates, ask your teacher if you can demonstrate how to make your product in class.

- Gather all the "how-to" explanations in your class and organize them into categories such as recipes, crafts, and decorations. Compile a "how-to" book and place it in your school's library.

Reflect on Your Explanation

Building Your Portfolio   Now that you are finished writing and publishing, take a moment and reflect on your "how-to" explanation. Remember your purpose for writing, and think about how your paper will achieve that purpose. Reflecting on a paper you have already completed will help make your next one better.

- Which step in your paper is the easiest to follow? What makes this step clear and easy to understand?

- You created a time line to list your steps in order. In what other types of writing would a time line be useful?

Finally, take time to examine all the papers in your portfolio. By doing so you can begin to recognize your strengths and weaknesses as a writer. What do you feel are your strengths? What is one goal you would like to work toward to improve your writing?

PRACTICE & APPLY 5   Proofread, Publish, and Reflect on Your Explanation

- Correct any grammar, usage, and mechanics errors. Pay attention to spelling and punctuation, particularly the use of commas in a series.

- Publish your paper so others can use your explanation.

- Answer the questions from Reflect on Your Explanation above. Include your responses in your portfolio.

RESOURCES

Writing Workshop

Assessment

- *Progress Assessment of Writing, Listening, & Speaking,* pp. 5–6, 34–36

Following Oral Instructions and Directions

Talk   Listen

"**A**ttention, students! All students with last names beginning with A through M should report to Room 206 at 10:15 A.M. for school pictures. Students with names beginning N through Z report to Room 208 at 10:45 A.M. Afterwards, please turn in order forms in Room 315."

Do announcements like this make your head spin? You can improve your ability to follow oral instructions by learning to listen. This workshop will help you learn valuable listening skills.

Follow Oral Instructions

The ability to follow oral instructions is a skill you need for life. Why is it sometimes hard to follow spoken instructions? Maybe you "tune out" for a minute, only to realize later that you have missed something important. Maybe the speaker uses terms that are not familiar to you, making the instructions difficult to understand.

Give Me a Clue   Most people *hear* what is being said, but they may not really *listen*. Listening is an active process. It involves trying to interpret the main points, as well as the speaker's *verbal* and *nonverbal cues*. **Cues** are hints or clues a speaker gives to help listeners follow his or her ideas. **Verbal cues** are spoken hints, including *how* the words are said. **Nonverbal cues** are unspoken hints such as movements, facial expressions, and gestures. The chart on the next page shows some common verbal and nonverbal cues.

WHAT'S AHEAD?

In this workshop you will learn how to follow oral instructions. You will also learn how to

- practice active listening skills
- take notes as you listen
- ask questions for understanding

Mini-Workshop

You may be asked to give or listen to a presentation that explains problems and solutions. For more information on **giving and listening to a problem-solution presentation,** see page 681.

Listening Workshop

PRETEACHING

Quotation for the Day

"Then I want to sit and listen and have someone talk, tell me things—. . . . Not to say anything—to listen and listen and be taught."

(Anne Morrow Lindbergh, 1906–2001, American author, married to the aviator Charles Lindbergh)

Write the quotation on the chalkboard. Then, ask students to reflect on their own listening skills. Do they pay close attention when someone is speaking, or do they find themselves "tuning out"? What do they do to help themselves stay focused when listening?

RETEACHING

Give Me a Clue

As you discuss verbal and nonverbal cues with the class, ask for volunteers to demonstrate some of the cues listed on the chart on page 546.

WORKSHOP RESOURCES

Listening Workshop
Planning
- *On Course: Mapping Instruction*
- *One-Stop Planner* CD-ROM
- *At Home: A Guide to Standards Mastery,* p. 15

- *At Home: In Five Languages*
- *Writing, Listening, & Speaking —Teaching Notes,* pp. 35–38

Differentiating Instruction
- *Lesson Plans for Language Development,* p. 228
- *Supporting Instruction in Five Languages*

Think Sheet
- *Writing, Listening, & Speaking,* WS. pp. 40, 42

Independent Practice
- *Writing, Listening, & Speaking,* WS. p. 39

(continued on p. 546)

DIFFERENTIATING INSTRUCTION

Special Education Students

To help students who may have difficulty listening and taking notes simultaneously, make copies of written instructions and give the copies to students. Then, ask a volunteer to read the instructions aloud. As students listen to the volunteer reading, have them work with a helper to highlight key words and phrases and to put question marks next to confusing sections.

 Resources Reminder

For more help with Special Education Students, see *Lesson Plans for Language Development.*

CRITICAL THINKING

Present students with a simple set of instructions in which you give both verbal and nonverbal cues. Ask students to take notes about the material they hear. Then, have students compare notes and share note-taking techniques. Discuss with students the verbal and nonverbal cues they cited, and have them share the strategies they used to analyze the cues.

COMMON VERBAL AND NONVERBAL CUES

Verbal Cues	Nonverbal Cues
clue words such as *first, next, last,* and *in conclusion* to help the listener follow along	"body language," or movements and facial expressions that show the speaker's mood or attitude
repetition of important phrases or ideas	demonstrating the activity or using hand movements to emphasize important points
emphasis on important information, such as speaking more loudly or stressing certain words	facial expressions or movements that ask for questions or encourage the listener's participation

Tricks for Tuning In In addition to using verbal and nonverbal cues, you should focus on the speaker to get the main points. You will miss important information if you are gazing out the window or doodling instead of taking notes. Try to avoid such distractions.

Jot It Down As you listen to oral instructions, you may need to take notes. Keep the following points in mind.

- Write down only key words and phrases.
- Abbreviate frequently used words or phrases. Just remember to make a key so you do not forget what your abbreviations mean.
- Jot down questions or put question marks by steps that confuse you. Look back to your notes if the speaker asks for questions.

Repeat After Me Use your notes to **restate** the instructions in your own words. If possible, read your restatement back to the speaker and ask him or her to check it. Here are one speaker's instructions and a listener's restatement of them.

> **Instructions:** To lock a bicycle securely, you need a U-lock and a cable. Place your bike next to a bike ring or a narrow pole. Open the U-lock and put it around the pole and the bike frame. Do not close the U-lock yet. First, attach one end of the cable to one side of the U-lock. Then, pass the cable through your front wheel, pulling the free end all the way through. Next, pass the cable through the back wheel. Finally, attach the free end of the cable to the other side of the U-lock and lock it.

 Listening and Speaking 1.3 Restate and execute multiple-step oral instructions.

WORKSHOP RESOURCES

(continued from p. 545)

Evaluation and Assessment

- *Writing, Listening, & Speaking,* WS. p. 41
- *Progress Assessment of Writing, Listening, & Speaking,* pp. 37–38
- *Diagnostic and Summative Assessments,* First-Quarter Test

Extension

- *Writing, Listening, & Speaking,* Videocassette, Segment 2

Restatement: Use a U-lock to secure the bike frame to a pole. Then, pass a cable through both wheels and attach each end to a different side of the U-lock. Close the lock.

Ask Questions As you listen to a speaker giving oral instructions, think about whether you are understanding what you hear. Ask questions to clarify anything you do not fully understand. Before you ask a question, though, you should know that there are "do's and don'ts" when it comes to asking questions. The chart below lists some of the most important "do's and don'ts" to remember when you need to ask a question.

GUIDELINES FOR ASKING QUESTIONS	
What to Do	**What Not to Do**
Wait until the speaker pauses before you ask a question.	Do not blurt out a question while the speaker is still talking.
Ask specific questions that show you have been listening.	Do not ask vague questions such as "What are you talking about?"
Ask in a clear, loud voice.	Do not mumble the question.
Read notes back to the speaker to make sure they are correct.	Do not assume you can figure out anything you did not understand.

PRACTICE & APPLY ⑥ **Follow Oral Instructions**

For this activity, work in a group of three or four students. Each of you will need several sheets of paper and a pen or pencil.

1. Draw a simple picture. Do not let anyone else in your group see it.

2. Describe your picture. Each of the other group members should listen, take notes, ask questions, then draw the picture.

3. Share your picture with the group. Discuss the similarities and differences of the pictures each group member created.

4. Complete the steps above using a picture and oral instructions from each member of the group. Then, talk about what group members learned about giving and listening to instructions.

Ask Questions
Read through the chart with students. Then, explain to students that you can think of additional "do's and don'ts" to add to the chart. Write an example of each on the board.

What to Do
Use polite wording in your question.

What Not to Do
Criticize the speaker in your question.

Have students demonstrate their understanding by suggesting additions to the lists, along with explanations.

PRACTICE & APPLY ⑥

Guided and Independent Practice
Monitor students' ability to follow oral instructions by giving them a set of directions that tells them how to meet in groups of three or four for the Practice and Apply activity. Have students meet in the groups and complete the activity as independent practice.

DIRECT TEACHING

REVIEW STANDARD

Follow Geographic Directions

The following activity is a review of the 5th-grade **Listening and Speaking Standard 1.4.**

Before students gather in groups to practice giving and following geographic directions, discuss with them the best way to organize geographic directions. Lead students to understand that spatial or logical organization will be most effective. To appeal to their audience of fellow students, remind them to mention landmarks with which other students are familiar. Using direction words like *north, south, east,* and *west* will also help their listeners who are sketching maps of the directions.

DIRECT TEACHING

Follow Geographic Directions

To locate maps of your city, you might try the city Chamber of Commerce, the city visitor's bureau, local businesses that sell maps, or a social studies teacher who teaches map skills.

PRACTICE & APPLY 7

Guided and Independent Practice

Before students complete **Practice and Apply 7,** have them practice taking notes while a partner gives a simple set of directions, such as directions to a room down the hall. Students can also practice restating the directions. When students have practiced giving and listening to directions, assign **Practice and Apply 7** as independent practice.

TIP Sketching a map of directions is helpful. If you can, show your map to the person giving you directions to make sure your understanding is accurate.

Follow Geographic Directions

Geographic directions are a specific kind of instructions that tell the way to a certain place. It is especially important to pay attention to verbal and nonverbal cues when listening to geographic directions. After all, if you miss a step or misunderstand, you could get lost. Whenever possible, you should take notes, ask questions, and restate the directions out loud to the person giving them. Look at the directions below and a listener's restatement of them.

> **Directions:** The trail starts just behind the lodge. Start by following the trail for about three miles. When the trail forks, bear left. When you reach the logging road, turn right. Stay on the logging road for about four miles. Just before you reach the summit, look for the sign for the Three Pines Trail on the right. Finally, take the Three Pines Trail back to the lodge.
>
> **Restatement:** Take the trail that starts behind the lodge for three miles, then bear left at the fork. Turn right on the logging road and follow it for four miles. Take the Three Pines Trail to the right and follow it to the lodge.

PRACTICE & APPLY 7   Follow Geographic Directions

For this activity, gather in a small group of three or four students. Your group will need a map of your town or city.

1. Have one student select a location, such as a public library or a park, without naming the place. Then, he or she should give directions out loud on how to get from your school to the place.

2. The other students should take notes, ask questions, and restate the directions.

3. The listeners should trace the directions along the map exactly as the directions were given and identify the final location.

4. If the place identified by the group is incorrect, discuss where the breakdown in oral communication happened. Then, have another person select a different place and repeat the procedure.

5. Each group should discuss what they learned about giving directions. Be prepared to share your findings with your class.

Listening and Speaking 1.3 Restate and execute multiple-step oral directions.

DIRECTIONS: Read the following paragraph from a draft of a student's "how-to" paper. Then, read the questions below it. Choose the best answer, and mark your answers on your own paper.

Easy and Fun Zesty Bagels

(1) Evenly spread 1 tablespoon of spaghetti sauce over the face of each bagel. (2) First, you will need to cut the six plain bagels in half and place the halves on a cookie sheet. (3) Then, sprinkle ¼ cup chopped black olives, 6 finely chopped mushrooms, and 1 cup grated Parmesan cheese evenly over the sauce. (4) Place the cookie sheet in a preheated oven and bake for 15–20 minutes. (5) When the bagels are done, remove them from the oven and let them cool for 5 minutes.

1. If you were revising the paragraph above to put the instructions in chronological order, which sentence would you move?
   A 2
   B 3
   C 4
   D 5

2. If the student wanted to add precise language to the paragraph, which of the following sentences would be appropriate?
   F You may add other toppings.
   G Your family will enjoy them.
   H The oven should be set at 350 degrees.
   J Prepare the bagels.

3. If the student wanted to add a transitional word to the beginning of sentence 5, which of the following would make the most sense?
   A However,
   B Meanwhile,
   C Since
   D Finally,

4. If you were listening to, rather than reading, the instructions, which of the following notes would best summarize the last step?
   F Remove from oven when done. Let cool 5 min.
   G Wash the dishes.
   H Sprinkle black olives, finely chopped mushrooms, and grated Parmesan cheese evenly over the sauce.
   J Pour sauce.

5. What is one question you might ask the speaker giving these instructions to clarify a specific point?
   A Did you get this recipe from a cookbook?
   B What type of spaghetti sauce do you recommend?
   C Do you think my little brother will like zesty bagels?
   D How many times have you made zesty bagels?

Standards Practice and Review **549**

RESOURCES

Exposition

Assessment
■ *Progress Assessment of Writing, Listening, & Speaking,* Wkshp. 2
■ *Diagnostic and Summative Assessments,* First-Quarter Test

Extension
■ *Writing, Listening, & Speaking,* p. 43

Standards Practice and Review

(Standards reviewed on this page: W 1.3, 1.2, 1.6, 2.2c; L&S 1.0. To read the standards, see pp. 526–527.)

Answers

1. A   4. F
2. H   5. B
3. D

APPLICATION

Technology
For homework, ask students to choose computer software with which they are familiar and to write a set of instructions telling how to use a specific feature of the software. Direct students to begin their instructions by describing the purpose and benefits of the software. Then, students should give their instructions, step by step. Finally, students should describe the desired outcome. Have students meet with partners to try out each other's instructions. You may want to assemble students' instructions in a computer manual the class can use as a **HOMEWORK** resource.

EXTENSION

Careers
Have students brainstorm a list of careers in which following oral instructions is an important everyday task. For example, students might list nurses, rescue workers, police officers, taxi drivers, and receptionists. Then, ask students to choose one of these careers and find out what types of oral instructions a person in this field must follow. Students can look in books in the library, use informational Web sites, or interview someone in the field. Ask students to share their findings with the class.

Program Organization

Holt Literature and Language Arts provides a complete curriculum for standards-based instruction in vocabulary, reading, literature, writing, speaking and listening, and media. The instructional content of the program is divided into quarters to enable teachers to anticipate and administer the quarterly assessments required by California.

About Workshop 3

Standards-based lesson plans and suggestions for linking instruction with Workshop 3 and the related instructional material are provided in *On Course: Mapping Instruction*.

- Workshop 3 focuses on responding to literature in writing, listening, and speaking. Chapter 3 connects to it by focusing on literary response to and analysis of theme.

- The related instructional material for Workshop 3 is shown on the chart. This material will also be covered in the second quarterly assessment. Specific teaching suggestions for the related material are found in Part 1 of this book and in the *Holt Handbook*.

Holt Literature And Language Arts

Pupil's Edition

Part 1, Chapter 3

The Heart of the Matter: Themes and Conclusions, pp. 114–169
- Reading Standards 1.2, 2.6, 3.6
- Writing Application **Writing a Response to Literature**

Part 2, Workshop 3

Response to Literature: Writing a Short Story Interpretation, pp. 552–569
- Writing Standard 2.4

  Giving and Listening to an Oral Response to Literature, pp. 570–574
- Listening and Speaking Standard 2.3

Part 2, Mini-Workshop 4

Writing a Movie Review, pp. 673–675
- Writing Standard 2.4

Holt Handbook

Chapter 5

Complements
- Written and Oral English-Language Conventions, Looking Ahead, Gr. 7 Standard 1.3, pp. 105–116

Chapter 6

Agreement
- Written and Oral English-Language Conventions Standard 1.2, pp. 124–140

Diagnostic and Summative Assessments: Midyear Test

Language Arts Content

This workshop uses the writing and listening and speaking strategies to enable students to master successfully the writing and speaking applications.

What standards are taught in Workshop 3?

In this workshop, students will master the following Grade 6 standards. They will also review several standards from an earlier grade.

Writing Strategies

1.0 Students write clear, coherent, and focused essays. The writing exhibits students' awareness of the audience and purpose. Students progress through the stages of the writing process as needed.

1.1 Choose the form of writing (e.g., review) that best suits the intended purpose.

1.2 Create multiple-paragraph expository compositions.

1.3 Use a variety of effective and coherent organizational patterns, including organization by categories and order of importance.

1.5 Compose documents with appropriate formatting by using word-processing skills and principles of design (e.g., tabs).

1.6 Revise writing to improve the organization and consistency of ideas within and between paragraphs.

Writing Applications

2.0 Students write expository texts of at least 500 to 700 words. Student writing demonstrates a command of standard American English and the organizational and drafting strategies outlined in Writing Standard 1.0.

2.2 Write expository compositions (e.g., explanation).

2.4 Write responses to literature.

Listening and Speaking Strategies

1.0 Students deliver focused, coherent presentations that convey ideas clearly and relate to the interests of the audience. They evaluate the content of oral communication.

1.1 Relate the speaker's verbal communication (e.g., pitch, feeling, tone) to the nonverbal message (e.g., posture, gesture).

1.2 Identify the tone conveyed in the oral communication.

1.4 Select a focus and an organizational structure matching the purpose, message,

occasion, and vocal modulation to the audience.

1.5 Emphasize salient points to assist the listener in following the main ideas and concepts.

1.6 Support opinions with detailed evidence.

1.7 Use effective rate, volume, pitch, and tone, and align nonverbal elements to sustain audience interest and attention.

Speaking Applications

2.0 Students deliver well-organized formal presentations employing traditional rhetorical strategies (e.g., exposition). Student speaking demonstrates a command of standard American English and

the organizational and delivery strategies outlined in Listening and Speaking Standard 1.0.

2.3 Deliver oral responses to literature.

Review Standards, Grade 5

Writing

2.2 Write responses to literature.

Listening and Speaking

2.3 Deliver oral responses to literature.

Instructional Planning and Support

Where do I locate lesson plans, additional resources, and other teaching aids?

- The Annotated Teacher's Edition and *On Course: Mapping Instruction* provide direction in planning and implementing a complete California standards–based curriculum. These components include instructions for administering diagnostic, progress, and summative tests; for presenting instruction of the standards; for differentiating instruction to provide universal access; and for locating and using the program's ancillaries.

- The program's resources are referenced at the beginning of each workshop, in the bottom margin of this teacher's edition: Writing a Short-Story Interpretation and Giving and Listening to an Oral Response to Literature.

- Reminders for using additional resources appear in this teacher's edition at point of use.

- The *One-Stop Planner* CD-ROM contains editable lesson plans and all print ancillaries, available in PDF format.

What if I don't have time to teach all of Workshop 3?

- Within this workshop, complete coverage of the application standards is provided by the following instructional features in the Pupil's Edition:
  - Read Your Short Story
  - Think About Purpose and Audience
  - Gather Details
  - Organize Details
  - A Writer's Framework
  - Evaluate and Revise Content
  - Proofread Your Interpretation
  - Plan Your Oral Response
  - Deliver Your Oral Response
  - Listen to an Oral Response

- Use Standards Practice and Review for a quick assessment and review of workshop standards.

What provisions have been made for students who have additional class time scheduled in language arts?

- *Universal Access: Writing, Listening, & Speaking,* Workshop 3 contains worksheets and transparencies that provide practice, reteaching, and extension of Workshop 3 standards. Each Practice and Apply exercise is supported by graphic organizers or practice activities for on-level learners, advanced learners, and learners having difficulty.

- *Universal Access: Lesson Plans for Language Development,* Workshop 3, provides alternative teaching strategies and additional worksheets designed specifically for English-language learners and special education students. Many of the suggestions and activities in this ancillary will also be helpful to students in the regular classroom who are having difficulty with particular skills.

Universal Access

How do I differentiate instruction to ensure that all my students master the standards?

Holt Literature and Language Arts provides comprehensive, differentiated instruction for all types of students.

- Most of the general instruction and teaching strategies in the Annotated Teacher's Edition are at grade level. These instructions will work well with the majority of your students.

- Advanced students have at least one activity for each workshop. The suggested activities are found in this teacher's edition at point of instruction. Point-of-use suggestions for learners having difficulty, English-language learners, and special education students are provided.

- *Universal Access: Writing, Listening, & Speaking,* Workshop 3, opens with Teaching Notes that suggest which worksheets and transparencies are appropriate for each of three levels of learners.

- *Universal Access: Lesson Plans for Language Development,* Workshop 3, offers teaching strategies and additional worksheets designed specifically for English-language learners and special education students.

- *Daily Language Activities Transparencies* and *Spelling: Lessons & Activities* provide ongoing review of and additional practice in a range of language arts skills.

- For every workshop, preselected Web sites and activities are available to provide enrichment, independent practice, and enhanced instructional opportunities.

Assessment

How do I determine whether or not my students are making progress in mastering the standards?

Progress Assessment

- Use the Standards Review at the end of Workshop 3 for an informal assessment of the writing, listening, and speaking standards taught in Workshop 3.

- Use Workshop 3 in *Progress Assessment of Writing, Listening, & Speaking* to test students' cumulative progress in mastering the standards taught in the workshop.

Summative Assessment

The content in *Holt Literature and Language Arts* has been divided into four quarters to allow you to administer the four summative tests required by California. Workshop 3 will be assessed in the second quarter of instruction. At the end of Workshop 3, you may ask students to take the Midyear Test in the *Diagnostic & Summative Assessments* booklet.

WORKSHOP 3

STANDARDS FOCUS

Writing

Prerequisite Standards

Grade 5

■ 2.2 Write responses to literature:

a. Demonstrate an understanding of a literary work.

b. Support judgments through references to the text and to prior knowledge.

c. Develop interpretations that exhibit careful reading and understanding.

Standards Coming Up in the Next Level

Grade 7

■ 2.2 Write responses to literature:

a. Develop interpretations exhibiting careful reading, understanding, and insight.

b. Organize interpretations around several clear ideas, premises, or images from the literary work.

c. Justify interpretations through sustained use of examples and textual evidence.

Response to Literature

Reading a work of fiction is just the first step in understanding it. When you read, you bring your own experiences and ideas to the text to form an **interpretation,** or understanding of it. In this workshop you will write and orally present an interpretation of a short story you have read. In the process you will practice these language arts standards.

WRITING WORKSHOP

Writing a Short-Story Interpretation

Page 552

LISTENING AND SPEAKING WORKSHOP

Giving and Listening to an Oral Response to Literature

Page 570

California Standards

Writing

1.0 Students write clear, coherent, and focused essays. The writing exhibits students' awareness of the audience and purpose. Essays contain formal introductions, supporting evidence, and conclusions. Students progress through the stages of the writing process.

1.1 Choose the form of writing (e.g., review) that best suits the intended purpose.

1.2 Create multiple-paragraph expository compositions:

a. Engage the interest of the reader and state a clear purpose.

b. Develop the topic with supporting details and precise verbs, nouns, and adjectives to paint a visual image in the mind of the reader.

c. Conclude with a detailed summary linked to the purpose of the composition.

1.3 Use a variety of effective and coherent organizational patterns, including organization by categories and order of importance.

1.5 Compose documents with appropriate formatting by using word-processing skills and principles of design (e.g., tabs).

1.6 Revise writing to improve the organization and consistency of ideas within and between paragraphs.

2.0 Students write expository texts of at least 500 to 700 words. Student writing demonstrates a command of standard American English and the organizational and drafting strategies outlined in Writing Standard 1.0.

2.2 Write expository compositions (e.g., explanation):

a. State the thesis or purpose.

go. hrw .com

GO TO: go.hrw.com
KEYWORD: HLLA6 W-3
FOR: Models, Writer's Guides, and Reference Sources

   c. Follow an organizational pattern appropriate to the type of composition.

   d. Offer persuasive evidence to validate arguments and conclusions.

2.4 Write responses to literature:

   a. Develop an interpretation exhibiting careful reading, understanding, and insight.

   b. Organize the interpretation around several clear ideas, premises, or images.

   c. Develop and justify the interpretation through sustained use of examples and textual evidence.

Listening and Speaking

1.0 Students deliver focused, coherent presentations that convey ideas clearly and relate to the background and interests of the audience. They evaluate the content of oral communication.

1.1 Relate the speaker's verbal communication (e.g., pitch, feeling, tone) to the nonverbal message (e.g., posture, gesture).

1.2 Identify the tone conveyed in the oral communication.

1.4 Select a focus and an organizational structure, matching the purpose, message, occasion, and vocal modulation to the audience.

1.5 Emphasize salient points to assist the listener in following the main ideas and concepts.

1.6 Support opinions with detailed evidence.

1.7 Use effective rate, volume, pitch, and tone and align nonverbal elements to sustain audience interest and attention.

2.0 Students deliver well-organized formal presentations employing traditional rhetorical strategies (e.g., exposition). Student speaking demonstrates a command of standard American English and the organizational and delivery strategies outlined in Listening and Speaking Standard 1.0.

2.3 Deliver oral responses to literature:

   a. Develop an interpretation exhibiting careful reading, understanding, and insight.

   b. Organize the selected interpretation around several clear ideas, premises, or images.

   c. Develop and justify the selected interpretation through sustained use of examples and textual evidence.

Listening and Speaking

Prerequisite Standards

Grade 5

■ **2.3** Deliver oral responses to literature:

   a. Summarize significant events and details.

   b. Articulate an understanding of several ideas or images communicated by the literary work.

   c. Use examples or textual evidence from the work to support conclusions.

Standards Coming Up in the Next Level

Grade 7

■ **2.2** Deliver oral summaries of articles and books:

   a. Include the main ideas of the event or article and the most significant details.

   b. Use the student's own words, except for material quoted from sources.

   c. Convey a comprehensive understanding of sources, not just superficial details.

Writing Workshop

PRETEACHING

Standards Starter

Motivate. Ask students to recall stories they have read that have important themes or messages. Have them list the elements in the story (setting, characters, and plot) that contribute to the story's meaning. Tell students that in this workshop they will read a short story and write an interpretation, an essay that shows how the elements of fiction help support a story's message.

Introducing the Workshop. To introduce the workshop, use the Journal Warm-up, Transparency 10, in *Writing, Listening, & Speaking*.

Quotation for the Day

"All good books are alike in that they are truer than if they really happened and after you are finished reading one you will find that all that happened to you and afterwards it belongs to you. . . ."

(Ernest Hemingway, 1899–1961, American writer)

Write the quotation on the chalkboard, and ask students to write journal entries about a book or a story they have read that made them feel as if they were part of the world portrayed. Tell students that part of their job in this workshop will be to explain how an author pulls the reader into a story.

WHAT'S AHEAD?

In this workshop you will interpret a short story. You will also learn how to

- preview a short story
- recognize elements of fiction
- develop insights about a character
- eliminate clichés from your writing
- correct run-on sentences

DO THIS

Reference Note
For more on **think sheets**, see page 495.

Writing a Short-Story Interpretation

You have just read a terrific short story that a friend recommended. When you discuss the story, you find that she has a very different take on, or *interpretation* of, the story than you do. Perhaps you think the main character is courageous when she chooses to face her fears. Your friend, on the other hand, might think the character is simply foolish to put herself in danger.

Whenever we read a story, we are invited to **interpret** it—to show an understanding or to explain its meaning. In this workshop you will read and then give your interpretation of a short story.

Professional Model: A Response to Literature

Some books you read, return to the library, and never think about again. Others, though, stick with you. In Louise Sherman's professional review on the next page, she examines one such book—*Number the Stars* by Lois Lowry.

As you read the response of a professional writer, create a **think sheet,** taking note of the author's interpretation and of what you can learn about responding to literature. Answering the numbered analysis questions next to the model will help you create a think sheet.

Writing 1.2 Create multiple-paragraph expository compositions. 2.2 Write expository compositions (e.g., explanation). 2.4 Write responses to literature.

552 (Workshop 3) **Response to Literature:** Writing a Short-Story Interpretation

WORKSHOP RESOURCES

Writing Workshop

Planning

- *On Course: Mapping Instruction*
- *One-Stop Planner* CD-ROM
- *Writing, Listening, & Speaking,* —Teaching Notes, p. 44

Differentiating Instruction

- *Lesson Plans for Language Development,* pp. 229–230

Practice

- *Writing, Listening, & Speaking,* Wkshp. 3

Reinforcement

- *Daily Language Activities*
- *Spelling*

A Review of Lois Lowry's

NUMBER THE STARS

by Louise L. Sherman

Annemarie's life in occupied[1] Copenhagen in 1943 seemingly is not much changed by the war—until the Nazi persecution of Danish Jews begins. Annemarie's family becomes involved in the Resistance[2] effort, helping a Jewish friend by having her pose as Annemarie's dead sister Lise. When an important packet must be taken to the captain of one of the ships smuggling Jews to neutral Sweden, Annemarie finds the courage needed to deliver it despite grave danger to herself. Later her Uncle Henrik tells her that *brave* means "not thinking about

1. Why does the reviewer begin with historical information?

2. Where does the summary of the story end and the author's interpretation begin?

the dangers. Just thinking about what you must do." Lowry's story is not just of Annemarie; it is also of Denmark and the Danish people, whose Resistance was so effective in saving their Jews. Annemarie is not just a symbol, however. She is a very real child who is equally involved in playing with a new kitten and running races at school as in the dangers of the occupation. *Number the Stars* brings the war to a child's level of understanding, suggesting but not detailing its horrors. It is well plotted, and period and place are convincingly recreated. An afterword answers the questions that readers will have and reiterates[3] the inspirational idealism[4] of the young people whose courage helped win the war.

3. What examples show that Annemarie is a realistic character?

"...brave means 'not thinking about the dangers. Just thinking about what you must do.'"

4. How does this quotation support the author's interpretation?

1. **occupied:** controlled by an enemy.
2. **Resistance:** the organized movement that opposes an occupying power.
3. **reiterates:** restates.
4. **inspirational idealism:** work for positive change that gives others hope.

Possible responses are given below.

1. Examples: Annemarie's courageous action and a quotation from the story. Descriptive words: *occupied, persecution,* and *grave danger.*

2. The idealism and courage of both young and old Danish people helped save the Jews and win the war.

3. It catches the reader's attention and provides convincing support for the reviewer's statement of the story's theme.

4. Purpose: to provide an interpretation and opinion of the novel *Number the Stars;* audience: students or teachers of young adult literature or school librarians.

   The author, Louise L. Sherman, begins her review by outlining the setting and plot of the novel. Sherman then discusses the main character, Annemarie, as a symbol and a real child who lives during the war. The reviewer next introduces her opinion that the novel makes the war easier for a child to relate to through the character of Annemarie. Sherman mentions that the plot and setting are convincing, and the novel's afterword is helpful and revealing.

Think About the Model

Working with a partner, discuss the following questions and write down your responses.

1. What examples and descriptive words does the author use to help the reader understand the book?

2. What does the reviewer think the theme, or meaning, of *Number the Stars* is?

3. Why do you think the reviewer sets one quotation apart from the rest of the review?

4. Write a summary of the review, noting the author's purpose and her audience.

Reference Note

For more on **summarizing,** see page 496.

Prewriting

Choose a Short Story

Ready to Read? For your interpretation you will read and analyze a short story. The first step is to find a story that you would like to understand better and that you think would interest your audience. Think about the types of characters or situations you like to read about. Then, look for a story with the type of character or situation that interests you most. To find a story, you might

- look in Part 1 of this book
- browse in bookstores—in person or online
- ask your friends or your teacher for recommendations
- ask a librarian or media specialist for suggestions
- look in magazines that publish stories
- read some reviews of short story collections

TIP In this workshop you will respond to literature by writing an interpretation of a short story. Your purpose will be to explain the story's meaning. A book review, like that of *Number the Stars,* is another way you can respond to literature. A review's purpose is to judge the value of the book. Depending on your purpose you may at some point want to write a review of literature, a movie, or a TV show. This book includes a Mini-Workshop on writing a review. Although that Mini-Workshop models a film review, you can use the guidelines to review a book, a short story, or even a TV show.

Mini-Workshop

See **Writing a Movie Review,** page 673.

 Writing 1.0 Students progress through the stages of the writing process as needed. 1.1 Choose the form of writing (e.g., review) that best suits the intended purpose.

Preview of Coming Attractions   Once you have found several short stories, **preview** each one to make a final decision. One student previewed "Boar Out There" by Cynthia Rylant by following the steps in the Thinking It Through below.

Reference Note

To read **"Boar Out There,"** see pages 501–502.

THINKING IT THROUGH   **Previewing a Short Story**

▶ STEP 1 **Study the title.** What do you think the story will be about?

It sounds like an adventure story about a boar, a kind of wild pig.

▶ STEP 2 **Look at the illustrations.** What hints do the illustrations give you?

There is a picture of a girl facing a wild boar. I think this is going to be an exciting story.

▶ STEP 3 **Skim some pages.** Does the main character seem likable? Do you see any interesting action taking place?

Jenny seems to be an imaginative person. She reminds me of my friend Dana. It looks as if she has an adventure in the woods.

▶ STEP 4 **Consider what you have found.** Does the story look interesting? Do you want to know more about the main character?

Yes, the story looks interesting. I want to know more about this character. I think that this is a good choice for me.

TIP   As you preview each story, keep in mind that your written response will be 500 to 700 words long. Therefore, it is important that you choose a story that will maintain your readers' interest throughout a paper of that length.

Read Your Short Story

KEY CONCEPT

Please Note . . .   As you read the short story you have chosen, **keep in mind that you will be writing about it later.** How can you organize your thoughts about the story as you are reading it? The first step is to analyze the basic **elements of fiction**—*setting, characters,* and *plot.* Remember, the **setting** is where and when the story takes place, the **characters** are the people or animals involved in the story, and the **plot** is the events that happen in the story.

Divide a sheet of paper into three columns. Label the columns *main character, setting,* and *plot.* Then, read your short story twice. First, read it to make sure that you understand what is happening in the story. The second time, read the story more closely, filling in the columns on your sheet by answering the questions in the chart on the next page.

Writing 2.0 Students write expository texts of at least 500 to 700 words.   **2.4a** Develop an interpretation exhibiting careful reading.

Read Your Short Story   **555**

QUESTIONS TO ASK

Main Character	Setting	Plot
▪ Who is the main character?	▪ Where does the story take place?	▪ What are the important events that happen in the story?
▪ What does the character look like?	▪ Does the setting affect the characters in the story?	▪ What problem, or conflict, does the main character face?
▪ How does the character act?	▪ How much time passes in the story?	▪ How does he or she deal with the problem?

REVIEW STANDARDS

The Point of It All

The following activity is a review of the 5th-grade **Writing Standard 2.2.**

Discuss with students a story with which they are familiar, and have students identify the story's theme or lesson about life. Then, ask students to list details from the story that support this theme. You might have students examine the literary elements of the story or answer the questions from the chart on this page to help them find details and textual references that support the theme.

CRITICAL THINKING

Tell students that stories have three basic types of conflicts: a person or persons against nature, a person or persons against another person or group of people, and a person against him- or herself. Have students analyze the conflicts in the stories they read.

The Point of It All After you have identified the basic elements of the short story, see if you can figure out its *theme*. The **theme** is the author's message or the lesson about life that the story reveals. Often, the author will not directly state the theme. Instead, you must figure it out by analyzing the story. Here are some suggestions.

- **Look at the title.** It can often give a hint about the theme.
- **Look at the events.** If you find repeated experiences, such as hardships or journeys, you might have a clue to the theme.
- **Look at how details of the story relate to real life.** In other words, try to determine how the details go beyond the story and mean something to you as the reader.

The student analyzing "Boar Out There" examined his responses to the questions in the chart above; then he wrote his notes for each element in a separate, short paragraph. Looking at those notes and the story, he determined the theme, as shown below.

TIP As you state the theme of your short story, keep in mind that themes often deal with emotions.

Main Character:	Jenny is the main character. She is afraid but eventually shows her bravery.
Setting:	The story is set in Glen Morgan and in the woods behind the old black Dodge. When Jenny is in the woods looking for the boar, the woods make her feel as if she is surrounded and trapped. The woods frighten her and add to the suspense of the story.
Plot:	Jenny wants to see the boar. Once she enters the woods, she is afraid. She is more afraid when she finds the boar, but then she realizes that it is as fearful as she is. It crashes away into the woods, and she wonders for a long time afterward if it is still afraid.
Theme:	The theme of "Boar Out There" is the power of sympathy and understanding over fear.

Choose and Read a Short Story

- Brainstorm a list of the types of short stories you like to read.
- Preview a few short stories by following the Thinking It Through steps on page 555.
- Choose one story. Then, read and re-read it, taking notes in a three-column chart based on your answers to the questions on page 556.
- Finally, write one or two sentences identifying the story's theme.

Think About Your Purpose and Audience

Why and Who?   You have read your story and are ready to tell people what you think of it. Before you begin, consider

- the **purpose** of your interpretation—why you are writing it
- your **audience**—the people who will be reading it

Your purpose, or reason for writing your interpretation, is to help your audience understand the story. Include in your introduction a **main idea statement,** or **thesis,** which directly states your purpose and the story's theme so that your readers know from the beginning why you are writing. To write a main idea statement, complete the sentence below just as the writer of the model on page 563 did.

> In my paper, I will show that *(title of short story)* by *(name of author)* is a story about *(theme of the story)*.

> In my paper, I will show that "Boar Out There" by Cynthia Rylant is a story about the power of sympathy and understanding over fear.

After writing a main idea statement, think about who will be the audience for your interpretation. Will it be just your teacher, or will it be the readers of an online student magazine? Once you have chosen an audience, ask yourself the following questions.

- What do my readers already know about this story and its subject?
- What about this story will most interest my audience? What will not interest them?
- How formal will my audience expect my interpretation to be?

TIP Remember your purpose for writing an interpretation is different from the purpose of the author who wrote the review on page 553.

Writing 1.0 Students write focused essays. The writing exhibits students' awareness of the audience and purpose. **1.2a** State a clear purpose. **2.2a** State the thesis or purpose.

Think About Your Purpose and Audience   **557**

Guided and Independent Practice

Monitor students' understanding by having them discuss the bulleted questions on p. 557 in small groups. Each group member should answer the questions aloud and support his or her answers. Encourage group members to share their opinions, and circulate among the groups to make sure students can answer each of the questions. Then, assign **Practice and Apply 2** for independent practice.

DIFFERENTIATING INSTRUCTION

Learners Having Difficulty

Some students may benefit from using tape recorders to record information about character, setting, and plot to use when writing summaries of their stories. Students can record important information and create oral notes while reading their stories. Suggest that students listen for relevant details and that they stop the tape while writing their inferences and insights about these details on a chart similar to the one shown on this page.

Advanced Learners

Acceleration. Share the following item with students to move them toward the 7th-grade **Writing Standard 2.2.**

Challenge students to provide textual evidence for every major point they make about the stories they read. Students should select the quotations based on their relevance, emotional impact, and brevity. Students may find that their papers will be too cluttered if they use all the quotations they note; however, each point they make should have specific support.

Write a main idea statement that includes your purpose and the theme of your short story. Answer the questions on page 557 to help you consider your audience.

Gather Details

Reference Note

For more on **developing an insight about a character,** see page 559.

Allow Me to Illustrate   To begin planning your interpretation, you will need to gather details from the story. These details will help you make **inferences,** educated guesses, and develop **insight** or understanding. The people who will read your interpretation will have no reason to accept your ideas unless you provide **evidence** and **examples** from the story to support them. You will also need to provide examples to support your main idea statement.

You can begin developing support for your ideas by looking back at the chart you made for Practice and Apply 1 on page 557. Based on your responses from the chart and the instruction on page 559, you can make inferences and develop insights about the story elements. Finally, you may need to gather from the story additional examples and **quotations,** word-for-word phrases or sentences, to prove to readers that your insights and inferences relate to the story's theme. Study the following **support chart** one student made for an interpretation of "Boar Out There."

Element	Inference or Insight	Example from Story
Main Character	Jenny wants to test her courage.	She faces the boar, silently looking at his scars and "ragged ears, caked with blood."
Setting	The setting of the woods is scary.	The trees are thick. The leaves are damp. The air presses around Jenny, making her feel trapped.
Plot	At the beginning of the story, Jenny is curious about the wild boar.	She looks over the fence and whispers "Boar out there."

Writing   1.0 Essays contain supporting evidence.   **1.2b** Develop the topic with supporting details.   **2.2d** Offer persuasive evidence to validate arguments and conclusions.   **2.4a** Develop an interpretation exhibiting understanding and insight.   **2.4c** Develop and justify the interpretation through sustained use of examples and textual evidence.

RESOURCES

Practice and Apply 2
Guided Practice
■ *Writing, Listening, & Speaking,* WS. p. 47

Developing an Insight About a Character

As you read a short story, you make **inferences,** or educated guesses, about the main character, setting, and plot. To make inferences, you combine clues the writer gives you with what you already know about the subject of the story. You may find these clues in the actions or words of a character or in the details or words that describe the setting or the action in the story.

In reading "Boar Out There," the student came across clues about Jenny: that she "forgot to breathe" and "stood stiff with wet eyes" when she heard the boar. He probably made the inference that Jenny was scared based on these clues and on his own reaction to a scary situation he experienced in the past.

As you read a short story, not only do you make inferences such as this, but you also develop *insights*. An **insight** is similar to an inference, but it is more meaningful. In a short-story interpretation an insight may reveal a deeper understanding of a character, the setting, or the plot—a meaning that lies further below the surface and is more important than an inference. To develop an insight about a character, follow the steps in the Thinking It Through below.

Developing an Insight About a Character

You may consider defining, providing examples of, or discussing the following terms with students before beginning **Mini-Lesson Critical Thinking:** *inference, insight, elements,* and *clues.*

THINKING IT THROUGH **Developing an Insight About a Character**

▶ **STEP 1** Think about how the character relates to the elements of the story—setting, characters, and plot.

Setting: In "Boar Out There," Jenny is afraid of the woods because they are dark. No one goes into the woods because a wild boar lives there.

Characters: At the beginning of the story, Jenny is fearful of the boar, but she still wants to see it. In the end of the story, Jenny's fear turns to pity for the boar when she realizes the boar is afraid and alone.

Plot: Jenny wants to see the boar, but she is also afraid of it. She faces her curiosity and her fears by entering the woods and facing the boar.

▶ **STEP 2** Reflect upon your responses to the story elements and your ideas about your own experiences. Develop an insight about what kind of person the main character is.

I think Jenny wants to test her courage. I know I test my courage sometimes. I'm afraid of heights, but just last year I rode a new roller coaster for the first time. Even though I was scared, I'm glad I did it because I actually had fun.

Writing 2.4a Develop an interpretation exhibiting understanding and insight.

RESOURCES

Mini-Lesson: Critical Thinking

Independent Practice
■ *Writing, Listening, & Speaking,* WS. p. 48

Guided Practice

(For independent practice, see Resources below on next page.)

Answers

Here are sample responses to the questions in the chart.

- *How the character relates to the setting:* Mary seems comfortable at Mrs. Yamamoto's house when she baby-sits Tim.

- *How the character relates to other characters:* Mary plays with Tim and is honest with Mrs. Yamamoto when she returns.

- *How the character relates to the plot:* Mary tries to attend to everything. She finds, however, that she is unable to watch everything and the picture frame breaks as the final result.

- *My related experiences:* I've baby-sat before and it is difficult to watch everything at the same time. It's almost like I need eyes in the back of my head to do a good job of monitoring everything.

- *My insight about the character:* Mary is a likable and believable character with a sense of right and wrong. She takes good care of a young child and owns up to her mistakes.

PRACTICE

Read the following passage. Then, fill in the chart that follows the passage to develop an insight about the main character, Mary. Use the steps in the Thinking it Through on page 559 to help you complete the chart.

Every Saturday Mary would baby-sit Mrs. Yamamoto's two-year-old son, Tim, while Mrs. Yamamoto ran errands. One Saturday, Mary was playing with Tim upstairs in his room when Tim threw a toy behind his bed. Mary retrieved it, but when she turned around, Tim was nowhere to be found. Mary walked out of the room just in time to see Tim toddling toward the stairs. Mary quickly rushed to grab him, but as she did she knocked over a glass picture frame that was sitting on a table in the hallway. The frame fell to the hardwood floor and shattered.

Mary was upset. What was she going to do? Should she tell Mrs. Yamamoto the truth, or could she blame the accident on Tim? She didn't have much time to think because at that moment she heard Mrs. Yamamoto calling her name.

Mary slowly carried Tim down the stairs. Mrs. Yamamoto could tell something was wrong. Mary would not look at her, and her face was bright red. "What is it, Mary?" Mrs. Yamamoto asked. With downcast eyes, Mary told Mrs. Yamamoto that she had broken the glass picture frame. Mrs. Yamamoto smiled and said, "It's all right. My husband bought the frame, but I didn't really like it. Now I can replace it with one that I do like."

How the character relates to the setting:	
How the character relates to other characters:	
How the character relates to the plot:	
My related experiences:	
My insight about the character:	

PRACTICE & APPLY 3 **Gather Details**

Create a support chart like the one on page 558 to develop insights and inferences about the story you read. Find examples from the story to support each inference or insight.

Organize Details

Taking Orders The main **organizational pattern** for your interpretation will be **order of importance,** in which you arrange details from most important to least important or from least important to most important. To organize the details of your interpretation in order of importance, follow the steps below.

1. First, decide which of the three elements—character, setting, plot—is the most important to your interpretation. Look at the support chart you created for Practice and Apply 3. You may choose the element that has the most details, or you may choose the element that has the most interesting insight.

2. Next, decide where you want to place the most important element in your interpretation. You can put the most important element first in order to give your readers the information they need to understand the other elements, or you can put the most important element last to leave your readers with your strongest point.

3. Once you have decided where you want to place the most important element, number the elements in your support chart in the order that you want to present them.

TIP Check to see that the ideas in your support chart are grouped together correctly. For example, all the details about character should be together. If they are not, rearrange the details so they are with the element they support. This will ensure that your ideas are unified, or **consistent**.

TIP When you begin writing your interpretation, add *transitional words* and *phrases* between and within your paragraphs. **Transitional words** and **phrases** will link your ideas together and give your interpretation **coherence,** or connectedness. Use transitions that show order of importance, such as *first, mainly, last,* and *most important.* For more on **transitions,** see pages 653–654.

PRACTICE & APPLY 4 **Organize Details**

Organize the details you have gathered in order of importance by following the steps above.

Writing **1.0** Students write clear, coherent essays. **1.3** Use a variety of effective and coherent organizational patterns, including order of importance. **2.0** Student writing demonstrates the organizational strategies outlined in Writing Standard 1.0. **2.2c** Follow an organizational pattern appropriate to the type of composition. **2.4b** Organize the interpretation around several clear ideas, premises, or images.

Organize Details **561**

PRACTICE & APPLY 3

Guided and Independent Practice

Using a story the class has read, monitor students' understanding by leading them through the process of developing insights and inferences. You may want to have students suggest supporting examples you can write on a transparency or the chalkboard. Then, assign **Practice and Apply 3** for independent practice.

DIRECT TEACHING

Taking Orders

You might turn back to Workshop 1 and point out transitions in the Professional Model "Boar Out There" (pages 501–502). This will give students an opportunity to see transitions in paragraphs.

PRACTICE & APPLY 4

Guided and Independent Practice

To monitor students' progress, you may circulate among students and randomly question *Which element do you plan to analyze?* and *Why did you choose this element over the others?* Then, students should complete **Practice and Apply 4** for independent practice.

RESOURCES

Practice and Apply 3

Guided Practice

■ *Writing, Listening, & Speaking,* WS. p. 49

Practice and Apply 4

Guided Practice

■ *Writing, Listening, & Speaking,* WS. p. 50

Quotation for the Day

"To note an artist's limitations is but to define his talent."

(Willa Cather, 1873–1947, American writer)

Write the quotation on the chalkboard. Point out to students that when they read they should notice a story's weak points as well as its strong ones. They can keep these strengths and weaknesses in mind when they write. Explain that analyzing a piece of literature for both its most and least successful qualities will allow students to make a more balanced assessment or a fuller interpretation.

A Writer's Framework

Short-Story Interpretation

Introduction
- Attention-getting opener
- Main idea statement

To get your audience's attention, you might open with a quotation, a question, or a description of a dramatic event from the story. Include a **main idea statement** that states your purpose and identifies the title, author, and theme of the story.

Body
- Plot details that support the main idea statement
- Setting details that support the main idea statement
- Character details that support the main idea statement

- Organize the body paragraphs of your interpretation by **categories**—plot, character, and setting. Make sure each detail in each paragraph is consistent with the main idea.
- Arrange the paragraphs in **order of importance,** starting or ending with the most important element.
- Use **transitional words** and **phrases** between sentences to give your paper **coherence.** (For more on **transitions,** see pages 653–654.)

Conclusion
- Summary
- Restatement of main idea

Leave your readers with no questions about your interpretation by making a detailed **summary** of the points you made. Also, **restate** your main idea. (For more information on writing **introductions** and **conclusions,** see pages 655–656.)

PRACTICE & APPLY 5

Guided and Independent Practice

Monitor students' understanding by discussing with them the different purposes, audiences, and methods of organization for a short-story interpretation. Have each student tell which purpose, audience, and method of organization he or she will use. Then, assign **Practice and Apply 5** for independent practice.

PRACTICE & APPLY 5 — Write a Short-Story Interpretation

Write a short-story interpretation. As you write, refer to the framework above and to the Writer's Model on page 563.

Writing **1.0** Essays contain formal introductions and conclusions. **1.2a** Engage the interest of the reader. **1.2c** Conclude with a detailed summary linked to the purpose of the composition. **1.3** Use a variety of effective and coherent organizational patterns, including organization by categories. **2.0** Student writing demonstrates the drafting strategies outlined in Writing Standard 1.0.

562 Workshop 3 **Response to Literature:** Writing a Short-Story Interpretation

RESOURCES

Practice and Apply 5

Think Sheet
- *Writing, Listening, & Speaking,* WS. p. 51

Template
- *Writing, Listening, & Speaking,* WS. p. 52

A Writer's Model

The final draft below closely follows the framework for a short-story interpretation given on the previous page. Notice the high-lighted transitional words and phrases the writer uses.

An Interpretation of
Cynthia Rylant's "Boar Out There"

Have you ever been face to face with something that you feared? If so, did you run or did you face your fear? In this paper, I will show that "Boar Out There" by Cynthia Rylant is a story about the power of sympathy and understanding over fear.

First, to support the message about fear, the plot of this story is suspenseful. From the beginning, you wonder whether Jenny will see the boar and what will happen if she does. She is curious about the boar and keeps looking over the fence and whispering "Boar out there." From this detail you can guess that she will look for the boar. Even though she is afraid, she goes into the woods. Suddenly the boar comes crashing through the trees, and Jenny does not have "time to scream or run." **Then,** just when it looks as if the boar will attack, he runs past her. Jenny never sees the boar again. It turns out that the boar is as afraid of her as she has been of it.

The story's suspenseful setting also adds to the story's message. The woods are mysterious and scary. An old black Dodge separates the forest from the rest of Glen Morgan, and Jenny knows that no one in town has gone beyond the rusted car. **Nevertheless,** Jenny enters the woods, scared but determined to find the boar. The trees are thick, the leaves are damp and brown, and the air presses against her. **As a result,** Jenny feels surrounded and trapped, but she continues her search.

Most important, Jenny's actions illustrate the theme of the story. When she hears the boar rushing toward her, Jenny is truly afraid. She forgets to breathe; she chokes and coughs, and she even cries. **However,** she is brave enough to fight her fear. **In fact,** she seems to want to test her courage. She does not run or scream. **Instead,** she stands silently looking at the boar's scars and "ragged ears, caked with blood." All at once, Jenny is not afraid. Her fear has been replaced with sympathy when she realizes that the boar is afraid and alone.

(continued)

INTRODUCTION
Attention-getting opener

Main idea statement

BODY
Plot details

GO TO: go.hrw.com
KEYWORD: HLLA6 W-3
FOR: A Student Model

Setting details

Character details

Insight about character

(continued)

CONCLUSION

Summary of points
made in the
interpretation

Restatement of
main idea

"Boar Out There" may seem like a simple story about a girl who enters a scary forest. In the story, though, is a lesson about fear: Maybe the animals (and people) we fear are more like us than they are different. Instead of being afraid, we should sympathize with them and understand their feelings.

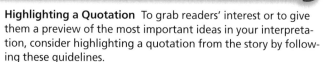

Designing Your Writing

Highlighting a Quotation To grab readers' interest or to give them a preview of the most important ideas in your interpretation, consider highlighting a quotation from the story by following these guidelines.

- Select a quotation by thinking about the main idea you are presenting in your essay. The quotation might illustrate the theme by describing the setting, a character, or the problem.
- Set the quotation apart from the rest of your interpretation by indenting it on both sides and by including one line of blank space before and after it. You may also use a different font to set the quotation apart further from the rest of the text.
- List the title and author of the story beneath the quotation, aligned with the right edge of the quotation. Here is an example.

> His large gray-black body shivered as he waited just beyond the shadow of the tree she held for support. His nostrils glistened, and his eyes; but astonishingly, he was silent. He shivered and glistened and was absolutely silent.
>
> "Boar Out There" by Cynthia Rylant
>
> Have you ever been face to face with something that you feared? If so, did you run or did you face your fear? In this paper, I will show . . .

COMPUTER TIP

Set **tabs** on your word processor to make indenting the left edges of a stand-alone quotation easier. Click your cursor on the bar at the top of the document to create a tab, and then press the tab key on your keyboard to begin typing at that point on each line. Set another tab to indent the title and author's name.

Writing 1.5 Compose documents with appropriate formatting by using word-processing skills and principles of design (e.g., tabs).

TECHNOLOGY TIP

W1.5

Discuss how to adjust margins and space correctly with students who are using computers. To change the margins, students can use the document-layout or page-setup feature. To change the spacing, students can use the format menu. The specific commands will vary, depending on the software students are using.

Evaluate and Revise Content, Organization, and Style

A Second Look Once you have written a first draft, you need to think about how to improve it. First, take a break from your interpretation and then read the draft twice. In the first reading, focus on your ideas. Do they make sense? Are they in a logical order? The guidelines below will help you decide. In the second reading, look at your words and sentences. The Focus on Word Choice on page 567 will help you.

First Reading: Content and Organization Use the following chart to evaluate and revise your short-story interpretation.

editor in charge

Short-Story Interpretation: Content and Organization Guidelines

Evaluation Questions	▶ Tips	▶ Revision Techniques
❶ Does the main idea statement include the title and author of the story and introduce the story's theme?	▶ **Put a check mark** next to the title and author of the short story and the introduction of the theme.	▶ **Add** the story's title and author's name, if necessary. **Add** a brief statement that introduces the story's theme.
❷ Is the interpretation supported in separate body paragraphs with information about the story's characters, setting, and plot?	▶ **Label** each paragraph with the element it discusses. **Highlight** details that elaborate on the characters, setting, or plot.	▶ **Rearrange** details into the appropriate paragraphs for **consistency**. **Elaborate** with details about the main character, setting, or plot events.
❸ Are the body paragraphs organized in order of importance? Are ideas connected with transitions?	▶ **Number** the elements labeled in #2 above in order of importance. **Circle** transitional words and phrases.	▶ **Rearrange** body paragraphs into order of importance, if necessary. **Add** transitional words or phrases if few are included.
❹ Does the interpretation end with a summary of the points made and a restatement of the main idea?	▶ **Underline** the summary. **Put a star** above the restatement.	▶ **Add** a summary and a restatement of the main idea, if necessary.

Writing 1.6 Revise writing to improve the organization and consistency of ideas within and between paragraphs.

Quotation for the Day

"I found that, having started writing books, I was always having to write one more to kind of make up for the deficiencies of the one I'd just completed."

(John Dos Passos, 1896–1970, American author)

Use this quotation to show students that most writers recognize the need to improve their work. Motivate students to improve their drafts by encouraging them to remember that even the work of professional authors needs to be evaluated and revised.

DIRECT TEACHING

Elaboration

To help students elaborate in the bodies of their essays, encourage them to use sensory words and details about the plot, setting, and characters of the stories they read.

First, suggest that students refer to the charts they made while reading their stories and taking notes about them. Then, ask students to look for vivid adverbs, adjectives, and sensory details to use in describing the plot, setting, and characters. Suggest that students add the most relevant and interesting details to their drafts.

Responding to the Revision Process

Answers

1. The writer added the phrase to provide a transition for the reader. The phrase alerts the reader that this is the most important idea.

2. The added sentence provides specific sensory details to elaborate on a main point.

3. The final sentence adds a restatement of the main idea of the interpretation.

DIRECT TEACHING

REVIEW STANDARD

Second Reading: Style
The following activity is a review of the 5th-grade **Writing Standard 1.6.**

Ask pairs of students to work together to evaluate their drafts. First, ask them to exchange papers and read each other's short-story interpretations. Then, direct them to the evaluation guidelines on p. 565 and the style guidelines on this page. Students should use the guidelines to assess the interpretations and to determine what information, if any, their partners might add, delete, or change to improve the meaning and focus of the writing. Students may write their comments in the margins of their partners' papers or on separate sheets of paper.

ONE WRITER'S REVISIONS This revision is an early draft of the short-story interpretation on page 563.

add — *Most important,* ∧Jenny's actions illustrate the theme of the story. When she hears the boar rushing toward her, Jenny is truly

elaborate — *She forgets to breathe; she chokes and coughs, and she even cries.* afraid. However, she is brave enough to fight her fear. In fact, she seems to want to test her courage. She does not run or scream. Instead, she stands silently looking at the boar's scars and "ragged ears, caked with blood." All at

add — *Her fear has been replaced with sympathy when she realizes that* once Jenny is not afraid. ∧ *the boar is afraid and alone.*

> **PEER REVIEW**
>
> As you evaluate a peer's paper, ask yourself the following questions.
> - Do I know the theme of the story?
> - Do details from the story support the theme?

Responding to the Revision Process

1. Why do you think the writer added the phrase to the beginning of the first sentence?

2. Why do you think the writer added the third sentence to the paragraph above?

3. Why do you think the writer added a sentence to the end of the paragraph?

▷ **Second Reading: Style** Now that you have looked at the big picture, it is time to focus on your individual sentences. There are many ways to edit sentences. One way is to eliminate *clichés.* **Clichés** are expressions that have been used so often they have lost their freshness. When you hear or read a cliché, you probably do not even bother to picture the image in your mind. The last thing you, as a writer, want is to have your readers ignore your ideas. The following guidelines will help you make your writing clear and original.

Style Guidelines

Evaluation Question	▶ Tip	▶ Revision Technique
Does the interpretation contain any clichés?	▶ **Put an X** through every word or phrase that you think is a cliché.	▶ **Replace** each cliché with precise words (nouns, verbs, and adjectives).

 Writing 1.2b Develop the topic with precise verbs, nouns, and adjectives to paint a visual image in the mind of the reader.

Clichés

When you are writing about a short story you have read, you may want to use certain familiar expressions. Clichés, however, will weaken the punch of your writing. Here are some examples of clichés. See if you can think of others.

Word Choice

Examples: raining cats and dogs   scared to death
tough as nails   butterflies in your stomach
cold as ice   busy as a bee

Replace clichés with more original wording to make your meaning clearer and more interesting. Use **precise verbs, nouns,** and **adjectives** to make your writing fresh and appealing.

The rain **pounded** the ground like a **jackhammer.**

She **zips** around all day like a **frantic** bee.

Reference Note

For more information on **precise verbs, nouns,** and **adjectives,** see page 534.

ONE WRITER'S REVISIONS

> Suddenly the boar comes~~ running like a maniac,~~ and *crashing through the trees*
>
> Jenny does not have "time to scream or run."

Responding to the Revision Process

How did replacing the cliché "running like a maniac" with more precise language improve the sentence above?

 PRACTICE & APPLY 6

Evaluate and Revise Your Short-Story Interpretation

- First, evaluate and revise the content and organization of your interpretation by using the guidelines on page 565.

- Next, replace any clichés in your writing. Use the style guidelines on page 566 and the Focus on Word Choice above to help you.

- If a peer evaluated your paper, think carefully about his or her comments before you revise.

 Writing 1.2b Develop the topic with precise verbs, nouns, and adjectives to paint a visual image in the mind of the reader.

Focus on Word Choice   **567**

Publishing

Proofread Your Interpretation

Getting It Right   Now you need to proofread your short-story interpretation. If you have too many errors in your interpretation, your readers may not take your ideas seriously. To make sure you catch every error, also have a classmate proofread your interpretation.

Grammar Link

Correcting Run-on Sentences

Sometimes when you write, your pencil cannot keep up with your thoughts. When this happens, you may write *run-on sentences*. A **run-on sentence** is really two or more sentences that are incorrectly written as one.

Mick loves old movies he also loves to read.

One way to correct a run-on sentence is to divide the sentences into separate sentences.

Mick loves old movies. He also loves to read.

You can also turn a run-on sentence into a compound sentence by adding a comma and *and, but,* or *or*.

Mick loves old movies. but he also loves to read.

> **PRACTICE**
>
> Correct the run-on sentences to the right. First, divide the run-on sentence into separate sentences. Then, rewrite the run-on sentence as a compound sentence by adding a comma and *and, but,* or *or*. If a sentence is correctly punctuated and is not a run-on, write C on your paper.

Example:

1. Last week I read an adventure story I really liked it.

1. Last week I read an adventure story. I really liked it.
   Last week I read an adventure story, and I really liked it.

1. "Boar Out There" is the title of the story it is about a girl named Jenny.

2. Jenny imagines that the wild boar that lives in the woods is a monster she wants to see it.

3. Everyone is scared to enter the woods Jenny goes into the woods alone to find the boar.

4. Jenny finds she cannot move, and she cannot breathe when she faces the boar.

5. The boar stared at Jenny he ran away when a blue jay startled him.

Reference Note

For more information and practice on correcting **run-on sentences**, see pages 388–391 in the *Holt Handbook*.

 Writing 2.0 Student writing demonstrates a command of standard American English.

Publish Your Interpretation

Read All About It   Finally, you have completed your short-story interpretation. Your goal was to write an interpretation that would interest other people in the story you read. How will you get your audience to read your interpretation? Here are some suggestions.

- Make a mobile that contains your interpretation. Each paragraph of your interpretation can be written on a separate piece of paper. Attach the papers to a hanger with string. You may want to add pictures to illustrate each element as well.

- Deliver your short-story interpretation as an oral response to the story. For more information on **giving an oral response,** see the Listening and Speaking Workshop on pages 570–573.

Reflect on Your Interpretation

Building Your Portfolio   Take time to think about writing your short-story interpretation. What did you learn from it? Good writers are always learning from their writing. You can, too, by answering the following questions.

- What did you find easy or difficult about writing an interpretation? Why?

- In what other school subjects might you develop an interpretation based on a few important elements?

- Which evaluation guideline (page 565) was most helpful in evaluating and revising your short story interpretation? Why?

> **PRACTICE & APPLY** 7 **Proofread, Publish, and Reflect on Your Writing**
>
> Wrap up your experience of writing a short-story interpretation by following the guidelines below.
>
> - Correct any spelling, punctuation, or grammatical errors in your short-story interpretation. Make sure that your interpretation does not include run-on sentences.
> - Publish your short-story interpretation so that others can read it.
> - Answer the Reflect on Your Interpretation questions above. Include your responses in your portfolio.

**Publish Your   W1.5
Interpretation**
You might advise students who have not yet entered their short-story interpretations into a word-processing document to do so before publishing their interpretations. Remind students to set tabs and include blank spaces to highlight a quotation within their interpretations, as mentioned in **Designing Your Writing** and **Computer Tip** on Pupil's Edition page 564.

▶ **Resources Reminder**
For help with writing assessment, see 6 Traits—Plus 1 in the "General Scales and Sample Papers" section of *Progress Assessment of Writing, Listening, & Speaking.*

English-Language Learners
Because students may not yet have developed the requisite skills to proofread for grammar, usage, and mechanics, you may assign peer tutors to help your English-Language Learners. Once you have read the paper the pair has proofread, list a focus area for each English-Language Learner.

▶ **Resources Reminder**
For more help with English-Language Learners, see *Lesson Plans for Language Development.*

PRACTICE & APPLY 7

Independent Practice

Answers
Some possible answers for the second reflection question include history, art, music, or drama.

Listening and Speaking Workshop

Talk   Listen

Listening and
Speaking
Workshop

PRETEACHING

Quotation for the Day

"Being specific sometimes involves no more than choosing the right word or phrase."

(Ronald Munson, 1939– , American author and teacher)

Write the quotation on the chalkboard. Ask several students to express it in their own words. Students can also freewrite their answer to this question: *How does this idea apply to an oral response to literature?* [Because listeners cannot re-read an oral response, speakers must be very precise in their presentations.]

DIRECT TEACHING

Plan Your Oral Response

Most students will adapt the written interpretations they wrote in the Writing Workshop into an oral response. If not, refer students to the Prewriting section that begins on p. 554 for choosing stories and developing interpretations.

Go by the Book

Discuss with students how they might use guide words to indicate important points or main ideas in their oral presentations. For example, students might use words like *first, second,* or *most importantly* to signal to their audiences that a main idea follows. Tell students to write these guide words down on their note cards so they will remember to use them in their presentations.

WHAT'S AHEAD?

In this workshop you will give an oral response to the short story you wrote about in the Writing Workshop. You will also learn how to

- consider your audience
- practice a clear speaking voice and eye contact
- listen for verbal and nonverbal messages
- evaluate the oral responses of others

Reference Note

For more on developing a **response to literature,** see pages 554–561.

Giving and Listening to an Oral Response to Literature

Imagine that you have just read a story, a play, or a novel. You really liked it and want to share it with others. You could share informally, sitting in the cafeteria talking to a friend, or you could share your ideas with a group—your class, for example. When you share information, you are giving an **expository presentation.** One type of expository presentation is an *oral response.* Giving an **oral response** allows you to share information about a written work. For this workshop you will adapt the written interpretation of a short story that you wrote earlier into an oral response.

Plan Your Oral Response

Writing vs. Speaking   To be an effective speaker, you will need to adapt your written interpretation instead of just reading it aloud. Listeners cannot re-read spoken words as they can written words. Therefore, it is important that you present the most important points of your interpretation clearly so that your audience can understand them.

Go by the Book   The first step in organizing an oral interpretation is to find the most important points in your written interpretation. As in your written response, your **focus** will be your interpretation of the story's theme. Read over your written response.

Listening and Speaking **1.0** Students deliver focused, coherent presentations that convey ideas clearly and relate to the background and interests of the audience. **1.4** Select a focus. **1.6** Support opinions with detailed evidence. **2.3a** Develop an interpretation exhibiting careful reading, understanding, and insight. **2.3b** Organize the selected interpretation around several clear ideas, premises, or images.

570   Workshop 3   **Response to Literature:** Giving and Listening to an Oral Response to Literature

Then, write brief sentences about the characters, setting, plot, and your **interpretation** of the theme on note cards to help you remember each idea you want to share. Include also **evidence** from your written response to support your ideas about the story's theme. (Leave plenty of space on each note card. You will need that space for other notes that will help you deliver your ideas effectively.)

Once you have your ideas on the note cards, you can **organize** them in a logical order. You can start with the most important idea, or you can end with the most important idea. Number your note cards in the order that you want to present your ideas.

Reference Note

For more on **order of importance,** see page 661.

Who's Listening? Since the **occasion,** or the situation that prompts you to speak, is a class assignment, your **audience** will be your teacher and classmates. To present your **message** in an effective way, you need to consider your audience's backgrounds and interests. For example, if your audience is not familiar with the short story you are sharing, you may want to provide more details about the plot or characters. If you know that your audience will not understand a particular word, you will want to define it. Making the content of your oral response match your audience will help you achieve your **purpose**—to share information.

TIP When you are speaking in front of your teacher and classmates, you should use **standard American English,** language that is grammatically correct, so that you will be understood.

Deliver Your Oral Response

Bringing It to Life To become a good public speaker, you must use more than just words. **Nonverbal** communication, or body language, adds to your message. The chart below lists some ideas on how you can include nonverbal elements in your oral response.

Quick guide!

USING NONVERBAL ELEMENTS

Nonverbal Element	Examples
Eye contact	Look into the eyes of your audience to keep your audience's attention.
Facial expression	Smile, frown, or raise an eyebrow to show your feelings or to emphasize parts of your message.
Gestures	Give a thumbs up, shrug, nod, or shake your head to emphasize a point or to add meaning to your speech.
Posture	Stand tall and straight to show that you are sure of yourself.

Listening and Speaking **1.4** Select an organizational structure, matching the purpose, message, and occasion to the audience. **2.0** Student speaking demonstrates a command of standard American English and the organizational strategies outlined in Listening and Speaking Standard 1.0. **2.3c** Develop and justify the selected interpretation through sustained use of examples and textual evidence.

Say It Like You Mean It

If students struggle with the concept of verbal and nonverbal elements, you may consider providing class time for students to practice making sure that nonverbal elements in their presentations match the verbal elements.

Have group members take turns using their notes to deliver fifteen or twenty seconds of their responses. After each group member's delivery, students should spend thirty seconds sharing constructive criticism and discussing each student's use of nonverbal and verbal elements. Students should move quickly around the circle and spend no more than thirty seconds discussing each member's presentation.

The fast pace of the exercise will keep students on task and encourage them to restrict their criticism to the use of verbal and nonverbal elements.

How you use your voice can also affect the message that you give your audience. Consider the **verbal elements** in the chart below as you practice and deliver your speech.

USING VERBAL ELEMENTS

Verbal Element	Explanation
Feeling	Even though you are providing information, you should not speak in a monotone, or dull voice. Instead, show enthusiasm through your voice so that your audience will become enthusiastic about your response.
Pitch (or vocal modulation)	Your voice rises and falls naturally when you speak. If you are nervous, your voice may get higher. To control your pitch, take deep breaths and stay calm as you give your speech. Capture the audience's attention by using the pitch of your voice to emphasize key points.
Rate (or tempo)	In conversations you may speak at a fast rate, or speed. When you make a speech, you should talk more slowly to help listeners understand you.
Tone (or mood)	Since you are sharing information, the mood of your presentation should be informative. Strive to maintain an objective point of view. The tone of your voice should show that you are knowledgeable about the short story.
Volume	Even if you normally speak quietly, you will need to speak loudly when giving your oral response. You shouldn't yell, but the listeners at the back of the room should be able to hear you clearly.

Putting the Two Together   You can help your audience understand your main idea by emphasizing important ideas with **nonverbal elements** and **verbal elements** that match. For example, if you are explaining how a main character develops sympathy for something she once feared, you might smile (nonverbal element) and speak with a soft voice (verbal element) at the same time.

Say It Like You Mean It   To help you remember all of the verbal and nonverbal elements you want to include in your oral response, make delivery notes. Consider writing your delivery notes on your note cards in a color different from that of your speaking notes. You can also draw an arrow from each delivery note to the exact place in your oral response where you will include a gesture or change in vocal expression. You might also underline words that you want to emphasize. On the next page you will see an example from a note card for an oral response to "Boar Out There."

Listening and Speaking 1.4 Match the vocal modulation to the audience.   **1.5** Emphasize salient points to assist the listener in following the main ideas and concepts.   **1.7** Use effective rate, volume, pitch, and tone and align nonverbal elements to sustain audience interest and attention.

(speak slowly for suspense)

When Jenny first sees the boar, it seems <u>threatening</u>.

(open eyes wide)

It is <u>covered</u> with <u>scars</u> and <u>blood</u>.

③

Finally, remember that the best way to get your ideas across and keep your audience's interest is by being yourself. Let your personality come through in your words, your delivery, and your enthusiasm.

Polish Through Practice   Practice your oral response out loud and standing up. Practice it over and over until all the words are familiar and you are comfortable with all the gestures, movements, and facial expressions you want to include. Practice with a friend or in front of a mirror, or use a tape recorder or videorecorder to figure out what parts of your presentation need work.

On the Spot   As much as you may plan and practice, be prepared for the unexpected during your presentation. If you are interrupted by a noise, speak louder or pause until the noise stops. If you forget a gesture, keep going. In addition, be flexible. Let your audience help you—pay attention to their responses, and adjust your delivery if your audience seems confused or bored. Remember that your goal is to give an interesting, entertaining, and informative talk.

PRACTICE & APPLY 8   **Plan and Deliver an Oral Response to Literature**

Use the guidelines on pages 570–573 to deliver an oral response.

- Write content and delivery notes on note cards.
- Practice your oral response.
- Deliver your oral response, making adjustments when necessary.
- Ask your audience for feedback.

Listening and Speaking 2.0 Students deliver well-organized formal presentations employing traditional rhetorical strategies (e.g., exposition). Student speaking demonstrates the delivery strategies outlined in Listening and Speaking Standard 1.0.   **2.3** Deliver oral responses to literature.

Deliver Your Oral Response   **573**

REVIEW STANDARD

Listen to an Oral Response

The following item is a review of the 5th-grade **Listening and Speaking Standard 1.2.**

Before beginning the oral presentations, remind students that listening is not a passive activity; they must be thinking all the time. To help students focus on listening, you may challenge them to articulate their ideas of a presentation that might earn a perfect score. Then, ask them what kinds of presentation flaws might lower that score. Urge presenters to keep these criteria in mind as they deliver their oral responses.

DIFFERENTIATING INSTRUCTION

English-Language Learners

Students who are less proficient in English may focus on a single aspect of delivery, such as volume and clarity of the presentation, rather than on content. Students can rate their ability to hear and understand everything the speaker is saying.

 Resources Reminder

For more help with English-Language Learners, see *Lesson Plans for Language Development.*

PRACTICE & APPLY 9

Guided and Independent Practice

Monitor students' comprehension by showing them a videotape of a presentation. Discuss the elements in the chart with students and make sure they can apply the concepts to the videotaped presentation. Then, assign **Practice and Apply 9** for independent practice.

Listen to an Oral Response

Sorting it Out   An effective listener considers not only the words being said, but also the speaker's verbal and nonverbal messages. When you listen to an oral response to literature, you can gain a deeper understanding of the story and evaluate the speaker's techniques at the same time.

As you listen to an oral response, make notes on content and delivery. You might use a chart like the following one.

EVALUATING AN ORAL RESPONSE

Content	Sample Response
What is the main idea in the speaker's response?	The main idea or message of "Boar Out There" is that people learn important lessons when they face their fears.
What support does the speaker provide for the main idea?	The speaker describes how the main character's fear of the boar turns to sympathy.
Delivery	**Sample Response**
Does the speaker talk loudly and clearly? Explain.	Yes. I can clearly understand everything the speaker is saying.
How would you describe the speaker's tone? Does it fit the speaker's purpose?	The speaker's tone is informative and objective. That tone fits with an informative presentation.
Do the speaker's nonverbal techniques (posture, gestures) relate to the speaker's verbal techniques (pitch, mood, tone)? Explain.	Yes. The speaker stands up straight, smiles, and sounds proud when describing how the main character learns to face her fears.
Does the speaker emphasize key points with his or her voice or gestures? Explain.	Yes, the speaker slows down and gestures to emphasize how frightened Jenny feels when she enters the woods.

PRACTICE & APPLY 9   **Listen to an Oral Response to Literature**

Listen to three of your classmates' oral responses, and make notes about content and delivery using a chart like the one above. Then, discuss your evaluations in a small group. Offer positive comments as well as constructive criticism.

 Listening and Speaking 1.0 They evaluate the content of oral communication.   **1.1** Relate the speaker's verbal communication (e.g., pitch, feeling, tone) to the nonverbal message (e.g., posture gesture).   **1.2** Identify the tone in the oral communication.

DIRECTIONS: Read the following paragraph from a student's short-story interpretation of a fairy tale. Then, read the questions below it. Choose the best answer, and mark your answers on your own paper.

> (1) Finally, the shoemaker's actions show that wisdom can come from simple places. (2) When the king calls a meeting for everyone in the kingdom, the shoemaker stands in the back of the room because he feels that he is "nobody important." (3) However, the shoemaker is important. (4) By asking the king simple and direct questions, he causes the king to offer the princess's hand in marriage and half his kingdom to anyone who can kill the troublesome dragon. (5) When the shoemaker's sons decide to accept the king's offer, he is wise again, offering them advice on how to kill the dragon. (6) The two older sons do not follow their father's advice and are eaten by the dragon, but the youngest one does. (7) He slays the dragon and receives half the kingdom and the princess's hand, but he wouldn't have been successful without the wisdom of his father. (8) The princess is happy that the youngest brother killed the dragon because she wants to marry the youngest brother.

1. What words did the writer use to let you know her insights about the shoemaker?
   A "important" and "wise"
   B "successful" and "happy"
   C "not important" and "simple"
   D "direct" and "troublesome"

2. What example, if added to the paragraph, would most likely support the idea that the shoemaker is wise?
   F a description of the middle son
   G the advice the shoemaker gives to his sons
   H the offer from the king
   J a quote by the youngest son

3. If you were revising this paragraph, which sentence might you delete because it does not support the idea that the shoemaker is wise?
   A 1
   B 4
   C 5
   D 8

4. During an oral response to the story discussed in the paragraph, what could the speaker do to help an audience unfamiliar with the story understand it?
   F speak quietly while smiling
   G have good posture by standing tall and straight
   H provide more details about the plot or characters
   J read from note cards

5. Imagine you were listening to the paragraph above as an oral response to literature. What would you identify as the main idea?
   A Wisdom can be found in unusual places.
   B Younger brothers are smarter than older brothers.
   C To become rich, one must kill a dragon.
   D People should not stand at the back of the room.

Answers

1. A
2. G
3. D
4. H
5. A

APPLICATION

Community Connections

Point out to students that newswriters and editors make interpretations of real events. Newswriters may concentrate on the characters, setting, and plot of an event—the *who, what, when, where, why,* and *how* of a story. They may also look for a deeper meaning, or theme, of the event: *How will the event affect the future?* For homework, have each student select a local event or development and report on the story. Students should cover the basic facts and also relate what they feel will be the long-term effects of the event.   **HOMEWORK**

EXTENSION

Technology

Have students post book, TV, and movie reviews on a class Web page. Remind students that, rather than just providing an interpretation of a work, a review evaluates a work and makes a recommendation. Students can provide links to related resources to accompany their reviews.

Internet resources are sometimes public forums, and their content can be unpredictable.

RESOURCES

Response to Literature

Assessment
- *Progress Assessment of Writing, Listening, & Speaking,* Wkshp. 3
- *Diagnostic and Summative Assessments,* Midyear Test

Extension
- *Writing, Listening, & Speaking,* p. 67

Program Organization

Holt Literature and Language Arts provides a complete curriculum for standards-based instruction in vocabulary, reading, literature, writing, speaking and listening, and media. The instructional content of the program is divided into quarters to enable teachers to anticipate and administer the quarterly assessments required by California.

About Workshop 4

Standards-based lesson plans and suggestions for linking instruction with Workshop 4 and the related instructional material are provided in *On Course: Mapping Instruction.*

- Workshop 4 focuses on expository research writing and the presentation and evaluation skills needed to present research reports. Chapter 5 connects to it by focusing on literary research.

- The related instructional material for Workshop 4 is shown on the chart. This material will also be covered in the third quarterly assessment. Specific teaching suggestions for the related material are found in Part 1 of this book and in the *Holt Handbook.*

Holt Literature and Language Arts

Pupil's Edition

Part 1, Chapter 5

Biography and Autobiography: Looking at Lives, pp. 240–325
- Reading Standards 1.4, 2.3, 3.5
- Writing Application **Writing a Research Report**

Part 2, Workshop 4

Research
Writing a Research Report, pp. 578–603
- Writing Standard 2.3

Giving and Evaluating a Research Presentation, pp. 604–608
- Listening and Speaking Standard 2.2

Using Electronic Texts, pp. 609–614
- Writing Standard 1.4

Part 2, Mini-Workshop 8

Creating Graphics, pp. 686–687
- Listening and Speaking Standard 1.6

Holt Handbook

Chapter 9

Using Modifiers Correctly
- Written and Oral English-Language Conventions
- Looking Ahead, Gr. 7 Standard 1.1, pp. 211–215
- Gr. 5 Review Standard 1.2, pp. 197–214

Chapter 10

A Glossary of Usage
- Written and Oral English-Language Conventions Standards 1.0, 1.5, pp. 221–234

Diagnostic and Summative Assessments: Third-Quarter Test

Language Arts Content

This workshop uses the writing and listening and speaking strategies to enable students to master successfully the writing and speaking applications.

What standards are taught in Workshop 4?

In this workshop, students will master the following Grade 6 standards. They will also review several standards from an earlier grade.

Writing Strategies

1.0 Students write clear, coherent, and focused essays. The writing exhibits students' awareness of the audience and purpose. Students progress through the stages of the writing process as needed.

1.1 Choose the form of writing (e.g., report) that best suits the intended purpose.

1.2 Create multiple-paragraph expository compositions.

1.3 Use a variety of effective and coherent organizational patterns, including organization by categories.

1.4 Use organizational features of electronic text to locate information.

1.5 Compose documents with appropriate formatting by using word-processing skills and principles of design (e.g., columns).

1.6 Revise writing to improve the organization and consistency of ideas within and between paragraphs.

Writing Applications

2.0 Students write expository texts of at least 500 to 700 words. Student writing demonstrates a command of standard American English and the research, organizational, and drafting strategies outlined in Writing Standard 1.0.

2.3 Write research reports.

Listening and Speaking Strategies

1.0 Students deliver focused, coherent presentations that convey ideas clearly and relate to the background and interests of the audience. They evaluate the content of oral communication.

1.1 Relate the speaker's verbal communication to the nonverbal message.

1.4 Select a focus, an organizational structure, and a point of view, matching the purpose, message, occasion, and vocal modulation to the audience.

1.5 Emphasize salient points to assist the listener in following the main ideas and concepts.

1.6 Support opinions with detailed evidence and with visual or media displays that use appropriate technology.

1.7 Use effective rate, volume, pitch, and tone, and align nonverbal elements to sustain audience interest and attention.

Speaking Applications

2.0 Students deliver well-organized formal presentations employing traditional rhetorical strategies (e.g., exposition). Student speaking demonstrates a command of standard American English and the organizational and delivery stages outlined in Listening and Speaking Standard 1.0.

2.2 Deliver informative presentations.

Review Standards, Grade 5

Writing

1.3 Use organizational features of printed text to locate relevant information.

2.3 Write research reports about important ideas, issues, or events.

Listening and Speaking

2.2 Deliver informative presentations about an important idea, issue, or event.

Instructional Planning and Support

Where do I locate lesson plans, additional resources, and other teaching aids?

- The Annotated Teacher's Edition and *On Course: Mapping Instruction* provide direction in planning and implementing a complete California standards–based curriculum. These components include instructions for administering diagnostic, progress, and summative tests; for presenting instruction of the standards; for differentiating instruction to provide universal access; and for locating and using the program's ancillaries.

- The program's resources are referenced at the beginning of each workshop in the bottom margin of this teacher's edition: Research and Giving and Evaluating a Research Presentation.

- Reminders for using additional resources appear in this teacher's edition at point of use.

- The *One-Stop Planner* CD-ROM contains editable lesson plans and all print ancillaries, available in PDF format.

What if I don't have time to teach all of Workshop 4?

- Within this workshop, complete coverage of the application standards is provided by the following instructional features in the Pupil's Edition:
  - Choose and Narrow a Subject
  - Ask Questions
  - Find and List Sources
  - Give a Research Presentation
  - Evaluate a Research Presentation
- Use Standards Practice and Review for a quick assessment and review of workshop standards.

What provisions have been made for students who have additional class time scheduled in language arts?

- *Universal Access: Writing, Listening, & Speaking,* Workshop 4, contains worksheets and transparencies that provide practice, reteaching, and extension of Workshop 4 standards. Each Practice and Apply exercise is supported by graphic organizers or practice activities for on-level learners, advanced learners, and learners having difficulty.

- *Universal Access: Lesson Plans for Language Development,* Workshop 4, provides alternative teaching strategies and additional worksheets designed specifically for English-language learners and special education students. Many of the suggestions and activities in this ancillary will also be helpful to students in the regular classroom who are having difficulty with particular skills.

Universal Access

How do I differentiate instruction to ensure that all my students master the standards?

Holt Literature and Language Arts provides comprehensive, differentiated instruction for all types of students.

- Most of the general instruction and teaching strategies in the Annotated Teacher's Edition are at grade level. These instructions will work well with the majority of your students.

- Advanced students have at least one activity for each workshop. The suggested activities are found in this teacher's edition at point of instruction. Point-of-use suggestions for learners having difficulty, English-language learners, and special education students are provided.

- *Universal Access: Writing, Listening, & Speaking,* Workshop 4, opens with Teaching Notes that suggest which worksheets and transparencies are appropriate for each of three levels of learners.

- *Universal Access: Lesson Plans for Language Development,* Workshop 4, offers teaching strategies and additional worksheets designed specifically for English-language learners and special education students.

- *Daily Language Activities Transparencies* and *Spelling: Lessons & Activities* provide ongoing review of and additional practice in a range of language arts skills.

- For every workshop, preselected Web sites and activities are available to provide enrichment, independent practice, and enhanced instructional opportunities.

Assessment

How do I determine whether or not my students are making progress in mastering the standards?

Progress Assessment

- Use the Standards Review at the end of Workshop 4 for an informal assessment of the writing, listening, and speaking standards taught in Workshop 4.

- Use Workshop 4 in *Progress Assessment of Writing, Listening, & Speaking* to test students' cumulative progress in mastering the standards taught in the workshop.

Summative Assessment

The content in *Holt Literature and Language Arts* has been divided into four quarters to allow you to administer the four summative tests required by California. Workshop 4 will be assessed in the third quarter of instruction. At the end of Workshop 4, you may ask students to take the Third-Quarter Test in the *Diagnostic & Summative Assessments* booklet.

Research

From sixth-graders to research scientists, people often need to find and share information with others. One way for people to share this information is by writing a research report. In this workshop you will research a subject and share your research in written and oral form. In the process you will practice these language arts standards.

GO TO: go.hrw.com
KEYWORD: HLLA6 W-4
FOR: Models, Writer's Guides, and Reference Sources

California Standards

Writing

1.0 Students write clear, coherent, and focused essays. The writing exhibits students' awareness of the audience and purpose. Essays contain formal introductions, supporting evidence, and conclusions. Students progress through the stages of the writing process as needed.

1.1 Choose the form of writing (e.g., report) that best suits the intended purpose.

1.2 Create multiple-paragraph expository compositions:

  a. Engage the interest of the reader and state a clear purpose.

  b. Develop the topic with supporting details and precise nouns to paint a visual image in the mind of the reader.

  c. Conclude with a detailed summary linked to the purpose of the composition.

1.3 Use a variety of effective and coherent organizational patterns, including organization by categories.

1.4 Use organizational features of electronic text (e.g., databases, keyword searches, e-mail addresses) to locate information.

1.5 Compose documents with appropriate formatting by using word-processing skills and principles of design (e.g., columns).

1.6 Revise writing to improve the organization and consistency of ideas within and between paragraphs.

2.0 Students write expository texts of at least 500 to 700 words. Student writing demonstrates a command of standard American

---

STANDARDS FOCUS

Writing

Prerequisite Standards

Grade 5

- 1.3 Use organizational features of printed text (e.g., citations, end notes, bibliographic references) to locate relevant information.

- 2.3 Write research reports about important ideas, issues, or events by using the following guidelines:

  a. Frame questions that direct the investigation.

  b. Establish a controlling idea or topic.

  c. Develop the topic with simple facts, details, examples, and explanations.

Standards Coming Up in the Next Level

Grade 7

- 1.4 Identify topics; ask and evaluate questions; and develop ideas leading to inquiry, investigation, and research.

- 1.5 Give credit for both quoted and paraphrased information in a bibliography by using a consistent and sanctioned format and methodology for citations.

- 2.3 Write research reports:

  a. Pose relevant and tightly drawn questions about the topic.

  b. Convey clear and accurate perspectives on the subject.

  c. Include evidence compiled through the formal research process (e.g., use of a card catalog, *Reader's Guide to Periodical Literature,* a computer catalog, magazines, newspapers, dictionaries).

  d. Document reference sources by means of footnotes and a bibliography.

English and the research, organizational, and drafting strategies outlined in Writing Standard 1.0.

2.3 Write research reports:

   a. Pose relevant questions with a scope narrow enough to be thoroughly covered.

   b. Support the main idea or ideas with facts, details, examples, and explanations from multiple authoritative sources (e.g., speakers, periodicals, online information searches).

   c. Include a bibliography.

Listening and Speaking

1.0 Students deliver focused, coherent presentations that convey ideas clearly and relate to the background and interests of the audience. They evaluate the content of oral communication.

1.1 Relate the speaker's verbal communication (e.g., word choice, pitch, feeling, tone) to the nonverbal message (e.g., posture, gesture).

1.4 Select a focus, an organizational structure, and a point of view, matching the purpose, message, occasion, and vocal modulation to the audience.

1.5 Emphasize salient points to assist the listener in following the main ideas and concepts.

1.6 Support opinions with detailed evidence and with visual or media displays that use appropriate technology.

1.7 Use effective rate, volume, pitch, and tone and align nonverbal elements to sustain audience interest and attention.

2.0 Students deliver well-organized formal presentations employing traditional rhetorical strategies (e.g., exposition). Student speaking demonstrates a command of standard American English and the organizational and delivery strategies outlined in Listening and Speaking Standard 1.0.

2.2 Deliver informative presentations:

   a. Pose relevant questions sufficiently limited in scope to be completely and thoroughly answered.

   b. Develop the topic with facts, details, examples, and explanations from multiple authoritative sources (e.g., speakers, periodicals, online information).

Listening and Speaking

Prerequisite Standards

Grade 5

■ 2.2 Deliver informative presentations about an important idea, issue, or event by the following means:

   a. Frame questions to direct the investigation.

   b. Establish a controlling idea or topic.

   c. Develop the topic with simple facts, details, examples, and explanations.

Standards Coming Up in the Next Level

Grade 7

■ 2.3 Deliver research presentations:

   a. Pose relevant and concise questions about the topic.

   b. Convey clear and accurate perspectives on the subject.

   c. Include evidence generated through the formal research process (e.g., use of a card catalog, *Reader's Guide to Periodical Literature,* computer databases, magazines, newspapers, dictionaries).

   d. Cite reference sources appropriately.

CALIFORNIA STANDARDS

Writing Workshop

Writing a Research Report

PRETEACHING

Standards Starter

Motivate. Discuss ways in which we all do research, formally or informally. For example, ask students how they would find out which store has the best prices on bicycles. Explain that researching and presenting a topic will help students learn interesting information.

Introducing the Workshop. To introduce the workshop, use the Journal Warm-up, Transparency 12, in *Writing, Listening, & Speaking.*

Quotation for the Day

"What one knows is, in youth, of little moment; they know enough who know how to learn."

(Henry Adams, 1838–1918, U.S. historian)

Write the quotation on the chalkboard or an overhead transparency, and explain that in this context the word *moment* means "importance." Then, ask students how the quotation applies to research. [Students may suggest that research is one way in which a person learns. Understanding how to research a question helps a person acquire knowledge.]

WHAT'S AHEAD?

In this workshop you will write a research report. You will also learn how to

■ **ask questions to guide your research**
■ **find and list authoritative sources**
■ **take organized notes**
■ **use precise nouns**
■ **capitalize and punctuate titles correctly**

| DO THIS

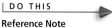

Reference Note

For more on **think sheets,** see page 495.

Have you heard about a snake that grows to be thirty feet long? Did you know that some gladiators in ancient Rome were women? When you find out an unusual fact, the first thing you want to do is tell someone about it. Writers of research reports feel the same way. They dig into subjects they are curious about; then, through writing, they share what they have learned. A research report can explore almost any topic, from hockey to hip-hop music to hot-air balloons. In this workshop you will have the opportunity to exercise your curiosity by researching a topic that interests you. Then, you will share what you discover with others by writing a research report.

Professional Model: An Informative Article

Examples of published research are everywhere. On the following pages is an informative article that was published in *Junior Scholastic.* The author began her research process by asking questions like "What is a gold rush? Who were the original Forty-Niners? Why is California known as the 'Golden State'?" You will find the answers to these questions and more as you read "The California Gold Rush."

As you read, create a **think sheet,** making note of the answers to the writer's research questions, support for her ideas, examples of formatting, and specific language. Answering on your think sheet the analysis questions that appear next to the article will help you find these items.

 Writing 1.2 Create multiple-paragraph expository compositions. **2.3** Write research reports.

578 Workshop 4 **Research:** Writing a Research Report

WORKSHOP RESOURCES

Writing Workshop
Planning
■ *On Course: Mapping Instruction*
■ *One-Stop Planner* CD-ROM
■ *At Home: A Guide to Standards Mastery,* p. 21
■ *At Home: In Five Languages*

■ *Writing, Listening, & Speaking,* —Teaching Notes, p. 68
Differentiating Instruction
■ *Lesson Plans for Language Development,* pp. 232–233
■ *Supporting Instruction in Five Languages*
Practice
■ *Writing, Listening, & Speaking,* Wkshp. 4

from Junior Scholastic

▪ THE CALIFORNIA ▪
GOLD RUSH

BY KATHY WILMORE

1 For seventeen years—ever since leaving his New Jersey home at age eighteen—James Wilson Marshall kept moving farther and farther west in search of a better life. In 1845, he went to California, which was part of Mexico then, and things finally seemed to turn around for him. A businessman named John A. Sutter gave him a job building a sawmill in a remote wilderness area in northern California. Build it, Sutter told him, and you can run the place for me. Sutter was looking

> **1.** Does this article start before, during, or after the California Gold Rush? How can you tell? Why does the author start here?

to make a tidy profit; Marshall was just hoping to make a living. But on January 24, 1848, Marshall was **momentarily** distracted from his work. A **glint** of light caught his eye—and sleepy California was never the same again.

"To See the Elephant"

In January 1848, California had a population of only 15,000 people. By the time December 1849 came around, the population was up to 100,000 and climbing. Why such a boom? Blame it on that glint that caught James Marshall's eye.

2

> **2.** To what does the blue heading above refer? Why do you think the author chose these words for the heading?

One cold and rainy day soon after, **3** Marshall arrived at Sutter's house with "some important and interesting news." Sutter studied the stuff that Marshall had brought and realized it was gold. He was not happy.

"I told [my employees] that I would **4** consider it as a great favor if they would keep this discovery secret only for six weeks, so I could finish [building] my large flour mill at Brighton. . . .

---

momentarily: for the moment or short time.
glint: gleam, brief flashing.

Professional Model

As students read, have them jot down any unusual facts that interest them or questions that they would like to explore further. Explain to students that using think sheets to summarize their notes from a reading serves two purposes. First, creating think sheets allows students to place their thoughts, observations, and questions on paper, which in turn helps increase reading comprehension. Second, the process of creating think sheets also provides students with ideas for their own writing, such as topics, structure, and word choice.

Professional Model Questions

Answers

1. The article includes information about James Marshall's early life before the California Gold Rush. The author begins the article with this information because James Marshall's discovery started the gold rush. Also, by initially focusing on one person's experiences, the author makes the story engaging.

2. The blue heading refers to the expression "I am going to see the elephant." This was an expression used by many Forty-Niners to indicate that they were traveling to California to see something wonderful and rare. The author probably chose this heading to catch the reader's attention and to sum up the fever surrounding the gold rush.

Reinforcement
- *Daily Language Activities*
- *Spelling*

Evaluation and Assessment
- *Test Generator (One-Stop Planner* CD-ROM)
- *Progress Assessment of Writing, Listening, & Speaking,* Wkshp. 4

- *Diagnostic and Summative Assessments,* Third-Quarter Test

Internet
- go.hrw.com
  (keyword: HLLA6 W-4)

3. John A. Sutter made this comment. The footnote at the bottom of the page indicates that this quotation came from an 1857 article called "The Discovery of Gold in California" in *Hutchings California Magazine*.

4. Students may say that the author includes these quotations because they add interest and authenticity to the report. These eyewitness accounts allow the reader to see what happened during the gold rush through the eyes of someone who experienced the events firsthand.

> **3. Who made this comment? Where did the author find this quotation? How can you tell?**

[I]nstead of feeling happy and contented, I was very unhappy, and could not see that it would benefit me much, and I was perfectly right in thinking so."[1]

5   Sutter's employees promised not to tell, but word leaked out—and reached Samuel Brannan.

6   Brannan, a newspaperman, knew a good story when he heard it. He also owned a general store not far from Sutter's Mill, and business was slow. After Brannan published news of Marshall's discovery, gold fever struck. Brannan soon had customers aplenty.

7   By 1849, the gold rush was on. People poured into California from all points of the compass. They arrived by ship or overland trails, crossing North America by wagon train, riding horses or mules, and even on foot.

8   These hopeful thousands, the first large wave of whom arrived in 1849, were known as Forty-Niners. Many had sold everything they owned to pay their way to California.

9   Ask a Forty-Niner why, and he or she was likely to reply, "I am going to see the elephant"—that is, to find something wonderful and rare.

"A Dog's Life"

10   Dreaming of gold was easy, but finding it was anything but. Miners faced hours of strenuous work. Some were able to reach out and pick up a gold-filled nugget, but that was rare.

11   Most miners spent hours slamming pickaxes into rocky soil, or scooping up panfuls of riverbed mud and rinsing it to find tiny grains of gold. They lived in rough, makeshift camps far from "civilization," with little shelter from cold mountain winds and rain. As William Swain described camp life in a letter sent home in 1850:

12   "George, I tell you this mining among the mountains is a dog's life. . . . [T]his climate in the mines requires a constitution like iron. Often for weeks during the rainy season it is damp, cold, and sunless, and the labor of getting gold is of the most laborious kind. Exposure causes sickness to a great extent for, in most of the mines, tents are all the habitation [home] miners have."[2]

> **4. Why do you think the author includes quotes such as this one in the article?**

Making a Go of It

13   Thousands of Forty-Niners made the trek to California with the idea of striking it rich, then returning home to spend their wealth. But for every Forty-Niner whose labor paid off handsomely, countless others had to find other ways of making a living.

14   Among those were thousands of Chinese. Word of "Gold Mountain"—the Chinese name for California—lit new hope among poverty-stricken

---

1. From "The Discovery of Gold in California" by Gen. John A. Sutter, *Hutchings California Magazine* (November 1857).
2. From a letter from California by William Swain, January 6 & 16, 1850.

> **5. Why do you think the author includes these statistics on the number of Chinese in California?**

15   peasants in China. In 1849, only 54 Chinese lived in California; by 1852, the number had risen to 14,000.

Chinese miners faced the resentment of many white Forty-Niners who saw them as unfair competition. . . . Looking for less risky ways of earning a living, many Chinese turned to service work: cooking meals, toting heavy loads, and washing clothes. Miners happily plunked down money for such services.

16   The Chinese were not the only Forty-Niners to make a go of things at something other than mining. One of the biggest success stories was that of a Bavarian immigrant named Levi Strauss. Strauss, a tailor, hoped to make his fortune by making and selling tents. But he found that another item he made was more popular: the heavy-duty work pants that became known as those "wonderful pants of Levi's." His blue jeans business prospered, and Strauss became one of the wealthiest men in California.

From Fortune to Misfortune

17   What of Sutter and Marshall, the men who started it all?

18   Sutter's workers all quit and poured their efforts into finding gold. When the first Forty-Niners arrived, they overran Sutter's land, wrecked his mills and farmlands, and even killed his cattle for food. As he later wrote:

19   "By this sudden discovery of gold, all my great plans were destroyed. Had I succeeded for a few years before the gold was discovered, I would have been the richest citizen on the Pacific shore; but it had to be different. Instead of being rich, I am ruined."[3]

20   Marshall's hope of earning a living by running the mill was destroyed when the workers quit and it was wrecked by treasure seekers. He became a drifter, then a poor farmer.

The Golden State

21   For California, however, the gold rush brought long-lasting benefits. California had become U.S. territory as a result of the treaty ending the Mexican War. That was signed on February 2, 1848—just eight days after Marshall spied that first glint of gold. California became the thirty-first state on September 9, 1850. In that short time, it grew from a place of scattered settlements to one of bustling seaports and boomtowns. Whether or not they ever had the thrill of "seeing the elephant," thousands of restless Forty-Niners found a place to call home. ■

> **6. Why do you think the author ends with information on what happened after the Gold Rush?**

---

3. See footnote #1.

Professional Model Questions

Answers continued

5. The author includes these statistics about Chinese immigrants to show the increase in population in California because of the gold rush and to show that many immigrants had to find other ways to earn a living besides mining.

6. The author gives information about what happened after the gold rush in order to provide a satisfactory conclusion and to give evidence to show how California changed as a result of the gold rush.

DIRECT TEACHING

Professional Model

After students read the model, ask them to identify its purpose and audience. [The purpose of the Professional Model is to provide information on the events that led to the start of the gold rush, insight into the people who participated in the gold rush, and details about the lives of the Forty-Niners. Students will probably say that the audience is young adult readers. The details in the article are aimed at a young audience, and many students will identify the source of the model, *Junior Scholastic,* as a young adult magazine.]

Think About the Model

Answers

1. The Gold Rush that began in 1849 brought thousands to a once sleepy territory and transformed it.

2. Students will likely say that the article contained enough information about the Forty-Niners and other immigrants who came to California to show how California changed as a result of the gold rush.

3. Footnotes at the bottom of the article show the sources for the quotations. The sources for the statistics and facts in the article are not included.

4. Students may say they found the blue headings helpful because the headings help guide readers by signaling what information will appear next.

5. Here is a sample summary. In January of 1848 James Marshall, an employee at a sawmill, discovered gold in California. Soon word spread and thousands of people began to pour into California in hopes of finding gold. These Forty-Niners, as they were called, found mining to be a hard life. To earn a living, many were forced to turn to other professions. Although the man who first discovered gold in California did not profit from his discovery, California benefited from the gold rush. By 1850, California was admitted as a state, and its economy was booming.

DIRECT TEACHING

Integrating with Grammar, Usage, and Mechanics

As students start their research reports, you may want to stop and review punctuating titles and fragments because these are concepts with which students often have trouble. See the Punctuation chapters and The Sentence chapter in the *Holt Handbook.*

Think About the Model

In a small group, discuss the following questions. Then, present your group's responses orally to the class.

1. What is the main idea of the article?
2. Do you think the article contained enough information to support its main idea?
3. Can you tell where the support came from? Why or why not?
4. Did you find the blue headings to be helpful as you read the article? Explain.
5. Write a one-paragraph summary of the article, noting the main points in the order in which they appear in the article.

<u>Reference Note</u>
For information on **summarizing,** see page 496.

Prewriting

Choose and Narrow a Subject

What Grabs You?   How did the Grand Canyon get there? Why do chipmunks hibernate? **Asking questions** like these can help you choose an interesting subject for your research report. Here are more strategies to help you brainstorm subjects.

- Make an "I wonder" log (*I wonder why cats purr, how helicopters fly, who discovered electricity. . . .*)
- Read published informative magazine articles, like the Professional Model that begins on page 579, to find interesting subjects (*people in the news, medical marvels, strange animals, space technology . . .*)
- Consider topics you have read about or discussed in other classes (*earthquakes, an ancient civilization, a musician . . .*)

TIP   Be sure to choose an interesting subject, one that will hold your readers' attention throughout a 500- to 700-word report. The subject should not only be one about which you are enthusiastic, but also one that many people have written about so that you can find plenty of information on it.

Writing **1.0** Students progress through the stages of the writing process as needed.   **2.0** Students write expository texts of at least 500 to 700 words.   **2.3a** Pose relevant questions with a scope narrow enough to be thoroughly covered.

Pin It Down   Once you have listed several possible subjects, you can choose the most interesting one. **You will need to focus on a part of the subject small enough to cover in one report.** For example, suppose that volcanoes fascinate you. Can you imagine the amount of research it would take to cover everything there is to know about volcanoes? To make it easier on yourself, you need to narrow that subject down to a focused topic. Your focused topic might be an active volcano in Hawaii. Here are more examples of narrowing a broad subject to a focused topic.

animals	astronomy	Olympics	Broad subject
↓	↓	↓	
birds	solar system	footraces	More narrow
↓	↓	↓	
green jay	asteroids	marathon	Focused topic

Here is how one writer narrowed a subject to a focused topic.

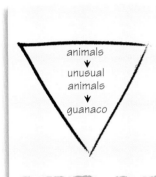

animals
↓
unusual animals
↓
guanaco

I like animals, but "animals" is too much to write about in a research report. I need to narrow this subject.

I want to write about an animal that most people have never heard of.

In an article about a wild animal ranch, I read about guanacos. I had never heard of a guanaco, and I doubt many other people have either.

TIP   Once you have your focused topic, make a plan to be sure you have enough time to complete your report. Divide the total time you are given among these activities.
- finding information (1/8 of total time)
- taking notes (1/4)
- organizing your notes (1/8)
- writing the first draft (1/4)
- revising (1/8)
- proofreading and publishing your report (1/8)

PRACTICE & APPLY 1   **Choose and Narrow a Subject**

Brainstorm some subjects that interest you, and choose one you want to research. Then, use an upside-down triangle to find a focused topic. Record your thoughts as you narrow your topic.

Writing 1.0 Write focused essays.

Choose and Narrow a Subject   **583**

DIFFERENTIATING INSTRUCTION

Learners Having Difficulty

To assist students who may have difficulty completing each stage of the research project on time, consider giving them frequent progress assignments. If you assign only a final deadline, students may find themselves with too much work to do at the last minute.

DIRECT TEACHING

Pin It Down

You may want to provide students with the following pronunciation guide to help them pronounce the word *guanaco*: gwä•nä′kō.

Spanish speakers may use the following pronunciation: hwä•nä′kō.

PRACTICE & APPLY 1

Guided and Independent Practice

To help you monitor and assess students' work, have them exchange triangles with partners. Have partners check to make sure that the topic lowest in the hierarchy is a focused topic and is narrower than the broad subject. If not, have the partners work together to narrow the broad subject to a focused topic.

RESOURCES

Practice and Apply 1

Guided Practice
- *Writing, Listening, & Speaking,* WS. p. 69

Reteaching and Modeling
- *Writing, Listening, & Speaking,* TP. 13

Reinforcement
- *Writing, Listening, & Speaking,* WS. p. 70

Think About Purpose and Audience

You may want to remind students that there is more than one form in which to present research. Some forms may be more appropriate depending on students' purpose and audience. For example, a letter or an e-mail might be an appropriate form in which to present information to a friend or another student. If the audience is a teacher, a formal research report is probably the most appropriate form for presenting information.

PRACTICE & APPLY 2

Guided and Independent Practice

To help you monitor and assess how realistic students are about their audience's interest in and knowledge of their topics, have them discuss with a small group of peers their answers to the three questions in the chart on this page. Students should take notes on peers' responses and, if necessary, revise their own answers.

DIFFERENTIATING INSTRUCTION

English-Language Learners

To help students improve their question-asking skills, review question words (*who, what, when, where, why, how*) and model using the words in questions related to a single topic. Then, have students work in small groups to brainstorm questions for their own topics.

▶ Resources Reminder

For more help with English-Language Learners, see *Lesson Plans for Language Development.*

Think About Purpose and Audience

The *Why* of It   Your **purpose** is your reason for writing. You have two purposes for writing a research report: to discover information for yourself, and to share what you learn with others.

The *Who* of It   The **audience** for your report will be people who share your interest in the topic but do not already know a great deal about it. In most cases, that audience will include your classmates and teacher. You need to think about your audience before you begin doing your research. Ask yourself the questions in the left-hand column of the chart below. One student's responses appear in the right-hand column.

1. What does my audience already know about my topic?	They probably know nothing more about the guanaco than I do.
2. What does my audience need to know?	what it is, where it lives, what it looks like, what it does
3. What kind of information would my audience find interesting?	any unusual or surprising facts that I discover

PRACTICE & APPLY 2   Think About Purpose and Audience

Your purpose is to discover information and share it with others. Answer the questions in the chart above to consider how you might communicate what you learn with your readers.

Ask Questions

TIP   You might discover new questions once you begin doing research. Add them to your chart only if they are **relevant,** or related to your topic. Discard any **irrelevant** questions, those that do not relate to your topic.

The K-W-L Method   When you think about your topic, you are probably full of questions. Research begins with questions. Of course, there are some things you already know about your topic.

You can use a K-W-L chart to list what you already **K**now about a topic, what you **W**ant to know about it, and what you **L**earned about it through research. Look at how one student organized his ideas in a K-W-L chart on the next page. As he finds answers to his questions, he will list them in the right-hand column.

 Writing 1.0 The writing exhibits students' awareness of the audience and purpose. 1.1 Choose the form of writing (e.g., report) that best suits the intended purpose. 2.3a Pose relevant questions with a scope narrow enough to be thoroughly covered.

RESOURCES

Practice and Apply 2

Guided Practice

■ *Writing, Listening, & Speaking,* WS. p. 71

What I Know	What I Want to Know	What I Learned
A guanaco is part of the camel family. It lives in South America.	What do guanacos look like? What do guanacos do? Do people use guanacos? Where do guanacos live?	

PRACTICE & APPLY 3 **Ask Questions**

Create a K-W-L chart like the one above on your own paper. In the left column, list everything that you already know about your topic. In the middle column, list the questions you have about your topic. Leave the right column of your chart blank. You will fill it out as you do your research.

Find Sources

Who Has the Answers? You now have a focused topic and a list of questions about it. What do you do next? Research! The best place to start your research is in the library, but that is just the beginning. You will look in several places to find answers to your questions. Some of the resources you can use include

- books, encyclopedias, and magazine and newspaper articles
- CD-ROM encyclopedias and dictionaries
- interviews and guest speakers
- library and online databases
- newsgroups and Web pages
- movies and videos

You will not find all of the information you need in a single source. You should plan to use at least three different kinds of sources. For example, you could find information on your topic in a book, in a magazine article, and on the Internet (a resource for information on all topics). Using a variety of sources will help you find complete answers to your research questions. If you have trouble finding sources **relevant,** or related, to your topic, go to the media center or ask your school's media specialist for help.

> **TIP** Some sources are better than others for research. Look for nonfiction sources created by people or organizations likely to know a great deal about the topic. In other words, look for **authoritative** sources. (For more on **evaluating sources,** see page 587. For more on **evaluating spoken information,** see pages 607–608.)

> **Reference Note**
> For more on **using electronic texts** to find information, see page 609.

 Writing 2.0 Student writing demonstrates the research strategies outlined in Writing Standard 1.0. **2.3b** Support the main idea or ideas with facts, details, examples, and explanations from multiple authoritative sources (e.g., speakers, periodicals, online information searches).

Find Sources **585**

PRACTICE & APPLY 3

Guided and Independent Practice
Students' research questions should be reasonable, specifically related to their topics, and easily answered with research. Circulate as students create their charts, and check that students' questions are logical enough to form the backbone of the report.

DIRECT TEACHING

Find Sources
Give students the following information to help them find sources in printed materials. You might also refer them to the Media Workshop on pp. 609–614 for help finding electronic sources.

- For books, remind students to use the table of contents and the index to help them locate specific information and to find starting page numbers for different sections.

- For reference sources, like encyclopedias, explain that articles are arranged alphabetically in different volumes.

- For magazines, the *Reader's Guide to Periodical Literature,* which is available online and in print, will help students locate articles in magazines. Once they find the magazine, students can refer to the table of contents to help them locate the article.

- For newspapers, remind students that newspapers are divided into sections, such as international and national, city and state, sports, business, and lifestyle. Students can locate articles by looking in the appropriate section. For example, an article about plans for a new city park would probably appear in the city and state section.

| KEY CONCEPT

Make a List of Sources

Who Said That? You will need to keep track of all of the sources you find that might be helpful in your research. In a numbered list, include information about each source. The following chart tells you what information you need to record for each type of source you might use in researching your topic.

INFORMATION ON SOURCES

Books: Author. <u>Title</u>. City where book was published: Name of Publisher, copyright year.

Ricciuti, Edward R. <u>What on Earth Is a Guanaco?</u> Woodbridge, CT: Blackbirch Press, 1994.

Magazine and Newspaper Articles: Author (if known). "Title of Article." <u>Name of Magazine or Newspaper</u> Date article was published: page numbers.

Lambeth, Ellen. "Here Comes Paco Guanaco: In the Hilly Grasslands of South America, a Camel Is Born." <u>Ranger Rick</u> Nov. 1996: 4-8.

Encyclopedia Articles: Author (if known). "Title of Article." <u>Encyclopedia Name</u>. Edition number (if known). Year published.

Franklin, William L. "Guanaco." <u>World Book Encyclopedia</u>. 2000.

Video Recordings: <u>Title</u>. Name of Director or Producer (if known). Format (videocassette or videodisc). Name of Distributor, year.

<u>The Living Edens: Patagonia</u>. Videocassette. PBS Home Video, 1997.

Internet Sources: Author (if known). "Title." <u>Name of Web site</u>. Date of electronic publication (if known). Name of Sponsoring Institution. Date you accessed information <Internet address>.

Sautner, Stephen. "Guanaco Numbers Continue to Dwindle." <u>Wildlife Conservation Society News</u>. 28 Jan. 1999. Wildlife Conservation Society. 30 Jan. 2003 <http://wcs.org/3422?newsarticle/3363>.

Other Electronic Sources: Author (if known). "Title." <u>Title of Database or CD-ROM</u>. Medium (CD-ROM or Database). Name of Publisher (if known). Copyright date.

Sentman, Everett. "Guanaco." <u>Grolier 2001 Multimedia Encyclopedia</u>. CD-ROM. 2000.

TIP The listings in the chart follow the Modern Language Association format, but your teacher may prefer that you use another format, such as the American Psychological Association format or your own school format. Whichever format you use, use it consistently. Remember, following a set format is important because it helps interested readers easily find more information on your topic.

 Writing 2.3c Include a bibliography.

MINI-LESSON CRITICAL THINKING

Evaluating Sources

Whenever you seek information about something, you need to start by making sure the information will be useful. Use the *4R* test to decide whether a particular source will be helpful. The sources you use should be **r**elevant, **r**ecent, **r**eliable, and **r**epresentative.

- **Relevant** A relevant source is one that directly addresses your topic. You do not want to skim an entire book only to find out that it barely mentions your topic. Begin by checking the table of contents or index of a book, skimming articles, or reading summaries of video- or audiotapes. Choose only the sources that look like they will provide a good deal of information on your topic.

- **Recent** If your topic is in a field that does not change quickly, such as medieval history or Greek mythology, using an older source may not be a problem. However, if you are writing on a fast-changing topic such as current movies or technology, you will need to look for sources published more recently.

- **Reliable** Consult only those sources you know are accurate. The producer of the source should have some **authority** in the subject area or be part of a respected institution. For example, if you are looking for authoritative information on soccer's World Cup, you might use a guide produced by FIFA, international soccer's governing body. Respected institutions with authority on a variety of topics include universities, government institutions, and nonprofit institutions.

In most cases, a source should also be **objective,** or not biased toward a certain point of view. For example, information on a political leader provided by his or her political party may be useful, but it will leave out anything negative about the politician. If you are not sure how authoritative and objective a source is, ask your librarian or teacher.

- **Representative** Finally, if your topic is controversial—for example, if public opinion on your topic is divided—you will need to find sources that address more than one side of the topic. Although your report will probably focus on a particular point of view, you should at least mention the other points of view.

PRACTICE

Working with a small group, choose a topic that interests all members. Then, each member should find two specific sources on the topic (for example, a magazine article and a Web site). Then, as a group, evaluate each source using the *4R* test. Present your group's three best sources to the class, and explain why these sources are the best. Also, share with the class the least useful source, and explain why it would not be helpful in research on your group's topic.

 Writing 2.3b Support the main idea or ideas with facts, details, examples, and explanations from multiple authoritative sources.

DIFFERENTIATING INSTRUCTION

Learners Having Difficulty

Some students may have difficulty determining how objective a source is. Give students the following examples and ask them to decide whether the source would be objective or biased and why.

- Information on skateboarding provided by an amateur skateboarder [This information might be biased because it is provided by someone who loves skateboarding. He or she might leave out anything negative about skateboarding.]

- Information about ancient Greece provided by Indiana University [This information would probably be objective because it is provided by a university and is not biased toward a certain point of view.]

MINI-LESSON CRITICAL THINKING

Guided Practice

(For independent practice, see Resources below.)

Answer

Once groups have decided on topics, check to see that the topics are appropriate and adequately narrowed. As students collect specific sources, make sure they record actual publication information. This will aid the groups in the evaluation process. As the groups evaluate their collected sources using the *4R* test, have each student record the group's comments concerning his or her two collected sources. Students can look back at these comments as they look for sources for their research reports.

Guided and Independent Practice

To facilitate monitoring of student progress, have students exchange lists and work in pairs to check the lists against the chart on p. 586. Ask partners to highlight any part of a citation that is incorrect. Then, discuss with the class common errors and problems and have students correct their source information.

DIRECT TEACHING

Take Notes

Remind students to check their K-W-L chart periodically during the note-taking stage to see which questions still need answers. Students may also decide to add new questions to their charts as they research their topics.

TIP Print sources are often more reliable than online sources. Some examples of print sources you can use are **periodicals** (magazines and newspapers) and **reference books** (encyclopedias and almanacs). For information on **finding periodicals and books using electronic sources,** see page 613.

Find and List Sources

Find and evaluate at least five sources you might use for researching your focused topic. Follow the instructions on page 586 to list information about these sources. Give each source a number to help you identify sources when you take notes later. For now, do not worry about the order of items in your list. You will alphabetize your source list later (by author's last name or by title, if no author is given).

Take Notes

Get the Facts Once you identify sources, look for answers to the research questions in your K-W-L chart. You will use the answers you find as support in your report. Types of support include *facts, examples, details,* and *explanations.* You can also use as support the expert opinions of people with special knowledge.

TYPES OF SUPPORT	
Type	**Example**
Facts are statements that can be proved true. They often include **statistics,** or information based on numbers.	Guanacos can be found from southern Peru to the tip of South America. (Where do guanacos live?)
Examples are specific instances of an idea. [The example to the right specifically states what guanacos do.]	With no warning at all, guanacos can accurately hit with smelly green spit whatever is annoying them. (What do guanacos do?)
Details are information that appeals to the five senses (sight, hearing, taste, touch, and smell), and measurement.	Guanacos are reddish brown with a dark gray head and a pale belly. (What do guanacos look like?)
Explanations make statements clear and easy to understand. [The example to the right explains why guanacos have no problems living in the mountains.]	Guanacos can be found in the hills of the Andes Mountains. Steep, rocky paths are no problem for guanacos because they are nimble and have thick, padded soles that protect their feet. (Where do guanacos live?)

Writing 1.0 Essays contain supporting evidence. 1.2b Develop the topic with supporting details. 2.3b Support the main idea or ideas with facts, details, examples, and explanations from multiple authoritative sources.

RESOURCES

Practice and Apply 4

Guided Practice

■ *Writing, Listening, & Speaking,* WS. p. 73

Jot It Down   You will need to record each answer you find, along with information about where you found it. The guidelines below will help you take notes.

- Use a separate note card or a sheet of paper for each new note.

- At the top of each note card, write the question that the notes on the card answer.

- Write the number of the source at the top of each note, so you will always be able to tell exactly where you found the information.

- **Summarize** important points of information explained in a long passage. (For more on **summarizing,** see page 496.) With shorter passages, **paraphrase,** or write all of the ideas in your own words. (For more on **paraphrasing,** see page 590.) If you copy exact words from a source, put them in quotation marks.

- If the information is from a printed book or article, put the page number at the end of your note.

   Here is an example of a student's note card.

TIP   While you research, keep your K-W-L chart handy. In the "What I Learned" column, write in the authors or titles of the sources where you found your answers. This will help you focus on using a variety of sources. It will also help you see quickly which of your questions still need answers.

TIP   When you write your report, you can either paraphrase (state in your own words) your source or quote your source word for word. Either way, you will need to include a **parenthetical citation** that lists the author's last name (or the title) and the page number (if available) where you found the information. Look at the following examples.

Paraphrase: Graham Harris of the Wildlife Conservation Society believes that, like the North American bison, the guanaco has a place in its continent's heritage (Sautner).

Quotation: According to Graham Harris of the Wildlife Conservation Society, the guanaco is "part of South America's heritage much like the bison is to North America" (Sautner).

MODELING AND DEMONSTRATION

Jot It Down
Explain to students that a summary is a restatement of the main idea of a passage. It is similar to a paraphrase because you restate someone else's words, but a summary is usually shorter than a paraphrase because you only note the most important points. Choose a passage in a science or social studies textbook, and model for students the process of creating a summary. Then, have student volunteers demonstrate their understanding by summarizing a different passage from the same textbook.

Paraphrasing

Explain to students that plagiarism is the use of someone else's ideas as your own. Therefore, even paraphrasing a source can constitute plagiarism if the writer does not acknowledge the source of those ideas in a Works Cited list.

Be aware of the common signs of plagiarism in student writing:

- sophisticated vocabulary that is not quoted or cited
- a number of sentences or a paragraph written in a different style from the rest of the writing
- information, opinions, and ideas not usually known by the average student and not attributed to any source

 MINI-LESSON   **WRITING**

Guided Practice

(For independent practice, see Resources below.)

Answers

1. Plagiarism: long strings of words are the same.

2. Paraphrase: the ideas are the same but most of the words are different.

MINI-LESSON **WRITING**

Paraphrasing

Paraphrasing means putting information from a source into your own words. Copying an author's words and presenting them as your own is **plagiarizing.** Plagiarizing is the same as stealing another writer's work. If you want to use a writer's exact words, put them in quotation marks and identify the source.

The passages below show the difference between paraphrasing and plagiarizing. Notice that the paraphrase on the left tells the ideas of the source passage in different words. The plagiarized passage on the right copies long strings of words which are printed in boldface.

> **Source Passage:** Guanacos, South American members of the camel family, lack the familiar humps of Asian and African camels. Slim and long-legged, guanacos move quickly and gracefully over the rugged terrain of their native Andes Mountains.
>
> **Paraphrase:** Although it is part of the camel family, the South American guanaco does not have a hump like its cousins in Asia and Africa do. It is slim, has long legs, and can run fast in its habitat, the Andes Mountains.
>
> **Plagiarism:** As **members of the camel family,** guanacos **lack the familiar humps of Asian and African camels.** They are able to **move quickly and gracefully over rugged terrain.** They live in the Andes Mountains.

PRACTICE

Read each source passage below, then the passage to its right. Tell whether the passage paraphrases or plagiarizes the source. Explain your answer in a sentence or two.

Source Passage

1. Manifest Destiny was the belief in the nineteenth century that the United States would eventually stretch across the entire continent, from the Atlantic Ocean to the Pacific Ocean.

2. The first settlers from the United States reached northeastern Texas in 1815, encouraged by the Mexican government, which controlled the territory at that time.

Paraphrase or Plagiarism?

1. People believed in the nineteenth century that the United States would eventually reach from the Atlantic Ocean to the Pacific Ocean. This belief was called Manifest Destiny.

2. The government of Mexico encouraged people from the United States to move to its territory of Texas. The first settlers moved to the northeast part of the state in 1815.

RESOURCES

Mini-lesson: Writing

Independent Practice

■ *Writing, Listening, & Speaking,* WS. p. 75

Research Your Topic and Take Notes

Using the sources you found earlier, locate answers for your research questions. Take notes from each source, using the instructions on page 589. Note the source of each piece of information you find by putting its source number on your note card.

TIP To make the most of your time, skim long passages looking for key words, ones that relate to your topic. Then, read only the sections that contain the key words.

Organize Your Information

Getting It Together A pile of notes will be about as useful to your readers as a box full of bicycle parts. Both need to be put together in a logical way to be of any use. Once you have gathered information from your sources, you will need to organize those ideas into **categories.** The questions you wrote on the top of your note cards will help you. Group together note cards that answer the same question. Each group of cards will become a paragraph in your report. If you find some note cards that do not seem to belong to any group, set them aside for now.

Outline Your Report

Planning It Out An **outline** is a plan for your report. It shows how you are grouping the information you have gathered and the order in which you will present the information. An outline will help you create a **coherent,** or clearly connected, report. One type of outline you can make is a *formal outline.* A **formal outline** lists a report's major **subtopics,** or categories of information related to your topic. It also lists the specific facts, examples, details, and explanations that make up each subtopic.

To identify the subtopics for your formal outline, first change the questions from your K-W-L chart into headings. A **heading** is a phrase that covers all the items listed below it. For example, the question "Where do guanacos live?" could be turned into the heading "Where Guanacos Live." As you turn your questions into headings, write each heading on a piece of paper, leaving several lines after it blank. Number each heading with a Roman numeral. Then, under each heading, write subheadings that will remind you of the information you will want to include in your report.

 Writing 1.0 Write clear, coherent essays. **1.3** Use a variety of effective and coherent organizational patterns, including organization by categories. **2.0** Student writing demonstrates the organizational strategies outlined in Writing Standard 1.0.

Outline Your Report **591**

Guided and Independent Practice

Monitor student progress by spot-checking to see if students' notes help answer the research questions and are written in the students' own words. Write any questions or suggestions you have for students on their note cards and draw a box around them so that students can easily separate queries from notes.

DIRECT TEACHING

Outline Your Report

Explain to students that the sample outline on the next page is an example of a formal outline, with Roman numerals for headings and capital letters for subheadings. Students may complete an informal outline by listing their headings and then jotting down the facts they want to include under each heading. An informal outline serves as an ordered reminder of what students want to include in their reports but is less heavily formatted than a formal outline.

RESOURCES

Practice and Apply 5

Guided Practice

■ *Writing, Listening, & Speaking,* WS. p. 76

Learners Having Difficulty

As students plan their reports, have them use a visual organizer such as the one below to help them shape their body paragraphs.

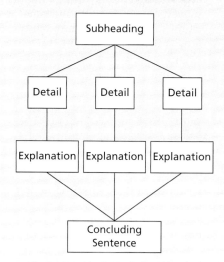

PRACTICE & APPLY 6

Guided and Independent Practice

After students turn their questions into headings, monitor their progress by having them turn in their K-W-L charts with their partial outlines. Check to see that students have developed appropriate headings that are in a logical order for the report. Keep in mind that students' questions may have changed since they made their K-W-L charts. Then, after students write their notes below each heading, have them talk through their outlines with partners. Encourage partners to query parts they don't understand as well as parts that need more or less detail.

TIP Review your outline to make sure you have at least two pieces of information under each body heading. If you don't, you may need to do a bit more research. You can also check any note cards you set aside to see if they fit under one of the headings. If not, you will not use those cards for this report.

The partial formal outline below shows the information the student writing about guanacos will use in his research report.

Body:

I. Where Guanacos Live
  A. Andes Mountains of South America
  B. How Guanacos Handle Their Habitat
  C. Protected Reserves

II. What Guanacos Look Like
  A. Similarities to Camels
  B. Differences from Camels

III. What Guanacos Do
  A. Spit Cud Accurately
  B. Run Fast and Early in Life
  C. Swim Across Streams and Between Islands

IV. How People Use Guanacos
  A. Carrying Loads
  B. Wool Used for Coats and Robes
  C. Hunted for Meat

TIP If, while outlining, you find that you have too many headings, you may need to narrow your topic. For example, the narrower topic "guanaco habitats" would focus only on where the guanaco lives. On the other hand, if you find that you have too few headings, you may need to broaden your topic. The broader topic "unique South American animals" would discuss jaguars and llamas in addition to guanacos.

PRACTICE & APPLY 6 — Organize Your Notes and Create a Formal Outline

Group your note cards based on the questions they answer. Then, create a formal outline by following these steps.

1. Turn questions into headings.

2. List your headings on a sheet of paper, leaving several blank lines after each. Number each heading with a Roman numeral.

3. Under each heading, write subheadings. Label each subheading with a capital letter.

RESOURCES

Practice and Apply 6
Guided Practice
■ *Writing, Listening, & Speaking,* WS. p. 77

Designing Your Writing

Creating Headings   To help readers see how your ideas are organized, include a descriptive heading before each section of your report. If you are writing on a computer, put your headings in boldface print or underline them. You may even want to use a font size for the headings that is larger than the rest of the text. If you are writing your report by hand, print the headings in capital letters or underline them.

Mini-Workshop

If you would like to add a visual to your research report, see **Creating Graphics** on page 686.

Write a Thesis

Tell It Like It Is   To help your readers understand your purpose and remember the major points about your topic, include a *thesis* in your introduction. A **thesis,** or **main idea statement,** tells readers the topic and the main points you will make about the topic. Here is how you can develop a thesis for your report.

THINKING IT THROUGH   Writing a Thesis

▶ **STEP 1** Identify the major points in your outline.

strange looking, unusual talents, useful to humans, threatened by hunting

▶ **STEP 2** Combine the major points in a single sentence about your topic.

Guanacos are strange-looking animals with unusual talents, and they are useful to humans but threatened by hunting.

▶ **STEP 3** If your step 2 sentence is long, condense the ideas into a more compact thesis.

Guanacos are unusual animals that are useful to humans but threatened by hunting.

PRACTICE & APPLY 7   Write a Thesis

Use the Thinking It Through steps above to develop a clear and compact thesis for your research report.

Writing   1.2a State a clear purpose.   **1.5** Compose documents with appropriate formatting by using word-processing skills and principles of design.

Write a Thesis   **593**

A Writer's Framework

Research Report

Introduction

- Attention-getting beginning
- Background information
- Thesis

One way to grab your readers' attention is to begin with a vivid description. Provide **background information** that will help explain the situation or give readers information they will need to understand the topic of your report. Your **thesis**, or **main idea statement**, should clearly identify your topic and the major points in your report. (For more information on writing **introductions**, see page 655.)

Body

- Heading 1 support
- Heading 2 support and so on

The headings in your formal outline represent subtopics. **Each subtopic will be covered in its own paragraph. Support** each subtopic with facts, details, examples, and explanations from your research. Present these ideas in a way that supports the main idea of your report.

Conclusion

- Restatement of thesis

In addition to restating your thesis, consider sharing interesting information that did not fit in the body of your report. The following Writer's Model, for example, tells what is being done to solve the problem discussed in the report. (For more information on writing **conclusions**, see page 656.)

List of Sources

- Alphabetized by author

A list of sources is also called a **Works Cited list** or **bibliography,** and should include at least three sources. List only the sources you actually used for your report. See the chart on page 586 for how to list different kinds of sources.

Writing 1.0 Essays contain formal introductions, supporting evidence, and conclusions. **1.2a** Engage the interest of the reader. **1.2c** Conclude with a detailed summary linked to the purpose of the composition. **2.0** Student writing demonstrates the drafting strategies outlined in Writing Standard 1.0. **2.3b** Support the main idea. **2.3c** Include a bibliography.

A Writer's Model

The final draft below closely follows the framework for a research report on the previous page and the MLA guidelines for research paper format.

The South American Guanaco

Visitors to the Andes Mountains may spot a creature resembling a tiny camel without a hump. This animal is the guanaco, a South American member of the camel family. Guanacos are unusual animals that are useful to humans but threatened by hunting.

For thousands of years, guanacos have grazed on tough grasses in the high plains and hills of the Andes Mountains. They can be found from southern Peru to the tip of South America (Burton 172). Their blood can handle the thin mountain air. Steep, rocky paths are no problem for guanacos because they are nimble like mountain goats and have thick, padded soles that protect their feet (Goodwin). Their only wild enemy is the mountain lion, but people have hunted the guanaco so much that the species is in danger. Some herds live in protected reserves in Argentina and Chile.

INTRODUCTION
Attention grabber

Background Information

Thesis

BODY
Heading 1:
Where Guanacos Live

Fact

Explanation

(continued)

REVIEW STANDARD

A Writer's Model
The following activity provides a review of the 5th-grade **Writing Standard 2.3.**

Remind students that readers will be drawing conclusions from the paragraphs in their research reports. Have students read **A Writer's Model** on this page, drawing conclusions and noting the facts, details, examples, and explanations that lead to the conclusions. Finally, ask them to review their own drafts, looking for facts, details, examples, and explanations that might help readers draw conclusions from the information in their reports.

DIFFERENTIATING INSTRUCTION

Learners Having Difficulty
Suggest that students use color-codes as they review their drafts. They may use one color to highlight the thesis statement and conclusion, another for the main ideas in the paragraphs, and a third color to highlight words that provide supporting details. By focusing on the colors, students can check the flow of their drafts.

TECHNOLOGY TIP

W1.5 As students begin to revise their papers, they need to be able to navigate within the document. To move among pages, students can use the mouse to move the pointer to the scroll bar on the side of the screen. Students can then move freely within the document by clicking and dragging the place marker, by clicking and holding the scroll button, or by clicking on the previous page or next page button. Students can move within a single page by moving the pointer and clicking or by using arrow keys to re-position the cursor. Text—once it is highlighted—can be copied, moved, modified, or deleted. Students who took notes in a word-processing document can copy text from their notes to their draft.

Heading 2:
What Guanacos
Look Like

Like other camels, the guanaco has long legs, two-toed hoofs, a long neck, and floppy lips. It can survive without water for long periods of time, just like a desert camel. The guanaco looks different from the humped camel, though. It has pointed ears and a slender neck and legs, and it stands less than

Facts

four feet high. The guanaco's body is about five-and-a-half feet long, and the average weight is almost 200 pounds (Sentman). In some ways it looks more like a deer or an antelope than a

Details

camel. It is reddish brown with a dark gray head and a pale belly.

Heading 3:
What Guanacos
Do

The guanaco has some strange talents. Like other kinds of camels, the guanaco helps its stomach digest grass by chewing it up again after it has been in the stomach for a while. This rechewed grass, or cud, comes in handy when another animal

Example

bothers the guanaco. With no warning at all, the guanaco can accurately hit with smelly green spit whatever is annoying it

Example

(Goodwin). The guanaco can also run fast and swim well. Almost as soon as they are born, guanacos can race to safety if

Fact

their mothers spot danger (Lambeth 7). Adult guanacos can run as fast as thirty-five miles an hour ("Guanaco"). Guanacos swim almost as well as they run. They easily cross cold, fast-running mountain streams. Believe it or not, they even swim in the ocean. They have been seen swimming from island to island off the coast of Chile in the Pacific Ocean.

Guanacos are helpful to people and are in trouble because of them. According to Graham Harris of the Wildlife Conservation Society, the guanaco is "part of South America's heritage much like the bison is to North America" (Sautner). People use guanacos to carry loads on the prairies and in the mountains of South America. Their wool is also used for making coats. These uses do not harm guanacos, but other human activities do. Newborn guanacos are often killed so that their silky wool can be made into beautiful robes called *capas*. The number of guanacos has also been reduced by hunters, who kill them for their meat.

To help the guanaco survive the threat of people hunting it for meat and hides, this unusual little camel will need to be protected. Some South American countries are already taking steps that may help guanacos to be plentiful again.

(continued)

A Writer's Model **597**

Fact

Heading 4:
How People
Use Guanacos

Example

Example

Example

CONCLUSION
Restatement of
thesis

DIRECT TEACHING

A Writer's Model **W1.0**
As students review **A Writer's Model,** remind them that they should link ideas within their essays with transitions to create coherence. Point out to students the following transitions that are used in **A Writer's Model** by listing, annotating, or highlighting them: *For thousands of years* (paragraph 2); *Like other camels* (paragraph 3); *Like other kinds of camels, when, also* (paragraph 4); and *also, but* (paragraph 5).

DIRECT TEACHING

A Writer's Model

Remind students that the Works Cited list should be alphabetized by the author's last name or by the source title if no author is given. As they prepare their source lists, students should use as models the entries on this page and those in the chart on page 586.

CRITICAL THINKING

Ask students to apply the *4R* test that they studied in the **Critical Thinking Mini-Lesson** on p. 587 to the sources used in **A Writer's Model.** One of the sources used for this report is from 1987. Discuss with students whether this is still a reliable source. [Students should say that many facts about guanacos, such as what they look like and what they do, will remain the same over time, so a source from 1987 is still reliable. Other information about the guanaco's habitat might need to come from a more recent source.]

PRACTICE & APPLY 8

Guided and Independent Practice

Monitor students' progress by spot-checking to be sure that they are following the framework on this page. If you wish to assign a length to the students' essays, suggest that drafts be 500 to 700 words long.

LIST OF SOURCES

GO TO: go.hrw.com
KEYWORD:
HLLA6 W-4
FOR: A Student Model

Works Cited

Burton, John A. The Collins Guide to the Rare Mammals of

the World. Lexington: The Stephen Greene Press, 1987.

Goodwin, George G. "Guanaco." Collier's Encyclopedia.

CD-ROM. 1997.

"Guanaco." Wildlife Gallery. Fota Wildlife Park. 26 Jan. 2003

<http://www.zenith.ie/fota/ wildlife/guanaco.html>.

Lambeth, Ellen. "Here Comes Paco Guanaco: In the Hilly

Grasslands of South America, a Camel Is Born."

Ranger Rick Nov. 1996: 4-8.

Sautner, Stephen. "Guanaco Numbers Continue to Dwindle."

Wildlife Conservation Society News. 28 Jan. 1999.

Wildlife Conservation Society. 30 Jan. 2003

<http://wcs.org/ 3422?newsarticle=3363>.

Sentman, Everett. "Guanaco." Grolier 2001 Multimedia

Encyclopedia. CD-ROM. 2000.

PRACTICE & APPLY 8 Draft a Research Report

Write the first draft of your report. Use the framework on page 594 and the Writer's Model on pages 595–598 to guide you.

RESOURCES

Practice and Apply 8

Think Sheet
■ *Writing, Listening, & Speaking,* WS. p. 79

Template
■ *Writing, Listening, & Speaking,* WS. p. 80

Revising

Evaluate and Revise Content, Organization, and Style

Double Duty   To make the information in your research report as clear as possible for your readers, read it at least twice. First, evaluate the content and organization using the guidelines below. Then, check your writing style using the guidelines on page 600.

▶ First Reading: **Content and Organization**   Use the following chart to evaluate the content and organization of your report. The tips in the middle column will help you decide how to answer the questions in the left column. If you answer *no* to any question, use the Revision Technique to improve that part of your writing.

Research Report: Content and Organization Guidelines

Evaluation Questions	▶ Tips	▶ Revision Techniques
❶ Does the introduction contain a thesis? Does the introduction include background information?	▶ **Highlight** the thesis. **Circle** the background information.	▶ If needed, **add** a thesis. **Add** background information, if necessary.
❷ Is each paragraph in the body consistent, explaining only one part of the topic?	▶ **Label** each body paragraph with the type of information it provides about the topic.	▶ **Rearrange** ideas so each paragraph covers only one part of the topic, or **delete** ideas that do not belong.
❸ Does each paragraph contain support that gives clear information about the topic?	▶ **Put a check mark** above each fact, detail, example, or explanation that elaborates on the topic.	▶ **Add** facts, details, examples, or explanations to any paragraph with fewer than two check marks.
❹ Does the conclusion restate the report's main idea?	▶ **Circle** the sentence that puts the thesis statement in different words.	▶ If needed, **add** a sentence that states the main idea in another way.
❺ Does the report include information from at least three sources?	▶ **Number** the items on the list of sources.	▶ **Elaborate** on the ideas in your report by using information from other sources as needed. Then, **add** the sources to the Works Cited list.

Writing 1.6 Revise writing to improve the organization and consistency of ideas within and between paragraphs.

Quotation for the Day

❝Blot out, correct, insert, refine, Enlarge, diminish, interline; Be mindful, When invention fails, To scratch your head, and bite your nails.❞

(Jonathan Swift, 1667–1745, Irish satirist)

Ask students to brainstorm in small groups lists of actions connected with revision. Then, share the quotation with the class and discuss how many of the actions the students listed are mentioned in the quotation. Students may have used different words, such as *elaborate* instead of *enlarge* or *insert* instead of *interline,* but the meanings will be similar. Emphasize that writers throughout history have performed these actions to improve their work.

DIRECT TEACHING

Elaboration

To help students elaborate with examples in their research reports, have them exchange papers with a peer. Ask the peer editors to look for and highlight sentences in which the addition of an example such as a fact, statistic, direct quotation, or expert opinion would further clarify the point the writer is making. Then, have students look through their notes to find additional information that they could use as examples. If students add an example from a source that is not listed in their Works Cited list or bibliography, remind them to add the source to their source list.

The guanaco can also run fast and swim well. Almost as soon as they are born, guanacos can race to safety if their mothers spot danger (Lambeth 7). Adult guanacos can run

delete

as fast as thirty-five miles an hour ("Guanaco"). ~~This is another way that they are like antelopes and deer.~~ Guanacos swim almost as well as they run. They easily cross cold, fast-running mountain streams. Believe it or not, they even

elaborate

swim in the ocean. *They have been seen swimming from island to island off the coast of Chile in the Pacific Ocean.*

GUIDED PRACTICE

Responding to the Revision Process

Answers

1. The passage flows better because each sentence now elaborates the idea of guanacos running and swimming.

2. The addition provides evidence that the guanacos swim in the ocean.

DIRECT TEACHING

Second Reading: Style

Suggest that students work with a partner to identify vague nouns in their reports. To make the task manageable for students, you may want to have them identify nouns in only one or two body paragraphs. Students can use the **Style Guidelines** to help them decide whether a vague noun needs to be replaced with a more precise one.

PEER REVIEW

As you read a classmate's report, ask yourself these questions.

- Is this information clear enough for me to tell someone else about this topic?
- What parts of this report caught my interest? Why?

Responding to the Revision Process

1. How did deleting a sentence improve the passage above?
2. Why was it important for the writer to add the final sentence?

Second Reading: Style   When sharing information with others, you should communicate your ideas as clearly as possible. One way to do this is to use *precise nouns* in your writing. **Precise nouns** name a person, place, thing, or idea in a specific way. Look for places in your writing where you can be more precise by changing a vague noun to one that is more specific. Use the guidelines below to help you identify where you already include precise nouns, and use the Focus on Word Choice on the next page to add more precise nouns.

Style Guidelines

Evaluation Question	▸ Tip	▸ Revision Technique
Does the report use specific words to name people, places, things, and ideas?	▸ **Highlight** each noun. **Put a star** above each specific noun.	▸ If the report has few stars, **replace** some vague nouns with more precise ones. (You may find more specific words in your notes.)

Writing 1.2b Develop the topic with precise nouns to paint a visual image in the mind of the reader.

Using Precise Nouns

Focus on

Word Choice

When you read the word *flower,* what image comes to mind? You might picture a daisy, while another reader might think of a buttercup or a daffodil. *Flower* is a vague noun because it lets the reader choose what to picture. When you write, give your readers the right picture by using *precise nouns* such as *honeysuckle* or *violet.* **Precise nouns** name people, places, things, or ideas in a specific way. Look at the sentences below. Which one tells you exactly what the writer had in mind?

Vague   The author Luis Valdez created a *program* for *people.*

Precise   The author Luis Valdez created a *theater company* for *farm workers.*

Replace vague nouns in your writing with more precise ones that will get your picture across. Precise nouns will help your readers learn about your topic.

TIP If you have trouble coming up with a precise noun, look up the vague noun in a **thesaurus.** Among the synonyms for the vague noun, you will often find more specific ones that you might use to revise your writing.

ONE WRITER'S REVISIONS

> For thousands of years, ~~the animals~~ *guanacos* have grazed on
> tough ~~plants~~ *grasses* in the high plains and hills of the *Andes* mountains.

Responding to the Revision Process

How do you think the changes the writer made improve the sentence above?

PRACTICE & APPLY 9 **Evaluate and Revise Content, Organization, and Style**

- Review the first draft of your report. Then, improve your report by using the Content and Organization Guidelines on page 599 and the Focus on Word Choice above.

- As you revise, carefully consider any peer comments you have received.

Writing 1.2b Develop the topic with precise nouns to paint a visual image in the mind of the reader.

Focus on Word Choice   **601**

DIRECT TEACHING

Using Precise Nouns

Suggest that students develop a fun way to practice using precise nouns. They can also share some of the facts discovered during the research and writing process. For example, students could create a crossword puzzle, a question-and-answer game show, or riddles. Students could share their games with other students as a warm-up or follow-up to their presentations.

GUIDED PRACTICE

Responding to the Revision Process

Answer

Adding the precise nouns *guanacos, grasses,* and *Andes* creates a clearer picture.

▶ Resources Reminder

For help with writing assessment, see 6 Traits—Plus 1 in the "General Scales and Sample Papers" section of *Progress Assessment of Writing, Listening, & Speaking.*

PRACTICE & APPLY 9

Independent Practice

Suggest that students read their revised reports out loud to a partner so that they can check for awkwardness, choppy sentences, and other organization and style issues. Have them record the partner's suggestions for improvements on their drafts.

RESOURCES

Focus on Word Choice

Independent Practice

- *Writing, Listening, & Speaking,* WS. p. 84 You may choose to assign this independent practice as homework.

HOMEWORK

Practice and Apply 9

Think Sheet

- *Writing, Listening, & Speaking,* WS. p. 81

Independent Practice

- *Writing, Listening, & Speaking,* WS. p. 83

Extension

- *Writing, Listening, & Speaking,* WS. p. 82

"He who hesitates is sometimes saved."

(James Thurber, 1894–1961, U.S. humorist, cartoonist, and author)

Have students discuss how stopping and looking for spelling, grammar, and mechanics errors during the publishing stage can "save" their reports. [Students may say that since these errors confuse and distract readers, they are worth correcting.]

DIRECT TEACHING

Integrating with Grammar, Usage, and Mechanics
If students create fragments or make errors in the punctuation of titles as they are proofreading, send them to The Sentence chapter or the Punctuation chapters in the *Holt Handbook.*

Capitalizing and Punctuating Titles
Review with students the **Information on Sources** chart on page 586, pointing out the capitalization and punctuation for each bibliographic format. Then, ask volunteers to write some entries on the chalkboard. Work as a class to correct any errors. For more information about format style, refer students to the *MLA Handbook for Writers of Research Papers.*

Grammar Link

Guided Practice
(For independent practice, see Proofreading Practice below.)

Answers
Underlined titles can also appear in italics.
1. "With a Song in His Heart"
2. The Giant Guide to the Internet
3. Freebie and the Bean
4. The Science of Lightning
5. "The Perfect Pearl"

Publishing

Proofread Your Report

Polish It You want your readers to focus on learning about your topic, not on finding errors. Look over your report carefully and correct any mistakes. Use the following Grammar Link to make sure your sources are written correctly.

Grammar Link

Capitalizing and Punctuating Titles

Sources of information for research reports are listed in a certain way. You may see the title of a source listed inside quotation marks, written in italics, or underlined. Some words are capitalized, and others are not. Here are three rules about how to write titles.

Titles of major works should be <u>underlined</u> or typed in *italics.* Major works include books, encyclopedias, magazines, newspapers, databases, Web sites, movies, and television series. <u>Underline</u> these titles when you type or write your report by hand. If you are using a computer, you can use the *italics* function.

Put titles of short works inside quotation marks. These include chapters of books; articles from encyclopedias, magazines, and newspapers; individual pages from Web sites; and titles of single episodes in a TV series.

Capitalize the important words in a title. The only words you will not capitalize in a title are articles (*a, an, the*), conjunctions (*and, but, or*), and prepositions with fewer than five letters (*to, for, with, in,* and so on). However, capitalize the first and last words of a title, no matter what they are.

PRACTICE

Rewrite the following titles. Capitalize each correctly and place it inside quotation marks or underline it.

Example:
1. Newspaper article: students stop disaster on playground
1. "Students Stop Disaster on Playground"

1. Magazine article: with a song in his heart
2. Book: the giant guide to the internet
3. Movie: freebie and the bean
4. Whole Web site: the science of lightning
5. Episode in a TV program: the perfect pearl

Reference Note
For more information and practice on **punctuating titles,** see pages 290 and 297 in the *Holt Handbook.*

Writing 2.0 Student writing demonstrates a command of standard American English.

RESOURCES
Grammar Link
Proofreading Practice
■ *Writing, Listening, & Speaking,* WS. p. 85 You may choose to assign this proofreading practice as homework.

HOMEWORK

Publish Your Report

Share the Wealth   Now you can share what you have learned with an audience. Here are some ideas.

- Make a display that includes your report and helpful illustrations. Place it in a hallway display case or the library.

- Adapt your report into a children's book that includes illustrations. Make sure you use language children can understand.

Designing Your Writing

Creating a Magazine With other students, create a magazine of research reports. To make the research reports look like magazine articles, format, type, or write them in **columns,** or vertical rows. Measure the width of a real magazine column, and make the width of the columns in each report the same size. Place the magazine in the classroom or library for everyone to enjoy.

Reflect on Your Report

Building Your Portfolio   Take some time to think about how you researched your topic and wrote your report. Consider the following questions.

- Where in your report do you think you did the best job of clearly answering a research question? Why do you think so?

- What kinds of information sources were useful? Would you use these types of sources for a future report?

PRACTICE & APPLY 10

Proofread, Publish, and Reflect on Your Report

- First, correct any errors in spelling, punctuation, and sentence structure. Be particularly careful about writing titles of sources correctly.

- Next, publish your report for an audience of interested readers.

- Finally, answer the Reflect on Your Report questions above. Include your responses in your portfolio.

COMPUTER TIP

You can use computer resources to help you proofread your report, such as grammar and spelling checkers. However, these resources are not always 100 percent accurate, so you will still need to proofread your work to avoid introducing errors.

Writing 1.5 Compose documents with appropriate formatting by using word-processing skills and principles of design (e.g., columns).

Reflect on Your Report   **603**

Listening and Speaking Workshop

PRETEACHING

Quotation for the Day

"We wholly conquer only what we assimilate."

(André Gide, 1869–1951, French writer)

Write the quotation on the chalkboard, and explain to students that *assimilate* means "to absorb into the mind." Then, ask students to discuss how this statement relates to prewriting. [Prewriting involves gathering facts and putting together data from various sources for their reports.] Lead students to understand that it is only when writers have assimilated the data they have collected that they are in control of their information and ready to present their reports.

DIRECT TEACHING

Plan Content

Remind students that just as they can go back to the prewriting stage at any point during the writing process—to gather more support, for example—they can do the same in the speaking process. Also, tell students to note the sources of their examples and other evidence on their speech note cards. The audience will find a speech more believable if they know the speaker has used reliable sources.

Talk   Listen

WHAT'S AHEAD?

In this workshop you will give and evaluate a research presentation. You will also learn how to

- turn your research report into notes for a speech
- practice formal speaking skills
- identify important parts of a presentation
- evaluate a speech

Reference Note

To develop a new subject into a research presentation, see pages 582–593.

Giving and Evaluating a Research Presentation

Researchers sometimes present their findings in a formal presentation or speech, in addition to sharing ideas in a written report. A research presentation tells an audience the important points a researcher has discovered. Here is your chance to share your research findings through an oral presentation and to discover what your classmates learned.

Give a Research Presentation

Even the most interesting report can sound dull if a speaker reads it word for word. A good speaker looks at the audience while presenting information. To make this possible, speakers use note cards to remind themselves of the points they want to make. They also practice their speeches until they are comfortable with what they are saying. To turn your research report into a research presentation, plan your **content,** or what you will say, and your **delivery,** or how you will say it. Use the guidelines on the following pages.

Plan Content   The ideas you present in your speech may not be exactly the same ideas your research report explained. For one thing, a time limit for your speech will limit the number of ideas and explanations you can present. To choose the content you will present, follow the suggestions on the next page.

Listening and Speaking 1.0 Students deliver focused, coherent presentations that convey ideas clearly and relate to the background and interests of the audience.   2.0 Students deliver well-organized formal presentations employing traditional rhetorical strategies (e.g., exposition).   2.2 Deliver informative presentations.

604   Workshop 4   **Research:** Giving and Evaluating a Research Presentation

WORKSHOP RESOURCES

Listening and Speaking Workshop
Planning
- *On Course: Mapping Instruction*
- *One-Stop Planner* CD-ROM
- *At Home: A Guide to Standards Mastery,* p. 15
- *At Home: In Five Languages*

- *Writing, Listening, & Speaking*
  — Teaching Notes, pp. 86–87
  — Project-Planning Guide, WS. p. 88

Differentiating Instruction
- *Lesson Plans for Language Development,* p. 234
- *Supporting Instruction in Five Languages*

Choose a Focus Focus on just a few of your research questions if you do not think you will have time to discuss all of them. Choose the research questions that you find most interesting or which your classmates will probably find most surprising.

Remember Your Purpose Because your **purpose** is to inform your listeners about your topic, the **message** should be informative, too. In an informative presentation, your **point of view** should be objective; that is, you should not appear to favor one side of an issue. If your research revealed widely varied opinions about your subject, share the different opinions with your audience.

Plan Your Support Look back at the outline you created for your research report. Identify the information you should use to answer the research questions on which your speech will focus. This information should include facts, details, examples, and explanations from a variety of sources.

Make Note Cards Create a separate note card for each outline heading that will be used in your speech. On each note card, neatly write words or phrases from your research notes, outline, or written report that will help you remember the ideas you want to share with your audience.

To keep your cards from becoming cluttered and difficult to read, write major ideas only, including key supporting evidence and examples. As you speak, you will elaborate on and clarify for listeners the ideas listed on your note cards.

- **Think of your audience** as you add key information to your note cards. Make sure that the words you choose and the ideas you share are appropriate for your listeners and appeal to their backgrounds and interests. Finally, be sure that all the information you share is from a variety of authoritative sources. (For information on **evaluating sources,** see page 587.)

- **Organize your ideas** (and number your cards) in a way that will hold your listeners' attention. You may want to organize your ideas by categories as you did for your written report. Beginning each section of your speech with a question might help your audience identify your main ideas. Asking questions may also hook your listeners' interest.

> **TIP** Add to your note cards the sources of any particularly unusual pieces of information. Telling your listeners where you found a surprising fact or detail will make your speech more believable.

Listening and Speaking **1.4** Select a focus, an organizational structure, and a point of view, matching the purpose and message to the audience.   **1.6** Support opinions with detailed evidence.   **2.2a** Pose relevant questions sufficiently limited in scope to be completely and thoroughly answered.   **2.2b** Develop the topic with facts, details, examples, and explanations from multiple authoritative sources.

Give a Research Presentation   **605**

DIRECT TEACHING

Choose a Focus
Most students will be adapting the research reports they wrote in the Writing Workshop. If not, refer students to the Prewriting section that begins on p. 582 for choosing and developing their topics for their presentations.

REVIEW STANDARD

■ **Organize your ideas**
The following activity is a review of the 5th-grade **Listening and Speaking Standard 1.4.**

Remind students of the different ways to organize informational presentations. Review with them the organizational patterns of order of importance, chronological order, and logical order. Suggest that students choose an organizational structure that will hook the audience's interest and be clear and easy to follow.

Think Sheet
■ *Writing, Listening, & Speaking,* WS. p. 89
Guided Practice
■ *Writing, Listening, & Speaking,* TP. 14
Independent Practice
■ *Writing, Listening, & Speaking,* WS. pp. 90, 91

Evaluation and Assessment
■ *Writing, Listening, & Speaking,* WS. p. 92
■ *Progress Assessment of Writing, Listening, & Speaking,* pp. 48–50
■ *Diagnostic and Summative Assessments,* Third-Quarter Test

Plan Delivery

If you have access to video recording equipment, have students videotape themselves as they practice their speeches. Students can replay the tape and evaluate the volume and rate of their speeches, their use of nonverbal elements, and the effectiveness of their visual or media displays.

Plan Delivery   Once you know what you will say, you need to plan how you will say it. Follow these suggestions.

■ **Practice your speech out loud.** Because the **occasion** for giving your speech is fairly formal, use **standard American English,** language that is grammatically correct. Avoid using slang or clichés. Consider your **volume** and **rate,** speaking loudly and slowly. Everyone in your audience—including people at the back of the room—should be able to understand you.

■ **Practice using your voice to add meaning to your ideas.** Slow down your rate of speech or change the **modulation** (pitch) of your voice to emphasize an important point. Make sure your **tone** of voice reflects a neutral **point of view** toward your subject.

■ **Use nonverbal elements** such as gestures and facial expressions that match **verbal elements** such as pitch and tone. Raising your voice while pointing a finger, for example, can cue your audience to listen for your most important point. Practice making eye contact as you rehearse your speech by making eye contact with a practice audience of friends or by moving your gaze from one object in the room to another if you prefer to practice alone.

Mini-Workshop

See **Creating Graphics,** page 686.

■ **Emphasize ideas in your speech by using a visual display or media display,** such as a map, chart, graph, slide show, or video segment. The design of the display should be clear and direct. Use the display to support the ideas you explain in your speech. Do not overuse visual displays; include only items that clearly support the important points, the main idea, or the purpose of the speech. Add a note to your cards to remind you when to use your visual during your speech.

> **TIP** Have a partner help you practice by answering these questions about your presentation.
> ■ Are there any points in the presentation that are not clear?
> ■ Does the visual (if one is used) help me better understand the information?

PRACTICE & APPLY 11

Guided and Independent Practice

As students practice their presentations, check that they are able to speak on their topics clearly and with little hesitation. Make sure that any conclusions they draw are clear and that their visuals are effective in presenting complicated facts or data or in giving helpful examples. Remind students to speak without reading their notes and to make eye contact with the audience.

PRACTICE & APPLY 11   **Give an Oral Research Presentation**

Follow the guidelines on pages 604–606 to present to your class information on your research report topic or a new topic.

Listening and Speaking **1.4** Match the occasion and vocal modulation to audience.   **1.5** Emphasize salient points to assist the listener in following the main ideas and concepts.   **1.6** Support opinions with visual or media displays that use appropriate technology.   **1.7** Use effective rate, volume, pitch, and tone and align nonverbal elements to sustain audience interest and attention.

Evaluate a Research Presentation

Why are some speeches more interesting than others? Speakers grab the audience's interest with *what* they say and *how* they say it. The what is the **content,** or the ideas a speaker presents. The *how* is the speaker's delivery. **Delivery** includes how the speaker talks, uses gestures, and makes eye contact with the audience. When you evaluate a presentation, you will look at the content of the speech and the speaker's delivery.

Get the Message   To evaluate the content of a research presentation, you will need to consider how clear and organized the speaker's information is. Monitor your understanding as you listen to the speech. If any ideas seem unclear, wait until the speaker is finished to raise your hand and ask a question for clarification. Also, answer the questions about content in the chart below as you listen.

Here is how one student evaluated the content of a classmate's speech.

ASKING QUESTIONS ABOUT CONTENT

Content	Comments
• What are the main ideas in the speaker's verbal message?	• He said guanacos are unusual animals that are in trouble.
• How does the speaker support the main ideas?	• He described what guanacos look like and what they do. He also talked about how they are being hunted.
• Does the speaker organize his or her ideas in a way that makes sense? Explain.	• Yes, he talked about what they looked like first so that we knew a guanaco was like a camel. He told us how they helped people last, which I thought was important.
• Does the speaker seem to understand the topic well? Explain.	• He really knew a lot about guanacos. I wish he would explain how they swim, though. Overall content: great

Special Delivery   A speaker who mumbles or says "um" frequently draws negative attention to his or her delivery. When you listen to a speech, you may only notice a speaker's delivery if there are problems such as these. When a speaker's delivery is good, you can focus on the content of the speech.

 Listening and Speaking   1.0 They evaluate the content of oral communication.

To identify good delivery, answer questions such as those in the chart below.

ASKING QUESTIONS ABOUT DELIVERY

Delivery	Comments
• Do the speaker's rate of speech, volume, vocal pitch, and tone of voice help him or her effectively communicate ideas? Explain.	• He talked a little too fast. He was loud enough except when he turned to the map. He sounded nervous at first because his voice was higher than normal, but then he calmed down. His serious tone of voice made me pay attention.
• Does the speaker look at the audience?	• He mostly looked at his notes.
• Do the speaker's verbal elements (word choice, pitch, feeling, and tone) and nonverbal signals (gestures, posture, and facial expressions) emphasize key ideas in the speech? Do they work well together to support meaning and hold audience interest? Explain.	• His face and voice showed that the issue was important. He did not smile, and his voice was serious. His language was also very formal. He seemed awkward, though. He did not stand up straight, and he moved his hands only to point at the map.
• If visuals are used, are they helpful? Do they help the speaker achieve an informative purpose? Explain.	• The map and picture told me where guanacos live and what they look like. Both helped me understand the topic better. *Overall delivery: good*

Put It All Together   As you listen to a speech, use charts like the one on page 607 and the one above to make notes about content and delivery. Considering both the content and the delivery of a presentation takes concentration, so try to limit your distractions. You may want to sit closer to the speaker and put away everything except your evaluation charts and a pen or pencil.

PRACTICE & APPLY 12   Evaluate an Oral Presentation

Evaluate a research presentation by one or more of your classmates.

■ First, create charts like those on page 607 and this page to evaluate both the content and delivery of each speech.

■ Then, share your comments with each classmate whose speech you evaluated. Point out what the speaker did well, and politely suggest ways the speaker could improve the presentation.

Listening and Speaking 1.1 Relate the speaker's verbal communication (e.g., word choice, pitch, feeling, tone) to the nonverbal message (e.g., posture, gesture).

Using Electronic Texts to Locate Information

Suppose you want to write a research report on giant pandas. You are short on time, so you decide to do your research on the World Wide Web. When you type the words *giant panda* into your favorite search engine, it produces hundreds of results, including sites on panda stamps and panda toys. Depending on how your search engine works, your search may even bring up sites on giant schnauzers and a sports team called the Giants! You know some of the Web sites contain useful information, but who has time to sort through hundreds of search results?

In this workshop you will learn efficient ways to navigate the Web and other electronic texts. You will also have the chance to use multiple electronic sources as you search for information about a topic of your choosing.

WHAT'S AHEAD

In this workshop you will use electronic texts to locate information. You will also learn how to

- choose an electronic text to fit your purpose
- use keyword searches to locate information
- identify the organizational features of electronic texts

Types of Electronic Texts

When you think of electronic sources of information, your first thought may be the Internet, but do not limit your searches to the Web alone. Explore the other electronic options at your library—the online library catalog, library databases, encyclopedias on CD-ROM, even e-mail. To choose the best source for your search, consider the purposes and limitations of each type of electronic text listed on the next page.

> **TIP** It may take practice to master using electronic sources. As you start to research a topic, focus on just *one* type of electronic text. When you are comfortable using one, then you can try the others.

 Writing 1.4 Use organizational features of electronic text (e.g., databases, keyword searches, e-mail addresses) to locate information.

Types of Electronic Texts **609**

Media Workshop

PRETEACHING

Quotation for the Day

❝The joy of life is variety.❞
(Samuel Johnson, 1709–1784, English lexicographer, critic, and writer)

Read this quotation out loud to students and ask students to tell ways they have seen information presented. You might prompt them by mentioning pamphlets and television shows. [Students might list textbooks, encyclopedias, magazines, newspapers, documentaries, or Web sites.] Tell students that in this lesson they will learn how to navigate and locate information in electronic sources.

DIRECT TEACHING

Types of Electronic Texts
You may want to set aside some class time for students to explore electronic options at your school library. If electronic resources are limited, ask students to print any useful information they find so that other students will have time to use these resources. Also, tell them that having a hard copy of their source materials will be useful if they need to take additional notes from the source or look back at source information.

WORKSHOP RESOURCES

Media Workshop

Planning
- *On Course: Mapping Instruction*
- *One-Stop Planner* CD-ROM
- *Writing, Listening, & Speaking*
  —Teaching Notes, pp. 93–95
  —Project-Planning Guide, WS. p. 96

Differentiating Instruction
- *Lesson Plans for Language Development,* p. 235
- *Supporting Instruction in Five Languages*

Think Sheet
- *Writing, Listening, & Speaking,* WS. pp. 97, 99

Guided Practice
- *Writing, Listening, & Speaking,* TP. 15

Independent Practice
- *Writing, Listening, & Speaking,* WS. p. 98

(Workshop Resources continued on p. 610)

Online Library Catalog Use an **online library catalog** to find information about the publications available in your specific library.
  Purpose: The online catalog will tell you whether a book is available for checkout and where in the library the book is located.
  Limitation: If your library's collection is small, you may not find much information in the catalog.

CD-ROM Encyclopedia Use a **CD-ROM encyclopedia** to find general background information about a topic and factual information, such as dates and definitions.
  Purpose: Use a CD-ROM encyclopedia for the same purpose as a printed encyclopedia. The only difference is that, using a CD-ROM, you can more easily move from one entry to another than you might with a large set of printed encyclopedias.
  Limitation: Like a printed encyclopedia, a CD-ROM encyclopedia may not include the most up-to-date information, depending on the date of the version you are using.

Library Databases Use a **library database,** such as a **periodical index,** to identify magazines, journals, and newspapers that contain articles about your topic.
  Purpose: A periodical index is a good place to start (and narrow) your search. It can direct you to the specific issue of a periodical that contains the information you need.
  Limitation: A database may include listings for a large pool of books or periodicals; you might find a listing for an interesting book but not find a copy of the book in your library.

Web Sites Use **Web sites** to find up-to-date news and information. Web sites contain text, audio, and video produced by just about anyone, from government officials to the eight-year-old next door.
  Purpose: The variety of sites available can help you find many different perspectives on your topic.
  Limitation: Web sites are not checked for accuracy. Try to stick with sites sponsored by trustworthy organizations, which often have addresses ending in *edu, gov,* or *org.*

E-Mail You can often find **e-mail** addresses for experts on your topic on Web sites that discuss your topic.
  Purpose: You can use e-mail to ask experts directly for information. For example, you might e-mail a zoologist in China to find out about the natural habitat of giant pandas.
  Limitation: Like Web sites, e-mail does not necessarily provide accurate information. Make sure anyone you consult really does know about your topic.

E-mail   **W. 1.5**

Students who communicate with experts via e-mail must be careful to enter e-mail addresses accurately, paying particular attention to upper- and lowercase letters. Also, students should include their own e-mail address in the texts of their requests because some e-mail programs do not automatically read addresses on received mail.

WORKSHOP RESOURCES

(continued from p. 609)

Evaluation and Assessment

- *Progress Assessment of Writing, Listening, & Speaking,* pp. 51–52
- *Diagnostic and Summative Assessments,* Third-Quarter Test

Extension

- *Writing, Listening, and Speaking,* Videocassette, Segment 4

Features of Electronic Texts

That's the Key When you use nearly any electronic text to search for information, you need to think of a *keyword*. A **keyword** is a word or phrase, such as *giant panda*, that identifies your specific topic. You may need to experiment with keywords in order to find the information you need. For example, if you begin searching for giant panda information by using the keyword *panda bear*, you might find little useful information. Switching to the keyword *giant panda* will provide better results. Any time you use an electronic source, be prepared to think of all the ways your topic might be listed in order to get the most useful information.

Our Feature Presentation Each type of electronic text is organized in a slightly different manner. To use electronic texts effectively, you need to understand the features of each type of text and the methods for using each type. Here are examples of four different types of electronic texts along with descriptions, explanations, and search tips.

Electronic Encyclopedia You might find this record by typing the keyword *panda* in the encyclopedia's search box.

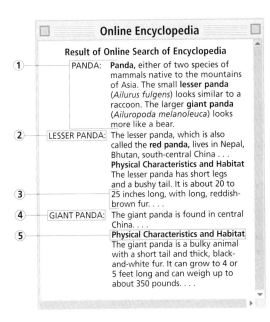

Online Encyclopedia

Result of Online Search of Encyclopedia

(1) PANDA: **Panda,** either of two species of mammals native to the mountains of Asia. The small **lesser panda** (*Ailurus fulgens*) looks similar to a raccoon. The larger **giant panda** (*Ailuropoda melanoleuca*) looks more like a bear.

(2) LESSER PANDA: The lesser panda, which is also called the **red panda,** lives in Nepal, Bhutan, south-central China . . . **Physical Characteristics and Habitat** The lesser panda has short legs and a bushy tail. It is about 20 to

(3) 25 inches long, with long, reddish-brown fur. . . .

(4) GIANT PANDA: The giant panda is found in central China. . . .

(5) Physical Characteristics and Habitat The giant panda is a bulky animal with a short tail and thick, black-and-white fur. It can grow to 4 or 5 feet long and can weigh up to about 350 pounds. . . .

(1) **First search result** finds two different entries about pandas.

(2) **Heading** for the entry about the first type of panda, the lesser panda

(3) Since you are interested in pandas with black-and-white fur, skip to the next entry.

(4) **Heading** for the entry about the second type of panda, the giant panda

(5) **Subheadings** introduce smaller sections of the entry. As you read, take notes. You can search for additional information by using details, such as names of places pandas inhabit, as keywords.

Web Site

Write the following topic on the chalkboard: "collecting baseball cards." Explain to students that a keyword search using only the word *baseball* will probably bring up too much information that is unrelated to the topic. Students can limit their search by using *baseball cards* AND *collect* or *baseball* AND *trading cards.* Remind students to look for additional search tips on a search engine's home page.

Have students demonstrate their understanding of how to limit searches by suggesting ways to search for information on the following topics: the history of football, damage to beaches from oil spills, and Egyptian pyramids.

DIRECT TEACHING

Web Site

Suggest that students open a word-processing document while they are searching the Internet. When they find relevant sources, they can highlight the source information (such as URL), choose copy from the edit menu, and paste the information onto the word-processing document. They can add a brief description of the source. This method will help prevent transcribing errors.

TECHNOLOGY TIP

W1.5 Students may use the bookmark feature in their browser to save an address and return to a site quickly. However, if that is not an option (school computers may become overloaded), remind students to type exact addresses in the location bar of the browser and hit return to go to the site. Caution students that browser commands may vary depending on the software they use.

Web Site You can use a *directory* or a *search engine* to find Web sites relevant to your search. A **directory** organizes sites into categories, such as sports. Each category is then broken down into smaller and smaller categories to help you narrow your search. A **search engine** allows you to type in your keyword and then provides you with a list of Web sites that include your keyword. In searching for information on giant pandas, you can eliminate irrelevant listings in most search engines by

- putting the words *giant panda* in quotation marks to find sites that include those words, next to each other and in that order
- using *AND* to find sites that include two terms (though not necessarily right next to each other), such as *computer AND games*
- using *NOT* to rule out irrelevant sites that commonly come up using your keyword. For example, in searching for sites on the human heart, you can eliminate the sites on romance by searching for *heart NOT love*

Here is an example of a Web page in a browser frame.

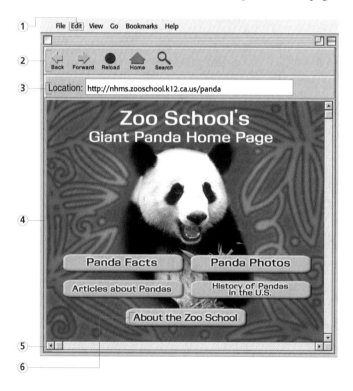

1. **Pull-down menu buttons** allow you to perform a variety of functions. Use the find command on the pull-down edit menu to locate quickly individual uses of a word in a text-heavy Web page.
2. **Toolbar buttons** help you navigate the Web.
3. The **Uniform Resource Locator** (URL) is the address of the Web page.
4. **Content area** of the Web page contains text, photos, and sometimes audio or video clips.
5. The horizontal and vertical **scroll bars** allow you to move side-to-side or up and down on a Web page.
6. When you click on underlined text or **hyperlink** buttons, your browser jumps to another part of the current page, a different page on the same Web site, or a page on a different Web site.

612 | Workshop 4 | **Research:** Using Electronic Texts to Locate Information

Online Library Catalog Like a traditional card catalog, an online catalog allows you to search for books and other information in the library by author, title, or subject. In most cases when you are doing research, you will search by subject. Look at the example of a subject entry below.

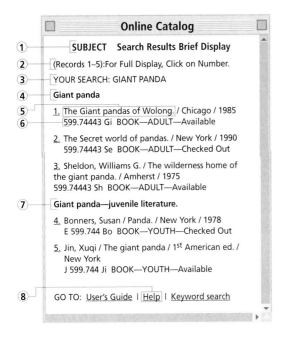

1. This line shows what kind of search (title, author, or subject) you performed. "Brief Display" means that just the basic information about each book is listed here.

2. Click on the number next to a listing to bring up a record containing more detailed information about the book.

3. The keyword you entered is noted here.

4. This is the first subject heading that matches your search request. (Compare it to item 7 below.)

5. This is the title of the first book on the subject of giant pandas.

6. This line notes the book's **call number**, which indicates where in the library the book is located and tells whether the book is available for checkout.

7. This next subject heading starts a section of children's books about giant pandas.

8. Click on the help button for instructions on using the library catalog. If on-screen help or an instruction sheet is not available, ask a librarian for help.

TIP If you search by **title**, leave off articles such as *The* or *A* when they are the first word in the title. If you search by **author**, type in the author's last name first, and check the spelling carefully.

Database Record from a Periodical Index Your library may carry hundreds of periodicals containing articles on every subject you can imagine. To search efficiently for articles about a particular topic in magazines, newspapers, or journals, refer to an online periodical index. You can search a periodical index, such as the *Readers' Guide to Periodical Literature,* to find a listing of magazine articles that fit your subject keyword. An example of a search result appears on the next page.

Online *Readers' Guide*

Readers' Guide Abstract results for **kw: Giant** and **kw: Panda**

(1) Record 1 of 51

DATABASE:	ReadersGuideAbs
(2) TITLE:	**Gentle giant.** death of Hsing-Hsing, panda at the National Zoo
(3) SOURCE:	*People Weekly* v. 52 no23 (Dec 13 1999) p.149
LANGUAGE:	English
(4) ABSTRACT:	Hsing-Hsing, Washington Zoo's beloved panda, has died at the age of 28. Hsing-Hsing and his companion Ling-Ling came to America in April 1972 as a gift from the People's Republic of China following President Nixon's historic visit there that February. The rare and beautiful pandas were an instant success, attracting as many as 20,000 visitors a day.
(5) SUBJECT(S):	Hsing-Hsing (Panda) Pandas—Mortality
(6) ARTICLE TYPE:	feature article

(7) Libraries   E-mail   Print   Help   Next Record

1. Your search for the keywords ("kw") *Giant* and *Panda* produced 51 records. This is the first record in the database.

2. Each line in a database is called a *field.* The **title field** contains the title of an article about giant pandas.

3. The **source field** indicates the name, issue number, and page number of the magazine in which the article was published.

4. An **abstract** gives you a summary of the article's contents.

5. The database shows **additional subject headings** related to your search.

6. Examining the **type of article** will also help you decide if the article will be useful for your research.

7. To see information about the next article that fits your search, click on the words *Next Record.*

Guided and Independent Practice

Check students' topic choices for appropriateness before they begin their searches. Suggest that they take notes from each type of source on separate sheets of paper so they can more easily compare the different types of electronic sources. After students summarize their findings, you might discuss with them which electronic source they found easiest to use and why.

Use Electronic Texts to Locate Information

- With a partner, choose a "fun" topic, such as a favorite sport, hobby, or hero, to research.
- Then, search for information about your topic in one of the four types of electronic texts explained in this workshop.
- After you feel comfortable navigating within one type of electronic text, search for information about your topic in the other three types of electronic texts. Take notes as you search.
- Finally, summarize your findings in a brief written report. In addition to sharing information about your topic, you and your partner's report should identify which types of electronic texts provided more thorough or unusual information on the topic.

Writing **1.4** Use organizational features of electronic text (e.g., databases, keyword searches, e-mail addresses) to locate information.

DIRECTIONS: Read the following paragraph from a student's research report on mound builders. Then, read the questions below it. Choose the best answer for each, and mark your answers on your own paper.

(1) One of the North American Indian groups who built mounds was the Adena. (2) They built the mounds as burial places in what is now southern Ohio. (3) Mounds made by other groups are found in Indiana, Michigan, Illinois, Wisconsin, Iowa, Missouri, and Canada. (4) The Adena buried most of their dead in simple graves within the mounds, covering the bodies with dirt and stone. (5) Leaders and other important people from the village were buried in log tombs before being covered with dirt and stones. (6) Gifts were often placed in the tombs. (7) A pipe made of clay or stone was a usual gift placed in the tombs. (8) Grave Creek Mound is one of the largest mounds built by the Adena. (9) At about seventy feet high, it is a mysteriously beautiful monument.

1. Which of the following research questions does the information in this paragraph best answer?
   A Why did the Adena build mounds?
   B How were the Adena leaders chosen?
   C When did the Adena build mounds?
   D Who are the other mound builders?

2. If the student wanted to add a fact to develop this paragraph, which of the following sentences would be most appropriate for a research report?
   F I saw a burial mound in Hillsboro, Ohio.
   G The mounds should be protected.
   H The Adena began to build mounds around 700 B.C.
   J It is amazing to think how the mounds were built.

3. If you were revising this paragraph to improve the coherence, which sentence might you delete or move to another paragraph?

   A 1
   B 3
   C 5
   D 8

4. Which of the following transitional words might be added to the beginning of sentence 5 to show the contrast of ideas between sentence 4 and sentence 5?
   F Therefore,
   G Finally,
   H Next,
   J However,

5. If you were to give the information above in a research presentation, which of the following visual displays would best support sentence 9?
   A a drawing of a clay or stone pipe
   B maps of the United States and Canada
   C a time line showing when mounds were built
   D a photograph of Grave Creek Mound

(Standards reviewed on this page: W1.0, 1.6, 2.3a, 2.3b; L&S 1.6. To read the standards, see pp. 576–577.)

Answers

1. A
2. H
3. B
4. J
5. D

APPLICATION

Social Studies
"The California Gold Rush" explores some of the reasons why people move from place to place. Discuss the article and have students brainstorm other reasons why people move. For homework, encourage them to research and report on either a historical migration, such as the westward expansion, or a current population shift, such as migration to the Sunbelt states. If possible, coordinate the research with the social studies teacher, who may be able to provide resources for students' research. **HOMEWORK**

EXTENSION

Listening and Speaking
Have students form a TV news team with two other classmates. Students can choose a local event on which to give an oral report. They might choose a holiday parade, a school basketball game, or a parent-teacher organization meeting. Each person on the team should attend the event and take notes. Then, the group should choose one member to present the report as if he or she were a reporter on a TV news program.

RESOURCES

Research

Assessment
- *Progress Assessment of Writing, Listening, & Speaking,* Wkshp. 4
- *Diagnostic and Summative Assessments,* Third-Quarter Test

Extension
- *Writing, Listening, & Speaking,* p. 100

Workshop 5 Persuasion

Program Organization

Holt Literature and Language Arts provides a complete curriculum for standards-based instruction in vocabulary, reading, literature, writing, speaking and listening, and media. The instructional content of the program is divided into quarters to enable teachers to anticipate and administer the quarterly assessments required by California.

About Workshop 5

Standards-based lesson plans and suggestions for linking instruction with Workshop 5 and the related instructional material are provided in *On Course: Mapping Instruction.*

- Workshop 5 focuses on using persuasion in writing and speaking and on the listening skills needed to evaluate a persuasive essay. Chapter 8 connects to this workshop by focusing on supporting a thesis in literary criticism.

- The related instructional material for Workshop 5 is shown on the chart. This related instructional material will also be covered on the fourth quarterly assessment. Specific teaching suggestions for the related material are found in Part 1 of this book and in the *Holt Handbook.*

Holt Literature and Language Arts

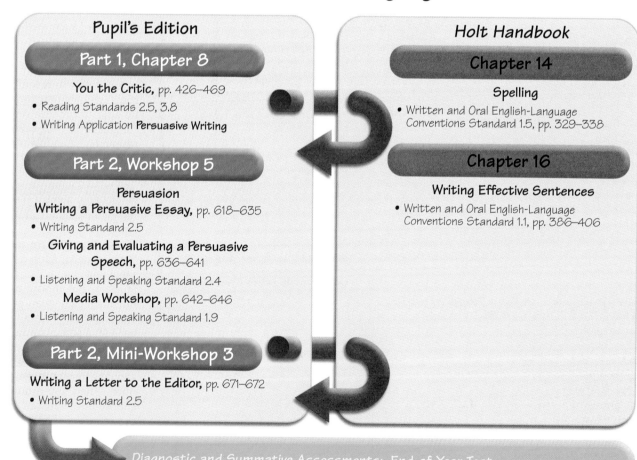

Pupil's Edition

Part 1, Chapter 8

You the Critic, pp. 426–469
- Reading Standards 2.5, 3.8
- Writing Application **Persuasive Writing**

Part 2, Workshop 5

Persuasion
Writing a Persuasive Essay, pp. 618–635
- Writing Standard 2.5
  Giving and Evaluating a Persuasive Speech, pp. 636–641
- Listening and Speaking Standard 2.4
  Media Workshop, pp. 642–646
- Listening and Speaking Standard 1.9

Part 2, Mini-Workshop 3

Writing a Letter to the Editor, pp. 671–672
- Writing Standard 2.5

Holt Handbook

Chapter 14

Spelling
- Written and Oral English-Language Conventions Standard 1.5, pp. 329–338

Chapter 16

Writing Effective Sentences
- Written and Oral English-Language Conventions Standard 1.1, pp. 386–406

Diagnostic and Summative Assessments: End-of-Year Test

Language Arts Content

This workshop uses the writing and listening and speaking strategies to enable students to master successfully the writing and speaking applications.

What standards are taught in Workshop 5?

In this workshop, students will master the following Grade 6 standards. They will also review several standards from an earlier grade.

Writing Strategies

1.0 Students write clear, coherent, and focused essays. The writing exhibits awareness of audience and purpose. Students progress through the writing process.

1.1 Choose the form of writing that best suits the intended purpose.

1.3 Use a variety of effective and coherent organizational patterns.

1.5 Compose documents with appropriate formatting by using word-processing skills and principles of design.

1.6 Revise writing to improve the organization and consistency of ideas within and between paragraphs.

Writing Applications

2.0 Students write persuasive texts of at least 500 words. Writing demonstrates a command of standard English and strategies outlined in Writing Standard 1.0.

2.2d Offer persuasive evidence to validate arguments and conclusions as needed.

2.5 Write persuasive compositions.

Listening and Speaking Strategies

1.0 Students deliver focused, coherent presentations that convey ideas clearly and relate to the background and interests of the audience.

1.1 Relate the speaker's verbal communication to the nonverbal message.

1.2 Identify the tone, mood, and emotion conveyed in the oral communication.

1.4 Select a focus, an organizational structure, and a point of view, matching the purpose, message, occasion, and vocal modulation to the audience.

1.5 Emphasize salient points to assist the listener in following the main ideas and concepts.

1.6 Support opinions with detailed evidence and with visual or media displays that use appropriate technology.

1.7 Use effective rate, volume, pitch, and tone, and align nonverbal elements to sustain audience interest and attention.

1.8 Analyze the use of rhetorical devices. Student speaking demonstrates a command of standard American English and the organizational and delivery strategies outlined in Listening and Speaking Standard 1.0.

1.9 Identify persuasive and propaganda techniques used in television, and identify false and misleading information.

Speaking Applications

2.0 Students deliver well-organized formal presentations employing traditional rhetorical strategies.

2.4 Deliver persuasive presentations.

Review Standards, Grade 5

Writing

2.4 Write persuasive letters or compositions.

Listening and Speaking

1.4 Organize information to achieve particular purposes and to appeal to the background and interests of the audience.

1.5 Clarify and support spoken ideas with evidence and examples.

Persuasion   Workshop 5   615B

Mastering the California Standards WORKSHOP 5

Instructional Planning and Support

Where do I locate lesson plans, additional resources, and other teaching aids?

- The Annotated Teacher's Edition and *On Course: Mapping Instruction* provide direction in planning and implementing a complete California standards–based curriculum. These components include instructions for administering diagnostic, progress, and summative tests; for presenting instruction of the standards; for differentiating instruction to provide universal access; and for locating and using the program's ancillaries.

- The program's resources are referenced at the beginning of each workshop in the bottom margin of this teacher's edition: Writing a Persuasive Essay and Giving and Evaluating a Persuasive Speech.

- Reminders for using additional resources appear in this teacher's edition at point of use.

- The *One-Stop Planner* CD-ROM contains editable lesson plans and all print ancillaries, available in PDF format.

What if I don't have time to teach all of Workshop 5?

- Within this workshop, complete coverage of the application standards is provided by the following instructional features in the Pupil's Edition:
  - Writing a Persuasive Essay
  - Choose an Issue
  - Consider Audience and Purpose
  - Addressing Counterarguments
  - Develop Reasons and Evidence
  - A Writer's Framework
  - Proofread Your Essay
  - Giving and Evaluating a Persuasive Speech
  - Relevant Reasons and Evidence
  - Putting It All Together

- Use Standards Practice and Review for a quick assessment and review of workshop standards.

What provisions have been made for students who have additional class time scheduled in language arts?

- *Universal Access: Writing, Listening, & Speaking,* Workshop 5 contains worksheets and transparencies that provide practice, reteaching, and extension of Workshop 5 standards. Each Practice and Apply exercise is supported by graphic organizers or practice activities for on-level learners, advanced learners, and learners having difficulty.

- *Universal Access: Lesson Plans for Language Development,* Workshop 5, provides alternative teaching strategies and additional worksheets designed specifically for English-language learners and special education students. Many of the suggestions and activities in this ancillary will also be helpful to students in the regular classroom who are having difficulty with particular skills.

Universal Access

How do I differentiate instruction to ensure that all my students master the standards?

Holt Literature and Language Arts provides comprehensive, differentiated instruction for all types of students.

- Most of the general instruction and teaching strategies in the Annotated Teacher's Edition are at grade level. These instructions will work well with the majority of your students.

- Advanced students have at least one activity for each workshop. The suggested activities are found in this teacher's edition at point of instruction. Point-of-use suggestions for learners having difficulty, English-language learners, and special education students are provided.

- *Universal Access: Writing, Listening,& Speaking,* Workshop 5, opens with Teaching Notes that suggest which worksheets and transparencies are appropriate for each of three levels of learners.

- *Universal Access: Lesson Plans for Language Development,* Workshop 5, offers teaching strategies and additional worksheets designed specifically for English-language learners and special education students.

- *Daily Language Activities Transparencies* and *Spelling: Lessons & Activities* provide ongoing review of and additional practice in a range of language arts skills.

- For every workshop, preselected Web sites and activities are available to provide enrichment, independent practice, and enhanced instructional opportunities.

Assessment

How do I determine whether or not my students are making progress in mastering the standards?

Progress Assessment

- Use the Standards Review at the end of Workshop 5 for an informal assessment of the writing and listening standards taught in Workshop 5.

- Use Workshop 5 in *Progress Assessment of Writing, Listening, & Speaking* to test students' cumulative progress in mastering the standards taught in the workshop.

Summative Assessment

The content in *Holt Literature and Language Arts* has been divided into four quarters to allow you to administer the four summative tests required by California. Workshop 5 will be assessed in the fourth quarter of instruction. At the end of Workshop 5, you may ask students to take the End-of-Year Test in the *Diagnostic & Summative Assessments* booklet.

Persuasion

Persuasion—convincing others to believe or do something—comes in many forms. A friend's spoken request, such as asking to borrow a CD, is usually casual and unplanned. The kind of persuasion you read and write, however, is so carefully constructed that it is sometimes called an art. In this workshop you will write a persuasive essay and give a persuasive speech. You will also analyze persuasive messages on TV. In the process you will practice these language arts standards.

STANDARDS FOCUS

Writing

Prerequisite Standards

Grade 5

- 2.4 Write persuasive letters or compositions:

  a. State a clear position in support of a proposal.

  b. Support a position with relevant evidence.

  c. Follow a simple organizational pattern.

  d. Address reader concerns.

Standards Coming Up in the Next Level

Grade 7

- 2.4 Write persuasive compositions:

  a. State a clear position or perspective in support of a proposition or proposal.

  b. Describe the points in support of the proposition, employing well-articulated evidence.

  c. Anticipate and address reader concerns and counterarguments.

WRITING WORKSHOP

Writing a Persuasive Essay Page 618

LISTENING AND SPEAKING WORKSHOP

Giving and Evaluating a Persuasive Speech Page 636

MEDIA WORKSHOP

Analyzing Propaganda on TV Page 642

GO TO: go.hrw.com
KEYWORD: HLLA6 W-5
FOR: Models, Writer's Guides, and Reference Sources

California Standards

Writing

1.0 Students write clear, coherent, and focused essays. The writing exhibits students' awareness of the audience and purpose. Essays contain formal introductions, supporting evidence, and conclusions. Students progress through the stages of the writing process as needed.

1.1 Choose the form of writing (e.g., letter to the editor) that best suits the intended purpose.

1.3 Use a variety of effective and coherent organizational patterns, including arrangement by order of importance.

1.6 Revise writing to improve the organization and consistency of ideas within and between paragraphs.

2.0 Students write persuasive texts of at least 500 to 700 words. Student writing demonstrates a command of standard American English and the research, organizational, and drafting strategies outlined in Writing Standard 1.0.

2.2 d. Offer persuasive evidence to validate arguments and conclusions as needed.

2.5 Write persuasive compositions:

   a. State a clear position on a proposition or proposal.

   b. Support the position with organized and relevant evidence.

   c. Anticipate and address reader concerns and counterarguments.

Listening and Speaking

1.0 Students deliver focused, coherent presentations that convey ideas clearly and relate to the background and interests of the audience. They evaluate the content of oral communication.

1.1 Relate the speaker's verbal communication (e.g., pitch, tone) to the nonverbal message (e.g., posture, gesture).

1.2 Identify the tone conveyed in the oral communication.

1.4 Select a focus, an organizational structure, and a point of view, matching the purpose, message, occasion, and vocal modulation to the audience.

1.5 Emphasize salient points to assist the listener in following the main ideas and concepts.

1.6 Support opinions with detailed evidence and with visual or media displays that use appropriate technology.

1.7 Use effective rate, volume, pitch, and tone and align nonverbal elements to sustain audience interest and attention.

1.8 Analyze the use of rhetorical devices (e.g., cadence, repetitive patterns, use of onomatopoeia) for intent and effect.

1.9 Identify persuasive and propaganda techniques used in television and identify false and misleading information.

2.0 Students deliver well-organized formal presentations employing traditional rhetorical strategies (e.g., persuasion). Student speaking demonstrates a command of standard American English and the organizational and delivery strategies outlined in Listening and Speaking Standard 1.0.

2.4 Deliver persuasive presentations:
  a. Provide a clear statement of the position.
  b. Include relevant evidence.
  c. Offer a logical sequence of information.
  d. Engage the listener and foster acceptance of the proposition or proposal.

Listening and Speaking

Prerequisite Standards

Grade 5

- 1.4 Select a focus, organizational structure, and point of view for an oral presentation.
- 1.5 Clarify and support spoken ideas with evidence and examples.

Standards Coming Up in the Next Level

Grade 7

- 1.4 Organize information to achieve particular purposes and to appeal to the background and interests of the audience.
- 1.5 Arrange supporting details, reasons, descriptions, and examples effectively and persuasively in relation to the audience.
- 2.4 Deliver persuasive presentations:
  a. State a clear position or perspective in support of an argument or proposal.
  b. Describe the points in support of the argument and employ well-articulated evidence.

CALIFORNIA STANDARDS

Writing Workshop

PRETEACHING

Standards Starter

Motivate. Ask students if they have ever convinced someone to take them somewhere or to help them do something. Have students work in pairs to reenact such a scene and to identify what they did or said that convinced the other person.

Introducing the Workshop.

To introduce the workshop, use the Journal Warm-up, Transparency 16, in *Writing, Listening, & Speaking*.

Quotation for the Day

"The chief danger in life is that you may take too many precautions."

(Alfred Adler, 1870–1937, Austrian psychiatrist)

Write the quotation on the chalkboard, and have students reflect on it by freewriting. Ask volunteers to share their thoughts. Point out that Adler is suggesting that people are often too afraid to take a stand. Briefly discuss with students how taking a stand can be a brave and exciting act.

WHAT'S AHEAD?

In this workshop you will write a persuasive essay. You will also learn how to

- state a clear position on a proposition or proposal
- support your position with relevant reasons and evidence
- address reader concerns
- eliminate stringy sentences
- punctuate possessives correctly

| DO THIS ➤

Reference Note

For more information on creating a **think sheet**, see page 495.

Writing a Persuasive Essay

When you were younger, did you ever try to **persuade,** or convince, someone to get you a special gift, such as a bicycle or video game? How did you go about persuading them? Did your efforts work? If so, you probably already know quite a bit about the art of persuasion.

Now that you are older, you have probably learned that persuasion can achieve more important results than a new bike. In fact, persuasion is one of the most effective tools you can use to make a difference in your world. In this workshop you will write a persuasive essay that can help you make positive changes in your school, neighborhood, or community.

Professional Model: A Persuasive Essay

Reading published persuasive essays can help you understand how writers use evidence to support their positions. The writer of the following essay, "The U.S. Has a Garbage Crisis," has a point to make. Can you figure out what it is?

As you read the essay, create a **think sheet,** making note of the writer's position, support the writer provides for his position, and the writer's responses to objections that some readers might have. Also, answer on your own paper the numbered analysis questions that appear next to the essay. These questions will help you create your think sheet.

Writing 2.5 Write persuasive compositions.

WORKSHOP RESOURCES

Writing Workshop

Planning

- *On Course: Mapping Instruction*
- *One-Stop Planner* CD-ROM
- *At Home: In Five Languages*
- *Writing, Listening, & Speaking* —Teaching Notes, p. 101

Differentiating Instruction

- *Lesson Plans for Language Development,* pp. 236–237
- *Supporting Instruction in Five Languages*

Practice

- *Writing, Listening, & Speaking,* Wkshp. 5

from The Environment:
Distinguishing Between Fact and Opinion

The U.S. Has a
GARBAGE CRISIS

BY WILLIAM DUDLEY

1   America is a "throwaway" society. Each year Americans throw away 16 billion disposable diapers, 1.6 billion pens, and 220 million tires. For the sake of convenience, we tend to throw these and other used goods away rather than repair or recycle them. The average American household generates 350 bags, or 4,550 gallons, of garbage per year. This comes out to a total of 160 million tons of garbage a year. We have to change our throwaway lifestyle before we are buried in it.

2   We are running out of places to put all the garbage we produce. About 80 percent of it is now buried in landfills. There are 6,000 landfills currently operating, but many of them are becoming full. The Environmental Protection Agency estimates that one-half of the remaining landfills will run out of space and close within the next five to ten years.

3   Can we simply build new landfills to replace the old ones? The answer is no. For one thing, we are running out of space. We cannot afford to use up land that is needed for farms, parks, and homes.

4   In addition, many landfills contain toxic[1] chemicals that can leak into and pollute underground water supplies. In New York City, over seventy-five wells had to be closed because of such toxic waste poisoning.

5   One suggested alternative to landfills is to burn the trash. In some states, large incinerators are used to burn garbage, and the heat that is generated is used to produce electricity. But this solution has drawbacks. Burning trash pollutes the air with dioxin and mercury, which are highly poisonous. Furthermore, burning does not completely solve the landfill problem. Leftover ash produced by burning is often highly toxic, and it still has to be buried somewhere.

---

1. **toxic:** poisonous.

1. What position does the writer express in this paragraph?

2. What reason does the writer give in this paragraph?

3. What alternative to landfills does the writer object to in paragraph 5?

4. What evidence supports the writer's reason that there are problems with burning trash?

DIRECT TEACHING

Professional Model

As students read, have them jot down any unusual facts that interest them or questions that they would like to explore further.

Explain to students that using think sheets to summarize their notes from a reading serves two purposes. First, creating think sheets allows students to place their thoughts, observations, and questions on paper, which, in turn, helps increase reading comprehension. The process of creating think sheets also provides students with ideas for their own writing.

Professional Model Questions

Answers

1. The writer's position is that Americans need to change their lifestyles so they do not throw away so much garbage.

2. He says there is less space to put garbage. Many landfills are almost full, and others will be full within the next five to ten years.

3. The writer objects to the alternative of burning trash.

4. Burning trash leads to air pollution and it produces toxic ash, which needs to be buried.

Reinforcement
- *Daily Language Activities*
- *Spelling*

Evaluation and Assessment
- *Test Generator (One-Stop Planner* CD-ROM)
- *Progress Assessment of Writing, Listening, & Speaking,* Wkshp. 5

- *Diagnostic and Summative Assessments,* End-of-Year Test

Internet
- go.hrw.com
  (keyword: HLLA6 W-5)

Answers continued

5. The quotation serves as a reason that proves the writer's point: Many people do not think that "the amount of garbage we produce" causes problems.

DIRECT TEACHING

Professional Model

You may ask students to identify the purpose and audience for the persuasive essay "The U.S. Has a Garbage Crisis." Students should explain their answers. [Possible purposes are to persuade or to inform. Based on the vocabulary and sentence structure, the intended audience is probably adults or mature readers. However, students could argue that anyone who throws away garbage is the target audience for the essay.]

6   The only real solution to the garbage crisis is for Americans to reduce the amount of trash they throw away. There are two methods of doing this. One is recycling—reusing garbage. Bottles can be washed and reused. Aluminum cans can be melted down and remade. Currently in the U.S., only 11 percent of solid waste is used again as something else. Japan, on the other hand, recycles about half of its trash. Environmentalist Barry Commoner estimates that we can reduce 70 percent of our garbage by recycling.

7   We must also reduce the amount of garbage we produce in the first place. We should use less plastic, which is hard to recycle and does not decompose[2] in landfills. Much garbage is useless packaging. Consumers should buy foods and goods that use less packaging. We also should buy reusable products rather than things that are used once and thrown away. . . .

8   A woman in California was asked about garbage. She replied, "Why do we need to change anything? I put my garbage out on the sidewalk and they take it away." Attitudes like hers must be changed. We have to face the inevitable question posed by Ed Repa, manager of the solid waste disposal program at the National Solid Waste Management Association: "How do you throw something away when there is no 'away'?"

5. How does the quotation from a woman in California help the writer support his position?

2. decompose: break down into basic parts.

Working with a partner, discuss the following questions and write down your responses.

1. What parts of the essay were most convincing to you? What parts were least convincing? Why?

2. How does the writer respond to possible objections that the audience might have? What sort of support does he offer for his responses?

3. What two specific solutions does the writer propose? How does he support those solutions?

4. Create a graphic organizer such as the one below, filling it in with examples from the first five paragraphs of the article.

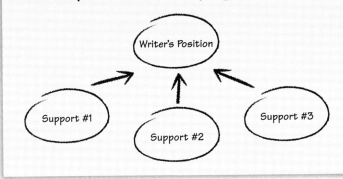

Prewriting

Choose an Issue

Dare to Care   Given a choice between soup or sandwiches for lunch, you might answer, "I don't care." For you, the kind of food you choose to eat is not an issue. In persuasive writing, though, *issues* are important. An **issue** is a topic with at least two sides about which people disagree. **In a persuasive essay the writer tries to make the reader agree with his or her position, or opinion, on an issue.** Persuasive essays also may ask readers to take action on an issue.

KEY CONCEPT

 Writing 1.0 Students progress through the stages of the writing process as needed.

Choose an Issue   **621**

Think About the Model

Answers
Possible answers are suggested below.

1. Most convincing: the exact numbers of diapers, pens, and tires thrown away and information about toxic waste poisoning. Least convincing: the uninformed attitudes of people who do not understand that there is a garbage crisis. The statistics helped me imagine the huge amount of waste. The toxic waste information convinced me that even I could be in danger.

2. The writer responds by asking an expert. The expert, Ed Repa, asks a question that reminds us that we cannot throw anything away. We must find a way to deal with the tons of garbage.

3. The author suggests reducing the amount of garbage by recycling and also by reducing the amount of garbage produced. The first solution is supported through facts and statistics. The second solution is supported through facts.

4. **Writer's Position:** Americans need to stop throwing away so much garbage.

   Support #1: There are fewer places to dispose of garbage—we are running out of landfill space.

   Support #2: We can't create more landfills because land is needed for farming, parks and homes.

   Support #3: Landfills pollute water with chemicals that leak underground.

   Support #4: We shouldn't burn trash because it gives off poisonous pollutants.

Integrating with Grammar, Usage, and Mechanics

As students start their persuasive essays, you may want to stop and review transitive and intransitive verbs and end marks, because these are concepts with which students often have trouble. See the Parts of Speech Overview and Punctuation chapters in the *Holt Handbook.*

DIFFERENTIATING INSTRUCTION

Special Education Students

You may need to give some students additional guidance in selecting issues that are neither too broad nor too narrow. Ask students to identify topics related to their issues. If they can list three or four topics, then their subjects are probably specific enough and can be covered adequately in a short persuasive letter. If students can list more than four or fewer than three topics, then their issues are probably too broad or too narrow.

 Resources Reminder

For more help with Special Education Students, see *Lesson Plans for Language Development.*

PRACTICE & APPLY 1

Guided and Independent Practice

Have students discuss issues and potential opinion statements with a partner. You can monitor progress by circulating among the pairs and working individually with students who need assistance with clarifying either their issues or their opinions. Then, assign **Practice and Apply 1** for independent practice.

TIP Make sure you choose an issue that gets people fired up, not just a topic. For example, "school hours" is a topic that can be explained, while "making the school day longer" is an issue about which many people disagree. Your issue should also be one that will maintain your readers' interest throughout a 500- to 700-word essay.

| KEY CONCEPT

TIP An opinion statement may also be called a **proposition** or a **thesis statement.**

Take Your Pick The issue you choose should be one that is important to you. If you do not feel strongly about an issue, how can you convince your readers to care about it? Ask yourself what issues most affect your world. Completing the following sentence starters will help you identify issues that matter to you.

My community would be a better place if _____.

I become upset when I see _____.

Little by Little You should choose an issue that is small enough for a local group to have an effect. For example, one student chose the issue of littering. Although she also felt strongly about the issue of homelessness, she felt that by taking on a smaller issue, she would be better able to make a difference. She also knew that choosing a local issue would make it easier for her to get real results and to find support for her ideas. Finally, she knew that an anti-littering campaign for her community soccer league would be an issue she could tackle in a clear, **focused** essay.

Write Your Opinion Statement

Take a Stand If you have chosen an issue that is important to you, you probably already know what your opinion on it is. You simply need to put that opinion into words. **An opinion statement should clearly state the issue and the writer's position on it.** Here is how one writer came up with her opinion statement.

> **issue:** litter at soccer games
>
> **+ how I feel about it:** soccer fields should be kept free of litter
>
> **opinion statement:** We need to start an anti-littering campaign to keep the soccer fields clean.

PRACTICE & APPLY 1

Choose an Issue, and Write an Opinion Statement

Brainstorm issues that might make your community a better place. Choose an issue that is both important to you and small enough to have an effect locally. Then, put the issue and your opinion together into a single clear sentence—your opinion statement.

Writing 1.0 Students write focused essays. 2.0 Students write persuasive texts of at least 500 to 700 words. 2.5a State a clear position on a proposition.

RESOURCES

Practice and Apply 1
Guided Practice
■ *Writing, Listening, & Speaking,* WS. p. 102

Reteaching and Modeling
■ *Writing, Listening, & Speaking,* TP. 17

Reinforcement
■ *Writing, Listening, & Speaking,* WS. p. 103

Practice and Apply 2
Guided Practice
■ *Writing, Listening, & Speaking,* WS. p. 104

Consider Purpose and Audience

To Whom It Concerns   Your **purpose** for writing a persuasive essay is to persuade your readers to care about the issue and do something about it. In persuasive writing, your specific purpose— exactly what you want your essay to accomplish—determines a great deal about what information you will include and how you will express your ideas to readers. Your purpose also helps you identify your audience.

Addressing your request, or proposal, to the right audience is an important part of your essay's effectiveness. Your **audience** should be a group of people who are interested in your issue and who also have the power to do what you want done. Although these people share your interest in the issue, they will not necessarily agree with your position on the issue. Notice how one student used the following questions to help identify her specific audience.

◄———— KEY CONCEPT

What part of your community does the issue involve?	Starting an anti-littering campaign at the soccer fields would involve the players, parents, and organizers of my soccer league.
What do you know about these people? (How old are they? What interests or concerns them?)	They are my peers and adults who are interested in soccer. I think they are all interested in keeping things running smoothly. They are also concerned about keeping fees low for players, so they may object to my idea if they think it will be expensive.

TIP   To achieve your purpose, you must be careful not to reverse your position. Instead, maintain a **consistent point of view**. For example, the student whose essay is modeled throughout this workshop would *not* argue that an anti-littering campaign is too much effort. However, the student could offer solutions to her audience's concern that an anti-littering campaign would be expensive. (For more on **audience concerns,** see page 624.)

PRACTICE & APPLY 2   **Consider Purpose and Audience**

Your purpose is to persuade readers to support your position. Use the questions in the chart above to figure out who that group of people is and to think about what you know about them.

Writing   1.0 The writing exhibits students' awareness of the audience and purpose.   **2.5c** Anticipate and address reader concerns and counterarguments.

Consider Purpose and Audience   **623**

Guided Practice

(For independent practice, see Resources below.)

Answers

Possible answers follow.

1. Possible counterargument: The principal is worried that the students involved with the after-school tutoring sessions will miss their transportation home. **Possible reason:** To ensure that students will not miss their transportation, tutors will be responsible for keeping sessions on schedule.

2. Possible counterargument: Parents might object to their children working with an individual that the parents do not know. **Possible reason:** To address parents' concerns, the school could provide an opportunity for parents to meet the tutors.

3. Possible counterargument: The older students might object to the extra time required to tutor. **Possible reason:** To provide additional motivation, tutors will receive extra credit for volunteering their time.

MINI-LESSON CRITICAL THINKING

Addressing Counterarguments

Imagine sweltering under the hot summer sun at the beach when a vendor selling mugs of steaming hot chocolate comes along. Are you tempted to buy? Of course not. The vendor has forgotten the basic rule of persuasion: **Appeal to your audience's concerns.** Once you know *your* audience's concerns, you can predict their main **counterargument,** or reason why they might disagree with you. Counterarguments often revolve around how much time or effort a proposed change would take, or how much the change would cost. By appealing to your audience's interests, you can make counterarguments such as these seem much less important.

TIP A counterargument is also called an objection.

THINKING IT THROUGH **Addressing Counterarguments**

You want to persuade the city council and community members to support a Latino cultural festival. Here's how to address their counterargument.

▶ **STEP 1** Identify the main reason your audience might disagree with you.

They might say that having a Latino cultural festival would be expensive.

▶ **STEP 2** Consider what is important to this audience.

- saving money
- bringing people together

▶ **STEP 3** Based on your audience's interests, identify a reason for your opinion that makes the audience's counterargument seem less important.

The festival can bring people together, and it can be inexpensive. To save money, volunteers can organize the festival, and vendors can pay a fee to sell food and crafts.

PRACTICE

You want to organize a tutoring program at your school. Older students would tutor younger students for one hour after school. Using the Thinking It Through steps above, identify a possible counterargument each of the audiences to the right might have. Then, list reasons that would address each audience's counterargument. Explain each reason.

1. the school principal
2. parents
3. students who would serve as tutors

Writing 2.5c Anticipate and address reader concerns and counterarguments.

RESOURCES

Mini-lesson: Critical Thinking

Independent Practice

- *Writing, Listening, & Speaking,* WS. p. 105

Develop Reasons and Evidence

Answering the Big Question Understanding your audience's interests will help you to answer their main question—"Why should I care?" **Your audience will want to know why they should accept your opinion.** You can answer their question by developing reasons and evidence.

◄ KEY CONCEPT

Building a Case Have you ever tried to build a human pyramid? The base of the pyramid needs to have more people, and stronger people, than the top does. Look at the following diagram of a persuasive essay. Notice that it looks like a pyramid.

The opinion in a persuasive essay is like the person at the top of a human pyramid. The *reasons* are like the people in the middle row. The *evidence* is like the group of people who form the base of a human pyramid. Persuasive writing must have support to be strong, just as a human pyramid needs strong supporters.

Reasons A **reason** explains *why* the writer holds a particular opinion. In a persuasive essay the writer will usually write one or two paragraphs supporting each reason.

Evidence The support for each reason is called **evidence,** the specific *facts* and *examples* that illustrate the reason. A **fact** is a statement that can be proved true, such as "Our soccer season is fifteen games long." An **example** is an event or illustration that shows one specific instance of a reason, for example, "On Saturday I saw a lot of trash on the ground at the soccer fields." The evidence you use to support your reasons may come from your own experience or from **research** on your issue.

> **TIP** Make sure your facts and examples are **relevant,** or clearly connected to the reasons.
> REASON: Sixth-graders should have their own dance *because dances provide a safe way to have fun.*
> IRRELEVANT EVIDENCE: Our school has funds for dances.
> RELEVANT EVIDENCE: The school has funds to hire an off-duty officer for safety at school dances.

 Writing 1.0 Essays contain supporting evidence. 2.0 Student writing demonstrates the research strategies outlined in Writing Standard 1.0. 2.2d Offer persuasive evidence to validate arguments and conclusions as needed. 2.5b Support the position with relevant evidence.

Develop Reasons and Evidence **625**

DIRECT TEACHING

Develop Reasons and Evidence

As students develop reasons and evidence, have them use a visual organizer such as the following to help them shape their body paragraphs.

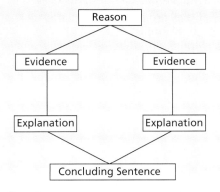

DIRECT TEACHING

Evidence

You may consider having group members work collaboratively to evaluate each other's supporting evidence. Arrange students in randomly assigned groups of five or six. Students may use the following questions to determine the appeal of each other's supporting evidence for a particular audience:

- Does the evidence suggest that the audience's life will be improved?
- Does the evidence suggest that the audience will save money or time?
- Does the evidence suggest that the audience will feel better?

Group members should provide feedback and discuss any points that are unclear.

Advanced Learners W2.5

Enrichment. Some students may want to contact outside sources in person for information about their topics. For example, if students are writing to the city council to address a particular issue, they might visit a city council meeting to see how decisions are made. If they are trying to convince the school administration to have a food drive, students might visit a local food bank to discover what the food needs are and how food is distributed.

You may want to obtain permission from parents or guardians and from the parties students intend to contact before beginning work on this assignment.

DIRECT TEACHING

Develop Reasons and Evidence W2.0

Students may need to perform research to find evidence to support their opinions. Some additional sources they may consult include a local library, CD ROM's, or experts on a particular issue.

Please be aware that Internet resources are sometimes public forums and their content can be unpredictable.

PRACTICE & APPLY 3

Guided and Independent Practice

Monitor student progress by spot-checking to see that each student has listed at least two reasons and that each reason is supported by evidence and an explanation of why the evidence is convincing. Then, assign **Practice and Apply 3** for independent practice.

In the chart below, a student lists reasons and evidence to begin an anti-littering campaign. In the right-hand column, she decides whether the support for her opinion will appeal to her audience.

Reasons	Supporting Evidence	Appealing to Audience?
Make people aware of the trash problem	My parents had to pick up trash left by others. That made them be more careful not to litter.	Yes. Most people want to enjoy the games and not worry about litter.
Earn money	By recycling, we can earn 32 cents for each pound of cans. This money can help pay for coaching clinics.	Yes. If we pay for clinics with recycling money, the league won't have to raise fees to cover these things.
Help players earn badges in Scouts	I can earn 2 badges.	No. This will help only a few of us.

From the chart above, you can tell that this student realized that the last reason might not appeal to everyone in her audience. The student thought about counterarguments her audience might have. Then, she came up with a new reason that addresses one concern.

New Reason	Supporting Evidence	Appealing to Audience?
Will not take much time or effort	Parents and players will make posters and collect the recycling containers.	Yes. This reason shows that picking up trash and recycling is not too much trouble, which I think might be their main concern.

PRACTICE & APPLY 3 — Develop Reasons and Evidence

Create a chart like the first one above, listing reasons and evidence to support your opinion. (Use your experiences, the library, or the Internet to find facts to support your reasons.) Also, decide whether each reason will appeal to your audience. Replace any reasons that will not appeal to most of your audience.

Writing 2.0 Student writing demonstrates the research strategies outlined in Writing Standard 1.0. 2.5c Anticipate and address reader concerns and counterarguments.

RESOURCES

Practice and Apply 3

Guided Practice

■ *Writing, Listening, & Speaking,* WS. p. 106

Practice and Apply 4

Guided Practice

■ *Writing, Listening, & Speaking,* WS. p. 107

Write a Call to Action

911 Means Action! When you dial 911, you are asking for help. In a way, your persuasive essay is also a 911 call because it includes a *call to action*. **A call to action tells readers how they can respond to your ideas.** To get your readers to take action, your call to action must be both *reasonable* and *specific*.

◀ KEY CONCEPT

A **reasonable** request is financially possible and within the audience's power. There is no point in asking an audience to spend trillions of dollars to end all wars. Instead, your call to action should focus on smaller actions, such as signing a petition or volunteering a few hours of time.

A **specific** request is clear and tells exactly what you want readers to do about an issue. How can a reader tell whether "Please do more for our children" is a call for more sidewalks or for a new playground? The specific call to action, "Start a tutoring program for elementary students," would be more effective.

THINKING IT THROUGH — Writing a Call to Action

Here is how to write a reasonable and specific call to action.

TIP A call to action may also be called a **proposal**.

STEP 1 Decide exactly what action you want to take place.	I want to see trash picked up and cans recycled at our soccer games.
STEP 2 State the call to action in specific terms.	I can ask the league to get recycling containers and put them at the soccer fields.
STEP 3 Address your call to action directly to the audience.	"The league should buy and place recycling bins for aluminum cans at the soccer fields. Then, we should ask teams to participate in the anti-littering campaign."

PRACTICE & APPLY 4 — Write a Call to Action

Use the steps above to write a reasonable and specific **call to action**. Remember that a call to action is a request, so be polite.

Writing 2.5a State a clear position on a proposal.

Write a Call to Action **627**

CRITICAL THINKING
Ask students to bring in examples of advertisements that have calls to action. Display the ads, and arrange the students in randomly assigned groups of five or six. Each group should choose and analyze one ad. Direct groups to identify the call to action and then decide whether it is reasonable and specific. If the call is not specific, you might ask the group to suggest ways to reword or revise it to make it specific.

PRACTICE & APPLY 4

Guided and Independent Practice
Offer students the following checklist to evaluate their own or a peer's call to action.

- Is the call reasonable or does it ask too much?
- What action does the call expect?
- How will the call motivate the audience?

Monitor students' progress by collecting these checklists and making sure each question is adequately answered. Schedule miniconferences with students who do not have adequate answers. Then, assign **Practice and Apply 4** for independent practice.

A Writer's Framework

Persuasive Essay

DIRECT TEACHING

REVIEW STANDARDS

Persuasive Essay
The following activity is a review of the 5th-grade **Writing Standard 2.4.**

Suggest that students form groups to collaborate on an essay. Students should state a clear position that reflects the group members' shared opinions. Following the plan in the framework on this page, students should collaboratively decide on relevant evidence to support their group's position. Finally, each member should read the essay for sense.

PRACTICE & APPLY 5

Guided and Independent Practice

Before students complete **Practice and Apply 5** for independent practice, use a sample topic to guide them through the framework. After students have completed their first drafts, have them annotate their drafts in the margins to show how each paragraph of their draft corresponds to a step of the framework. Use students' marginal notes to help you monitor their progress.

Introduction

- Attention-grabbing opening
- Opinion statement

Body

- Reason #1
  Evidence supporting reason #1
- Reason #2
  Evidence supporting reason #2
  and so on

Conclusion

- Summary of reasons
- Call to action

Grab your readers' interest right away with an **interesting beginning.** For example, you could begin your essay with an anecdote (a brief story) or a question. Next, include a clear **opinion statement** that tells your audience exactly what you think about the issue you have chosen. (For more information on writing **introductions,** see page 655.)

- Support your opinion and address your readers' **counterarguments** with at least two good reasons. Write a **paragraph for each reason.** You can arrange your body paragraphs in **order of importance,** starting with the most important reason and ending with the least important reason or vice versa. (For more organizational ideas, see the Professional Model on pages 619–620.)

- Support each of your reasons with at least one specific **fact** or **example.**

- Use **transitions** between paragraphs to give your essay **coherence.** (For a list of transitions, see page 654.)

Remind your audience why this issue is important by **summarizing** your reasons in a single sentence. Tell readers what they should do about the issue with a reasonable and specific **call to action.** (For more on writing **conclusions,** see page 656.)

PRACTICE & APPLY 5 Draft Your Persuasive Essay

Now, it is your chance to write a first draft of a persuasive essay. As you write, refer to the framework above and the Writer's Model on the next page.

Writing 1.0 Students write coherent essays. Essays contain formal introductions, supporting evidence, and conclusions. **1.3** Use a variety of effective and coherent organizational patterns, including arrangement by order of importance. **2.0** Student writing demonstrates the organizational and drafting strategies outlined in Writing Standard 1.0. **2.5b** Support the position with organized evidence.

628 Workshop 5 **Persuasion:** Writing a Persuasive Essay

RESOURCES

Practice and Apply 5
Think Sheet
- *Writing, Listening, & Speaking,* WS. p. 108

Template
- *Writing, Listening, & Speaking,* WS. p. 109

A Writer's Model

The final draft below closely follows the framework for a persuasive essay on the previous page.

Put Litter in Its Place

My soccer team won its game last Saturday. I was happy and excited until I started walking toward the parking lot. I passed cups and candy wrappers left in the stands and six trash cans overflowing with aluminum cans. Seeing all the trash that people did not throw away and the cans that could be recycled bothered me. With the help of players and parents, we can improve the Eastside Soccer League. We need to start an anti-littering campaign to keep the soccer fields clean.

An anti-littering campaign would help people become aware of the trash problem. Since I talked to my family about the problem, they have noticed how bad the trash is, too. After last Saturday's game, they made sure they picked up their trash so that they were not contributing to the problem. Letting people know there is a problem is the first step toward solving it.

Some people may not like the idea of the league spending money on things like additional trash cans or supplies for making anti-littering posters. However, if we make recycling a part of the plan, the anti-littering campaign could actually earn money for the Eastside Soccer League. By recycling all the aluminum cans that we are currently sending to the city landfill, the league could earn thirty-two cents per pound from the Central City Recycling Center. There are twelve trash cans at the soccer fields, and each can holds about two pounds of aluminum cans. The season is fifteen games long, so we could earn as much as $115.20 each season. In addition to financing the anti-littering campaign, this money could be used to pay for clinics to train new coaches and referees. That way, more people could get involved in the league because training would be available.

I have heard people say that keeping the soccer fields neat would take too much time and effort. To those asking, "Who's

(continued)

INTRODUCTION
Attention-grabbing opening

Opinion statement

BODY
Reason #1: Help people become aware

Evidence (example)

Counterargument

Reason #2: Earn money

Evidence (facts)

GO TO: go.hrw.com
KEYWORD: HLLA6 W-5
FOR: A Student Model

DIRECT TEACHING

A Writer's Model W1.0

As students review **A Writer's Model,** remind them that they should link ideas within their essays with transitions to create coherence and show order of importance.

Point out to students the following transitions that are used in **A Writer's Model** by listing, annotating, or highlighting them: *until* (paragraph 1); *Since, After* (paragraph 2); *However, so, In addition, That way* (paragraph 3); *If, Also, Since, Once* (paragraph 4); *Then* (paragraph 5).

Counterargument

Reason #3: Easy to do

Evidence (examples)

CONCLUSION

Summary of reasons

Call to action

going to do the dirty work?" I say, "Everyone!" If parents and players all pitch in, no one will have to work more than a few minutes. Each team will make posters encouraging people to be responsible for their trash. Also, the two teams playing the last game on a field will pick up the trash left in the stands and empty the recycling containers located at their field. Since the teams already rotate playing times, a different team will be responsible for this chore every week. Once the recycling containers are emptied, one parent can take the aluminum cans to the recycling center on the way home.

An anti-littering campaign will help people become aware of the trash problem at our soccer fields. It will also earn money for the league without becoming a time-consuming or expensive project. The benefits of this campaign will go beyond making money, though. The players, parents, and other participants in the Eastside Soccer League will gain a sense of pride and accomplishment by taking control of the litter problem. The league should buy and place recycling bins for aluminum cans at the soccer fields. Then, we should ask teams to participate in the anti-littering campaign.

Revising

Evaluate and Revise Content, Organization, and Style

Twice Is Nice Double the persuasive power of your essay by giving it at least two readings. In the first reading, focus on the content and organization of your first draft. The guidelines below can help. In the second reading, look at the individual sentences using the Focus on Sentences on page 633.

First Reading: Content and Organization When you **edit** your essay, you evaluate what you have written and revise it to make it better. In this section you will edit your essay to make it more persuasive. Use the following guidelines to improve the organization and consistency of ideas within and between paragraphs.

Persuasive Essay: Content and Organization Guidelines

Evaluation Questions	▶ Tips	▶ Revision Techniques
❶ Does the introduction have a clear opinion statement?	▶ **Underline** the opinion statement.	▶ **Add** an opinion statement, or revise a sentence to state the opinion clearly.
❷ Does the essay give at least two reasons to support the opinion? Are there any reasons that do not support the opinion?	▶ **Put stars** next to the reasons that support the opinion.	▶ **Add** reasons that support the opinion. If necessary, **delete** reasons that support an opposing point of view.
❸ Does at least one piece of evidence support each of the reasons?	▶ **Circle** evidence that supports each reason. **Draw a line** to the reason each piece of evidence supports.	▶ If necessary, **add** facts or examples to support each reason. **Rearrange** evidence so it is close to the reason it supports.
❹ Are paragraphs arranged in order of importance?	▶ **Number** each body paragraph according to how important the reasons are.	▶ **Rearrange** paragraphs if the numbers do not indicate that they are arranged from least important to most important, or vice versa.
❺ Does the conclusion include a specific and reasonable call to action?	▶ **Draw a wavy line** under the call to action.	▶ **Add** a call to action, or **revise** the call to action to make it more specific and reasonable.

Writing 1.6 Revise writing to improve organization and consistency of ideas within and between paragraphs.

Evaluate and Revise Content, Organization, and Style **631**

Quotation for the Day

"There should be no distinction between what we write down and what we really know."

(Allen Ginsberg, 1926–1997, American poet)

Read the quotation aloud, and ask students to brainstorm how the writing process helps them to clarify and organize their thoughts. Point out that the revising stage allows writers to fine-tune their writing and to express clearly what they know.

DIRECT TEACHING

Elaboration

Remind students that they should elaborate by explaining why their evidence is convincing. If students' evidence needs elaboration, you might suggest that they read their facts or examples to a partner and then state their explanations aloud while their partner takes notes. Students can then use these notes to help them compose their explanations.

GUIDED PRACTICE

Responding to the Revision Process

Answers

1. The sentence was not a clear opinion statement. The revised sentence is more specific.

2. The sentence provides support for the reason.

DIFFERENTIATING INSTRUCTION

English-Language Learners

Some students may have trouble identifying stringy sentences. One way to illustrate the effects of stringy sentences is to read examples aloud to the class. Exaggerate breathlessness and overemphasize each conjunction while reading.

 Resources Reminder

For more help with English-Language Learners, see *Lesson Plans for Language Development*.

ONE WRITER'S REVISIONS This revision is an early draft of the essay on pages 629–630.

revise

With the help of players and parents, we can improve the Eastside Soccer League. *We need to start* An anti-littering campaign *to keep the soccer fields clean* ~~would help~~.

An anti-littering campaign would help people become aware of the trash problem. Since I talked to my family about the problem, they have noticed how bad the trash is,

add

too. *After last Saturday's game, they made sure they picked up their* Letting people know there is a problem is the first step toward solving it. *trash so that they were not contributing to the problem.*

PEER REVIEW

As you read a peer's persuasive essay, ask yourself these questions.

- Who is the target audience for this essay? Does the writer appeal to their interests?
- What is the strongest piece of support? What makes it stand out?

Responding to the Revision Process

1. Why did the writer revise the sentence at the end of the first paragraph?

2. Why did the writer add a sentence to the second paragraph?

 Second Reading: Style You have taken a look at the big picture of your essay. In your second reading, you will look at the pieces of that picture by focusing on the sentences. One way to improve your writing is to make stringy sentences more compact. Use the following guidelines and the Focus on Sentences on the next page.

Style Guidelines

Evaluation Question	▶ Tip	▶ Revision Technique
Does the writer avoid long sentences made up of strings of ideas connected by *and, but,* **or** *so***?**	Highlight long sentences that use *and, but,* or *so* to join two or more complete thoughts—ideas that can stand alone.	Break a long sentence with two or more complete thoughts into two shorter sentences.

Writing 1.0 Students write clear essays.

Eliminating Stringy Sentences

When your purpose is to persuade, your style should also be persuasive. Avoid using stringy sentences. Reading long, stringy sentences is like listening to a person who goes on and on. They bore readers, and a bored reader is an unconvinced reader. To eliminate stringy sentences, follow these steps.

- First, find the conjunctions *and, but,* or *so* in a very long sentence. Put a slash mark before each conjunction.

- Then, see if each part of the sentence has a subject and a verb. If each part has both a subject and a verb and expresses a complete thought, then it can stand alone.

- Revise a stringy sentence by breaking it into two or more separate sentences. Each complete thought may have its own sentence.

ONE WRITER'S REVISIONS

> My soccer team won its game last Saturday, ⊙so I was
>
> happy and excited until I started walking toward the park-
>
> ing lot ⊙and I passed cups and candy wrappers left in the
>
> stands and six trash cans overflowing with aluminum cans.

Responding to the Revision Process

How did breaking the sentence above into three sentences improve the passage?

Sentences

Reference Note

For more on **conjunctions,** see page 66 in the *Holt Handbook.*

TIP If part of the sentence does not express a complete thought, that part will not be able to stand alone in its own sentence. For more on **complete sentences,** see page 4 in the *Holt Handbook.*

PRACTICE & APPLY 6

Evaluate and Revise Your Persuasive Essay

Use the guidelines on page 631 and page 632 to evaluate and revise the content, organization, and style of your essay. If a peer reviewed your essay, consider his or her comments as you revise.

Writing 1.0 Students write clear essays.

Focus on Sentences **633**

RESOURCES

Focus on Sentences
Independent Practice
- *Writing, Listening, & Speaking,* WS. p. 113 You may choose to assign this independent practice as homework.

  HOMEWORK

Practice and Apply 6
Think Sheet
- *Writing, Listening, & Speaking,* WS. p. 110

Independent Practice
- *Writing, Listening, & Speaking,* WS. p. 112

Extension
- *Writing, Listening, & Speaking,* WS. p. 111

DIRECT TEACHING

Eliminating Stringy Sentences

Tell students that they should select a style appropriate to their purpose. Because stringy sentences can sound like spoken language, they may be appropriate if the purpose is to express or entertain. For the purpose of persuading, advise students to avoid stringy sentences. Instead, encourage them to choose other stylistic elements, such as the use of analogy (concrete comparisons to explain and emphasize important points) or the use of vocabulary (active verbs and vivid adjectives to create a dynamic sounding, persuasive style).

GUIDED PRACTICE

Responding to the Revision Process

Answer

Each sentence now contains one complete thought. Also, in this case, three sentences are easier to read and understand.

PRACTICE & APPLY 6

Independent Practice
To assess students' use of the **Content and Organization Guidelines** on Pupil's Edition p. 631, ask students to list on the backs of their drafts the evaluation questions they used during the revision process, along with the specific actions they took as a result of their evaluations.

Quotation for the Day

"A good book is the best of friends, the same today and forever."

(Martin Tupper, 1810–1889, English writer)

Read the quotation aloud to students. Discuss with students how their own writing is a permanent record of what they are thinking at a given time.

DIRECT TEACHING

Integrating with Grammar, Usage, and Mechanics

If students make mistakes with transitive and intransitive verbs and end marks, send them to the Parts of Speech Overview and Punctuation chapters in the *Holt Handbook*.

Grammar Link

Guided Practice

(For independent practice, see Proofreading Practice below.)

Answers

1. Recycling helps meet the city's goals as outlined in its long-range plan.

2. C

3. Theirs are successful. Ours still needs the council's approval.

4. The county's landfill is quickly filling up from the four towns' trash.

5. Voters' signatures filled page after page of one group's petition.

Publishing

Proofread Your Essay

Edit for Oomph Careless mistakes decrease the persuasive power of your essay. Proofread your essay for mistakes in grammar, spelling, and punctuation.

Grammar Link

Punctuating Possessives Correctly

The **possessive** form of a noun or pronoun shows ownership. Using possessives helps writers make their points more concisely. Notice that the second example below states the idea in the first example more concisely.

the playground equipment at our school

our school's playground equipment

Here are four rules to remember about possessives.

To form the possessive case of a singular noun, add an apostrophe and an *s*.

girl's sweatshirt   car's bumper

To form the possessive case of a plural noun ending in *s*, add only the apostrophe.

books' pages   stores' signs

Do not use an apostrophe to make a noun plural. If you are not sure when to use an apostrophe, ask yourself, "Does the noun possess what follows?" If you answer *yes*, you need an apostrophe.

Do not use an apostrophe with possessive personal pronouns. These pronouns include *its, yours, theirs, his, hers,* and *ours*.

The dog missed **its** owner.

PRACTICE

Write the following sentences on your own paper, adding apostrophes where they are needed. If a sentence is correct, write *C* next to the sentence on your paper.

Example:

1. In visitors eyes, our towns trash is its biggest problem.

1. *In visitors' eyes, our town's trash is its biggest problem.*

1. Recycling helps meet the citys goals as outlined in its long-range plan.

2. Other towns have recycling programs.

3. Theirs are successful. Ours still needs the councils approval.

4. The countys landfill is quickly filling up from the four towns trash.

5. Voters signatures filled page after page of one groups petition.

Reference Note

For more information and practice on possessives, see page 300 in the *Holt Handbook*.

Writing 2.0 Student writing demonstrates a command of standard American English.

RESOURCES

Grammar Link

Proofreading Practice

■ *Writing, Listening, & Speaking,* WS. p. 114 You may choose to assign this proofreading practice as homework.

HOMEWORK

Publish Your Essay

Finding a Forum You have carefully developed a persuasive message targeted at a specific audience. To get that audience to read your essay, try one of these suggestions.

■ Post your essay to a community Internet site to see how readers respond to your ideas.

■ Convert your essay to a **letter to the editor** and submit it to your school newspaper or to a local newspaper.

■ Turn your essay into a persuasive speech, and deliver it to members of your chosen audience or to your class. (Use the instruction in the Listening and Speaking Workshop on pages 636–641 to adapt your essay into a speech.)

Mini-Workshop
For more information on this publishing option, see **Writing a Letter to the Editor,** page 671.

Reflect on Your Essay

Building Your Portfolio Take time to reflect on both the process of persuasion and the process of writing an essay. Answer these questions.

■ What is the strongest reason in your essay? Explain.

■ How does your essay achieve its persuasive purpose?

Then, reflect on your entire portfolio by answering the following questions.

■ What are your strengths as a writer? What did you do well in this piece and in other pieces in your portfolio? Which piece was your best or favorite? Why?

■ What writing skills do you need to work on? If you had the chance, what would you do differently in this piece or in other pieces in your portfolio? Why?

■ What are your goals as a writer now? What kinds of writing does your portfolio seem to be missing? What would you like to try next?

PRACTICE & APPLY 7 **Proofread, Publish, and Reflect on Your Essay**

First, correct mistakes in grammar, usage and punctuation. Next, publish your essay. Finally, answer the Reflect on Your Essay questions above.

 Writing 1.1 Choose the form of writing (e.g., letter to the editor) that best suits the intended purpose.

Reflect on Your Essay **635**

RESOURCES

Writing Workshop
Assessment
■ *Progress Assessment of Writing, Listening, & Speaking,* pp. 13–15, 53–55, 95–103

TECHNOLOGY **TIP**
W1.5
Advise students to publish their essays using a word processor if they haven't been working on one up to this point. You might also suggest that students try using the shading feature to make strong points, such as a quotation from an expert, stand out in their persuasive essays. To shade a selection, highlight the selection. Then, select Borders and Shading from the Format menu. Select Shading, and choose the desired features.

DIRECT TEACHING

Finding a Forum
Be aware that students who choose to post their essays to a community Internet site may encounter unpredictable content, as Internet resources are sometimes public forums.

Resources Reminder
For help with writing assessment, see 6 Traits—Plus 1 in the "General Scales and Sample Papers" section of *Progress Assessment of Writing, Listening, & Speaking.*

PRACTICE & APPLY 7

Independent Practice
If students typed their essays on a computer, remind them to use the spellchecking and grammar-checking functions to help them proofread their essays. Remind students to double-check the spelling since spellchecking by computer may leave some errors.

If students have written their essays by hand, have them exchange essays with partners who can check for the legibility of their cursive or manuscript handwriting. Emphasize to students that papers which are neatly presented and free of errors are more persuasive.

Reflect on Your Essay **635**

Listening and Speaking Workshop

Listening and Speaking Workshop

PRETEACHING

Quotation for the Day

"The vital, successful people I have met all had one common characteristic. They had a plan."

(Marilyn Van Derbur, former Miss America)

Use the quotation above to illustrate the importance of planning for a speech. Remind students that having a plan will make their speeches clearer and more effective and their finished products more focused.

DIRECT TEACHING

Adapt Your Essay

Most students will be adapting the persuasive essays that they wrote in the Writing Workshop into a speech. If not, refer students to the Prewriting section that begins on p. 621 for choosing an issue and developing support.

Talk   Listen

WHAT'S AHEAD?

In this workshop you will present and evaluate a persuasive speech. You will also learn how to

- relate your message to your audience
- support your opinion with evidence and visual and media displays
- analyze a speaker's persuasive techniques, delivery, and credibility

TIP To explore a new topic in your persuasive speech, refer to the Prewriting instruction on pages 621–627.

TIP Understanding the relationship between purpose, audience, and occasion will give your speech a clear **focus.**

Giving and Evaluating a Persuasive Speech

Writing is certainly not the only way to get your opinions across to your intended audience. You may prefer to share your views by delivering a persuasive speech. Giving a speech may seem as simple as reading out loud the persuasive essay you wrote in the Writing Workshop, but there is much more to it. In this workshop you will adapt your persuasive essay to create a persuasive speech that you will deliver to your classmates. You will also listen to and evaluate persuasive speeches delivered by your classmates.

Adapt Your Essay

The **position** (or **point of view**) at the heart of your speech will be the same one you took in your essay. Your specific **purpose** for arguing your position may change, depending on your speech **audience.** Before you adapt your essay, consider the **occasion,** or situation that prompts you to speak. Since the occasion for your speech is a class assignment, you know your audience will be your classmates. To match your specific purpose to this audience, ask yourself,

- Will my audience tend to agree or disagree with my opinion?
- Are they willing to get involved in a cause?

The answers to these questions will help you figure out whether you should push for action on your issue or simply try to open your audience members' minds.

Listening and Speaking 1.4 Select a focus and a point of view, matching the purpose, message, and occasion to the audience. **2.4a** Provide a clear statement of the position.

WORKSHOP RESOURCES

Listening and Speaking Workshop Planning
- *On Course: Mapping Instruction*
- *One-Stop Planner* CD-ROM
- *At Home: A Guide to Standards Mastery,* p. 15

- *At Home: In Five Languages*
- *Writing, Listening, & Speaking*
  —Teaching Notes, pp. 115–116
  —Project-Planning Guide, WS. p. 117

Differentiating Instruction
- *Lesson Plans for Language Development,* p. 238

Whatever your specific purpose and occasion, you will need to **engage your audience.** To grab their attention and make them care about your issue, you can use the following strategies.

- Choose support that will appeal to your audience's interests and backgrounds.
- Create eye-catching visual and media displays.
- Use rhetorical devices like *repetition* and *onomatopoeia.*
- Place your strongest points in an attention-grabbing location.

The guidelines on the following pages explain the strategies above. Following the guidelines will help you construct a speech that will interest, and possibly persuade, your chosen audience.

Relevant Reasons and Evidence If your classmates were not part of the audience for your persuasive essay, you may need to change elements of your **message** to appeal to their interests and backgrounds. For example, suppose you wrote your persuasive essay on the issue of extending the passing period, or time between classes. Because an important member of the audience for your essay was your teacher, you explained how an extended passing period would benefit teachers. However, this reason may not convince a listening audience of your classmates. Instead, you should think of reasons that will be **relevant,** or related to them.

Visual and Media Displays You can make your speech more convincing by using visual and media displays. These displays may be made by hand or with technology. The chart below explains some types of visual and media displays and their purposes.

Reference Note

For more information on **evidence,** see pages 625–626.

Mini-Workshop

See **Creating Graphics,** page 686.

VISUAL OR MEDIA DISPLAYS

Type	Purpose
Charts, including pie charts	To show how different pieces of information relate to each other
Graphs, including bar graphs and line graphs	To show changes over a period of time
Tables	To show numbers and statistics
Illustrations and photographs	To show an item or event that is unfamiliar or hard to describe
Video segments	To show the sights and sounds of a real event

Listening and Speaking **1.0** Students deliver focused presentations that convey ideas clearly and relate to the background and interests of the audience. **1.6** Support opinions with detailed evidence and with visual or media displays that use appropriate technology. **2.4b** Include relevant evidence. **2.4d** Engage the listener and foster acceptance of the proposition or proposal.

Adapt Your Essay **637**

Advanced Learners

Acceleration. Use the following activity to move students toward the 7th-grade **Listening and Speaking Standard 1.5.**

Advanced students can use this opportunity to focus on reaching a specific audience. Since their audience is their classmates, students can use their classmates as "experts in residence." Assign students to design a simple survey or poll that they can give to their classmates. They should incorporate the results into their speeches. Additionally, they can incorporate classmates' quotes into their speeches.

CORRECTING MISCONCEPTIONS

Explain to students that visual or media displays may not always be a positive addition to an oral presentation. If a display does not communicate specific information related to the topic, if it is difficult to read or hear, or if it is displayed at inappropriate times (too soon or too late in the presentation), it will be distracting and detract from the presentation.

MODELING AND DEMONSTRATION

Visual or Media Displays
You may bring in published photographs to demonstrate emotional impact. If possible, mount them simply on construction paper. Model for students the proper citation for photographs—including the photographer's name, the publication name, date, and page number. Students should be aware that printed pictures are easily reproducible, but are also very likely copyrighted.

- *Supporting Instruction in Five Languages*

Think Sheet

- *Writing, Listening, & Speaking,* WS. pp. 118, 119, 120

Evaluation and Assessment

- *Writing, Listening, & Speaking,* WS. p. 121
- *Progress Assessment of Writing, Listening, & Speaking,* pp. 56–58
- *Diagnostic and Summative Assessments,* End-of-Year Test

Repetitive Patterns

Most students will be familiar with Dr. Martin Luther King, Jr.'s phrase "I have a dream." Have students ask their family members to share with them other phrases they remember from famous speeches. Have students write these down, along with the speakers' names, and bring them back to class to share. Possibilities include Sojourner Truth's "Ain't I A Woman?" and former president George H. W. Bush's "a thousand points of light."

Putting It All Together

If students struggle with ordering information in their speeches, illustrate for them how strong support should be placed at the beginning or end of a speech to be most effective.

Tell your class that they are going to participate in a tug-of-war contest with another class. Choose three members randomly from the class by having them draw marbles or having them choose numbers. Have those three come to the front of the room, and have your class determine in which order the three contestants should hold the rope to ensure a win. The class will probably determine, or may already know, that the strongest member of the team should be placed at the back to anchor the rope, and another strong member should be at the front.

Make Every Word Count You want your message to be clear, but you also want it to be memorable. **Rhetorical devices,** effective writing and speaking techniques, can help you emphasize your major points and develop a memorable message. As you plan your message, think about where you might include one or more of the following devices.

- **Cadence** refers to the rhythmic rise and fall of your voice as you speak. Varying your sentence lengths will allow you to achieve a rhythmic cadence. Without cadence, your voice may become a monotone, and your words may sound dull and uninteresting.

- **Repetitive patterns** are words or phrases that are repeated to stress their importance. By repeating a word or phrase throughout a speech, you make it easier for your audience to remember your main points.

- **Onomatopoeia** is the use of words that imitate sounds, such as *whiz, pop,* or *clang.* You can use such words to draw attention to a point or to help your audience understand an idea.

> **TIP** It is important to use *standard American English* in your speech. **Standard American English** follows the rules and guidelines found in grammar and composition books and is used in most school and business situations. Since standard American English is widely used and accepted, it allows people from many different regions and cultures to communicate clearly with one another.

Reference Note

For more information on **order,** see page 653.

Putting It All Together You have a clear opinion, relevant evidence to support it, and rhetorical strategies to make your points memorable. Now you will need to be sure your information is organized in a way that will persuade your audience. Whether your speech includes reasons and evidence from your essay or new information, plan to place your most appealing reasons at the point in your speech where they will pack the biggest punch. You can either

- begin with your most important reason and supporting evidence to grab your listeners' attention or

- end with your most important reason and supporting evidence to leave your listeners with a strong impression

Also, plan to make your ideas **coherent,** or clearly connected, for listeners by using **transitions,** such as *for this reason* and *most important.*

Listening and Speaking **1.0** Students deliver coherent presentations. **1.4** Select an organizational structure. **1.8** Analyze the use of rhetorical devices (e.g., cadence, repetitive patterns, use of onomatopoeia) for intent and effect. **2.0** Student speaking demonstrates a command of standard American English. **2.4c** Offer a logical sequence of information.

Develop Your Delivery

Your ideas may not be persuasive if you do not deliver them effectively—for example, if you get rattled by distractions, mumble, or have trouble operating the audio or visual equipment. To avoid these types of problems, practice your speech before delivering it. As you practice, concentrate on using *nonverbal* and *verbal elements*, using visual and media displays, and handling distractions.

The Way That You Say   When you speak, you communicate a message not only with the words you say, but also with **verbal elements** (how your voice expresses those words) and **nonverbal elements** (what your face and body do as you say the words). Aligning these elements by matching your voice and movements can add to the impact of your message and make you a more effective and persuasive speaker.

Verbal Elements   *Rate, volume, pitch,* and *tone* are all examples of verbal elements. When you give a persuasive speech, it is important to speak at a slow **rate** so your audience can keep up with what you are saying. You should also speak at a loud enough **volume** so the people in the back of the room can hear you. Varying your **vocal modulation,** or **pitch**—the high or low notes of your speaking voice—can help keep your audience interested. Adjusting the **tone,** or attitude, of your voice to match your message helps the audience know your feelings about the issue. When giving a persuasive speech, your tone should be enthusiastic and believable so your audience will accept your opinion.

Nonverbal Elements   Your **posture, eye contact** with the audience, **gestures,** and **facial expressions** are examples of nonverbal elements. Standing tall while looking directly at your audience shows that you are confident, and using appropriate gestures and facial expressions can **emphasize** important ideas. For example, if you were to ask a question such as "Is this the best way to solve the problem?" you could demonstrate your own uncertainty by shrugging your shoulders and raising your eyebrows.

> **TIP**   If possible, practice in front of a small group of friends or family members so you can get used to speaking in front of a group. Ask the group for feedback, and make note of any trouble spots mentioned.

 Listening and Speaking   **1.4** Match the vocal modulation to the audience   **1.5** Emphasize salient points and assist the listener in following the main ideas and concepts.   **1.7** Use effective rate, volume, pitch, and tone and align nonverbal elements to sustain audience interest and attention.

Develop Your Delivery   **639**

REVIEW STANDARD

Oh Say, Can You See?
The following item is a review of the 5th-grade **Listening and Speaking Standard 1.6.**

Sound and visual checks generally take place before any audience members arrive. Students may not realize that before a presentation, professional speakers carefully check all areas of a room or auditorium to make sure audience members can hear and see the presentation.

Place students in random groups of three or four, and let the teams check the room for sound and visuals. One member can present a mock speech with visual displays while other team members move throughout the room performing sight and sound checks.

PRACTICE & APPLY

Guided and Independent Practice

As students complete their speeches, monitor their progress by checking that they have prepared an outline or note cards from which to make their presentations. Allow students to choose partners and go through "dress rehearsals" that include not only delivering the speech, but also manipulating any media displays.

Oh Say, Can You See? Visual and media displays can make a powerful case for your opinion. Use these tips as you prepare to deliver your speech.

- Make sure all audience members can see your displays.
- Make sure you have all the audio and visual equipment that you need and that it is working properly. Cue your video or audio clips to the correct starting point ahead of time.
- Use an easel, if available, for graphs, charts, and other hand-held visuals.
- If you use presentation software, make sure your computer is loaded with the necessary program. Make sure the computer and program are running properly.

Dealing with Distractions Try not to let your plans for a focused message with a strong delivery be affected by distracting noises or unexpected events. Here are some suggestions.

- If you hear continuing, low background noise, ignore it and speak louder. For a more noticeable noise or distraction, pause until the noise subsides, and then go on.
- If you drop a note card or a visual or forget to mention a point that is not very important in your speech, try to go on as if nothing happened. If the dropped item is important, quickly pick it up and continue. If the point you skipped is important, tell where it fits into your speech organization, explain it, and then return to the part of the speech where you were when you stopped.

PRACTICE & APPLY 8 **Deliver a Persuasive Speech**

Adapt your persuasive essay into a focused, coherent speech that will appeal to an audience of your classmates. Include visual or media displays to support your ideas, and deliver your speech effectively.

Listen and Evaluate

As your classmates deliver their speeches, listen carefully. Your purpose for listening to a persuasive speech will be to understand the speaker's position and evaluate his or her ideas. To listen effectively, you must consider the *content* and *delivery* of the speech.

Listening and Speaking 1.0 They evaluate the content of oral communication. **2.0** Students deliver well-organized formal presentations employing traditional rhetorical strategies (e.g., persuasion). Student speaking demonstrates organizational and delivery strategies outlined in Listening and Speaking Standard 1.0. **2.4** Deliver persuasive presentations.

What's That, You Say?   As you listen to the speeches of your classmates, ask yourself the following questions about the **content** of the speech, and note your responses on a piece of paper.

- What is the speaker's opinion? Is it clearly stated?
- How effectively does the speaker support his or her opinion with relevant evidence and visual or media displays? How strong is the evidence? How well do the visuals support the message?
- Which rhetorical devices, such as **cadence, repetitive patterns,** and **onomatopoeia,** does the speaker use? How do these devices help the speech achieve its purpose?
- How is the speech organized? Does this organization seem logical to you? Why or why not?

Reference Note

For more on **cadence, repetitive patterns,** and **onomatopoeia,** see page 638.

How's That, You Say?   As you listen to your classmates' speeches, you will also need to evaluate their **delivery** skills. Ask yourself the following questions about each speaker's delivery, and note your responses on a piece of paper.

- Does the speaker talk loudly and slowly enough?
- How effectively does the speaker vary the **pitch** of his or her voice?
- What is the speaker's **tone,** or attitude toward the issue? How well does the tone match the speaker's message?
- Do the speaker's **posture** and **eye contact** show confidence and make the message seem believable?
- How well do the speaker's nonverbal messages, such as **gestures** and **facial expressions,** match the verbal message?

PRACTICE & APPLY 9

Evaluate a Persuasive Speech

- Listen to your classmates' persuasive speeches, and take notes on content and delivery using the questions above. Afterward, review your notes and add further explanations while the speech is still fresh in your mind.
- Then, use the information in your notes to write a brief evaluation of one classmate's speech. You might share your evaluation with the speaker as feedback.

TIP   If other students evaluate the same speech, compare your impressions in a small group.

?   Was the speaker effective? Why or why not?

Listening and Speaking   1.0 They evaluate the content of oral communication.   **1.1** Relate the speaker's verbal communication (e.g., pitch, tone) to the nonverbal message (e.g., posture, gesture).   **1.2** Identify the tone conveyed in the oral communication.   **1.8** Analyze the use of rhetorical devices (e.g., cadence, repetitive patterns, use of onomatopoeia) for intent and effect.

Listen and Evaluate   **641**

PRACTICE & APPLY 9

Guided and Independent Practice

Divide students into four-person evaluation teams. When a student from another group presents a speech, each member from the other groups will evaluate one of the four content elements. Allow two to three minutes after each speech for group members to share their ideas. After all speeches have been presented, have each group select one speech about which to write a brief evaluation.

You may monitor students' progress by circulating among the groups to ensure all members are contributing.

PRETEACHING

Quotation for the Day

"I dearly love to persuade people. There can hardly be a greater pleasure (of a selfish kind) than to feel you have brought another person around to your way of thinking."

(James Hinton, 1822–1875, English philosopher)

Read the quotation aloud to students. Then, reread the final sentence. Ask students to comment upon the art of persuasion as a selfish art. [Responses may include persuading people to do favors for you or to participate in a cause you support.]

Then, turn the tables. Ask students when the art of persuasion is not a selfish act. [Responses may include persuading a friend not to engage in harmful behavior or persuading someone to follow a dream.]

CORRECTING MISCONCEPTIONS

Write this definition for *propaganda* on the chalkboard: a focused, widespread attempt to promote certain beliefs or ideas. Point out that the definition does not limit propaganda to negative or untrue information. Then, write the word *connotation* on the chalkboard along with the following definition: the emotional meaning that a word carries.

Explain that *propaganda* often carries a negative connotation, though its literal definition says only that *propaganda* is an organized attempt to spread certain beliefs. You may share that the word *propaganda* is often used when referring to political and wartime messages.

WHAT'S AHEAD?

In this workshop you will analyze propaganda techniques on television. You will also learn how to

- **distinguish between persuasive techniques and propaganda techniques**
- **identify false and misleading information on TV**

Analyzing Propaganda on TV

Persuasive messages are not limited to essays, letters, and speeches. You also find them in television, radio, and movies. The persuasive messages you listen to and view usually contain *persuasive techniques* or *propaganda techniques*. **Persuasive techniques,** such as the information you included in your persuasive essay for the Writing Workshop, convince an audience by providing sound reasons. These reasons persuade through strong, relevant supporting evidence. **Propaganda techniques,** though, appeal primarily to an audience's emotions and may contain false or misleading information. When you unquestioningly listen to or view messages that contain propaganda techniques, you may make poor decisions. This workshop will help you identify persuasive and propaganda techniques, including false and misleading information. These skills will help you make well-informed decisions when watching TV.

Persuasive Techniques

As you learned in the Writing Workshop, to be persuasive you must make sense. Signs of persuasive techniques include

- a clearly stated opinion or claim
- logical reasons for the opinion supported by relevant evidence
- an appeal to the interests and backgrounds of a particular audience

Watch for these signs as you view, but don't automatically accept a message that includes them. First, check for propaganda techniques.

Listening and Speaking 1.9 Identify persuasive techniques used in television.

WORKSHOP RESOURCES

Media Workshop
Planning
- *On Course: Mapping Instruction*
- *One-Stop Planner* CD-ROM
- *At Home: A Guide to Standards Mastery,* p. 23

- *Writing, Listening, & Speaking*
  —Teaching Notes, pp. 122–123
  —Project-Planning Guide, WS. p. 124

Differentiating Instruction
- *Lesson Plans for Language Development,* p. 239
- *Supporting Instruction in Five Languages*

Propaganda Techniques

Propaganda techniques appeal more to your emotions than to common sense or logic. Like persuasive techniques, they are used to convince you to think, feel, or act a certain way. The difference is that a **propagandist,** a person who uses propaganda techniques, does not want you to think critically about the message.

For example, when you hear the name of a product or see its logo associated with your favorite football team, your excitement for that team is being used to sell that product. If you connect your excitement about the team with the product enough times, this propaganda technique, known as **transfer,** may eventually persuade you to buy the product. Your decision would be based not on logical reasons for buying the product but on your emotional response to the propaganda technique.

The following chart gives definitions and examples of other common propaganda techniques found in television ads and programs. As you watch TV, look for the given clues to identify these techniques in every kind of programming you watch.

TIP A persuasive message that includes propaganda techniques may be sound—as long as it also provides strong and accurate supporting evidence. The term *propaganda* describes a message that relies too heavily on propaganda techniques. Propaganda may also contain false or misleading information. (See pages 644–645.)

PROPAGANDA TECHNIQUES USED ON TELEVISION

Techniques	Clues	Examples
Bandwagon tries to convince you to do something or believe something because everyone else does.	Listen for slogans that use the words *everyone, everybody, all,* or in some cases, *nobody.*	While being interviewed on a talk show, an author might encourage viewers to join the thousands of other people who have benefited from his new diet book.
Loaded language uses words with strongly positive or negative meanings.	Listen for strongly positive or negative words, such as *perfect* or *terrible.*	*Wake-up Juice is a fantastic way to start your day!*
Product placement uses brand-name products as part of the scenery. The products' companies may pay producers for this seemingly unintended advertising.	As you watch TV, keep your eyes peeled for clearly visible brand names. Ask yourself if the brand names have anything to do with the plot of the show.	In the middle of a TV movie, an actor may drink a bottle of juice. The juice is not an important part of the plot, but the brand name of the juice is clearly visible.
Snob appeal suggests that a viewer can be special or part of a special group if he or she agrees with an idea or buys a product.	Listen for words, such as *exclusive, best,* or *quality.* Look for images of wealth, such as big houses, expensive cars, and fancy boats.	*Treat your cat like a queen; give her the cat food preferred exclusively by discriminating cats.*

(continued)

Listening and Speaking 1.9 Identify propaganda techniques used in television.

Think Sheet
- *Writing, Listening, & Speaking,* WS. p. 128

Independent Practice
- *Writing, Listening, & Speaking,* WS. pp. 125, 126, 127

Evaluation and Assessment
- *Progress Assessment of Writing, Listening, & Speaking,* pp. 59–60
- *Diagnostic and Summative Assessments,* End-of-Year Test

Extension
- *Writing, Listening, and Speaking,* Videocassette, Segment 5

REVIEW STANDARD

Propaganda Techniques
The following activity is a review of the 5th-grade **Listening and Speaking Standard 1.7.**

- Assign students to groups of four or five.
- Ask each group to think of a television commercial with which they are familiar.
- Then, have the students write a script for a new commercial which reveals truths that manufacturers keep hidden. For example, students may choose a commercial for fast food. Their script may include the fact that nutritionally, the fast food promoted in the commercial is not healthful.
- Have students present their scripts to the rest of the class and follow each skit with a brief discussion of the elements the manufacturer of the product did not want consumers to know.

RETEACHING

Propaganda Techniques
To reteach the concept of propaganda techniques, use the following activity. Divide the class into six even groups. Assign each group one of the six propaganda techniques from the chart on pp. 643–644. Provide each group with a stack of old magazines, and have the members search the magazines for examples of their assigned propaganda technique. Have them cut out the examples and paste them onto a sheet of colored paper to form a collage. Allow each group to share a few examples from their completed collage with the class.

Techniques	Clues	Examples
Symbols associate the power and meaning of a cultural symbol with a product or idea.	Look for flags, team mascots, state flowers, or any other symbol that people view with pride.	A political candidate might use a national flag as a backdrop for a speech on TV.
Testimonials use knowledgeable or famous people to endorse a product or idea.	Look for famous actors, athletes, politicians, and experts. Listen for their names or titles as well.	*TV star Zen Williams actively supports alternative energy research—shouldn't you?*

PRACTICE & APPLY 10 · Identify Persuasive and Propaganda Techniques

- View a TV advertisement, infomercial, or other program, and identify what the TV message wants you to do, buy, or think.
- Then, identify whether the message uses the persuasive techniques mentioned on page 642 or any of the propaganda techniques in the chart on pages 643–644.
- Finally, write a paragraph explaining what you found.

False and Misleading Information

Are You Sure About That?   As mentioned earlier, a propagandist counts on you to be led by your emotions and not by your intelligence. Even if you wanted to think critically about a propagandist's message, you would not have much to go on because propaganda is so strongly **biased**. That is, it favors one point of view and ignores information that supports another point of view.

However, any persuasive message can be misleading, not just those containing the propaganda techniques listed on pages 643–644. Here are some signals that a persuasive message contains misleading information.

Presenting Opinions as Facts **Opinions** are beliefs, judgments, or claims that cannot be tested and proved true. Watch out for opinions presented as if they were facts. For example, a news report may quote an expert who says, "Space exploration is necessary for the future of human survival." How could such a statement be proved? Opinions presented as facts, and not supported with evidence, can be misleading.

 Listening and Speaking 1.9 Identify misleading information.

Missing Information A persuasive message may downplay or leave out negative information. For example, car commercials often downplay the high price of the car. Instead, the commercials focus on the comfort, design, speed, and other positive features of the car. Information on pricing is usually included in small print or announced very quickly at the end of the commercial. As you watch TV, ask yourself, "What is missing? What facts or points of view are not being included?"

The Moon Is Made of Green Cheese While some persuasive messages may include misleading information, others may present falsehoods as if they were true. This type of information may sound perfectly logical, so it is much more difficult to detect than other propaganda techniques. For example, a talk show guest promoting his diet book might say, "With other plans, ninety percent of people gain back at least three-fourths of the weight they lost." This might sound convincing, but because it would be difficult to track down these statistics, and because the speaker is trying to sell his own book, you should have a few doubts.

To avoid believing false information, consider the source of any fact or statistic. An authoritative source such as a respected research institution—for example, the Smithsonian Institution—probably provides accurate facts. If the information comes from a source you suspect may be strongly biased—for example, an oil company providing information that "proves" environmental regulations don't work—look for a more reliable source that can confirm the facts before you accept them.

> **TIP** Entertainment programs may also show bias. Think of programs that address controversial topics. Do these programs present equal, nonjudgmental information on both sides of a topic? Or do they show one side as correct or at least preferable to another?

THINKING IT THROUGH — Analyzing False and Misleading Information

The following steps will help you identify and analyze examples of false and misleading information on TV.

▶ STEP 1 **Focus on a specific program or advertisement. Briefly describe the message you have chosen and how it makes you feel.** You might pick an interview on a talk show, a segment of a newscast, a sports broadcast, or a commercial shown during your favorite TV program. I watched an ad for a water park. The ad shows kids having a lot of fun on the park's rides. Some of the kids even say how great it is. This water park looks like a lot of fun to me.

(continued)

Listening and Speaking 1.9 Identify false information.

(continued)

▶ **STEP 2** **Identify the main message or claim of the program or ad.** *The advertisement says that this is the #1 water park in North America because it is the biggest and has the best rides.*

▶ **STEP 3** **Ask yourself, "Is the claim a fact, which can be proved true, or is it someone's opinion?"** Remember that scientific-sounding words do not necessarily point to factual information. *I am not sure what the commercial means when it claims that this is the "biggest" park. Does that mean it has the largest attendance? the biggest area? the most rides? When the ad says that this is the "#1 water park," does that mean because of attendance, or was there a poll where water parks were ranked? These claims confuse me. Also, the kids say, "This park is the best!" This is an opinion that really cannot be proved. I wonder if these kids are actors paid to say positive things about the park.*

▶ **STEP 4** **Ask yourself, "What is missing from the message?"** Is there any information you still do not know after watching the program or advertisement? Are there other parts of the event, product, service, or idea that were not presented? *The commercial does not say how much tickets to this water park cost. How long are the lines for the rides? Can I bring a lunch, or do I have to buy one there?*

▶ **STEP 5** **Using your answers from the previous questions, decide whether or not you think the TV program or advertisement is misleading. Explain your answer.** *I think the commercial is misleading. The commercial presents opinions as facts and leaves out some important information. Although at first this water park looked like a lot of fun, I should probably get more information before I decide whether to go.*

TIP If you choose to analyze a TV program, make sure that the program has a persuasive message, whether it advertises a product or takes sides on an issue.

PRACTICE & APPLY 11

Guided and Independent Practice

In order to monitor students' understanding of the process of analyzing media, you may wish to have small groups analyze a print ad in class using the **Thinking It Through** steps on pp. 645–646 before completing **Practice and Apply 11** for independent practice.

Not all students may have access to a television at home. You may provide a videotape of a variety of advertisements or short pieces that they can analyze at school.

PRACTICE & APPLY 11

Analyze False and Misleading Information

- Choose a TV program or advertisement, and take notes as you watch it.
- Using the Thinking It Through steps that begin on page 645, identify false or misleading information, if any.
- Write a paragraph that sums up your findings, and illustrate your points with examples from the televised message.

Listening and Speaking 1.9 Identify false and misleading information.

(Standards reviewed on this page:
W1.0, 2.5a, 2.5b, 2.5c; L&S1.6, 2.4a.
To read the complete standards,
see pp. 616–617.)

DIRECTIONS: Read the following paragraph from a student's persuasive letter in a school newspaper. Then, read the questions below it. Choose the best answer, and mark your answers on your own paper.

> (1) The Helping Hands Community Assistance Program needs our school's help. (2) The supplies of clothing, shoes, and blankets are very low and will not be enough to help everyone who seeks assistance. (3) Only four coats, six blankets, and one pair of shoes are available. (4) Also, winter is coming soon. (5) The cooler winter temperatures always bring a higher demand for warm clothing. (6) Last winter some families left without supplies because the supplies were gone.

Answers

1. D   4. J
2. F   5. B
3. C

1. Which of the following sentences, if added to the paragraph, would provide evidence proving that supplies are low?
   A Helping Hands is a nonprofit organization.
   B The Helping Hands Community Assistance Program has low supplies.
   C You can tell winter is approaching because the temperatures are cooler.
   D The program needs clothing for twenty adults and ten children.

2. How might the writer address the concern of some readers that helping the program may cost money they do not have?
   F by suggesting that they donate used supplies instead of buying new ones
   G by telling them to borrow money to purchase the supplies
   H by providing them with a list of stores that have the supplies on sale
   J by ignoring this concern since not all readers may share it

3. Which of these sentences presents a **reasonable** and **specific** call to action?
   A Everyone should write the governor of our state and ask her to give coats, blankets, and shoes to the program.
   B The Helping Hands Community Assistance Program needs help now!
   C Our school should organize a clothing and blanket drive to help the program gather supplies.
   D The people of our community should consider doing their part.

4. If you were presenting this paragraph in a persuasive speech, what type of visual or media display might you use to persuade listeners that their help is needed?
   F a table showing the number of workers the program employs
   G a graph showing average temperatures for each month of the year
   H a photograph of the building in which the program is located
   J a video segment showing empty containers that usually hold supplies

5. If the paragraph above were part of a persuasive speech, which sentence would best summarize the speaker's opinion?
   A Last year, people had to leave without any supplies.
   B The Helping Hands Program needs help to collect supplies.
   C During cold weather, many people want coats, shoes, and blankets.
   D The program has four coats, six blankets, and one pair of shoes.

Standards Practice and Review **647**

APPLICATION

A Donation, Please

Explain to students that each year manufacturers and corporations donate merchandise to individuals and groups. For homework, students should write a persuasive letter to a company official explaining why the company should make a particular donation. For example, a student may write the president of a bicycle manufacturer and ask for a donation of a road bike that would be ridden across the state in an effort to raise money for cancer research. Letters could be addressed to real or fictional people and companies.

HOMEWORK

EXTENSION

Commercial Appeal

Divide the class into groups of four. Instruct each group to choose a product and design a thirty-second television commercial for the product. Groups should prepare a script, secure necessary props and costumes, and finally, present the commercial to the class or videotape it for later viewing. Have the students in the audience evaluate the effectiveness of the commercials by commenting on specific persuasive techniques used in the commercials.

RESOURCES

Persuasion

Assessment
■ *Progress Assessment of Writing, Listening, & Speaking*, Wkshp. 5
■ *Diagnostic and Summative Assessments*, End-of-Year Test

Extension
■ *Writing, Listening, & Speaking*, p. 129

Workshop 6 Learning About Paragraphs

Program Organization

Holt Literature and Language Arts provides a complete curriculum for standards-based instruction in vocabulary, reading, literature, writing, speaking and listening, and media. The instructional content of the program is divided into quarters to enable teachers to anticipate and administer the quarterly assessments required by California.

Workshop 6 is designed to teach and reinforce writing strategies to promote students' success in writing.

Language Arts Content

This workshop uses the writing strategies to enable students to master successfully the writing application.

What standards are taught in Workshop 6?

In this workshop, students will master the following Grade 6 standards.

Writing Strategies

1.0 Students write clear, coherent, and focused essays. Essays contain formal introductions, supporting evidence, and conclusions.

1.2 Create multiple-paragraph expository compositions.

1.3 Use a variety of effective and coherent organizational patterns, including comparison and contrast; organization by categories; and arrangement by spatial order, order of importance, or climactic order.

1.6 Revise writing to improve the organization and consistency of ideas within and between paragraphs.

Writing Application

2.2 Write expository compositions (e.g., description, explanation, comparison and contrast, problem and solution).

Instructional Planning and Support

Where do I locate lesson plans, additional resources, and other teaching aids?

- The Annotated Teacher's Edition and *On Course: Mapping Instruction* provide direction in planning and implementing a complete California standards-based curriculum. These components include instructions for administering diagnostic, progress, and summative tests; for presenting instruction of the standards; for differentiating instruction to provide universal access; and for locating and using the program's ancillaries.

- The program's resources are referenced at the beginning of each workshop in the bottom margin of this teacher's edition.

- Reminders for using additional resources appear in this teacher's edition at point of use.

- The *One-Stop Planner* CD-ROM contains editable lesson plans and all print ancillaries, available in PDF format.

Universal Access

How do I differentiate instruction to ensure that all my students master the standards?

Holt Literature and Language Arts provides comprehensive, differentiated instruction for all types of students.

- Most of the general instruction and teaching strategies in the Annotated Teacher's Edition are at grade level. These instructions will work well with the majority of your students.

- Advanced students have at least one activity for each workshop. The suggested activities are found in this teacher's edition at point of instruction.

- *Universal Access: Writing, Listening, & Speaking,* Workshop 6, opens with Teaching Notes that suggest which worksheets and transparencies are appropriate for each of three levels of learners.

- *Universal Access: Lesson Plans for Language Development,* Workshop 6, offers teaching strategies and additional worksheets designed specifically for English-language learners and special education students.

- *Daily Language Activities Transparencies* and *Spelling: Lessons & Activities* provide ongoing review of and additional practice in a range of language arts skills.

- For every workshop, preselected Web sites and activities are available to provide enrichment, independent practice, and enhanced instructional opportunities.

Assessment

How do I determine whether or not my students are making progress in mastering the standards?

Progress Assessment

- Use the Standards Review at the end of Workshop 6 for an informal assessment of the writing standards taught in Workshop 6.

- Use Workshop 6 in *Progress Assessment of Writing, Listening, & Speaking* to test students' cumulative progress in mastering the standards taught in the workshop.

WORKSHOP 6

Learning About Paragraphs

A paragraph is a group of related sentences that focus on a *main idea*. Often a paragraph is part of a longer piece of writing. For example, in a paper about a visit to a wildlife park, one paragraph might focus on the apes and monkeys. Each of the other paragraphs in the paper could each focus on another type of animal. In this way, the paragraphs would give readers a clear idea of what they might experience at the wildlife park.

In this workshop you will learn how to write focused, coherent paragraphs. In the process you will practice the following language arts standards.

STANDARDS FOCUS

Writing

Prerequisite Standards

Grade 5

- **1.0** Students write clear, coherent, and focused essays. Essays contain formal introductions, supporting evidence, and conclusions.

- **1.2a** Establish a topic, important ideas, or events in sequence or chronological order.

- **1.2b** Provide details and transitional expressions that link one paragraph to another in a clear line of thought.

- **1.2c** Offer a concluding paragraph that summarizes important ideas and details.

- **1.6** Edit and revise manuscripts to improve the meaning and focus of writing by adding, deleting, consolidating, clarifying, and rearranging words and sentences.

Standards Coming Up in the Next Level

Grade 7

- **1.0** Students write clear, coherent, and focused essays. Essays contain formal introductions, supporting evidence, and conclusions.

- **1.1** Create an organizational structure that balances all aspects of the composition and uses effective transitions between sentences to unify important ideas.

- **1.2** Support all statements and claims with anecdotes, descriptions, facts and statistics, and specific examples.

- **1.7** Revise writing to improve organization after checking the logic of the ideas.

California Standards

Writing

1.0 Students write clear, coherent, and focused essays. Essays contain formal introductions, supporting evidence, and conclusions.

1.2 Create multiple-paragraph expository compositions:
- **a.** Engage the interest of the reader and state a clear purpose.
- **b.** Develop the topic with supporting details and precise verbs, nouns, and adjectives to paint a visual image in the mind of the reader.
- **c.** Conclude with a detailed summary linked to the purpose of the composition.

1.3 Use a variety of effective and coherent organizational patterns, including comparison and contrast; organization by categories; and arrangement by spatial order, order of importance, or climactic order.

1.6 Revise writing to improve the organization and consistency of ideas within and between paragraphs.

2.2 Write expository compositions (e.g., description, explanation, comparison and contrast, problem and solution):
- **a.** State the thesis or purpose.
- **b.** Explain the situation.
- **c.** Follow an organizational pattern appropriate to the type of composition.

GO TO: go.hrw.com
KEYWORD: HLLA

WORKSHOP RESOURCES

Planning
- *One-Stop Planner* CD-ROM

Differentiating Instruction
- *Lesson Plans for Language Development,* pp. 240–241
- *Supporting Instruction in Five Languages*

Practice
- *Writing, Listening, & Speaking,* Wkshp. 6

Assessment
- *Progress Assessment of Writing, Listening, & Speaking,* Wkshp. 6

Internet
- go.hrw.com (keyword: HLLA6 W-6)

The Paragraph

The Parts of a Paragraph

Paragraphs are not all alike, but many of them have the same parts. Most paragraphs have a *topic sentence* that states the *main idea* of the paragraph, and *supporting sentences.*

The Main Idea and Topic Sentence   All of the sentences in a paragraph usually point to a single main idea. This **main idea** is the main point, or **focus**, of the paragraph. An author frequently states the main idea in a **topic sentence**. When a paragraph has a topic sentence, it is often the first sentence of the paragraph, as in the following example.

> Unlike domestic cattle today, the wild buffalo on the plains were very hardy animals. They lived and thrived when other animals, especially cattle, might have died. When winter blizzards hit the plains and prairies, the buffalo did not drift with the storm like cattle. Instead, they faced into the storm, either standing still waiting for the storm to pass or slowly heading into it. In this way the storm passed faster for the buffalo than it did for cattle, who would drift with the storm and frequently die from the elements.
>
> David A. Dary, *The Buffalo Book*

Sometimes, the topic sentence comes in the middle or at the end of the paragraph. In the following paragraph, the topic sentence comes at the end.

> He thought he had failed in his life's work. Others agreed with him. He died poor and bitterly disliked. To us today, this rejection seems strange. He had helped to free five South American countries from Spanish rule. He had won major
>
> *(continued)*

 Writing 1.0 Students write focused essays.

WHAT'S AHEAD

In this workshop you will develop coherent, focused paragraphs. You will also learn how to

- write a topic sentence that expresses a main idea
- develop supporting details
- use transitional words and phrases
- write introductions and conclusions

PRETEACHING

Standards Starter

Motivate. Tell students you will reveal the secret of making the perfect peanut-butter-and-jelly sandwich. Then, give them the following steps: *put jelly on one slice of bread; match slices, filling on the inside, and cut in half; finally, spread a thin layer of peanut butter on the other slice of bread.*

Students will protest that they cannot add peanut butter to the sandwich once it has been made and cut. The final step is out of order. Point out to students that the confusion they felt at the steps being out of order is the same a reader will feel if a paragraph he or she is reading is not properly organized. Tell students that they will learn how to write paragraphs to avoid such confusion.

Quotation for the Day

"The paragraph is a convenient unit; it serves all forms of literary work. As long as it holds together, a paragraph may be of any length—a single, short sentence or a passage of great duration."

(E. B. White, 1899–1985, American humorist, essayist, and novelist)

Discuss the quotation with students and challenge them to come up with their own definition of the word *paragraph.* [A possible response is that a paragraph is a unit of writing of varying length that contains one main idea.]

Ask for volunteers to share their ideas with the class. Have students write their definitions and save them for review after completing the chapter, so they may see if their ideas have changed or expanded.

Learners Having Difficulty

Allow students to work together to practice finding the main idea or topic sentence in a passage. You can use paragraphs from a reading selection in one of the earlier chapters in this book.

One way to help students identify a topic sentence is to tell them to look for the central sentence in a paragraph, the sentence without which the paragraph would seem vague or incomplete.

You can also draw on the chalkboard the graphic organizer below, in which the main idea or topic sentence is the hub of a wheel, with the supporting ideas the spokes. Have groups share their results.

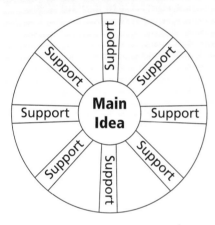

PRACTICE & APPLY **1**

Guided Practice
(For independent practice, see Resources below.)

Answer
The following topic sentence is a sample answer.

Last night's game was our team's best of the season.

(continued)

victories on the battlefield. He was anything but a failure. Over time, people began to accept the truth. Monuments were built to honor him. People started to celebrate his birthday. Today, Simón Bolívar is regarded as one of Latin America's greatest heroes.

Some paragraphs do not have topic sentences. However, when you are writing, it is helpful to use them. Writing a topic sentence helps you focus on the main idea of your paragraph. It also helps readers know what to expect from your paragraph. The types of paragraphs that often do not have topic sentences are paragraphs that describe a series of events or that tell a story. Read the following paragraph closely. You will notice that although it does not have a topic sentence, all the sentences focus on one main idea—Roberto Clemente loved playing baseball whether he played in a great stadium or on a muddy field.

It was a warm tropical evening in Puerto Rico. Roberto Clemente was playing with a group of boys on a muddy field in Barrio San Antón. It was nothing at all like the great stadium in San Juan. There were bumps and puddles, and the outfield was full of trees. The bat in Roberto's hand was a thick stick cut from the branch of a guava tree. The bases were old coffee sacks. The ball was a tightly-knotted bunch of rags.

Paul Robert Walker, *Pride of Puerto Rico*

PRACTICE & APPLY **1**   **Write a Topic Sentence**

Read the following paragraph carefully. Then, write a topic sentence that states the main idea. Remember, you may place the topic sentence at or near the beginning or end of the paragraph.

During last night's basketball game, our players made great passes to open teammates. They shot field goals and free throws better than they have all season. They made fewer mistakes than in any other game this season. They also played their best defensive game. They forced the other team into losing the ball and taking bad shots. They kept pressure on them for the entire game.

650   Workshop 6   **Learning About Paragraphs**

RESOURCES

Practice and Apply 1
Independent Practice
- *Writing, Listening, & Speaking,* WS. p. 130

Practice and Apply 2
Independent Practice
- *Writing, Listening, & Speaking,* WS. p. 131

Supporting Sentences Supporting **sentences** contain details that develop the topic by supporting, explaining, proving, or elaborating upon the main idea. The elaboration provided by supporting sentences may be in the form of *facts, examples,* or other kinds of details such as *sensory details.*

- **Facts** are statements that can be tested and proved true. They can be checked in reference books or through firsthand observations. They often include **statistics,** or information based on numbers.

- **Examples** are specific instances of an idea. T-shirts and sunglasses are examples of things you wear.

- **Sensory details** are details that you see, hear, taste, touch, or smell. To paint a picture in the mind of the reader with sensory details, use **precise nouns, verbs,** and **adjectives.**

In the following paragraph, notice that the writer uses all of the types of elaboration listed above. The supporting sentences explain the main idea that is stated in the first sentence.

> Your bones resist breaks in two ways. Not only are they as strong as steel, but they also have the ability to stretch like a rubber band. Bone is made of hard mineral crystals. These crystals give bone enough strength to <u>withstand</u> thousands of pounds of weight without breaking. Also in bone is a stretchy material, called <u>fiber</u>, which prevents bone from easily snapping when bent.

Topic sentence
Example
Sensory detail
Fact
Fact
Precise verb
Fact
Precise noun

PRACTICE & APPLY 2 **Collect Supporting Details**

To practice gathering details about the main idea of a paragraph, choose one of the main ideas below. Then, make a list of three or four details that support it. Try to use at least one fact, one example, and one sensory detail. Also, use precise language.

1. Skateboarding (or another sport) requires skill.

2. My room is always messy (or neat).

3. I cannot stand snakes (or spiders, worms, or storms).

Writing **1.0** Essays contain supporting evidence. **1.2b** Develop the topic with supporting details and precise verbs, nouns, and adjectives to paint a visual image in the mind of the reader.

The Parts of a Paragraph **651**

TIP The kind of support you will use to develop a paragraph will depend on which of the four types of paragraphs you are writing.

- A **narrative paragraph** tells a story or explains a series of events.

- A **descriptive paragraph** describes a person, scene, or object.

- An **expository paragraph,** such as the one on this page, provides information, including facts, instructions, and definitions.

- A **persuasive paragraph** tries to convince others to accept the writer's opinion or take action.

MODELING AND DEMONSTRATION

Supporting Sentences
Model for students how to find facts, examples, and sensory details for a main idea of your choice. Write your ideas on the chalkboard in a three-column chart with the headings *Facts, Examples,* and *Sensory Details.* Then, ask volunteers to demonstrate finding their own supporting details for a main idea of their choosing. Write their ideas on the same chart.

PRACTICE & APPLY 2

Guided Practice
(For independent practice, see Resources below.)
Answers
The following are sample answers.

1. Skateboarding requires skill.
Fact: It took me three years to perform only simple tricks.
Example: Bumpy surfaces can make you lose your balance.
Sensory detail: Elizabeth, the best skateboarder I know, is covered with scrapes from falling off her board.

2. My room is always messy.
Fact: I keep my clean and dirty clothes in two piles on the floor.
Example: When my friend Yan came over to see my new model airplane, he said, "When did the hurricane hit?"
Sensory detail: My closet is full of sports equipment that spills into the room.

3. I cannot stand snakes.
Fact: Whenever I am around snakes, I start to hyperventilate.
Example: Once I saw a picture of a snake in an encyclopedia and I nearly jumped out of my seat.
Sensory detail: Even the thought of snakes makes me feel a cold sweat and a prickling on the back of my neck.

The Parts of a Paragraph **651**

Unity

One way for students to make sure their paragraphs have unity is to check that each sentence of their compositions supports the main idea. Students can keep their main ideas a priority by writing them on a notecard or separate sheet of paper that they keep in view while composing or revising.

PRACTICE & APPLY 3

Guided Practice
(For independent practice, see Resources below.)

Answer
The following sentence destroys unity.

Fishing for catfish is popular, too.

The Makings of a Good Paragraph

Unity   When every sentence in a paragraph supports the topic sentence or main idea, the paragraph has **unity,** or **consistency of ideas.** A paragraph without unity can make readers wonder what the real point of the paragraph is. For example, if you are writing a paragraph on your most embarrassing moment at school, you would not want to include a sentence on your proudest moment at school. Such a sentence would destroy the unity of the paragraph by introducing a new idea to it. When you write a paragraph, be sure that every sentence supports the main idea.

Read the following paragraph closely. Notice that each sentence tells you something more about the main idea of the paragraph stated in the first sentence.

> Comets, asteroids, and meteors are the speed demons of the solar system. The average comet moves at 129,603 miles per hour; an asteroid's average speed is 39,603 miles per hour. Using radar, astronomers have clocked one meteor whizzing along at 164,250 miles per hour.
>
> Time-Life Books, *Forces of Nature*

PRACTICE & APPLY 3   Find a Sentence That Destroys Unity

The following paragraph contains one sentence that destroys the paragraph's unity. See if you can find it.

> Bass fishing has become the most popular type of freshwater fishing in the southern part of the United States. From Texas to Florida, the roads are filled with vehicles towing bass boats of every description (and every price, too). Surf the channels at practically any hour of the day or night, and you will find a television show devoted to bass fishing and sponsored by makers of bass fishing gear. Fishing for catfish is popular, too. Look on the newstands, and you will find entire magazines devoted to bass fishing. Bass fishing tournaments are held on lakes throughout the south for both amateurs and professionals.

Writing 1.6 Revise writing to improve the consistency of ideas within and among paragraphs.

RESOURCES

Practice and Apply 3
Independent Practice
■ *Writing, Listening, & Speaking,* WS. p. 132

Coherence A good paragraph needs more than a clear main idea, supporting sentences, and unity. It also needs to have *coherence*. **Coherence** occurs when the details in a paragraph are arranged and connected in a way that makes sense to the reader. One way you can create coherence is by arranging your details in an organizational pattern that fits your purpose and is clear to your readers. Organizational patterns for paragraphs are similar to those for whole compositions. Some of the more common patterns are shown in the chart below.

COMMON ORGANIZATIONAL PATTERNS

Organizational Pattern	Where Applied
Chronological order: Ideas and details are arranged in time order.	"How-to" explanations (See page 533.) Personal narratives (See page 676.)
Organization by categories: Ideas and details are arranged by the categories to which they belong.	Research reports (See page 591.)
Spatial order: Ideas and details are arranged by location—for example, from top to bottom or left to right.	Descriptive essays (See page 667.)
Climactic order: Ideas and details are arranged so that they build toward a climax, or moment of highest tension.	Short stories (See page 508.)
Order of importance: Ideas and details are arranged in increasing (or decreasing) order of importance.	Persuasive essays (See page 628.)
Comparison and contrast: Usually, ideas and details about one subject are discussed in one block (most likely a paragraph) and then compared or contrasted to ideas about a subject discussed in another block.	Comparison-contrast (See page 662.)

Transitional Words and Phrases Another way to create coherence is to use special words or phrases to help show how ideas are related. These words and phrases are called **transitional words and phrases.** They are connectors that tie one idea to another, one sentence to another, or one paragraph to another. For example, if you were writing a personal narrative in chronological order, you would want to use transitional words and phrases, such as *when, later, after,* and so on to help your reader follow the sequence of events in your narrative. The chart on the next page lists some common transitional words and phrases.

Writing **1.0** Students write clear, coherent essays. **1.3** Use a variety of effective and coherent organizational patterns, including comparison and contrast; organization by categories; and arrangement by spatial order, order of importance, or climactic order. **2.2c** Follow an organizational pattern appropriate to the type of composition.

REVIEW STANDARD

Transitional Words and Phrases

The following tip is a review of the 5th-grade **Writing Standard 1.2b.**

Transitional words and phrases are one way for students to create unity and coherence in paragraphs; however, as students write their compositions, you may want to provide these additional strategies:

- Before drafting, organize ideas using a cluster diagram and cross out ideas that are not related to the main idea.
- Use precise words consistently. In a paragraph about types of terriers, the writer should include specific words such as *cairn terrier* more often than vague words such as *dog.*

DIFFERENTIATING INSTRUCTION

Learners Having Difficulty

Allow students to practice using transitions by arranging students in small groups for a brief activity. Create a short passage or paragraph and supply groups with copies in which the transitions have been replaced with blanks. Then, have group members work together to fill in the blanks with the correct words from the chart. When groups are finished, ask them to discuss with one another why they placed the transitional words where they did.

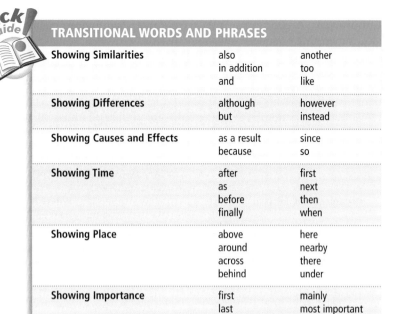

TRANSITIONAL WORDS AND PHRASES

Showing Similarities	also in addition and	another too like
Showing Differences	although but	however instead
Showing Causes and Effects	as a result because	since so
Showing Time	after as before finally	first next then when
Showing Place	above around across behind	here nearby there under
Showing Importance	first last	mainly most important

The following paragraph is about Babe Didrikson Zaharias, the greatest female athlete of her time. In 1932, she was the entire winning track "team" for an insurance company in Dallas, Texas. Notice how the underlined transitional words connect the ideas, helping give the paragraph coherence. Notice, too, that the transitional words all show time, which tells you that the paragraph is arranged in chronological order.

Even <u>as</u> the teams entered the stadium, the loudspeakers were calling them for the parade onto the field. <u>When</u> the Illinois Women's Athletic Club was called, twenty-two athletes marched forward. A second club fielded fifteen girls, another twelve. All in all there were more than 200 female athletes on the field. <u>Then</u> they called the team of the Employers' Casualty Insurance Company of Dallas, Texas . . . . One lonely girl marched bravely down the field. The crowd roared.

Harry Gersh, *Women Who Made America Great*

Writing 1.6 Revise writing to improve the organization of ideas within and between paragraphs.

Identify Transitions

The transition words in the following paragraph show how one idea is related to another. Identify the transitions in the paragraph. Use the chart on page 654 to help you.

> Building an igloo calls for skill and experience. First, the builder locates a site in firmly packed snow. Next, while standing in the outlined igloo, the builder cuts the snow into blocks of different sizes. Large blocks are used for the bottom layer, and thinner blocks are used for the walls. After the blocks are cut, the builder trims the top edge of each block to help the walls slope inward. Finally, the blocks are stacked to create a dome.

Special Types of Paragraphs

Introductions   Paragraphs that introduce essays must catch the attention of readers. There are several ways you do this.

- Begin with a surprising or unusual fact. *You may not think you can build a house, but with teamwork, people can quickly build, paint, and landscape a house.*

- Start with a personal anecdote or a funny story. *House painting has always been something I do well, so when I showed up at the volunteer building site, I was ready to paint. Little did I know that my friend Joaquin was ready to paint me!*

- Ask a question. *Do you wonder what to do with all of your free time after school and on the weekends?*

Next, an introduction must state the **purpose** or the **thesis** (main idea) of the essay. In other words, it must name the topic and, directly or indirectly, tell the reader what the essay will say about it.

Statement of purpose: In this essay, I will explain the valuable lessons I learned from volunteering to build homes.

or

Thesis statement: Volunteering to build homes taught me to respect all kinds of people, to work hard, and to challenge myself.

In some cases, the introduction will also *explain the situation* that led the writer to write on a particular topic.

Reference Note

For information on stating a **main idea**, see pages 649–650.

TIP Explaining the **situation** is required most often in persuasive or problem-solution writing. For example, before proposing adding a stop sign at a busy intersection, a problem-solution writer would need to explain that a number of accidents had already occurred at that intersection.

 Writing **1.0** Essays contain formal introductions.   **1.2a** Engage the interest of the reader and state a clear purpose.   **2.2a** State the thesis or purpose.   **2.2b** Explain the situation.

Special Types of Paragraphs   **655**

PRACTICE & APPLY 4

Guided Practice
(For independent practice, see Resources below.)

Answer
The following transition words are located in the paragraph: *First, Next, and, After,* and *Finally.*

DIRECT TEACHING

Special Types of Paragraphs
When discussing introductory and concluding paragraphs, offer students the image of a sandwich. Suggest that the introductory and concluding paragraphs are like the bread, and the paragraphs in between, which supply the supporting details, are like the filling.

RETEACHING

Introductions
Review the elements of paragraph structure by emphasizing purpose. Pair students and have each partner deliver orally an urgent message to the other, such as *A tornado has been spotted! Students should follow the practiced procedures as quickly and calmly as possible.* The other partner should record the message in writing.

Point out to students that a writer will always have a purpose that necessitates clear, organized writing to get his or her point across. The writer should give the main idea as concisely as possible, without any unnecessary details, so that the audience understands immediately the writer's purpose. Next, the writer should give details that support the main idea.

Students can review their urgent messages to see how similar they are, in miniature, to well-written paragraphs.

Conclusions   The concluding paragraph of an essay provides a detailed summary of the essay that reminds readers of the purpose of the essay. Look at the following suggestions for making your conclusion as interesting as your introduction.

- Finish what you started in the introduction. If you asked a question, answer it. If you began with an anecdote, finish it. If you began with a surprising fact, comment on it.

- Restate your main idea in a different, thought-provoking, or amusing way. *I now know that by giving up a few Saturdays, I did not miss out on fun. I had a great time and felt that my day was spent in an important way.*

- **Summarize** the main idea of each body paragraph in your essay, and connect those ideas back to your purpose. *What are the valuable lessons I learned? Volunteering to build homes taught me practical skills like preparing wood for painting, but more important, I learned to work with all kinds of people and to challenge myself.*

- Follow up on the ideas you have presented. For example, if you wrote about an experience that taught you a lesson about life, conclude by saying how that lesson will affect your attitude and behavior in the future. *I enjoyed my Saturday of painting so much that I have decided to spend one day each month volunteering in some way.*

Guided and Independent Practice

Before students complete **Practice and Apply 5** for independent practice, remind them to use a variety of details to support their main ideas. You may also point out that they do not need to include transition words or phrases in every sentence.

PRACTICE & APPLY 5   **Write an Original Paragraph**

Choose a topic that interests you. Then, consider the following questions, and write a paragraph on your topic.

- Will your paragraph be narrative, descriptive, expository, or persuasive? (See the tip on page 651 for definitions, or refer to the Writing Workshops for instruction.)

- What will be the main idea of your paragraph? How can you express that idea in a topic sentence? (See pages 649–650.)

- What kinds of details will you use to support your main idea? (See page 651.)

- How will you organize ideas and details? (See page 653.) What kinds of transitions might you use to connect your ideas? (See pages 653–654.)

Writing   **1.0** Essays contain conclusions.   **1.2c** Conclude with a detailed summary linked to the purpose of the composition.

RESOURCES

Practice and Apply 5

Guided Practice

- *Writing, Listening, & Speaking*, WS. p. 134

(Standards reviewed on this page: W1.0, 1.6. To read the complete standards, see p. 648.)

DIRECTIONS: Read the following paragraph. Then, choose the best answer for each question below it. Mark your answers on your own paper.

> (1) Guide dogs for the blind are more than just pets. (2) They go almost everywhere with their owners. (3) Unlike most pets, guide dogs wear special harnesses that help them direct their owners safely through unfamiliar places. (4) Guide dogs are trained to ignore strangers unless the strangers are in their owners' way. (5) You should not pet them while they are working.

1. Which of the following transitional words could you add to the beginning of sentence five to improve the coherence of the paragraph?
   A Before,
   B Therefore,
   C Also,
   D Finally,

2. Which sentence would destroy the unity or consistency of the paragraph above?
   F Even if a guide dog does not appear to be working, you should always ask the owner for permission to pet it.
   G Some service dogs are trained to help people with Parkinson's disease avoid falling and get back up after a fall.
   H Also, ask permission before you pet guide dogs wearing special vests rather than harnesses.
   J Many guide dogs are shepherds or retrievers, but collies and standard poodles also perform this service.

3. If this paragraph were part of an essay on service animals, which of the following sentences might the writer include in the introduction?
   A Dogs work for people in many ways: guiding the blind, pulling wheelchairs, and serving as support.
   B Millions of Americans have pets, including dogs, cats, fish, birds, gerbils, and many more exotic pets.
   C Among the dogs that work as guides for the blind are German shepherds, golden retrievers, and collies.
   D Guide dogs must be intelligent, cooperative, and thoroughly trained before beginning service.

4. How might you organize an essay about different types of service animals?
   F in chronological order, explaining the process involved in training a service animal
   G in comparison-contrast order, explaining why dogs are more suited than cats for service work
   H in logical order, discussing guide dogs for the blind, the hearing-impaired, and people with other disabilities
   J in spatial order, elaborating on how the dog uses its head, body, and paws to provide services

5. Which of the following sentences might the writer include in the conclusion of an essay about service animals?
   A Clearly, the assistance provided by service animals enriches the lives of many people.
   B A guide dog for the blind can work for many years and can become a pet when it is too old to work.
   C Animals make people's lives better by playing with them, listening to them, or curling up with them.
   D Only certain types of animals are suited to service so you are unlikely to see a Chihuahua in service.

Answers
1. B
2. G
3. A
4. H
5. A

APPLICATION

Model Search
Have students form small groups of three or four to search for exemplary paragraphs in magazines or newspapers. Groups should find one each of the following paragraph types: narrative, descriptive, expository, and persuasive. Remind students that paragraphs should have clear topic sentences that state main ideas and a variety of support. Students can refer to these model paragraphs as they work on their own writing throughout the school year.

EXTENSION

Careers
Explain the following scenario to students: You are a scientist who has recently discovered a new species of plant or animal. While at a conference with other scientists, you will have the opportunity to share this new species with your colleagues. For homework, have students create one or two paragraphs describing their new species. Remind students that their paragraphs should have main ideas accompanied by plenty of support. You may allow students to present their species to classmates in a conference format. **HOMEWORK**

RESOURCES

Assessment
■ *Progress Assessment of Writing, Listening, & Speaking,* pp. 16–20

Program Organization

Holt Literature and Language Arts provides a complete curriculum for standards-based instruction in vocabulary, reading, literature, writing, speaking and listening, and media. The instructional content of the program is divided into quarters to enable teachers to anticipate and administer the quarterly assessments required by California.

Mini-Workshop 5 in *Holt Literature and Language Arts* is to be covered in the first quarter of Grade 6; Mini-Workshops 1 and 4 are to be covered in the second quarter; Mini-Workshops 2 and 8 in the third quarter; and Mini-Workshops 3, 6, and 7 in the fourth.

About the Mini-Workshops

Standards-based lesson plans and suggestions for linking instruction with the mini-workshops and the related instructional material are provided in *On Course: Mapping Instruction.* For each mini-workshop specific teaching suggestions for the related material is found in Part 1 of this book and in the *Holt Handbook*.

- Mini-Workshop 1 focuses on writing a comparison-contrast essay. This material is also covered in the second quarterly assessment.

- Mini-Workshop 2 focuses on writing a descriptive essay. Chapter 6 connects to this mini-workshop by focusing on literary devices. This material is also covered in the third quarterly assessment.

- Mini-Workshop 3 focuses on writing a letter to an editor. Workshop 5 connects to this mini-workshop by focusing on persuasion. This material is also covered in the fourth quarterly assessment.

- Mini-Workshop 4 focuses on writing a movie review. Workshop 3 connects to this mini-workshop by focusing on responding to literature. Chapter 3 connects to this mini-workshop by covering theme. This material is also covered in the second quarterly assessment.

- Mini-Workshop 5 focuses on writing a personal narrative. Workshop 1 connects to this mini-workshop by focusing on narration. Chapter 1 connects to this mini-workshop by focusing on plot and setting. This material is also covered in the first quarterly assessment.

- Mini-Workshop 6 focuses on writing a problem-solution explanation. This material is also covered in the fourth quarterly assessment.

- Mini-Workshop 7 focuses on giving and listening to a problem-solution presentation. This material is also covered in the fourth quarterly assessment.

- Mini-Workshop 8 focuses on creating visuals. This material is also covered in the third quarterly assessment.

Language Arts Content

These mini-workshops use the writing and listening and speaking strategies to enable students to master successfully the writing and speaking applications.

What standards are taught in the mini-workshops?

In these mini-workshops, students will master the following Grade 6 standards. They will also review several standards from an earlier grade.

Writing Strategies

1.0 Essays contain formal introductions, supporting evidence, and conclusions.

1.2 Create multiple-paragraph expository compositions.

1.3 Use a variety of effective and coherent organizational patterns, including order of importance and organization by categories.

1.6 Revise writing to improve the organization and consistency of ideas within and between paragraphs.

Writing Applications

2.0 Students write narrative, expository, persuasive, and descriptive texts of at least 500 to 700 words in each genre.

2.2 Write expository compositions.

2.5 Write persuasive compositions.

Listening and Speaking Strategies

1.0 Students deliver focused, coherent presentations that convey ideas clearly and relate to the background and interests of the audience. They evaluate the content of oral communication.

1.1 Relate the speaker's verbal communication to the nonverbal message.

1.2 Identify the tone, mood, and emotion conveyed in the oral communication.

1.4 Select a focus, an organizational structure, and a point of view, matching the purpose, message, occasion, and vocal modulation to the audience.

1.6 Support opinions with detailed evidence and with visual or media displays that use appropriate technology.

1.7 Use effective rate, volume, pitch, and tone, and align nonverbal elements to sustain audience interest and attention.

Speaking Applications

2.0 Students deliver well-organized formal presentations employing traditional rhetorical strategies.

2.5 Deliver presentations on problems and solutions.

Review Standards, Grade 5

Writing

1.2 Create multiple-paragraph expository compositions.

1.6 Edit and revise manuscripts to improve the meaning and focus of writing by adding, deleting, consolidating, clarifying, and rearranging words and sentences.

Listening and Speaking

1.2 Interpret a speaker's verbal and nonverbal messages, purposes, and perspectives.

1.4 Select a focus, organizational structure, and point of view for an oral presentation.

1.5 Clarify and support spoken ideas with evidence and examples.

1.6 Engage the audience with appropriate verbal cues, facial expressions, and gestures.

2.1b Show, rather than tell, the events of the story.

2.2 Deliver informative presentations about an important idea, issue, or event.

2.4a State a clear position in support of a proposal.

2.4b Support the position with relevant evidence.

Instructional Planning and Support

Where do I locate lesson plans, additional resources, and other teaching aids?

- The Annotated Teacher's Edition and *On Course: Mapping Instruction* provide direction in planning and implementing a complete California standards–based curriculum. These components include instructions for administering diagnostic, progress, and summative tests; for presenting instruction of the standards; for differentiating instruction to provide universal access; and for locating and using the program's ancillaries.

- The program's resources are referenced at the beginning of each workshop in the bottom margin of this teacher's edition.

- Reminders for using additional resources appear in this teacher's edition at point of use.

- The *One-Stop Planner* CD-ROM contains editable lesson plans and all print ancillaries, available in PDF format.

What provisions have been made for students who have additional class time scheduled in language arts?

- *Universal Access: Writing, Listening, & Speaking,* Mini-Workshops, contains worksheets and transparencies that provide practice, reteaching, and extension of mini-workshop standards. Each Practice and Apply exercise is supported by graphic organizers or practice activities for on-level learners, advanced learners, and learners having difficulty.

- *Universal Access: Lesson Plans for Language Development,* Mini-Workshops, provides alternative teaching strategies and additional worksheets designed specifically for English-language learners and special education students. Many of the suggestions and activities in this ancillary will also be helpful to students in the regular classroom who are having difficulty with particular skills.

Universal Access

How do I differentiate instruction to ensure that all my students master the standards?

Holt Literature and Language Arts provides comprehensive, differentiated instruction for all types of students.

- Most of the general instruction and teaching strategies in the Annotated Teacher's Edition are at grade level. These instructions will work well with the majority of your students.

- Advanced students have at least one activity for each workshop. The suggested activities are found in this teacher's edition at point of instruction. Point-of-use suggestions for learners having difficulty, English-language learners, and special education students are provided.

- *Universal Access: Writing, Listening, & Speaking,* Mini-Workshops, opens with Teaching Notes that suggest which worksheets and transparencies are appropriate for each of three levels of learners.

- *Universal Access: Lesson Plans for Language Development,* Mini-Workshops, offers teaching strategies and additional worksheets designed specifically for English-language learners and special education students.

- *Daily Language Activities Transparencies* and *Spelling: Lessons & Activities* provide ongoing review of and additional practice in a range of language arts skills.

- For every mini-workshop, preselected Web sites and activities are available to provide enrichment, independent practice, and enhanced instructional opportunities.

Assessment

How do I determine whether or not my students are making progress in mastering the standards?

Progress Assessment

- Use the Standards Review at the end of the mini-workshops for an informal assessment of the writing and listening standards taught in the mini-workshops.

- Use the mini-workshops in *Progress Assessment* to test students' cumulative progress in mastering the standards taught in the mini-workshops.

Summative Assessment

The content in *Holt Literature and Language Arts* has been divided into four quarters to allow you to administer the four summative tests required by California. These mini-workshops will be assessed in the quarterly tests in the *Diagnostic & Summative Assessments* booklet. The tests will be administered separately, after the chapters, workshops, and mini-workshops pertaining to a quarter have been completed.

Mini-Workshops

STANDARDS FOCUS

Writing

Prerequisite Standards

Grade 5

- 1.2 Create multiple-paragraph expository compositions.

- 2.1b Show, rather than tell, the events of the story.

- 2.4a State a clear position in support of a proposal.

- 2.4b Support a position with relevant evidence.

Standards Coming Up in the Next Level

Grade 7

- 1.2 Support all statements and claims with anecdotes, descriptions, facts and statistics, and specific examples.

- 1.3 Use strategies of notetaking, outlining, and summarizing to impose structure on composition drafts.

- 2.1c Use a range of appropriate strategies (e.g., dialogue; suspense; naming of specific narrative action, including movement, gestures, and expressions).

- 2.4a State a clear position or perspective in support of a proposition or proposal.

- 2.4b Describe the points of support of the proposition, employing well-articulated evidence.

Mini-Workshops

In this section you will find several brief workshops. These mini-workshops will help you learn to

- write a comparison and contrast essay
- write a descriptive essay
- write a letter to the editor
- write a movie review
- write a personal narrative
- write a problem-solution explanation
- give and listen to a problem-solution presentation
- create graphics

You will practice these language arts standards.

California Standards

Writing a Comparison-Contrast Essay, pages 660–664

Writing

1.2 Create multiple-paragraph expository compositions.

1.3 Use organizational patterns, including comparison and contrast.

2.2 Write expository compositions (e.g., comparison and contrast).

Writing a Descriptive Essay, pages 665–670

Writing

1.2b Develop the topic with supporting details and precise verbs, nouns, and adjectives to paint a visual image in the mind of the reader.

1.3 Use arrangement by spatial order.

2.0 Students write descriptive texts of at least 500 to 700 words.

2.2 Write expository compositions (e.g., description).

Writing a Letter to the Editor, pages 671–672

Writing

1.1 Choose the form of writing (e.g., letter to the editor).

1.5 Compose documents with appropriate formatting.

GO TO: go.hrw.com
KEYWORD: HLLA

2.0 Students write persuasive texts.

2.2b Explain the situation.

2.5a State a clear position on a proposition or proposal.

2.5b Support the position with organized and relevant evidence.

Writing a Movie Review, pages 673–675

Writing

1.1 Choose the form of writing (e.g., review).

1.3 Use organization by categories.

2.4 Write responses to literature.

Writing a Personal Narrative, pages 676–677

Writing

1.1 Choose the form of writing (e.g., personal letter, narrative).

2.0 Students write narrative texts.

2.1b Include sensory details and concrete language.

2.1c Use a range of narrative devices (e.g., dialogue).

Writing a Problem-Solution Explanation, pages 678–680

Writing

1.2a Engage the interest of the reader and state a clear purpose.

1.3 Use arrangement by order of importance.

2.2 Write expository compositions (e.g., problem and solution).

Giving and Listening to a Problem-Solution Presentation, pages 681–685

Listening and Speaking

2.5 Deliver presentations on problems and solutions:

    a. Theorize on the causes and effects of each problem and establish connections between the defined problem and at least one solution.

    b. Offer persuasive evidence to validate the definition of the problem and the proposed solution.

Creating Graphics, pages 686–687

Listening and Speaking

1.6 Support opinions with visual or media displays that use appropriate technology.

CALIFORNIA STANDARDS

Listening and Speaking

Prerequisite Standards
Grade 5

- 1.5 Clarify and support spoken ideas with evidence and examples.

- 2.2 Deliver informative presentations about an important idea, issue, or event.

Standards Coming Up in the Next Level
Grade 7

- 1.5 Arrange supporting details, reasons, descriptions, and examples effectively and persuasively in relation to the audience.

- 2.4a State a clear position or perspective in support of an argument or proposal.

- 2.4b Describe the points in support of the argument and employ well-articulated evidence.

Writing a Comparison-Contrast Essay

You and your best friend both wear the same brand of tennis shoes, save your allowances, and spend too much time on the phone. You and your friend share many similarities, but you also have differences, such as your messy room and her clean one. Whenever you recognize that two things are both alike and different, you are comparing and contrasting. In this Mini-Workshop you will write an essay comparing and contrasting two subjects.

Choose Two Focused Subjects To plan your essay, choose two subjects you know well enough to explain in detail. These subjects should have basic similarities as well as differences. Consider choosing two TV shows, two people, two hobbies, or two animals. Make sure your two subjects are narrow enough to explain in an essay. For instance, you could compare apples and oranges in a short essay, but to compare fruits and vegetables, you would need to write a book.

> **TIP** One way to choose two subjects for a comparison-contrast essay is to pick a category first. Then, select two subjects within that category. For example, apples and oranges are part of the same category—fruit. Apples and motorcycles are from two different categories—food and transportation—so comparing them would be difficult.

Identify Purpose and Audience To determine a specific **purpose** and **audience** for your essay, first ask *why* you are comparing and contrasting the two subjects. Then, ask yourself *who* would be able to use the information. Once you have identified your purpose and audience, you can decide what background information you should include to help your readers get useful ideas from your essay.

The notes below show how one student identified her purpose and audience. She first brainstormed answers to her questions and then put check marks by the answers she wanted to address in her essay.

Subjects: dogs and hamsters

Purpose: What is the reason for comparing and contrasting dogs and hamsters?

✓ to help people choose a family pet

to help students from other countries understand two American pets

Audience: Who would be able to use this information?

✓ students and families who want a pet

students from other countries who do not have dogs or hamsters as pets

---

Writing 1.0 The writing exhibits students' awareness of audience and purpose. **2.2** Write expository compositions (e.g., comparison and contrast). **2.2a** State the thesis.

Standards Starter

Motivate. Activate thinking about comparing and contrasting by having students work in pairs to compare their favorite sports. Ask them to think about characteristics to compare, such as skills, strategies, and methods of scoring. After partners complete their comparisons, have volunteers share the results with the class. Discuss with students how comparing items helps them make decisions and judgments.

Identify Purpose and Audience

Students may have difficulty determining what background information their audience already has and what needs to be provided. Explain to students that they can conduct a simple, informal survey with their intended audience to determine the extent of the audience's background. For example, if a student is comparing road bike racing to mountain bike racing and the target audience is classmates, the student could ask his or her classmates the following questions:

Have you ever ridden a bicycle?

Do you know the difference between a mountain bike and a road bike?

Have you seen a mountain bike race or a road race in person or on television?

Have you ever ridden in a bicycle race?

RESOURCES

Writing Mini-Workshop
Planning
■ *On Course: Mapping Instruction*
■ *One-Stop Planner* CD-ROM
■ *Writing, Listening, & Speaking* —Teaching Notes, p. 135

Differentiating Instruction
■ *Lesson Plans for Language Development,* p. 242
■ *Supporting Instruction in Five Languages*
Template
■ *Writing, Listening, & Speaking,* WS. p. 136

Choose and Gather Support How are your two subjects alike? How are they different? As you answer these questions, begin to notice the larger areas in which you find both similarities and differences. These areas will be the **points of comparison** that will help you organize your essay. For example, in an essay about dogs and hamsters as pets, the kind of care each pet requires might be a useful point of comparison. Similarities in needs would include food and water. Differences would include outdoor exercise versus exercise inside a cage. List as many details as possible to support each point of comparison. Just be sure each detail relates directly to its point of comparison. If it does not, it will weaken, not support, your point.

TIP To plan for a vivid, interesting comparison, use **precise verbs, nouns,** and **adjectives** as you list details. For example, in the Venn diagram below the writer uses precise words such as "chase" and "fetch."

A **Venn diagram** can help you organize your details. To make a Venn diagram, draw two overlapping circles like the ones in the student's example below. In the example, the points of comparison are listed to the left of the circles. Each circle represents one of the subjects. The overlapping section includes the details that the subjects have in common. The sections that do not overlap include the details that make each subject different.

Writing **1.2b** Develop the topic with supporting details. **1.3** Use a variety of effective and coherent organizational patterns, including comparison and contrast. **2.0** Student writing demonstrates a command of the organizational strategies outlined in Writing Standard 1.0.

Writing a Comparison-Contrast Essay **661**

Mini-Workshop 1 • Writing a Comparison-Contrast Essay

DIRECT TEACHING

REVIEW STANDARD

Choose and Gather Support
The following lesson is a review of the 5th-grade **Writing Standard 2.3c.**

Researching their subjects thoroughly will help students as they work to add details, facts, and explanations to their essays. For example, the writer of this essay may conclude that it will cost more to feed a dog than a hamster. In order to add detail to the essay, the writer should research actual costs and provide examples in the essay. For example, the writer could compare the actual cost of feeding a large dog such as a Golden Retriever with the cost of feeding a hamster.

Evaluation
- *Writing, Listening, & Speaking,* WS. p. 137

Assessment
- *Progress Assessment of Writing, Listening, & Speaking,* p. 61
- *Diagnostic and Summative Assessments,* Midyear Test

DIFFERENTIATING INSTRUCTION

Special Education Students

Tell students that a thesis statement presents the essay's subjects, purpose, and points of comparison. Here is an example.

Subjects: fiction books and comic books
Purpose: helping readers learn more about forms of fiction writing
Points of Comparison: how fiction books and comic books are organized and how they tell stories
Main Idea Statement: Fiction books and comic books are both entertaining forms of storytelling, but they are different in how they are organized and in how they tell stories.

 Resources Reminder

For more help with Special Education Students, see *Lesson Plans for Language Development.*

MODELING AND DEMONSTRATION

Plan Your Essay

Explain that the block style works well for comparison-contrast essays, but the author needs to make use of words and phrases in the second paragraph that remind the reader of points from the first paragraph. Write this thesis statement on the board: "Basketball and soccer are both fun and fast-paced, but they are different in how the players handle the ball and score points."

Draw two large boxes on the board, one under the other. Write "basketball" in the top box and "soccer" in the bottom box. In the lower box write "Unlike basketball players, soccer players . . ." Tell students this is the type of transition that keeps both subjects in the reader's mind.

Ask volunteers to demonstrate understanding by suggesting words or phrases that will tie these two subjects together. [Possible responses: however; but; another difference between basketball and soccer]

Plan Your Essay   Map out the parts of your comparison-contrast essay by creating a graphic organizer that contains the following information about your topic.

INTRODUCTION

- **Involve readers** by connecting their interests to your topic.

- State your **thesis**, or main idea. This statement will identify the two subjects and your points of comparison, and it should directly relate to your **purpose** for writing.

- If necessary, briefly note any **background information** readers will need to know in order to understand your comparison.

BODY

Choose an **organizational pattern** for arranging details about your two subjects, in either *block style* or *point-by-point style.*

- **Block style** explains all of the points of comparison for the first subject and then, in the same order, all of the points of comparison for the second subject.

EXAMPLE	Subject 1: Dogs	• How they relate to people
		• What they need
	Subject 2: Hamsters	• How they relate to people
		• What they need

- **Point-by-point style** alternates between subjects, explaining first how they are alike and different for one point of comparison, then another, and so on. The subjects should be presented in the same order for each point of comparison.

EXAMPLE	Point of comparison 1:	How they relate to people
		• Dogs
		• Hamsters
	Point of comparison 2:	What they need
		• Dogs
		• Hamsters

CONCLUSION

Briefly **sum up** your comparison, and link your summary to your **purpose** for writing.

Writing 1.0 Essays contain formal introductions, supporting evidence, and conclusions. **1.2a** Engage the interest of the reader and state a clear purpose. **1.2c** Conclude with a detailed summary linked to the purpose of the composition. **2.2a** State the thesis or purpose. **2.2c** Follow an organizational pattern appropriate to the type of composition.

662   Mini-Workshop 1   Writing a Comparison-Contrast Essay

Give It a Go To draft a comparison-contrast essay, use the ideas in your Venn diagram and your graphic organizer to give your audience a clear picture of the similarities and differences between your two subjects. Here is an example. As you read, decide whether this essay is organized in block style or point-by-point style.

Writer's Model

Puppy Love or Hamster Heaven?

Your friends have one, maybe even two or three. The neighbors have one. Does it seem that everyone has one but you? No, it is not the latest video game, but something much more fun—a family pet. Dogs and hamsters both make good family pets, but they are different in the way they relate to people and in their needs.

Dogs and hamsters are both fun to hold and pet, but they relate to people in different ways. For instance, dogs enjoy human contact. They love to play fetch, chase, and tug-of-war with their owners. Dogs like to be petted, and most dogs will roll over to have their bellies rubbed. Dogs are also affectionate and love licking their owners' faces. However, dogs need lots of care, too. They need fresh food and water every day, and they need regular exercise. They also need someone to take care of them when their owners go out of town.

Hamsters are very different from dogs. Having contact with people is not important to them. They like to sleep when people want to play. Unlike dogs, hamsters do not like being petted. Many will hide when their owners want to pick them up. Hamsters are also very independent. They like to spend their time exploring. Hamsters may be low on affection, but they need less daily care than dogs do. They need food and water just as dogs do, but an owner usually fills up the food and water dishes only once a week. Hamsters need exercise, too, but they get their exercise by running on wheels in their cages. If their owners go out of town, hamsters can be left alone.

Dogs and hamsters both make good pets. Dogs provide plenty of affection, but they are also high maintenance. Hamsters are definitely low maintenance, but they are also less cuddly. The choice is yours.

INTRODUCTION
Attention-getting beginning

Thesis

BODY
Subject 1: First point of comparison

Subject 1: Second point of comparison

Subject 2: First point of comparison

Subject 2: Second point of comparison

CONCLUSION
Summary of comparison

Connection to purpose

Give It a Go
Point out to students the phrases "Unlike dogs, hamsters do not" and "need less daily care than dogs do" and "need food and water just as dogs do." Tell them that these are the types of phrases that tie the two subjects together when the block style is used.

DIRECT TEACHING

Fine Tuning

Consider pairing students who have chosen very different topics. Students should take turns evaluating each other's points of comparison. Students may indicate in the margins if the points are clear to them or, if necessary, mark areas that need more details.

Fine Tuning Most good writers are never satisfied with their first drafts. They study their drafts carefully to find ways to improve content, organization, and style. Once you have drafted your comparison-contrast essay, take a step back and think about how you might improve it. Then, trade papers with a classmate. Use the questions in the chart below to help you revise your own essay and offer revision suggestions to your classmates.

REVISING A COMPARISON AND CONTRAST ESSAY	
Introduction	Does the writer catch the interest of the reader immediately? Does the writer include a clear thesis, or main idea, statement? Is the writer's purpose for writing the essay clear?
Body (Organization)	What organizational pattern does the writer use—block or point-by-point? What changes might he or she make for clearer organization?
Body (Content)	Are the points of comparison and contrast well supported? Explain. Does the writer use precise language to communicate points of comparison and contrast?
Conclusion	Does the writer effectively summarize the main points of comparison or contrast? Is the summary linked to his or her purpose? Explain.

PRACTICE & APPLY

Guided and Independent Practice

Before students begin writing their essays, have them write down their purpose and a thesis statement. Briefly check each student's purpose and thesis statement to make sure that the thesis matches the purpose, that the two subjects are appropriately balanced, and that the subjects can be adequately compared within an essay. As students plan their essays, spot-check to see that they are organizing their papers correctly in the block or point-by-point style.

PRACTICE & APPLY **Write a Comparison-Contrast Essay**

Follow the guidelines on pages 660–664 to

- plan, write, and revise a comparison-contrast essay about two subjects of your choice
- proofread your essay
- give helpful feedback to improve a classmate's essay

Finally, publish your essay by posting it on a bulletin board, reading it aloud, or giving it directly to a reader.

Writing **1.0** Students progress through the stages of the writing process as needed. **1.6** Revise writing to improve the consistency of ideas within and between paragraphs.

Writing a Descriptive Essay

Have you ever read a description that was so rich in detail that you formed a vivid picture of the subject in your mind? If so, the description you read accomplished its purpose. When you **describe**, you help readers create a mental picture.

In this section you will write a descriptive essay that examines a person, pet, or object. You will describe details about that subject that you can gather through your five senses—plus your thoughts and feelings about those details. Through those details, your readers will be able to identify your **dominant impression**—what you think and how you feel—about the subject.

The Pick of the Litter   Choose a subject for your description by first listing the people you know well, pets belonging to you or someone you know, and objects with which you are very familiar. As you look over your list of possible subjects,

make sure you can answer yes to each of the following questions. If your answer to any of them is no, you may have a difficult time describing the subject.

1. Do you know the subject well?

2. Can you can study the subject closely, or have you been around the subject enough to remember important details?

3. Do you have strong thoughts and feelings about the subject that you are willing to share with readers?

Do You See What I See?   To help your readers visualize your subject, use two kinds of descriptive details: *sensory details* and *factual details*. The following chart provides definitions and examples from one writer's brainstorming list about his cat.

Quick guide

DESCRIPTIVE DETAILS

Type	Examples
Sensory Details: details that express what you experience through your five senses	**sight**—light gray with darker stripes, blue eyes, thin body **hearing**—purrs, hisses, meows **taste**—(does not apply) **touch**—soft, silky fur; sharp claws **smell**—dusty, litter box smells <u>awful</u>
Factual Details: details about the person, place, or thing that can be proved true, often involving measurements, numbers, and names	four legs, streaks through the house, ears hear everything, eyes see everything (even in the dark), eats human food and cat food (and bugs!), five years old, named Chaz, weighs eight pounds, tail indicates his emotions

Writing 1.0 Students progress through the stages of the writing process as needed. **2.2** Write expository compositions (e.g., description).

PRETEACHING

Standards Starter

Motivate. Before beginning the workshop, ask a volunteer to describe aloud for the class any object of his or her choice (a musical instrument, for example, or a building, or exotic animal). The student should describe the object as completely as possible and then call on classmates to guess what the object is. List sensory details and factual details on the chalkboard as they are used, and point out to students how the descriptive words and phrases the student used help listeners to picture the object. Then, refer students to the chart of descriptive details on this page.

MODELING AND DEMONSTRATION

The Pick of the Litter

Model for students the process involved in choosing a subject for a description. You may want to write your answers to the questions on the chalkboard. Then, ask a volunteer to use the same steps to demonstrate choosing a topic of his or her own.

RESOURCES

Writing Mini-Workshop
Planning
- *On Course: Mapping Instruction*
- *One-Stop Planner* CD-ROM
- *Writing, Listening, & Speaking* —Teaching Notes, p. 135

Differentiating Instruction
- *Lesson Plans for Language Development,* p. 243
- *Supporting Instruction in Five Languages*
Template
- *Writing, Listening, & Speaking,* WS. p. 138

Evaluation
- *Writing, Listening, & Speaking,* WS. p. 139
Assessment
- *Progress Assessment of Writing, Listening, & Speaking,* p. 62
- *Diagnostic and Summative Assessments,* Third-Quarter Test

DIFFERENTIATING INSTRUCTION

English-Language Learners

Arrange students in small groups with native English speakers. Have group members work together to come up with other examples of similes, metaphors, and personification. Group members can use the sensory and factual details in their essays to create before and after charts like the one on this page. Have groups share their results with the class.

 Resources Reminder

For more help with English-Language Learners, see *Lesson Plans for Language Development.*

DIFFERENTIATING INSTRUCTION

Advanced Learners   W2.1b

Enrichment. Encourage students to explore the concept of the extended metaphor, in which a writer compares an object or idea with another object or idea on more than just one point. Students can look for examples of extended metaphors in their favorite poems. Then, have students practice writing their own extended metaphors on the subjects of their choice.

When expressing details, use **precise language**—nouns, verbs, adjectives, and adverbs that are specific. For example, instead of "My cat plays with stuff," the writer of the model on pages 669–670 says "Chaz ferociously tears into his catnip mouse, table-tennis balls, and yarn."

Further Embellishment   Elaborate on your description by adding **figurative language**—descriptive language that compares one thing to another. Figurative language, such as *similes, metaphors,* and *personification,* will bring your subject to life.

- **Similes** compare two unlike things using *like* or *as.*
- **Metaphors** compare two unlike things by saying one *is* the other.

- **Personification** uses human characteristics to describe something nonhuman.

Similes, metaphors, and personification are called figurative language because the comparisons they make do not mean exactly what they say. For example, when the writer who is describing his cat says, "His ears are radar dishes," he means only that his cat's ears are very sensitive, like radar dishes, not that his cat's ears are electronic detection devices.

To create figurative language, look at the sensory and factual details in your essay to see what comparisons you can make. The following examples show how the writer who described his cat turned ordinary sensory and factual details into more imaginative images.

SIMILE

Before	After
You can be very quiet. . .	You can be as quiet as a classroom on the first day of summer vacation. . .
His body is very thin.	He is not solidly built, like a truck, but is slender and built for speed, like a race car.

METAPHOR

Before	After
His ears can hear anything.	His ears are radar dishes.
Chaz's claws are very sharp.	Chaz's claws are sharp, deadly daggers.

PERSONIFICATION

Before	After
He especially likes to trip people . . .	He laughs when he manages to trip a foolish person who tries to fumble through the house in the dark.

 Writing 1.2b Develop the topic with supporting details and precise verbs, nouns, and adjectives to paint a visual image in the mind of the reader.

Make a Good Impression After brainstorming a list of details, you will need to decide which details to keep and which ones to leave out. Think about the dominant impression, the main idea or feeling, that you want your readers to get from your description. For example, the writer who described his cat wanted to show that his cat is amazing to him. He decided not to include the sensory details related to smell, since for him the litter box is a disadvantage of owning a cat, nor did he include the sensory details related to taste, since those details are not relevant to cats.

> **TIP** Remember that the essay you write should be 500 to 700 words in length. This means that you have to be careful in your selection of details and in the amount of elaboration you provide for each of those details. Do not include so many details that you have no room to elaborate upon them. On the other hand, do not use so few that you cannot meet the length requirement.

First Things First Once you have decided how to describe your subject, consider how you will introduce it to your audience. The introduction to your essay should catch your readers' attention. Ask a question or make a bold statement that will really draw in your readers. Include a **thesis statement** of one or two sentences that clearly states your dominant impression and gives your audience some sense of your **purpose**—to describe a subject. For example, in response to the question "How can you love a cat?" the writer who described his cat wrote the following thesis statement.

> *In this essay I hope to answer that question by showing what an amazing animal my cat, Chaz, is—from the tops of his ears to the tip of his tail.*

> **TIP** For this workshop, you should be creative and expressive because the person, pet, or object you describe is close to you. A **subjective description** provides details in a way that shows your thoughts and feelings on the subject. In a subjective description you may want to speak directly to your reader, using the words *I, me,* and *you.* You will also use more figurative language in a subjective description. However, when your purpose is only to inform your readers about your subject, you can create an *objective description.* An **objective description** gives a factual, realistic picture of the subject without revealing your feelings about it.

Call to Order Next, you will need to decide in what order you will present the details you have selected. An effective pattern of organization for describing physical objects is **spatial order,** organizing details according to their location. You might describe your subject from right to left, from top to bottom, or from far away to close up. Following a clear order will help you focus your essay in a logical and **coherent** way.

Make sure you use transitional words and phrases to tell where each detail is located. Some useful transitions for explaining location are *below, beside, down, on top, over, next to, to the right,* and *to the left.* (See page 654 for more **transitional words** and **phrases.**)

Writing 1.0 Students write clear, coherent, and focused essays. **1.2a** Engage the interest of the reader and state a clear purpose. **1.3** Use effective and coherent organizational patterns, including arrangement by spatial order. **2.0** Students write descriptive texts of at least 500 to 700 words. **2.2a** State the thesis or purpose. **2.2c** Follow an organizational pattern appropriate to the type of composition.

Writing a Descriptive Essay **667**

REVIEW STANDARD

Call to Order
The following activity is a review of the 5th-grade **Writing Standard 1.2a.**

Students may need help deciding which spatial order to use in their essays. Suggest that carefully studying a visual representation of their subject will help them determine the best spatial order to use. To help them visualize their subjects, students can draw a rough sketch, create a labeled diagram, or take a snapshot. After studying the image and deciding on the best spatial order, students can gather accurate sensory and factual details to help them write their essays.

Mini-Workshop 2: Writing a Descriptive Essay

DIFFERENTIATING INSTRUCTION

Learners Having Difficulty

Point out to students how the writer of the model on p. 669 incorporated the details from the chart on this page into the **Writer's Model.** You might ask students to note how the writer turned the sensory and factual details into imaginative images and how the writer ordered the details to present a clear, coherent essay.

Other Possibilities   If you are focusing on your thoughts and feelings about a subject instead of its physical qualities, you might choose to organize your ideas in *chronological order, order of importance,* or *climactic order.* In **chronological order** you arrange your thoughts and feelings about the subject in the order in which you experienced them. In **order of importance** you arrange your thoughts and feelings from most to least important or vice versa. In **climactic order** you build from your least intense thoughts and feelings about the subject to your most intense.

To help organize your details in the organizational pattern that you choose, list them in a chart as you study your subject. The spatial order chart below shows one writer's top-to-bottom description of his cat.

SPATIAL ORDER	DETAILS
Head (top)	Ears—triangular, slightly to sides of head, hear everything: trouble, fun, food
	Eyes—beautiful, blue, catch anything his ears do not, can see in the dark, can see small things (bugs, tiny pieces of food, lost toys); returns your gaze thoughtfully
Body (middle)	Body—gray, striped, thin (eight pounds); soft, silky fur; eats cat food and human food (and bugs!)
	Legs—keep him in shape; runs fast, sneaks silently
	Claws—very sharp; tears up his toys
Tail (bottom)	a mood indicator; does the talking for him
	happy = sticks straight up in the air, slight curl at end
	angry = carries it low, swishes it back and forth
	scared = the hairs all stand out

Ready, Set, Write   Once you have organized the details about your subject, you are ready to write a descriptive essay. Write complete sentences using the details that you listed. Your chart can serve as an informal outline for your first draft.

In your **conclusion,** sum up briefly the most important ideas in your essay, and remind your readers why you wrote your essay. For example, the writer who described his cat concludes his description by writing, "I hope you can now see why I think Chaz is an amazing animal."

Writing **1.2** Create multiple-paragraph compositions. **1.2c** Conclude with a detailed summary linked to the purpose of the composition. **2.0** Student writing demonstrates the organizational and drafting strategies outlined in Writing Standard 1.0.

Now Picture This The following is a final draft of a descriptive essay about a pet cat. Do you see how the combination of sensory and factual details, figurative language, and spatial order helps readers better understand the subject and form a mental image of this pet?

Writer's Model

My Cat Chaz

Some people ask me, "How can you love a cat?" I say, "How can I not?" In this essay I hope to answer that question by showing what an amazing animal my cat, Chaz, is—from the tops of his ears to the tip of his tail.

As you look at Chaz from top to bottom, the first things you notice are his ears. They are little triangles that sit slightly to the sides of his head. His ears are the radar dishes Chaz uses to detect trouble, fun, or, most important, the sound of food. Even while Chaz is sound asleep half the house away, you can be as quiet as a classroom on the first day of summer vacation and he will hear you whenever food is involved. He never misses the hiss that a can makes when the can opener first punctures it or the crinkle of his treat bag being opened.

Lower down the front of his head are his beautiful, blue eyes. If anything could possibly escape Chaz's ears, you can bet his eyes would not miss it. Cats can see in the dark, which allows Chaz to play tricks on his less-gifted human friends. He especially likes to trip any person who foolishly tries to fumble through the house with the lights off. His eyes can also locate bugs, tiny dropped pieces of food, and lost cat toys that our human eyes cannot find. When you look into his eyes, though, he returns your gaze, as if he is looking deep to say, "I'm glad we're friends."

Working downward from Chaz's head to his gray, striped body, you have to wonder—How does he stay so thin? Beneath his soft, silky fur he weighs only eight pounds, despite eating his recommended daily amount of cat food; human food he has stolen, begged, or found; and whatever bugs he finds. He is

(continued)

INTRODUCTION
Attention-getting opener

Thesis statement

BODY
Description begins with head

Figurative language—simile

Sensory details (hearing)

Factual details

Description continues with body

Sensory details (sight and touch)

Factual details

Writing 1.0 Essays contain formal introductions, supporting evidence, and conclusions.

Writing a Descriptive Essay **669**

DIRECT TEACHING

Be Wise: Revise!

Have students review one another's descriptions in small groups. Each student should answer one of the peer-review questions as he or she reviews the other group members' descriptions. Group members can meet in a circle and pass their descriptions repeatedly in one direction until they are returned their own descriptions, with the other group members' comments attached.

Mini-Workshop 2 • Writing a Descriptive Essay

(continued)

not solidly built, like a truck, but is slender and built for speed, like a race car. Maybe this is why he uses his legs to propel himself through the house at breakneck speed. Those legs can also be used to sneak up on his toys, and the claws at the end of those legs are sharp, deadly daggers. Chaz ferociously tears into his catnip mouse, table-tennis balls, and yarn.

At the very end of Chaz is his remarkable tail. His tail is a mood indicator. He lets it do the talking for him. When he is happy, his tail will stick straight up in the air, with a slight curl at the end. When he is angry, he will carry it low and swish it back and forth. When he has been scared, the hairs of his tail will all stand out, puffing up like a giant, hairy caterpillar.

I hope you can now see why I think Chaz is an amazing animal. His ears hear everything, his eyes see everything, his claws shred everything, and his tail tells you everything you need to know. I wonder if he thinks that I am as amazing as I think he is?

Figurative language—
metaphor
Precise language
Description ends
with tail
Sensory details (sight)

CONCLUSION
Restated thesis
Summary of points

Be Wise: Revise! When you have finished writing your first draft, you will want to re-read it to see if your dominant impression has come through. Have a peer editor answer the following questions about your draft.

- What is the **dominant impression** that this essay expresses?
- Does the essay follow a clear, focused, **organizational pattern**?

- Are there more **details** that you would like to know about this subject? If so, what are they?
- Are the comparisons made through **figurative language** clear and imaginative?

After incorporating your peer reviewer's comments into your essay, re-read your essay, proofreading for correct spelling, punctuation, and grammar.

PRACTICE & APPLY

Guided and Independent Practice

Lead the class in a group description of the classroom. Check for understanding by making sure each student takes part in selecting details and suggesting ways to organize the description. Then, assign this Practice and Apply for independent practice.

PRACTICE & APPLY **Write and Revise a Descriptive Essay**

Use the instructions on pages 665–670 to write and revise a descriptive essay about a person, pet, or object. Then, share your descriptive essay with others.

Writing 1.6 Revise writing to improve the organization of ideas within and between paragraphs.

Writing a Letter to the Editor

Many newspapers and magazines publish letters from readers. The letters are addressed to the editor but are aimed at an **audience** of all of the publication's readers. The **purpose** of writing a letter to the editor is to persuade readers to do or believe something. Here are reasons you might write a letter to the editor.

- You disagree with a magazine or newspaper's position, or stand, on an issue.
- You want to persuade people in your community to take a certain action on an issue.

In this Mini-Workshop you will write a persuasive letter to the editor on an issue important to you.

Who Wants to Know? Where you send your letter depends on the issue about which you are writing. For example, if the issue you want to deal with is the problem of trash-covered community soccer fields, the community newspaper would be the right place to send the letter. The people who care about this issue are likely to read the local paper.

After choosing a publication to which to send your letter, look for the name and address of its editor. You can usually find this information on the page where letters and editorials appear. Many newspapers and magazines also include guidelines for you to follow when writing your letter.

Explain Yourself In the opening of your letter, explain the **situation** or issue that prompts you to write. For example, you might want to explain that the young people who play soccer are tired of playing on trash-covered soccer fields. Then, state your **position** on the issue or your **proposal** for solving the problem. Next, present your case in support of the proposal. Finally, in your conclusion, include a **call to action,** telling readers how to respond to your ideas.

The Perfect Fit Because space is limited in the editorial section of the newspaper, your letter must be short and direct—one hundred to two hundred words. (Your entire letter should fit on one page.) State your position directly and use only your most convincing supporting evidence.

I Mean Business Using a formal business letter format will show that you take the issue seriously. The parts of a formal letter are labeled in all capitals in the model on the next page. Notice that the **heading** includes the writer's address and the date, while the **inside address** includes the name and address of the audience for the letter.

The model is formatted correctly in the **block form.** Every part of the letter begins at the left margin of the page. A blank line is left between paragraphs, which are not indented.

Writing 1.0 The writing exhibits students' awareness of the audience and purpose. **1.1** Choose the form of writing (e.g., letter to the editor). **2.0** Students write persuasive texts. **2.2b** Explain the situation. **2.5** Write persuasive compositions. **2.5a** State a clear position on a proposition or proposal. **2.5b** Support the position with organized and relevant evidence.

Writing a Letter to the Editor   Mini-Workshop 3   **671**

PRETEACHING

Standards Starter

Motivate. Ask students to bring to class a number of newspapers. Have groups of students work together to read opinion articles and find an issue or position with which they do not agree. Point out to students that one way to express their own opinions on the issue is to write letters of their own.

RETEACHING

REVIEW STANDARD

Explain Yourself

The following activity is a review of the 5th-grade **Writing Standard 2.4.**

Remind students that a letter with a clear call to action will have a stronger effect on an audience than a letter simply expressing a difference in opinion. Have students meet with partners to tell each other the action they want to persuade their audience to pursue. If students have difficulty thinking of an action, they can describe the subject of their letters and partners can brainstorm for actions.

DIRECT TEACHING

I Mean Business

Point out to students that they cannot always tell from a first name whether a person should be addressed as Mr. or Ms. (consider "Kelly," "Stacey," and "Robin"), just as they cannot tell if a person should be addressed as Mrs., Ms., or Miss. An acceptable salutation in a business letter is to use first and last name, as in "Dear Shawn Lockhart."

DIFFERENTIATING INSTRUCTION

Learners Having Difficulty

Students may have trouble editing their letters to the editor for space constraints. Have students meet with two or three other students to read each other's letters. Group members can mark the opinion statements in the letters and rank the best three supporting points in order, from 1 for the most convincing to 3 for the least convincing. Students can use their group's feedback to decide what material is essential for their letters.

PRACTICE & APPLY

Guided and Independent Practice

Before students complete this Practice and Apply for independent practice, refer them to the **Writer's Model** on this page. After students have completed their first drafts, have them compare their work to the model. Suggest that they notate their drafts in the margins to show how each part of their draft corresponds to a part of the model. You can use students' marginal notations to help you monitor their progress.

Writing a Letter to the Editor (continued)

Writer's Model

HEADING
325 Main Street #12
Elton, CA 91217
February 25, 2003

INSIDE ADDRESS
Mr. Wayne Matsuo, Editor
The Elton Ledger
15 Madison Avenue
Elton, CA 91217

SALUTATION
Dear Mr. Matsuo:

BODY
Situation
Position statement
The Elton community soccer teams are tired of playing on ugly, trash-filled fields. We players want to start an anti-littering campaign to keep the fields clean and recycle the litter.

Reasons to support proposal
If the fields were kept clean of trash, more families would enjoy coming to games. Recycling the aluminum cans that litter the fields (at 32 cents a pound), we could likely earn over $100.00 a season, which could be used to train new coaches. Most important, citizens would be proud of our beautiful fields.

Call to action
During March, Elton soccer players will collect donations at games for the purchase of trash cans and recycling bins. We urge community members to give generously and to take responsibility for trash and recyclables when attending games.

CLOSING
Sincerely,

SIGNATURE
La Vonne Barton
La Vonne Barton

PRACTICE & APPLY **Write a Letter to the Editor**

Write a letter to the editor on an issue important to you. Format your letter correctly, and send it to an appropriate publication.

672 Mini-Workshop 3 Writing a Letter to the Editor

RESOURCES

(Continued from p. 671)

Evaluation
- *Writing, Listening, & Speaking*, WS. p. 141

Assessment
- *Progress Assessment of Writing, Listening, & Speaking*, p. 63
- *Diagnostic and Summative Assessments*, End-of-Year Test

672 Mini-Workshop 3 Writing a Letter to the Editor

Writing a Movie Review

In the Writing Workshop on pages 554–569, you responded to a story by writing an interpretation. Another way to respond to stories—in books, on TV, or on film—is to write a review.

Similar but Different   In some ways, a review is similar to an interpretation. Both identify specific elements of character, setting, and plot. However, when you write a review, your purpose is to tell readers your judgment, or opinion, of the subject of your review and give reasons for your opinion.

In a **movie review,** you can look at a movie's unique elements, such as special effects, the mood created by music, and so on. However, to keep this assignment simple, you will evaluate only the elements of character, setting, and plot.

An Appetizer   Focus your review by writing a **formal introduction.** Your introduction should catch the interest of your readers. An attention-grabbing opening may be a quotation, a short dialogue, or a description of action from the movie. You should also include the title of the movie in the introduction and explain what **genre,** or type, of movie it is. Telling your audience whether a movie is a western or a comedy can help them decide whether to see it.

> **TIP**   If you are handwriting your review, remember to underline the movie's title. If you are typing your review, you can use italics, as the writer of the model on page 675 did.

The Main Course   To help your readers understand what the movie is about, give a short explanation of the movie's characters, setting, and plot.

Characters   One important element of a movie review is the discussion of characters. Who are the central characters? Tell your readers about the characters' ages, personalities, strengths, and weaknesses. You should also tell your audience the names of the actors who portray the characters in the movie.

Setting   The setting of a movie is important. For example, a child's backyard is very different from a deserted island in the Pacific Ocean. A movie set in the present is vastly different from a movie set on the American frontier in the 1870s.

Let your audience know when and where the story told in the movie takes place. Also, give your readers some idea of how much time passes from the beginning to the end of the movie—hours, months, or years. When you watch a movie, be on the lookout for clues about the movie's setting—where and when the events in the movie take place.

Plot   After introducing your audience to the characters and setting, you can summarize the plot. Follow chronological order, telling what happens in the beginning and the middle of the movie. Be careful not to give away the ending of the movie.

 Writing 1.1 Choose the form of writing (e.g., review). 2.4 Write responses to literature. 2.4a Develop an interpretation exhibiting understanding and insight. 2.4b Organize the interpretation around several clear ideas, premises, or images.

Writing a Movie Review   Mini-Workshop 4   **673**

Writing Mini-Workshop
Planning
- *On Course: Mapping Instruction*
- *One-Stop Planner* CD-ROM
- *Writing, Listening, & Speaking* —Teaching Notes, p. 135

Differentiating Instruction
- *Lesson Plans for Language Development,* p. 245
- *Supporting Instruction in Five Languages*
Template
- *Writing, Listening, & Speaking,* WS. p. 142

(Continued on p. 674)

Standards Starter
Motivate. Ask students for their opinions of the best movie ever made. Write students' answers on the chalkboard, and point out that not every film listed can be labeled "the best." Point out that an evaluation of a film is a matter of opinion, based on certain criteria. Discuss with students the qualities that make a good movie, and ask them how they might share their opinion about a specific film.

Writing a Movie Review
Consult a book of movie reviews for ratings and content to make sure students choose appropriate films to review. You may want to make a list of suitable film titles for students or even show a film in class that students can review.

Advanced Learners
Acceleration. Use the following activity with students to move them toward the 7th-grade **Writing Standard 2.2.**

Encourage students to analyze their movie's unique elements, such as the editing, soundtrack, pacing, and use of special effects and voiceovers. Students can find a glossary of relevant terms in a film encyclopedia. You may want to bring in professional examples students can use as models. Have students compare the use of film techniques in a movie with the use of literary techniques in a written story. Which techniques are similar, and why? How do they affect the audience's understanding and appreciation of the story?

MODELING AND DEMONSTRATION

Dessert

Model for students the process involved in evaluating a movie. You may want to write your responses to the three bulleted steps on the chalkboard. Then, ask a volunteer to use the same steps to demonstrate evaluating a movie of his or her choice. Make sure the volunteer provides support for his or her evaluation.

DIRECT TEACHING

A Perfect Pattern

Point out to students that they can use the graphic organizer both as a checklist (to make sure they have all the elements of a movie review) and as a framework (to make an outline).

Remember that readers will want to know more than just what happens in the movie. They will want at least a hint about *why* the events in the movie happen. Therefore, after you describe the basic situation, provide some details about the most important events.

You may want to elaborate on the movie's **conflict**—the problem faced by the main character or characters. Keep in mind that conflict can take on many forms. For example, a character may be struggling with a difficult decision, or a character may be trying to survive in a jungle or save the universe from evil. Whatever the conflict, it keeps moviegoers interested. It will also keep your readers interested.

Dessert   Save the best part of your review for last. Conclude with your evaluation of the movie. In an evaluation, you

- tell readers your opinion—whether you like or dislike the movie
- give reasons for your opinion
- include a recommendation to see or not to see the movie

It is not enough simply to say you liked or disliked the movie. You need specific **evidence** for your opinion. For example, you might have disliked the movie because the characters were unrealistic or the plot was confusing. Use specific **details** from the movie to show where the movie failed or succeeded.

Finally, make it clear to readers whether you recommend that they see the movie or skip it. Remember to think of your audi-

ence when you make your recommendation. Would everyone like this movie, or just certain groups of people? For example, you may think the plot is too simple for teenagers, but it may be just right for elementary-age children.

A Perfect Pattern   You should organize your review in the familiar introduction, body, and conclusion pattern. The body of your review should be organized by **categories.** In a simple review, the categories are the elements of the movie—characters, plot, and setting. In longer reviews, however, you might include other categories such as special effects. Use a graphic organizer like the one below to organize your review.

Introduction
- Attention-grabbing opening
- Movie's title
- Type of movie (genre)

Body
- Details about characters
- Details about setting
- Details about plot

Conclusion
- Opinion/judgment
- Reasons
- Recommendation

Writing 1.3 Use a variety of effective and coherent organizational patterns, including organization by categories. **2.4c** Develop and justify the interpretation through sustained use of examples and textual evidence.

RESOURCES

(Continued from p. 673)

Evaluation
- *Writing, Listening, & Speaking*, WS. p. 143

Assessment
- *Progress Assessment of Writing, Listening, & Speaking*, p. 64
- *Diagnostic and Summative Assessments*, Midyear Test

Writer's Model

A Review of *Chicken Run*

Do you want to change forever how you look at chicken potpie? Do you want to laugh all the while? Then go see the clay-animation movie *Chicken Run*. This wonderful movie is at the same time a romance, a comedy, and a drama.

Ginger (voice of Julia Sawalha) is the central character, one of many hens cooped up in an egg farm owned by the villain of the film, Mrs. Tweedy (voice of Miranda Richardson). Some of the chickens, who have been held prisoner for a long time, dream of freedom. Ginger tries again and again to escape. She always fails and eventually gets put into solitary confinement in a dumpster for her efforts.

Help falls out of the sky in the form of Rocky the Rhode Island Red Rooster (voice of Mel Gibson), who has just escaped from a traveling circus. Rocky has a rough landing and ends up with an injured wing. Ginger and friends nurse him back to health. Meanwhile, they discover that the evil Mrs. Tweedy has dangerous plans. She is planning to kill all the chickens and turn them into potpies.

They have only a short time to escape from the egg farm. Rocky says he can help them escape by teaching them how to fly. Will they succeed or become potpies? You will have to see the movie to find out for yourself.

Chicken Run is excellent. The story is humorous and suspenseful—at a couple of points I laughed so hard I nearly fell off the edge of my seat. The characters are believable and funny. The settings are colorful. I strongly recommend *Chicken Run* as a movie that both kids and adults can enjoy. Don't miss it!

INTRODUCTION
Attention-grabber

Statement of title
Type of movie
BODY
Character and setting details

Plot details

Conflict details

CONCLUSION
Opinion
Reasons
Recommendation

PRACTICE & APPLY   Write a Movie Review

> Now it is your turn to write a movie review. As you write, keep your audience in mind, and refer to the graphic organizer on page 674 and the Writer's Model above.

DIRECT TEACHING

REVIEW STANDARD

Writer's Model
The following activity is a review of the 5th-grade **Writing Standard 1.2b.**

Have students pay special attention to the vivid details the writer uses to provide specific support in the review. What are the benefits of the details? You may want to give students sticky notes to put at the appropriate places on the model so that they may mark the specific elements of the review. Encourage students to use vivid details in their own writing.

PRACTICE & APPLY

Guided and Independent Practice
Monitor students' progress by discussing with the class the different parts of the model and by making sure students show a familiarity with the elements of a movie review. Then, assign this Practice and Apply for independent practice.

Standards Starter

Motivate. Ask students if they enjoy hearing stories about themselves when they were very young from adults in their family. Most will probably respond positively. Then, you might share one of your own stories or ask a student to share one. Explain that these true stories fall into the category of personal narrative because they are autobiographical in nature.

MODELING AND DEMONSTRATION

Events

Remind students that they should "show" rather than "tell." One way to do this is by providing detailed sensory descriptions. To help students include sensory details in their personal narratives, draw lines on the chalkboard to create five columns. Above the columns, place these headings: *Sight, Sound, Taste, Touch, Smell.* In each column, begin a list of words that students can refer to as they write their narratives. For example, you might place the words *glittering, fluorescent,* and *gargantuan* in the Sight column. Have students demonstrate their understanding by creating their own lists of ten or more words in each column that relate to their personal narratives. Encourage them to be imaginative.

RETEACHING

And the Moral of the Story Is . . .

Explain to students that their reason for narrating their experience is the same as their purpose. As they begin thinking of topics, tell them to write down their reasons for choosing each topic. Have them be more specific than "It was fun." Encourage them to be exact: "I learned that I was really good at something I'd been afraid to try before."

Writing a Personal Narrative

Some of the best stories come from real life. When you write a **personal narrative,** your topic is **autobiographical**—a true story from your own life. The main purpose of a personal narrative is to express your own thoughts and feelings about your experience. In this Mini-Workshop you will write a personal narrative in the form of a letter to a specific person.

Let Me Tell You   A personal narrative is a natural way to share an experience with someone. Even so, what you say to your Aunt Keisha would probably be different from what you would say to Letty, your best friend. Keep in mind that when you write a personal narrative in letter form, you choose details that would make the experience interesting to your audience.

Getting Personal   To choose a topic for a personal narrative, select an experience that is meaningful to you. Think about times in your life you would describe as being the happiest, saddest, most frightening, most embarrassing, or most challenging. If you choose an experience that sticks out strongly in your memory, you will have an easier time recalling details about it. Remember: Choose a topic that you feel comfortable sharing.

You Had to Be There   You can help your reader feel as if he or she is reliving the experience with you by using plenty of **details**. Include details about people, events, and feelings.

- **People** Who are the main people in your experience? Include details about appearance, personality, and behavior to make the people come alive.
- **Events** Make sure your reader can visualize the events of your experience. Use **concrete language,** such as action verbs and precise nouns and adjectives, to describe events that occurred, rather than just summarizing them. Include **sensory details** to describe what you saw, heard, tasted, felt, and smelled.
- **Feelings** Describe details about your thoughts and feelings throughout the body of your letter. You can describe your feelings directly, such as *I was really afraid.* However, you may want to reveal your feelings through **dialogue** and **action details**—what you said and did.

And the Moral of the Story Is . . . There has to be a reason for narrating a specific experience. Maybe you were incredibly homesick at camp. Did that experience help you appreciate your family? Did it teach you how to make new friends? Be sure that your reader knows how you felt about the experience and what it taught you.

Order Counts   You should tell your personal narrative in **chronological order**—the order in which the events happened. Your readers will be able to follow your story more easily if you begin with the first event and end with the last event.

Writing 1.0 The writing exhibits students' awareness of the audience and purpose. **1.1** Choose the form of writing (e.g., personal letter, narrative). **1.3** Use a variety of effective and coherent organizational patterns. **2.0** Students write narrative texts. **2.1** Write narratives. **2.1b** Include sensory details and concrete language. **2.1c** Use a range of narrative devices (e.g., dialogue).

RESOURCES

Writing Mini-Workshop
Planning
- *On Course: Mapping Instruction*
- *One-Stop Planner* CD-ROM
- *Writing, Listening, & Speaking* —Teaching Notes, p. 135

Differentiating Instruction
- *Lesson Plans for Language Development,* p. 246
- *Supporting Instruction in Five Languages*
Template
- *Writing, Listening, & Speaking,* WS. p. 144
Evaluation
- *Writing, Listening, & Speaking,* WS. p. 145

Express Yourself   Read the personal narrative below. Notice that the writer briefly introduces the subject of her letter. She describes her thoughts and feelings and includes dialogue. She concludes her letter by explaining the meaning of the experience. You can use the same techniques in your personal narrative.

Writer's Model

Dear Margaret,

    You asked how things are going since I moved. Let me give you an idea by telling you about my first day at Oakridge Middle School.

    I was so scared my legs were shaking. As a new kid, I was afraid to speak to anyone. No one spoke to me either, but two girls smiled at me.

    The principal gave me a class schedule and a locker number. Then, she called a boy into her office and said, "Sam will be your guide today, Rosa. He lives in your apartment building. I thought you'd like to meet a new friend and neighbor." I was embarrassed and couldn't speak because my throat felt so dry. Sam rescued me by asking where I was from and if I had any brothers or sisters. It felt good to meet someone who wanted to know me.

    Now Sam is one of my best friends. I have many other friends, too. Being a new kid is painful for a while, but it does not last very long. I still miss you and my other friends there, but I'm glad that Sam was willing to help a scared new kid feel at home. Now I will do the same for other new kids I see at Oakridge.

                         Your friend,

                         Rosa

INTRODUCTION
Topic

Attention-grabber

BODY
Dialogue

Sensory details

Feelings

CONCLUSION

Meaning of experience

PRACTICE & APPLY

Write a Personal Narrative in Letter Form

Write a personal narrative in letter form using the instructions on pages 676–677 and the model above. Then, mail the letter or share it with your class.

Writing 2.0 Student writing demonstrates the organizational and drafting strategies outlined in Writing Standard 1.0.

CRITICAL THINKING
Rosa ended her letter with this sentence: "Now I will do the same for other new kids I see at Oakridge." Ask students what that sentence reveals about Rosa's personality. Ask for suggestions of other closing sentences that would reveal a different personality. For example, the sentence "I have begged my parents never to move again" may indicate that Rosa is still fearful and lacks confidence.

PRACTICE & APPLY

Guided and Independent Practice
Monitor students' progress by having them share with you individually the incidents they will write about, the main events they will include, and the effects the incident had upon them. As they write, encourage them to refer back to the framework for a short story on p. 510.

Assessment
- *Progress Assessment of Writing, Listening, & Speaking,* p. 65
- *Diagnostic and Summative Assessments,* First-Quarter Test

Standards Starter

Motivate. Begin a discussion about the large number of advice columnists who offer a solution to any kind of problem. Ask students what they think about this type of advice. Explain that it is more helpful and rewarding to work toward personal solutions to personal problems than to depend on an advice columnist. Mention also that individuals may sometimes share relevant experiences with others that they trust.

CORRECTING MISCONCEPTIONS

Students may make the mistake of thinking that making connections between problems and their solutions simply involves restating the problem in a different way. For example, students may write, "Respecting each other more will help siblings overcome their rivalry, because disrespect is often at the source of sibling rivalry." Point out that such an argument is circular. That is, it does not answer the question of *how* to create respect among siblings but simply restates the problem. Emphasize to students that they should be as specific as possible in presenting solutions, that they should give substantive support, and that they should not leave important reader questions unanswered.

Writing a Problem-Solution Explanation

At the track meet, you race to victory in the 200-meter dash. After the finish, you look for your older sister, but you can't seem to find her. When you do, you try to tell her about the race, but she gets angry and stomps off. Your best friend tells you about a similar situation with her little brother. That starts you thinking: How can arguments with brothers and sisters be avoided? You might explore this question by writing a problem-solution explanation.

What's the Problem? A problem-solution explanation is a kind of exposition. The purpose of **exposition** is to inform the reader. A **problem-solution**

explanation informs the reader about a problem and gives some possible solutions to the problem. Problem-solution writing shows readers that the problem is real and that the solutions are workable—meaning readers can use the solutions.

A problem-solution explanation has at least four parts, as shown in the following graphic organizer. Some problem-solution writing tries to persuade the reader to adopt a particular solution. However, in this assignment you will not promote one solution over another. Instead, you will provide information, so be sure to **state your purpose** clearly in your introduction.

Introduction
- State the purpose
- Explain the situation—the causes and effects of the problem

Solution 1
- Explain the first solution
- Make connections with the problem
- Give support showing that the solution is workable

Solution 2
- Explain the second solution
- Make connections with the problem
- Give support showing that the solution is workable

Conclusion
- Summarize the problem and solutions

Writing 1.2 Create multiple-paragraph expository compositions. **1.2a** State a clear purpose. **2.0** Students write expository texts. **2.2** Write expository compositions (e.g., problem and solution). **2.2a** State the purpose.

RESOURCES

Writing Mini-Workshop

Planning
- *On Course: Mapping Instruction*
- *One-Stop Planner* CD-ROM
- *Writing, Listening, & Speaking* —Teaching Notes, p. 135

Differentiating Instruction
- *Lesson Plans for Language Development,* p. 247
- *Supporting Instruction in Five Languages*

Template
- *Writing, Listening, & Speaking*, WS. p. 146

Evaluation
- *Writing, Listening, & Speaking*, WS. p. 147

Explain the Situation Your introduction should also give readers information about the **causes** and **effects** of the problem. To analyze the causes and effects of the problem, you may need to do a little research in addition to thinking about your own experience. For example, you might remember what caused a conflict with your brother, but you might need to read a book on sibling rivalry to find out about the effects of this type of conflict. Focus only on the one or two most important causes and effects of the problem in your essay.

Organization In the body of your essay, you will explain two possible solutions. You may discover solutions yourself or find them through research. The best **organizational pattern** for a problem-solution essay is **order of importance,** in which you discuss the solution you think is most important first.

Make sure your explanation of each solution answers these two questions.

■ *Does the solution address the cause of the problem?* For example, if sibling rivalry is

caused by feelings of competition, a good solution must reduce these feelings of competition.

■ *Does the solution fix the effects of the problem?* For instance, an effect of sibling rivalry is disrespect between siblings. A good solution must help siblings respect one another.

In the graphic organizer on page 678, notice that the arrows point from the solutions back to the problem explained in the introduction. These arrows mean that you should explain how each solution addresses the problem's causes or effects.

Support Your identification of the causes and effects of the problem and your explanation of each solution must have support. Use facts, examples, statements made by experts, and other **evidence** from research and from your own experience with the problem.

Problem Solved Below is an example of a problem-solution explanation on sibling rivalry.

Writer's Model

> "She started it!" "No, I didn't! He did!" Often, brothers and sisters fight. Sibling rivalry—the name for the intense competition between young family members—can be a serious problem. Experts say that sibling rivalry can hurt children's feelings and even cause permanent emotional damage. Also, siblings who do not get along as children might miss out on the fun and comfort of having a good relationship with a brother or
>
> *(continued)*

INTRODUCTION

Effects of the problem

Writing **1.2b** Develop the topic with supporting details. **1.3** Use a variety of effective and coherent organizational patterns, including arrangement by order of importance. **2.2b** Explain the situation. **2.2c** Follow an organizational pattern appropriate to the type of composition. **2.2d** Offer persuasive evidence to validate arguments and conclusions as needed.

Assessment

■ *Progress Assessment of Writing, Listening, & Speaking,* p. 66
■ *Diagnostic and Summative Assessments,* End-of-Year Test

DIRECT TEACHING

REVIEW STANDARD

Support
The following lesson is a review of the 5th-grade **Writing Standard 2.4b.**

Give students the following mnemonic device to help them remember different ways to elaborate when writing a problem-solution explanation:

Naughty **d**ogs **e**at **c**at **t**reats.

Numbers

Descriptive words

Exact verbs

Comparisons (simile, metaphor)

Transitions

Explain to students that adding some or all of these elements will not only make their explanations clearer and easier to follow, but will also give them an air of authority.

DIFFERENTIATING INSTRUCTION

Advanced Learners

Acceleration. Use the following activity with students to move them toward the 7th-grade **Writing Standard 1.2.**

Ask students to add anecdotes, descriptions, facts, statistics, or specific examples to the model to support the descriptions of the problems and solutions. Students can either do research to find such support or use examples and anecdotes from their own lives. Tell students to be prepared to defend how their additions strengthen the model's problem-solution explanation.

DIFFERENTIATING INSTRUCTION

Learners Having Difficulty

Arrange students in pairs. Have partners work together to make sure that their explanations contain all the criteria listed in the four-part graphic organizer on p. 678. Students should label the parts of their explanations that match the criteria in the organizer. If students are missing some information, the partners can work together to revise or add to their explanations.

PRACTICE & APPLY

Guided and Independent Practice

Monitor students' understanding by choosing a sample problem and presenting solutions. Then, have students work together to make sure the problem-solution explanation answers the questions on p. 679. You may want to present your problem-solution explanation in outline form on the chalkboard while students answer the questions. Then, assign this Practice and Apply as independent practice.

(*continued*)

Causes of the problem	sister as adults. According to experts, there are two causes for sibling rivalry. The first cause is that children feel they are not getting the same amount of attention from their parents. The second cause is that siblings are competing to find their own talents, activities, and interests. Here are two possible solutions siblings might try to solve the problem of sibling rivalry.
Statement of purpose	
BODY Solution 1 Support	First, siblings can focus on each other's strengths. Instead of picking on faults, they can praise what they like or admire about the other sibling. They can ask for the sibling's help with something he or she knows about. By focusing on each other's strengths, brothers and sisters can help one another find their talents and abilities.
Solution 2 Support	Second, siblings can open up to one another. Sharing thoughts and feelings helps reduce competitiveness between siblings. This kind of sharing gives brothers and sisters something in common and makes them less likely to work against each other in a competitive way.
CONCLUSION Summary of problem Summary of solutions	Sibling rivalry is disruptive, and it can ruin relationships that should last a lifetime. However, siblings can help end rivalry. By focusing on each other's strengths and sharing openly, siblings can become partners, not rivals, in discovering who they are.

Check It Out After you have written a draft of your problem-solution explanation, use the graphic organizer on page 678 to evaluate the content and organization of your draft. If necessary, revise your draft by adding or elaborating information or by rearranging ideas. Finally, proofread your revised essay, and correct any errors you find in spelling or punctuation.

PRACTICE & APPLY

Write a Problem-Solution Explanation

Write a problem-solution explanation using the instructions on pages 678–679. Proofread your explanation before sharing it with a small group of classmates.

Writing 1.0 Students write clear, coherent, and focused essays. Essays contain formal introductions, supporting evidence, and conclusions. **1.6** Revise writing to improve the organization of the ideas within and between paragraphs.

Mini-Workshop 6 · Writing a Problem-Solution Explanation

Giving and Listening to a Problem-Solution Presentation

"You get along so well with your sister. Could you come talk to my scout troop about sibling rivalry?" If you were asked to give a problem-solution presentation, would you be prepared?

A **problem-solution presentation** is a type of **oral exposition**—an explanation given out loud to an audience. In this Mini-Workshop you will not only deliver a problem-solution presentation, but also listen to and evaluate a classmate who does the same. (For additional help in developing the content for your problem-solution presentation, see pages 678–680.)

What's the Problem?   The first step in planning a problem-solution presentation is to identify a problem. Follow the guidelines below in selecting a problem.

- The problem should directly affect your audience.
- The solutions you propose should be ones your listeners can use.

Avoid selecting a problem your listeners are not affected by or cannot help solve.

Define the Problem A focused problem-solution presentation should define the problem and provide **evidence** to validate, or prove, the existence of the problem. You can research the problem by interviewing people, viewing Web sites, and reading newspaper and magazine articles.

Explain Causes and Effects Once you have defined the problem, identify the problem's most important **causes** and **effects**. To identify causes and effects, think about or research the problem. Make note of one or two causes of the problem as well as the one or two most common or noticeable effects of the problem. For example, the problem of overcrowded lunchrooms might be caused by scheduling too many students for lunch at one time. This problem might have the noticeable effect of students being tardy to class after lunch because they spent so much time waiting in the cafeteria line.

Solve It!   After explaining the problem and its causes and effects, plan to provide your listeners with two solutions that they could use themselves. A good solution should

- limit the causes of the problem, or
- reduce the effects of the problem

In order for listeners to accept your solutions, you will need to support your explanation of each solution with **evidence**. Evidence includes facts, examples, descriptions, and statements made by experts. You can find evidence by doing research and by thinking of your own experience with the problem.

Listening and Speaking **1.4** Select a focus. **1.6** Support opinions with detailed evidence. **2.5** Deliver presentations on problems and solutions. **2.5a** Theorize on the causes and effects of each problem and establish connections between the defined problem and at least one solution. **2.5b** Offer persuasive evidence to validate the definition of the problem and the proposed solution.

Giving and Listening to a Problem-Solution Presentation   Mini-Workshop 7   **681**

RESOURCES

Listening and Speaking Mini-Workshop

Planning
- *On Course: Mapping Instruction*
- *One-Stop Planner* CD-ROM
- *Writing, Listening, & Speaking*
  —Teaching Notes, p. 135
  —Project-Planning Guide, WS. p. 148

Differentiating Instruction
- *Lesson Plans for Language Development*, p. 248
- *Supporting Instruction in Five Languages*

Evaluation
- *Writing, Listening, & Speaking*, WS. p. 149

(Continued on p. 682)

Standards Starter

Motivate. Ask students to name problems they have noticed at school or around their neighborhoods, such as littering in certain areas. Write students' suggestions on the chalkboard and ask students how they could share their proposed solutions for the problems. How would they present their solutions? Who would listen? Tell students that in this workshop they will learn how to give and listen to a problem-solution presentation.

MODELING AND DEMONSTRATION

Explain Causes and Effects
Model for students the process of explaining the causes and effects of a problem by using a flow chart on the chalkboard to illustrate the causes and effects of a sample problem. An example is provided below. Then, have a volunteer demonstrate using the same graphic organizer to map the causes and effects of his or her own problem.

Causes	Problem	Effects
• pollution by local businesses • dumping by area residents • runoff from a development	• pollution in Wood Creek	• declining water quality • litter • dying fish •unpleasant odor

DIRECT TEACHING

Solve It!

Have students spend two minutes brainstorming for possible solutions to the problems they have chosen. Encourage students to write down every solution they think of, no matter how ridiculous or impractical they think it is. At this stage, students should focus only on thinking creatively, not critically. After they have finished brainstorming, students can review their lists of solutions and choose the best two.

682 Mini-Workshop 7 Giving and Listening to a Problem-Solution Presentation

DIRECT TEACHING

A Plan of Action

Students may be at a loss as to what facts and evidence to use if their problems are local and not well documented. Tell students that just because their problem is local does not mean that no one else has worked on a similar problem elsewhere. Students can use the Internet and a periodical index, with the subject of their problem as a keyword in the search, to gather data from wide-ranging sources. Also alert students that there may be area experts that they may quote in their presentation. You may want to approve of students' interview subjects before students contact them. Also be aware that the Internet serves as a public forum and that its content may be unpredictable.

RETEACHING

REVIEW STANDARD

A Plan of Action

The following activity is a review of the 5th-grade **Listening and Speaking Standard 1.4.**

Discuss with students the contemporary TV and radio news practice of presenting with their stories "sound bites," or brief, focused quotations. Point out to students that a short, direct comment saves time in the news broadcast and is also easier for the audience to remember and understand.

Encourage students to review their problem-solution explanation and to distill the matter of their presentation into a single memorable sound bite. Students may or may not want to use the sound bite in their presentations, but they should make sure their presentations are as clear and as focused as they can possibly be, and that their audience never loses sight of their main point.

Avoid trying to persuade the audience to choose a particular solution, though; your **purpose** for speaking is simply to provide information.

A Plan of Action Your next step in planning a presentation is to organize the problem, causes, effects, solutions, and evidence you have gathered. Consider creating note cards or a graphic organizer such as the example below.

In the introduction, explain the problem's causes and effects. In the body, provide evidence, as shown in blue in the example below. To leave listeners with a strong impression, put the best solution last. (This organizational structure is known as **reverse order of importance.**) Finally, conclude your presentation by summarizing your problem and your solutions. You may also want to explain the benefits of solving the problem.

Introduction
  Problem: sibling rivalry
    example of typical behavior
  Causes: feelings of competition; parent favoritism
    facts from book: Siblings Without Rivalry
  Effects: hurt feelings; loss of adult relationship w/ sibling
    quote from Siblings. . . on emotional damage

Solution 1: share feelings
  describe behavior
  • reduces competitiveness
    opinion of school counselor
  • strengthens relationships
    anecdote from experience

Solution 2: focus on strengths
  describe behavior
  • reduces competitiveness
    anecdote from experience
  • makes sibling feel better, not worse
    make comparison

Conclusion
  • summary of the problem and solutions

Consider Your Listeners As you organize your presentation, think about your **audience.** If the audience is not familiar with the problem, you will have to explain it in more detail. For example, if you are talking to teachers about the poor condition of your school's tennis courts, you should explain the problem and its effects in depth. If your listeners are members of the tennis club, however, they will already understand the problem from their own experiences.

Listening and Speaking **1.0** Students deliver focused, coherent presentations that convey ideas clearly and relate to the background and interests of the audience. **1.4** Select an organizational structure, matching the message to the audience.

RESOURCES

(Continued from p. 681)

Assessment

■ *Progress Assessment of Writing, Listening, & Speaking*, p. 67
■ *Diagnostic and Summative Assessments,* End-of-Year Test

Going Through the Motions Run through your speech several times, relying only on your graphic organizer or note cards and your memory to practice elaborating on the ideas you have noted. Once you are comfortable with the content of your presentation, it is time to rehearse as if you were delivering that content to your audience.

Voice and Body Language To give an interesting presentation, use your voice and body. The following chart describes verbal and nonverbal techniques you can use to enhance your presentation. **Verbal elements** relate to how you use your voice. **Nonverbal elements** refer to how you use your body language.

VERBAL ELEMENTS	
Element	**Explanation**
Rate of speech: how fast you talk	Keep your rate slow enough for listeners to understand but not so slow that you bore them.
Volume: how loudly you speak	Speak loudly enough for everyone to hear, but avoid shouting.
Pitch: how high or low your voice is; also called **vocal modulation**.	Changes in pitch give listeners a clue to pay special attention. Vary your pitch to emphasize important ideas, lowering it to say something serious and raising it to show excitement.
Tone of voice: how you express your overall attitude	Your tone should match what you are saying. For instance, to explain a serious problem, use a concerned tone.

NONVERBAL ELEMENTS	
Element	**Explanation**
Gestures: your body movement, such as pointing or nodding	Emphasize key points with gestures. As you make a gesture, add emphasis by decreasing your **rate** or raising your **pitch**.
Posture: the position of your body	Use your posture to add to the attitude expressed by your **tone**. For example, lean forward when you feel strongly about something. Avoid slouching, which may communicate boredom.
Facial expressions: the look on your face	Facial expressions show how you feel about what you say. Match your expression and **vocal modulation**, raising your **pitch** when your face shows excitement, for example.
Eye contact: looking at your audience	Frequently look at your listeners. When you make an important point, look at the audience, not at your notes.

Listening and Speaking 1.5 Emphasize salient points to assist the listener in following the main ideas and concepts. 1.7 Use effective rate, volume, pitch, and tone and align nonverbal elements to sustain audience interest and attention.

Giving and Listening to a Problem-Solution Presentation **683**

Right column content

DIRECT TEACHING

Going Through the Motions

You may want to allow students time to rehearse their presentations in class. Consider arranging students in three or four groups and having every student present the first part of his or her explanation to each group. Practicing for a smaller group will help students ease into the idea of speaking for an audience, and the repetition will help students polish their introductions.

Voice and Body Language

Show the class a videotape of a successful presentation or speech. Stop the tape partway through and mute the sound to have students pay attention to the speaker's gestures and body language. Discuss the speaker's techniques with students, and then play the rest of the presentation with the picture blacked out to have students pay attention to the speaker's voice. Then discuss with students how all of the speaker's techniques work together to make for an effective presentation.

CORRECTING MISCONCEPTIONS

Students may pay close attention to the verbal elements in their presentations but not nearly enough attention to the nonverbal elements, believing them to be less important. Point out that the two are often interrelated. For example, maintaining a good posture may help a student better project his or her voice. Also tell students that a great deal of face-to-face communication comes through body language. Being aware of the importance of body language and using it to one's advantage will help a presentation be much more successful.

Mini-Workshop 7 · A Problem-Solution Presentation

DIRECT TEACHING

Ears Front and Center

Before students begin giving their presentations, discuss with the class the behavior they expect from someone listening to their presentations. You may want to write students' suggestions on the chalkboard and leave them posted for students to refer to during the presentations. Point out to students that they should hold themselves to their own standards as others are speaking.

TECHNOLOGY TIP

Encourage students to prepare on a computer a spreadsheet or chart similar to the one on p. 685. Students can print out copies of their charts so they can take notes as the presenters speak.

Add It Up   Adding the techniques in the chart on page 683 to the content of your speech will take some work. Try to build the techniques into your rehearsals gradually. Start by adding gestures and facial expressions to your content, for example. Then, you can add vocal modulation the next time through, and so on, until your presentation includes all of the elements listed in the chart.

In the Spotlight   Once you have practiced both content and delivery, you are ready to deliver your presentation to a small group or to your entire class. Even if speaking in front of a group makes you nervous, your rehearsals and the notes on your graphic organizer or note cards should help you deliver a smooth, effective presentation.

Ears Front and Center   Your job is not finished when your presentation ends. You should listen carefully and politely to your classmates' presentations in order to learn from them. As you watch and listen to your classmates' presentations, notice both **content**—what the speaker says—and **delivery**—how the speaker says it.

Content   A speaker's ideas should be clear, well supported, and appropriate to the audience—in other words, his or her ideas should matter to listeners. A speaker addressing the school board about the problem of a shadeless, too-hot recess area might explain the problem's negative effects on student health. If the same

speaker were talking to classmates, though, discussing or mentioning the effect of smelling sweaty after a break might have a greater impact on the audience.

Delivery   A good speaker provides a strong message and uses his or her voice and body language together effectively to present that message. Pay attention to each speaker's **verbal** and **nonverbal elements**. Refer to the chart on page 683 if you need to review these elements.

On a High Note   You will listen to many presentations, but you will need to select one classmate's presentation to evaluate. Listen to the presentation you have chosen to evaluate, thoroughly and thoughtfully. As you listen, identify the speaker's **tone,** or attitude toward the topic. Watch for the speaker to use voice and body language together. For example, the speaker may raise the pitch of his or her voice and use facial expressions to create a certain feeling at a particular point in the presentation. The speaker's posture can also help you identify the tone.

Creating a chart like the one on the next page can help you organize your ideas about a classmate's presentation. You might refer to the chart on page 683 and the instruction on pages 681–682 to come up with additional criteria for evaluating the content and delivery of a presentation. As you listen, add to your chart your notes about how well the speaker meets those criteria.

Listening and Speaking 1.0 They evaluate the content of oral communication. 1.1 Relate the speaker's verbal communication (e.g., pitch, feeling, tone) to the nonverbal message (e.g., posture, gesture). 1.2 Identify the tone conveyed in the oral communication.

EVALUATION QUESTIONS

Content Questions	• How clear was the explanation of the problem and its causes and effects?	He explained the causes and effects well, with evidence from experts.
	• How useful and well supported did the solutions seem to you?	The first solution wasn't well supported. I could use the second solution, though.
Delivery Questions	• What was the speaker's tone?	He seemed serious.
	• How effective was the speaker's use of verbal and nonverbal elements such as volume, rate, facial expressions, and eye contact?	He could have made more eye contact, but his voice was loud enough, and he spoke clearly and expressively.
	• What techniques did the speaker use to emphasize important points?	He raised the pitch of his voice and pointed when he explained the most important ideas.

To decide how effectively your classmate delivered his or her presentation, use the notes you took and think about your overall impression of the presentation.

Then, write a one-paragraph evaluation explaining how effective you found your classmate's presentation based on the criteria in the chart above.

PRACTICE & APPLY — Give and Evaluate a Problem-Solution Presentation

- Choose a focused problem. Then, prepare and deliver a presentation to a small group of classmates or to the class as a whole. You might want to include ideas from your problem-solution essay if you completed the Mini-Workshop on pages 678–680.

- Listen to your classmates' presentations. Take notes on one speaker's content and delivery, answering the questions in the chart above. Then, write a helpful one-paragraph evaluation of your classmate's presentation.

Listening and Speaking 2.0 Students deliver well-organized formal presentations employing traditional rhetorical strategies (e.g., exposition). Student speaking demonstrates the organizational and delivery strategies outlined in Listening and Speaking Standard 1.0.

Giving and Listening to a Problem-Solution Presentation **685**

DIRECT TEACHING

Give and Evaluate a Problem-Solution Presentation

Remind students to be courteous as they write their evaluations. Have students first point out positive aspects of the speaker's presentation before they point out the problems. Ask students to make suggestions about the ways that a speaker might improve his or her presentation.

PRACTICE & APPLY

Guided and Independent Practice

Monitor students' progress by checking their charts or outlines for completion and for clarity and by circulating among groups as students rehearse their presentations. Then, have students give their presentations to the class or to a group of classmates.

Standards Starter

Motivate. Remind students that graphics often serve to complement by further explaining or illustrating ideas in written or spoken text. You might ask them if they have ever looked at a map, chart, or other graphic in a textbook that helped deepen their understanding of a difficult concept or idea. Tell students that in this Mini-Workshop they will learn how to create graphics to complement texts.

DIFFERENTIATING INSTRUCTION

Learners Having Difficulty

Allow students to work in small groups to determine places in their written compositions where a graphic would be helpful or interesting to the reader. Each student should highlight one place. Group members can review one another's choices either to agree and brainstorm for an appropriate type of visual or to disagree and suggest a better place for inserting a graphic. Have students draw quick sketches of their graphics and share them with the group before spending time creating the final versions.

DIRECT TEACHING

Get the Picture

To help students determine if they should seek permission before using a selection, you may want to refer to the AAP guidelines for Fair Use in the Classroom at the Library of Congress's Web site.

Creating Graphics

Showing Them Think back to the time when you were first learning to read. Remember how the books had pictures? You used the pictures to figure out what was being said. **Graphics** help readers and listeners of all ages understand the topic better. In this section you will learn how you can boost your audience's understanding by creating or finding a graphic to include in a piece of writing of your choice.

The most obvious kind of graphic is a photograph or drawing. A writer who wrote a research report on guanacos (a species of the South American llama), for example, found this photograph in a book. He photocopied it and included it in his report, giving credit to its source.

Make a Choice Before you create a graphic, you must first decide two things: what information you are going to show and how you are going to show it. To decide what information to show as part of a written composition, read the piece to find anything your audience may need help understanding. Then, decide how you can put that information in a graphic. The chart on the next page gives you some examples.

Get the Picture Once you have made your decision about what kind of graphic will be most helpful for your audience, you will need to create or find it. You might use one of the following ideas.

- Draw it freehand.
- Trace it, using tracing paper or an overhead projector.
- Photocopy it if you have access to a copier and permission to use it. (Check with your teacher to make sure that you can use an image created by someone else.)
- Cut it out of a magazine or newspaper if you have permission.
- Create it in a computer program.
- Download it from an Internet source if you have permission to do so.

When you create your own graphics, use color carefully. In general, use no more than three colors in a graph, chart, or time line. Color attracts attention, but too many colors distract the reader and make information hard to find. A map, however, may need more than three colors, for example, to contrast all adjoining states and countries.

TIP If you will use your graphic in a **multimedia presentation,** look at it from the back of the room. Make sure the graphic is easy to read and understand even from across the room. Do some lines need to be bolder? Do some words need to be bigger? Would color help?

Listening and Speaking 1.6 Support opinions with visual or media displays that use appropriate technology.

RESOURCES

Media Mini-Workshop

Planning
- *On Course: Mapping Instruction*
- *One-Stop Planner* CD-ROM
- *Writing, Listening, & Speaking*
  —Teaching Notes, p. 135
  —Project-Planning Guide, WS. p. 150

Differentiating Instruction
- *Lesson Plans for Language Development,* p. 249
- *Supporting Instruction in Five Languages*

Reinforcement
- *Writing, Listening, & Speaking,* WS. p. 151

HOW TO CHOOSE A GRAPHIC

To show . . .	Use a . . .
changes or trends over time Examples: • a baseball player's batting average over several seasons • **the number of students tutored through a volunteer program**	bar graph
statistics: facts that involve numbers Examples: • **the percentage of people who ride bicycles** • number of votes received by each student council candidate	chart such as a pie chart
an area's physical features, political divisions, or other geography-related topics Examples: • the mountains, valleys, lakes, and rivers of Utah • **the location of one of Canada's provinces—Prince Edward Island**	map

PRACTICE & APPLY **Create a Graphic**

Use these steps to create a graphic for a piece of your writing.

■ Decide what information to show and the best graphic to use.

■ Create or find your graphic, making sure it is large and clear.

■ List the source if you have copied, cut out, or downloaded the graphic. For a reminder about how to list sources, see page 586.

Creating Graphics **687**

DIFFERENTIATING INSTRUCTION

Special Education Students

Have students work with a helper to determine what kind of graphic would be most effective for their reports. After brainstorming ideas, the helper could sketch one or two graphics and work with the student to choose and refine one of the ideas.

▶ Resources Reminder

For more help with Special Education Students, see *Lesson Plans for Language Development.*

PRACTICE & APPLY

Guided and Independent Practice

Monitor students' progress by checking to make sure that students have chosen an appropriate place in their reports to include a graphic and that each student has a rough sketch of his or her idea. Then, have students create their graphics as independent practice, reminding them to list the sources for their graphics, if necessary.

Assessment

■ *Progress Assessment of Writing, Listening, & Speaking,* p. 68

■ *Diagnostic and Summative Assessments,* Third-Quarter Test

Resource Center

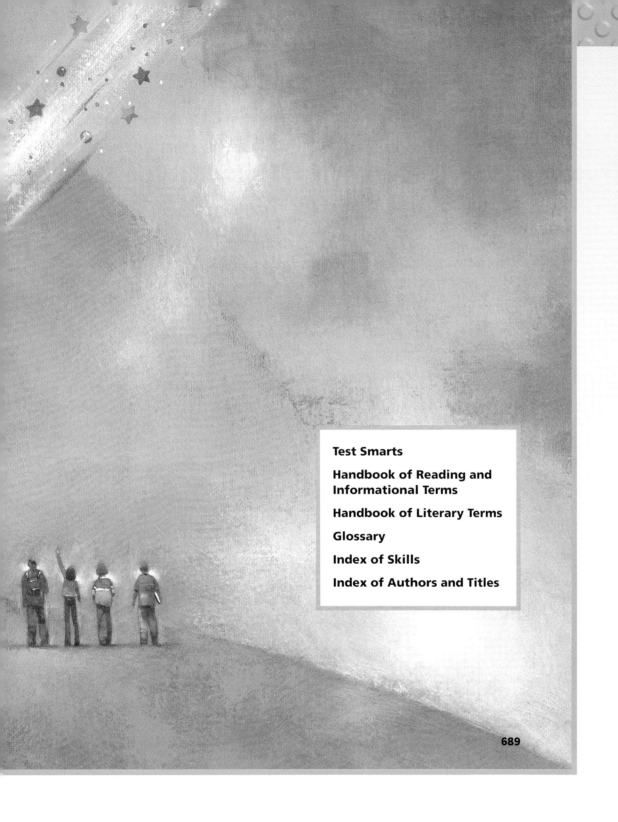

689

Test Smarts *by* Flo Ota De Lange and Sheri Henderson

Strategies for Taking a Multiple-Choice Test

If you have ever watched a quiz show on TV, you know how multiple-choice tests work. You get a question and (usually) four choices. Your job is to pick the correct one. Easy! (Don't you wish?) Taking multiple-choice tests will get a whole lot easier when you apply these Test Smarts:

T rack your time.

E xpect success.

S tudy the directions.

T ake it all in.

S pot those numbers.

M aster the questions.

A nticipate the answers.

R ely on 50/50.

T ry. Try. Try.

S earch for skips and smudges.

Track Your Time

You race through a test for fear you won't finish, and then you sit watching your hair grow because you finished early, or you realize you have only five minutes left to complete eleven zillion questions. Sound familiar? You can avoid both problems if you take a few minutes before you start to estimate how much time you have for each question. Using all the time you are given can help you avoid making errors. Follow these tips to set **checkpoints:**

- How many questions should be completed when one quarter of the time is gone? when half the time is gone?
- What should the clock read when you are halfway through the questions?
- If you find yourself behind your checkpoints, you can speed up.
- If you are ahead, you can—and should—slow down.

Expect Success

Top athletes know that attitude affects performance. They learn to deal with their negative thoughts, to get on top of their mental game. So can you! But how? Do you compare yourself with others? Most top athletes will tell you that they compete against only one person: themselves. They know they cannot change another person's performance. Instead, they study their own performance and find ways to improve it. That makes sense for you too. You are older and more experienced than you were the day you took your last big test, right? So review your last scores. Figure out just what you need to do to top that "kid" you used to be. You can!

What if you get anxious? It's OK if you do. A little nervousness will help you focus. Of course, if you're so nervous that you think you might get sick or faint, take time to relax for a few minutes. Calm bodies breathe slowly. You can fool yours into feeling calmer and thinking more clearly by taking a few deep breaths—five slow counts in, five out. Take charge, take five, and then take the test.

Study the Directions

You're ready to go, go, go, but first it's wait, wait, wait. Pencils. Paper. Answer sheets. Lots of directions. Listen! In order to follow directions, you have to know them. Read all test directions as if they contained the key to lifetime happiness and several years' allowance. Then, read them again. Study the answer sheet. How is it laid out? Is it

1

2

3

4

or

1   2   3   4 ?

What about answer choices? Are they arranged

A   B   C   D

or

A   B

C   D ?

Directions count. Be very, very sure you know exactly what to do and how to do it before you make your first mark.

Take It All In

When you finally hear the words "You may begin," briefly **preview the test** to get a mental map of your tasks:

- Know how many questions you have to complete.
- Know where to stop.
- Set your time checkpoints.
- Do the easy sections first; easy questions are worth just as many points as hard ones.

Spot Those Numbers

"I got off by one and spent all my time trying to fix my answer sheet." Oops. Make it a habit to

- match the number of each question to the numbered space on the answer sheet every time
- leave the answer space blank if you skip a question
- keep a list of your blank spaces on scratch paper or somewhere else—but *not* on your answer sheet. The less you have to erase on your answer sheet, the better.

Master the Questions

"I knew that answer, but I thought the question asked something else." Be sure— very sure—that you **know what a question is asking you.** Read the question at least twice before reading the answer choices. Approach it as you would a mystery story or a riddle. Look for clues. Watch especially for words like *not* and *except*—they tell you to look for the choice that is false or different from the other choices or opposite in some way. If you are taking a reading-comprehension test, read the selection, master all the questions, and then re-read the selection. The answers will be likely to pop out the second time around. Remember: A test isn't trying to trick you; it's trying to test your knowledge and your ability to think clearly.

Anticipate the Answers

All right, you now understand the question. Before you read the answer choices, **answer the question yourself. Then, read the choices.**

If the answer you gave is among the choices listed, it is probably correct.

Rely on 50/50

"I . . . have . . . no . . . clue." You understand the question. You gave an answer, but your answer is not listed, or perhaps you drew a complete blank. It happens. Time to **make an educated guess**—not a *wild* guess, but an *educated* guess. Think about quiz shows again, and you'll know the value of the 50/50 play. When two answers are eliminated, the contestant has a 50/50 chance of choosing the correct one. You can use elimination too.

Always read every choice carefully. **Watch out for distracters**—choices that may be true but are too broad, too narrow, or not relevant to the question. Eliminate the least likely choice. Then, eliminate the next, and so on until you find the best one. If two choices seem equally correct, look to see if "All of the above" is an option. If it is, that might be your choice. If no choice seems correct, look for "None of the above."

Try. Try. Try.

Keep at it. **Don't give up.** This sounds obvious, so why say it? You might be surprised by how many students do give up. Think of tests as a kind of marathon. Just as in any marathon, people get bored, tired, hungry, thirsty, hot, discouraged. They may begin to feel sick or develop aches and pains. They decide the test doesn't matter that much. They decide they don't care if it does—there'll always be next time; whose idea was this, anyway? They lose focus. Don't do it.

Remember: The last question is worth just as much as the first question, and the questions on a test don't get harder as you go. If the question you just finished was really hard, an easier one is probably coming up soon. Take a deep breath, and keep on slogging. Give it your all, all the way to the finish.

Search for Skips and Smudges

"Hey! I got that one right, and the machine marked it wrong!" If you have ever—ever—had this experience, pay attention! When this happens in class, your teacher can give you the extra point. On a machine-scored test, however, you would lose the point and never know why. So, listen up: All machine-scored answer sheets have a series of lines marching down the side. The machine stops at the first line and scans across it for your answer, stops at the second line, scans, stops at the third line, scans, and so on, all the way to the end. The machine is looking for a dark, heavy mark. If it finds one where it should be, you get the point. What if you left that question blank? A lost point. What if you changed an answer and didn't quite get the first mark erased? The machine sees two answers instead of one. A lost point. What if you made a mark to help yourself remember where you skipped an answer? You filled in the answer later but forgot to erase the mark. The machine again sees two marks. Another lost point. What if your marks are not very dark? The machine sees blank spaces. More lost points.

To avoid losing points, take time at the end of the test to make sure you

- did not skip any answers
- gave one answer for each question
- made the marks heavy and dark and within the lines

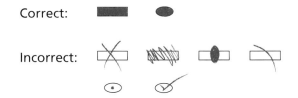

Get rid of smudges. Make sure there are no stray pencil marks on your answer sheet. Cleanly erase those places where you changed your mind. Check for little stray marks from pencil tapping. Check everything. You are the only person who can.

Reading Comprehension

Many tests have a section called **reading comprehension.** The good news is that you do not have to study for this part of the test. Taking a reading-comprehension test is a bit like playing ball. You don't know where the ball will land, so you have to stay alert to all possibilities. However, just as the ball can come at you in only a few ways, there are only a few kinds of questions that can be used on reading-comprehension tests. This discussion will help you identify the most common ones.

The purpose of the reading comprehension section is to test your understanding of a reading passage. Be sure to keep these sug-gestions in mind when you read a selection on a test:

- **Read the passage once** to get a general overview of the topic.

- If you don't understand the passage at first, keep reading. **Try to find the main idea.**

- Then, **read the questions** so that you'll know what information to look for when you **re-read the passage.**

Two kinds of texts are used here. The first one is an informational text. The second is an updated fairy tale.

DIRECTIONS: Read the following selection. Then, choose the best answer for each question. Mark each answer on your answer sheet in the square provided.

Call of the Wild

Baffin Island, a remote, wild region of Canada, is home to a group of canids that survive on their own, obeying no master but their ancient instincts. (*Canid* is a term that covers all doglike creatures, including dogs, wolves, jackals, foxes, and coyotes.) Scientists went to Baffin Island to observe a group of five adult wolves that functioned as a family. The group included a litter of seven young wolves whose parents were the leaders of the clan. The group occupied a series of five dens (shelters the wolves dig in the earth) on hills near a river. The dens were just about halfway between the summer and winter ground of the wolves' main prey, caribou, large deer that live in tundra regions like Baffin.

Like humans, the wolves use division of labor to provide for the needs of the group. While one wolf goes out on a long, wearying search for food, another stays behind to guard the pups. When the designated hunter returns, giving out meat to the hungry pups and preparing for a long nap—sometimes up to eighteen hours—the "baby sitter" sets out on the long journey across the tundra in search of more caribou meat.

ITEM 1 asks for vocabulary knowledge.

1. In the first sentence of the passage, the word <u>remote</u> means —

   A tiny

   B filthy

   C bustling

   D faraway

Answer: Look at the surrounding sentences, or **context,** to see which definition fits.

A is incorrect. If the area is wild, it is unlikely to be tiny.

B is incorrect. Wild areas are not likely to be filthy.

C is incorrect. Wild areas are not bustling. *Bustling* is a word usually applied to a place where there are crowds of people.

D is the best answer. Wild regions are usually faraway from towns and cities.

ITEM 2 asks you to use context clues to determine the meaning of a word.

2. What is the meaning of the italicized word *canids*? Look for a context clue.

   F It is a term that covers all doglike creatures.

   G It is a word for animals that live in Canada.

   H It is another word for a dog.

   J It is another word for a wolf.

Answer: Look at the context to see which answer makes sense.

F is correct. The definition of *canids* is given in parentheses in the next sentence.

G is incorrect. This definition is not close.

H is incorrect. *Canid* refers to animals other than just dogs.

J is incorrect. *Canid* refers to animals other than just wolves.

ITEM 3 asks you to identify the meaning of a word with multiple meanings.

3. In the phrase "a litter of seven young wolves," the word *litter* means —

   A cover with bits of trash

   B a stretcher

   C bits of trash

   D a family of baby animals

Answer: Try out each meaning in the context of the sentence.

A is incorrect. Although the word *litter* can be a verb meaning "scatter bits of trash," as in "litter halls with garbage," this meaning does not fit the context.

B is incorrect. Although the word *litter* can mean "a stretcher," as in "an injured person lay on a litter," this meaning does not fit the context of the sentence.

C is incorrect. Although the word *litter* can be a noun meaning "bits of trash," as in "streets full of litter," this meaning does not fit the context of the passage.

D is correct. In references to mammals, a *litter* is a "family of young animals," as in "a litter of seven young wolves" in this passage.

ITEM 4 asks for close reading. Read carefully to see if the answer is stated directly in the text.

4. Why did these scientists go to Baffin Island?

   F To rescue a litter of wolves threatened by the cold

   G To observe a group of five adult wolves that functioned as a family

   H To prove that wolves are just like dogs

   J To follow the wolves for a year

Answer: Read the passage carefully to see if the answer is directly stated.

G is the correct answer. It is a direct quote from the passage. Once you find this, you know that **F, H,** and **J** are incorrect.

ITEM 5 asks for close reading. Read carefully to see if the answer is stated directly in the text.

5. How are the wolves like humans?

    A They use division of labor to provide for the group's needs.

    B They take good care of their young.

    C They gather more food than they need.

    D They use baby sitters to search for food.

Answer: Read the passage carefully to see if the answer is directly stated.

A is the correct answer. It is cited in the text. Once you find the answer cited directly in the text, you know you can eliminate all the other answer choices.

ITEM 6 asks for an inference.

6. What statement *best* sums up the main point of this passage?

    F Baffin Island is a remote, wild region in Canada.

    G Canids obey no master.

    H The wolves' main prey is caribou.

    J Wolves work together to provide for the needs of the group.

Answer: Ask yourself which statement covers the passage as a whole.

F is incorrect. It is only one detail in the passage.

G is incorrect. It also is only one of many details in the passage.

H is incorrect. It also is only one of many details in the passage.

J is the best answer. It covers almost all the details in the passage.

DIRECTIONS: Read the following selection. Then, choose the *best* answer for each question. Mark each answer on your answer sheet in the space provided.

Technologically Correct Fairy Tales: Little Red Riding Hood

One summer morning, Little Red Riding Hood was on her way to her grandmother's house when, on the path through the woods, she met Mr. Canis Lupus. Her mother had warned her not to speak to anyone, but this wolf looked friendly.

"Where are you going, little girl?" quizzed Mr. Lupus, otherwise known as Gray Wolf. He squinted his shifty eyes. He was a hungry wolf.

"I'm taking some fresh rolls and butter to my grandmother," Little Red Riding Hood answered.

"I bet I know who your grandmother is," cried Mr. Lupus, and off he ran without so much as a catch-you-later.

Reaching Grandmother's cottage first, Wolf tied up Grams and put her in the closet. Then he changed into one of her outfits, pulled out his new laptop, and started a game of hearts.

When Little Red Riding Hood arrived, she said, "Why, Grams, what a big scanner you have."

"All the better to digitize you with, my dear," said Wolf in a high-pitched voice.

"Why, Grams, how many chips you have!" exclaimed Little Red Riding Hood.

"All the better to remember you with, my dear," snorted Wolf.

"Why, Grams, what a lot of megahertz you have," cried Little Red Riding Hood.

"All the better to process you with, my dear," hooted Wolf, and he sprang at Little Red Riding Hood, ready to have her for dinner.

Just then a Webmaster appeared in the doorway. Seeing disaster about to happen, the techie deleted Wolf's program and re-fused to let him boot up again until he had released Red Riding Hood, untied Grams, and traded in his hearts for a heart.

ITEM 1 is a vocabulary question.

1. In the selection above, the underlined words <u>Canis Lupus</u> mean —

   A character

   B gray wolf

   C fox

   D dog

Consider the surrounding sentences, or context, to identify the best definition.

A is incorrect. Mr. Canis Lupus *is* a character in the story, but that is not what the term means.

B is the best answer. The next sentence in the story states that Mr. Canis Lupus was also called Gray Wolf.

C is incorrect. A fox is not a character in the story.

D is incorrect. A dog is not a character in the story.

Now, try **ITEM 2** on your own. It is another vocabulary question.

2. In the selection above, the word <u>chips</u> means —

   F memory capacity in a computer

   G salty snack made of potatoes

   H places where small pieces have been broken off

   J wooden shavings from a block

F is the best answer. G, H, and **J** are all definitions of *chips*, but not as the word is used in this story.

ITEM 3 asks you a factual question.

3. Where does Little Red Riding Hood meet Mr. Lupus?

   A Far, far from home

   B On her way to Grandfather's

   C Under the birches

   D On the path through the woods

A is incorrect. The story never says that Little Red Riding Hood is far, far from home.

B is incorrect. There is no grandfather character.

C is incorrect. There are woods, but the type of tree is not identified.

D is the best answer. This is where Little Red Riding Hood meets the wolf.

Now, try **ITEM 4** on your own. This factual item asks you to fill in the blank.

4. Little Red Riding Hood is bringing her grandmother —

   F her cloak to repair

   G a basket of cookies

   H an apple pie

   J rolls and butter

J is the best answer. None of the other choices are mentioned in the story.

ITEM 5 is another factual question, but you may have to look a little harder to find the answer.

5. What words or phrases does the writer use to give a glimpse of the wolf's character?

   A grim, sneaky, evil

   B shifty eyes

   C grand, decisive, heroic

   D little, meek, polite

A is incorrect. Although you may think of the wolf as having a grim, sneaky, and evil character from other versions of the story you know, the question asks for words the writer uses. These words are not used in the story.

B is the best answer. These words are used to describe the wolf's eyes. Shifty eyes suggest a deceitful person.

C is incorrect. These words are not in the story.

D is incorrect. These words are not in the story.

Now, try **ITEM 6** on your own. This is an interpretation question, so you'll have to think about it.

6. The wolf puts on one of Grandmother's outfits because he —

    F is cold

    G wants a disguise

    H is having a bad hair day

    J is afraid of the Webmaster

G is the best answer. The wolf is pretending to be Little Red Riding Hood's grandmother. The other answers do not fit the plot of the story.

ITEM 7 is another interpretation question.

7. Which character's actions determine what happens at the end of the story?

    A The Webmaster's

    B The grandmother's

    C The wolf's

    D Little Red Riding Hood's

A is the best answer. The Webmaster prevents further disaster from happening and makes the wolf change his ways.

B is incorrect. The grandmother is present but is tied up in the closet.

C is incorrect. The wolf would not have ruined his own plans.

D is incorrect. Little Red Riding Hood is present but doesn't say or do anything at the end of the story.

ITEM 8 asks a vocabulary question.

8. Which statement about the word megahertz is *most* accurate?

    F It has to do with wolves.

    G It means "courage."

    H It refers to food.

    J It has to do with computers.

J is correct. The story uses other computer terms in this dialogue: *scanner, digitize,* and *chips.* Little Red Riding Hood's third remark to the wolf-grandmother also has to do with computers. The other choices don't make sense.

ITEM 9 is another interpretation question.

9. Which is the *best* statement of the story's main message?

    A Computers are dangerous.

    B All wolves are evil.

    C Children should obey their elders.

    D Old people should not live alone.

C is the best answer. None of the other choices are even suggested in the story.

Strategies for Taking Writing Tests

Writing a Fictional or Autobiographical Narrative

Sometimes a prompt on a writing test may ask you to write a narrative, or story. The following steps will help you write a **fictional** or **autobiographical narrative**. The responses are based on this prompt.

Prompt

Describe an experience you had that changed your perspective—made you see the world or yourself differently.

THINKING IT THROUGH

Writing a Fictional or Autobiographical Narrative

▶ **STEP 1** **Read the prompt carefully.** Does the prompt ask you to write a fictional story (a story that is made up) or an autobiographical story (a story of something that really happened to you)?

The prompt asks me to write about my own experience.

▶ **STEP 2** **Outline the plot of your narrative.** What is the sequence of events that makes up your story?

1. Some kids in my class were teasing Joel. 2. Suddenly, I found myself walking up to one of the bullies and yelling, "Stop!" 3. It got really quiet. 4. The bullies left, looking embarrassed. 6. Joel left, too, but later thanked me. I realized I was stronger than I thought.

▶ **STEP 3** **Identify the major and minor characters.** What do they look and act like? How do they sound when they speak?

Joel is tall but very gentle. He is also quiet. The ringleader of the bullies is small but mean. He yells at people a lot. I am shy and not that tall. I don't consider myself brave.

▶ **STEP 4** **Identify the setting of your narrative.** Where and when does your story take place?

on the soccer field, near the bleachers, right after school, in the month of May

▶ **STEP 5** **Draft your narrative, adding dialogue, suspense, and sensory details.** Dialogue, the actual words characters or people say, will add interest to your story; suspense will hold readers' attention; sensory details will bring your story to life.

▶ **STEP 6** **Revise and proofread your narrative.** Make sure the events in your story are presented in a logical order. To show the sequence of events, use transitions, such as *first, then, next, before,* and *later.*

Writing a Summary

Prompt

Summarize the article "The California Gold Rush," by Kathy Wilmore.

As you progress through school, you may take tests that ask you to write a **summary**. In summary writing, you read a passage and then rewrite in your own words its main idea and significant details. How would you answer the prompt to the right?

The following steps will help you write a summary in response to such a prompt. The student responses are based on only four paragraphs in the reading selection "The California Gold Rush" on pages 579–581. On a test, though, the student would summarize the entire selection.

THINKING IT THROUGH

Writing a Summary

STEP 1 Read the passage carefully. Identify the main idea, and restate it in your own words. If the main idea is not directly stated, look at all the details and decide what point the writer is making about the general topic of the passage.

Forty-Niners, including Chinese and other immigrants, rushed to California to find gold, but many were forced to do other jobs.

STEP 2 Identify important details to include in the summary. Which details directly support the main idea of the selection? Look for at least one key idea or detail in each paragraph.

—thousands of Forty-Niners
—Chinese called California "Gold Mountain"
—Chinese faced prejudice
—Levi Strauss, a Bavarian immigrant, started a blue jeans business

STEP 3 Write the main idea and most important details in a paragraph, using your own words. Give details in the order in which they are presented in the passage, and use transitions between the ideas.

Thousands of Forty-Niners traveled to California in search of gold, but many did not find gold and had to find other jobs. Many Forty-Niners were poor Chinese, who called California "Gold Mountain." Because of prejudice, many Chinese ended up doing service work rather than mining for gold. Other immigrants also started businesses. One of these was Levi Strauss, a Bavarian immigrant, who created blue jeans.

Writing a Response to Literature

On a writing test, you might be asked to read a work of literature and to write a response to that work. Such test questions evaluate your reading, thinking, and writing abilities. The following steps will help you write a **response to literature.** The examples are based on the prompt to the right.

Prompt

Identify the theme, or underlying message, of "The Sneetches" by Dr. Seuss. Support your interpretation with examples from the poem.

THINKING IT THROUGH ○ **Writing a Response to Literature**

▶ STEP 1 **Read the prompt carefully, noting key words.** Key words might include a verb—such as *analyze, identify,* or *explain*—and a literary element—such as *plot, characters, setting,* or *theme.* In the sample prompt above, the key words are *identify* and *theme.*

▶ STEP 2 **Read the selection carefully, keeping the key words from the prompt in mind.** Consider the overall meaning of the work, as well as the specific elements identified in the prompt.

▶ STEP 3 **Write a main idea statement.** Your main idea statement should give the title and author of the work and should directly address the prompt. A main idea statement in response to the prompt above could be: *The theme of "The Sneetches," by Dr. Seuss, is that all people are equal, regardless of what they look like or wear.*

▶ STEP 4 **Skim the selection to find examples and details from the literary work that support your main idea.** To support the main idea statement above, you might discuss how no one could tell the difference between the Star-Belly Sneetches and Plain-Belly Sneetches when the Plain-Belly Sneetches got stars put on their tummies.

▶ STEP 5 **Draft, revise, and proofread your response.** Be sure to include transitions—*for instance, however, as a result, most important*—to show the relationships among ideas. When you have written your draft, re-read it to make sure that you have presented your ideas clearly and in a logical order. Double-check to make sure you have addressed all the key words in the prompt. Finally, proofread to correct mistakes in spelling, punctuation, and capitalization.

Writing a Persuasive Essay

Some writing tests ask you to choose and support an opinion on an issue. Your response may be a **persuasive letter** or **essay**. If the prompt at the right appeared on a test, how would you approach it?

Prompt

The city council has a limited budget for a new park. It is trying to decide between spending money for large shade trees or for an in-line skating path. Decide how you think the money should be spent. Then, write a letter asking the city council to vote in favor of your decision. Give three reasons for your opinion.

THINKING IT THROUGH ✎ Writing a Persuasive Essay

▶ **STEP 1** **Identify the task the prompt is asking you to do.**

The prompt asks me to decide how the council should spend the money. I have to write a letter stating my opinion and giving three reasons to support it.

▶ **STEP 2** **Decide on your opinion.**

I like in-line skating, but I think trees are more important.

▶ **STEP 3** **Develop three reasons to support your opinion.** Be sure your reasons address any concerns readers might have.

1. More people will enjoy trees.
2. Trees give shade, which makes the park more comfortable.
3. Trees take time to grow, so we need to plant them now. A skating path can be added anytime.

▶ **STEP 4** **Develop evidence (facts and examples) to support your reasons.**

1. All people appreciate trees. The only people I know who skate are my age.
2. Summer temperatures are in the 90s. Shade will keep the park cool.
3. We planted a tree when I was six, and it is still not as tall as our house.

▶ **STEP 5** **Write your essay. Include your opinion in the introduction, make each reason a paragraph—with support—and give a call to action in your conclusion.**

▶ **STEP 6** **Edit (evaluate, revise, proofread) your essay.**

Handbook of Reading and Informational Terms

For more information about a topic, turn to the page(s) in this book indicated on a separate line at the end of the entry. To learn more about *Cause and Effect,* for example, turn to page 224.

On another line there are cross-references to entries in this Handbook that provide closely related information. For instance, *Chronological Order* contains a cross-reference to *Text Structures.*

AUTHOR'S PURPOSE The author's purpose may be to **inform,** to **persuade,** to **express feelings,** or to **entertain.** An author may create a **text,** which is any written work, with more than one purpose in mind. One of the purposes is usually more important than the others. Once you've identified the author's purpose, you'll have a pretty good idea of how to read the text. If you're reading an **informational text,** you may need to read slowly and carefully. You may also want to complete a think sheet like the one below on the left or take notes. If you're reading a text that the author wrote mostly for you to enjoy, you can read at your own pace—any way you want.

See also *Note Taking; Reading Rate.*

Question Sheet for Informational Texts

1. What is the topic?_____

2. Do I understand what I'm reading? _____

3. What parts should I re-read? _____
_____

4. What are the main ideas and details?

    Main idea: _____ Main idea: _____

    Details: _____ Details: _____

    Main idea: _____ Main idea: _____

    Details: _____ Details: _____

5. Summary of what I learned:
_____
_____

CAUSE AND EFFECT A **cause** is the *reason* something happens. An **effect** is *what happens* as a result of the cause. The cause happens first in time. The *later* event is the effect. In most stories, events in the plot are connected by cause and effect. Look for a **cause-and-effect text structure** in informational materials. Watch out! Sometimes writers put the effect first even though that event happened as a result of (and after) the cause. For instance, consider the following sentence:

> Bears come out of their dens when the winter snow melts.

The *cause* is the melting snow. The *effect* is that bears come out of their dens. Some of the clue words that signal cause-and-effect relationships are *because, since, so that, therefore,* and *as a result.*

See page 224.
See also *Text Structures.*

CHRONOLOGICAL ORDER Most narratives are written in **chronological** or **time order,** the order in which events happen in time. When you read a story, look for time clues—words and phrases like *next, then, finally,* and *the following night.* Writers use time clues as signals to help you follow the **sequence,** or order, of events. Sometimes writers break into the sequence with a **flash-back,** an event that happened earlier. Look for chronological order in any kind of text where the order of events is important. For instance, in an article explaining how to make something, the steps are usually listed in chronological order.

See pages 193, 286.
See also *Text Structures.*

COMPARISON AND CONTRAST When you **compare,** you look for **similarities,** ways in which things are alike. When you **contrast,** you look for **differences.** In a comparison-contrast text, the features looked at are called **points of comparison.** The points of comparison are usually organized in either a **block pattern** or a **point-by-point pattern.** When you read a comparison organized in a block pattern, you find the points of comparison about each subject presented separately, first one, then the other. Here is a **block-pattern** paragraph comparing Mary's and Roger's ways of surviving Ta-Na-E-Ka (page 55):

> Mary survived by getting help from other people. She borrowed money from a teacher and used it to pay for food at Ernie's restaurant. Ernie gave her warm clothes to wear and a place to stay at night. In contrast, Roger survived on his own in the traditional Kaw way. He ate berries and maybe even grasshoppers. He lost weight during Ta-Na-E-Ka and was never warm and comfortable.

A writer who uses the **point-by-point pattern** goes back and forth between the two subjects being compared, like this:

> Mary ate well, but Roger lost weight. Mary ate good food at a restaurant while Roger lived on berries. Mary got help from others, but Roger survived by himself. Both passed the test; however, Roger survived in the traditional way. Mary found a new way of surviving.

Some of the clue words that signal comparison and contrast are *although, but, either . . . or, however,* and *yet.*

See pages 54, 189, 203.
See also *Text Structures.*

CONTEXT CLUES You can often find clues to the meaning of a word you don't know by looking at its **context,** the words and sentences around it. Here is the beginning of a paragraph from "The Dog of Pompeii" (page 432):

> The water—hot water—splashing in his face revived him. He got to his feet, Bimbo steadying him, helping him on again.

If you don't know the meaning of *revived* in the first sentence, look at the context. The beginning of the second sentence, "He got to his feet," helps you figure out that *revived* means "brought back to life."

See pages 16, 41, 129, 233, 261, 285.

EVALUATING EVIDENCE When you read informational and persuasive texts, you need to weigh the **evidence** that writers use to support their ideas. That means you need to read carefully and decide whether the writer has presented evidence that's **adequate, appropriate,** and **accurate.** *Adequate* means "sufficient" or "enough." You make sure there's enough evidence to prove the writer's points. Sometimes one example or one fact may be adequate. Other times the writer may need to provide several facts and maybe even statistics. A direct quotation from a well-respected expert in the field can often be convincing. Make sure that the writer chooses *appropriate* evidence that relates directly to the writer's idea. To be sure that evidence is *accurate*, or correct, make sure it comes from a source you can trust. Don't assume that everything you see in print is accurate. If a fact, example, or quotation doesn't sound right, check out the magazine or book that it came from. Is the magazine or book a trustworthy and reliable source? What is the author's background?

> See pages 130, 144, 157, 338, 412–418.
> See also *Fact and Opinion.*

EVIDENCE **Evidence** is the support or proof that backs up an idea, conclusion, or opinion. When you're reading an informational or persuasive text, you look for evidence in the form of examples, quotations from experts, statistics (information expressed as numbers), and personal experiences.

FACT AND OPINION A **fact** is something that can be proved true.

> **Fact:** Abraham Lincoln was the sixteenth president of the United States.

An **opinion** expresses a personal belief or feeling. An opinion cannot be proved true or false.

> **Opinion:** Abraham Lincoln was the best president the United States has ever had.

A **valid opinion** is a personal belief that is strongly supported by facts. When you read "The Mysterious Mr. Lincoln" (page 331), look for the facts that Russell Freedman uses to back up his opinions.

> See page 157.
> See also *Evidence.*

GENERALIZATION A **generalization** is a broad statement based on several particular situations. When you make a generalization, you combine evidence in a text with what you already know to make a broad, universal statement about some topic. For example, after reading "Wartime Mistakes, Peacetime Apologies" (page 79), you might want to make a generalization about the treatment of Japanese Americans during World War II.

> See page 135.
> See also *Evidence.*

GRAPHIC FEATURES Headings, design features, maps, charts, tables, diagrams, and illustrations are all **graphic features.** They present information visually. Shapes, lines, and colors combine with words to help you understand a text.

A **heading** is a kind of title for the information that follows it. Size and color set off the heading from the rest of the text. A repeated heading like "Bonus Question" in this textbook is always followed by the same type of material.

Some of the **design features** you may find in a text are colors, borders, boldface and italic type, type in different styles (fonts) and sizes, bullets (the dots that set off items in a list), and logos (like computer icons). The Quickwrite heading (see page 6 for an example) always appears with the pencil logo, for instance. Design features make a text look more attractive. They steer your eyes to different types of information and make the text easier to read.

Graphic features such as **maps, charts, diagrams, graphs,** and **tables** communicate complex information with lines, drawings, and symbols. The following elements help to make them effective:

1. A **title** identifies the subject or main idea of the graphic.

2. **Labels** identify specific information.

3. A **caption** is the text (usually under a photo or another kind of illustration) that explains what you're looking at.

4. A **legend** or **key** helps you interpret symbols and colors. Look for a **scale,** which helps you relate the size or distance of something on the graphic to real-life sizes and distances.

5. The **source** tells where the information in the graphic came from. Knowing the source helps you evaluate the graphic's accuracy.

Charts and **diagrams** use symbols, lines, and numbers to explain or to display information. They are used to compare ideas, show steps in a process, illustrate the way something is made, or show how the parts of something relate to the whole thing. A **pie graph,** for instance, shows proportions. It's a circle divided into different-sized sections, like slices of pie.

Pie Graph

A **flowchart** shows you the steps in a process, a sequence of events, or cause-and-effect relationships. See page 224 for an example of a flowchart.

Graphs, including bar graphs and line graphs, show changes or trends over time. Notice that the same information is presented in the following bar graph and line graph.

Bar Graph

Line Graph

A **table** presents facts and details arranged in rows and columns. It simplifies information to make it easy to understand.

Table

Number of Volunteers in the Peer-Tutoring Program	
First year	15
Second year	10
Third year	8

Viewing Tips: When you come across graphic features, use the tips below.

1. Read the title, labels, and legend before you try to analyze the information.

2. Read numbers carefully. Note increases or decreases. Look for the direction or order of events and for trends and relationships.

3. Draw your own conclusions from the graphic, and compare them with the writer's conclusions.

See page 342.

INFERENCE An **inference** is an educated guess. You make inferences all the time in real life. For instance, if you see pawprints crossing the snow, you can **infer** that an animal walked there. The pawprints are the **evidence.** On the basis of your experience with animal tracks, you might be able to infer that the animal was a rabbit, a cat, a dog, or a raccoon.

Readers **make inferences** on the basis of clues writers give them and experiences from their own lives. When you make inferences, you read between the lines to figure out what the writer suggests but does not state directly.

Read this passage from Avi's story "What Do Fish Have to Do with Anything?" (page 348).

During the twenty minutes that Willie watched, no one who passed looked in the beggar's direction. Willie wondered if they even saw the man. Certainly no one put any money into his open hand.

A lady leading a dog by a leash went by. The dog strained in the direction of the man sitting on the crate. The dog's tail wagged. The lady pulled the dog away. "Heel!" she commanded.

Here are some **inferences** you might draw from the passage: People don't want to look at the man who is begging. It's as if he doesn't exist for them. The dog is friendlier than the people.

See pages 17, 90, 262, 347, 363, 430.

MAIN IDEA The most important idea in a piece of nonfiction writing is the **main idea.** There may be more than one main idea in a nonfiction story or article. Sometimes the writer states a main idea directly; at other times the writer only **implies,** or suggests, the main idea. Then the reader must **infer** or guess what it is.

To infer the main idea, look at the **key details** or **important events** in the text. See whether you can create a statement that expresses the idea that these details or events develop or support. In a nonfiction text the writer may state the main idea more than once and use different words for each statement. Look especially for a **key passage** near the end of the piece. That's where the writer often emphasizes or sums up a main idea.

See pages 64, 244, 254, 262, 269, 300.
See also *Outlining.*

NOTE TAKING Taking notes is important for readers who want to remember ideas and facts. It's especially useful when you read **informational texts.** You can jot down notes in a notebook or on note cards. Notes don't have to be written in complete sentences. Put them in your own words; use phrases that will help you recall the text. You may want to put each important idea at the top of its own page or note card. As you read, add details that relate to that idea. Put related ideas on the same page or card as the main idea they support.

Whenever you copy a writer's exact words, put quotation marks around them. Write down the number of the page that was the source of each note. Even though no one but you may see your notes, try to write clearly so that you'll be able to read them later. When you finish taking notes, review them to make sure they make sense to you.

See pages 64, 78, 442.
See also *Author's Purpose*.

OUTLINING Outlining an informational text helps you identify important ideas and understand how they are connected or related to each other. Once you've made an outline, you have a quick visual summary of the information. Start with the notes you've taken on an article. (See *Note Taking*.) You should have each **main idea** with **supporting details** in one place, either on a page or on a card. Many outlines label the main ideas with Roman numerals. You need to have at least two headings at each level. Three levels may be all you need. A four-level outline is arranged like this:

I. First main idea

  A. Detail supporting first main idea

    1. Detail supporting point A

    2. Another detail supporting point A

      a. Detail supporting point 2

      b. Another detail supporting point 2

    3. Another detail supporting point A

  B. Another detail supporting first main idea

II. Second main idea

See page 64.
See also *Main Idea*.

PARAPHRASING When you **paraphrase** a text, you put it into your own words. You can check how well you understand a poem, for instance, by paraphrasing it, line by line. When you paraphrase, you follow the author's sequence of ideas. You carefully reword each line or sentence without changing the author's meaning or leaving anything out.

PERSUASION Persuasion is the use of language or visual images to get you to *believe* or *do* something. Writers who want to change your mind about an issue use **persuasive techniques.** Learning about these techniques will help you evaluate persuasion.

Emotional appeals get the reader's feelings involved in the argument. Some writers use vivid language and give reasons, examples, and anecdotes (personal-experience stories) that appeal to basic feelings such as fear, pity, jealousy, and love.

Logical appeals make sense because they're based on correct reasoning. They appeal to your brain with reasons and evidence. (See *Evidence*.) When you're reading a persuasive text, make sure that the writer has good reasons to support each opinion or conclusion. Evidence such as facts, personal experiences, examples, statistics, and statements by experts on the issue should back up each reason.

Logical fallacies are mistakes in reasoning. If you're reading a text quickly, an argument based on **fallacious reasoning** may look as if it made sense. Watch out for these fallacies.

1. **Hasty generalizations.** Valid generalizations are based on solid evidence. (See *Generalization*.) Not all generalizations are valid. Here's an example of a hasty generalization, one made on the basis of too little evidence.

> "The Sneetches" is a poem that rhymes.
> "John Henry" is a poem that rhymes.
> **Hasty generalization:** All poems rhyme.

Sometimes hasty generalizations can be corrected by the use of **qualifying words,** such as *most, usually, some, many,* and *often.* After you've read all the poems in this textbook and considered all the evidence, you could make this generalization:

> **Valid generalization:** Some poems rhyme.

2. **Circular reasoning.** This example illustrates circular reasoning, another kind of logical fallacy:

> We have the greatest football team because no other school has a team that's as fantastic as ours.

Someone using circular reasoning simply repeats an argument instead of backing it up with reasons and evidence.

3. **Only-cause fallacy.** This fallacy assumes that a problem has only one cause. It conveniently ignores the fact that most situations are the result of many causes. The **either-or fallacy** is related to the only-cause fallacy. The either-or fallacy assumes that there are only two sides to an issue.

> **Only-cause fallacy:** I didn't do well on the test because it wasn't fair.
>
> **Either-or fallacy:** If your parents don't buy this set of encyclopedias for you, they don't care about your education.

Persuasion tends to be most interesting—and effective—when it appeals to both head and heart. However, it's important to be able to recognize logical fallacies and emotional appeals—and to be aware of how they can mislead you.

See pages 412–414.

PREDICTING Making **predictions** as you read helps you think about and understand what you're reading. To make predictions, look for clues that the writer gives you. Connect those clues with other things you've read, as well as your own experience. You'll probably find yourself **adjusting predictions** as you read.

See pages 69, 174, 450.

PRIOR KNOWLEDGE *Prior* means "earlier" or "previous." **Prior knowledge** is what you know about a subject when you're at the starting line—before you read a selection. **Using prior knowledge** is a reading skill that starts with recalling experiences you've had, as well as what you've learned about the subject of the text. Glancing through the text, looking at the pictures, and reading subtitles and captions will help you recall what you already know. As you focus on the subject, you'll come up with questions that the text may answer. Making a **KWL chart** is one way to record your reading process. Here is part of a KWL chart for Mildred D. Taylor's "The Gold Cadillac" (page 175).

K	W	L
What I **Know**	What I **Want** to Know	What I **Learned**
A Cadillac is an expensive car.	How would someone feel in a gold Cadillac?	

See page 330.

PROPAGANDA Propaganda is an organized attempt to persuade people to accept certain ideas or to take certain actions. Writers sometimes use propaganda to advance a good cause. However, most writers of propaganda use emotional appeals to confuse readers and convince them that the writers' opinions are the only ones worth considering. Propaganda relies on emotional appeals rather than on logical reasons and evidence. Here are some common propaganda techniques:

1. The **bandwagon** appeal suggests that you need something or should believe something because everyone else already has it or believes it. It's an appeal to "join the crowd, climb on the bandwagon, and join the parade."

2. A **testimonial** uses a famous person, such as an actor or an athlete, to promote an

idea or a product. People who use **snob appeal** associate the product or idea they're promoting with power, wealth, or membership in a special group.

3. Writers who use **stereotypes** refer to members of a group as if they were all the same. For instance, an article stating that all professional wrestlers have limited intelligence unfairly stereotypes wrestlers. Stereotyping often leads to prejudice, or forming unfavorable opinions with complete disregard for the facts.

4. People who engage in **name-calling** offer no reasons or evidence to support their position. Instead, they attack opponents by calling them names, such as "busy bodies," "nitpickers," or "rumormongers."

See pages 415–418.

READING RATE Readers adjust the rate at which they read depending on their purpose for reading and the difficulty of the material. The following chart shows how you can adjust your reading rate for different purposes.

Reading Rates According to Purpose

Reading Rate	Purpose	Example
Scanning	Reading quickly for specific details	Finding the age of a character
Skimming	Reading quickly for main points	Previewing a science chapter by reading the headings
Reading slowly and carefully	Reading for mastery (reading to learn)	Reading and taking notes from an article for a research report
Reading at a comfortable speed	Reading for enjoyment	Reading a novel by your favorite writer

See also *Author's Purpose.*

RETELLING Retelling is a reading strategy that helps you recall and understand the major events in a story. From time to time in your reading—for instance, after something important has happened—stop for a few moments. Review what has just taken place before you go ahead. Focus on the major events. Think about them, and retell them briefly in your own words.

See page 6.

SUMMARIZING When you **summarize** a text, you restate the author's main points in your own words. You include only the important ideas and details. A **summary** of a text is much shorter than the original, while a paraphrase may be the same length as, or even longer than, the original text.

When you're summarizing, stop after each paragraph you read. Try to restate in one sentence what the author wrote. If you're summarizing a story, look for the major events in the **plot,** the ones that lead to the **climax.** If you're summarizing an **essay,** look for the important ideas. Here is a summary of Maya Angelou's "Brother" (page 263):

> Bailey was the person who was most important to the writer when she was a child. She loved Bailey because he was smart, generous, kind, and full of life. He always defended her whenever anyone insulted her. He always came up with ideas to have fun. The author says that Bailey was someone she trusted and loved with all her heart.

See pages 86–87, 118, 130, 274.

TEXT STRUCTURES Understanding the way a text is structured, or organized, can help you follow the writer's ideas. **Analyzing text structures** will help you understand the information you're reading. The five patterns of organization that writers use most often are

Handbook of Reading and Informational Terms **709**

cause and effect, chronological order, comparison and contrast, listing, and **problem solution.** Some texts contain just one pattern; others combine two or more patterns. The following guidelines can help you analyze text structure:

1. Look for words that hint at a specific pattern of organization. (See *Cause and Effect, Chronological Order,* and *Comparison and Contrast.*)

2. Look for important ideas. See whether these ideas are connected in an obvious pattern.

3. Draw a graphic organizer that shows how the text is structured. Compare your graphic organizer with the following five diagrams, which illustrate the most common text structures.

A **cause-and-effect pattern** focuses on the relationship between causes and effects. The **causal chain** below shows how the city of Pompeii was destroyed.

Causal Chain

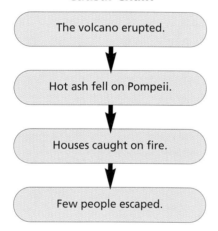

Chronological order shows events in the order in which they happen. The **sequence chain** below is a list of steps for making salsa.

Sequence Chain

A **comparison-and-contrast pattern** focuses on similarities and differences between things. The Venn diagram below compares and contrasts Mary's and Roger's experiences during Ta-Na-E-Ka (page 55).

Venn Diagram

An **enumeration** or **list pattern** organizes information in a list by order of importance, size, or location or by another order that makes sense. The list below organizes after-school jobs by ranking them in order of difficulty. (You might not agree with this order!)

List
1. Baby-sitting (most difficult)
2. Walking dogs
3. Lawn and garden work

A **problem-solution pattern** focuses on a problem and solutions to the problem. The cluster below shows a problem and some possible solutions:

Cluster

See pages 189, 193, 203.
See also *Cause and Effect, Chronological Order, Comparison and Contrast.*

Handbook of Literary Terms

For more information about a topic, turn to the page(s) in this book indicated on a separate line at the end of the entries. To learn more about *Alliteration*, for example, turn to pages 378–379.

On another line are cross-references to entries in this Handbook that provide closely related information. For instance, *Autobiography* contains a cross-reference to *Biography*.

ALLITERATION The repetition of the same or very similar consonant sounds in words that are close together. Alliteration usually occurs at the beginning of words, as in the phrase "*b*usy as a *b*ee." It can also occur within or at the end of words. The following poem repeats the sounds of *s* and *p*:

> **January**
> In January
> it's so nice
> while slipping
> on the sliding ice
> to sip hot chicken soup
> with rice.
> Sipping once
> sipping twice
> sipping chicken soup
> with rice.
>
> —Maurice Sendak

Alliteration can establish a mood and emphasize words. If you've ever twisted your tongue around a line like "She sells seashells by the seashore" or "How much wood could a woodchuck chuck if a woodchuck could chuck wood?" you have already had some fun with alliteration.

See pages 378–379.

ALLUSION A reference to a statement, a person, a place, or an event from literature, history, religion, mythology, politics, sports, or science. Writers expect readers to recognize an allusion and to think, almost at the same time, about the literary work, person, place, or event that it refers to. The cartoon below makes an allusion you will recognize right away.

"*Someone's been sleeping in my bed, too, and there she is on Screen Nine!*"

Danny Shanahan © 1989 from The New Yorker Magazine Collection. All Rights Reserved.

AUTOBIOGRAPHY The story of a person's life, written or told by that person. Maya Angelou's account of her childhood experiences, called "Brother" (page 263), is taken from her autobiography *I Know Why the Caged Bird Sings*.

See pages 242, 262, 274–275, 297.
See also *Biography*.

BIOGRAPHY The story of a real person's life, written or told by another person. A classic American biography is Carl Sandburg's life of

Abraham Lincoln. A biography popular with young adults is Russell Freedman's *Lincoln: A Photobiography* (see page 331). Frequent subjects of biographies are movie stars, television personalities, politicians, sports figures, self-made millionaires, and artists. Today biographies are among the most popular forms of literature.

> See pages 242–243, 286–287, 297.
> See also *Autobiography.*

CHARACTER A person or an animal in a story, play, or other literary work. In some works, such as folk tales, animals are characters (see "He Lion, Bruh Bear, and Bruh Rabbit" on page 225). In other works, such as fairy tales, fantastic creatures, like dragons are characters. In still other works, characters are gods or heroes (see "Medusa's Head" on page 210). Most often characters are ordinary human beings, as in "The All-American Slurp" (page 119).

The way in which a writer reveals the personality of a character is called **characterization.** A writer can reveal character in six ways:

1. by describing how the character looks and dresses

2. by letting the reader hear the character speak

3. by showing the reader how the character acts

4. by letting the reader know the character's inner thoughts and feelings

5. by revealing what other people in the story think or say about the character

6. by telling the reader directly what the character's personality is like (cruel, kind, sneaky, brave, and so on)

> See pages 4, 15, 26, 76, 90, 106, 142, 201, 252, 297, 428–429, 430.

CONFLICT A struggle or clash between opposing characters or opposing forces. An **external conflict** is a struggle between a character and some outside force. This outside force may be another character, a society as a whole, or a natural force, like bitter-cold weather or a ferocious shark. An **internal conflict,** on the other hand, is a struggle between opposing desires or emotions within a person. A character with an internal conflict may be struggling against fear or loneliness or even being a sore loser.

> See pages 4–6, 15, 106, 163, 187, 193.

CONNOTATIONS The feelings and associations that have come to be attached to a word. For example, the words *inexpensive* and *cheap* are used to describe something that is not costly. The dictionary definitions, or **denotations,** of these words are roughly the same. A manufacturer of DVD players, however, would not use *cheap* in advertising its latest model, since the word *cheap* is associated with something that is not made well. *Inexpensive* would be a better choice. Connotations can be especially important in poetry.

> See pages 362, 369.

DESCRIPTION The kind of writing that creates a clear image of something, usually by using details that appeal to one or more of the senses: sight, hearing, smell, taste, and touch. Description works through **images,** words that appeal to the five senses. Writers use description in all forms of writing—in fiction, nonfiction, and poetry. Here is a description of a famous character who has found a place in the hearts of readers everywhere. The writer's description appeals to the sense of sight, but it also gives a hint of the girl's character. Viewing this lone figure in a deserted train station, an "ordinary observer" would see

Handbook of Literary Terms

a child of about eleven, garbed in a very short, very tight, very ugly dress of yellowish gray wincey. She wore a faded brown sailor hat and beneath the hat, extending down her back, were two braids of very thick, decidedly red hair. Her face was small, white, and thin, also much freckled; her mouth was large and so were her eyes, that looked green in some lights and moods and gray in others.

—L. M. Montgomery,
from *Anne of Green Gables*

See pages 262, 267, 373.

DIALECT **A way of speaking that is characteristic of a particular region or of a particular group of people.** A dialect may have a distinct vocabulary, pronunciation system, and grammar. In a sense, we all speak dialects. The dialect that is dominant in a country or culture becomes accepted as the standard way of speaking. Writers often reproduce regional dialects or dialects that reveal a person's economic or social class. For example, the animal characters in "He Lion, Bruh Bear, and Bruh Rabbit" (page 225) use an African American dialect spoken in the rural South. In the passage below, a spunky young girl gets up the courage to ask her uncle a hard question (she is speaking an African American urban dialect).

So there I am in the navigator seat. And I turn to him and just plain ole ax him. I mean I come right on out with it. . . . And like my mama say, Hazel—which is my real name and what she remembers to call me when she bein serious—when you got somethin on your mind, speak up and let the chips fall where they may. And if anybody don't like it, tell em to come see your mama. And Daddy look up from the paper and say, You hear your mama good,

Hazel. And tell em to come see me first. Like that. That's how I was raised.

So I turn clear round in the navigator seat and say, "Look here, . . . you gonna marry this girl?"

—Toni Cade Bambara,
from "Gorilla, My Love"

DIALOGUE **Conversation between two or more characters.** Most plays consist entirely of dialogue. Dialogue is also an important element in most stories and novels. It is very effective in revealing character and can add realism and humor to a story.

In the written form of a play, such as *Blanca Flor* (page 91), dialogue appears without quotation marks. In prose or poetry, however, dialogue is usually enclosed in quotation marks.

DRAMA **A story written to be acted in front of an audience.** A drama, such as *Blanca Flor* (page 91), can also be appreciated and enjoyed in written form. The related events that take place within a drama are often separated into **acts.** Each act is often made up of shorter sections, or **scenes.** Many plays have two or three acts, but there are many variations. The elements of drama are often described as **introduction** or **exposition, complications, conflict, climax,** and **resolution.**

See also *Dialogue.*

ESSAY **A short piece of nonfiction prose.** An essay usually examines a subject from a personal point of view. The French writer Michel de Montaigne (1533–1592) is credited with creating the essay. Robert Fulghum, a popular essayist, is represented in this book (page 234). "Go for Broke" (page 88) and "Separate but Never Equal" (page 190) are examples of essays on historical topics.

FABLE A very brief story in prose or verse that teaches a moral, a practical lesson about how to succeed in life. The characters of most fables are animals who behave and speak like human beings. Some of the most popular fables are those thought to have been told by Aesop, who was a slave in ancient Greece. You may be familiar with his fable about the sly fox who praises the crow for her beautiful voice and begs her to sing for him. When the crow opens her mouth to sing, she lets fall from her beak the piece of cheese that the fox had been after the whole time.

See pages 172, 224.
See also *Folk Tale, Myth.*

FANTASY Imaginative writing that carries the reader into an invented world where the laws of nature as we know them do not operate. In fantasy worlds, fantastic forces are often at play. Characters wave magic wands, cast spells, or appear and disappear at will. These characters may be ordinary human beings—or they may be Martians, elves, giants, or fairies. Some of the oldest fantasy stories, such as "The Emperor's New Clothes" (page 137), are called **fairy tales.** A newer type of fantasy, one that deals with a future world changed by science, is called **science fiction.** "All Summer in a Day" (page 18) is Ray Bradbury's science fiction story about life as he imagines it on the planet Venus.

FICTION A prose account that is made up rather than true. The term *fiction* usually refers to novels and short stories.

See also *Fantasy, Nonfiction.*

FIGURATIVE LANGUAGE Language that describes one thing in terms of something else and is not literally true. Figures of speech always involve some sort of imaginative comparison between seemingly unlike things. The most common forms are **simile** ("My heart is like a singing bird"), **metaphor** ("The road was a ribbon of moonlight"), and **personification** ("The leaves were whispering to the night").

See pages 129, 134, 329, 387–388, 410.
See also *Metaphor, Personification, Simile.*

FLASHBACK A scene that breaks the normal time order of the plot to show a past event. A flashback can be placed anywhere in a story, even at the beginning. There, it usually gives background information. Most of the play *The Diary of Anne Frank* is a flashback.

See page 193.

FOLK TALE A story with no known author, originally passed on from one generation to another by word of mouth. Folk tales generally differ from myths in that they are not about gods and they were never connected with religion. The folk tales in this book include "Little Mangy One" (page 162) and "He Lion, Bruh Bear, and Bruh Rabbit" (page 225). Sometimes similar folk tales appear in many cultures. For example, stories similar to the old European folk tale of Cinderella have turned up in hundreds of cultures.

See pages 173, 224.
See also *Fable, Myth, Oral Tradition.*

FORESHADOWING The use of clues or hints to suggest events that will occur later in the plot. Foreshadowing builds suspense or anxiety in the reader or viewer. In a movie, for example, strange, alien creatures glimpsed among the trees may foreshadow danger for the exploring astronauts.

See also *Suspense.*

FREE VERSE Poetry that is "free" of a regular meter and rhyme scheme. Poets writing in free verse try to capture the natural rhythms

Handbook of Literary Terms

of ordinary speech. The following poem is written in free verse:

The City
If flowers want to grow
right out of the concrete sidewalk cracks
I'm going to bend down to smell them.

—David Ignatow

See pages 378–379.
See also *Poetry, Rhyme, Rhythm.*

IMAGERY Language that appeals to the senses—sight, hearing, touch, taste, and smell. Most images are visual—that is, they create pictures in the mind by appealing to the sense of sight. Images can also appeal to the senses of hearing, touch, taste, and smell. They can appeal to several senses at once. Though imagery is an element in all types of writing, it is especially important in poetry. The following poem is full of images about rain:

The Storm
In fury and terror
the tempest broke,
it tore up the pine
and shattered the oak,
yet the hummingbird hovered
within the hour
sipping clear rain
from a trumpet flower.

—Elizabeth Coatsworth

See pages 328, 329, 368.

IRONY A contrast between what is expected and what really happens. Irony can create powerful effects, from humor to horror. Here are some examples of situations that would make us feel a sense of irony:

- A shoemaker wears shoes with holes in them.

- The children of a famous dancer trip over their own feet.

- It rains on the day a group of weather forecasters have scheduled a picnic.

- Someone asks, "How's my driving?" after going through a stop sign.

- A Great Dane runs away from a mouse.

- Someone living in the desert keeps a boat in her yard.

- The child of a police officer robs a bank.

- Someone walks out in the midst of a hurricane and says, "Nice day."

LEGEND A story, usually based on some historical fact, that has been handed down from one generation to the next. Legends often grow up around famous figures or events. For example, legend has it that Abraham Lincoln (see page 331) was a simple, ordinary man. In reality, Lincoln was a complicated man of unusual ability and ambition. The stories about King Arthur and his knights are legends based on the exploits of an actual warrior-king who probably lived in Wales in the 500s. Legends often make use of fantastic details.

See pages 172–173.

LIMERICK A humorous five-line verse that has a regular meter and the rhyme scheme *aabba.* Limericks often have place names in their rhymes. The following limerick was published in Edward Lear's *Book of Nonsense* in 1846, when limericks were at the height of their popularity:

There was an old man of Peru
Who dreamt he was eating a shoe.
    He awoke in the night
    With a terrible fright
And found it was perfectly true!

MAIN IDEA The most important idea expressed in a piece of writing. Sometimes the main idea is stated directly by the writer; at other times the reader must infer it.

See pages 40, 67, 84, 109, 252, 254, 262, 267, 269, 272, 300, 314, 336.

METAPHOR A comparison between two unlike things in which one thing becomes another thing. An **extended metaphor** carries the comparison through an entire work. A metaphor is an important type of figure of speech. Metaphors are used in all forms of writing and are common in ordinary speech. When you say about your grumpy friend, "He's such a bear today," you do not mean that he is growing bushy black fur. You mean that he is in a bad mood and is ready to attack, just the way a bear might be.

Metaphors differ from **similes,** which use specific words, such as *like, as, than,* and *resembles,* to make their comparisons. "He is behaving like a bear" is a simile.

The following famous poem compares fame to an insect:

Fame is a bee.
It has a song—
It has a sting—
Ah, too, it has a wing.

—Emily Dickinson

See pages 129, 134, 329, 330, 336, 368, 387–388, 410.
See also *Figurative Language, Personification, Simile.*

MOOD The overall emotion created by a work of literature. Mood can often be described in one or two adjectives, such as *eerie, dreamy, mysterious, depressing.* The mood created by the poem below is sad and lonely:

Since Hanna Moved Away
The tires on my bike are flat.
The sky is grouchy gray.

At least it sure feels like that
Since Hanna moved away.

Chocolate ice cream tastes like prunes.
December's come to stay.
They've taken back the Mays and Junes
Since Hanna moved away.

Flowers smell like halibut.
Velvet feels like hay.
Every handsome dog's a mutt
Since Hanna moved away.

Nothing's fun to laugh about.
Nothing's fun to play.
They call me, but I won't come out
Since Hanna moved away.

—Judith Viorst

MYTH A story that usually explains something about the world and involves gods and superheroes. Myths are deeply connected to the traditions and religious beliefs of the cultures that produced them. Myths often explain certain aspects of life, such as what thunder is or where sunlight comes from or why people die. **Origin myths,** or **creation myths,** explain how something in the world began or was created. Most myths are very old and were handed down orally for many centuries before being put in writing. The stories of the hero Perseus (page 208) and of the decent couple Baucis and Philemon (page 150) are famous Greek myths.

See pages 172, 208, 222.
See also *Fable, Folk Tale, Oral Tradition.*

NARRATION The kind of writing that relates a series of connected events to tell "what happened." Narration (also called **narrative**) is the form of writing storytellers use to tell stories. Narration can be used to relate both fictional and true-life events.

See pages 187, 193.

NONFICTION Prose writing that deals with real people, events, and places without

changing any facts. Popular forms of non-fiction are the autobiography, the biography, and the essay. Other examples of nonfiction are newspaper stories, magazine articles, historical writing, travel writing, science reports, and personal diaries and letters.

See also *Fiction*.

NOVEL A long fictional story that is usually more than one hundred book pages in length. A novel includes all the elements of storytelling—**plot, character, setting, theme,** and **point of view.** Because of its length, a novel usually has a more complex plot, subplots, and more characters, settings, and themes than a short story.

See page 174.

ONOMATOPOEIA The use of a word whose sound imitates or suggests its meaning. Onomatopoeia (än'ō·mat'ō·pē'ə) is so natural to us that we begin to use it at a very early age. *Boom, bang, sniffle, rumble, hush, ding,* and *snort* are all examples of onomatopoeia. Onomatopoeia helps create the music of poetry. The following poem uses onomatopoeia:

Our Washing Machine
Our washing machine went whisity whirr
Whisity whisity whisity whirr
One day at noon it went whisity click
Whisity whisity whisity click
click grr click grr click grr click
    Call the repairman
    Fix it . . . quick.

—Patricia Hubbell

See also *Alliteration*.

ORAL TRADITION A collection of folk tales, songs, and poems that have been passed on orally from generation to generation.

See pages 172–173, 224.
See also *Folk Tale*.

PARAPHRASE A restatement of a written work in which the meaning is expressed in other words. A paraphrase of a poem should tell what the poem says, line by line, but in the paraphraser's own words. A paraphrase of a work of prose should briefly summarize the major events or ideas. Here is the first stanza of a famous poem, followed by a paraphrase:

Once upon a midnight dreary, while I
    pondered, weak and weary,
Over many a quaint and curious volume of
    forgotten lore—
While I nodded, nearly napping, suddenly
    there came a tapping,
As of someone gently rapping, rapping at
    my chamber door.
"'Tis some visitor," I muttered, "tapping at
    my chamber door—
    Only this, and nothing more."

—Edgar Allan Poe,
from "The Raven"

Paraphrase: One midnight, when I was tired, I was reading some interesting old books that contain information no one learns anymore. As I was dozing off, I suddenly heard what sounded like someone tapping at the door to the room. "It is someone coming to see me," I said to myself, "knocking at the door. That's all it is."

Notice that the paraphrase is neither as eerie nor as elegant as the poem.

PERSONIFICATION A special kind of metaphor in which a nonhuman or nonliving thing or quality is talked about as if it were human or alive. You would be using personification if you said, "The leaves danced along the sidewalk." Of course, leaves don't dance—only people do. The poem below personifies the night wind:

Rags
The night wind
rips a cloud sheet
into rags,
then rubs, rubs
the October moon
until it shines
like a brass doorknob.

—Judith Thurman

In the cartoon below, history and fame are talked about as though they were human.

"*While you were out for lunch, History passed by and Fame came knocking.*"

Edward Koren © 1969 from The New Yorker Magazine Collection. All Rights Reserved.

See pages 129, 329, 387–388, 410.
See also *Figurative Language,*
Metaphor, Simile.

PLOT **The series of related events that make up a story.** Plot tells "what happens" in a short story, novel, play, or narrative poem. Most plots are built on these bare bones: An **introduction** tells who the characters are and what their **conflict,** or problem, is. **Complications** arise as the characters take steps to resolve the conflict. When the outcome of the conflict is decided one way or another, the plot reaches a **climax,** the most exciting mo-

ment in the story. The final part of the story is the **resolution,** when the characters' problems are solved and the story ends.

See pages 4–5, 98, 106, 135, 224, 428–429.
See also *Conflict.*

POETRY **A kind of rhythmic, compressed language that uses figures of speech and imagery to appeal to emotion and imagination.** Poetry often has a regular pattern of rhythm, and it may have a regular pattern of rhyme. **Free verse** is poetry that has no regular pattern of rhythm or rhyme.

See pages 378–379, 387–388.
See also *Free Verse, Imagery, Refrain,*
Rhyme, Rhythm, Speaker, Stanza.

POINT OF VIEW **The vantage point from which a story is told.** Two common points of view are the omniscient (äm·nish′ənt) and the first person.

1. In the **omniscient,** or all-knowing, **third-person point of view,** the narrator knows everything about the characters and their problems. This all-knowing narrator can tell us about the past, the present, and the future. Below is part of a familiar story told from the omniscient point of view:

> Once upon a time in a small village, there were three houses built by three brother pigs. One house was made of straw, one was made of twigs, and one was made of brick. Each pig thought his house was the best and the strongest. A wolf—a very hungry wolf—lived just outside the town. He was practicing house-destroying techniques and was trying to decide which pig's house was the weakest.

2. In the **first-person point of view,** one of the characters, using the personal pronoun *I,* is telling the story. The reader

Handbook of Literary Terms **719**

becomes familiar with this narrator and can know only what he or she knows and can observe only what he or she observes. All information about the story must come from this one narrator. In some cases, as in the following example, the information this narrator gives may not be correct:

> As soon as I found out some new pigs had moved into the neighborhood, I started to practice my house-destroying techniques. I like to blow down houses and eat whoever is inside. The little pigs have built their houses of different materials—but I know I can blow 'em down in no time. That brick house looks especially weak.

See pages 69, 244, 252, 260, 262, 267, 284, 286, 297, 298, 319.

PROSE **Any writing that is not poetry.** Essays, short stories, novels, news articles, and letters are written in prose.

REFRAIN **A repeated word, phrase, line, or group of lines in a poem or song or even in a speech.** Refrains are usually associated with songs and poems, but they are also used in speeches and some other forms of literature. Refrains are often used to create rhythm. They are also used for emphasis and emotional effects.

See page 404.

RHYME **The repetition of accented vowel sounds and all sounds following them.** *Trouble* and *bubble* are rhymes, as are *clown* and *noun*. Rhymes in poetry help create rhythm and lend a songlike quality to a poem. They can also emphasize ideas and provide humor or delight.

End rhymes are rhymes at the ends of lines. **Internal rhymes** are rhymes within lines. Here is an example of a poem with both kinds of rhymes:

> In days of *old* when knights caught *cold*,
> They were not quickly *cured*;
> No aspirin *pill* would check the *ill*,
> Which had to be *endured*.
>
> —David Daiches,
> from "Thoughts on Progress,"
> from *The New Yorker*

Rhyme scheme is the pattern of rhyming sounds at the ends of lines in a poem. Notice the pattern of end rhymes in the poem in the cartoon below.

See pages 378–379, 380.

RHYTHM **A musical quality produced by the repetition of stressed and unstressed syllables or by the repetition of other sound patterns.** Rhythm occurs in all language—written and spoken—but is particularly important in poetry. The most obvious kind of rhythm is the repeated pattern of stressed and unstressed syllables, called **meter**. Finding this pattern is called **scanning**. If you scan or say the following lines aloud, you'll hear a strong, regular rhythm. (Crowns, pounds, and guineas are British currency.)

> When I was one-and-twenty
> I heard a wise man say,
> "Give crowns and pounds and guineas
> But not your heart away."
>
> —A. E. Housman, from
> "When I Was One-and-Twenty"

See pages 378–379, 380, 399.
See also *Free Verse, Poetry.*

SETTING The time and place of a story, a poem, or a play. The setting can help create mood or atmosphere. The setting can also affect the events of the plot. In some stories the conflict is provided by the setting. This happens in "The Dog of Pompeii" (page 432) when the characters' lives are threatened by a volcano. Some examples of vivid settings are the gloomy planet where it rains for seven years in "All Summer in a Day" (page 18), the snow-covered countryside in "Zlateh the Goat" (page 451), and Ernie's Riverside restaurant in "Ta-Na-E-Ka" (page 55).

See pages 4, 5, 15, 17, 26, 43, 47.

SHORT STORY A fictional prose narrative that is about five to twenty book pages long. Short stories are usually built on a **plot** that consists of these elements: **introduction, conflict, complications, climax,** and **resolution.** Short stories are more limited than novels. They usually have only one or two major characters and one setting.

See pages 174, 193.
See also *Conflict, Fiction, Novel, Plot.*

SIMILE A comparison between two unlike things using a word such as *like, as, than,* or *resembles.* The simile (sim'ə·lē') is an important figure of speech. "His voice is as loud as a trumpet" and "Her eyes are like the blue sky" are similes. In the following poem the poet uses a simile to help us see a winter scene in a new way:

> **Scene**
> Little trees like pencil strokes
> black and still
> etched forever in my mind
> on that snowy hill.
>
> —Charlotte Zolotow

See pages 129, 134, 201, 329, 387–388, 410.
See also *Figurative Language, Metaphor.*

SPEAKER The voice talking to us in a poem. Sometimes the speaker is identical to the poet, but often the speaker and the poet are not the same. A poet may speak as a child, a woman, a man, an animal, or even an object. The speaker of "Things to Do If You Are a Subway" asks the reader to imagine that he or she is a subway train and to act like one.

> **Things to Do If You Are a Subway**
> Pretend you are a dragon.
> Live in underground caves.
> Roar about underneath the city.
> Swallow piles of people.
> Spit them out at the next station.
> Zoom through the darkness.
> Be an express.
> Go fast.
> Make as much noise as you please.
>
> —Bobbi Katz

See pages 297, 298, 389, 403.

STANZA In a poem, a group of lines that form a unit. A stanza in a poem is something like a paragraph in prose; it often expresses a unit of thought.

Handbook of Literary Terms   721

Handbook of Literary Terms

SUSPENSE The anxious curiosity the reader feels about what will happen next in a story. Any kind of writing that has a plot evokes some degree of suspense. Our sense of suspense is awakened in "The Gold Cadillac" (page 175), for example, when the narrator and her family begin their trip to Mississippi. The anxious and fearful warnings of the family's friends and relatives make us eager to read on to see if the journey will prove dangerous.

See page 450.
See also *Foreshadowing, Plot.*

SYMBOL A person, a place, a thing, or an event that has its own meaning *and* stands for something beyond itself as well. Examples of symbols are all around us—in music, on television, and in everyday conversation. The skull and crossbones, for example, is a symbol of danger; the dove is a symbol of peace; and the red rose stands for true love. In literature, symbols are often more personal. For example, in "The Gold Cadillac," the Cadillac stands for success in the eyes of Wilbert.

See pages 329, 347, 357.

TALL TALE An exaggerated, fanciful story that gets "taller and taller," or more and more far-fetched, the more it is told and retold. The tall tale is an American story form. John Henry (page 405) is a famous tall-tale character. Here is a short tall tale:

> When the temperature reached 118 degrees, a whole field of corn popped. White flakes filled the air and covered the ground six inches deep and drifted across roads and collected on tree limbs.
>
> A mule that saw all this thought it was snowing and lay down and quietly froze to death.

THEME A truth about life revealed in a work of literature. A theme is not the same as a subject. A subject can usually be expressed in a word or two—*love, childhood, death.* A theme is the idea the writer wishes to reveal about that subject. A theme has to be expressed in a full sentence. A work can have more than one theme. A theme is usually not stated directly in the work. Instead, the reader has to think about the elements of the work and then make an inference, or educated guess, about what they all mean. One theme of "The Emperor's New Clothes" (page 137) can be stated this way: People are often afraid to speak the truth for fear that others will think them stupid.

See pages 116–117, 118, 128, 135, 142, 149, 155, 167, 187, 357, 373.

TONE The attitude a writer takes toward an audience, a subject, or a character. Tone is conveyed through the writer's choice of words and details. The tone can be light and humorous, serious and sad, friendly or hostile toward a character, and so forth. The poem "The Sneetches" (page 381) is light and humorous in tone. In contrast, Francisco X. Alarcón's "In a Neighborhood in Los Angeles" (page 392) has a loving and respectful tone.

See pages 84, 389, 394, 400.

Glossary

The glossary that follows is an alphabetical list of words found in the selections in this book. Use this glossary just as you would use a dictionary—to find out the meanings of unfamiliar words. (Some technical, foreign, and more obscure words in this book are not listed here but instead are defined for you in the footnotes that accompany many of the selections.)

Many words in the English language have more than one meaning. This glossary gives the meanings that apply to the words as they are used in the selections in this book. Words closely related in form and meaning are usually listed together in one entry (for instance, *compassion* and *compassionate*), and the definition is given for the first form.

The following abbreviations are used:

adj.	adjective
adv.	adverb
n.	noun
v.	verb

Each word's pronunciation is given in parentheses. A guide to the pronunciation symbols appears at the bottom of this page. For more information about the words in this glossary or for information about words not listed here, consult a dictionary.

A

aghast (ə·gast′) *adj.:* shocked; horrified.

alien (āl′yən) *n.:* foreigner.

ambitious (am·bish′əs) *adj.:* eager to succeed.

animation (an′i·mā′shən) *n.:* liveliness.

anonymous (ə·nän′ə·məs) *adj.:* unknown; unidentified.

audacity (ô·das′ə·tē) *n.:* boldness; daring.

avenge (ə·venj′) *v.:* get even for; get revenge for.

C

chaos (kā′äs′) *n.:* total confusion or disorder.

cleft (kleft) *adj.:* split; divided.

contemplate (kän′təm·plāt′) *v.:* study carefully.

controversial (kän′trə·vʉr′shəl) *adj.:* debatable; tending to stir up argument.

crusade (kro͞o·sād′) *n.:* struggle for a cause.

D

defiant (dē·fī′ənt) *adj.:* disobedient; boldly resisting.

defy (dē·fī′) *v.:* resist; oppose.

descend (dē·send′) *v.:* move to a lower place; come down.

determine (dē·tʉr′mən) *v.:* decide.

devastate (dev′ə·stāt′) *v.:* cause great damage. —**devastating** *v.* used as *adj.*

diagnosis (dī′əg·nō′sis) *n.:* act of identifying a disease by examining symptoms.

diligence (dil′ə·jəns) *n.:* steady effort.

disengage (dis′in·gāj′) *v.:* unfasten.

---

at, āte, cär; ten, ēve; is, īce; gō, hôrn, look, to͞ol; oil, out; up, fʉr; ə *for unstressed vowels, as* a *in* ago, u *in* focus; ′ *as in* Latin (lat′′n); chin; she; zh *as in* azure (azh′ər); thin; *th*e; ŋ *as in* ring (riŋ)

E

elude (ē·lōōd') *v.:* escape the notice of; avoid detection by.

emit (ē·mit') *v.:* give out; send forth.

etiquette (et'i·kit) *n.:* acceptable manners and behavior.

evacuate (ē·vak'yōō·āt') *v.:* remove from an area.

evident (ev'ə·dənt) *adj.:* obvious.

exposure (ek·spō'zhər) *n.:* state of being unprotected.

exude (eg·zyōōd') *v.:* give off.

F

feral (fir'əl) *adj.:* untamed; wild.

formidable (fôr'mə·də·bəl) *adj.:* fearsome.

forsaken (fôr·sā'kən) *adj.:* abandoned; deserted.

furtive (fur'tiv) *adj.:* done in a sneaky or secretive way.

G

gawky (gô'kē) *adj.:* clumsy; awkward.

gorge (gôrj) *v.:* fill up; stuff (oneself).

grating (grāt'iŋ) *adj.:* irritating.

grimace (grim'is) *v.:* twist the face to express pain, anger, or disgust.

H

hallucination (hə·lōō'si·nā'shən) *n.:* sight or sound of something that isn't really there.

hazardous (haz'ər·dəs) *adj.:* dangerous; risky.

heedful (hēd'fəl) *adj.:* attentive; keeping in mind.

hover (huv'ər) *v.:* remain suspended in the air.

I

ignorance (ig'nə·rəns) *n.:* lack of knowledge.

inexplicable (in·eks'pli·kə·bəl) *adj.:* not explainable.

infest (in·fest') *v.:* inhabit in large numbers (said of something harmful).

intent (in·tent') *adj.:* closely attentive. —**intently** *adv.*

intern (in·turn') *v.:* imprison or confine.

J

jubilant (jōō'bə·lənt) *adj.:* joyful.

L

laud (lôd) *v.:* praise highly.

lavish (lav'ish) *adj.:* generous; plentiful. —**lavishly** *adv.*

legitimate (lə·jit'ə·mət) *adj.:* here, reasonable; justified.

listless (list'lis) *adj.:* lifeless; lacking in interest or energy.

lofty (lôf'tē) *adj.:* noble; high.

lure (loor) *v.:* tempt; attract.

M

marvel (mär'vəl) *v.:* wonder.

melancholy (mel'ən·käl'ē) *adj.:* mournful; gloomy.

milestone (mīl'stōn') *n.:* significant event.

mortify (môrt'ə·fī') *v.:* make ashamed; embarrass deeply. —**mortified** *v.* used as *adj.*

N

nurture (nur'chər) *v.:* promote the growth of; nurse.

O

omen (ō'mən) *n.:* thing believed to be a sign of future events.

P

paramount (par'ə·mount') *adj.:* main; most important.

penetrate (pen'i·trāt') *v.:* pierce; make a way through.

perpetual (pər·pech'ōō·əl) *adj.:* permanent; constant.

perplexity (pər·plek′sə·tē) *n.:* bewilderment; confusion.

placate (plā′kāt′) *v.:* calm or soothe (someone who is angry).

ponder (pän′dər) *v.:* think over carefully.

precision (prē·sizh′ən) *n.:* exactness; accuracy.

proverb (präv′ərb) *n.:* short traditional saying that expresses a truth.

prudent (proo͞′dənt) *adj.:* wise; sensible.

R

recess (rē′ses) *n.:* inner place.

regain (ri·gān′) *v.:* recover.

repose (ri·pōz′) *n.:* state of rest or inactivity.

resilient (ri·zil′yənt) *adj.:* springy; quick to recover.

reticent (ret′ə·sənt) *adj.:* reserved; tending to speak little.

revive (ri·vīv′) *v.:* awaken; bring back to life.

rural (roor′əl) *adj.:* having to do with country life.

S

savor (sā′vər) *v.:* delight in.

servitude (sur′və·too͞d′) *n.:* condition of being under another person's control.

shrewd (shroo͞d) *adj.:* sharp; clever. —**shrewdest** *adj.* used as *n.*

sinewy (sin′yoo͞·ē) *adj.:* strong; tough.

slacken (slak′ən) *v.:* lessen; slow down. —**slackening** *v.* used as *adj.*

spectacle (spek′tə·kəl) *n.:* remarkable sight.

surge (surj) *v.:* move in a wave.

T

tolerant (täl′ər·ənt) *adj.:* patient; accepting of others.

U

urgency (ur′jən·sē) *n.:* pressure; insistence.

V

vague (vāg) *adj.:* not clear or definite; general. —**vaguely** *adv.*

vapor (vā′pər) *n.:* gas; fumes.

W

wily (wī′lē) *adj.:* sly; clever in a sneaky way.

Acknowledgments

For permission to reprint copyrighted material, grateful acknowledgment is made to the following sources:

Arcade Publishing, New York, NY: "A balmy spring wind" from *Haiku: This Other World* by Richard Wright. Copyright © 1998 by Ellen Wright.

Archaeology's Dig: Magazine cover from *Archaeology's Dig,* vol. 2, no. 2, April–May 2000. Copyright © 2000 by Archaeology's Dig.

Atheneum Books for Young Readers, an imprint of Simon & Schuster Children's Publishing Division: "The Bracelet" by Yoshiko Uchida from *The Scribner Anthology for Young People,* edited by Anne Diven. Copyright © 1976 by Yoshiko Uchida. "Since Hanna Moved Away" from *If I Were in Charge of the World and Other Worries* by Judith Viorst. Copyright © 1981 by Judith Viorst.

Estate of Toni Cade Bambara: From *Gorilla, My Love* by Toni Cade Bambara. Copyright © 1971 by Toni Cade Bambara.

Bancroft Library, University of California, Berkeley: From *Desert Exile: The Uprooting of a Japanese American Family* by Yoshiko Uchida. Copyright © 1982 by Yoshiko Uchida.

Catherine Beston Barnes: "The Storm" by Elizabeth Coatsworth.

Susan Bergholz Literary Services, New York: "Eleven" from *Woman Hollering Creek* by Sandra Cisneros. Copyright © 1991 by Sandra Cisneros. Published by Vintage Books, a division of Random House, Inc., New York, and originally in hardcover by Random House, Inc. All rights reserved.

The Estate of Gwendolyn Brooks: "Cynthia In the Snow" from *Bronzeville Boys and Girls* by Gwendolyn Brooks. Copyright © 1956 by Gwendolyn Brooks Blakely.

Candlewick Press Inc., Cambridge, MA: "What Do Fish Have to Do with Anything?" from *What Do Fish Have to Do with Anything?* by Avi, illustrated by Tracy Mitchell. Copyright © 1997 by Avi.

CBS, a division of Viacom Inc.: From "One Child's Labor of Love" from *60 Minutes II,* October 5, 1999. Copyright © 1999 by CBS, a division of Viacom Inc.

Children's Express Foundation, Inc.: From "Too Much TV Can Equal Too Much Weight" by Jamie Rodgers from *Children's Express,* accessed September 22, 2000, at http://www.cenews.org/news/200007obesetv.htm. Copyright © 2000 by Children's Express Foundation.

Chronicle Books, San Francisco: "In a Neighborhood in Los Angeles" from *Body in Flames/Cuerpo en Llamas* by Francisco X. Alarcón. Copyright © 1990 by Francisco X. Alarcón.

Clarion Books/Houghton Mifflin Company: "The Mysterious Mr. Lincoln" from *Lincoln: A Photobiography* by Russell Freedman. Copyright © 1987 by Russell Freedman. All rights reserved.

Cobblestone Publishing Company, 30 Grove Street, Suite C, Peterborough, NH 03458: "Wartime Mistakes, Peacetime Apologies" by Nancy Day from *Cobblestone: Japanese Americans,* April 1996. Copyright © 1996 by Cobblestone Publishing Company. All rights reserved. From "Making a Flying Fish" by Paula Morrow from *Faces: Happy Holidays,* vol. 7, no. 4, December 1990. Copyright © 1990 by Cobblestone Publishing Company. All rights reserved.

Coffee House Press: "Forty-one Seconds on a Sunday in June, in Salt Lake City, Utah" from *Choruses: Poems* by Quincy Troupe. Copyright © 1999 by Quincy Troupe.

Don Congdon Associates, Inc.: Quote by Ray Bradbury from *Something About the Author,* vol. 40. Copyright © 1976 by Gale Research Company Inc. "All Summer in a Day" by Ray Bradbury. Copyright © 1954 and renewed © 1982 by Ray Bradbury.

David Daiches: From "Thoughts on Progress" by David Daiches from *The New Yorker,* August 28, 1954. Copyright © 1954, 1982 by David Daiches.

Dial Books for Young Readers, an imprint of Penguin Putnam Books for Young Readers, a division of Penguin Putnam Inc.: Author's note and "The Gold Cadillac" from *The Gold Cadillac* by Mildred D. Taylor. Copyright © 1987 by Mildred D. Taylor.

Gwen Everett: From *John Brown: One Man Against Slavery* by Gwen Everett. Text copyright © 1993 by Gwen Everett.

Farrar, Straus & Giroux, LLC: From *A Day of Pleasure: Stories of a Boy Growing Up in Warsaw* by Isaac Bashevis Singer. Copyright © 1969 by Isaac Bashevis Singer.

Don Foley: Illustration for "What Will Our Towns Look Like? (If We Take Care of Our Planet)" from *Time for Kids,* January 21, 2000. Copyright © 2000 by Don Foley.

The Gainesville Sun: Text and photo from "Suit Helps Girl Enjoy Daylight" by Lise Fisher from *The Gainesville Sun,* January 31, 1999. Copyright © 1999 by The Gainesville Sun.

The Gale Group: From "Olivia Coolidge" and "Virginia Hamilton" from *Something About the Author,* vol. 4, edited by Anne Commire. Copyright © 1976 by Gale Research Company. All rights reserved. From "Huynh Quang Nhuong" from *Contemporary Authors,* vol. 107, edited by Hal May. Copyright © 1983 by Gale Research Company. All rights reserved.

Greenhaven Press, Inc.: From "The U.S. Has a Garbage Crisis" from *The Environment: Distinguishing Between Fact and Opinion* by William Dudley. Copyright © 1990 by Greenhaven Press, Inc.

Grolier Publishing Company, a division of Scholastic, Inc.: From "Nilou" from *Newcomers to America: Stories of Today's Young Immigrants* by Judith E. Greenberg. Copyright © 1996 by Judith E. Greenberg.

Harcourt, Inc.: From "Words from the Author" by Russell Freedman from *HBJ Treasury of Literature: Beyond Expectations* by Roger C. Farr and Dorothy S. Strickland. Copyright © 1993 by Harcourt Brace & Company. "La Bamba" from *Baseball in April and Other Stories* by Gary Soto. Copyright © 1990 by Gary Soto. From "Letter to Kids" by Gary Soto from a promotional for *Local News.* "Ode to Mi Gato" from *Neighborhood Odes* by Gary Soto. Copyright © 1992 by Gary Soto.

HarperCollins Publishers: From *The Land I Lost* by Huynh Quang Nhuong. Copyright © 1982 by Huynh Quang Nhuong. "Zlateh the Goat" and an excerpt from *Zlateh the Goat and Other Stories* by Isaac Bashevis Singer, illustrated by Maurice Sendak. Text copyright © 1966 by Isaac Bashevis Singer. "January" from *Chicken Soup with Rice: A Book of Months* by Maurice Sendak. Copyright © 1962 and renewed © 1990 by Maurice Sendak.

Henry Holt and Company, LLC: "The Emperor's New Clothes" by Hans Christian Andersen from *Michael Hague's Favorite Hans Christian Andersen Fairy Tales* by Michael Hague. Copyright © 1981 by Henry Holt and Company.

The Horn Book, Inc., 56 Roland Street, Suite 200, Boston, MA 02129, (617) 628-0225: From "The Common Ground" by Ann Petry from *The Horn Book Magazine,* April 1965.

Houghton Mifflin Company: "Baucis and Philemon" and "Medusa's Head" from *Greek Myths* by Olivia Coolidge. Copyright © 1949 and renewed © 1977 by Olivia E. Coolidge. All rights reserved.

Jet Propulsion Laboratory, California Institute of Technology: From the NASA Solar System Exploration Web site, accessed July 21, 2000, at http://sse.jpl.nasa.gov /features/planets/venus/venus.html and http://sse.jpl.nasa .gov. Copyright © 2000 by Jet Propulsion Laboratory, California Institute of Technology.

Bobbi Katz: "Things to Do If You Are a Subway" by Bobbi Katz from *Upside Down and Inside Out: Poems for All Your Pockets.* Copyright © 1973 by Bobbi Katz. Bobbi Katz controls all reprint rights.

Alfred A. Knopf, a division of Random House, Inc.: "Motto" and "Poem" from *Collected Poems* by Langston Hughes. Copyright © 1994 by the Estate of Langston Hughes.

Alfred A. Knopf Children's Books, a division of Random House, Inc.: "He Lion, Bruh Bear, and Bruh Rabbit" and an excerpt from *The People Could Fly* by Virginia Hamilton. Copyright © 1985 by Virginia Hamilton.

Edward Lueders: "Your Poem, Man . . ." by Edward Lueders from Some *Haystacks Don't Even Have Any Needle: And Other Complete Modern Poems,* compiled by Stephen Dunning, Edward Lueders, and Hugh Smith. Copyright © 1969 by Scott, Foresman and Company; copyright renewed © 1997 by Edward Lueders.

Margaret K. McElderry Books, an imprint of Simon & Schuster Children's Publishing Division: "Hard on the Gas" from *Behind the Wheel: Poems About Driving* by Janet S. Wong. Copyright © 1999 by Janet S. Wong.

Alice P. Miller: "All Aboard with Thomas Garrett" by Alice P. Miller from *Cobblestone,* vol. 2, no. 2, February 1981. Copyright © 1981 by Alice P. Miller.

Lensey Namioka: "The All-American Slurp" by Lensey Namioka from *Visions,* edited by Donald R. Gallo. Copyright © 1987 by Lensey Namioka. All rights reserved by the author.

North Shore Animal League, Port Washington, NY: North Shore Animal League Pet Adoption Application. Copyright © 2000 by North Shore Animal League.

Pantheon Books, a division of Random House, Inc.: "Little Mangy One" from *Arab Folktales* by Inea Bushnaq. Copyright © 1986 by Inea Bushnaq.

Penguin Books Ltd.: "Winter rain" by Nozawa Bonchō and "Bad-tempered, I got back" by Ōshima Ryōta from *The Penguin Book of Japanese Verse,* translated by Geoffrey Bownas and Anthony Thwaite, Penguin Books, 1964. Translation copyright © 1964 by Geoffrey Bownas and Anthony Thwaite.

People Weekly: From "Brave Hearts" (retitled "Trial by Fire") by Dan Jewel and Sophfronia Scott from *People Weekly,* July 14, 1997. Copyright © 1997 by Time Inc. All rights reserved.

Pets.com: "Animal Instincts" by Gina Spadafori from *Pets.com, The Magazine for Pets and Their Humans,* vol. 1, issue 4, June 2000. Copyright © 2000 by www.pets.com.

Random House, Inc.: From *All I Really Need to Know I Learned in Kindergarten* by Robert L. Fulghum Copyright © 1986, 1988 by Robert L. Fulghum. Excerpt

(retitled "Brother") from *I Know Why the Caged Bird Sings* by Maya Angelou. Copyright © 1969 and renewed © 1997 by Maya Angelou.

Random House Children's Books, a division of Random House, Inc.: "The Sneetches" from *The Sneetches and Other Stories* by Dr. Seuss. TM and copyright © 1953, 1954, 1961 and renewed © 1989 by Dr. Seuss Enterprises, LP. "Just Once" by Thomas J. Dygard from *Ultimate Sports,* edited by Donald R. Gallo. Copyright © 1995 by Donald R. Gallo.

Marian Reiner: "An old silent pond" by Bashō from *Cricket Songs: Japanese Haiku,* translated by Harry Behn. Copyright © 1964 by Harry Behn; copyright renewed © 1992 by Prescott Behn, Pamela Behn Adam, and Peter Behn.

Marian Reiner on behalf of Patricia Hubbell: "Our Washing Machine from *The Apple Vendor's Fair* by Patricia Hubbell. Copyright © 1963 and renewed © 1991 by Patricia Hubbell.

Marian Reiner on behalf of Judith Thurman: "Rags" from *Flashlight and Other Poems* by Judith Thurman. Copyright © 1976 by Judith Thurman.

Russell & Volkening as agents for Ann Petry: "A Glory over Everything" from *Harriet Tubman: Conductor on the Underground Railroad* by Ann Petry. Copyright © 1955 and renewed © 1983 by Ann Petry.

The Saturday Review: "The Path Through the Cemetery" by Leonard Q. Ross from *Saturday Review of Literature,* November 29, 1941. Copyright © 1941 by General Media International, Inc.

Scholastic Inc.: From "The California Gold Rush" by Kathy Wilmore from *Junior Scholastic,* December 1, 1997. Copyright © 1997 by Scholastic Inc. "Ta-Na-E-Ka" by Mary Whitebird from *Scholastic Voice,* December 13, 1973. Copyright © 1973 by Scholastic Inc. "A Civil War Thanksgiving" by Timothy Kelley from *The New York Times Upfront,* vol. 133, no. 6, November 13, 2000. Copyright © 2000 by Scholastic Inc. and The New York Times Company.

School Library Journal: From a book review of Lois Lowry's *Number the Stars* in *School Library Journal,* vol. 35, no. 7, March 1989. Copyright © 1989 by Cahners Business Information, a division of Reed Elsevier Inc.

Robert Silverberg: From "Pompeii" from *Lost Cities and Vanished Civilizations* by Robert Silverberg. Copyright © 1962 and renewed © 1990 by Agberg, Ltd.

Simon & Schuster Books for Young Readers, an imprint of Simon & Schuster Children's Publishing Division: Quote by Avi from *Avi Bradbury Press Promotional Brochure.* Copyright © 1992 by Avi. From "Boar Out There" from *Every Living Thing* by Cynthia Rylant. Copyright © 1985 by Cynthia Rylant. Excerpt (retitled "Storm") from *Woodsong* by Gary Paulsen. Copyright © 1990 by Gary Paulsen.

Gary Soto: Comment on "Summer School" by Gary Soto. Copyright © 1993 by Gary Soto.

Stone Soup, the magazine by young writers and artists: "The Brother I Never Had" by Gim George, thirteen years old, from *Stone Soup, the magazine by young writers and artists,* vol. 21, no. 5, May–June 1993. Copyright © 1993 by the Children's Art Foundation.

Teacher Ideas Press, Englewood, CO, (800) 237-6124: Adapted from *Blanca Flor/White Flower* from *¡Teatro! Hispanic Plays for Young People* by Angel Vigil. Copyright © 1996 by Teacher Ideas Press.

Third Woman Press and Susan Bergholz Literary Services, New York: "Good Hot Dogs" from *My Wicked, Wicked Ways* by Sandra Cisneros. Copyright © 1987 by Sandra Cisneros. Published by Third Woman Press and in hardcover by Alfred A. Knopf. All rights reserved.

Picture Credits

The illustrations and/or photographs on the Contents pages are picked up from pages in the textbook. Credits for those can be found either on the textbook page on which they appear or in the listing below.

Illustrations

Index of Skills

The boldface page numbers indicate an extensive treatment of the topic.

LITERARY RESPONSE AND ANALYSIS (INCLUDING READING SKILLS AND STRATEGIES)

Index of Skills   **731**

READING: WORD ANALYSIS, FLUENCY, AND SYSTEMATIC VOCABULARY DEVELOPMENT

INDEPENDENT READING

Index of Skills

Index of Authors and Titles